D0970530

SAFIRE'S
NEW
POLITICAL
DICTIONARY

SAFIRE'S
NEW
POLITICAL
DICTIONARY

The Definitive Guide to the
New Language of Politics

BY WILLIAM SAFIRE

RANDOM HOUSE NEW YORK

This work was originally published in 1968 as *The New Language of
Politics* by Random House, Inc. Two revised editions were published in
1972 and in 1978 as *Safire's Political Dictionary*.

Library of Congress Cataloging-in-Publication Data

Safire, William, 1929-
  Safire's new political dictionary / by William Safire. — 1st ed.
    p.   cm.
  Rev. and enl. ed. of: Safire's political dictionary. 3rd ed.
c1978.
  Includes index.
  ISBN 0-679-42068-1
  1. United States—Politics and government—Dictionaries.
I. Safire, William, 1929– Political dictionary. II. Title.
III. Title: New political dictionary.
JK9.S2 1993
320'.03—dc20   93-14554   CIP

Manufactured in the United States

Book design by Janet Tingey

New York Toronto London Sydney Auckland

With words we govern men.

—DISRAELI

For Mark Safire

TABLE OF CONTENTS

INTRODUCTION   xiii

POLITICAL DICTIONARY   1

RESEARCH, METHODOLOGY,
AND CREDITS   897

INDEX   903

INTRODUCTION

This book is the culmination of twenty-five years of recording the language of politics, with emphasis on contemporary American political usage. There were three previous editions, each stacked upon the other. The first edition, titled *The New Language of Politics: An Anecdotal Dictionary of Catchwords, Slogans & Political Usage*, was published by Random House in 1968. The second and third, updated and retitled *Safire's Political Dictionary*, a name I like much better, appeared in 1972 and 1978.

In the fifteen years that have passed since the last edition, the political landscape has again been transformed. Consider only these: the advent of three new Administrations, the end of the Cold War, the dissolution of Soviet-type Communism. Each of these changes, along with many others, has introduced new terms and usages into political discourse. Moreover, a certain number of older terms (*junta, cloture, conventional wisdom*) that had been left out of the earlier editions were crying for inclusion. That called for the publication of a completely updated edition, which is what this book is. The "new" in its title, *Safire's New Political Dictionary*, is intended to signal the reader that much of the content has been revised and updated, many new articles have been introduced, and old gaps have been freshly filled—all to make this book a comprehensive guide to the language of politics through the remaining years of this fast-talking century.

WHAT IS THE LANGUAGE OF POLITICS?

The new, old, and constantly changing language of politics is a lexicon of conflict and drama, of ridicule and reproach, of pleading and persuasion. Color and bite permeate a language designed to rally many men and women, to destroy some, and to change the minds of others.

Part of it is the private argot politicians use in talking to other insiders, when they *take him to the mountaintop* and wonder if the *smell of magnolias* will cause a *bullet vote*. Another part is the language about politics, from *smoke-filled room* and *whistlestopping* to a *passion for anonymity*. Finally, there is the public language used by political figures, from a needling *barefoot boy from Wall Street* to a descriptive *gridlock* to an evocative *just and lasting peace*.

The language of politics is vivid. *Gutfighters* with an *instinct for the jugular* and *hatchetmen* adept at *nut-cutting* prowl the political jungle. An anonymous voice becomes a *voice from the sewer*, a bigot an *apostle of hate*, a pessimist a *nattering nabob of negativism*, a censor a *bookburner* or perpetuator of *political correctness*; those who enter the political *arena* with *foot-in-mouth disease* leave in a *hail of dead cats*.

The best of the phrases in politics paint word pictures: you can see the *man on the wedding cake*; you can almost feel the *wave of the future*. And the lexicon delights in disaster: *landslides, prairie fires, firestorms,* and *avalanches* are the goals of *whirlwind campaigns*. Politicians pray that *lightning may strike*.

The language dips into the Bible for *all things to all men* (now *to all people*), *Eleventh Commandment, fight the good fight,* and *Armageddon;* turns to church terms for *party faithful, party elders, bleeding heart,* and *gray eminence;* to poetry for Shakespeare's *strange bedfellows,* Wordsworth's *Happy Warrior,* T. S. Eliot's *wasteland;* to the American Indian for *sachem, mugwump, muckey-mucks,* and *off the reservation;* to horse racing for *dark horse, running mate, front runner, bolt,* and *shoo-in;* and to the military for *campaign, boom, spoils system, rally, regular, hundred days, man on horseback, war horse,* and *old fogy,* as well as war-gaming words like *escalation* and other products of *Foggy Bottom* and the *think tanks*.

It encompasses the jargon of the news media (*off the record, authoritative sources, backgrounder, dope story, leak, plant, not for attribution, sound bite, Walter time*) and the language of the civil rights movement (*black power, white power structure, Freedom Now, backlash, We Shall Overcome, soul, tokenism, Uncle Tom, Jim Crow, segregation, stand in the doorway*).

The political zoo offers the most metaphors of all. *Doves* and *hawks* fly in its aviary, along with emblematic *bald eagles,* as *lame ducks eat crow* on the *rubber-chicken circuit* and all look warily at the *floo-floo bird,* lowest in the *pecking order.* The menagerie features the familiar *elephant* and *donkey,* with a big cage for *tigers* (*Tammany* and *paper*) who enjoy *twisting the lion's tail.* The *mossback* ignores the racket of the *watchdog committees* and the *bird dogs* and *kennel dogs* yapping at the *fat cats,* who in turn hunger for a *red herring* and long to hear *shrimps whistle.* The willing *gofer* and the *coon,* whose skin is a prize for Presidential walls, shudder at the ominous silence from the *dinosaur wing,* where *copperheads* slither and *gerrymanders* abound. In the candidates' stable, the *dark horse,* the *wheelhorse,* and the *stalking horse* are hitched in a *troika,* as the old *war horse* awaits the *man on horseback.* All this causes a *feeding frenzy* on the *zoo plane*.

This is a dictionary of the words and phrases that have misled millions, blackened reputations, held out false hopes, oversimplified ideas to appeal to the lowest common denominator, shouted down inquiry, and replaced searching debate with stereotypes that trigger approval or hatred.

This is also a dictionary that shows how the choice of a word or metaphor can reveal sensitivity and genius, crystallize a mood and turn it to action; some political language captures the essence of an abstraction and makes it understandable to millions.

NOT IN THIS DICTIONARY

As defined here, the language of politics does not include much of the language of government. If a word has a good definition available in most dictionaries, this is not the place to look for it. "Amendment" is not here, though *rider* is; "assistant majority leader" is not, but *whip* is; "Vice President" is not, though *veep, Throttlebottom,* and *heartbeat away from the Presidency* are; "President" is not, but *awesome burden, loneliest job in the world,* and *Presidential initials* are; "diplomat" is not, but *nonstarter, shirtsleeve diplomacy, striped-pants diplomacy,* and *cookie pusher* are.

In the same way, this dictionary concerns itself not with the historical event, but with the language that comes out of it: there is no "Marshall Plan," "Point Four Program," or "Monroe Doctrine" here, though there is an entry on *doctrines;* no "Atlantic Charter," but an entry on *four freedoms;* no "Geneva conference," but entries on *summitry* and *spirit of;* no "Army-McCarthy hearings," but entries on *point of order* and *junketeering gumshoes;* no "government agencies," but an entry on *alphabet agencies* and *acronyms.* The *Bay of Pigs* is included because of its use of *fiasco,* and the Cuban missile crisis of 1962 is listed under *eyeball to eyeball.*

OLD PHRASE, NEW CONTEXT

A linguistic view of history offers more than a few insights. Promises and appeals to blacks and whites took the shape of slogans like "vote yourself a farm," *forty acres and a mule,* "three acres and a cow," *full dinner pail,* and *black power.* For diplomats, there is a lesson in Kennedy's choice of *quarantine* to describe a blockade, taken from the preconditioning of the word by FDR before World War II; in the same way, McKinley used the revered *manifest destiny* to justify his acquisition of Hawaii.

Most of the seemingly "new" language is surprisingly old: Henry IV's *chicken in every pot,* Al Smith's cooing *doves* and Thomas Jefferson's *war hawk* accusation, Henry Clay's struggle against the *can't-win technique,* Alf Landon's borrowing of *New Frontier* from Henry Wallace, Teddy Roosevelt's blast at the *lunatic fringe*—all are old and have been used as new.

There is the longevity of the terms *advice and consent, vox populi,* Aristotle's *political animal* and Bacon's *Presidential timber,* and the use of *Hottentots* as a symbol of the underdeveloped nations. There is a sisters-under-the-skin relationship between Louis XIV's *L'état c'est moi* and Frank Hague's *I am the law*, and subtle differences between a *kitchen cabinet*, a *brain trust*, and a *privy council*.

Some words are freshly minted: in the thirties, *boondoggle* and *gobbledygook* were neologisms that stayed with us; in the sixties, *clout*, *crunch*, and *charisma* took on new political meaning; in the seventies, *convention bounce* and *power curve* appeared; the eighties saw *evil empire*, *empowerment*, and *defining moment;* the nineties spread the use of *ankle-biters*, the *bubba vote*, and everything-*bashing*.

The political language is constantly changing: *gutter flyer* replaces *roorback*, *angry young men* edges aside *Young Turks*, *swing voter* takes over for *floater*, *opportunist* for *trimmer*, *plum* for *persimmon*, *barnacle* for *hanger-on*, *henchman* for *fugleman*. (See OBSOLETE POLITICAL TERMS.) But some die and are born again: *snollygoster* and *mossback* were Harry Truman favorites, and *Philippic* makes an occasional reappearance.

Phrases are sharpened in use; longer statements by Jefferson and Cleveland became "few die and none resign" and *public office is a public trust*. Bismarck's "iron and blood" wound up as "blood and iron," and Churchill's "blood, toil, tears and sweat" (with a long history of its own) was popularized as *blood, sweat, and tears*.

CHORUS COINAGE, PHANTOM COINAGE

Sometimes a word or phrase pops into the political language spontaneously, without an individual coiner. "As Maine goes, so goes the nation" was a well-known slogan; when only Maine and Vermont went for Landon in 1936, it was natural for hundreds of politicians to say "As Maine goes, so goes Vermont" in a chorus coinage.

More mysterious, however, is the phantom coinage: a word like *backlash*, more apt than "backfire" or *boomerang* or "reaction," subtly carrying the slavemasters' whip, appears to have entered the language by osmosis. It was quickly accepted because it filled a linguistic need. The coinage of *Medicare*, also dwelt on at length here, is included because it shows how the right word will triumph over governmental obstacles. The coiner of *Medicare* was neither famous nor had an important national forum: his word grew slowly and inexorably until it could not be stopped. So did *infrastructure*, despite Churchill's scorn.

BOOSTING

The technique of "boosting"—changing a word or phrase slightly to add irony or a fresh meaning—is as old as phrasemaking. Some abolitionists in 1850 called themselves the Know Somethings, providing an antonym for the *Know-Nothings;* the ambivalence of the nineteenth-century "pax Britannica" has been transatlantically resurrected in our own *pax Americana*.

When Adlai Stevenson suggested the Republican slogan should be "throw the rascals in," or Richard Nixon accused Lyndon Johnson of launching a "war on prosperity," they were boosting—playing on familiar phrases. This is a useful device for making a point, and the strength of a phrase can often be determined by how many *turnarounds* have been given it. Allan Nevins's *too little and too late*, for example, went through "enough and on time," to "too much too soon," and is not dead yet.

In this way, Lyndon Johnson made *let us continue* an early theme of his Administration, boosting on John Kennedy's "let us begin"; *peacenik* and *Vietnik* (see -NIK SUFFIX) grew out of *beatnik*; "scrambled eggheads" appeared as a refinement of the original word; and FDR talked of a "sixth column" of gossips and defeatists. Every current phrase offers ammunition for boosting: *black power* spawned dozens of other powers, including "blackboard power" for militant teachers and "gay power" for militant homosexuals.

Since the weight of a word can tip political balances, politicians are wise to concern themselves with usage. In his final campaign FDR said, "This Administration has made mistakes. That I freely *assert*. And I hope my friends of the press will not change that to *admit*." Sherman Adams, searching for the right word to characterize his dealings with industrialist Bernard Goldfine, rejected "unwise" and "wrong" to select "imprudent." Harry Truman used *red herring* with impunity, as Al Smith did before him, until he agreed to its use in a Communist context, when suddenly it became a terrible *blooper*.

DISPUTES

When two distinguished sources say the other is "in error," which do you believe? When the conflicting sources are books, there is recourse to other sources, original letters, or manuscripts. A reference in the *winds of change* entry is made to Milton, as quoted in *Bartlett's:* "Though all the winds of doctrine were let loose to play upon the earth, so Truth be in the field, we do ingloriously by licensing and prohibiting to misdoubt her strength." But the *Oxford Dictionary of Quotations* substitutes "injuriously" for "ingloriously." Who's right? A check of the original text gives the nod to "injuriously."

But when flesh-and-blood eyewitnesses disagree, there is no resolving the claims. When Professor Raymond Moley and Judge Samuel Rosenman each state flatly that he gave *New Deal* to Franklin Roosevelt to coin, citing date and place, the historian has to throw up his hands. Both Professor Moley and Judge Rosenman were responsive to the author's queries on a number of items, and I am grateful to them; the reader can see what each source says and make his or her own decision. Similarly, there were conflicting credits given to the coinage of *New Frontier;* in that case, however, the author was given enough background to suggest a judgment.

The reader will find no gleeful "Hah! He was wrong" comments from the author regarding inaccurate entries in venerable sources about political sayings. The reason is that new information is constantly turning up showing earlier uses. Harold Ickes is credited with *government by crony*, which he used four days after it had appeared in an Arthur Krock column credited to a "press gallery wit," who Krock admitted to the author was himself. That made Krock the coiner—until somebody comes up with an earlier use. There were also varying reports on the context of Dean Rusk's *eyeball to eyeball* remark, two of which are reported under that entry.

PRESIDENTS AND THEIR PHRASES

The memories of an era can be evoked by a look at its inventory of political phrases. Some are coined by a President, some by his cabinet, others coined for use against him. Here is a balance sheet of phrases by Administration, with popularizations included under coinages. First, FDR:

coinages	descriptions	attacks
again and again and again	alphabet agencies	boondoggle
arsenal of democracy	brain trust	clear it with Sidney
day of infamy	dollar-a-year man	court-packing
economic royalists	hundred days	indispensable man
fellow immigrants	nine old men	spend and spend…
fireside chat	pump-priming	that man in the
forgotten man	voice from the sewer	White House
four freedoms		traitor to his class
Good Neighbor Policy		
Happy Warrior		
iffy question		
Martin, Barton and Fish		
my friends		
New Deal		
nothing to fear but fear itself		
one third of a nation		
quarantine [the aggressor]		
rendezvous with destiny		

The Roosevelt era's phrase record offers a sharp contrast with Harry Truman's:

coinages	descriptions	attacks
do-nothing [80th] Congress	Marshall Plan	five percenter
Fair Deal	Point Four Program	government by crony
give 'em hell, Harry	Truman Doctrine	Had Enough?
red herring		influence peddler
		soft on Communism

The Eisenhower years included many from John Foster Dulles and Woodrow Wilson:

coinages	*descriptions*	*attacks*
agonizing reappraisal	Eisenhower Doctrine	bird dog...kennel dog
atoms for peace	new look	brinkmanship
bigger bang for a buck		Eisenhower syntax
curl your hair		security in prison
domino theory		what's good for
engage in personalities		General Motors...
[I shall] go to Korea		
massive retaliation		
modern Republicanism		
open-skies proposal		
spirit of		
unleash Chiang		

Of these coinages, *agonizing reappraisal, bigger bang for a buck, massive retaliation,* and *unleash Chiang* were used for attacks.

A different pattern appears for John F. Kennedy:

coinages	*descriptions*	*attacks*
Alliance for Progress	Bailey Memorandum	absentee Senator
ask not	Camelot	managed news
I am a Berliner	Irish Mafia	
New Frontier	Kennedy Round	
profiles in courage		
rising tide lifts all the boats		
victory has a thousand fathers		

The balance sheet for Lyndon Johnson:

coinages	*descriptions*	*attacks*
chronic campaigner	Johnson treatment	big daddyism
coonskin on the wall	smell of magnolias	credibility gap
creative federalism		daisy spot
Great Society		Macbird
let us continue		
Nervous Nellies		
no wider war		
pressing the flesh		
that dog won't hunt		
war on poverty		

Here are the major coinages or popularizations by the Administration during the early Nixon years:

black capitalism	instant analysis
bring us together	lift of a driving dream
effete snobs	linkage
game plan	nattering nabobs of negativism
hack it	New Federalism

Nixon Doctrine	strict constructionist
old wine in new bottles	Vietnamization
radic-lib	wilderness years
silent majority	workfare

Here are the descriptive phrases that came from outside the Administration that gained currency in that span:

heartland	quality of life
machismo	reordering priorities
Middle America	social issue
new politics	winding down
psephology	women's lib

And here are the phrases that were most often used in early attacks on Nixon:

benign neglect
Nixonomics
secret plan
Southern strategy
used car salesman

Compare the above to the eruption of coinages produced by the Watergate scandal in only two years, 1973 and 1974. Politicians and historians will deal with that period in their own ways, but to lexicographers, the era of the Watergate vocabulary was a Golden Age of Political Coinage.

Some of the expressions fixed in the public tongue in those days were nonce words—*shredding* has already lost its sinister connotation—but a survey of Watergate lingo makes the point that this time had no precedent in its political linguistic fecundity:

at that point in time	hardball
big enchilada	inoperative
cover-up	laundered money
CREEP	nobody drowned at Watergate
deep-six	plumbers
dirty tricks	Saturday Night Massacre
enemies list	smoking gun
executive privilege	stonewalling
firestorm	twisting slowly, slowly in the wind
-gate construction	

This list ignores the phrases that had already been part of the colloquial tongue ("break-in," "caper," "paper the file," "team player"); locutions unfamiliar to laypeople but that had lives in the law ("obstruction of justice," "abuse of power," "misprision of a felony"); and phrases that seemed unforgettable for the nonce but now have become frozen in time (*third-rate burglary*, "sinister force," "expletive deleted," "Deep Throat," "Huston plan," "candyass," *limited modified hangout*). The list includes some phrases that have a long history in American slang: *dirty tricks* had nineteenth-century usage and was recently applied to the CIA's covert operations before assuming its current political meaning of foul play, or the extreme of *hardball*; *deep-six* was naval slang, meaning to jettison after the call of six fathoms; *laundered money* and *cover-up* were familiar to con men; and *inoperative* was used in an important Lincoln statement. A legal phrase, *executive privilege*, was rooted in the Eisenhower years.

But the Watergate investigation leading to the resignation of President Nixon not only popularized expressions that had been little known, but spawned new language likely to be used for generations: *cover-up*, loosely applied to any obstruction of justice (or used by any reporter denied access to information), is a political charge that now carries weight; *stonewalling*, an Australian cricket term given new meaning as refusal to comment, seems here in politics to stay; and *twisting slowly, slowly in the wind* is likely to be used whenever Presidents let their nominees go without support.

The Watergate coinage was followed by a two-year linguistic silence: Gerald Ford's presidency was unique in this century for not producing a single memorable phrase. "Our long national nightmare is over" was received with relief but not recognition; Mr. Ford's most newsworthy action, the pardon of his predecessor, contained no phrase that became part of the political language. His "WIN button"—for "Whip Inflation Now"—was derided and soon forgotten. Reflecting his caretaker presidency, Mr. Ford's language provided a time for lexicographers to digest the tumult of the 1973–74 period and to prepare for a return to normal phrase production.

However, during the decline of Nixon and the subsequent service of President Ford, a new producer of coinage came forward: Henry Kissinger and his circle of articulate aides at the National Security Council and the State Department gave us *quiet diplomacy, shuttle diplomacy, back channel, bargaining chip,* and *step by step*.

Phrasemaking under Jimmy Carter was on a par with the Truman and Kennedy years:

coinages	descriptions	attacks
born again	Jimmy who?	one-term President
ethnic purity	Magnolia Mafia	steel magnolia
moral equivalent of war (MEOW)	running against Washington	
three-martini lunch		
zero-base budgeting		

But wordsmithing rebounded during Ronald Reagan's two-term tenure:

coinages	descriptions	attacks
are you any better off	let Reagan be Reagan	amen corner
cautiously optimistic	Reagonomics	amiable dunce
evil empire	supply-side economics	October surprise
fatally flawed	Teflon-coated	sleaze factor
keister	Presidency	
level playing field		
make my day		
morning in America		
star wars		
stay the course		
supply-side		
there you go again		

And for a President whose garbled syntax came frequently under attack, George Bush left a legacy of a few memorable phrases:

coinages	description	attacks
draw a line in the sand	empowerment	Velcro Presidency
inside the Beltway		vision thing
kinder and gentler nation		
like ugly on an ape		
moving the goalposts		
new world order		
read my lips		
thousand points of light		
voodoo economics		

Bill Clinton's campaign and his first half year in office produced surprisingly few neologisms. A campaign slogan, *It's the economy, Stupid,* was widely quoted and *Clintonomics* was boosted from *Nixonomics* and *Reagonomics.* "Clintonites" rallied around him, but his *new covenant* never got off the ground. He used *gridlock,* but that was Ross Perot's popularization.

Except for the extraordinary spurt of coinage resulting from Watergate during Nixon's second term, FDR's thirteen-year span produced more phrases than any of the other, shorter administrations. The quality and staying power of the coinages and popularizations of FDR stand out over his successors as well. There are at least six landmark catch phrases of FDR (*New Deal, Good Neighbor Policy, four freedoms, day of infamy, fireside chat, nothing to fear but fear itself*) as against one for Truman (*do-nothing Congress*); three for Eisenhower, two of which were Dulles's (*domino theory, agonizing reappraisal, massive retaliation*); two for Kennedy (*New Frontier, ask not*); two for Johnson (*Great Society, war on poverty*); two for Nixon (*silent majority, Middle America*); two for Ford, which were Kissinger's (*shuttle diplomacy, bargaining chip*); two for Carter (*born again, three-martini lunch*); three for Reagan (*supply-side, evil empire, star wars*); and one for Bush (*thousand points of light*). Clinton's score is too early to call.

Major phrases associated with candidates who lost in this period include Wendell Willkie's *one world, loyal opposition*, and *campaign oratory*, with *barefoot boy from Wall Street* against him; Dewey's *time for a change* with *idiot engineer* and *man on the wedding cake* against him; Stevenson's *dinosaur wing*, "talk sense to the American people," *numbers game*, and *nuclear proliferation*, with *egghead* against him; Nixon's *kitchen debate, Checkers speech*, and *cloth coat*, with the last two also used against him; and Goldwater's *defoliate, extremism* [*in defense of liberty*], and *no-win policy*, all of which were also used against him in addition to *trigger-happy, nuts and kooks*, and *little old ladies in tennis shoes*. Walter Mondale used "where's the beef?" in 1984 and Gary Hart was bedeviled by the *character issue* in 1988.

The most popular target for phrases in the postwar period was Senator Joseph McCarthy, who popularized "I have in my hand," *security risk*, and *point of order*, and was hit with *guilt by association, character assassin, McCarthyism, big lie*, and *junketeering gumshoes*.

There was a relatively arid period in the twenties. Hoover coined *rugged individualism* and *noble experiment*, with *chicken in every pot* and "prosperity is just around the corner" thrown at him. Al Smith came up with good uses for *baloney, Santa Claus, laundry ticket*, and *lulu*. Coolidge's "the business of America is business" is generally forgotten, though he can be credited with *against sin*. Harding coined *normalcy* and was associated with *smoke-filled room*.

Woodrow Wilson and Theodore Roosevelt, however, were great phrasemakers. Wilson coined *New Freedom, little group of wilful men, too proud to fight, watchful waiting, open covenants, peace without victory, make the world safe for democracy*, and *self-determination* [*of nations*], with *war to end wars* unduly credited to him.

Compare the type of Wilson phrases with the type of Theodore Roosevelt's: *lunatic fringe* and *hat in the ring*, in active political usage today; *bully pulpit*, [*stand at*] *Armageddon, big stick, malefactors of great wealth, pussyfooting, weasel words, mollycoddle, muckraker, parlor pink, Square Deal*, and "100% American."

The other giants of political coinage were Abraham Lincoln (*just and lasting peace*, "malice toward none," *don't change horses*, possibly *Presidential bug* and *you can't beat somebody with nobody*, and just about every other line of the *Gettysburg address*), Thomas Jefferson (*entangling alliances*, "few die and none resign," and "life, liberty and the pursuit of happiness"), and English Conservative Edmund Burke, who coined such necessary words as "colonial," "diplomacy," *electioneer, federalism*, and "municipality." Winston Churchill's *blood, sweat, and tears,* "pumpernickel principality," *sheep in sheep's clothing, special relationship,* crowned by *iron curtain*—which, alongside Herbert Bayard Swope's *cold war,* was the major postwar coinage—carried on the Burke tradition.

Though political phrases are most often coined by politicians, they are also the province of journalists (William Allen White's *tinhorn politician,* Arthur Krock's *government by crony,* Walter Lippmann's *Atlantic Community,* Stewart Alsop and Charles Bartlett's *hawks* and *doves*), professors (Raymond Moley's possible coinage of *New Deal,* Allan Nevins's sure coinage of *too little and too late,* John Kenneth Galbraith's *affluent society* and *conventional wisdom*), judges (*curse of bigness,* "clear and present danger," *with all deliberate speed*), generals ("unconditional surrender," *no substitute for victory,* "vote as you shot"), and voices in a crowd (*give 'em hell, Harry* and *tell it like it is*).

HIDDEN ENTRIES

Every lexicographer is faced with the problem of writing entries he knows nobody is ever going to look up. He puts them in anyway, hoping a browsing reader will trip over them. Some of these, like "son of a bitch" and *baloney,* have had interesting political usage even though they are not political expressions. Others are *great, black, wall,* and *new,* and suffixes like *-nomics, -word, -bashing,* and *-ocracy.* Speech constructions are also hidden entries, and the reader is directed to *"I see" construction* for a brief history of visionary statements, *contrapuntal phrases* and *turnarounds* for a brief look at how to make a phrase more memorable, as well as *Gettysburg address* for a look at poetic use of images and repetition of words.

Phrases are entered the way they are most often remembered or quoted and not necessarily the way they were spoken. "The only thing we have to fear is fear itself," for example, is entered as *nothing to fear but fear itself.*

Euphemisms are hidden in an entry by themselves, but clichés are tagged as such when they appear individually. *Madison Avenue techniques* are always "high-powered," images are always "projected," there are *gaps* for everything, and the cliché that bounds along most merrily on election-night television is *tantamount to election.*

Words used to describe language have their own problems of fuzzy usage. "Jargon," as used herein, is synonymous with "cliché" and "bromide," as is illustrated in the *Pentagonese* entry; "argot" is used when a word in a specialized vocabulary has not been abused; "lingo," which used to be quite close to "argot," is now used loosely as being synonymous with "language," "tongue," "lexicon," and "vocabulary." *Cant,* however, preserves its meaning as slang used by insiders with intent to confuse outsiders, as in *strike a blow for freedom,* except when it refers to unintentional repetition, as illustrated in the entry *cant.*

SOMETHING BORROWED

A prime purpose of this book is to make readily available the words that worked for politicians. By showing from what these words were derived (or on what analogy they were coined), I hope to have removed a certain guilt about borrowing in phrasemaking. The political subdivision of the English language has been in business too long for almost any phrase to be totally original; some of the best are twists of others. The many quotations herein, necessary to show usage, are also possible springboards for better usage. The best entries are those put together from the words of others that will suggest more apt words from others to come. Winston Churchill, as he wrote of fighting on the beaches, in the hills, and in the streets of wartime England, was familiar with Clemenceau's defiance in 1918: "I shall fight in front of Paris, within Paris, behind Paris." An apt quotation may make a point, but an apt alteration of a good phrase makes a speech and helps in the making of a leader.

LOVE'S LABOR NOT LOST

This tome is now approaching 550,000 words, with 1,800 terms defined in over 1,100 entries. Since the original edition, the lexicographer has undergone several metamorphoses: from a public relations man in the early sixties—see *flak, selling candidates like soap, Madison Avenue techniques*—to a White House aide in the early seventies—see *speechwriter, ghostwriter*, and creations like *nattering nabobs of negativism, workfare*, and (gulp) *CREEP*—to a columnist for the *New York Times* today (see *pundit, thumbsucker*).

In each incarnation I have kept a hand in the development of this labor of love, collecting citations for new words, digging further into the origins of other entries, filling in gaps of words that should have been covered in the beginning.

Therefore, this edition contains new economic terms like *dead-cat bounce, dip/double dip, Rosie Scenario, soft landing*, and *supply-side* while filling in a term missed in earlier editions, *animal spirits;* it stays up to date with political terms like *Beltway bandits, bubba factor, defining moment, face time*, and the new sense of *gridlock*, while reaching back to pick up *city on a hill; blood, sweat and tears; dustbin of history; full disclosure;* and the *redheaded Eskimo bill*. It stays on top of the new (*ankle-biters*) while picking up the old (*advisers*); it covers *no more Mr. Nice Guy, family values*, and *spending cap* while retrieving *forty acres and a mule*. The updating includes new usages like Reagan's *evil empire*, Bush's *thousand points of light*, and Gorbachev's *glasnost* and *perestroika*, while going back to retrieve Disraeli's *side of the angels*, Stalin's *scorched earth*, Ike's *go to Korea*, and JFK's *rising tide lifts all the boats*. The *thought police* of the *politically correct* may be accused of *pushing the envelope*, but the *short list* of *happy campers* with *sharp elbows* makes a *quick fix* to avoid falling behind the *power curve*.

As a newspaper columnist, I have become more opinionated and polemical in my writing, but partisanship stops at the dictionary's edge: as a lexicographer, I have tried—God, how I've tried—to remain nonpartisan, or at least bipartisan. Although the practice of politics pits Democrat against Republican, liberal against conservative, the tough-minded against the tender-hearted, the study of politics divides the house differently: into the politically active and the politically inert. That is why politically active people of all persuasions, and certain ex-colleagues of unfortunate convictions, have responded willingly to queries about who coined what and when.

Normal political differences and tensions were suspended; in tracking the etymology of political language, we are all lexicographers. And even blunders can help. For an example of the way mistakes lead to new discoveries, take *thunder on the left*. In my *New York Times* column I misattributed the phrase to G. K. Chesterton; a reader wrote in to point out a 1925 book with that title by Christopher Morley. I ran a correction, which caused a retired professor to write in with another correction: he sent a page from the 11th edition of *Bartlett's Quotations* that cited the first use of *thunder on the left* in a 1640 tract by "Sir Eustace Peachtree." Grimly, I ran another correction, which brought a letter from a Kit Morley fan who was able to prove that Mr. Morley, while one of the editors of *Bartlett's* in the forties, perpetrated a small hoax: he playfully attributed his own phrase to a nonexistent sage of three centuries ago. It's all straightened out in here, thanks to that series of forward fumbles.

THE DISAPPEARING ART

In studying the derivation of political phrases, the lexicographer digging through early drafts of famous speeches can pick up an insight on the evolution of speechwriting. The craft of ghosting is hardly new—President James Madison, for example, wrote the speeches given by his Secretary of State—but the willingness of some of the greatest orators to accept suggestions from colleagues is rarely considered. One reason the political speech is a declining art today is that most modern politicians turn to speechwriters for the complete job, and do not collaborate closely in the preparation of the expression of what is—or should be—in their own minds.

In researching *musical metaphors*, I stumbled across the derivation of Lincoln's "the mystic chords of memory," which illustrates the way a political leader can take a thought contributed by an aide and shape it to his own style.

The Civil War had not yet begun. In his draft of his first inaugural address, President-elect Lincoln had planned to conclude with a message to his "dissatisfied friends" in the South that the choice of "peace or the sword" was *in your hands,* and not in his. William Seward, whom Lincoln had beaten for the Republican nomination and after the election had appointed Secretary of State, suggested in a letter that this note of defiance be tempered with "a note of fraternal affection," and submitted language for the penultimate paragraphs:

> I close. We are not, we must not be, aliens or enemies, but fellow countrymen and brethren. Although passion has strained our bonds of affection too hardly, they must not, I am sure they will not, be broken. The mystic chords which, proceeding from so many battlefields and so many patriot graves, pass through all the hearts and all hearths in this broad continent of ours, will yet again harmonize in their ancient music when breathed upon by the guardian angel of the nation.

Lincoln accepted Seward's idea of seeking to evoke the sentimental ties that could help bind the nation together, and he used Seward's musical metaphor as well. But he rewrote the suggested passage, lifting it from oratory to poetry:

> I am loath to close. We are not enemies, but friends. We must not be enemies. Though passion may have strained, it must not break our bonds of affection. The mystic chords of memory, stretching from every battlefield and patriot grave, to every living heart and hearthstone, all over this broad land, will yet swell the chorus of the Union, when again touched, as they surely will be, by the better angels of our nature.

Do users of political language today make that kind of effort to persuade and inspire? I think not. If they did, would it work? Styles change with the times, and Seward's florid style may seem excessive to us now, but Lincoln's improvement produced a soaring simplicity that I believe has what we now call impact.

In using the *bully pulpit* of the White House in this century, Theodore Roosevelt tried strenuously, and often succeeded; Taft did not try; Wilson succeeded; Harding failed; Coolidge and Hoover did not try; FDR succeeded; Truman did not try; Eisenhower succeeded only in his farewell; Kennedy succeeded; Johnson and Nixon tried and sometimes succeeded; Ford went out of his way not to try; Carter contributed an accent but few phrases; Reagan tried and succeeded; Bush seemed not to try but succeeded modestly; Clinton is trying and it is too soon to tell.

Oratorical success does not ensure political success, as can be seen, but those among us who love the political language—and realize what it can to do uplift and lead—hold out the hope that it helps.

abolitionist one who advocates the abolition of an institution; a politically loaded word.

Originally (as early as 1790) applied to those who sought the abolition of slavery, more recent use refers to those who advocate the abolition of capital punishment.

Spelled with an initial capital, the term was applied most widely during the nineteenth century to fierce opponents of slavery such as the journalist William Lloyd Garrison, the author Harriet Beecher Stowe, who wrote *Uncle Tom's Cabin*, and the BARNBURNERS of New York State.

In the 1920s, *abolitionist* was revived as the term of choice for opponents of the death penalty. The abolitionist philosophy was summed up in a letter published in the *Edmonton* (Alberta) *Journal* on June 9, 1979: "Abolitionists are convinced that the evidence does not indicate that capital punishment serves as a deterrent or is otherwise useful but is, in fact, simply retribution or revenge."

Countries that have abolished the death penalty, such as Canada, are often called *abolitionist states*, a term used in the earlier sense during the Civil War. After limiting capital punishment in 1972, the Supreme Court reapproved it in 1976, and most states of the U.S. still practice it. The District of Columbia has no death penalty.

Abominable No-man sobriquet of Sherman Adams, Eisenhower's chief of staff, who took on the onus of unpleasantness produced by the President's negative decisions.

By becoming the "no-man," the flinty former New Hampshire governor assumed the role of lightning rod for resentment that would ordinarily have been directed at the Chief Executive. Critics said Adams usurped a portion of the Presidential decision-making power by "insulating" Eisenhower. Friends said he permitted himself to be a scapegoat: "the yesses come from Eisenhower, the no's from Sherman Adams."

This term has also been applied to other politicians. In 1980, for instance, the *Washington Post* wrote of "former Rep. H. R. Gross (R.-Iowa), known and feared on Capitol Hill as the 'Abominable No Man' for his resourceful opposition to virtually everything."

The term was also applied to John Sununu, President Bush's Chief of Staff, when he became the target of press criticism in 1991.

Jack Watson, at one time Jimmy Carter's Chief of Staff, called the job "Javelin Catcher."

The phrase is a play on the "Abominable Snowman of the Himalayas," legendary monster known as the Yeti whose tracks are "found" and shuddered at by occasional mountain climbers.

See PALACE GUARD; GRAY EMINENCE.

above politics a stance taken most often by generals and businessmen dissociating themselves from partisan strife, often in the hope of attracting political support from opposing sides.

Nonpartisan connotes no controversy at all; *above politics* implies that partisanship exists and there is an individual above it. Applied to issues and not to individuals, however, *nonpartisan* and *above politics* are synonymous.

Politicians occasionally place themselves above politics when they feel they no longer need political allies, when they are ready to become elder statesmen, or when they have reached a point described by Francis Bacon in 1612 in his essay "In Great Place": "All rising to great place is by a winding stair; and if there be factions, it is good to side a man's self whilst he is in the rising, and to balance himself when he is placed."

Among U.S. Presidents, Eisenhower was one of the few able to place himself above politics on many occasions. Another military hero, Admiral George Dewey, was less successful. When asked his party affiliation, the hero of Manila Bay smiled: "I am a sailor. A sailor has no politics." To his amazement, he soon found himself with no support from either political party.

See BIPARTISAN; NONPARTISAN; PARTISAN; WATER'S EDGE.

abuse of power. See ARROGANCE OF POWER.

academic freedom the right of scholars and students to conduct their studies and express their findings or opinions free of institutional, political, or sectarian control.

Who first used the phrase is uncertain, but it has been a rallying cry for many decades; it is one of those ideas to which few will admit opposition. The magazine *World's Work* wrote in 1901: "Every right-thinking man will stand firmly for academic freedom of thought."

Nationally, academic freedom became a subject of argument during the McCarthy-influenced 1950s. There was pressure not only against leftists, liberals, and dissenters in general, but also against the presence of their books in publicly sponsored libraries. In 1953 President Dwight Eisenhower, speaking at Dartmouth, made his widely quoted response: "Don't join the BOOKBURNERS. Don't think you are going to conceal faults by concealing evidence that they ever existed." In the sixties, the passions of the McCarthy period had cooled, but the academic freedom controversy found its central forum at the University of California's Berkeley campus.

In 1967 the brouhaha was over the Central Intelligence Agency's subsidization of student groups. After the first round of investigations, Senator Richard Russell, chairman of the Armed Services Committee, said, "all this clamor about impairing academic freedom . . . is a lot of hogwash."

access. See INFLUENCE PEDDLER.

accommodation compromise; relaxation of international tensions after a conciliatory, usually unilateral gesture.

Woodrow Wilson used the word in its present political sense in his "Peace Without Victory" speech early in 1917: "Difficult and delicate as these questions are, they must be faced with the utmost candor and decided with a spirit of real accommodation if peace is to come with healing in its wings, and come to stay."

When labor leader John L. Lewis split with American Federation of Labor chieftain William Green in 1935 to form the Committee (later Congress) of Industrial Organizations, Arthur Krock wrote in the *New York Times*: "After all, as Huck Finn realized when he heard the Child of Calamity and the other braggart on the raft tell what they would do to each other—and didn't—the most-publicized impasses are those which are surest accommodated. Yet this one looks less soluble in an era of realignments." Ultimately, the AFL and CIO reached their "accommodation."

In 1951 Dr. Edward Corwin wrote in the *New Republic* that Congress and President Truman, in the midst of a constitutional dispute over sending troops to Europe to serve in the North Atlantic Treaty Organization, should undertake "a decent consultation and accommodation of views."

As PEACEFUL COEXISTENCE began to be talked of during the post-Stalin era, the terms *accommodation, reconciliation, realignment*, and DÉTENTE became popular in many liberal journals, and the SOFT ON COMMUNISM attack lost some of its appeal.

The proponents of a policy of accommodation are quite serious, but the word was introduced to the political vocabulary by a comic writer, Artemus Ward (Charles Farrar Browne), in 1866: "My pollertics, like my religion, being of an exceedin' accommodatin' character. . . ."

See DOVES.

accountability. See OVERSIGHT; SIGN OFF ON.

acronyms, political words formed from the initials of agencies, programs or phrases.

Military acronyms have led the way.

A.W.O.L. (Absent Without Leave) is a much-used Army term. *Snafu* (in bowdlerized form, "Situation Normal: All Fouled Up") was used by U.S. Secretary of State Dean Acheson on a visit to England in 1952 to apologize for an administrative error: "It is only as the result of what in the United States is known as a *snafu* that you were not consulted about it." (Churchill pronounced it snay-foo.) Derivatives were *fubb* (Fouled Up Beyond Belief) and *tuifu* (The Ultimate In Foul-Ups). *WAVEs, WACs,* and *WRENs* became well-known words, as did *radar* and *sonar*. Troops of the Republic of Korea soon were known as *ROKs*.

VEEP was first applied to Vice President Alben Barkley and then came to mean the vice president of any organization.

UNIVAC (Universal Automatic Computer) became a familiar friend on election night. When President Eisenhower spoke to ACTION (American Committee To Improve Our Neighborhoods), he wondered which came first—the initials or the name.

Former Secretary of Defense Robert A. Lovett ("the Bald Eagle of Foggy Bottom") told the National Institute of Social Sciences in 1952 that he frankly advocated the use of what he termed "initialese." Time was saved by referring to the Commander in Chief, Far East, as CINCFE, and to his counterpart in Europe as CINCEUR. CINCUS (Commander in Chief, U.S. Fleet) was shudderingly dropped when naval officers pronounced the acronym. As for his own position as Secretary of Defense, the initialese was SECDEF rather than the more obvious S.O.D. "S.O.D. was abandoned," Lovett explained, "because it would require the most careful enunciation in order not to be excessively accurate as a description of the Secretary of Defense."

Often political acronyms are designed to be humorous. "MOM and POP briefings," reported Scripps-Howard in 1967, "are all the rage at Peace Corps Headquarters here. These are acronyms for 'Memo on Marriage' and 'Policy on Pregnancy.'" However, the War on Poverty lent itself to an ethnic slur.

During the Nixon Administration, top-secret studies were labeled "National Security Study Memoranda" and called by an awkward acronym, NSSM, pronounced "Nissim." When Zbigniew Brzezinski took over as National Security Adviser in the Carter Administration, he wanted all vestiges of Kissingerese removed; accordingly, the word "Presidential" was substituted for "National Security" in these memos: Presidential Study Memorandum. However, after one day of "PISSIMs," the name was further changed to "Presidential *Review* Memoranda," and became known throughout the Carter Administration as more prim PRMs.

Acronyms flourished during the Reagan years. To replace SALT, START became National Security Adviser Richard Allen's acronym for Strategic Arms Reductions Talks. OPEC stood for Organization of Petroleum Exporting Countries (with "OPEC nations" a redundancy similar to "SALT talks").

A deliberately jocular acronym making the rounds in the 1980s was BOGSAT (sometimes spelled BOGSATT), used to describe the process by which a President chooses his team. In 1986, the *New York Times* reported that, according to Congressman Les Aspin, "an old Pentagon hand with a penchant for acronyms," policy-making in the Pentagon was "really no more than BOGSATT . . . 'Bunch of guys sitting around the table.'"

Financial terms such as DINK ("double income, no kids") and variations of YUPPIE ("young urban professional") flourished in the late 1980s, and George Bush helped introduce spookspeak initialese. Acronyms of security clearance include LIMDIS ("limited distribution"), EXDIS ("exclusive distribution"), and NOFORN ("no foreign dissemination"). Operation Desert Storm helped popularize such older military acronyms as SAM ("surface-to-air missile"), and arms controllers clung to MIRV ("multiple independently targetable reentry vehicle").

With the advent of the Clinton Administration, an acronym surfaced for Hillary Rodham Clinton: TMPWA, pronounced "TUMP-wah," refers to "the most powerful woman in America."

The last word on acronyms, though, belongs to a cartoon in *Punch* (September 28, 1977), showing two angry people marching under a banner titled "COCOA—Council to Outlaw Contrived and Outrageous Acronyms."

See MEGO; GULAG; CREEP; RIF; SALT.

activist as a noun, a person willing to work for a cause, to take direct action to accomplish or dramatize its aims; as an adjective, the attitude of that person.

At the turn of the twentieth century, *activist* was the name of a philosophy of realism, akin to "pragmatist," assuming the active existence of everything. By 1920 the adjective's meaning changed to a description of a policy of energetic action; German intellectuals called political engagement *Aktivismus*.

Activist as a noun, with its current meaning, was set forth in 1954 by Arthur Koestler, in *Invisible Writing*: "He was not a politician but a propagandist, not a 'theoretician' but an 'activist.'"

The word seems to have replaced *agitator*, which is now a quaint derogation of a labor organizer. This word came into popularity when a high-level committee of English army officers was organized in 1647 to kidnap King Charles I, called "the Adjutators" (from adjutant, or assistant); the Presbyterians promptly nicknamed them the Agitators, as shakers-up of the status quo. In 1842 "the Agitator" was the sobriquet of Daniel O'Connell, advocate of Irish freedom.

In modern times, organized labor has not given up on the word. Lane Kirkland, Secretary-Treasurer of the AFL-CIO, told his convention in 1977: "The founders of the American labor movement left us all with one central theme and doctrine: 'Agitate, Educate, Organize.'" Mr. Kirkland, in the same speech, defined "militancy" as "an attention-getting device most successfully and easily employed by spearing one's colleagues for the titillation of the press."

Militant is a calibration more active than "activist." In England in the thirties, the word was often applied to labor leaders holding out for high wage demands; by 1960, London's *Economist* was describing "a 'more-militant-than-thou' attitude" on the part of some trade union leaders. In the late sixties the word became popular in the U.S. as a label, usually intended to be pejorative, but not taken that way by those so described, for a demonstrator with "non-negotiable demands." Most of the time, "militant" implied a lack of reasonableness: ironically, militants usually displayed a distaste for anything military, whether National Guard troops or military service in Vietnam.

Professor Leopold Labedz, in the 1977 *Fontana Dictionary of Modern Thought*, held that *militant* "refers properly to the degree of radicalism in a person's politics" and *activist* merely to "the degree of involvement in politics," but such a nice distinction is

rarely made in current American political use.

In the vocabulary of verbal representation, an *advocate* is a persuasive spokesman, and has a positive connotation, as in the title assumed by Ralph Nader, "consumer advocate"; an *apologist* is a propagandist, once meaning an explicator of God's word but now only used to mean a slavish mouthpiece; a *spokesman* or *spokeswoman* or *spokesperson* is a neutral term for one who presents a point of view for another, often on television.

In the lexicon of activism, an *activist* is one who presses for the idea of direct action; a *lobbyist* is a derogatory description of a paid activist on the other side; a *supporter* is a less active member of the troops, giving rise to the vogue term "supportive"; a *demonstrator* or *protester* is one who participates in street action and may be derogated as a *rioter*; a *dissident* is a heroic description of a demonstrator, noisier than a *dissenter*; and a *militant* is a fierce and uncompromising believer in a cause who—when endowed with leadership qualities—can be called a *firebrand*. Both *rabble-rouser* and *agent provocateur* are obsolescent.

adamant for drift. See LOYAL OPPOSITION.

administration regime; the government of a specific leader.

European and United States usages differ on this word. In Europe, "government" is used to describe a particular leader's time in power; the Callaghan government replaced the Wilson government. When, as in France, a government "falls," only the leadership falls—the structure of government, of course, continues.

In the U.S., the word *administration* is used to designate the term of a president, while *government* is used to mean the ongoing constitutional organization. "Administration officials" and "administration policy" are U.S. government men and policies, but the use of the temporary word stresses the temporary tenure of U.S. elected officials.

Regime is the loosest word of the three and can be used for the power-span of an individual ("the Brezhnev regime") or a mode of government (*l'ancien régime*). This is a European word, however; in the U.S. it is mainly applied to foreign governments or eras. Thus, Englishmen in 1978 thought of "the Carter government" in the U.S., and Americans talked of "the Callaghan administration" in Great Britain, each applying his own usage to the other's political system; both, however, referred to a "Gaullist regime," as did the French. In U.S. usage, *regime* is slightly pejorative; Senator George McGovern derogated the Saigon government in 1972 as "the Thieu regime."

A second use of "administration" is in subcabinet-level government agencies, as "National Recovery Administration," "Federal Housing Administration." In recent years there has been a tendency to substitute *agency* for *administration* in these titles. A *commission* differs from an administration or agency in that it is a quasi-judicial board; an *authority* is an organization set up by legislative act, one step removed from political influence or likelihood of change as an administration (in its first, overall sense) changes.

advance man   one who arranges for publicity, protocol, transportation, speaking schedules, conferences with local government officials, and all the details smoothing the way for a political figure.

Preparations for a campaign trip are known as "advancing." Members of the advance party usually move into a city three or four days ahead of the candidate. At least one professional writer is on hand to draft "local inserts" for the candidate's speeches, and might prepare specific data on how the regional economy was suffering under the opposition administration, or scan local newspapers for issues on which the candidate might comment. Such a writer would also develop a humorous introduction that would have special meaning for local voters or politicians.

Advance men work with local party leaders to plan the schedule, determine the motorcade route, decide on platform sites and seating, help get the crowds to turn out, handle police and press, distribute press kits, flags, buttons and banners, and arrange for "spontaneous" hand-lettered signs, etc.

President Dwight D. Eisenhower's advance man at the Republican convention in San Francisco in 1956 was the resourceful Tom Stephens, who, in this note to Sherman Adams, concerned himself with the probable weather:

> If the President arrived some time between 8:30 and 9:30 at night I believe it would be most helpful to him. While it is not cold here in the evening, it does get cool, and if you will look at the weather reports for the last couple of years, which I am enclosing, you will find that it has never gone below 50 degrees and seldom over 60 degrees between 8:30 and 9:30 around the 22nd, 23rd or 24th of August.

There are all kinds of "advance men" in politics, from those who attend to relatively small but important details to those who influence policy. And the advance man will occasionally make news himself: Eisenhower press secretary James Hagerty, advancing a presidential trip to Japan (that never took place), found himself in the center of riots and left-wing demonstrations.

A sign frequently displayed in rooms where experienced advance men teach the trade to neophytes reads: "If you arrive with the candidate, you're not advancing."

The predecessor phrase of "advance man" appears to have been "advance agent"; in 1897, the circus term was politically applied by Tennessee Congressman H. R. Gibson who lauded "that great priest and apostle of protection, and that great advance agent of prosperity, William McKinley." See BANDWAGON.

In the special lingo of advance men, *newsies* (which include *wires, reels,* and *stills*) and *staffers* make up the *caravan* following *the man*. Sometimes included are *surrogates*, a half-dozen VIPs who can speak for the candidate before, after, or instead of a personal appearance. The advance staff can schedule, or *pencil in*, a hasty *drop-by*, or a *visual*, which is a *photo opportunity*, even if this means *lunching him out*, or denying the candidate a midday meal; ears are cocked at the rally for the *wrap-up*, or standard peroration, which is the signal for a mad dash to buses to beat the crowd out of the hall.

In 1973, during the Watergate investigation, the term "black advance" was used to describe the darker side of advance work. Presidential aide Richard Moore, acting as an investigative counsel, drafted a memo dated March 22, 1973, detailing what he found in interviews with aides Dwight Chapin and Gordon Strachan regarding the disruptive activities of Donald Segretti: "They made reference to Dick Tuck [a Democratic prankster] and cited the kind of harassment of the campaign activities of opposition candidates which Tuck has engaged in over the years. At one point, Strachan described the type of activity as 'black advance,' a term used in political campaigning to describe the planning of measures to harass the opposition or to detect and guard against harassment by the opposition." Segretti served a

jail term for campaign infractions, and Chapin (who advanced the 1972 Nixon trip to China) was sentenced for perjury; suddenly, political advance work learned its limits.

advice and consent the phrase in the U.S. Constitution (Art. II, sec. 2) enabling the Senate to act as a check on the appointive and treaty-making powers of the president.

This ancient phrase was popularized in 1959 when it was used as the title of a novel by Allen Drury, later made into a motion picture. The title was *Advise and Consent*—not *advice*—taken from Senate Rule 38: "the final question on every nomination shall be, 'Will the Senate advise and consent to this nomination?'"

However, most earlier expressions of the phrase used the noun "advice" rather than the verb "advise." In current use, the verb is preferred and automatically changes the companion word, "consent," from a noun to a verb. A frequent play on the phrase, especially after Senate opposition to the Vietnam War became outspoken, is "advise and dissent."

In its original form, advice and consent is one of the oldest English phrases in current political use. In A.D. 759 King Sigiraed gave lands to Bishop Eardwulf "with the advice and consent of my principal men." In 1184, Henry II issued the Forest Assize "by the advice and consent of the archbishops, bishops, barons, earls, and nobles of England," and Henry III ascended the throne "by the common advice and consent of the said king and the magnates."

The English colonies in America preserved the phrase and the concept, with the executive acting "by and with the advice and consent" of whatever the legislative body happened to be named. The old statute book of North Carolina began with the phrase: "Be it enacted by his Excellency Gabriel Johnson, Esq., Governor, by and with the advice and consent of His Majesty's Council and General Assembly . . ."

At the 1787 Constitutional Convention, it was natural for the English-trained lawyers to use the phrase in describing the action of the Senate to review appointments: "He [the President] shall nominate, and by and with the advice and consent of the Senate shall appoint ambassadors, other public ministers, and consuls, etc."

The "advice" function soon atrophied and was merged into "consent," and though the phrase survives intact, in practice its meaning has been halved: the Senate checks, but usually does not share, the presidential power of appointment. See BLUE SLIP.

An omission in the Constitution led to a century-long battle between the executive and legislative arms of the U.S. government: Need the President seek the advice and consent of the Senate in the removal of appointed officials? Though Jefferson grumbled about the offices packed with Federalists when he came to power in 1800 ("few die and none resign"), he displaced only 39; Andrew Jackson, when the Senate refused to amend the civil-service laws to make places for his followers, proceeded to replace more than a thousand political appointees in his first year and the Senate did not take up the strong President's gauntlet. See SPOILS SYSTEM.

Weaker Presidents followed Jackson, however, and "senatorial courtesy" soon encroached on both powers of appointing and removing. See PERSONALLY OBNOXIOUS. The Tenure of Office Act of 1867 seized enormous power from Andrew Johnson's hands by limiting removal of public officials to reasons of "misconduct or crime." Only slightly modified, the law rankled Presidents Grant, Hayes, and Garfield, but not until 1887 was a President—Grover Cleveland—able to have the act repealed and permanently wrest the power of consent from the Senate. Said Cleveland to the Senate: ". . . my duty to the Chief Magistracy which I must preserve unimpaired in all its dignity and vigour compels me to refuse compliance . . ."

The most dramatic case of the Senate's withholding advice and consent was its rejection of the League of Nations, despite Woodrow Wilson's pleas; this is inaccurately identified with the LITTLE GROUP OF WILFUL MEN. During the Eisenhower Administration, the refusal to confirm the appointment of Admiral Lewis Straus as Secretary of Commerce was a surprising defeat. In 1969, the Senate rejection of Supreme Court nominees Clement Haynsworth and G. Harrold Carswell was widely interpreted as a reassertion of the "advice" function, as was the 1977 resistance to the Carter nomination of Theodore Sorensen to be Director of Central Intelligence, which caused him to withdraw.

During the 1980s, Ronald Reagan's nomination of Judge Robert H. Bork was defeated in the Senate (see BORK). George Bush's nominee, Judge Clarence Thomas, was confirmed, but only after nationally televised hearings into charges of sexual harassment made against Thomas by Professor Anita Hill.

advisers 1. political consultants; 2. assistants who wish to upgrade the title of "aide"; 3. military personnel sent in to train a friendly army, or a euphemism for those armed forces to conceal their combat role.

The agent-noun *adviser* dates back to 1611 for "one who gives counsel or advice." A modifying term, as in *legal adviser* or *security adviser*, identifies the authority's area of expertise.

Military use began in 1915, when *adviser* first served as a euphemism for combat soldier, particularly one sent to help a foreign army. The 1915 *Handbook of the Turkish Army* described reserve divisions formed by "Turkish military authorities and their German military advisers," and a 1939 text on Soviet policy stated, "The Russians have kept a number of 'advisers,' military and otherwise, in Sinkiang for several years."

The military assistance of advisers provided to Vietnam in the 1960s and El Salvador in the early 1980s drew sharp criticism. Walt W. Rostow, Lyndon B. Johnson's national security adviser during the Vietnam War, told the *Washington Post* in 1982: "We already have military advisers on the scene in El Salvador—though we have renamed them 'trainers.' Trainers, advisers, whatever—they are our tribute, our tangible contribution meant to make our commitment look good." Rostow added, "Of course, advisers in Vietnam proved inadequate to the task at hand, a task that wasn't carefully measured before the commitment was made."

The term is sometimes spelled *advisor*, on the *-or* analogy of *bettor*, influenced by *supervisor*, but the primary spelling is with an *e*.

affirmative action.   See QUOTA.

affluent society   an economic condition of the U.S.: rich and booming, with undertones of unrest from those not participating in the affluence.

The publisher's blurb on a reprint of John Kenneth Galbraith's 1958 book reads, "*The Affluent Society* has added a new phrase to our language." It has. Positioned between Walter Lippmann's *The Good Society* and Lyndon Johnson's GREAT SOCIETY, Galbraith's phrase was taken up by critics of America's effort to come to grips with

poverty at home. Yet his theme was not pessimistic:

> The affluent country which conducts its affairs in accordance with rules of another and poorer age also forgoes opportunities. . . . The problems of an affluent world, which does not understand itself, may be serious, and they can needlessly threaten the affluence itself. But they are not likely to be as serious as those of a poor world where the simple exigencies of poverty preclude the luxury of misunderstanding but where, also and alas, no solutions are to be had.

Just as "austerity" was the vogue word in England after 1945, "affluence" took the lead in 1958. "The Conservatives turned 'austerity' into a dirty word," wrote British author John Montgomery, "the Socialists said that 'affluence' was an upper-class word and that in any case Britain was not really affluent."

The most typical use of the phrase was made by Dr. Martin Luther King, Jr., in a 1963 letter written to ministers from a Birmingham jail: ". . . when you see the vast majority of your twenty million Negro brothers smothering in an air-tight cage of poverty in the midst of an affluent society . . . then you will understand why we find it difficult to wait." The phrase has been largely replaced in the 1990s by "the rich."

African-American.   See BLACK, POLITICAL USE OF.

again and again and again   an oratorical device of FDR's.

During the 1940 campaign, Wendell Willkie's charge that FDR was leading the nation into war annoyed the President and worried his advisers. Bronx boss Ed Flynn wired his demand that Roosevelt reassure the public that he was not going to send Americans into foreign wars.

"But how often do they expect me to

say that?" Roosevelt asked Harry Hopkins and speechwriter Robert E. Sherwood. "It's in the Democratic platform and I've repeated it a hundred times."

"Evidently," said Sherwood, "you've got to say it again—and again—and again."

Roosevelt liked the phrase, especially since his own pronunciation of "again" was distinctive in U.S. speech, rhyming with "rain" rather than "when." The sentence, "Your boys are not going to be sent into any foreign wars," was written, and Judge Samuel Rosenman wanted to add, as FDR had often before, "except in case of attack." Roosevelt disagreed: "If we're attacked it's no longer a foreign war." This was a mistake that he was later to regret.

In a famous Boston speech (see MARTIN, BARTON AND FISH) the President said: "I have said this before, but I shall say it again and again and again: Your boys are not going to be sent into any foreign wars."

Four years later, in the campaign against Republican Thomas E. Dewey, FDR found himself on the defensive because he had not used the "except" clause Rosenman had recommended. The President turned a minus to a plus by repeating the phrase originally associated with the statement: "I am sure that any real American would have chosen, as this government did, to fight when our own soil was made the object of a sneak attack. As for myself, under the same circumstances, I would choose to do the same thing again, and again, and again." The crowd, remembering, roared its approval.

The phrase continued to reverberate after Roosevelt's death in 1945. The *Chicago Tribune*, an arch-foe of FDR, recalled it in 1948 while lambasting somebody else: "The Great I Am, old Again and Again and Again himself, couldn't possibly have done a better job of bunking the American people. . . ."

against sin. See RUNNING AGAINST HOOVER.

ageism. See SEXISM.

agitprop obvious propaganda.

In a 1977 theater review in *Time*, T. E. Kalem wrote of a play by Bertolt Brecht: "One word of joyous warning. In *Happy End*, Brecht has dropped agitprop. The show has no redeeming social value save delight."

The word is a *Time* favorite. In 1935 the newsmagazine reported: "Far more serious, far more earnest is the Depression-born movement of workers' theaters which are currently putting on 'agit-prop' (agitational propaganda) plays in 300 U.S. cities."

Since the 1930s, the word has lost its hyphen in most dictionaries and in journalistic use. In a May 22, 1992, review of the film *American Dream*, Sam Roberts wrote in the *New York Times*: "Ms. Kopple [the director] insists that 'American Dream' is not agitprop but rather a tale of people fighting to preserve a value system that began to erode when worker loyalty was rewarded not with a raise but with a pay cut."

Like "apparatchik" (bureaucrat), the word has a nicely sinister foreign tone and is frequently used in newsmagazine description of political propaganda, in the U.S. and abroad. It comes from *agitatsiya propaganda*, which was a department of the Central Committee of the Communist Party in the former Soviet Union dealing with political persuasion.

agonizing reappraisal reassessment; phrase used by Secretary of State John Foster Dulles in December 1953, hinting at a possible change in U.S. policy toward its European allies.

By "agonizing reappraisal" Dulles meant that any basic change in American foreign policy that would weaken the position of American allies in Europe would be very painful to the U.S.; however, since the U.S. had growing commitments in Asia, Africa, and Latin America, it might have to shift its area of primary concern from the European continent to one of the other major areas of East-West conflict. He told the National Press Club: "When I was in Paris last week, I said that . . . the United States would have to undertake an agonizing reappraisal of basic foreign policy in relation to Europe. This statement, I thought, represented a self-evident truth."

The mouth-filling nature of the phrase has kept it in the political language long after its specific Europe-to-Far East meaning died. In 1965, Yale professor and leading "dove" (see DOVES) Staughton Lynd called presidential adviser McGeorge Bundy "that unagonized reappraiser."

Trying to persuade Israel to offer more concessions in his SHUTTLE DIPLOMACY, Secretary of State Henry Kissinger called for a "reassessment" of U.S. support, a word Jimmy Carter exploited in a 1976 debate with President Ford.

For other Dulles coinages, see BRINKMANSHIP; MASSIVE RETALIATION.

aide-mémoire. See POSITION PAPER.

alarmist one who attempts to arouse fear; sometimes a person who is easily frightened and transmits panic to others.

The word has been used many times in American history, especially prior to and during wartime. Of French origin (*alarmiste*), the word was coined during the French Revolution. It is attributed to Bertrand de Barère de Vieuzac, French lawyer and revolutionist who defended the Terror. It was used in England in 1794 by the Irish dramatist and orator, Richard Brinsley Sheridan, in a speech in Parliament: "Will the train of newly titled alarmists . . . thank him for remarking to us how profitable his panic has been to themselves, and how expensive to the country?"

In the U.S. the word was employed in 1840 by Representative White of Kentucky, quoted in the *Congressional Globe*: "Sir, open and bold usurpations never alarm me. I fear no danger of the perpetuity of this government, from the assaults of the manly tyrant or despot. I can look with some forbearance upon the unjust pretensions to power, asserted and defended upon principle yet, whilst I protest, I am no alarmist."

The word is current. "Alarmist cries about the lack of civilian control of the military," said Truman's Secretary of Defense Robert Lovett, ". . . deal with a strawman issue."

The retaliatory words are usually "smug" and "complacent," using the symbol of an ostrich with its head in the sand.

alienation disengagement and withdrawal from a society felt to be so oppressively paternal and centralized as to be suffocating to the individual. The word was popular as part of the terminology of the New Left.

The "Establishment"—especially the "Liberal Establishment"—is the foundation of the "power structure" (see WHITE POWER STRUCTURE), the shibboleth of New Leftese. A rejection of centralized, remote government and a hatred of Big Brother in business, university, and political life caused the new radical to disengage.

Historians of "The Movement" Paul Jacobs and Saul Landau explain that "'alienation' was used to describe the society's effects on its citizens, and American society was seen as the source of injustice and suffering everywhere."

The word broadened to a general sense of malaise and helplessness. Irving Howe, the late editor of *Dissent* and a critic of the new radicals, wrote that "alienation is not some metaphysical equivalent of the bubonic plague which constitutes an irrevocable doom; it is the powerlessness deriving from human failure to act. . . . Each time the civil rights movement brings some previously mute Negroes into active political life, each time a trade union extends its power of decision within a factory, the boundaries of alienation are shrunk."

Conservatives, hard-liners, and silent majoritarians have long considered the word alien to their taste, or the sort of language used by alienists, or "shrinks." *Washington Post* columnist Roger Rosenblatt caught this distinction in a July 1978 piece about the cultural differences of Democrats and Republicans, providing this table to show the different terms used for the same things:

DEMOCRATS	REPUBLICANS
total	corporate
influence	clout
truth	bottom line
disturbed	sloshed
innovations	software
alienated	jerk
hostile	jerk
defensive	jerk
sensitive	jerk
chairperson	"chairperson"

all deliberate speed.   See WITH ALL DE-LIBERATE SPEED.

Alliance for Progress   the name of John F. Kennedy's Latin American policy, first used by him in a campaign speech at Tampa, Florida, in October 1960.

Speechwriter Richard Goodwin re-

calls that the phrase was born while he was riding in a campaign bus rolling through Texas in September 1960. Trying to think of the words which would express for Kennedy what GOOD NEIGHBOR POLICY had expressed for Franklin D. Roosevelt, Goodwin's eye caught the title of a Spanish-language magazine left on the bus in Arizona: *Alianza.*

Kennedy agreed that "alliance" should be part of the phrase; but alliance for what? Goodwin telephoned Karl Meyer, one of the editors of the *Washington Post*, for suggestions. Meyer, in turn, called Ernesto Betancourt, a Cuban who had broken with Fidel Castro and was working for the Pan American Union in Washington. "Betancourt said to Meyer," Goodwin informs the author, "that it should be Alliance for something, and proposed several alternatives including 'development,' 'freedom,' 'progress,' etc., from which the final version was selected."

Ted Sorensen offers a slightly different version: "I suggested 'Alianza,' assuming that it had broader meaning than 'alliance' because it was the name of an insurance cooperative organized by some of our Mexican-American supporters in Arizona. A Cuban refugee and Latin America expert in Washington, Ernesto Betancourt, suggested through Goodwin the addition of 'para el progreso' (although for some time we mistakenly dropped the 'el'). The candidate liked it—and the Alliance for Progress was born."

In his Tampa speech Kennedy outlined the Alliance, which included "unequivocal support to democracy" and opposition to dictatorship; provision of "long-term development funds, essential to a growing economy"; stabilization of the prices of the principal commodity exports; aid to programs of land reform; stimulus to private investment and encouragement of private business "through mixing capital with local capital, training local inhabitants for skilled jobs, and making maximum use of local labor."

The Alliance for Progress was launched officially on March 13, 1961, before the Latin American diplomatic corps assembled for the occasion in the White House.

"I have called on all people of the hemisphere," said President Kennedy, "to join in a new Alliance for Progress—*Alianza para Progreso*—a vast cooperative effort, unparalleled in magnitude and nobility of purpose, to satisfy the basic needs of the American people for homes, work and land, health and schools. . . . Let us once again transform the American continent into a vast crucible of revolutionary ideas and efforts."

Any grand title lends itself to ridicule. Asked Senator Everett Dirksen in 1967: "Where is the Alliance? Where is the Progress?"

The Alliance for Progress was phased out as a program in the early 1970s.

alliteration repetition of the same consonant or sound in consecutive words; a device, when used obviously, to coin a slogan or catch phrase; when used subtly, to create a mood rather than a phrase.

"Apt alliteration's artful aid," a 1763 turn of phrase by Charles Churchill always used in discussing alliteration, has been neatly disposed of in Fowler's *Usage*: "not as good an example of alliteration as it looks, since only the first two a's have the same value."

When a Member of Parliament made a snide reference to "fancy franchises," Benjamin Disraeli replied: "Alliteration tickles the ear and is a very popular form of language among savages . . . but it is not an argument in legislation."

The careful culling of consonants to pack a punch in politics has long been in U.S. common use, for good and evil. An early Ku Klux Klan slogan: "Kill the Kikes, Koons, and Katholics." In the 1876 campaign: "Hayes, Hard Money and Hard Times." In 1884: "rum, Romanism, and rebellion."

In the twenties, politicians tried to emulate the alliterative success of Warren G. Harding, who made history with "not heroics but healing, not nostrums but NORMALCY, not revolution but restoration, not agitation but adjustment, not surgery but serenity, not the dramatic but the dispassionate, not experiment but equipoise, not submergence in internationality but sustainment in triumphant nationality."

In 1952 Adlai Stevenson, stung by the "Korea, Communism and Corruption" slogan of the Republicans (see K_1C_2), attacked all the alliterative phrases: ". . . each of the following words will appear at least once: crime, corruption and cronies; bossism, blundering and bungling; stupidity and socialism . . ."

"Words can do more than convey policy," John F. Kennedy wrote in 1961, using alliteration to show what he meant: "They can also convey and create a mood, an attitude, an atmosphere—or an awakening."

President Johnson, whose corniness of style offended many intellectuals, addressed a joint session of Congress five days after the Kennedy assassination and used alliteration subtly and effectively: "I profoundly hope that the tragedy and the torment of these terrible days will bind us together . . ."

Vice President Agnew, campaigning in 1970 to elect Republican congressmen, used "pusillanimous pussyfooters" and "vicars of vacillation" against Democrats, reaching a crescendo with NATTERING NABOBS OF NEGATIVISM. In so doing, he made alliteration a campaign issue, but the technique was contagious—Senator George McGovern denounced the Vice President's "foaming fusillades."

Ronald Reagan used EVIL EMPIRE. George Bush said America had "more will than wallet." In the 1992 debates, Bill Clinton trotted out "heartbreak and hope, more pain and more promise," while George Bush reached for "deadbeat dads," but muffed the alliteration with "deadbeat fathers."

all-out war. See TOTAL WAR.

all things to all men   deliberate ambivalence; two-facedness.

The phrase is used against a politician who makes conflicting promises in an effort to win an election or gain political advantage. But it can also be used to describe public speculation about an unknown quantity. Jonathan Daniels, former press secretary to President Roosevelt, wrote of the reaction to Harry Truman's ascension to the presidency when Roosevelt died: "He seemed all things to all men and all men including New Dealers and anti-New Dealers, Roosevelt friends and Roosevelt enemies, old friends and new ones, Pendergast politicians, Truman committee members, the eager and the ambitious, seemed to expect that he would be all things to them."

Deliberately seeking to be all things to all men is universally condemned but widely practiced; oddly, the phrase is related to concepts like "beauty is in the eye of the beholder" and "a face only a mother could love." In a work of art, varying interpretations of the same object is a mark of greatness; in diplomacy, a studied ambiguity is often admired; but in politics, a man who seeks to be all things to all men runs the risk of being nothing to anybody, and the practitioner can be attacked as "fuzzy" or for being "tall in the STRADDLE."

In 1826 Benjamin Disraeli entitled a chapter of his novel *Vivian Grey* "All Things to All Men," using the phrase in its current sense.

The duplicity in being all things to all men is readily admitted by the Christian saint who coined the term and perfected the art. In I Corinthians 9:20, Paul the Apostle says: "And unto the Jews I became as a Jew, that I might gain the Jews . . ." On that principle he ordered the circumcision of Timothy, to recommend his ministry to the Jews, despite Christianity's substitution of baptism for circumcision as a religious rite. He continues two verses later: "To the weak became I as weak, that I might gain the weak: I am made all things to all men, that I might by all means save some." He justifies the means by the end in 10:32–33: "Give none offense, neither to the Jews, nor to the Gentiles, nor to the Church of God: even as I please all men in all things, not seeking mine own profit, but the profit of many, that they may be saved."

The technique of being all things to all men has an effect not only on the voter but often on the candidate. "No man, for any considerable period," Nathaniel Hawthorne wrote, "can wear one face to himself, and another to the multitude, without finally getting bewildered as to which may be the true."

Unlike *one person, one vote* for ONE MAN, ONE VOTE, the male reference has not yet been replaced by a sex-neutral word; perhaps this is because the phrase is rooted in the King James translation of the Bible.

alphabet agencies   term used to describe, and mildly derogate, the succession of new agencies created by the early Franklin D. Roosevelt Administration.

New administrations, authorities, and corps appeared in sudden profusion in 1933: NRA (National Recovery Administration), TVA (Tennessee

Valley Authority), CCC (Civilian Conservation Corps), and AAA (Agricultural Adjustment Administration) were among the best-known.

The term was originally "alphabetical agencies," used in this manner by Bronx Democratic boss Ed Flynn: "A small informal committee was formed, however, consisting of [James] Farley, [Frank] Walker, [Louis] Howe and myself. We were primarily interested in taking care of the original group of people who had started out with us in the campaign prior to the convention in Chicago. This group became known as the 'FRBC': 'For Roosevelt Before Chicago.' Perhaps this was the first of the New Deal alphabetical agencies."

The alphabet-agency phrase gave color to the charge of excessive bureaucracy. Democrat Al Smith, disenchanted with Roosevelt, described the government as "submerged in a bowl of alphabet soup," and Republican campaigners at their 1936 convention carried an Alfred Landon banner that read "UP WITH ALF—DOWN WITH THE ALPHABET!"

Of course, the use of initials in describing government acts and agencies did not originate with the New Deal. In World War I, Great Britain's Defence of the Realm Act was called DORA, and the American Expeditionary Force was the AEF. In Germany in the twenties, *Nationalsozialistische* was shortened to Nazi, and in Russia the *Obyedinennoe Gosudarstvennoe Politicheskoe Upravlenie* (United Government Political Administration) was known as the OGPU. See ACRONYMS, POLITICAL.

Today, most commonly used, with mild amusement, is *alphabet soup*, named after a favorite soup of children, with noodles cut in the shape of letters of the alphabet. A September 1984 ad in *Business Week* informs the reader: "WATS, MCI, SPC, AT&T, RCA, USTC, ITT, WU, SBS . . . our brochure unscrambles the alphabet soup facing every cost-conscious company seeking the best mix of long distance communications services." In a book review on the KGB, *Time* magazine describes in October 1990 the spy agency's evolution "through an alphabet soup of designations (GPU, OGPU, NKVD, NKGB, MGB, MVD) to the present [KGB]."

always falling, never fallen. See ADMINISTRATION; SPLINTER GROUP; BUREAUCRACY.

amateurs professional politician's scornful word for citizens inexperienced in political campaigns and who show up near election time only, but without whom most campaigns would be doomed.

The obvious difference between an amateur and a professional in politics is the degree of experience. More important, however, is the willingness to work in what politicians call "the vineyards" on a year-round basis, without the glamour and excitement of a campaign.

Amateurs should not be confused with VOLUNTEERS, lower-level campaign workers who are recruited for canvassing, poll-watching, letter-writing, coffee-klatsch-giving, and clerical work. In a professional politician's eyes, amateurs include those top-level businessmen, labor leaders, attorneys, advertising and public relations people who are highly paid and highly successful in their own fields. Many have excellent political judgment and skills beyond most political pros; their enthusiasm and the transient nature of their politicking are their strengths, because they can speak their minds freely. Moreover, they are unaware of obstacles that the professional knows exist; through sheer ignorance of previous failure amateurs sometimes scale heights no sensible pol would ever attempt.

On the other hand, many of these high-level amateurs enter politics with a distaste for the pros, or "hacks" (see HACK) as they call them, and reject out of hand the experience and sensitivity leaders have to the often useful TROOPS.

Because there are a great many more amateurs than pros, the public image of the amateur is that of a fresh-faced, civic-minded citizen out to do battle for a cause he believes in, versus the cigar-chomping image of the political professional. For this reason, many candidates call themselves "amateurs." Adlai Stevenson kept referring to himself and his close associates as "amateurs" long after he and they had acquired solid professional standing. In the seventies, the wisest politicians were the "antipoliticians."

The appearance of being an amateur, then, is something to be coveted; the act of doing political work amateurishly is something to be avoided. "An important maxim to remember is 'Don't be an amateur,'" said Henry Cabot Lodge in 1951, when he was the unofficial campaign manager for Eisenhower in battle against the "pros" behind Robert Taft. "The job of being a professional politician, in spite of the odium which some persons have falsely attached to it, is a high and difficult one," Lodge continued. In that instance, as in others, amateurs acting professionally, in tandem with pros, were able to capture the nomination.

See VOLUNTEERS; for antonyms, OLD PRO; PROFESSIONAL.

amen corner automatic support; political followers who echo the party line.

The phrase *amen corner* predates the Civil War. *Harper's Magazine* commented in 1860 that "the Reverend Judson Noth, a local Methodist preacher, . . . was one of the best 'scotchers' that occupied the 'Amen Corner.'" The term applied to the part of a church or meetinghouse in which believers sat to respond regularly with "amen" to the preacher's words.

By 1884, a transferred sense was recorded in the *Congressional Record*: "When commiserated upon the fact that he was compelled to go to what is commonly known here as the amen corner, [he] frankly said that any seat in the Senate was better than none." The same publication referred a decade later to "those saintly Republican monopolists who sit in the 'Amen corner' of protected privilege."

Although the term was in decline by the late 1970s, it was revived and popularized by Patrick Buchanan before his 1992 Presidential campaign. A conservative columnist and former aide to Richard Nixon and Ronald Reagan, Buchanan criticized plans for Operation Desert Storm in a 1990 comment: "There are only two groups that are beating the drums for war in the Middle East—the Israeli Defense Ministry and its amen corner in the United States."

This position triggered charges that Buchanan was imputing a dual loyalty to Jewish American commentators and was thus anti-Semitic. The term, now usually lowercased, sparked a smaller controversy when the British television journalist David Frost interviewed Patrick Buchanan. Mr. Frost pronounced the interjection as AH-men; Buchanan countered with a long-A pronunciation of *amen*.

American boys orator's reference to American troops, now with a corny or chauvinistic connotation.

"We want to get the boys out of the trenches," said Henry Ford in 1915, explaining the purpose of his Ford Peace Ship. He did not add, Gilbert Seldes insists, "by Christmas," nor was he referring to "American boys" who were not yet fighting. Nevertheless, the idea of "getting the boys home by Christmas" has become a phrase used in every U.S. war since.

Isolationist Senator Burton K. Wheeler, on January 12, 1941, infuriated FDR by stating, "The lend-lease-give program . . . will plow under every fourth American boy." Roosevelt called this remark "the rottenest thing that has been said in public life in my generation."

In the Korean War, General Douglas MacArthur, dismissed by President Harry Truman, told a Senate investigating committee in May of 1951: "You can't just say 'Let that war go on indefinitely while I prepare for some other war,' unless you pay for it by the thousands and thousands and thousands of American boys."

Secretary of State John Foster Dulles made what Sherman Adams termed "an unfortunate blunder" in using the term during Senate testimony on the "Eisenhower Doctrine" in 1957. Senator Wayne Morse wanted to know why England and France were not brought into the U.S. stand in the Middle East so that "American boys won't have to fight alone." Dulles replied: "If I were an American boy, as you term it, I'd rather not have a French and a British soldier beside me, one on my right and one on my left." He regretted the undiplomatic remark immediately.

Lyndon Johnson probably regretted a "boys" statement made during the 1964 campaign that came back to haunt him. Urging a policy of restraint in Vietnam, on August 12 the President attacked those pressing for escalation: "They call upon us to supply American boys to do the job that Asian boys should do."

The use of "boys," rather than "men" or "troops," is obviously used to play on the emotions of parents; the word stresses the youth of the troops, thereby seeking to increase the public's

desire to protect them from bloody warfare. The word is so obviously loaded, however, that there has been a tendency in recent years to steer away from its use for fear of appearing demagogic. With the increase in the number of women in the armed services—and their resistance to being referred to as "girls"—the term "boys" is likely to fall into disuse.

Without the word "American," the word "boys" acquires a different political meaning. The boys are "the boys in the backroom"—the political bosses, a usage still current that can be traced at least as far back as 1879: "Stalwartism" [see STALWART], wrote *The Nation*, ". . . includes indifference or hostility to civil-service reform, and a willingness to let 'the boys' have a good time with the offices."

American Dream the ideal of freedom and opportunity that motivated the Founding Fathers; the spiritual strength of the nation.

Compared with the AMERICAN WAY OF LIFE or AMERICANISM, the American Dream is much less often satirized or considered corny. The American System is considered the skeleton and the American Dream the soul of the American body politic. The phrase has not crossed the usage line from sacred to sacrosanct.

In 1893 Katherine Lee Bates wrote in *America the Beautiful* of a "patriot dream that sees beyond the years." In 1960 the poet Archibald MacLeish, debating "national purpose," said: "There are those, I know, who will reply that the liberation of humanity, the freedom of man and mind, is nothing but a dream. They are right. It is. It is the American dream."

The American Dream, to some, stresses opportunity. Historian Matthew Josephson wrote of Thomas Alva Edison: "The rise of the former trainboy and tramp telegrapher from rags to riches was an enactment of the American Dream."

The black writer Louis Lomax applied it to equality: "It is the segregationists who are wielding the iron pipes and unleashing the savage dogs . . . if the law-abiding rather than the lawbreakers must cease and desist, then the American promise is but a cruel joke on humanity and the American dream dissolves to the most God-awful nightmare."

Both novelist Norman Mailer and playwright Edward Albee have attacked the phrase in titles. Richard Cornuelle, before becoming executive director of the National Association of Manufacturers, wrote a book in 1965 about the "private sector" called *Reclaiming the American Dream*. In it he said: "We wanted, from the beginning, a free society, free in the sense that every man was his own supervisor and the architect of his own ambitions. . . . We wanted as well, with equal fervor, a good society—a humane, responsible society in which helping hands reached out to people in honest distress. . . . For a long time it seemed that the free society and the good society could be realized together in America. This, I think, was the American dream."

The phrase defies definition as much as it invites discussion. As a force behind government philosophy, it seems to be interpreted by most users as a combination of freedom and opportunity with growing overtones of social justice. In the personal sense, its present meaning can be inferred from Richard Nixon's words accepting the Republican nomination in 1960: "I can only say tonight to you that I believe in the American dream because I have seen it come true in my own life."

See "I HAVE A DREAM"; LIFT OF A DRIVING DREAM; VISION OF AMERICA; "I SEE" CONSTRUCTION.

Americanism a patriotic political philosophy, sometimes abused by chauvinists; also, a word or phrase peculiarly American.

Theodore Roosevelt popularized "Americanism" in 1909 as "a question of principle, of purpose, of idealism, of character; it is not a matter of birthplace or creed or line of descent." It was Roosevelt who introduced or propagated the phrases "100% American" and "hyphenated American," and he often returned to this theme: "Americanism means the virtues of courage, honor, justice, truth, sincerity and hardihood—the virtues that made America."

The KNOW-NOTHINGS of the 1840s and 1850s used the word Americanism with a different meaning. They were opposed, for example, to waves of immigration and especially to Irish Catholics. Progressives, however, used the word in the opposite sense—to urge assimilation of immigrants into the U.S. social system.

Editor William Allen White wrote of the McKinley-Bryan campaign of 1896: "The election will sustain Americanism or it will plant Socialism." Huey P. Long, U.S. Senator and Governor of Louisiana, frequently accused of secret ambitions to become a dictator, once said that "if fascism comes to America it would be in a program of Americanism." See UN-AMERICAN.

In its linguistic sense, the word *Americanism* was first used in 1781 by John Witherspoon, a signer of the Declaration of Independence and president of the College of New Jersey, which became Princeton University:

> The first class I call Americanisms, by which I understand an use of phrases or terms, or a construction of sentences, even among people of rank and education, different from the use of the same terms or phrases, or the construction of

similar sentences in Great Britain. It does not follow, from a man's using these, that he is ignorant, or his discourse upon the whole inelegant; nay, it does not follow in every case that the terms or the phrases used are worse in themselves, but merely that they are of American and not of English growth. The word *Americanism*, which I have coined for the purpose, is exactly similar in its formation and significance to the word *Scotticism*.

H. L. Mencken, in *The American Language*, wrote: "The first American colonists had perforce to invent Americanisms, if only to describe the unfamiliar landscape and weather, flora and fauna confronting them."

American system   the private enterprise system; occasionally used as a euphemism for capitalism.

"Let the thirteen states," wrote Alexander Hamilton in *The Federalist* Number II, ". . . concur in erecting one great American system, superior to the control of all transatlantic force . . ." Twenty years later Jefferson wrote: "The history of the last twenty years has been a sufficient lesson for us all to depend for necessaries on ourselves alone; and I hope that twenty years more will place the American hemisphere under a system of its own . . ."

In 1824 Henry Clay applied the phrase in a speech defending the protective tariff of that year. To the Kentucky senator, the "American system" meant nationwide economic improvements combined with high tariffs that would reduce America's dependence on imports and expand its domestic market. Hamilton, Jefferson, and Clay used "American system" as a contrast to and defense against the European economy and polity. In the twentieth century the phrase lost its protective-tariff meaning and has been used in the sense of a political and economic philosophy of life. As Herbert Hoover said in 1945: "The American system of life is unique in the world . . . our American system also holds to economic freedom . . . we have proved the American system by raising the standards of life higher than any nation on earth." FDR, accused by Hoover of replacing this system with "regimentation," referred in 1936 to "the American system of private enterprise and economic democracy."

In a 1929 interview, underworld overlord Al Capone used the phrase in the current sense: "Don't get the idea that I'm one of these goddam radicals. Don't get the idea that I'm knocking the American system."

For more modern usages, see SYSTEM, THE; TWO-PARTY SYSTEM; PROCESS, THE.

American way of life   phrase now used mainly in FOURTH OF JULY oratory; earlier, a patriotic characterization of the free enterprise system. Often shortened to "the American Way."

One of the Alf Landon slogans in the campaign of 1936 was "Save the American Way of Life," an appeal against the then-radical measures of the New Deal. Telephone operators at the switchboard of the *Chicago Tribune* answered calls with "only—more days to Save the American Way of Life."

Writing in the *New York Times* in 1958, American diplomat and motion-picture executive Eric Johnston felt the phrase was a euphemism and attacked it head-on: "And the word is capitalism. We are too mealy-mouthed. We fear the word capitalism is unpopular. So we talk about the 'free enterprise system' and run to cover in the folds of the flag talk about the American Way of Life."

In *The Republican Establishment*, Stephen Hess and David Broder described the subjective reaction to the phrase in 1967: "Like Romney, there is in Nixon a small-town or Western accent on 'the American way' and 'the things that made America great' that seems stodgy to some and pleasantly nostalgic to others."

In the 1980s, the television producer Norman Lear used the phrase in the title of his liberal group, People for the American Way.

"Life style," a 1929 coinage of psychologist Alfred Adler, is a current substitute for "way of life."

amiable dunce pleasant but incompetent leader; comic or inept politician.

Clark Clifford, the Washington lawyer and former Secretary of Defense, originated this clownish configuration when he described President Ronald Reagan in 1981 as "an amiable dunce" with policies that would be "a hopeless failure." (Clifford's comments, secretly recorded at a Democratic PAC meeting in Averell and Pamela Harriman's Washington home, were reported in the *Wall Street Journal* by James M. Perry.)

A decade later the charge surfaced again in attacks on Dan Quayle. Martin Schram of *Newsday* commented in early 1992: "The Washington Post has birthed a study—in-depth, up-close and personal—which makes a case that Vice President Dan Quayle really isn't an amiable dunce. What Quayle seems to be, on a scale of 1 to 10, is an amiable deuce."

Levelers of the charge, however, are open to countercharges. Molly Ivins, political analyst for the *Dallas Times Herald*, asked at the end of Reagan's second term: "If, in fact, the President of the United States for the past eight years has been . . . an 'amiable dunce,' what does it say about the performance of the press that he's leaving office with one of the highest popularity ratings anyone can remember?"

The phrase bit its coiner in 1990. Mr.

Clifford, accused of wrongdoing as a director of a bank controlled by the corrupt Bank of Commerce and Credit International, asserted that he had been the unwitting dupe of the overseas bankers. A columnist noted that the superlawyer's defense against charges of venality was that he had merely been an "amiable dunce."

anaphora. See "I SEE" CONSTRUCTION.

angry young men a dissatisfied, impatient group of younger people in a party.

When John F. Kennedy achieved his nomination in 1960, he sought to heal the wounds within the party, especially those of older Democrats like Truman and Averell Harriman, who would have preferred Symington or Stevenson. The nominee explained why he wanted Harriman to second his nomination: "It will be useful for me to have someone who serves as a link to the Roosevelt and Truman administrations; also an older man. I don't want the Convention to think we're just a collection of angry young men."

The "anger" in the phrase was popularized by British dramatist John Osborne, whose 1956 play *Look Back in Anger* articulated a restlessness and disgust, a rebellion against the "old boy" philosophy prevalent in British politics and business, where young men were trained for careers that they later rejected or that the "Establishment" did not permit them to pursue. After the general use of this phrase began to wane, the political lexicon made "angry young men" its own.

Earlier, in 1951, the religious philosopher Leslie Allen Paul had entitled his autobiography *Angry Young Man*, but it was Jimmy Porter, the hero of Osborne's play, and Lucky Jim, the hero of Kingsley Amis's novel of that name, who became the prototypes of angry young men. The phrase crystallized a mood. Wrote critic Kenneth Allsop: "It was as if the pin-table ball that many young people feel themselves to be today, ricocheting in lunatic movement, had hit the right peg. Lights flashed. Bells rang. Overnight 'angry' became the code word."

Allsop went on to define the phrase with some eloquence:

The phrase Angry Young Man carries multiple overtones which might be listed as irreverence, stridency, impatience with tradition, vigour, vulgarity, sulky resentment against the cultivated and a hard-boiled muscling-in on culture, adventurousness, self-pity, deliberate disengagement from politics, fascist ambitions, schizophrenia, rude dislike of anything phoney or fey, a broad sense of humour but low on wit, a general intellectual nihilism, honesty, a neurotic discontent and a defeated, reconciled acquiescence that is the last flimsy shelter against complete despondency—a wildly ill-assorted agglomeration of credos which, although without any overall coherence, do belong to this incoherent period of social upheaval.

"Don't clap too hard, we're in a very old building," goes one Osborne passage. "Yes, very old. What about *that?* *(Pointing to Britannia)* What about her, eh—Madam with the helmet on? I reckon she's sagging a bit if you ask me."

In America, the phrase for a time eclipsed YOUNG TURKS, with which it is synonymous.

animal. See POLITICAL ANIMAL; BIRD DOG . . . KENNEL DOG.

animal spirits willingness to take risks; the entrepreneurial urge.

The term was first used in English by Bartholomew Traheron, in his 1543 translation of a text on surgery: "There ben thre kindes of spirites, *animal*, *vital* and *naturall*. The animal spirite hath his seate in the brayne, facultie of

movynge, and feelynge. It is called *animal*, bycause it is the first instrument of the soule, whych the Latins call *animam*."

By the eighteenth century, *animal spirits* was used in economics. William Wood reported in his 1719 *Survey of Trade* on "The Increase of our Foreign Trade . . . whence has arisen all those Animal Spirits, those Springs of Riches which has [sic] enabled us to spend so many millions for the preservation of our Liberties."

The economist John Maynard Keynes picked up this phrase and used it three times in his 1936 masterwork, *The General Theory of Employment, Interest, and Money.* Lord Keynes supported this risk-taking: "If the animal spirits are dimmed and the spontaneous optimism falters, leaving us to depend on nothing but a mathematical expectation, enterprise will fade and die."

Today's use of the term by political economists varies from "risk-taking investment" to "undue optimism," as in the following statement by economist Larry Kudlow, quoted in the October 15, 1990, issue of the *National Review*: "Most of all, the problem with current economic conditions is a decided lack of risk-taking and entrepreneurship. Instead of animal spirits, business and consumers seem possessed by a highly defensive belt-tightening strategy." The primary sense, however, connotes courage, the nerve that Daniel Defoe celebrated in his 1719 novel, *Robinson Crusoe*: "That the Surprise may not drive the Animal Spirits from the Heart."

ankle-biters annoying or small-minded bureaucrats; pettifogging aides.

This hyphenated term replaces the 1970s *munchkins* or the 1980s *weenies* (as well as the *mice* of the later Reagan years). It refers specifically to low-level workers who use minor details and bureaucratic red tape to hamper or annoy superiors.

Usually used in the plural, the noun *ankle-biters* comes from the name for trousers patterned after the fifteenth-century Hungarian pants of the Hussars, who wore the bottoms tucked inside stockings at the ankle. Since 1960, the term has been used as a slang term for young children, similar to the mock put-down of *rug rats* and *curtain climbers*.

By the early 1980s, the expression *ankle-biters* was used for adults as well. A 1981 *New York Times* report on changes being made at West Point stated that the general in charge "had enough prestige 'to keep the ankle-biters away.'"

From military use, the term was soon transferred to law and then politics. In 1990, Prince Bandar bin Sultan, serving as the Saudi Ambassador to the United States, told *Defense News* of his message to American troops in his country: "Don't let the ankle-biters get to you . . . You are defending your national interest and also you are defending great principles."

Sometimes two words, sometimes one word without a hyphen, the term *ankle-biters* is meant to demean the person being labeled as both small and irritating.

annuit coeptis.   See UNITED WE STAND.

antithesis.   See CONTRAPUNTAL PHRASES.

anti-Washington.   See RUNNING AGAINST HOOVER.

apartheid.   See SEGREGATION.

apostle of hate   one who espouses bigotry; a racist.

In the post–Civil War era, those who revived bitter memories of the war to advance their own political fortunes were accused of preaching a "gospel of hate." See BLOODY SHIRT. In 1876 *Harper's Magazine* rejected the use of the phrase: ". . . anybody in this centennial year . . . who does not confine himself to rejoicing over our happy reunion, but looks to see the facts, is [called] an apostle of hate, delighting to dabble his fingers in the gore of the bloody shirt."

At the 1950 convention of the Congress of Industrial Organizations held in Cleveland five years before the union's merger with the American Federation of Labor, the leaders of most of the member unions delivered attacks on the Communists in their ranks. Philip Murray, who was president of the CIO, called the Communists "apostles of hate" who lied "out of the pits of their dirty bellies." He was primarily attacking the Communists who had seized control of the United Electrical, Radio and Machine Workers Union.

Lyndon B. Johnson, in his speech to a joint session of Congress on November 27, 1963, five days after the assassination of President John F. Kennedy, made a moving plea for unity in dealing with racial bigotry and intolerance:

> The time has come for Americans of all races and creeds and political beliefs to understand and to respect one another. So let us put an end to the teaching and preaching of hate and evil and violence. Let us turn away from the fanatics of the far left and the far right, from the apostles of bitterness and bigotry, from those defiant of law and those who pour venom into our nation's bloodstream.

See RACISM.

appeasement   a policy of acceding to the demands of aggressors, which often leads to more demands and greater concessions; an attack word against those opposing intervention in the affairs of another country.

The word was first used in its pejorative political sense by Philip Henry Kerr, Marquess of Lothian, in a letter to the *Times* of London in 1934, objecting to "a limitation of armaments by political appeasement." The word had no negative implications for British Prime Minister Neville Chamberlain. When President Franklin D. Roosevelt wanted to call an international conference in Washington on peaceful relations (an idea of Sumner Welles's), Secretary of State Cordell Hull urged him to check it out first with Chamberlain. The British leader, whose tightly rolled umbrella became the symbol of appeasement in the thirties (see UMBRELLA SYMBOL), wrote the President that such a plan would undermine his own efforts at what he termed "a measure of appeasement" of Italy and Germany.

At the Munich conference on September 29, 1938, the Sudetenland and all vital Czechoslovakian fortresses were yielded to Germany. Chamberlain proclaimed "PEACE FOR OUR TIME" on his return, as Winston Churchill warned: "Britain and France had to choose between war and dishonour. They chose dishonour. They will have war."

Fowler's *Modern English Usage* includes appeasement in a group of "worsened words" whose meaning has gained a new stigma: collaborator, imperialism, colonialism, and academic. "There is no hint in the *OED* definitions of anything discreditable or humiliating about the word [appeasement]. No one thought any the worse of Aeneas for letting Cerberus [dog guarding the gates of Hades] have his usual sop."

The *Domesday Dictionary* gives an appropriately horrible example of the nature of appeasement in this selection from Leonardo da Vinci: "Of the bea-

ver one reads that when it is pursued, knowing this is to be on account of the virtue of its testicles for medicinal uses, not being able to flee any farther it stops and in order to be at peace with its pursuers bites off its testicles with its sharp teeth and leaves them to its enemies."

But Churchill, the man most identified as a foe of appeasement (see MUNICH ANALOGY; IRON CURTAIN), made these remarks to the House of Commons in 1950:

> It [no appeasement] is a good slogan for the country . . . however . . . it requires to be more precisely defined. What we really mean, I think, is no appeasement through weakness or fear. Appeasement in itself may be good or bad according to circumstances. Appeasement from weakness and fear is alike futile and fatal. Appeasement from strength is magnanimous and noble and might be the surest and perhaps the only path to world peace.

arena   place of political combat for the clash of ideologies and personalities.

The original Latin sense of arena is "a sandy place," the center of an amphitheater where sand was scattered to absorb the blood of gladiators.

Henry Clay of Kentucky, a three-time loser for the presidency, wrote in 1837 of being "again forced into the presidential arena"; William Jennings Bryan, destined to be a three-time loser, used the exact words sixty years later. Supreme Court Justice Charles Evans Hughes, asked to run against Woodrow Wilson in 1916, declared: "One who has accepted a seat on the Supreme Court has closed behind him the door of political ambition. It is such a man's duty to refuse any proposal to serve in the presidency, and no patriotic citizen would urge him to cast off the judicial ermine in order to enter political arena." Yet, he ran, lost, served as Harding's and Coolidge's

Secretary of State, and was appointed Chief Justice by Hoover.

A representative assembly, wrote John Stuart Mill in *Considerations on Representative Government* in 1861, has a responsibility "to be at once the nation's Committee of Grievances and its Congress of Opinions; an arena in which not only the general opinion of the nation, but that of every section of it, and, as far as possible, of every eminent individual whom it contains, can produce itself in full light and challenge discussion; where every person in the country may count upon finding somebody who speaks his mind as well or better than he could speak it himself . . ."

The word's use has been broadened in recent years to include all political and ideological spheres. President Lyndon Johnson defined Asia as "the crucial arena of man's striving for independence and order." President Eisenhower passed along to friends a copy of a quotation of Theodore Roosevelt's that returned the metaphor to the gladiator's blood-smeared pit:

> It is not the Critic who counts, not the one who points out how the strong man stumbled or how the doer of deeds might have done them better.
>
> The credit belongs to the man who is actually in the arena, whose face is marred with sweat and dust and blood; who strives valiantly; who errs and comes short again and again; who knows the great enthusiasms, the great devotions, and spends himself in a worthy cause; who, if he wins, knows the triumph of high achievement; and who, if he fails, at least fails while daring greatly, so that his place shall never be with those cold and timid souls who know neither victory nor defeat.

After his defeat in 1960, Richard Nixon sent reprints of his "Man in the Arena" quotation to hundreds of his friends; since that time, supporters of candidates who have lost elections have frequently sent it to their leaders in lieu of a condolence letter. The *Boston Globe* commented in 1992 on George Bush's use of the metaphor: "The man-in-the-arena tactic, pioneered by G.O.P. consultant Roger Ailes for Richard Nixon's 1968 campaign, served Bush well in his comeback victory in New Hampshire in 1988."

"Politics," wrote John F. Kennedy in *Profiles in Courage*, "merely furnishes one arena which imposes special tests of courage. In whatever arena of life one may meet the challenge of courage, whatever may be the sacrifices he faces if he follows his conscience—the loss of his friends, his fortune, his contentment, even the esteem of his fellow men—each must decide for himself the course he will follow."

See HAT IN THE RING.

are you any better off . . . ? question to measure voter satisfaction (or to trigger dissatisfaction) with political leadership.

The question evolved from a statement in declarative form, usually expressed in the negative. Bill Peterson, writing in the *Washington Post* in 1977, quoted a 1976 comment by Arnold Miller on the reform movement in miners' unions: "I don't think coal miners are any better off than they were three years ago."

The question, first of a series, was burned into the political lexicon by Ronald Reagan at the conclusion of his October 28, 1980, televised debate with President Jimmy Carter in Cleveland, Ohio. "Next Tuesday all of you will go to the polls," said candidate Reagan. "You'll stand there in the polling place and make a decision. I think when you make that decision, it might be well if you would ask yourself, are you better off than you were four years ago? Is there more or less unemployment in the country than there was four years ago? Is America as respected throughout the world as it was? Do you feel that our security is as safe, that we're as strong as we were four years ago?"

Richard Bryan, Nevada's Democratic attorney general, challenged campaign audiences in 1982 to consider the influence of a Republican Administration: "Are you any better off than you were four years ago? For the first time in 50 years the administration in Carson City has failed to protect us from the effects of a national recession."

Six years later, George Bush recalled the phrase as an indicator of comparative comfort in a campaign commercial. Broadcast on the eve of Election Day in 1988, the spot featured Bush saying, "Americans are better off than they were eight years ago, and if you elect me President, you will be better off four years from now than you are today."

The phrase came back to haunt him early in the 1992 campaign against Bill Clinton, as the economy headed into the "double dip" of recession. A poll in *Newsweek* on September 21, 1992, asked, "Are you better off now than you were four years ago?" The response showed 38 percent saying "yes," 58 percent "no." That was very close to the ultimate vote for and against President Bush.

The simplistic wording of the question has provoked some criticism. Michael McKeon, a political pollster, told the *Los Angeles Times* in 1989 that yes-or-no questions fail to reveal "big-time disenchantment," adding, "It's nothing you can put a number on, but there is a resentment out there that the lower middle class, and their children, aren't going to be any better off than they were."

Armageddon a great, final conflict between the forces of good and evil.

The term was popularized in a polit-ical sense by Theodore Roosevelt in 1912. At the time he formed the Bull Moose party so that he could run as an independent candidate for president, thus effectively splitting the Republican ranks (which supported Roosevelt's handpicked choice as successor, William Howard Taft) and enabling Democrat Woodrow Wilson to win. At the Bull Moose party's Chicago convention on August 5, 1912, amid singing of "Onward, Christian Soldiers" and other stirring hymns, "Teddy" thundered: "We stand at Armageddon, and we battle for the Lord!"

The reference, of course, was Biblical; in Revelation, chapter XVI, we read that at a place called Armageddon "there were voices, and thunders and lightnings; and there was a great earthquake, such as was not since men were upon the earth . . . and every island fled away, and the mountains were not found . . . and there fell upon men a great hail out of heaven . . ." Babylon was destroyed, Satan was cast into Hell, and "they were judged every man according to their works."

Geographically, the place is probably the mount of Megiddo, where the Canaanites fought and Josiah was slain; the associations of the spot are suitably warlike.

With the development of nuclear power, the possibility of total annihilation loomed larger. The word was thus used more and more often to describe World War III, and was the title of a novel by Leon Uris about the threat of war in Berlin. General Douglas MacArthur, accepting the Japanese surrender on the deck of the battleship *Missouri* in Tokyo Bay, September 2, 1945, used the word in its current sense, a battleground that would mean the end of civilization: "Military alliances, balances of power, leagues of nations, all in turn failed, leaving the only path to be by way of the crucible of war. The utter destructiveness of war now blocks out this alternative. We have had our last chance. If we will not devise some greater and more equitable system, Armageddon will be at our door."

armchair strategist one who pontificates about world events; a sofa sophist.

The phrase is similar to PARK-BENCH ORATOR, though the armchair strategist might be less inclined to take public positions. The similar phrase *Monday morning quarterback* implies carping criticism with the advantage of hindsight, but an armchair strategist might be enthusiastic as well as critical.

The armchair is a place of comfort from which to make discomfiting remarks; it can also be used as a symbol for laziness. Architect Frank Lloyd Wright claimed in 1938 that "armchair education" was the reason Americans did not realize how discredited their culture was in the eyes of the world.

Wrote *New York Times* correspondent Max Frankel in 1967:

> In most wars, the armchairs are full of generals refighting every battle, recasting every strategy, second-guessing every field commander. But Vietnam, being different in virtually every other sense as well, has also produced a new kind of kibitzer—the armchair diplomat. The galleries in this war are crowded mostly with mediators who second-guess, not the warriors but the negotiators, and spin many an intricate design not for winning the war but for ending it.

arrogance of power the theme of a school of criticism of U.S. foreign policy in the 1960s, questioning the basis of U.S. intervention in some conflicts abroad.

Senator J. William Fulbright of Arkansas, a Democrat, an intellectual, and the chairman of the Senate Foreign Relations Committee, had already raised questions about U.S. foreign policy for some time, as in his speech and book on "old myths and new realities." In 1966, he gave a series of lectures sponsored by the Johns Hopkins School of Advanced International Studies. One of them was entitled *The Arrogance of Power*, as was his subsequent book containing the same material.

Fulbright was skeptical about more than U.S. involvement in Vietnam and the Dominican Republic. He cast doubt on the validity of the nation's general posture in foreign affairs: "For lack of a clear and precise understanding of exactly what these motives [for going to war] are, I refer to them as the 'arrogance of power'—as a psychological need that nations seem to have . . . to prove that they are bigger, better or stronger than other nations." At another point, he elaborated: "One wonders how much the American commitment to Vietnamese freedom is also a commitment to American pride—the two seem to have become part of the same package."

In the debate over Vietnam, Martin Luther King, Jr., said in 1967:

> . . . honesty impels me to admit that our power has often made us arrogant. We feel that our money can do anything. We arrogantly feel that we have everything to teach other nations and nothing to learn from them. We often arrogantly feel that we have some divine, messianic mission to police the whole world. We are arrogant in not allowing young nations to go through the same growing pains, turbulence and revolution that characterizes our history . . .

In many of the attacks on Fulbright from both parties, the word "arrogant" was seized upon, as in this comment from Democrat James Farley: "It is arrogant indeed for a Senator to indict the character of the American people in time of war, or in the terms used by their enemy."

The phrase spawned other book titles: *The Limits of Power* by Eugene McCarthy, *The Abuse of Power* by Theodore Draper, *LBJ: The Exercise of Power* by Rowland Evans and Robert Novak, and *The Accountability of Power* by Walter Mondale, and may have had a hand in Stokely Carmichael's BLACK POWER.

Fulbright might have picked up the phrase from John F. Kennedy, who said in 1963: ". . . when power leads a man towards arrogance, poetry reminds him of his limitations . . ."

See POWER CORRUPTS.

arsenal of democracy   the role of the U.S. in supplying munitions to the nations opposing the Axis powers in World War II.

The phrase was coined by Jean Monnet, French ambassador to the United States, in a conversation with Supreme Court Justice Felix Frankfurter. Monnet was describing what would be the most effective assistance the U.S. could provide in the struggle against tyranny.

Frankfurter, struck by the forcefulness of the phrase, told Monnet it was precisely the sort that should be given world currency by President Roosevelt. He asked Monnet not to use it again, lest some other statesman pick it up. The Monnet phrase also came to the attention of John J. McCloy, an Assistant Secretary of War, and it was submitted in a draft speech sent by General Edward S. Greenbaum, executive officer of Undersecretary of War Robert Patterson, to FDR speechwriter Samuel I. Rosenman.

Roosevelt used it on December 29, 1940: "We must be the great arsenal of democracy. For us this is an emergency as serious as war itself. We must apply ourselves to our task with the same resolution, the same sense of ur-

gency, the same spirit of patriotism and sacrifice we would show if we were at war."

art of the possible   a frequent definition of politics stressing the need for compromise, asking not "what must be done" but "what can be done."

Political figures, under fire for falling short of attaining lofty goals promised in campaigns, often fall back on the phrase, "the art of the possible," as a useful defense. It emphasizes the practical nature of political rule, with its built-in checks and balances.

Ironically, the source is rarely quoted: the Chancellor of Prussia, Otto von Bismarck (1815–1898), defined politics as "the doctrine of the possible, the attainable . . . the art of the next best."

Adlai Stevenson called Lyndon Johnson "a master of the art of the possible in politics," citing Johnson's own stated philosophy on the subject: "Frequently in life I have had to settle for progress short of perfection. I have done so because—despite cynics—I believe that half a loaf is better than none. But my acceptance has always been conditioned upon the premise that the half-loaf is a step toward the full loaf—and that if I go on working, the day of the full loaf will come."

For another definition, see WHO GETS WHAT, WHEN, AND HOW.

as is well known.   See REPORTEDLY.

ask not.   See CONTRAPUNTAL PHRASES.

Atlantic Community   defined variously as "the Western world," the members of the North Atlantic Treaty Organization, or in its most limited sense, the U.S., Great Britain, and Canada.

Walter Lippmann popularized and

possibly coined the expression in his book, *U.S. War Aims*, published in 1944. According to Lippmann, the Atlantic Community includes not merely the U.S., the United Kingdom and France, but all of the South American and Central American nations, Mexico, Canada and Cuba, Spain, Portugal, Italy, Greece, Switzerland, Belgium, the Netherlands, Eire and Iceland, the Union of South Africa, Australia, New Zealand and the Philippines.

In May 1945, *Fortune* magazine commented: "If her rehabilitation results in prosperity, western Europe will merge with what Walter Lippmann, for lack of a better word, baptized the Atlantic Community."

The use of "community" in the sense of a group of nations with mutual interests can be traced to 1888, when English statesman Henry Molyneux Herbert, Earl of Carnarvon, made the prophetic observation: "We are part of the community of Europe, and we must do our duty as such."

See WEST, THE.

at that point in time a circumlocution for "then," carrying a spurious specificity.

In the mid-sixties, "at that point in time" and "in point of fact" were academic-bureaucratic vogue phrases. In a 1968 memo to his political colleagues, the author urged the Nixon campaign to eschew such words as "at that point in time," "exacerbate" and "eschew."

As the televised Watergate hearings began, young bureaucrats of the Nixon Administration's campaign committee (see CREEP) popularized the phrase, which is a combination of "at that point" and "at that time" and seemed more precise than the other vogue term "in that time frame."

But Raven McDavid of the University of Chicago wrote to *American Speech* magazine: "Since the beginning

of the Watergate extravaganza, academicians have amused themselves with the recurrent phrase *at that point in time* . . . however, much as it embarrasses me, it seems clear that the burrocrats [the misspelling was intentional] were following the lead of the intellectuals." He provided three citations, one from a 1970 *Daedalus*, an early 1973 use in the *American Anthropologist*, and a 1963 selection from Cleanth Brooks's literary criticism of William Faulkner: "he takes us back to a point in time three years before Isaac's act of renunciation."

The phrase was introduced at least a half-century earlier. The novelist Jack London wrote in *John Barleycorn* in 1913: "I did just what I did. I did what millions of men all over the world were doing at that particular point in time."

But the phrase was closely associated with Watergate language, and was used ironically by minority counsel Fred Thompson as the title of his book on the hearings. In 1977 a *Washington Star* editorialist was complaining about the disuse into which the plain words "now" and "then" had fallen. "Even as 'at this (or that) point in time' became an ungainly scrub for now or then, there was the sudden, curious intrusion of 'presently.' In the old days it meant 'in a short while' but now, we take it, means 'at this point in time' or, if you will pardon the expression, now."

Au H_2O = 1964 bumper-strip slogan advocating Barry Goldwater for President in 1964.

Much earlier Goldwater support came from young conservatives on college campuses; in all likelihood, a politically minded chemistry student came up with the formula Au (symbol for gold) H_2O (water) equals victory in 1964.

Anti-Goldwater people, pressing the TRIGGER-HAPPY charge, countered with bumper-strips or snipes reading "AuH$_2$O + 1964 = ♀ "

For a similar symbol, see K$_1$C$_2$.

austerity. See AFFLUENT SOCIETY.

autarkic adj., economically viable; in noun form, as "autarky," a nation able to claim self-sufficiency.

This word is most often confused with its homonym, "autarchy," which means autocratic or totalitarian rule. Autarky with a "k" is a nation able to take care of itself, its state of economic affairs brought about by a policy aimed at avoiding dependency on neighboring nations.

The word is old: Samuel Ward in *Balme from Gilead* wrote in 1617 of "the autarchie and selfe-sufficiencie of God." The spelling changed in the late seventeenth century to separate the word from its autocratic confuser.

The connotation of the word changed from good (self-sufficient) to bad (isolationist, selfish), especially during the early sixties, when "declarations of interdependence" became the vogue. In the seventies the word was frequently used in the foreign economic policy addresses of Henry Kissinger.

authoritarian. See TOTALITARIAN.

authoritative sources the screen behind which a political figure airs his views without being directly quoted or identified.

Authoritative sources, informed circles, and *a source close to* are all signals that a BACKGROUNDER has taken place.

The single most authoritative source is called the *highest authority*. He is the President of the United States wearing a beard and dark glasses.

See BACKGROUNDER; NOT FOR ATTRIBUTION; OFF THE RECORD; LEAK; DOPE STORY; SOURCES.

automobile metaphor frequently used economic word-picture.

The metaphor first appeared very soon after the introduction of the automobile; in 1907, *Emporia Gazette* editor William Allen White referred to Indiana Senator (and highly regarded orator) Albert Beveridge as "a geared-up speedster, a show car." Woodrow Wilson was reported to have said "the way to stop financial joy-riding is to arrest the chauffeur, not the automobile."

Adlai Stevenson, in the 1952 presidential campaign, used the metaphor to describe what he felt was a schism in the Republican party: "It is an ancient political vehicle, held together by soft soap and hunger, and with front-seat drivers and back-seat drivers contradicting each other in a bedlam of voices, shouting 'go right' and 'go left' at the same time. I don't envy the driver and I don't think the American people will care to ride in his bus very far."

The metaphor was used in an economic context by Richard M. Nixon in a 1965 speech to the National Association of Manufacturers:

This Administration has adopted a completely contradictory policy in dealing with the threat of inflation. It has tried to replace the market's law of supply and demand with Johnson's law of Comply and Expand: Business complies and government expands. But a policy that requires business to slam on the price brakes while government steps on the spending accelerator will in the end only produce a collision—and the family budget will be the casualty.

See OVERHEATED ECONOMY; USED CAR SALESMAN.

availability candidate potential; one who has all of the generally accepted qualifications for public office and would offend no significant voting bloc or region. Derogatory when used to describe overeagerness on the part of an unannounced candidate.

Harold J. Laski, the British political philosopher, wrote: "Out of all this complexity [of preconvention maneuvering] there has emerged the doctrine of 'availability.' The party needs a candidate who, positively, will make the widest appeal and, negatively, will offend the least proportion of the electorate. . . . He ought not to possess any nostrum which can be represented as extreme."

Warren G. Harding, the dark-horse candidate who became the Republican nominee for the presidency in 1920 after Governor Frank Lowden of Illinois and General Leonard Wood deadlocked the convention, was considered eminently available, ultimately offering "not nostrums but NORMALCY." He was a senator who had offended no one, from a large midwest state, personable, handsome, and in accord with the prevailing conservative Republican philosophy.

Hubert H. Humphrey was one of many possible vice-presidential candidates considered by Lyndon B. Johnson in 1964. When newsmen asked him almost daily whether he was in the running, Humphrey would say: "Nobody has to woo me. I'm old reliable, available Hubert." He added: "I'm like the girl next door—always available but you don't necessarily think about marriage."

In courtship, "available" is several cuts below "eligible" in terms of attractiveness; an available girl is one not often dated. In Al Capp's "Li'l Abner" comic strip, a character named Available Jones was constantly ready—for a small fee—to go anywhere and do anything. The pejorative sense appeared as early as 1837, in the *Baltimore Commercial Transcript*: "The New York papers are discussing whether the most talented, or the most available man, shall be re-elected as candidate for the next presidency."

Incumbent first-term Presidents traditionally seek to disguise their obvious availability to create suspense. William McKinley stated a position of qualified availability which has been restated often: "The question of my acquiescence will be based absolutely upon whether the call of duty appears to me clear and well-defined."

The best play on the word came around the time of its earliest political use. Scorning the selection of William Henry Harrison and John Tyler by the Whigs in 1840 without even the pretense of a party platform, Senator Thomas Hart Benton of Missouri said, "Availability was the only ability sought by the Whigs."

See JOB SEEKS THE MAN.

avalanche   staggering ballot majority; thunderous downpour of votes.

Avalanche, like *landslide* and *tidal wave*, is a word of natural disaster applied to political disaster. Early use, especially in the "Log Cabin and Hard Cider" campaign of 1840 of Harrison against Van Buren, applied to large crowd turnouts: "It was another of those glorious and enthusiastic Avalanches of the people," said a Harrison handout, "that distinguish this contest from any other in our National History." Later the word came to mean votes rather than people, and the New York *Tribune* wrote in 1888 of the Vermont Democrats being "buried under an avalanche of Republican ballots." This is the use that is current today.

Avalanche refers specifically to votes; *landslide* refers to an election as well as to votes. An election in which the popular-vote differential is not large, but the electoral-vote difference is considerable, is a landslide without an avalanche.

See DISASTER METAPHORS.

average man. See JOHN Q. PUBLIC; COMMON MAN, CENTURY OF THE.

awesome burden. See LONELIEST JOB IN THE WORLD.

axis an alliance of powers; specifically, the Axis Powers (Rome, Berlin, later Tokyo just before and during World War II).

The word comes from the imaginary line that can be drawn through a body, and around which that body could revolve. In its political context, the phrase is attributed to Benito Mussolini who said in 1936 that the German-Italian agreement was "an axis round which all European states, animated by the will to collaboration and peace can also assemble." In 1937, he added: "We have forced the axis to Berlin and Rome. That is the beginning of European consolidation."

The Rome-Berlin axis, around which Europe presumably was to revolve, became a familiar phrase in 1938; the *New York Times* wrote, "There was a triangle in 1914—Berlin-Vienna-Rome. There is an axis in 1938—Berlin-Rome." *Newsweek* added: "Central Europe regards the Rome-Berlin axis as an artificial structure."

Adolf Hitler made reference to the axis in his Sportspalast speech in Berlin while the Munich Pact was being negotiated, as he assured the world he had no more territorial demands: "This relation [between Germany and Italy] has long left a sphere of clear economic and political expediency and over treaties and alliances has turned into a real, strong union of hearts. Here an axis was formed represented by two peoples . . ."

With the entry of Japan into the war, the "axis" lost its metaphoric meaning as the alliance became—as it had been in the First World War—a triangle. But the Axis Powers were the opponents of the Allied Powers; "axis" for a generation meant only "Hitler-Mussolini-Tojo," and has only recently begun to regain its original meaning of any two powers in alliance, as in "a London-Washington axis."

When the link between two cities is a function of geography or trade rather than political alliance, the word "corridor" is preferred, unless a new name is devised; the "Boston-Washington corridor" is sometimes called "Boswash," sometimes extended to "Bosnywash" to include a third city, New York.

B

backbencher a legislator of low seniority; a steadfast supporter of party leaders.

In Great Britain's House of Commons, where this expression originated, a backbencher is one who goes down the line in regular support of the party leadership at the front bench of the House.

As the expression is used in the U.S., the "party regularity" emphasis is dropped, and the "low seniority" aspect is emphasized. In discussing the dark-horse possibilities of freshman Senator Charles Percy, *U.S. News & World Report* wrote in 1967: "Senator John F. Kennedy of Massachusetts was still a 'backbencher' in 1960 when he took the Democratic nomination away from older and more experienced figures in his party."

Reporting Republican Congressman Newt Gingrich's battles with the Democrats in the House of Representatives, the *New York Times Magazine* described in August 1992 his efforts to push the House Ethics Committee into "stiffer sanctions against various Democrats and one Republican, Representative Dan Crane of Illinois, who was censured for having sex with a House page. He put less formal pressure on two other backbench Republicans to resign."

See SHADOW CABINET.

back channel a secret or informal method at passing "sensitive" information, circumventing normal procedures.

At U.S. embassies around the world, the Central Intelligence Agency has long maintained a secret communications network designed to bypass normal State Department cable traffic. This is called "the back channel."

Such an officially unofficial, or discreet, mode is often useful in diplomacy. For example, when the government of Italy did not want Lieutenant General Vernon Walters to be President Nixon's official translator on a state visit to that country (because the Italians suspected General Walters of having financed a right-wing coup attempt with CIA funds), this request was passed by presidential advance men to the CIA in Rome, and back to CIA headquarters in Washington, rather than through regular diplomatic channels.

When National Security Adviser Henry Kissinger called a Nixon speechwriter into his office to discuss a presidential announcement of the failure of secret Paris negotiations with the North Vietnamese, he introduced the subject with a dramatic: "We have had a back channel in Paris."

Thanks to the Kissinger usage in matters other than the particular CIA back channel at embassies, the phrase became national security jargon for any clandestine method of reporting. In the White House in 1971 and later, a "series check" was the classified term for a method of monitoring embarrassing political information gathered by the National Security Agency in the process of eavesdropping on international communications. These data, of political rather than national security significance (such as a foreign leader's personal opinion of a traveling U.S. official), were screened out of the intelligence system and not passed to the CIA. Such reports entered a "back channel" in the White House, with distribution limited to the National Security Adviser, his deputy, and sometimes the President.

The phrase is now used in diplolingo to describe any alternative routing. In 1977, after Mr. Kissinger had left office, the *Washington Post* wrote: "Soviet Ambassador Anatoly Dobrynin confers often on the phone with Kissinger—a 'back channel' arrangement that reportedly has annoyed some at the White House."

But the original use is still basic CIA-ese. Reporting on corporate spying, *Time* magazine wrote on February 22, 1992: "Although the Agency is forbidden to provide information directly to private companies, it will usually pass on tips through back channels when it stumbles across foreign schemes to steal commercial secrets."

backer political supporter, especially a financial contributor.

One who will talk about you admiringly is a *fan*; one who will ring doorbells for you is a *worker*, or one of the TROOPS; one who believes in a cause is an *adherent*; one who will put his money where his vote is, is a *backer*—in substantial sums, a FAT CAT. A general term covering all these activities is a *supporter*, or a (name of candidate) *man*. The collective term is *following*.

According to William Riordan in 1905, George Washington Plunkitt of Tammany Hall explained how to begin to get backers: "I had a cousin, a young man who didn't take any particular interest in politics. I went to him and said: 'Tommy, I'm goin' to be a politician, and I want to get a followin'; can I count on you?' He said, 'Sure, George.' That's how I started in business. I got a marketable commodity—one vote."

backgrounder a press conference, or interview with a single reporter, where the information is on the record but the news source cannot be revealed precisely. See NOT FOR ATTRIBUTION; THUMBSUCKER; DOPE STORY; SOURCES.

Theodore Sorensen explained the John F. Kennedy rationale for backgrounders:

> During his Christmas holiday in Palm Beach, both in 1961 and 1962, he invited the two dozen or so regular White House correspondents accompanying him to a free-wheeling three-to-four hour "backgrounder". . . dividing each session into domestic and foreign affairs discussions. Year-end "think pieces" (which would have been written anyway, he reasoned) were in this way better informed of views attributable to "the highest authority" or "sources close to the administration." Although these phrases deceived no one in the know, it made for a freer and fuller exchange than would have been true of a regular press conference or a larger background group in Washington.

If the technique of the backgrounder is overused, the news media will be overloaded with phrases like "a spokesman said," "a source close to the White House revealed," "political circles are buzzing with the rumor that," etc. This leaves the impression that the top official concerned does not wish to stand up and be counted, which is true enough, but it is not the impression he wants to leave at all. During the 1966 dispute between the Kennedy family and the publishers of William Manchester's book, *The Death of a President*, there were daily Kennedy family backgrounders throughout the crucial week before serialization, causing columnist Murray Kempton to comment: "One always departs with his gratitude for a Kennedy backgrounder somewhat diluted by the wish that it hadn't left the foreground so foggy."

In December 1971 the *Washington Post* decided this technique was being abused; editor Benjamin Bradlee said "the public has suffered from this collusion between the government and the press." Particularly offensive was the "deep backgrounder" in which no source at all could be given. Presidential press secretary Ronald Ziegler promptly agreed: ". . . over the years, to some degree, government has misused backgrounders." Newsmen were cautious in their criticism, however, lest the pendulum swing back too far; the abolition of backgrounders would dry up important sources of news, especially in the foreign policy area.

A cartoon in *Frontier* magazine showed a dais of faceless men with a faceless master of ceremonies speaking at a podium labeled "Washington Press Banquet" and saying: "It's an honor this evening to present the nation's Highest Authority, who will be introduced by a Spokesman Close to the President, following remarks by a Highly Placed Official and A Usually Reliable Source . . ."

A speech delivered in May 1993 by Peter Tarnoff, Assistant Secretary of State for policy, to forty journalists on background was duly reported with no attribution. Because it was a departure from policy, the Secretary of State, Warren Christopher, disavowed it—without revealing the name of the official.

Lloyd Grove of the *Washington Post* reported reaction to the incident:

"This is a classic example of how Washington stands itself on its head because of allegiance to some really ridiculous rule about attribution," said Washington Post Co. Vice President Benjamin C. Bradlee, who as the paper's executive editor was a continual critic of backgrounders—once running a photo of then–Secretary of State Cyrus Vance to accompany a story based upon such a briefing, with a caption identifying Vance as "a senior State Department official traveling on the secretary's plane."

"Everybody knows who he is," Bradlee added, referring to the current anonymous briefer. "Who are we supposed to be keeping secrets from now that we don't have the Commies? It's the American people."

When a reporter files a story from a region or city not recently covered, he sometimes reports on the background of events in that area, but that is properly called a *situationer* and not a "backgrounder."

backlash civil rights recoil: the reaction by whites against the advancement of blacks when its implications—especially in job competition—hit close to home.

For eighty-three days—from February 10 to June 19, 1964—the Senate debated the Civil Rights bill passed by the House. During that time, "backlash" was given political meaning.

American Speech magazine has provided two leads as to its first use. This sentence appeared in the *Nation's Business* magazine (April 1964): "This sensitivity for such pocketbook issues has politicians of both parties jittery over the possible backlash from civil rights developments." Tait Trussell, managing editor of the business magazine, tracked down the writer of the line, John Gibson. "I talked to John about the source of the word 'backlash,'" Trussell writes of the author. "He believes it was used by Richard Scammon, the director of the Census. However, both John and I seem to recall that the word was being bandied about elsewhere at the time."

Scammon's recollection: "Maybe Oliver Quayle started it; maybe I did. But most likely it just crept into conversations from several sources, like the 'As Maine goes, so goes Vermont' phrase of election night, 1936."

The second lead was in the *New York Times*, on April 9, 1964. Reporter Earl Mazo wrote: "In the immediate aftermath of the Wisconsin voting it is obvious that a backlash against the current civil-rights drive has materialized." Mazo responded to a query: "I remember using it, of course, but my mind is hazy as to how it came about. I know I was reaching for a word more vivid than 'reaction' that meant reaction. I believe, in that regard, I occasionally used the words 'boomerang' and 'backfire.' I have no idea, Bill, whether I had heard or seen 'backlash' elsewhere before using it myself."

The reason for dragging the reader up and down these blind alleys is to illustrate the "phantom coinage" phenomenon, when a word or phrase seeps into the language without a single source, apparently by osmosis.

However, until another researcher comes up with earlier usage, credit for the word's popularization belongs to Washington columnists Rowland Evans and Robert Novak. After the Birmingham, Alabama, riots in the summer of 1963, President Kennedy's depressed-areas bill was defeated in the House. In the June 16, 1963, *New York Herald Tribune*, Evans and Novak wrote that this defeat was due to other causes and was not "the first backlash of civil rights turmoil." The columnists used the word frequently afterward, and—like Walter Lippmann with Herbert Bayard Swope's COLD WAR and the Alsops with EGGHEAD and PECKING ORDER—were the popularizers.

Mr. Novak tells the author they took the word from a usage earlier that summer of 1963 by economist Eliot Janeway, which Mr. Janeway corroborated. He had been discussing the impact of automation on white and black workers, and pointed out that in any economic downturn there was likely to be a breakup in the longtime political alliance between civil rights groups and labor unions, as white workers "lashed back" at competition from blacks for the remaining jobs.

Writing in *Look* in September 1964, Fletcher Knebel gave one derivation of the term: "'This Thing' was the now famous backlash, a word long used by sports fishermen. The angler casts his lure, watches it fly in a silver arc across the water. Suddenly the lure stops and whips backward toward the fisherman, while a snarl of line fouls his reel. . . . Transferred to the world of politics, the white backlash aptly describes the resentment of many white Americans to the speed of the great Negro revolution, which has been gathering momentum since the first rash of sit-ins in early 1960."

An angrier definition was provided by Brad Cleaveland of the University of California's Free Speech Movement: ". . . the phrase 'white backlash' is the simplest way to say 'the bigotry of the majority' . . . the real meaning of 'white backlash' is 'Don't bug me nigger . . . you're buggin' me with that civil disobedience . . . now stop that or we'll show you who has the tear gas, cattle prods, and shotguns!!!'"

The word was used frequently in the 1964 presidential campaign; a SILENT VOTE motivated by the white backlash was supposed to materialize, but never did to the extent some expected. "For every backlash the Democrats lose," said Lyndon Johnson, "we pick up three frontlash."

backup candidate. See FALLBACK POSITION; DARK HORSE.

bafflegab jargon providing more obfuscation than enlightenment, as is often found in government reports and other official statements.

Bafflegab began appearing in newspapers and conversation in the early 1950s. In a 1952 newspaper interview, Milton Smith, then assistant general counsel of the U.S. Chamber of Commerce, claimed authorship. Smith explained: "I decided we needed a new and catchy word to describe the utter incomprehensibility, ambiguity, verbosity and complexity of government regulations." Before hitting on *bafflegab*, Smith said, he considered "burobabble" and "gabbalia."

Smith's contribution surfaces from time to time, as in a 1967 column by Sylvia Porter, the economics writer. She relegated to "this year's batch of bafflegab" such phrases as "healthy slowdown" and "rolling readjustment." Other euphemisms for recession include "crabwise movement," "high-level stagnation," "period of basic readjustment," and "minislump."

Time magazine in 1968 published a "baffle-gab thesaurus" (unnecessarily hyphenating the word) based on a Royal Canadian Air Force collection of fuzzy phraseology. A ringing, three-word phrase, guaranteed to impress, can be assembled from the spare parts in each of these three categories:

	A	B	C
0)	Integrated	Management	Options
1)	Total	Organizational	Flexibility
2)	Systematized	Monitored	Capability
3)	Parallel	Reciprocal	Mobility
4)	Functional	Digital	Programming
5)	Responsive	Logistical	Concept
6)	Optional	Transitional	Time-Phase
7)	Synchronized	Incremental	Projection
8)	Compatible	Third-Generation	Hardware
9)	Balanced	Policy	Contingency

In popular usage, *bafflegab* runs behind GOBBLEDYGOOK and OFFICIALESE. Also see PENTAGONESE; ECONOMIC JARGON; CIA-ESE.

bagman intermediary in a political payoff; one who carries the bribe from the beneficiary of a corrupt deal to the grafter. Not to be confused with "black bag job" (see CIA-ESE).

The courts have decided that the word is libelous. Harlem Congressman Adam Clayton Powell described Mrs. Esther James as a "bagwoman" in the policy racket, but chose to make the charge outside the libel-proof halls of Congress. The woman sued for libel and was awarded damages. The congressman spent years avoiding payment and ducking service of subpoenas, requiring him to reside outside his district and country, ultimately followed by House exclusion.

In the administration of Mayor William O'Dwyer of New York, a minor officeholder named James Moran was widely reputed to be the bagman, and went tight-lipped to prison. Newsmen Norton Mockridge and Robert Prall wrote in *The Big Fix*: "Nobody believed, either, that Jim Moran kept all the money he collected. For many years he had been known as a bagman, which in political jargon, is literally the man who carries the bag or boodle for somebody higher up. And the bagman never gets to keep the big money."

Another, more recent, use of bagman is as the military officer who follows the President, carrying the "football." See FOOTBALL, POLITICAL.

Bailey Memorandum document alleged to have been written by John Bailey, Connecticut Democratic State Chairman (later National Chairman), demonstrating how useful a Catholic could be on the national ticket.

The Bailey Memorandum was used in an attempt to gain the 1956 vice-presidential nomination for John F. Kennedy, who lost to Senator Estes Kefauver. Contrary to the belief at the time, the document was written by Theodore Sorensen, Kennedy's closest aide.

The sixteen-page memorandum of statistics, quotations, analyses, and arguments sought to answer Democratic fears of "anti-Catholic" votes by raising hopes of recapturing a greater share of the votes of Catholics, especially among conservatives in urban areas who had voted for Eisenhower in 1952. The memo held that a vice-presidential nominee of the Catholic faith would do more to swing states with large electoral-vote totals into the Democratic column than any non-Catholic candidate from the south or farm belt.

When the word of the document spread to newsmen and politicians, Kennedy arranged Bailey's assertion of authorship to avoid being accused of personally injecting a religious issue.

The memorandum controversy again mushroomed during the 1960 presidential election when Republicans reprinted it as an example of a blatant appeal to "Catholic voting blocs." Kennedy, fearing a "Protestant bloc,"

instructed his aides not to talk publicly in terms of Catholic voting strength.

Sorensen wrote in 1965: "The Bailey Memorandum oversimplified, overgeneralized and overextended its premise in order to reach an impressive conclusion." Many Republicans sadly disagreed.

balanced ticket a slate of candidates nominated so as to appeal to as many voter groups as possible. Typical considerations in balancing a ticket: the nominees' geographic origin, race or religion, type of experience, position on specific issues, and COLORATION.

In American Presidential politics, the home state of the candidates for President and Vice President was, historically, the weightiest item on the scale. More than local chauvinism was involved; whether the issue was slavery or free silver, tariffs or manifest destiny, sectional interests came into play. As national politics grew more complicated—and sophisticated—so did the question of balance. Joe Martin, former House Republican Leader, recalled his 1940 sales presentation to Wendell Willkie on behalf of Senator Charles McNary as a vice-presidential candidate. "You are known as a utilities man; McNary has sided with the public power boys. You're supposed to represent big business interests; McNary was the sponsor of the McNary-Haugen farm bill. You aren't supposed to know much about the legislative process; McNary is a master of it. I think you'd make a perfect team." Neither Willkie nor McNary liked the other's politics, but in the spirit of balance they ran together.

The phrase has even been applied to foreign politics where no election in the American sense is involved. In 1962, Averell Harriman of New York, then Assistant Secretary of State for Far Eastern Affairs, was attempting to establish a coalition government for

Laos that would both bring stability to that country and satisfy the great and interested powers. His controversial solution: a TROIKA consisting of rightists, neutralists, and pro-Communists. President John Kennedy defended Harriman's efforts, saying: "He's putting together a New York State balanced ticket."

Geographical balance is often sought on a Presidential ticket, but it is useless. In 17 out of 24 national elections since the Civil War, vice-presidential candidates on the losing ticket failed to carry their home states. Within recent years, Henry Wallace could not deliver Iowa for Roosevelt in 1940, Estes Kefauver failed to swing Tennessee for Stevenson in 1956, Earl Warren did not carry California for Dewey in 1948, and Henry Cabot Lodge lost Massachusetts to Kennedy in 1960. In 1992, Bill Clinton of Arkansas ignored the tradition to choose Al Gore of Tennessee; the success of the Clinton-Gore ticket further eroded the idea of geographical balance.

In local politics, balance is struck between religion, national origin, and, more recently, race. Most big cities remain not-very-melted pots in which as many lumps as possible must be appealed to. Edward Costikyan, the former leader of Tammany Hall, spoke for the politicians' consensus when he defended the practice of giving the public a *"representative* representation." In *Behind Closed Doors*, Costikyan recalled the apocryphal DREAM TICKET for the Upper West Side of Manhattan when that section was a prosperous ghetto: "one reform Jew, one orthodox Jew and one agnostic Jew."

balance of power the theory that peace is best ensured when rival groups are equal in strength.

An object of international diplomacy for centuries, the term was in use as early as 1700. Alexander Pope wrote a poem entitled "The Balance of Europe" in 1715: "Now Europe's balanc'd, neither side prevails;/For nothing's left in either of the scales." The British, in particular, sought to apply it to maintain a relatively durable peace from 1871 to 1914, with a balance between the Triple Alliance (Germany, Austria, Italy) and the Triple Entente (Britain, France, Russia).

In the U.S., political writers often use the expression to discuss the CHECKS AND BALANCES among the states of the Union or the three branches of government. "Every project," wrote John Adams in 1789, "has been found to be no better than committing the lamb to the custody of the wolf, except that one which is called a balance of power." Before the Civil War, it referred to a balance between the slaveholding and the free states.

The phrase is also applied to disputes among the branches of the government. Franklin D. Roosevelt said in 1937, while discussing his plan to pack the Supreme Court (see NINE OLD MEN), that over the last half-century "the balance of power between the three great branches of the Federal Government has been tipped out of balance by the courts in direct contradiction of the high purposes of the framers of the Constitution."

Occasionally it has been scorned as a shaky way of keeping peace. Thus, Winston Churchill, in his famed Fulton, Missouri, IRON CURTAIN speech in 1946, declared that if the English-speaking Commonwealth joined forces with the U.S., "there will be no quivering, precarious balance of power to offer its temptation to ambition or adventure. On the contrary, there will be an overwhelming assurance of security." In his 1961 inaugural, John F. Kennedy called on both sides in the Cold War to "join in creating a new endeavor—not a new balance of power, but a new world of law, where the strong are just and the weak secure and the peace preserved."

Kennedy later came to see the balance of power as the only real way of minimizing the temptation to adventure, as Churchill put it. During the Cuban missile crisis, Kennedy said: "If we suffer a major defeat, if they suffer a major defeat, it may change the balance of power." Such a change, he said, "also increases possibly the chance of war."

With the advent of nuclear weaponry, another phrase was often used in place of balance of power—"balance of terror," coined by Canadian Prime Minister Lester Pearson in 1955.

bald eagle the national symbol of the United States; frequent nickname of baldheaded political leaders.

Though references to bald eagles can be traced to 1836, the first patriotic reference is found in the June 19, 1873, *Newton Kansan*: "Let patriots everywhere . . . prepare to do the clean thing by Uncle Sam and his bald-headed eagle."

The bald eagle has been on the Great Seal of the United States since 1782, an olive branch with thirteen olives in its right claw, thirteen arrows in the left (after the thirteen original colonies), and a banner in its beak saying "E Pluribus Unum" (From Many, One). It can be found on the back of every dollar bill. Kennedy aide Ted Sorensen used it metaphorically in 1963: "How does a President choose, for example, in a moment of crisis, between the olive branch of peace (clutched in the right talon of the eagle on his Seal) and the arrows of war (which are clutched in the left)?"

The symbol has also been called "the spread eagle" because of its outstretched wings. The *North American Review* after the Civil War defined "spread-eaglism" as "a compound of

exaggeration, effrontery, bombast, mixed metaphors, platitudes, defiant threats thrown at the world, and irreverent appeals to the Supreme Being."

Of course, the "bird of Washington" is only white-headed, not bald; but James M. Husted was cited by Charles Ledyard Norton in 1890 as "the Bald Eagle of Westchester County"; Robert A. Lovett, Secretary of Defense under Truman and a State Department veteran, was the "Bald Eagle of Foggy Bottom" (see FOGGY BOTTOM).

The bald eagle on the Presidential Seal has had a curious history. Heraldic custom calls for eagles on coats of arms to be facing to the right, so that the bird will be facing forward, toward the flagstaff, when flown on a flag ahead of marching troops. During the Administration of President Rutherford B. Hayes, when the Presidential Seal originated, a designer became confused copying the Great Seal of the United States, and turned the presidential eagle's head to the left—looking backward, as it were, while the nation marched ahead.

This national embarrassment could have continued without rectification were it not for President Franklin Roosevelt's concern about the number of stars on the Commander in Chief's flag. As a White House release of October 25, 1945 delicately put it: "It seemed inappropriate to President Roosevelt for the flag of the Commander in Chief to have only four stars when there were five stars in the flags of Fleet Admirals and Generals of the Army, grades which had been created in December 1944."

As this oversight was being corrected, Arthur E. DuBois, chief of the Heraldic Section of the Office of the Quartermaster General of the Army, pounced on the wrong-headed eagle that had been troubling heraldic specialists for years. He designed a new Presidential Coat of Arms, Seal and

Flag, with the bald eagle facing toward the right. In heraldry, that is the "direction of honor," which has no ideological right-left significance but has to do with the way the eagle is facing on the flag of honorably marching troops (and, presumably, is why a hostess seats her guest of honor on her right, and why diplomatic protocol calls for guests at a State dinner to speak first to the dinner partner on the right).

The new flag and seal were completed after President Roosevelt's death. President Truman, who unfurled it for the first time publicly on October 25, 1945, called attention to a more important symbolic change. "Now raise that flag up, there," he said to his military aide, General Harry Vaughan, who was holding the previously used presidential flag. "This flag here—in President Wilson's time there were two flags for the President, an Army flag with a red star and a Navy flag for the President with a blue star. President Wilson ordered a single flag for the President, and this was the result of that [*General Vaughan displays flag*] with the white eagle facing toward the arrows, which is the sinister side of the heraldic form, and no color." "This new flag [*to General Vaughan*] if you will raise that one up, now you will see—you can see the difference. . . . This new flag faces the eagle toward the staff which is looking to the front all the time when you are on the march, and also has him looking at the olive branches for peace, instead of the arrows for war; and taking the 4 stars out of the corner and putting 48 stars around the Presidential seal."

In the abbreviated version of this story told to visitors on White House tours, President Roosevelt is said to have had the seal changed so that the eagle would be facing the olive branch of peace rather than the arrows of war. That is true as far as it goes, but it was Harry Truman who caught the war-to-

peace significance of the turning of the head of the American eagle.

See PARTY EMBLEMS; UNCLE SAM.

Balkanization.   See VIETNAMIZATION.

ballbuster.   See NUT-CUTTING.

balloon goes up   signal of impending campaign; indication of political excitement to begin.

The release of a hot-air balloon signaled to British forces in 1915 that the artillery should begin firing.

The phrase floated over into American military slang and became the term to indicate the start of any activity. In advertising, for example, "The balloon goes up next week" would signal the start of a new ad campaign.

Two centuries ago, the phrase *political balloon* referred to empty or inflated discourse in politics. *Gentleman's Magazine* of London commented on such inflated claims in 1784: "All these are political squibs, or balloons, filled with inflammable air, which have been dispersed *gratis* in town and country, and having now evaporated, will probably be assigned to oblivion." See TRIAL BALLOON.

The use of *balloon goes up* has not strayed too far from its military origins, however. When the United States prepared to attack Iraq in 1991, Secretary of State James A. Baker 3d duly informed Bandar bin-Sultan, the Saudi Ambassador, of the military action: "The balloon is going up. This is your notification."

ballot-box stuffing   vote fraud; originally, the illegal insertion of paper votes into the ballot box, with or without the connivance of local election officials.

The practice flourished in the days of Boss Tweed and the heyday of Tammany Hall in New York City. With the introduction of voting machines the practice was curtailed, however, leaving the phrase to mean any attempt to falsify the vote count.

Both practice and phrase appear to have started in San Francisco just after the Gold Rush. An advanced form of ballot-box stuffing was described in the House of Representatives in 1882 by Benjamin Butterworth of Ohio:

> They had been accustomed to have a box so constructed that the lid would pull out in a groove part of the way, and on election morning pulling the lid part way back, so the bottom of the box could be seen, the judge, or one of them, would say, "You see there is nothing in the box." The box would be closed, and the balloting proceed. True, the box would appear to be empty, while under the lid in the top of the box two or three hundred tickets would be fastened. The box being shut with a thud, the tickets would fall down.

Some historians say that ballot-box stuffing in New York City may have cost James G. Blaine, Republican, the presidency of the United States in 1884. Blaine lost New York State by a margin of 1,143 votes for Grover Cleveland, the Democratic candidate, out of more than 1,100,000 cast. In the Electoral College, Cleveland obtained 219 votes to 182 for Blaine; had Blaine received New York's 36 electoral votes, he would have been elected. According to Henry L. Stoddard, editor and publisher of the *New York Evening Mail*, Tammany politicians arranged for "Battle Ax" Paddy Gleason in Long Island City and John Y. McKane in Coney Island to stuff the ballot boxes to make up Cleveland's 1,143 vote margin of victory.

In the Kennedy-Nixon campaign of 1960, Nixon campaign chairman Leonard Hall was incensed at what he considered flagrant ballot-box stuffing in Texas, some other parts of the South, and particularly Cook County, Illinois. Since a switch of these narrowly won states would have swung the election to Nixon, Hall urged that Nixon declare the election "stolen" and dispute the result, which Nixon declined to do.

In the January 16, 1966, *New York Post*, writer Paul Hoffman recounted the classic story about ballot-box stuffing, updating it to make his central figure "Uncle Dan" O'Connell, a veteran political leader of Albany: "'Uncle Dan,' President Johnson, and Lady Bird were sailing down the Potomac all alone when their boat sprang a leak. Each grabbed for the lone life preserver. "Let's settle this the American way, by secret ballot," suggested the President. "Uncle Dan won it the Albany way . . . his vote was 17 to 2."

See CEMETERY VOTE.

ballyhoo as a verb, to create enthusiasm; to promote colorfully; to "beat the drums"; to tout. As a noun, the material of such efforts.

"Last of the professions on the Midway," wrote *World's Work* in 1901, "are those of the 'barker,' 'ballyhooer' and 'spieler.'" The circus origin now applies to stunts, "pseudo-events," and exploitation, both commercial and political, using more modern techniques. Warned FDR in his second fireside chat: "We cannot ballyhoo our way to prosperity." The *Atlantic Monthly* in March 1948 wrote of candidates that are "ballyhooed, pushed, yelled, screamed and in every way propagandized into the consciousness of the voters."

Wilfred Funk believes the word is traceable to the village of Ballyhooly, in Cork County, Ireland, where, according to the March 1934 *Congressional Record*, "residents engage in a most strenuous debate . . . and from the violence of those debates has sprung forth a word known in the English language as ballyhoo."

Eric Partridge agrees: "In Erse, *bally* (or *bal*) means 'a dwelling, a village' and it occurs in scores of Celtic place-names. The precise relationship to this glorified village is uncertain: but American colloquial and slangy speech is 'full of' references to Irish joviality and noisy high-spirits."

A synonym is HOOPLA, which politicians regard as a necessary evil to generate artificial fervor that hopefully ignites genuine fervor. See BANDWAGON. An early edition of *Bartlett's Quotations* indicates "hoopla" as having been a driver's hurrying-up to his horse, a meaning that survives in the political sense of a stimulus to excitement.

baloney nonsense, malarkey; stronger than blarney, more politically palatable than unprintable expletives.

"No matter how thin you slice it," said Alfred E. Smith in 1936, "it's still baloney."

It was one of the New York governor's favorite words. Ten years before, when asked by a cameraman at a cornerstone-laying ceremony to actually lay a brick for the movies, he had snarled, "That's just baloney. Everybody knows I can't lay bricks." Expressing his opposition to FDR's rumored plan to take the U.S. dollar off the gold standard in 1933, he was widely quoted as saying, "I am for gold dollars as against baloney dollars."

This was not the last baloney attack on New Dealers. Clare Boothe Luce, ridiculing Vice President Henry Wallace's foreign policy proposals in 1943 (see HOTTENTOTS, MILK FOR), used the Smith construction with a new twist: "Much of what Mr. Wallace calls his global thinking is, no matter how you slice it, still Globaloney."

President Harry Truman picked it up again in 1948, to ridicule Thomas E. Dewey's unity campaign: "In the old days, Al Smith would have said: 'That's baloney.' Today, the Happy Warrior would say: 'That's a lot of hooey.' And if that rhymes with anything it's not my fault . . ."

As early as 1943, George Allen wrote to General Eisenhower: "How does it feel to be a candidate?" In his memoirs, Eisenhower recalled his answer: "Baloney!"

When a colleague of Winston Churchill stated in 1953 that "economic planning is baloney," the British statesman was called upon to explain his associate's remark in the House of Commons. Majestically, he evaded the question with "I should prefer to have an agreed definition of the meaning of 'baloney' before I attempted to deal with such a topic."

The word, in its political usage, is current and used in the best circles. James Reston, Washington correspondent of the *New York Times*, wrote in 1964: "More harm is done by swallowing political baloney in this country than by swallowing arsenic or smoking reefers."

The original meaning, however, prevails. *U.S. News & World Report* of May 28, 1990, quotes someone saying, with undisguised pride, "One of my best things is baloney . . . I'm a good liar."

The word is spelled baloney, bolony, balony, bologna, and in various other ways, but no matter how you spell it . . .

For better or wurst, see SALAMI TACTICS.

bandwagon a movement appealing to the herd instinct of politicians and voters to be on the winning side in any contest.

The word was used in P. T. Barnum's *Life*, published in 1855, to describe a difficult chapter in the life of the circus: "At Vicksburg we sold all our land conveyances excepting four horses and the 'bandwagon.'"

The humor magazine *Puck* in 1884 depicted Chester Arthur driving a bandwagon carrying other presidential hopefuls, and in 1896 it published a similar cartoon showing a McKinley bandwagon.

Songs have also helped popularize the notion of bandwagons. A song published in 1851, written by W. Loftin Hargrave, titled "Wait for the Wagon, A New Ethiopian Song and Melody," was still a favorite in 1900.

In 1900, too, the Prohibitionists helped popularize a temperance song called "The Prohibition Bandwagon," with the words:

And our friends who vote for gin,
Will all scramble to jump in,
When we get our big bandwagon,
some sweet day.

From 1902 onward the word became well established in American political terminology. In Albert Shaw's cartoon history of Theodore Roosevelt's career, a wagon is shown with Roosevelt's friends making musical noises in his favor but the main character—Senator Thomas C. Platt—is shown running after the wagon frantically trying to jump aboard, with a whip in his hand indicating that he would like to be in the driver's seat.

Most extensive use of a real bandwagon in modern times was the "Eisenhower-Nixon Bandwagon" of 1952, a project conceived by Arthur Gray, Jr., and C. Langhorne Washburn. Three 25-ton trailer trucks, each with a three-man crew, "advanced" Eisenhower appearances throughout the campaign. Each gaily decorated truck contained helium tanks for barrage balloons, twelve "Ike" dresses in sizes ten and twelve with parasols and hats, thousands of buttons and pieces of literature, Navy bosun's whistles, and a jeep with a loudspeaker.

In 29 cities over 32 days, the bandwagon rolled ahead of the candidates to organize parades and major receptions, giving a colorful focal point to local activity. Each night, the campaigners set up what they called an "Ethereal Nocturnal Splendor": powerful searchlights played on the barrage balloons with their "Ike" signs, a sight which could be seen from ten miles away. After taking office, President Eisenhower kept one of the bosun's whistles from the bandwagon in the Oval Office as a memento.

The expression is in use in Great Britain as well. Wrote the *Daily Mirror* in 1966, establishing its independent position: "The *Mirror* . . . does not jump on bandwagons . . . it isn't, never has been, and never will be, a tin can tied to a political party's tail."

See HYMIE'S FERRYBOAT.

banner district   the voting unit in which a party or candidate makes a better showing than anywhere else in a single election; also, the section of a larger constituency in which a politician or party has the strongest support.

Crediting an area with banner status was common practice in political reportage and speechmaking during much of the nineteenth century. Political usage seems to have originated in the 1840 presidential election in which the incumbent democrat, Martin Van Buren, was challenged by William Harrison, a Whig. In the course of the colorful "log cabin and hard cider" campaign, a Whig group in Louisiana promised a banner to the state giving the most impressive vote to Harrison. The subsequent controversy over which state won outlived Harrison—who died of pneumonia one month after being inaugurated—and helped popularize the phrase.

Historically, a commander's banner or standard served as a rallying point and symbol of success to come. Much of this meaning has been preserved whether banner is used as a noun or adjective in a figurative sense. Politically, the term has acquired an antique flavor; STANDARD-BEARER, however, is still current. See MILITARY METAPHORS.

ban the bomb. See BETTER RED THAN DEAD.

barefoot boy from Wall Street description of Republican presidential candidate Wendell L. Willkie by FDR's Interior Secretary, Harold L. Ickes. Ickes derided a "humble" image of the Indianan by reminding voters of Willkie's success in finance.

Ickes, "the old curmudgeon" (see CURMUDGEON), laced into Willkie soon after the candidate's 1940 acceptance speech. The Secretary characterized the Republican candidate as "the rich man's Roosevelt; the simple, barefoot Wall Street lawyer," which later was shortened to "the barefoot boy from Wall Street." He added later that the candidate was a "one-spur leather puller who does not even pretend to know anything about the West." Ickes was a master at the art of colorful insult (see MAN ON THE WEDDING CAKE; INVECTIVE, POLITICAL), and occasionally was himself on the receiving end: Governor Huey Long called him "the Chicago chinch bug."

bargain and corruption. See KINGMAKER.

bargaining chip a prospective concession; an arms program justified on the theory that it can be used as a device to induce an adversary to give up an equivalent strategic weapon.

This was SALT lingo, popularized by members of the National Security Council staff during the early seventies, when Henry Kissinger was National Security Adviser, later adopted by congressmen and writers on the SALT and START talks. Some diplomatic reporters tell the author they first heard the phrase in the mid-sixties. Fred R. Shapiro of Yale Law School found a 1965 use in a *Boston Globe* column by Chalmers Roberts on LBJ: "Mr. Johnson had by then won a massive election victory, but he had just ordered the first bombing of North Viet Nam in an effort to bring Hanoi to a conference table where the bargaining chips on both sides would be more closely matched."

In the April 1973 issue of the *Friends' Committee Washington Newsletter*, the term was used instead of its predecessor, "trade-off": "Regarding the SALT negotiations, 14 Republican congressmen appealed to President Nixon to go slow on the 'bargaining chip' idea, calling for restraint in development of weapons such as the B-1 bomber and the Trident submarine at this time." In the *New York Times Magazine* a year later, the term was again defined: "Bargaining from strength calls for arms programs that can serve as 'bargaining chips' to trade for concessions that the other side might not otherwise make . . . The pursuit of hedges and chips brings about an intensification of the arms race just to keep 'bargaining-chip gaps' from developing."

The phrase evokes the metaphor of high-stakes poker and was a favored Kissingerism, along with "STEP BY STEP," "QUIET DIPLOMACY," and "SHUTTLE DIPLOMACY." As such, it was attacked as a "foolish approach" by Jimmy Carter in his 1976 campaign. On July 6 Charles Mohr of the *New York Times* reported: "Mr. Carter argued against the possibility of a limited nuclear war and the 'bargaining chips' approach to nuclear negotiations—both central tenets of the [Ford] Administration. These considerations have provided the main justification for building new systems of nuclear weapons."

In the Spring 1977 *Political Science Quarterly*, Robert Bresler and Robert Gray wrote: "The bargaining chip, like the DOMINO THEORY of the 50s and 60s, has become one of the most voguish ideas in the field of weapons development. Yet the concept is perhaps as old as arms competition itself. . . . Bargaining chips that enhance trust, signal a desire not to let technology get out of hand, and are kept clear of projected force postures, may, in the final analysis, be the only ones we should play." As Senator Gary Hart warned about the MX missile in 1985, "The MX is a weak weapon, and weak weapons make weak bargaining chips."

See SALT.

Barnburners persons demonstrating uncompromising determination, even at risk of total loss; practitioners of the art of the impossible.

The word originally designated the antislavery wing of the Democratic party in New York State in the 1840s led by Martin Van Buren and his son, John. The name was devised by the "Hunkers," a Democratic opposition faction, to ridicule Van Buren's radical approach "in the manner of the Dutch farmer who burned his barn to destroy the rats."

The Barnburners played an important role in the presidential election of 1848. They bolted from the Democratic National Convention and joined the Free-Soilers; their combined vote swung the election to Whig Zachary Taylor. The antislavery views led them into the Republican party in the mid-1850s.

The term *Barnburners* is not in current use, but the concept reappears from time to time. A letter sent to President Hoover after his term of office included an affirmative appraisal of his policies: "We are grateful during your occupancy of the White House you never got the idea of burning down the temple of our fathers in order to destroy a few cockroaches in the basement."

Warning of the danger of MCCARTHY-ISM in meeting the threat of Communist subversion, Adlai Stevenson said in 1952: "We must take care not to burn down the barn to kill the rats."

A *Washington Post* editorial on January 6, 1977, continued the use into recent times: "Canadian radicals and barn-burners of various denominations have titillated themselves for years with talk of resorting to arms in Quebec."

The expression can be traced to a sermon by Thomas Adams in 1629: "The empiric to cure the fever, destroys the patient; so the wise man, to burn the mice, set fire to his barn."

barnstorm to take an extended electioneering trip with many brief stops.

Barnstorming has been widely used at least since the nineteenth century, deriving from the old custom of using a barn for performances by itinerant players; because politicking was something of a rural amusement, the transfer was simple and logical. The term has since been supplemented by "whistlestop." See WHISTLESTOPPING.

Although politicians rarely speak in barns any longer, the usage persists. In October 1944, for instance, the *Chicago Daily News* wrote: "President Roosevelt indignantly denies that his New York and Chicago barnstorming trips violate his pledge not to campaign in the usual sense." Samuel Rosenman later explained that under pressure from Thomas Dewey's strong campaign, "the President soon began to realize that it was necessary for him to get out and fight hard. He also realized that it was up to him to prove that he could stand the physical and mental rigors of a political campaign."

The term can also be used more loosely, as in *Time* magazine in 1947: "Barnstorming Presidential Candidate Harold Stassen whirled through Belgium in one day."

See NONPOLITICAL TRIP; CHAUTAUQUA CIRCUIT.

-bashing excessive criticism; a combining form to derogate rhetorical attacks on a person, group, or principle.

The combining forms of *-bashing* and *-basher* began in Britain. *Bash*, the eighteenth-century verb that led to these forms, may have been onomatopoeic (a word that imitates a sound) or a blend of *bang* and *smash*. British lexicographer Eric Partridge noted the nineteenth-century use of *basher* for a boxer or professional criminal. By 1940, the peeling of potatoes was known as *spud-bashing*.

Probably the driving force behind this counterattacking combining form is *The Economist*, a London weekly. In 1975, this publication coined *Commie-basher* for Jacques Chirac, the French Gaullist leader, and Senator Henry Jackson was labeled "a veteran Russia-basher."

Recent use in the United States has hit upon numerous objects of vituperation, from *male-bashing* to *Japan-bashing*. When the Reagan Administration blamed the Federal Reserve Board for rising interest rates, the *Wall Street Journal* reported that "Reagan aides hope their 'Fed-bashing' will pressure the central bank to ease its tight grip on the nation's credit."

Other *bashing* terms include "blame game" and "finger-pointing."

Bay of Pigs fiasco the abortive invasion of Cuba in 1961 by U.S. supported anti-Castro refugees.

Few phrases of recent coinage are so powerfully fused together as "Bay of Pigs" and "fiasco." The invasion is never referred to as the Bay of Pigs *di-saster*, or the Bay of Pigs *tragedy* or *failure, flop, botch*, or even *snafu*. Always *fiasco*, of the same root as "flask," often of wine, which probably caused *fiasco* to gain its connotation of a drunken, ridiculous attempt to accomplish a pretentious feat that falls flat on its face.

The criticism of Kennedy following the invasion attempt soon after his inauguration was vicious: "Caroline is a cute kid, but we shouldn't let her plan any more invasions." But no matter whether the comment came from critics or Kennedy supporters (said Theodore Sorensen: "The Bay of Pigs fiasco had its influence"), the use of "fiasco" was universal. Substituting another word would be as jarring to the ear as saying "the *attack* of the Light Brigade."

In politics and in other fields, a "Bay of Pigs" now means a monumental flop with an overtone of ultimate redemption (as Kennedy redeemed himself in the confrontation with Khrushchev over Cuba a year after the Bay of Pigs, uh, fiasco). Broadway showman David Merrick closed a show in 1966 called *Breakfast at Tiffany's* before opening night, at a loss of $450,000, with the remark: "It's my Bay of Pigs."

In April 1993, when a Clinton aide sought to minimize the President's responsibility for an FBI attack that led to a large death toll in Waco, Texas, early in his administration, he said, "This was not a Bay of Pigs."

beanbag what politics ain't.

"His early experience," wrote Finley Peter Dunne of his creation, saloon-keeping philosopher Mr. DOOLEY, "gave him wisdom in discussing public affairs. 'Politics,' he says, 'ain't beanbag. 'Tis a man's game; an' women, childher, an' pro-hybitionists'd do well to keep out iv it.'"

The above quotation is taken from the preface to *Mr. Dooley in Peace and*

War, published in 1898; it had been used earlier by Dunne, on October 5, 1895, in an essay in the *Chicago Evening Post*.

A beanbag is a cloth bag partly filled with beans (or, more recently, with plastic beads), easily catchable, used in a children's game of the same name. In Mr. Dooley's use, the child's play made a dramatic comparison with a man's game, and has been used for that purpose ever since (though the "man's game" has recently been replaced by HARDBALL).

"Carter's flaw as a political leader," wrote Jack Germond and Jules Witcover in a column that appeared in the *Washington Star* on September 14, 1977, "has always been his massive self-assurance, his total confidence that no one would believe him capable of political knavery or personal weakness. But in the Bert Lance case, what was in question was his sophistication. And, as Mr. Dooley told us long ago, politics ain't beanbag."

bean counter   accountant; keeper of financial records or statistics; in recent usage, a derogation of one who seeks to hold politicians to perceived promises of racial or sexual quotas.

This phrase, sometimes hyphenated, comes from the image of a person carefully keeping track of the number of individual beans. A 1975 issue of *Forbes* magazine referred to one number-cruncher as "a smart, tightfisted and austere 'bean-counter' accountant from rural Kentucky."

Both the quotation marks and the attributive use before *accountant* were dropped by 1980. The *New York Times* reported in June 1980: "Businessmen hang lively monikers on each other's specialties. A bean counter is, as aspiring bookkeepers know, an accountant."

The term was extended from business into military usage by the early 1980s. George C. Wilson of the *Washington Post* questioned our military readiness in 1980, pointing out that "the Pentagon's bean counters have rated six of the nation's stateside divisions far from ready to fight."

Frequently in political usage *bean counter* carries a connotation of disapproval or dismissal. Senate Appropriations Committee chairman Mark Hatfield criticized the Office of Management and Budget for derogating a 1982 plan; according to Senator Hatfield, "By no responsible account can this be called a budget buster, as it has been characterized by the bean counters at the OMB."

Dr. Frank Young, Food and Drug Administration commissioner in 1989, also used the negative connotation, saying, "I reject the characterization that our employees are just bureaucrats and bean counters."

On occasion, though, *bean counter* is given a positive twist. Douglas A. Brook, who became acting chief of the Office of Personnel Management in 1992, told the *Washington Post* about his earlier Army job in financial management: "If I've learned one thing from that [job], it's how you can use the bean counters to drive culture changes."

As President Bill Clinton was naming his Cabinet choices during the 1992–93 interregnum, he came under critical attack from women's groups for not appointing enough women. He responded angrily at a news conference in Little Rock on December 21, 1992, calling them "bean counters" more interested in quotas than ability. He was irritated because two of his appointees—to head the Council of Economic Advisers and the Environmental Protection Agency—were not being treated as top-level appointments by advocates of women's advancement because they were not Cabinet posts. "If I had appointed

white men to those jobs," he said,
". . . they would have been counting
those positions against our Administration, those bean counters who are
doing that."

This usage gave a new sense to the
relatively recent derogation of accoun-
tants: one who puts mere numbers
ahead of other substantive evidence.

beatnik. See -NIK SUFFIX.

beauty contest. See CATTLE SHOW.

bedsheet ballot a ballot with a lengthy
list of candidates, often confusing to
voters.

This phrase is most often used pejoratively, as if an attempt is being made
to bamboozle voters with complexity;
in modern times, it has frequently been
used in connection with voting in primaries for delegates to a convention.

A synonym is "blanket ballot"; both
phrases use the analogy of bed-cover-
ings to evoke a picture of an enormous
piece of paper, capable of handling a
bewildering multiplicity of names or
propositions.

before April 9th men. See CUFFLINKS
GANG; ALPHABET AGENCIES.

bellwether a trend-setter; or, a district
with a history of reflecting a nationwide vote; or, a STALKING HORSE.

In 1878 *Harper's Weekly* said the unthinking crowd would "follow the
bellwether over any wall and into any
pasture, but the independent sheep
would not."

Literally, a wether is a male sheep; the
leading sheep of the flock sometimes
wears a bell. Thomas Jefferson used
the term in describing critics of his
published writing: "Their real fear is
that this popular and republican pamphlet . . . is likely . . . to wipe out
all the unconstitutional doctrines

which their bellwether, Davilla, has
been preaching for a twelve-month."

The Judas-goat or stalking-horse
meaning remains: Cabell Phillips, after
describing the machinations within
the Democratic party to dump Henry
Wallace from the vice presidency in
1944, wrote that James Byrnes felt indignant because the party leadership
"had deceived him and used him as a
bellwether to undermine Wallace and
to create an opening for Truman."

The trend-setting meaning is taking
over, however. John Kennedy, fighting
to hold down prices in 1961, described
the steel industry as "a bellwether, as
well as a major element in industrial
costs." A 1988 *New York Times* listing
offers "estimates for Treasury's bellwether bonds."

Beltway bandits computer consultants and scientists who thrive on federal government contracts.

The term for these consultants, who
primarily work for the defense industry, is based on proximity to the Capital Beltway around Washington, D.C.
(*Beltway* is a 1951 word for what the
British call a *ring-road.*) This circumferential highway, which cuts through
Maryland and Virginia suburbs, speci-
fies the geographical location of these
Washington area "think tanks," a term
coined in the late 1960s.

Beltway bandits is jocular usage with
a sharp edge; its source was probably
the early 1970s usage for thieves who
would strike homes near the Beltway
and use the high-speed road to make
their escape.

In defense contracting, this alliterative phrase first surfaced in print in the
Washington Post on January 25, 1978:
"Some 'Beltway bandit' ought to be
hired to put one team of computer experts to work designing crime-proof
defenses." The term's appearance in
quotation marks suggests earlier usage.
See INSIDE THE BELTWAY.

benign neglect   a suggestion to allow tensions to ease, interpreted as a plot to abandon the civil rights movement.

Nixon's urban affairs adviser, Daniel Patrick Moynihan, had a predilection for transmitting his advice in long and literate memoranda. On occasion, the President directed that Moynihan memos be circulated to Cabinet members, who then passed copies throughout their departments. On March 2, 1970, this casual method of transmission backfired.

"The time may have come," wrote Moynihan, "when the issue of race could benefit from a period of 'benign neglect.'"

In context, Moynihan's meaning was that blacks would profit if extremists on both sides of the race issue were to lower their voices. But, as *Newsweek* wrote, "to black leaders and their allies, 'neglect'—benign or malign—seemed precisely to describe everything the Administration was and was not doing about race. And they responded with a fury . . ."

Moynihan was quoting the Earl of Durham, who wrote Queen Victoria in 1839 that Canada had done so well "through a period of benign neglect" by the mother country that she ought to be granted self-government.

The oxymoronic overtone of the phrase made it memorable, but the mischief that its misinterpretation could cause made it a tempting morsel to leak to the *New York Times*.

The leak twisted the meaning of Moynihan's advice and hurt him in the liberal community. It did not damage him within the Administration; as the *New Republic*'s John Osborne wrote, "The insiders judged the incident to be an example of how outsiders misjudge insiders and fail to comprehend the intricacies of Presidential counseling and communications."

Columnist Max Lerner could not resist observing, "If anything, he might have used Holmes' 'intelligent neglect.'"

Mr. Moynihan, as a Democratic Senator from New York, could take heart, however, in seeing the phrase used in 1978—without reference to him and in the sense it was originally intended—by a *New York Times* editorialist in January 1978: "Early this month, the Carter Administration abandoned its 'benign neglect' of the dollar."

Berlin Wall.   See WALL, POLITICAL USE OF.

best man, the   object of a convention choice; claim by all candidates on the basis of qualifications.

Like ARENA and HAT IN THE RING, the phrase is closely associated with boxing, when the referee concludes his instructions to the fighters with "and may the best man win."

Gore Vidal used the phrase as the title of a play, later a motion picture, about the selection of a presidential candidate.

In 1964, when President Lyndon Johnson was faced with the choice of a running mate, proponents of Hubert H. Humphrey used a subtle slogan to soft-sell their candidate: "The Next Best Man."

Better Red Than Dead   slogan of the British nuclear disarmament movement.

English philosopher Bertrand Russell wrote in 1958 that if "no alternative remains except communist domination or the extinction of the human race, the former alternative is the lesser of the two evils." This was sloganized into "Better Red Than Dead" and became part of the "Ban the Bomb" demonstrations.

John F. Kennedy, speaking at the University of Washington in 1961, took note of the phrase: "It is a curious fact that each of these two extreme opposites resembles the other. Each believes that we have only two choices: appeasement or war, suicide or surrender, humiliation or holocaust, to be either Red or dead."

An obvious turnaround was used by British author Stanley Reynolds in 1964, in a book urging an anti-Communist crusade entitled *Better Dead Than Red*. This effectively sabotaged the slogan; after a while, most people did not know which slogan came first or who was for what. Thermonuclear thinker Herman Kahn (see UNTHINK-ABLE THOUGHTS) wrote:

If somebody says, "I would rather be Red than dead," he is a coward, and I think properly an object of contempt and scorn. But if somebody says, "I would rather have everybody Red than everybody dead," he is taking a reasonable position with which I agree.

While I would rather have everybody Red than everybody dead, we must not allow a situation to develop in which such a choice is the only one we have.

between a rock and a hard place.
See ROCK AND A HARD PLACE, BETWEEN A.

Big Apple New York City.
In his 1938 book, *Hi De Ho*, bandleader Cab Calloway defined "apple" as "the big town, the main stem, Harlem." In a 1976 conversation with the author, Mr. Calloway explained further that "The Big Apple"—the name of a Harlem nightclub in the mid-thirties—was a mecca for jazz musicians. A dance which *Life* magazine in 1937 called "a loose-hipped, freehand combination of 'truckin' and the square dance" was named "The Big Apple," an appellation taken from the nightclub, according to Calloway.

Robert Gold, author of *Jazz Talk*, published in 1975, points to a 1966 speculation in *Record Research* as the likely etymology: "My suspicion [is] that *Big Apple* is a transliteration of the older Mexican idiom *'manzana principal'* for the main square of the town or the downtown area."

However, American Dialect Society Publication #16 (November 1951) says that "big apple" comes from "racetrack argot: in big time racing, New York City had a tradition of high purses, excellent tracks, fine horses." Why racetrack people would use the phrase "big apple" was unexplained, unless the fruit was a reward for a horse.

Professor Gerald Cohen of the University of Missouri at Rolla has tracked the term to a 1909 book, *The Wayfarer in New York*, by Edward Martin: "It [the Midwest] inclines to think that the big apple gets a disproportionate share of the national sap." Mr. Calloway may have been on the right track about the term's popularization: the phrase was black-English jazz talk in the mid-thirties. Mr. Gold also cites *Dan Burley's Original Handbook of Harlem Jive* (1944), defining "apple" as "the earth, the universe, this planet. Any place that's large. A big Northern city." Evidently the apple is the symbol of the earth, and by synecdoche, New York is taken to be that center—and thus the "big" apple.

In the mid-seventies, with New York City in great financial difficulty, the Convention and Visitors Bureau made an attempt to "sell" the city by popularizing the phrase as the city symbol, which seemed more apt than its predecessor, FUN CITY.

big casino the center ring, grand arena, place of major action.
Ronald Reagan introduced this gaming expression to politics, referring in 1974 to the race for the presidency as "the big casino." A casino was originally a public dancing and meeting

hall, later a place for gambling; the word is also used for a card game. (The term beginning with a capital *C* was used in another sense by John Wayne, dying of cancer, who sought to defeat "the big Casino.")

Wendell Rawls Jr. wrote in the *New York Times* of January 29, 1978, that a Republican candidate for governor of Pennsylvania, Richard Thornburgh, had "helped remove a complacent federal prosecutor in Philadelphia and encouraged the replacement, Mr. [David] Marston, to look upon the city as the 'big casino' of political crime."

See CARD METAPHORS.

big-character posters. See GRAFFITI; SNIPE.

Big Daddy. See GREAT WHITE FATHER.

big enchilada the top man, or main target; in Watergate terminology, former Attorney General John Mitchell.

An enchilada is a Spanish-American word for a tortilla enclosing chopped meat, topped with a chili-flavored sauce (the root of the en*chil*ada is chili).

"I coined the phrase," former White House aide John Ehrlichman informed the author from his incarceration in 1977. "I've cooked my own enchiladas for years. My California upbringing. Could have said 'big fish,' or 'top dog' or 'big cheese,' I guess."

The comedian Steve Allen questioned Ehrlichman's claim to the coinage of "the big enchilada." He wrote to *Newsweek* in 1978, "The original version of the phrase, 'the whole enchilada,' was common in the West Coast 'Madison Avenue' talk of the 1940's."

The phrase was heard on the March 27, 1973, Nixon tape in connection with giving the President's pursuers a substantial prize, in the hope they would be satisfied. Of John Mitchell,

H. R. Haldeman said, "He is as high up as they've got," and Ehrlichman replied, "He's the Big Enchilada."

The popular food is also used as a synecdoche for the world, or "the entire situation," similar to "the whole ball of wax." After the election victory of Jimmy Carter in 1976, former California Governor Ronald Reagan said that the Democrats, long in control of Congress, would no longer be able to share responsibility for difficulties with Republicans. "For the first time," Reagan said, "the Democrats cannot fuzz up the issue by blaming the White House. They've got the whole enchilada now."

big foot columnist or celebrated journalist; a derogation of a "media biggie" by envious or bemused colleagues.

This jocular term applies to any columnist or editor who temporarily joins the regular staff on a press bus following a Presidential candidate. The image suggests an outsider who will trample the territory of reporters who normally cover that beat.

During the Presidential campaign of 1980, T. R. Reid of the *Washington Post* first used the sobriquet in print. He was describing Hedrick Smith, then the Washington correspondent of the *New York Times*, who wore a large cast on a broken ankle for several months.

Media superstars may be pushed beyond this label. Reid writes, for example, of Walter Cronkite's entrance: "The traveling reporters, who have divided political journalists into two categories—junior reporters, known as 'little feet,' and senior political analysts, or 'big feet'—have given Cronkite a designation all his own: 'Ultra Foot.'"

Big foot (usually written as two words, but on occasion *bigfoot*) is based on the 1960s nickname for Sasquatch, the large, hairy, humanlike creature that supposedly lives in the Pacific Northwest. Purported evidence of the presence of the creature has been fearsome footprints supposedly left by *Big Foot*. See ABOMINABLE NO-MAN.

bigger bang for a buck more efficient use of defense appropriations, relying largely on nuclear deterrents.

Secretary of State John Foster Dulles laid down the policy of MASSIVE RETALIATION in 1954 and told the Council on Foreign Relations this policy "permits of a selection of military means instead of multiplication of means. As a result, it is now possible to get, and share, more basic security at less cost."

Defense Secretary Charles E. Wilson promptly dubbed the policy the NEW LOOK (after a fashion phrase describing lower hemlines) and said it would provide "a bigger bang for a buck."

Historian and naval expert Samuel Eliot Morison analyzed it this way: "To strengthen American retaliatory power, to 'get a bigger bang for a buck' as the phrase ran, the defense department built up a long-range 'strategic' air force, with a stockpile of atomic bombs, but neglected both navy and ground forces."

Ultimately, the doctrine of massive retaliation was modified to allow for "brushfire wars" or LIMITED WARS and defense budgets allotted more to ground and naval forces, presumably a smaller bang for a buck but useful when smaller bangs avoid nuclear wars. President Kennedy summed up his approach to the budgetary problem during his Administration with a similar counterphrase: "There is no discount price on defense."

big government an attack phrase on centralized federal authority and massive taxation and expenditure.

The phrase probably stemmed from "Big Business," which also spawned

"Big Labor" (both usually capitalized) but the concern about the size and power of the federal authority began with the birth of the nation. Reformer Samuel Tilden, fighting Boss William Marcy Tweed in New York, harked back to the problems of Thomas Jefferson in 1801: "A grasping centralism, absorbing all functions from the local authorities, and assuming to control the industries of individuals by largesses to favored classes from the public treasury . . . were then, as now, characteristics of the period." Tilden called for a return to Jefferson's way: "He repressed the meddling of government in the concerns of private business."

But the rise of populism (see POPULIST) and the advent of the trust-busters showed that the public felt that "bigness" was a greater threat from business than from government. Lawyer Louis Brandeis inveighed against the CURSE OF BIGNESS in business. He was countered later with William Howard Taft's statement: "Mere size is no sin." As a Supreme Court Justice, Brandeis kept up his campaign against bigness in both business and government. When the Court unanimously decided to strike down the National Industrial Recovery Act in 1935— Black Monday, New Dealers called it—Brandeis warned Roosevelt aide Thomas Corcoran: "Tell the President we're not going to let this government centralize everything."

"Maybe it's unfortunate," wrote an editor of the *New Republic*, "but about the only counterweight the little man has to Big Business is Big Government." Republicans and conservative Democrats sharply disagree. Thomas E. Dewey stated the case against big government in 1950: "All-powerful, central government, like dictatorships, can continue only by growing larger and larger. It can never retrench without admitting failure. By absorbing more than half of all the taxing power of the nation, the federal government now deprives the states and local governments of the capacity to support the programs they should conduct . . . it offers them in exchange the counterfeit currency of federal subsidy."

Dwight Eisenhower deplored what he called "the whole-hog mentality," which "leans toward the creation of a more extensive and stifling monopoly than this country has ever seen . . . you don't need more supergovernment."

Republican House Minority Leader Gerald Ford, in 1966, blamed it all on the Democrats, labeling them "the party of Big Business, of Big Government, of Big Spending, of Big Deficits, of Big Cost of Living, of Big Labor Trouble, of Big Home Foreclosures, of Big Scandals, of Big Riots in the Streets and of Big Promises."

"The truth about big government," said John F. Kennedy in 1962, "is the truth about any other great activity: it is complex. Certainly it is true that size brings dangers, but it is also true that size also can bring benefits."

A favorite Ronald Reagan line was "Government is not the solution to the problem; government is the problem."

big lie   a falsehood of such magnitude and audacity that it is bound to have an effect on public opinion even if it is not given credence by a majority; a propaganda technique identified with Adolf Hitler.

Hitler wrote in *Mein Kampf*:

The size of the lie is a definite factor in causing it to be believed, for the vast masses of a nation are in the depths of their hearts more easily deceived than they are consciously and intentionally bad. The primitive simplicity of their minds renders them a more easy prey to a big lie than a small one, for they themselves often tell little lies but would be ashamed to tell big ones. . . .

Something therefore always remains and sticks from the most impudent lies, a fact which all bodies and individuals concerned with the art of lying in this world know only too well, and hence they stop at nothing to achieve this end.

In the U.S. during the 1950s, Senator Joseph R. McCarthy's critics accused him of using the big lie technique to intimidate his opponents in and out of the Senate. An example is this editorial in the *St. Louis Post-Dispatch* of 1951: "Gloomy Washington prophets are forecasting a period of 'the big lie,' of the furtive informer, of the character assassin, of inquisition, eavesdropping, smear and distrust. They lump the whole under the term MCCARTHYISM."

A Senate committee headed by Millard Tydings of Maryland, following a four-month investigation of McCarthy's charges that there were 81 card-carrying Communists in the State Department, castigated him in terms rarely used about a Senate member: "We are constrained to call the charges, and the methods used to give them ostensible validity, what they truly are: a fraud and a hoax perpetrated on the Senate and the United States and the American people. They represent perhaps the most nefarious campaign of half truths and untruth in the history of this Republic . . . the totalitarian technique of the 'big lie' on a sustained basis." McCarthy's efforts helped defeat Senator Tydings in the next election.

Social scientists in the mass communications field have found that the size of a requested opinion or behavior change is important in the degree of change effected. Herbert Adelson, of Opinion Research Corporation, observed: "The more extreme the opinion change that the communicator asks for, the more actual change he is likely to get . . . communications that advocate a greater amount of change from an audience's view in fact produce a greater amount of change than communications that advocate a position that is not much different from the position that the audience already holds."

bigot. See REDNECK; REVERSE BIGOTRY.

big stick. See DETERRENT.

big tent the theory that a political party is a spacious home for debate, and not a cozy bungalow that permits only a narrow political ideology.

TRUE BELIEVERS hold that a political party must "stand for principle" and not muddy up its philosophy with ME TOO ideas held by the opposition.

On the contrary, say the advocates of the big tent: there is plenty of room for divergence of opinion within any party, which should be a device for getting into power. They point to Jefferson's statement "Not every difference of opinion is a difference of principle."

After his 1976 defeat, Gerald Ford called a meeting of Republican leaders John Connally, Ronald Reagan and Nelson Rockefeller and said pointedly: "The Republican tent is big enough to encompass the four individuals who were here today."

In the late 1980s, Lee Atwater, the Republican National Chairman known for his slashing style in the 1988 Bush campaign, mellowed and advocated "a big tent approach" to overcome the split in the party caused by the abortion issue.

In 1993, the metaphor was extended by Massachusetts State Senator William R. Keating. At a groundbreaking ceremony for a new mosque, the guests included ministers, priests, rabbis and local officials, all of whom huddled under a white tent when it started to rain; said Keating, "In this world we are all under one tent."

The phrase is derived from the circus; the big tent has several arenas which can put on separate shows.

The current synonym is "politics of inclusion."

bigwig party leader; humorous or sardonic reference to the higher-ups.

Probably derived from the British law courts, where persons of importance (judges, barristers) wear large white wigs. Charles Dickens referred to them, defending a man "spoken of by the bigwigs with extreme condescension."

In current political use, the term is most often included in a phrase like "all the party bigwigs were there"; it is used often by reporters but rarely by politicians. In the mid-seventies the word achieved vogue as "biggies," and was extended to "ad biggies" and "media biggies."

See MUCKEY-MUCKS.

bipartisan interparty cooperation on a matter that is essentially political; NONPARTISAN means interparty cooperation on matters nonpolitical.

In bipartisanship, politicians set aside differences to work together on political matters; in nonpartisanship, politicians work together as individuals, as in philanthropic, patriotic or civil causes.

"Bipartisanship" in foreign affairs is most closely associated with Senator Arthur Vandenberg, Michigan Republican, an outspoken isolationist of the thirties. A month after the German invasion of Poland, he was saying: "This so-called war is nothing but about 25 people and propaganda." World War II and a trip to blitzed London changed his thinking, and the ranking Republican in the Senate Foreign Relations Committee made a dramatic speech in 1945 that laid the groundwork for foreign-affairs bipartisanship: "I do not believe that any nation hereafter can immunize itself by its own exclusive action. . . . I want maximum American cooperation. . . . I want a new dignity and a new authority for international law. I think American self-interest requires it."

The Vandenberg switch shattered nascent postwar isolationism and the United Nations Charter was approved with only two senatorial votes against it, a far cry from the furor over the League of Nations after World War I. Vandenberg was hailed by most of the U.S. press for his new stand. At the birth of the Truman Doctrine, which aided the Greeks and Turks in combating internal Communism, "Vandenberg," wrote Truman later, "championed this program in a truly bipartisan manner." But the senator was nagged by his own worry about bipartisanship being carried dangerously far. "To me," he wrote a constituent in 1950, "'bipartisan foreign policy' means a mutual effort under our indispensable two-party system to unite our official voice at the water's edge so that America speaks with maximum authority. . . . It does not involve the remotest surrender of free debate in determining our position. On the contrary, frank cooperation and free debate are indispensable to ultimate unity."

Within a few months, Vandenberg was asking if "bipartisanship meant more Chinas and more Hisses and more messes with Russian bombs hanging over us," a position not all that far from Robert Taft's blast at "the wreckage that is our Far Eastern policy." Thomas E. Dewey, whose own internationalist position insured bipartisanship in foreign affairs in the 1944 wartime campaign, reasserted the need for such a united front in war but qualified his position with, "I am not prepared to assert that, in a normal,

peaceful world, foreign policy should always be bipartisan."

The tension underlying any bipartisanship in foreign policy can never really be relieved: on one hand is the need for a single American voice to the world, on the other hand a need for self-examination and criticism that is the obligation of LOYAL OPPOSITION. In fact, what goes under the heading of bipartisanship is usually a coalition of like-minded men in both parties; Dwight Eisenhower found that Democratic votes put across his foreign policy and foreign-aid programs no fewer than 48 times in 1953.

Vandenberg, often called the "architect of the bipartisan foreign policy," preferred a different word: unpartisan. Presumably, this meant nonpartisan, but experience has shown that foreign policy in times short of all-out war must include "dissent."

See ABOVE POLITICS; PARTISAN; NON-PARTISAN; WATER'S EDGE.

bipolar. See POLARIZE; MULTIPOLAR WORLD.

Bircher a member or supporter of the John Birch Society, which in the 1960s was the best known and probably most active of the ultraconservative, militantly anti-Communist splinter groups.

Secrecy is a Birch tenet and the society did little to publicize itself as an organization. After its founding in 1958, it was more or less discovered gradually by a number of journalists, particularly after the writings of retired candy manufacturer Robert Welch, Jr., founder of the society, became known. Among other things, Welch called Dwight Eisenhower a willing tool of the Communist conspiracy. Welch and his followers are often identified as being on the RADICAL RIGHT, or in Alan Barth's phrase, "rampageous right."

On the derivation of the title, at least, there is no argument. Captain John Birch was an otherwise obscure USAF officer killed by Chinese Communists in 1945, and is sometimes referred to as "the first casualty of the Cold War." The Chinese Red forces were nominally our allies against the Japanese, and his murder, according to the society, was hushed up by Communist agents in the U.S.

Arthur M. Schlesinger, Jr., described the Birch Society's mood as "one of longing for a dream world of no communism, no overseas entanglements, no United Nations, no federal government, no Negroes or foreigners—a world in which Chief Justice Warren would be impeached, Cuba invaded, the graduated income tax repealed, fluoridation of drinking water stopped and the import of Polish hams forbidden."

A question often asked of Republican candidates in the sixties was "Do you accept or reject support of the Birchers?" In the 1962 California gubernatorial primary, Richard Nixon specifically rejected them; he won the nomination and lost the election. In 1966, Ronald Reagan refused to take this position, holding that people who supported him bought his views, not he theirs. Reagan—who carefully applied State Chairman Gaylord Parkinson's ELEVENTH COMMANDMENT, which states, "Thou shalt not speak ill of fellow Republicans"—won by close to a million votes, though there is no telling how much of this was the effect of the Bircher straddle.

bird dog . . . kennel dog one who works to earn his keep (bird dog), rather than one who depends on others (kennel dog).

In 1954, pockets of serious unemployment were distressing the Eisenhower Administration; in Flint, Michigan, 22 percent of the labor force was idle. When Secretary of Defense Charles E. Wilson held a press conference in nearby Detroit, he was asked why his department did not allocate more defense contracts to depressed areas. Wilson suggested that unemployed workers would do better to move to those areas where labor shortages existed, and in reaching for a metaphor came up with the political blooper of the year: "I've always liked bird dogs rather than kennel dogs myself. You know, one who will get out and hunt for food rather than sit on his fanny and yell."

Coming just before an off-year election, the remark was seized upon as an example of a heartless Administration run by unfeeling big businessmen. Union leaders said that workingmen "wear no leash and will not be muzzled." Wilson promptly apologized: "I admit that I made a mistake . . . by bringing up those bird dogs at the same time I was talking about people." See FOOT-IN-MOUTH DISEASE. But the damage was done; other Administration officials were told to keep silent. In his memoirs Sherman Adams wrote: "Learned that the newspapers had [been] expecting me to say something about Wilson and his dogs. Remembering the President's advice, I did not miss that opportunity to keep my mouth shut."

For another Wilson remark that was turned against the Administration, see WHAT'S GOOD FOR GENERAL MOTORS. The former president of GM had an aptitude for raising the hackles of some of his listeners with his turn of phrase. He once told a Senate committee: "The trouble with you men is that you don't understand the problem." Referring to U.S. senators as "you men"—as if they were a group of his employees—did not sit well.

Wilson's bird-dog remark recalls other canine roots in political terminology. A "still hunt"—a method of hunting stealthily, with the dogs muted—was adopted by Tilden supporters in 1876, who boasted that their man conducted a secret "still hunt" of Boss Tweed.

Davy Crockett said: "Are the people like my hounds, that bark when I tell them, and leave off when I stamp my foot at them?" The idea of a dog trailing at his master's heels was probably the derivation of WARD HEELER, and Petroleum V. Nasby used the simile in 1866: "The bold shivelrous Southner . . . and the Dimokrat uv the North foller'n, like a puppy dog, at his heels, takin sich fat things ez he cood snap up." *American Speech* reported an 1888 definition of *bird dog*: "a dog which accompanies a bird-hunter for the purpose of scenting the game and picking it up after it falls."

Speaker Champ Clark of Missouri, whose presidential hopes were sabotaged by Wilson-supporter William Jennings Bryan at the 1912 Democratic convention, was plagued by an old song:

Ev'ry time I come to town
The boys keep kickin' my dog aroun';
Makes no difference if he is a houn',
They gotta quit kickin' my dog aroun'.

In British politics, Harold Wilson received a bad press in 1966 when he mocked Conservative leader Edward Heath's Common Market efforts as "rolling on his back like a spaniel at any kind gesture from the French." Perhaps the most effective use of a canine simile was by Winston Churchill, after being invited by the Chamberlain cabinet to meet German Ambassador Joachim von Ribbentrop: "I suppose they asked me to show him that, if they couldn't bark themselves, they kept a dog who could bark and might bite."

"Bird-dog," used as a verb, has an entirely different meaning: to hunt down, or ferret out, facts, or to follow through on a project until it is successfully completed. Usage: "I don't want this bogged down in red tape—bird-dog it and tell me when it's done." *Newsday* reported in July 1992 that "CBS News President Richard Salant said he was 'embarrassed' by Dan Rather's live convention floor bird-dogging of a G.O.P. official." See HONCHO.

For Chinese Communist use of "running dogs," see FELLOW TRAVELER. For other snarling similes, see POLITICAL ANIMAL and THAT DOG WON'T HUNT.

bird metaphors. See FLOO-FLOO BIRD; PECKING ORDER; WAR HAWKS.

bite the bullet commit to a difficult course of action; make a tough decision.

Lyndon Johnson popularized—and simultaneously stigmatized—the phrase by using it in connection with the hard decisions of the Vietnam War. Criticizing Congress for inaction on a bill to raise taxes, President Johnson said on May 3, 1968: "But I think the time has come for all the members of Congress to be responsible and, even in an election year, to bite the bullet and stand up and do what ought to be done for their country."

In 1975 President Ford said: "Some have said that instead of asking Congress and the nation to bite the bullet, I have offered only a marshmallow," adding that the Congress "wouldn't even chew that marshmallow."

Mr. Ford's metaphoric extension caused Columnist David Braaten of the *Washington Star* to analyze "that recent favorite of literary gourmets, the bite-size bullet" in these terms: "Originally, one bit a bullet to distract oneself from the pain of drastic surgery when no anesthetic was available. It supposedly kept the patient from biting his tongue, or screaming so loud the surgeon was unsettled. From that simple beginning, bullet-biting has come to be used in the quite opposite sense of taking one's medicine. It has replaced the bitter pill as something to be swallowed . . ."

The author queried *American Heritage* on the etymology; Oliver Jensen (perhaps influenced by Rudyard Kipling's "The Soldiers and Sailors Too") gave this first impression: "I think I have always misunderstood the phrase, thinking it had something to do with an old style of bullet that had to have something bitten off it to free the powder for the spark—indicating, so to speak, that you were making the crucial decision to be ready to shoot. But I begin to lose faith in that theory now." Mr. Jensen wrote to Civil War historian Bruce Catton, who sent him this reply:

I can't give you a definite quotation, but it most certainly comes from before the Civil War; I believe it originated with the British army as early as the 18th Century. Here is how it came into being:

It dated from pre-anesthetic days, when a wounded soldier in a field hospital had to have a painful operation, usually the amputation of a limb. (What with the saw and everything, having that done without chloroform, ether or morphine would obviously be pretty agonizing). When they were ready to go, the afflicted soldier (who was either strapped down or held firmly in place by two or three husky comrades) would be given a round, soft-lead bullet and told to bite on it. This would help him to get through the ordeal without screaming; the fact that the bullet was of soft lead would make it possible for him to clamp down hard without breaking his teeth. So—to "bite the bullet" meant to endure something extremely bad with suitable stoicism and without making unmanly outcries.

This could not be Civil War in origin. First place, in most cases they had anesthetics in that war. They did have to bite the *cartridge*—not the bullet—when

loading those muzzle-loading rifles. The bullet was a cylindro-conoidal bit of lead with a tube of paper attached to the base; paper was full of powder, with the lower end crimped. To load his rifle, the soldier bit off the crimped paper, poured the powder down the barrel, rammed the bullet down after it, and was all ready to operate.

The ammunition-munching metaphor, after a flurry of use in the late sixties, has settled into a political language that needs alternatives to "make difficult decisions." An unnamed member of President Carter's Cabinet was quoted in 1978 by *New York Times* Washington correspondent Hedrick Smith as observing of Mr. Carter: "He's still not ready to admit that some of these things—like 4 percent unemployment and 4 percent inflation and a balanced budget—are irreconcilable. It's terribly painful for him . . . There's a reluctance on his part to bite the bullet and make the hard choices."

A more hopeful attitude was expressed in a comment printed in *National Review* of September 17, 1990: "We expect [President Bush] to bite the bullet of military action when he judges the time is right to reduce Iraq's power to harm."

black, political use of black civil rights militants reintroduced the term "black" to replace "Negro" in the sixties. A century before, BLACK REPUBLICAN had been used to describe the party of abolition and reconstruction, but in the twentieth century the word was used in its racial sense to describe African natives and as a racial slur to imply that American Negroes were close to their ancestors "in the jungle."

To avoid giving offense, white writers and politicians have referred to blacks as: *Negroes, colored people, nonwhites* (a statistician's word including Puerto Ricans, Mexicans, Chinese, American Indians, etc., but politically a euphemism for blacks), and most euphemistic of all, *minority group*. When a politician speaks of minority groups, he is mainly concerned with blacks; when he speaks of ethnic groups, he is usually speaking of Jews, or of Italian, German, or other nationality groups.

Blacks have never used the counterterm "majority group" to apply to whites, choosing recently "WHITE POWER STRUCTURE" and the slang terms "whitey," "honkie," and "Mister Charlie" (see CHARLIE). When comparing blacks and whites, white is not capitalized, Caucasian usually is.

As black racial pride increased, civil rights leaders frequently compared "white men and black men" and looked on marketers of skin-whitening and hair-straightening products with disdain. Martin Luther King, Jr., launched a poster campaign around the slogan "Black is beautiful" in 1967. White usage of "black" lagged until the emergence of "BLACK POWER" as a slogan in 1966.

Political leaders opposing integration prefer "separation of races" to the harsher term "SEGREGATION"; some politicians go to the extreme of substituting "indigenous" for "native" whenever it appears, though none has gone so far as to say "my indigenous land."

The fear of an unintentional racial slur is real. When New Jersey Governor Richard Hughes held an angry press conference during the 1967 riot in Newark, he said, "We have determined that the line between a jungle assault on law and order may as well be drawn here as anywhere else in America," later repeating his condemnation of "jungle law." Wrote the *New York Post*: "While gubernatorial assistants tried to explain that Hughes was referring to 'the law of the jungle' as opposed to 'civil order,' and meant no racist connotations, the damage had been done."

In 1970, semanticist (later California Senator) S. I. Hayakawa quoted a letter written in 1928 by W. E. B. DuBois to a young man who wanted to stop the use of the word Negro:

> Historically, of course, your dislike of the word Negro is easily explained: "Negroes" among your grandfathers meant black folk; "colored" people were mulattoes. The mulattoes hated and despised the blacks and were insulted if called "Negroes." But we are not insulted—not you and I. We are quite as proud of our black ancestors as our white. And perhaps a little prouder. . . . Your real work as a Negro lies in two directions: First, to let the world know what there is fine and genuine about the Negro race. And secondly, to see that there is nothing about that race that is worth contempt; your contempt, my contempt, or the contempt of the wide, wide world.

In a 1974 *Psychology Today* article about bigotry in language, Paul Chance listed a few phrases in which "black" is used positively: Black Beauty, black belt (karate), black gold (oil), black tie, black soil, black pearls. "White," which is usually used metaphorically for "good," has some reverse connotations: white trash, whitewash, white flag, white feather, white slave, white elephant.

Cartoonist Jules Feiffer, alert to language changes (see DISADVANTAGED), pictured a bearded black intellectual in 1967 describing the ring-around-the-Rosie of the political use of the word: "As a matter of racial pride we want to be called 'blacks.' Which has replaced the term 'Afro-American'—Which replaced 'Negroes'—Which replaced 'colored people'—Which replaced 'darkies'—Which replaced 'blacks.'"

By the 1990s, the preferred term had become *African-American*.

black advance. See DIRTY TRICKS.

black capitalism a 1968 campaign phrase pledging government encouragement to blacks starting their own businesses.

In the middle of his primary campaign, Richard Nixon felt the need to address at some length—and in a positive tone—the problem of racial division in America. In two radio addresses, the first on April 25, 1968, entitled "Bridges to Human Dignity," he outlined his desire to go beyond programs "that feed the stomach and starve the soul."

In the first six drafts of the April 25 speech, one of the ideas he put forward was "black entrepreneurship." Ray Price, the writer working most closely with the candidate on the development of the speech, felt this phrase was awkward and sought an alternative.

In the radio studio where the speech was to be recorded, the author recalled the New York Stock Exchange's recapture of the word "capitalism" from Communist terminology in their "people's capitalism" advertising campaign. Three alternatives—black entrepreneurship, black enterprise, and black capitalism—were suggested to the candidate, who chose the last.

"A third bridge," he said, "is the development of black capitalism. By providing technical assistance and loan guarantees, by opening new capital sources, we can help Negroes to start new businesses in the ghetto and to expand existing ones."

The phrase and the idea received some attention, which posed a problem for Democratic candidate Hubert Humphrey when he later advocated a similar program. After the campaign, one of the Humphrey writers told this writer, "We couldn't use Nixon's phrase, black capitalism, so we had to go with black entrepreneurship, which is a mouthful, and is hell to fit into a headline."

black hats villains; "heavies."

The extension of the Western-movie metaphor to politics is most pronounced when a simplistic "us-against-them" mood dominates the political scene. The users of the phrase are conscious of the satire implicit in its usage: in the shades-of-gray real world of political compromise, few hats are all-black, and all-white hats soon become scuff-marked.

A related phrase is "good guys," easy to spot in a six-gun epic, which writer Jimmy Breslin appropriated for a book title about the Watergate affair: *How the Good Guys Finally Won.*

Elliot Richardson, who as Nixon Attorney General was regarded by many as a white hat in a black-hatted White House, used the phrase in a talk to business leaders in 1977: "Isolated in the corporate fortress, too many businessmen have cast their argument in terms of the traditional interests—profit and capital for investment. But these are the terms of the black hats. They translate, of course, into jobs, prices, consumer satisfaction—even, given responsible political decision-making, into satisfaction of collective wants and ultimately the improved 'quality of life.' But these are all terms which have been expropriated by those now confidently postured in white hats."

See WHITE HATS.

blacklist. See GUILT BY ASSOCIATION.

black power a deliberately ambiguous slogan, meaning antiwhite rebellion to some, the use of black political and economic "muscle" to others.

The phrase was used in June 1966 by Stokely Carmichael, then head of the Student Nonviolent Coordinating Committee (SNCC), on the occasion of a SNCC-organized march through Mississippi. It appeared in the *New York Times* on June 18, 1966, in a report that Carmichael was teaching marchers the use of the slogan.

Two weeks before, on May 30, Harlem Congressman Adam Clayton Powell used the phrase in a speech to students at Howard University: "To demand these God-given rights is to seek black power . . ." There may be other previous uses in the black community, but the phrase was made famous in a dramatic context by Carmichael.

Dr. Nathan Hare, Carmichael's sociology professor at Howard University, called the slogan not antiwhite, but "anti-antiblack." He added: "'Power' is the ability to influence another person—even against his will, if necessary . . . 'black power' means the exercise by black people of influence on the forces which oppress us. . . . Assimilation has not worked. . . . As Malcolm X [the late Black Muslim leader] said, 'We've been praying when we should have been preying, or playing when we should be flaying—you know, skinning alive.'"

Floyd McKissick, head of the Congress of Racial Equality (CORE), told Senator Robert Kennedy in 1967: "I believe that black power will be accepted just like Irish power has been accepted." This was using the phrase in its non-violent, political-power sense, and liberal columnist Max Lerner argued its fallacy: ". . . while the Irish and the Jews . . . acted as political appeal groups, they never raised the slogans of 'Irish Power' or 'Jewish power,' nor implied hatred for the majority groups. Nor did they ever scorn to share power with non-Irish or non-Jews, even in the big cities where they were heavily represented."

James Farmer, former head of CORE, tried to moderate the expression: "Black power, whatever the coiners of this slogan mean, to me means shared power—otherwise it leads to an illusion."

To the Black Muslims, Black Panthers, and other extremist groups, the phrase was a rallying cry for guerrilla warfare. When riots erupted in several cities in the summer of 1967, the phrase's more ominous side became apparent.

H. "Rap" Brown, Carmichael's successor at SNCC, began to arouse audiences with his extension of black power to "get you some guns." In Jacksonville, Florida, Governor Claude Kirk showed up unexpectedly at a Brown appearance, appealed to "the Negro pride aspect of black power," drawing the line "at any talk of guns."

In July 1967, the *New York Times* analyzed the meaning of the phrase:

> Many believe the slogan means only that Negroes should take pride in their race and organize themselves for political and economic action. Others view it as an antiwhite rallying cry. Still others see it as a sort of para-military slogan that leads to riots and rebellion . . . the very ambiguity of the phrase is its major strength as a rallying cry for Negroes.

The slogan was important enough to be quoted in a Supreme Court decision a year after its coinage. The Court upheld (5 to 4) the contempt conviction of Dr. Martin Luther King, Jr., for defying a court injunction against a march he led in Alabama. The dissent was written by Justice William Brennan: "We cannot permit fears of 'riots' and 'civil disobedience' generated by slogans like black power to divert our attention from what is here at stake—arming the state courts with the power to punish as a 'contempt' what they otherwise could not punish at all."

Sometimes the term is combined with *power base*. A South African meeting in 1989 was described in the *Washington Post* by Steven Friedman, policy research manager of the South African Institute of Race Relations: "What you are dealing with is an acknowledgment by a government authority that they are going to negotiate with an organized black power base."

Along with "escalate" (see ESCALATION), black power became one of the major coinages of the sixties. A rhyming variation was "flower power," a slogan of the hippies who used flowers as a symbol of love. "Power" was used as the phrase-making device for a variety of groups, including "blackboard power" or "teacher power" for militant educators, "gray power" for senior citizens, and "gay power" for the increasingly militant homosexual community.

black Republican used as a political imprecation by Southerners and some northern Democrats before and during the Civil War in an attempt to label the new Republican party as fanatically pro-Negro.

Stephen Douglas, who was to be Lincoln's chief antagonist six years later, began denouncing "black Republicans" as early as 1854, when what was to become the Grand Old Party had barely hatched. Other orators used it as well. By 1855–56, when the Republicans and abolitionists generally took "BLEEDING KANSAS" as a war chant, Democrats and proslavery interests answered with "black Republicans." The *Lancaster* (Ohio) *Eagle* in 1855 condemned "black Republicans with their woolly heads."

By 1860 it was so common a curse that candidate Abraham Lincoln devoted part of his address at Cooper Union in New York City to rebuttal. He repeated his party's opposition to slavery but argued that illiterate slaves were largely unaware of the party's stance. Thus, the party could not be responsible for unrest and violence among blacks. Lincoln said that to dramatize their case, enemies of the new party defined black Republicanism as "insurrection, blood and thunder among the slaves."

Lincoln's defense did no good. He was nominated for the presidency three months after the Cooper Union speech, and in the acrimonious campaign that followed, Lincoln heard himself often attacked as a black Republican. Jefferson Davis used the term in private correspondence.

The phrase might have been adapted from one used in Europe earlier—red republicans—to describe radicals in the revolutionary movements of the 1840s. In this country, many considered the overthrow of slavery just as radical as many Europeans viewed the death of monarchy.

White officer John Pershing led the 10th Negro Cavalry during the Spanish-American War. Because of his service with black troops, he acquired the nickname "Black Jack."

Although no longer used seriously in modern American politics—indeed the Republicans' big problem has been to retrieve black support—black Republicanism is still employed occasionally in a bantering way. Joe Martin, the former House Republican leader, recalled requesting of Franklin Roosevelt a new federal road for Massachusetts. Roosevelt promptly instructed an aide to call the appropriate official "and tell him I am sending down a black Republican and I want . . . to give him a road."

blame America first. See SAN FRANCISCO DEMOCRAT.

blanket ballot. See BEDSHEET BALLOT.

bleeding hearts an ultraconservative view of ultraliberals, as those whose "hearts bleed" for the poor, who are "suckers" for every "sob story," and who place tax burdens on all in a mistaken effort to cure social ills.

The liberal who is so labeled considers the one who calls him a "bleeding heart" to be reactionary. See DINOSAUR WING; RADICAL RIGHT; MOSSBACK. The conservative who urges a cutback of welfare programs often prefaces his remarks with, "This will be met with cries of anguish from the bleeding hearts, but . . ."

The expression was introduced into political usage in the thirties by columnist Westbrook Pegler. See INVECTIVE, POLITICAL. Its origin may be the Order of the Bleeding Heart, a semireligious order of the Middle Ages honoring the Virgin Mary, whose "heart was pierced with many sorrows."

England's *New Statesman* in 1966 showed a cartoon of President Lyndon Johnson in a Christmas sleigh, captioned with a vitriolic poem:

> Bedecked with olive branch, he showers
>   blessings on Hanoi:
> The gift of an ephemeral life for every
>   girl and boy.
> But do not judge him harshly if he scatters fire and germ,
> You have to steel your bleeding heart to
>   clinch a second term. . . .

By the 1990s the term was applied more broadly and, not without irony, even to ultraconservatives. In April 1990, *U.S. News & World Report* described New York Federal Judge Robert Sweet as being "no bleeding heart when it comes to meting out tough sentences." And in *The Nation* of November 9, 1990, Eric Alterman had this to say about ultraconservative Pat Buchanan: "This bleeding heart for the suffering of West Bank Palestinians is uncharacteristic."

Jack Kemp, Secretary of Housing and Urban Development in the Bush Administration, characterized himself as "a bleeding-heart conservative." See LIBERAL.

bleeding Kansas   the guerrilla skirmishing, rioting, and other disorders that shook ante-bellum Kansas as proslavery and antislavery factions competed for control.

Which newspaper or political orator first referred to "bleeding Kansas" is unknown, but the phrase appeared in many headlines and speeches when the fighting became serious in 1855–56. Both sides were guilty of atrocities, which included a minor massacre perpetrated by John Brown. In the propaganda war, however, it was the abolitionists who used "bleeding Kansas" as a war cry across the North, especially during the 1856 elections.

Kansas's agony was not the first case of civil strife to be called "bleeding." In the seventeenth century, for instance, it was "bleeding Ireland." The usage has remained largely historic, although bleeding Kansas can be used to describe a minor conflict that presages a much larger one involving roughly the same issues. Historian Samuel Eliot Morison juxtaposes bleeding Kansas and the subsequent Civil War with the Spanish Civil War and the subsequent World War II.

Reporter John Gunther wrote in his 1947 *Inside U.S.A.*: "Does 'Bleeding Kansas' still bleed? Will it still rise to fight injustice? I asked this question generally, and one answer I got was, 'Oh, we still have a hemorrhage once in a while.'"

blitz.   See DEWEY BLITZ.

bloc   a group of citizens or organizations gathered to promote some special interest, as "the farm bloc."

The French popularized the term, applying it to those temporary and shifting combinations of parties in the Chamber of Deputies during the Third Republic. Clemenceau's *Bloc des Gauches*, formed after the Dreyfus Affair, was one example, and Poincaré's

Bloc National, formed in 1919, was another.

In the U.S., the term has been used to convey the idea of selfish interests as well as special ones. Conferring with his advisers soon after his election to the presidency in 1920, Warren G. Harding asked the question that every one of his successors has had to confront since then: "What shall we do about the farm bloc?"

Adlai Stevenson, during his 1952 presidential campaign, deplored another kind of bloc: ". . . the myth of monolithic voting—the idea that all the votes in a bloc go one way or the other in response to the candidate's willingness to go along with the official positions of the bloc." In a similar vein, John F. Kennedy said during his dramatic confrontation with the Greater Houston Ministerial Association in 1960 that he believed in an America "where there is no Catholic vote, no anti-Catholic vote, no bloc voting of any kind." See BAILEY MEMORANDUM. As the Vietnam War grew, its opponents coalesced into what was called the "Peace Bloc."

For Americans, the word long had another association—in the phrase, "Sino-Soviet bloc," similar to an earlier use of Rome-Berlin AXIS. With the growing split between Moscow and Peking in the 1960s, however, many experts urged abandonment of the phrase as an inaccurate oversimplification. As historian Arthur Schlesinger, Jr., wrote in a memo to the State Department in 1963, when he was serving as a White House aide: "In view of what is going on currently in Moscow, could not the Department bring itself to abolish the usage, 'Sino-Soviet bloc'? The relationship of that phrase to reality grows more tenuous all the time."

blockade. See QUARANTINE.

blocks of five. See SWING VOTER.

bloodbath a feared extermination of allies.

During the Vietnam War, one of the reasons advanced for the U.S. to continue supporting the South Vietnamese forces was that a pull-out of Americans would lead to a "bloodbath"—the killings of tens of thousands of American allies by the North Vietnamese. The word was popularized by California Governor Ronald Reagan.

After the Vietnam War ended, the predicted bloodbath did not materialize in South Vietnam, but it did in Cambodia, where an estimated million citizens died after the Khmer Rouge took over in Phnom Penh.

The word is a political extension of "massacre," and is a calque of the German *Blutbad*. According to Eric Partridge, German soldiers called the 1916 Battle of the Somme "the bloodbath," and it was adopted by Allied soldiers in World War I to describe any engagement in which casualties were heavy.

For the ultimate in destruction, see HOLOCAUST, THE.

blood, sweat, and tears promise of an all-out effort; giving everything possible.

This expression is a truncated and rearranged version of Winston Churchill's words. In his first speech as Prime Minister, Churchill told the House of Commons on May 13, 1940, "I would say to the House, as I have said to those who have joined this government, 'I have nothing to offer but blood, toil, tears and sweat.'"

Earlier versions conjoining the three bodily fluids have been traced to the poets John Donne and Byron, but Churchill's words popularized the expression, which was used in the late 1960s to name a popular rock group.

The phrase is often used today to derogate lesser sacrifices suggested by the speaker. A 1990 *Washington Post* editorial on George Bush compared that President's rhetoric to the "Churchillian rejection of appeasement. But Churchill went on to promise blood, sweat and tears. Bush promises a cut in the capital gains tax."

This phrase still resonates, though, in international affairs. Alistair Horne, writing in the *National Review* in 1990 on U.S.-Soviet negotiations, observed, "If I had been one of those grim [Soviet] generals that faced me at the Institute, I think I would be feeling puzzled and bitter at how much that had been won, with our blood, sweat and tears in 1945, was now being given away."

bloody shirt waved or shaken rhetorically for nearly three decades after the Civil War; an appeal to old wartime emotions to equate Democrats with the Confederacy, and the south with warmongering.

Even before the war, the political antecedents of radical Republicans used the bloody shirt, both literally and in oratory, as a call for retribution. Abolitionist James Baird Weaver recounted how in the 1850s he acquired the stained and shredded linen of a preacher who had been flogged for inflaming slaves. "I waved it before the crowds," said Weaver, "and bellowed: 'under this bloody shirt we propose to march to victory.'"

The term came into wide use in the 1860s and '70s. Both Democrats and moderate Republicans who sought a conciliatory policy used it when attempting to debunk wilder statements of the hard-peace Republicans. Horace Greeley had been a Union man and an abolitionist, but in 1872, when he broke with the Republicans to run for President as an independent, he denounced his former friends for "waving the bloody shirt." Four years later Republican Senator John Logan of Illinois said in a typical speech: "It has come to be a saying . . . that we are

shaking the bloody shirt if we call attention to brutal wholesale murder of colored Republicans. . . . When Democrats will stop staining the shirt with blood, we will quit shaking it."

The association of an "ensanguined garment" with vengeance and a debt of blood is ancient. In Shakespeare's *Julius Caesar*, Mark Antony whipped up the fury of his fellow Romans by waving his murdered leader's toga. Gibbon mentions that when the Caliph Othman of Damascus was murdered in A.D. 656, his stained clothes were displayed. It appears in literature and in history—in Scotland (a 1603 massacre by the Clan MacGregor), Corsica, France, and eighteenth-century America, where Patrick Henry displayed a victim's clothing in a court case. Abraham Lincoln was said to have employed a similar trick in an Illinois murder trial where he was assisting the district attorney, saying, ". . . it is better to wave the bloody shirt than to waive justice."

Commenting on American politics in 1880, *Punch* magazine wrote of candidate James G. Blaine:

> There was an old stalwart named Blaine,
> Who hailed from the region of Maine.
> When he felt badly hurt
> He would cry "Bloody Shirt"—
> And slay over the already slain.

In 1942, writer Carey McWilliams characterized anti-Orientalism on the West Coast—resulting in the imprisonment of American citizens of Japanese descent during World War II—as "California's Bloody Shirt."

blooper an exploitable mistake; a slip of the tongue, or unthinking comment, that can be seized upon by the opposition.

A *blooper* is worse than a *goof* or *boner*, more adult than a *boo-boo*, not as serious as a *flub* or *blunder*, equivalent to a *gaffe*. Repeated commission of any results in a description of having FOOT-IN-MOUTH DISEASE.

Nelson Rockefeller was asked, as he campaigned for re-election as New York governor in 1966, about his campaign promise of 1962 not to raise taxes. His seemingly casual reply was the result of many strategy meetings of aides, who worried about how to meet the most serious opposition charge. The decision was to admit it had been a mistake. Said Rockefeller: "That was the biggest blooper I ever made."

Blooper is a recent coinage, probably adapted from radio announcers' slang for a spoonerism or slip of the tongue. ("Ladies and gentlemen," said NBC's Harry Von Zell, "the President of the United States, Hoobert Heever.") But the act of blooping has been in politics since the game, science, business, or art began. "Hancock the Superb"—General Winfield Scott Hancock—had a good chance to beat James Garfield in 1880. When asked about tariffs, he replied "The tariff is a local issue," and was pleased that he did not get embroiled in the issue. "The Republicans, however," wrote editor Henry Stoddard, "made much ado about a soldier's ignorance of economics. Hancock's long dream of the Presidency dissolved in these five inopportune but truthful words." Stoddard suggested that it was only a blooper.

Winners' bloopers are seldom remembered; losers' bloopers gain in importance with the years. In the Truman-Dewey campaign of 1948, Truman's whistlestop appearances were seldom on time and Democratic scheduling was less than airtight. See WHISTLESTOPPING. But the Dewey "Victory Special" campaign train rolled on with awesome efficiency, schedules met, speech texts promptly available. At one of the local stops, the Dewey train suddenly jerked away from the station, such a change from the usual smooth start that the candidate exclaimed: "What's the matter with that idiot engineer?"

"This turned out to be a magnificent blooper," wrote Cabell Phillips of the *New York Times.* "In the skilled hands of the Democratic propagandists, it became overnight a jeering anti-Dewey slogan in railroad roundhouses and Union halls all across the country."

A British example: In the General Election of 1964, Conservative Prime Minister Sir Alec Douglas-Home faced a tough interrogation on BBC television. In answering a question about a proposed supplement for older pensioners, Sir Alec used the word "donation." Labor supporters of Harold Wilson seized the usage, cartoonists illustrated it, and it was used throughout the campaign to exploit the apparently patrician attitude of the Conservatives.

An American example: In the summer of 1971 Senator Ed Muskie told a group of black leaders that he did not believe the American electorate was ready yet for a black on the national ticket. Wrote Milton Viorst, a liberal columnist: "Judged by the conventional political code of conduct, Muskie committed a blooper, perhaps a serious one."

On the international scene, diplomatic errors may be serious (see MISCALCULATION) or amusing, as when U.S. Ambassador to the UN, Warren Austin, hoped during the 1948 war in Palestine that the Jews and the Arabs would settle their differences "like good Christians."

See BRAINWASH.

bloviate to orate pompously.

Warren G. Harding popularized this word; his biographer, Francis Russel, claimed it was an old Ohio term meaning "to loaf," and, as Harding said, "The world has no use for a loafer."

Perhaps Harding used "bloviation" in that sense; however, it soon became applied to his own oratory, and today is best remembered as a description of Harding's forensic fatuousness.

In fact, the word has had that empty-oratory meaning for more than a century. In its October 23, 1909, edition, *Literary Digest* derided a proposal to create a separate state of Southern California by quoting a *Louisville Courier-Journal* suggestion to make Los Angeles a state, an arrangement "which would rid California of a maximum of bluster and bloviation and a minimum of territory."

This meaning of "bloviate" was cited by Albert Barrère and Charles G. Leland in their 1889 *Dictionary of Slang, Jargon and Cant*: "Bloviate (American): a made up or 'factitious' word, which has been used since 1850, and is perhaps older. It is irregularly used to signify verbosity, wandering from the subject, and idle or inflated oratory or blowing, by which word it was probably suggested, being partially influenced by 'deviate.'"

In current usage, that definition stands. A recent example of "bloviation" appeared in September 1992 in an article by Susan Lee in the "Hers" column of the *New York Times Magazine*: ". . . men in Washington talk too much. Everywhere you look, there are men talking. It's like a giant Bloviation Bee." The derivation, as Barrère and Leland suggest, is from "blow," which has an old slang meaning of loud and empty talk, and is also the root of the related "blowhard."

blowback. See CIA-ESE.

blue book. See WHITE PAPER.

blue ribbon panel   a jury or committee chosen on the basis of intelligence or special experience to investigate particularly complex or important matters.

Denoting exclusivity, the term comes from the ribbons worn by members of the Order of the Garter in Great Britain, and the *cordon bleu* of the ancient order of *St. Esprit* in France, as well as from the ribbons awarded to prize-winners, animal and human alike. Though properly applied to juries, "blue ribbon panel" has become something of a cliché for any government-appointed committee. Practically every major investigative or reform group, from the postwar Hoover Commission that recommended sweeping reforms in the U.S. executive branch, to Lyndon Johnson's commission on the draft, has been described in the press as a blue-ribbon panel.

Columnist Art Buchwald spoofed the phrase in 1967: "While Art Buchwald is taking a few days off, a blue ribbon panel has selected some of his articles from the past . . ."

In 1992, Hillary Clinton called her panel for health care legislation a TASK FORCE, broken down into "work groups."

blue slip   an individual senator's approval of a presidential nomination, the lack of which, in some cases, results in withdrawal of a nomination.

The "blue slip" is the currency of SENATORIAL COURTESY. If a senator objects to a nomination the President has made, he can cast a blackball by simply not returning the approval forms sent out by the Majority Leader. If the appointee is from the senator's state, and if the senator and the appointee, or the senator and the President, are in the same party, the likelihood of a further Senate consideration is small.

Here is the text of a blue slip, 1978 vintage, from the Committee on the Judiciary, Senator James Eastland (D-Miss.) chairman:

"Dear Senator: Will you kindly give me, for the use of the Committee, your opinion and information concerning the nomination of [blank]. Under a rule of the Committee, unless a reply is received from you within a week from this date, it will be assumed that you have no objection to this nomination. Respectfully . . ."

The second sentence is understood by sender and recipient to be the opposite of the truth. If the blue slip is not returned, a committee secretary calls the senator who has not returned it, to make sure the slip did not get lost in the mail; if the senator's office says, simply, that the senator has not yet acted upon it, the blackball has been cast and the nominee has been "blue-slipped."

See PATRONAGE; PERSONALLY OBNOXIOUS.

board of education a House of Representatives leadership group that gathered on occasion to persuade less senior members of the leadership's wisdom.

In a profile of the new Speaker of the House in 1962, the *New York Times* headline read: "Rayburn's 'Board of Education' Keeps Role Under McCormack." Citing evidence that John McCormack of Massachusetts was a conservative on preserving traditions, the January 29 story pointed out: "The latest is his decision to continue the 'Board of Education.' Under Speaker Rayburn, the group—partly social, partly political and entirely private— met about sundown in an out-of-the-way room on the ground floor of the Capitol . . . Under Speaker McCormack, the same room is used, and the same customs, including the pouring of bourbon and scotch, are maintained." Members included Representative Carl Albert (who succeeded McCormack as Speaker) and Lewis Deschler, parliamentarian of the

House. "The only new member," wrote the *Times* reporter, introducing a future Speaker, "as far as non-members have been able to determine, is Rep. Thomas P. O'Neill of Massachusetts. He is a longtime close friend and political associate of Speaker McCormack." See STRIKE A BLOW FOR FREEDOM.

body politic any group governed by any means; a governmental system, with the word "body" used in the same sense of "body of laws" or "body of facts."

An early use occurred in Thomas Hobbes's *Leviathan*, published in 1651: "Of systems subordinate, some are political and some private. Political (otherwise called bodies politic and persons in law) are those which are made by authority from the sovereign power of the Commonwealth."

The metaphor linking the human anatomy to the system of government can be found in Plato's *Republic*. In Jean-Jacques Rousseau's *Discourse on Political Economy*, the metaphoric use was extended: "The body politic, taken individually may be considered as an organised, living body, resembling that of a man. The sovereign power represents the head; the laws and customs are the brain . . . commerce, industry and agriculture are the mouth and stomach . . . the public income is the blood . . . the citizens are the body and the members, which make the machine live, move and work. . . ." Rousseau held that "the body politic, therefore, is also a moral being possessed of a will." In *Social Contract* he wondered, "Has the body politic an organ to declare its will?" and warned, "The body politic, like the human body, begins to die from its birth, and bears in itself the causes of its own destruction." (In other translations, the famous phrase reads "seeds of its own destruction.")

The comparison to the human body offered many American politicians an opportunity to be eloquent. James Garfield, a future President speaking just after the Civil War, pressed for the Negro's right to vote: ". . . the inequality of rights before the law, which is now a part of our system, is more dangerous to us than to the black man whom it disenfranchises. It is like a foreign substance in the body, a thorn in the flesh; it will wound and disease the body politic."

In more recent times, the phrase has been used metaphorically by some, straight by others. Chief Justice Charles Evans Hughes said: "In the great enterprise of making democracy workable we are all partners. One member of our body politic cannot say to another: 'I have no need of thee.'" Dwight Eisenhower helped his audience by defining it: "As we see difficulties and defects in the body politic, in the social order, we must never attempt before our own consciences to dodge our own responsibilities."

Columbia University, conferring its Doctorate of Laws on Adlai Stevenson in 1954, took an extreme metaphoric route: "Physician extraordinary to the body politic, skilled in diagnosis, bold in prognosis, forthright in prescription, buoyant of bedside manner . . ."

Franklin Roosevelt discarded the phrase and used the idea. "A nation, like a person, has a body," he said in his Third Inaugural Address in 1941, which must be fed and housed and clothed in accordance with American standards, and "a nation, like a person, has a mind" which must be kept informed and be understanding. Finally, "a nation, like a person, has something deeper, something more permanent, something larger than the sum of its parts. It is that something that matters most to its future. . . . It is a thing for which we find it difficult—even im-

possible—to hit upon a single simple word. And yet, we all understand what it is: the spirit . . . the faith of America . . ." Like Rousseau, FDR found in the body politic "a moral being possessed of a will."

boll weevil   a Southern conservative Democrat.

Boll in this phrase refers to the seedpod of a plant, such as cotton. *Boll weevil*, first used in 1895, is a small beetle with a prolonged snout; the bug, which can be controlled but not eliminated, infests and destroys cotton plants.

The name of this Southern pest became a self-applied label by conservative Democrats in the 1950s. During Eisenhower's Administration, Representative Howard Smith of Virginia and, later, Representative Omar Burleson of Texas advanced the boll weevil as the symbol of their unstoppable group.

In the 1980s, Representative Charles Stenholm, a Democrat from Texas, reapplied the term, linking himself with other tenacious conservative Democrats: "People have been trying to eradicate boll weevils for a long, long time."

The use of insects for nicknames has also been tried by moderate Northern Republicans, who in the early 1980s began to call themselves *gypsy moths*. First used during the Reagan Administration by Representative Lawrence DeNardis of Connecticut, the term contains a promise of change; as DeNardis told columnist David Broder, "The gypsy moth goes through a unique metamorphosis from worm to fly."

bolt   to desert one's party or faction; as a noun, the act of such desertion.

Bolt is venerable in political usage, going back deep into the nineteenth century, and possibly further, which isn't surprising because the term goes to the heart of party politics: the never-ending cycle of sundering and solidifying loyalties. In 1884 the *Boston Journal* posed this definition: "a bolter's one . . . who can't command and won't obey." That, of course, spoke for the viewpoint of PARTY LOYALTY. Many have upheld the primacy of personal principle. Raymond Moley, who bolted the Democratic party after the 1936 election of Franklin Roosevelt, gave the classic reply: "I was frequently asked why I left the Democratic party. My answer was that the Democratic party had left me."

The term has kept its original meaning, as well as its currency, perhaps because there is no real difference between its political or figurative sense and its literal or physical meaning (the horse bolted out of control). Harry Truman, discussing the defection in 1948 of the Progressives on the left and the Dixiecrats on the right, said, "I was confronted not with one major defection in the Democratic party but with two bolts . . ." A more colloquial term, dropped into the political vocabulary in 1936 by Alfred E. Smith when he publicly broke with Roosevelt, is to TAKE A WALK. Walter "Red" Barber, then the broadcaster for the Brooklyn Dodgers, was able to tie baseball, domestic politics, and the Cold War together during the United Nations' early years when the Russian delegation, led by Andrei Gromyko, occasionally bolted, or took a walk. Barber would say of a recipient of a base on balls: "He's taking a Gromyko."

In British political usage, "to bolt a bill" is to pass it without close consideration, which in American usage is "railroad it through."

For other horse-racing metaphors in politics, see DARK HORSE; SHOO-IN; FRONT RUNNER. For a milder form of bolting, see OFF THE RESERVATION; for organized bolting, see SPLINTER GROUP and DIXIECRAT.

bombing pause a temporary cessation of bombing to determine whether the opponent wishes to negotiate; a concession to create an atmosphere for negotiation.

The phrase was probably introduced into debate about the war in Vietnam by Canadian Prime Minister Lester Pearson, in a speech in Philadelphia on April 2, 1965. Pearson, who as Canada's Minister of External Affairs had won a Nobel Peace Prize, suggested that President Johnson ought to order a "pause" in bombing North Vietnam, which might bring about peace talks.

The phrase gave focus, and the sponsor gave weight, to much previous pressure from what was called the "Peace Bloc" to halt the bombing. On May 13, 1965, the first "bombing pause" began, lasted for six days, and was followed by longer and shorter pauses in subsequent years. DOVES said the pauses were too temporary and too short; "hawks" (see WAR HAWKS) said the pauses were a show of weakness, allowing the North Vietnamese to regroup and resupply.

"Pause" is a word with a curious history in politics. President James Buchanan remarked on the eve of the Civil War, "Let us pause at this momentous point and afford the people an opportunity for reflection"—by which he meant a general election that would relieve him of responsibility.

German propagandists in 1941 described the lull in fighting after the Nazi conquest of Crete as a "creative pause." *Time* magazine in 1942 referred to any cessation of hostilities as the "creative pauses of Adolf Hitler." The phrase was an ominous one, implying a build-up of power for a fresh attack (and offering a good excuse for inactivity).

The word hurt the Conservatives in the 1964 general elections in Great Britain. Chancellor of the Exchequer

Selwyn Lloyd, in an effort to meet Britain's balance-of-trade crisis, said of wages and salaries: "There must be a pause until productivity has caught up." The "pay pause" was used by Labour to attack the government; after Labour had won, the "pause" went into effect and became known as a "freeze."

In a book by Richard V. Allen on peaceful coexistence, published by the American Bar Association, the Russian word *peredyshka* is defined: "Breathing Space (Peredyshka)—Period of rest in which forces are regrouped in preparation for another offensive against the West, which usually occurs after a Communist advance has been halted and the 'enemy' has become alert to further Communist aggression; a period designed to relax the enemy's defenses so as to facilitate the next offensive. 'Peredyshka' means 'pause.'"

During the Gorbachev era in the Soviet Union, this *peredyshka* was contrasted to the more famous PERESTROIKA, "restructuring."

bomfog   a high-sounding, glittering generality.

The word comes from reporters' shorthand covering Governor Nelson Rockefeller's speeches in his 1964 campaign against Barry Goldwater in the New Hampshire primary, which resulted in an upset victory in New Hampshire for Henry Cabot Lodge.

Nancy Shea, of Rockefeller's staff, informed the author:

> Bomfog was originated by Hy Sheffer who was at one time the Governor's stenotypist. Hy told me he started using it in the late 1959–60 national effort. Since the Governor used the phrase "the brotherhood of man under the fatherhood of God," so often, Hy began to simplify it on the stenotype machine. *Bomfog* took only two strokes on the machine compared to several more

strokes for the whole phrase. The reporters traveling with the Governor's party picked it up and made it famous.

"Brotherhood of man, fatherhood of God" is part of the Rockefeller family credo, a speech by John D. Rockefeller, Jr., etched in marble near the statue of Prometheus in New York's Rockefeller Center: "These are the principles upon which alone a new world recognizing the brotherhood of man and the fatherhood of God can be established."

The initials had an appeal as a political word because it seemed to combine "bombast" with "fog," or amorphous oratory. Its use is no longer limited to critics of Nelson Rockefeller.

boneless wonder.   See INVECTIVE, POLITICAL.

boodle   graft; illicit profit derived from holding public office, usually in the form of bribes; more loosely, loot of any type.

This durable word of several meanings came into wide political use in New York during the early 1880s, when the construction of the Brooklyn Bridge was hotly debated. A number of publications used the term around the same time and with the same meaning. Typical was *Puck's* Dooley-esque spoof in 1883, quoting an unnamed alderman: "They say there's a power of boodle in the building av it; so yous needn't bother about what they'll do wid it." The following year the *New York World* said of the lobbyists' activities: "It has been a double-barrelled shotgun of boodle."

Boodle went national in the presidential election of 1884 and was used most tellingly against James G. Blaine, the unsuccessful Republican candidate. When he attended a Delmonico's dinner in his honor—given by some of the country's richest men—the newspapers dubbed the event the "boodle banquet." A Thomas Nast cartoon depicted Blaine defending "Fort Boodle." Benjamin Harrison, the Republican nominee four years later, absorbed similar attacks, but won anyway. Said the *New York Times* when Harrison took Indiana: "There seems to be no good reason to doubt that boodle and bulldozing have carried the state for Harrison."

At the 1948 Republican convention, Illinois Governor Dwight Green lambasted the Democrats as an alliance of "bosses, boodle, buncombe and blarney."

Although the word's etymology is perfectly proper (it comes from the Dutch *boedel*, meaning property), its American use seems always to have had a larcenous or facetious connotation. At least three decades before it became synonymous with political swag, it was used to denote counterfeit money. Although GRAFT, *fix, payoff*, and *bribe* are more frequently used words, *boodle* is still current. "Each time there was a payment," wrote *Life* magazine in a 1968 story on organized crime in New York, "there was this ritual cutting up of the boodle."

In an era of electronic eavesdropping, another synonym is a "wordless word": in lieu of the question "Can he be bribed?" the potential briber says nothing but rubs his thumb against his index and middle finger and raises his eyebrows.

See REACHED; LITTLE TIN BOX.

bookburners censors; self-appointed guardians of what may and may not be read; anti-intellectuals.

The burning of books considered offensive to the group in power had often occurred in the Middle Ages, but "bookburning" became a political word on the evening of May 10, 1933, less than five months after Hitler came to power. William L. Shirer described the scene in Berlin:

At about midnight a torch light parade of thousands of students ended at a square on Unter den Linden opposite the University of Berlin. Torches were put to a huge pile of books that had been gathered there, and as the flames enveloped them more books were thrown on the fire until some twenty thousand had been consumed. Similar scenes took place in several other cities. The book burning had begun.

Propaganda Minister Joseph Goebbels addressed the students in the light of the pyre: "The soul of the German people can express itself. These flames not only illuminate the final end of an old era; they also light up the new." (See NIGHT OF THE LONG KNIVES.)

FDR, in a message to the American Booksellers Association in 1942, wrote: "We all know that books burn—yet we have the greater knowledge that books cannot be killed by fire. . . . in this war, we know, books are weapons."

Senator Joseph McCarthy, investigating the State Department's predecessor to the U.S. Information Agency, sent two of his assistants, Roy M. Cohn and G. David Schine, abroad to investigate alleged inefficiency and cases of doubtful loyalty. Their tour (see JUNKETEERING GUMSHOES) aroused controversy; subsequently the State Department excluded "the works of all Communist authors" from U.S. libraries abroad. One news report chose the slanted word "burned" rather than "removed," evoking memories of the Nazi experience.

President Eisenhower, who refused to ENGAGE IN PERSONALITIES, made this observation on the campus of Dartmouth College: "Don't join the bookburners! Don't think you are going to conceal faults by concealing evidence that they ever existed. Don't be afraid to go in your library and read every book as long as that document does not offend your own ideas of decency. That should be the only censorship."

History's first recorded bookburning was ordered by the first emperor of the Ch'in dynasty in China around 220 B.C. The emperor, who was responsible for the completion of the Great Wall, not merely burned books but also buried alive a few hundred scholars in pits mainly to suppress Confucianism. In China "bookburning and scholar pitting" has become a familiar phrase.

boom (boomlet)   a well-publicized movement to promote a political candidate.

Booms may be artificially induced, but those that have voter appeal often turn into the real thing. The word gained political currency in the late 1870s when it was used to describe the noise and hullabaloo associated with the growing sentiment for General Ulysses S. Grant for another Republican presidential nomination. An 1879 story in the *San Diego Daily Union*: "Mr. McCullagh, editor of the *St. Louis Globe-Democrat*, who first applied the word 'boom' to the Grant movement, says he used the term in the sense that it is applied to a sudden and irresistible rise in a river. He wanted a term to imply that the Grant movement was sweeping everything before it, and he chose the word 'boom.'"

The magazine *Puck* speculated in 1879 about the origin of the phrase: "Lately has been added to our American political vocabulary the word 'boom,' which sprang up nobody knows where, and means nobody knows exactly what. The term may have arisen from the system of booming great rafts of logs on our rivers; or the term may refer to the boom which is spread out from the mast to extend the canvas to the favoring breeze. Our opinion is that it is the 'boom' of cannon which has given rise to the phrase." A year later *Puck* posed the question that puzzles practical politicians to this day: "Can a boom once boomed be reboomed, or does it boom itself out at the first boom?"

A boomlet is a boom that makes only a plaintive, popping sound. Boomlets are started for candidates with little real hope of achieving a nomination. Generally they die out and the man for whom the boomlet was launched throws his support to someone else, possibly in return for a place on the ticket—which might have been the reason for the boomlet all along.

An economic boom is similar in meaning to a political boom: both are off and running, though there is less connotation of manipulation in an economic boom.

boom and bust   severe cyclical movement of an economy; apparent prosperity followed by extreme depression; a manic-depressive economy.

The phrase always means something to be shunned. In his 1948 State of the Union message, President Harry Truman used the familiar phrase calling for a comprehensive anti-inflation program "to protect our economy against the evils of boom and bust."

Eisenhower economic adviser Arthur Burns said in 1960: "The American people have of late been more conscious of the business cycle, more sensitive to every wrinkle of economic curves, more alert to the need for contracyclical action on the part of government, than ever before in our history." Unfortunately for the Republicans, economic expansion programs were not pressed at that time and the 1960 election was held in the midst of an economic slump.

The NEW ECONOMICS of John Maynard Keynes did much to encourage the public to believe that government action could indeed eliminate the wide swings of boom and bust. Walter Heller, economic adviser to Presidents Kennedy and Johnson, held that economists had to go beyond contracyclical planning. "Policy thinking," he wrote in criticism of the Eisenhower years, "had been centered more on minimizing the fluctuations of the business cycle than on realizing the economy's great and growing potential."

But the new economists' goal of steady economic growth relieved of sharp movements in either direction was not easily achievable. The boom of the 1980s ended in a major recession, ominously depicted in the January 8, 1990, issue of *U.S. News & World Report*: ". . . developers and property owners who forgot they were in a boom-and-bust business in the buoyant decade just ended may not be around to enjoy the 1990's."

boomerang a political statement or policy that unexpectedly damages its perpetrator; a disastrous reaction.

In the 1936 presidential campaign, many companies printed flyers for insertion into pay envelopes opposing Roosevelt's Social Security program. "The whole campaign of propaganda turned out to be a boomerang," wrote Samuel Rosenman. "There may have been a time . . . as in the Bryan campaigns, when the workers of the nation, either willingly or unwillingly, took political advice from their employers; by 1936 they were voting on their own."

The derivation of boomerang is familiar: the crescent-shaped hunting weapon used by Australian Aborigines. When hurled, it comes back to the thrower. The metaphor was probably introduced by poet Oliver Wendell Holmes in 1845: "Like the strange missile which the Australian throws/ Your verbal boomerang slaps you on

the nose." Cartoonist Thomas Nast used it politically in 1877 against Carl Schurz, who made a politically unwise protest against the sale of arms to France. Nast showed Schurz firing a gun which explodes in his face, with the caption: "Carl's Boomerang. Little Children Should Not Investigate (French) Firearms."

In political usage, the word differs from BLOOPER, *blunder, goof, fluff,* and *gaffe*, which are more slips of the tongue than errors in judgment; a boomerang connotes a conscious policy willingly undertaken that turns out to be mistaken because of the unexpected adverse reaction.

Defense Secretary Charles E. Wilson, victim of several bloopers (see BIRD DOG . . . KENNEL DOG; WHAT'S GOOD FOR GENERAL MOTORS . . .), learned late in his career to be more careful of his statements. Treading carefully in a 1957 press conference, he ducked a question by observing, "I somehow feel there's a boomerang loose in the room."

In 1967 Alan Otten wrote an article titled "The Grating Society" and observed: "Slogans are an established ingredient of political public relations. Probably they are initially helpful in selling a program. But they have a way of wearing out their welcome, even boomeranging. They begin to sound contrived or corny; they provide a rallying cry for a program's foes as well as friends."

For a boomerang with racial overtones, see BACKLASH.

boondoggle any project on which government funds are wasted through inefficiency or political favoritism; originally a make-work project, using government funds to stimulate the economy.

When New York City's Board of Aldermen (now City Council) was investigating relief payments in 1935, they discovered money was being spent for the teaching of tap dancing, manipulation of shadow puppets, and the geographical distribution of safety pins. One Robert Marshall told the aldermen he was paid for teaching "boon doggles."

The word livened up the hearings, and Marshall explained to the *New York Times*: "Boon doggles is simply a term applied back in the pioneer days to what we call gadgets today . . . no, it is not named for Daniel Boone . . . it is spelled differently."

The word's origin is obscure. Most sources attribute its coinage to an American scoutmaster, R. H. Link, who in 1925 applied the word to the braided leather lanyard made and worn by Boy Scouts. The *Chicago Tribune* wrote that "to the cowboy it meant the making of saddle trappings out of odds and ends of leather, and they boon doggled when there was nothing else to do on the ranch."

The word has lost its Depression-born connotation of keeping the idle busy with government funds, though it always implied waste of money. Now the word is used in attacks on government bureaucracy on all levels, and has acquired a new connotation of favoritism. The Defense Department's "TFX" bomber program was denounced as a "huge boondoggle," and in 1966, a full-page advertisement appeared in the *New York Times* attacking a proposal for the construction of government-owned merchant ships as "a $2 billion government-aerospace boondoggle."

"Boon" means gift, or favor, and might have played a role in the word's formation; "doggle," however, appears to be the operative verb and can be used to make the term more specific. For example, when the American Legion in 1966 pressed for an expansion of national cemeteries to include all Vietnam veterans and their families, the *New Republic* headlined their comment: "The Gravedoggle."

An even more cynical definition appeared in the *Los Angeles Times Magazine* of May 31, 1992: "*Boondoggle, n.* Business trip whose location is chosen for travel/vacation motives."

boring from within infiltration of a group or society by agents dedicated to its overthrow; a FIFTH COLUMN.

Communists have long been accused of using a technique of takeover borrowed from nature: a tree-destroying beetle embeds its eggs as deeply as it can in a notch in the tree's bark, and the hatching insect instinctively bores its way through the wood.

In *Suite 3505*, published in 1967, Goldwater organizer F. Clifton White wrote about "how Communist agents and their dupes incessantly bore from within in their untiring efforts to destroy our democratic society . . ." Nelson Rockefeller, in 1963, accused the Goldwater men of doing exactly the same within the Republican party, in his first MAINSTREAM statement: ". . . the vociferous and well-drilled extremist elements boring within the party utterly reject these fundamental principles of our heritage."

A "borer" is an obsolete term for political lobbyist; the *Cincinnati National Republican* wrote in 1923 that Pennsylvanians "have applied to each other the elegant appellations of logrollers and borers . . ."

The accusation has not been limited to Communists and extremists. *Chicago Tribune* publisher Robert McCormick, America's leading Britain-hater in the forties, explained his estimate of the reason behind Rhodes scholarships: "The infamous Cecil Rhodes conceived the plan to give free education to Americans in Oxford and make them into English cells, boring from within."

bork attack viciously a candidate or appointee, especially by misrepresentation in the media.

A contemporary example of eponymy (using proper names to create words) like *lynch* and *boycott*, this verb is based on the name of Judge Robert H. Bork, whose nomination to the U.S. Supreme Court in 1987 by Ronald Reagan was rejected by the Senate after an extensive media campaign by his opponents.

The verb first appeared in print in 1988, enclosed in quotation marks, as in the *Chicago Tribune* of November 20, 1988: "Honest disagreement is one thing: 'borking' is something else."

In February 1989, Republican Senator M. Wallop of Wyoming commented on "CBS This Morning": "I feel strongly that he [Senator John Tower] is being borked. . . . The charges that have been leveled at him have all proved groundless, baseless." On the same program on July 9, 1990, it was reported that "an opponent of Judge Clarence Thomas said yesterday, 'We're going to bork him.'"

The verb is also proving useful to right-wingers seeking to retaliate for Judge Bork's defeat. A recent *New Republic* essay by Ruth Shalit discusses Democratic nominees to the Supreme Court and is headlined "Borking Back," with the subhead "The right gets even."

In other contexts, users of the verb sometimes allude or refer to the word's eponymous source, as in the article in the *Los Angeles Times* of August 23, 1992: "Perhaps . . . Hillary Clinton is being 'borked'—attacked in the same orchestrated manner which ultimately undermined the U.S. Supreme Court nomination of Judge Robert H. Bork."

The word is similar to an earlier eponymous verb, to *burke*, originally meaning "to murder someone by suffocation, especially in order to sell the body for dissection," and later used figuratively to mean "to smother or suppress (a book, a debate, an issue, etc.)." The verb was taken from the name of William Burke, a notorious criminal who was executed in Edinburgh in 1829 for smothering his victims so as to leave no mark on their bodies that would make them unacceptable for anatomical dissection. At his execution, the spectators shouted, "Burke him, Burke him! Give him no rope!"

To *burke* is to murder someone; to *bork* is to murder someone's character, to become a CHARACTER ASSASSIN.

born again in its new political sense, freshly convinced; or, newly returned to the fold.

"Born again" is a phrase central to Evangelical Christianity, meaning a spiritual experience resulting in a commitment to Christ. Convicted White House Counsel Charles Colson used the phrase in that sense as the title of his 1976 bestseller. When Jimmy Carter became a serious contender for the Democratic Presidential nomination, questions were raised about his religiosity: he freely asserted that he was a "born-again Christian" and his sister, Ruth Stapleton, was an eminent Evangelist. This strong assertion of religious belief was regarded by some politicians as a negative, since it was met with suspicion by some voters and with guilt by others.

But the threat of "too much religion" in the candidate turned out to be a political old wives' tale, similar to the shibboleth that no Catholic could run successfully for President, which persisted until John Kennedy won.

The phrase "born-again," however, was taken into the political terminology: Democrats returning to the party were hailed as "born-again Democrats," and liberals reluctant to make difficult spending decisions that required new taxation were dubbed "born-again conservatives."

The phrase is now used in politics with no religious meaning, but with an ironic Carteresque connotation, to mean "newborn" or suddenly converted. Anthony Lake, who was a member of the national Security Council staff in the late sixties and who broke with Henry Kissinger in 1970 to become an outspoken DOVE, became a top policy planner in the Carter State Department. In 1978 the State Department found it necessary to dissociate itself from some of the extremely dovish positions taken by UN Ambassador Andrew Young; although continuing to espouse noninvolvement, Lake "put some daylight" between himself and Young. This led to his being identified by columnists Evans and Novak in June 1978 as a "born-again hawk."

In its theological sense of "being born of God" or becoming a child of God, the phrase first appeared in English in John Wyclif's 1382 translation of the Bible: "But a man schal be born agen."

Bosnywash. See AXIS.

boss, bossism party leader who may not hold public office himself but who, through his control of the party organization, exerts great power over those of his party who do; bossism is a political system so organized. Both terms are almost always used in a pejorative sense.

"Bosses" and "bossism" had their first major impact on the lexicon in the mid-nineteenth century, as big-city political organizations came into vogue. There were many political bosses of course, both urban and rural, but William Marcy Tweed of New York's Democratic party became nationally notorious as "Boss Tweed." A statement generally attributed to him

sums up the boss's credo: "You may elect whichever candidates you please to office, if you allow me to select the candidates." He also stole still-uncounted millions in public funds, although recent research disputes this. Upon entering prison he gave his occupation as "statesman."

Few bosses before or since have equaled Tweed in either avarice or self-esteem. But they have played a crucial part in American politics, both in their function of building strong party organizations on the county, city, and state levels, and as a recurrent election issue and target for reformers.

Just as the nation is a federal union, each major American party is really a collection of state and local party organizations. The men who tend the machinery get as their principal wage— unless they personally hold public office—power. This power is tangible in the form of PATRONAGE, influence on nominations for great and small posts, and such matters as where a new road is to be built. But one thing that leaders of this kind rarely obtain is a good public face. Regardless of their honesty, they are often thought of as the gross, evil, Tweed type or as the insatiable tiger clawing over his victims' bodies, as Thomas Nast drew the TAMMANY TIGER in Tweed's day.

The relatively unknown Woodrow Wilson was nominated for governor of New Jersey in 1910 largely through the efforts of boss James Smith of Newark and the state's lesser Democratic captains. Even before he took office, Wilson cooled toward Smith and, as James MacGregor Burns tells it, pictured Smith "not as he really was—a run-of-the-mill party boss—but as evil personified, a party despot, a symbol of corruption and predatory control. . . . Frantically Smith charged Wilson with dishonesty . . . but few would take the word of a boss over the word of a high-minded professor."

There have been many other such instances. Mayor Robert Wagner of New York won nomination for a third term (and then re-election) on a beat-the-boss platform. The irony was that the principal boss, Tammany's Carmine De Sapio, had himself come to power as something of a reformer, had liberalized Tammany's internal practices, and had been a much-valued ally of Wagner's for years. The moral was clear: De Sapio was stripped of power by the very processes he introduced. At the same time in neighboring Bronx County, the late Charles Buckley retained power until his death although he lost his congressional seat to the reformers. Buckley, unlike De Sapio, had never sanctioned the direct election of local party officials.

Since World War II, it has often been said that bosses and tightly held political machines are in such bad health that only political coroners should care. Ed Flynn, a Buckley predecessor in the Bronx, wrote the apologia in his 1947 book, *You're the Boss*. Harry Truman said sarcastically in 1959: "When a leader is in the Democratic Party, he's a boss; when he's in the Republican Party, he's a leader."

bounce. See CONVENTION BOUNCE.

Boy Scout a naive politician; one with a head-in-the-clouds approach to government.

"Boy Scout" is a derisive comment, made by cynical reporters or politicians, about those who do not bear the scars of compromise.

The best definition is Disraeli's remark about Gladstone: ". . . honest in the most odious sense of the word." An early political use was by Frank Kent of the *Baltimore Sun*, describing the parade of planners and Ph.D.s into the new Roosevelt Ad-ministration in 1933: "Boy Scouts in the White House . . . a government by Pink Pollyannas, first-name slingers, mothers' little helpers."

At a ball given by New York newspaper reporters soon after the election of John Lindsay as mayor, the new mayor was played onstage by a reporter (Edward O'Neill of the *Daily News*) in a Boy Scout uniform. After Michigan Governor George Romney visited New York's City Hall, Lindsay confided to associates: "You know, they call me a Boy Scout. If I am, Romney's an Eagle Scout."

In *The Arrogance of Power* (1967), Senate Foreign Relations Committee chairman J. William Fulbright used Boy Scouts in a story illustrating America's misplaced missionary zeal: "I am reminded of the three Boy Scouts who reported to their scoutmaster that as their good deed for the day they had helped an old lady to cross the street. 'That's fine,' said the scoutmaster, 'but why did it take three of you?' 'Well,' they explained, 'she didn't want to go.'"

Politicians who make an important point about integrity in government during their campaigns, or who frequently use the word "reform," are often tagged with the title of the current comic-strip or television hero (Lindsay, for example, was often called "Batman"). Another similar appellation is "Mr. Clean," the name of a household detergent. *Newsweek* wrote of Ronald Reagan in November 1967: "At times as governor he comes on like Mr. Clean and Captain Nice rolled into one." A month later, when a kickback scandal embarrassed the Lindsay administration, columnist William F. Buckley Jr. wrote: "It is always piquant when it turns out that Mr. Clean never bathes." See MR. NICE GUY.

The political derogation of Boy Scout had its effect; in 1977 the Boy

Scouts of America changed its venerable name to "Scouting/USA."

boys in the backroom. See AMERICAN BOYS.

bracketing   organized opposition to a candidate before and after each campaign stop; surrounding of a campaign visit by a "truth squad."

The gerund *bracketing* comes from the 1580 noun *bracket*, used in architecture for a projecting piece that holds weight or gives support. Writers use brackets inside quotation marks to add information or to verify accuracy with [*sic*].

The political sense of *bracketing* first appeared during the Presidential race of 1988, when surrogates for George Bush tracked the Dukakis campaign. A Republican "truth squad," staking out cities in which Governor Dukakis was scheduled to appear, would offer questions in advance about the candidate's record and remain after his departure to challenge his remarks.

An unidentified Bush aide told the *Washington Post* that, by using the technique of "bracketing," the Bush campaign intended to "be in front" of Dukakis at rallies until the last day of the campaign.

See TRUTH SQUAD.

Brahmin   aloof elite; a social, intellectual, or political aristocracy which manipulates power from non-elective positions.

The Brahmans of India were members of the highest Hindu caste, at the other end of the scale from the "untouchables"; Brahmanism is the word for the often-attacked but never really removed caste system in that country.

When the word arrived in Boston in the late nineteenth century, the spelling was changed. Oliver Wendell Holmes was the importer of the word in *Elsie Venner*: "He comes of the Brahmin caste of New England. This is the harmless, inoffensive, untitled aristocracy referred to, and which many readers will at once acknowledge."

Irish politicians in Boston took the "harmless" and "inoffensive" out of the word and used it as an epithet. Boston Mayor James M. Curley's biographer headed one chapter "The Boston Brahmin-baiter" and quoted a Curley-watcher as saying: "Jim can make the term 'blue blood' sound like the vilest epithet known to man. He shows the people why it would be a catastrophe to permit the 'Brahmins,' as he terms the wealthy and socially prominent, to obtain a foothold in politics."

"The Brahmins today," wrote John Gunther in 1947, "make a wonderfully close-knit archaic group, which nothing in the United States quite rivals. Harvard and trusteeships; the world placidly revolving around Back Bay; the Apley-Pulham spirit; aridity and charm and a Bloomsbury cultivation; above all, profound family interweavings."

The term is no longer limited to Boston; Brahmins are everywhere, raising money and pulling strings, being occasionally denounced as part of the EASTERN ESTABLISHMENT by those who are not "in." An October 1990 piece in *U.S. News & World Report* uses the word pejoratively: "[William] Weld's biggest challenge is to overcome the perception that he's a Brahmin out of touch with the average citizen." But a Brahmin is a power, and it is generally no longer considered an insult to be called one.

brain drain   the siphoning of scientific and technical talent from one country to another, or from one academic institution to another.

The phrase probably originated in 1963 in British newspapers concerned with an exodus of English scientists drawn to the U.S. by the higher salaries of U.S. corporations and universities.

One U.S. company—American Gauge and Machine Co. of Chicago—attacked the subject head-on with an advertisement in a London newspaper headed "Brain Drain—or the Chance of a Lifetime." The company sought a foundry manager, four draftsmen, and three machine-shop foremen.

Britons were most indignant when this kind of raid was made on their educated professional class. A government committee warned that "this deliberate and planned recruitment should not be allowed to go too far without remedial action." Labour party chairman John Boyd claimed that the brain drain had brought a windfall savings of $1 billion in education and training costs to the U.S.

Trying to smooth over this international irritant, Vice President Hubert Humphrey sought to emphasize one facet of the problem: the students who come to the U.S. with the expectation of returning home with training, but who remain here instead. "There are thousands of young scientists and engineers working in the United States who came to learn, but stayed here to earn," he said in 1966. "These are precious human resources [the developing countries] cannot afford to lose. We can help by working with the developing countries to insure that too high a percentage of their students do not come to the United States to acquire skills which have no relation to the priorities at home."

But England was no "developing country," and the English were concerned with what they considered the outright piracy of home-trained brainpower. Lyndon Johnson appointed an Inter-Agency Council on International Education and Cultural Affairs in 1965; after two years of study, the Council reported "some brain drain" but said it posed "no serious threat" to other countries.

However, a *New York Times* dispatch by John Darnton from Lagos, Nigeria, on October 31, 1976, described "the 'brain drain' of developing nations, a new class of émigrés who are not political refugees, but self-exiles . . . They concentrate in fields of study that would be useful back home, and then they discover that there is a ready market for their skills in the industrial countries—and a much more pleasant existence."

Britain continued to suffer from brain drain into the 1980s and beyond. According to the December 4, 1989, issue of *The New Republic,* "The brain drain from Thatcherite Britain has taken on the coloring of the exodus of Jews, liberals, and socialists from Germany and central Europe in the late 1930s. . . . The British government estimates that about 200 scholars a year leave Britain for overseas universities."

When the Soviet Union suffered a grain shortage in 1972 and 1973, its wheat purchases from the West—which was not aware of the Russian shortfall—was later termed "The Great Grain Robbery," a play on "train robbery," as well as "the grain drain."

brain trust   a group of advisers to a candidate or incumbent, prized more for their expertise in particular fields and intimacy with their patron than for their official position or rank.

Sperber and Trittschuh found its first use in academic circles: "If I went up before that brain trust in the faculty room once more . . . " wrote George Fitch in *At Good Old Siwash* in 1911. In 1928 *Time* headlined an article on a meeting of the American Council on Learned Societies "Brain Trust." To speculate: this could have been a play on "beef trust," which in the early

1900s meant a monopoly on meat but later was a jocular reference to hefty chorines.

The press popularized *brain trust* during the 1930s and the BBC imported the phrase as the title for a British equivalent of an American radio program, "Information Please." The BBC show followed the original American usage—*brains trust*—but the cumbersome *s* fell by the verbal wayside in the United States.

The phrase was first applied to the group of university professors whose brains Franklin Roosevelt picked and trusted during the 1932 presidential campaign. Raymond Moley, one of the original "brain trusters," says that James Kieran, a *New York Times* reporter, coined the phrase. But Samuel Rosenman, who advised Roosevelt to recruit academic help, contends that Louis Howe, Roosevelt's earliest close adviser, used the term derisively in a conversation with the chief. Rosenman says Roosevelt himself then used it at a press conference. In any event, it caught on and stuck through the New Deal and beyond with little change in meaning. Roosevelt himself had preferred calling the original group his "privy council." Critics called it, among other things, "the Professoriat."

See KITCHEN CABINET, IRISH MAFIA and PALACE GUARD for other views of advisers, and EGGHEAD for a derogation of intellectuals.

brainwash to change drastically someone's outlook and opinion pattern; to convince thoroughly, usually through nefarious means.

In current political use, totally committed supporters of an opponent's point of view are derided as "brainwashed"; that is, it is a waste of time to try to convince them of another cause. It is a scare word used in political argument, a frequent warning against being converted. When the American Medical Association chose Dr. Edward Roland Ennis to "answer" President Kennedy on the subject of MEDICARE, the doctor claimed that "the American public is in danger of being blitzed, brainwashed and bandwagoned into swallowing the idea that the King-Anderson Bill is the only proposal . . ."

The word first began to appear in 1950 to describe the technique of mental and physical torture and concentrated indoctrination of prisoners of war held in Communist countries. "In the newly authoritarian countries," wrote the *American Journal of Psychiatry* in February 1951, "the term 'brainwashing' is born to indicate this systematic breaking down of old loyalties and paternal ties." Wrote the *New York Times* in March: "In totalitarian countries the term 'brainwashing' has been coined to describe what happens when resistance fighters are transformed into meek collaborators . . . [Cardinal] Mindszenty was spiritually softened until he became putty in the hands of his persecutors."

The word—a translation from a Chinese term for "thought reform"—gained currency during prisoner-of-war exchanges at the conclusion of the Korean conflict. Americans were shocked when 21 U.S. soldiers expressed a wish not to be repatriated. Subsequently, a new code of conduct for U.S. armed services personnel was issued to clarify a prisoner's responsibilities under the inducements and threats of "brainwashing." (For a 1941 use by a Chinese leader, see Theodore H. White's memoir under CONSCIOUSNESS-RAISING.)

Michigan Governor George Romney's use of the term, in September 1967, illustrated its power. "When I came back from Vietnam [in 1965]," he told a TV interviewer, "I had just had the greatest brainwashing that anybody can get when you go over to Vietnam . . . not only by the generals but also by the diplomatic corps over there, and they do a very thorough job . . ." He had intended to imply that the reason for his change of position about the war in 1967 was that he had been misled two years before. But Romney's use of "brainwash" was in his campaign manager Len Hall's words "not a plus"; ally Jacob Javits called it "inartistic"; Eugene McCarthy said "a light rinse would have been sufficient"; and the *Chicago Daily News* used several current synonyms as they asked whether the U.S. "can afford as its leader a man who, whatever his positive virtues, is subject to being cozened, flimflammed and taken into camp." See BLOOPER.

brass collar Democrat one who slavishly follows the party line; used mainly in the southern U.S.

Reader's Digest editor Earl Mazo, in a 1972 letter to the author disclaiming coinage of BACKLASH, referred to "brass collar Democrat" as his favorite bit of political slang. A possible allusion is to those newly freed blacks in Reconstruction days who did not vote Republican. An early slang dictionary (Barrère and Leland, 1895) defines "Big Dog with the Brass Collar" as a leader, now shortened to "top dog." See YELLOW DOG DEMOCRAT.

Bravo Zulu job well done; a commendable performance.

Bravo Zulu was popularized by National Security Adviser Robert C. McFarlane's use of the phrase in documents widely quoted during the Irancontra hearings. "Bravo Zulu on Jenco's release," Colonel McFarlane wrote to Vice Admiral John M. Poindexter after the freeing of an American held hostage in Lebanon in late July of 1986. McFarlane again used the phrase in ending a memo to praise

the performance of Lieutenant Colonel Oliver L. North.

Taken from Navy signal code, the word *Bravo* stands for the letter *B*, and *Zulu* for Z. These signals started with semaphore, using flags to indicate the letters. It remains unclear why this particular combination of *B* and Z is used to represent "job well done."

Originally, *Bravo Zulu* was expressed as *Baker Zebra*. The North Atlantic Treaty Organization changed the code words in 1952, choosing to represent Z with *Zulu*, for a member of the Bantu-speaking people of South Africa. More appropriate to the message is *Bravo*, an interjection based on Italian for "brave, excellent" and used in English since the eighteenth century to applaud or praise.

bread-and-butter issue a POCKETBOOK ISSUE, one that affects voters' personal budgets.

Bread and butter, the staff of life slightly greased, had a stronger political meaning in 1840 when an Ohio politician named John Brough switched his vote on a bill with the explanation: "I have my bread and butter to look after." Earlier, Washington Irving had referred to these "little, beardless bread-and-butter politicians." The phrase is obviously related to "knowing which side your bread is buttered on."

"The Bread and Butter Brigade" was the derisive term applied to the appointees of President Andrew Johnson. Senator Zachary Chandler of Michigan lashed into Johnson in 1867: "[These offices] were filled by Mr. Lincoln with good, responsible, reliable Union Republicans. [They] were removed by Andrew Johnson to make place for unreliable, irresponsible Copperheads in most cases, or bread-and-butter men, who are worse." Theodore Roosevelt, in his Bull Moose campaign, wrote: "They represent the bread-and-butter politicians and the office holders. And we stand for the future."

Bread-and-butter politician fell into disuse in recent years, and when the phrase reappeared as *bread-and-butter issue*, the pejorative meaning had disappeared. It is still in current political use, though its meaning is more usually expressed as *pocketbook issue*, or one that hits the voter where it hurts. Neither is as strong as the PARAMOUNT ISSUE phrase of the late nineteenth century, or the GUT ISSUE or HOT-BUTTON issue of today.

break all the china   carry out an order regardless of obstacles.

"'Break all the china in this building,'" counsel Charles Colson wrote that President Richard Nixon told him, "'but have an order for me to sign on my desk Monday morning.'"

This favorite Nixon locution was probably based on "a bull in a china shop" and was taken by some aides to mean "cut through the red tape and usual objections," by other aides to mean "march over a cliff."

The phrase is occasionally used without reference to the Nixon period to describe a bureaucratic shaker-upper, with a connotation of insensitivity: "Criticism of [Director of Central Intelligence Stansfield] Turner as a breaker of china in his own agency," wrote columnists Evans and Novak in December 1977, "is hurting him in the administration."

Brezhnev Doctrine.   See DOCTRINES.

bridge building   measures to reduce the tensions and dangers of the cold war, both between the United States and the Soviet Union and, more generally, between any peoples of differing ideologies.

The bridge as a symbol of peaceful intercourse has a long history; "bridging the bloody chasm" was a phrase used by post–Civil War leaders. Its applications to American foreign policy came into wide use after Lyndon Johnson became President in 1963. In his first State of the Union message, Johnson said: "We must develop with our allies new means of bridging the gap between east and west." He and other officials repeated the phrase often enough—although with variations—to give it wide currency. Senator William Fulbright phrased it this way: "Bridges can be built across the chasm of ideology."

The expression reflected the specific and limited agreements sought, and sometimes achieved, during the Eisenhower, Kennedy, and Johnson Administrations. The partial nuclear test-ban treaty of 1963, the consular treaty ratified in 1967, increased trade relations with Eastern Europe, and other measures were significant, but they hardly constituted a general settlement.

Newspaper use of the phrase without explanation indicated its general acceptance, as when the *New York Times* said in 1967: "The Senate Foreign Relations Committee advanced the Administration's East-West bridge-building program today by approving the United States–Soviet consular treaty." Like so many political terms, bridge building can be overused, as Soviet Premier Nikita Khrushchev pointed out: "Politicians are the same all over. They promise to build a bridge even where there is no river."

Foreign relations applications of the metaphor declined after the Johnson Administration left office. But Richard Nixon, in the campaign of 1968, titled two of his key speeches "Bridges to Human Dignity" and used the phrase from time to time in his Administration to describe welfare reform and BLACK CAPITALISM.

After the 1969 episode at the Chappaquiddick bridge involving Senator

Edward Kennedy, the bridge metaphor gained a tragic connotation and was temporarily dropped from political discourse.

The word now preferred is *dialogue*.

briefing book political game plan; notes to prepare a candidate or politician on wide-ranging subjects.

This alliterative term dates in Presidential usage to the mid-1970s. Before Jimmy Carter's inaugural in 1977, the *Washington Post* commented on the nation's capital and "the real U.S. government here, something that isn't in any of the briefing books and transition papers that have been developed for him."

The term became embroiled in controversy after Carter's failed second Presidential campaign. A briefing book that had been prepared for President Carter in 1980 to help in a debate came into the hands of the Reagan campaign. In 1983, the "debategate" story surfaced, and at first Reagan commented, "Is it stolen if someone gives it to you?" Subsequent public pressure led Reagan to order a Justice Department investigation into the matter.

Still in use, *briefing book*—shorter and punchier than a collection of "position papers"—is particularly prominent during election years. In September 1992, *Newsday* reported that "Budget Director Richard Darman already has debate briefing books in the works" for the Bush campaign, and that Clinton's staff "has begun collecting facts and figures and drafting witty rejoinders for the briefing books."

This term, though, can also suggest a crutch, indicating a candidate's need for coaching in areas of weakness (see HANDLERS). Lawrence J. Haas, writing for the *National Journal* in 1987, implied this negative connotation in complimenting David Stockman of the Reagan Office of Management and Budget: "On Capitol Hill, longtime budget experts say that, yes, Stockman could be sly, but his knowledge was phenomenal. In testimony, he rarely consulted briefing books."

bring us together a closing-ranks theme used by President-elect Nixon on the day after the election, which critics later interpreted as a promise and frequently derided.

"I saw many signs in this campaign," said Richard Nixon on the morning after he had been elected President. "Some of them were not friendly and some were very friendly. But the one that touched me the most was one that I saw in Deshler, Ohio, at the end of a long day of whistle-stopping, a little town, I suppose five times the population was there in the dusk, almost impossible to see—but a teenager held up a sign, 'Bring Us Together.' And that will be the great objective of this Administration at the outset, to bring the American people together. This will be an open Administration, open to new ideas, open to men and women of both parties, open to the critics as well as those who support us. We want to bridge the generation gap. We want to bridge the gap between the races. We want to bring America together."

It was Richard Moore, a California communications lawyer, culling "local color" items for the candidate on the campaign trail, who got off the train in Deshler to mingle with the crowd listening to Nixon speak from the rear platform. He spotted a girl with the sign, hand-lettered and obviously not produced by the local Republican organization, and called it to the candidate's attention.

Nixon first used the phrase at the conclusion of a Madison Square Garden speech in New York City on October 31, 1968, recollecting it as "Bring us together again."

This phrase, briefly used and relatively unnoticed, was not used again in the campaign's final weekend. National unity was not the dominant theme of either candidate, as the country was so torn at the time that such a theme would have been received with scorn. (The initial Democratic posters, "United with Humphrey," were quickly scrapped.)

On Election Day, flying from California to New York aboard the *Tricia*, while the nation's citizens voted below, and frustrated at having no writing assignment after months of heavy production, the author drafted a victory statement. To have sent it to the candidate would have been an invitation to bad luck, so it was passed to Communications Director Herb Klein, who was sure to be around Nixon before he went in front of the cameras the next day.

Just before taking the Waldorf-Astoria elevator down to the press room, Nixon glanced at the draft. The "Bring Us Together" suggestion registered.

The *New York Times* headed the transcript "Statement by Nixon Pledging to 'Bring America Together,'" and the Inaugural Committee promptly made it the theme of their festivities. Several Nixon staff aides, this writer included, objected to this, pointing out that while "Bring Us Together" was appropriate for a victory statement, the need for unity should not suddenly be placed ahead of the need for progress; also, the phrase was a call *to* a candidate rather than a call *from* a President. The solution was "Forward Together," which served as the inaugural slogan, but which did not catch on.

The *Times* had sent a reporter and photographer to Deshler to find the little girl; they came up with Vicki Lane and a picture of the sign. The reporter quoted her as saying she saw it lying on the ground and held it up when Nixon was speaking. Since there was no reason to doubt her claim, she was brought to Washington with her family for the inaugural.

As might have been expected, whenever President Nixon took an action that aroused sharp differences of opinion, a common critical refrain was "He promised to bring us together." The phrase was used in this sarcastic sense as the title of a book by Leon Panetta and Peter Gall, once again proving that a phrase with an emotional charge can charge both ways. (Mr. Panetta became Bill Clinton's director of the Office of Management and Budget.)

brinkmanship   a national security policy dictating that the nation be willing to risk large-scale—or even total—war in order to force an adversary to back down during a confrontation; when used derisively by the policy makers' critics, a reckless gamble or hollow bluff.

During the 1956 presidential campaign, Democrats led by Adlai Stevenson accused the Eisenhower Administration, and particularly Secretary of State John Foster Dulles, of "brinkmanship."

Dulles coined only part of the term in an interview with correspondent James Shepley published by *Life* in January 1956. Said Dulles: "The ability to get to the verge without getting into the war is the necessary art. If you cannot master it, you inevitably get into war. If you try to run away from it, if you are scared to go to the brink, you are lost." Citing the 1953 Korean peace-talk crisis and the 1954 threats of major war over Formosa and Indochina, Dulles said: "We walked to the brink and we looked it in the face."

The Republicans won the election, but the debate over brinkmanship went on, keeping alive the new term. Even Sherman Adams, Eisenhower's White House aide, questioned Dulles' argument. "I doubt," Adams wrote after leaving office, "that Eisenhower was as close to the brink of war in any of these three crises as Dulles made him out to be."

The metaphor depicting nations falling into war as if plunging over the edge, or brink, of a cliff is old and much used. In 1850 Henry Clay, appealing in the U.S. Senate for amity between North and South over the slavery issue, said, "Solemnly I ask you to pause at the edge of the precipice."

Adding the -*manship* to construct a "facetious formation" is contemporary. Fowler's *Dictionary of Modern English Usage* (2nd edition) compares *brinkmanship* with earlier Stephen Potterisms such as *one-upmanship* and *gamesmanship*. However, Fowler's takes brinkmanship seriously as a word, if not a foreign policy, on the grounds that it is a necessary addition to the vocabulary. Webster's *New International Dictionary* (3rd edition) also accepts it as standard English rather than slang. John Kennedy referred to "the brink" after his 1961 meeting in Vienna with Nikita Khrushchev and went to the brink the following year during the Cuban missile confrontation. See EYEBALL TO EYEBALL.

Use of the term has been extended over the years to less earthshaking issues. When Senator Patrick Moynihan proposed in 1990 to cut the Social Security payroll tax, the February 12, 1990, issue of *The Nation* used the term to attack his proposal: ". . . Moynihan is playing fiscal brinkmanship. His aim is to reveal the true size of the deficit, which is hidden on paper by the Social Security reserve."

At the 1964 Republican convention in San Francisco, some hawkish Goldwater placard carriers waved the slogan "Better brinkmanship than chickenship."

brokered convention   a party convention at which many key delegations are committed to FAVORITE SONS, thus cutting down the first-ballot strength of the serious contenders for the nomination, and resulting in bloc bargaining.

Such a convention is dominated by factional party leaders and favorite sons, who deal directly or through "neutral leaders" (see POWER BROKERS) and throw their delegate strength to one or another candidate in return for promised positions on the ticket or in the cabinet, or simply to be with the winner.

The opposite of a *brokered convention* is an OPEN CONVENTION in which individual delegates are free to vote their personal choice. In a *locked-up* or *rigged convention*, the outcome is rarely in doubt, as when an incumbent president is a candidate for renomination or when one candidate is known to "have the tickets" or majority of delegates.

Most conventions are brokered to some degree; only when two or more candidates show real strength and when no STAMPEDE can be started does a genuine brokered convention take place.

By 1972, the proliferation of primaries and erosion of the "unit rule" made brokerage more difficult, though not impossible.

brother Jonathan   early symbol for the U.S.

George Washington referred to his adviser Jonathan Trumbull, governor of Connecticut, as "brother Jonathan" recalling the second book of Samuel in the Old Testament. He may have taken this from the 1787 play *The Contrast*, by Royall Tyler, in which a character named "brother Jonathan" is portrayed as a Yankee trader.

Since a nation needs a symbol for its citizens collectively, or its average man—as the British have "John Bull" and the French "Marianne"—"brother

Jonathan" became the first appellation of the typical American.

James Russell Lowell contrasted Englishmen and Americans in 1848 in this way: "To move John you must make your fulcrum of solid beef and pudding; an abstract idea will do for Jonathan."

Rarely used now, the phrase has been replaced by UNCLE SAM.

brouhaha.   See UNFLAPPABLE.

brown derby symbol.   See TAKE A WALK.

bubba factor   the potential influence of Southern conservatives on an issue or election.

Bubba is a noun of direct address (a name or nickname for the person being spoken to). It comes from *bub*, a century-old term of endearment formed from a shortening of *brother*. The *u* in *bubba* is short, pronounced as in *cub* and *rub*.

The *Dictionary of American Regional English* reports primary use of *bubba* among blacks, particularly in Southern usage. Professional football players, such as Bubba Smith of the Baltimore Colts, helped popularize the name.

Although the term is widely used by blacks, the political *bubba factor* primarily takes into account the influence of Southern conservative whites. When applied to poor rural whites in the South, *bubba* may be used as a synonym for *cracker, redneck*, and *good ol' boy*.

A step beyond the *bubba factor, bubba vote* denotes the political power of Southern white conservatives, primarily rural males.

When George Bush's campaign for reelection was challenged from the far right by television commentator Pat Buchanan, *Newsweek* commented in December 1991 that "the media

. . . wondered whether the president could still speak to the all-important 'Bubba vote.'"

In early 1992 the *Wall Street Journal* reported that Pat Buchanan was "making inroads into the 'Bubba' vote— conservative whites, many of them Democrats." A follow-up bulletin from the *Journal* added: "Now the word appears to apply to Southern good ol' boys in general. It is akin in meaning to 'redneck,' and it may connote bigotry, but not necessarily."

A new publication, *Bubba Magazine*, offers a quotation from Bill Clinton on the Clinton-Gore ticket in 1992: "There's a little Bubba in both of us—in the sense that we both come from small towns, where people have old-fashioned values and want their country to be the best country in the world—and I don't think that's all bad."

In its Spring 1993 issue, *American Speech* reports other variants of the term, including *bubba ticket* for a pairing of white Southern male candidates; *bubbacracy* for the ruling system (for other uses of the combining form, see -OCRACY); and *bubbette*, a 1990 word for "white Southern female of the same class as the *bubba*."

buck stops here, the   the motto of President Harry S. Truman, who kept a sign with these words on his desk.

The motto meant that the presidency was, in Calvin Coolidge's words, "the place of last resort." It was especially appropriate for Truman, who had to make some momentous decisions: to drop the first atomic bomb; to order U.S. forces to South Korea; to fire General Douglas MacArthur.

Arthur Schlesinger, Jr., writing about John F. Kennedy, observed that "the Constitution made it clear where the buck stopped," and quoted Kennedy as saying: "The President bears the burden of the responsibility. . . . The advisers may move on to new advice." In a BBC interview soon after taking office, Kennedy said, "President Truman used to have a sign on this desk which said: 'The buck stops here'—these matters which involve national security and our national strength finally come to rest here."

Truman's close association with "the buck stops here" led to its present use as a synonym for final responsibility. Tom Wicker wrote in the *New York Times* in 1967: "Thus, in heightening the pressure on Hanoi, Lyndon Johnson is increasing it on himself as well. He makes the choices, and he knows where the buck stops."

The motto comes from the phrase "passing the buck," which is a poker-playing expression. See CARD METAPHORS. The buck was a marker to show who next had the deal; the buck could be passed by someone who did not want the responsibility of dealing to the man on his left. (The marker was occasionally a silver dollar, which, by the way, is how the dollar became known as a buck.)

The motto was adopted by President Jimmy Carter, who placed a small sign with those words on a table near his desk in the Oval Office.

In 1990, the *National Review* reminded its readers of the price sometimes paid for not passing the buck. "Back in 1987, John Poindexter told Congress and the nation: 'The buck stops here with me.' Three years and twenty million special prosecutor's dollars later, a jury ratified the former admiral's judgment, finding him guilty on five counts of deceiving Congress about the Iran arms sale. . . ." (The decision was reversed on appeal.)

In 1992, the phrase was used by Clinton Administration Attorney General Janet Reno in assuming responsibility for the failure of the FBI to avoid cas-

ualties in ending the siege of a religious cult in Waco, Texas.

bug as a verb, to eavesdrop by means of a concealed transmitter; as a noun, the tiny device used for that purpose.

"Does it have the bug?" That was a question asked by campaign managers of their advertising and printing aides, to make sure that the "union bug"— the oval emblem of the printers' union—was on all campaign literature.

This innocent meaning has been replaced by the more sinister slang meaning of "electronic eavesdropping." According to Stuart Berg Flexner, since 1889 a "bug" was a card stuck by a gambler to the underside of the gambling table, to be substituted when profitable for a card in hand; the concealed-item meaning was switched over to the little microphone-transmitters, which bore some resemblance to an insect of the same name.

Another slang meaning, the verb "to bug," means "to annoy"; when Attorney General John Mitchell spoke at a press dinner in 1970, he said facetiously, "If you quit bugging me, I'll quit bugging you." The quip, containing both senses of the term, turned out to be the opposite of prophetic.

In 1993, a White House tape made four days after the Watergate burglary was released. On the tape, Richard Nixon used *bug* as a verb to make a shortsighted prediction: "I don't think you're going to see a great, great uproar in this country about the Republican committee trying to bug the Democratic headquarters."

See TAPS AND BUGS.

bullet vote one in which the voter enters the booth determined to pull the lever for one candidate and no other on the same or any competing ticket.

Such a vote is based on personal magnetism and voter service within the district rather than ideology. According to *New York Herald Tribune* reporter Tom O'Hara, left-wing New York Congressman Vito Marcantonio claimed a large portion of his support came from "bullet votes." Voters with no interest in the candidates for other offices (and who probably would not have voted at all) lined up to cast their ballots for their favorite congressman. As a result, Marcantonio's total in the forties bulged beyond the others on his ticket. After voting for Marcantonio, many voters then left the American Labor party line to choose Republican or Democratic candidates for other offices, or else cast no other votes for other offices at all. When they cast other votes on other lines, they became *split-ticket voters* (see SPLIT TICKET); when they cast no other votes they were considered *bullet voters*.

A *Boston Globe* article in 1991 repeated the expression. During a local election, the *Globe* wrote, "Operatives were watching closely to see how many 'bullet' votes—votes for only one candidate on the ballot—were cast." A year earlier, *Newsday* turned the term into a verb, reporting that a local candidate "is asking residents to 'bullet vote' by casting ballots only for him, rather than for two candidates."

Political leaders may plan bullet voting campaigns in runoffs or in at-large elections. When a voter has a selection of six out of twelve candidates to vote for, or when there are weights assigned to his first, second, and third choices, he may be directed to choose only one, giving no assistance to any other candidate running.

bully pulpit active use of the Presidency's prestige and high visibility to inspire or moralize.

Theodore Roosevelt, a President of expansive character, took an unrestricted view of his job. In the many controversies during his two administrations, he never hesitated to take his case directly to the people from a Presidency he called a "bully pulpit."

The image of the White House as a pulpit with the whole nation as congregation—linked with the zesty adjective "bully," meaning first-rate, or admirable—has been frequently used ever since. It has special pertinence in the seemingly endless analysis of active Presidents, or those who take the largest possible view of their office and powers, versus the more restrained chief executives. James MacGregor Burns, discussing the influences that helped form Franklin Roosevelt's political views, says: "T.R. and Wilson were both moral leaders . . . who used the presidency as a pulpit." FDR used the theme in 1932, calling the Presidency "preeminently a place of moral leadership."

Douglass Cater recalls that John Kennedy liked to quote the "bully pulpit" phrase. "Among the multitudinous roles a president must fill," says Cater, "his greatest challenge and greatest power must be a blending of those of poet and preacher." In *A Thousand Days*, his memoir of the Kennedy Administration, Arthur M. Schlesinger, Jr., entitled one chapter "The Bully Pulpit."

Since the 1960s, the phrase has been widely applied to positions of power and influence other than the Presidency. For example: ". . . a Senator is better able to make use of the bully pulpit than a House member" (*The Nation*, April 1991), and "The prime ministership has rarely been a bully pulpit" (*Time* magazine, October 1990).

But the Presidency remains the most important of all bully pulpits, and some Presidential critics have taken to use "bully" not in the original sense of "first-rate," but in the sense of "intimidating, bullying." *Washington Post* columnist Mark Shields, anticipating in September 1990 President Bush's use of television to persuade Americans to accept his tax proposals, said on the *MacNeil/Lehrer NewsHour,* "He's going to use the bully pulpit to bully the people."

bunk pretentious nonsense; claptrap; a long-winded oration meant for hometown consumption.

"Religion is all bunk," declared Thomas Alva Edison.

"History is bunk," stated his friend Henry Ford.

Bunk is an Americanism with a history almost as rich and colorful as "OK." It is a shortening of *bunkum,* which is an altered shortening of *Buncombe,* a county in North Carolina that made up part of the district represented by Felix Walker, who sat in the House of Representatives in 1820. Walker interrupted a debate on the Missouri Compromise with a long, dull, irrelevant speech, apologizing to his impatient colleagues with the statement "I'm talking for Buncombe." In 1828, according to *Niles Weekly Register,* "talking to (or for) Buncombe" was well known. The *Wilmington* (N.C.) *Commercial* referred in 1849 to "the Buncombe politicians—those who go for re-election merely," and British author Thomas Carlyle showed that the expression traveled the Atlantic with its meaning intact: "A parliament speaking through reporters to Buncombe and the twenty seven millions, mostly fools."

The word was clipped to "bunk" toward the end of the nineteenth century, and in George Ade's *More Fables in Slang,* published in 1900, it appeared as "he surmised that the Bunk was about to be handed to him." In 1923 William E. Woodward wrote a book titled *Bunk,* and introduced the verb, to *debunk.* A school of historians were named "debunkers" for the way they tore down the myths other historians

had built up. "Hokum," according to the *OED,* is a blend of hocus-pocus and bunkum.

Another verb occasionally used is "to bunko" or "to be buncoed," which means to be cheated or swindled. The well-meaning politician from Buncombe is not the villain here; more likely, the evil meaning comes from the Spanish *banco,* or game of cards. Senator Frank Brandegee of Connecticut, one of the anti-Wilson LITTLE GROUP OF WILFUL MEN, said in the League of Nations debate: "I am not to be buncoed by any oleaginous lingo about 'humanity' or 'men everywhere.'"

bureaucracy administrative agencies of government (or large private institutions) manned for the most part by career personnel and characterized by rigid adherence to rules and established procedure; almost always used in a derogatory sense.

Bureaucratic is a nineteenth-century label that has stuck for a phenomenon that goes back at least to ancient Rome and old Cathay. King or president, mayor or mandarin, every ruler needs help running things. The first echelon below the top has typically been a kind of aristocracy, whether by appointment, heredity, or election. Below that comes the civil service, or bureaucracy.

In impact on both vocabulary and life, the bureaucracy looms ever larger as the functions of government multiply. The bureaucracy is supposed to administer laws and policies framed by its superiors, but often the manner of administration looms more important than the policy handed down. "The executive bureaucrat," wrote sociologist C. Wright Mills, "becomes not only the center of decision but also the arena within which major conflicts of power are resolved or denied resolution."

The term comes from *bureau,* the French word for office, and was commonly applied to government agencies. After Napoleon's reign, a relatively permanent and quasi-autonomous civil service took firm hold in France and is generally credited with maintaining government functions through the upheavals at the top that make up so much of French history ("always falling, never fallen"). But the French system also produced the evils generally ascribed to bureaucracy. "Wherever possible," said sociologist Max Weber, "political democracy strives to shorten the term of office by election and recall. . . . Thereby democracy inevitably comes into conflict with the bureaucratic tendencies which, by its fight against notable (i.e., patrician) rule, democracy has produced."

A bureaucrat is a self-stopper. But the criticism of public servants, as they call themselves, is often politically inspired: Alben Barkley, in the 1948 Democratic convention keynote address, said "a bureaucrat is a Democrat who holds a job a Republican wants."

Bureaucrats speak *bureaucratese*, which is often called GOBBLEDYGOOK, BAFFLEGAB, PENTAGONESE, or BUZZ-WORDS. Adjectives most frequently associated with bureaucracy's noun are "entrenched," "swollen," and "bloated." A favored form of communication is "touching base." When they cannot be reached, they are "in the field." For their most frequent method of self-protection, see C.Y.A.

burning question. See TOPIC A; PARAMOUNT ISSUE.

business as usual complacency; unconcern for imminent danger; or, determination to carry on despite danger.

Winston Churchill, speaking at the Guildhall in London in the opening days of World War I, said, "The maxim of the British people is 'Business as usual.'" This carried the same kind of

bravery-in-adversity message that he restated more eloquently in the early days of World War II.

In the generation between the wars, however, the meaning of the phrase changed radically. During the Depression "no business as usual" was a wry slogan. As war approached again, a "business-as-usual policy" was denounced as unworthy of a people aware of the unusual requirements of a wartime economy. Traces of the previous defiant meaning lingered on, however; during the Battle of Britain, with London under almost constant bombardment, a small sign in the Piccadilly window of A. A. Julius, jeweler, read: "Business as Usual."

In current use, the phrase is synonymous with complacency. The 1962 "Port Huron Statement" of Students for a Democratic Society derogated the "familiar campus" as "a place of commitment to business-as-usual, getting ahead, playing it cool." Richard Neustadt in *Presidential Power* (1960) characterized the Truman-Eisenhower years as "emergencies in policy with politics as usual."

busing to achieve racial balance the phrase that became the battleground between forces believing in the primacy of the "neighborhood school" versus those who held that physical transportation of students was necessary to break down segregation.

The most controversy-laden CODE WORD of the late sixties and early seventies was "busing." (The spelling with one *s*, which looks as if it could rhyme with "confusing," triumphed over "bussing," which is synonymous with "kissing.") To many supporters of desegregation in theory, busing meant carrying the battle for civil rights into their own neighborhoods, and affected their own children; some activists felt cognitive dissonance at that point, and many parents who had been lukewarm about desegregation felt the abandonment of the tradition of keeping children in schools close to their residences was a serious mistake.

The crucial part of the phrase was "racial balance." In the legislative history of Title IV of the 1964 Civil Rights Act, the phrase first appeared (as "racial imbalance") in a message from President John F. Kennedy of June 19, 1963, recommending federal technical and financial assistance to schools which were "engaged in the process of meeting the educational problems flowing from desegregation or racial imbalance . . ."

In the House hearings on this bill, Congressman William Cramer (R-Fla.) tried to get witnesses to define "racial imbalance" with no success; accordingly, the House on January 31, 1964, adopted an amendment he submitted to provide that any definition of "desegregation" in the Civil Rights Act "shall not mean the assignment of students to public schools in order to overcome racial imbalance."

In the Senate, Hubert Humphrey (D-Minn.)—after an 83-day debate had made clear that "busing to achieving racial balance" would have to be sacrificed if any civil rights bill was to be passed—said on June 4 that the amendments dealing with busing "preclude an inference that the title confers new authority to deal with 'racial imbalance' in schools, and should serve to soothe fears that Title IV might be read to empower the Federal Government to order the busing of children around a city in order to achieve a certain racial balance or mix in schools."

The Supreme Court, in *Swann* v. *Charlotte-Mecklenburg Board of Education*, held in 1971 that this language limiting the Civil Rights Act foreclosed the granting of new powers to the courts to redress *de facto* segrega-

tion (caused by residential patterns), but did not withdraw from the courts "their historic equitable remedial powers" to strike down *de jure* segregation (caused by discriminatory action by state authorities).

In most of the political debate on the issue of busing, only the most dedicated civil rights activists defended the idea of transporting students to overcome the segregation brought about by living patterns. Changing *de facto* segregation was described as "integration," while most public opinion preferred "desegregation," which stopped short of "busing to achieve racial balance."

A litmus test of the political leanings of the speaker could be found in the adjective used to describe busing. Liberals used "involuntary busing"; conservatives or anti-busing liberals preferred "forced busing."

The word first came into the language with the double-*s* spelling, and was usually associated with military transport: "They were instructed in march-discipline," wrote Rudyard Kipling in 1923, ". . . as well as bussing and de-bussing against time into motor-buses."

See SEGREGATION; SEPARATE BUT EQUAL.

buttonhole to stop a moving delegate, engage his attention, and press for the support of a candidate or cause; in more general terms, to electioneer.

The verb is colorful because it describes the act of holding on to the persuadee's button, lapel, or any grabbable part of his clothing. The *OED* reports a pre-political usage: "Charles Lamb, being buttonheld one day by Coleridge . . . cut off the button."

The word was adopted by politicians in the mid-nineteenth century. Mark Twain, in *The Gilded Age*, recorded a friend who "bussed and 'buttonholed'

Congressmen in the interest of the Columbia River scheme."

In recent years, the word is being limited in application to delegates on a convention floor. In the raucous 1940 Republican convention that nominated Wendell Willkie, the Willkie supporters who overflowed onto the convention floor (see PACKING THE GALLERIES) caused the head of the New Hampshire delegation to shout into the microphone: "Mr. Chairman! I call the attention of the chair to the fact that many people are in the aisles and buttonholing delegates, who have no right to be on the floor of the convention." The chairman's gavel cut off the buttonholers.

A related phrase is "nickel-and-diming," the pursuit of support down to the small change of personal persuasion of individual delegates by the candidate. Gerald Ford's press secretary, Ron Nessen, wrote in his 1978 memoir *It Sure Looks Different from the Inside* of the 1976 Republican delegate hunt:

> Ford . . . appealed to individual uncommitted delegates by phone. He invited many delegates to the White House. . . . it was called "nickel-and-diming," trying to win the necessary delegates one by one . . .
>
> A joke went around illustrating how some uncommitted delegates played hard-to-get. It seems one delegate from New Jersey received a phone call from the President inviting him to a reception and state banquet for Queen Elizabeth at the White House. There was a long pause of indecision and then, according to the gag, the delegate asked Ford, "What's for dinner?"

buttons, campaign a device for a shy voter to communicate his preference; one of the few "absolute musts" in a campaign budget that managers agree is largely a waste of money; a stimulus to enthusiasm of workers.

When the wearing of campaign buttons was spoken of as inelegant in 1900, Congressman E. L. Hamilton of Michigan angrily rose to his feet in the House of Representatives. "The wearing of a campaign button is a harmless sort of decoration," he began, "but a social condition that dictates to a man what kind of a button he shall wear approaches a condition of tyranny, and makes a man want to stick campaign buttons all over him, and protect his privilege with a Gatling gun!"

With the freedom to wear buttons given this First Amendment umbrella, their use proliferated. Button manufacturers like Emanuel Ress ("The Button King") recalled an upsurge in 1940 ("Eleanor Start Packing—The Willkies Are Coming," "No Third Term," "Two Good Terms Deserve Another").

Rhyme has always been important to button-makers. "I Like Ike" appeared on buttons manufactured in 1947 (as Eisenhower began to be spoken of as a possible Democratic nominee); "Who Else but Nelse" (Rockefeller), "Madly for Adlai" (Stevenson), "All the Way with LBJ" (Johnson), "Who but Hubert" (Humphrey), and "The Grin Will Win" (Carter) followed.

The style of button showing the candidate's picture and name with some patriotic symbol was replaced by the picture-plus-slogan button in the forties, and gradually the use of pictures on buttons has declined. In 1964, anti-Goldwater forces sported "Extremism in the Pursuit of Vice Is No Virtue." When General Eisenhower told that convention to beware of "sensation-seeking columnists," button men within three hours turned out "Sensation Seeking Press" buttons for reporters, along with "Stamp Out Huntley-Brinkley."

In the 1965 John Lindsay campaign for mayor of New York, Adam Mark Lawrence came in with "a great idea for a Lindsay button," which was a button with the copy "Lindsay button." This was followed by buttons that simply said "Button" ("for the sort of people who like to call their dog 'dog'").

Gold lapel pins and cufflinks, advanced forms of buttonry, are often used as fund-raising devices. "The most successful 'button,'" wrote Ted Sorensen, "was a tie clasp in the form of Kennedy's old PT boat. It became a popular badge for Kennedy supporters and a fast-selling item in the 'Dollars for Democrats' drive." See CUFFLINKS GANG.

There was a tendency in the mid-sixties to use campaign buttons when there was no political campaign. Many carried a social rather than political message: "Make Love Not War," "I Am a Human Being: Do Not Fold, Spindle or Mutilate," "Turn On, Tune In, Drop Out." A wide variety of gag buttons were sold: "Support Mental Health or I'll Kill You," "Kill a Commie for Christ," "Leisure Suits Make You Sterile." A 1970s favorite was "Agnew and Eagleton—Nobody's Perfect."

Many hardened political operatives who would never be caught wearing any button cannot resist one sold at the end of campaigns: "Good Job, Kid . . . Now Get Lost."

buzzword jargon; or, a vague vogue word intended to trigger a stereotyped response.

A buzzword can be a CODE WORD that appeals to the emotions. When President Carter, angered at the congressional mangling of his energy proposals in October 1977, lashed the oil-industry lobbyists in tones reminiscent of Harry Truman, American Gas Association president George Lawrence replied, "While buzzwords like 'war profiteers' and 'rob' and 'ripoff' might prove successful in inflaming public opinion, they cannot substitute for the production incen-

tives so flagrantly lacking in the Administration's energy plan."

The more common meaning of "buzzword" comes from the derivation of "buzz" as a verbalized hum or hiss: a sense-dulling bit of jargon that puts the outsider to sleep. ("The buzz" represents the latest word or rumor.) In a 1974 book, *Buzzwords*, Robert Kirk Mueller defined the word on the cover as "words, phrases or zingo-lingo used by an ingroup, a cult, or the cognoscenti for rapid communication within the group . . . it refers also to the verbal, intellectual one-upmanship of the cant, slang, jargon, argot and pseudo-tribal language, used by relatively small groups for their own benefit and to help isolate the group from the hoi polloi . . . a sort of pro's prose." He credits the word's coinage to Professor Ralph Hower of Harvard, who "used the label *buzzwords* for those phrases that have a pleasant buzzing sound in your ears while you roll them on your tongue and that may overwhelm you into believing you know what you're talking about when you don't."

Some buzzwords listed in that book are "conceptual framework" (a grand-design favorite of Henry Kissinger's); "going toes up" or "going down the tubes" (to fail); "junior angel" (euphemism for the euphemism "senior citizen"). For others, see PENTAGONESE; BAFFLEGAB; GOBBLEDYGOOK; CIA-ESE.

According to *Regardie's* magazine of March 1990, "The buzzword for the nineties is *treatment*. There is a program for everything: drug abuse, gambling abuse, embezzlement, infidelity, cellulite—you name it."

by-election an election in a locality between general elections.

This is British usage; Americans prefer "special election" to describe a race that takes place when an incumbent dies or resigns. "By-electioneering" is campaigning by or for candidates during these times, and it is interpreted as a test for the popularity of the party in power.

Byzantine Machiavellian; characterized by scheming, double-crossing, backbiting and similarly nefarious behavior often attributed to the denizens of the center of power; or, labyrinthine, arcane, mysteriously complex.

The word was probably introduced to politics by Theodore Roosevelt about 1916, criticizing President Woodrow Wilson as a "Byzantine logothete." Since a logothete in Byzantium was an accountant, or collector of revenues (from the Greek "to put to account"), former President Roosevelt was derogating President Wilson as one who fiddled with a pencil while World War I called for American intervention.

But "Byzantine" in that phrase only located the main word, which was "logothete"; the Machiavellian nature of the word "Byzantine" did not appear until later.

Arthur Koestler was fond of using this word to describe intricate political workings: "In the old days people often smiled at the Byzantine structure of the Spanish Army," he wrote in 1937, adding in another work eight years later: "The antidote to Eastern Byzantinism is Western revolutionary humanism." That Koestler use is the meaning in Britain today; the 1972 supplement to the *OED* defines the word as "the spirit of Byzantine politics. Hence, intricate, complicated; inflexible, rigid, unyielding."

A different, if related, meaning prevails in the U.S. "Was French party politics," Peter Braestrup wrote in the *New York Times* in 1966, "with its

Byzantine maneuvers and its feuding factions, really en route to a transformation?" To most U.S. political writers, the synonym for Byzantine is "devious." This sense of the word is used in a September 1991 *Los Angeles Times* review of a book about J. Edgar Hoover and the FBI. In it, the book's author describes Hoover as using his political knowledge "with a brilliant skillfulness to both establish and maintain his Byzantine power structure against all enemies for nearly five decades."

To a churchman, "Byzantinism" has an altogether different meaning: the denial of religious freedom, or the belief that the civil power controls the spiritual power.

The adjective comes from the city of Byzantium, later Constantinople, now Istanbul, which became the capital of the Roman Empire around A.D. 330, and for seven hundred years was the main repository of Roman and Greek civilization.

However, the court of the emperor—usually named Constantine—was marked by rivalries, duplicity and violence, giving the city and the word a bad name today. In fairness, it should be pointed out that this moral decay notwithstanding, the empire was enlarged, civilization spread despite the Visigoths and Vandals, and Russia was converted to Christianity. Notes the *Columbia Encyclopedia*, looking for the brighter side of the maneuvering: "In the unceasing struggle between the great landowners and the small peasantry, most of the emperors favored the peasants. Economic prosperity was paralleled by a new golden age in science, philosophy and architecture."

For the complete story of the fall, see Gibbon.

C

cabal group hatching a dark political plot; always carries a sinister connotation.

Derived from the Hebrew word *qabbalah*, the mystical interpretation of Scripture said to be handed down to the rabbis by Moses, the word came to mean in French and English "any secret or mystical tradition," then "a secret or private meeting," and finally "a group engaged in secret or private intrigue."

An inner group of advisers to Charles II of England was known as the "Cabal," legend has it, because the initials of their last names—Chudleigh, Ashley, Buckingham, Arlington, and Lauderdale—formed the word.

John Quincy Adams wrote in his diary of 1821: "I would take no one step to advance or promote pretensions to the Presidency. If that office was to be the prize of cabal and intrigue, of purchasing newspapers, bribing by appointments, or bargaining for foreign missions, I had no ticket in that lottery."

George Brinton McClellan Harvey, editor of *Harper's Weekly*, used the term to describe the group of "irreconcilables" (including Senators Lodge, Brandegee, and McCormack) who opposed Woodrow Wilson's League of Nations just after World War I.

William Allen White of the *Emporia Gazette* believed a cabal was responsible for Warren Gamaliel Harding's nomination during the 1920 Republican National Convention. He wrote: "Oil controlled the convention of 1920. It worked through the 'Senate cabal' whose members were so busy hating Wilson that they became easy victims of the greed for oil."

Former President Dwight D. Eisenhower refused to join what he termed a cabal organized prior to the 1964 Republican convention. Refuting newspaper statements claiming he was supporting Governor William Scranton of Pennsylvania for the Presidential nomination, the General informed Governor Scranton that he would be no part of a "stop Goldwater" movement forming within party ranks: the movement promptly collapsed.

Caesarism. See ELEPHANT, REPUBLICAN.

calculated risk action taken when inaction or an alternate course offers greater possibilities of danger; a step soberly taken after the likely consequences have been assessed.

This is believed to be a World War II

phrase of Army Air Force origin; risks of possible bomber losses were calculated before missions were decided upon. A play by Joseph Hayes, *Calculated Risk*, appeared on Broadway in 1961. Mrs. Omar Bradley told the author in 1978 that the phrase was coined by her husband in a wartime briefing.

Whenever a political figure takes a chancy step, he often labels it a "calculated risk," indicating he fully understands what he is likely to suffer. In a sense, it is a pre-alibi statement.

Humorist James Thurber, writing in *Punch*, put it this way: "I have made some study of the smoke-screen phrases of the political terminologists, and they have to be described rather than defined. Calculated Risk, then, goes like this: 'We have every hope and assurance that the plan will be successful, but if it doesn't work we knew all the time it wouldn't and said so.'"

"With what he [President Kennedy] privately acknowledged to be a 'calculated risk,'" wrote Ted Sorensen, "he named a panel of conservative private enterprise skeptics to review his 1963 AID request. That panel, under General Lucius Clay, recommended cuts while strongly defending the program. [Appropriations Subcommittee Chairman Otto] Passman and Company ignored the defense, accepted the cuts and made still more cuts—and Kennedy's gamble backfired."

Camelot   an idealization of the Administration of President John F. Kennedy; now usually used in irony.

Camelot, in the legend of King Arthur, was the city that was home to the Knights of the Round Table. A Lerner-Loewe musical drama of that title starring Richard Burton and Julie Andrews was popular on Broadway at the beginning of the Kennedy Administration, and its evocation of excellence, hope, taste and high courage was seized upon as symptomatic of the ide-

alism of the "new generation" to whom the torch had been passed in Washington, D.C.

Satirist Vic Gold defined the word in 1969 as "mythical U.S. Liberal era" when all men were equal, all women were beautiful, witty, well-groomed, and *Republicans knew their place*. By the 1980s, in light of revelations of peccadilloes and Mafia relationships, *Newsweek* was referring to "Camelittle." See also GOVERNMENT-IN-EXILE.

CHARISMA was much spoken of at the time, but the years brought a sober reassessment. "Lyndon Johnson suffered to the end," wrote Russell Baker in 1974, after the Nixon resignation, "from the suspicion that he lacked both 'charisma' and 'style,' and often seemed deluded by the notion that but for their lack he could have raised a higher 'Camelot.'" Deriding the public relations style of the Nixon men and alluding to the development of this kind of "p.r." in the Kennedy days, Baker observed: "Politicians will not revive 'Camelot' for a while now. Every disaster has its bright side." When Bill Clinton spoke glowingly of his chance as a teenager to meet JFK in Washington, Curtis Wilkie wrote in the *Boston Globe:* "That was the last summer of Camelot, when Washington seemed to young Democrats to be suffused with earnest enthusiasm and perpetually decorated with cherry blossoms."

In the seventies, especially after the revelations of the Senate Select Committee on Intelligence in 1975, the political fashion was to denigrate the "false hopes" of the Kennedy years, and to use the term "Camelot" in so doing. When a woman friend of President Kennedy was revealed to have been simultaneously seeing a Chicago mobster, *Newsweek* headlined the story "Cloud over Camelot."

The vision of the seat of government as a citadel of hope will probably reappear one day, possibly with the Camelot connotation, because it is so deeply rooted in the American self-image. "The eyes of all people are upon us," John Winthrop said in 1630, at the founding of the Massachusetts Bay Colony. ". . . we shall be made a story and a byword throughout the world . . . we shall be a City upon a Hill." The theme of a CITY ON A HILL was adopted by John Kennedy and used often in speeches by Ronald Reagan.

campaign as a noun, the term is applied to virtually all phases of an effort to win any kind of election, but most particularly the phase involving open, active electioneering; as a verb, to strive for a political nomination or office.

This term has been part of American politics at least since the turn of the nineteenth century. In Massachusetts, John Quincy Adams observed that the 1816 "parliamentary campaign hitherto has been consumed in one laborious effort to suppress the reformers." To provincial journals far inland, the term was already familiar.

"Campaign" comes from the French word for open, level country and evolved from there into the military vocabulary, where it was first used to denote the amount of time an army was kept in the field, and later a particular military operation. In seventeenth-century England, the term was extended to politics and usually meant a session of a legislative body. The meaning further changed in transatlantic passage and has since expanded in meaning as the business of getting elected to public office has grown more complex. But the idea that politics is a form of combat remains. See ARENA. When he accepted the Democratic nomination for President in 1932, Franklin Roosevelt told the convention: "This is more than a political campaign. It is a call to arms."

For other political terms with military origins, see ON THE POINT and MILITARY METAPHORS.

campaign oratory exaggerated charges, promises, or claims made during the heat of a campaign, expected by the speaker to be taken with a grain of salt, to be deprecated and softened after the campaign is over.

Thomas Macaulay once observed: "The object of oratory alone is not truth, but persuasion." Theodore Roosevelt told Henry L. Stimson, in regard to William Howard Taft's campaigning: "Darn it, Harry, a campaign speech is a poster, not an etching!" Stimson got the point, and later wrote: "A man's campaign speeches are no proper subject for the study of a friendly biographer." Theodore Sorensen agreed: "John Kennedy would not want to be measured solely by the speeches we ground out day and night across the country—and neither would I . . . some, particularly near the close, were overly caustic and captious in their criticism of Nixon."

Arthur Schlesinger, Jr., made the same point: "[Kennedy] began by appearing to adopt the thesis that the State Department should have listened to its pro-Batista ambassadors and recognized the revolution as a communist conspiracy from the outset. This differed markedly from his interpretation in *The Strategy of Peace*. Doubtless it was campaign oratory."

The phrase was firmly fixed in the political lexicon by Wendell Willkie during the campaign of 1940. His hoarse voice had rasped: ". . . if the present Administration is restored to power for a third term our democratic system will not outlast another four years." And "on the basis of his past performance with pledges to the people, you may expect war by April, 1941 if he [FDR] is elected." After his defeat, Willkie traveled to England, held long talks with Winston Churchill, and returned to the U.S. to urge that the U.S. send Britain all available bombers. In Lend-Lease hearings, Senator Gerald P. Nye (R-N.D.) asked how he could square that position with his earlier charges against FDR. Willkie took a long pause in his testimony, grinned and shrugged: "It was just a bit of campaign oratory."

Representative Joseph P. Martin, then Republican National Chairman, recalls: "Republicans in Congress were particularly incensed . . . it undermined all the criticism that had been made of the President's foreign policy in the campaign."

Just as there is an unwritten law that takes for granted campaign exaggerations, there is also an unwritten law that a candidate may not afterward disown his campaign statements and leave his supporters in exposed positions.

campaign promises pledges made by a candidate to gain certain things for his constituents after election.

This is probably the oldest form of politicking since elections began. Said a sign on a first-century Roman wall: "Genialis urges the election of Bruttius Balbus as duovir [commission member]. He will protect the treasury." A candidate's promises, like a party platform, are rarely taken as literal commitments. Often they seem part of a game in which candidates outpromise each other, accuse each other of making rash promises and cite the opposition's unfulfilled promises left over from previous elections.

Occasionally a particular promise takes on major—even historic—importance. One such was Dwight Eisenhower's pledge to go to Korea if elected in 1952. But for the most part, Bernard Baruch's admonition seems valid. "Vote for the man who promises

least," said Baruch. "He'll be the least disappointing."

The classic campaign-promise story was recounted by Senator Russell Long (D-La.) about his uncle, Governor Earl Long. He had promised voters the right to elect their local sheriffs, but once in office, went in the opposite direction. When a delegation came to "Uncle Earl's" office to protest, Senator Long told the author, "Uncle Earl told his right-hand man, 'I don't want to see 'em—you see 'em.' His aide said, 'What'll I tell 'em?' And Uncle Earl said, right out, 'Tell 'em I lied!'"

campaign songs ditties using the candidates' names, usually putting words to melodies already popular and whipped up for use at rallies, conventions and similar events; occasionally, a tune and set of lyrics adopted whole as a candidate's theme.

Although few major campaigns run their course today without producing a song or two, political music had its zenith in the nineteenth century, when not only was one's candidate boosted, but the opposition roundly and rhythmically knocked. William Henry Harrison became famous in the Indian battle of Tippecanoe, Indiana Territory, in 1811. Thus the song when he ran for President against the more citified Martin Van Buren in 1840: "Old Tip he wears a homespun coat./He has no ruffled shirt-wirt;/But Mat he has a golden plate,/And he's a little squirt-wirt-wirt." Said a contemporary journalist: "It was a ceaseless torrent of [Whig] music. . . . If a Democrat tried to speak, argue or answer . . . he was only saluted with a fresh deluge." When Harrison's grandson Benjamin ran in 1888, the Republicans sang: "Yes, Grandfather's hat fits Ben—fits Ben;/He wears it with dignified grace, oh yes!"

The "Battle Hymn of the Republic" provided music for songs both pro and con. The opposition in 1872 sang: "We'll hang Horace Greeley to a sour apple tree . . ." Four years later, the Republican supporters of Rutherford Hayes and William Wheeler offered this chorus: "Glory, glory Hayes and Wheeler./As we go voting on." Candidates generally grin and bear the songs invented for them. Growled U. S. Grant: "I know but two tunes; one of them is Yankee Doodle and the other isn't."

Ring Lardner wrote a number called "Teddy, You're a Bear" in honor of Bull Mooser Theodore Roosevelt. Some of the most famous campaign songs of the twentieth century were Al Smith's theme, "Sidewalks of New York," FDR's "Happy Days Are Here Again" and Eisenhower's "I Like Ike" by Irving Berlin. The rousing tune of "Hello, Dolly" became "Hello, Lyndon" for political purposes in 1964; when Goldwater enthusiasts tried "Hello, Barry," producer David Merrick, a Democrat, threatened to sue.

Political headquarters are deluged with campaign songs to this day. In the 1961 New York mayoralty campaign, a songwriter came up with "Lefkowitz, Gilhooley and Fino," an original ditty which when translated and sung in Spanish for the city's Puerto Rican residents was astonishing in its lack of impact.

Rather than create new songs—which must be learned—managers now prefer to adapt and identify with popular music. Robert Kennedy started this trend with "This Land Is Our Land"; Bill Clinton continued it with Fleetwood Mac's "Don't Stop Thinking About Tomorrow," sung at the 1992 convention that nominated him.

campaign trail. See STUMP; HUSTINGS.

campaign train a caravan on rails, containing candidate, political advis-

ers, press, local candidates, and supporters, with an aura of "going to the people."

There are no free train rides for candidates, including Presidents who are campaigning. The Interstate Commerce Commission in the Taft Administration laid down the rule to stop "deadheading" by politicians. This rule was bent slightly in the case of Presidents requiring Secret Service accompaniment, after Calvin Coolidge decided to save some money by traveling to the Black Hills of South Dakota as a drawing-room passenger.

FDR, not especially remembered for his railroad campaigning, covered more than 350,000 miles in 399 railroad trips during his presidency, many on campaign jaunts. "On his trips," wrote White House correspondent Charles Hurd, "Roosevelt normally had to buy from six to eight tickets—for himself, Mrs. Roosevelt or other family members, and for two or three actual staff members. Newspapers were billed for the transportation of their representatives. The Treasury Department paid for the Secret Service agents. . . . Thus in pinch-penny luxury the President toured the country in what was euphemistically described as 'The Presidential Special Train.'"

Thomas E. Dewey called his campaign train "The Victory Special," and it was the scene of a grievous error (see BLOOPER); Harry Truman popularized a new political word (see WHISTLE-STOPPING) in his 21,000-mile, 300-speech GIVE 'EM HELL campaign of 1948; Barry Goldwater named his train the *"Baa Hozhnilne"* (Navaho for "To Win Over"), and Lyndon Johnson, campaigning for Vice President in 1960, cut a swath through the South in his "Corn Pone Special."

The pressures of life on a campaign train were described by PERENNIAL CANDIDATE Harold Stassen, explaining why General Eisenhower in 1952 allowed himself to be persuaded to remove a statement about General George Marshall from a speech in an area friendly to Senator Joseph McCarthy. "It's easy to judge harshly," Stassen said, "sitting back here in New York and not knowing the pressures that go on inside that insane campaign train. You are trapped there. There are just a few people near you whom you trust. You don't have a chance to get out in the clean air and think things through. . . . And when all of them around you gang up, to insist you do this or that, it is just about impossible to fight back."

A campaign train, in an era of television and jet airplanes, symbolizes the old virtues of face-to-face personal campaigning, of "life on the campaign trail," of "being out on the hustings." A candidate seeking votes in this manner shows he is trying, proves that he is a real campaigner; since television crews accompany the train, the "whistlestop" audiences are not really small. In modern times, the campaign train has become a useful, expensive "prop" or backdrop for speeches.

Camp David. See SPIRIT OF.

candidate   "*a* candidate" is an office seeker, often the object of scorn; "*the* candidate" is the party's chosen standard-bearer, cherished and adulated by his supporters, a worrisome threat to opponents.

Candidates for high office come in all sizes, from James Madison (five feet four inches, 100 pounds) to Abraham Lincoln (six feet four inches) to William Howard Taft (332 pounds); and with a good education (only 9 Presidents never attended college; of those who did, 9 were Phi Beta Kappa).

The word comes from the Latin *candidatus*, wearer of a white toga, which the Roman office seekers always wore

as a symbol of purity. The same root gave the language "candor" and "incandescence," qualities that candidates occasionally have.

Candidates have a variety of styles and methods of campaigning (see WHISTLESTOPPING; FRONT-PORCH CAMPAIGN; WHIRLWIND CAMPAIGN; even WHISPERING CAMPAIGN) and surround themselves in different ways (see BRAIN TRUST; PALACE GUARD).

Few candidates will confess that they hate the idea of meeting people (see PRESSING THE FLESH) or attending dinners (see RUBBER-CHICKEN CIRCUIT). All claim to find campaigning exhilarating and a "great opportunity to meet the people"; some actually find it so. Many have to grit their teeth to crack a smile and some would rather shake a fist than shake a hand.

In Shakespeare's *Coriolanus*, the proud Roman general becomes a candidate for consul and must submit to the indignity of soliciting votes from common citizens. He puts on the white toga and asks a citizen: "Well then, I pray, your price of the consulship?" The imperious general is startled by the citizen's mild, perceptive reply: "The price is to ask it kindly."

Candidates may be *undeclared* (example: Edmund Muskie in 1971) or DARK HORSE (James Polk in 1844, Wendell Willkie in 1940); *perennial* (see PERENNIAL CANDIDATE); they may be *reluctant*, as Adlai Stevenson was described in 1952, or *captive* (see CAPTIVE CANDIDATE), as Stevenson called Eisenhower in 1952; they may style themselves as *unbossed* candidates or *no-deal* candidates, or be styled by their opponents as "the candidate of the *far right* (or the *far left*)." In current use an *undeclared* candidate needs only a formal announcement, at which point he becomes an *avowed* candidate.

At a Republican governors conference in 1967, Nelson Rockefeller declined to hold a press conference because, as he said, "I am not a candidate." When reporters complained that another noncandidate, Ronald Reagan, had held a press conference earlier that week, Rockefeller smiled and said, "Well, he's a different kind of not-a-candidate."

canine metaphors. See BIRD DOG . . . KENNEL DOG; THAT DOG WON'T HUNT.

cannibalism. See IDEOLOGY.

cant favorite words of public figures.

Eighteenth-century English theologian William Paley observed: "There is such a thing as a peculiar word or phrase cleaving, as it were, to the memory of a writer or speaker, and presenting itself to his utterance at every turn. When we observe this, we call it a cant word or cant phrase."

A word that keeps popping up in Thomas Jefferson's writings is "boisterous": "Timid men . . . prefer the calm of despotism to the boisterous sea of liberty." "The whole commerce between master and slave is a perpetual exercise of the most boisterous passions." And Theodore Roosevelt, exponent of "the strenuous life," used the word "strenuous" repeatedly.

Adlai Stevenson had an addiction for "felicitous"; his friend, Arthur Schlesinger, Jr., turns often to "odious." John F. Kennedy used "vigor" so often and with such a distinctive Boston accent ("vigah") that it became the butt of jokes; Dwight Eisenhower harped on "deeds"; Lyndon Johnson probably used "must" more often than any other President (thirty-one times in his 1964 message to Congress alone); and Richard Nixon liked to say "let me make one thing perfectly clear" until it became too much of a trademark. Jimmy Carter laid great stress on his aversion to "disharmonious-

ness" and "incompatibility." One of Ronald Reagan's favorites was "quiet diplomacy," which suited the good-natured side of his personality, whereas George Bush had a thing about "thing" (see VISION THING). And Bill Clinton tried hard to sell "covenant"; later he made "infrastructure" the underpinning of his economic policies.

can't-win technique a method of pouring cold water on a hot candidacy; an appeal to delegates to set aside affection and loyalty and even their judgment of ability, to concentrate on the man with "winnability," the best chance to win.

"Perhaps the most important single influence in the decision of the delegates," observed Thomas E. Dewey in 1950, "is whether they believe a candidate can win if he is nominated."

Henry Clay was among the first to find that out. As a national figure in 1840 and as leader of one of the Whig factions opposing Martin Van Buren and the Jacksonian Democrats, the senator from Kentucky had considerable delegate strength. Thurlow Weed of New York, a powerful behind-the-scenes political figure, decided on the anti-Clay strategy: "Clay can't win." To undermine Clay's support, Weed organized a "triangular correspondence": men professing to be Clay supporters wrote to other state leaders hoping they were having better luck drumming up Clay support than the writer. The men who received the letters were also in on the plot: they in turn showed the letters to genuine Clay supporters with a sorrowful "we like him, but Clay can't win." It worked.

In more recent times, Ohio Senator Robert A. Taft—"Mr. Republican"— lost the nomination to Willkie in 1940, let Ohio John Bricker make the race in 1944 (on the Dewey ticket), lost to

Dewey in 1948, and lost his last chance to Eisenhower in 1952.

Taft had been given a taste of the "Taft can't win" treatment in 1948, and tried to bury it forever in a landslide senatorial victory in 1950. He carried Ohio by 430,000 votes that year, in the teeth of vigorous labor opposition; despite the impressive demonstration, he was met in the 1952 convention with the same headshaking—"Taft can't win."

What is called today a "loser image" is a hard thing to shake, and has roots deep in the convention system. "While there are doubts as to my fitness for President," muttered one of the earliest Republicans, Horace Greeley, "nobody seems to deny that I would make a capital beaten candidate."

To be accused of being "one of life's losers" is a hard charge to shake off, especially in a field where the graceful acceptance of defeat is not widely admired. ("Show me a good loser, and I'll show you a loser" was a saying attributed to Henry Kissinger in 1974.) Only election victory can dispose of a loser image; curiously, a triumph over a "can't win" charge in gaining a nomination is itself a long step toward establishing "winnability." Richard Nixon showed that in his comeback of 1968; he was later accused of being a "sore winner."

Canucks   French Canadians.

In the primary campaign of 1972, Democratic Senator Edmund Muskie of Maine, campaigning in the snows of New Hampshire, was hit by a charge scrawled in a letter to the *Manchester Union Leader* that the candidate, while in Florida, had laughed at a description of French Canadians as "Canucks."

The "Canuck letter" is now judged to have been spurious, and the Florida incident denied; a White House aide was charged with the DIRTY TRICK, and

denied it. But the Canuck charge, along with printed derogation of his wife, brought a reaction from Muskie that was seen as excessively tearful and cost him much support.

The author, in a *New York Times* column, used "Canuck" in passing and received an objection from a fellow writer who said it was a racial or national slur. The *Oxford English Dictionary* labels it "in U.S. usage, generally derogatory." A query to the *Régie de la Langue Française* in Quebec brought this response from Jacques Robichaud, Secretary:

> French-Canadians do not use the word "Canuck." English-speaking Canadians use it sparingly in familiar speech, for example: "The Vancouver Canuck Hockey Team." I am personally unaware that the use of this word by Canadians of either language offends Canadians of French descent.
>
> I must therefore refer you back to the original or present general users of the word. As mentioned in the excerpt from a *Canadian Encyclopedia* attached to your letter, those who have coined this expression were thus referring to English-speaking Canadians originally. It is quite likely that, as a result of the migration of some one and a half million French-Canadians to the New England States in the second half of the 19th Century, the word "Canuck" became primarily associated with them during that period. Today, as suggested in that same encyclopedia, the word refers to any Canadian of either French or English ancestry.
>
> In the final analysis, the context in which a word is used is the only, the real guide as to whether or not it is derogatory.

The Prime Minister of Canada, Pierre Trudeau, queried, responded in 1977:

> As with all slang, and especially that of nationality, the implications of the word vary a great deal according to the context and the intent of the speaker or

writer. Opinion also varies as to who exactly is designated by the word Canuck. Many Canadians feel it refers to all Canadians, some believe it is Eastern Canadians, others that it is French Canadians, while the majority have rarely heard it used in any context. Although much less widely used than the word "Yankee," its connotations have more or less the same range. We have a hockey team called the Vancouver Canucks, as you have a baseball team called the New York Yankees. "Johnny Canuck" was the personification of an English Canadian war hero in a comic strip. The Yankee of "I'm a Yankee doodle dandy . . ." is not the same as 'Yankee, go home.' Thus, you can see that the question you have posed is not easily answered. Whether or not you committed an ethnic slur would depend entirely on the way the word was used.

You asked more precisely about French Canadians' attitude to this word. Personally, I have never heard it used pejoratively in connection with French Canadians, nor have I ever heard or read the term being used by French Canadians.

These comments are not intended as an official definition but rather as my own feelings in this regard. I think that in closing I might mention that, to me, a slang term applied to a nationality by a person of a different nationality could, under certain conditions, be construed as a slur.

Mitford Mathews, editor of the *Dictionary of Americanisms,* wrote in *American Speech* magazine in 1974 that he suspected the word came from the South Sea Island *kanakas,* as reported by Richard Henry Dana in his 1840 *Two Years Before the Mast.* He cites M. Schele de Vere's 1872 entry in *Americanisms: the English of the New World:* "*Canacks, Canucks* and *K'nucks* are slang terms by which the Canadians are known in the United States and among themselves." Mr. Mathews adds: "If *Canack* instead of *Canuck* had become the current spelling, we might have been spared any puzzlement about its

source. It is clearly the shortened form of *Kanaka.*"

canvass as a verb, to determine the degree of support for a candidate, and sometimes in so doing, to solicit support for the candidate; as a noun, an election or a survey.

The meaning of this word is in the process of changing. The root may be the Old French *canabasser,* to scrutinize, or literally to sift through canvas. For many years, the political meaning of the noun *canvass* was the final scrutiny of an election count, resulting in certification or if necessary re-count. Lord Bryce used this meaning in 1888. "If all the returns have not been received, the canvass must be postponed." The noun also used to mean "election," as in Theodore Roosevelt's use in a boast to Henry Cabot Lodge that he had made "a rattling canvass, with heavy inroads into the Democratic vote."

Within recent years, a second meaning for both noun and verb has been developing: finding out voter sentiment before the votes are cast. Pollsters canvass voters to find out their attitudes. The third—and newest—meaning carries over some of the polling connotation: "canvassers" in current usage are supporters of a candidate who survey other voters with the intent of persuading the doubtful and making sure the "committed" get a reminder telephone call to turn out on Election Day. Frances Costikyan, a Manhattan district leader and wife of the former leader of Tammany Hall, described some of the techniques of canvassing:

. . . canvassing in person is infinitely more effective than a telephone campaign. As any salesman can tell you, it is much harder for people to say "no" face to face. A personal visit gives the voter a chance to size up the worker, to ask questions that bother him in a quiet conversational tone. . . . Most captains have discovered that those who live in the lower floors of the walk-ups (which are the slightly more expensive apartments) and the lower floors of the high-rise buildings (which are the slightly less expensive apartments) are much easier people to talk to. The very poor on the top floors of the walk-ups and the very rich on the top floors of the elevator buildings are too reluctant to commit themselves to anything as public or "controversial" as politics, or too uninterested, to be bothered with us.

A British canvasser is a "knocker-up."

cap. See FENCE; SPENDING CAP.

capitalism. See AMERICAN WAY OF LIFE; FREE ENTERPRISE.

captive candidate one who is under the domination of others; an attack phrase used when the opponent is too well liked for direct assault.

The phrase came into prominence during the 1952 presidential campaign. Republicans first attacked Adlai Stevenson as being "the captive of the big-city bosses," particularly Jake Arvey of Chicago. Stevenson took up the phrase and turned it around:

> They describe me as a "captive" candidate. They say I am the "captive" of the big city bosses, and then of the CIO, and then of the Dixiecrats, and then of Wall Street, and then of an organization called A.D.A. . . . I had no idea I was so popular, and I hope I can bear this multiple courtship and captivity with becoming modesty . . . meanwhile, it's not too uncomfortable to be captured by most everybody—except the Republican Old Guard!

After General Eisenhower had won the 1952 Republican nomination in Chicago and had a unity meeting with his opponent, Senator Robert A. Taft (see SURRENDER ON MORNINGSIDE HEIGHTS), Democrats pressed hard on the "captive" idea, since it was difficult to attack Eisenhower directly. "I am beginning to wonder who won at Chicago," said Stevenson. "Perhaps there is a six-star general somewhere in the Republican party." In 1984, Walter Mondale tried hard to counter Republican attacks that he was a captive of organized labor.

The phrase harks back to images of Harding manipulated by the predatory men around him; it has been used on all levels of politics when a popular candidate offers little chance for an attack.

card-carrying committed; firmly a member of; dedicated.

The phrase gained currency in the thirties, used to differentiate "hard-core" Communist party members from FELLOW TRAVELERS, "left-wingers," and others without actual membership who sympathized with Communist party aims.

Senator Joseph McCarthy revived the phrase in the early fifties with his charge that there were "card-carrying Communists" in the State Department.

The phrase was adopted, in a jocular way, to describe dedicated, ROCK-RIBBED Republicans; ". . . one Chicago newspaperman last week characterized him [Robert A. Taft]," wrote a *New York Times* reporter in 1952, "as a 'card-carrying Republican.'" Syndicated columnist William S. White wrote in 1967 of Richard Nixon that "he is still Mr. Republican to the regular and, so to speak, card-carrying Republicans." The new use cannot be applied to liberals, but can be used to describe conservatives, because of the sharpness of the contrast.

A candidate who has suffered through defeats or has labored for the party is said to have "paid his dues."

card metaphors "The bizarre world of cards," wrote Ely Culbertson, bridge expert active in public affairs, is "a world of pure power politics where rewards and punishments were meted out immediately. A deck of cards was built like the purest of hierarchies, with every card a master to those below it, a lackey to those above it. And there were 'masses'—long suits—which always asserted themselves in the end, triumphing over the kings and aces."

Because of the play of power in card games, the metaphor has been applied to politics for centuries. A German poet in 1521 talked of rearranging the affairs of men by "shuffling the cards in a better way," and Thomas Hobbes, in his *Leviathan* (1651) wrote: ". . . there is no honour military but by war, nor any such hope to mend an ill game, as by causing a new shuffle."

In U.S. politics, John Quincy Adams referred to Henry Clay, a renowned poker player, as "a gamester in politics as well as cards." A poker player a century later, Warren G. Harding, explained his own selection as a candidate in the SMOKE-FILLED ROOM in these terms: "We drew to a pair of deuces and filled."

FDR pointed to Mark Twain's *Connecticut Yankee* as the source of the best-known card metaphor, "new deal": " . . . in a country where only six people out of a thousand have any voice in the government," says Twain's Yankee, "what the 994 dupes need is a new deal." But the phrase was used in a political context throughout the nineteenth century. See NEW DEAL; SQUARE DEAL.

Cardplaying, while not the sport of kings, has often been the recreation of Presidents. Dwight Eisenhower enjoyed bridge, especially with General Alfred Gruenther as his partner; Harry Truman enjoyed poker-playing with his friends, who were promptly labeled "poker-table cronies"; poker, for some reason, connotes gambling more than bridge. A slight dispute exists about the outcome of a poker game played by Truman, Winston Churchill, and others on the train home from Fulton, Mo., in 1946 after Churchill's "iron curtain" speech. "Churchill took [Truman] for a few shillings on the train ride," wrote *Washington Post* correspondent Edward Folliard. "Truman didn't find out until the game was over that old Winston had learned the rudiments in the Boer War." Clark Clifford, who was there, recalls the game differently: "Churchill was rather an indifferent poker player, and had such a rough time that night that the President cautioned those in the game the next day to 'go easy on old Winnie, boys. I don't think he's in our league.'"

Terms like "ace in the hole," a "fast shuffle," "dealing from the bottom of the deck," "up his sleeve," "call a bluff," etc., are all card expressions used as commonly in politics as in everyday speech. "Wheeler-dealer," however, seems limited to big business and national politics, and Lyndon Johnson was attacked by Michigan Governor George Romney in 1967 as he compared the New Deal and Fair Deal with "the Fast Deal."

When President Carter's National Security Adviser, Zbigniew Brzezinski, picked up a term several Washington columnists were using in 1978 to describe the leverage on the Soviets of a move toward Peking, Soviet leader Leonid I. Brezhnev charged that "attempts are being made lately in the U.S.A., at a higher level and in a rather cynical form, to play the 'Chinese card' against the USSR."

See STAND PAT; BUCK STOPS HERE, THE; GO-IT-ALONE; SLEEPER; FINESSE; BIG CASINO.

caretaker one placed in power only to protect the position for another; a seatwarmer.

Despondent Democratic leaders in 1948, certain that Truman could not defeat Dewey, insisted that Senator Alben W. Barkley go on the Truman ticket as vice-presidential nominee, so that—in Arthur Krock's words—"he would be in a position to act as 'caretaker' of the Democratic organization during four and perhaps eight years out of power."

When John F. Kennedy was elected President, Governor Foster Furcolo of Massachusetts appointed Benjamin Smith II to replace him as senator; columnists pointed out that it was common knowledge that Smith was acting as "caretaker" of the seat to be sought later by Ted Kennedy.

Meanwhile, the same word was used to needle President Johnson, as the President who would simply warm the seat of power until another Kennedy (Robert) could run for the office. By quickly adopting his own style and asserting the "LBJ brand" of leadership, he dispensed with the notion that he would ever be a "caretaker president." The word was used to disparage Gerald Ford in 1976.

carpetbagger an outlander moving into a new area to seek political power at the expense of the native politicians.

The term "carpetbagger" gained wide currency in the South during the Reconstruction period. With the help of federal troops and discriminatory laws, Northerners of the period were able to control many public offices. English writer George Rose in 1868 described "what the Southerners call carpetbaggers, men traveling with little luggage and less character, making political capital out of the present state of affairs." Congressman S. S. Cox of New York said in 1875, "The carpetbagger had little to go on and much to get. He made out of Negro credulity a living and he made the Negro his prey. He began as a sharper

and was reconstructed into a statesman."

The carpetbag was a symbol of the man who traveled light, and hence of the man on the make. Before the Civil War, a carpetbagger was an itinerant banker with meager assets who operated in sparsely settled areas. Even during Reconstruction, the term began to be applied outside the South to any nonnative politician. Representative James Brooks found it necessary to defend himself in 1868 with this statement: "I was born in the State of Maine and went to New York with a trunk 30 years ago. I did not go there three months ago with a carpet bag." In 1964, another New Englander went to New York and found himself accused of being a carpetbagger. Robert Kennedy was so freshly arrived in the state when he ran for senator that he was repeatedly spoofed: one gag had him appearing before an audience of New Yorkers saying, "Fellow New Yorkites . . ." and another had him asking, "Where *are* the Bronx?" He won anyway.

Alan Otten, chief of the *Wall Street Journal*'s Washington bureau, wrote on April 29, 1970, about the decline of the carpetbagger issue. One case in point was young Jay Rockefeller, who campaigned in 1968 for secretary of state of West Virginia, not exactly known as Rockefeller family territory. To blunt the charge, the candidate told audiences of a phone call he made to advise his uncle Nelson of his intention to introduce Robert Kennedy at a Charleston rally. "There was a long pause at my uncle's end of the line, so I asked him whether he had anything against the senator. There was another long pause at my uncle's end of the line, till finally he said, 'Well, you know he *is* a carpetbagger.' And then there was a long pause at my end of the line."

Otten concluded: "Jay Rockefeller won handily, and perhaps this disarming anecdote helped. Or perhaps people are not quite so concerned any more about voting for men who weren't born and bred right in the locality. . . . In short, 'carpetbagger' just doesn't seem as dirty a word as it once was."

catchword a word that crystallizes an issue, sparks a response; a technique condemned by those not imaginative enough to master it.

"Normalcy" was a *catchword;* "not nostrums but normalcy" a *catch phrase;* "back to normalcy" a *slogan.*

Catchwords and catch phrases can be dead serious, as FDR's use of DAY OF INFAMY and STAB IN THE BACK illustrates; they may take a popular expression and give it political application: "YOU NEVER HAD IT SO GOOD," "HAD ENOUGH?" Or they may build upon previous phrases, as Lyndon Johnson's "LET US CONTINUE" was built upon John F. Kennedy's "Let Us Begin."

At their best, catch phrases used as slogans summarize and dramatize a genuine appeal, the way "Vote As You Shot" did for Civil War veterans. At their worst, they are plain silly—"We Polked You in 1844, We Shall Pierce You in 1852" tried too hard.

A slogan need not contain a catchword to be effective, as "He Can Do More for Massachusetts" proved for two Kennedys, and a catchword need not be sloganized with a verb (see LEBENSRAUM).

Catch phrases rely heavily on alliteration ("Burn, Baby, Burn!"; "Tippecanoe and Tyler, Too"; "Rum, Romanism and Rebellion") and both catch phrases and slogans often make use of rhyme ("All the Way with LBJ"; "I Like Ike"; "Jim Crow Must Go"; and Jimmy Carter's "The Grin Will Win"). For a more thorough analysis of these techniques, see SLOGAN and ALLITERATION.

At the turn of the century, Epiphanius Wilson wrote:

To make the effect of an oration lasting in the memory of the hearers it is good to use some telling phrase or catchword in which the point of the contention is summarized or suggested. Unlettered people carry all their knowledge or wisdom in short rhymes and proverbs, which are delightful even to the most cultivated as being portable, racy, and seasoned with a kind of wit. As models of this sort of watchword we may point to the "Peace with honor" of Beaconsfield, the "toujours l'audace" [always to dare] of Danton, "the Cross of Gold" of W. J. Bryan, the "Plumed Knight" of Ingersoll, and the "iridescent dream" of Ingalls.

The word "catchword" comes from printing. To make reading easier, John de Spira in 1469 printed at the foot of each page the first word of the next page, a boon to those who read aloud to their families. This was called the catchword; the main entry words in a dictionary were also printed in bold type or capital letters to catch the eye, as "catchword" is at the start of this entry. In the theater, it has occasionally been used as a substitute for "cue."

The greatness of a catchword or catch phrase is often its ambivalence, leaving it open to controversial interpretations for years. "A good catchword," said Wendell L. Willkie in a 1938 Town Hall debate, "can obscure analysis for fifty years." (For one obscure analysis, see ONE WORLD; also MAN IN THE STREET.)

Catholic candidate. See BAILEY MEMORANDUM.

cattle show public gathering of Presidential candidates during a primary.

This derisive term has been a favorite of politicians and the media since the late 1970s. In February 1980 *The Atlantic* poked light fun at "another of those Saturday Republican 'cattle shows' where all the G.O.P. contenders . . . make brief speeches to the assembled throngs." In 1983, the TV show *Good Morning America* reported, "Democrats gathered . . . for the first cattle show of the 1984 campaign."

On March 3, 1983, the *New York Times* described such an event in satirical terms: "In a cattle show, national candidates are herded into a ballroom, which then becomes a kind of stockyard-showcase. Local politicians poke them to see if their flesh is pressable; national pundits prod them to find variances in their views; the local party profits on ticket sales."

When Republican Senator Robert Dole considered running for the Presidency in 1984, he decided to consult with former President Richard Nixon about the strategy he should use as a candidate. *Time* magazine described in August 1985 Dole's visit to Nixon: "Dole went up to New Jersey . . . and found the old campaigner with candidate lists and vote projections. He advised Dole to keep his job in the Senate and stay away from the candidate 'cattle show.' Dole loved it all."

The predecessor term was *beauty contest.*

caucus a closed meeting of party policy makers, originally to nominate candidates and now, more typically, to agree on a legislative program; as a verb, so to meet.

In the early days of the Republic, party machinery was rudimentary and even presidential nominations were decided in small meetings, usually of a party's congressional delegation. What is a partisan's chief duty? an Ohio paper asked rhetorically: "To obey the decrees of King Caucus." It was common to ascribe monarchical attributes to powerful institutions: King Cotton controlled the South's agricultural economy and the first King Cong was not an ape, but the Continental Congress.

Andrew Jackson helped start the convention system that took the caucus down several notches in importance, although small groups can sometimes still control a convention. The term itself seems to be genuinely American, deriving from an Indian word meaning "elder," or "counselor." John Adams in 1763 noted the existence of a discussion group in Boston called the Caucus Club.

A group of black civil rights leaders organized the Black Caucus in the late 1960s; this is a meeting of black congressmen and congresswomen who try to influence national policies at political conventions and in Congress.

See SACHEM.

cautiously optimistic having a guarded sense of well-being; the hopeful politician's straddle.

This phrase restricts the adjective *optimistic* by modifying it with the wary adverb *cautiously*. President Reagan, asked how he felt about the possibility of approval for his sale of AWACS aircraft to Saudi Arabia, often answered, "cautiously optimistic."

Overused by politicians who picked up Reagan's use, *cautiously optimistic* has become a cliché to reflect an upbeat attitude that is not imprudent. In contrast, "cautiously pessimistic" is almost never used.

cell a secret unit of political activity, taking direction from a central authority but not directly connected to other units.

The word was closely identified with the Communist party; exposés of membership in "Communist cells" were frequent in the thirties and forties, culminating in the Chambers-Hiss confrontation of 1948.

Stephen Shadegg, an early Goldwater supporter, discussed the value of a cellular political structure in *How to Win an Election.* He pointed to Mao

Tse-tung's statement "Give me just two or three men in a village and I will take the village" and adapted "The Cell Group" to Barry Goldwater's 1952 and 1958 Senate campaigns:

The individuals we enlisted became a secret weapon possessing strength, mobility, and real impact. They were able to infiltrate centers of opposition support, keep us informed of opposition tactics, disseminate information, enlist other supporters, and to do all these things completely unnoticed by the opposition. . . . Mao Tse-tung might have been able to take a village with just two or three men. I have learned that to guarantee success in the political effort it is desirable to have three to five per cent of the voting population enlisted in the Cell Group.

The cell imparts a sense of conspiracy to its members, a greater receptivity to ideological discipline, and a direct organizational control from the top to workers at the grass roots. In the 1990s, it became the favored organizational device of worldwide terrorist groups controlled by Iran. See BORING FROM WITHIN.

cemetery vote specifically, a fraudulent vote cast in the name of a voter who has died, but who continues to be listed on the registration rolls; generally, any example of BALLOT-BOX STUFFING.

It is a collective phrase, similar to "suburban vote" or "upstate vote." Politicians will jokingly say, "He's out jotting down the names from the tombstones." Vote fraud was long treated lightly by many politicians; "Vote early and often" is a familiar phrase on Election Day.

Franklin D. Roosevelt was elected governor of New York in 1928 by a margin of 25,000 votes out of a total of 4,235,000. On election night he told Samuel Rosenman, "I have an idea that some of the boys upstate are up to their old tricks of delaying the vote and stealing as many as they can from us." Worried about the "cemetery vote" and illegal tampering with the results of voting machines, he put in a call to several sheriffs in upstate counties. "This is Franklin Roosevelt," he said, ". . . the returns from your county are coming in mighty slowly, and I don't like it. . . . If you need assistance to keep order or to see that the vote is counted right, call me here at the Biltmore Hotel and I shall ask Governor Smith to authorize the State Troopers to assist you."

Rosenman points out that this was pure bluff: "There was really little that Roosevelt could do if those instructions were not followed, especially if he were not elected. But it worked—the returns began to come in more quickly. And they were better."

Few modern get-out-the-vote campaigns can compare with the results of the drive in New York in 1844. There were 41,000 people qualified to vote that year. Allowing for those who were ill that day, the turnout was heartwarming—55,000. "The dead filled in for the sick," explained Bruce Felknor of the Fair Campaign Practices Committee.

In the 1964 presidential campaign, Lyndon Johnson was under severe attack regarding previous vote-stealing episodes that both worked for him and against him. The old cemetery-vote joke, traceable back to Rutherford B. Hayes, was used again. Little boy is asked why he is crying. "For my poor dead father," he replies. "But your father's been dead for ten years." Sobbing, the boy answers, "Last night he came back to vote for Lyndon Johnson and he never came to see me."

Warren Moscow, in *Politics in the Empire State,* tells of Hudson Valley political boss Lou Payne, who admitted that he sometimes voted tombstones, but added, "We never vote a man unless he would have voted our way if he were still alive. We respect a man's convictions."

censure. See VOTE OF CONFIDENCE; QUOTED OUT OF CONTEXT.

center of power. See POWER BROKER; OVAL OFFICE.

centralized government. See BIG GOVERNMENT; CREEPING SOCIALISM.

centrist an ideological position between extremes within a party; a member of a center party; or one closely attuned to the thinking of the majority.

Colloquial definition is MIDDLE-OF-THE-ROADER, comfortable with the CONSENSUS, in the MAINSTREAM. Sometimes mistakenly used to mean a believer in centralized government.

During the Truman Administration, political scientist Julius Turner wrote: "Only a Democrat who rejects a part of the Fair Deal can carry Kansas, and only a Republican who moderates the Republican platform can carry Massachusetts."

Centrist is of relatively recent political coinage, and is gaining in use as a more sophisticated self-definition than middle-of-the-roader. A similar phrase is *the vital center*, coined in 1949 by Arthur Schlesinger, Jr., as the place for pragmatic liberals to be.

The term is now used to define the area where the swing voter lies and where the big decisions are made; a politician who is a centrist can attract both mildly liberal and mildly conservative votes, and can develop a pattern of positions that encompass points on both sides of an ideological fence. But Clinton Rossiter held that a concern for this kind of centrism need not stultify debate between parties: "The unwritten laws of American politics command that the differences between the parties be relatively few and mod-

est, but it does not follow that those differences also be obscure. Let the parties compete for the millions of Americans in the vital center by offering alternatives that do not wrench our minds too violently in one direction or the other, but let them also offer us alternatives that can be clearly grasped."

Politicians have more than one center. When Bill Clinton decided to drop his controversial nomination of Lani Guinier to become the Justice Department's civil rights chief in 1993, he announced: "This has nothing to do with the political center. This is about *my* center."

See MIDDLE OF THE ROAD; OPPORTUNIST.

century of the common man. See COMMON MAN, CENTURY OF THE.

chameleon on plaid. See UNHOLY ALLIANCE.

changing horses. See DON'T CHANGE HORSES.

channels. See RED TAPE.

character assassin one who wages political warfare by seeking to destroy his adversary's reputation, usually by scurrilous means.

The phrase, or variations of it, is probably as old as the tactic—that is, ancient—but it was most recently in vogue during the early 1950s, when Senator Joseph McCarthy's red-hunting forays brought down game of many hues. Besides calling the Communists-in-government issue a RED HERRING, Harry Truman, in a 1950 speech to the American Legion, denounced "scandalmongers and character assassins." Although McCarthy was a fellow Republican, Dwight Eisenhower later criticized those who "assassinate you or your character from behind." See PHILIPPIC. Toward the end of McCarthy's period of influence, his feud with the Army itself became the subject of a congressional investigation. Joseph N. Welch, an attorney retained by the congressional committee, was shocked when the senator related how a young lawyer in Welch's firm had belonged to a tainted organization. At a poignant moment of the televised hearings, Welch replied, "Let us not assassinate this lad further, Senator. Have you no sense of decency, sir? At long last, have you left no sense of decency?"

The congressional committee has often been a forum for character assassination. Courtroom rules of evidence do not apply. Defamation laws offer no protection because nothing said during official proceedings is actionable. Thus as early as 1876 one member of Congress complained of critics who "say that our committees of investigation are intended to strike down some loyal men, or assassinate character." The Democratic senators who began probing the Teapot Dome situation soon after the death of Warren G. Harding were described by the *New York Tribune* as "the Montana scandalmongers," by the *New York Post* as "mud-gunners," and by the *New York Times* as "assassins of character." Over the years, their stock rose as Harding's fell.

George Bush, who pushed the CHARACTER ISSUE, had this destructive term aimed at him during the 1992 campaign. Thomas Oliphant wrote in the *Boston Globe* of Bush's body language during the televised debates: "In St. Louis, the character assassin had trouble looking straight at the camera; in Richmond, the off-his-game, disengaged President kept looking at his watch."

character issue the moral uprightness of a candidate; or, a euphemism for an attack on a candidate for philandering.

Almost always used in a verbal attack, *character issue* insinuates a negative evaluation of a candidate's personal background. The raising of this issue is meant to stimulate suspicions of a politician's ability to lead, based on information and innuendo about his or her private life. The attacker usually claims the issue is not whether the candidate committed some ethical slip or moral sin, but whether he or she lied about it—when, of course, forthright admission of a peccadillo would sink the candidacy.

The modern phrase has ancient roots, demonstrated by Shakespeare's study of a leader's aloofness in *Coriolanus*. The noun *character*, used attributively in this noun phrase, comes from ancient Greek for "engraving tool," its meaning extended to the mark that a person makes, or the distinguishing qualities of an individual.

Character issue first appeared in *Newsweek* magazine in October 1979, when an unnamed Democrat warned against Senator Edward M. Kennedy's challenge to President Jimmy Carter's renomination: "If Kennedy is the nominee, the 'character' issue will be 'fair game for the Republicans in the fall.'"

Other political phrases employing *issue* abound. These terms include *burning issue* (William Jennings Bryan's forceful replacement in the campaign of 1900 for *leading issue* and PARAMOUNT ISSUE), the 1964 GUT ISSUE (a visceral appeal to emotions), BREAD-AND-BUTTER ISSUE (a basic or economic issue, described by the 1836 attributive noun phrase *bread-and-butter*), SWITCHER *issue* (a controversial topic such as gun control or abortion that causes a voter to switch to the opposition), SOCIAL ISSUE (the 1970 coinage of sociologists Ben J. Wattenberg and Richard M. Scammon for the replacement of economic concerns by changing morality and social concerns), HOT-BUTTON *issue* (a 1980s term for issues that incense voters, such as perks for politicians), and the newest term, WEDGE ISSUE (an issue used to divide coalitions).

charisma political sex appeal, that "certain something" that campaign managers look for: a combination of attractiveness, charm, and sincerity that turns a candidate into The Candidate.

Charisma is the ancient Greek word for gift (and is pronounced with a *k*). In theology, it is defined as a grace, such as the power to heal or to prophesy.

In medieval Byzantium, charisma referred to those in a state of maniacal passion—berserk or drugged or in a convulsive fit—who were maintained as a kind of weapon in warfare to inspire loyal troops and frighten the opposition. Earlier in history, charismatic ascetics and "holy men," relying on begging for support, troubled the early Christians; St. Paul's warning "If a man does not work, neither shall he eat" was directed against the alarming spread of charismatic missionaries.

Charisma (the "gift") determined the fate of Chinese monarchs. If war, flood, or famine afflicted the land, it was a sign that the monarch did not possess the charismatic virtue, that he was not indeed a "son of Heaven." Max Weber, in a chapter on charismatic authority in *The Theory of Social and Economic Organization,* wrote: "The term 'charisma' will be applied to a certain quality of an individual personality by virtue of which he is set apart from ordinary men and treated as endowed with supernatural, superhuman, or at least specifically exceptional powers or qualities."

A politician with charisma can build a personal following outside his party, while developing special attachments within his party. Both Roosevelts had it, Eisenhower had it, Kennedy had it. It is less spiritual than "vision" and more elemental than "style."

In 1967 a group of celebrities tried to define charisma for writer Leon Harris in *This Week.* "The person I think who had the most was Malcolm," said Lena Horne, speaking of Malcolm X, the assassinated Black Muslim leader. "I never met him and yet I felt him and still feel him. Malcolm had the thing and Stokely Carmichael hasn't."

Thomas P. F. Hoving, when director of the Metropolitan Museum of Art, said:

> The man with the most charisma I ever saw, is Muñoz Marín of Puerto Rico. The minute he walks into the room, you feel it whether you know who he is or not. The same is true of Picasso, of Haile Selassie, and de Gaulle and Chiang. Pope John had it and Pope Paul doesn't. Khrushchev had it and Stalin didn't.

Columnist Stewart Alsop, covering Ted Kennedy's Massachusetts campaign for the Senate in 1962, spoke of the candidate's charisma to a woman reporter, and reported her reply: "Charisma, hell. It's just plain old sex appeal." A psychological study in the *Washington Post* in 1992 tied *charisma* to sexual energy: "Indeed, a candidate's ability to generate the kind of political charisma some people crave may be psychologically inseparable from an aggressive sex drive."

Charles River Gang a jocular derogation of the academic-political-scientific "community" in Boston.

Both Harvard College and the Massachusetts Institute of Technology have, in recent generations, been the source of valued counsel to Administrations in Washington, D.C.—most often, but by no means exclusively, Democratic. In the mid-seventies the power of this intellectual-technological establishment was recognized by hard-liners on the staff of the Senate Armed Services Committee, led by Richard Perle, who dubbed it "the Charles River Gang."

The Charles River, about 47 miles long, has an estuary which separates Boston from Cambridge.

Other uses of *gang* in politics include the *Ohio gang*, cronies of Warren G. Harding (see SMOKE-FILLED ROOM), and the Chinese *Gang of Four*, a group that sought to gain control in Peking after Mao's death.

Charlie name used to designate the letter *C;* also, black nickname for whites.

Three uses of "Charlie" have been prevalent in recent years.

1. "Checkpoint Charlie," in Berlin, was the key point of interchange between the American and Soviet sectors. It was named as part of the normal Army use of words to designate letters clearly, as Able, Baker, Charlie, Dog, etc. The significance of this particular checkpoint, plus the alliteration, made the name famous.

2. Members of the armed forces in Vietnam referred to the Viet Cong as "VC" or "C," which naturally became "Victor Charlie," or simply "Charlie." Correspondent Kuno Knoebl wrote a book in 1967 called *Victor Charlie: The Face of War in Vietnam.*

3. In the lexicon of the civil rights movement, "Mr. Charlie" was a derisive nickname for the white man. Author James Baldwin used the phrase in one of his most important works, *Blues for Mr. Charlie.* There appears to be no connection with the letter *C* in this use, although there might have been a derivation from "white Charley," the name for right-wing Whig party members. The *Congressional Globe* of 1842 reported: "There seems to me as much prospect of the ultra-Whigs—the 'White Charlies'—co-

alescing with the Democrats, as there is of Tyler and his friends."

Other common men's names that have acquired special meanings include George (for good), Jack (I'm all right), and Sam (for UNCLE SAM), a nickname given members of the American, or KNOW-NOTHING, party.

Charlie Regan a straw man used to absorb resentment in political campaigns.

Every headquarters must turn down a certain number of well-meaning volunteers without offending them. Horrible campaign songs, meaningless slogans, and painful pamphlets are submitted, and must be rejected in a way that will not diminish enthusiasm. At other times, strategic delays are necessary. That is why this phrase is so often heard:

"I'll give you a firm go-ahead just as soon as Regan gets back."

Charlie Regan never does get back, for he is the little man who isn't there. He is a fiction, a secret known only to the three or four people at the helm of the campaign. He has a place on the Table of Organization, in a little box near the top, but off to the side (title: "General Campaign Coordination and Liaison"), a desk, a telephone, a listing in the mimeographed directory at headquarters. He has a raincoat, which is sometimes draped over his chair, sometimes neatly hung up.

But there is no Charlie Regan. Whenever anybody calls, he is "down at the printer's." Somehow, being down at a political printer's shop implies exploration of the Mindanao Deep: nobody questions its importance or total inaccessibility.

At the end of the campaign, like all the other top headquarters personnel, Charlie Regan receives a spiritually uplifting letter from the candidate, win or lose. ("Have I ever met Regan? I just can't visualize him." "Oh, you've been in a dozen meetings with him, the little balding guy with the cigar." "Sure, I remember now.") Countless public officials throughout America think they owe a favor to a man named Charlie Regan, and countless frustrated candidates blame their losses entirely on him.

James Hagerty, White House press secretary under Eisenhower, told the lexicographer, "Our Charlie Regan went by the name of Frank Pierce."

The device might have been derived from "George Spelvin," the name a hungry actor adopts as a pseudonym when he accepts a role so minor that playing it under his own name would hurt his reputation, or the name an impecunious producer uses in a program when the same actor is playing two parts.

Chautauqua circuit   old-fashioned BARNSTORMING; speaking to culturally active groups in small towns.

On the shores of Lake Chautauqua, New York, Methodist clergyman John Vincent and Lewis Miller called an assembly in the summer of 1874 to promote Bible study in Sunday school. In a few years a permanent summer camp was formed which led to home-study courses in a variety of subjects. The institution was widely imitated, and after 1900, a "traveling Chautauqua" was begun—a series of lectures and concerts held in tents around the country—which lasted until the Depression.

The word came to connote grass roots intellectualism and mobile speechifying. In *The Economist* in 1931, the capitalization was dropped as the word became generic: "The Chequers [the Prime Minister's residence] conversations proved to be the first of a series of statesmen's chautauquas in the capitals of Europe." While in Britain the word has a Sunday-school flavor, in the U.S. the meaning is more political. "It seems only fitting," wrote the *Atlantic* about Hubert Humphrey in 1968, "that the boy from behind the drug counter in Huron, South Dakota, should wow a Chamber of Commerce convention, that the Chautauqua tent and Grange hall Populist can make a Deep Southern audience jump to its feet."

The word is evocative of a bygone era, campaigning to listening audiences with neither the tedium of the RUBBER-CHICKEN CIRCUIT nor the phoniness of the MEDIA EVENT.

chauvinist.   See JINGOISM; WOMEN'S LIB.

Checkers speech   the address Richard Nixon gave on nationwide television to defend himself against charges that he was the beneficiary of a "secret" political fund; now, any such emotionally charged speech.

During the 1952 campaign the Republicans were having a field day with Truman Administration scandals when word got out of the existence of a "secret Nixon fund," as the Democratic *New York Post* called it. The reaction was noisy—and even included demands that Nixon resign his candidacy. Dwight Eisenhower at first appeared to give Nixon little support. Nixon decided on a television rebuttal, and in a 30-minute speech successfully explained that the collection was neither secret nor sinister, but an open and well-audited fund to pay legitimate political expenses such as travel costs. The reaction from both the country and Eisenhower was favorable.

In the course of the speech, however, Nixon tugged at a few heartstrings. He pointed out that he was too poor for his wife to have anything but a cloth coat. He also admitted his family had accepted a present—a cocker spaniel puppy named Checkers. "And you know," he went on, "the kids, like all kids, loved the dog, and I just want to say this, right now, that regardless of what they say about it, we are going to keep it."

In his 1962 book, *Six Crises,* Nixon wrote: "It was labeled as the 'Checkers speech,' as though the mention of my dog was the only thing that saved my career. Many of the critics glided over the fact that the fund was thoroughly explained, my personal finances laid bare, and an admittedly emotional but honest appeal made for public support."

But many felt that Nixon's approach was overly emotional and corny. Wrote Nixon later:

A distinguished political science professor, after making a thorough study of the 1960 election, stated his considered judgment that if it had not been for the fund broadcast I would have been elected President of the United States. It was a neat theory, brilliantly supported by facts and figures, but like most classroom theoreticians he had not faced up to the hard reality of the alternative. If it hadn't been for that broadcast, I would never have been around to run for the presidency.

Nixon took the idea of injecting Checkers into his speech from Franklin Roosevelt's FALA SPEECH of 1944. The Republicans accused FDR of sending a destroyer to fetch his Scots terrier. Roosevelt did more than deny the charge; he turned it around to make it seem a libel on a poor dumb animal. Fala, he concluded, "has not been the same dog since."

Great men do well to have small dogs. Thomas E. Dewey's Great Dane did not help project his master as a warm human being; Winston Churchill's brown poodle, Rufus, was the kind of endearing small animal that appeals to the public. George Bush did well with a spaniel, Millie; Bill Clinton was the first to reach out to cat lovers, with Socks.

checks and balances   the limitations on the powers of each branch of government—and on the government as a whole—provided for in the federal and state constitutions.

The federal Constitution's authors feared concentrations of power of all kinds, from monarchism to mob rule. During the nationwide debate over creating a federal union in the 1780s, "checks and balances" emerged as the Federalists' prescription for protecting all sectors of the pluralistic American society.

The term was probably coined by seventeenth-century British political philosopher James Harrington. Among the early users was James Madison, one of the great Federalist advocates, as when during the ratification fight he explained how the landed gentry's rights would be protected: ". . . our government ought to secure the permanent interests of the country against innovation. Landholders ought to have a share in the government, to support these invaluable interests, and to balance and check the other [numerically larger groups]."

This explained the government's diversity. The House of Representatives was popularly elected but the Senate was not. The President could veto congressional action, but only Congress could appropriate funds for him to spend. Federal judges depended on the President for appointment and on Congress for money, but the judges serve for life.

Because it describes simply a fundamental and enduring principle of the American system, "checks and balances" has survived as a term, too. It appears frequently in the statements of judges, politicians and historians. James MacGregor Burns described the "system of checks and balances that would use man's essential human nature—his interests, his passions, his ambitions—to control itself."

chicken in every pot an easily attackable Republican slogan created and exploited by Democrats.

King Henry IV of France (1553–1610) was easily the champion phrasemaker of his era. He was responsible for "the white plume" or "plumed knight" expression used by supporters of James Blaine in the late nineteenth century; he coined "Le Grand Dessein," the "great design" for world peace that Franklin Roosevelt appropriated (see GRAND DESIGN); and as a result of his statement *"Je veux qu'il n'y ait si pauvre paysan en moi royaume qu'il n'ait tous les diamanches sa poule au pot"* ("I wish that there would not be a peasant so poor in all my realm who would not have a chicken in his pot every Sunday"), he was given the sobriquet of *le Roi de la poule au pot* ("King of the chicken in the pot").

Herbert Hoover never said it. He did say, on October 22, 1928, "The slogan of progress is changing from the 'FULL DINNER PAIL' to the full garage." The former President's secretary wrote to quote-collector George Seldes in 1958: "No one has ever been able to find, in Mr. Hoover's speeches or writings, of which a very careful file has been kept over the years, the expression 'a chicken in every pot.' Mr. Hoover also never promised or even expressed his hope of two cars in every garage."

The repopularization of the phrase, and Hoover's supposed connection with it, can be traced to a Republican campaign flier of 1928 titled "A Chicken In Every Pot." Democratic candidate Al Smith, in a Boston campaign speech, held up the flier and quoted from it:

"Republican prosperity has reduced hours and increased earning capacity."

And then it goes on to say Republican

prosperity has put a chicken in every pot and a car in every backyard to boot. . . . Here's another good one for you. "Republican efficiency has filled the working-man's dinner pail and his gasoline tank besides, and placed the whole nation in the silk stocking class.". . . Now just draw on your imagination for a moment, and see if you can in your mind's eye picture a man working at $17.50 a week going out to a chicken dinner in his own automobile with silk socks on.

By 1932, reminders of promises of prosperity were particularly embarrassing to Republicans; Hoover's passing reference to a "full garage" was combined with Smith's characterization of the Hoover campaign flier to manufacture a Hoover promise: "A chicken in every pot and two cars in every garage."

Democratic campaigners do not let it die. In 1960 John F. Kennedy misquoted the phony quotation in Bristol, Tennessee: "It is my understanding that the last candidate for the presidency to visit this community in a presidential year was Herbert Hoover in 1928. President Hoover initiated on the occasion of his visit the slogan 'Two chickens for every pot,' and it is no accident that no presidential candidate has ever dared come back to this community since."

Comedian Dick Gregory played on a more recent meaning of "pot" with this turnaround in 1972: "A chicken in every pot will probably not be revived as a campaign slogan. With the eighteen-year-old vote now in effect, some folks feel the new battle cry is more likely to be 'some pot in every chicken.'"

chief of staff. See ABOMINABLE NO-MAN.

chilling effect an action or situation that inhibits free speech, or threatens to intimidate or dispirit the press.

Justice William Brennan, author of the Supreme Court's 1965 opinion in *Dombrowski* v. *Pfister* (380 U.S. 479), popularized the phrase in its current meaning. A civil rights group in Louisiana protested that the state's Subversive Activities and Communist Control Law subjected its members to harassment by local authorities. Instead of deciding on the basis of bad-faith harassment, the Court found intimidation inherent in "the existence of a penal statute susceptible of sweeping and improper application . . . the chilling effect upon the exercise of First Amendment rights may derive from the fact of the prosecution, unaffected by the prospects of its success or failure."

"Chilling effect" made its next appearance in 1967, in *Walker* v. *City of Birmingham*, this time in a dissent by Justice Brennan to a majority opinion written by Justice Potter Stewart. Since the lexicographer heard that the phrase might have stemmed from Justice Stewart's decision, a letter to that jurist elicited this letter from Justice Brennan to Justice Stewart dated March 7, 1974, describing the derivation:

> There is a note in 69 Columbia Law Review 808–842 (1969) entitled "The Chilling Effect in Constitutional Law." That Note traces the concept of "chilling effect" to a concurring opinion by Felix Frankfurter in *Wieman* v. *Updegraff*, 344 U.S. 183, 195 (1952) where Felix, joined by Bill Douglas, said of a teacher's loyalty oath:
> "Such unwarranted inhibition upon the free spirit of teachers affects not only those who, like the appellants, are immediately before the Court. It has an unmistakable tendency to *chill* that free play of the spirit which all teachers ought especially to cultivate and practice; it makes for caution and timidity in their associations by potential teachers."
> . . . Frankly, I have no recollection of bottoming the phrase on Felix's *Wie-*

man opinion nor upon the opinions of lower courts dating back to 1939 and cited in footnote 2 of the Law Review Note. I would suppose that the Note would help meet Mr. Safire's desire for its history.

And so it does, showing how the term "chilling" had been used since 1939 in cases regarding judicially regulated sales. The metaphor can be traced to the sixteenth century to mean "to affect as with cold": the *OED* cites Hooker's *On the Laws of Ecclesiastical Polity* with "chilleth . . . all warmth of zeal." According to the *Columbia Law Review*, the author of this article, written in 1969, was New York attorney Herbert T. Weinstein, and his conclusions in that piece show how the Court has used Brennan's phrase to extend the First Amendment:

> At first blush, the doctrine seems merely to indicate a rational relationship between constitutionally protected conduct and the law sought to be held unconstitutional. But if this is the function of the chilling doctrine, the words "deters" and "inhibits" would serve as well as the word "chills." It appears, however, that the Court uses the chilling doctrine for more far-reaching purposes. First it uses the doctrine to justify activism in restricting and eliminating laws which proscribe protected conduct. Here the chilling effect reverses the usual presumption of federalism that federal courts should defer to state courts and open their doors only when state judicial and administrative procedures have been exhausted.
> The second function of the chilling effect doctrine is to indicate the abridgement of a constitutional right. Here the chilling effect appears to emphasize a presumption in favor of the protected conduct and against the state regulation which deters it.

In current political, rather than legal, use, the phrase is used by reporters who complain that others—not themselves—might be intimidated by "leak-plugging" efforts of government officials. See PLUMBER. In 1992, *Roll Call* discussed stricter codes on sexual harassment: "If and when this policy is adopted, it will have a chilling effect on free speech around the Capitol Dome."

China lobby attack phrase used against those urging support of Chiang Kai-shek against Mao Tse-tung, and later pressing for aid to Chiang on Taiwan.

In February 1946 a mission to China headed by General George Marshall had arranged for a cease-fire and a co-alition government, which began to break up within three months. General Patrick Hurley, in an angry resigna-tion from his ambassadorial post, warned that "subversives" in the State Department were secretly plotting a Communist victory. "Around the country," wrote Cabell Phillips in *The Truman Presidency,* "a 'China lobby' was forming, controlled largely by zealots of the right beating the gongs of public opinion to 'save' China."

General Marshall returned from his mission in January 1947, and Ameri-can aid to the Chiang government soon began to dry up. Friends of Chiang in the U.S. bitterly criticized this decision, and President Truman in July 1947 sent General Albert Wedemeyer to China for another look. Wedemeyer filed an ambivalent re-port, which the Truman Administra-tion suppressed, further whipping up the attacks of Chiang's American sup-porters.

After Chiang retreated from the mainland to Taiwan, the efforts of the "China lobby" were directed to his support on Formosa and the rejection of any attempt to replace the Chiang government in the UN by the Com-munist Chinese.

Finley Peter Dunne's "Mr. Dooley" (see DOOLEY, MR.) expressed a skepti-cism toward the Chinese government that existed among many Americans well before the turn of the twentieth century:

"He's th' Chinee ministher," said Mr. Dooley, "an' his business is f'r to supply fresh hand-laundhried misinformation to the sicrety iv state. . . .

"Th' Westhren civilization, Hin-nissy—that's us—is a pretty good liar, but he's a kind iv rough-an'-tumble at it. . . . How in th' wurruld can we compete with a counthry where ivry lab'rer's cottage projooces lies so deli-cate that th' workment iv th' West can't undherstand thim? We make our lies be machinery; they tur-rn out theirs be hand. . . .

"They can't hurt us with their lies," said Mr. Hennessy of our Western civi-lization. "We have th' guns an' we'll bate thim yet."

"Yes," said Mr. Dooley, "an' 'twill be like a man who's had his house desthroyed be a cyclone gettin' up an' kickin' at th' air."

During the Eisenhower Administra-tion, Senate Minority Leader William Knowland of California was often at-tacked as a captive of the "China lobby" and was labeled "the Senator from Formosa." When mainland China replaced Taiwan in the UN in 1971, and Richard Nixon paid his pres-idential visit to Peking in 1972, the in-fluence of the China lobby was seen to have been overrated. When President Nixon arranged for "liaison offices" in Peking and Washington, the name of the "China lobby" began to change to "supporters of Taiwan." The vogue phrase became "normalization of rela-tions" with the PRC, which President Carter pledged to carry forward in his campaign, based on the Nixon-Mao "Shanghai Communiqué," a 1972 agreement which cleverly recognized that Chinese on both sides of the For-mosa Straits agreed there was but "one China."

By the mid-seventies, another "lobby"—again carrying the pejorative connotation of manipulation—was spoken of in the U.S. This was the "Israel lobby," which gained much attention when the Chairman of the Joint Chiefs of Staff, General George Brown, said in 1976 that Jewish groups made their influence felt on U.S. policy makers, who considered the defense of Israel "a burden." In Great Britain the "Israel lobby" is called, even more pejoratively, "the Jewish lobby," as in this *Financial Times* usage in 1977: "In Washington, the 'Jewish lobby' has already reacted powerfully and angrily." The phrases that most distressed supporters of Israel in 1977 and 1978 were "imposed solution" (forced upon Israelis by the U.S.) and "legitimate rights" (code words for demands for an independent Arab state on the Jordan River's west bank).

In the 1980s, as Egyptian and Saudi Arabian embassies in Washington became more sophisticated in dealing with U.S. public opinion, hiring lobbyists for that purpose, a counterphrase began to appear: the "Arab lobby."

China watchers   outside observers of political customs inside Communist China; sifters of official statements for hidden meanings.

This phrase is probably derived from "bird watching" with its connotation of intense concentration, intricate analysis and observation from a distance. It has replaced OLD CHINA HANDS—reporters and businesspeople who made their careers in the Far East before the rise of Communism there.

A synonym for China watcher was "Pekingologist," coined on the analogy of KREMLINOLOGIST—those who made their living trying to decipher the puzzles of the former Soviet government. The creed of the China watcher and Kremlinologist was summed up by Winston Churchill's description of the Soviet Union: "It is a riddle wrapped in a mystery inside an enigma."

The work of China watchers, unlike that of Kremlinologists, did not stop in the post–Cold War period, especially after the crushing of the democracy movement at Tiananmen Square, Beijing, in 1989.

"China watching" is a construction that has been borrowed for use to describe any group of analysts who laboriously pick over the movements of their subject for hidden meanings—thus, "Bobby watchers" (Kennedy), "Clinton watchers," etc.

choice, not an echo   attack on "metooism" (see ME TOO), a call for a division of parties along ideological lines.

"We think the American people want a clear-cut choice," said Peter O'Donnell, chairman of the Draft Goldwater Committee in April 1963, "between the New Frontier of the Kennedys and Republican principles."

On January 3, 1964, candidate Goldwater announced: "I will offer a choice, not an echo. This will not be an engagement of personalities. It will be an engagement of principles."

Phyllis Schlafly chose the phrase for her best-selling paperback book *A Choice Not An Echo*, published soon afterward; this was called (by Democrats) one of the "three dirty books" of the campaign. The others were *None Dare Call It Treason* by John Stormer and *A Texan Looks at Lyndon* by J. Evetts Haley.

At the 1964 Republican convention, Pennsylvania Governor William Scranton, taking the liberal baton after Nelson Rockefeller's defeat in the California primary, played on the phrase: "I have come here to offer our party a choice. I reject the echo we have thus far been handed . . . the echo of fear, or reaction . . . the echo from the

Never Never Land that puts our nation backward to a lesser place in the world of free men."

The Goldwater strategy relied on the presence of a strong SILENT VOTE that had stayed home up to now because Republicans had not drawn a sharp ideological line with Willkie, Dewey or Nixon. The desire for such a reconstruction (called a restructuring in some circles) of the two-party system has not been limited to conservatives. Felix Frankfurter, explaining his vote for third-party candidate Robert La Follette in 1924, quoted English observer James Bryce's comparison of the two American parties: "Both have certainly war cries, organizations, interests enlisted in their support. But those interests are in the main getting or keeping the patronage of the government. Distinctive tenets and policies, points of political practice have all but vanished."

FDR flirted with the idea in conversations after the 1940 campaign with Wendell Willkie. Moderates of both parties, however, point out that such a polarization would result in the "left" winning most of the time, and the danger of a drastic wrench when conservatives, through the popularity of an individual or war or depression, finally turned the tables.

See TWO-PARTY SYSTEM; BIG TENT; IDEOLOGY; TRUE BELIEVER; DIME'S WORTH OF DIFFERENCE.

Christmas tree bills. See RIDER.

chronic campaigner characterization of Richard Nixon by President Lyndon Johnson, in angry rebuttal to a Nixon analysis of Vietnam policy.

In the 1966 congressional campaign, former Vice President Richard Nixon was the foremost campaigner for Republican candidates nationally. He carried the attack to President Johnson, who pursued the same strategy he had used so successfully two years earlier on Barry Goldwater: to remain above the battle. With the polls showing his popularity dropping, Johnson chose to make a dramatic trip to Southeast Asia, including a visit to U.S. troops in Vietnam, two weeks before election. Nixon held his fire during the President's trip, but on Johnson's return put out a closely reasoned, critical analysis of the Manila Communiqué issued by Johnson and the Southeast Asia leaders.

The *New York Times* decided to run the text of the Nixon critique, which gave it national importance; the next morning, at the President's news conference, Johnson startled his audience by losing his temper. He called Nixon "a chronic campaigner" who was "playing politics with peace."

Johnson's "chronic campaigner" phrase focused national attention on Nixon's role in the campaign and gave him a superb opportunity to counter with almost presidential calm.

A similar attack, though less emotional, was made by John Quincy Adams on Henry Clay: "His opposition to Monroe and myself arises out of a disappointed ambition, a determination to run down the administration and become president by hook or crook in 1824."

See PERENNIAL CANDIDATE.

CIA. See INVISIBLE GOVERNMENT; DIRTY TRICKS.

CIA-ese spookspeak; the language of the intelligence community (formerly the intelligence establishment), selected from a glossary compiled in 1976 by the Senate Select Committee to Study Governmental Operations with Respect to Intelligence Activities:

asset: Any resource—a person, group, relationship, instrument, installation or supply—at the disposition of an intelligence agency for use in an operational or support role. The term is normally applied to a person who is contributing to a CIA clandestine mission, but is not a fully controlled agent of the CIA.

backstopping: A CIA term for providing appropriate verification and support of cover arrangements for an agent or asset in anticipation of inquiries or other actions which might test the credibility of his or its cover.

bigot lists: Using the term *bigot* in the sense of "narrow," this is a restrictive list of persons who have access to a particular and highly sensitive class of information.

black bag job: Warrantless surreptitious entry, especially an entry conducted for purposes other than microphone installation, such as physical search and seizure or photographing of documents.

bug: A concealed listening device or microphone, or other audiosurveillance device; also, to install the means for audiosurveillance of a subject or target.

code word: A word which has been assigned a classification and a classified meaning to safeguard intentions and information regarding a planned operation.

cover: A protective guise used by a person, organization or installation to prevent identification with clandestine activities and to conceal the true affiliation of personnel and the true sponsorship of their activities.

covert action: Any clandestine activity designed to influence foreign governments, events, organizations, or persons in support of United States foreign policy. Covert action may include political and economic action, propaganda and paramilitary activities.

cut-out: A CIA term referring to a person who is used to conceal contact between members of a clandestine activity or organization.

double agent: A person engaging in clandestine activity for two or more intelligence or security services who provides information to one service about the other, or about each service to the other, and who is wittingly or unwittingly manipulated by one service against the other.

executive action: This term is generally a euphemism for assassination, and was used by the CIA to describe a program aimed at overthrowing certain foreign leaders, by assassinating them if necessary.

informant: A person who wittingly or unwittingly provides information to an agent, a clandestine service or police. In reporting such information, this person will often be cited as the source.

informer: One who intentionally discloses information about other persons or activities to police or a security service (such as the FBI), usually for a financial reward.

notionals: Fictitious, private commercial entities which exist on paper only. They serve as the ostensible employer of intelligence personnel, or as the ostensible sponsor of certain activities in support of clandestine operations. (Not to be confused with "nationals," citizens of a given country.)

plumbing: A term referring to the development of assets or services supporting the clandestine operations of CIA field stations—such as safe houses, unaccountable funds, investigative persons, and surveillance teams.

proprietaries: A term used by the CIA to designate ostensibly private commercial entities capable of doing business which are established and controlled by intelligence services to conceal governmental affiliation of intelligence personnel and/or governmental sponsorship of certain activities in support of clandestine operations.

safe house: An innocent-appearing house or premises established by an intelligence organization for conducting clandestine or covert activity in relative security.

sanitize: The deletion or revision of a report or document so as to prevent identification of the intelligence sources and methods that contributed to or are dealt with in the report.

sheep dipping: The utilization of a military instrument (e.g., an airplane) or officer in clandestine operations, usually in a civilian capacity or under civilian cover, although the instrument or officer will covertly retain its or his military ownership or standing. The term is also applied to the placement of individuals in organizations or groups in which they can become active in order to establish credentials so that they can be used to collect information of intelligence interest on similar groups.

source: A person, thing or activity which provides intelligence information. In clandestine activities, the term applies to an agent or asset, normally a foreign national, being used in an intelligence activity for intelligence purposes. In interrogations, it refers to a person who furnishes intelligence information with or without knowledge that the information is being used for intelligence purposes.

sterilize: To remove from material to be used in covert and clandestine actions any marks or devices which can identify it as originating with the sponsoring organization or nation.

target of opportunity: A term describing an entity (e.g., governmental entity, installation, political organization or individual) that becomes available to an intelligence agency or service by chance, and provides the opportunity for the collection of needed information.

United States country team: The senior, in-country, U.S. coordinating and supervising body, headed by the chief of the U.S. diplomatic mission (usually an ambassador) and composed of the senior member of each represented United States department or agency.

watch list: A list of words—such as names, entities, or phrases—which can be employed by a computer to select out required information from a mass of data.

Curiously, in the committee report the phrase *plausible denial* was listed but not defined: it is a cover story which enables high government officials to disclaim knowledge of an intelligence activity. (Asked about the oversight committee's oversight, a staffer said merely, "We closed out the report in such a rush we just forgot that definition," which is a plausible denial.)

Another intelligence agency word is *mole*, an operative planted in another country's intelligence community, a specific form of *agent in place.* This is either reportage or coinage by novelist David Cornwell, whose pen name is John le Carré; whether or not a fictional fancy, *mole* has burrowed its way into intelligence jargon. Former CIA chief Richard Helms tells the author he never heard *mole* used in his tenure; the word used for that most feared prospect was "penetration."

Fluttering is giving a lie-detector test to one's own agents to find out if they are telling the truth. Rudy Maxa wrote in the October 9, 1977, *Washington Post Magazine:* "Investigators for the Church committee learned—but never revealed—that many of the journalists who had cooperated with the CIA were given lie-detector tests. In the spy business that's called 'fluttering,' and some reporters were fluttered more often than regular agency employees to test their loyalty."

Synecdoche is a word also used by intelligence professionals. The word (pronounced sin-EK-do-key) means a rhetorical device that uses a part to stand for the whole, or a small thing to symbolize a big thing: the BIG APPLE, a nickname for New York City, uses an apple as a synecdoche for the world. The CIA Inspector General in 1967, Lyman Kirkpatrick, said in an internal report dealing with assassination: "The point is that of frequent resort to synecdoche—the mention of a part when the whole is to be understood, or vice versa. Thus, we encounter repeated references to phrases such as 'disposing of Castro,' which may be read in the narrow literal sense of assassinating him, when it is intended that it be read in the broader figurative sense of dislodging the Castro regime.

"Reversing the coin," the CIA man continued, "we find people speaking vaguely of 'doing something about Castro' when it is clear that what they have specifically in mind is killing him."

Another CIA favorite is *blowback,* coined on the analogy of the automotive "blow by" and the electronic "feedback," or perhaps from the windshift danger in the use of poison gas. In what was called "psychological warfare" in the fifties, the Soviets pioneered in "disinformation"—falsehoods, widely disseminated, distinguished from "misinformation" by the intent to misinform—and U.S. "black propaganda" has done the same, notably in the implantation of bogus material in Khrushchev's "secret speech" in 1956 denouncing Joseph Stalin. The danger of such a farrago of lies being picked up by U.S. correspondents abroad and sent back to the U.S. as the truth is called "blowback"; its CIA synonyms are *fallout* and *domestic replay.*

Family jewels is a jocular CIA phrase for its own most embarrassing secrets. When James Schlesinger was appointed Director of Central Intelli-

gence in 1973, he asked employees to come forward with information about activities "which might be construed to be outside the legislative charter of this agency." Wrote Schlesinger's successor, William Colby, in his 1978 book *Honorable Men:* "Presented to the Director so that he would know about them, they were promptly dubbed by a wag the 'family jewels'; I referred to them as 'our skeletons in the closet.' Among them were the Chaos Operation against the antiwar movement, the surveillance and bugging of American journalists in hope of locating the sources of leaks of sensitive materials, and all the connections with the Watergate conspirators and White House 'plumbers.'" (The phrase "family jewels" has a longtime taboo slang use meaning "testicles," which are a source of pride as the source of progeny.)

Witting describes anybody who has been let in on a secret plan; somebody uninformed plays an *unwitting* role, and anybody partially informed is *half witting.*

Code word is still current. In 1987, the *Washington Post* reported florid terms for attacks on Libya: "In the White House and N.S.C., the top-secret plan to oust Gadhafi was given the code word 'Flower'; a C.I.A. component to undermine Gadhafi covertly was called 'Tulip,' and the plan for a U.S.-Egyptian military action was 'Rose.'" For other uses of this term, see CODE WORDS.

The retired CIA employee, still on the payroll and readily available, is an *annuitant.* Another recent example of spookspeak is *U.P.S.,* "uncontested physical searches," updating *black bag job.*

See DESTABILIZE.

cigarette-holder symbol cartoonists' political symbol for Franklin Delano Roosevelt.

Reporters found it an infallible press-conference barometer. Wrote Associated Press White House correspondent Jack Bell, "If the cigarette in his holder was pointed toward the ceiling and his head was thrown back, the news would be good. If he was hunched over his desk and the cigarette pointed downward, look out, somebody was going to get hell."

Jonathan Daniels, a Roosevelt press aide, described Roosevelt's exultation after triumph at the polls in 1936: "His cigarette holder seemed not merely a scepter but a wand." (In 1993, the Clintons banned smoking in the White House.)

Other cartoonists' symbols include Churchill's cigar, Senator Joseph Mc-Carthy's "five o'clock shadow," John F. Kennedy's rocking chair, John L. Lewis's eyebrows, Senator Everett Dirksen's "basset" jowls, Lincoln's stovepipe hat, Theodore Roosevelt's teeth, Coolidge's high collar, Grant's cigar stub, Hitler's and Stalin's mustaches, Al Smith's brown derby, Gerald Ford's Band-Aid (from bumping his head), Jimmy Carter's teeth, Lyndon Johnson's Stetson, and Bill Clinton's round jaw.

circumlocution. See RED TAPE.

citizen of the world an internationalist as opposed to an isolationist; more loosely, one concerned with universal issues, whether they apply at home or abroad.

Historian Richard Hofstadter credits Woodrow Wilson with being the first major American figure to urge Americans to be "citizens of the world." Both during World War I and the ensuing fight over U.S. membership in the League of Nations, Wilson constantly tried to combat the isolationist argument that European affairs were no concern of this country. Wilson contended that American principles were not "the principles of a province or of a single continent . . . [but] the principles of a liberated mankind."

Neither the sentiment nor the phrase, of course, was original with Wilson. In 1762 Oliver Goldsmith wrote a satire entitled *Citizen of the World* and the phrase was used in the fourth century B.C. by Socrates. American abolitionist William Lloyd Garrison wrote: "My country is the world; my countrymen are mankind." Franklin Roosevelt, who also had problems with isolationists, said in his last inaugural address: "We have learned to be citizens of the world, members of the world community." John Kennedy expanded the phrase still further in a parallel to his famous "ask not" passage when at his inaugural he said, "My fellow citizens of the world, ask not what America will do for you, but what together we can do for the freedom of man."

citizens committee a pseudo-independent organization set up by a political party to provide a "home" for independents and members of the opposition party; in other cases a genuine nonpartisan committee set up for civic action.

During campaigns it is necessary to enlist the enthusiasm and political activity of people who have no interest in year-round partisan political work. To provide an umbrella for these citizens who "vote for the man and not the party," the device of the citizens committee was created. In addition, all radio and television commercials and newspaper advertisements must carry the name of the political sponsor; it is considered more palatable to use a citizens committee imprimatur on these advertisements than a political party's. The citizens committee often raises its own money by subdividing itself into "Lawyers for (candidate)," "Professors for (candidate),"

"Businessmen for (candidate)," etc. The money raised is then spent at the direction of the party chairman or campaign manager, although there is occasionally some friction between the professionals and the citizens' groups. See AMATEURS.

There was a Communist governmental counterpart to this American political technique. In an article on Yugoslavian Marxism, C. P. McVicker wrote: ". . . new institutions were created which do serve to bring the ordinary Yugoslav into local government affairs. 'Citizens' councils' are permanent or *ad hoc* bodies of local citizens whose experience and talents make them especially well qualified to advise their people's committee in the various specific areas of its competence."

See VOLUNTEERS; CREEP.

City Hall. See GO FIGHT CITY HALL.

city on a hill the ideal or shining example; a paragon of civic success or virtue.

St. Matthew's Gospel introduced this well-worn metaphor. In Matthew 5:14, Jesus tells his followers during the Sermon on the Mount, "Ye are the light of the world. A city that is set on an hill cannot be hid."

John Winthrop, aboard the *Arabella* bound for the New World, included the expression in a 1630 sermon. The founder of the settlement that became Boston warned his fellow settlers of the Massachusetts Bay Colony that "we shall be as a city upon a hill, the eyes of all people are upon us."

John Kennedy, who must have seen that quotation on the pedestal of the statue of Winthrop on Boston Common, used the expression repeatedly in his stump speeches. Ronald Reagan also had success in describing the city as "shining," although New York Governor Mario Cuomo turned that image against him at the 1984 Democratic Convention, pointing out that "the hard truth is that not everyone is sharing in this city's splendor and glory."

See CAMELOT.

civil disobedience a doctrine requiring the individual to act against the law, accepting the law's punishment, if he believes the law is morally wrong or politically unjust.

English utilitarian philosopher Jeremy Bentham expressed the position clearly: that it was "allowable to, if not incumbent on, every man . . . to enter into measures of resistance . . . when . . . the probable mischiefs of resistance (speaking with respect to the community in general) appear less to him than the probable mischiefs of obedience."

In the Declaration of Independence, Thomas Jefferson carried the thought to its political extreme: ". . . that whenever any Form of Government becomes destructive of these Ends it is the Right of the People to alter or abolish it, and to institute new Government . . ."

Political philosophers have long held that a "natural law" or HIGHER LAW exists that has precedence over the man-made laws, and when these come in conflict the individual has the duty to disobey and resist the man-made laws. But this means that the law may be legally disobeyed, a contradiction in terms that has led to bloody dispute. William Seward of New York said in 1850: "There is a higher law than the Constitution," and his words became an abolitionist rallying cry.

The phrase "civil disobedience" was popularized in the U.S. by Henry David Thoreau's 1848 essay of that title, and in India by Mohandas K. Gandhi in his long battle against British rule. It became one of the cornerstones of the civil rights movement and was expressed eloquently by the Rev. Martin Luther King, Jr., in his "Letter from a Birmingham Jail":

> I submit that an individual who breaks a law that conscience tells him is unjust, and willingly accepts the penalty by staying in jail to arouse the conscience of the community over its injustice, is in reality expressing the very highest respect for law.
>
> Of course there is nothing new about this kind of civil disobedience. . . . It was practiced superbly by the early Christians. . . .
>
> We can never forget that everything Hitler did in Germany was "legal" and everything the Hungarian freedom fighters did in Hungary was "illegal.". . .

Wrote Stewart Alsop in *Newsweek* in 1971: "'Civil disobedience'—a euphemism for breaking those laws in which the law breaker does not believe—has become both respectable and relatively safe. The civil-rights movement of the early sixties began to make it respectable, and the increasing unpopularity of the Vietnam war has helped to make it safe as well as respectable."

civilian review describing a semijudicial board made up of citizens who are not police officers, to investigate complaints made against the police.

"Police brutality" was one of the earliest and most impassioned phrases of the civil rights movement. Photographs of police dogs being loosed on black demonstrators caused a national revulsion that lent impetus to the movement; it also lent credibility to unfair charges of brutality against police officers enforcing the law.

In an effort to lessen racial tensions, several cities adopted civilian review boards to assure minorities of an independent control of police activities. In New York City, the issue of civilian review was put to the voters in 1966, with the concept enthusiastically endorsed by Senators Javits and Kennedy and Mayor John Lindsay. The proposal was overwhelmingly defeated. The police had argued that their own civil liberties were being violated by such a board. However, the vote was attributed to BACKLASH by the civil rights groups.

An amateur videotape of Rodney King, a speeding motorist, being beaten by a quartet of Los Angeles policemen brought the issue of police brutality to the fore in 1992; after a state trial of the officers resulted in acquittal, the worst riot of the century in the United States ensued, leaving 50 dead. The accused were tried again under a federal civil rights statute, and two were convicted.

civil rights those rights guaranteed to an individual as a member of society; most often applied to the movement for black equality.

Civil rights refers to positive legal prerogatives—the right to equal treatment before the law, the right to vote, the right to share equally with other citizens in such benefits as jobs, housing, education, and public accommodations. In their *Cyclopedia of American Government* (1914), A. C McLaughlin and A. B. Hart defined civil rights as "those which belong to the individual as a result of his membership in organized society, that is, as a subject of civil government."

The term is sometimes substituted for *civil liberties,* which refers to more negative rights—that is, those things an individual is legally free to do without government interference. Spelled out in the Constitution and the Bill of Rights, the more notable civil liberties include freedom of speech, press, assembly and religion, and protection against unreasonable searches and seizures.

Virtually interchangeable with civil rights is the seldom-used *civic rights,* though the latter is somewhat broader. At the 1924 Democratic convention, for example, liberals who wanted to condemn the Ku Klux Klan for its discrimination against Jews and Catholics as well as blacks, introduced a plank opposing any attempts "to limit the civic rights of any citizen or body of citizens because of religion, birthplace, or racial origin." The plank was narrowly defeated by Southern Democratic votes, and the issue has been a bitterly divisive one in the Democratic party ever since.

Civil rights, however, is a term more closely associated with the struggle of blacks for equal treatment since the Civil War (though for a time it was used often by labor union organizers). In 1875, Congress passed a Civil Rights Act outlawing discrimination in public accommodations. By 1883, a reaction had set in, and the Supreme Court found key sections of the act unconstitutional. Not until 1957 was another Civil Rights Act passed.

See SEPARATE BUT EQUAL; WE SHALL OVERCOME; FREEDOM RIDERS; HUMAN RIGHTS.

clean sweep a smashing, across-the-board victory; a wide-ranging change of officeholders.

In current usage, *landslide* refers more often to a great individual victory; *avalanche* refers to a great number of votes; *clean sweep* refers to a wide party victory with many successful candidates belonging to a single party.

The phrase stems from the expression "a new broom sweeps clean," an English proverb traceable to 1546. In Andrew Jackson's presidential campaigns, "Old Hickory" promised that his hickory broom would sweep out the "Augean stables" of corruption—specifically the "corrupt bargain" of

John Quincy Adams and Henry Clay. In 1840 Clay was quoted as saying, "General Jackson was a bold and fearless reaper carrying a wide row, but he did not gather the whole harvest; he left some gleanings to his faithful successor, and he seems resolved to sweep clean the field of power."

Soon after Jackson's inauguration, the phrase's meaning changed. The SPOILS SYSTEM entered American politics and a "clean sweep" came to mean a total change of appointive officeholders. In the twentieth century, however, the meaning reverted to its original sense of broad party victory.

clear it with Sidney a statement of FDR's used by his critics to illustrate how strongly the President was dominated by organized labor.

Arthur Krock reported in the *New York Times* on July 25, 1944, that Roosevelt had said "Clear everything with Sidney" in connection with the choice of a Vice President in 1944. (The choice turned out to be Harry Truman to replace Henry Wallace. Others being considered at the time were James Byrnes, William O. Douglas, Sam Rayburn, Paul McNutt, Scott Lucas, Alben Barkley, and John G. Winant.)

"Sidney" was Sidney Hillman, head of the Political Action Committee of the CIO, a Roosevelt adviser. The remark was officially denied, but in a book published fourteen years later James F. Byrnes said the remark was made between July 15 and 17, 1944.

Hillman strongly urged that Wallace be kept on the ticket, but it never "cleared" FDR. Truman was Hillman's second choice. The attack on Hillman, Samuel Rosenman felt, "was obviously an unvarnished, unabashed appeal to anti-Jewish prejudices. . . . The President did not try to defend Sidney Hillman, or say that there was no truth to the charge that things had to be 'cleared with Sidney.' Instead, he carried the attack right to his opponent." Roosevelt's attack came early in the campaign, slamming into religious intolerance in a Boston speech: ". . . big as this country is, there is no room in it for racial or religious intolerance . . . and there is no room for snobbery."

Writing about Hillman a decade later, C. Wright Mills gave the phrase sociological significance, ". . . his awareness of himself as a member of the national elite, and the real and imagined recognition he achieved as a member ('Clear it with Sidney') signaled the larger entrance, after the great expansion of the unions and after the New Deal, of labor leaders into the power elite."

In the Eisenhower Administration, a frequent remark was "Clear it with Sherm" (Sherman Adams; see ABOMINABLE NO-MAN). In 1967, a *New York Times* story began: "The 'clear it with Hubert' order was issued by the President at a cabinet meeting last Wednesday."

In current usage, "run it past" is overtaking "clear it with."

cloakroom   congressional meeting places just off the Senate and House floors, where members of Congress confer, trade, and gossip.

As far back as 1868, English observer George Rose wrote to his countrymen about "a rush to the cloakroom amid the shouts and laughter of the House." The "cloakrooms" of the Capitol came to mean not a place to hang a hat but a place to bargain. "In the quiet councils of committee rooms and cloakrooms," wrote former White House correspondent Charles Hurd in 1965, "they negotiate, compromise and trade their votes."

The sense of trading in the cloakrooms appears to be switching more to a sense of gossiping. "The cloakrooms of Congress resounded with a lurid account," reported the *Chicago Daily News* in 1947, "of what General Eisenhower there proposed as a solution." Congressional cloakrooms are tending to become synonymous with "rumor mill" and "rumor factory."

See LOBBY.

closed shop   a place of work where only union members may be employed.

The "closed shop"—so called because it excludes unorganized workers from the workshop—goes back to labor troubles in Philadelphia's shoe industry in the early nineteenth century. But it was not really used widely until the early twentieth century. Unionists prefer "union shop," because it sounds less restrictive. As the publication *American Federationist* wrote in 1904: "The object of the union shop is not to create a monopoly of opportunity. *It is not a closed shop.*" But the phrase has stuck. In a 1948 article, for example, the *Chicago Daily News* wrote, "A 'closed shop' violates the fundamental rights of the individual."

Recent usage has extended the term to professional sports. In 1989, *Newsday* reported on negotiations by teams seeking to sign Dallas Cowboys running back Herschel Walker: "Until they heard Walker had vetoed a deal with the Vikings on Wednesday, said a source close to the negotiations, 'A lot of them thought it was a closed shop.'"

See RIGHT TO WORK.

closed society.   See OPEN SOCIETY.

closing ranks   the act of healing wounds after a battle for nomination and achieving party unity in the general election.

After a particularly bitter primary, there are always those who will speak up for the importance of the two-party system and the need to close ranks.

Customarily, the victor in a nomination fight extends the invitation to his previous opposition; many political analysts were astounded at Barry Goldwater's 1964 acceptance speech at the Republican convention, when no such invitation was offered.

Like many other political expressions (see ON THE POINT), this is a MILITARY METAPHOR, referring to the scattering of troops during a skirmish and the subsequent need to close ranks to become a cohesive fighting force once again.

The act of forcing a smile and supporting the man who defeated you or your candidate is a difficult and humbling experience. Two Republicans who opposed William McKinley's nomination in 1896—Henry Cabot Lodge and Theodore Roosevelt—traveled to Canton, Ohio, where the candidate was conducting his FRONT-PORCH CAMPAIGN and made the necessary obeisances. Statesman John Hay wrote: "Cabot and Teddy have been to Canton to offer their heads to the axe and their tummies to the harikari knife."

cloth coat. See CHECKERS SPEECH.

clothespin vote   a vote cast without enthusiasm or with outright displeasure.

A *clothespin* is a wooden peg or clip used to fasten wet clothes to a line for drying. This type of pin has long been used to signal disgust; cartoons from the turn of the twentieth century show a person's nose clamped tight with a clothespin to keep from inhaling unpleasant odors.

Clothespin is an Americanism first found in print in 1846. Its attributive use in the noun phrase *clothespin vote* is of recent origin. This type of vote is often cast by those who find the ticket noxious but decide to stick with their party despite its candidate (see YEL-

LOW DOG DEMOCRAT) or because the alternative seems to them even worse. See HOBSON'S CHOICE.

cloture   the cutting off of debate; the forced ending of discussion to produce a vote.

Based on a French noun with a circumflex over the *o*, this term denotes the closing of debate in the French Assembly by majority vote. The *Edinburgh Review* wrote in 1871 of the prolonged debate "before the establishment of the cloture in the French Chamber."

An etymological relative of *cloister* and *claustrophobia* (the fear of enclosed spaces), *cloture* comes from French based on the Latin *clausere*, "to close."

Before its 1882 introduction into the British House of Commons, cloture caused political observers to fear the effects of cutting short debate. *The Spectator* commented in 1881, "Might not an unscrupulous party chief . . . use the cloture to arrest necessary discussion." Following its introduction, this method of shutting off debate became known in England as *closure*, spelled with an *s*.

Cloture entered American politics during the First World War. On March 8, 1917, the Senate adopted the cloture rule, which allowed the will of a majority to end debate; however, any Senator was allowed to speak for an hour after the rule was invoked.

Still invoked in the 1990s, the *cloture rule* can lead to a *cloture vote*. Senator Warren Rudman, Republican of New Hampshire, told television interviewer Larry King in June 1992 about the result of debate on balancing the budget: "Well, this is actually a procedural vote, Larry. It's a so-called cloture vote, and if 60 votes are achieved, then we will have a final vote tomorrow on the balanced budget amendment." Two months later, Democratic Senator

Harris Wofford of Pennsylvania expressed the hope on Cable News Network for "the cloture votes, beyond the 57 [Democratic votes], to get something on the floor of the Senate."

Cloud-Cuckoo-Land dream world; an area of unrealistic expectations and foolish behavior.

The eponym of this unreal world is the *cuckoo*, a thirteenth-century noun that imitates the bird's call. The cuckoo's common European species is a grayish-brown bird that builds no nest and instead expects other birds to hatch and raise its young.

Cloud-Cuckoo-Land comes from the Greek *Nephelokokkygia*, the name for a dream world in Aristophanes' ancient comedy *The Birds*. The Greek term was translated into English in 1824 as *Cuckoocloudland*; however, the British journalist Richard Whiteing reworked the name in his 1899 novel, *No. 5 John Street*: "All his thinking processes fade off into the logic of Cloud Cuckoo Land."

Variations include a 1903 comment in the *Daily Chronicle* about "our new school of economists (sort of cloud-cuckoo-town)," but nowadays the term most often used is *Cloud-Cuckoo-Land*, capitalized and hyphenated.

In 1988, when George Bush proposed an expensive child-care plan during his first presidential campaign, Michael Dukakis countered that the Republican plan belonged in "financial Cloud-Cuckoo-Land."

cloud no bigger than a man's hand. See STRAW POLL.

clout power, or influence.

Clout means political *power* when applied to a candidate or public political personage; it means *influence* when applied to a political leader not in the public eye, a large contributor, or member of a palace guard.

Since it can be used to define both political influence and political power, the word has a fuzzy meaning—because there is a difference between power and influence.

Clout, in its power sense, applies to the ability of an individual or group to put across a program, decide a nomination, sway votes. In its influence sense, clout means the ability to reach and persuade those in power; it is one step removed from the power source.

The political use of the word is believed to have originated in Chicago in the 1940s, taken from the baseball phrase "What a clout!," meaning "a powerful hit" or "a long hard drive."

Another possibility is a derivation from cloth, or specifically handkerchief. Atcheson Hench, in *American Speech* magazine (October 1959), pointed out that a "clouter" was originally a handkerchief thief, the noun "clout" later covering any petty thievery. In current underworld lingo, "to clout heaps" means to steal automobiles. It is a short jump from thievery to political influence; still, most politicians think the word comes from a baseball slugger.

Columnist Irv Kupcinet, in the *Chicago Sun-Times*, December 14, 1958, said: "Defendants in Chicago, as in Los Angeles, are found innocent on the age-old legal premise of 'reasonable doubt'—not, as the judge insinuated, 'reasonable clout.'"

A member of the U.S. Office of Education said mournfully in 1972: "We just don't have the clout we would have with specific legislation, and what we need more than anything else right now is some muscle to get this thing moving." Theodore M. Bernstein, in his word-watching column syndicated by the *New York Times*, provided a nice distinction between "clout" and "muscle": "The two words mean virtually the same thing: power or effectiveness, particularly in the areas of government or business. But . . . there is a shade of difference between the two. The accumulation of *muscle* leads to the possession of *clout.*"

An early citation of this vivid political term was supplied the author by writer Paul Hoffman of New York, who found a use in Harold Gasnell's *Machine Politics,* published in 1937, quoting a Chicago precinct captain: "No one gets anywhere in politics or business on his merits. He has to have the 'clout' from behind."

See JUICE.

club. See INNER CLUB.

coalition a grouping of often disparate political elements into a major party, or of several minor parties into a working majority.

"A political aspirant in the United States," Alexis de Tocqueville wrote, "begins by discovering his own interest, and discovering those other interests which may be collected around and amalgamated with it." According to political scientist James MacGregor Burns, "Tocqueville was describing one of the oldest and simplest acts of politics—the effort of the Greek magistrate or the Roman senator, of the Russian revolutionary or the British squire, to piece together a following big enough to win power in a legislative assembly or a political party or a popular election."

One example is the formation of the Republican party. It drew its strength, as Clinton Rossiter wrote in *Parties and Politics in America,* from "almost every party and group on the American scene—from the Whigs, yes, but also from the Democrats, Free-Soilers, Abolitionists, Know-Nothings, local third parties and, lest we forget, the temperance movement."

This is the essence of U.S.-style coali-

tion. In multiparty nations abroad, a coalition involves the fusion of a number of individual parties into a working majority. West Germany's "Grand Coalition" of the Socialist and Christian Democratic parties is an example. In the U.S., by contrast, the major parties are themselves coalitions, combining liberals, moderates, and conservatives, and helping Democrats and Republicans to avoid extremes. For this reason, most politicians instinctively reject suggestions that U.S. politics be realigned into liberal and conservative parties.

Former NBC News president Richard Wald noted the danger in the decline of coalition politics in a 1978 *Esquire* interview with reporter Richard Reeves: "Old politicians were looking for part of the audience, for a coalition. They were looking at problems and saying, 'Look, this is a common problem for many of you. I"ll represent you in dealing with it.' The new politicians are looking for chords. They float above the problems. They strike responsive chords. What they really want to do is cloud men's minds."

The word was incorporated into a political movement in the 1980s, as part of Jesse Jackson's "Rainbow Coalition," a reference to people of different colors. (See PEOPLE OF COLOR.)

Words of praise for coalitions are BIG TENT and UMBRELLA; attack phrases are STRANGE BEDFELLOWS and UNHOLY ALLIANCE.

coattails political carrying power; the ability to attract and hold support, not only for oneself but for other members of a ticket.

Congressman Abraham Lincoln popularized the phrase in a speech in the House on July 27, 1848, after the metaphor had been introduced by Alfred Iverson of Georgia:

> But the gentleman from Georgia further says, we have deserted all our prin-

ciples, and taken shelter under General Taylor's military coat tail. . . . Has he no acquaintance with the ample military coat tail of General Jackson? Does he not know that his own party have run the last five Presidential races under that coat tail, and that they are now running the sixth, under the same cover? . . . Mr. Speaker, old horses and military coat tails, or tails of any sort, are not figures of speech, such as I would be the first to introduce into discussions here; but . . .

The military connotation soon fell by the wayside and coattails came to mean an inducement to straight-ticket voting.

In the 1960 presidential campaign, Kennedy supporter Adlai Stevenson said of the Republican nominee, "Nixon is finding out there are no tails on an Eisenhower jacket." In the 1966 congressional campaign, when Nixon achieved a political comeback stumping the country for congressional candidates, he also found use for the metaphor, attacking Lyndon B. Johnson's sagging popularity: "There is a new fashion sweeping the country: skirts are shorter, pants are tighter and the LBJ coattails are going out of style."

See HYMIE'S FERRYBOAT.

code words a charge that particular phrases, innocuous in themselves, are intended to transmit hidden meanings.

Charles P. Taft, chairman of the Fair Campaign Practices Committee, said in 1968:

> . . . candidates who would never use the word "nigger" nor any of its slurring variations, are using other terms which apparently carry a similar connotation. They are using the racial shorthand in areas of the country where an outright expression of racism would bring immediate social—and political— ostracism. . . .
>
> These forms suggest rather than state, the campaigner's intent. For instance,

instead of saying he is opposed to open housing, the sophisticated racist proclaims, "YOUR HOME IS YOUR CASTLE," and leaves the rest unsaid. We cannot prevent voters from casting ballots based on racist sentiment, but we can spotlight those campaigners who appeal to that sentiment. We can, that is, if we point to an objective study of the understood meanings of the campaign code words—the current shorthand of racial bigotry.

Among the words considered part of the "code" at that time were LAW AND ORDER, CRIME IN THE STREETS, and "forced" BUSING.

Undoubtedly, in many cases the use of these words was intended to, and did, cloak appeal to racial prejudice. However, they were also often used in good faith to discuss controversial topics, and the "code word" charge could be, and was, used as a smear.

The code is sometimes only in the eye of the beholder. In a few areas, for example, whenever the phrase "Roman Catholic" is used rather than "Catholic," anti-Catholic prejudice is suspected—since "Roman" (as in "Rum, Romanism and Rebellion") is occasionally perceived as a word intended to show domination from abroad.

Wrote Max Lerner in the *New York Post* on September 20, 1972:

> Every campaign becomes, at some point, a battle of coded words and ideas . . . in which the issues are somehow scooped out and only the verbal husk remains. [Senator George McGovern's] code words are "precious young lives" and "dying far from home for a corrupt dictatorship." Another is "SPECIAL INTERESTS." . . . The code vocabulary of the Republicans is much longer, richer, more available. Take President Nixon's quick visit to an Italian American festival in Prince George's County, Md. All he had to do was use the words "work" and "family" and everybody got the message. He was talk-

ing of the WORK ETHIC as against "getting something for nothing." He was talking of family loyalties as against the uprooted and alienated "kids." "QUOTAS" became a coded signal at the Republican convention. It is working overtime for Nixon among the "ETHNICS," and has become one of the major symbols in the areas of Jewish voters.

Although *code word* is sometimes used to mean "euphemism," most often the phrase is an attempt to impugn the motive of the speaker, by imputing a racist, sexist, anti-youth or anti-intellectual overlay to what may (or may not) be intended.

In the *Wall Street Journal* on July 18, 1977, Irving Kristol objected to the use of biased code words in news broadcasts:

> There are "ultraconservatives" on TV news (e.g., Cardinal Lefevre, Senator Jesse Helms) but when was the last time you encountered an "ultraliberal"? Apparently there is no such species. Nor are there any "extremists" to the left of center—only "militants" or "activists." An "extremist" is someone who passionately holds the wrong views, while a "militant" is someone who is immoderately pursuing the "correct" ends.
>
> . . . But the neatest ploy of all is the selective use of the word "controversial"; legislation to regulate the price of natural gas is not controversial. Anita Bryant is "controversial"; leaders of Gay Rights groups are not. This is the subtlest code word of them all. Watch for it.

The language of diplomacy is rife with code words. In the Middle East, the phrase "defensible borders" is taken by Israelis and Arabs to mean not returning much of the land taken by Israel in the 1967 war. The phrase "legitimate rights of the Palestinian people" is seen as a commitment to the "right" to a sovereign state, and its use by President Carter in 1977 angered many supporters of Israel, who would have preferred "legitimate in-

terests" (Mr. Carter countered by saying he did not say "legitimate *national* rights").

To whites in South Africa, "majority rule" is a code phrase for black takeover (see ONE MAN, ONE VOTE); among Eurocommunists, "proletarian internationalism" was shorthand for domination by Moscow.

In 1970 the author, preparing a speech for President Nixon, slipped up on a diplomatic code word. In Europe, the U.S. and the Soviet Union have been negotiating in a desultory fashion about the removal of each other's troops. The Americans call this Mutual and Balanced Force Reduction (MBFR); the Soviets call it Mutual Force Reduction (MFR). In the speech, the writer left out "and balanced"; Secretary of State William Rogers called to ask that the two words be inserted in the written version of the speech as finally released for publication. The reason is that the U.S. thinks the removal of one American across the Atlantic Ocean should be "balanced" by the removal of more than one Russian from nearby Europe—as Secretary Rogers put it, "those two words could mean a couple hundred thousand troops." The dispute continues, and some European countries—wanting to offend neither superpower—referred to the talks in 1978 as "M (B) FR" talks.

In 1977, writing in *The New Yorker* about the victory of Ed Koch in New York City's mayoral race, Andy Logan quoted the mayor-elect as saying, "The code word of my Administration will be 'reality.'" The writer added parenthetically, "'code' word is now itself a kind of code word." The mayor probably intended an up-to-date version of "byword."

FAMILY VALUES became code words in 1992 for opposition to homosexuality and abortion; after the attack on the phrase, Republicans behind George

Bush and Dan Quayle preferred to use "traditional values."

coffee-klatsch campaign   a method of campaigning in urban areas where the candidate meets small groups of voters at a "coffee hour."

Cocktail parties lend themselves to fund-raising, but less to campaigning with the candidate present; they tend to degenerate into bona fide cocktail parties, noisy, and inattentive. The coffee klatsch (*Klatsch* is German for noise, akin to the English "clatter") offers a candidate an opportunity to meet about twenty-five people personally, make a brief talk, and move on. The coffee klatsch is usually given by one of the voters. It costs the host little and has proven an effective technique for apartment-house dwellers.

The German word, sometimes used in full, is spelled *kaffeeklatsch*—one word, lower case, no hyphen.

cold war   nonmilitary conflict; ideological hostilities; now used to indicate outmoded or unwanted policies.

Capitalized, *the* Cold War refers to international tension and jockeying for power between the former Soviet Union (and its satellites) and the Western nations; lower case, a cold war is any adversarial activity short of open conflict; behind-the-scenes struggle; tension and deadlock beneath the political surface, as "the cold war between the Johnsons and the Kennedys."

The phrase was minted by Herbert Bayard Swope, publicist, three-time winner of the Pulitzer Prize, and occasional speechwriter for elder statesman (and Port Washington, N.Y., neighbor) Bernard Baruch. In 1946, about the time Churchill was speaking of an IRON CURTAIN, Swope used "cold war" in a draft speech for Baruch to describe U.S.-Soviet relations (as contrasted to the recent "hot" or "shooting" war).

Baruch felt it was too strong, but used it one year later in a speech at Columbia, South Carolina: "Let us not be deceived—today we are in the midst of a cold war." He repeated the phrase, by that time picked up and popularized by columnist Walter Lippmann, to the Senate War Investigating Committee on October 24, 1948.

Since *cold war*, along with *iron curtain*, is one of the great coinages of the post–World War II period, its birth deserves a close examination. The late Mr. Swope's secretary, Kathleen Gilmour, provided the author with a file of correspondence on the coinage. From Bernard Baruch to Swope, August 17, 1949:

> The first time I ever heard the expression "cold war" was when you first said it some time about June 1946. We decided not to use it at that time. I first used the phrase in April 1947 on the occasion of the presentation of my portrait to South Carolina. This was the first time it was given currency or was publicly uttered so far as I know. Immediately afterward, it was very much commented upon, especially in an editorial in the *New York Daily News*. I then called Mr. [Reuben] Maury and told him I had gotten it from you. Later on, he wrote an editorial giving you credit. In other words, you coined the expression and I gave it currency.

Baruch freely credited Swope with the coinage in several interviews; the probable reason Swope elicited the credit in writing was that Walter Lippmann was being given credit as coiner rather than as disseminator. Lippmann, after a while, mentioned to Swope that he recalled a French expression in the thirties, *la guerre froide,* and on May 10, 1950, Swope wrote Lippmann to set him straight:

> The first time the idea of the cold war came to me was probably in '39 or '40 when America was talking about a "shooting" war. I had never heard that

sort of qualification. To me "shooting" war was like saying a death murder—rather tautologous, verbose and redundant.

I thought the proper opposite of the so-called hot war was cold war, and I used that adjective in the early '40's in some letters I wrote, before our war.

I may have been subconsciously affected by the term cold pogrom which was used to describe the attitude of the Nazis toward the Jews in the middle '30's. I never heard the French expressions to which you refer.

The description became timely again when the Russians were putting pressure on us for the second front, but I used it first in a little talk I made in '45, just before the war ended. Then in '46 at the time BMB made his speech to the United Nations on the American attitude toward the atomic bomb, I used the phrase in the first draft of his speech that I prepared in March or April. Baruch, Eberstadt and Hancock thought it was too severe to describe our relations with the Russians, even though they had been attenuated for a long time, so it was taken out of the speech.

But the words were put in an important speech which Baruch delivered at the end of '46 or the beginning of '47 at the State Capitol in South Carolina when his portrait was unveiled. . . .

I hope this answers your question. I've always believed that I happened to be the first to use the phrase.

A part of the American political language, the phrase gained international currency when Deputy Premier Nikolai Bulganin used it in his opening speech at the Big Four Conference in Geneva on July 18, 1955. Calling for a lessening of international tensions in accord with the "spirit of Geneva" (see SPIRIT OF), Bulganin spoke of the Soviet "desire for a settlement of the outstanding international problems and for the termination of the 'Cold War.'"

Sir Ernest Gowers, who attributes the phrase to Walter Lippmann in his revision of Fowler's *Modern English*

Usage, makes this point on its usage: ". . . the metaphor places politicians in a dilemma when they try to follow it up. Are they to advocate a rise or a fall in the temperature of the cold war? The latter would seem to intensify an already alarming crisis; the former to bring the hot war a stage nearer. This problem has to be dodged by doing violence to the metaphor. *In an atmosphere of 'live and let live' for a generation the cold war may well become less turbulent."*

The problem was solved by the use of "a thaw in the Cold War," which indicated a melting of the frozen positions without the increased danger of a hot war.

Cold warrior became a term of derogation used by supporters of DÉTENTE. Conservative writer Richard Whalen used "Cold War II" in the mid-seventies to describe a hardening of Soviet attitudes, which froze over in 1978 and caused Mr. Carter's National Security Adviser, Zbigniew Brzezinski, to be labeled by many U.S. "doves" as a "cold warrior."

"We won the Cold War," said George Bush in 1992, following the demise of Communism in Europe and the breakup of the Soviet Union. This led to "post–Cold War."

collateral damage. See SALT; EUPHEMISMS, POLITICAL.

College of Cardinals. See POWERHOUSE.

color. See PEOPLE OF COLOR.

coloration ideological identification based on political associations, record and statements.

This has remained an inside political word because its use has been relatively narrow. When a political team is being set up around a candidate, or a ticket is being balanced (see BALANCED

TICKET), consideration is given to coloration: RIGHT WING, LEFT WING, private or public power, EASTERN ESTABLISHMENT, Southern Conservative or other region, known for any beliefs or slogans, etc.

Coloration is purely appearance, not necessarily substance; many times, honest, outspoken men acquire—through region, association, family name—a coloration totally different from their point of view.

"The most striking discovery one makes in examining the Johnson history," wrote Selig Harrison in the *New Republic* in 1960, "is how little he has changed. Unlike Kennedy—whose political coloration is not at all what it was ten years ago—Johnson seems to have been from the beginning more or less what he is today."

color metaphors BLACK REPUBLICANS referred to those who supported Negro causes in the mid-nineteenth century. See BLACK, POLITICAL USE OF. The Black and Tans were opposed by the Lily-Whites, and BLACK POWER emerged in the 1960s.

White is also most often used racially, with a "white hope" stemming from the attempts of white boxers to defeat black champion Jack Johnson. And the word CANDIDATE comes from the Latin "white toga," the color symbolizing purity of motive.

However, issues are not all black and white; "*gray* areas" are known to exist, often providing the best atmosphere for a GRAY EMINENCE like a monk who controls a cardinal who controls a king. The gray uniforms of the Confederate soldiers led to the phrase "the grays and the blues" with blue the Union color.

Blue has a sexual overtone. Blue jokes offend bluenoses, who pass blue laws closing stores on Sundays.

Green is the color of the amateur, the newcomer; the greenhorn was carefully cultivated by big-city machines,

which also provided cash, or "long green," or "greenbacks." However, the Green Berets of the U.S. Special Forces gave the color professionalism.

Purple symbolizes royalty. The color also is a sign of apoplexy; insulted politicians turn purple.

Yellow stands for cowardice, and there is no baser charge than having "a yellow streak"; yellow journalism deals in sensationalism, derived from the papers that carried the comic strip "The Yellow Kid"; and the dangers in Asia used to be called "the yellow peril."

Brown, as in Brownshirt, connotes fascism to some; *orange* is often used in describing atomic explosions, and radical *red* has a separate entry herein.

Red stood for Communism; after its collapse, the color returned to its original symbol of radicalism in general.

For "color-blind," see QUOTA.

colossus of the north. See GOOD NEIGHBOR POLICY.

come now, and let us reason together
a Biblical saying identified with Lyndon B. Johnson's CONSENSUS.

Adlai Stevenson, introducing a book of Johnson speeches, wrote: "'Come now, and let us reason together' is Lyndon Johnson's favorite quotation and his best characterization. I can't recall when I first heard him use these words from Isaiah. But for the thirty years I have known him—as a Congressional secretary, Congressman, Senate Majority leader, Vice President, and now President—reasoning together, face to face, has been his method and his strength."

Arthur Schlesinger, Jr., later wrote of a meeting between Johnson and Philip Graham, then publisher of the *Washington Post* in the hectic days before the 1960 Democratic convention: "Graham had meanwhile arranged to lunch that day with Johnson in the double hope of persuading him to release Stevenson from his neutrality pledge in order to nominate Kennedy and also of persuading Johnson to accept the Vice Presidency. But he found the Senate leader far from Isaiah and in no mood for reasoning together." The paragraph is footnoted "Isaiah 1:18, L.B.J., *passim.*"

From time to time, when Republicans were attacking Johnson's assumption of the centrist position and difficult-to-assail consensus, they pointed to more of the same Isaiah quotation, a prophet's threat: "If ye be willing and obedient, ye shall eat the good of the land; but if ye refuse and rebel ye shall be devoured with the sword."

The prophet's words were used derisively against memories of the Johnson Administration in the early seventies, but were recalled with affection by Senator Hubert Humphrey in October 1977, as the former Johnson Vice President, dying of cancer, addressed the Senate: "What a wonderful place this is, where we can argue, fight, have different points of view, and still have a great respect for one another and, many times, deep affection . . . now my plea to us is, in the words of Isaiah, as a former President used to say,—and I mean it very sincerely—'Come, let us reason together.'"

committed   cliché for dedicated, involved, a believer in; opposite of alienated, disengaged.

"Participatory democracy" was a catch phrase of the New Left, meaning citizen involvement in the affairs that affect him: the poor involved in the administration of poverty programs, students in the administration of schools, workers in the management of business. Only in this way, the new radicals held, could ALIENATION be overcome and people be given incentive to become "committed." The word was popularized in modern politics by French leftist philosopher Jean-Paul Sartre, who urged *engagement* in a 1946 book: "What counts is total commitment."

The word was also used in the negative, referring to the "uncommitted nations," synonym for NEUTRALISTS or THIRD WORLD. In politics, a commitment meant a pledge or promise (see CONTRACT). In the sixties, however, the new meaning of the word took hold and was especially useful because it did not label the one described to any single political belief.

Russell Baker, the "Observer" of the *New York Times,* imagined a dialogue between a jargon doctor and a man who felt that being described as a "liberal" meant that he was no longer "with it."

> "Ideally," said the doctor, "you should have people say of you, 'He is committed.' When that happens, and word gets about that you have 'made a commitment,' your return to a gratifying sense of moral superiority should follow quite rapidly."
>
> "But what am I supposed to get committed to?"
>
> "What a silly question! When you were a liberal, you didn't feel that you had to be liberal about anything in particular, did you? The comfort derived from feeling the word snugly wrapped about you. It is the same with being 'committed.' In political unthink, nothing much changes but the words."

Curiously, in its noun form, the word assumed a conservative cast: "to honor commitments" became a hardliner's plea.

common man, century of the
utopian ideal popularized by Henry A. Wallace in a 1942 speech.

"The century on which we are entering can be and must be the century of the common man," said Wallace, who was FDR's Vice President at the time he made the speech. "Everywhere the common people are on the march."

In the middle third of the century, the "common man" was the subject of some lavish flattery. Even Adolf Hitler sought to embrace him. "National Socialism," said the Nazi dictator, "is the revolution of the common man." But political thinkers soon began recalling that commonness had not always been a cherished value—far from it. "The superior man," Confucius said, "thinks always of virtue; the common man thinks of comfort."

In 1956, former President Herbert Hoover warned that "we are in danger of developing a cult of the Common Man, which means a cult of mediocrity." Essayist Joseph Wood Krutch wrote:

> From defending the common man we pass on to exalting him and we find ourselves beginning to imply not merely that he is as good as anybody else but that he is actually better. Instead of demanding only that the common man be given an opportunity to become as uncommon as possible, we make his commonness a virtue and, even in the case of candidates for high office, we sometimes praise them for being nearly indistinguishable from the average man in the street.

To Lyndon Johnson, speaking at the Tufts University commencement in 1963, "it seems no longer adequate to describe this as the Century of the Common Man." For, he explained, a "revolution of education" was underway that was "changing the capabilities of the common man," so much so that the period "should henceforth be known as the Century of the Educated Man."

Still, the idea of the common man has not entirely lost its appeal, particularly for politicians. After Richard Nixon's 1952 CHECKERS SPEECH, Scripps-Howard columnist Robert Ruark wrote: "Tuesday night the nation saw a little man, squirming his way out of a dilemma, and laying bare his most private hopes, fears and liabilities. This time the common man was a Republican, for a change."

Communist terminology There are separate entries in this dictionary for PROLETARIAT, PARTY LINE, PEACEFUL CO-EXISTENCE, and WAR OF NATIONAL LIBERATION. The following smattering of Communist terms is adapted from a glossary prepared by Richard V. Allen in *Peace or Peaceful Co-Existence?*, published by the American Bar Association in 1966.

adventurism: "excess revolutionary zeal" that leads to taking unnecessary risks and increases the possibility of error.

bourgeoisie: originally the middle class, as distinguished from the very wealthy; Lenin later enlarged this group to include all property owners. In current use it can mean all non-Communists.

class enemy: a class that holds political power or which stands between the proletariat and its achievement of power; also, anti-Communists within Communist countries.

class struggle: from Marx and Engels in their "Communist Manifesto"— "The history of all hitherto existing society is the history of class struggles." Communist doctrine holds that classes must seek to destroy each other until the proletariat is victorious.

counterrevolution: opposing an accomplished Communist revolution or seeking to crush a developing Communist revolution.

oppressed peoples: citizens of colonial or nonself-governing areas, as well as those emerging nations which maintain too close ties with their former developers.

For a group of Communist terms about deviation from the party line, see REVISIONISM. For post-Communist terms, see GLASNOST and PERESTROIKA.

community a kindly lumping together of related organizations, instilling by euphemism a sense of shared purpose rarely present.

The "defense establishment" was a term used by defenders of expanded budgets for the armed services who were derided by critics of the MILITARY-INDUSTRIAL COMPLEX. However, when "establishment" became pejorative—as in EASTERN ESTABLISHMENT—military people and their supporters began talking (in the early sixties) of the "defense community," probably taken from Walter Lippmann's mid-forties ATLANTIC COMMUNITY.

"Community" had a less cliquish connotation, and had been a favored term of home builders, who had changed "tract developers" to "community developers." Similarly, the term "business leaders" was followed by "the business community" as arbiters of whether an Administration possessed "business confidence."

The "community" euphemism came to the rescue of the beleaguered members of the spying profession in the seventies. The "cloak-and-dagger crowd," also known as the "intelligence establishment," became the "intelligence community." As in real communities, resentments soon developed among people living on different sides of the tracks.

A related word, "set," is always used pejoratively in politics, from the isolationist "Cliveden set" in Great Britain before World War II to the "Georgetown cocktail party set" in Washington in the sixties and seventies. "Wine and cheese set" and "brie and chablis set" were tried during John Anderson's 1980 campaign.

See WEST, THE.

compact of Fifth Avenue an agreement between Governor Nelson Rockefeller and Vice President Richard Nixon before the Republican convention in 1960, temporarily healing a breach between liberal and conservative wings in the party on the subjects of civil rights and national defense.

The platform committee, headed by Charles Percy, had drafted a platform acceptable to Republican conservatives and middle-of-the-roaders, but the Rockefeller forces let it be known that—unless the document was changed—they would launch a floor fight. Without informing his Chicago convention staff, Nixon went to Rockefeller's New York apartment; over dinner, he offered the governor the vice-presidential nomination, which was declined, and then the two men went over a draft memo submitted by Rockefeller's staff.

The 14-point "compact" that emerged advocated increased defense expenditures, took a cautiously liberal view on health care for the aged and education, and a forthright civil rights position. When the manifesto was passed on to the delegates in Chicago, many were furious at Rockefeller's "high-handedness," others charged Nixon with a SELLOUT. To many conservatives, this appeared to be the opposite side of the coin minted eight years before between Eisenhower and Taft at the SURRENDER ON MORNINGSIDE HEIGHTS.

In fact, those positions advocated in the compact were on the whole those taken by Nixon before and since; he took personal charge of selling the platform committee on the changes needed, and the furor died, though Senator Goldwater had branded the compact "the Munich of the Republican party." See MUNICH ANALOGY. President Eisenhower felt that the defense suggestions were an affront to his administration, although Nixon had removed Rockefeller's proposal that $3 billion in additional defense expenditure was immediately necessary. As with all successful platforms, compromises were made; the term "sit-in," part of the Rockefeller statement, was left out of the final plank, but the plank was strongly enough worded to satisfy the liberals. With the help of Representative Melvin Laird of Wisconsin, an accomplished parliamentarian who took over Charles Percy's chair on the 103-member platform committee, the "compact of Fifth Avenue" reshaped the 1960 platform.

Comsymp Communist sympathizer; FELLOW TRAVELER.

This was a coinage of Robert Welch, founder of the John Birch Society, who held that the leadership of American corporations, universities, foundations, communications media, and government was riddled with Communists and those who agreed with Communist aims.

The word was useful to Birchers because it avoided having to say if any particular person under attack was a Communist party member or not. The technique of compression was used by Vice President Spiro Agnew in 1970, attacking "radical liberals" as "RADIC-LIBS."

See PINKO; BIRCHER.

concession speech remarks of a candidate in the process of being defeated, recognizing the inevitable loss and permitting the winner to make his victory speech.

The two men with the greatest opportunity to refine Presidential concession speeches reacted quite differently. Henry Clay said, "I would rather be right than be President" (see I'D RATHER BE RIGHT), which had the flavor of sour grapes. William Jennings Bryan, after his third defeat, said, "I am reminded of the drunk who, when

he had been thrown down the stairs of a club for the third time, gathered himself up, and said, 'I am on to those people. They don't want me in there.'"

To show that defeat need not mean failure, politicians who lose often turn to the comments of sportsmen. Sportswriter Grantland Rice produced this classic: "For when the One Great Scorer comes to mark against your name, he writes—not that you won or lost—but how you played the game." (Green Bay Packer coach Vince Lombardi, in a succeeding generation, took a harder line: "Winning is not the most important thing about football—it's the only thing.")

Napoleon, after Waterloo, said, "My downfall raises me to infinite heights." Winston Churchill began an aphorism with "In defeat, defiance"; Ernest Hemingway, after a serious air crash in 1954, remarked, "I am a little beat up, but I assure you it is only temporary," a modern version of John Paul Jones's "I've just begun to fight."

Although the speech conceding defeat is as old as politics, the modern concession speech began to come into its own with network radio election coverage and blossomed fully in the atmosphere of television. Rapid reporting and analysis of election returns on election night, with computerized "decisions" by commentators (with propagation of phrases like "probable winner" and "too close to call"), has resulted in the opportunity to have both concession and victory statements on the same night.

The televised concession speech can be poignant (Hubert Humphrey after his West Virginia primary defeat by John F. Kennedy in 1960, with a folk singer strumming a melancholy song) or even nonexistent (Nixon in 1960, with the tide appearing to turn in his favor after midnight, as West Coast results made the race one of the closest in U.S. presidential history, but prompting Kennedy's caustic comment: "No class").

One of the most eloquent of the televised concession speeches was Adlai Stevenson's in 1952; after reading his congratulatory telegram to General Eisenhower, he concluded: "Someone asked me, as I came in, down on the street, how I felt, and I was reminded of a story that a fellow-townsman of ours used to tell—Abraham Lincoln. They asked him how he felt once after an unsuccessful election. He said he felt like a little boy who had stubbed his toe in the dark. He said that he was too old to cry, but it hurt too much to laugh."

condition, not a theory. See PRACTICAL POLITICS.

confederate as a verb, to form an alliance that acts more as a coalition of interests than as a single sovereignty.

Federate, based on the Latin *foedus*, "compact, league," means "to form a union that acts as one," but *confederate* (the older verb in English) means "to create an alliance that acts as a group, not as a single entity."

The Founding Fathers moved from the Articles of Confederation, in effect from 1781 to 1789, to a more unified Constitution that would federate, or more thoroughly combine, the states. Southerners preferred *Confederacy* during the Civil War to emphasize the looser alliance of the Southern states.

The nouns corresponding to these verbs are also not exact synonyms. *Federation* refers to a single sovereignty; a *confederation*, in which each participating power holds onto its sovereignty, is weaker than a *federation*.

Of the political ties that bind, the most tightly binding words are *union* and *united*; then comes *federation*, followed by the looser *confederation*, the association of independent states called a *commonwealth*, and the loos-

est of all, *league*. The "United States" and "United Kingdom" are unions; the "United Nations" is a league.

conflict of interest the dilemma of a person trying to serve two masters.

"As a phrase, 'conflict of interest' is a relative newcomer to the American lexicon of wrongdoing," wrote *Newsweek* in January 1969. "But as a political problem, it is as ancient as public servants with private incomes, secret holdings or conveniently placed kin." Senator Daniel Webster's 1832 letter to Bank of the United States president Nicholas Biddle was cited: "I believe my retainer has not been renewed or refreshed as usual." At the time of Webster's dunning, the Senate and the bank were in a battle over the bank's charter.

The phrase was probably born, or at least gained currency, during World War II. In a letter to the Secretary of War on March 31, 1942, Acting Attorney General Charles Fahy gave an opinion about the suggestion that an Army officer be permitted to maintain liaison with a corporation in which he held stock. "Conflict between the interests of the U.S.," wrote Fahy, "the interests of the corporation and the interests of the Army officer as an officer and stockholder of the corporation are more than likely to arise." The Justice official quoted Section 41 of the Criminal Code and a statute forbidding government employees from accepting salary from outside sources for government work, adding: "Both are intended to prevent a conflict between self-interest and the interests of the government."

The phrase has been adopted in the criminal code: Chapter 11 of Title 18 of the U.S. Code is entitled "Bribery, Graft and Conflicts of Interest."

As the phrase became more current, columnist Les Whitten made it the title of a novel in the mid-seventies.

consciousness-raising   inciting to enthusiastic involvement; awakening the need for political activity; a recognition of suppressed resentments which call for redress.

"Consciousness," wrote John Locke in his 1690 *Essay on Human Understanding*, "is the perception of what passes in a Man's own mind." That quality of perception—of being awake—is usually involved in the many uses of the word.

Although moral philosophers, and later psychologists, popularized the term, in the mid-twentieth century politicians made it their own. It has early Communist associations; former Moscow correspondents have reported to this lexicographer of its frequent use in ideological discussions in the fifties, and Theodore H. White, in his 1978 book *In Search of History,* writes of an interview held in 1941, in the Chinese Communist redoubt in Yenan, with P'eng Te-hai, a close ally of Mao Tse-tung: "The men who came in from the field, he said . . . had to have their minds washed out, had to be remolded in ideology. [See BRAIN-WASHING.] At first he thought this could be done in only three months; he had now learned that a full year was necessary to 'remold the brain' before they could go on to study military matters, or economics, or heal, or administration. His interpreter and I searched for a word better than 'brain remolding' and finally the interpreter came up with the phrase 'raising the level of consciousness.' This was the first time I heard that phrase, which, over the years, moved out of China and on to the streets and fashions of America in the 1960's."

Whether it stemmed from Chinese or Russian use, or another origin, the idea of "raising" the level of consciousness (as distinct from "expanding" consciousness through the use of psychedelic drugs) came into use strongly in the sixties in the U.S., in the civil rights movement and most especially in the women's liberation movement. It may have been influenced by its use in psychology: "encounter groups" and "sensitivity training" also used "consciousness-raising" in their terminology.

By the mid-seventies, the word had been taken over by the women's movement—see WOMEN'S LIB and SEX-ISM—and the use by Locke in this entry would be frowned on.

consensus   a broad agreement which, while not necessarily all-embracing, does embrace enough elements to form a sizable majority.

Though Lyndon B. Johnson put his special brand on the term "consensus," politicians and thinkers have been pondering its uses and abuses for centuries. Some twenty centuries ago, the Roman orator Cicero declared, "The consensus of opinion among all nations, on whatever matter, may be taken for the law of nature." Sir Francis Bacon, in his essay *Of Faction,* wrote: "When factions are carried too high and too violently, it is a sign of weakness in princes, and much to the prejudice both of their authority and business."

Not everybody considers the quest for consensus the best *modus operandi.* Activist liberal advisers urged on John F. Kennedy the "superiority of the politics of combat as against the politics of consensus."

Nonetheless, consensus has its clear uses in a nation as diverse as the U.S. Dwight Eisenhower said in 1954: "If we are to build and maintain the strength required to cope with the problems of this age, we must cooperate one with the other, every section with all others, each group with its neighbors." Four years later, he found himself forced to back down from a proposed reform of the Pentagon because "my personal convictions, no matter how strong, cannot be the final answer. There must be a consensus reached with the Congress, with the people that have the job of operating the services."

Consensus is not total agreement. "When President Johnson speaks about seeking a consensus he is not saying that he expects every one to vote for him and to agree with him," wrote Walter Lippmann. "But he is saying that the great internal problems cannot be solved successfully and satisfactorily until and unless they have the support of a very big majority. In the American political tradition, a very big majority is taken to lie between 60 and 75%. An American consensus is more than a bare 51%." What Johnson was seeking to do, wrote Jack Bell in *The Johnson Treatment*, was to effect cooperation among "the liberals, who believed in big government, the conservatives, who wanted federal power diffused, the representatives of big business, big labor, the minorities most vocally represented by the Negroes and the poverty-stricken." (This would more accurately be termed a coalition.)

After the Republican party's big gains in the 1966 elections, New York's Governor Nelson Rockefeller urged the twenty-five GOP governors to work toward a consensus on their objectives before worrying about picking a candidate for the 1968 presidential race. Michigan's Governor George Romney, flying to Puerto Rico for a meeting with Rockefeller, took umbrage at his host's remark. Consensus? "That is Rockefeller's word," snapped Romney. "I associate it with someone else"—namely Lyndon Johnson—"who hasn't fared too well with leadership." Later Romney and Rockefeller made up, and Romney apologetically explained his outburst by saying, "I was just a little allergic to the previous association of the word."

Even with its connotation of evasiveness, the word is still able to bring about confrontations. The school of political historians who disputed the long-held "conflict" school—which held that the study of U.S. history was in the conflict between institutions and ideas—called itself the "consensus" school.

See COME NOW, AND LET US REASON TOGETHER.

conservation. See ENVIRONMENTALIST.

conservative a defender of the status quo who, when change becomes necessary in tested institutions or practices, prefers that it come slowly, and in moderation.

In modern U.S. politics, as in the past, "conservative" is a term of opprobrium to some, and of veneration to others. Edmund Burke, the early defender and articulator of the conservative philosophy, argued that the only way to preserve political stability was by carefully controlling change and seeking a slow, careful integration of new forces into venerable institutions. In his *Reflections on the Revolution in France*, he wrote: "It is with infinite caution that any man ought to venture upon pulling down an edifice which has answered in any tolerable degree for ages the common purposes of society, or on building it up again without having models and patterns of approved utility before his eyes." Abraham Lincoln called it "adherence to the old and tried, against the new and untried."

The philosophy has had some famous detractors as well. Disraeli, who was to become a Tory Prime Minister, wrote in his sprightly novel *Coningsby:* "Conservatism discards Prescription, shrinks from Principle, disavows Progress; having rejected all respect for antiquity, it offers no redress for the present, and makes no preparation for the future." Lord Bryce was of two minds about it in *The American Commonwealth*: "This conservative spirit, jealously watchful even in small matters, sometimes prevents reforms, but it assures the people an easy mind, and a trust in their future which they feel to be not only a present satisfaction but a reservoir of strength."

The political origin of the word can be traced to the *Sénat Conservateur* in the 1795 French Constitution, and was used in its present English sense by British statesman, later Prime Minister, George Canning in 1820. J. Wilson Croker, in the *Quarterly Review* of January 1830, made the concrete proposal: "We have always been conscientiously attached to what is called the Tory, and which might with more propriety be called the Conservative party." It was soon applied in America to the Whigs, amid some derision: *"The Pennsylvania Reporter,"* wrote the *Ohio Statesman* in 1837, "speaking of a probable change in the name of the opposition, from Whig to 'Conservative,' says the best cognomen they could adopt would be the 'Fast and Loose' party."

Today the more rigid conservative generally opposes virtually all governmental regulation of the economy. He favors local and state action over federal action, and emphasizes fiscal responsibility, most notably in the form of balanced budgets. William Allen White, the Kansas editor, described this type of conservative when he wrote of Charles Evans Hughes as "a businessman's candidate, hovering around the status quo like a sick kitten around a hot brick."

But there exists a less doctrinaire conservative who admits the need for government action in some fields and for steady change in many areas. In-stead of fighting a rearguard action, he seeks to achieve such change within the framework of existing institutions, occasionally changing the institutions when they show need of it.

See NEOCONSERVATIVE; HIDEBOUND; ROCK-RIBBED; LEFT WING, RIGHT WING.

constituent   voter or elector; formal term for resident of a represented district.

Since 1622, this word has been used for anybody who appoints another as a proxy or representative. A century later, the term took the specific meaning of "one who elects another to public office," particularly a representative to a legislature.

From the Latin *constituere*, "to constitute," the political noun (more formal than *voter*) is related to *constituency*, an elected official's district or the voters that one represents, and the equally political *Constitution*.

Republicans are especially fond of the term. In 1992, Gene Randall of Cable News Network said to Transportation Secretary Andrew Card, "Mr. Secretary, when Lee Atwater was the head of your party, he had a self-appointed role, opening up the party to new constituents; he called it a 'BIG TENT.'"

A spokesman for the 1992 Connecticut delegation to the Republican National Convention used the word in a way that suggested that constituents were to be communicated with, but their views were not necessarily to be followed: "We encourage candidates to talk to their constituents, elected officials to talk to their constituents—and vote their conscience."

See FENCE MENDING.

containment   policy of limiting the aggressive expansion of Communism by military means, in the hope that its failure to expand will weaken and eventually destroy the Communist system.

In February 1946 George F. Kennan, a little-known scholar of Russian history who was counselor of our embassy in Moscow, wrote an 8,000-word treatise on Russia for his State Department superiors that was to change the course of U.S. foreign policy.

Kennan's memo, later printed in the July 1947 issue of *Foreign Affairs* under the title "The Sources of Soviet Conduct," stated:

> . . . Soviet pressure against the free institutions of the western world is something that can be contained by the adroit and vigilant application of counterforce at a series of constantly shifting geographical and political points, corresponding to the shifts and maneuvers of Soviet policy, but which cannot be talked or charmed out of existence. . . .
>
> . . . no mystical, Messianic movement—and particularly not that of the Kremlin—can face frustration indefinitely without eventually adjusting itself in one way or another to the logic of that state of affairs.

The policy of containment—to establish "situations of strength" around the world so as to stop Soviet expansion—came to encompass the establishment of U.S. military bases in friendly countries, the Marshall Plan, the Point Four aid to underdeveloped countries, and a rebuilding of U.S. military power.

But containment was essentially a defensive policy with little political appeal. Ultimate victory was decades away. There was no clean-cut, decisive end to the problem of aggressive Communism. With the loss of China to the Communists in the late forties, American restlessness with containment increased. In the 1952 presidential campaign, General Eisenhower's foreign policy adviser, John Foster Dulles, expounded a policy that went beyond containment—LIBERATION OF CAPTIVE PEOPLES. After Eisenhower's victory, Secretary of State Dulles explained it to the Senate Committee on Foreign Relations: ". . . a policy which only aims at containing Russia . . . is bound to fail because a purely defensive policy never wins against an aggressive policy. . . . It is only by keeping alive the hope of liberation . . . that we will end this terrible peril . . ."

When no liberations took place, a general disillusionment set in about "liberation," and "containment" gained the upper hand. The word and policy has, of course, drawn fire. Said Senator George Aiken of Vermont in 1967 regarding Communist China: "I don't know how you go about containing an idea. I also don't know how you go about containing 700 million people."

Curiously, the appeal of "containment" as a geopolitical philosophy, more than a policy, was undermined in the Administration that might have been expected to espouse it. Earl Ravenal wrote in *Foreign Policy* (Winter 1977–78) that Nixon policies in the early seventies had helped transform the international system from "bipolar confrontation" to a more diffused balance of power. "If Nixon and Kissinger did not quite end 'containment,' at least they devalued it, making it an item of strategy rather than ideology, blurring its once-sharp focus of hostility, and generalizing it into the more neutral concept of international 'stability.'"

In the late eighties, the White House chose "Beyond Containment" as the label for George Bush's foreign policy. A 1953 book of that title, written by William Henry Chamberlin, was published by Regnery in Chicago.

After the Soviet Union's breakup, Jack H. Watson, Jr., Jimmy Carter's chief of staff, wondered in *Newsday* in

1993 about what would follow containment: "Without the yardstick of communist containment to rely upon, what principles should govern U.S. foreign aid and economic development policies . . . ?"

Perhaps to avoid the historic resonance of "containment," President Clinton in 1993 said that his purpose in suggesting intervention in the war among Serbs, Croats, and Bosnians in the former Yugoslavia was "to confine the conflict."

contract an agreement to deliver a political favor; an accepted political assignment.

The *Dictionary of American Slang* defines "contract" as "a political or business favor; a bribe; the fix. 1958: 'Contract—any favor one policeman says he'll do for another.'—G. Y. Wells, *Station House Slang*."

In underworld lingo, *contract* is an assignment to a *torpedo* to make a *hit;* that is, a contract to commit a murder. That probably explains the sinister connotation in the nonpolitician's mind when he hears the more innocent use of contract by a politician.

In current political use, the "fix" connotation is disappearing; contract now is used as a legitimate promise to perform, with no bribe implied. A contract is not a "deal"; a deal clearly implies a two-way transaction, while a contract is merely an assignment accepted with no specific return favor demanded.

Sample: "You'll sit me on the dais next to the Governor?" "I'll try." "No—make it a contract." "Okay, it's a contract, you'll sit there."

For an 1893 usage, see DELIVER.

contrapuntal phrases a phrase-making technique that uses a repeated rhythm with an inversion or substitution of words for emphasis; rhetorical antithesis.

Good speechwriters reach for contrapuntal phrases. "We have fought side by side to make America free," wrote Alexander Hamilton; "let us hand in hand struggle to make her happy." Gilbert Highet pointed out in an analysis of the Gettysburg Address that Lincoln was especially fond of antithesis: "The world will little note nor long remember what we say here; but it can never forget what they did here."

This contrapuntal description of Harry Truman has been attributed to Speaker Sam Rayburn: "Right on all the big things, wrong on most of the little ones."

FDR in his Four Freedoms speech said, "As men do not live by bread alone, they do not fight by armaments alone." In the contrapuntal use of a single word, the possibility for oratorical error is a danger: when, in 1933, FDR shaped a sentence that read "Hard-headedness will not so easily excuse hard-heartedness," he drew a tiny picture of a head over the first word on the reading copy of the speech, and a heart with an arrow through it over the balance word.

John F. Kennedy used the device more than any other U.S. President. "Let us never negotiate out of fear, but let us never fear to negotiate." "A willingness to resist force, unaccompanied by a willingness to talk, could provoke belligerence—while a willingness to talk, unaccompanied by a willingness to resist force, could invite disaster." "While we shall negotiate freely, we shall not negotiate freedom." And, of course, "Ask not what your country can do for you—ask what you can do for your country." (That last line may have been modeled on a phrase in an 1884 Memorial Day address delivered by Oliver Wendell Holmes in Keene, New Hampshire: ". . . it is now the moment . . . to recall what our country has done for each of us, and to ask ourselves what we can do for our country in return.")

The "Sorensen style" used by Kennedy did not go unnoticed. Columnist William F. Buckley, Jr., writing in 1967 about the Communist world revolution, obliquely referred to a single form of contrapuntal inversion: "And unless we learn how to cope with it, it will—as Theodore Sorensen would put it—cope with us."

"In Ted Sorensen," observed *Washington Star* editorialist Edwin M. Yoder, Jr., in February 1978, "Mr. Kennedy had a speechwriter of excellent style with a fondness for antithesis, so that it became a sort of rhetorical tic. Like all the rhetorical devices that we inherit from Latin by way of the 18th Century, antithesis needs a strict sense of occasion. It can be absurdly trivialized: 'Always close the door before you leave, but never leave after you have opened the window.'"

See TURNAROUNDS.

contrarian one who deliberately opposes or goes against the trend.

Humphrey Neill, the financial adviser who wrote the 1954 *Art of Contrary Thinking*, began using *contrarian* in the 1960s to promote financial investment against the current of general investor thinking. Elizabeth M. Fowler wrote in the *New York Times* in 1966 that "Mr. Neill, who calls himself a contrarian, which means he tends to act just the opposite of the crowd or general public, now advises caution."

A builder used this new sense in commenting to the *New York Times* about his company's increased activity after the 1987 stock-market crash: "We took a contrarian view. We decided to go full steam ahead. We figured that if other developers were holding back, there would be less competition."

Based, like *contrary*, on the Latin *contra*, "opposite," the term *contrarian* has moved from financial jargon to political term as both noun and adjective. It is applied to pollsters who defy conventional wisdom and to candidates who run against the ideological grain of their party. *Contrarian*, however, differs from the merely opposing *contrary;* the longer word suggests opposing popular opinion in order to make a profit or to profit politically from being a MAVERICK.

controversial. See CODE WORDS.

convention. See SPONTANEOUS DEMONSTRATION; PACKING THE GALLERIES; VOICE FROM THE SEWER; BROKERED CONVENTION.

conventional wisdom generally accepted but sometimes wrong ideas; stodgy consensus.

The economist John Kenneth Galbraith coined the term in a chapter title of his 1958 book, *The Affluent Society:* "The Concept of the Conventional Wisdom." Galbraith wrote that "the hallmark of the conventional wisdom is acceptability. It has the approval of those to whom it is addressed."

To indicate the pejorative sense of the term, Galbraith added, "Ideas need to be tested by their ability, in combination with events, to overcome inertia and resistance. This inertia and resistance the conventional wisdom provides."

This phrase, which flourished for a while with the neutral sense of "general view," was probably bottomed on a phrase in ecclesiastical use, *received wisdom,* from a 1382 phrase *received custom,* meaning "the teaching of tradition"; today, both *received* and *conventional* as modifiers of *wisdom* carry the negative connotation that Galbraith intended.

Usually derogated in the phrase "contrary to the conventional wisdom," the term has been popularized by *Newsweek* magazine in its "Conventional Wisdom Watch." *Newsweek* indicates whether political figures are up or down according to current estimates, but the implication is clear that the conventional wisdom is changeable.

convention bounce a temporary rise in opinion polls following widespread coverage of a party's national convention.

Following the Democratic National Convention in the summer of 1992, Bill Clinton took a realistic and expectation-dampening view of his rising ratings in the polls: "It's partly a convention bounce." After the Republican National Convention in August, George Bush's ratings also improved, and the *Christian Science Monitor* commented, "It represents a routine convention bounce." *Newsweek* asked in its "Conventional Wisdom Watch," "Why does the CW worry about the 'convention bounce' if the CW also says the bounce dissipates within two weeks?"

The term was coined as early as 1980, when it was used by Jody Powell, President Carter's spokesman. Powell described the psychological lift from Carter's increase in ratings as "the post-convention bounce we hoped for." (The prefix *post-* is no longer used with the phrase.)

A related term is *New Hampshire bounce*, describing a candidate's short-term increase in popularity following a successful showing in that state's early Presidential primary. The *Washington Post* commented in February 1988 on Bob Dole's showing in Iowa: "Dole's victory may set up a New Hampshire bounce over Bush."

In both phrases, the noun *bounce* has become more popular than its variant, *bump*.

cookie pusher an effete, or "striped-pants" diplomat; a foreign service pharisee concerned with form rather than substance; opposite of SHIRT-SLEEVE DIPLOMAT.

The phrase graphically describes one who attends social teas, and presumably cocktail parties; it was popularized by New York Democratic Congressman John J. Rooney, chairman of the House subcommittee on appropriations that oversees State Department spending. "While I have used the expression 'cookie pusher' many times during my years in the U.S. House of Representatives," Congressman Rooney wrote the author, "I cannot at all claim authorship, and I have no idea who it was that coined it."

Adlai Stevenson's biographer, Kenneth S. Davis, says the lifted-pinkie phrase was used against Stevenson and his associates in the Committee to Defend America by Aiding the Allies in 1940: "Nor could [Stevenson] fail to resent being dubbed, with his colleagues, a 'cookie pusher,' a 'professional bleeding heart,' a 'warmonger,' day after day in [Chicago] *Tribune* news and editorial columns . . ."

cooling-off period in labor disputes, a time allowed management and labor to negotiate with neither strikes nor lockouts permitted.

The "cooling-off" period became locked into the political language with the passage of the Taft-Hartley Act of 1947. The law specified that sixty days' notice must be given before a labor contract can be changed or terminated; if no agreement is reached within thirty days, the Federal Mediation and Conciliation Service steps in. When a dispute threatens what the president considers to be the national welfare, he is authorized to seek a court injunction to maintain the status quo for eighty days. At the end of this eighty-day cooling-off period, a strike or lockout is permitted.

The phrase has earlier usage in diplomacy. William Jennings Bryan, Woodrow Wilson's Secretary of State in 1913, took the initiative in providing for a method of arbitration on all international disputes, referring these to a permanent investigating commission. He negotiated agreements with thirty-one nations which became known as "Bryan's 'cooling off' treaties."

President Woodrow Wilson, campaigning for the League of Nations in 1919, used an eloquent metaphor in the last major speech before his stroke:

> With a cooling space of nine months for human passion, not much of it will keep hot. I had a couple of friends who were in the habit of losing their tempers, and when they lost their tempers they were in the habit of using very unparliamentary language. Some of their friends induced them to make a promise that they never would swear inside the town limits. When the impulse next came upon them, they took a street car to go out of town to swear, and by the time they got out of town they did not want to swear. They came back convinced that they were just what they were, a couple of unspeakable fools, and the habit of getting angry and of swearing suffered great inroads upon it by that experience. Now, illustrating the great by the small, that is true of the passions of nations. It is true of the passions of men however you combine them. Give them space to cool off.

cooling the rhetoric. See RHETORIC.

coonskin on the wall   symbol of victory; similar to "scalp."

At Cam Ranh Bay in South Vietnam, just before the November 1966 elections in the U.S., President Johnson visited U.S. troops in the field and told them, "I salute you. Come home with that coonskin on the wall."

The expression jarred many members of the President's party, as limited objectives and limited war were the basis of diplomatic feelers, and the President's colorful remark appeared

close to the MacArthur NO SUBSTITUTE FOR VICTORY statement.

Commented Walter Lippmann three months later: ". . . Lyndon Johnson is a complicated human being. There are at least two spirits wrestling within him. One is that of the peacemaker and reformer and herald of a better world. The other is that of the primitive frontiersman who wants to nail the coonskin to the wall. . . . It is this second spirit which is now tempting him, and on the outcome of the ordeal depends more than it is pleasant to contemplate."

The hide of the raccoon or opossum has had a long background in American speech, and was the symbol of frontiersman Daniel Boone. Estes Kefauver, senator from Tennessee and Democratic vice-presidential candidate in 1956, wore the coonskin cap for photographers and used it as a symbol on many of his handshaking tours. "The irony of Kefauver," wrote Russell Baker of the *New York Times*, "was that the coonskin cap, by which the country at large knew him, was a fraud. It implied a log cabin rustic bred to the cracker barrel circle, but it concealed one of the authentic eggheads of American politics."

co-opt   to convert by absorption; or, to subvert by suffocating agreement.

In the dictionaries, "co-opt" as a verb, or "co-optation" as a noun, refers to the election to a group of an outsider by a vote of the membership.

In its new political meaning, however, "to co-opt" is to ensnare the victor. Subtly, the Establishment reaches out for the election winner, or the bureaucracy enfolds its supervisory appointee, and in the guise of wanting to help or offering to educate, takes him over by changing his cultural or political outlook. The absorption of outlook is rarely dramatic; on the contrary, it seems to occur by osmosis, as the "outsider" thinks he is convincing or changing the "insiders."

"Co-opt" was used frequently in discussions about the incoming Carter Administration—held to be "anti-Washington"—by congressional Democrats in 1977.

Both sides of the hyphenated word came from voguish forebears. "Co-" has been used frequently in recent years, with "co-host" a popular television term, and "co-equal" taken to mean more equal than the usual equal. OPT is the vogue form for "choose," without its impulsive differential.

In the January 1978 issue of *Foreign Affairs*, Jean-François Revel wrote: "As long as the Western communist parties remain organized according to the so-called schema of 'democratic centralism,' meaning a Politburo recruited by co-optation . . . it is ridiculous to think of de-Stalinization."

"If you can't lick 'em, join 'em" is an old political axiom; in the case of "co-opt," the axiom appears to be "If you can't lick 'em, flatter 'em, and they'll join you." For an earlier form of stealing the opposition's clothes, see DISH THE WHIGS.

copperhead   near-traitor; DEFEATIST; spokesman for an unpopular cause.

The copperheads were those Northerners who opposed the Union cause during the Civil War. The copperhead snake is considered by many to be the lowest of a low breed: it strikes without warning, contrasted with the fair-minded, noisy rattlesnake.

The word was used in America preceding the Civil War as a synonym for "sneaky," but in the off-year elections of 1862 it became the epithet for Southern sympathizers in the North. The Lawrence (Kan.) *Republican* surveyed the epithet list: "That faction of the Democracy who sympathize with the rebels are known in Ohio as 'Vallandinghamers,' in Illinois as 'guerrillas,' in Missouri as 'butternuts,' in Kansas as 'jayhawkers,' in Kentucky as 'bushwhackers,' and in Indiana as 'copperheads.'"

The word atrophied after the Civil War resentments died down, though the progressive politicians at the turn of the century were derided as "copper-streaked" by their enemies. Franklin Roosevelt renewed its use in 1938, at the suggestion of Thomas Corcoran, to apply it to those Democrats who wished to drag their feet on New Deal legislation: "Never in our lifetime has such a concerted campaign of defeatism been thrown at the heads of the President and Senators and Congressmen as in the case of this Seventy-Fifth Congress. Never before have we had so many Copperheads—and you will remember that it was the Copperheads who, in the days of the War between the States, tried their best to make Lincoln and his Congress give up the fight . . ."

Roosevelt liked the word and used it again just before World War II as a label for Colonel Charles A. Lindbergh and the America Firsters. When a form of isolationism was articulated in 1990 by Patrick Buchanan, opposed to U.S. intervention in the Persian Gulf, some of his official targets (see AMEN CORNER) retaliated with a charge of "Copperhead."

cordon sanitaire.   See IRON CURTAIN.

corn pone   symbol of folksiness and Southern voter appeal.

Mark Twain wrote in his essay "Corn Pone Opinions": "You tell me whar a man gits his corn pone, en I'll tell you what his 'pinions are."

Corn pone can be a bread made of corn meal, milk, and eggs; or a cereal whose alternative name is hominy grits; or a cakelike bakery product made of pounded corn, pounded sunflower seeds, and boiled beans. Pone can be a wide variety of products made from corn, and can stir as many heated debates about what it is and how it is made as "egg cream" in New York City.

Governor Huey Long brought it into politics as part of his lighthearted but effective campaign to identify himself with rural voters in Louisiana. He started a debate over the proper method of eating corn pone with pot liquor, a juice that remains in the pot after turnip greens are boiled with a piece of salt pork. "Kingfish" Long solemnly held that the pone should be "dunked" in the pot liquor, and not "crumbled" in and then elegantly eaten with a spoon. Governor Franklin Roosevelt of New York wired the *Atlanta Constitution* that he sided with the "crumblers," and Oklahoma's "Alfalfa Bill" Murray called for a wider investigation to include "poke" salad and hog jowl. The matter reached the Solomon's Temple of Emily Post, who decreed: "When in Rome, do as the Romans do."

Corn pone has come to mean "sweet talk," and gentle persuasion. See SMELL OF MAGNOLIAS. Non-Southerners tend to consider it synonymous with "corny" or "cornball," cloyingly folksy, but in the South there is a more gallant political connotation. In 1960 Lyndon Johnson named his CAMPAIGN TRAIN, which did so much to hold the South for the Kennedy-Johnson ticket, "The Corn Pone Special."

Time magazine in 1968 wrote that the nation's cartoonists had pictured President Johnson as "macaw-beaked, jug-eared and two-gunned, a tragicomic, corn pone character."

corporate state. See FASCIST; TRAINS RAN ON TIME.

correct. See POLITICALLY CORRECT.

corridors of power. See POWER BROKER.

cost-benefit analysis study of cost efficiency; assessment of a project's cost in relation to its benefits or value.

A phrase from the early 1960s, *cost-benefit analysis* is based on a 1928 term from industrial management, *cost-benefit*. By 1963, economists had introduced the longer term in studying social projects; a *Times* of London article explained, "Cost-benefit analysis . . . constitutes an endeavour to bring into relationship with 'the measuring rod of money' all the social consequences either of introducing a new project or removing an old one."

In the 1970s, such studying of efficiency was sometimes the subject of criticism. The *National Journal* reported in 1979 on a regulatory agency's negative reaction when Jimmy Carter's executive order limited its powers: "It objected particularly to cost-benefit analysis in the areas of safety, health and the environment, arguing that the order 'impedes, rather than strengthens, a sound regulatory process.'"

The phrase, along with such variations as *cost-benefit calculations* and *cost-benefit study*, has been used in political attacks. In 1988 Stephen Kurkjian of the *Boston Globe* discussed the views of George Bush's critics on his environmental background, adding: "They stressed that during the early months of the Reagan Administration, Bush played a key role in bringing 'cost-benefit analysis' to the field of federal regulation. No longer would the environmental impact be the sole measure of whether a regulation should take effect."

In 1992, British Prime Minister Margaret Thatcher was profiled in the *Washington Post* by Glenn Frankel, who wrote that although "Thatcher showed great reverence for the throne as the repository of Victorian values, many of her followers tend to apply a rigid cost-benefit analysis, in which the royals come out looking like a luxury that Britain can no longer afford."

Not every cost undergoing analysis can be measured in monetary units. The *San Francisco Chronicle* in July 1992 assessed Bill Clinton's choice of Al Gore as his running mate; the study was introduced by "Here is a quick cost-benefit analysis on the major issues."

During the Kennedy Administration, Defense Secretary Robert McNamara introduced to the Pentagon the related term *cost-effective.* Henry Brandon of London's *Sunday Times* wrote in his 1988 book, *Special Relationships,* about the passing of this term from American to British English. When members of the British defense staff visited Washington during the Kennedy years, John Thompson, a defense aide to the British Ambassador, sought to explain this new usage.

"At a dinner he gave for them," Brandon wrote, Thompson "therefore served three different red wines and asked them to tell him how, according to their taste, they rated each. After they had done that, he told them how much each cost and then he asked them which, taking the cost into consideration, they would buy."

Brandon added, "The wine samples did what wine does not always do, it cleared their minds, and thus *cost-effectiveness* entered the English vocabulary."

cost of living.   See HIGH COST OF LIVING.

cost-push.   See INFLATION.

countdown   period of crisis before a decision or event; the last few days before an election.

The word was popularized as the na-

tion watched televised rocket blast-offs from Cape Canaveral, Fla., and announcers in ominous tones said: "Countdown four minutes, thirty seconds and counting," or "two minutes, twenty seconds and holding," with the last ten seconds counted backward to "Ignition. Blast-off."

In 1959 Majority Leader Lyndon Johnson was quoted as saying "The countdown has begun" in regard to pending legislation; in 1960 General John Medaris wrote a book titled *Countdown for Decision* about the confusion in the missile program; the *New York Times Book Review* headlined a review in 1967 "Countdown for the Minds of Men."

Political headquarters in campaigns managed by John A. Wells (New York mayoralty in 1961, senatorial in 1962, Rockefeller for President in 1964 and for governor in 1966) featured large signs titled "Countdown—Days to Go" with the number of days changed daily, a constant reminder of the number of days left until Election Day.

For a time the word was used in lieu of "roll call" by television commentators (many of whom covered the astronaut blastoffs) as the states were called at national conventions. An AP dispatch in July 1960 said that "they professed to believe that Kennedy would lose support in Indiana, Maryland and Ohio in a second countdown."

Subsequently the word enjoyed considerable popularity; comedians spoke of a child who came home after learning "the New Math" counting "10 . . . 9 . . . 8 . . . 7 . . ." But the word settled into the political language quietly and is now used to describe the last tense moments of a campaign.

counterculture   an amalgam of dropouts, professional dissenters, anti-intellectuals, experimenters with drugs, as well as thoughtful and literate critics of American society in the sixties.

Drug culture is a critical description; *youth culture* neutral; and *counterculture* usually a self-description. The use of "counter" is superior to "anti" because it carries the connotation of offering an alternative.

The word gained circulation in the late sixties as dissident groups began making use of national holidays and local festivities as foils for their own activities. In 1969 a protest demonstration in Washington, D.C, was called a "counter-Inaugural."

The new word, probably based on counterrevolution and counterintelligence, added prestige as it was adopted by social critics and analysts who prepared "counterbudgets" and the like. By treating disparate anti-Establishment groups and individuals as a new culture, the word dignified what had been thought of mainly as a motley crew, and was embraced by those who would not be caught dead in a silent majority.

British author Kingsley Amis and poet Robert Conquest defined the word in the January 10, 1971, *New York Times Magazine* as "(1) Socially: living off bourgeois society without paying literal or metaphorical taxes to it. (2) Artistically: creativity, which, whether using bourgeois materials (words, pigments, etc.) or other materials or none, does not admit of the elitist application of divisive criteria showing one work to be 'better' than another."

As a selling term, it is effective; some of the best fighters in the ring are counterpunchers.

Here is a brief review of the vocabulary of the counterculture (also called "hippie language"), drawn largely from the research of rock music reviewer Mike Jahn:

bummer: bad experience
bust: arrest
cosmic: significant
down: negative experience
far out: superlative
gig: occupation
goof on: make fun of
groove on: enjoy
heavy: powerful
into: interested in
off: kill
organic: vital
outasight: fantastic
pig: police
put down: insult
put on: tease
rap: extended conversation
rip off: steal
shuck: trick
spaced: distracted
speed: amphetamine
stoned: high on drugs
strung out: addicted
together: well-adjusted
trip: experience
up: positive experience
vibrations: impressions

Most of these words were dropped long ago from counterculture usage, but lingered on in the pitiable efforts of squares to appear "with it."

One of the central expressions of the counterculture is "do your thing," which means "establish your own identity," or "follow your star"; critics of the individualistic life style find this the height of self-indulgence. Unlike most of the rest of counterculture vocabulary, the source of the phrase is specific: Ralph Waldo Emerson, in his *Essay on Self Reliance,* wrote: "If you maintain a dead church, contribute to a dead Bible-Society, vote with a great party either for the government or against it . . . under all these screens, I have difficulty to detect the precise man you are. . . . But do your thing, and I shall know you."

cover-up any plan to avoid detection of wrongdoing; or, an act to conceal a mistake; specifically, the conspiracy to obstruct justice in the Watergate case.

Mystery writer Raymond Chandler, in *Black Mask* magazine in 1935, gave a character this line: "I don't have to tell you how a police department looks at that kind of a cover-up on a murder." The law enforcement slang soon crossed into the political language, to mean a general—not necessarily illegal—concealment of the truth. In a telephone conversation with financier Louis Wolfson in 1968, Supreme Court Justice Abe Fortas told his former law client (who was recording the call) that a conflict-of-interest charge could be made if their relationship was misconstrued: "That your giving me and my accepting the foundation post was nothing but a cover-up and that what was really happening was that I was taking a gratuity from you . . . and that is very bad."

In the Watergate case, the charge of cover-up (usually hyphenated, though sometimes one word) gained currency early in the spring of 1973. On April 30, according to a transcript of a taped conversation with former Attorney General John Mitchell in the Oval Office, President Nixon said: "I want you all to stonewall it, let them plead the Fifth Amendment, cover-up or anything else, if it'll save it—save the plan."

That transcript was released in the summer of 1974, and the words were used on the July 22, 1974, cover of *Newsweek*. In an interview with David Frost in 1977, the former President allowed as how a reasonable person could construe his actions "as a cover-up," but denied that the concealment had involved criminal action on his part.

Because of its Watergate connotation, the word is now frequently used to attach sinister implications to any attempt to withhold information. To HANG TOUGH is permissible; to STONEWALL implies grounds for suspicion; to

cover up, or to engage in a *cover-up,* imputes improper concealment or unlawful obstruction.

Bush Administration Attorney General William Barr was attacked as the "Coverup-General" by a columnist in the *New York Times* exercised by the refusal to permit independent counsel in "Iraqgate."

cover your ass. See C.Y.A.

cowboy a political rebel, usually one opposed to party discipline.

"Cowboy" never enjoyed the political currency of such synonyms as MAVERICK and MUGWUMP and is only occasionally heard today. Its most famous use was upon the death of President William McKinley. Senator Mark Hanna, the leading Republican strategist while McKinley lived, said of Theodore Roosevelt: "Now look, that damned cowboy is President of the United States!"

It is uncertain precisely how Hanna applied the term because Roosevelt had actually lived and worked in cattle country for a time, and was also considered most unfaithful by orthodox GOP chiefs. In fact, it was their attitude that made him President. He was serving as governor of New York in 1900, assiduously earning the enmity of the Republican organization with his reforms. The vice presidency was vacant and the New York Republican leadership promoted Roosevelt's candidacy, some say to get him out of the state. He won the nomination when men favored by McKinley pulled out. "We did our best," Hanna told McKinley, "but they nominated that madman. Now it's up to you to live."

"Cowboy" took on unpleasant connotations during the American Revolution. Tory irregulars in the New York area were called cowboys while rebel marauders were known as "skinners." The idea of a cowboy being someone unreliable stuck. Senator James G. Blaine in 1879 explained his dislike for "those fellows who are between the parties" by saying that "they are the cowboys of modern days."

After the election of Ronald Reagan in 1980, the European press wrote that the U.S. had elected a "cowboy"; the image was reinforced by Reagan's role as host of the TV series *Death Valley Days*. The cowboy charge slowly wore off.

See LONER.

cow-waddle. See FILIBUSTER.

crackdown the use of harsh disciplinary action; repression through suddenly severe enforcement of laws.

This noun, along with its verb phrase *to crack down*, first appeared during the Depression. The phrase appeared in a 1933 article in *Newsweek* about the National Recovery Administration: "The 'cracking down' phase of the Blue Eagle's career opened last week." In 1935, the *Washington Post* used the word in writing about the "threat of a 'crack-down' by the middle-class group against those who put forward the legislation for abolishing public utility holding companies."

Now written without a hyphen, the noun *crackdown* is less powerful than *purge* (the Russian *chistka*) but more forceful than *strong measures* (or *zhostkiye mery*). Evoking Stalin, the Russian term *zheleznaya ruka*, or "iron hand," is that language's closest equivalent to *crackdown*.

cradle-to-the-grave total security: a phrase used to attack welfare statism.

Cradles and graves are mentioned in the same breath as far back as the early seventeenth century. Joseph Hall, Bishop of Norwich, wrote: "Death borders upon our birth and our cradle stands in the grave."

Poet John Dyer wrote in 1726:

A little rule, a little sway,
A sunbeam in a winter's day,
Is all the proud and mighty have
Between the cradle and the grave.

This was parodied by Samuel Hoffenstein in the 1930s:

Babies haven't any hair; old men's heads
*   are just as bare;—*
Between the cradle and the grave lies a
*   haircut and a shave.*

A 1931 political use was by District Attorney Crain of New York, inveighing against racketeers who "have their hands in everything from the cradle to the grave—from babies' milk to funeral coaches."

Throughout the 1930s, "cradle-to-the-grave" was used to attack the New Deal's social security measures. Democratic candidate Adlai Stevenson referred to these attacks in the campaign of 1952: "Republican leadership has opposed us almost every step of the way and now, while adopting everything and proposing to repeal nothing, at least publicly, their orators still sneer at everything we now have and shout about socialism. They call our lives of pride and dignity 'cradle-to-the-grave rides through the welfare state.'"

Other spoofs have included "womb to tomb," the most extreme being "erection to resurrection."

See WELFARE STATE.

creative federalism federal stimulation and encouragement of state and local action to meet human needs, rather than by direct federal action.

Governor Nelson Rockefeller of New York put forth the idea of a modified form of federalism in a series of lectures and a 1964 campaign document (distributed as a paperback book) called *The Future of Federalism*.

The word "federalism," with its Founding Father connotation overshadowing its too-much-centralization connotation, was thus given new currency and next appeared as the "creative federalism" concept of President Johnson. *Fortune* magazine editor Max Ways wrote a piece on the subject in 1966.

Both the phrase and the concept appeared to be a defense against the charge of BIG GOVERNMENT domination of American life; the new, "creative" approach enhances the role of those state and local governments that are willing to undertake responsibilities assumed in recent years by the federal government.

Its proponents considered it an advance into new areas with the localities serving as the cutting edge; critics like Raymond Moley said, "The expression 'creative federalism'. . . serves as an impressive screen to cover the retreat of those who, since the presidency of the first Roosevelt, have urged the projection of federal authority into the areas traditionally reserved to the state and local governments."

As for the phrase, President Johnson took something old (the federalism of Jefferson, Hamilton, Jay, and Madison, resuscitated by Rockefeller) and something new ("creative"). In California in 1966, Ronald Reagan took "creative," added it to the mature "society" from Johnson's Great Society, and came up with "the creative society." Rockefeller then countered with an inaugural speech on "the just society." And so it went.

Federalism itself was coined by British conservative Edmund Burke, who also minted diplomacy, expenditure, municipality, and electioneer.

See NEW FEDERALISM; CONFEDERATE.

credibility gap the chasm that sometimes exists between public office and the public's trust.

The term first came into widespread use in early 1965 when American GIs in South Vietnam began sporting buttons reading "Ambushed at credibility gap." President Johnson actually suffered from a bit of a credibility gap when he came to his office; a long career as Senate majority leader, during which he was known as a master manipulator and a crafty compromiser, was responsible for that.

Only a few weeks after becoming President, he opened the gap wider when he hinted to newsmen that his first budget would probably exceed $102 billion, then produced a budget of under $98 billion. A number of other actions opened it into a yawning abyss (most abysses yawn): the excessive secretiveness and frequent overoptimism surrounding the Vietnam War; his charade in 1964 over his choice of a running mate, which he insisted was not decided until only minutes before he selected Hubert Humphrey; his scheduling a campaign swing in 1966 on the eve of the election, then canceling it and insisting that he had never really planned the trip at all.

Coinage of the phrase in print probably belongs to an anonymous *New York Herald Tribune* headline writer. On May 23, 1965, reporter David Wise wrote a piece that had the word "credibility" in the same lead with the word "gap" though not tied together. The headline read "Dilemma in 'Credibility Gap.'" The phrase was given currency by *Washington Post* reporter Murray Marder on December 5, 1965, in a story about "growing doubt and cynicism concerning Administration pronouncements. . . . The problem could be called a credibility gap."

In a whimsical mood on the eve of his departure as White House press secretary, Bill Moyers remarked that "the credibility gap . . . is getting so bad we can't even believe our own leaks." In a more somber mood, Moyers defined the gap as "the difference between what the President says and what the people would like him to say or what they think he should say."

Walter Lippmann, a less sympathetic observer, wrote in 1967 that "the credibility gap today is not the result of honest misunderstanding between the President and the press in this complicated world. It is the result of a deliberate policy of artificial manipulation of official news." The *Baltimore Sun's* Henry L. Trewhitt defined it as "the degree of refusal by the public to accept at face value what the government says and does." *New York Times* columnist James Reston wrote: "The most serious problem in America today is that there is widespread doubt in the public mind about its major leaders and institutions. There is more troubled questioning of the veracity of statements out of the White House today than at any time in recent memory."

The credibility gap developed into a major political issue and was accordingly seized upon by leading Republican contenders for the 1968 presidential nomination. "For years now," said Michigan's Governor George Romney, "we haven't been told the whole facts, and when you begin to find yourself in the position where you can't have confidence in what those who have a public trust are saying about fateful and vital situations, well, you are really in a tough spot."

"Credibility" has also assumed a more significant meaning in the geopolitics of the postwar world. The "credible deterrent" or "military credibility" refers to the degree to which a country convinces a potential enemy of its strength. See GAP.

CREEP the discredited Nixon campaign committee of 1972.

The story of how CREEP came into being was recounted in the author's 1975 book, *Before the Fall: An Inside*

View of the Pre-Watergate White House:

. . . My only real contribution to the committee had been a recommendation to stress Nixon's incumbency in its title. When Jeb Magruder came into my office in late 1971, the President had not yet publicly chosen Agnew as his running mate again. . . . Magruder said, "We can't call it 'Citizens for Nixon-Agnew' because that announces Agnew, and we can't call it 'Citizens for Nixon,' because that will be seen as throwing Agnew overboard, so what do we call the committee?" I remembered the 1966 Rockefeller campaign in New York, when the slogan was "Governor Rockefeller for Governor". . . and I suggested, simply, the Committee to Re-elect the President. "That's the best you can do?" Magruder inquired. I started to remind him that I was charging clients $90,000 a year for advice when he was selling pancake makeup for a local cosmetics house, but then I thought for a moment: any acronym problem? You always have to watch that. C, R, P. Democrats would have to try to stick an "A" in there to make fun of it, which would be in bad taste and they wouldn't try that; if you made it C, R, E, P, using the "election" as a non-hyphenated capital, you would have a french pancake, and that's even too effete for snobs. It would be safe, solid, and stress the incumbency. And so CREEP was created.

The CRP was dubbed "CREEP" not by a Democrat, but by Republican National Committee Chairman Robert Dole, who felt the RNC was being shunted aside by the brash young men of the Nixon White House. An early printed reference was in the September 15, 1972, issue of *Life:* "The CRP—or 'CREEP,' as some members of the Republican National Committee call it— occupies five floors of one building and spills across the street onto three floors [of another]." On May 21, 1973, *Time* wrote: "But during the campaign he [Dole] fought many a gallant losing battle with the Committee for the Re-Election of the President; in fact it was he who dubbed it CREEP."

Senator Dole's crack had been aimed at the play on the word "creep," which is taken from a person who gives one "the creeps" or who causes the flesh to crawl—a derogation that can be found in a 1930 James T. Farrell story. But after it was discovered that the Nixon committee had financed the break-in to Democratic headquarters at the Watergate office complex, "CREEP" gained a different and far more sinister connotation—as one who enters by stealth—and what had begun as an intraparty gibe became a weapon in the hands of everyone who was anxious to attack anything associated with the 1972 Nixon victory.

creeping socialism measures increasing the sphere of government activity that are accused of having the cumulative effect of undermining private enterprise.

Republicans during Franklin Roosevelt's New Deal and Harry Truman's Fair Deal frequently used "creeping socialism" to describe Democratic programs, especially in the economic and social welfare areas. Historian Samuel Eliot Morison observed later: "Republican orators played this theme in elections and in Congress . . . [but] postwar developments, especially under Eisenhower, justify the quip that instead of creeping socialism, galloping capitalism emerged from the New Deal and the war."

Indeed, "creeping socialism" survives as a term not so much because of Republican or conservative affection for it, but because liberals find it an easy target. See Adlai Stevenson's gibe under DINOSAUR WING. Walter Lippmann, for instance, wrote in 1962: "The so-called socialism which is supposed to be creeping up on us is in fact nothing more than the work of making

life safe and decent for a mass society collected in great cities." When Dwight Eisenhower used the phrase in 1953 ("in the last 20 years creeping socialism has been striking in the United States"), one of his aides wrote him a memo saying it had been "the hallmark of the Old Guard Republicans" and that modern Republicans should have "their own idiom." Eisenhower agreed.

The word "socialism" was first used politically in 1835 in England by followers of Robert Owen.

The word "creeping" is now a jocular form of "incipient," not limited to ideology, and can be applied to any "ism" for a piquant effect. "After all the amateurish, impromptu diplomacy," wrote columnists Evans and Novak in 1978 about President Carter's use of carefully prepared remarks upon returning from his first trip abroad, "it could be a sign of creeping professionalism."

crime in the streets initially, urban crime; later a phrase used to derogate the emphasis of "law and order" as an issue.

For a full discussion of the LAW AND ORDER issue, see that entry. Although the words "law and order" were described for a time in the late sixties as "code words for racism," the severe increase in crime—of special concern to black victims in slums—soon erased the pejorative connotation. However, "crime in the streets" was used not so much to describe the situation itself as the political issue arising from it, and this has come to mean "making a political issue out of law enforcement." "Law and order" ceased to be regarded as code words by 1971, while "crime in the streets" retained the political, though not especially racist, connotation.

The term is still used in the 1990s. A rhyming derogation of white-collar crime was expressed in a 1993 White House briefing as "crime in the suites as well as crime in the streets."

Language expert Mario Pei offered this interesting sidelight in *Modern Age: A Quarterly Review*, in 1969: "'Crime in the streets' is a very ancient phenomenon, widespread even in such a world-renowned city as imperial Rome. It gave rise, curiously, to French *crier*, which in turn has become English 'cry.' The root word is *'Quirites!'* 'Citizens!' a cry of distress corresponding to our 'Help!' used by Romans attacked in the streets."

See CODE WORDS.

cronyism. See GOVERNMENT BY CRONY.

crossover vote a theory that a primary in one party can be affected substantially by the votes of members of an opposition party.

During the 1976 Republican primaries, supporters of President Ford explained several losses in state primaries in this way: in those states with no party-registration requirement, many Democratic voters—who would ultimately vote for the Democratic candidate in November—were "crossing over" to vote for Ronald Reagan in the Republican primaries.

"Among those who described themselves as Republicans," wrote R. W. Apple, Jr., in the *New York Times* on May 5, 1976, describing a post-primary poll, "Mr. Reagan and President Ford fought on almost equal terms, but the California conservative swept the Democratic crossover voters and beat the President by about 3 to 2 among the independents."

The crossover theory holds that the crossover voter is fickle, or mischievous, or only interested in voting in the more hotly contested primary, and intends to come "home" to the party

in which he is registered later in the general election. The theory was challenged by Michael Barone, writing in the *Washington Post* under the headline "That 'Crossover' Nonsense!" "All but an insignificant number of the people who will vote for Gerald Ford or Ronald Reagan or Jimmy Carter or Morris Udall in Michigan," he argued, "will be people who are quite ready to vote for them in the general election. In that sense, and it is the only one that matters, they will be legitimate Republican and Democratic voters, not mischievous 'crossovers.' The 'crossover' theory is nonsense."

But as the influence of the state primary grows in the selection of presidential candidates, the idea of the crossover vote will be offered as an explanation or an excuse by primary losers, who will insist they were defeated by a vote that did not really reflect the wishes of regular party members.

See NOVEMBER REPUBLICANS.

cross the street. See TAKE A WALK.

crowdsmanship. See NUMBERS GAME.

crunch high-pressure squeeze; a period of tension that becomes a political or economic moment of truth, when participants display courage or cowardice.

The verb *to crunch*, probably of imitative origin (as "the ship crunched through the ice"), was given an extra definition in the mid-sixties. Businessmen, editorialized the *New York Times* in 1967, "will lose their fears of a credit crunch when it becomes clear that we are not headed for another 1966 [credit crisis]."

Squeeze is almost exclusively an economic word for tightening; *pinch*, as in Shakespeare's use of "necessity's sharp pinch," is a generalized type of stress, and *in a pinch* is a time of mild hardship; NUT-CUTTING implies action in a crisis toward an individual; *moment of truth,* with its bullfighting origin, has acquired a literary connotation; the *clutch,* with a baseball derivation, is the decisive moment in a close contest; the *crunch* is the pressure of a political or economic nutcracker.

The word was given new meaning when it was changed from its familiar verb form. Another example of this is "hurting"; to *hurt* or to *be hurt* means inflicting or receiving physical pain, while *hurting* (Dean Rusk in 1967: "the North Vietnamese are hurting") means to be in political or military difficulties. And when the crunch comes, a lot of fence-sitters find themselves hurting.

An alliterative phrase, *credit crunch,* has reinforced the political and economic use of the term. The *Boston Globe* wrote of George Bush's Treasury Secretary Nicholas F. Brady in 1991: "He labeled the credit crunch the Administration's 'number one economic priority.'"

crusade a political movement characterized by moral fervor; a word used to endow an effort with a religious-moral tone.

Most Americans today identify the word with Dwight D. Eisenhower, but it has had a long political history. "A crusade against ignorance" was urged by Thomas Jefferson in 1786. "Spend and be spent in an endless crusade," Theodore Roosevelt exhorted his supporters. Franklin D. Roosevelt agreed; on the day of his first inauguration, March 4, 1933, he not only called for a "new deal," but issued "a call to arms . . . a crusade to restore America to its own." Three years later, in a cabinet meeting, FDR talked about prospects for re-election: "We will win easily next year, but we are going to make it a crusade."

FDR's 1940 opponent, Wendell Willkie, took a page from "that man's" book; in his speech accepting the Republican nomination, Willkie pledged: "We go into this campaign as into a crusade . . . on the basis of American liberty, not on the basis of hate, jealousy or personalities."

Eisenhower first used the word, in its traditional moral-military context, in his June 6, 1944, "Order of the Day" to the Allied troops poised to invade Europe: "Soldiers, sailors and airmen of the Allied Expeditionary Force: You are about to embark upon a great crusade, toward which we have striven these many months. . . . The hopes and prayers of liberty-loving people everywhere march with you."

The general entitled his best-selling memoirs *Crusade in Europe,* and it was natural for his political advisers to seize on the word so closely identified with their candidate. Throughout the campaign of 1952 he reiterated the word, perhaps most dramatically in his "I shall go to Korea" speech on October 24: "I do not believe it a presumption for me to call the effort of all those who have enlisted with me—a crusade. I use that word only to signify two facts. First: We are united and devoted to a just cause of the purest meaning to all humankind. Second: We know that—for all the might of our effort—victory can come only with the gift of God's help. In this spirit—humble servants of a proud ideal—we do soberly say: This is a crusade."

That Detroit speech was prepared by Emmet Hughes, and its use of "crusade" was limited to the quest for peace, a narrowing down of its earlier use by Eisenhower to apply to anything on the domestic scene as well. Wrote Hughes later: "I struck from the current vocabulary any use of 'Crusade' on the national scene, and 'liberation' on the world scene. Their presumption seemed to me offensive, and they nowhere appeared in any passage of any speech that I prepared for the rest of the campaign." This attitude might have been in response to Adlai Stevenson's gibes about Eisenhower's oft-repeated dedication to a crusade: "The General has dedicated himself so many times, he must feel like the cornerstone of a public building."

John F. Kennedy used the word in an odd, effective context in 1961: "Let our patriotism be reflected in the creation of confidence in one another, rather than in crusades of suspicion."

BBC correspondent Alistair Cooke, writing in *The Listener* in 1963, made an astute observation about crusades and Presidents: "All Presidents start out pretending to run a crusade, but after a couple of years they find they are running something much less heroic, much more intractable: namely, the Presidency."

The word's moral fervor is built in; its literal meaning is "taking the cross," coined in the eleventh century to describe the first military expedition by European Christians to recover the Holy Land from the Mohammedans.

C three C 3. See K₁C₂.

cufflinks gang a group of supporters of FDR in his run for the vice presidency in 1920, tied together later by the postcampaign gift of gold cufflinks from the candidate.

White House aide Marvin McIntyre wore his cufflinks throughout the thirties, symbol of his membership in the "original" group; later Bronx Democratic boss Ed Flynn echoed the sentiment by forming an FRBC Club (For Roosevelt Before Chicago) of those who supported FDR before the 1932 Chicago convention. Twenty years before, Theodore Roosevelt's manager, Senator Joseph Dixon of Montana, used "Before April 9th Men" to hail Roosevelt supporters who spoke up for him before the April 9, 1912, Illinois primary brightened his chances.

Mementos like the cufflinks are cherished by the recipients as a badge of being an early insider, with presumably some slight prerogative over the Johnny-come-latelies. John F. Kennedy gave his aides a PT-109 tieclasp, which became the highest status symbol of the New Frontier.

Cufflinks and tieclasps, chosen for these gifts because of their high visibility and portability, are customarily presented by winners (Nelson Rockefeller's post-1966 gubernatorial campaign gift was a pair of cufflinks with a tiny "rock of Gibraltar" embedded in each). After the 1952 campaign Vice President Richard Nixon presented "Order of the Hound's Tooth" scrolls to his intimates, suitable for framing, and KITCHEN CABINET scrolls to those who accompanied him to the KITCHEN DEBATE in Moscow in 1959. After his 1960 defeat, Nixon sent a desk memento to one hundred key men: a clay replica of the life cast taken of Abraham Lincoln's right hand. Ironically, most of these were not wrapped securely and arrived broken in the mail, and the aide responsible (author of this dictionary) spent six miserable months apologizing, having new ones made and reshipped to impatient, fuming recipients. After his successful campaigning for congressional candidates in 1966, Nixon aides, who had learned a lesson, sent out unbreakable Churchill crowns to helpers across the nation with a quotation from Churchill about the dangers of appeasement.

cult of personality promotion of personal adulation, as contrasted with collective leadership.

At a secret session of the Communist Party Congress on February 25, 1956, Party Secretary Nikita Khrushchev rose to denounce Joseph Stalin, startling the world and leading to a drastic revision of Soviet history books. Leaked reports of the meeting, distributed by the CIA, quoted Khrushchev as saying that a "cult of personality" had been promoted by Stalin after Lenin's death, and that Stalin had abused his personal prestige by using it to undermine collective leadership of the Presidium. *Pravda* followed up a month later with: "Stalin's disregard of the principle of collective leadership, and the frequent decisions taken by him personally, led to the distortion of party principles and party democracy, to the violation of revolutionary law, and to repression."

There was criticism in Communist circles in later years of a cult of personality growing up around Khrushchev, and some analysts think this contributed to his own downfall. In the Western world, the phrase is occasionally used in an ironic or joking way.

The idea of extending power through a personality cult, of course, was not original with either Stalin or Khrushchev. Alexander Hamilton, in an 1802 letter, outlined a plan for a "Christian Constitutional Society," appealing to people "through a development of a 'cult' of Washington and benevolent activities." The cult that Hamilton had proposed was formed in 1808—the Washington Benevolent Society—too late to help the sagging Federalists.

Columnist Murray Kempton, writing in 1967 about the first U.S. press conference of Stalin's daughter, Svetlana Alliluyeva, commented: "Of all Russians, the daughter of Joseph Stalin is the one to remind his replacements that the Cult of Personality can no more decently be employed to lay all the guilt on one man than it can be to give him all the credit."

Cultural Revolution political and social upheaval in the People's Republic of China, fostered by Mao Tse-tung to forestall bureaucratization and to preserve the purity of the revolution as he knew it.

What troubled Party Chairman Mao when he launched the "Great Proletarian Cultural Revolution" was the growing gap in China between city and village, intellectual and peasant. Instead of devotion to the cause, there were signs of REVISIONISM, "backsliding," and "bureaucratism," along with yearnings for such bourgeois things as comfort, status, and education. As *Toronto Star* correspondent Mark Gayn wrote in the January 1967 issue of *Foreign Affairs*, Mao sought "nothing less than the rejuvenation of a great revolution, the rebirth in middle age of the drive, the passion, the selflessness and the discipline it had in its youth a third of a century ago."

The revolution began in November 1965 when a Shanghai newspaper attacked the deputy mayor of Peking, Wu Han, for writing historical plays rather than modern ones. The following year Mao and his then heir-apparent, Marshal Lin Piao, created the Red Guards as instruments to restore purity. Patterned after the peasant youth movement of Hunan in the late 1920s, the Red Guard movement created a reign of terror with public humiliations of those who opposed Mao, kangaroo trials, beatings, and killings.

The faction described as "antiradical" in the West ultimately made a comeback under Teng Hsiao-ping. After Mao's death a short, fierce struggle took place between the "Shanghai radicals" led by Mao's widow and the successor to Mao, Hua Kuo-feng, who had the army's backing. As a result, the group that had gained power during the Cultural Revolution was arrested and denounced as "the gang of four," while Teng agreed to serve under Hua, whom he soon pushed aside to become what was called "paramount leader."

curmudgeon a likeably irascible old man. In politics, a cantankerous, outspoken older politician with a talent for invective.

FDR's Interior Secretary, Harold Ickes, earned the title "The Old Curmudgeon." More recently, New York Parks Commissioner Robert Moses was often identified as a curmudgeon, but the word still evokes memories of "Harold the Ick." Among his memorable blasts, he tagged Wendell Willkie as "the simple, BAREFOOT BOY FROM WALL STREET," and is sometimes credited with labeling Thomas E. Dewey as "the little man on the wedding cake"; Alfred Landon was "a strong but silenced man." When Huey Long called Ickes "the Chicago Chinch-Bug," Ickes replied, "The trouble with Senator Long is that he is suffering from halitosis of the intellect. That's presuming Senator Long has an intellect." He denounced opponents of academic freedom as "intellectual Dillingers," proponents of the Liberty League as "vestal virgins," and Governor Talmadge of Georgia as "His Chain Gang Excellency." He intended to deliver a speech about Martin Dies, head of the House Un-American Activities Committee entitled "A Case of Loaded Dies," but Roosevelt restrained him.

A curmudgeon may expect to be attacked in kind. Ickes was described as "the New Deal blackjack squad," "blunderbuss Ickes," and (by Joe Martin) "Comrade Harold L. Ickes, Overlord of the Interior and Commissar of the P.W.A."

The archaic definition of curmudgeon as one who is "grasping" and "avaricious" (Samuel Johnson thought it may have come from *coeur méchant*, or wicked heart) does not apply in politics; "irascible" and "cantankerous" are the right adjectives. The curmudgeon is liked because he is a throwback to the days when politicians had fewer advisers telling them to soften their words.

In 1969, *Life* magazine columnist Hugh Sidey referred to publisher John Knight, seventy-five, as "an old curmudgeon." Knight looked up the definition in Webster's *New International Dictionary* (3rd edition) and was distressed to see "a miser; churl" among other disparagements. Sidey quickly wrote one of Knight's perturbed associates: "Word meanings are fluid, like history. Dictionaries are often inaccurate guides to the moment. William Safire's book, *The New Language of Politics,* . . . says 'Curmudgeon—a likeably irascible old man.' That is precisely how I feel about Mr. Knight. I believe he is a splendid journalist, a delightful skeptic, a wonderful human being. Nothing you wrote changes my opinion of this old curmudgeon."

Knight replied to Sidey: "I guess that calls for a drink" and wrote this author: "I have had a lot of fun with being called a 'curmudgeon' but I much prefer your definition to the one in Webster's."

curse of bigness an attack phrase on monopoly, unlawful combinations, and the power of large corporations.

Labor unrest and violence shocked the nation in 1911, culminating in the dynamiting of the then antilabor *Los Angeles Times* by three union officials. Boston attorney Louis D. Brandeis (later a Supreme Court Justice) wrote the editor of the magazine *Survey* on December 30, 1911: "Is there not a causal connection between the development of these huge, indomitable trusts and the horrible crimes now under investigation? Is it not irony to speak of equality of opportunity in a country cursed with bigness?"

Brandeis's phrase caused a stir; he used it again as the title of an essay published in *Harper's Weekly:* "The Curse of Bigness."

The classic answer to Brandeis's phrase is one of the few memorable phrases of President William Howard Taft: "Mere size is no sin against the law." Both phrases are used in discussions of antitrust cases; David Lilienthal switched the Brandeis phrase around in the 1950s in discussing the "curse of smallness."

cutting edge. See ON THE POINT.

C.Y.A. the initialized euphemism for "cover your ass," sometimes further euphemized as "posterior protection"; the bureaucratic technique of averting future accusations of policy error or wrongdoing by deflecting responsibility.

Rear Admiral John M. Poindexter testified at the Iran-contra hearings that he destroyed a secret Presidential finding, which "had been prepared essentially by the C.I.A. as a—what we call a C.Y.A. effort."

C.I.A. (usually spelled CIA, without periods) is the Central Intelligence Agency; C.Y.A. is a military-bureaucratic abbreviation defined by Democratic Senator Sam Nunn of Georgia during the same hearings: "Isn't this cable in effect a C.Y.A. cable? . . . They were covering their rear end back in Washington, weren't they?"

This use of initialese—always capitalized and usually used with periods—stands for an imperative clause and points to the fuzzing of responsibility. A bureaucrat adept at C.Y.A. (a) likes to employ passive constructions ("Mistakes were made"), (b) follows up a meeting or phone call with a self-serving *memcon*—"memorandum of conversation," (c) routes memos to and through as many other bureaucrats as possible, thereby spreading the risk, and (d) "papers the file" with memoranda supporting and sometimes contradicting his or her position.

D

daisy spot political advertising; antiwar commercial.

This term, in which "spot" is used in the advertising sense of "announcement," comes from a campaign commercial used by Lyndon B. Johnson in his 1964 Presidential campaign. To torpedo his Republican opponent Barry Goldwater, Johnson used an advertisement aimed at underscoring the challenger as a warmongering extremist.

The ad showed a young girl counting as she picked petals from a daisy. A military voice begins a different type of countdown, leading to a nuclear explosion that mushrooms across the screen, and LBJ's voice is heard discussing "the stakes" of the election.

Shown only once, on September 7, 1964, the commercial drew immediate outcries from Republicans about its unfairness. Republican National Committee chairman Dean Burch complained, "This horrible commercial is designed to arouse basic emotions," and it was immediately withdrawn, but its impact lingered.

The ad's creator, political consultant Tony Schwartz, was quoted in *Newsday* in 1992 that the daisy spot "was the first national Rorschach test," with its implications that Goldwater, who wasn't even mentioned, would start a third world war.

Said Schwartz:

> When this commercial was shown, it was against a backdrop of what was out in the environment about Goldwater, that he had spoken for the use of nuclear weapons to defoliate the jungles of East Asia, and for letting field commanders use them at their discretion. . . . People say political commercials manipulate viewers, but viewers have to participate in the manipulation—projecting their own frames of reference onto commercials, filling in the message's blanks.

In current usage, negative advertising is often measured against the impact of, and fierce reaction to, the *daisy spot*.

dark horse a long-shot candidate for nomination, usually the second or third choice of many delegates, whose best chance for selection lies in a deadlock of the leading candidates.

The first "dark horse" appeared at one of the earliest Democratic conventions. Indeed, the choice of James Polk of Tennessee proved the usefulness of political party conventions. An impasse had been reached between former President Martin Van Buren of New York and Lewis Cass of Michigan in the convention held in Baltimore in 1844. On the eighth ballot, with neither leader willing to give way to the other, a compromise of Polk was suggested. He received 44 votes, Cass 114, Van Buren 104, Calhoun and Buchanan 2 each, with 134 needed to nominate. On the ninth ballot, the convention stampeded to the "dark horse." Polk received all 266 votes.

Like most compromise candidates who followed him, Polk was not well known nationally. "Who's Polk?" became a slogan of the 1844 campaign, in which Polk narrowly defeated the Whigs' Henry Clay. The next dark horse to win was Franklin Pierce, who was not considered as a candidate until the 35th ballot, winning on the 49th. The Democrats' slogan then became "We Polked You in 1844, We'll Pierce You in 1852." He, too, defeated the Whig candidate, General Winfield Scott. In 1876, Rutherford B. Hayes was another successful dark horse.

In more recent times, Warren Gamaliel Harding of Ohio was the most successful dark horse. Army hero Leonard Wood and Governor Frank Lowden of Illinois deadlocked the Republican convention of 1920 for nine ballots. In a suite on the top floor of Chicago's Blackstone Hotel, party leaders selected Harding, a man with no enemies. See SMOKE-FILLED ROOM.

Wendell Willkie in 1940 began his campaign for the nomination as a dark horse against the favorites, Thomas E. Dewey and Robert A. Taft. William Allen White extended the metaphor in a profile in the *New Republic:* "What sort of man personally is this unknown dark horse who is being groomed in the Augean stables of our plutocracy?" See CLEAN SWEEP.

The phrase was used in a novel by the young Benjamin Disraeli, *The Young Duke,* published in 1831: "A dark horse which had never been thought of, and which the careless St. James had never even observed in the list, rushed past the grandstand in sweeping triumph." In politics, it probably first entered the language after Polk and before Pierce. Hans Sperber and Travis Trittschuh find its first printed reference in a quotation from New York's Hamilton Fish, speaking for Lincoln in 1860: "We want a log-splitter, not a hair-splitter; a flat-boatman, not a flat-statesman; log cabin, coonskin, hard cider, old Abe and dark horse—hurrah!"

Reviewing the first edition of this dictionary in *Encounter* magazine in 1968, historian Sir Denis Brogan added: ". . . in a moment of patriotic pride, I should like to suggest that the most brilliant use of the term 'dark horse' was made by John Morley (known to good Radicals as 'honest John Morley,' no doubt to distinguish him from his colleagues); he called Lord Rosebery (who was as proud of having won the Derby as of having been Prime Minister) 'a dark horse in a loose box.' (The term 'loose box' was also used to describe the special accommodation provided for the mistresses of Edward VII at his coronation in Westminster Abbey in 1902.)"

In 1967, "backup candidate" came into use as a more specific form of dark horse, one that would get the support of a group if its own candidate failed. See FALLBACK POSITION.

Other horse-racing metaphors common to politics are BOLT, SHOO-IN, RUNNING MATE, and FRONT RUNNER. Winners take the reins of government; losers are known as "also-rans."

day of infamy Franklin Roosevelt's reference to the attack on Pearl Harbor on December 7, 1941, asking for a declaration of war on Japan.

The speech was drafted by Roosevelt himself, without the aid of either Robert E. Sherwood or Samuel Rosenman, his speechwriters at that time. The first draft's first sentence read: "Yesterday, December 7, 1941, a date which will live in world history, the United States was simultaneously and deliberately attacked by naval and air forces of the Empire of Japan." In the second draft, FDR crossed out "world history" and substituted "infamy"; he crossed out "simultaneously" and used "suddenly."

The third draft includes insertions in FDR's handwriting: "Last night Japanese forces attacked Hong Kong. Last night Japanese forces attacked Wake Island. This morning the Japanese attacked Midway Island." While the President was preparing to go to Congress, he added the latest news as it came in. Harry Hopkins suggested a sentence, which Roosevelt approved, expressing confidence that we would "gain the inevitable triumph—so help us God."

"The remarkable thing," wrote Rosenman later, "is that on one of the busiest and most turbulent days of his life he was able to spend so much time and give so much thought to this speech." Secretary of State Cordell Hull had argued for a long speech, detailing the history of Japanese-American relations. Roosevelt said that he would go into detail in a fireside chat the next day, and decided on his own six-minute dramatic message to Congress.

Roosevelt's revision from "world history" to "infamy" is intriguing; the word was aristocratic and little-used (Voltaire had written to a friend in 1760: "I wish that you would crush this infamy"), but the change of the word made the phrase memorable.

dead-cat bounce an aborted economic recovery.

A *dead-cat bounce* suggests a slight rise after an economic decline, fol-lowed in fast order by a second decline. This metaphor is a graphic depiction of what economists call a "double dip" (see DIP/DOUBLE DIP).

Usually hyphenated, *dead-cat bounce* first appeared in the *Financial Times* of December 7, 1985, without a hyphen; in this article, investment experts in the Far East described a slight rise in economic indicators as "partly technical and cautioned against concluding that the recent falls in the market were at an end. 'This is what we call a dead cat bounce,' one broker said flatly."

The Associated Press reported the term's use in New York a year later, when a broker, Raymond DeVoe, Jr., warned, "Beware the dead-cat bounce." He offered a definition for the term: "This applies to stocks or commodities that have gone into free-fall descent and then rallied briefly. If you threw a dead cat off a 50-story building, it might bounce when it hit the sidewalk. But don't confuse that bounce with renewed life. It is still a dead cat."

See HAIL OF DEAD CATS.

dead end, political the mayoralty of any large city; supposedly a thankless job that makes major enemies and aborts a political career.

When New York Congressman John V. Lindsay was being urged to run for mayor, his friends pointed to the careers of Fiorello La Guardia and Robert Wagner as evidence that the job was "a political dead end." Vice President Hubert Humphrey's rise from mayor of Minneapolis, Minnesota, was dismissed as an exception that proved the rule, but it was not.

Wrote *Newsweek* in 1967: "Democrat Richardson Dilworth won national acclaim during the 1950s as Mayor of Philadelphia only to learn the hard way that City Hall is more often a dead end than a steppingstone for promising political careers."

The phrase is derived from the Sidney Kingsley play *Dead End;* its movie version starred a group of tough-talking young actors who became known as "the Dead End Kids." The title was taken from a traffic sign that indicates no exit at the far end of the street, and was used to symbolize the lack of opportunity available to young men from poor neighborhoods. See DISADVANTAGED.

The vice presidency is occasionally referred to as a political dead end. President Eisenhower in 1956 asked Vice President Richard Nixon whether he felt that a cabinet post would be more helpful in furthering his own career. "The President explained to Nixon," reported Sherman Adams, "that history had shown the vice presidency to be somewhat of a political dead end; no vice president in this century had gone on to the presidency except through accidental succession . . ." But with the accidental succession to power of Harry Truman, Lyndon Johnson, and Gerald Ford, the phrase is rarely used today in relation to the office a HEARTBEAT AWAY FROM THE PRESIDENCY.

See GRAVEYARD; STEPPINGSTONE.

deal a political trade of favors or support. When either discovered or imagined, an effective attack word that turns what some consider an honorable arrangement into what others consider a bribe.

In 1824, the "era of good feeling" began to sour when John Quincy Adams made a deal with Henry Clay. Andrew Jackson had won a plurality of the popular and electoral votes, but not a majority, and the election had to be decided in the House of Representatives. Speaker of the House Clay threw his support behind Adams, who then won, and promptly named Clay his Secretary of State. In the 1828 election, Jackson's slogan

was "Bargain and Corruption" and he won handily.

After that, deals became something to be denounced by all candidates, especially regarding cabinet posts and other appointments, a point that rarely discouraged campaign managers from dealing in realities. Lincoln wired his convention floor manager in 1860, David Davis: "Make no deals in my name." Davis is reported to have remarked, "Hell, we're here and he's not," and dealt freely with the Blair and Cameron forces. As President, Lincoln fulfilled the promises made by Davis, who was rewarded with a seat on the Supreme Court.

At the Republican convention of 1880, former President U.S. Grant went a little too far in denying a deal. "It was my intention, if nominated and elected, to appoint John Sherman Secretary of the Treasury. Now you may be certain I shall not. Not to be President of the United States would I consent that a bargain should be made." No bargain, no support; James Garfield was nominated.

Probably the most monumental deal in U.S. political history occurred in the disputed election between Rutherford B. Hayes, Republican of Ohio, and Samuel J. Tilden, Democrat of New York, in 1876. Tilden had won a majority of the popular vote and led Hayes in the electoral vote 184 to 165, with 185 the necessary majority. Twenty votes, from "carpetbag" governments in Florida, Louisiana, and South Carolina, as well as one from Oregon, were in dispute. The Republican-controlled Senate and the Democratic-controlled House could not agree on how the disputed votes were to be counted. An electoral commission was appointed, with seven men from each party plus one "independent"—Supreme Court Justice David Davis, the same man who made the convention deals for Lincoln. He resigned in favor of an eighth Republican, who threw the election, predictably, to Hayes.

Why did the Democrats hold still for this decision to substitute a Republican for the independent swing man? Because the Republicans agreed to a simple deal: the election of Hayes, in return for the withdrawal of federal troops from the "carpetbag" states, ending Reconstruction governments and giving the Democrats control of the South. In the long run, the Democrats got the better of the deal.

William Randolph Hearst received the Democratic nomination for governor of New York in 1906 from the hands of Tammany Leader Charles Murphy, whom Hearst papers had attacked a few months before as "The Colossus of Graft" and "The Black Hand." Suspecting a deal, writer Edmund Wetmore put into poetry what Hearst might have said:

"So I lashed him and I thrashed him in my hot reforming zeal,/Then I clasped him to my bosom in a most artistic deal."

More recently, at the 1948 Republican convention, Robert Taft (beaten by Thomas E. Dewey for the nomination) agreed to the vice-presidential nomination of his fellow Ohioan, John Bricker, in return for the pledge of Bricker forces for active support of Taft in 1952 (which was forthcoming, though Taft lost to Eisenhower).

As a noun, "deal" takes its coloration from its adjective: a "square deal" is good and a "fast deal" is bad. Its definition depends on the point of view: what is a "cynical bargain" to your adversary is an "honorable compromise" to you. The late Oklahoma Democratic Senator Robert Kerr, a noted wheeler-dealer, liked to say: "I'm against any deal I'm not in on."

decision-making process the way a political executive makes up his mind;

a cliché used by press secretaries to block access to information about the conflicting pressures leading to a decision, or used by reporters to describe whatever inside information they can get about what advice was given.

Author Victor Navasky described his 1971 book, *Kennedy Justice,* as "a series of forays into what is forbiddingly known as the Decision-making Process, a look at how an institution makes up its mind . . ."

In the sense used above, the process is institutional, used to show how the man at the top cannot be totally blamed or credited with his conclusions. In this sense, the phrase has a negative connotation, as a difficult-to-penetrate wall, or bureaucratic maze.

The phrase has been used positively as well in the politics of participation, as "we must involve more of the people in the decision-making process."

A typical fifties usage was by Attorney General William P. Rogers to a Senate judiciary subcommittee on March 6, 1958, about EXECUTIVE PRIVILEGE: "I appreciate the opportunity . . . to present my views as to the extent of the inquiry which can be made by the legislative branch of the Government concerning the decision-making process and documents of the Executive Branch."

The process itself can be amorphous and mysterious, as in President Truman's decision to drop the atom bomb, or formally laid out with options, projected consequences, and recommendations, as in many of the decisions that are made through the present National Security Council system. Or it can represent the workings of one man's mind, little influenced by staff.

There is commercial value to its understanding. "The regulatory process in Washington is influenced by political factors," former Deputy Attorney General Laurence Silberman told reporter Steven Roberts of the *New York Times* in 1978. "It's awfully important to understand the nature of the decision-making process, to know what is decided at what level and by whom."

The cliché most commonly associated with "decision-making process" is "input," a term from computer technology.

See TICK-TOCK; BITE THE BULLET; PROCESS, THE.

decouple   separate, split up, unlink.

This verb became popular in the late 1970s as a strategic synonym for *disjoin*. In 1979, Fred Kaplan wrote in the *New York Times Magazine* about the suspicion that "America was 'decoupling' its own defense from that of NATO."

As Vice President, George Bush used the term to warn against division in alliance: "The Soviet Union, having already deployed sufficient missiles to intimidate Western Europe, is now trying to decouple our security from each other." Secretary of Defense Caspar W. Weinberger commented a year later, "There's not the slightest possibility that America would be decoupled from Europe by the pursuit of this vital initiative."

First used in 1602, the word *decouple* (from the French verb *decoupler*) gained prominence as a railroad term for unhooking train cars. Scientists and economists picked up the word in the 1970s before its rise in popularity as military-diplomatic lingo.

deeds not words   a platitudinous attack on platitudes; a demand for specific action instead of oral or written assurances.

In modern politics, the phrase is mostly identified with Dwight Eisenhower, who used it often in speeches. Returning from his promised trip to Korea after his 1952 election, he told

reporters: "We face an enemy whom we cannot hope to impress by words, however eloquent, but only by deeds—executed under circumstances of our own choosing." Before the American Society of Newspaper Editors in 1953, he said: "We welcome every honest act of peace. We care nothing for mere rhetoric. We are only for sincerity of peaceful purpose attested by deeds." He returned to the theme again and again, as in a UN speech in 1953 after a Bermuda Conference: "These are not idle words or shallow visions. . . . These are deeds of peace."

The phrase can be found in Samuel Butler's "Hudibras," a poem satirizing the Puritans, with these lines written before the execution of King Charles I in 1649: ". . . we must give the world a proof/ Of deeds, not words."

Shakespeare's Richard III said, "Talkers are no good doers"; Hamlet, asked what he was reading, replied, "Words, words, words." British Prime Minister Neville Chamberlain used the word "words" in the same derisive sense in a rebuff to Franklin Roosevelt in 1938: "It is always best and safest to count on nothing from the Americans but words." In 1966, the British Conservative party slogan was "Action not words."

The long form of "deeds not words" was used by President Grover Cleveland: "It is not the mere slothful acceptance of righteous political ideas, but the call to action for their enforcement and application, that tests the endurance and moral courage of men." A common variation on the phrase is "in deed as well as word," as used by Mao Tse-tung: "Whoever sides with the revolutionary people in deed as well as in word is a revolutionary in the full sense."

Word and deed have gone hand in hand throughout history. "Deeds are males, words females are," written by

John Davies in 1610, was adopted in Italian by the first Baron Baltimore (*fatti maschii; parole femine*) and is the motto of the state of Maryland. A proverb traced to 1546 goes: "That deede without woords shall driue him to the wall." The Roman Catholic confession, traceable to 1075 in something like its present form, talks of sinning "in thought, word and deed." And Plautus, in *Pseudolus,* written about 190 B.C., said, "Let deeds match words."

The state of Maryland motto was re-translated in 1993: "Strong deeds, gentle words." That translation, however, renders a different Latin saying (in reverse order), which was Dwight Eisenhower's motto: *Suaviter in modo, fortiter in re.*

deep background. See NOT FOR ATTRIBUTION.

deep freeze. See INFLUENCE PEDDLER.

deep-six to dispose of, with emphasis; to destroy or deliberately lose.

In Watergate testimony on June 25, 1973, former White House counsel John Dean attributed the use of the phrase to John Ehrlichman: "He told me to shred the documents and 'deep-six' the briefcase. I asked him what he meant by 'deep-six.' He leaned back in his chair and said: 'You drive across the river on your way home at night, don't you? Well, when you cross over the bridge on your way home, just toss the briefcase into the river.'"

Before entering prison in 1976, John Ehrlichman disputed Dean's testimony in this interview in the *Washington Post's Potomac Magazine* with reporter Nick Thimmesch: "The specific acts by me were supposed to be the conversations with Dean where he said I told him to get Howard Hunt out of the country, and later to 'deep-six' the contents of Hunt's safe. A con-

versation with Herbert Kalmbach was the basis of another charge. Those conversations never took place."

"Deep-six" is naval slang. "As an ex-Navy type," Joseph Ross of the Congressional Research Service wrote in answer to the author's query, "I know that this is Navy talk, meaning to jettison. It comes from the leadsman's (fellow who took the soundings) call for six fathoms (36 feet) of depth: 'by the deep six.'" Lexicographer Peter Tamony has supplied a 1927 citation in *A Glossary of Sea Terms,* by Gershom Bradford: "Deep six—overboard."

Thus, to deep-six anything is to throw it overboard with an eye toward making its recovery unlikely. When used as a noun, the phrase is not hyphenated; as a verb, it takes a hyphen, contrary to COVER-UP, which is hyphenated only as a noun.

defeatist attack word against those urging caution, or withdrawal from what they consider indefensible positions.

Defeatism may be a state of mind about a social program, or a specific position (so labeled by the opposition) on a particular policy. In his 1936 campaign, Franklin Roosevelt recalled "the many cruel years" of the "era of tooth and claw" when poverty was accepted by "the defeatist attitude."

Charles A. Lindbergh and the America First group, with their worries about the invincibility of Nazism in Europe in the late thirties, were attacked as "defeatist." Then, as in the sixties, the word was often used in conjunction with "appeasers" (see APPEASEMENT); the word has never again reached the currency it had in the thirties, but it has occasionally appeared as an attack on the DOVES in U.S. Far Eastern policy.

See COPPERHEAD; NATTERING NABOBS OF NEGATIVISM; GLOOM AND DOOM, PROPHETS OF.

defining moment   significant action or event that illustrates character.

The phrase was first used in print by Howell Raines of the *New York Times*, in a 1983 article on John Glenn: "Confronted by Glenn and his 'constituency of the whole' candidacy, Walter Mondale has rallied the Democratic establishment. It is a defining moment."

Howell Raines provided the lexicographer with this definition of the term: "*Defining moment* is that point at which the essential character of a candidate or campaign stands revealed to the individual or political organization and to the external world."

Used frequently during the 1988 campaign, *defining moment* was usually applied to the character of an individual. By the time Secretary of State James A. Baker 3d appeared before the House Foreign Affairs Committee in 1990, however, the phrase was being used as a plural and applied to larger contexts. "The Iraqi invasion of Kuwait," Secretary Baker testified, "is one of the defining moments of a new era. . . . If we are to build a stable and more comprehensive peace, we must respond to the defining moments of this new era."

During the early 1990s, the widespread use of the phrase elevated the status of the participle "defining" to a full-fledged adjective, spawning such collocations as "defining event" (as in "the defining event of mid-20th-century America"), "defining achievement," and so on. On January 29, 1991, President George Bush began his State of the Union message with ringing words that lengthened the moment, crossing it with *shining hour:* "I come to this house of the people to speak to you and all Americans, certain that we stand at a defining hour."

defoliate   to expose jungle supply lines with the use of atomic, chemical, or incendiary weapons; one of the words used by Senator Goldwater in the 1964 presidential campaign that damaged him most.

Several times in the course of the presidential primaries of 1964, Barry Goldwater raised the possibility of "defoliating the jungle with low-yield atomic weapons" to interdict supplies to the Viet Cong from North Vietnam. When he repeated the point in a television interview, he added that he did not think it was a course the United States should follow. Democrats who were pressing the TRIGGER-HAPPY charge overlooked the senator's reservation in quoting his statement of the possibility of defoliation, and Goldwater adherents cried foul play and QUOTING OUT OF CONTEXT. However, the senator's previous references to the possibility without the reservation gave the charge credence.

At the Republican convention in San Francisco in 1964, civil rights demonstrators marched in front of the Cow Palace carrying signs that included "Defoliate Goldwater."

As the Vietnam War developed, napalm was used to defoliate areas suspected of covering trails or Viet Cong emplacements. In early 1967 the *Saturday Evening Post* reported the "slogan of the Air Force's flying defoliators: 'Only you can prevent forests.' "

New York Times correspondent Max Frankel used the word in 1967 in the sense of removing "confusing verbiage": "Every day someone is urging one side or the other to escalate or to de-escalate, to de-augment and to disinfiltrate, to pause temporarily or unconditionally and, above all, to negotiate. On paper, at least, it is time to defoliate. . . . The semantic defoliation might best begin with the genus negotium, the Latin root of 'negotiate,' meaning 'not easy.' "

deliberate speed.   See WITH ALL DELIBERATE SPEED.

deliver to make good on a political promise, especially the promise to turn out a vote for a candidate.

"Heaven help the legislator who does not deliver," said Illinois Democratic Senator Paul Douglas, shortly after his defeat by Charles Percy in 1966. He was talking about the PORK BARREL and the need for a legislator to promise and get federal projects built in his state.

The first recorded use of the word in a political sense was in a November 16, 1893, issue of *The Nation:* "No man is so fierce in his Americanism as . . . a boss who has 'delivered' the vote of his district as per contract." In that sense, to "deliver the vote" was similar to "deliver the goods," a phrase traceable to 1879. But a pejorative connotation was added when "the vote" did not mean all the votes in an area, but an individual vote or another man's influence. "The basis of the break," wrote the *Brooklyn Union* in 1904, "is said to have been a charge that Shevlin 'delivered' Boss McLaughlin in some deal without the latter's knowledge."

Politicians treat the word with enormous respect, because it touches on the essence of power. "There are no alibis in politics," said Kansas City boss Thomas Pendergast. "The delivery of votes is what counts. . . . All the ballyhoo and showmanship such as they have at the national conventions is all right. It's a great show. It gives folks a run for their money. It makes everybody feel good. But the man who makes the organization possible is the man who delivers the votes, and he doesn't deliver them by oratory. Politics is a business, just like anything else."

In its broader sense—to keep a political pledge—the word was used in the 1948 presidential campaign. Republican Thomas E. Dewey said, "The 80th Congress delivered as no other Congress ever did for the future of our country." President Harry Truman quoted that line to his "whistlestop" (see WHISTLESTOPPING) audiences, and punched: "I'll say it delivered. It delivered for the private power lobby. It delivered for the big oil company lobby. It delivered for the railroad lobby. It delivered for the real estate lobby. That's what the Republican candidate calls delivering for the future. Is that the kind of future you want?"

Senate Majority Leader Lyndon Johnson in 1958 used the word (in its deliver-the-vote sense) in international relations. After Johnson's statement on outer space to the UN Political Committee, India's V. K. Krishna Menon commented, "I wish that your country would give as much time to disarming as you give to preparations for arming." Johnson was not intimidated. "Well now, Mr. Ambassador, we're ready," he shot back. "We'll disarm tomorrow. Can you deliver the disarmament of the Communist bloc?"

Deliver is the put-up-or-shut-up word of politics. It calls the bluffs of political leaders and calls to account big-promising candidates. Reporter John Gunther, covering the unpredictable state of Ohio in his 1947 *Inside USA*, wrote: ". . . nobody is ever sure of Ohio. Once the manager of a presidential candidate, arriving in Columbus, asked the local boss if he could 'deliver' Ohio. The legend is that the local boss took a deep protesting breath, curled up his toes, and on the spot died of heart failure."

demagogue one who appeals to greed, fear, and hatred; a spellbinding orator, careless with facts and a danger to rational decision.

This is one of the enduring, slashing attack words of politics, in use since the American republic began. John Adams in 1808: "It is to no purpose to declaim against 'demagogues.' . . . Milo was as much an agitator for the patricians as Clodius for the plebeians; and Hamilton was as much a demagogue as Burr."

Being denounced as a demagogue is a sure sign to a speaker that he is making powerful points with some part of the public. In different historical periods, those most often denounced were Ben Butler, William Jennings Bryan, Huey Long, and Senator Joseph McCarthy. Reverend Thomas Dixon's attack on Bryan was typical: "a slobbering, mouthing demagogue, whose patriotism is in his jawbone." At one time, "slobber" was an operative verb for demagogue's noun. When Wilson's Secretary of War Newton Baker appealed for support of the League of Nations by referring to "the closed eyes of soldiers in American uniform who were dying and who whispered to me messages to bring to their mothers," Senator Key Pittman of Nevada replied, "The speaker who spoke before here, with his wild burst of oratory, with tears in his eyes and his brokendown, slobbering body across this rail, is trying to appeal to your sympathies, not to your judgment."

Theodore Roosevelt and William Howard Taft, after their falling-out, exchanged charges of "fathead" and "demagogue." Roosevelt observed in a letter to Henry Cabot Lodge: "When there is a great unrest, partly reasoning and partly utterly unreasoning and unreasonable, it becomes extremely difficult to beat a loudmouthed demagogue, especially if he is a demagogue of great wealth."

The appeal to emotion is not the only hallmark of the demagogue; an appeal to class is often included. When Democrat Al Smith broke with FDR, he made this point in words reminiscent of the earlier Roosevelt-Taft break: "I will take off my coat and fight to the end against any candidate who persists in any demagogic appeal to the masses of the working people of this country to destroy themselves by setting class against class and rich against poor!"

The word has had its defenders. It is from the Greek demagogos (leader of the people), which referred to the popular leaders who appeared in Athens during its period of decay. English journalist George Steevens, writing about the U.S. in 1897, held that "in a free country every politician must be something of a demagogue. Disraeli and Gladstone were both finished demagogues, and until we have two more great demagogues in England, politics will continue to be as dishwater." Muckraker Lincoln Steffens wrote in his autobiography: "I had begun to suspect that, whenever a man in public life was called a demagogue, there was something good in him, something dangerous to the system."

But the popular conception of the word was given most eloquently by a President not known for his eloquence, Calvin Coolidge: ". . . the final approval of the people is given not to demagogues, slavishly pandering to their selfishness, merchandising with the clamor of the hour, but to statesmen, ministering to their welfare, representing their deep, silent, abiding convictions."

The word has retained all of its original sting. Relations between Presidents Truman and Eisenhower permanently cooled when Truman referred to Eisenhower's "I shall GO TO KOREA" statement as "a piece of demagoguery." In 1992 George Bush used the word as a verb: "We can't demagogue this."

The final g in the adjective demagogic is soft; the more difficult-to-pronounce and spell demagoguery, with its final g hard, is more commonly used in the U.S. than demagogy, final g soft, which is British usage.

demand-pull. See INFLATION.

Democrat a member of one of the two major U.S. political parties, or "democrat with a small *d*": one who favors strong governmental action for the welfare of the many.

It was under Andrew Jackson that the Democratic party, founded in 1828, began using its present name, but "democrat" was current long before that. "Washington," wrote John Adams scornfully toward the end of the eighteenth century, "appointed a multitude of democrats and jacobins of the deepest dye. I have been more cautious in this respect." Others shared his low esteem. A popular poem in the early days of the Republic was Fessenden's "Democracy Unveiled":

> *And I'll unmask the democrat,*
> *Your sometimes this thing, sometimes that,*
> *Whose life is one dishonest shuffle,*
> *Lest he perchance the mob should ruffle.*

The Federalists sneered at Thomas Jefferson's Republicans as "democrats"—panderers to the mob; they in turn scorned the Federalists as "aristocrats." Still, by 1856 the Middletown (N.Y.) *Banner of Liberty* could write that "the name Democrat has become so honorable that all sorts of isms and new-fangled parties claim the name."

In 1955 Leonard Hall, a former Republican National Chairman, began referring to the "Democrat" rather than the "Democratic" party, a habit begun by Thomas E. Dewey. Hall dropped the "ic," he said, because "I think their claims that they represent the great mass of the people, and we don't, is just a lot of bunk." The University of Virginia's Atcheson L. Hench said of this usage in *American Speech* magazine: "Whether they have meant to imply that the party was no longer democratic, or whether they banked on the harsher sound pattern of the new name; whether they wanted to strengthen the impression that they were speaking for a new Republican party by using a new name for the opposition, or whether they had other reasons, the fact remains that . . . highly influential speakers . . . used the shorter adjective."

Some Democrats suggested retaliating by shortening REPUBLICAN to Publican, but the National Committee overruled them, explaining that Republican "is the name by which our opponents' product is known and mistrusted."

Probably the best-known modern quote involving the word comes from Will Rogers: "I belong to no organized party. I am a Democrat."

Republican Theodore Roosevelt, campaigning in the Deep South, supposedly told the classic why-I'm-a-Democrat story. When asked why he was a Democrat, a Southerner replied, "Because my father was a Democrat and my grandfather was a Democrat." A Northerner countered, "What if your father was a horse thief and your grandfather was a horse thief, what would you have been then?" The Southerner's reply: "In that case, I guess I'd have been a Republican."

demonstration. See MARCH ON WASHINGTON.

deniability. See SIGN OFF ON.

Depression party recurrent Democratic attack against the Republican party since the 1932 campaign; considered demagogic now, often compared to the Republican charge that Democrats are the WAR PARTY.

After Herbert Hoover had been defeated largely by the "Depression party" charge, some Republicans in 1933 sought to attach the Depression label on the Democrats. The feeble effort was devastated by FDR: ". . .

although I rubbed my eyes when I read it, we have been told that it was not a Republican depression but a Democratic depression. . . . Now, there is an old and somewhat lugubrious adage that says: 'Never speak of rope in the house of a man who has been hanged.' In the same way, if I were a Republican leader speaking to a mixed audience, the last word in the whole dictionary that I think I would use is that word 'depression.' "

Harry Truman took up the Depression party charge in his GIVE 'EM HELL campaign of 1948, especially relating it to the DO-NOTHING CONGRESS: "The Republican party has shown in the Congress of the last two years that the leopard does not change its spots. It is still the party of the Harding-Coolidge boom and Hoover depression."

Republican Dwight Eisenhower deplored what he felt was an outmoded and unfair attack on his party. In his memoirs he wrote: "For more than twenty years economic depression had been the skeleton in the Republican closet, locked in by demagogues. In many minds [in 1954] the suspicion lurked that this problem might once again prove to be the party's undoing."

See RUNNING AGAINST HOOVER.

depth polling   motivation research; pollsters' questions that go beyond voting intention.

A man's current attitudes and opinions, studied alongside his previous voting behavior and his social and ethnic background, help behavioral scientists predict the way he will vote and—more important—what political appeals may get him to vote another way.

"Depth polling" has been adopted as the operative phrase by some political communications experts because "motivation research" has acquired such a bad image. The latter phrase, used by Dr. Ernest Dichter and others, excori-

ated by author Vance Packard in *The Hidden Persuaders,* led to criticism like this by Professor (later Senator) S. I. Hayakawa, a leading linguist: "Motivation researchers are those harlot social scientists who, in impressive psychoanalytic and/or sociological jargon, tell their clients what their clients want to hear, namely, that appeals to human irrationality are likely to be far more profitable than appeals to rationality."

Polling pioneer Dr. Elmo Roper answered the author's query: "The phrase which is usually used is 'polling in depth' and what that means is nothing more than a check to learn the difference in attitude by various sub-groups in the population and even more particularly, *why* they hold whatever attitude they do hold. As a matter of fact, the first term applied generally to this type of probe was 'depth interview.' Apparently the newspapers insist on the word 'poll,' and 'depth interview' became 'polling in depth.' "

Dr. George Gallup responded as well, also resisting depth polling, the phrase used by laymen: "Usually the expression is 'interviewing in depth'— or this may be shortened to 'depth interviewing.' This term goes back to 1935. Dr. Paul Lazarsfeld introduced this concept into American research. It typically refers to the long cross-examination of a person with many questions to get at his thinking on a given issue. Today many persons use the term 'depth interviewing' when they have asked more than a few questions on the same subject."

Three levels of polling are currently used, occasionally by the same pollsters: the STRAW POLL or NOSE COUNT; *issues polls,* indicating voter feelings about specific issues; and *depth polls.* See POLLSTER. More recently, *focus groups* have been assembled by pollsters to measure reactions.

None of these should be confused with *exit polls,* taken chiefly by members of the news media, in which people leaving the voting booth are asked how they voted. Exit polls have been taken since the late 1960s and are useful in projecting winners but regarded by some as interfering with the orderly voting process.

When a pollster's forecast is accurate, it is not news; when it is wrong, the words of Jesus to the Pharisees (Matthew 16:3) are recalled: "O ye hypocrites, ye can discern the face of the sky; but can ye not discern the signs of the times?"

deserving Democrats party workers worthy of patronage reward.

Three-time candidate William Jennings Bryan, when he became Woodrow Wilson's Secretary of State, tried to take care of a few old friends. He wrote to the receiver-general of the Dominican Republic, Walter W. Vick, on August 20, 1913, asking if he could find some places in the customs administration of that country. Bryan's letter contained the phrase in the following question: "Can you let me know what positions you have at your disposal with which to reward deserving Democrats?"

The letter was indiscreet; Republicans denounced it as an attempted extension of the SPOILS SYSTEM into the administration of a foreign country under U.S. domination.

Democrat Felix Frankfurter explained in 1924 why he was bolting to vote for a third party: "The Republican party is frankly standpat—things are all right. To the Democrats, also, things are all right, only those who administer them are not. What the country needs is 'honest' Democrats and, doubtless, William J. Bryan would add, 'deserving Democrats.'"

The phrase has long ago lost its sting and is now used affectionately; Republicans appeal to "discerning Democrats" for crossover support.

destabilize euphemism for "overthrow."

Director of Central Intelligence William Colby disclosed to a congressional committee in April 1974 that the CIA had spent $8 million in Chile between 1970 and 1973 in an effort to make it difficult for Marxist Salvador Allende Gossens to govern.

"The goal of the clandestine CIA activities," wrote Seymour M. Hersh in the *New York Times* on September 8, 1974, ". . . was to 'destabilize' the Marxist government . . ."

Since the word was a freshly coined euphemism, and since it appeared to conflict with sworn testimony by Secretary of State Kissinger that "the CIA had nothing to do with the coup," the term was used with savage glee by critics of covert U.S. activities.

Curiously, the word was used again, in a positive sense, early in the Carter Administration. U.S. Ambassador to the UN Andrew Young (see POINT MAN) discussed Cuban intervention in Africa as possibly proving to be a "stabilizing force." As Cuban troop strength grew in Africa in 1978, critics of the Carter foreign policy used "stabilizing force" against the Carter men, much as critics of Mr. Kissinger had used "destabilization" against him.

See CIA-ESE.

détente an improvement in relations between nations, warmer than accommodation, cooler than rapprochement.

Woven through the history of the post–World War II period is the word *détente,* or such rough equivalents as *thaw,* ACCOMMODATION, *normalization of relations,* or *opening to the East.* When President Eisenhower met the Soviet Union's dual leaders, Nikolai Bulganin and Nikita Khrushchev, at Geneva in July 1955, he told them, "We have come to find a basis for accommodation which will make life safer and happier not only for the nations we represent but for the people elsewhere."

The thaw begun at Geneva later froze over; during the Cuban missile crisis of 1962, President Kennedy wrote Khrushchev: "If your letter signifies that you are prepared to discuss a détente affecting NATO and the Warsaw Pact, we are quite prepared to consider with our allies any useful proposals." In his *Kennedy*, Ted Sorensen described the subsequent search for areas of agreement as "the emerging détente." He added: "The breathing spell had become a pause, the pause was becoming a détente and no one could foresee what further changes lay ahead."

Ahead lay the escalation of the war in Vietnam; not until 1971, with the progress of arms-limitation talks and the announcement of a visit to mainland China, did détente become an active possibility.

The heyday of "détente," in policy and in usage, was in 1972 and 1973, as U.S. and Soviet leaders held summit conferences and launched arms-control agreements. After the Nixon resignation, President Ford found both policy and word becoming a burden, as hard-liners previously kept at bay by Nixon attacked détente as a SELL-OUT, GIVEAWAY, and a "one-way street." Henry Kissinger's policy was described as "like going to a wife-swapping party and coming home alone."

The Soviet Union resented the attack on the word, rightly interpreting it as an attack on the Brezhnev policies. On January 4, 1976, *Pravda* denounced those in the U.S. who were critical of "one-way advantages" won by the Soviets. "Some people with weak nerves," said the Soviet official organ, "losing self-control, are even speaking in extremes. The pseudo-oracle William Safire, who spread himself across the pages of the *New York Times* on

New Year's Eve, croaked: 'Détente is dead. The second cold war has begun.'"

President Carter in 1977 tried to take some of the onus off the now-controversial word by defining it in a Notre Dame speech as "progress toward peace." In a *Foreign Affairs* piece (December 1977) gutsily titled "Russia, America and Détente," former Ford State Department counselor Helmut Sonnenfeldt wrote: "Some of our debates about Soviet policy have tended to turn more on the definition of the labels that have been attached to it than on substance. 'CONTAINMENT,' 'COLD WAR,' 'an era of negotiation,' 'détente' . . . all caught elements of the complex realities . . . but over time they came to obscure rather than illuminate them."

The word has had its tongue-in-cheek defenders. David Braaten of the *Washington Star* wrote in 1973: "In the world of clichés, it is always comforting to have a reliable, steady favorite like détente." Pointing to its use in Bizet's eighteenth-century translation of Herodotus about a period preceding the Spartan sack of Athens, and to its resuscitation by *New York Sun* editorialist Mortimer Lovelace rhapsodizing the Locarno Pact in the twenties, Braaten added: "It meets all the requirements: it is French, and therefore impossible for Americans to pronounce with any degree of certainty; it is short enough to fit in a one-column headline, should that unfortunate necessity arise, yet full-bodied enough to add solidity and a sense of importance to a four-column head-cum-kicker; its meaning is only hazily grasped by its users, and, perhaps most important of all, it means nothing whatever to the reader."

Strangely, a cousin of "détente" is rarely used, except among diplomats: *démarche* means "step forward," or improvement of relations, and clichémarkers can hope that its day will come.

In the late 1980s, *détente* was lightly referred to around Washington as the "D-word" (see -WORD).

deterrent   a military force or weapons system whose strength, real or feigned, is capable of forestalling an enemy attack by the threat of devastating retaliation.

"The major deterrent is in a man's mind," wrote Admiral Arleigh Burke in 1960. "The major deterrent in the future is going to be not only what we have, but what we do, what we are willing to do, what they think we will do. Stamina, guts, standing up for the things that we say—those are deterrents."

The concept of preparedness as a deterrent is an old one. In his first annual address to both houses of Congress, George Washington said in 1790: "To be prepared for war is one of the most effectual means of preserving peace." James Monroe, for one, argued otherwise. "Preparation for war," he said in 1818, "is a constant stimulus to suspicion and ill-will." But many agreed with Washington. "Speak softly and carry a big stick," Theodore Roosevelt said in 1901. "You will go far."

In 1940, FDR defended the draft by saying: "Your boys are not going to be sent into any foreign wars. They are going into training to form a force so strong that, by its very existence, it will keep the threat of war far away from our shores." (See AGAIN AND AGAIN AND AGAIN.)

Nuclear weapons were believed by many to be the most powerful deterrent of all against a major war. Though they did not prevent minor wars, they kept them from "escalating" into major conflicts. "What has really happened," Walter Lippmann wrote of the Korean truce in 1953, "is that both sides and all concerned have been held within a condition of mutual deterrent."

Israeli Foreign Minister Abba Eban gave a new wrinkle to the definition in 1966 after his country attacked a Jordanian town in an effort to halt Arab terrorism. He called it "demonstrative deterrence"; a year later the Israelis preferred "pre-emptive strike." This was, however, short of PREVENTIVE WAR—an idea put forward as a means of preventing China from growing too menacing. See MASSIVE RETALIATION; DOOMSDAY MACHINE; SALT.

deviationism.   See REVISIONISM.

Devil is in the details   the smallest particulars may prove the most troubling; a need to attend to the tiniest details.

The nitpickers' creed, *the Devil is in the details* has become a key clause in arms negotiations. It appeared as early as 1978 in economic reporting, when Hobart Rowen of the *Washington Post* was told by a source in Bremen, "There is an old German saying that the Devil is in the details."

By 1987, the saying was being used by Max M. Kampelman, the United States arms negotiator; he acknowledged to Reuters that agreement with the Soviets was being reached on intrusive verification, but he added, "You know the Devil is in the details." Used frequently during 1987, this expression was described by *Newsweek* that year as "the old arms-negotiation maxim, 'The Devil is in the details.'"

Written sometimes with a small *d*, *Devil* is usually capitalized to signify the figure of Satan, not some minor vexation. The Devil, however, may not have been part of this quotation's source.

A variant form of this saying is *God is in the details*. That version was used by the German Bauhaus architect

Ludwig Mies van der Rohe and is sometimes attributed to the nineteenth-century French novelist Gustave Flaubert, but no citation for Flaubert's use of the expression has been found.

devolution   transfer of power from a central government to a region or locality; sometimes used as a euphemism for secession or separation.

In a general sense, *devolution* is a synonym for "power sharing," a movement that grew popular in the sixties and seventies as charges of "bureaucracy" were often leveled at centralized authority.

Frequent use of the word began in connection with HOME RULE in Ireland, and extended to the calls for "more local say" to outright independence, from Scotland to Quebec. Most early citations in the seventies are from the *Times Literary Supplement*.

In 1975 the *Wall Street Journal* described British Prime Minister Harold Wilson's moves to meet Scottish demands: "The government policy is called 'devolution'—the decentralizing of many government powers and functions." In 1976 columnist C. L. Sulzberger of the *New York Times* wrote: "Arguments over 'devolution' versus local 'nationalism' rage in non-English sections of the United Kingdom including Scotland, Wales and Northern Ireland. It is not merely a matter of reviving relatively little-used languages like Gaelic and Welsh but of actually shifting major authority including title to mineral wealth into regional hands."

In Canada, the separatists of Quebec—who wanted to withdraw from English-speaking Canada and to set up their own French-speaking state—used "devolution" as a less revolutionary-sounding word than "secession." The word seems closer to "evolution" than "revolution," and is

useful to those who want to maintain a moderate-sounding position before demanding or declaring "independence."

Dewey blitz   the second-ballot pressure by the Dewey forces that enabled them to wrest the nomination from Senator Robert Taft in the 1948 Republican convention.

Three Republican candidates led the field in 1948: Dewey, Taft, and Harold Stassen. 548 convention votes meant nomination. On the first ballot, Dewey received 434, Taft 224, and Stassen 157. The favorite-son delegations of Senator Arthur Vandenberg (Michigan) and Governor Earl Warren (California) were considered least likely to change on the second ballot; the favorite-son delegations of Illinois and Tennessee were likely to switch to Taft. That meant Dewey had to pick up other favorite-son delegations, plus strength from Stassen, to hold his momentum.

Led by New York attorney Herbert Brownell, the Dewey organization "leaned on" (see FEET TO THE FIRE) the Stassen voters; important defections were achieved from the Iowa, Maryland, Nebraska, and South Dakota delegations. Though Stassen picked up scattered votes elsewhere, his second-ballot total dropped to 149; Dewey's increased to 515 and Taft's to 274. Thus, the Dewey second-ballot increase was 81 to Taft's 50—and the STAMPEDE was on.

If liberal columnist Max Lerner did not coin the phrase "Dewey blitz," he was at least an early user. Lerner wrote that Dewey won the nomination "not because he had principles or even appeal, but because he had a machine. The machine was ruthless and well oiled, run by a group of slick and modern operators. It combined the age-old methods of power politics with the newest strategies of blitz warfare and the precision tools of American industry and administration."

The word *Blitz* (German for "lightning") was still relatively new in its military context and referred to fast-moving mechanized warfare carried out by Nazi armored divisions in early World War II. In 1941 the Birmingham (U.K.) *Sunday Mercury* asked: "If the last war's *strafe* is this war's *blitz*, what will it become in the war after next?"

In its English form—lightning—the word enjoyed a brief political vogue in the 1880s. Alabama Democrats adopted a "lightning creed" in 1880, to turn out the Reconstruction Republicans and Negroes. "No man can be appointed (in Alabama) to hold a precinct election," Illinois Representative J. H. Rowell told the House in 1890, "unless he is known to be a 'lightning man,' a ballot-box stuffer, a false counter."

The Dewey blitz brought the word into U.S. politics; the phrase is still used by politicians to refer to excellent convention organization, and "blitz" has been adopted to describe saturation television campaigns.

A "TV blitz" in politics is a concentration of advertising in the last week of the campaign, aimed at the "undecided" and at turning out the vote of the committed. Since 1952, when admen Al Hollender and Rosser Reeves created the Eisenhower "spot" campaign, half-hour speeches have given way to spots of one minute, twenty-, or ten-second duration, selling hard to huge audiences. But like all MADISON AVENUE TECHNIQUES, they are troubling. "These new techniques," wrote James Perry in the *National Observer*, "are so overwhelming, so terribly effective. Some day, maybe they will elect a truly dangerous and sinister man to high office."

dial back reduce or lower the controls; decrease the pressure.

A favorite *Newsweek* locution, the phrase *dial back* appeared in the newsmagazine in late 1980: "As a result, 'Kemp-Roth will be dialed back in the Republican-controlled Senate as well as in the House,' says one well-wired Congressional tax expert." In that same issue of *Newsweek* was this comment on Massachusetts Governor Edward King: "King has dialed back on his tax-cut pledges and watched his popularity plummet."

Rich Thomas, a *Newsweek* reporter, pointed to engineering controls as the metaphor's source, adding, "When you get too much steam in a boiler, you move the pressure dials back." Others disagree with this etymology, however, contending that to "move the dials back" does not reduce steam pressure; instead, the pressure-relief valve must be opened, an action that differs from dialing back.

dialogue genuine two-way communication, or the pretense thereof.

The phrase "national dialogue" was popularized by Adlai Stevenson in his 1952 campaign as part of his theme, "let's talk sense to the American people." The word appealed to John F. Kennedy, who used it often, as in a 1962 Yale speech: ". . . the dialogue between the parties—between business and government—is clogged by illusion and platitude . . ."

In current political usage, the word has an intellectual, slightly wistful connotation; a *dialogue* is more pointed than a *discussion*, less heated than an *argument*, less formal than a *debate*. It is used to describe the establishment of wary communication between divergent groups; when modified by "meaningful," the word becomes meaningless. See ISSUES, THE.

diaper in the ring. See HAT IN THE RING.

diehards dwindling handful committed to a losing cause, fighting long after hope of victory is gone.

In 1911 British Prime Minister Herbert Henry Asquith was determined to reduce the veto power of the House of Lords over the House of Commons. He extracted a trump card from the previous King, Edward VII, and held George V to it as well: if the House of Lords would not go along with a reduction of power, the King would appoint as many new peers to that House as necessary to get the deciding vote.

A substantial group in the House of Lords, led by Lord Halsbury, refused to go along; they said they would "die in the last ditch," and became known as the "Diehards." Wrote R. J. Minney in a history of 10 Downing Street: "Behind the scenes the 'Diehards' held angry meetings over dinner and exchanged letters in one at least of which violence was advocated if necessary." But other peers were not prepared to die hard; they accepted a two-year veto compromise and deserted the "Diehards." The King recorded in his diary: "The Halsburyites were, Thank God, beaten. It is indeed a great relief to me—I am spared any further humiliation by a creation of peers."

The British political use of diehard was taken from the nickname of the Middlesex Regiment, the 57th Foot; at the Battle of Albuera in 1811, Colonel William Inglis was badly wounded and refused to be taken to the rear, crying "Die hard, men, die hard!" The phrase was reinforced in America because George Washington's last words were reported to be "It is well. I die hard, but am not afraid to go."

See ROCK-RIBBED.

dime's worth of difference, not a a minor-party sneer at the similarity between the two major parties.

The phrase was central to the presidential campaigns of Alabama Governor George Corley Wallace, who stressed the need to SEND THEM A MESSAGE—"them," in Governor Wallace's eyes, being the "pointed-headed professors" in Washington who dominated the planning of both the Democratic and the Republican parties.

Governor Wallace informed the author in 1976: "I do not recall the exact date that we first used the phrases 'dime's worth of difference' and 'pointed-headed.' Both of these, I am sure, were used initially in 1967 as we were preparing for the third party campaign and gaining ballot positions. To the best of my knowledge, both of these expressions were original with me and something that I just thought of and put into an extemporaneous speech. The expressions were received well by the crowds and I continued to use them."

See ME TOO.

dinosaur wing an attack term against extreme conservatives.

A parenthetical remark by Adlai Stevenson in a speech at the Mormon Tabernacle, Salt Lake City, Utah, October 14, 1952, either coined or popularized the phrase: "Yet the same Republicans (the dinosaur-wing of that party) who object to service from our Government—who call everything 'creeping socialism' . . . who hint darkly of 'dictatorship'—these same men begin to hint that we are 'subversive,' or at best the tools of our country's enemies, when we boast of the great strides toward social justice and security we have already made . . ."

It is possible that Stevenson saw the word used in the *New York Times* the day before: "Anybody who gets indignant [over corruption] is a hypocritical old dinosaur." A similar metaphor was used in the mid-nineteenth century to describe former Whigs, "the fossil remains of an extinct party."

The predecessor phrase was "Neanderthal wing." The Truman Library has an unsigned memorandum dated June 29, 1948, probably written by Judge Samuel Rosenman, urging Truman to call back Congress after the Democratic convention because "it would keep a steady glare of publicity on the Neanderthal men of the Republican party . . ." Columnists Evans and Novak used "Stone Age Republican" in this sense.

In a story on Chicago Mayor Richard J. Daley, the *Saturday Evening Post* in 1964 gave the word a bipartisan connotation: "The last dinosaur wins again."

The dinosaur made another foray out of extinction in American business lingo when George Romney, then president of American Motors, launched a compact-car campaign attacking the "gas-guzzling dinosaurs" of the road. When he entered politics, it was just a question of time before he adapted his best-known phrase, and the time came in spring of 1967 when he told a political audience "the Great Society has become a tax-guzzling dinosaur."

The word "dinosaur" was coined by Sir Richard Owen in 1841 from the Greek *deinos* (fearful) and *sauros* (lizard) before it was discovered that the beast would have registered as a vegetarian.

See RADICAL RIGHT; BIRCHER; LITTLE OLD LADIES IN TENNIS SHOES; KOOKS, NUTS AND; TROGLODYTIC. In the other direction, see PINKO; FELLOW TRAVELER; FLAMING LIBERAL.

dip/double dip economic decline; with "double," a return to recession.

Dip began as a verb in Old English, akin to Germanic words for *"deep."* By 1599, *dip* was used as a noun, usually for a brief plunge or dive into water. That downward movement led to an economic sense of "financial downturn."

Two downturns in quick succession form a *double dip*, often used as a hyphenated term to modify *recession*. In February 1975, *Business Week* attributed the first use to an unidentified economist in the Ford Administration: "What is now likely is a 'double-dip recession,' as one Administration economist puts it." Three months later, the same publication offered a financial view that "portrays a double-dip recession in which the economy recovers in the second half of 1975 but lapses into decline again in 1976," but this double dip did not occur.

The alliterative term returned in late 1991, when a manufacturing executive commented on his colleagues' view of the economy: "Interestingly, only 3 percent expect a double dip, so I think while they see a weaker than expected recovery, manufacturers don't expect us to fall back in recession." That double dip, and George Bush's belated reaction to it, became the central issue of the 1992 campaign.

Double dip began as a sign not of decline but of lavish or excessive offering. An ice-cream store clerk, to provide a double dip, would place two scoops on a single cone. Such excess probably led to the popularization of *double dipping* for "the taking of income from two government sources simultaneously."

For a graphic example of *double dip*, see DEAD-CAT BOUNCE.

diplomacy when used as the second element in a phrase, a disparagement of the handling of negotiations between nations.

This word, which dates back to 1796, comes from the Greek *diploma*, meaning "folded paper," a letter folded so that its contents remain secret. Within the last century, however, it has become the basis of noun phrases, usually derogatory, that reflect various approaches to international relations.

Dollar diplomacy first appeared in *Harper's Weekly* in 1910; during the Taft Administration, Secretary of State Philander C. Knox was criticized for throwing money at politicians in Honduras. By 1912, though, William Howard Taft spoke in favor of "substituting dollars for bullets" in a talk that became known as his "Dollar Diplomacy" speech.

Gunboat diplomacy was first used in 1927. This phrase referred to the use of military force for Western domination of China in the early twentieth century, when American and British interests were protected by the threatened force of gunboats. (See GUNBOAT DIPLOMACY.)

Media diplomacy, which can denote the use of satellite telecasts for diplomatic meetings of opposing nations, is more often used to cast aspersion on the attempts of diplomats to use television interviews to conduct foreign relations.

Ping-Pong diplomacy named the first efforts to open relations between China and the West. *Ping-Pong*, a trademark for table tennis, is the game whose players were used in 1970 Sino-American diplomatic moves.

Public diplomacy appeared by early 1976 in the Republican party's platform. Richard Allen, the foreign-policy analyst, used the term in the platform's section on national security: "A strong and effective program of global public diplomacy is a vital component of U.S. foreign policy." Flourishing during the Reagan Administration, *public diplomacy* was defined by Gilbert A. Robinson, President Reagan's first deputy director of the United States Information Agency, as a different form of media diplomacy; according to Robinson, "Governments are learning that while bilateral diplomacy has its place, a television special on a given policy can often have more impact on a foreign government's actions than a host of traditional diplomatic exchanges."

Quiet diplomacy was Henry Kissinger's preference. This phrase, with its suggestion of diplomatic activity behind the scenes, was also used on occasion by President Reagan.

Shuttle diplomacy appeared in 1973. *Time* magazine reported a year later that Kissinger traveled to the Middle East "for another round of 'shuttle diplomacy.'" This term may have been based on the National Aeronautics and Space Administration's "space shuttle," then in the news, or the earlier Eastern Airlines shuttle service between New York and Washington, although *shuttle* as a verb dates back to the fourteenth century.

dirty politics unethical practices in campaigning: ballot-box stuffing, mudslinging, character assassination, and other chicanery.

Franklin D. Roosevelt, Jr.'s, characterization of Hubert Humphrey as a "draft-dodger" in the 1960 West Virginia primary (while Roosevelt was campaigning for John F. Kennedy) was described by the *Washington Star* as "a new low in dirty politics." Bruce Felknor, executive director of the Fair Campaign Practices Committee, in 1966 compiled a volume of low tricks, smears, and unethical attacks entitled *Dirty Politics*.

American slang includes *dirty pool, dirty wash, dirty linen, dirty work,* and *dirty word*. With a small addition of water, dirt becomes *mud*, leading to *political mudbaths,* MUDSLINGING, and *mudsills*.

Oddly, there is no antonym for dirty politics: clean politics is not a phrase in use. PRACTICAL POLITICS carries a connotation of cynicism, *power politics* and *smart politics* slightly more, and *dirty politics* the most.

Each phrase is purely subjective. Often a campaign manager will wire a protest about his opposition's radio or TV spots to the station manager just before an election, with a copy to the FCC, threatening a suit for libel. Unless the spots are in the candidate's own voice, the station will ordinarily take them off the air for at least several hours until a decision is made or the spots modified. The spots might have been accurate or innocuous, but the protest knocks them off for a while. To the party pulling the trick, it is smart politics; to the party on the receiving end, it is dirty politics.

dirty tricks as "Department of Dirty Tricks," the nickname of the covert operations of the Central Intelligence Agency; since the Watergate scandals, a disapproving term for campaign smears and disruptive activities of a "black advance."

In the sixties, applied to the CIA, the phrase had a ring of derring-do, since it was felt that democracies had to fight cold-war fire with fire of their own: a *Time* cover story on Richard Helms (February 24, 1967) described a post he had held as "deputy chief of the plans division, the so-called 'dirty tricks' department . . ." Soon after criticism mounted of our support of South Vietnam, columnist Walter Lippmann began to wonder about those activities: "The question before us today is whether the activities of the CIA which are outside genuine intelligence, that is to say its black propaganda, its interventionist operations, its 'dirty tricks,' are truly in the national interest."

The phrase "dirty trick" can be traced back to 1674, but was rarely used politically, and if so, not in the way it was applied to the CIA: a lighthearted description of serious, sometimes murderous, acts. In 1972 it was used in a general sense by Margaret Truman in a biography of her father: "Along with the smears and lies Dad

was continually rebutting, the Republicans threw in a few dirty tricks aimed specifically at our campaign train. A 'TRUTH SQUAD' followed us around the country, issuing statements that supposedly countered Dad's speeches. In Buffalo they hired a horde of school children who tried to drown out Dad with screams and catcalls, anticipating by twenty years the Students for a Democratic Society."

In March of 1973, however, the phrase in the CIA sense was applied to politics in the Watergate scandals. "Money from the safe, it is alleged," wrote the *National Observer* on March 10, "was used to finance Republican 'dirty tricks' during the campaign." The *New York Times* on April 29: "Last week, it was disclosed that a third private treasury of about $600,000 [was] used to finance a variety of dirty tricks." In the July 23 *New Yorker,* Common Cause president John Gardner told reporter Elizabeth Drew that the activity could not be minimized by using the ironic phrase: "'Some of the highest officials of this nation carried on a sustained and systematic attempt to destroy our form of government. It wasn't "dirty tricks" within the system—it was an attempt to subvert the system . . .'"

Although Nixon speechwriter Patrick Buchanan sought to draw distinctions between time-honored pranks and illegal campaign practices (see HARDBALL), the phrase "dirty tricks" lost its smirk and became a serious term for criminal, or at least obviously unethical politicking. Right after the Watergate scandal, *New York Times* reporter Seymour Hersh broke the CIA scandal, and the new seriousness with which outside-the-law activities were perceived underscored the new meaning of "dirty tricks." As the bridge between the Watergate and CIA investigations, the phrase became embedded in the vocabulary of unethical dealing and is likely to be used as an attack phrase in the future—which, in itself, is a mild form of "dirty trick."

See SMEAR; ROORBACK; GUTTER FLYER.

disadvantaged   a euphemism for "poor," replacing "underprivileged" in social workers' jargon.

As a result of the civil rights movement of the fifties and sixties, it was felt that no citizen was "privileged," though many were "advantaged," thus the substitution. Since "underadvantaged" is cumbersome, "disadvantaged"—without the advantages of education and opportunity—was selected.

In the same way, what used to be called a "slum" is now delicately referred to as "a culturally deprived environment."

A cartoon by Jules Feiffer published in 1965 shows a man saying to himself: "I used to think I was poor. Then they told me I wasn't poor, I was needy. They told me it was self-defeating to think of myself as needy, I was deprived. Then they told me underprivileged was overused. I was disadvantaged. I still don't have a dime. But I have a great vocabulary."

disaster metaphors   natural catastrophe is commonplace in political language. Beginning with a mild GROUNDSWELL (a heavy rolling sea due to a distant storm), a candidate's fortunes may move forward like a *prairie fire,* his headquarters *flooded* with telegrams of support, leading him to a WHIRLWIND CAMPAIGN, but a *tidal wave* or FIRESTORM of criticism after a scandal has *erupted* may lead to an AVALANCHE of votes against him and an electoral LANDSLIDE for his opponent, leaving him *snowed under* and wondering how he could have been *blitzed* (German for "lightning," which candidates hope will strike) by a threat that seemed, at the beginning,

like a cloud no bigger than a man's hand (I Kings 18:44).

Typical of a political disaster comment was William Allen White's assessment of the defeat of Alfred Landon in 1936: "It was not an election the country has just undergone, but a political Johnstown flood."

disgrace to the human race.   See THREE-MARTINI LUNCH.

dish the Whigs   to steal the opposition's clothes; to win by reversing long-held stands.

In nineteenth-century English slang, "to dish" was to defeat decisively, especially by trickery; the term probably came from the notion of cooking something and serving it well-done, though there is also speculation that it is derived from the Old English "disherit," now "disinherit": to take away one's inheritance.

When England's Conservative party surprised itself and the world by passing the radical Reform Bill of 1867—thereby enfranchising two million workingmen, a goal of its Whig opposition for many years—the Prime Minister, Lord Derby, said delightedly, "Don't you see we have dished the Whigs?" With the aid of Benjamin Disraeli, who was to succeed him as head of the Tories, Derby had indeed won support that had been taken for granted by the opposition.

The British phrase was a favorite of *Newsweek* columnist Stewart Alsop's, and is still used by history buffs to describe a flip-flop: "Seldom in Western politics since Disraeli's Reform Bill of 1867," declared a *New York Times* editorial about Nixon summiteering on February 10, 1972, "—when Lord Derby boasted, 'We've dished the Whigs'—has a national leader so completely turned his back on a lifetime of beliefs to adopt those of his political opponents."

The Derby reference was especially piquant, since his only other famous remark was: "When I first came into Parliament, Mr. Tierney, a great Whig authority, used always to say that the duty of an Opposition was very simple—it was, to oppose everything, and propose nothing." That statement has been shortened to "the duty of an Opposition is to oppose" and, ironically, is attributed to the politician who won by adopting the tenets of his opposition.

disinformation. See PROPAGANDA.

disintermediation. See ECONOMIC JARGON.

dissent. See PRESIDENT OF ALL THE PEOPLE; ACTIVIST.

divorce issue the question raised about the "morality" of a candidate who has been divorced.

The *youth issue* has died; the *divorce issue* is dying. The marriage of Andrew Jackson to divorcee Rachel Donelson Robards caused a stir, particularly since her divorce was in question; and Wallis Simpson's divorced status made it necessary for King Edward VIII to abdicate in order to marry her.

The first divorced man to run for President was James Cox in 1920. According to some accounts, a deal was suspected: the GOP would not mention Cox's divorce, and the Democrats would not whisper about Harding's mistresses.

In modern times, divorce itself is not the issue; Adlai Stevenson had been divorced when he ran for President in 1952, and that fact was never very important. It is remarriage after a divorce that rankles a portion of the public, and "home-wrecking" is considered the worst sin of all.

Nelson Rockefeller was divorced in 1961; he was re-elected governor of New York in 1962 by a comfortable half-million votes. Before the election, social critic Cleveland Amory observed that "he's certain to get the divorce vote and remember that's one in four these days." But in May 1963 he married Margaretta Fitler ("Happy") Murphy, herself recently divorced, and without assured custody of her five children; there was a measurable reaction.

"People will forgive a politician they love almost any sin," wrote Theodore White, "—as witness James Michael Curley, Huey Long, Adam Clayton Powell, Jimmy Walker, and a score of others; in matters of romance, particularly, they will forgive him almost any peccadillo . . . so long as the peccadillo is not flaunted. But the frank and open acceptance of a new marriage was a breach with the general indulgence of the hypocrisy of politics . . ."

In the crucial California primary against Barry Goldwater in 1964, the divorce issue hurt Rockefeller—but until the final weekend, the polls showed him ahead. That weekend, "Happy" Rockefeller bore the candidate a son; the newspapers were filled with the story of Rockefeller's flying visit to the hospital, a fresh reminder of the divorce and remarriage. An insidious slogan, "Elect a leader, not a lover" was pressed home by word of mouth, and Rockefeller lost by a narrow margin. A Rockefeller campaign worker, later looking at a picture of robust Nelson, Jr., playing with his toys, sighed, "If only that little boy were three days younger, he'd be the son of the President of the United States." See FAMILY VALUES.

Dixiecrat Southern Democrats who bolted the national party in 1948 in opposition to President Truman's civil rights platform.

In a fiery speech to the 1948 Democratic convention, Hubert Humphrey posed the central issue to face his party in the decades ahead: "It is time for the Democratic party to step out of the shadow of state's rights—and to walk forthrightly into the bright sunshine of HUMAN RIGHTS." Most Democrats followed his lead (although, twenty years later, many liberals—angered by the Vietnam policy of Lyndon Johnson, whom Humphrey served as Vice President—were reluctant to support him).

The States Rights Democrats from Alabama, Mississippi, Louisiana, and other Southern states held a convention of their own in 1948, nominating Senator J. Strom Thurmond as their candidate for President. The votes lost to the Democrats in the South were probably offset by votes Democrats gained in the North, no longer embarrassed by their party's civil rights divisions.

Coinage has been attributed to William Weismer, telegraph editor of the *Charlotte* (N.C.) *News,* who squeezed States Rights Democrats into a headline. *American Speech* magazine lists another headline on May 5, 1948, using the word in the *Birmingham News.* Alabama Governor Frank Dixon did not like the new nickname: "Dixiecrats leaves the wrong impression," he complained. "Our contention is that we are returning to the original concepts of the founding fathers of our nation and the Democratic party."

Harry Truman was having none of that. He wrote: "The States Rights Democrats claim that this was not a bolt from the Democratic party. They said they represented the true Democrats of the Southland. It was a BOLT."

The technique of label-formation using one half of Democrat or GOP as an acronym lingers on. Derivations include "Dixiegop," for Southern Republican, and in 1966 Democratic supporters of Republican candidate for Florida governor Claude R. Kirk called themselves "Demokirks."

See TAKE A WALK; OFF THE RESERVATION; OUTSIDE WORLD.

doctrines policies that have hardened with acceptance.

When the word is applied in retrospect, it usually sticks; when it is announced with a policy, it usually fades. President Monroe's decision to deny European influence in the Americas was not laid down as the *Monroe Doctrine;* it became known as that many years later. On the other hand, most Americans do not remember what was contained in the *Truman Doctrine* (aid to Greece and Turkey to fight Communism) or the *Eisenhower Doctrine* (same kind of containment in the Middle East).

Two of the most hotly debated doctrines in American history have faded from the language today: the *Freeport Doctrine* of Stephen Douglas, which held that the people of a territory could exclude slavery prior to the formation of a state constitution, and John Calhoun's *Doctrine of Non-Interference,* declaring that federal intervention on the slavery issue in a state was illegal.

In what used to be the Communist world, the *One Glass of Water Doctrine* is still remembered, but more in the breach than the observance. This held that good Communists should regard sexual desire as being no more important than a glass of water. Lenin revoked this doctrine after the Bolsheviks took power, but it remained for many years as gospel to Chinese Communists under the name *Pei-shui-chu-i.* It was the cause of some disaffection among the Viet Cong in South Vietnam.

The *Brezhnev Doctrine,* expounded by Leonid Brezhnev on November 12, 1968, after Soviet arms had crushed a turning toward freedom in Czechoslovakia earlier that year, held that "the Socialist community as a whole"—

that is, the Soviet Union—had the right to intervene in otherwise sovereign states when it detected a tendency toward capitalism subverting an already Communist state. This asserted Soviet military control of its satellites: "to protect Communist regimes even if it means the use of force."

"The Carter approach to foreign policy," said the State Department's Leslie Gelb in 1977, "rests in a belief that not only is the world far too complex to be reduced to a doctrine, but there is something inherently wrong in having a doctrine at all."

See NIXON DOCTRINE.

dog metaphors.   See BIRD DOG . . . KENNEL DOG; THAT DOG WON'T HUNT.

do-gooder politician's derisive name for reformers and civic-action nonpartisans.

The phrase "do-goods" can be traced back to 1654 *(OED)*, and the use of the compound word in a political context can be found in a 1923 issue of *The Nation:* "There is nothing wrong with the United States except . . . the parlor socialists, uplifters, and do-goods." Tracing the use of "good" back in political history, the pattern seems to be "Good Government Clubs," "goo-goos," "goody-goody"—with a separate branch for "holier than thou."

The City Club of New York came up with a district-level network of local action groups called "Good Government Clubs" in the 1890s. Promptly dubbed the "goo-goos" by the *New York Sun,* the reformers raised the ire of Theodore Roosevelt: "The Republican machine men have been loudly demanding a straight ticket; and those prize idiots, the Goo-Goos, have just played into their hands by capering off and nominating an independent ticket of their own."

Like so many reform groups, the Good Government Clubs atrophied and died in a few years; the Democratic and Republican machines skillfully redistricted the city, and the reformers no longer knew which club they belonged to.

Just before the rise of the goo-goos, "holier-than-thou" was the name given the independent Republicans in 1884. This was derived from Isaiah 65:5, in which the prophet derisively quotes hypocrites: "Stand by thyself, come not near to me; for I am holier than thou."

dollar diplomacy use of U.S. military and political power to further the interest of U.S. entrepreneurs in Latin America; or, enticement of foreign nations to follow U.S. political leadership with promises of economic aid.

Early in the twentieth century, under the Roosevelt Corollary to the Monroe Doctrine, U.S. Marines helped U.S. businessmen open up new markets in Latin America and protected those interests; protectorates were established over Cuba, Haiti, Nicaragua, and Santo Domingo. *Harper's Weekly* in 1910 referred to the phrase as it was then being applied to Secretary of State Philander C. Knox: "An attempt is made, necessarily sketchy, to outline simply and clearly what is meant by the term 'Dollar Diplomacy' as it has come to be commonly applied to certain of the activities of Secretary Knox as manifested in Honduras, in Liberia, and in negotiations now in progress looking to the participation of American capital in railway construction in the Far East."

President William Howard Taft, in his annual message on December 3, 1912, defended the philosophy in what came to be known as the "Dollar Diplomacy" speech: "The diplomacy of the present administration has sought to respond to modern ideas of commercial intercourse. This policy has been characterized as substituting dollars for bullets. It is one that appeals alike to idealistic humanitarian sentiments, to the dictates of sound policy and strategy, and to legitimate commercial aims."

Dollar diplomacy became a term of criticism used by Latin American diplomats who resented economic arm-twisting. In its more general sense, the phrase has come to mean the dangling of economic plums in front of a hungry neutral or unfriendly nation. In 1965 President Lyndon Johnson offered a billion-dollar investment program in Southeast Asia if only the Communists would replace aggression with "peaceful cooperation." Wrote Arthur Krock in the *New York Times:* "Only from members of the small Republican minority . . . was any question raised . . . of the political psychology of a proposal reminiscent by its attendant circumstances of the crude era of American 'dollar diplomacy.'"

In late 1971, the phrase was used in derogation of hard-bargaining Treasury Secretary John Connally, but temporarily lost its pejorative connotation after a realignment of currency rates favorable to the U.S.

For related terms, see DIPLOMACY.

domino theory the concept that if one strategically placed nation in an area goes Communist, the others will quickly follow.

Dwight Eisenhower used the Joseph Alsop metaphor politically in 1954, in explaining his decision to offer economic aid to the South Vietnamese government of Ngo Dinh Diem. "You have a row of dominoes set up," said the President at a press conference, "you knock over the first one, and what will happen to the last one is that it will go over very quickly. So you have the beginning of a disintegration that would have the most profound influences." The theory derives from

what historian Arthur Schlesinger, Jr., describes as "a popular construction, or misconstruction, of the MUNICH ANALOGY." In any event, the idea was accepted widely. As Eisenhower told Churchill: "We failed to halt Hirohito, Mussolini and Hitler by not acting in unity and in time."

John F. Kennedy had reservations about the theory. Columnist Arthur Krock wrote after an interview with him: "I asked him what he thought of the 'falling domino' theory—that is, if Laos and Vietnam go Communist, the rest of Southeast Asia will fall to them in orderly succession. The President expressed doubts that this theory had much point any more because, he remarked, the Chinese Communists were bound to get nuclear weapons in time, and from that moment on the nations of Southeast Asia would seek to be on good terms with Peking."

Some of Kennedy's closest advisers, nevertheless, accepted the theory. His former Chairman of the Joint Chiefs of Staff, General Maxwell Taylor, told a House subcommittee shortly after Kennedy's death that if the U.S. withdrew from Vietnam, the country would quickly go Communist, and "the remainder of Southeast Asia would very shortly thereafter go neutralist, possibly even Communist. Burma would be affected, India also. Indonesia would soon line up with the Communists. We would be pushed out of the Western Pacific back to Honolulu."

One of the most persistent critics of the theory, Senate Foreign Relations Committee Chairman J. William Fulbright, wrote in *The Arrogance of Power:* "The inference we have drawn from this is that we must fight in one country in order to avoid having to fight in another, although we could with equal logic have inferred that it is useless to fight in one country when the same conditions of conflict are present in another." A graphic meta-phoric attack was made by novelist Norman Mailer during a 1965 anti-Vietnam demonstration at the University of California at Berkeley: "They are not dominoes but sand castles. Sand castles. And a tide of nationalism is on the way in."

U.S. News & World Report in 1968 termed the phrase "a cornerstone of U.S. reasoning about Vietnam since the Eisenhower years."

The phrase has currency. A 1993 letter to the editor in the *Washington Post* commented on an op-ed piece whose authors called for American intervention in Bosnia's civil war: "Their arguments remind one of the domino theory for intervention in Vietnam in 1965: That failure to act will lead to a wider European war, perhaps war between Europe and the Muslim world."

The phrase was parodied in 1968 by columnist Art Buchwald. He held that BRINKMANSHIP was named after a man named Brinkman, and the domino theory after one Sam Domino, who explained how he coined it: "Well, one evening we were having a buffet and there were about twenty people lined up with plates waiting for some chicken cacciatore when my uncle, who was first in line, slipped and fell backward. He knocked over my aunt standing in back of him and she, in turn, knocked over my cousin, who knocked over my son and so on until all twenty people were on the floor. It suddenly occurred to me that if this could happen to people, it could happen to countries."

donkey, Democratic symbol of the Democratic party.

The donkey gained its acceptance as the Democratic symbol in 1874 as a result of Thomas Nast's cartoons (see EL-EPHANT, REPUBLICAN), supported by Ignatius Donnelly's remark in the Minnesota Legislature: "The Demo-

cratic party is like a mule—without pride of ancestry or hope of posterity."

The donkey has provided cartoonists and speechwriters with an invaluable metaphor. For example, when the Democrats at their 1928 Houston convention nominated Al Smith (who favored repeal of Prohibition) and Senator Joseph T. Robinson of Arkansas (who favored Prohibition), the wisecrack was "the Democratic donkey with a wet head and wagging a dry tail left Houston."

Nast exercised good judgment in his selection of symbols. Clinton Rossiter writes that the difference between the two parties "is caught vividly in the choice of beastly emblems that was made for all of us long ago: the slightly ridiculous but tough and long-lived Donkey—the perfect symbol of the rowdy Democrats; the majestic but ponderous Elephant—the perfect symbol of respectable Republicans. Can anyone imagine the Donkey as a Republican and the Elephant as a Democrat?"

do-nothing Congress Harry Truman's epithet for the 1947–48 Republican-controlled session that rejected much of his program.

"Do-nothing" is associated with Truman's criticism of the 80th Congress, since it was so instrumental in giving him an upset victory over Thomas E. Dewey in 1948. But the term was in use as early as the sixteenth century, and Franklin Roosevelt used it in referring to the "do-nothing policy of Hoover." In his memoirs, Truman quoted Will Rogers's addition to an old slogan: "Keep Cool with Coolidge and Do Nothing."

Truman picked it up when, crossing the U.S. in June 1948, he found audiences responding to his attacks on "the good-for-nothing, do nothing, Taft-Hartley 80th Congress" and the "worst Congress" ever. When he accepted the Democratic nomination, he declared: "On the 26th day of July, which out in Missouri we call 'Turnip Day,' I am going to call that Congress back in session, and I am going to ask them to pass some of these laws they say they are for in their platform. Now, my friends, if there is any reality behind that Republican platform, we ought to get some action out of the short session of the 80th Congress. They could do this job in 15 days if they wanted to. . . . What that worst 80th Congress does in its special session will be the test. The American people will decide on the record."

Dominated by Robert A. Taft and his disappointed followers, the special session accomplished nothing, and Truman was able to continue campaigning on what he considered its obstructionism and on the fact that he had to use the veto 62 times against it. It was a bold move for, as Democratic adviser Clark Clifford recalls: "We were on our own 20-yard line. We had to be bold. If we kept plugging away in moderate terms, the best we could have done would have been to reach midfield when the gun went off. So we had to throw long passes."

Instead of the traditional defense of the record of the Administration in power, the Truman strategy was to turn its own frustrations and defeats into an asset by furiously attacking those who had effectively hamstrung the Administration. The strategy worked. In recent times, both Ross Perot and Bill Clinton attacked legislative impasse by complaining of GRIDLOCK.

don't change horses an expression urging voters to continue an Administration during a period of crisis.

The metaphor was Lincoln's, spoken at the Republican convention of 1864, to a delegation from the Union League Club which had hailed the action of the convention in nominating Lincoln.

Reported Nicolai and Hay: "The President answered them more informally, saying that he did not allow himself to suppose that either the Convention or the League had concluded that he was either the greatest or the best man in America, but rather that they had decided it was not best to 'swap horses while crossing the river.'"

Sperber and Trittschuh traced the origin to an 1846 newspaper: "There is a story of an Irishman who was crossing a stream with mare and colt when finding it deeper than he expected, and falling off the old mare, he seized the colt's tail to aid him in reaching the shore. Some persons on the bank called to him, advising him to take hold of the mare's tail, as she was the ablest to bring him out. His reply was, that it was a very unseasonable time for swapping horses."

The expression was edited by usage into "Don't change horses in midstream," or "Don't swap horses while crossing the stream." In recent times, its best-known use was in the Roosevelt campaigns of 1940 and 1944.

Republican Chairman Joe Martin remained convinced that the unwillingness to shift leadership in a crisis was the root cause of the Willkie defeat in 1940: "The fall of France and the imminent danger to Britain filled the American people with a fear of switching administrations. 'Don't change horses in the middle of the stream' was never a more potent argument in American history than it was then. Not even the third-term issue could prevail against it."

"The Democrats could not seem to fight their way out of the hard crust of inertia in Washington," wrote Irving Stone of the Roosevelt-Dewey campaign, "and the only effort they cared to make was the negative cry of 'Don't change horses in midstream.' " Dewey's slogan was "TIME FOR A CHANGE," and public opinion polls showed him closing the gap on the President. Dewey's 1944 campaign (in contrast to 1948) was slashing and vigorous; Roosevelt supporters, viewing the erosion of their margin of safety, urged FDR to drop his above-the-battle stance and hit hard. The FALA SPEECH soon followed, infuriating the Republicans and reminding independents that the Old Master had not lost his political touch.

The phrase is current. The *New York Times* editorialized in 1967: "President Johnson . . . clearly intends to run as the commander-in-chief appealing to patriotism and national unity in a time of war and crisis. This approach has numerous precedents, including Lincoln's 'don't swap horses in the middle of the stream' in 1864 and Franklin Roosevelt's 1940 and 1944 campaigns."

Heavy use of the phrase was made in the Hoover-Roosevelt campaign of 1932. The *New Republic* characterized the Republican campaign theme as "Don't change barrels while going over Niagara." Roosevelt supporters said, "Swap horses or drown!"

don't let them take it away an unofficial Democratic campaign slogan of 1948 and 1952.

The phrase appeared in the *New York Journal-American* of December 28, 1946, as a kind of belated answer to the Republican "HAD ENOUGH?" that had been so successful in the 1946 off-year elections. It was used in the 1948 Truman campaign, though not nearly as much as "DO-NOTHING CONGRESS."

In 1952, Adlai Stevenson treated it lightly: "There have been times when I have wondered whether you, my friends here in Illinois, couldn't have found some easier way of getting rid of me. In fact, before the Convention I wrote a song about it, only the Democratic party took the song and changed the words. My song was called 'Don't Let Them Take Me Away.' "

This is a defensive slogan, similar to the British Conservative party's 1964 slogan: "It's your standard of living—keep it with the Conservatives." That did not catch on, either. For one that did, see YOU NEVER HAD IT SO GOOD.

don't waste your vote slogan of a major party attempting to win back support lost to splinter parties; usually accompanied by the statement "A vote for [splinter party candidate name] is a vote for [major opposition party name]."

President Harry Truman, fighting his uphill battle in 1948, knew that Henry Wallace's Progressive party was drawing votes from people who would ordinarily be Democratic. As Truman ripped into the DO-NOTHING CONGRESS and its MOSSBACK committee chairmen, he said in Los Angeles: ". . . a vote for the third party plays into the hands of the Republican forces of reaction whose aims are directly opposed to the aim of American liberalism."

A classic example of a double don't-waste-your-vote effort was the four-way New York gubernatorial race in 1966. Republican Rockefeller was urging members of the splinter Conservative party not to waste their votes on Paul Adams, while Democrat Frank O'Connor was urging Liberal party members not to waste their votes on Liberal candidate Franklin D. Roosevelt, Jr. At the last minute, word was passed to Liberal district leaders that their party members should switch to the Democrat, though too few did so to influence the result.

Reformer William Evarts, who helped break up New York's Tweed ring, was running for U.S. Senator in 1884 and came up with a phrase to dissuade New Yorkers from paying attention to the man running on the Prohibition ticket. He called it "voting in the air."

In the 1992 Presidential election, both major parties revived the expression. Republicans staunchly for George Bush as well as Democrats wanting Bill Clinton to garner the votes of the dissatisfied argued that votes for Ross Perot would be wasted, although Perot's forces denied it.

The answer to the don't-waste-your-vote plea is, of course, a stand on principle. Said Hearst's *San Francisco Examiner* in support of a hopeless cause in 1908: "The vote for principle is never thrown away. It is the only vote that isn't thrown away." Felix Frankfurter, explaining his vote for Robert La Follette in 1924, agreed: "If clarification of American politics through the formation of a new party is required to make our politics more honest and more real, then all the talk of 'throwing one's vote away' is the cowardly philosophy of the BANDWAGON."

A question in the minds of many American voters is: "Is my vote really needed?" Third parties play on this nagging doubt by urging voters to "make your vote count" by registering a protest. Major parties appeal on these grounds as well. Recalling the importance of "a single vote in each election district" in the 1960 election, they point out that each vote is important and the front runner could lose if that particular voter did not turn out.

Worry about the wasted vote is particularly strong in Japan. "For some reason," wrote Nobutake Ike in 1958, "Japanese voters do not like to 'waste' their votes. They are therefore reluctant to vote for a candidate who clearly has no chance to win. By the same token, if they believe that a particular candidate will win by a wide margin, they might shift their vote to someone else. They feel that 'he is going to win anyway, so why shouldn't I make my vote count by giving it to another candidate.'"

For the opposite appeal, used by both George Wallace and Ross Perot, see SEND THEM A MESSAGE.

Dooley, Mr. a fictional creation of author Finley Peter Dunne, who made sage political observations in a thick Irish brogue.

Mr. Dooley first appeared in a Chicago newspaper in the 1890s and dispensed his wisdom up to World War I.

Dunne lifted his character out of his hometown Chicago sixth-ward commentary in the Spanish-American War, and gained national recognition in 1896 by commenting on the William Jennings Bryan campaign. Skepticism kept his epigrams astringent: "I see grreat changes takin' place ivry day, but no change at all ivry fifty years." His best-known line, now used after being rendered into proper English, was: "No matther whether th' Constitution follows th' flag or not, th' Supreme Coort follows th' iliction returns." See SUPREME COURT FOLLOWS THE ELECTION RETURNS.

A typical Dooley comment is this view of the vice presidency: "Ye can't be sint to jail f'r it, but it's a kind iv a disgrace. . . . It is princip'lly because iv th' vice-prisidint that most iv our prisidints have enjoyed such rugged health. Th' vice-prisidint guards th' prisidint, an' th' prisidint, afther sizin' up th' vice-prisidint, con-cludes that it wud be betther f'r th' counthry if he shud live yet awhile."

The tradition of political humor in dialect is that of Petroleum V. Nasby and Artemus Ward. Mark Twain placed political observations in the mouths of Huck Finn, Tom Sawyer, and Pudd'nhead Wilson. Will Rogers carried the torch for a while, and more recently, without dialect, the field has been dominated by Art Buchwald, Russell Baker, and Dave Barry.

See BEANBAG.

Doomsday Machine a computer programmed to set off a nuclear war based on another nation's actions; carrying DETERRENT to the extreme.

The Doomsday Machine, properly constructed, should be capable of wiping out life on earth. It sits in the nation that built it, but its behavior is controlled by an enemy nation.

This means that the enemy nation knows that certain actions will trigger the machine, and that no fears or false hopes in the nation that built the machine can stop its use. The enemy is thus provided with a list of restraints which have been programmed into the computer and knows where the line is drawn. One such restraint could be "You may not build a Doomsday Machine."

"Although it is most unlikely that any nation would build such a device in the next ten to twenty years," admits Herman Kahn, author of *On Thermonuclear War*, "there clearly are some circumstances in which a nation might wish it had built one."

A related expression, the Doomsday Clock, has led to the use of the urgent phrase "two minutes to midnight." Since 1947, the Doomsday Clock appears monthly on the cover of the *Bulletin of the Atomic Scientists*. Powered by mankind's activities regarding atomic energy, the clock ticks toward the world's midnight when, presumably, all bets are off.

The *Domesday Dictionary* was published in England in 1964, defining the more frightening nuclear words in a deadpan manner; *domesday* is pronounced *doomsday*, and refers to the survey of England for taxing purposes made by William the Conqueror in 1085, which was recorded in the *Domesday Book*.

doorbell-ringing   house-to-house canvassing for votes; personal persuasion by party workers of individual voters, hallmark of a well-organized campaign.

A doorbell-ringing campaign is one in which the party's workers are mobi-lized to make a personal appeal to individuals in their residence. Some of the rules: (1) an index-card file must be prepared of all registered voters, with party preference checked, and need for babysitter or transportation on election day indicated; (2) no calls before 8 A.M. or after 9 P.M.; (3) teams of men and women to do the actual doorbell-ringing, to reassure the voter of his safety and to provide for the safety of canvassers.

A follow-up to, but not a substitute for, a doorbell-ringing campaign is a telephone blitz—calls made from a "boiler room" to remind favorably inclined voters to turn out on election day.

Theodore White, in *The Making of the President 1964*, held that it was the influence of strangers ringing the doorbells of lonely newcomers in California that tipped the scales from Rockefeller to Goldwater in the closing days of the 1964 primary campaign that decided the Republican nomination.

See CANVASS.

dope story   information leaked to a reporter and published as his own analysis; useful method of launching TRIAL BALLOONS or conditioning public opinion.

A good example of this technique was the way President Harry Truman handled the special session of what he termed the "DO-NOTHING CONGRESS" in the campaign of 1948. A President's special message to Congress is ordinarily handled as top secret, but in this case presidential press secretary Charles Ross leaked its contents the week preceding its delivery. "Thus the Truman program got double exposure in the nation's press," wrote biographer Cabell Phillips, "first in the provocative form of 'dope stories,' and again when the message was made officially public. As a publicity gimmick, it was a small triumph."

Dope has a dual root in American slang. As a synonym for narcotics, it is extended to one who appears drugged or stupid, as "dopey." As slang for information, it spawned "inside dope," "dope out," "dope sheet," and "dope story." The narcotic meaning appears to come from the Dutch word *doop*, with a current meaning of "baptism" but an earlier one of "sauce"—and opium smokers deal with a gooey substance. ("On the sauce" is current slang for alcoholism.) But no plausible explanation has been given for the root of dope as "data," to the author's knowledge. It is not new; the *Dictionary of Americanisms* has an entry dating to 1901, from a book by George Hobart: "I've known Tommy for a long time, so he feels free to read his dope to me."

Richard Nixon was the first President to use the phrase publicly; on January 28, 1969, he told a large group of State Department employees: "I have been reading some dope stories lately about the rivalries that may develop between the various Departments in government . . ."

The term is current. A *Washington Post* editorial in late 1992 cautioned President-elect Clinton against appointing Cabinet members based solely on "help from the press, dope stories fed by various sources and the lobbying groups themselves."

A conflict of meanings exists; in Washington, D.C., a man who knows no inside dope is considered fairly dopey.

See BACKGROUNDER; NOT FOR ATTRIBUTION; LEAK; PLANT; THUMBSUCKER.

double digit inflation of 10 percent or over.

A digit, from the Latin *digitus*, is a finger. Children start counting on their fingers, which is how the word for "finger" became the word for "number." "Double digit" means two numbers, like 10 or more.

The phrase began as "double-figure inflation" in England in the sixties, taken from "double figures" in cricket scores. In the U.S. the coinage of the phrase "double digit" belongs to Leonard Silk, then a member of the editorial board of the *New York Times*, who wrote this lead editorial on March 22, 1974:

"For American consumers, it is slaughter at the checkout counters and the gasoline pumps. Food and fuel prices soared again in February, giving another big thrust to skyrocketing consumer prices. With last month's increase of 1.3 percent, the cost of living has climbed 10 percent in the past twelve months—the first double-digit rate of inflation in consumer prices since the Korean War."

Mr. Silk recalls: "I remember coming up with the phrase and noticing how fast it was picked up afterward. Of course, we all know that coincidences happen, but I'd be surprised if there was prior publication, since my piece was right on the news, when the digits went double."

Though the phrase is usually confined to inflation, it can be used to describe any high, or inflationary, price. In an essay in the *Washington Post* about the casual names given expensive places, Frank Mankiewicz wrote in 1977: "Joe's Place, which used to guarantee . . . a friendly roadhouse with live music on Saturday nights, now could signal anything from an elegant boutique to a restaurant with double-digit entree prices."

See HIGH COST OF LIVING; INFLATION; OVERHEATED ECONOMY.

double dipping income, in the form of salary or pension, from two government sources.

A more complete definition was given to the author by CPA P. K. Seidman: "The practice of collecting a government salary or other money benefit on top of a pension from the same government, or using the same salary as the base of securing two pensions from related governments such as state and county."

Civilian employees who retire and then return to government service in a different capacity forfeit their pension during their working years. But this does not apply to members of the armed forces. A *New York Times* editorial on April 12, 1977, argued: "Double dippers are members of the military who retire young, then take civilian jobs with the Federal government and collect both a military pension and a civilian salary. There are already 150,000 of them . . . Double dipping is indefensible."

The defense put forward by some is that retired soldiers ought not to be penalized by losing their pension income for the "crime" of entering the civilian labor force of the government. On September 19, 1977, Harry W. Quillian wrote a letter to the *Washington Post* making this point: "As one who has no prospect of becoming a 'double dipper' I suggest that term be banished from reporting on and discussion of the dual compensation controversy. The implication it seems to carry—that it is reprehensible to earn a salary while receiving a pension—is absurd and doubtless painful to some honorably retired people supplementing their pensions by working at a second job."

The phrase comes from the ice cream parlor: a cone with two scoops of ice cream is a double dip. Additional pension benefits have not yet been termed "sprinkles."

See also DIP/DOUBLE DIP.

doves believers in ACCOMMODATION as the route to peace, who reject the "appeasement leads to war" argument of the "hawks" (see WAR HAWKS).

The dove, perched on the arm of Aphrodite, Greek goddess of love and beauty, has been a symbol of peace and gentleness since ancient times. When modern painter Pablo Picasso lent his prestige and his palette to the Communist movement, the dove was seized upon as the symbol of peace used in Communist posters and at international conferences.

In the Soviet-American confrontation over the placement of missiles on Cuban soil in 1962, the "dove versus hawk" metaphor came to the fore. In the deliberations of the Kennedy cabinet, UN Ambassador Adlai Stevenson was represented as a "dove" by reporters Stewart Alsop and Charles Bartlett; Robert Kennedy, Dean Rusk, and McGeorge Bundy were identified as the leading "hawks." Since a firm U.S. line resulted in a Russian backdown, subsequent identification as a dove in this crisis was in essence an attack at unwise softness, and friends of Stevenson objected strenuously to such leaks.

Concurrently, debate on the U.S. position in Vietnam was beginning. Those who wished to extricate the U.S. from what they felt was a hopeless quagmire were labeled *doves,* and those who felt it necessary to contain Communism and resist the new "wars of national liberation" at the South Vietnamese border were called *hawks.* With many exceptions, most liberals favored what came to be known as a "dovelike position," and most conservatives, with a history of attacking liberals as SOFT ON COMMUNISM, willingly identified themselves as hawks. (Senator George Aiken of Vermont preferred to describe himself as an owl.)

In the 1966 elections, many conservative candidates found it possible to adopt far more liberal domestic positions without losing their conservative support, as long as they held to a "hard line" in Vietnam; and vice versa.

Edmund Burke's address to Parliament on "conciliation with America" in 1775 made a basic point that applied to the position of the doves of the 1960s: "Terror is not always the effect of force: and an armament is not a victory. If you do not succeed, you are without recourse; for, conciliation failing, force remains; but, force failing, no further hope of reconciliation is left."

McGeorge Bundy, after he resigned as Johnson's chief adviser on national security matters to head the Ford Foundation, made a dovelike (or dove-ish, usually spelled dovish) differentiation for one so intimately identified with the hawks: "The real choice is not between 'doves' and 'hawks.' It is between those who would keep close and careful civilian control over a difficult and demanding contest, and those who would use whatever force is thought necessary by any military leader in any service." In this manner, he sought to label the center position as "dovelike," pushing "hawk" over to the extreme military-solution position. This would put the "moderate hawks" into dove's feathers, but it never caught on.

POLARIZED positions are traditional in U.S. politics: the *hards versus softs, lily-whites versus black and tans*, and *doves versus hawks* are summed up in this analysis of the *tough-minded and tender-minded* by philosopher William James:

> The tough think of the tender as sentimentalists and softheads. The tender feel the tough to be unrefined, callous, or brutal. Their mutual reaction is very much like that that takes place when Bostonian tourists mingle with a population like that of Cripple Creek. Each type believes the other to be inferior to itself; but disdain in the one is mingled with amusement, in the other it has a dash of fear.

Before its recent usage, "dove" was best known for the use New York Democratic Governor Al Smith made

of a remark by his opponent in 1926 in which the luckless Republican said: "If I am elected Governor, I will get along with the Legislature like a cooing dove." Replied Smith: "Had I gotten along with the Legislature like a cooing dove, there would have been no automobile regulation. . . the people of New York want clear-headed, strong-minded fighting men at the head of the government and not doves. Let the doves roost in the eaves of the Capitol—not in the Executive Chamber. So much for the doves . . ."

Appropriately, the goddess Aphrodite, referred to at the beginning of this entry, is associated with two symbols: the dove and the "apple of discord."

Doves whose concern for the protection of human rights overcomes their reluctance to use force are called *dawks*.

For the British equivalents of *doves*, see WETS.

do your own thing. See COUNTER-CULTURE.

draft, Presidential a demand by a party that a man not seeking the nomination accept it; upon rare occasion, applies to one who did not encourage his own candidacy.

The most recent authentic draft was at the Democratic convention of 1952. At that time a reluctant Adlai Stevenson, who was President Harry Truman's early choice, was drafted by the delegates who felt uncomfortable with Senator Estes Kefauver (who led on the first two ballots). Historian Richard Morris contends that "Stevenson, who did not seek the nomination, was the first Presidential nominee to be drafted since Garfield (1880)."

The Garfield draft (see PRESIDENTIAL FEVER) was a classic example of a man putting himself forward without appearing to do so. Supporters of former President U. S. Grant, led by party leader Roscoe Conkling, had the most strength; James Blaine of Maine and John Cooper of Ohio trailed close behind. Before the balloting began, a floor fight broke out over the seating of delegates who refused to take a party-loyalty pledge. Congressman James Garfield of Ohio, in a graceful speech, suggested a face-saving compromise. As he agreed to the compromise, Conkling sent Garfield a note on his potential nomination for the presidency.

The three-man deadlock lasted for 34 ballots when Wisconsin, whose votes had been scattered between Grant, Blaine, and Cooper, suddenly cast 16 votes for Garfield. Garfield jumped up to exclaim, "No man has a right, without the consent of the person voted for, to announce that person's name, and vote for him in this Convention." But Garfield had not objected when two Pennsylvania delegates voted for him on 30 previous ballots; his sudden protestation of unavailability triggered more support. On the 36th ballot, Garfield was drafted.

FDR felt he had to be drafted in 1940 by the Democratic convention, to prove he had no dictatorial ambitions and to blunt the third-term issue. For his technique in arranging the draft, see VOICE FROM THE SEWER. Though FDR used the word "muster" rather than draft when referring to military conscription, he embraced the word "draft" in his acceptance speech in 1940: "Only the people themselves can draft a president. If such a draft should be made upon me, I say to you, in the utmost simplicity, I will, with God's help, continue to serve . . ."

As a political word, *draft* remains best known for military conscription, and the "Draft Riots" in New York during the Civil War locked the word in the lexicon. In 1966, students chalked walls and wore buttons that played on another meaning of the word: "Draft beer not men."

draw a line in the sand   set a limit; a dramatic figure of speech to conjure the phrase "this far, no farther."

After Iraq's invasion of Kuwait in 1990, George Bush announced in a televised speech that "a line has been drawn in the sand," which, despite the passive construction, presented a vivid figurative marker of limits in the Arabian Desert. The *New York Times* followed the President's usage with a headline that read "Worried Nation Backs U.S. Line in the Sand."

The infinitive phrase *to draw the line* means to mark a limit or boundary, as in a children's game that dares opponents to cross a line. This expression may have come from the lines of farm boundaries that were plowed in medieval England or from the lines of tennis courts that were established in fourteenth-century France. The phrase first appeared in print in 1793, in *The Trial of Fyshe Palmer*: "It is difficult . . . to draw the line."

The figurative *line in the sand* may have come from a literal use of the phrase. Among the Texas legends of the Alamo, besieged by the Mexican army in 1836, is the story that William Barret Travis used his sword to draw a line in the ground (or sand). Travis said, "Those prepared to die for freedom's cause, come across to me," and 189 of the 190 Texas fighters did; the 190th lived to tell the story.

dream ticket   politician's vision of a combination of candidates with an unbeatable appeal, simultaneously unifying the party's divergent wings; rarely comes true.

"GOP Dream Ticket" *Newsweek* headlined in 1967, "Reagan and Brooke." Dreamily, the magazine continued: "Some professional Democrats now say privately that the strongest team the GOP can field in '68 is one headed by Ronald Reagan and Edward Brooke. The Negro Senator from Massachusetts might cost the ticket some Southern votes, they admit. But these would be more than offset by the votes he could capture for Reagan in the populous industrial states of the U.S. where elections are usually won or lost . . ."

A dream ticket not only balances geography, ideology, age, and religion but also puts together two personalities that are famous—neither of which is ever likely to accept the other at the top of the ticket. Republicans in 1960 talked of a dream ticket of Nixon and Rockefeller, and Nixon did urge the New York governor to be his running mate; Rockefeller, as most realists predicted, turned it down. See COMPACT OF FIFTH AVENUE.

The dream ticket means one that is especially strong; *a* dream ticket is one that is striking in its juxtaposition of personalities. Many Democrats thought Clinton and Gore to be both *the* and *a* dream ticket in 1992.

Dr. Fell syndrome a voter's inexplicable distaste for a candidate whose positions would ordinarily command his or her support.

Stewart Alsop, writing in *Newsweek* in 1970, identified the "Dr. Fell Syndrome" as the cause of President Nixon's greatest political weakness— many of the people who liked what he stood for didn't like the way he stood.

The phrase is from the poem by Thomas (Tom) Brown written while he was a student at Christ Church, Oxford, during the 1600s. It is a loose translation of some lines in Martial's *Epigrammata*, written in the first century A.D.:

I do not love thee, Dr. Fell.
The reason why I cannot tell;
But this alone I know full well,
I do not love thee, Dr. Fell.

A real Dr. Fell, a seventeenth-century English divine, was able to maintain Church of England services despite Cromwell and was made dean of Christ Church after the Restoration. Though he was generally acknowledged to be a man of courage, rectitude, and vision, some people just couldn't warm up to him.

drop-by. See ADVANCE MAN; FACE TIME.

duck. See PROVERBS AND AXIOMS, POLITICAL.

dump. See JOE SMITH; KINGMAKER.

dustbin of history relegation to oblivion; lack of historical significance or fame.

Leon Trotsky popularized the term, when he shouted after the Mensheviks departing from the 1917 Congress of Soviets, "Go to the place where you belong from now on—the *dustbin of history*!" This expression, transliterated as *musornyi yashchik*, appeared in the English translation of Trotsky's autobiography.

Synonyms for *dustbin* are used in various translations. In 1982, for example, Ronald Reagan used the term in a London speech: "The march of freedom and democracy . . . will leave Marxist Leninism on the *ash heap of history*." A year later, the Soviet leader Yuri Andropov used the expression with a different synonym in the Tass translation: "Those who encroached on the integrity of our state . . . found themselves on the *garbage heap of history*."

Dust heap was the original term used in English by the British essayist Augustine Birrell, who coined the expression in *Obiter Dicta*, his 1887 collection of essays: "that great dust heap called 'history.'" As the Soviet Union disintegrated more than a century later, the *International Herald Tribune* provided a synonym familiar to both British and American readers in a 1991 headline: "Scrap Heap of History."

dyed-in-the-wool   descriptive of an all-out partisan, proud of his party label; most often used about Democrats.

The expression comes from the coloring of textiles while the material is in a raw, unfinished state; wool so dyed is likely to be more colorfast than that with color added later in the process.

The use can be traced to 1830, and likely originated earlier; in current use, alliteration has consigned *dyed-in-the-wool* to Democrats, and ROCK-RIBBED to Republicans. *Whole hog* (Jacksonian origin) is applied mainly to Democrats, *staunch* to Republicans; HIDEBOUND belongs to extreme conservatives.

Senator Huey Long had some fun with the phrase. "I am a dyed-in-the-wool party man," he told the Senate in 1935. "I do not know just what party I am in right now, but I am for the party."

dynamic conservatism   Eisenhower's attempt to define his approach to the economic and social needs of the nation.

The President and the more conservative Republican congressmen became more and more disillusioned with one another as his Administration drew on. He found that Democratic votes were often needed to save measures he thought necessary; the Republicans found a New Deal-ish tinge to many of those same measures. The result was a President who thought many of his party members were too Republican to be progressive, and a number of conservatives who found him too progressive to be a very good Republican.

The President, in 1955, was looking for a phrase which would have the right sound and sum up his basic philosophy. One he liked was "conservative dynamism." In his speech before the finance committee of the Republican National Committee on February 17, 1955, President Eisenhower turned it around before using it: "I have said we were 'progressive moderates.' Right at the moment I rather favor the term 'dynamic conservatism.' I believe we should conserve on everything that is basic to our system. We should be dynamic in applying it to the problems of the day so that all our 165,000,000 Americans will profit from it."

But this term, too, failed to satisfy his desires and went the way of "progressive moderation" and "moderate progressivism."

To Adlai Stevenson, this fuzzy sloganeering was the subject of a 1955 Chicago press conference: "I have never been sure what progressive moderation means, or was it conservative progressivism? I have forgotten and I am not sure what dynamic moderation or moderate dynamism means. I am not even sure what it means when one says that he is a conservative in fiscal affairs and a liberal in human affairs. I assume what it means is that you will strongly recommend the building of a great many schools to accommodate the needs of our children, but not provide the money."

dynasty   the recurrence of political power in generations of a single family; previously, the passing of power among a small group of the political elite.

In the U.S., the first "dynasty" to be denounced was the Virginia Dynasty—the succession of power from Jefferson to Madison to Monroe. The Jacksonian Democrats tagged a "dynasty" label on what was then an Establishment, and on their second try for national power, broke it up.

The dynasty charge, sometimes called "the nepotism issue," was an important part of the election of Benjamin Harrison, grandson of President William Henry Harrison. In 1888 the Democratic song was "Grandpa's pants won't fit Benny," and the Republican refrain went "Yes, Grandfather's hat fits Ben—fits Ben."

For his study of *American Political Dynasties,* Stephen Hess chose the following families: Adams, Lee, Livingston, Washburn, Muhlenberg, Roosevelt, Harrison, Breckenridge, Bayard, Taft, Frelinghuysen, Tucker, Stockton, Long, Lodge, and Kennedy.

Sociologist C. Wright Mills pointed out: "There are of course political dynasties in elite American politics—the Adams family being only the outstanding and best known. Yet, it can be safely said that throughout U.S. history well over half of the American political elite have come from families not previously connected with political affairs. They come more frequently from families highly placed in terms of money and position than political influence."

A startling cover of *Esquire* magazine in March 1967 capsuled the hopes and worries of many Americans about the Kennedy "dynasty." It showed four men in rocking chairs—John F. Kennedy, 35th President; Robert Kennedy, 37th President; Ted Kennedy, 38th President; and John-John Kennedy (John F.'s son) 39th President. This kind of frightening satire has long been associated with the Kennedy clan. John F. Kennedy was quoted as saying: "Joe [Junior] was supposed to be the politician. When he died, I took his place. If anything happened to me, Bobby would take my place. If something happened to Bobby, Teddy would take his place."

Despite two assassinations, because of their willingness and ability to have a great many children, the Kennedys had an especially strong chance at creating a dynasty. When Mrs. Robert F. (Ethel) Kennedy had her tenth child in 1967, her mother-in-law, Rose Kennedy, commented, "If I knew there was going to be a contest, I never would have stopped at nine."

E

eagle symbol. See BALD EAGLE.

Eastern Establishment a cluster of legal, financial, and communications talent centered in New York, generally liberal Republican in politics; not an organized group but influential all the same.

The late Senator Robert A. Taft spoke of the Eastern Establishment when, after losing the 1952 GOP nomination, he complained: "Every Republican candidate for president since 1936 has been nominated by the Chase National Bank." Barry Goldwater was another critic—as evidenced by his frequent, only half-jesting remark during the 1964 campaign that he would like to "saw off the Eastern seaboard" and set it adrift in the Atlantic.

Historian Arthur Schlesinger, Jr., offered an apt description of the Eastern Establishment—sometimes known as the "Eastern kingmakers" or simply as the "Establishment"—in *A Thousand Days:*

He was little acquainted in the New York financial and legal community— that arsenal of talent which had so long furnished a steady supply of always orthodox and often able people to Democratic as well as Republican Administrations. This community was the heart of the American Establishment.

Its household deities were Henry L. Stimson and Elihu Root; its present leaders, Robert A. Lovett and John J. McCloy; its front organizations, the Rockefeller, Ford and Carnegie Foundations and the Council on Foreign Relations; its organs, *The New York Times* and *Foreign Affairs.* Its politics were predominantly Republican; but it possessed what its admirers saw as a commitment to public service and its critics as an appetite for power which impelled its members to serve Presidents of whatever political faith.

In *The Making of the President 1964,* Theodore White wrote:

. . . how intertangled is the maze of the Eastern Establishment, even to a New Yorker—and how much more so to the primitives out beyond the mountains . . .

From beyond the Alleghenies, the Eastern Establishment seems to inhabit a belt that runs from Boston through Connecticut to Philadelphia and Washington. Its capital is New York, a city shrouded in symbolic words like "Wall Street," "international finance," "Madison Avenue," "Harvard," "*The New York Times,*" "The Bankers Club," "Ivy League prep schools," all of which seem more sinister and suspect the farther one withdraws West or South.

"Eastern Establishment" is a specific political term; "establishment" alone is a general sociological term, originally coined in Great Britain by Henry Fairlie. See ANGRY YOUNG MEN. The *National Observer* objected to the overuse of the general term at the end of 1967: "If someone wishes to complain about something but hasn't a very clear idea of what, all he needs do is blame the problem on the 'establishment' and people will sagely wag their heads. . . . It is one of the great blessings of America that it has no 'establishment.'"

In 1987, *Newsweek* commented that "Bush's native political tribe—the Eastern-establishment wing of the G.O.P.—is nearly extinct today."

With *American* as its modifier, however, the noun continues in international political jargon. In January 1993, an official Kremlin International News broadcast commented, "The American establishment is linking the success of Russia's reform and the prospects of democracy in Russia to the political fate of Boris Yeltsin." A month later, the *Times* of London wrote of "the American establishment already alarmed by Mrs. Clinton's forthright display of her political power."

See COMMUNITY.

eat crow to admit freely a bad mistake and to offer to accept the consequences.

The *San Francisco Picayune* of December 3, 1851, printed a story that had been making the rounds about a man who boasted he could eat anything: "The bet was made, the crow was caught and nicely roasted . . . he took a good bite, and began to chew away. . . . 'Yes, I can eat a crow! . . . but I'll be darned if I hanker after it.'" This joke's punch line became a part of American folklore.

The political use of the phrase appears to have taken hold in 1872, when a splinter group calling themselves Liberal Republicans bolted to the Democrats and persuaded them to nominate renegade Republican Horace Greeley to run against Republican President Ulysses Grant. "Mr. Greeley appears to be 'boiled crow' to more of his fellow-citizens," wrote *The Nation*, "than any other candidate for office in this or any other age . . . boiled crow he is to his former Republican associates; and now the Democrats are saying in a curious way that to them also he is boiled crow." By 1885, the *Magazine of American History* was saying: "'To eat crow' means to recant, or to humiliate oneself. To 'eat dirt' is nearly equivalent."

While the expression has been adopted throughout the language, it appears to have a special place in politics. The *New York World* in 1881 reprinted the original story and gave it a political base: ". . . the delectable old story of the political sneak who, having been caught and convicted of slander and fed upon his own words, looked up piteously from the unsavory meal and murmured: 'I hev eat crow, and I kin eat crow, but I don't hanker arter crow.'" Its use in a cartoon without the complete punch line indicates its widespread use in 1900; Carl Schurz and his friends were shown eating a "silver" crow with the caption "We can eat it, but—"

In recent use, "boiled" has been dropped and the phrase used mostly about "experts" who have been wrong in political prognostications. The most poll-shaking example of this came in 1948, when Harry Truman amazed the pundits by defeating Thomas E. Dewey. As Truman and Vice President–elect Alben Barkley rode up Pennsylvania Avenue in their "homecoming" celebration, they saw a sign hung from the *Washington Post* building that read: "Mr. President, we are ready to eat crow whenever you are ready to serve it." Truman wrote in his memoirs: "I sent that great newspaper word that I did not want anyone to eat crow, that I was not elated or in a mood myself to crow over anyone."

That was a nice turn of phrase; "crow over" is another use of the image of the tough, raucous black crow. For another use, see JIM CROW.

ecology. See ENVIRONMENTALIST.

economic jargon
Stagflation: ". . . applause and acclaim awaits the creator of the newest star of economic slang: 'stagflation,'" wrote *Washington Post* reporter Robert J. Samuelson on September 19, 1971. "The word is everywhere these days—in the London *Economist,* in speeches, in newspaper columns." But no claimant to the coinage came forward; Peter Jay, financial editor of the *Times* of London and late ambassador to the U.S., used the term in a 1969 article, but thought it came from the U.S.; economists here are inclined to attribute the word to a British use. The word describes a situation of unrelenting inflation combined with low (stagnant) economic growth and high unemployment—often called "the worst of both worlds." A related blend is *slumpflation,* in which unemployment and decreased productivity are accompanied by an increase in inflation.

Nixonomics: A pejorative term used to label the economic policy of the Nixon Administration, coined by Walter Heller in the summer of 1969, and popularized by columnists Rowland Evans and Robert Novak, with an assist from Larry O'Brien, chairman of the Democratic National Committee. O'Brien's definition: "Nixonomics means that all the things that should go up—the stock market, corporate profits, real spendable income, productivity—go down, and all the things that should go down—unemploy-

ment, prices, interest rates—go up." Ironically, the neologism had been independently suggested by this writer in early 1969 as a catch phrase to replace "gradualism," but was turned down as too contrived. Presidents whose names end in *n* have ever since been identified, or burdened, by the "-omics" suffix. Reaganomics was followed by Clintonomics. See -NOMICS.

Liquidity crisis: Along with "credit crunch," this describes a lack of ready cash in banks for lending to companies. In the summer of 1970, with the Federal Reserve restraining the growth of the money supply to combat inflation, there were fears this would lead to a drying up of the funds needed for the conduct of business; at a White House dinner at that time, Federal Reserve Chairman Arthur Burns told a group of businessmen in plain terms, "There will be no liquidity crisis," and there was not.

Disintermediation: This word was popularized in 1969, and again in 1971, by Federal Reserve Governor Andrew Brimmer and Assistant Budget Director Maurice Mann. When interest rates are rising, and the rates that may be paid by banks and savings and loan associations are restricted by legal ceilings, investors shift their funds from banks and S&Ls to bonds and other financial instruments that pay higher rates.

"Intermediation" is the process by which lenders use an intermediary in passing funds to a borrower; an individual puts his money in a bank, and the bank lends it to a home buyer. Disintermediation cuts out the middleman, or bank, as the lender lends his money directly to the borrower by purchasing a bond. The process, however, is not always viewed favorably; in 1989, the *New York Times* wrote of an incentive plan that would restrict family savings to federal savings products: "The disintermediation and market-damaging effects caused by such accounts would have a negative impact on competition and innovation."

See BAFFLEGAB; HOLD THE LINE; IN-FLATION; GAME PLAN; JAWBONING; NEW ECONOMICS; GUIDELINES; WE ARE ALL; OVERHEATED ECONOMY; SNAKE IN THE TUNNEL; HIGH COST OF LIVING; DOUBLE DIGIT; DEAD-CAT BOUNCE; DIP/DOUBLE DIP.

economic royalists President Franklin D. Roosevelt's description of those people with great financial wealth who hoped to control the activities of government.

In his acceptance speech, following the 1936 Democratic convention in Philadelphia, Mr. Roosevelt said: "The economic royalists complain that we seek to overthrow the institution of America. What they really complain of is that we seek to take away their power."

The speech was written by Samuel I. Rosenman and Stanley High, although Judge Rosenman gives credit for the phrase—much repeated thereafter—to Mr. High. However, FDR fund-raiser Sidney Weinberg recalled that "economic royalist" was originally suggested by Robert Jackson, who later became a Supreme Court Justice.

The phrase awakened memories of "MALEFACTORS OF GREAT WEALTH," "robber barons," and VESTED INTER-ESTS. See RUNNING AGAINST HOOVER.

In 1977 President Carter lambasted oil-industry lobbyists for "the greatest rip-off in history" in opposing his energy proposals. His selection of an amorphous, faceless villain—rather than an opponent like Senator Russell Long—recalled the FDR tactic to many. "A President enters a slanging match," editorialized the *Washington Star,* "with the 'economic royalists' of the moment at his own risk, although most Democratic chief executives find the temptation to do so irresistible."

edifice complex a monumental desire by a politician to leave behind great buildings.

When the Albany Mall was under construction in the sixties, New York Governor Nelson Rockefeller came under fire for spending too much taxpayer revenue on Ozymandian buildings. The governor, who in his youth helped manage Rockefeller Center in New York City, was accused of having an "edifice complex."

In a 1990 interview about his record, New York Governor Mario Cuomo said, "If I had wanted to be the guy with the edifice complex . . . I could have talked only about the state university building I've rebuilt and the roads and bridges I've rebuilt."

The pun is, of course, a play on "Oedipus complex," the yearning a child feels toward a parent of the opposite sex.

effect when used as the second element in a phrase, a change effected in something due to its being observed or studied.

Scientific parlance has contributed several phrases employing *effect* to the study of politics. Used in general application by analogy, phrases such as *Heisenberg effect* and *Hawthorne effect* refer to the influence of observation on the objects being observed.

The *Heisenberg effect,* formally known as the *Heisenberg uncertainty principle,* came from the German physicist Werner Karl Heisenberg, who died in 1976. Applications of his effect in financial marketing and media studies led to its political usage. The columnist Richard Reeves of the *New York Times* applied it to President Jimmy Carter's activities in 1977: "No one does or can do the same things onstage that he does unobserved. It's the popularized Heisenberg effect: the act of observing inevitably changes the process under observation."

Opinion polls taken immediately after the first Reagan-Mondale debate in 1984 showed Mondale the winner by a small margin; the discussion of the debate by political commentators vastly increased that margin in later polls. To explain the increase, George Church wrote in *Time* magazine, "This seemed to be a political application of what in physics is known as the Heisenberg uncertainty principle: the very act of measuring a phenomenon changes the phenomenon being measured in such a way as to make future readings unpredictable."

The *Hawthorne effect* offers a similar conclusion. This effect came from experiments during the 1920s at the Western Electric Company's Hawthorne Works of Cicero, Illinois. The performance of workers, according to this effect, will be affected by the study of that performance. When lights were turned up, worker productivity increased; when lights were lowered, productivity again increased—both primarily from the effect on workers of being included in the experiment.

effete snobs   a more recent term for EGGHEAD; a derogation of the arrogance of pseudo-intellectuals.

"A spirit of national masochism prevails," Vice President Agnew told a dinner at New Orleans on October 19, 1969, "encouraged by an effete corps of impudent snobs who characterize themselves as intellectuals."

Headline writers dropped "corps of impudent" to compress the epithet to "effete snobs," which is how it is generally remembered today. One reason the phrase caused such a fierce reaction was that many readers interpreted "effete" to mean "effeminate," which is not its meaning—"enervated," "wrung out," "intellectually barren" define the term properly and fit the context of his remarks.

The New Orleans speech was a lengthy, fairly dull exposition of the Nixon Administration's foreign and economic policies; however, the opening—including the controversial phrase—was prepared by speechwriter Pat Buchanan for the Vice President and gripped the audience. In it, he took care to blunt the charge of anti-intellectualism: "Persuasion through speeches and books is too often discarded for disruptive demonstrations aimed at bludgeoning the unconvinced into action. . . . Subtlety is lost, and fine distinctions based on acute reasoning are carelessly ignored in a headlong jump to a predetermined conclusion. Life is visceral rather than intellectual, and the most visceral practitioners of life are those who characterize themselves as intellectuals."

The term was used by Agnew critics as an example of polarization, "escalating the rhetoric," and—as expected—anti-intellectualism.

egghead   an intellectual; a highbrow. When used derogatively, an effete, bookish person with intellectual pretensions; when used affirmatively, a person with brains.

The term, which dates back to the early 1900s, appears in a circa-1918 letter by the poet Carl Sandburg. The letter, in the Toledo, Ohio, public library, is from the poet to his former newspaper boss, Negley Dakin Cochran: "'Egg heads' is the slang here for editorial writers. . . . I have handed in five editorials on Russia and two on the packers, voicing what 95 percent of the readers of The News are saying on the [trolley] cars and in the groceries and saloons but they have been ditched for hot anti-bolshevik stuff. . . . At that it isn't so much the policies of the papers as the bigotry and superstition and flunkeyism of the Egg Heads."

Stewart Alsop, in his syndicated column, reported in September 1952:

After [Adlai] Stevenson's serious and rather difficult atomic energy speech in Hartford, Conn., this reporter remarked to a rising young Connecticut Republican that a good many intelligent people, who would be considered normally Republican, obviously admired Stevenson. "Sure," was the reply, "all the eggheads love Stevenson. But how many eggheads do you think there are?"

Alsop went on to define the word as "what the Europeans would call 'intellectuals' . . . [someone] interested in ideas and in the words used to express those ideas." Years later he revealed that the "rising young Connecticut Republican" was his brother, John (not Joe): "John says the word sprang unbidden into his mind, with the mental image of a thin outer shell with mushy white stuff underneath." *Newsweek* quoted the source, John Alsop, as recalling "Egghead . . . dredged up out of my unconscious . . . is a visual picture of speech, tending to depict a large, oval head, smooth, faceless, unemotional but a little haughty and condescending."

Stewart Alsop had not intended to attack Stevenson seriously, but there was a need for a new word to crystallize the prevailing anti-intellectualism. Novelist Louis Bromfield soon defined it as "a person of intellectual pretensions, often a professor or the protégé of a professor . . . superficial . . . feminine . . . supercilious . . . a self-conscious prig . . . a BLEEDING HEART." The *Baltimore Sun* observed: "Writers on the lower levels of the trade have sought in vain for a new way of saying 'highbrow.' 'Loftydome' was about the best they could do, until 'egghead' came along."

Stevenson tried to laugh it off. To a University of Wisconsin audience in October of 1952, he said: "For a few minutes I took this egghead talk personally in injured silence. But I couldn't stand it and summoned up the courage to ask them what an egghead was. The answer, I discovered, is that an egghead is anyone who has gone to college! So at least today I have a lot of company." Later he quoted Professor Madison Priest's Latin joke *Dura est ovicipitum via,* which translates freely into "The way of the eggheads is hard." He bravely kidded: "Eggheads of the world, unite; you have nothing to lose but your yolks."

But, as the MAN ON THE WEDDING CAKE hurt Dewey, and the BAREFOOT BOY FROM WALL STREET hurt Willkie, *egghead* hurt Stevenson. The familiar image had long gone unnamed, but was nonetheless etched in many minds. From the huge, bald head of the scientist in the comic strip "Buck Rogers" to the description of an intellectual by Mao Tse-tung ("swollen in head, weak in legs, sharp in tongue but empty in belly"), a stereotype existed of a balding, top-heavy head bulging with brains and shaped like an egg.

For a while, subdivisions were made of eggheads that included "scrambled eggheads" for the confused variety to "hard-boiled eggheads" for the more tough-minded type. In 1992, *Barron's* magazine attacked those "so-called intellectuals" who criticized Vice President Dan Quayle for objecting to the values of the television sitcom *Murphy Brown.* "Nothing better illustrates what's wrong with those scrambled eggheads," wrote *Barron's.* "You can't knock something you've never seen? Since when?"

President Eisenhower, when asked about a Latin motto on his desk, *Suaviter in modo fortiter in re* ("Gentle in manner, strong in deed"), replied, "That proves I'm an egghead."

In the late sixties George Wallace sharpened the top of the egg to label his target "pointy-headed professors." See SEND THEM A MESSAGE.

eight millionaires and a plumber
description of the original Eisenhower cabinet.

In selecting his original cabinet, President Eisenhower turned for administrative talent to the business community. Democrats naturally sniped at the business-weighted cabinet. When it came to choosing a Labor Secretary, Eisenhower later wrote: "I hoped to find a satisfactory man from the ranks of labor itself. Long before, the old Department of Commerce and Labor had been divided, and Commerce was now traditionally headed by a businessman; I thought as a counterbalance the Labor Department should be headed by one actually experienced in the labor movement."

Adviser Herbert Brownell suggested Martin Durkin, a Chicago Democrat, head of the Journeyman Plumbers and Steamfitters Union. The contrast of Durkin with the other cabinet members only served to accentuate the business orientation; Richard Strout, under the pseudonym "TRB" in the *New Republic,* wrote in the issue of December 15, 1952: "The next four years may see the biggest lobby drive since Grant's day to loot the public domain, reverse history and crown big business. Ike has picked a cabinet of eight millionaires and a plumber."

The phrase caught the public fancy; writing a follow-up on February 2, 1953, Mr. Strout observed: "We often ask ourselves how much influence a weekly column like ours has, and we still don't know the answer, though it is curious to note the following. In the December 15 issue of this magazine we commented casually, 'Ike has picked a cabinet of eight millionaires and one [*sic*] plumber.' The result was rather astonishing. We find the comment still traveling outward after being included by such excellent columnists as Alsop, Childs, Stokes, Fleeson and goodness knows how many others; it bounded

the Atlantic into the London *Economist* and bounced back to America again in the *St. Louis Post-Dispatch.* Well, good luck, little quip—keep flying! Everybody in Washington, of course, likes to see his ephemeral comment take into the air and buzz away; no question of paternity is ever asked."

Asked about its paternity in 1977, Mr. Strout recalled: "It came to me in the bar of the National Press Club and I carefully husbanded it, knowing that if I loosed it there it would be around before I had reached 14th Street."

Oddly, the phrase is now usually misquoted as "nine" millionaires and a plumber, perhaps because of the growth of the cabinet. A pundit writing about the Clinton cabinet singled out Health and Human Services Secretary Donna Shalala with "fourteen New Democrats and a multiculturalist."

Eisenhower Doctrine. See DOCTRINES.

Eisenhower syntax convoluted extemporaneous remarks; ad libs that appear confused.

Spoken English differs from written English. Good secretaries rephrase their bosses' dictation before presenting it for signature. John Steinbeck was one of the rare authors who occasionally dictate rather than write or type their prose. Journalists have often "covered" for extemporaneous speakers by adding punctuation and rearranging sentences.

Dwight Eisenhower had his good days and bad days with unprepared remarks. His off-the-cuff addition to a speech before the American Society of Newspaper Editors in 1956 was a model of clarity; in many press conferences, however, the written transcript was both fuzzy and contorted. (Earlier Presidents refused to permit direct quotation, and newsmen had to edit their sentences.)

Oliver Jensen, later an editor of *American Heritage,* rewrote the GETTYSBURG ADDRESS as Eisenhower would have ad-libbed it, satirizing both Eisenhower syntax and vocabulary:

> I haven't checked these figures, but 87 years ago, I think it was, a number of individuals organized a governmental setup here in this country. . . . Well, now of course we are dealing with this big difference of opinion, civil disturbance you might say, although I don't like to appear to take sides or name any individuals. . . . But if you look at the overall picture of this, we can't pay any tribute—we can't sanctify this area—we can't hallow, according to whatever individual creeds or faiths or sort of religious outlooks are involved, like I said about this particular area. It was those individuals themselves, including the enlisted men—very brave individuals—who have given this religious character to the area. . . . We have to make up our minds right here and now, as I see it, they didn't put out all that blood, perspiration and—well, that they didn't just make a dry run here, that all of us, under God, that is, the God of our choice, shall beef up this idea about freedom and liberty and those kind of arrangements, and that government of all individuals, by all individuals and for the individuals shall not pass out of the world picture.

Columnist Arthur Krock observed that this kind of criticism dimmed the Eisenhower glory. "One reason is that glory withers in the controversial fires of politics. Others were supplied by the General himself: his frequent revelations at news conferences that he had not done his homework, his often blind and always labyrinthian syntax when extemporizing. These were gleefully seized on by the articulate 'liberals' who were his principal critics to lampoon him as an old fogey . . ."

It may be surprising to some that Eisenhower was a sharp and accurate editor of written copy; speech texts corrected by him show sensible tightening and clarifying. His first official words, following a brief prayer, spoken after taking his oath of office on January 20, 1953, were: "The world and we have passed the midway point of a century of continuing challenge." He had written on the margin of a draft: "I hate this sentence. *Who* challenges *whom? About what?*" He resisted the rhetoric, then agreed to use it. The author picked up a copy of an Eisenhower speech in 1952 after the General had edited it. Here is a typical sentence: "The Federal Government can make a tremendous contribution ~~through~~ ^{s including} the example it sets in ~~how it~~ ^{the} conducts ^{of} its business."

Reporter Tom Wicker, reviewing William Manchester's *Death of a President,* showed that rambling ad libs were not confined to the Eisenhower era: "Kennedy gets only the best of verbs, adjectives and similes. Thus, a certain day was 'as clear and crisp as a Kennedy order'; this may be an allowable descriptive, but not to those who tried to decipher a large part of the Kennedy syntax as recorded at many news conferences."

elder statesman an older politician or adviser to Presidents, who is treated with much public respect and some veneration.

"You can always get the truth," said abolitionist Wendell Phillips in 1860, "from an American statesman after he has turned seventy, or given up all hope of the Presidency."

As a dead or retired reporter becomes a "journalist," many politicians who leave the arena become known as "statesmen"; and those who grow old in this often active limbo are sometimes dubbed "elder statesmen."

The term was originally applied to the *genro,* Japanese political leaders who after their retirement from office unofficially controlled the emperor's privy council, especially in the period 1898–1914.

Like PUNDIT, the phrase was popularized in the U.S. by *Time.* An early use in that publication was September 16, 1929: "Last spring Elihu Root, gray Elder Statesman of U.S. diplomacy, good friend of Herbert Hoover, went to Geneva . . ."

Best known of the breed was financier Bernard Baruch, who in his Wall Street days gave new respectability to the word "speculator." A typical accolade was Arthur Krock's in 1943:

Though others have titles, he has none. Yet he is the President's counselor, philosopher and guide. . . . He is an honored visitor at the Pentagon, the Navy Department, the Department of State. . . . His rooms at the Carleton and the Shoreham, and the bench in Lafayette Square where he likes to warm his old bones in the sunshine, are the gathering places for all those with problems growing out of the State's business. . . . He is the nation's elder statesman. He is Bernard Mannes Baruch.

President Harry Truman had a more acerbic view of B.M.B. "He had always seen to it that his suggestions and recommendations, not always requested by the President, would be given publicity. . . . Baruch is the only man to my knowledge who has built a reputation on a self-assumed unofficial status as 'adviser.'"

Elder statesmen are occasionally PARTY ELDERS as well; Harry Truman and Herbert Hoover, in their later years, qualified for both. But normally, an elder statesman is "above" partisan politics; he is turned to for advice and photographs by Presidents who wish to show the breadth and depth of their brainpicking, and he lends his prestige to projects like international arms control and efficiency in government.

Eleanor Roosevelt, writing about her husband's soul-searching before deciding to run for a third term, showed how the elder-statesman role has a powerful appeal: ". . . it became clearly evident to me, from little things he said at different times, that he would really like to be in Hyde Park, and that the role of elder statesman appealed to him. He thought he would enjoy being in a position to sit back and offer suggestions and criticisms." Unlike Theodore Roosevelt, who left the presidency and then changed his mind about being an elder statesman, Franklin Roosevelt decided that the edge of power was no substitute for the center of power.

elect a leader, not a lover. See DIVORCE ISSUE.

electioneer to campaign crassly; to appear to intrigue or try too hard to get votes.

The word was probably coined by English conservative Edmund Burke, used at the time of the Revolutionary War and later to connote a too narrowly partisan approach to the polls. "The whole judicial authority," wrote John Adams in 1798, "as well as the executive, will be employed, perverted and prostituted to the purpose of electioneering."

To this day, the word's negative connotation—similar to "profiteer"—is reinforced by signs posted some fifty yards from voting places by Boards of Elections that read: "No Electioneering between this point and the Polls."

Attacking Lyndon Johnson's diplomacy, reporters Edward Weintal and Charles Bartlett set forth their version of a meeting between the President and the British Prime Minister, Harold Wilson: "The President blasted the

Prime Minister in no uncertain terms. 'I won't have you electioneering on my doorstep,' he stormed. 'Every time you get in trouble in Parliament you run over here with your shirttail hanging out . . . '"

electronic eavesdropping. See TAPS; BUGS.

elephant, Republican symbol of the GOP, born in the imagination of cartoonist Thomas Nast and first presented in *Harper's Weekly* on November 7, 1874.

An 1860 issue of *Railsplitter* and an 1872 cartoon in *Harper's Weekly* connected elephants with Republicans, but it was Nast who provided both parties with their symbols.

Oddly, two unconnected events led to the birth of the Republican elephant. James Gordon Bennett's *New York Herald* raised the cry of "Caesarism" in connection with the possibility of a third-term try for President Ulysses S. Grant. The issue was taken up by Democratic politicians in 1874, halfway through Grant's second term and just before the midterm elections, and helped disaffect Republican voters.

While the illustrated journals were depicting Grant wearing a crown, the *Herald* involved itself in another circulation-builder in an entirely different, nonpolitical area. This was the Central Park Menagerie Scare of 1874, a delightful hoax perpetrated by the *Herald*. They ran a story, totally untrue, that the animals in the zoo had broken loose and were roaming the wilds of New York's Central Park in search of prey.

Cartoonist Thomas Nast took the two examples of *Herald* enterprise and put them together in a cartoon for *Harper's Weekly*. He showed an ass (symbolizing the *Herald*) wearing a lion's skin (the scary prospect of Caesarism) frightening away the other animals in the forest (Central Park). The caption quoted a familiar fable: "An ass, having put on a lion's skin, roamed about in the forest and amused himself by frightening all the foolish animals he met with in his wanderings."

One of the foolish animals in the cartoon was an elephant, representing the Republican vote—not the party, the vote—which was being frightened away from its normal ties by the phony scare of Caesarism. In a subsequent cartoon on November 21, 1874, after the election in which the Republicans did badly, Nast followed up the idea by showing the elephant in a trap, illustrating the way the Republican vote had been decoyed from its normal allegiance. Other cartoonists picked up the symbol, and the elephant soon ceased to be the vote and became the party itself; the jackass, now referred to as a donkey, made a natural transition from representing the *Herald* to representing the Democratic party that had frightened the elephant. See DONKEY, DEMOCRATIC.

Why the choice of an elephant? New York State Senator N. A. Elsberg in Francis Curtis's 1904 book, *The Republican Party*, explains: "Among the elephant's known characteristics are cleverness and unwieldiness. He is an animal easy to control until he is aroused; but when frightened or stirred up, he becomes absolutely unmanageable. Here we have all the characteristics of the Republican vote . . ."

A less sympathetic explanation came from Adlai Stevenson: "The elephant has a thick skin, a head full of ivory, and as everyone who has seen a circus parade knows, proceeds best by grasping the tail of its predecessor."

Eleventh Commandment "Thou Shalt Not Speak Ill of Fellow Republicans."

When Dr. Gaylord E. Parkinson, a San Diego obstetrician, became California State Republican Chairman, he inherited a party that had been torn apart with internecine warfare every two years.

Just before the contest between actor Ronald Reagan and San Francisco Mayor George Christopher for the Republican gubernatorial nomination in 1966, Parkinson laid down the rule that he named the "Eleventh Commandment." Reagan, who had most to lose in a bitter battle and whose strategy was to "unify the party behind a candidate who can win," accepted the rule with alacrity; Christopher followed along and never really joined the "inexperience" issue.

In the 1988 primaries, George Bush announced his intention not to badmouth Bob Dole. Said Bush: "I'm going back to being the old George Bush. I'm going to be the nice, benign guy that I was, an 11th-commandment guy; never say anything bad about another Republican and all that stuff."

Party chairmen traditionally try to heal breaches in primaries before they become so irreparable as to make a nomination valueless. Boss Frank Hague of Jersey City, plumping for Al Smith against FDR for the Democratic nomination in 1932, declared that Franklin Roosevelt would not carry a single state east of the Mississippi. FDR's manager, Jim Farley, made a mild reply, calculated to win the respect of the professionals: "Governor Roosevelt's friends have not come to Chicago to criticize, cry down or defame any Democrat from any part of the country."

Calling a truism a commandment, or endowing a fiat with commandment status, gives a jocose weight to any political advice. In July 1977 Vernon Jordan, head of the National Urban League, criticized President Carter for "not living up to the first commandment of politics—help those who help you."

elitism leadership by an aristocracy—whether of the intelligent, the wealthy, the tastemaking, the meritorious, or the merely powerful.

In the Nixon attempt to identify and rally a cross-party "silent majority," a useful *bête noire* was "elitism." In 1968 Alabama Governor George Wallace had successfully exploited the resentment of lower-middle-class voters against unseen forces in faraway Washington that manipulated their lives; in the congressional campaign of 1970 President Nixon directed Vice President Spiro Agnew to "crack those elitists" who ran the power centers most critical of his Administration: the media, the academy, the foundations. This was an attempt at a turnabout: the liberal philosophy, which espoused the redistribution of income for the benefit of the greatest number of people, could be attacked as being guided by a small clique. The target was the leadership, not the recipient of liberalism's liberality.

The word, which had been popularized in sociology by C. Wright Mills (see POWER ELITE) gained its -ist and -ism forms in the early fifties in the writings of sociologist David Riesman. Freud, he wrote in 1950, "shared with . . . Nietzsche and Carlyle elements of an elitist position."

Although some conservatives preferred "illuminati," the term "elitist" became current as an attack word; defenders of the idea shied away from the word, which is definitely pejorative, and countered with "meritocracy."

In 1972 the editors of the *Public Interest,* a quarterly, surveyed the emergence of the new political-sociological favorite:

Elitist, of course, is closest to the surface. Perhaps it has already lost its esoteric quality. Who knows, any longer, that it derives from Mosca, Michels, and Pareto, and achieved a bastardized American birth through the midwifery of Harold Lasswell, James Burnham, and C. Wright Mills. But in a populist society, elitist is a handy stick for all sides and for all seasons. In the *New York Times* Op-Ed page, that elitist sounding board for the vox populi, Jeffrey St. John denounces "public broadcasting" as appealing only to elitists, and concludes that therefore the U.S. Government should not provide a subsidy. . . . Not to be outdone, President Nixon, in responding to the report of the Environmental Council, according to the *New York Times*, "said at one point that the environment was in danger of becoming an 'elitist' issue and that the Council should 'reach down and include the fellow who never went to college.'" And, in the letters column of the *Village Voice*, that Miss Lonelyhearts of the counterculture, a transsexual person denounces lesbian Jill Johnston for her "transvestite-hating . . . elitist and authoritarian stance."

By 1978 the word had become a standard blast at anyone with an undue regard for excellence as a criterion for the receipt of money or power. Next to "racism" and "sexism," the charge of "elitism" had to be vigorously resisted by those tagged. A good example was in this letter to the *Washington Star* from Michael Straight, deputy chairman of the National Endowment for the Arts:

> Now that four-letter words have become respectable, we need new epithets, and "elitist," like "racist," has slid into frequent and careless employment. Like "racist," it confuses thought in an area that demands precision.
>
> If "elitism" means anything in cultural terms, it means adherence to the position set forth by T. S. Eliot in his "Notes Towards a Definition of Culture." Eliot argued that "culture" could only be understood and transmitted by a small minority of well-educated citizens, and that the majority was and always would be incapable of appreciating the arts.
>
> I happen to have spent eight years denouncing Eliot's position, which to me is wholly antithetical to the nature and purpose of the National Endowment for the Arts. I happen to believe that public funding for the arts is justifiable only on the assumption that they may and will be enjoyed by the majority of our citizens.

In the 1992 Presidential campaign, Dan Quayle and his Chief of Staff, William Kristol, introduced the term "cultural elite"; *Newsweek* promptly published its choices for that list.

empowerment   the gaining of power; moving into a position of control, or gaining the feeling thereof.

Dating back to 1849, the noun *empowerment* is built on the seventeenth-century verb *empower,* "to give legal power or authority to."

This forceful noun has gained political and economic overtones since its adoption by the Students for a Democratic Society in the 1960s. Especially resonant among blacks, the word was used in 1976 by Vernon E. Jordan Jr., when he headed the National Urban League: "That goes to economic security, income maintenance, economic empowerment—the real basic issues of equal opportunity."

In politics, the term has been applied in voter registration as *electoral empowerment.* Pat Caddell, the political pollster, offered the word in a wistful commentary after Reagan's reelection: "The issue was the empowerment of a generation. . . ."

George Bush employed the word in 1990, during an awards ceremony in the Rose Garden. "Each of these seven Americans," said Bush, "provides a definition of the word that I have learned to respect so much, learned from Jack Kemp—empowerment."

Foremost among the word's supporters in Washington has been Jack F. Kemp, Bush's Secretary of Housing and Urban Development. A 1993 *New York Times Magazine* article described the use of the term by Kemp and James Pinkerton in economic messages: "Debating the meaning of 'empowerment' was one of the more consuming activities of the Bush domestic planners. When pressed, Kemp and Pinkerton would fall back on a familiar roll call of policies: enterprise zones; vouchers that let parents choose their children's schools; tax credits for the poor; and the HOPE program."

Here is Kemp's own definition of *empowerment*: "Giving people the opportunity to gain greater control over their own destiny through access to assets of private property, jobs and education."

Five prominent Republicans—Theodore J. Forstmann, William J. Bennett, Jack Kemp, Jeane J. Kirkpatrick and Vin Weber—recently joined in an organization known as Empower America, which many thought was meant to lay the basis for the 1996 Presidential campaign.

empty chair a phrase dramatizing an opponent's refusal to debate.

When John Foster Dulles ran unsuccessfully against incumbent New York Senator Herbert Lehman, he was unable to draw Lehman into debate. To make his point, Dulles traveled with a "prop"—an empty chair he debated in lieu of Lehman.

The origin of this oratorical technique was provided the author by historian George Johnson. In 1924, while running for Vice President on Robert La Follette's Progressive ticket, Burton K. Wheeler attacked President Calvin Coolidge in a way Wheeler described in his *Yankee from the West*:

"In Des Moines, I hit on an original showmanship gimmick. The hall was jammed to the rafters . . . I said,

'You people have a right to know how a candidate for President stands on issues, and so far President Coolidge has not told you where he stands on anything . . . so I am going to call him before you tonight and ask him to take this chair and tell me where he stands.' People in the auditorium began to crane their necks to see if Coolidge really was somewhere on the premises. I pulled a vacant chair and addressed it as though it had an occupant. 'President Coolidge,' I began, 'tell us where you stand on Prohibition.' I went on with rhetorical questions in this vein, pausing after each for a short period. Then I wound up: 'There, my friends, is the usual silence that emanates from the White House.' The crowd roared in appreciation."

In the four-man gubernatorial race in New York in 1966 (Rockefeller, O'Connor, Adams, and Roosevelt, Jr.), negotiations for a debate appeared interminable to Frank O'Connor's representative, Peter Straus. Straus threatened John Trubin, Rockefeller's representative and a law partner of Senator Jacob Javits, that O'Connor would go on alone and debate an empty chair. Trubin shook his head. "That's against FCC regulations," he said with a straight face. "This is a four-man race. You'd have to debate *three* empty chairs."

The symbol is not limited to the United States. Gaby Rado of Independent Television News reported in June 1991 on Soviet newspapers and their criticism of Boris Yeltsin: "Yeltsin's also been criticized for refusing to take part in last night's pre-election TV debate. An empty chair was pointedly left for him on the studio floor."

See EQUAL TIME.

enemies list originally, Nixon counsel John Dean's roster of Administration opponents to be harassed; now used as a counterattack by any person considering himself targeted for criticism by those in power.

"This memorandum," Dean wrote on August 16, 1971, "addresses the matter of how we can maximize the fact of our incumbency in dealing with persons known to be active in their opposition to our Administration. Stated a bit more bluntly—how we can use the available federal machinery to screw our political enemies."

George Bell, an aide to presidential counsel Charles Colson, compiled a list in response to Dean's memo, which Colson forwarded to Dean under the heading "Opponents List." However, when Dean revealed his own memo and its answer in testimony before the Senate Watergate Committee, he called it an "enemies list"; the word "enemies," which he had used in his original memo, carried a far more savage connotation than "opponents." Curiously, the revulsion at this device exempted its author, Dean, and concentrated on Nixon, Colson and the rest of the "President's men." Among those on the list were a fund-raiser (Arnold Picker of United Artists Corp.), a large contributor (Howard Stein of the Dreyfus Corporation), a labor leader (Leonard Woodcock of the United Auto Workers), a black congressman (John Conyers, D-Mich.), and "a real media enemy" (Daniel Schorr, CBS).

The "enemies list" became one of the phrases associated with the abuses of power charged during the Watergate investigation. Colson argued that it had been compiled "for the use of the social office" to exclude opponents from White House dinners, but it was apparent that the intent was to use the power of government to punish political adversaries.

William Sullivan, a former deputy to J. Edgar Hoover at the FBI, insisted that the idea "originated in the Bureau. In the Bureau it was called the 'No Contact List' . . . On the No Contact List went all individuals who had criticized the Bureau or Hoover personally."

In September 1977, when supporters in the Senate of President Carter's natural-gas program were filibustering against deregulation, and were unexpectedly abandoned by the White House, Senator James Abourezk (D-S.D.) cracked: "This Administration doesn't have an enemies list—it has a friends list."

As Watergate memories recede, the phrase has been used in gentle spoofs. On April 10, 1978, a *New York Times* editorial stated: "We have been compiling an enemies list: uppity words . . ." The ten on the list were *absent* ("when disguised as a synonym for 'without'"), FEEDBACK, *governance* ("except when accompanied by ELDER STATESMEN"), *hold harmless, in place, massive* ("except in case of nuclear attack"), OPTION, *posture, thrust,* and *viable.*

Other political lists include HIT LIST, for those targeted for dismissal; WATCH LIST, a list of potential problems; *wish list,* a compilation of legislative desires; and SHORT LIST, those being seriously considered for appointment.

engage in personalities phrase used to evade direct or personal political clash, always disappointing to news reporters.

The phrase is most closely associated with Dwight Eisenhower, and is consistent with his frequent ABOVE POLITICS stance. At one of the early press conferences of his 1952 campaign, he was reminded of his comment that the loss of China must not be repeated, and asked on whom he would pin responsibility for that loss. "I am not . . . going to engage in personalities in anything I have to say. I believe in certain principles, certain procedures and methods that I will discuss with anybody at any time. I am not going to talk personalities."

In office, Eisenhower held to his rule. Looking over a draft of a presidential message to Congress that implied criticism of some congressional leader's motives, he is reported to have said, "Look here, you and I can argue issues all day and it won't affect our friendship, but the minute I question your motives you will never forgive me."

A good many Democrats questioned Eisenhower's motives in refusing to tangle with Senator Joseph McCarthy in the tumult of McCARTHYISM. In his memoirs, Eisenhower answered this criticism: "McCarthyism was a much larger issue than McCarthy. This was the truth that I constantly held before me as I listened to the many exhortations that I should 'demolish' the Senator himself. . . . Lashing back at one man, which is easy enough for a President, was not as important to me as the long-term value of restraint, the due process of law, and the basic rights of free men." See PHILIPPIC.

In *At Ease*, he wrote: "I make it a practice to avoid hating anyone. If someone's been guilty of despicable actions toward me, I used to write his name on a piece of scrap paper, drop it in the lowest drawer of my desk, and say to myself: 'That finishes the incident . . . and that fellow.' The drawer became over the years a sort of private wastebasket for crumbled-up spite and discarded personalities."

By steadfastly refusing to "engage in personalities," Eisenhower did what many campaigners often promise but seldom observe. Wendell Willkie, who later engaged FDR forcibly, said: "We go into this campaign as a crusade. We shall fight the campaign on the basis of American liberty, not on the basis of hate, jealousy or personalities."

The phrase, as it stands, is confusing; it is a shortening of "engage in a discussion of personalities," and really means "You won't get me in the gutter with that guy."

Current synonyms are *finger-pointing* and the *blame game.*

enlightened self-interest the theory that actions taken seemingly at variance with personal benefit can benefit society, including the individual, in the long run.

Self-interest, sometimes written without the hyphen, dates back to the mid-1600s. Primarily used in religious contexts, the term suggested sinful self-absorption in contrast to Christian charity.

Edmund Burke, the Irish-born political writer and British statesman, coined the longer phrase in his 1790 *Reflections on the Revolution in France.* In refusing to support the French Revolution, Burke wrote of "an enlightened self-interest, which, when well understood, they tell us, will identify with an interest more enlarged and publick."

Within a decade the longer term was being used to rationalize personal benefit or profit. *Farmer's Magazine* in 1801 wrote of "an enlightened sense of self-interest."

In this context, the past participle *enlightened* can suggest persuasion or pressure. George Beall, a Baltimore attorney and former prosecutor, told the *Washington Post* in 1977 about business deals being cut with cooperating witnesses. According to Beall, those witnesses cooperated out of "enlightened self-interest. It's not a very nice business—it's a dirty business."

On Cable News Network in 1992, the enlightening phrase was used by Michael Young, spokesman of the U.S. delegation to an environmental summit: "It's enlightened self-interest that will produce precisely the kinds of technical breakthroughs that we need to save the environment. Business is part of the problem, but business is also a very good part of the potential solution."

Enlightened is a political modifier of nouns that might otherwise draw criticism. In 1989, former Senator Gary Hart proposed "enlightened engagement," justifying selective intervention to those who, a generation ago, had opposed Vietnam involvement. Secretary of State James A. Baker 3d, unaware of the source, picked up the term in speeches.

entangling alliances a phrase of Jefferson's that is threaded through American history, most often used to justify a policy of ISOLATIONISM.

George Washington, who many people think first used "entangling alliances," only came close to using the phrase in his Farewell Address in 1796: "It is our true policy to steer clear of permanent alliances with any portion of the foreign world." In the same speech he also said: "Why, by interweaving our destiny with that of any part of Europe, entangle our peace and prosperity in the toils of European ambition, rivalship, interest, humor, or caprice?"

Two years later Thomas Jefferson wrote to T. Lomax: "Commerce with all nations, alliance with none, should be our motto." He reworked this sentence for his inaugural address in 1801: "Peace, commerce, and honest friendship, with all nations; entangling alliances with none."

Jefferson's crystallization of Washington's point became a rock of American foreign policy for over a century. When Woodrow Wilson tried to persuade Americans to accept the League of Nations, he addressed himself to the one phrase that most stood in his way, and tried to identify himself with it: "I am proposing that all nations henceforth avoid entangling alliances which would draw them into competitions of

power. . . . There is no entangling alliance in a concert of power."

The phrase was handled just as gingerly by Franklin Roosevelt and his Secretary of State, Cordell Hull, in the mid-thirties. While denouncing *entanglements* (which everybody is automatically against) they had to lay the groundwork for *alliances* (which most people more or less favor). FDR said in 1935: "Our national determination to keep free of foreign wars and entanglements cannot prevent us from feeling deep concern when ideals and principles that we have cherished are challenged." Hull added in 1936: "While carefully avoiding any political entanglements, my Government strives at all times to cooperate with other nations to every practical extent in support of peace objectives . . ."

"Entanglement" has lost none of its effectiveness as an attack word. Walter Lippmann (see ATLANTIC COMMUNITY) wrote in 1965 that if Lyndon Johnson's conception of the Great Society were to fail, "it would not be because the conception is false. It would be because of some external cause—possibly because we had become diverted by some entanglement in another continent."

A serious threat of entanglement is now called a "quagmire."

entitlement a right to benefits that ought to be provided by government or, to opponents of the growth of federal spending, a euphemism for "welfare."

The term appeared in a law passed by Congress in 1944: ". . . it should be clearly provided that entitlement to pay and allowances is not to be terminated on the actual date of death. . . ." After a few decades of limited use, the word was revived by Congressional aides in the late 1960s, at the end of the GREAT SOCIETY, to defend against attacks on "welfare cheats."

The word was used synonymously for *welfare,* which was once a euphemism for *relief;* a generation after its introduction, though, *welfare* became a pejorative term because of its abuses. (In New York City, "Welfare Island" was renamed "Roosevelt Island.")

In the mid-1970s centrists preferred to adopt the term *entitlement* in discussions about cutting spending. The *New York Times* wrote about Representative Brock Adams: "He indicated a belief that something had to be done to hold down the growth of programs, granting an automatic 'entitlement' to eligible individuals. Among these are food stamps, welfare and health-care financing."

Not everybody accepts the equating of *entitlement* and *welfare.* Ceil Frank at the Office of Family Assistance in Washington said in 1982: "Entitlement includes both earned benefits and unearned benefits. Social Security and veterans' benefits are earned benefits, and unearned benefits are what *welfare* refers to."

While certain criteria have to be met for anyone applying for an entitlement, the very existence and spread of entitlements came into question during the Reagan Administration. A 1981 *New York Times* editorial, entitled "Charity," quoted Budget Director David Stockman as saying, "I don't think people are entitled to any services."

In response, the *Times* editorial, while admitting that "the budgeteers' word 'entitlements' certainly does sound arrogant," went on to say that "there are some things people should not have to beg for. Food, for instance, or safe housing, or a lawyer when there's trouble. . . . To say 'no entitlements' or 'let the states do it,' or 'let the private sector do it' is a barely varnished way of saying 'Don't do it.' And that is not a

war against inflation. It is a war against the poor."

Liberals prefer to differentiate between *welfare* as being "public assistance" and *entitlements* as being earned or deserved. Conservatives prefer to lump the two together and call for SPENDING CAPS; Ross Baker, a political science professor at Rutgers, called *entitlements* "tenure for the UNDERCLASS."

In a June 1993 speech in Milwaukee, as his policies were being criticized as too liberal, Bill Clinton attacked what he chararacterized as the Reagan era's "politics of abandonment" and juxtaposed that extremist position with *entitlement* as the opposite extreme: "We have to move beyond entitlement and abandonment. I ran for President basically on the same things that I found had worked for me when I was a governor—not entitlement, not abandonment, but EMPOWERMENT. . . ."

environmentalist an anti-pollutionary; one who puts the values of the preservation of the earth and its atmosphere ahead of economic development.

At the turn of the twentieth century, an environmentalist was a scientist who believed that a human being's behavior was determined more by his surroundings than by his genetic inheritance.

Until the sixties, the battle of heredity vs. environment colored the use of the word. However, another battle was beginning that gave the word new surroundings. Keith Mellanby, in *Pesticides and Pollution* in 1967, wrote of pesticides "which have recently been shown to constitute such an important contribution to environmental pollution." In 1970 a group of marine biologists wrote the *Times* of London that "we are actively involved in various facets of environmental science—a less emotive and more encompassing term than pollution studies."

By the seventies, "environmental impact" became a rallying phrase for a loose alliance of scientists and political activists who were worried about the encroachments of immediate comfort upon the long-term life of man; the word "ecology," which had meant a balance in nature of organisms and their environment, became a vogue term around 1970. "Ecologist," a term coined in 1873 by biologist Ernst Haeckel to describe the relationship of organisms to their environments, may replace "environmentalist" in time. However, "ecologist" has a more scientific connotation, and "environmentalist" still encompasses people who don't like chemicals in their drinking water or the smell of cigarette smoke in airplanes.

"Conservationist," the predecessor term, survives; perhaps it has been avoided by liberals interested in the restraint of technology because of its resemblance to "conservatism." George Reiger, conservation editor of *Field & Stream*, wrote the *New York Times* on January 10, 1978: ". . . you should permit the record to be set straight on conservation, a word popularized in America by Gifford Pinchot (a hunter) after it had been used in Great Britain for half a century to describe 'the wise use of renewable resources.' . . . People who believe that no creatures should be killed, that no forests should be cut, that, in fact, the goldfinch that comes to their feeder this winter is the very same bird that visited them a decade ago should be called ultra-preservationists, radical environmentalists, unrealistic extremists, or residents of the twilight zone, but please, please, don't call them conservationists. They are not."

An old geneticist might say that political environmentalism inherited a natural schizophrenia: a stance that is outspokenly anti-development, pro-wilderness, and suspicious of technology's "advances" (which is seen as anti-business) also comes directly into conflict with the development of new jobs, and is thus attacked by organized labor as ELITIST.

"If there's ever a flat choice between smoke and jobs," said President Nixon to this speechwriter in 1970, "tilt toward jobs." The environmentalists, toward the end of the seventies, had succeeded in many of their goals of ensuring the consideration of the impact of polluting atmosphere and water on many business and governmental plans, but began to develop a backlash among those who felt their efforts limited the growth of the job market.

Demanding "a more vigorous approach to supply expansion," the NAACP issued a statement at the end of 1977 saying: "We cannot accept the notion that our people are best served by a policy based on the inevitability of energy shortage and the need for the government to allocate an ever-diminishing supply among competing interests." (See ZERO SUM GAME.)

Republican Ronald Reagan seized on this statement as indicative of the "elitism" of environmentalists, whose best-known publication was *The Limits to Growth*. "The limits-to-growth people," said Reagan, "who are so influential in the Carter Administration are telling us, in effect, that the American economic pie is shrinking, that we all have to settle for a smaller slice . . . the best way . . . is for government to get out of the way while the rest of us make a bigger pie so that everybody can have a bigger slice."

Environmental activists are known the world over as *greens;* it became the name of a German political party.

E Pluribus Unum.   See UNITED WE STAND.

eponymy. See QUISLING; MAVERICK; GERRYMANDER; SOLON; PHILIPPIC; BORK.

equal time a doctrine requiring radio- and television-station licensees to exercise fair play in making air time available to opposing candidates for public office or views differing from the station's editorial policies.

Curiously, the phrase "equal time" does not appear in any of the statutes or decisions of the Federal Communications Commission, the agency charged with regulating stations. In a 1968 letter to the author, FCC Secretary Ben F. Waple explained:

As you point out, in Section 315 of the Communications Act of 1934, as amended (47 U.S.C. 315), the phrase "equal opportunities" is used in reference to broadcasts by candidates for public office. The same phrase is used in the Commission's Rules regarding that subject (47 CFR 73.-120). The term "equal time" is used popularly in the broadcasting industry as an equivalent to "equal opportunities." "Equal time" has no official status and does not appear in the Commission statute, rules, or interpretive rulings; however, it may appear in press releases for the Commission's Office of Reports and Information.

(For an example of reluctant official adoption of a popular phrase, see MEDICARE.)

In essence, "equal time" requires stations to make provision for all candidates if they make their airwaves available to any, *unless* the coverage is part of a regularly scheduled news broadcast, interview, documentary, or on-the-spot coverage of a news event. To be on the safe side, most stations lean backward to provide equal time on interviews and regularly scheduled news broadcasts (over a period of time) as well.

Under its "historical notes," the FCC does use "equal time" to describe the special provision made in the 1960 presidential campaign to permit the Kennedy-Nixon debates without offering time to the splinter-party candidates.

The phrase, as used today, applies only to free, public service time proffered by stations and networks; on purchased time, candidates can and do obtain unequal time, depending on the financial capability and media choices of the parties. However, if one party "reserves the time" in a period shortly before election day, and the opposition decides to spend some money that night, stations must bend every effort to make equal "commercial" time available for sale, even though it might already be sold to others.

The equal time law, aimed at protecting minority rights to be heard, can be used as a shield for abuses. Jack Gould, television critic for the *New York Times*, showed how campaign strategists in 1964 used the law to their advantage:

In the last Presidential race, for example, established TV news programs sought appearances by President Johnson and Sen. Barry Goldwater. Virtually all the overtures were rejected by the White House, allegedly because the Democratic party saw no point in giving free exposure to the Republican aspirant. Unless both candidates agreed to appear, the networks were open to violation of the principle of equal time. In effect, therefore, if one candidate feels he is better known than his rival he can exert a veto power over his opponent's free appearance and force him to buy time. This strategic attitude also accounts for the invariable nonsense over challenges and counter-challenges on the subject of TV debates, which do not involve any campaign costs. One candidate, usually the one enjoying the publicity advantage of being an incumbent, sees no purpose in putting a rival on an equal stature in the public eye.

Era of Good Feeling the years 1817 to 1825, when James Monroe was President of the United States, and there was, in effect, no political opposition.

The term was probably first used by Benjamin Russell in the *Columbian Centinel* in 1817 while Monroe was making a northern tour. Russell, speaking for the defeated Federalists, expressed a wish that the Federalist faction, now practically defunct, should be treated as though past differences had never existed.

The "Good Feeling" was more apparent than real. Monroe's victory was largely the product of political organization, the Federalists' complete loss of credit because of their opposition to the War of 1812, and an attempt in New England to secede during that war. The result had been the sweeping Monroe victory in 1820 in which only one elector voted against him.

During the Era, factions were forming which eventually gave rise to political parties as we know them today. At that time there was the "Adamite" faction, Eastern-oriented, looking toward Europe and the sea. They were merchants and the new manufacturers, followers of John Quincy Adams, who would soon become the Whigs. Then there were the Jacksonites, farmers and frontiersmen, who were soon to become the leaders of the Democratic party.

The term has been continually revived. Victorious Northern Republicans used it after the Civil War, meaning by an "Era of Good Feeling," the hope that the Democrats and the South would accept their defeat gracefully.

Franklin D. Roosevelt used it in 1928 when, upon being elected New York governor, he described ". . . a period in our history known in all our school books as the 'era of good feeling.' It is my hope that we stand on the threshold of another such era in this State."

As President, Roosevelt called in his second inaugural address for "a genuine period of good feeling." And Lyndon Johnson, after his overwhelming victory over Senator Barry Goldwater in 1964, expressed the hope that a new Era of Good Feeling would result.

It did not; and under conditions of political democracy, it never does for any appreciable length of time. Even in the days of Monroe there was continual conflict between individual supporters of John Quincy Adams and Andrew Jackson. President Johnson's hopes were based on the continued success of his policy of CONSENSUS and this, too, was frustrated.

See PRESIDENT OF ALL THE PEOPLE; DEAL.

erring brethren. See EUPHEMISMS, POLITICAL.

escalate the rhetoric. See RHETORIC.

escalation an increase in military activity, either in preparation for or during an armed conflict; by extension, acceleration of effort in any kind of campaign.

Escalation is one of the linguistic products of the COLD WAR and the nuclear age. Scientists and strategists began writing what they called SCENARIOS of how nuclear war might occur and how it might be avoided. Herman Kahn, one of the most articulate of the thermonuclear thinkers, put it this way: "War by miscalculation might also result from the process . . . called 'escalation.' A limited move may appear safe, but set into motion a disastrous sequence of decisions and actions." Kahn even postulated a sixteen-step "escalation ladder" leading from "subcrisis disagreement" to the aftermath of "all-out war." Through the writings of Kahn and others in the 1950s, the term came into wide use as one of the relatively unusual cases in which both experts and laymen could share the same snippet of jargon. "But wars, large or small, are fought for victory," wrote *The Nation* early in 1961. "That means you pound the enemy with every available lethal assistance, with the inevitable result—to use the fancy new term—of escalation to all-out war."

Centuries ago, there had been another military term for an elevating device or act. *Escalade,* from the French, was used as a verb meaning to scale a wall or fortification. As a noun, *escalade* means the ladder used for this purpose. Sir Ernest Gowers in Fowler's *Modern English Usage* explains the preference for escalation over the older term by pointing out that escalation "has the advantage of novelty and a more native look, and a moving staircase provides a more up-to-date metaphor than a scaling ladder."

Escalation gained its widest currency not because of nuclear conflict but because of the war in Vietnam. Each time one side or the other introduced reinforcements or a type of weapon previously unused in the war, the act was branded as escalation. In the U.S., the word took on political overtones and a pejorative shading first because Washington was pledged to seeking peace rather than "widening" the war, and second because it gave opponents of the war a universally understood term with which to attack the Administration. Official spokesmen, said the *New York Times,* "have generally shied away from describing each new expansion of the air war as 'escalation' because of political sensitivity . . . [they] prefer to say that the air war is being widened, that pressure is being increased or that the war is being increased."

Time magazine lost all patience with the term in April 1967, calling it in a lead article "one of those windy words that are foisted on the public by mili-tary bureaucrats, interminably parroted by the press and kept in the vernacular long after losing any real meaning." Nonetheless, escalation seemed too deeply entrenched for exorcism. Dr. Martin Luther King, Jr., an opponent of the war, called on his followers for "an escalation of our opposition to the war in Vietnam."

Although real escalators run both up and down, the political term heads only upward. The antonym is *de-escalate,* which is awkward, or *descalate,* which the *New York Times* proposed on May 31, 1967, as a word for mutual reduction of military activity but which did not catch on.

When escalation of troop levels in Vietnam ceased to be an issue in the U.S., the word became part of a new cliché, "don't escalate the rhetoric," an admonition honored largely in the breach. See WINDING DOWN; VIETNAMIZATION.

establishment. See EASTERN ESTABLISHMENT.

ethnic cleansing the mass murder or removal of an ethnic group from an area by another ethnic group.

In the late 1980s, this term for genocide was popularized. The Armenians and Azerbaijanis were fighting for control of the autonomous enclave of Azerbaijan called Nagorno-Karabakh in 1988; according to Serbo-Croatian sources, Soviet officials used this term—in Russian, *etnicheskie chistki,* "ethnic purges"—to describe the attempts of one group to drive out the other.

In an April 1993 news conference, President Clinton was questioned about conflicts in Bosnia. He responded, "The principle of ethnic cleansing is something we ought to stand up against."

The phrase "ethnically clean" was first used in Yugoslav politics in an

April 1987 speech by Slobodan Milosevic, then head of the Communist party in Serbia and later Serbia's President, in the town of Kosovo Polje. Discussing efforts by ethnic Albanians to drive Serbs and Montenegrins from Kosovo, where Albanians predominate, he said, "Albanian separatists and nationalists are counting on the time factor and that conditions are working for them. . . . There is the political view that is very prominent that the request for an ethnically clean Kosovo is justified and possible."

See FINAL SOLUTION.

ethnic purity cultural or racial solidarity of a community; a phrase, conceded to be impolitic, used by Jimmy Carter in his presidential campaign.

"I have nothing against a community," said Jimmy Carter in April of 1976 as he approached the Democratic nomination, "that's made up of people who are Polish, Czechoslovakians, French Canadians or blacks who are trying to maintain the ethnic purity of their neighborhood. This is a natural inclination on the part of people."

The remark—intended to assuage Southern fears that the former Georgia governor was in favor of "forced busing" and other drastic remedies for segregation—instead ignited resentment among blacks and Northern liberals distrustful of the Carter candidacy. At first the candidate tried to explain what he meant, but the pressure soon caused him to withdraw the phrase and apologize for it. During this flap Congressman Andrew Young, a Carter supporter (later U.S. Ambassador to the UN) worked hard to allay black suspicions and earned the candidate's gratitude.

The phrase, like BENIGN NEGLECT, is occasionally used to remind voters of an old error. In August 1977 William Raspberry wrote in the *Washington*

Post: "Despite his repeated, embarrassed, back-tracking attempts to explain, it never became clear just what Jimmy Carter meant by that 'ethnic purity' remark. I suspect the candidate himself didn't fully understand it. Some of us thought the phrase meant hardly anything at all, except possibly as veiled opposition to the establishment of public housing in white working-class neighborhoods.

"He should have visited Chicago. Ethnic purity is alive and well in this city that has earned its reputation as the most segregated city in America."

In 1993, the term became linked internationally to the issue of ETHNIC CLEANSING. The *Washington Post* reported in February 1993 on Vojislav Seselj, the Serb leader in the former Yugoslavia, who increased "his demands for ethnic purity. He says he wants at least 360,000 ethnic Albanians to clear out of Kosovo."

ethnics Americans who take pride in their national origin; now broadening to any group conscious of a cultural heritage that is not White Anglo-Saxon Protestant or black.

"Ethnic" began as an adjective, meaning "pagan" or "heathen"; a confusion with the Greek etymology gave rise to the mistake that it stems from "heathenic." At the start the meaning was limited to people neither Jewish nor Christian; later, in social science, the meaning was "racial," or ethnological; in 1941, sociologists W. Lloyd Warner and Paul S. Lunt, in *The Social Life of a Modern Community,* used the adjective for the first time as a noun, calling attention to their coinage by using quotation marks: "These groups . . . we have called 'ethnics.'"

By 1970, as the white BACKLASH took political form, a word was needed for lower-middle-class whites who felt threatened by the advancement of minorities. In a 1973 promotional piece for the *American Heritage Dictionary,* associate editor Alma Trinor wrote: "There is among many groups in the population a new sense of group identity and pride that has given rise to changes in nomenclature. Now we read not about hyphenated Americans, second-generation Americans, or religious minorities, but about *ethnics.*"

David Guralnik, when he was editor of *Webster's New World Dictionary,* recalled: "Originally the term was created to refer specifically to Jews, Italians, and Irish in the large cities, but in Cleveland it is now pretty well restricted to people of central European extraction, but specifically excluding Jews."

As "ethnic groups" changed to a breezier "the ethnics," the term at first took on an anti–civil rights connotation and then lost it. In 1972 *Newsweek* columnist Stewart Alsop wrote of the rules of television situation comedies: "The rules are: 'ethnics' are okay, Jews are okay, blacks are very okay, white Anglo-Saxon Protestants are a bunch of bigoted boobies."

By the presidential campaign of 1976, every campaign had ways of reaching the ethnics. In a televised debate on foreign policy, President Ford blundered by insisting that the East European nations were not under Soviet domination; the "captive nations" spokesmen denounced this as inaccurate. At the inauguration of President Carter, an inaugural official used two vogue words in his complaint: "There's no outreach to the ethnics."

In current use, "ethnics" is a slightly clinical, neutral, and inoffensive way of identifying national groups, though it carries a note of condescension to some ears. In a 1974 *Atlantic Monthly* article, Henry Fairlie, coiner of "Establishment," drew a useful distinction between the polemically loaded "ethnic" and the more clinical "ethnic group." "One *belongs* to an ethnic group, one *is* an ethnic, and there is a world of difference. To say that someone is a member of an ethnic group is implicitly to say that one is describing only one of his characteristics. To say that he is an ethnic is to imply that this is the most important characteristic about him, the determining characteristic . . ."

See HYPHENATED AMERICANS.

eunuch rule   provision in state constitutions forbidding governors from succeeding themselves, except after the lapse of another term.

In most states, particularly in the South, governors are rendered impotent—lame ducks from the moment they enter the Statehouse—by the "eunuch rule." This was designed to prevent four-year governors from building long-lasting machines. (In two-year term states, like Texas and Arkansas, succession is permitted.)

Wherever the eunuch rule applies, the governor starts thinking about (1) running for senator, (2) laying the groundwork for a career in private business, or (3) "modernizing" the state constitution to permit reelection.

Alabama Governor George Wallace, unable to achieve the necessary modernization that would have enabled him to succeed himself, beat the system by running his wife, Lurleen, in his place in 1966. She was elected, and the state received "two Governors for the price of one." Wallace himself was later re-elected.

euphemisms, political   avoidance of hard words; or, obvious avoidance to underscore a cliché with ironic humor.

The classic political euphemisms come out of the Civil War, which was delicately referred to as "the late unpleasantness" by humorist Petroleum

V. Nasby. The Confederate states were sarcastically called "our erring brethren" by Northerners, or "our wayward sisters" (a phrase of General Winfield Scott's). After the war, the BLOODY SHIRT was called "the ensanguined undergarment." (A fine euphemistic difference is still drawn about this war. Northerners say "Civil War," but many Southerners say "The War Between the States," a phrase which carries less stigma of rebellion.)

During the Cold War Pentagon officials estimated that World War III would cause 120 million deaths in the U.S., and more than 120 "megadeaths" (million deaths) in the Soviet Union; the euphemism for this cataclysm was an "All-Out Strategic Exchange," similar to a "future unpleasantness." Similarly, Hitler's genocidal campaign against the Jews was called the FINAL SOLUTION.

On the domestic scene, politicians dealing with the problem of the aged shy away from "old people," "the aged," or even "the elderly." An *Esquire* cartoon showed one of these people shouting at a television set: "Call me Gramps, call me an Old Fogy—call me anything except a Senior Citizen!"

The most derided euphemism of 1970 was "protective reaction," a military term for bombing raids against anti-aircraft installations, followed in a few years by "termination with extreme prejudice," a CIA term for assassination. In South Africa, "apartheid" was given the name of "plural relations."

In 1976 the influx of "illegal aliens" into the U.S. was recognized as a problem; since most of these were Mexicans, formerly derogated as "wetbacks" (from having to swim the Rio Grande), many Americans felt they should be given legal status and changed their appellation to "noncitizens"; that still did not remove the stigma, and was further euphemized with "undocumented persons." (Spanish-speaking Americans usually eschew the euphemisms and call them *ilegales.*)

A U.S. Department of Labor dictionary of job definitions, published at the end of 1977, enshrined euphemism in a government document. To eliminate sex and age references, occupational analysts changed "busboy" to "dining-room attendant"; "batboy" to "bat handler"; "governess" to "children's tutor"; "repairman" to "repairer." Faced with deciding what to call people who wait on tables, the Labor Department came up with "waiter-waitress."

The Gulf War of 1990–91 produced its own spate of euphemisms: "collateral damage" (civilian casualties resulting from bombing military targets); "assets" (weapons); "discriminate deterrence" (pinpoint bombing); "blue on blue" (friendly fire, itself a euphemism of the Vietnam War; the phrase with "blue" alludes to the Civil War); and "persons in transit" (refugees).

Other recent euphemisms include "optimize the labor structure" or "downsize" (to fire workers) and President Clinton's use of "contribution" to mean tax.

See DISADVANTAGED; POLICE ACTION.

Eurocommunism the form of uninternational Communism espoused in the 1970s by leaders in West European nations who purported to be independent of the line set forth by the Communist party in the Soviet Union.

"The striking fact about Eurocommunism," said anti-Titoist Yugoslav Milovan Djilas in 1977, "is that for the first time opposition to Moscow flows from the democratic process."

Eurocommunism received its biggest boost in Italy, where political pluralism was embraced by Italian Communist leader Enrico Berlinguer, who recommended a HISTORIC COMPROMISE whereby Communists could share power in the national government of Italy. In France, Communist party chief Georges Marchais set back the cause of Eurocommunism in September 1977 by dramatically breaking with the Socialists, driving a wedge in the "Union of the Left" with a demand for specifics in the nationalization of industry; as a result, the right was able to turn back the challenge from the left in 1978.

everyman. See JOHN Q. PUBLIC.

every man a king slogan of Louisiana Governor Huey P. Long.

This was the trigger phrase of Governor Long's Share-the-Wealth program, which he espoused from 1928 until his assassination in 1935. It was taken from William Jennings Bryan's "Cross of Gold Speech" to the 1896 Democratic National Convention.

Long held that 10 percent of the people in the U.S. owned 70 percent of the wealth, taking most of his populist ideas from Senator S. J. Harper. The full slogan used "Every Man" as one word: "Everyman a King, but No Man Wears a Crown."

evil empire a moral attack on the worldwide corruption of Communism, criticized as simplistic when made but now accepted as a sound historic judgment.

Ronald Reagan introduced this alliterative-looking phrase on March 8, 1983. Speaking at a National Association of Evangelists convention in Orlando, Florida, Reagan delivered what amounted to a political sermon on the sources of evil in the modern world. In the speech's peroration he stressed his anti-Soviet theme: ". . . in your discussions of the nuclear freeze propos-

als, I urge you to beware the temptation of pride—the temptation blithely to declare yourselves above it all and label both sides equally at fault, to ignore the facts of history and the aggressive impulses of an evil empire."

Western accommodationists found the phrase extreme, and the liberal historian Henry Steele Commager labeled this speech "the worst ever given by a President." Reagan and his aides, however, had managed to couch the U.S.–Soviet superpower geostrategic competition in stark moral terms: "the struggle between right and wrong, good and evil."

Anthony R. Dolan, Reagan's chief speechwriter, provided him with *evil empire* to denounce Soviet totalitarianism. Writing for *The American Enterprise* a decade after the speech, Dolan observed: "The President's critics and many foreign-policy analysts were vastly uncomfortable with conservatives like Reagan who used such words as 'evil' about a regime toward which their own priorities were ordered not so much by a concern for moral distinctions as by the pursuit of a modus vivendi—an accommodation with Soviet power." (The phrase's importance is underscored in the title of a 1993 book by Dolan, *Undoing the Evil Empire: How Reagan Won the Cold War.*)

The *empire* of this phrase may have been influenced by the repressive regime featured in the popular "Star Wars" films by George Lucas. *The Empire Strikes Back,* a sequel to the 1977 *Star Wars,* appeared in 1980, and that "empire" was fought again in the 1983 *Return of the Jedi.* (See STAR WARS.)

An earlier origin, however, is possible. Rabbi Emeritus Michael M. Szenes of Schenectady writes of a Biblical source, adding that *"mamlacha hachata'a* in Amos 9:8 is usually translated as the 'Sinful Kingdom.' In an unpublished manuscript, I found the translation 'The Wicked Empire.'"

Other political voices continue to echo the Reagan usage. Richard Nixon stated in *Time* magazine in 1992, "The nations of the former evil empire lost faith in communism both because of its inhumanity and because it did not work." That same year, William E. Odom wrote in the *Washington Post* of the Democrats' reaction to Reagan's words: "Some were horrified at the 'evil empire' speech, although they surely did not believe it was a 'virtuous empire.'"

exchange rates.   See SNAKE IN THE TUNNEL.

executive privilege   the right claimed by a President to withhold information from Congress or the judiciary.

"The doctrine of Executive privilege is well established," President Nixon said publicly on March 12, 1973, as the Watergate case was about to break. Citing its use since George Washington, he said that both members and former members of his White House staff "shall follow the well-established precedent and decline a request for a formal appearance before a committee of the Congress."

Historian and former Kennedy aide Arthur Schlesinger, Jr., took sharp issue with this in the March 30, 1973, *Wall Street Journal:* ". . . the very term 'Executive privilege' seems itself to be of fairly recent American usage . . . You will look in vain for it as an entry in such standard reference works as the Smith-Zurcher *Dictionary of American Politics,* or the *Oxford Companion to American History* or Scribner's *Concise Dictionary of American History.* It is not even to be found, I was dismayed to discover, in *The New Language of Politics,* compiled by William Safire of Mr. Nixon's very own White House staff."

To correct that omission from the earlier editions, here is the history of the phrase taken from Schlesinger's observations, a tracking of the term in *American Speech* (Fall-Winter 1973), and a contribution by an early user.

"In May 1954," Schlesinger recounted, "in the midst of the Army-McCarthy hearings, President Eisenhower instructed employees of the Department of Defense that, if asked by the McCarthy Committee about internal exchanges within the Department, they were 'not to testify to any such conversations or communications or to produce any such documents or reproductions.' This was an unprecedently sweeping denial to Congress. But it had a certain moral justification in the atrocious character of the McCarthy inquisition, and it was given legal color by an accompanying memorandum from Herbert Brownell, the Attorney General . . ."

That was a point that was to trouble many scholars: if Mr. Eisenhower's evocation of "executive privilege" (the idea, not the phrase) was constitutionally right in the case of withholding data from the "atrocious" Senator McCarthy, how could Mr. Nixon's repetition of that maneuver be constitutionally wrong in withholding information from a Congress operating with more public support? Judge John Sirica supplied the answer. As *Time* reported in 1973, Sirica "noted that the Supreme Court in 1953 had recognized an Executive privilege for military secrets . . . But he made it clear that Executive privilege does not cover conversations relevant to a criminal investigation and not involving performance of official duties."

The practice of withholding information from Congress, without the modern phrase, did begin with Washington. In the 1792 House inquiry into the St. Clair expedition, President Washington gave the House the documents it requested, and sent his cabinet members to testify, but—according to

Thomas Jefferson's diary—agreed with his cabinet officers that "the Executive ought to communicate such papers as the public good would permit, and ought to refuse those, the disclosure of which would injure the public; consequently were to exercise a discretion."

The phrase grew out of the use of the word "privilege" in law, to mean "the royal prerogative," or privilege of clergy, or the privilege of Parliament. The 1953 citation by Judge Sirica was in the Supreme Court decision of *U.S. v. Reynolds,* when the Court referred to the government's "privilege against revealing military secrets." On May 17, 1954, Attorney General Herbert Brownell wrote: "Presidents have established, by precedent, that they and members of their Cabinets, and other heads of executive departments have an undoubted privilege and discretion to keep confidential, in the public interest, papers and information which require secrecy." Raoul Berger, in his 1974 *Executive Privilege: A Constitutional Myth,* traced the phrase to a 1958 article by Conrad D. Philos in the *Federal Bar Journal* (14:113) titled "Executive Privilege and the Release of Military Records," and a Federal Supplement (157:943/2), "The position taken rests on the claim of executive privilege."

The earliest judicial use of the term was tracked down by Fred R. Shapiro, editor of the *Oxford Dictionary of Legal Quotations* (1993), to August of 1940, in an opinion handed down by the U.S. Court of Appeals in *Glass v. Ickes.* The court held that Harold Ickes, FDR's Secretary of the Interior, was immune from the charge of defamation because "a communication, released generally to the press, [was] within this executive privilege."

The earliest use of the phrase by a high official of government that this lexicographer can find is in testimony by William P. Rogers (who, as Deputy Attorney General under Herbert Brownell, helped draft the 1954 memorandum) before the Senate Judiciary Subcommittee on Constitutional Rights on March 6, 1958, objecting to new disclosure requirements on administrative procedure legislation. The phrase was used three times in Mr. Rogers' summary:

"(1) the executive privilege applies to the executive functions of the independent agencies; (2) the executive privilege obviously does not apply to judicial functions; similarly (3) legislative inquiry into the legislative functions of the independent agencies is not limited by any executive privilege, but there are other restraining considerations . . ."

Coincidentally, Mr. Rogers was Richard Nixon's Secretary of State when the dispute arose in 1973 over the Nixon use of the separation-of-powers doctrine to keep Congress from digging into Administration actions about the Watergate affair. When Mr. Nixon turned to Mr. Rogers for legal support of his claim of executive privilege, Rogers advised that in having already directed aides to testify on related matters, the President had waived his claim to privilege.

Because its use was discredited in Watergate, the phrase (with the *e* not capitalized, as it should be if referring to the Office of the President) is rarely chosen by White House officials or cabinet officers as a cause for withholding information from the Congress now, although Bush's national security adviser, Brent Scowcroft, cited executive privilege in declining to testify before the Senate banking committee in 1992 about prewar exports of American technology to Iraq. When public opinion once again resists some congressional inquiry, as it did in the Joseph McCarthy era, the practice may reappear under a different name, such as "presidential privacy."

But not even the Watergate-tarnished phrase escaped commercialization: Bloomingdale's department store brought out a gift for Christmas, 1973, which it called "Executive Privilege": an electric paper shredder with a smoky Plexiglas shell to catch the shreds.

exit polls. See DEPTH POLLING.

extremism a position at the end of an ideological spectrum; home of the politically far-out.

Senator Barry Goldwater, accepting the Republican nomination for President in 1964, drew a roar from his adherents and a gasp from his opponents in the party with this line in his acceptance speech: "I would remind you that extremism in the defense of liberty is no vice. And let me remind you also that moderation in the pursuit of justice is no virtue!"

In his text, Goldwater underlined the two sentences. (Authorship of these CONTRAPUNTAL PHRASES has been attributed to speechwriter Karl Hess.) In their campaign Democratic speakers underlined it as well, stunned—almost—at their luck in garnering from their chief opponent's own mouth a phrase unequaled in its service to the enemy since a Blaine supporter's condemnation of "Rum, Romanism and Rebellion."

Supporters of Goldwater, and the Senator himself, had been annoyed at the "extreme" label applied to them by the Republican MODERATES in the primary campaign. Some saw Goldwater's use of "extremism" as a way of "rubbing it in" to the defeated liberals; others felt it was an affirmation of his personal identity and point of view, as opposed to the usual unity approach after a difficult division. "My God,"

cried a reporter, "he's going to run as Goldwater!"

Republican Nelson Rockefeller, leader of the liberal wing, issued this statement the following day: "To extol extremism whether 'in defense of liberty' or 'in pursuit of justice' is dangerous, irresponsible and frightening. Any sanction of lawlessness, of the vigilante and of the unruly mob can only be deplored. . . . I shall continue to fight extremism within the Republican party. It has no place in the party. It has no place in America."

Richard Nixon, who sat on his hands during the enthusiastic demonstration after Goldwater's line, sought some unifying clarification from Goldwater three weeks later. Nixon and others pointed out to the candidate that his statement was being construed as a blanket endorsement of extremism. In a letter to Nixon, Goldwater backtracked to this extent: "If I were to paraphrase the two sentences in question in the context in which I uttered them I would do it by saying that wholehearted devotion to liberty is unassailable and that half-hearted devotion to justice is indefensible."

But the original statement could not be glossed over. Lyndon B. Johnson hammered it home at the conclusion of the campaign: "Extremism in the pursuit of the Presidency is an unpardonable vice. Moderation in the affairs of the nation is the highest virtue."

Extremism today remains as frowned upon by most people as in this 1639 English proverb: "Extremity of right is wrong." See RADICAL RIGHT; CODE WORDS.

eyeball to eyeball a direct international confrontation; a diplomatic crisis with war a distinct possibility.

In 1962 Senator Kenneth B. Keating (R-N.Y.) charged that Russian missiles were being established in Cuba. Within weeks, the "Cuban missile crisis" had come to test the will of the Kennedy Administration, which was still smarting from its earlier Cuban errors. See BAY OF PIGS FIASCO.

Reconstructing the events that led to the strong stand by the U.S. writers Charles Bartlett and Stewart Alsop, in the *Saturday Evening Post*, quoted Secretary of State Dean Rusk as saying: "We're eyeball to eyeball and the other fellow just blinked." Roger Hilsman of the State Department reported that the statement was made by Rusk to ABC newsman John Scali, who had helped in the negotiations, and the words used were: "Remember when you report this—that, eyeball to eyeball, they blinked first." See WAR HAWKS; DOVES.

The metaphor, closer than *face-to-face*, with its vivid picture of two men, foreheads pressed together, glaring into each other's eyes, soon became synonymous with "confrontation" and was as well known as BRINKMANSHIP in the Eisenhower years.

In current usage, an eyeball-to-eyeball situation is something that farsighted diplomatic policy seeks to avoid. However, both the idea of confrontation and the phrase that so vividly describes it are not likely to disappear. In September of 1977, when U.S. Secretary of State Cyrus Vance became embroiled with eye patch–wearing Israeli Foreign Minister Moshe Dayan in dispute over the makeup of a Geneva conference, columnist Joseph Kraft wrote: "They're eyeball to eye patch, and you can't tell who blinked." Charles Bierbauer of Cable News Network reported in early 1993 that "Iraq and the United States have gone eyeball to eyeball again, and Baghdad may have blinked."

The expression has a military origin, and is a contribution of black English. General Harold Johnson, U.S. Army Chief of Staff in the mid-sixties, tells the author he first heard the term used—and widely quoted—in November 1950, during the Korean conflict. Before President Truman desegregated the armed forces, the 24th Infantry Regiment was all-black; after a counterattack had caused a retreat of U.S. forces, MacArthur's headquarters sent an inquiry to the 24th Regiment, which was expected to bear the brunt of the fighting: "Do you have contact with the enemy?" The reply: "We is eyeball to eyeball."

F

face time brief face-to-face meeting with someone important; being noticed by a significant audience; impressing a superior or employer by being in his or her presence.

U.S. News & World Report wrote in 1978 that Jimmy Carter "drops by the White House press room . . . guaranteeing himself a few precious seconds of 'face time' on the evening TV news." Quotation marks around that use suggest an earlier spoken usage.

In 1981, Lois Romano of the *Washington Post* wrote that Presidential adviser Ed Meese attended a book party "for what is commonly referred to in Washington as 'face-time.'" She defined the quoted term as "a handshake, a walk around the room and one drink." (In political jargon, that appearance is known as a *dropby*.)

That sense of appearing in person rather than on television was mentioned by Jeffrey Schmalz in a *New York Times* article about the 1983 hockey season at Cornell University: "'Going to the games is positive face time,' said Alan Baren, a senior. (Translation: Having your face seen at the right place, at the right time, with the right people.)"

The lexicographer included the phrase in a 1985 survey of college slang: "Happily, a recent term for necking—*sucking face* —is on the decline, replaced by the more romantic *doing face time*." Kara B. Kerker, then a senior at Cornell, disputed that definition, defining *face time* as "the art of seeing and being seen." She wrote that undergraduates collected FTUs (face time units) in various ways, including "occupying the window seat in a popular town bar and throwing dead fish at the Harvard players during their hockey team's annual visit to Ithaca."

In Pentagonese, the term took on a sense of "apple-polishing." Major General Perry M. Smith provided a glossary of insider lingo at Fort Fumble in the 1989 book *Assignment: Pentagon*. He defined *face time* as "time spent near big bosses in attempts to impress them with your diligence and loyalty," adding that *night face* (after-hours contact) counts double and *weekend face* counts triple.

Campaign staffs use the term to derogate aides who think they can do best by being close to the candidate: "out of sight, out of mind" is the apple-polishers' fear. The less personal sense of televised time, however, persists. During Persian Gulf War preparations in 1990, Maureen Dowd of the *New York Times* was told that a White

233

House aide, being thrust into the limelight, was "getting a lot of face time on national television."

For the face time of television anchors, see WALTER TIME.

fact-finding trip a serious effort to obtain firsthand information, or a ploy designed to impress the folks back home with a spurious interest in foreign affairs.

An overseas tour by a congressman or candidate is described by him as a *fact-finding trip*, and as a *junket* by his opponents, who usually add "at the taxpayer's expense."

A good test of whether a trip abroad is politically motivated is whether it covers "the three I's": Ireland, Italy, and Israel, points of origin or antecedence for many urban voters.

The appeal to voters of an "I want to see for myself" attitude was demonstrated by Eisenhower's "I shall go to Korea" pledge, which was heightened by the fact that he was a general going to study a war. But it works for civilians as well, and the year before a national convention, world leaders find their calendars filled with visits by aspiring U.S. politicians.

Another important use of a fact-finding trip is to keep a national political figure out of trouble for weeks at a time; when he returns for a ship- or plane-side interview, he is "fresh" news copy.

Massachusetts Attorney General Edward McCormack, campaigning (unsuccessfully) against Ted Kennedy for the Senate Democratic nomination in 1962, tried to dampen the effect of a Kennedy trip to Ireland by quoting— to Irish voters—a story in the *Dublin Sunday Independent:* "Arriving in Ireland today is Mr. Edward 'Ted' Kennedy, age thirty. . . . Why is he coming to Ireland? He's coming because later this year he is due to be involved in a political fight back home in Mas-

sachusetts. . . . You do not spend your time campaigning in your own little patch . . . you go out in the world far far afield, hit the headlines, hit the American voters in the right way. I think the trips are more political than fact-finding."

In labor negotiations, parties who do not wish to be bound by arbitration occasionally agree to a fact-finding panel, or one may be imposed by government.

On rare occasions the phrase is used in its past tense, as in this 1967 comment by Jacques Barzun, provost of Columbia University, on the subject of the spread of social research studies: "Judging from what is being studied, researched, and fact-found all over the world, it is clear that as a civilization we no longer know how to do anything . . . we repeatedly analyze the familiar and suspend action." See NONPOLITICAL TRIP; JUNKETEERING GUMSHOES.

fail-safe a retaliatory strike that can be recalled if the original signal was a mistake; a system whereby bombers may be launched on an ambiguous warning.

During the Cold War, bombers operating on a "fail-safe" system could take off if an enemy attack appeared to be under way, fly to a point of no return, and there get instructions from a central control whether or not to continue on to target. "In this way," wrote Herman Kahn, "the central authorities have additional time to confirm or deny the validity of the original warning."

UPI disclosed the existence of "fail-safe" in a story of the Strategic Air Command's operations in the Arctic, soon followed by a book and motion picture on the sensational subject. "It should have been possible," wrote Douglass Cater, later a White House aide, "to describe our military precautions without resorting to the phoney dramatics about bombers headed toward Moscow which alarmed our allies and provided propaganda material for the Soviets."

Fail-safe refers to a system with two signals: one to take off, the other to verify. If bombers headed for enemy territory "fail" to receive a confirmation signal, they return home, placing the communications failure on the "safe" side.

Fair Deal the theme of President Truman's State of the Union message in 1949, updating the "New Deal" inherited from Roosevelt.

During his first eighteen months in office, President Truman worked under the shadow and confining legacy of Franklin Roosevelt's New Deal policies.

Truman needed a phrase and an image of his own. These he established in his first message to the 81st Congress: "Every segment of our population and every individual has a right to expect from his government a fair deal."

The press picked up the phrase—a natural progression from the New Deal of FDR—and used it to label the domestic policies of the Truman Administration. Two generations before, Woodrow Wilson had used "Fair Deal" as a counterpart to Theodore Roosevelt's "Square Deal."

In 1967 Michigan's Republican Governor George Romney made a punning reference to the progression of "the Deals": "There was the New Deal of Franklin Roosevelt, the Fair Deal of Harry Truman and the ordeal of Lyndon Johnson."

See CARD METAPHORS.

faithful. See PARTY FAITHFUL.

Fala speech a Franklin D. Roosevelt campaign speech in 1944 that marked a return to partisan politicking from a previous "above the battle" posture.

In the summer of 1944 many Republican newspapers were printing a rumor that President Roosevelt's Scottie, Fala, had been left in Alaska after a presidential visit and that an American destroyer had to be turned around and sent back for him. More serious charges were being made, but FDR seized on this one to ridicule and cast doubt on all the others.

In a campaign speech to the Teamsters Union in Washington, President Roosevelt answered the Republican attacks this way:

> . . . Republican leaders have not been content with attacks on me, or my wife, or on my sons. No, not content with that, they now include my little dog, Fala. Well, of course, I don't resent attacks, and my family doesn't resent attacks, but Fala does resent them. You know, Fala is Scotch, and being a Scottie, as soon as he learned that the Republican fiction writers in Congress and out had concocted a story that I had left him behind on the Aleutian Islands and had sent a destroyer back to find him— at a cost to the taxpayers of two or three or eight or twenty million dollars—his Scotch soul was furious. He has not been the same dog since.
>
> I am accustomed to hearing malicious falsehoods about myself. . . . But I think I have a right to resent, to object to libelous statements about my dog.

The rest of the "Fala speech" was a serious enumeration of the problems facing the U.S. and those points had considerable effect on the campaign of '44. However, the Fala reference made the speech come alive; speechwriter Samuel Rosenman, in retrospect, felt it was FDR's most effective single political speech.

The Democratic National Committee said after the speech: "The race is between Roosevelt's dog and Dewey's goat." See CANINE METAPHORS; CHECKERS SPEECH; DEWEY BLITZ.

fallback position an agreed-upon line of retreat.

"Fallback position" came into political use late in 1966, as Republican liberal leaders sought to avoid the divisions of 1964 that led to the nomination of a conservative. New York's Governor Rockefeller announced his support of Michigan's Governor George Romney, urging all Republican MODERATES to do the same. Romney pegged his campaign on his "winnability," a dangerous route presupposing no slump in his popularity rating. When the slump came in early 1967, there was talk of a secret DEAL on a "fallback position"; *New York Times* reporter Warren Weaver referred to Illinois freshman Senator Charles Percy as "the backup candidate." This implied no active support for him unless Romney faltered, at which point the combined liberal forces would move— in impossibly disciplined fashion—to a second candidate.

A year before the 1968 convention, Senator Jacob K. Javits used the phrase in an interview with *Time*, reiterating his and Rockefeller's support of Romney. Obviously recognizing the weakening effect of the admission of any secret second choice, he insisted: "We have no fallback position. There are no alternatives." *Time* added: "None, that is, unless Romney happens to stumble." When he did, it became apparent that Rockefeller had occupied the fallback position. See PENTAGONESE.

Jimmy Carter was the first President to use the phrase in diplomatic negotiation. In July 1978 he warned Israel that if direct negotiations between Egypt and Israel did not produce results, the matter could be placed in the anti-Israel UN: "The Geneva conference is . . . the basic framework for peace and that is always a fallback position if we fail as an intermediary or mediator."

The expression is based on the phrase *to fall back*, which can be twisted into a transitive verb. In 1992, the *Washington Post* quoted Albert R. Wynn, a newly elected Representative from Maryland, on committee assignments for freshmen: "I'll be part of the scramble for Energy and Commerce. My fallback position is a seat on the Public Works Committee. But I shouldn't say that, or they'll fall me back."

fallout unfortunate side effects of a political policy or event; unanticipated negative reaction.

Senator William Fulbright wrote in 1966: ". . . the Vietnamese war thus far has had three major 'fallout' effects on East-West relations: first, it has generated a degree of mistrust and antagonism toward the United States . . . second, it has weakened the drive of the Eastern European countries toward greater independence of the Soviet Union; third, it has put a severe strain on the Soviet-American detente . . ."

The political use is an extension of the scientific term coined after the explosion of the first atomic bombs in 1945. "Fallout" is defined in the April 1953 issue of the *Bulletin of the Atomic Scientists* as "the descent of the [radioactive] particles back to earth—[that] may occur in the immediate vicinity of the detonation or as far as several thousand miles away . . . although it is heaviest near the site."

Political usage should not be confused with "falling-out," or disagreement.

family jewels. See CIA-ESE.

family values the unifying power of traditional home life in American culture; or, code words to counter supporters of abortion and homosexual rights.

The Reverend Andrew M. Greeley and Peter H. Rossi wrote in their 1966 book, *The Education of Catholic Americans,* that "marriage and family values do show some relationship with Catholic education; however, the relationship is in most instances not a strong one."

Political use of the phrase began a decade later. The 1976 Republican party platform stated, "Divorce rates, threatened neighborhoods and schools and public scandal all create a hostile atmosphere that erodes family structures and family values."

New York Governor Mario Cuomo used *family* and *values* in a warm, positive sense during his speech to the 1984 Democratic National Convention.

Used together, though, the words became the GOP attack term of the 1992 campaign. Pat Robertson, the religious broadcaster who campaigned in 1988 for the Presidency, spoke out against the Democratic use of the term: "When Bill and Hillary Clinton talk about family values, they are not talking about either families or values. They are talking about a radical plan to destroy the traditional family and transfer its functions to the federal government."

The traditional family is that of father and mother (of opposite sexual orientation), legally married, with children under 18 at home. In 1992, according to the Census Bureau, 26 percent of American households met this definition, labeled the *nuclear family* by the anthropologist George P. Murdock in 1949.

Implicit in the phrase's celebration is that the opposite side takes a permissive attitude regarding abortion and homosexual rights, undermining the institution of the family. *Family values* echoes the use of "social issue" (see PSEPHOLOGY; ISSUES, THE) for concern about the drug culture and changing moral standards.

This powerful campaign theme, however, can backfire. At the Republican convention, nominees Bush and Quayle gathered their families to assert traditionality (while, unknown to them, the background music playing was "The Best of Times" from *La Cage Aux Folles,* a Broadway musical about accepting homosexuality). After Patrick Buchanan's hard-right convention speech declaring "cultural war" seemed harsh to many centrist Republicans, the Bush-Quayle campaign team backed away from the phrase *family values,* which was drawing fire from Democrats as a code phrase for intolerance, and adopted instead "traditional values."

fascist   originally, a believer in the corporate state; now a derogation imputing totalitarianism to the far right.

Fascio is the Italian word for "bundle," or "group"; in 1895 a political organization called itself *fasci dei lavoratori,* and in 1915 the *fascio interventista* were called the *fascisti.* The movement grew in the early twenties as an especially brutal alternative to Communism, and under Benito Mussolini, controlled Italy from 1922 to 1943.

In current use, the word is an epithet directed often from the far left toward anyone on the right; in Communist terminology, it was the worst insult short of "revisionist." In the demonstrations of the sixties in the U.S., the phrase "fascist pig" was used so often that the word lost some of its sting.

See TRAINS RAN ON TIME.

fatally flawed   containing too much error for correction; damaged beyond repair.

This treaty-knocking cliché began to be overused when Ronald Reagan charged that the Carter Administration's SALT II treaty was fatally flawed, unable to reduce the numbers of large Soviet land-based missiles. Reagan repeated the alliterative term in 1987 when President Oscar Arias Sanchez of Costa Rica proposed a plan in Guatemala; a *New York Times* editorial countered, "The Guatemala plan, whatever its weaknesses, is not fatally flawed."

Dun's Review used the phrase in print in 1975 when a job-hunter wrote, "He said my resume was fatally flawed because it failed to tell a prospective employer what I could do for him." By the early 1980s, the hyperbolic term had become trite. In 1983, for example, the United States Ambassador to UNESCO, Jean Gerard, recommended leaving the organization that had become "so skewed, so far off course, so fatally flawed."

The term is a participial phrase, with an adverb (*fatally*) modifying a past participle (*flawed*). Also frequently used is *seriously flawed*, but the adverb *seriously* is weaker than *fatally* and implies the possibility of overhaul and correction.

Fatally flawed is derived from the noun phrase *fatal flaw*. Merriam-Webster offers a 1916 use by Sir Arthur Quiller-Couch in "On the Art of Writing," in which the famed stylist criticizes a work for "the one fatal flaw that it imports emotion into a theme which does not properly admit of emotion." Perhaps *fatal flaw* is patterned after *tragic flaw*, known as *hamartia* in Greek tragedy, the inescapable weakness that leads to a tragic hero's downfall.

fat cat a man of wealth, particularly an important contributor to political campaigns. The phrase is both derogatory and respectful, since few politicians can go far without such supporters.

The phrase was popularized by Frank R. Kent of the *Baltimore Sun* in his 1928 book, *Political Behavior:* ". . . these capitalists have what the organization needs—money to finance the campaign. Such men are known in political circles as 'fat cats.'"

In politics, "fat" means "money." The word was used back in the last century: high-pressure fund-raising was called "fat-frying" in the campaign of 1888. Publisher Henry L. Stoddard wrote historian Mark Sullivan: "[Mark] Hanna was *a* fat-fryer. *The* fat-fryer was John P. Forster, President of the League of Young Republican Clubs. It was in 1888 that he wrote a letter suggesting 'to fry the fat out of the manufacturers.'"

The word is not always used in the campaign contributor sense. FDR in 1937 wrote to Ambassador Bowers in Spain: "All the fat-cat newspapers—85% of the whole—have been utterly opposed to everything the Administration is seeking . . ."

By the forties, politicians had developed a taste for biting the hand that fed them. Republican Party Finance Chairman Ernest T. Weir tried to oust National Chairman Joe Martin after the Willkie defeat in 1940 by putting on a financial "freeze." At a private luncheon in the Capitol, in 1941, Wendell Willkie said, "The thing I like about Joe Martin is that he has the guts to tell those fat cats to go to hell."

Fund-raisers for John F. Kennedy organized "The President's Club" with a membership gained by a donation of $1,000. This was denounced by Republicans as evidence of "fat cats with axes to grind" getting contracts as special recognition for their contributions to Kennedy's campaign. Despite the negative publicity, "Governor's Clubs," "County Chairman's Clubs," etc., were formed by both parties to give the fat cats a warm hearth and a feeling that their purrings were heard by the man at the top. Since that time, "campaign finance reform" has become the label for legislation to limit the influence of fat cats.

See GREASE.

fat-frying. See SLUSH FUND; FAT CAT.

favorite son   a candidate who holds a state's votes together at a convention for brokerage purposes; not a serious candidate for the presidency, but one who seeks a trading position with a chance as a compromise candidate or Vice President.

The phrase was first applied to George Washington as "Freedom's Favorite Son" in the late 1780s. Probably its first use in a more partisan sense applied to Martin Van Buren, "New York's favorite son" in the 1830s, and Henry Clay, "Kentucky's favorite son" a decade later.

In current use, a state's political leader often announces his intention of going to a convention as a favorite son. In that way he appears not to be seeking the nomination seriously; he can be promoting the interests of his own state (Hiram Fong's demonstration at the 1964 Republican convention extolled the delights of Hawaii on national television), avoiding a divisive primary fight in his home state, or simply holding his delegates in line to act more influentially as a bloc.

The favorite-son candidacy gives an alibi to the potentially serious candidate for refusing to withdraw his name from preferential primaries in other states—such a disavowal would be "inconsistent" with being a favorite son. Because of its usefulness, the scornful implication of the phrase, prevalent in the later part of the nineteenth century, has disappeared.

Though "favorite son" is understood throughout the political U.S., "native son" is also used to mean the same, particularly in the Midwest. Harry Truman wrote in his memoirs: "I re-called the 1928 Democratic convention in Houston. There were two or three native-son nominations that year, including Jim Reed of Missouri . . ."

Jokingly, but prophetically, John F. Kennedy said in Arizona during his 1960 campaign that "if we keep working, we will just take Arizona out of Barry Goldwater's bag. In any case, we will make it easy for him to be a candidate in 1964. That is the least we can do for a favorite son."

-feasance   accountability in public office; the taking of public responsibility.

Without a prefix, the noun *feasance* is labeled "obsolete" in dictionaries. It was first used in a 1538 translation of *Littleton's Tenures:* "This is nat proued that the fesaunce of the condycion . . . oughte to be made vppon the lande." Nouns from *feasance* are primarily formed by adding negative prefixes: *misfeasance, malfeasance,* and *nonfeasance.*

Misfeasance is wrongdoing of minor proportions; the prefix *mis-* means "badly" or "wrongly." Reckless decisions by those in power may raise questions of *misfeasance* but not of outright corruption. For example, a public company that dumps waste materials out of ignorance may be guilty of *misfeasance.*

Mal-, on the other hand, is the French prefix for "evil," and the noun *malfeasance* refers to deliberate acts of serious wrongdoing, as in illegal dumping of waste materials despite knowledge of the law. Somebody who commits *misfeasance* may be unsuitable for public office, but a deliberate abuse of public office, bordering on criminal activity, is covered by the more serious term *malfeasance.*

Nonfeasance means "a failure to carry out one's responsibility," not acting when one has a duty to act. Not filing a tax return is an example, and a

President who fails to fulfill the duties of office may also be held responsible for *nonfeasance*. When some pundits telephone politicians and are asked by officious gatekeepers, "What is this in reference to?" they sometimes respond, "Nonfeasance"; it usually gets a call back quickly.

federalese. See PENTAGONESE; GOBBLEDYGOOK.

federalism. See CREATIVE FEDERALISM; NEW FEDERALISM.

feedback response; voter reaction; information resulting from a TRIAL BALLOON.

A modern word, perhaps originating in the radio engineers' vocabulary, feedback describes the loud squeak that jars the nerves of an audience when loudspeakers are misplaced in such a way that they feed sound waves back into the microphone. In automation, feedback is the essence of automatic control, the return to input of part of the output of a machine, system, or process.

In politics, feedback is the information a candidate gets when he has probed in a given direction. It can be approving or critical, but it gives him the first test reaction before a major commitment. Example: "Put out a rumor that I'm supporting so-and-so and see what kind of feedback we get."

A second political meaning is negative reaction, similar to FALLOUT. The Suffolk (L.I.) *Sun* headlined its column of complaints and protests from readers "Feedback."

A *New York Times* editorial on April 10, 1978, included feedback as one of its ten least-liked words "except in analyses of computer or stereo performance."

See FLAK.

feeding frenzy intense media interest; excessive attacks by the media.

This derogation of oppressive press and broadcast reporters began in the 1970s. An Associated Press article of March 9, 1977, reported a speech by Gerald L. Warren, who was editor of the *San Diego Union* and a former Nixon press secretary. In the speech, he called for the end of "jugular journalism" that leads some reporters to behave like "sharks in a feeding frenzy."

The literal sense dates back to *Shark Attack*, a 1958 book by V. M. Coppleson, who discusses "slow feeding" as "distinct from 'collective behavior' or 'frenzied feeding,' seen under somewhat rare conditions. In this case, sharks compete with others for possession of the prey and attack everything within range."

The figurative *feeding frenzy* was picked up by Wall Street. Thomas P. Murphy, commenting on the business use of the term, wrote in *Forbes* magazine in 1983: "A feeding frenzy, in case you are not a fisherman, occurs when bait is thrown to a school of hungry fish. They go wild, slashing at the bait, each other and anything else with the temerity to move."

Political use of the phrase resurfaced in 1988, after Dan Quayle was introduced as George Bush's Vice Presidential candidate. Don Kowet wrote in the *Washington Times* about what he perceived as the media's savaging of Quayle: "In a piranha-like feeding frenzy, yesterday television news tossed away any pretense of fairness."

feet to the fire pressure to fulfill a commitment.

The phrase is customarily used in regard to persuading delegates to convention to honor their promises, and often implies economic coercion. "Who knows his banker? Who's his boss? Who does he do most of his business with? Put his feet to the fire."

Governor Ronald Reagan of California said in 1967 he would approve a withholding system of taxation only if "they held a hot iron to my feet." Senator Stephen Young told of a colleague who had switched his vote, and was congratulated by a friend for having "seen the light." The reply: "I didn't see the light, but I felt the heat."

The *New York Times* in 1968 used the phrase in this way: "Senator Robert F. Kennedy has been squirming rather uncomfortably at the edge of the national arena of late, and the man who has been putting his feet to the political fire has been his supposed comrade-in-arms, Senator Eugene F. McCarthy of Minnesota."

In 1980, *Business Week* reported that while President Carter's proposed economic program would meet congressional opposition in 1981, Administration officials were saying, "All we can do is hope to hold Congress' feet to the fire."

Admonitions of political pressure begin with a mild *talk to him,* rise to *twist his arm,* then *get his attention,* then *lean on him,* and finally *put his feet to the fire.*

See LEVERAGE.

fellow countrymen. See MY FRIENDS.

fellow immigrants an ironic reminder to bluebloods of a common revolutionary past.

This salutation, which can be more grating than ingratiating, is used to hail one's compatriots, drawn from various ethnic backgrounds.

Franklin Delano Roosevelt's April 21, 1938, speech to the Daughters of the American Revolution is remembered as the "My fellow immigrants" speech, although FDR—often derided as "a traitor to his class"—did not use the salutation.

FDR first reminded the audience that he was one of them: "It so happens, through no fault of my own, that I am descended from a number of people who came over in the *Mayflower*." Then he made the point that modern aristocrats must not forget their non-aristocratic heritage; the closest he came to "my fellow immigrants" was this passage: "Remember always that all of us, and you and I especially, are descended from immigrants and revolutionists."

The purpose of the ad-libbed remark, made the day after the upper-class audience had adopted resolutions denouncing his leftist proposals, was to assure his "class" that his New Deal was not traitorous to its immigrant heritage, and to suggest gently that the members of the DAR not forget their roots.

Variants of the phrase have also been tried. Dan Quayle, addressing the American-Israeli Political Action Committee in 1992, used *fellow Zionists.*

The original phrase was coined after Roosevelt's speech as a play on "my fellow Americans," or more directly in FDR's case, the salutation "my friends."

See MY FRIENDS.

fellow traveler one who accepts most of the Communist doctrines, but is not a member of the Communist party; or one who agrees with a philosophy or group but does not publicly work for it.

Leon Trotsky was angered by some Russian authors of the twenties who were only interested in the Bolshevik Revolution, not dedicated to it. He made the distinction: "They are not the artists of the proletarian revolution, but only its artistic fellow travelers." The word in Russian is *poputchik.*

Max Lerner, in an article in *The Nation* in 1936 titled "Mr. Roosevelt and his Fellow Travelers," explained: "The term has a Russian background and means someone who does not accept all your aims but has enough in common with you to accompany you in a comradely fashion part of the way."

After World War II, the term was most often applied to those who were (or were accused of being) in general agreement with the Communist party.

In literal translation, Soviet Sputniks are fellow travelers: something (satellite) traveling with a traveler (the earth).

"Fellow traveler" has been an attack phrase on Communists; the Communist attack phrase on the same subject, especially prevalent in China, has been "running dogs." See "ducks" under PROVERBS AND AXIOMS, POLITICAL.

feminazi. See WOMEN'S LIB.

fence to place restrictions on; to limit by using conditions or requirements.

This verb began in the fifteenth century with the literal sense of "to enclose with a fence." The most popular of the verb's various figurative senses has been "to sell stolen property to a fence," the slang term for a receiver of stolen goods.

In political use, the verb *fence* took on a new figurative sense of "to limit." During the Reagan Administration, Senator John Tower of Texas announced that "funding for production of the MX missile would be retained in the bill but would be fenced." Linda Hill, explaining the Senator's words, said, "In Senator Tower's statement, the word *fence* was used to mean 'restrict.' The money for the MX was to be approved, but before it could be used, certain requirements had to be met—that was the restriction, or the fence." Senator Tower's usage was probably dialectal, similar to that of the popular Western song "Don't Fence Me In."

Almost synonymous with *fence* is the verb *cap*, which politicians borrowed from the oil industry's use of "to place a cap on," as in capping a gusher. *Cap* means "to restrict in height" and is usually used with amounts of money in spending; *fence* restricts in width by applying conditions or requirements that must be met.

fence, on the undecided; unwilling to take a position; straddling.

In its original use, "on the fence" meant refusing to take a firm stand for or against a candidate or issue and was an attack phrase. That sense continues, but a new use has arisen: to be "on the fence" is not all bad, because it shows that a political figure is considering all the alternatives.

The term blossomed in 1828 and was probably in use before then. The *Ohio Journal* in that year summed up the Senate split between supporters of President John Quincy Adams and Andrew Jackson:

Administration 22
Jackson 13
On the fence 1

The *Georgia Journal* in 1840 suggested a position that was later termed ALL THINGS TO ALL MEN to politicians of the time: "Our advice to all politicians who have a hankering after the praise of all . . . is to take a position near the fence, on the fence, or above the fence."

Carl Schurz, insisting on political independence, described his position (according to James Blaine) "as that of a man sitting on a fence, with clean boots, watching carefully which way he may leap to keep out of the mud."

This defense of fence-sitting remains a secondary meaning of the phrase: the best place to be before all the facts are in. Daniel Moynihan told the Americans for Democratic Action in 1967:

President Johnson is said to be fond of relating the experience of an out-of-work school teacher who applied for a position in a small town on the Texas plains at the very depths of the depression. After a series of questions one puckered rancher on the school board looked at him and asked, did he teach that the world was round or that the world was flat. Finding no clues in the faces of the other members of the board, the teacher swallowed hard and allowed he could teach it either way.

Johnson's Texas background led to his being criticized as "tall in the straddle," a play on "saddle," when he took a position on the fence. "Straddle," its political use traced to 1843, carries a more negative connotation than being "on the fence."

fence mending looking after interests in one's political POWER BASE; taking care of the folks back home.

When Senator John Sherman of Ohio made a trip home in 1879, ostensibly to look after his farm but actually to see to his political interests, he insisted to reporters that he was home "only to repair my fences."

The following interchange took place in the House of Representatives on August 16, 1888:

Mr. Dougherty:—I presume [the absent members] are at home seeking renomination or looking after their fences. . . .

Mr. Weaver:—I have "fences" as well as other gentlemen; but my friends will look after my "fences" while I am here. . . .

Mr. Springer:—I am very anxious that the public business would be dispatched as early as possible, and that we may return to our constituents; and then, if there are any "fences" to be mended, . . . we shall have our own time in which to attend to such matters.

A deeper sense of fence mending was given in Robert Frost's poem, "Mending Wall." In it the poet explains the comradeship and sense of mutual respect between two men who recognize each other's limitations:

Before I built a wall I'd ask to know
What I was walling in or walling
*   out . . .*
Something there is that doesn't love a
*   wall,*
That wants it down . . .
He only says, "Good fences make good
*   neighbors."*

Fences have an important place in politics. Fence mending—talking to local politicians, contributors, workers, and newsmen—is considered good and necessary, but *sitting on the fence* is often considered cowardly and *fence straddling* is opportunistic. See FENCE, ON THE. The underworld use of "fence"—as an intermediary for stolen goods—is not used in politics; however, a baseball metaphor, *hitting it over the fence*, is occasionally used in politics to describe a successful speech, and politicians parry questions while *fencing* with reporters.

The British equivalent to fence mending is "nursing a constituency."

fetcher bill a legislative proposal designed to attract a bribe to bury it.

Like RIPPER BILL, this is statehouse lingo. Frank Trippet, in *The States: United They Fell* (1967), defined a fetcher bill as "a measure that, by threatening to curtail some commercial interest, provides incentive for a payoff to obtain the death of the bill."

The American political phrase is probably of English slang origin. The *OED* has a meaning for "fetch," beyond the usual verb "go get," as a noun to mean contrivance, stratagem, or trick. A 1745 citation reads: "This might be another of their politick Fetches." A fetcher bill is one that fetches—or elicits, or goes and brings back—a bribe.

fiasco. See BAY OF PIGS FIASCO.

field expedient an alteration in plans made on the stump without consulting campaign headquarters.

A field expedient is an army term for a makeshift substitute; an ingenious device, made from materials at hand, to take the place of a manufactured item. A rifle barrel can be cleaned with a government-issue item consisting of a small lead weight, a chain, and a square of chamois cloth. When this is lost, soldiers come up with a "field expedient" of a small pebble, a string, and a piece of shirttail.

When General Eisenhower was campaigning through upstate New York in 1952, he was scheduled to broadcast to a New York City fund-raising dinner from Governor Thomas E. Dewey's mansion in Albany. A microphone and loudspeaker were set up in Dewey's office for the two-way broadcast of a conversation between dinner chairman Paul Hoffman in New York City and Eisenhower and Dewey in Albany.

A moment before the broadcast was to begin, the line went dead. In desperation, the author, then an Eisenhower volunteer, made a telephone call to the Grand Ballroom of the Waldorf-Astoria, got Hoffman on that end of the line, and jammed earphones on the heads of Dewey and Eisenhower. The earphones were too small for Dewey and hurt his head; angrily, he muttered, "Save us from AMATEURS."

Eisenhower, who had been tense at the sudden change in technical setup and worried looks of the engineer and director, immediately relaxed when the volunteer explained, "Field expedient, General." "Nothing to worry about," the nominee reassured Dewey. "This is a field expedient." Since the General seemed to expect him to understand the term, Dewey stopped glaring and coolly proceeded to introduce the broadcast.

fifth column any secret group of traitors or sympathizers with an enemy, prepared to rise up and strike on his behalf at the most propitious moment.

The term was coined by Emilio Mola, a rebel general in the Spanish Civil War. Javier Gaytan de Ayala, director of the Spanish Library of Information, says he believes the term was first used during an interview granted by General Mola while his troops were advancing on the then Loyalist-held capital of Madrid in October 1936. Mola described how four rebel columns were converging on the city; when asked by a reporter which column he believed would actually capture the city, he replied, "the fifth."

The phrase was used again and elaborated on in a radio broadcast on October 16, 1936. The exact words have been lost, but General Mola made it clear that by a fifth column he meant sympathizers of the Franco cause who would rise within the city at the appropriate time. General Mola died in an airplane crash on June 3, 1937, before the fifth column of which he boasted achieved the results he had predicted.

The world, wrote *Time* in 1947, "pounced on the phrase with the eagerness of a man who has been groping for an important word."

Ernest Hemingway titled his only play *The Fifth Column* and it was presented in a 1937 performance at Madrid's Florida Hotel, a center for foreigners sympathetic with the Loyalist cause.

The phrase was later used to describe the secret Hitler sympathizers in Western Europe, then to identify almost any hidden group of enemies. *Chicago Daily News* correspondent Leland Stowe, covering the fall of Norway to the Nazis in World War II, broadcast a description of that country's collapse in which he charged

Norway had fallen "to its fifth column of Quislings and others."

President Roosevelt used "sixth column" to describe the "gossips and defeatists" during World War II.

In his 1946 IRON CURTAIN speech, Winston Churchill described Communist parties in Western countries as "Communist fifth columns [that] are established and work in complete unity and absolute obedience to the directive they receive from the Communist center."

Fifty-Four Forty or Fight. See WAR HORSE.

fighting the problem   refusal to come to grips with a situation that requires action; pettifogging delay.

This military expression is gaining some currency in political life. An army recruit who explains to the mess sergeant that unpeeled potatoes have more vitamins and better flavor than peeled potatoes is "fighting the problem": sooner or later, he will have to peel the potatoes.

"As Secretary of State," writes Harry Truman in his memoirs, "[General George C.] Marshall had to listen to more staff talk than when he was Chief of Staff. He would listen for a long time without comment, but when the debates between members of his staff seemed destined to go on interminably and he could stand it no longer, he would say, 'Gentlemen, don't fight the problem; decide it.'"

Defense Secretary Robert Lovett used another line in the same kind of situation: "Gentlemen, as one rat said to the other, 'To hell with the cheese, let's get out of the trap.'"

fight the good fight   to stand up for one's convictions; a lifelong battle for principle.

The Bible is referred to as "the good book," and "the good fight" is an eth-

ical fight. The outcome is less important to the definition than the idea of taking a stand on a question of principle. The phrase comes from the second epistle of Paul to Timothy (4:7): "I have fought a good fight, I have finished my course, I have kept the faith."

Senator George Norris of Nebraska, a leader in battles to overthrow the arbitrary rule of House Speaker "Uncle Joe" Cannon, to introduce federal power in the Tennessee Valley, and to abolish the LAME DUCK Congress with the Twentieth Amendment, put it this way toward the end of his life: "I have fought the good fight with all that was in me. Now there is no strength left. Other hands must take up the burden. Remember, the battle against injustice is never won."

Adlai Stevenson titled his final television appeal of the 1952 campaign "The Good Fight." In political use, it has come to connote a worthwhile but losing battle and is the title of a 1993 book by former Senator Gary Hart.

filibuster   a technique by which a minority of senators attempts to defeat or alter a measure favored by the majority through the device of continuous talking, or when a senator dramatically calls public attention to a bill he considers is being "railroaded through."

The entire process rests upon the Senate's pride in itself as the world's foremost chamber of enlightened debate. The vehicle is Rule 22, which provides for unlimited debate on any measure before it can be brought to a vote. Such debate is not possible in the House of Representatives where the rules limit the duration of any individual's right to speak, or in Great Britain's House of Commons, where Rule 20 permits the Speaker to direct a member "who persists in irrelevance" to "discontinue his speech."

The usual strategy is for the group of senators involved in a filibuster to follow one another in planned succession. As the vocal cords or imagination of one begins to tire, he yields to a successor. Subject matter need not be relevant—a common phrase is *reading the telephone book;* a synonym is *talkathon,* or marathon talk.

The word was first used to describe the sixteenth-century English and French privateers who began by raiding Spanish treasure ships in the waters of the Caribbean, then known as the Spanish Main, and who ended up, more often than not, as pirates.

The word is derived from the Dutch *vrijbuiter* (*vrij,* "free," and *buiter,* "booter") or "freebooter," a word commonly used to describe pirates. Freebooter was translated into French as *flibustier* and into Spanish as *filibustero,* and then back to English as "filibuster."

Whatever the origin, the term was already common in American politics in its present sense by the time of the Civil War. James Blaine claimed its first appearance occurred when a minority of senators succeeded in delaying the Kansas-Nebraska Act in 1854. In recent years it has most commonly been used in connection with civil rights legislation, the modern outgrowth of the slavery issue.

Until 1957, Southern senators were able to defeat proposed civil rights legislation by filibustering, and often merely by threatening to filibuster. The countermeasures employed by the majority were round-the-clock sessions, intended to wear the minority down, and cloture (more often used than "closure"), a two-thirds vote to end debate. In this manner the 1957 Civil Rights Bill was finally passed; today, only a three-fifths vote is required to invoke cloture.

The all-time champion filibusterer is Republican—formerly Democratic—Senator Strom Thurmond of South Carolina, who talked for more than twenty-four hours in the battle against the 1957 bill. The man considered to be his closest challenger was Democratic—formerly Republican—Senator Wayne Morse of Oregon. However, Senator Morse rejected the role, claiming his most strenuous long-talking efforts made in opposition to the Kennedy Administration's space satellite communication bill was not filibustering but merely "education."

In 1967 Senator Albert Gore (D-Tenn.), attempting to stop the tax checkoff measure for financing political campaigns, protested a delaying action taken by Louisiana Senator Russell Long. Long (whose father Huey set the then-record of sixteen hours in 1935) replied with an expression reminiscent of *Alice in Wonderland*'s "curiouser and curiouser." "When the Senator talks about delaying tactics," he said, "he is speaking as one filibusterer to another filibusterer."

Early in President Bill Clinton's Administration, the Republicans staged a successful filibuster to stall the President's much-vaunted economic stimulus package on the grounds that it was full of "pork" (see PORK BARREL). Taken by surprise, the President wondered "whether this is all just political posturing to prove that a minority can paralyze the federal government." He was, in his own way, defining a filibuster.

A similar technique in the Japanese Diet is the "cow-waddle," used to delay a vote and express minority displeasure. As the vote is called, opposition members individually waddle—with infinite slowness, stopping to chat along the way—to the ballot box on the rostrum.

See GRIDLOCK.

Final Solution Hitler's planned extermination of the Jews; now used to mean any plan whose carrying-out would lead to a neat, if morally monstrous, conclusion.

This euphemism for mass murder was used by Reinhard ("The Hangman") Heydrich, then head of the Reich Security Police, in a letter of November 6, 1941, to the Nazi Quartermaster General. He had previously used the term (in German, *Endlösung*) in a secret report about Polish Jews to the German military officials in Poland in September of 1939.

"At the Nuremberg trials," Charles Whittier of the Library of Congress informs the author, "a memorandum from Hermann Göring to Heydrich, dated July 31, 1941, was cited: Göring claimed that *Endlösung* in that memo meant 'total' solution and not 'final' (*Gesamtlösung*, rather than *Endlösung*)."

Another user of the phrase was Franz Stuckart, who drafted the Nuremberg decrees in 1938, but in his use probably did not mean what has come to be called "genocide": Stuckart recommended the deportation of all Jews from Germany so as to make the Reich *"Judenrein,"* or free of Jewish taint.

The earliest use the author can find is in the March 10, 1920, *Völkischer Beobachter* ("Racial Observer"), using the term *Endziel,* or "final goal," and proposing concentration camps for Jews.

The phrase is now used ironically in the U.S., as an example of the furthest reach of euphemism. It was widely recalled when a phrase used by CIA bureaucrats surfaced: "termination with extreme prejudice," the polite term for murder.

See HOLOCAUST; ETHNIC CLEANSING.

finding the decision that allows a President to suspend a law secretly.

Finding is a gerund (a noun ending in *-ing*) that was first used in the fourteenth century for "the act of locating." Shoemakers picked up the term and applied it to parts and materials, such as laces and buckles, in the making of shoes.

An 1829 essay by the German dramatist Johann Wolfgang von Goethe uses this gerund in translation: "The artist may be well advised to keep his work to himself till it is completed, because no one can readily help him or advise him with it . . . but the scientist is wiser not to withhold a single finding or a single conjecture from publicity." By 1859, the word had received a legal sense: "the result of an official inquiry or investigation; a judicial decision."

From that judicial sense comes the political use of *finding,* often capitalized in security use. The National Security Act of 1947 allows a President to make the decision about when to obey or to suspend a law, but requires the Chief Executive to report the finding to the Congress in timely fashion. Presidents and congressional leaders traditionally differ on the meaning of "timely."

Ronald Reagan's Finding on arms sales to Iran was released almost a year after its signing. This Finding, signed by the President and backdated to January 17, 1986, stated in part: "I hereby find that the following operation . . . is important . . . and direct the Director of Central Intelligence to refrain from reporting this Finding to the Congress." See C.Y.A.

finesse as a verb, to use a stratagem of applying only as much power as is absolutely necessary to accomplish a political goal, yet not so much power as to induce a counterattack; as a noun, style (as viewed by an ally), trickiness, guile (as seen by an enemy).

In establishing the right of judicial review, Chief Justice John Marshall finessed President Thomas Jefferson. At the start of Jefferson's Administration, the Supreme Court was packed with

Federalists appointed by John Adams. Jeffersonian Republicans let it be known that if the Court tried to invalidate important Republican measures, the President would defy the judges, thereby denying the Court the power to declare laws unconstitutional.

Marshall selected the case of *Marbury* v. *Madison* to finesse the President. He invalidated a minor part of a bill that, ironically, would have given certain technical powers to the Supreme Court. Had he chosen an important Republican measure to declare unconstitutional, Jefferson would have joined the issue and disputed judicial review. But this was a minor, technical matter at hand, without even a specific court order for Jefferson to refuse to obey. The President was finessed, and the vital precedent was set.

On the point of applying "just enough" power, a common political expression is: "You don't use an elephant gun to shoot a rabbit."

The word entered political language through cardplaying (as did "new deal"). In bridge, a finesse is an attempt to take a trick with a lower card (while holding a higher card) in the hope that one's right-hand adversary holds an intermediate card of that suit. Also, in croquet, an opponent is finessed by placing the ball in a difficult position for him to make a shot, which is precisely what Marshall did to Jefferson. See CARD METAPHORS.

finger on the button   ready to launch a nuclear war; a scare phrase used in attacking candidates who complain of a NO-WIN POLICY.

President Lyndon Johnson, campaigning on television in 1964, let the nation know that he considered Barry Goldwater TRIGGER-HAPPY: "You must have strength, and you must always keep your guard up, but you must always have your hand out and be willing to go anywhere, talk to anybody, listen to anything they have to say, do anything that is honorable, in order to avoid pulling that trigger, mashing that button that will blow up the world."

Former President Dwight Eisenhower, in a televised conversation with candidate Goldwater, did what he could to refute the implication: "This is actual tommyrot . . . you're not going to be doing those things that are going to be—what do they call it?—push button, you're not going to push a button here and start a war."

In a 1954 press conference, Eisenhower gave a more eloquent explanation of the restraints a President must keep on himself: "In many ways the easy course for a president, for the administration, is to adopt a truculent, publicly bold, almost insulting attitude. A president experiences exactly the same resentments, the same anger, the same kind of sense of frustration almost, when things like this occur to other Americans, and his impulse is to lash out."

Sorensen called the President "custodian of the nuclear trigger." "Trigger" and "button" are interchangeable in this sense, in both the U.S. and Britain. In the 1951 British election, the Labour party accused the Conservatives of being warmongers, an attack led by the *Daily Mirror*'s article, "Whose Finger on the Trigger?"

The derivation of trigger is from the Western "hair-trigger," as explained in the entry on "trigger-happy"; button, as in push-button war, is becoming preferred, and is probably derived from the "panic button" of World War II. Writing in *American Speech* magazine, Lt. Col. James L. Jackson, USAF, suggests:

The actual source seems probably to have been the bell system used in bombers (B-17, B-24) for emergency procedures such as bailout and ditching. In case of fighter or flak damage so extensive that the bomber had to be abandoned, the pilot rang a "prepare-to-abandon" ring and then a ring meaning "jump." The bell system was used since the intercom was apt to be out if there was extensive damage. The implications of the phrase seem to have come from those few times when pilots hit the panic button too soon and rang for emergency procedures over minor damage, causing their crews to bail out unnecessarily.

The phrase has affected Presidential campaigns. Eddie Mahe, an adviser to the Reagan campaign, was quoted by the *New York Times* in 1992 about his candidate's success: "The only thing he had to prove to people was that they did not have to be scared if he had his finger on the button. . . . When he proved that, it was over."

Soon after taking office in 1969, Richard Nixon removed an electric push-button window-opener from his White House bedroom, which had been installed by President Johnson. "I took that out," said President Nixon, "because I was afraid if I pushed the button, I'd blow up the world."

Finlandization persuading or intimidating a neighboring nation into adopting a foreign and defense policy of accommodation.

This word first appeared, with a British spelling, in the *Manchester Guardian Weekly* on May 22, 1969: "There is a foreign policy called Finlandisation, which allows more independence than Rumania has."

Capitalized and spelled with a *z* in American English, *Finlandization* takes its name from Finland, a country that maintained a foreign policy of neutrality to keep its independence from the former Soviet Union. This policy of neutrality was considered supportive of the neighboring superpower.

From the noun came a 1972 verb, *Finlandize.* C. L. Sulzberger wrote in the *New York Times* in 1972 about North Atlantic Treaty Organization nations: "The voters want comfort more than protection; their governments worry about letting this area gradually become 'Finlandized.'"

Although Finns dispute the accuracy of the term, *Finlandization* usually connotes domination. A new and more positive sense, however, emerged with the relaxing of Soviet control throughout Eastern Europe. In the *New York Times* in 1989, James M. Markham wrote from Bonn: "The talk is of the decay of the Soviet Union's western empire that could, in optimistic scenarios, lead to the 'Finlandization' of swaths of Eastern Europe."

Other foreign policies have also relied on the suffix *-ization.* Among these terms are *Balkanization* (describing the breakup of an empire or a region into small, usually hostile units and in the 1990s applied to the breakup of Yugoslavia); VIETNAMIZATION; and a 1983 coinage by Shimon Peres, Israel's Labor party leader, when his country's troops were removed from Lebanon: *Lebanonization.*

fire in the belly an unquenchable thirst for power or glory; the burning drive to win a race or achieve a goal.

As a political phrase, the expression is usually used to indicate a Presidential candidate's desire to win, particularly the willingness to endure the long contest. It first appeared in print in 1882, in an essay by Robert Louis Stevenson, in which he compared historians Thomas Carlyle and Thomas Babington Macaulay. "Carlyle," wrote Stevenson, ". . . had a fire in his belly so much more hotly burning than the patent reading-lamp by which Macaulay studied, that it seems at first sight hardly fair to bracket them together."

The source of the expression is not known. Perhaps this metaphor for ambition comes from stoking a potbellied stove or from the fiery sensation of heartfelt heartburn.

When Senator Howard Baker, a laid-back and unflappable politician, campaigned for the Republican nomination in 1984, he responded to questions about his willingness to go the distance with this cliché: "I have the fire in the belly."

How to turn the cliché upside down was demonstrated in 1989 by Dianne Feinstein, then mayor of San Francisco. At the start of her campaign for the governorship of California, her longtime political consultant resigned from the campaign, claiming that she lacked "fire in the belly." When shortly afterward she underwent a hysterectomy, Feinstein quipped, "I had a fire in the belly and had it removed."

fireside chat a warm, informal talk by a political leader to a few million of his intimate friends.

In 1938, President Roosevelt wasn't sure just how the term "fireside chat" began to be applied to his radio talks. "The name 'fireside chat,'" he said, "seems to be used by the press even when the radio talk is delivered on a very hot mid-summer evening."

Roosevelt's first fireside chat as President was made on March 12, 1933, dealing with the opening of banks the next day. However, he had used radio talks in the same way during his first term as governor of New York State, principally to woo upstate Republicans who received most of their information from Republican newspapers.

The title of the first speech made no mention of firesides; it was "An Intimate Talk with the People of the United States on Banking." In a letter dated October 30, 1933, FDR recalled the audience he had in mind: "I tried to picture a mason at work on a new building, a girl behind a counter, and a farmer in his field." As Joseph Abrell points out in an unpublished study of Roosevelt's radio usage, ". . . the term 'Fireside Chat' was not applied to his first such address but in promoting the second. Harry C. Butcher, who in 1933 was head of the CBS office in Washington, D.C., suggested the name, and from then on they were identified as such by everybody from the 'girl behind the counter' to Roosevelt himself."

Will Rogers thought the talk had so simply explained banking that "even bankers understood it." The *New York Times* editorialized: "His use of this new instrument of political discussion is a plain hint to Congress of a recourse which the President may employ if it proves necessary to rally support for legislation which he asks for and which the lawmakers might be reluctant to give him." Backhanded testimony came from defeated Republican candidate Alf Landon in 1938: "The Presidency is primarily an executive office, not a broadcasting station."

Roosevelt was so effective as a radio speaker that succeeding Presidents were urged by their advisers to give more radio and TV reports to the nation.

President Kennedy's journalist friends urged him so strongly to use the airwaves more often that he commented, "People seem to think Roosevelt gave a fireside chat once a week." Kennedy's staff found that Roosevelt gave only thirty fireside chats during his twelve years as President; before World War II, he averaged only two a year. See OVEREXPOSURE.

The phrase was used as the basis for a gag in 1976 about Senator Henry Jackson's lackluster speech delivery, and since then about Senators Sam

Nunn and Bill Bradley: "If he gave a fireside chat, the fire would go out."

When President Carter made a televised "fireside chat"—complete with crackling fire—in 1977, he included a wrinkle of his own: a cardigan sweater.

firestorm sudden, fierce controversy; a surge of public fury.

"Richard Nixon clung tenuously to office last week," wrote *Newsweek* in its issue of November 5, 1973, "in the face of the most devastating assault that any American President has endured in a century—a nationwide rebuke of such magnitude that one of Mr. Nixon's principal aides described it as 'a fire storm.'"

The anonymous aide who so described it was White House chief of staff Alexander Haig, a lifelong Army officer accustomed to the vocabulary of military catastrophe. The following April, *Newsweek* reprised the word to describe the scene: "It was a full five months since the Saturday-night massacre—the firing of Special Prosecutor Archibald Cox, the resignation of Attorney General Elliot Richardson and the ouster of his deputy, William Ruckelshaus—touched off the fire storm of public outrage that made the impeachment of a U.S. President a real possibility."

General Haig was familiar with the term since its use in the language of atomic warfare. After a heavy incendiary attack, or the dropping of an atomic bomb, rising hot air creates a vacuum that causes a "storm" of air to rush in, causing further devastation. In 1959 the *New York Times* estimated casualties in an atomic attack in this way: "Nearly half of these could be expected to die instantly, killed by blast or incinerated in the fire-storms caused by the explosions." (The *OED* tracks the word back to 1581 in a curiously similar upward-sucking metaphor: "Helias . . . was taken up into Heaven in a fire storme.")

Although the word has occasionally been used in its political sense before Watergate (columnist James J. Kilpatrick wrote in 1970 that "the next revolutionary who strikes a match in Seattle may ignite a political firestorm"), its association with the most crucial moment in the Nixon decline annealed it to political crisis terminology. Hence, when President Gerald Ford issued his surprise pardon of Mr. Nixon, CBS correspondent Bruce Morton quoted a congressman as saying he predicted "a firestorm of criticism," a calibration more than criticism's usual storm. The *Wall Street Journal* used the same word for the same event the next month: "It may well be, as some of Mr. Ford's oldest and closest advisers say privately, that the President will soon recover from the fire storm that followed the Nixon pardon."

As in most catastrophic metaphors—from PRAIRIE FIRE to AVALANCHE—the new word was soon trivialized. When Secretary of Agriculture Earl Butz made a racial slur in a joke told privately during the 1976 campaign, John Fialka wrote in the *Washington Star:* "What began as a casual conversation among three airline passengers—John Dean, Pat Boone and Earl Butz—has ended in a political firestorm that has cost Butz his job . . ."

In this way, firestorm (now usually one word, sometimes hyphenated) has almost become synonymous with FLAP, which is unfortunate, since a word for a sudden public-opinion rage is useful. See DISASTER METAPHORS.

first in war "To the memory of the man," read the resolution presented to the House of Representatives by Henry (Light Horse Harry) Lee on the death of George Washington in 1799, "first in war, first in peace, first in the hearts of his countrymen."

The line is as famous as any in American history primarily because of the circumstances in which it was spoken; at the death of a great president, the nation is attuned to a memorable phrase (Stanton on Lincoln: "Now he belongs to the ages").

The line also scans in three-syllable beats like the hoofbeats of a galloping horse: first-in-war/first-in-peace/first-in-the/hearts-of-his/coun-trymen/. This rhythm has led to parroting, which overlooks the truth in the phrase: Washington was indeed the man who was most responsible for winning the Revolutionary War, for setting up a republic, and refusing a monarchy, and was the most popular American.

Like almost every familiar line, it has been parodied. When Tammany Hall scandals began to embarrass New York Governor Franklin Roosevelt in 1931, *Time* magazine wrote of Tammany: "First in war, first in peace, first in the pockets of its countrymen."

And in 1967, cartoonist Conrad in the *Los Angeles Times* pictured a colonial-looking Lyndon Johnson as "First in War, second in Peace, and 46% in the Polls of his countrymen."

first lady the wife of the President of the U.S.

British war correspondent William Howard Russell (who coined the phrase "thin red line" in his [London] *Times* coverage of the Crimean War) used "first lady" in *My Diary North and South,* published in 1863. "The gentleman who furnished fashionable paragraphs for the Washington paper has some charming little pieces of gossip about 'the first Lady in the Land.'"
His use of the phrase in quotations indicates an earlier usage than this reference (in the *Dictionary of Americanisms*) to Mary Todd Lincoln. Carl

Sferrazza Anthony points out a possible coinage in his book *First Ladies,* when President Zachary Taylor eulogized Dolley Madison in 1849: "She will never be forgotten, because she was truly our First Lady for a half-century." The British novelist Edward Bulwer-Lytton used the expression in his 1853 book *My Novel:* "She looked like the first lady in the land."

American poet and novelist Mary Clemmer Ames used the phrase in describing the inauguration of President Rutherford B. Hayes on March 5, 1877. It became part of the language when playwright Charles Nirdlinger wrote a comedy about Dolley Madison in 1911, entitled *The First Lady in the Land,* which enjoyed a good run at New York's Gaiety Theatre. She was the first Presidential wife also to be a public figure. In recent Administrations, Nancy Reagan was noted (and occasionally criticized) for her influence on White House business, and Hillary Rodham Clinton's active role in health care legislation has earned her the title of TMPWA (see ACRONYMS, POLITICAL) for "the most powerful woman in America."

When the President dies, the first lady ceases to be "first," but may remain a celebrity. Eleanor Roosevelt was consistently on the "most admired American" lists after 1945 and was often introduced as "First Lady of the World." Jacqueline Kennedy remained the center of some attention after Lady Bird Johnson became first lady in 1963.

Recently, the wives of governors and mayors have been referred to as first ladies; as this usage grows, the words describing the wife of the President are likely to be capitalized, to set her off from the pack.

The term is particularly popular in show business. Helen Hayes, who died in 1993, was eulogized as "the first lady of the American theater."

When John J. O'Connor, television critic for the *New York Times*, wrote about Roseanne Barr in 1991, he called her "the First, er, Lady of Prime-Time Television."

In the 1980s, the wife of the Vice President began to be called "the second lady," perhaps on the analogy of Air Force Two.

fiscal integrity the "motherhood" of money—everybody is for it.

Fiscal policy has to do with budgeting the government's taxes against its expenditures; *monetary* policy concerns itself with the interest rates that reflect and guide the flow of funds in a nation. A *balanced* budget and *deficit financing* are phrases in the fiscal area; *tight money* and *hard money* belong in the monetary area.

Fiscal integrity, then, has been used most often to describe a balanced budget. It is stressed more often by conservatives, who charge liberals with recklessness and "fiscal irresponsibility." With the advent of Lord Keynes (see NEW ECONOMICS), the rules appeared to change on fiscal integrity: if balanced budgets could lead to depressions, then perhaps fiscal integrity required deficit financing.

"I think the virtues of a 'balanced budget' can at times be exaggerated," wrote Harry Truman. "Andrew Jackson paid off the national debt entirely, and the budget was balanced when the unprecedented Panic of 1837 struck. Even the depression following the crash of 1929 overtook a government which was operating in the black."

Such a comment would have been considered heresy for a politician only a generation before. Its acceptance as a position without blinking now indicated that "fiscal integrity" was shifting away from balancing the budget and toward some amorphous "doing the right thing for the economy to en-

sure prosperity, full employment and no inflation." In his 1992 campaign, Bill Clinton pledged only to "cut the deficit in half" by the 1996–97 fiscal year, a pledge he amended soon after taking office. See PAY AS YOU GO.

fishing expedition investigation without a specific goal; a probe undertaken usually by a committee dominated by one party into the affairs of another party, for the purposes of unearthing whatever "bait" might be useful in a campaign.

The phrase is used as a defensive smear of a legitimate investigation. Thomas L. Stokes wrote in 1940 about the Harding–Teapot Dome investigation of 1924: ". . . many voters, undoubtedly, were willing to accept the Republican explanation that it was just a 'political fishing expedition.'"

In a 1955 Eisenhower cabinet meeting, Philip Ray, general counsel to the Department of Commerce, explained why he refused to turn over department records to the House Judiciary Anti-Trust subcommittee, headed by Democrat Emanuel Celler. Ray said that Celler seemed bent on a "fishing expedition," and Eisenhower agreed that the department should draw a line between what could and could not be released to a committee of Congress. According to reporter Robert Donovan's reading of the minutes of that meeting, Eisenhower said "he was never going to yield to the point where he would become known as a President who had practically crippled the Presidency."

Other fishing metaphors in politics include the familiar *fish or cut bait*, the graphic *floundering around*, and a fishing expression unique to politics, *going fishing*, which means *sitting out a campaign*, or not quite *bolting* (see BOLT) but refusing to help.

The July 2, 1876, *Cincinnati Commercial* wrote: "There has been a great deal of inquiry as to whom Carl Schurz was going for in the presidential campaign. Perhaps he is not going for anybody, but is going a-fishing."

Writing on California Republican politics in the *New Republic* in 1967, Andrew Kopkind observed: "[Senator Thomas] Kuchel supported [Mayor George] Christopher against [candidate for Governor Ronald] Reagan, and 'went fishing' in the general election."

To *fish for votes* is a common construction, leading to this frequent admonition to candidates too willing to spend time on citizens too young to vote or too deeply committed to either side: "Fish where the fish are."

In the seventies, the expression's sharp edge of unwarranted intrusion was blunted by a frequent use meaning "feeler" (see PEACE FEELER) or TRIAL BALLOON. After Carter aides had sounded out television executives to find out if they would telecast a routine Fourth of July speech, Tom Shales wrote in the June 29, 1978, *Washington Post:* This practice of testing the waters to gauge possible interest—'a fishing expedition,' one NBC executive calls it—has been common practice . . ." Defending the White House right to "think out loud," another executive—Sanford Socolow of CBS—used a locution that is the farthest-out form of fishing expedition: "Those guys are entitled to blue-sky once in a while."

five percenter   one who claims to know government officials in high places and can be "helpful" for five percent of a contract.

Republicans, notably Senator Joseph McCarthy of Wisconsin, popularized the phrase in the friends-in-high-places scandals during the Truman Administration.

A New England furniture manufacturer, Paul Grindle, triggered a congressional investigation of influence peddlers in Washington. Grindle, a former reporter for the *New York Herald Tribune,* alleged that James V. Hunt, a management counselor in Washington, assured him that he could introduce him to influential people for $1,000 down, $500 a month and five percent of any contract.

Grindle closed the deal and then put the *Tribune* on to the story. The newspaper story started a Senate investigating committee on Hunt's trail. Subsequent investigations uncovered other emoluments: the wife of an examiner of loans for the Reconstruction Finance Corporation received a $10,000 mink coat after the RFC had approved a loan for a Florida motel; Major General Harry Vaughan, President Truman's military aide, and other Washington notables received deep freezers as gifts. Remaining aloof from the controversy, Truman refused to get drawn into a detailed discussion of the five-percenter investigations. Vaughan said he was "bewildered and baffled" by the uproar about doing a few favors for friends.

As a result of the Senate investigations, the RFC was reorganized and there were some purges in both the Department of Justice and the Internal Revenue Service.

See BELTWAY BANDITS; INFLUENCE PEDDLER; MESS IN WASHINGTON.

flak   opposition, especially noisy opposition to a new idea or program. To "run into flak" means to encounter some unexpected but not devastating criticism.

The word was coined in World War II to describe anti-aircraft gunfire, an acronym for the German *Flieger* (aircraft) *Abwehr* (defense) *Kanone* (gunfire). In politics, flak serves to bring down TRIAL BALLOONS.

The puffs of smoke of the exploding anti-aircraft shells may have also given rise to another meaning of "flak": press agent, or government public information officer. The puffs refer derogatorily to "puffed-up" or inflated, exaggerated information; "puff pieces" are articles that flatter and swell the head of the subject. Fred R. Shapiro of Yale Law School, however, has traced the eponymous *flack* to a note in the June 1939 issue of *Better English* magazine: "That alert weekly, *Variety*, birthplace of numerous Americanisms, is trying to coin the word 'flack' as a synonym for publicity agent. The word is said to be derived from Gene Flack, a movie publicity agent. Something *Variety* may have overlooked, however, is that a Yiddish word similar in sound means 'one who goes around talking about the other fellow's business.'"

The two meanings came together in a small footnote to history. While working on a speech in the White House one day in 1969, the author received a call from David Young, an assistant to Henry Kissinger (who later went on to some fame as the coiner of PLUMBER). The young aide wanted to know what "flack" meant.

Since the first rule of bureaucratic survival is not to pass out any information without knowing its intended ultimate use, the speechwriter deliberately misinterpreted the question and gave an answer that explained the German derivation of the acronym "flak."

Moments later the aide called back to say, "Dr. Kissinger doesn't need you to teach him German, but he says Joe Kraft just called him 'an Administration flack' and he wants to know whether he should take offense."

With the background understood, I passed along the current meaning of "flack" with a *c*—apologist, or paid proponent, with its pejorative but sometimes madcap connotation. To cheer up Dr. Kissinger, the thought was added that the role, if not the word, could be an honorable one, since a skilled advocate was needed to explicate foreign policy.

However, when next Dr. Kissinger passed by, he gloomed: "I decided to take offense." Perhaps he was wrong to worry about "flack"; in a few years he was to learn what it was to be the object of "flak" without a *c*, from this writer and others.

"Flak" continues to be useful in political commentary. The *National Journal* reported in February 1993 on the line-item veto that "Clinton took some flak for his views"; a week earlier, the *Los Angeles Times* commented on Hillary Rodham Clinton that "If she's going to catch flak . . . she might as well catch flak over something that matters, and health care does."

flaming liberal   attack word on a member of the political left; more vivid than "radical."

Fire is often used to characterize radicalism. A *fiery* orator, or *firebrand*, *fires up* his audience; with *fire in his eyes*, he *inflames* their passions to *heated* argument about his *infernal* opinions. (Smoke, on the other hand, implies deviousness: see SMOKE-FILLED ROOM and SMOKE SCREEN.) The color of fire is red, and red is the name of everything radical. Some issues "burn"; others are merely "hot."

The phrase might have arisen parallel to the "flaming youth" of the twenties. All-encompassing labels like LIBERAL require adjectives to make a description more exact. During Prohibition, those who went along with repeal were called "Wets," and they opposed the "Drys"; but those who felt strongly about repeal were labeled "dripping Wets." (See WETS.) Similarly, liberals are tagged KNEE-JERK liberals (who react without thinking), *professional* liberals (a favorite Harry Truman criticism of those who only talked liberalism), or *flaming* liberals.

A flyer put out by an extreme right-wing group in 1964 attacked "Hubert Humphrey The Flaming Liberal" as a member of "a semisecret, New York-based, Communist-appeasing group called the Council on Foreign Relations." The flyer did not add that other members of this group included Dwight Eisenhower, Lucius Clay, Edward Teller, and several of Barry Goldwater's foreign policy advisers.

flap. See UNFLAPPABLE.

flat-out a maximum effort applied from the beginning, with no consideration given to rest, overexposure, or saving a last burst of energy and money for the end.

The phrase is probably derived from auto racing, where it means maximum speed, accelerator flat on the floor.

Opposite of *flat-out* is PEAKING, planning a campaign so that all activity, expenditure, and voter interest reach a crescendo just before election day. In the campaign of 1960, Kennedy began as the underdog and ran a flat-out campaign, as an underdog must do; Nixon, who dropped back after the first debate on television, came on with a rush at the end, "peaking" just a few days too late to win. Wrote Arthur Schlesinger, Jr.: "Some close to Kennedy believed that, if the campaign had gone on three days more, he would have been beaten. The candidate himself knew the tide was shifting."

FDR believed in peaking, though the phrase was not current in his time. He began the 1936 campaign by going on a leisurely two-week cruise, allowing the Republicans to take center stage; his time would come nearer the decision date. "The Republican high command," he wrote his running mate, John Nance Garner, "is doing altogether too much talking at this stage of the game." See OVEREXPOSURE.

The flat-out campaigner runs the risk of being spent, physically and financially, on the crucial weekend before election; the campaigner concerned with peaking runs the risk of having energy and money left over when it is too late to use them.

The phrase, now current, is often misused for the shorter word *flat*. When Robert Kennedy and FBI Chief J. Edgar Hoover began trading charges in 1966 on who was responsible for electronic eavesdropping, one former Justice Department aide accused Hoover of "a flat-out lie." Lies and denials can be *flat* or *out-and-out;* campaigns and races are *flat-out.*

San Francisco Mayor George Christopher, Nelson Rockefeller's Northern California chairman in the 1964 Republican primary ultimately won by Barry Goldwater, gave this description of what it is like to be involved in an intense, flat-out campaign: "This morning I was sitting on the edge of the bed just holding a sock in my hand. My wife asked me what I was doing. I told her I was trying to figure out whether I was getting up or going to bed."

flatteries of hope. See GLOOM AND DOOM, PROPHETS OF.

flip-flop a U-turn, or reversal of position; a sudden shift of opinion.

Both noun and verb have become common in political attacks. In supporting a tax increase, President Reagan was asked whether he had "flip-flopped on the tax issue"; he replied, "There is not any flip-flop on this at all."

The reduplication *flip-flop* has been used in English for more than four centuries. Its original senses, describing large ears or imitating the sound of slippers as they slap the floor, were replaced by the image of a somersault. George Lorimer applied that somersault image in 1902: "When a fellow's turning flip-flops up among the clouds, he's naturally going to have the farmers gaping at him." By the 1940s, a metaphorical use described romantic fickleness as "heart flip-flops."

Richard Nixon dismissed a charge of flip-flopping in his 1971 decision to impose wage and price controls with the curt "circumstances change," but its use in political vituperation has continued. In the 1988 campaign, Governor Michael Dukakis pointed to Representative Richard Gephardt and said, "There's a flip-flopper over here," adding, "I'm not a flip-flopper."

Although the term is always pejorative and brings an irate denial, a refusal to flip-flop in the light of changing circumstances can be a sign of rigidity; a willingness to flip-flop is expressed by supporters as evidence of flexibility.

floater. See SWING VOTER.

floo-floo bird a bird that flies backward, more interested in where it has been than where it is going; liberal's description of a conservative.

Frank Lloyd Wright referred to this curious creature in a 1938 speech to architects in Washington, D.C.:

> The cultural influences in our country are like the "floo floo" bird. I am referring to the peculiar and especial bird who always flew backward. To keep the wind out of its eyes? No. Just because it didn't give a darn where it was going, but just had to see where it had been. Now, in the "floo floo" bird you have the true symbol of our Government architecture . . . and in consequence, how discredited American culture stands in the present time. All the world knows it to be funny except America.

Frank Lloyd Wright did not hyphenate the floo-floo bird in his written remarks. Proper usage requires the hyphen, which looks both ways.

Just after Dwight Eisenhower's reelection in 1956, Senate Majority Leader Lyndon Johnson said the country supported the President because it felt that Eisenhower "was more interested in where he is going than where he has been." The lack of wisdom present in backward-looking was expressed by baseball pitcher Satchel Paige, who counseled: "Never look back. Someone may be gaining on you."

Other birds in the mythical heavens include the "worry bird," a small desk ornament that does the worrying for executives; the "gooney bird," or weekend Air Force reservist flying around for practice; and the extinct dodo, subject of the expression, "dead as a dodo." The Johnson family's names (wife "Lady Bird" and daughter Lynda Bird) gave rise to some satire, as in the play *MacBird!* (produced in New York in 1966), parodying Shakespeare's *Macbeth*.

For the political menagerie's complete aviary, see this dictionary's Introduction.

floor fight an argument, usually about platform demands or delegate credentials, that cannot be settled in committee and is taken to the floor of the convention for decision.

Floor fights are despised by most political professionals: compromise has failed, and sections of the party will consider themselves losers at the convention and may go home and sit on their hands.

Historian Stefan Lorant tells of the day in 1896 when a man burst into Republican boss Mark Hanna's St. Louis hotel room and announced: "Mr. Hanna, I insist on a positive declaration for a gold-standard plank in the platform."

Hanna looked up and said, "Who the hell are you?" The man replied, "Senator Henry Cabot Lodge of Massachusetts."

"Well, Senator Henry Cabot Lodge

of Massachusetts, you can go plumb to hell. You have nothing to say about it."

"All right, sir," bristled Lodge. "I will make my fight on the convention floor." Replied Hanna: "I don't care a damn where you make your fight." But cooler heads prevailed, and a floor fight was averted. When it became known that the Democrats would declare for free silver, the platform committee placed the Republicans dead against it. ("Avert a floor fight," as used above, is a cliché. For a modern example of how to stop a floor fight before it starts, see COMPACT OF FIFTH AVENUE.)

A floor fight in the 1952 Republican convention over contested credentials swung the nomination away from Taft to Eisenhower (see THOU SHALT NOT STEAL); a floor fight on ideological grounds in the 1948 Democratic convention resulted in the bolt of the DIXIECRATS. Democrats averted a floor fight about the abortion issue in the 1992 convention by refusing to give podium time to Pennsylvania Governor Robert Casey, a pro-life advocate in a pro-choice hall; this was exploited in the subsequent Republican convention.

The meaning of "floor" as "forum," or "right to speak," predates American political history and comes from English parliamentary tradition. See HUSTINGS.

flugie   a rule that only benefits the maker of the rule, and can be changed to avoid having it benefit his opponent.

When Senator Russell Long (D-La.) wanted to get special legislation passed for a constituent, and a fellow senator objected, Senator Long would explain patiently that his proposal was "just like a flugie." When the objector wondered what that was, Senator Long would eagerly tell the story:

Two men are playing poker; one gets a full house and starts to gather in the winnings, when another player—with not even two of a kind in his hand—stops him. "This is my pot," says the full-house man, "you don't have a thing." "Ah," says his opponent, "but nothing is a 'flugie.' Read the sign on the wall behind me." Sure enough, the sign says: "A Flugie Beats Everything." The man with nothing in his hand takes in the pot.

On the next hand, the man who just held the full house comes up with nothing, and starts to rake in his pot. "Wait," says the flugie expert, who this time has a pair. "Read the sign behind you." On the wall, the sign reads: "Just One Flugie Per Evening."

Washington Star reporter James Dickenson, recounting this in 1977, added: "The widespread notion of the U.S. Senate is that when it comes to tax legislation Long really wants, which very often benefits oil and gas producers, he consistently gets the only flugie of the evening."

The slang term "flugie"—or its variants "floogie," "floozie," "floosy"—usually describes a woman of loose morals. The World War II ditty "Flatfoot Floogie with a Floy-Floy" was said to mean, to the cognoscenti, a streetwalker with a venereal disease. This is evidently not the meaning Senator Long had in mind.

flyer   a small handbill or circular with a brief political message.

Political literature includes *handbills, handcards, doorknob-hangers, flyers, brochures, reprints,* and *mailers.*

In current use, *flyer* and *handbill* are used interchangeably to mean a cheap circular about an issue or one calling attention to an upcoming event or visit; a *handcard* is a picture of a candidate on heavier stock paper with a brief description of his background and occasionally a summary of his platform; a *brochure* is an expanded version of the handcard, often using pictures of the candidate in action and with improved graphic design, usually more elaborate than a flyer; a *door-knob-hanger* is a flyer saying that a volunteer called and giving some brief information about a candidate, with the top of the flyer slit or shaped so that it can be hung on a doorknob; a *reprint* is a photo-offset reproduction of a favorable article about the candidate, in flyer form to be handed out; a *mailer* (or *self-mailer*) is a brochure designed, with space left for address and stamp, to be mailed without an envelope.

Relatedly, a *bumper sticker* is a self-adhesive rectangle affixed to an auto bumper or signpost. The message must be short; supporters of Jay Rockefeller in a West Virginia Senate race chose "Too rich to steal."

Circular is no longer in current use in politics; HANDOUT is rarely used in this sense; its current meanings are a welfare payment or a press release.

Flyer (when not used to mean aviator or small venture in the stock market) is the most frequently used word in political literature. It can be traced to an 1888 speech in the House by Congressman T. E. Tarsney of Michigan: "[My opponent] placed upon every doorstep of every house in the city [of Saginaw] a flyer. 'Do not vote for Tim Tarsney: he is a freetrader.'"

For examples of how flyers can get far more vicious than the kind Tarsney complained about, see GUTTER FLYER; ROORBACK.

FOB. See IRISH MAFIA.

Foggy Bottom the State Department.

Robert A. Lovett, who served as Secretary of Defense in the Truman Administration, had been dubbed "the Bald Eagle of Foggy Bottom" (see BALD EAGLE) from his earlier State Department days. State Department offices were built on land that had

originally been called Foggy Bottom, and the name was reapplied because it recalled a fogginess of official language.

New York Times columnist James Reston told the lexicographer that the reporter who first applied the phrase to the State Department was Edward Folliard of the *Washington Post.* "Eddie grew up down by the gasworks, between what is now the New State Department building and the K Street bridge," Reston recalls. "The coinage took place soon after State moved out of the building across the street from the White House, that's now the Old Executive Office Building."

The Library of Congress provided the author with a description of the derivation, from George R. Brown's 1930 book, *Washington.*

> Over in the old First Ward of an earlier day . . . where originally had been the little town of Hamburgh, which existed before Washington was even conceived, was—and still is—Foggy Bottom, lying west of Twenty-third Street and extending to Rock Creek and stretching from the river nearly to Pennsylvania Avenue. In its southern reaches it was formerly a section of swamps and flats, from which arose at night miasmatic vapors which gave to it its colorful cognomen.
>
> Indeed, that whole region which extends from the river to the White House, south of Pennsylvania Avenue, the western extremity of which is still known to the old families as "Foggy Bottom," became in time a fashionable neighborhood . . . which afterwards, however, declined, and is only just now experiencing a renaissance somewhat similar to that which Georgetown has enjoyed, as people of means and culture have flocked there . . .

As people in the foreign service flocked to the "western extremity," the State Department came to be known by the mildly mocking name. Wrote

Arthur Schlesinger, Jr., in *A Thousand Days:* "The State Department sent over a document. . . . In addition to the usual defects of Foggy Bottom prose, the paper was filled with bad spelling and grammar."

The phrase should not be confused with *Puzzle Palace*, the nickname for the Pentagon.

following. See BACKER.

football, political an innocent civic or philanthropic project used to make a political issue.

Pity the low-flying, nonpolitical bird that finds itself the shuttlecock in a game of political badminton. This, to mix a SPORTS METAPHOR, is the political football, and it means "unfair use of a pure project for crass partisan gain." As can be seen, the phrase itself is an attack phrase, drawing sympathy to the nonpartisan ball that is getting kicked.

In 1800 Abraham Bishop wrote in *Connecticut Republicanism:* "Multitudes of rational men are for destroying that kind of religion which is made a football or stalking horse, and which operates only to dishonor God and ruin man."

Fiorello La Guardia, former New York City mayor who headed the United Nations Relief and Rehabilitation Administration, got into a debate with Adlai Stevenson in 1946 over methods of providing emergency relief. Taking the offensive, the "Little Flower" accused Stevenson of "making a political football out of food." In the same way, Harry Truman said of Dwight Eisenhower's actions in the campaign of 1952: "Hard as it was for us to understand this side of Eisenhower now revealed to us, it was even more of a jolt to see our foreign policy used as a political football."

Mobster Charles "Lucky" Luciano, in a 1953 interview with the author, sat in a Naples bar and gloomily reviewed the causes of what he felt was his persecution: "I was sent to jail, I was sprung, and I was deported, all because I was a political football."

A recent, more ominous use of "football" refers to the small, thirty-pound metal suitcase containing codes that can launch a nuclear attack. It is carried by a military aide to the President and follows the Chief Executive wherever he goes. See BAGMAN. For the use of football terminology in politics, see GAME PLAN.

foot-in-mouth disease tendency to blunder when ad-libbing; error-prone.

The day after Eisenhower's Defense Secretary Charles E. Wilson made his famous BIRD DOG . . . KENNEL DOG comparison, he admitted his error and told reporters that some of his cabinet colleagues "seem to think I have foot-in-mouth disease."

This is a combined colloquialism of interesting parentage, now almost exclusively applied to political figures.

To put one's foot in it, presumably to step into a foul substance or tread heavily on thin ice, has long been a colloquial expression for a misstep or mistake. On matters verbal, the expression was narrowed to *put your foot in your mouth.* This was closely akin to the cattleman's problem, *foot-and-mouth disease* (or hoof-and-mouth disease), a contagious disease of livestock, especially of cloven-hoofed animals. "Foot and mouth" and "foot in mouth" sound identical when spoken quickly, thus spreading the political "disease."

The metaphor can be mixed. Newbold Morris, wealthy reform associate of Fiorello La Guardia and at one time president of New York's City Council, was derided as a man "born with a silver foot in his mouth."

Medical metaphors (see BODY POLITIC) offer political writers vast opportunities; in 1967, a *New York Post* editorial writer was able to pack five medical words into a single sentence: "After consultation with his political doctors, Governor Romney of Michigan has resolved to refrain from further comment in the near future on Vietnam; this self-imposed quarantine may help arrest his virulent attack of foot-in-mouth disease."

Prince Philip, the Duke of Edinburgh, coined the pseudo-medical term *dontopedalogy* for foot-in-mouth disease. The word, made up of Greek *dontos*, "teeth," and Latin *pedalis*, "of the foot," was too infelicitous to catch on even among the royals.

Foot-in-mouth disease should not be confused with *logorrhea*, which means speaking on and on past the point of no interest. To apologize in advance for a long speech and to avoid the appearance of verbal diarrhea, politicians often use the self-deprecating line: "This reminds me of the little girl who claimed she knew how to spell 'banana' but she didn't know when to stop."

See BLOOPER.

footnote to history   a seemingly insignificant detail, contributed long afterward to a great event or a historic person's life.

Samuel Rosenman felt that the story of Roosevelt's use of language was important, "not only as a footnote to history, but as an aid to the better understanding of the leadership exercised by Franklin D. Roosevelt." By designating his information as a footnote to history, the contributor strikes a modest pose; in addition, he calls attention to the detail—most people, like it or not, find their eyes dragged down to the bottom of a page by a footnote.

The phrase is from a book of that title by Robert Louis Stevenson.

Criteria for a footnote to history are that it be (1) hitherto unpublished, (2) from firsthand knowledge, (3) illustrative of character or mood, and (4) unpretentious. See the Kissinger story under FLAK, or the Eisenhower story under FIELD EXPEDIENT, as examples.

foreign wars.   See AGAIN AND AGAIN AND AGAIN.

forgotten man   single image for the millions left in economic desperation by the Depression.

Governor Franklin D. Roosevelt of New York, campaigning in 1932 for the Democratic presidential nomination, used this phrase in a short speech containing several ideas which would become basic during the first years of his presidency. The theme of this address was the need to come up with plans that "rest upon the forgotten, the unorganized but the indispensable units of economic power . . . that build from the bottom up and not from the top down, that put their faith once more in the forgotten man at the bottom of the economic pyramid."

The party's 1928 presidential candidate, former New York Governor Alfred E. Smith, saw it as a radical attack on business: "At a time like this, when millions of men, women and children are starving throughout the land, there is always a temptation to some men to stir up class prejudice . . ."

To the man out of work, already suffering or fearful of what lay ahead, the "forgotten man" was himself; the phrase played a part in Roosevelt's victory over Smith at the Democratic convention and then over Hoover.

The future President was not the man who coined the phrase, nor was Professor Raymond Moley, though he picked it up and inserted it in that initial speech. A sociologist at Yale University, William Graham Sumner, first used the phrase in an article written in

1883. Far from intending it to describe the destitute, Sumner had in mind the sturdy middle-class citizen who bears society's greatest loads: "Such is the Forgotten Man . . . he is not in any way a hero (like a popular orator); nor a problem (like tramps and outcasts); nor an object of sentiment (like the poor and weak); nor a burden (like paupers and loafers) . . . therefore, he is forgotten. All the burdens fall on him . . ."

Just how important FDR's use of the phrase was at the time is shown by a bitter verse printed in the *New York Sun*, a paper whose unyielding Republicanism was never in doubt, after Roosevelt's victory and just before his inauguration. The President had gone on a fishing cruise on Vincent Astor's yacht, the *Normahal*. The party included other well-to-do friends, which inspired the newspaper's poet to write:

> They were just good friends with no
>   selfish ends,
> To serve as they paced the decks;
> They were George and Fred and the
>   son of Ted
> And Vincent (he signed the checks);
> On the splendid yacht in a climate hot
> To tropical seas they ran;
> Among those behind they dismissed
>   from mind
> Was the well-known Forgotten Man!

In 1972, on the 90th anniversary of Roosevelt's birth, the *New York Times* editorialized: ". . . to anyone under the age of 40, his name is likely to evoke nothing more than the shadow outline of a wartime statesman . . . Roosevelt is in danger of himself becoming America's greatest 'forgotten man.'"

For Roosevelt Before Chicago. See CUFFLINKS GANG.

forty acres and a mule   illusory political promise to secure black votes.

This Civil War term, an offer by dishonest politicians, began as *ten acres and a mule*, which the lexicographer Stuart Berg Flexner reported in use as early as 1862. Northern propagandists offered a promise, later broken, that Southern plantations would be confiscated and divided among the slaves after the Civil War. The acreage increased after Union General William Tecumseh Sherman issued a special field order on January 16, 1865: "Every family shall have a plot of not more than forty acres of tillable ground."

Forty acres, one-sixteenth of a *section*, appeared frequently as a measure of land, even shortened to *forty* —as in "the back forty"—in the mid-nineteenth century. By 1871, the longer phrase appeared in print, when the *Congressional Globe* stated, "The slaves only appreciated the advantages of fighting for freedom when this privilege was accompanied with a present bounty or future prospect of 'forty acres and a mule.'"

This expression was featured in *Gone With the Wind*. The 1939 film, based on the Margaret Mitchell novel, showed a carpetbagger on a soapbox addressing a group of freed blacks in Atlanta; identified in the script as the Orator, he pledges, "We're goin' to give every last one of you forty acres and a mule. . . . Because we're your friends and you're going to become voters—and you're going to vote like your friends do."

Modern uses of the phrase point back to the Reconstruction promises. In 1978, the *Washington Post* commented on the plight of black businessmen in securing loans for small business: "Success would redeem government's post–Civil War pledge of '40 acres and a mule' for blacks."

The phrase has been revived by the minority group as a symbol of broken promises and dashed expectations.

The production company for black filmmaker Spike Lee's *Malcolm X* in 1992 was 40 Acres and a Mule Filmworks.

Not only blacks, however, have been disappointed by broken pledges. John Powers of the *Boston Globe* commented in a 1992 essay on a series of American political promises to entice or bamboozle voters: "We elect politicians who vow to make every man a king, who promise us 40 acres and a mule, a chicken in every pot and a car in every garage."

Founding Fathers   a group of revolutionaries willing to take their chances on treason to pursue the course of independency—now viewed as sage, stately signers of the documents of U.S. freedom.

Although the phrase has the feel of an early Americanism, it is of twentieth-century origin.

At the instigation of Richard Hanser, television writer and phrase hunter, the Library of Congress researched the subject and came up with an unlikely originator: Warren Gamaliel Harding.

On George Washington's birthday in 1918, then-Senator Harding told the Sons and Daughters of the American Revolution: "It is good to meet and drink at the fountains of wisdom inherited from the founding fathers of the republic." He repeated it in his campaign for the presidency in 1920 and used the phrase again in his inaugural address: "I must utter my belief in the divine inspiration of the founding fathers."

As it often happens, however, the *Oxford English Dictionary* provided an earlier date for the term in the title of a book by K. B. Umbriet: *Founding Fathers: Men Who Shaped Our Tradition*, published in 1914.

Without capitalization, the phrase now means the originator of any movement or organization; capitalized, the reference is primarily to the men who gathered at the Constitutional Convention in Philadelphia in 1787.

Richard Whelan used the phrase in a dynastic sense as the title of his 1964 biography of Joseph P. Kennedy.

Harding was fond of matching up words with the same beginning letter (see his "not nostrum but normalcy" line-up under ALLITERATION) and Founding Fathers functioned as the fulfillment of his forensic fancy.

four freedoms   objectives of U.S. policy as summarized by President Franklin D. Roosevelt in his message to Congress, January 6, 1941: freedom of speech, of religion, from want, and from fear.

In his State of the Union message, eleven months before the U.S. entered World War II, President Roosevelt suggested the Lend-Lease program to supply Great Britain with war equipment to fight the Axis Powers. He also outlined the "four freedoms":

> In the future days, which we seek to make secure, we look forward to a world founded upon four essential human freedoms.
> The first is freedom of speech and expression—everywhere in the world. The second is freedom of every person to worship God in his own way—everywhere in the world.
> The third is freedom from want—which, translated into world terms, means economic understandings which will secure to every nation a healthy peaceful life for its inhabitants—everywhere in the world.
> The fourth is freedom from fear—which, translated into world terms, means a worldwide reduction of armaments to such a point and in such a thorough fashion that no nation will be in a position to commit an act of physical aggression against any neighbor—anywhere in the world.

President Roosevelt, his speech writers, and his personal secretary, Dorothy Brady, were working over the fourth draft of his 1941 State of the Union message when FDR turned to his secretary and asked her to take down an addition. The addition was the passage he must have had in mind since the previous July, when he briefly mentioned the four freedoms in a news conference.

One of the speechwriters who was present at the meeting, Samuel Rosenman, later wrote that only a few words were changed from the way FDR dictated the four-freedoms passage to the final draft as it was delivered.

In his dictation, Roosevelt added "everywhere in the world" only to the first two freedoms.

Harry Hopkins suggested that "everywhere in the world" covered a lot of territory. He doubted that the American people were interested in "the people in Java."

President Roosevelt answered, "They'll have to be some day. The world is getting so small that even the people in Java are getting to be our neighbors now." In the final draft Roosevelt added "everywhere in the world" and "anywhere in the world" to the last two freedoms. The four freedoms were later incorporated into the Atlantic Charter.

fourth estate   the press; now outdated and used ironically.

Books of quotations usually credit Edmund Burke with coinage, thanks to a citation by historian Thomas Carlyle in *Heroes and Hero-Worship,* written in 1839: "Burke said that there were three estates in Parliament; but, in the Reporters' Gallery yonder, there sat a Fourth Estate more important far than them all." When diligent research failed to turn up the phrase in anything Burke said or wrote, some quotation

detectives assumed Carlyle was referring to Lord Macaulay, who said in 1828: "The gallery in which the reporters sit has become a fourth estate of the realm."

"Fourth estate" had been used much earlier in both England and France, usually in reference to "the mob" (the other estates being the king, the clergy and the commons, all powers whose agreement was necessary for legislation). The *OED* suggests that Lord Brougham used it in Commons in 1823 applied to the press, "and at that time it was treated as original."

The vote of this lexicographer for the coiner of the phrase as a definition of the press goes to English essayist William Hazlitt, who wrote on the character of William Cobbett in an 1821 *Table Talk.* Cobbett was a vituperative pamphleteer and editor, and the only man ever prosecuted for libel in both England and America. Hazlitt wrote of him: "One has no notion of him as making use of a fine pen, but a great mutton-fist; his style stuns his readers . . . He is too much for any single newspaper antagonist; 'lays waste' a city orator or Member of Parliament, and bears hard upon the government itself. He is a kind of *fourth estate* in the politics of the country."

The phrase was used to put the press on an equal footing with the greatest powers in a nation; in the twentieth century it was taken up by many editors in descriptions of the importance of journalism. The phrase lost its vividness as the other "estates" faded from memory, and now has a musty and stilted connotation. In current use "the press" usually carries with it the aura of "freedom of the press" enshrined in the U.S. Constitution, while press critics usually label it, with a sneer, "the MEDIA."

For a related etymology, see THIRD WORLD.

Fourth of July speech an emotional speech appealing to the spirit of patriotism; a flag-waver.

A speech made on the Fourth of July is expected to be patriotic; when the term "Fourth of July speech" is used to describe a speech made on any other day, it is derogatory.

The expression dates far back in American history. Ohio Senator Stanley Matthews, on Feb. 13, 1879, asked his fellow senators: "Has the oratory that is peculiar to the Fourth of July come to be a hissing and a byword, a scorn and a reproach . . . is it enough to smother opposition and put down argument, to say that that is merely the sentimentality of a Fourth of July oratory?"

One example of how Fourth of July oratory came to have a bad name can be seen in this excerpt from a speech on July 4, 1827, by Edward Everett, Massachusetts governor, U.S. Secretary of State, and Harvard president (best known for his forgotten speech before Lincoln spoke at Gettysburg): "Let us then, as we assemble on the birthday of the nation, as we gather upon the green turf, once wet with precious blood, let us devote ourselves to the sacred cause of Constitutional Liberty! Let us abjure the interests and passions which divide the great family of American freemen! Let us resolve . . ." etc.

James Russell Lowell, a poet who served as ambassador to England, abjured that approach in his Independence Day speech in London in 1883: "Now the Fourth of July has several times been alluded to, and I believe it is generally thought on that anniversary the spirit of a certain bird known to heraldic ornithologists—and I believe to them alone—as the spread eagle, enters into every American's breast, and compels him, whether he will or no, to pour forth a flood of national self-laudation." Lest his English listeners think him unpatriotic, Lowell added: "I ask you, is there any other people who have confined their national self-laudation to one day in the year?"

Although Americans are traditionally self-conscious about excessive displays of patriotism (see SUPERPATRIOTS), and will deride such excess as "Fourth of July," there are limits to which derision is allowed. When Rufus Choate denounced the "glittering and sounding generalities that make up the Declaration of Independence" in 1856, Ralph Waldo Emerson snapped back with "Glittering generalities! They are blazing ubiquities."

freebie a gift; a free pass.

This slang noun dates back to the 1920s; it is first found in print in Rudolph Fischer's 1928 novel *The Walls of Jericho*, where it is spelled *freeby*. This spelling and the variant *freebee* are recorded in Berrey and Van den Bark's 1942 *American Thesaurus of Slang*. Louis Armstrong defined it in his 1954 autobiography: "That meal was a freebie and didn't cost me anything."

The two-syllable word uses a popular *-ie* ending, with the *b* inserted between the vowels to ease the pronunciation (this insert is a "paragogic infix"). *Lesko's Info-Power* by Matthew Lesko was described by a 1990 news release as a book on "how to tap into the thousands of freebies and cheapies" among "30,000 government goodies." (The earlier *cutie* is now considered sexist; Reagan campaigners in 1980 stirred up feminist sentiment against the Democratic incumbent by passing out "Cuties for Carter" buttons.)

By 1990, the term had entered the political lexicon. When President Bush was asked whether preparations for the Persian Gulf War would change his projections on cutting the budget deficit, he replied, "It may cause for a re-arrangement in how money is spent, because this is not a freebie."

freedom fighter. See CIVIL DISOBEDIENCE; ACTIVIST; TERRORISM.

Freedom Now slogan of the civil rights movement, stressing impatience with delay in achieving equality in fact after achieving it in law.

"To the Negro demand for 'now,'" wrote Murray Friedman in the *Atlantic Monthly* in 1963, "to which the deep South has replied 'never,' many liberal whites are increasingly responding, 'later.' But the Negro will accept nothing short of first-class citizenship, now."

"Now" became one of the "in" words of the mid-sixties, probably stemming from its use in "Freedom Now," a militant civil rights slogan that preceded Stokely Carmichael's BLACK POWER. Its structural sloganeering predecessor was Clarence Streit's pre–World War II call for an international federation, "Union Now." In 1966, there were "now" dresses (miniskirts), "now" dances, and the "Now Generation" (from the "Lost Generation" via the "Beat Generation").

"Freedom," like democracy, justice, and peace, is a Humpty Dumpty word, meaning whatever the user chooses it to mean. In phrases, it was used in "freedom fighters" in Hungary in the early fifties, and FREEDOM RIDERS in the U.S. a decade later.

Theodore White wrote in 1965: "Perhaps the most necessary intellectual operation in American life is some redefinition of the word 'freedom.' I have attended as many civil-rights rallies as Goldwater rallies. The dominant word of these two groups, which loathe each other, is 'freedom.' Both demand either Freedom Now or Freedom for All. . . . It is quite possible that these two groups may kill each other in cold blood, both waving banners bearing the same word."

freedom of the press. See RIGHT TO KNOW.

freedom riders groups of blacks and whites who rode buses through the South in the summer of 1961 testing the segregation of public facilities in interstate bus terminals.

In February 1960, four black students attempted to sit and eat at a lunch counter in Greensboro, North Carolina. They were evicted. For the next year, the director of the Congress of Racial Equality (CORE), James Farmer, raised money to hire buses and recruited black and white volunteers to ride them through the South to demand the right to sit and eat in a public place or to use facilities which the general public was permitted to use. CORE dubbed the buses "freedom buses," those who rode them "freedom riders." See FREEDOM NOW.

During the summer of 1961, the freedom riders did most of their riding and testing in Alabama. Riders were beaten in Birmingham; a bus was burned in Anniston. Attorney General Robert Kennedy sent more than 600 deputy federal marshals to Alabama. There were only a few minor incidents during the rest of the summer.

"The most nightmarish day of our freedom ride," wrote CORE's James Peck, who took 53 stitches after a beating, "was Sunday, May 14, Mother's Day. I identify the date with Mother's Day because when Police Chief Connor was asked why there was not a single policeman at the Birmingham Trailways terminal to avert mob violence, he explained that since it was Mother's Day, most of the police were off-duty visiting their mothers."

In September 1961, the Interstate Commerce Commission desegregated all facilities in terminals used in interstate bus travel and the Justice Department ordered the desegregation of public transportation. See SEGREGATION.

The phrase became secure enough to be parodied. When a New York State law threatened to invalidate "quickie" Mexican divorces, a stampede of unhappy spouses poured into Juarez, Mexico, before the law took effect. "Most of the New Yorkers flocking here are women," wrote the *Wall Street Journal* in 1967, "and many arrive on American Airlines flight 295 (which they call 'the Freedom Riders Special') . . ."

free enterprise the practice of capitalism under representative government.

The Republican platform in 1936 charged President Roosevelt with having displaced "free enterprise with regulated monopoly." FDR fired back: "Private enterprise, indeed, became too private. It became privileged enterprise, not free enterprise."

A British economist, Alfred Marshall, wrote in 1890 of tracing "the growth of free enterprise in England." Woodrow Wilson used it in 1913 at the time the Federal Reserve System was being set up to help "resourceful businessmen . . . deal with the new circumstances of free enterprise . . ."

The term, used also as "freedom of enterprise" by Wilson in 1913, has been most popular with those who find the capitalistic system challenged by government regulation. For example, *Newsweek* wrote in 1938: "Management leaders representing the world's democratic countries agreed that free enterprise, not government control, is the key to better times."

Roosevelt felt the need to reaffirm his faith in 1944: "I believe in free enterprise—and always have. I believe in the profit system—and always have."

The term became more popular after 1936, primarily as a euphemism for *laissez-faire* which some no longer considered politically acceptable. See AMERICAN SYSTEM; AMERICAN WAY OF LIFE; BLACK CAPITALISM.

free lunch as to which there is no such thing.

Nobel economics laureate Milton Friedman has published articles, a book and lectures using the title "There Is No Such Thing as a Free Lunch." His meaning is that everything, even what is seemingly "free," must be paid for by somebody in some way and that there is no sense in hiding that fact.

Reached by letter, Dr. Friedman replied that he had no idea where his much-quoted phrase comes from: "I wish I did, but if wishes were horses . . . " (An allusion to the saying "If wishes were horses, beggars would ride," to which novelist Vladimir Nabokov once replied, "I'd wish for Pegasus.")

Slanguist Stuart Berg Flexner offered the author this help: "*Free lunch* dates from the 1840s and was supposed to have moved from the West to the East, getting fancier as it approached eastern bars and hotels, so sometime after the late 1840s I can just see some bartender slapping the hands of a customer and asking him to buy that 5¢ beer before shoveling in the victuals—though whether it was ever used in that literal way or not by bartenders, I don't know. It sure is a great conservative line, though."

Thanks to the Friedman popularization, and to the seventies trend toward a fresh acceptance of conservative ideas, the phrase's use mushroomed. When a bill favoring the maritime industry was defeated in a surprise vote in Congress in 1977, Common Cause president David Cohen explained: "The maritime industry has had a free lunch on Capital Hill before this, because there'd been no publicity." In November 1977, reporter Fox Butterfield wrote in a *New York Times Magazine* article about an improbable welfare state in Micronesia, especially on the island of Yap: "Yap is a living refutation that there is no such thing as a free lunch," a U.S. official was quoted as saying. "Here it's a smörgåsbord."

The phrase was popularized by science fiction writer Robert A. Heinlein in his 1966 novel *The Moon Is a Harsh Mistress.* Heinlein coined "tanstaafl" (there ain't no such thing . . .), the long acronym for the phrase.

For a 1964 Goldwater use, see SANTA CLAUS, NOBODY SHOOTS AT.

free ride a campaign undertaken by an officeholder who runs for a higher office without giving up his own; if he loses, he continues to serve in the first office.

Senators, serving six-year terms, have the best opportunity for "free rides" running for governor of their states, or on a national ticket. In the election of 1960, for example, Senator John F. Kennedy, whose term did not expire until 1964, had a free ride; in 1964 Senator Barry Goldwater, whose term expired that year, did not. Lyndon Johnson solved the problem in 1960 by running simultaneously for both Senator and Vice President.

A generation earlier, California Democratic Senator Sheridan Downey was a possible gubernatorial nominee. "Downey would be getting a 'free ride,'" wrote Leo Katcher, "in that, if he lost, he would continue as Senator. Nothing is dearer to a politician's heart than such a free ride . . ."

In a more general sense, the phrase means any effort that requires no sacrifice. Robert F. Kennedy, announcing his 1968 challenge to Lyndon Johnson's renomination, said, "I can't believe that anybody thinks that this is a pleasant struggle from now on, or that I'm asking for a free ride . . . I'm

going into primaries . . . I'm not asking for a free ride . . ." In July 1992, the *Washington Post* commented, "This is an odd time in the campaign, providing something of a free ride for the Democratic ticket before the Republican National Convention is held next month."

The term continues to be used outside of politics. The *New York Daily News* headlined "When Hollywood Makes Movies in New York," with the subhead "Film Makers Get Free Ride."

Free Soil, Free Men, Fremont. See REPUBLICAN.

free world in the eyes of the Western democracies during the Cold War, any nation not under Communist domination.

The "free world" probably was in use as a phrase during both world wars, to describe the nations not under German or Axis control, but it gained currency in the late nineteen forties and early fifties as realization of the Communist expansion dawned. A 1955 Marcus cartoon was typical: an upstanding-looking gentleman labeled "free world," with his arm in a sling labeled "violation of Yalta agreements," is spurning the blandishments of a bear labeled "Russian honor," with the caption "Once bitten, twice shy."

Dwight Eisenhower used the phrase frequently: "I believe that the situation and actions best calculated to sustain the interests of ourselves and the free world . . ." (memo to John Foster Dulles, 1955).

Its constant use by Western orators made it uniquely an anti-Communist phrase that could not be turned around, as the Communists did with the phrase "people's democracy." This was revealed in Chairman Nikita Khrushchev's preface of the phrase with a SNEER WORD in an address to the

21st Congress of the Communist party, January 27, 1959: "The so-called free world constitutes the kingdom of the dollar . . ."

The breakup of the Soviet Union has changed the perception of the phrase. In 1992, *Newsday* discussed the success of Clinton's campaign: "He portrayed Bush as a man who sees the world locked in a struggle between communism and the free world, and implied that Bush was unable to make the transition to the post–Cold War world." But the "post–Cold War world" is an unwieldy, transitional phrase, based on the "postwar world" that described the time after World War II and was a source of confusion after the wars in Korea and Vietnam. If the world was no longer divided into the Free World, the Communist bloc, and the Third World, what was the new world to be named?

"The very phrase 'the world community,'" wrote Harvard professor Samuel P. Huntington in 1993, "has become the euphemistic collective noun (replacing 'the Free World') to give global legitimacy to actions reflecting the interests of the United States and other Western powers." He footnoted: "Almost invariably Western leaders claim they are acting on behalf of 'the world community.' One minor lapse occurred during the run-up to the Gulf War. In an interview . . . British Prime Minister John Major referred to the actions 'the West' was taking against Saddam Hussein. He quickly corrected himself and subsequently referred to 'the world community.' He was, however, right when he erred."

See WEST, THE.

freeze   stop or halt; the discontinuance or suspension of action.

Freeze began as an Old English verb and took the sense of "to become solid or congealed by cold." Police jargon picked up the imperative use of "Freeze!" to stop suspects from fleeing.

The noun *freeze*, first used in the fifteenth century, gained modern prominence in the phrase *nuclear freeze*, used by supporters to express an end to the arms race. Opponents of that freeze, however, argued against conceding Soviet superiority.

In 1983, the National Conference of Catholic Bishops eschewed the political controversy of *freeze* in a long pastoral letter. After a series of drafts, however, the Roman Catholic bishops chose the dovish synonym *halt* in place of the restraining *curb*.

Economic uses of the noun date back to the October 1942 use of *price freeze*, based on a 1930s concept of price control. From that use of the term comes *COLA freeze*, a 1980s attempt to end the cost-of-living adjustment of Social Security benefits.

After a freeze has been in effect for a while, critics of the policy usually want to *unfreeze* or to *lift* the freeze or, in extended imagery of ice, to *thaw*.

Friends of Bill.   See IRISH MAFIA.

front-porch campaign   originally, a dignified campaign technique, eminently successful; now, a pompous approach to voters by a lazy candidate.

"McKinley stayed at home," wrote Harry Truman, "and spoke only to such delegations as came to his house from time to time. This was the first of the 'front porch' campaigns. I do not approve of 'front porch' campaigns. I never liked to see any man elected to office who did not go out and meet the people in person and work for their votes."

Although Harry Truman, in his 1948 campaign (see WHISTLESTOPPING) laid to rest for modern campaigners any thoughts of relaxed campaigning at home, his historical analysis is open to debate. There were three front-porch campaigns—Harrison in 1888, McKinley in 1896, and Harding in 1920—and the last two resulted in landslides for the front-porcher. McKinley, especially, had good reason to stay at home and entertain delegations to Canton, Ohio—he was not the stemwinding orator that his opponent, William Jennings Bryan was. It made more political sense to play to his strength, which was a homely, conservative, heartland-of-America stability.

Benjamin Harrison made speeches from his front porch in 1888, narrowly defeating Cleveland, and repeated the technique in 1892, losing to Cleveland. But it was McKinley's campaign that perfected the technique and coined the phrase. The delegations to Canton organized by Mark Hanna's Republican organization included railroad excursion fares, which made such a trip, in the *Cleveland Plain Dealer*'s disgusted opinion, "cheaper than staying at home." Though the candidate said he was "averse to anything like an effort being made to bring the crowds here," the delegations were met at the depot by a gaily uniformed escort of horsemen, conducted to the McKinley home in a noisy parade, and treated to a fine display of rustic Americana; they returned home with excellent word-of-mouth to pass on about the charming gentleman who shook each visitor's hand.

In his next campaign, in 1900, McKinley felt more confident about Bryan's opposition, and agreed to travel more. In 1920, the Harding managers thought it would be safer to keep their man mainly at home and out of the kind of trouble possible in a STUMP campaign.

What makes a front-porch campaign impossible today is that a candidate must never seem remote and inaccessible. But McKinley's accessibility—to those who would take the trouble to travel to see him—added to his appeal. English journalist George Steevens wrote: "If you want to see a Presidential candidate you ring the bell and walk in and see him. That is what he is there for. I rang and walked in; Mr. McKinley was sitting on a rocking-chair not ten feet from the door . . . he is gifted with a kindly courtesy that is plainly genuine and completely winning."

front runner the leading contender for a nomination.

Another racing term describes the front runner: "shows early foot." This means that the horse (or candidate) is capable of getting out of the starting gate well and sets the pace for the others in the field. Occasionally his lead becomes insurmountable, as Barry Goldwater's nomination race showed in 1964, and Jimmy Carter's capture of many convention states and early primaries showed in 1976, but the phrase as used today in politics carries ominous overtones of a likelihood of fading in the homestretch.

FDR, the front runner in 1932, received this letter from Robert W. Wooley about his leadership so early in the campaign: "Herein lies the danger . . . automatically you become the target of the other candidates, real and potential. There isn't a single favorite son whose delegation won't be held out of the Roosevelt column so long as there is a reasonable chance of getting something for that favorite son, even at your expense."

Ted Sorensen echoed this point about Kennedy a generation later: "There were disadvantages in being the 'front runner.' The Senator's critics became more open and vocal and his every word was politically interpreted."

The front runner must come thundering into the convention increasing his speed and with enough "kick" left for a final spurt. "When the balloting starts," wrote Thomas E. Dewey, "every candidate wants to show enough strength to be one of the leaders on the first ballot. He also wants to have enough strength in reserve so he can gain on the psychologically important second ballot. For example, in 1940, I led on the first three ballots out of six—the wrong three. I lost ground on the second ballot. That was the beginning of the end and everybody knew it." See DEWEY BLITZ.

Despite all the protestations of danger in being the front runner, candidates prefer that position to DARK HORSE because it has a greater chance of victory. However, the racing analogy is not complete. In 1953, a sports page of the *New York Times* pictured a victorious jockey completely splattered with mud. The caption explained that "it is evident McCreary's mount had to come from way back to win—front runners stay clean." Not so in politics.

frying the fat. See FAT CAT.

fudge factory. See WAFFLE.

full-court press an all-out effort.

"Something dramatic was in order," wrote *Time* in October 1977, describing Carter Administration plans for a counterattack on opponents of its energy legislation. "[Vice President Walter] Mondale spoke up and, using a basketball image, urged a 'full-court press' on energy. Carter liked the idea."

"Full-court press" became White House lingo in the late sixties; one of its most frequent users was counsel Charles Colson. In politics, the term has come to mean a strenuous effort to get legislation passed, probably because of its resemblance to "all-out pressure."

In basketball, however, the phrase is used only to describe a defense. When a professional team takes the ball into play from behind its own basket, it has ten seconds to cross mid-court; the defense sometimes employs a "full-court press" to harass and otherwise delay the offense from bringing the ball across. Other "presses" are half-court and (in college ball) zone; in each case, the meaning is to concentrate delaying pressure on the offense (in hockey, this is known as a forecheck).

However, in political usage the defensive image has dribbled away, and only the aggressiveness remains. The Associated Press reported in March 1993 that "President Clinton promised a 'full-court press' against Bosnian Serbs to secure their agreement to the peace plan."

See SPORTS METAPHORS.

full dinner pail symbol of prosperity, turn-of-the-century equivalent of a cornucopia, or horn of plenty; slogan of the 1900 McKinley campaign.

"Hurrah for a full ballot-box, a full dinner-pail, and continued prosperity!" The *Review of Reviews* in 1900 showed a picture of a large dinner pail featured in a Youngstown, Ohio, parade, with a caption: "Four more years of the Full Dinner Pail."

William Jennings Bryan, in his second campaign against McKinley, stressed imperialism as the PARAMOUNT ISSUE: "Immediate Freedom for the Philippines" was the Democratic slogan. The Republicans emphasized prosperity, with vice-presidential candidate Theodore Roosevelt doing much of the campaigning, assuring the workingman that Republicanism and high tariffs would continue to keep the dinner pails full.

The dinner pail had long been a symbol in the growing labor movement. Thomas Nast used it in an 1880 *Harper's Weekly* cartoon, and Theodore Roosevelt wrote a friend in 1894: "I hear all around that the working men intend to vote 'for the policy of the full dinner pail'. . ."

In 1928 Herbert Hoover tried to update the phrase, holding the symbol for the "party of prosperity": "The slogan of progress is changing from the full dinner pail to the full garage." (See CHICKEN IN EVERY POT.) Writing about his defeat a year later, Democrat Al Smith described Republican strategy that had "brought down from the garret the old full dinner pail, polished it up and pressed it into service."

Since the Depression, Republicans have stayed away from symbols of prosperity in campaigning, though they have used the word prosperity itself; Democrats have hammered away at the "chicken in every pot"—which Hoover never said—denying Republicans the full dinner pail as a symbol. Since dinner pails are blue-collar rather than white-collar, the symbol may be expected to reappear in a more modern form.

full disclosure   complete candor; total release of information.

This revealing phrase has appeared in all areas of governmental information, the release of which has been governed by both the Freedom of Information Act of 1966 and the Privacy Act of 1974. Its use of the modifier *full* suggests the built-in skepticism about the willingness to disclose information.

The Securities and Exchange Commission provides the origin of the term. It first appeared in the preamble to the Securities Act of 1933: "An act to provide full and fair disclosure of the character of securities sold in interstate and foreign commerce and through the mails, and to prevent frauds and the sale thereof, and for other purposes."

Environmentalist William Futrell, a Sierra Club spokesman, commented in the *National Journal* in 1977 that "the full disclosure of the impact statement is our most valuable tool for environmental coalitions."

Almost a decade later, Ronald Reagan urged Congress to give limited immunity to John Poindexter and Oliver North for their Iran-contra testimony. Reagan's statement read in part, "There is an urgent need for full disclosure of all facts surrounding the Iranian controversy."

In 1992, Peter Canellos of the *Boston Globe* reviewed Richard Nixon's "Checkers" speech from four decades earlier. Canellos echoed the skepticism of the phrase in his appraisal of Nixon: "He spoke of slanders and slights from his many opponents and promised a full disclosure of the fund. But the disclosure turned out to be a statement from an accounting firm hired by the Republicans to assess the fund."

The lexicographer used the phrase as the title of a 1977 novel about the 25th Amendment, concerning a blinded President's inability to carry out his duties.

full generation of peace   the central theme and highest ideal of the Nixon presidency.

President Nixon attributed the phrase to Jawaharlal Nehru. As Vice President in 1953, on his first trip to India, he asked the Indian Prime Minister what was his nation's greatest single need. According to Nixon, Nehru replied, "The greatest need for India, and for any newly independent country is for twenty-five years of peace—a generation of peace."

Six months earlier (on May 11, 1953) soon after the death of Stalin, Winston Churchill had told the House of Commons that a "conference on the highest level" should be convened: "At the worst, the participants in the meeting could have established more intimate contacts, and at best we might have a generation of peace."

On his arrival in India on July 31, 1969, President Nixon referred to the Nehru observation, and made it his own theme: "It is essential, absolutely essential, that we have a generation of peace for Asia and the world."

By using the phrase again in his speech to the 25th anniversary of the United Nations, and repeating it in the 1971 State of the Union message, the President made it plain that he had found his central theme.

There was one thing odd about the concept, however; "only" one full generation of peace was a limited ideal, retaining the possibility of war in a later generation—considerably short of the idea of "permanent peace," or in Lincoln's phrase a JUST AND LASTING PEACE. This writer and others pointed out the need for an explanation of the limited nature of the goal, and the President addressed the subject in an appropriate forum, the dedication of the Woodrow Wilson International Center for Scholars in Washington, D.C., on February 18, 1971:

> Every war-time President since Woodrow Wilson has been tempted to describe the current war as "the WAR TO END WARS." But they have not done so because of the derision that the phrase evoked, a reminder of lost dreams, of lights that failed, of hopes that were raised and dashed.
>
> What I am striving for above all else, what this nation is striving for in all that we do is something America has never experienced in this century, a full generation of peace. . . . That is why I have set our sights on a span of time that men in positions of power today can cope with, just one generation, but one long step on the path away from perennial war.

Fun City   a sardonic reference to New York City.

Woody Klein, who was Mayor John Lindsay's first press secretary, wrote the author:

> As for the origin of "Fun City," I believe that the Mayor himself originated this term early in 1966, or possibly in late 1965 when he participated in an advertisement for an airline and he was asked about New York. His reply contained the phrase "Fun City." It was Dick Schaap, columnist for the *World Journal Tribune*, who publicized the term with his regular columns entitled "What's new in Fun City."

Columnist Schaap turned the mayor's innocent remark into his regular lead for stories on pollution, traffic congestion, and everything wrong with a metropolis.

The adjectival use of the mass noun "fun" has been noted in *Webster's Third International,* which cites "a fun hat" and "have a fun time." Linguists have been observing its use as an adjective like astronomers watching the sky, certain that a new star has to appear in a given spot.

Dwight Bolinger of Harvard explained in the journal *American Speech:* "There was a hole in the semantic pattern. Other nouns of emotion have their corresponding adjectives meaning 'productive of': joy: joyful, joyous; fear: fearful; excitement: exciting. The noun fun had the disadvantage of seeing its adjective *funny* put to the irrelevant uses of 'laughable' and 'odd.'" Since *funny* did not mean "filled with fun," the noun *fun* had to double in brass as an adjective, the way the word "good" does.

University of Georgia professor John Algeo explained: "Since the substantive fun is a mass noun, it often occurs in the predicate position without a determiner. In this position the word looks like an adjective, and thus analogy operates: 'That thing is good': 'That thing is fun': 'That is a good thing': 'That is a fun thing.'" Professor Algeo added solemnly: "The future development of adjectival *fun* needs watching . . . we may even anticipate being told that one car is funner than another, and that will be the funnest thing of all."

For the successor of *Fun City*, see BIG APPLE.

fur ball fierce dogfight; a difficult political tangle.

As military aviation slang for close aerial combat, this phrase gained popularity during the Persian Gulf conflict. In January 1991, the Associated Press reported its use by military pilots as meaning "the hectic tangle of air-to-air dogfights."

As early as 1984, however, the term was used in conjunction with aircraft. An April 1984 issue of *Aviation Week & Space Technology* quoted an expert on air traffic who was describing a "fur ball of airplanes, so many that Patrick radar approach control can't handle them."

Within three years, the term was also used for the engagement of enemy aircraft. Mike Spick wrote in *Defense & Foreign Affairs* in June 1987 about the improved training of aerial fighters: "Should they get trapped in the fur ball, and there are no absolutes in air combat, then they are better equipped both to win and to survive than their predecessors."

An extension of the metaphoric *dogfight*, the term *fur ball* (sometimes written solid as *furball*) suggests any tangle, military or political, too tight for the participants to be differentiated. (A related expression for fighting, *to make the fur fly*, began in American slang in the early nineteenth century. The *Niles Register* of 1814 warned, "Smugglers look out, or you will soon see 'the fur fly.'")

By extension, *fur ball* has also been used for any difficulty. Junette A. Pinkney wrote in the *Washington Post* in 1984: "The only fur ball in the whole business was that Brenno had to get an allergy shot."

fusion coalition before election; a combination of minority parties to defeat the majority party.

Coalition is used to describe the alliance of different political groups who combine to form a government after an election, and therefore is mainly a word to describe non-American politics. *Fusion,* on the other hand, is a welding of interests before an election in the U.S. and particularly in big cities.

As a young novelist, Benjamin Disraeli described the usage in the 1840s in England: "Political conciliation became the slang of the day, and the fusion of the parties the babble of the clubs."

Edward Costikyan, the new-breed Tammany leader in 1964 who managed the 1977 Ed Koch campaign for mayor of New York, offered this definition: "'Reformer' was a term of opprobrium within the machine, and reformers looked . . . to the occasional creation of an *ad hoc* political force which would sporadically 'throw the rascals out' and enjoy four years or so of steadily deteriorating governmental power, until the machine returned to power. In New York, this tradition became known as 'fusion.'"

New York fusion succeeded four times: in 1901, when Seth Low became a one-term mayor; in 1913, when John Purroy Mitchel became a one-term mayor; in 1933, Fiorello La Guardia for three terms; in 1965, John Lindsay. Lindsay was fond of quoting La Guardia's appeal to nonpartisanship when speaking to voters registered Democratic: "There is no Republican way or Democratic way to clean the streets."

A *fusion* need not always be an alliance of minority parties. As the *New York Times* of November 8, 1981, reported, "With his re-election last week as the candidate of both the Republican and Democratic parties, Mr. Koch, a lifelong Democrat, joined the slender ranks of New York's fusion mayors." In this case, even without the fusion, the Mayor would still have headed the majority party.

Bronx boss Ed Flynn expressed the feeling of the Democratic organization politician in New York for the two groups that caused him the most trouble: ". . . the 'other party,' which in New York is the Republican party; and the motley mob of political hacks that cluster periodically about benign old jurists and smart young boy gangbusters who raise the flag of 'Fusion.'"

future and it works. See WAVE OF THE FUTURE.

fuzziness. See ALL THINGS TO ALL MEN.

G

gaffe. See BLOOPER.

gag rule a parliamentary device or resolution to limit debate.

Both in England and America, sedition acts at the end of the eighteenth century were labeled "gags" by critics. The most famous American example of "gag rule" was a resolution passed by the House of Representatives in 1836 to cut off debate on the subject of abolishing or curtailing the institution of slavery.

In 1833 the American Anti-Slavery Society was founded. The House of Representatives was deluged by thousands of antislavery petitions and proposed measures, particularly bills demanding the abolition of slavery in the District of Columbia.

The answer of the slaveholding interests, operating within the Democratic party, was the "gag rule." The measure was actually proposed by a Northerner, Mr. C. G. Atherton of New Hampshire; and Northerners within the Democratic ranks supported it. It tabled any measures dealing with the subject.

Former President John Quincy Adams, who had entered the House as a representative after his term as Chief Executive, opposed it at the beginning of every session of Congress, writing later: ". . . then came Atherton of New Hampshire, the man of the mongrel gag."

In 1844 the "gag" was finally defeated, but not before it had become a national issue publicizing the antislavery forces. Adams was anathematized by some; however, John F. Kennedy in his *Profiles in Courage* refers to the Adams fight against the measure as "the brightest chapter of his history."

Action to limit debate by the device of cloture in Britain's House of Commons is usually referred to by the minority as "using the gag." The usual reaction of any parliamentary minority, faced with an attempt by the majority to limit debate, is to complain that they are being subjected to a "gag rule." See MUZZLE.

Rule is a word that harkens back to the American distaste of monarchy, and is almost invariably used pejoratively in politics. In addition to *gag rule*, there is *mob rule*, which usually means anarchy following a breakdown of law and order but occasionally is used in regard to organized racketeering; *boss rule*, the object of reformers' scorn; *rule-or-ruin*, from English poet John Dryden's "resolved to ruin or to rule the state," used in the U.S. in 1836 against the Whigs and now a condemnation of sore losers and bolters in primaries or conventions; *one-man rule,* first used against "King Andrew" Jackson; and *one-party rule,* the *bête noire* of the advocates of a TWO-PARTY SYSTEM. In Great Britain the sovereign *reigns but does not rule;* a positive use of the word is in *majority rule,* but even that came under attack with Tocqueville's "tyranny of the majority." About the only rules held sacred are the Golden Rule, the RULE OF LAW, and HOME RULE.

game plan   strategy; a plan with the ultimate goal permeating all tactics.

Paul McCracken, chairman of the Council of Economic Advisers, told the American Statistical Association on August 21, 1969: "There is one thing that perhaps the Council Chairman can do. That is to outline for you the Washington game plan for economic policy."

The game plan was to use both monetary and fiscal policy to restrain inflation; then, even before the results of that policy of tightening became fully apparent, to restimulate the economy and thereby avert a recession. The ultimate goal was a new steadiness of prosperity, not controlled by government, that would produce full employment and a stable dollar.

That was the plan; despite setbacks like more unemployment than the Administration expected and too slow a slowing of inflation, that remained the game plan. Halfway through the four-year term, the Nixon economists pointed out that inflation was indeed being curbed, that the mildest recession after a major inflation was already over, and a strong surge of the Gross National Product could be expected. Critics blamed the Administration for not using various forms of controls, for causing unemployment to rise to

the average level of the Kennedy years, and for not slowing inflation soon enough; the central metaphor for their derision was the "game plan."

McCracken had used a phrase that was current in Administration circles because the President used it often in private conversation with his aides, usually as a verb: "We have to game-plan this." This was natural enough, as he was both an avid football fan and a believer in the GRAND DESIGN.

The expression proceeded to become hackneyed. Every suggestion had to be "game-planned" and those who suggested the term be banned were told sympathetically to submit a game plan on how this was to be done. When this writer used the phrase in a draft of an economic speech, the President struck it out—enough was enough.

Alan Otten wrote in the *Wall Street Journal* on December 23, 1970: "Government also tends to become infatuated with a phrase, and then abuse or misuse it. Thus officials in both foreign and economic policy areas have too eagerly embraced the 'game plan' image of the sports world. They now constantly project their 'economic game plan' or 'Vietnam game plan,' even though the phrase carries overtones of fun and frivolity that don't quite suit the serious business of ending the war in Southeast Asia or restoring economic vigor at home."

In the 1980s, use of the cliché slackened. The *American Banker* wrote in 1985 about a trend "away from political game plans and toward business strategies."

Gang of Four.   See CULTURAL REVOLUTION; OPPORTUNIST.

gap   a phrasemaking word, overused, to illustrate shortage, lack, insufficiency, a falling short, or a gulf between.

The original gap was the MISSILE GAP,

a Democratic charge in 1959 and 1960; educators have used "reading gap," businessmen have used "experience gap," and many have used CREDIBILITY GAP against Lyndon Johnson, who talked of "bridging the gap between East and West" in his 1964 State of the Union message. See GENERATION GAP.

Russell Baker, the "Observer" of the *New York Times,* needled the gapsters in a 1967 column, calling attention to

the so-called gap gap, one of the most pressing problems confronting the Government today. Several of Washington's most important Cabinet officials illustrate the enormous range of gaps that have already been dealt with in intensive, two-year studies conducted by the nation's leading universities, and make a convincing argument that if the present rate of two-year studies is maintained the country will be out of gaps to keep its blue-ribbon committees employed by the end of 1969. The inescapable sociologist, Sean Moynihan, controversial as always, proposes solving the problem by lengthening all two-year gap studies to four years.

garden-hose analogy FDR's homely parable to explain Lend-Lease to the American people.

Late in 1940, Prime Minister Churchill wrote a 4,000-word letter to President Roosevelt reviewing Britain's military and financial position, and hoping that the U.S. would not "confine the help which they have so generously promised only to such munitions of war and accommodations as could be immediately paid for." At a press conference in Washington on December 17, 1940, Roosevelt pointed out that the more supplies Britain took—paid or not—the more quickly our own productive capacity would grow, and the war materials were more useful "if they were used in Great Britain, than if they were kept in storage here."

He went on extemporaneously telling a kind of parable:

Suppose my neighbor's home catches fire, and I have a length of garden hose four or five hundred feet away. If he can take my garden hose and connect it up with his hydrant, I may help him to put out his fire. Now, what do I do? I don't say to him before the operation, "Neighbor, my garden hose cost me $15; you have to pay me $15 for it." What is the transaction that goes on? I don't want $15—I want my garden hose back after the fire is over.

After the fire is put out, he puts the garden hose back, and if it is damaged beyond repair in putting out the fire, he (my neighbor) says, "All right, I will replace it."

Now, if I get a nice garden hose back, I am in pretty good shape.

The plain words about lending a garden hose to a neighbor to put out a fire—which, incidentally, might well spread to your own home—and later getting the garden hose back, or a duplicate, was Lend-Lease in its simplest terms. As complex a scheme as Lend-Lease turned out to be, it could not have been more simply or effectively placed before the American people.

Of course, the hose was never returned, nor did FDR ever expect it would be.

garrison state. See WELFARE STATE.

-gate construction a device to provide a sinister label to a possible scandal.

After WATERGATE, a scandal in France dealing with the adulteration of Bordeaux wines was promptly dubbed *Winegate.* This led to the adoption of the *-gate* suffix as a scandalizer in other fields.

When it became known in 1976 that an investigation had been launched into corruption of members of Congress by the South Korean CIA, this writer started referring automatically to *Koreagate*.

Similarly, when President Carter's Director of Management and Budget, Bert Lance, was charged with taking a SWEETHEART LOAN it was natural to label it *Lancegate;* and when mayoral candidate Mario Cuomo attacked New York Mayor Abe Beame for seeking to suppress an SEC report on the finances of the BIG APPLE—New York City—he called it *Applegate*. More aptly, charges leveled at Congressman Daniel Flood in 1978 were called *Floodgate*.

The floodgates did indeed open for *-gate* in the 1980s. Billy Carter's shady Libyan connection during his brother Jimmy's Presidency was naturally called *Billygate*. A tasteless war between competing televangelists was appropriately named *Pearlygate*. The notorious Iran-contra affair, in which money from the sale of arms to Iran was illegally diverted to support the rebel forces in Nicaragua, earned the name *Irangate*, while *Iraqgate* was the name given in 1989 to the controversy about grain credits being used to furnish Iraq with rocket technology. The 1993 move to dismiss the White House travel staff and blacken their reputation in favor of hiring Bill Clinton's distant cousin was dubbed *travelgate*. The 1991 controversy about rubber checks and the abuse of the bank in the House of Representatives was labeled *rubbergate*. The *-gate* construction was extended to the criticism of President Clinton in 1993 for a $200 haircut by a hairdresser called Christophe of Beverly Hills, while Air Force One held up air traffic in Los Angeles, an incident that came to be known as *scalpgate*.

Clearly, the *-gate* construction is too useful to be slammed shut.

generation gap   a frustrating lack of communication between young and old; or, a useful stretch of time that separates cultures within a society, allowing them to develop their own character.

Generation gap was not sired by *missile gap* out of *credibility gap*, though gapsmanship in general reinforced all three. The originator was Sir Winston Churchill, who wrote in *My Early Life* (1930): "Come on now, all you young men, all over the world. You are needed more than ever now to fill the gap of a generation shorn by the war . . ."

Churchill went on to write: "Don't take no for an answer, never submit to failure. Do not be fobbed off by mere personal success or acceptance. You will make all kinds of mistakes; but as long as you are generous and true, and also fierce, you cannot hurt the world or even seriously distress her. She was made to be wooed and won by youth."

See GAP.

genocide.   See HOLOCAUST; FINAL SOLUTION; ETHNIC CLEANSING.

geopolitics.   See HEARTLAND; LEBENS-RAUM.

gerrymander   drawing of political lines by the party in power so as to perpetuate its power; designing a district to fit a voting pattern.

This is one of the most triumphant political expressions, traceable to the early days of the Republic and still in current use.

Charles Ledyard Norton selected a picture of a gerrymander for the cover of his 1890 book, *Political Americanisms,* and detailed the derivation:

> The term is derived from the name of Governor [Elbridge] Gerry, of Massachusetts, who, in 1811, signed a bill readjusting the representative districts so as to favor the Democrats and weaken the Federalists, although the last named

party polled nearly two-thirds of the votes cast. A fancied resemblance of a map of the districts thus treated led [Gilbert] Stuart, the painter, to add a few lines with his pencil, and say to Mr. [Benjamin] Russell, editor of the Boston *Centinel,* "That will do for a salamander." Russell glanced at it: "Salamander?" said he, "Call it a Gerrymander!" The epithet took at once and became a Federalist war-cry, the map caricature being published as a campaign document.

Gerry's name was pronounced with a hard *g;* but because of the similarity of the word with "jerrybuilt" (meaning rickety, no connection with gerrymander) the letter *g* is pronounced as *j.*

Governor Gerry, a signer of the Declaration of Independence and later one of James Madison's Vice Presidents, has become—thanks to linguistics— one of the villains of American history. Actually, he never sponsored the redistricting bill and is said to have signed it reluctantly. But his name has been perpetuated in denunciations like this: "See where the hateful serpent of the gerrymander has wound his sinuous course," said an Indiana congressman in 1893. "See where in his glittering folds he has strangled the life out of the spirit of liberty."

In 1993, the *Los Angeles Times* printed this comment on a school board redistricting plan: "A gerrymander by any other name is still a gerrymander. This is one of the problems of the board. Too much self-interest instead of interest where it ought to be—the education of our children."

The construction, with the governor's name up front, can be made more current. Critics of New York State's reapportionment in 1961 called it "Rockymandering" after Nelson Rockefeller.

Gerrymandering created some odd-looking districts, such as the "Monkey-Wrench" district of Iowa, the "Dumb-bell" district of Pennsylvania, the "Horseshoe" district of New York, and the "Shoestring" district of Mississippi. The Supreme Court held in 1993 that such perversions of compactness and contiguity could not be tolerated even in pursuit of the goals of the Voting Rights Act. For a modern use of the ancient technique, see ONE MAN, ONE VOTE. For other examples of eponymy, see MAVERICK, SOLON, PHILIPPIC, BORK, and QUISLING.

Gettysburg address the Sermon on the Mount of politics, often quoted, seldom understood.

To most Americans, Lincoln's Gettysburg address is a string of revered catch phrases, beginning with "fourscore and seven years ago" (a solemn way of saying eighty-seven) and ending with the familiar "of the people, by the people and for the people." See IDEAS. Some who memorized it in grammar school will also recall "the last full measure of devotion" and "that these dead shall not have died in vain." The back-of-the-envelope legend is recalled, along with a satisfying memory that the main speaker's address has been forgotten while the President's modest remarks are immortal.

The Gettysburg address is a poem based on the theme of national resurrection. Its opening sentence contains four images of birth—of a nation *"conceived* in liberty"—*"brought forth"* (born) by "our *fathers"* with all men *"created* equal." The speech then uses the forum of a national cemetery and the images of death ("final resting place," "brave men, living and dead") to symbolize purification and resurrection—that out of this scene of death, "this nation, under God, shall have a *new birth* of freedom."

Rather than addressing himself at length to the dead men in that cemetery, Lincoln used the occasion to recount the conception, birth, death, and rebirth of the nation. But the metaphor, central to Christianity, is never labored.

In his 266 words, Lincoln used the word "dedicate" five times. The first and second times refer to the nation's dedication to an ideal—"that all men are created equal." The third use refers to the specific purpose of the occasion, honoring the dead men buried at Gettysburg—"to dedicate a portion of that field as a final resting place." The fourth and fifth times refer to the ideals—"to the unfinished work" and "to the great tasks remaining before us."

The structure of this speech can be based on these uses of "dedicate"—a strong dedication to ideals first, then a passing dedication of ground for the dead, and finally a ringing rededication to the ideals.

The speech is so deceptively simple that it spawned the "jotted-on-the-back-of-an-envelope" legend. Most speechwriters feel that it was far too carefully constructed to have been written so casually.

For a parody, see EISENHOWER SYNTAX.

get with the program conform or adapt to a new regimen; modify behavior to fit another style.

Business lingo uses the term to emphasize the need to conform, and political party members use it to argue against deviation from the party line. The all-purpose phrase, which may sound like computerese, has been used from sports to international diplomacy.

This *program*, however, is unrelated to computers and instead suggests "routine"; in the 1972 *Black Jargon in White America*, David Claerbaut defines *program* as "lifestyle, behavior pattern." Citations for the phrase date back to its repeated use by Sharon Davis, a Republican campaign worker in Santa Barbara, California, during the 1968 Presidential election.

In sports, the primary sense is "to repress individual ambition and serve as a useful team member." The basketball coach Pat Riley commented in 1991 in the *New York Times* about his style with the Knicks: "I'm very easy to get along with as long as you accept the spirit of the team. The most difficult thing to teach players is how to get away from being themselves and get with the program."

In international relations, the phrase means "to adapt to current opportunity." *Time* magazine, in a 1991 article about a worldwide push for stronger laws of copyright and trademarks, wrote, "Countries that don't get with the program are asking for trouble."

ghostwriter one who writes another's speeches, articles, and planned "ad libs."

Seven categories of ghost (or "spook") haunt the political scene:

1. *Speechwriter,* a ghost who operates out in the open. Only a President, who the public has come to recognize is too busy to prepare all his own messages, can afford to permit it to become known who writes his speeches (see SPEECHWRITER).

2. *Ghostwriter,* or *ghost,* one who surreptitiously prepares written and oral messages for public figures below the highest levels.

3. *Phrasemaker,* one who improves upon speeches already drafted, who "punches up" or adds impact to remarks that contain no quotable passages.

4. *Wordsmith,* in current usage a hack ghostwriter, with the ability to transcribe thoughts into speakable English but with no ideas of his own.

5. *Sloganeer,* which can be a pejorative word for phrasemaker, or an advertising copywriter whose assignment is to create slogans and define issues in a short headline.

6. *Research assistant,* who can be one

ferreting out the facts on which to base a speech or with which a general speech can be made more specific; or a ghost or wordsmith on the public payroll whose euphemistic title conceals his public-relations or writing activities.

7. *Press aide,* or *press secretary* (called *press agent* or *flack* by the press), also writes material for his employer, though the higher the public office becomes, the less likely the press aide is to handle the speechwriting function.

Campaigning in support of Republican congressional candidates in 1970, Vice President Spiro Agnew suggested that network news commentators be quizzed on the air by elected officials, to reveal their biases. Eric Sevareid of CBS fired back: "Unlike the Vice President, we don't possess a stable of ghost writers. Come to think of it, if there are mysteries around, unseen spirits motivating the public dialogue, maybe that's the place that could use the glare of public scrutiny—that stable of anonymity."

See OFFICIAL FAMILY.

giveaway attack word against proponents of private development of natural resources, made by those who feel that public development would be more in the public interest.

If there is any counter to the conservative's charge of CREEPING SOCIALISM, it is the liberal's charge of "giveaway." The word became popular in the controversy in 1953–55 over who should provide power to the city of Memphis, Tenn.: the public Tennessee Valley Authority (proudest product of the New Deal), or a combine of private companies called "Dixon-Yates" after the names of the two company presidents.

Democrats charged that the Dixon-Yates proposal would "give away" some $5 million in profits annually to private enterprise, which could be "saved" if the TVA did the job. "Give-away," "SELLOUT," and "steal" were the words most often used in the attack. Eisenhower in 1954 attempted to explain his position: "The issue is not . . . public power versus unregulated private power. The issue posed to us is federal monopoly of power, as against public or regulated power, freely chosen in each instance by the citizens of each area, with the federal government coming in as a cooperating partner where this seems necessary or desirable."

However, after a contract had been signed with Dixon-Yates, it was revealed that a consultant to the Bureau of the Budget was also an official of the banking firm that was to finance the deal, and the City of Memphis decided to build its own power plant.

Democrats felt they had a good campaign issue against the Eisenhower policy on power and conservation, but it became confused when the "natural gas lobby" overstepped the bounds of propriety in fighting for their bill in 1956. While agreeing with the purpose of the natural gas bill, Eisenhower vetoed it because of the nature of the lobbying, which left Majority Leader Lyndon Johnson, who supported the bill, holding the bag. After that, "giveaway" lost its bite, and Dixon-Yates gave way to new issues.

Some conservatives finally found use for the word in 1977: they charged that the Panama Canal treaty was a "giveaway" of U.S. sovereignty.

give 'em hell, Harry a Truman battle cry in 1948, now used to characterize a slugging campaign.

Enthusiasm for Harry Truman's candidacy was lacking among Democrats early in the 1948 campaign; signs at the convention read: "I'm just mild about Harry."

On September 17, as he began barnstorming the country (see WHISTLE-STOPPING), Truman recalls he told his running mate, Alben Barkley: "I'm going to fight hard. I'm going to give them hell." As he ripped into the "gluttons of privilege" (see VESTED INTERESTS) and the DO-NOTHING CONGRESS, the crowds responded to the scrappiness of the underdog with welcome interruptions of "Give 'em hell, Harry!"

"I never give them hell," Truman smiled as he reviewed his technique in 1956. "I just tell the truth, and they think it is hell."

The phrase became closely identified with the former president in an affectionate way. When Oxford University presented him with an honorary degree in 1956 ("to Harricum Truman, Doctors in Iure Civili") the student cheer was "Harricum! Harricum! Give 'em hell, Harricum!"

The current generic use of the phrase is illustrated by this passage from Sherman Adams's memoirs: "[Len] Hall and I realized that it was futile to expect Eisenhower as the head of the party to make a 'give 'em hell' tour of the countryside . . ."

glacis buffer state; a defensive barrier between potential enemies.

Sahabzada Yaqub-Khan, Foreign Minister of Pakistan, used the term in 1982 to discuss the country that lay between the Soviet Union and Persian Gulf interests: "Afghanistan might one day be intended by the Soviets to be a glacis."

Pronounced GLAY-sis, this term is derived from the Old French verb *glacier*, "to slip or slide." The English noun was first used in 1672 for a gentle slope or inclined embankment; that sense soon led to the more specific use for a fortification that slopes to ground level.

Its figurative sense, however, developed in the mid-1950s. The *Times* of London reported in 1955 that East Germany was seen "as part of Russia's defensive glacis"; in 1960, *The Observer* commented that Eastern European countries "form the glacis between the Soviet Union and the West."

The phrase *glacis state* indicates a barrier of defense, but it suggests more than *buffer state*, which merely separates two powers. A *glacis* also separates powers, but it serves additionally as part of the defense of one of those powers.

glasnost openness; public release of information.

Translated fom the Russian as "openness" or "publicity," *glasnost* refers to the declared policy of the former Soviet Union of allowing freedom of speech and the press. Primarily identified with Mikhail Gorbachev, the word emphasized his attempts to reform the Soviet image of suppressing free speech.

This term, derived from the Russian word *glas*, meaning "voice," was in use long before Gorbachev popularized it. In *Deception: The Invisible War Between the K.G.B. and the C.I.A.*, Edward Jay Epstein notes that Lenin used the term more than forty times in his writings.

In carrying out occasional purges, Lenin would use *glasnost* to force local officials into confessing their own errors and indicating the mistakes of others; his urging of *glasnost* strengthened the dictatorship and at the same time offered the appearance of a movement toward free speech. Lenin's eloquent expression of this policy stated that "*glasnost* is a sword which itself heals the wound it inflicts."

glass ceiling invisible barrier to women or minorities in corporate promotions.

This image of an unexpected see-through obstruction was coined in the mid-1980s. Alice Sargent, a Fortune 500 consultant and author of *The An-*

drogynous Manager, told the *Washington Post* in 1987 that women in corporate America are "bumping their heads on the glass ceiling. Women are looking up at the top and not making it into the board room or the executive suites."

Women are not alone in discovering this barrier; minority males have experienced the same prejudicial treatment. Theresa Hong Bailar reported in *East/West News* in 1988, "*The glass ceiling. The broken ladder. The great wall.* These are terms used to describe promotional barriers faced by Asian Americans in the workplace today— whether as a journeyman plumber or a rising star in an established company like Hewlett Packard."

Perhaps patterned on *price ceiling* for a solid upper limit, *glass ceiling* is primarily a barrier to upper management. Television reporter and producer Linda Ellerbee defined the term for *USA Today* in 1989: "There's a ceiling you didn't know was there because you can see through it. You get to a certain place where you would reasonably expect that the next executive producer job will be yours, for example. Then you see younger, less qualified men promoted over you."

A tougher variant of the breakable *glass ceiling* is *Lucite ceiling*. These terms, applied outside of hiring policy, tend to be trivialized. A 1991 *Los Angeles Times* report on the American beer market, for example, states that analysts "question whether adding new brands has reached a glass ceiling of success for breweries."

Anna Quindlen emphasized the discriminatory policy in a 1991 column for the *New York Times*. "The glass ceiling," she wrote, "gets more attention, but it's good to remember the cement floor, to remember that there are still places that might as well have signs: Girls Keep Out! It serves to remind you of the bad old days, and of

the fact that there's nothing cute about trying to be treated fairly."

glitch a mechanical or electronic failure that afflicts campaigns and can rattle campaigners.

A monkey wrench that finds its way into a "well-oiled political machine"; the piercing sound of feedback when a speaker reaches a climactic moment in a speech; the loss of baggage on a campaign tour—all these come under the heading of "glitches," a term with electronic-error connotations.

A glitch, the mischief of a computerized gremlin, fills a linguistic need for an annoying and usually inexplicable failure of normal operations which results in a candidate's toe-stubbing or diplomatic gaffe.

On Jimmy Carter's first trip abroad as President in December of 1977, he was unexpectedly troubled by a State Department interpreter's mistranslation of his "desire" to be in Poland as "lust" for Poles, and of his "leaving" the U.S. as "abandoning" the U.S. This was followed in India by the world wide coverage of Mr. Carter's whispered, private suggestion to Secretary of State Cyrus Vance that he send a "cold, very blunt" letter to the Indian Prime Minister upon their return to the U.S.; unknown to the President, a microphone was open nearby during a "photo opportunity," and the Presidential whisper required fast backtracking by the press secretary, Joseph L. Powell.

"That private talk with Vance," wrote Vernon A. Guidry, Jr., of the *Washington Star* on January 2, 1978, "is now likely to become a source of embarrassment to Carter. It became public through another one of the glitches that have plagued the President's foreign tour . . ." A *Star* copy editor, unfamiliar with "glitches," changed the word in the second edition to "snafus."

The word probably originated in the German *glitsche* and Yiddish *glitsh*, meaning "slip." According to the *Polyglot's Lexicon,* it entered the language in 1966, as a false signal, mishap, or malfunction in spacecraft.

It still carries weight in political campaigns. During the Presidential election of 1992, the *Los Angeles Times* wrote: "What if an advance man stumbles? What if the sound system fails, a setting sun makes the candidate squint, the motorcade breaks down or passing air traffic drowns out a speech? . . . One such glitch can stain or spoil a campaign appearance, leaving a poor impression that can be hard to shake."

For a locomotive glitch, see the "idiot engineer" who undid candidate Thomas E. Dewey, under BLOOPER.

glittering generalities. See FOURTH OF JULY SPEECH.

globaloney. See BALONEY.

gloom and doom, prophets of the dismissal by the "Ins" of the viewing-with-alarm of the "Outs."

"My theory has always been," wrote Thomas Jefferson, "that if we are to dream, the flatteries of hope are as cheap, and pleasanter than the gloom of despair." Not so to a group of political pundits, or to almost any candidate running for another man's seat. The man seeking to oust the incumbent must convince voters that all is not rosy, that we are indeed in grave danger of a variety of catastrophes that could only be averted by a change of administration or representation.

Incumbent Democrats described Republicans in the campaign of 1936 as "disciples of despair" floundering in a "fountain of fear"; during the Eisenhower years, Republican Clare Boothe Luce denounced Democrats as "troubadors of trouble and crooners of catastrophe," and Bill Clinton in 1993 derided the "preachers of pessimism." Most common, however, is prophets of, or peddlers of, "gloom and doom."

One of the leading prophets, consistent through changes in Administrations, was columnist Joseph Alsop. After World War II ended, Alsop predicted to Harvard's Signet Club that the cause of Western man was lost; he urged free men to emulate the brave action of the Spartans at Thermopylae, to "comb their golden hair in the sunlight and prepare to die bravely."

The *Miami News* in 1967 wrote about the *Miami Herald:* "A gloom-and-doom piece in a Sunday newspaper here is rather typical of the nitpicking . . ." See NATTERING NABOBS OF NEGATIVISM.

gluttons of privilege. See VESTED INTERESTS.

gnomes of Zurich international bankers.

This phrase, used in foreign economic policy coverage, was popularized by British Foreign Secretary George Brown in 1964. It paints a picture of busy elves in the Swiss financial capital, and was aimed at derogating the speculators who by questioning Great Britain's credit standing forced unpopular austerity measures on the government. Brown felt the "gnomes of Zurich" were out to make a killing at the expense of the pound sterling.

Reporter Paul Hoffman points out: "The term is a misnomer, since George Brown was actually referring to the Bank for International Settlements, which is in Basel."

The word "gnome" was coined by Philippus Aureolus Paracelsus, a sixteenth-century Swiss alchemist and physician, while investigating the mechanics of mining and the diseases of miners; the word is from the Greek *genomos,* earth dweller, and originally meant a misshapen being who guarded the mines and quarries of the inner earth, able to move through earth as a fish moves through water.

The mining derivation of gnome made Brown's phrase especially apt: in Zurich, the gnomes deal in gold, a metal that was the quest of the alchemists.

Unlike MALEFACTORS OF GREAT WEALTH and ECONOMIC ROYALISTS, *gnomes of Zurich* has a manipulative rather than a predatory connotation. By 1968, the phrase had gained the top rank of bogeymen, as in this use in the *Wall Street Journal:* "Frankly, we had enough to worry about with the MILITARY-INDUSTRIAL COMPLEX, the Establishment, the gnomes of Zurich, the illuminati and the POWER ELITE. Now the arbiters of instant demonology have added the jet set."

George J. W. Goodman, using the pseudonym "Adam Smith" in *The Money Game* in 1968, called one character the Gnome of Zurich. His pessimistic credo: since men cannot long manage their affairs rationally, politicians make costly promises, trade surpluses evaporate, gold reserves trickle away, and a "dollar crisis" periodically results.

The term is current. James Pinkerton, a Bush adviser now at the Manhattan Institute, commented in January 1993 on President Clinton's first week: "The gnomes of Zurich and Tokyo are all tuned in, and they react in ways that clearly are catching Clinton by surprise."

go along. See HOLD STILL . . . GO ALONG.

goals. See QUOTAS.

gobbledygook the stilted circumlocution of official directive, sometimes intended to be hard to comprehend but usually the result of a lazy lapse into legalese. Synonyms are OFFICIALESE, "federalese," PENTAGONESE, and BAFFLEGAB.

The coiner of this classic Americanism was Texas Congressman Maury Maverick, whose grandfather Samuel lent his name to the word for "rambunctious loner" (see MAVERICK).

"People ask me where I got gobbledygook," Representative Maverick wrote in the *New York Times Magazine* on May 21, 1944. "I do not know. It must have come in a vision. Perhaps I was thinking of the old bearded turkey gobbler back in Texas, who was always gobbledy gobbling and strutting with ludicrous pomposity. At the end of this gobble there was a sort of gook."

The Congressman defined the term as "talk or writing which is long, pompous, vague, involved, usually with Latinized words. It is also talk or writing which is merely long, even though the words are fairly simple, with repetition over and over again [*sic*], all of which could have been said in a few words."

In his seminal article, Maverick quoted Lewis Carroll's *Alice in Wonderland:* "'Speak English,' said the Eaglet. 'I don't know the meaning of half these long words, and, what's more, I don't believe you do, either.'" And the Congressman found a text from the Bible: ". . . except ye utter by the tongue words easy to be understood, how shall it be known what is spoken? for ye shall speak into the air."

He discovered metaphoric arrogance in one cant phrase: "The Gobbledygookers are forever talking about 'levels' of government, as though the Federal Government, for which they work, is in the High Place." And he called for "a new language development in America which will rescue our present language from the curse of confusion. We must stop dragging in the corpses of dead languages. A man's language is a very important part of his conduct. He should be held morally responsible for his words just as he is accountable for his other acts."

Maverick must have been using the word in late 1943; it appeared in *American Notes and Queries* in April 1943 as "Maury Maverick's name for the long high-sounding words of Washington's red-tape language," and in *Time* on April 10, 1944: "Maury Maverick . . . railed against what he called Washington's 'gobbledygook' language."

Eric Partridge, in his introduction to the 1952 *Chamber of Horrors,* speculated on what might have been going through Maverick's mind: "When a term is so devastatingly apposite as *gobbledegook* [here Partridge uses an alternative spelling], it walks unquestioned into the vocabulary, as *quisling* had done four years earlier in Britain. The allusion is to the gobbling noise made by a turkey cock; probably the word was an unconscious yet none the less inspired adaptation of '*gobble* of *the* turkey *cock*,' *the* becoming *de* in imitation of stage foreigners' pronunciation, and *cock* becoming *gook* by assimilation to the *g* of *gobble,* and *gock* becoming *gook* perhaps under the influence of *goon.*"

In 1975 the *Washington Star* began a series called "Gobbledygook" regularly exposing to ridicule some blatant examples of federal prose. With the word thus regularly featured, President Carter enshrined it in the language in 1978 as part of his first State of the Union address: "We have made a good start on turning the gobbledygook of federal regulations into plain English that people can understand, but we still have a long way to go."

gofer one who will "go for" coffee and run errands in a political headquarters.

Political novices are sometimes star-tled by the caliber of people willing to act as "gofers" in the final stages of a campaign. Officeholders, district leaders and fat cats, anxious to be seen at headquarters by the candidate and his managers, will often willingly assume menial tasks. The word is often spelled "go-fer"; an alternative spelling "gopher" is from association with the rodent.

Just after John Lindsay took office as New York's mayor in 1966, a minor controversy arose when it was charged that policemen were being used as "gofers"—to bring coffee into the Lindsay offices.

The need for gofers, and the sustenance they bring harried workers, was recognized in 1712 by Alexander Pope in *The Rape of the Lock* when the British poet wrote of "coffee, which makes the politicians wise."

In Philadelphia in the first part of the nineteenth century, tradesmen who lobbied were called "coffeehouse politicians." Coffee remains in the political lexicon (see COFFEE-KLATSCH CAMPAIGN).

The word was used in this doggerel by Fred Bruhn in the *Wall Street Journal* in 1974, commenting on a proposal for a permanent special prosecutor for top officials:

> It's not the big black cars with chauffeurs,
> It's not the maids, the aides, the go-fers,
> It's not the top floor corner space
> It's not the horsy country place
> What stamps a man of power and wealth:
> A prosecutor for himself.

In Texas the word used for a "gofer" is "Billy-do-boy." A similar-sounding word, coined on the same analogy as "gofer," is "two-fer," which originally meant two tickets for the price of one, and in politics is used to indicate that an appointee is both black and a woman, thereby pleasing two constituencies.

go fight City Hall   an expression of helplessness in the face of bureaucracy; a shrugging acceptance of the insuperable difficulties of organized society.

The expression, which probably originated in New York City, is not to be taken literally and assumed to be a call to action. On the contrary, it means that you *cannot* fight City Hall. The speaker is really saying, "Don't bother me with your problem, take it up with the powers that be in government—and you won't get anywhere with them, either." The expression implies the same futility as "tilting at windmills," a reference to the foolish gallantry of Don Quixote.

In 1967, when Senator Albert Gore (D-Tenn.) was able to get enough votes to attach a rider calling for repeal of a campaign fund measure favored by Majority Whip Russell Long (D-La.), a Gore aide was quoted as saying happily, "You don't beat City Hall too often."

A *Wall Street Journal* headline illustrates the range of government "City Hall" refers to: "Fighting City Hall: Public Employees Turn Militant, Go On Strike to Back Wage Demands/ New Jersey Teachers Force a Town to Curtail Classes; Firemen Stage a Slowdown."

When the phrase is used to mean the real city hall, it is a joke, as in this 1967 *Newsweek* usage about New York City's crackdown on diplomatic parking abuses: "For the smouldering diplomats, the encounter was a new lesson in international relations. Around the U.N., the word was being passed that you can say what you like about the United States, but you can't fight City Hall."

A frustrated characterization of organized society began with *City Hall*, and progressed to *Establishment, power structure,* and *System*. Ross Perot, in his third-party campaign for President in 1992, chose GRIDLOCK—a traffic term—to describe paralysis caused by legislative and executive disagreements.

go fishing.   See FISHING EXPEDITION.

go-it-alone   to stand by oneself as a person or a nation.

American politicians have been either proud of themselves or critical of others for "going-it-alone" since about 1850, when cardplayers began using the phrase to describe one who wanted to play the game of euchre single-handed. In the card game of four-handed euchre (not three-handed, or "cutthroat" euchre), a player's point total is doubled if he takes in his tricks by rejecting the help of a partner and "goes it alone."

In 1874 Senator G. F. Edmunds of Vermont said, "Our forefathers [did not act] upon the idea that a member of Congress was to take his carpet-bag and go it alone [in Washington]."

Early in 1953, Ohio Republican Senator Robert A. Taft suggested that "the U.S. might as well forget the United Nations as far as the Korean war is concerned. I believe we might as well abandon any idea of working with the United Nations in the East and reserve to ourselves a completely free hand." President Eisenhower didn't like Taft's idea and said so at a news conference on May 28, 1953: "If you are going to go it alone in one place, you have to go it alone everywhere." Taft later denied that he was advocating a policy of "go-it-alone."

Senator Charles Mathias (R-Md.) used the synonym for isolationism in 1978, with an ironic twist: "No matter how ready the rest of us are for a bipartisan foreign policy, we cannot go it alone. The President must provide the leadership."

See CARD METAPHORS; ISOLATIONISM; UNILATERALISM.

good fight.   See FIGHT THE GOOD FIGHT.

good guys.   See MR. NICE GUY; WHITE HATS.

Good Neighbor Policy   Franklin Roosevelt's program for relations with Latin American nations.

FDR set forth the phrase "good neighbor" in his inaugural address drafted by brain truster Raymond Moley in March 1933: "In the field of world policy I would dedicate this nation to the policy of the good neighbor—the neighbor who resolutely respects himself and, because he does so, respects the rights of others." A month later he told the Pan-American Union: "Never before has the significance of the words 'good neighbor' been so manifest in international relations. Never have the need and benefit of neighborly cooperation in every form of human activity been so evident . . ."

The time was ripe for a fresh approach to Latin American relations. Phrases like "colossus of the north," "Yankee imperialists," and DOLLAR DIPLOMACY were in common use in Central and South America to show resentment toward the "big brother" in the north. At a conference in Montevideo, Uruguay, on December 26, 1933, Secretary of State Cordell Hull supported a pact declaring, "No state has the right to intervene in the internal or external affairs of another." FDR added two days later: "The definite policy of the U.S. from now on is one opposed to armed intervention."

There was some sniping from the opposition; the Republican candidate in 1936, Alfred Landon, commented, "We can be a good neighbor without giving away the latch-key to our door." But the Latin American policy turned out to be the least controversial of all Roosevelt's foreign policies, supported by both isolationists and internationalists. The internationalists felt that a united hemisphere was useful in maintaining world peace; isolationists held that cross-hemispheric relations fell within a kind of "regional isolationism."

The policy was bolstered by the Act of Chapultepec in 1945, the Rio Treaty of 1947 (both pacts of mutual military assistance), and the creation of the Organization of American States. The policy was strained in U.S. dealings with dictators like Argentina's Juan Perón and, later, Cuba's Fidel Castro.

President Eisenhower felt it necessary to amend the phrase. "Our Good Partner Policy," he said in 1960, "is a permanent guide encompassing nonintervention, mutual respect and juridical equality of States." The phrase never took hold.

John F. Kennedy, reported Theodore Sorensen, "requested suggestions for a policy label as meaningful for the sixties as Roosevelt's 'Good Neighbor Policy' had been for the thirties. I suggested 'alianza.' . . ." See ALLIANCE FOR PROGRESS.

The neighborhood is being extended. At a Defense Department briefing in April 1993, Bob Hall described joint military training with the Royal Thai Armed Forces, "conducted under Thailand's good neighbor policy with observers from other countries in the region."

good ole boy.   See REDNECK.

good soldier   a politician willing to place the good of the party first; one who swallows personal pride and falls in line.

The phrase is often preceded by a gulp. In 1956, Ohio favorite son Michael Di Salle announced that he was throwing his support to Senator John Kennedy for vice-presidential nominee (he lost to Senator Estes Kefauver). William Coleman, Ohio state chairman, did not like Di Salle's decision but decided to go along. A *Columbus Dispatch* reporter asked him, "Mr. Coleman, is Senator Kennedy really your choice?" The grim-faced state chairman replied, "I am a good soldier."

He was echoing a phrase made famous by Missouri Senator James Reed at the 1932 Democratic convention. Reed, who had bitterly opposed Franklin Roosevelt, sat on the platform with what was described as "an expressionless face" while the final ballot showed 945 votes for Roosevelt, 190½ for Al Smith. The convention chairman asked him to address the convention in a display of unity, and he refused. FDR aide Arthur Mullen went to him and said, "We're all Democrats, Jim." Reed went to the microphone and calmed the disappointed Smith supporters: "At a time like this, every man who claims to be a Democrat should banish from his heart all feeling of disappointment, all sense of chagrin, and like a good soldier, fall in line, salute the colors and face the enemy."

Speaker of the House Sam Rayburn also used the phrase at a convention. In 1960, when John Kennedy urged him to convince his fellow Texan, Lyndon Johnson, to take second spot on the ticket, "Mr. Sam" replied, "Well, there is always the thought in a fellow's mind that he might get to be President. Lyndon is a good soldier, and he will hear the call of duty."

Good soldier is a high accolade among politicians, a decoration for regularity. The ringing phrase must not be confused with *old soldier,* a funky cigar butt, or *dead soldier,* an empty whiskey bottle. See OLD SOLDIERS NEVER DIE; MILITARY METAPHORS.

goo-goo. See DO-GOODER; REFORM.

GOP   Republican; initials for the Grand Old Party.

In the 1870s, "grand old party" and "gallant old party" were in use, mostly referring to Republicans. Meanwhile, in England, Prime Minister William Gladstone was being dubbed "the Grand Old Man," first used in 1882. Soon after, Gladstone was "the G.O.M." Soon after that, GOP made its bow. "'The G.O.P. Doomed,' shouted the *Boston Post,*" wrote the *New York Tribune* on October 15, 1884; nobody has yet found the earlier *Boston Post* use.

In early motorcar days, the letters also stood for "get out and push"; in the sixties, the Republican National Committee launched a modernization program for the old acronym, referring to themselves as "the GO-Party," and in 1972 pointed to "Generation of Peace." Harry Truman said the initials meant "Grand Old Platitudes."

gopher.   See GOFER.

gospel of hate.   See APOSTLE OF HATE.

go to Korea   confront a problem directly and personally; promise a hands-on approach to difficulty.

Dwight Eisenhower introduced this phrase in a statement he made in Detroit during his first Presidential campaign. Although General Omar Bradley had testified to the Senate in 1951 that widening the Korean conflict "would involve us in the wrong war, at the wrong place, at the wrong time and with the wrong enemy," the conflict did escalate, and in October 1952 truce talks were indefinitely postponed. Eisenhower, however, promised action in his stump speech, pledging, "I shall go to Korea."

The political power of the phrase, however, has not been limited to Eisenhower or to Republican Administrations. In 1977, the *Washington Post* described new American policy toward Korea during the Carter Administration and added, "A representative of the State Department, Phil Habib, and the Chairman of the Joint Chiefs of Staff, General Brown, would go to Korea to explain this policy."

Hodding Carter III, who served as Carter's assistant secretary of state for public affairs, used the phrase in a 1992 *Newsday* piece. Recounting foreign policy during Presidential elections, Hodding Carter wrote, "Franklin D. Roosevelt pledged he would never send American boys to die on foreign soil. Dwight Eisenhower promised he would 'go to Korea' if elected."

This phrase was adopted by the Democrats in the 1992 election. Bill Clinton reminded listeners in a July 1992 address at the New Orleans Superdome: "President Eisenhower didn't complain that the Korean problem was a problem he inherited. He said, 'Vote for me. I will go to Korea.'" (Clinton's interpolation of *will* for Eisenhower's *shall* replaced the earlier President's simple intention with a stronger verb of determination, but the sense of hands-on problem solving remains the same.)

go to the well   expect public revenues to finance; look to the public treasury for support.

Unlike GO TO KOREA, this phrase does not promise immediate addressing and correcting of a problem. Instead, *go to the well* often suggests a negative solution to financially draining problems.

As a water-filled symbol of plenty, the well as metaphor dates back to Biblical times. "The mouth of a righteous man," says Proverbs 10:11, "is a well of life."

The political use of the phrase became popular during Ronald Reagan's Administration. In May 1988, the *National Journal* reported on the financing of public services, adding that "privatization supporters say that as government officials go to the well to pay for new constituent services, they are discovering that the well is dry and are beginning to see the wisdom of private-sector initiatives."

As that usage indicates, the phrase is usually negated by a suggestion of the well's diminishing resources. Representative Byron L. Dorgan, Democrat of North Dakota, repeated that image in a 1991 House Ways and Means Committee hearing on middle-class tax cuts; he described the nation's financial crisis as "a very precarious position with fundamental structural problems in the economy," adding, "and we can go to the well with stimulus."

By adding the word *with*, the phrase's meaning changes. Lyndon Johnson was reported to have asked of potential aides, "Is he someone you can go to the well with?" This is a Southwestern phrase, rooted in pioneer days when the danger from Indians required two men to get water from wells far from the house. One person would draw the water, and the other would stand guard; the phrase came to mean "someone who can be trusted."

governance.   See PUNDIT.

government.   See ADMINISTRATION.

government by crony   an Administration in which advisers qualify not by experience or talent but by their long-time friendship with the Chief Executive.

Washington columnist Arthur Krock, in a February 9, 1946, piece titled "Government by Crony," wrote: "During the Truman administration, New Dealers and Conservatives found themselves together in opposition to what a press gallery wit has called a 'government by crony.'"

Krock suggested that many New Dealers held over from the Roosevelt Administration "opposed many of Truman's intimate White House circle because, they say, they are of courthouse caliber."

The columnist added: "Government by crony is not new in Washington. President Roosevelt appointed many persons of doubtful competence or eligibility because of personal relationships."

Soon after Krock's use of the phrase, Secretary of the Interior Harold Ickes (see CURMUDGEON) resigned with a blast at Truman: "I am against government by crony."

The author suspected that the anonymous "press gallery wit" quoted by Krock might be similar to "Western observer"—the reporter himself. Mr. Krock replied to a query from his neighbor at the Washington Bureau of the *Times:* "As I recall, I was referring modestly to myself in that reference to 'a press gallery wit,' though I couldn't document that I am the originator. But I, too, have seen no previous use of the expression in the public prints."

"Government by" phrases used in the pejorative sense include: "Government by organized money" (FDR in referring to the Republican Administration before 1932); "Government by epilepsy" (Brazilian President Janio Quadros describing Fidel Castro's Cuba in 1961); "Government by injunction" (John L. Lewis after the U.S. government found him guilty of abrogating the United Mine Workers contract with the government in 1946); "Government by golly" (anti-Eisenhower); "Government by Irish Mafia" (anti-Kennedy); "Government by Texans" (anti-Johnson).

Most of the "government by" phrases of the last century were probably coined to compare unfavorably with the phrase Lincoln popularized, "government of the people, by the people, for the people." For the derivation of that phrase, see IDEAS.

government-in-exile   a description of the Kennedy family, and their close associates, during the Administration of President Lyndon Johnson.

"On Capitol Hill," wrote William Manchester in 1967, "the two brothers [Robert and Ted Kennedy] inevitably came to be regarded as the nucleus of a government-in-exile."

Although President Johnson asked most of the Kennedy men (see IRISH MAFIA) to stay on after the assassination of John F. Kennedy ("I need you more than he ever did"), most left the White House to write books and form a coterie around other Kennedys. Ted Sorensen, Arthur Schlesinger, Jr., Richard Goodwin, Kenneth O'Donnell, Stephen Smith, and others of the "Clan" formed a circle around Robert, Ted, and Jacqueline Kennedy; Postmaster General Lawrence O'Brien, Poverty War head Sargent Shriver, and Defense Secretary Robert McNamara refrained from going into "exile."

The use of the phrase indicated an estrangement that grew within the Democratic party, which author Manchester was accused of exaggerating in *The Death of a President.*

In its traditional use, a "government-in-exile" has either been forced out by revolution or usurpation, or invaded and taken over by another nation, with the "legitimate" government taking refuge elsewhere. The use of the phrase in the Johnson-Kennedy context served to further polarize the situation.

A typical reflection of the tension between the two groups which led to a nomination fight in 1968, is the description of White House adviser John Roche (see INTELLECTUAL-IN-RESIDENCE) in a 1967 *New York Times* article: "He plainly enjoyed the recent row about the 'government in exile' at Harvard and candidly confesses that he has never had anything in common with 'that crowd of cold Kennedy cats operating exclusively on the star system.'"

After its nonce use in the Johnson Administration, the phrase was applied to the usually liberal Brookings Institution during the Nixon-Ford and Reagan-Bush years, and then to the conservative American Enterprise Institute and Heritage Foundation in the Carter and Clinton years.

government of laws, not of men

a maxim that suggests there is little human weakness in the administration of justice; or, that all stand equal before the bar.

The idea can be found in Baron Montesquieu's *Spirit of Laws,* a work written in 1748 that influenced many of the framers of the U.S. Constitution: "The rulers of republics establish institutions, and afterwards the institutions mould the rulers."

John Adams, in his preamble to the Massachusetts Constitution in 1778, used the phrase as his ultimate political goal: "In the government of the Commonwealth of Massachusetts the legislative, executive and judicial power shall be placed in separate departments, to the end that it might be a government of laws, not of men."

Chief Justice John Marshall picked up the Adams phrase in his decision in the landmark *Marbury* vs. *Madison:* "The government of the United States has been emphatically termed a government of laws, and not of men."

In England the phrase for the same idea is alliterative: MEASURES, NOT MEN. In the U.S. the phrase is often replaced by the august RULE OF LAW. During the year preceding Richard Nixon's resignation in 1974, the phrase was used both as an admonishment to the Nixon men (for putting themselves above the law) and as a spur to the forces favoring impeachment (holding the law above the elected officials). Its most dramatic use came on the night of October 20, 1973, when Special Prosecutor Archibald Cox—just fired by the President in what came to be known as the SATURDAY NIGHT MASSACRE—issued a statement from his home: "Whether ours shall continue to be a government of laws and not of men is now for Congress and ultimately for the American people."

gradualism. See TOKENISM; SALAMI TACTICS.

graffiti slogans and messages scrawled on walls.

"Cuba Sí—Yanqui No" and "Ami Go Home," in paint or chalk on walls in the U.S. and abroad, first brought this ancient art to the attention of U.S. politicians. The word originally applied to all scrawled messages, from "Kilroy Was Here" to the names of a boy and a girl with an arrow and heart, to outright smut, but its meaning has narrowed to messages with some social or political content.

A 1967 advertisement for "Books USA," a government-endorsed project to mail books abroad, showed a picture of a U.S. soldier standing next to graffiti that read "Go Home Yankee Dog," with this copy: "Read any good walls lately? Probably not. Few flattering things have ever been written on walls about anyone. And the unflattering truth is that there are walls like this in many countries, covered with words written in anger, mistrust and ignorance . . ."

A collection of *Graffiti: Selected Scrawls from Bathroom Walls* was made in 1967 by Robert Reisner, and included political graffiti like "Yankee Go Home (via Pan Am)," "Peace is a cool scene," "Bomb Saigon," "Half the Way with LBJ," "Dulles Lives," "Unleash Chiang Kai-shek." Often, graffiti are in the form of a dialogue, with answers or comments scrawled below, as: "What happened to all the high class graffiti?" "It got read." "Better read than dead."

The word is the plural of *graffito*, which refers to a method of ornamenting architectural plaster surfaces by scratching the top coat to reveal colored layers underneath, used in ancient cultures and refined in fifteenth-century Italian decorative art.

The spreading of slogans by graffiti is not unlike the dissemination of news via wall posters in China. "Posters written in big characters," said Mao Tse-tung, "are an extremely useful new type of weapon." See SNIPE. During the upheavals of the CULTURAL REVOLUTION, *dazibao*, or big-character posters, served as the best way of getting news to the people and is still an approved form of communication in the People's Republic of China.

A combination of wall-poster news and commenting graffiti is to be expected. Reported KREMLINOLOGIST Harry Schwartz in 1967: "A traveler who recently returned from Hong Kong reports that among the graffiti he saw there was the assertion: 'Mao Tse-tung is a Hippie.' The suspicion must be strong that the author was a frustrated China watcher expressing his conviction that only a user of LSD or marijuana could have been responsible for this past year's convulsions in China."

Graffiti were supplemented in the eighties and nineties by the use of messages on T-shirts, some outrageously sexist, like "Wanted: woman who can cook, keep house, and has boat. Send picture of boat."

graft money or property gained through political corruption.

A grafter is the one who receives the money, or seeks the payment. Standard English construction would ordinarily make him the *graftee*, and the one who makes the payment the *grafter;* this is not current usage, because the corrupter is considered less sinful than the official who "betrays a public trust."

The word is traceable as thieves' argot back to a *Police Gazette* of 1865: "'Twas handy that we were so related, as, when about a 'graft,' or 'doing stur,' both sisters could keep each other company." Josiah Flynt in his *Tramping with Tramps* (1899) and *World of Graft* (1901) defined the word as "a generic slang term for all kinds of theft and illegal practices generally."

St. Louis circuit attorney Joseph W. Folk gave the word its political flavor soon after the turn of the century, and his war on what he called "grafters" took him to the governorship of Missouri in 1905. As politics took over the word, thieves' argot shifted to "grift."

Richard Leche, Louisiana governor who succeeded Huey Long, turned out to have an income in 1938 of $282,000 on a salary of $7,500. Shortly before he went to jail, Leche earned his place in political history with the comment: "When I took the oath as Governor, I didn't take any vows of poverty." However, outright bribery of major officials is now becoming rare.

Graft is specific, *corruption* general; graft is the currency of corruption. In 1914 Walter Lippmann overlooked the differentiation in explaining the emerging meaning of both words:

> We can see, I think, what people meant by the word graft. They did not mean robbery. It is rather confused rhetoric to call a grafter a thief. His crime is not that he filches money from the safe but that he betrays a trust. The grafter is a man whose loyalty is divided and whose motives are mixed. A lawyer who takes a fee from both sides in some case; a public official who serves a pri-

vate interest; a railroad director who is also a director in the supply company; a policeman in league with outlawed vice; these are the relationships which the American people denounce as "corrupt." The attempt to serve at the same time two antagonistic interests is what constitutes "corruption."

See HONEST GRAFT; BOODLE; WHIPSAW; REACHED; GREASE.

grand design a diplomatic master plan; a broad strategy to shape historical forces.

This phrase comes from the French, *Les Grands Desseins,* and "grand" is translated as "great" or "grand." The phrase, from the time of the French King Henry IV, was reintroduced by Franklin D. Roosevelt at the Teheran Conference in Iran, December 1943, where Stalin, Churchill, and Roosevelt planned an envasion of France and received a commitment from Stalin that Russia would enter the war against Japan. Roosevelt used "Great Design" and Churchill, in his war memoirs, "Grand Alliance" (after the English-Dutch-Hapsburg "Grand Alliance" of 1701).

At the 1944 Republican convention, former President Herbert Hoover traced the derivation: "During the past month Forrest Davis has published a circumstantial account of the Teheran Conference. It is said to have been authorized. It has not been denied. It relates to President Roosevelt's new peace method, called by him, the Great Design. A peace method under this same name, the Great Design, was proposed by Henry the Fourth, a French monarch, some 350 years ago. It has some similarities to Mr. Roosevelt's idea. . . . The American people deserve a much fuller exposition of this Great Design." This point was indicative of a Republican charge of "secret agreements" made after later Big Three conferences, especially Yalta.

FDR might have taken the phrase from its use by Theodore Roosevelt, who received a letter from some prominent Frenchman congratulating him on his efforts in international conciliation. TR later wrote: "They believe that the action of President Roosevelt, which has realized the most generous hopes to be found in history should be classed as a continuance of similar illustrious attempts of former times, notably the project for international concord known under the name of 'The Great Design of Henry IV' in the memoirs of his Prime Minister, the Duke de Sully."

Sully's memoirs refer to vague *Grands Desseins* based on the King's wish to avoid another European war. Until recently, a grand design kept that method-for-peace connotation; of late, it has taken on more of a means-of-defense meaning, not exactly the same.

For another contribution to American political terminology by Henry IV, see CHICKEN IN EVERY POT.

grandpa's pants won't fit Benny. See DYNASTY.

grants-in-aid. See TAX SHARING.

grapevine rumor factory; word-of-mouth communication of political secrets or background; inside gossip.

The grapevine is falling into disuse because reporters learn and print most rumors before politicians have a chance to pass them along. "I hear by the grapevine" between politicos has been almost altogether replaced by Mr. DOOLEY's "I see by the papers." The phrase persists mainly in the hints of jobs available and personnel shifts.

Hans Sperber thought the word may have had its origin in an episode told by Charles Howard Shinn, in a mining book about the Great Comstock lode in Nevada:

That curious and vivid Western phrase, "grapevine telegraph," originated in 1859. Colonel Bee constructed a telegraph line between Placerville and Virginia City, attaching the wire to the trees; their swaying stretched it until it lay in loops on the ground, resembling the trailing California wild grapevines. Frequent breaks occurred from falling trees and avalanches, till the line became almost useless, being sometimes beaten into Sacramento by the Pony Express. California and Nevada papers took it up, and whenever a journalist wished to cast doubts on the freshness of his opponent's news he forthwith accused him of running a grapevine telegraph.

The phrase was used before 1859, however, in connection with the Underground Railroad, the abolitionists' method of aiding escaped slaves. The grapevine was their communications system, and was often used interchangeably with "the clothesline telegraph." Grapevines, it may be assumed, were used as a substitute for rope and the two phrases came into being together. Union captain John Truesdale, in an 1867 collection of Civil War anecdotes called *The Blue Coats,* showed how the clothesline could be used as an intelligence device: clotheslines were used as visual transmitters of espionage, with shirts of different colors hung out to dry used as a code to reveal the order of battle of the Confederate troops.

grassroots the ultimate source of power, usually patronized, occasionally feared; the rank and file of a party, or voters not normally politically active.

The term began with a rural flavor, implying simple virtues of the land as against city-slicker qualities. Recently the anti-big-city connotation has been disappearing, leaving only an anti-boss, up-from-the-people meaning. Accordingly, politicians seek support "from the grassroots and the sidewalks of the nation" to cover everybody.

The word has its own roots in mining terminology, used in 1876 to mean the soil just beneath the surface. An early metaphoric use was by Rudyard Kipling, in *Kim,* published in 1901: "Not till I came to Shamlegh could I meditate upon the Course of Things, or trace the running grassroots of Evil." (Why "running"? Philip Howard of the *Times* of London wrote in 1977 that Kipling was probably referring to "*Agropyron repens,* the common couch or twitch grass, whose long creeping root-stalks or rhizomes run below the surface and make it a pestilential and ineradicable garden weed.")

An early political use was in 1912, when Senator Albert J. Beveridge told the Bull Moose convention in Chicago: "This party comes from the grass roots. It has grown from the soil of the people's hard necessities." The Farmer-Labor party used it as a slogan in 1920.

The term came into prominence with a Republican effort to organize a massive thrust to unseat FDR. In Springfield, Ill., on June 10, 1935, the Grass Roots Conference was held. "Issues are hard to find," reported *Common Sense,* "and the 'Grass Roots' Conference in Springfield, Illinois, found itself stumped." Three decades later, Republican Chairman Ray Bliss called a similar conference to mobilize grassroots (by now one word) support in the big cities, and claimed better results.

The word has become an adjective, meaning "of or among ordinary citizens," as in *grassroots lobbying* or as used in this excerpt from the August 6, 1990, issue of *U.S. News & World Report:* "A spontaneous grassroots movement has sprung up . . . aimed at squashing the despised property tax." Most candidates now claim to run *grassroots campaigns,* where they get out to meet the people, just the opposite of a FRONT-PORCH CAMPAIGN. However, the best way to reach the grassroots is from a television studio, posing a semantic problem. Senator George McGovern used the word as the title of his memoirs in 1977.

Reporting on Attorney General Robert Kennedy's trip to the Far East in 1962, *Newsweek* came up with a good play on the phrase: "He sought to make U.S. policies understandable at the rice-roots level."

grass will grow in the streets a threat of financial ruin if the opposition is elected, and specifically if a protective tariff is removed.

The phrase was made famous in this century by Herbert Hoover in the campaign of 1932 as he was defending the Smoot-Hawley tariff against a suggested Democratic tariff proposal: "The grass will grow in the streets of a hundred cities, a thousand towns; the weeds will overrun the fields of millions of farms if that protection is taken away." This was fairly colorful language for Hoover, but it came with the election only a week away and did little good. Roosevelt used it in 1936, however, reminding responsive audiences: "I look for the grass which was to grow on city streets."

The grass-in-the-streets prophecy was a part of the most famous of all convention speeches: William Jennings Bryan's 1896 "Cross of Gold" address, which had a strong agrarian flavor. "Burn down your cities and leave our farms, and your cities will spring up again as if by magic," he orated, "but destroy our farms and the grass will grow in the streets of every city in the country."

Bryan, and later Hoover, only rephrased a metaphor used frequently before, especially in regard to tariffs. The October 13, 1892, issue of *The Nation* warns that an argument for a protective tariff "is the old 'howling wilderness' and 'grass-in-the-streets' argument for protection."

The earliest use found so far was in a speech by Jefferson Davis, shortly after his inauguration as President of the Confederate States of America. He predicted a short, victorious war, because soon "Grass will grow in the Northern cities."

The phrase is now obsolescent, partially because so many park-hungry urbanites would welcome grass wherever it grew within a city's limits.

See GLOOM AND DOOM, PROPHETS OF.

gratitude, political favors done now in anticipation of return favors to come.

Unlike normal gratitude, political gratitude looks forward and not backward. The phrase is used usually when a politician turns down a request from someone who helped him in the past. The rejected former helper, understandably cynical, murmurs "That's political gratitude," meaning the politician will be "grateful"—receptive—only to those who can help him in the future.

President Kennedy is reported to have said that "politicians do not have friends, they have allies." This was an adaptation of "the British Empire has no friends, only interests."

Newsweek columnist Raymond Moley wrote: "Sam Rayburn once told me that whenever he secured a job for a political applicant, he 'made nine enemies and one ingrate.'"

Rayburn was passing along a comment of Louis XIV, in Molière's *Siècle de Louis Quatorze:* "Every time I fill a vacant office I make ten malcontents and one ingrate." Thomas Jefferson in 1807 increased the enemies as he quoted obliquely: "Every office becoming vacant, every appointment made, *me donne un ingrat, et cent ennemis.*"

Essayist William Hazlitt ascribed to English man of letters Horace Walpole the following maxim, similar to one of La Rochefoucauld's: "The gratitude of place expectants is a lively sense of future favors."

graveyard top secret; an unbreakable confidence; or, a DEAD END.

Political secrets are often transmitted with the prefatory admonition: "This is graveyard." It appears to have gained currency in the 1950s and is common political usage today, although it rarely, if ever, is seen in print. Presumably the metaphor connotes a place of darkness, whispers, and trepidation, the proper atmosphere for a political confidence.

A second meaning of the word is "final political resting place," or "dead end." A reporter in 1967 asked New York Mayor John Lindsay, "Isn't the mayor's office a political graveyard?" Lindsay replied with a reference to two New York mayors who departed office under a cloud, James Walker and William O'Dwyer: "Some mayors have gone on to international fame. One went to Europe, one went to Mexico . . ."

gravitas. See HEFT, POLITICAL.

gray eminence from the French, *l'éminence grise;* a shadowy figure who exercises power through another; in current use, a manipulative adviser.

Armand Jean du Plessis, Duc de Richelieu, French statesman and cardinal, wore a red habit (unique at the time) that made him known as *L'Éminence Rouge,* "The Red Cardinal." As Prime Minister, he controlled Louis XIII, directing both foreign and domestic policy, successfully shifting the balance of power from the Hapsburgs to the Bourbons.

Cardinal Richelieu's private secretary, Père Joseph de Trembley, attired in a gray habit, became known as *L'Éminence Grise*—"the Gray Cardinal," who, while not a Cardinal at all, often exercised the power of a prince of the Church because of his influence on Richelieu.

The title's ghostly connotation made it eminently suitable for political use; a gray eminence is now used to describe any POWER BEHIND THE THRONE or KINGMAKER who has the ear of a political leader but does not often appear publicly.

The description was often applied to Louis Howe, a brilliant, gnomelike, lifelong adviser and confidant of Franklin Roosevelt. "Roosevelt's election," wrote Jonathan Daniels, "was, of course, Howe's final, unique triumph. He was to be remembered as the long-time friend, the Warwick, the alter ego, *l'éminence grise.*"

Other figures have also received this description. The late newsman Eric Sevareid was called "an in-house wise man and gray eminence of CBS News" in the *Washington Post* in 1992, and the *National Journal* referred to Brent Scowcroft in 1989 as "Washington's preeminent 'gray eminence' on national security."

Japanese Liberal party leader Tsuji Karouki, a behind-the-scene power, was described as a *kuromaku,* or "black curtain." See RUSTLING BEHIND THE JALOUSIES.

grease as a verb, to smooth the way by bribery; as a noun, the money used in such corruption.

"Cash . . . is a necessary article in their business," wrote the *Columbian Centinel* in 1797, "and without daily application of this specific grease their wheels must roll heavily on."

Grease can be used in a meaning limited to money ("We must have grease to run a campaign," Democratic leader John Thompson told the Ohio Central Committee in 1881) but the overtone that the money is corruptly obtained is more often present.

After a period in which the word was considered an archaism, it appears to be making a comeback: "U.S. Attorney Thomas P. Sullivan said yesterday," went a UPI report from Chicago in 1977, "a federal investigation is under way on charges that Mayor Michael A. Bilandic 'greased' an 11.7 percent city taxi fare increase last summer."

For the derivation of the monetary meaning of "fat," see FAT CAT: another, earlier use of "grease" is "to grease the fat pig," or to give to those who need it least, a proverb found in John Heywood's 1566 collection of sayings.

great, political use of   great, in the sense of GREAT SOCIETY, means *fine and magnanimous;* in the sense of GREAT UNWASHED, it means *a large body;* in the sense of GREAT DEBATES, it means *important;* as an adjective modifying "statesman" or "leader," it means *eminent.*

Historians who compare the greatness of Presidents use a wide variety of criteria, especially the ability to meet crises, make progress, and verbally exalt and inspire the nation. In this connection, they have created the comparative word "near-great."

In its political use, the word cannot be used as a synonym for "big": Big Government is not at all Great Government, and Great Business and Great Labor are never used, indicating that the political meaning of "Great" does not usually include the idea of size.

As an adjective in introductions, the word is intended to mean "noble" or "outstanding," but the meaning has been prostituted by its frequent application to nonentities and hacks.

Bitterness at its overuse in convention oratory was illustrated in this passage by novelist John Dos Passos

about jobless men sleeping on the streets in 1932. "Try to tell one of them that the *gre-eat* Franklin D. Roosevelt, Governor of the *gre-eat* state of New York, has been nominated by the *gre-eat* Democratic party. . . . Hoover or Roosevelt, it'll be the same cops."

In diplomacy, *greater,* capitalized in front of the name of a country, is a way of warning of plans for expansion beyond territorial lines. Secretary of State James Baker's reference in 1989 to a "Greater Israel" troubled many supporters of the Jewish state; in 1993, the *Washington Post* warned of threats to Bosnia posed not only by "aggressive Serbs seeking a Greater Serbia but also by treacherous Croats seeking a Greater Croatia."

great debates   in recent times, the series of televised debates between Kennedy and Nixon, Carter and Reagan, and Bush and Clinton; earlier, the debates between Calhoun, Clay, and Webster.

Because "great" rhymes with "debate," there is a tendency to label important national discussions as "great debates." The first known widely by this title was the Senate debate of Henry Clay's package of compromises regarding slavery, including admission of California as a free state, and no restrictions on slavery in the territory acquired from Mexico.

In the debate that lasted through February and March 1850, Clay occupied the middle position, Daniel Webster spoke for the Union without slavery, John C. Calhoun (enfeebled by illness, his final speech read by another) advocated the halting of agitation on the slavery issue and opposed the compromise. During this debate Webster said, "I wish to speak today not as a Massachusetts man, not as a Northern man, but as an American. . . . I speak today for the preservation of the Union. 'Hear me for my cause.'"

Oddly, the debates between Lincoln and Douglas were not known as "great debates," simply as the Lincoln-Douglas debates. In recent times, a "great debate" was held at the United Nations in 1946 over the adoption of the Baruch plan for atomic control.

Senator Blair Moody, a Michigan newsman serving out the unexpired term of Senator Arthur Vandenberg in 1952, had the idea of a national confrontation of major presidential candidates. This failed to interest either Eisenhower or Stevenson in 1952; Stevenson was said to feel that a challenge to Eisenhower would be regarded as a gimmick. And Section 315 of the Federal Communications Act requiring EQUAL TIME for all candidates stood in the way. In August 1960, however, Congress temporarily suspended Section 315, and on the night of Richard Nixon's nomination, NBC board chairman Robert Sarnoff offered Democrats and Republicans eight hours of prime time for what he called "The Great Debate." Kennedy, lesser known, promptly accepted; four days later, Nixon did the same.

Nixon's gaunt appearance surprised many viewers on the first debate of four; "Was Nixon Sabotaged by TV Make-Up Artist?" asked the *Chicago Daily News*. When asked "Who won?" after the first debate, viewers tended to go along with the candidate they had previously supported, and radio listeners gave Nixon the edge. But the first debate gave the Kennedy campaign a powerful boost, and in retrospect, many viewers later said they thought Kennedy "won" the first debate.

"As they approached this brave new frontier of television," wrote Douglass Cater years later, "the two candidates were far more concerned about their images than their arguments. Both proved remarkably adaptable to the new art form. They were marvels at extemporization, wasting none of their precious time by reflective pauses . . . the flowering of television in politics had coincided with the flowering of politicians particularly adapted to its special demands."

Pollster Samuel Lubell found "the overwhelming majority responded in terms of how the candidates looked and handled themselves rather than in terms of the issues that were argued about."

According to Theodore White, what the debates did best "was to give the voters of a great democracy a living portrait of two men under stress and let the voters decide, by instinct and emotion, which style and pattern of behavior under stress they preferred in their leader." White added: "The salient fact of the great TV debates is not what the two candidates said, nor how they behaved, but how many of the candidates' fellow Americans gave up their evening hours to ponder the choice between the two."

The televised debates between Gerald Ford and Jimmy Carter in 1976 were not billed as "great," but a lengthy pause due to a GLITCH was labeled "the Great Silence." The most memorable lines in the Reagan-Carter debates of 1980 were "ARE YOU ANY BETTER OFF than you were four years ago?" and "THERE YOU GO AGAIN," both spoken by Mr. Reagan. In 1988, the most memorable line occurred in the vice-presidential debate, when Democratic candidate Lloyd Bentsen told Dan Quayle, "Senator, you're no Jack Kennedy." (See YOU'RE NO JFK.) In 1992, the most telling moment came when George Bush was capured by the camera looking at his watch, as if he had something better to do.

Great Leap Forward   a Chinese Communist plan for dramatic economic advance, notable for its failure; now, any dramatic diplomatic move in the Far East.

Mao Tse-tung's "Great Leap Forward" began to be mentioned in the Chinese media in 1957, not as part of any five-year plan, but as a special effort to dramatically advance the Chinese economy. It was officially adopted at the second session of the eighth Party Congress between May and July of 1958, and is generally considered to have ended in mid-1960.

Westerners regarded the "leap" as a colossal failure, and the expression was used in derision throughout the sixties. However, when President Nixon announced his acceptance of the invitation of the People's Republic of China to visit Peking, U.S. media turned to the phrase and set aside its previously pejorative connotation.

Max Frankel in the *New York Times:* "President Nixon's success in arranging a trip to China evoked the widespread judgment here today that American policy, in Mao Tse-tung's phrase, was taking a great leap forward."

Columnist Mary McGrory: "Some are saying the trip to China is merely a step in the right direction. For Richard Nixon it could be the 'great leap forward' that could not only bring a long-deferred encounter with reality, but also carry him back to the White House."

Newsweek: "After years of fighting each other, castigating each other, fearing each other—and just plain wondering about each other—the most powerful nation in the world and the most populous nation in the world had decided to recognize each other's existence. And that alone represented a great leap forward."

In a related terminological development, President Nixon began substituting "mainland China" for "Red China" or "Communist China" in pri-

vate meetings in 1970. In a toast to Rumanian President Ceausescu in the White House State Dining Room on October 26, 1970, the President used "People's Republic of China" for the first time publicly, in a way that hindsight makes clear he was hinting at his own future plans: "It happens that in the world today because of the divisions, there are times when the leader of one nation does not have adequate communication with the leader of another. But as I was saying to the President earlier today, he is in a rather unique position. He heads a government which is one of the few in the world which has good relations with the United States, good relations with the Soviet Union, and good relations with the People's Republic of China."

In his report to the Congress on foreign policy of February 25, 1971, the President used the official name again, and this time it was noticed: "Each of the major powers of the Pacific region—Japan, the USSR, the People's Republic of China, and the United States—is faced with difficult decisions in adjusting its policies to the new realities of East Asia." In a spoken summary of this long document, he chose to use the official term again, which was taken as a gesture of respect by those who had been previously known in the U.S. as the Red Chinese.

great seal of U.S. See UNITED WE STAND; BALD EAGLE.

Great Society slogan of the administration of President Lyndon B. Johnson.

President Johnson's first approach to the theme was made three months after he took office. When asked on a television program if he had a slogan as yet, he replied, "I haven't thought of any slogan, but I suppose all of us want a better deal, don't we?"

He tried "Better Deal" a few times in

subsequent speeches, but it didn't catch on. The SQUARE DEAL-NEW DEAL-FAIR DEAL lemon had been squeezed dry.

Meanwhile Richard Goodwin, a Kennedy speechwriting holdover, suggested "Great Society." He prepared a draft of a speech presenting the first Eleanor Roosevelt Memorial Award to Judge Anna M. Cross on March 4, 1964. Jack Valenti, then the President's chief speechwriter, preferred another draft without the phrase, but held the thought for later trial.

When the "better deal" fizzled, the "Great Society" began popping up in Johnson speeches; the President was obviously anxious to drop the label "Kennedy-Johnson programs." At a White House ceremony on March 17, 1964, he tried: "We want to have the glorious kind of society." He asked a group of editors on April 21, to "accept with me the responsibility of developing a greater society." He told a Democratic fund-raising dinner on April 23: "We have been called upon— are you listening?—to build a great society of the highest order, a society not just for today or tomorrow, but for three or four generations to come."

Johnson liked the feel of the phrase and he used it at least sixteen times publicly thereafter. Goodwin, who was writing the May 22 speech at graduation exercises of the University of Michigan, then developed it in detail. The advance tests of the speech capitalized the phrase—"Great Society"— a clear signal to the press that the President had found his slogan.

. . . in your time, we have the opportunity to move not only toward the rich society and the powerful society, but upward to the Great Society.

The Great Society rests on abundance and liberty for all. It demands an end to poverty and racial injustice. . . . The Great Society is a place where every child can find knowledge to enrich his mind and to enlarge his talents. It is a place where leisure is a welcome chance to build and reflect, not a feared cause of boredom and restlessness. It is a place where the city of man serves not only the needs of the body and the demands of commerce but the desire for beauty and the hunger for community. . . .

But most of all, the Great Society is not a safe harbor, a resting place, a final objective, a finished world. It is a challenge constantly renewed, beckoning us toward a destiny where the meaning of our lives matches the marvelous products of our labor.

Republican researchers promptly pounced on a previous use of the phrase by English Fabian socialist Graham Wallas, in a book titled *The Great Society,* published in 1914. Wallas told one of his Harvard students, Walter Lippmann, that the book was "an analysis of the general social organization of a large modern state . . ." Lippmann later amended the title for a more influential book of his own, *The Good Society.* Goodwin had never heard of Wallas's work.

Wallas, in turn, probably never read another use of the phrase in *Blackstone's Commentaries* of the 1760s, "Of the Nature of Laws in General":

Man was formed for society; and, as is demonstrated by the writers on the subject, is neither capable of living alone, nor indeed has the courage to do it. However, as it is impossible for the whole race of mankind to be united in one great society, they must necessarily divide into many, and form separate states, commonwealths, and nations, entirely independent of each other, and yet liable to a mutual intercourse.

In 1931 English socialist Harold Laski, in his *Introduction to Politics,* titled a chapter "The Place of the State in the Great Society."

Sir William Blackstone and Harold Laski used "great" as meaning "whole," or "total"; Wallas and later

Johnson meant it as "noble" or "grand."

Adaptation is the sincerest form of recognition; Ronald Reagan used the phrase "creative society" in his campaign for California governor in 1966, Nelson Rockefeller used "a just society" after his reelection as governor of New York that year, and Senator J. William Fulbright said in 1967 that our preoccupation with Southeast Asia was making the U.S. a "sick society." Since then, the most successful use has been the title of a comic strip, "The Small Society."

The term is still used, although not always in appreciation of its legacy. In December 1992, conservative economist Thomas Sowell wrote in *Forbes* magazine about the impending start of Clinton's Presidency: "Long after those first hundred days are history . . . the taxpayers and the economy will still be carrying the burden, as they are today still carrying the burden of Great Society and New Deal programs."

great unwashed condescending view of the lower classes; now used ironically and not publicly by politicians.

Current use is typified in this passage from black novelist James Baldwin's *The Fire Next Time* (1963): ". . . as long as we in the West place on color the value that we do, we make it impossible for the great unwashed to consolidate themselves according to any other principle."

The phrase is now used to show how the WHITE POWER STRUCTURE is supposed to treat those beneath them with disdain, although it is rarely used by any member of any elite group, unless in an ironic sense.

The phrase was used in 1864 to describe the English lower classes of an earlier time by English novelist James Payn: "There were no such things as 'skilled workmen' or 'respectable arti-

sans,' in those days. The 'people' were 'the Great Unwashed.'"

The phrase is said to have been used before that by Edmund Burke. In the U.S., political observer George Julian wrote in 1884 about the Polk-Clay race that the Whigs "insisted that . . . the larger element of ignorance and 'unwashed' humanity, including our foreign-born population, gave victory to Mr. Polk."

Throughout the nineteenth century the phrase was used to mean Democratic voters, and was often a self-description of some pride. A *Cleveland Leader* headline in 1884 read: "Thomas A. Hendricks Addresses The Great Unwashed at Cincinnati." William Allen White used the word in its Democratic sense as late as 1946: "When election time came around, this black abolition Republican, who was my mother, and this Stephen Douglas Copperhead Democrat, who was my father, still unwashed, still voting for Jackson, had their purple moments."

In current use, the phrase has dropped its specific party affiliation. Broadcasting executives and admen often refer to their audiences as "the great unwashed," in an effort to explain why they aim at a low common denominator.

The term is also used in self-reference. Susan Trausch of the *Boston Globe* opined in February 1993 that "the lobbyists in nice suits may be lining up outside Congressional offices, but the people— that great, unwashed, unregistered bulk of us who represent our grandchildren —are lining up behind an idea."

See VAST WASTELAND; SILENT MAJORITY; MIDDLE AMERICA.

Great White Father a term ridiculing the paternalism of the President of the United States.

Just after the 1936 Democratic convention, publicist Herbert Bayard Swope wrote to his friend Felix Frankfurter: "Probably you and I are the only ones left who have no hope of reward, or fear of punishment, from the Great White Father." (Frankfurter was rewarded with a Supreme Court Justiceship three years later; Swope—see COLD WAR—never found a government role.)

The phrase is used either in a spirit of mild affection, which was Swope's usage, or in a blast at all-powerful, centralized government. "It is devouring the substance of self-supporting people," wrote *Reader's Digest* in 1949, "to render them self-supporting no longer and to establish a condition of universal reliance upon the biased paternalism of a Great White Father."

In the early days of the Republic, the Great White Father was the name given the president by the Indians subjugated by the new nation, and the treatment was paternal indeed. President Thomas Jefferson, in 1808, nearing his retirement told a group of Indian chiefs gathered to bid him farewell:

> Sensible that I am become too old to watch over the extensive concerns of the seventeen states and their territories, I requested my fellow citizens to permit me to live with my family, and to choose another President for themselves, and father for you. . . . Be assured, my children, that he will have the same friendly dispositions towards you which I have had, and that you will find in him a true and affectionate father. . . . Tell your people . . . that during my administration I have held their hand in mine; and that I will put it into the hand of their new father, who will hold it as I have done.

In political campaigns, donning an Indian headdress for photographers has become as encrusted a tradition as kissing babies. In his memoirs, General Eisenhower told this story about some unfortunate Indian campaigning by his rival for the 1952 nomination, Senator Taft: "The day before the Minnesota primary a Navajo medicine man conferred an Indian blessing on Senator Taft. Unhappily, however, he left his turkey-feather wand at home and at the site of the ceremony had to improvise one of chicken feathers. When reporters asked the medicine man afterward how he estimated Taft's chances, he replied glumly, 'Wand had chicken feathers instead of turkey feathers. Now Taft is finished.'"

An often-told political joke is that of the politician addressing a large crowd of Indians, who shouted "Oompa!" in response to his promises. Pleased with the enthusiastic reception, the politician began to move off the platform, only to be warned by an aged chief, who indicated a pile of manure, "Don't step in the oompa."

The phrase is probably associated with "Big Daddy" (the name of a character in Tennessee Williams's *Cat on a Hot Tin Roof*), which was used by critics of Lyndon Johnson. "Big Daddyism" means stiflingly paternalistic government.

The tag was a natural for President Johnson because he frequently used the word himself, as when he claimed FDR had been "like a daddy to me." In California, the term was most often applied to the Democratic Speaker of the Assembly, Jesse M. Unruh. In 1968, after Unruh had reduced his weight from 285 to 200 pounds, Governor Ronald Reagan remarked, "It seems like it takes more than a tailor to change the image of Big Daddy," a comment that Unruh felt was "sort of poor taste on his part."

Political analyst Morton Kondracke used the phrase recently on "The McLaughlin Group." Discussing the civil rights movement, he said, "They look to the Great White Father, the President, to somehow bail out the black community." The novelist James Baldwin was quoted in *The New Republic* in 1992 as saying of his earlier activism, "I was, in some way, in those years, without entirely realizing it, the Great Black Hope of the Great White Father."

greens. See ENVIRONMENTALIST.

greetings. See MY FRIEND.

gridlock a legislative logjam.

This highway engineering term for a massive automobile traffic jam gained notoriety during a transit strike in New York City in April of 1980. It entered the language of politics in the same year. In the wake of the 1980 Presidential election, the *Chicago Sun Times* used the word prophetically: "The instant analysis of election night raised the possibility of political gridlock, a government unable to function because of the division between the Republican President-Senate and the Democratic House of Representatives."

Throughout the Reagan and Bush Administrations, legislative gridlock, brought on by the tug of war between the Republican executive branch and the liberal Democratic Congress, blocked the passage of many crucial bills.

In 1992, Ross Perot capitalized on this issue with his third-party campaign, using the word *gridlock* to make his point and pledging to put an end to the impasse that had characterized the government for twelve years. After Bill Clinton's election, even before his "honeymoon" period had been consummated, he was confronted by the very bugbear he had joined Perot in pledging to eliminate: gridlock. In April 1993, Republican Senators staged a filibuster to stop passage of Clinton's economic-stimulus bill which they described as a PORK BARREL bill. "The Ad-

ministration has earnestly shouted 'gridlock,'" reported the *New York Times* on April 19, ". . . saying Republicans were thwarting efforts to create jobs."

The Republicans, led by Bob Dole, had the last word. "If you're against something," he told some editors in Concord, New Hampshire, "you'd better hope there is a little gridlock." See GO FIGHT CITY HALL.

groundswell popular support; enthusiasm for a policy or candidate from the lower levels of a party or from the general public.

To a sailor, a groundswell is a heavy undulation of the ocean, caused by a far-off gale or earthquake. The sense of depth and inexorability is kept in the political metaphor; when a genuine groundswell develops for one candidate, all the others are in choppy water.

"A ground swell, however," wrote President-to-be James Buchanan in 1856, ". . . among a noble people who had sustained me for more than thirty years forced me reluctantly into the field."

In March 1968, the *New York Times* observed: "By the politico-meteorological standards of New Hampshire, the sudden Rockefeller candidacy not only failed to qualify as a ground swell, but fell considerably short of a frost heave."

In current use, the two words are usually wedded, as with the similar GRASSROOTS; the word continues to refer to an unled, unmanipulated public opinion. For examples of other natural phenomena used in politics, see DISASTER METAPHORS.

guaranteed annual wage. See LIVING WAGE.

guidelines (guideposts)   a general standard of measuring wage and price increases to determine whether they are in what the federal government considers to be the national economic interest.

The national wage-price guidelines (suggesting a limit of 3.2 percent rise per year) were promulgated by President Kennedy in 1962; he resisted the charge that wages and prices were none of his business by pointing out "when things go badly . . . if we have another recession, the President of the United States is to blame. So I think it is our business."

Walter Heller called the guidelines (which he usually termed "guideposts") "the jawbone method" of holding wages and prices down, since they were founded on no statute and included no specific sanction to violators. Kennedy never picked up the usage, probably suspecting that some critic would point out that Samson used "the jawbone of an ass."

Heller informs the author that he felt the word guidelines sounded "too interventionist—guideposts seemed to me less constricting." However, the press and public preferred the more activist "guidelines."

The rationale for the guidelines was that high wage demands, passed on as price increases, would inflate the economy and dissipate any real wage increase. Opponents argue that government intervention here was in effect wage-price control and a long step toward a "managed economy."

As guidelines began to erode in 1966, Heller took a more modest view of their intent: "First, the guideposts have been a useful moderating influence in 1961–1965. Second, since they are designed to function as a supplement rather than an alternative to overall fiscal monetary policy, they should not be expected to carry the burden of stabilization—nor should they be judged by the performance of wages and prices—in a period of excessive total demand."

"Guidelines" was not a new word in the use of presidential power; Eisenhower told a cabinet meeting in 1954 that he wanted guidelines laid out for departmental handling of congressional requests for information.

Franklin Roosevelt used another word for a more limited economic purpose than Kennedy's wage-price guidelines. Before he became President, he called for public competition with private power utilities, "at least as a yardstick." As President, he demanded that the Tennessee and Columbia rivers be the sites of federal power projects for use as "yardsticks" in measuring private utility services and costs.

The guideline phrase traveled. In the British general election of 1964, the Conservatives were saddled with a "pay pause" phrase that one of their leaders had mistakenly used; Labour Minister John Hare announced that any pay pause would soon give way to a more flexible "guiding light."

guilt by association   a SMEAR technique, implying wrongdoing by a person because of the wrongdoing—or extremist connections—of those with whom he associates.

The phrase was used by civil libertarians against what they considered the WITCH HUNTS of the early fifties, when blacklists such as "Red Channels" cast doubts on the loyalty of many who belonged to Communist or Communist-front organizations, or were associated with or related to those who did.

The Supreme Court, however, in *Adler* v. *Board of Education,* 342 US 485 (1952), noted that people are indeed often judged by the company they keep, and a person's associations may be considered in determining loyalty. See SECURITY RISK.

The charge of using "guilt by association" was most often made against Senator Joseph McCarthy, when he headed the Senate Subcommittee on Permanent Investigations. J. B. Matthews, staff director, wrote an article for the *American Mercury* magazine in 1953 charging that "the largest single group supporting the Communist apparatus in the United States today is composed of Protestant clergymen." Though McCarthy was not aware of the article in preparation, he was obliged to stick by his appointee. There was protest from areas that had earlier kept silent about McCarthy; Eisenhower denounced the attack in a telegram to clergymen, and Matthews resigned.

"There was irony in this, too," wrote Robert Donovan, "because McCarthy, so far as anyone knows, had nothing whatsoever to do with Matthews' article. He was simply trapped in a case of guilt by association, which had been his own favorite snare for catching others."

Those who rely too heavily on character references are sometimes accused of seeking "innocence by association." See LOVED FOR THE ENEMIES HE MADE.

The phrase is secure enough to resist punning: during hearings to confirm Nelson Rockefeller as Vice President in 1974, it was revealed that he forgave large loans to his former government aides. This was dubbed "gilt by association."

Gulag acronym for the Soviet slave labor camps.

When Russian novelist Alexander Solzhenitsyn published *The Gulag Archipelago 1918–1956* in Paris in 1973, the word "gulag" entered the English language.

The word is an acronym for the main administration of correctional labor camps—in Russian, *Glavnoye Upravleniye Ispravitelno-trudovykh Lagerei.* When the U.S. State Department referred to this system, the acronym was spelled as an acronym

ought to be—all in caps—but in most other use, the word was merely capitalized as "Gulag," as if it were a place. This led to a widespread assumption that the Gulag was a large prison, or an island chain. But the metaphor Solzhenitsyn had in mind was a series of islands—or camps—in the sea of the USSR.

The term was soon linked to almost any discussion of forced labor or the absence of human rights in the former Soviet Union. See SAMIZDAT.

This expression is not often used in humor. In April 1993, however, Bruce W. Nelan wrote in *Time* magazine that a Russian referendum of Boris Yeltsin has been "a listless campaign in which both candidate and voters have acted as if a week in the Gulag would be preferable to enduring one more speech."

gumshoe campaign. See JUNKETEERING GUMSHOES.

gunboat diplomacy the iron fist of threatened force inside the velvet glove of diplomatic relations.

The expression is always derogatory, and has always been used in the sense of those days being over. "It has been said that the days of 'gunboat diplomacy' in China are over," goes an *OED Supplement* citation from proceedings of the U.S. Naval Institute dated February 1927. In the United Nations in 1961, an Iraqi delegate termed a British action in Kuwait "gunboat diplomacy at its worst."

The phrase began in a description of Western domination of China in the early twentieth century, with U.S. and British interests maintained by gunboats on the main rivers and patrolling harbors. In 1937 the "*Panay* incident" took place when a Japanese bomber sank a U.S. gunboat 27 miles north of Nanking on the Yangtzse River, but that was an example of a gunboat being on the receiving end of force.

The gunboat has a long tradition in American naval history. The "gunboat system"—small armed craft manned by local seamen—was preferred by Thomas Jefferson to a more expensive regular navy for the defense of U.S. harbors, and in the war of 1812 defended New Orleans from the British until Andrew Jackson arrived. But the term gained an oppressive or imperialistic connotation from its Chinese experience.

Now the phrase is used exclusively to express dismay at what is considered JINGOISM. In 1976, when Republican Ronald Reagan charged that the Ford Administration's advocacy of black majority rule in Rhodesia "risks increased violence and bloodshed," Senator Joe Biden (D-Del.) commented: "There is a good deal of gunboat rhetoric that is misleading the American people."

A *Washington Post* editorial in 1992 criticized George Bush's attempts at this form of diplomatic relations, despite his defeat of Saddam Hussein: "He has fared poorly in developing intermediate policies that persuade or coerce other nations to avoid looming confrontation. He is not a skillful practitioner of gunboat diplomacy, in an era when that talent would be of great utility."

For a rundown of the way "diplomacy" has been used to make phrases, see DIPLOMACY and SHUTTLE DIPLOMACY.

gung ho enthusiasm undampened by experience, often shown by a political volunteer; as an adjective, showing such enthusiasm.

When a political operative is "gung ho," he is willing to undertake the impossible cheerfully, often overcoming obstacles that "old pros" consider too difficult to attack.

"Gung ho" was used by Allied armed forces in World War II to express a spirit of cooperation and enthusiasm, popularized by Colonel Evans F. Carlson's marine raiders. The word was drawn from the Chinese, roughly meaning "work together," the name of the industrial cooperatives set up by missionaries in China in the mid-thirties.

Nym Wales, an authority on Chinese affairs, wrote in 1938:

. . . the Gung Ho industrial cooperatives were to be neutral politically—to start co-ops for both Kuomintang and communists to help win the war—and to bring about the industrial revolution in the village, not in the treaty-port cities, as before.

Would Henry Luce sponsor the Gung Ho industrial cooperatives? This was a vital question. *Time* did give publicity to the infant Gung Ho cooperatives and Henry Luce agreed to be on the advisory board of the America Committee in Aid of Chinese Industrial Cooperatives along with Mrs. Franklin Roosevelt . . .

The phrase may be used derisively, as a modernization of Talleyrand's advice to diplomats: "Above all, not too much zeal."

Used attributively, the term is now *gung-ho*, with a hyphen, and generally means "overly zealous or militant." Joseph Sobran, writing in the *National Review* of October 15, 1990, chastised critics of dovish conservatives for "an unworthy attempt to marginalize fellow conservatives and hustle us all into gung-ho unanimity."

guns before butter the strain placed on consumer products and social-welfare projects by a nation that must place a higher priority on war supplies.

The phrase is generally attributed to Hermann Göring, who said in a radio broadcast in 1936: "Guns will make us powerful; butter will only make us fat." Earlier that year, Nazi Propaganda Minister Joseph Goebbels had said: "We can do without butter, but, despite all our love of peace, not without arms. One cannot shoot with butter but with guns."

The "guns before butter" slogan came to mean the domestic economic sacrifices any nation must face in preparing for war. In the U.S., however, the phrase has changed to "guns *and* butter," which is a charge that the President is refusing to face up to the sacrifices required. Senator Lyndon Johnson made this charge against President Harry Truman in the early stages of the Korean conflict; he was on the receiving end during his own presidency.

In his 1966 State of the Union message, Johnson told the joint session of Congress: "Time may require further sacrifices. If so, we will make them. But we will not heed those who will wring it from the hopes of the unfortunate in a land of plenty. I believe we can continue the Great Society while we fight in Viet Nam." No signal was needed; editorial writers and Johnson critics across the country called this "a guns and butter policy." A year later, following a House Appropriations Committee's gentle handling of a public-works-project (PORK BARREL) bill, the *New York Times* asked: "If the nation can't afford guns and butter, can it afford guns and pork?"

The phrase is current. In 1993, Ariel Cohen of the Heritage Foundation told Reuters' Steve Holland of the need for American aid to the former Soviet Union: "We can pay a little bit now, or we can pay hundreds of billions of dollars later for a new arms race. It's better to send butter to Russia now, than to build guns against Russia later."

guru. See RABBI.

gutfighter a tough, no-holds-barred political operative always ready to go for the jugular vein of his opponent.

Wrote *Times* reporter Cabell Phillips: "The people voted for the homely, rumpled, irrational gutfighter, Harry Truman."

Curiously, *gutfighter* is generally used admiringly, unlike *mudslinger* or CHARACTER ASSASSIN, and is not to be confused with *gutter fighter,* which means one who drags a campaign down to the low level of the gutter.

Gutfighter is an inside political word, not yet fully taken up by the general public; politicians consider a gutfighter to be one who is totally committed, intensely loyal, and willing to do almost anything for his cause or candidate. Gutfighters are at their best dealing with GUT ISSUES.

Typical use in 1967 was by political writer John Hopkins, in the *Fort Lauderdale News:* "Florida's Democratic party is shadow-boxing when it should be gut-fighting . . . today they search for the knife-wielder who has not shown up yet."

As an antonym of this term, the polite *gentleman* has been suggested. Robert Goodman, a Baltimore-based media consultant, said in the *National Journal* of a 1986 campaign, "I think you have two gentlemen here who aren't really gutfighters."

See INSTINCT FOR THE JUGULAR; HATCHETMAN; HARDBALL.

gut issue a political-campaign theme that reaches beyond rational discussion and affects the emotions of the voter; a topic that engenders a visceral reaction.

Examples of gut issues are war-fever and war-weariness; depression or inflation; fear of crime or resentment of minority groups. A "switcher issue" is a gut issue to a limited group of voters, such as abortion and gun control, which can cause that group to abandon normal political alliances. "Non-gut issues" include fiscal integrity, better highways, state constitution modernization. A "burning issue" is always discussed; a gut issue may be discussed or not.

A peripheral issue in one campaign can be a gut issue in another; urban renewal leaves the suburban voter cold while "slum clearance" can be a gut issue in a city. Restraint in foreign policy dealings was hardly a gut issue until the Johnson forces in 1964 tagged Goldwater as TRIGGER-HAPPY, and the fear of nuclear adventurism became a gut issue.

In modern campaigns, DEPTH POLLING is often used to determine what lies beneath the articulated problems worrying voters; this will often turn up the gut issue that can either be brought out into the open or alluded to subtly. In the 1966 Rockefeller campaign for governor, a gut issue that surprised politicians turned out to be a fear of crimes committed by narcotics addicts in poorer city neighborhoods. Rockefeller forces promptly gave major billboard space and television time to the governor's program to "get the addicts off the streets," a theme that had not even been considered early in the campaign.

Both "gut" and "guts" refer to the entrails, bowels, belly, intestines. While "gut" has come to mean emotionally or psychologically underlying, "guts" in current usage connotes courage and stamina. In World War II General George Patton was known as "Old Blood and Guts."

Fiorello La Guardia's radio signoff—"Patience and Fortitude"—recalled to many the "intestinal fortitude" of the scrappy mayor.

Author Louis Adamic offered the following definition in *A Study in Courage:* "There is a certain blend of courage, integrity, character and principle which has no satisfactory dictionary name but has been called different things at different times in different countries. Our American name for it is 'guts.'"

A gut issue, now more often called a HOT BUTTON issue, should not be confused with the leading rational issue of a campaign. The *leading issue,* or *key issue,* of imperialism was called by William Jennings Bryan the *burning issue* and the PARAMOUNT ISSUE in 1900. But in 1970, it was hard to tell whether the *social issue* or the *economic issue* was the gut issue. The gut issue in the 1992 campaign for President was economic; George Stephanopoulos, Bill Clinton's press chief, put up a sign in his Little Rock headquarters quoting campaign strategist James Carville: "IT'S THE ECONOMY, STUPID!" See ISSUES, THE.

gutter flyer   the lowest variety of political literature, vicious and not traceable.

The "coffin handbill" of 1828 was the first important example of this genre. The one-page flyer recounting "some of the Bloody Deeds of General Jackson," was decorated with coffins, illustrating the murders of soldiers and others while he was commanding troop. Philadelphia publisher John Binns was credited later with the authorship of the handbill, which contained the text of the execution order for six men signed by Lieutenant Colonel (later Senator) Thomas Hart Benton and approved by Jackson. Most of the "victims" represented by coffins had been court-martialed for mutiny or desertion. One man Jackson had slain himself; the general had been tried, pleaded self-defense, and was acquitted. The handbill was effective, but Jackson won.

Another, more recent, gutter flyer was the "Nixon deed" used in the 1960 campaign. This was a blowup of the deed of the house in which Richard

Nixon lived in Washington; like all other houses in that area, it contained a restrictive covenant. The flyer, clearly implying a racial bias by the candidate, was distributed widely in black neighborhoods in New York, Philadelphia, Detroit, and other urban areas. Democratic headquarters claimed no knowledge of the effort, but it appeared too well organized and financed to be the work of a single vicious entrepreneur. To force a halt, a young Republican volunteer thought of getting a similar deed on Kennedy-family homes in the Washington area, most of which contained a similar restrictive covenant.

But wherever he looked in the town records, the sheet had been destroyed; the organizer of the "Nixon deed" plot had thought ahead.

In November 1963, John F. Kennedy was welcomed to Dallas with a gutter flyer in the form of a Bertillon police poster, with front and side views of Kennedy and the headline "Wanted for Treason."

In most cases, gutter flyers are unsigned. A federal law prohibits the use of unsigned literature in a campaign for federal office.

For an early example, see ROORBACK; for recent episodes, see DIRTY TRICKS.

H

hack attack word on a long-time politician; a political drudge.

The word is derived from the hackney horse in England, a horse that was let out for hire, usually mistreated, and became dull, broken-down, and exhausted. See HOBSON'S CHOICE. The word was especially apt for politics because political hacks were disciplined by a party whip.

After the death of William Pitt in 1806, England was governed by a star-studded "Ministry of All the Talents," as the administration headed by Lord Grenville was dubbed. However, this was followed in 1807 by a less eminent—if more practical—group, soon derided as "All the Hacks."

The English word made the transition to American politics in the earliest days of the new nation; in 1828 the *New York Enquirer* said that other publications were calling those "friendly to Gen. Jackson 'political hacks.'"

A *hack*, in current usage, is one who works mechanically; he differs from a HENCHMAN, who works under clear direction, a HATCHETMAN, who works ruthlessly, and a *hanger-on*, who does not work at all.

A hack writer, disdained in intellectual circles, is sometimes sought after in politics despite his hackneyed prose. "Find me a good hack writer," one local candidate told the author, "who will put down what I think, and you can keep all your Sorensens and Emmet Hugheses with their fancy ideas." For the PECKING ORDER of political writers, see SPEECHWRITER; GHOSTWRITER.

hack it to succeed; to come through after a struggle.

In a news conference on March 4, 1971, President Nixon used a phrase he attributed to General Creighton Abrams: "His evaluation after three weeks of fighting is that—to use his terms—the South Vietnamese can hack it . . ."

Several weeks later, commentator Howard K. Smith, in a televised conversation with the President, observed, "You also said that the Laos operation showed the South Vietnamese could hack it by themselves." The President again used the phrase in his reply: "When I use the term 'hack it' . . . we have now concluded, and this is General Abrams' assessment, that the South Vietnamese have now passed a milestone in their development."

Garry Trudeau, in a January 1981 *Doonesbury* cartoon, used the phrase to parody a Presidential nominee's arrogant response to a senator's helpful remark: "Well, thanks, Senator, but frankly, I can hack it without anybody pulling punches. We're here to determine my fitness, so stop whimpering and give me your best shot."

The phrase appears to be an offshoot of "cut it," a shortened form of "cut the mustard."

"Had Enough?" Republican campaign slogan in the off-year elections of 1946.

The phrase "had enough," with a modern variant "had it," is an old expression of mild disgust. When Theodore Roosevelt decided not to run for a third term in 1908, he said, "I don't want it. I've had enough . . ."

In 1946 Harry Truman was in trouble. The cost-of-living index was climbing rapidly, more unions were striking than usual, shortages of meat, autos, and housing were continuing. The White House was the scapegoat. The creation of an advertising slogan that reflected the public mood—"Had Enough?"—is credited to the Harry M. Frost agency of Boston.

Wrote Eric Goldman: "A nation which had quite enough of inflation and the Russians, of strikes, shortages, and the atom bomb, of everlasting maybe's about peace and prosperity, rose up in a hiss of exasperation and elected the first Republican Congress since the far-distant days of Herbert Hoover."

See DON'T LET THEM TAKE IT AWAY.

hail of dead cats criticism accompanying the exit of an unpopular figure from public life.

The National Recovery Administration, a New Deal project, ran into severe criticism soon after Roosevelt's HUNDRED DAYS had ended, and was frequently labeled "the National Run-Around."

A series of strikes, especially in the textile industry, required National Guard action that resulted in a list of dead and wounded on the labor front. In the fall of 1934 General Hugh Johnson, controversial head of the NRA, resigned in what he called "a hail of dead cats."

Precipitation has an affinity for resignations. A "rain (or flood or deluge) of complaints" leads to a resignation "under a cloud"; a "storm of criticism" is followed by the most colorful expression of all, "a hail of dead cats."

The expression is probably not related to the "dead cats" of the circus (nonperforming lions and tigers) but may be akin to "catcall," a raucous noise expressing disapproval.

For another use of a fatal-feline image, see DEAD-CAT BOUNCE.

half-breeds. See STALWART.

half-truth a statement accurate enough to require an explanation; and the longer the explanation, the more likely a public reaction of half-belief.

Senator Joseph McCarthy was often accused of using "half-truths, innuendos and smears." On the other hand, one defense of a charge that might be largely true was to label it a half-truth and denounce "McCarthy-type tactics" (except in areas where McCarthy had a strong following).

Alexander Gilchrist, in his *Life of William Blake*, quoted the English poet-artist-mystic as referring to "the great half-truth, Liberty." In Blake's *Auguries of Innocence*, this couplet appears:

A truth that's told with bad intent
Beats all the lies you can invent.

Philosopher Alfred North Whitehead wrote: "There are no whole truths. All truths are half-truths. It is trying to treat them as whole truths that plays the devil."

A political adage attributed to nobody is: "Half a truth is like half a brick—you can throw it twice as far." And the evasiveness of a half-truth is recognized in court oaths swearing in witnesses: "The truth, the whole truth, and nothing but the truth."

See BIG LIE.

handlers managers of political candidates; aides who "handle" candidates.

In the 1300s, *handlers* were moneychangers, those who handled silver. A century later, the word was used figuratively in criticizing a preacher as "an unreverent *handler* of God's word."

By the nineteenth century, the term was used in animal fighting; a *handler* held a fighting dog or gamecock. During the twentieth century, the word was applied to the *handler* of dogs at dog shows, somebody who shows off the best points of the dog to the judges.

The word had entered boxing by mid-century, labeling the seconds who offer backrubs and advice between rounds. Jack Dempsey wrote in 1950, "His *handlers* threw in the towel," meaning the seconds "asked the referee to stop the fight."

As a political term, *handlers* first became prominent during the 1988 Presidential campaign. This sense, however, suggested negative control and manipulation of the candidate. A. M. Rosenthal wrote in the *New York Times:* "I do not believe in the genius of the handlers. They are all brilliant during the campaigns. How come 50 percent of them turn out to be so wrong on election night, when their man loses?"

Dan Quayle, in his first campaign for the Vice Presidency, sought to avoid the appearance of being robotically "programmed," and he announced: "Now it's my turn. I'm my own handler."

President George Bush rankled at the suggestion that White House *handlers* were in charge of political nominees. Bush said in 1991 he considered it demeaning "to suggest that handlers are telling everybody what to say or not to say," and showed his knowledge of the term's etymology by adding, "Somehow I don't like the word *handlers.* Like the prizefighter—O.K., go in there and slug him again."

Newsweek used the term in reporting on George Bush's insistence on wearing a loud red-white-and-blue necktie: "'You're in full-throttle handler revolt,' Mary Matalin, his favorite handler, told him one day. 'You're still wearing that horrible tie.'"

Those in the business of coaching political figures never call themselves *handlers;* they prefer *consultants* or *advisers.*

handout a welfare payment; or, a press release; or, a handbill.

"Handout" is an attack word on welfare payments. A political cliché is "People want a hand up, not a handout." The word has connotations of begging; the usage began in the late nineteenth century as hobo lingo, referring to the bundle of clothes or plate of food given at the back door. See HOTTENTOTS, MILK FOR.

A press handout is a story written by a political figure's press aide, or by himself, to be given to reporters at a press conference to save them the trouble of taking notes or asking questions. Good reporters profess to ignore "handouts" and dig for themselves; however, an informative handout can be helpful and timesaving. A *handout* is usually directly given by press agents to reporters; a *release* may either be handed out or mailed. Bush press secretary Marlin Fitzwater called a press statement read for the cameras a *readout.*

Handout is also an infrequently used word for political handbill. See FLYER.

hand-picked a candidate chosen or an appointment made by a powerful person; an allusion to boss rule.

Hand-picked is always an attack word; in the 1958 Democratic convention in New York State, the choice of District Attorney Frank Hogan for senatorial candidate was dictated by Tammany chief Carmine De Sapio. Hogan was promptly depicted by Republicans as "Boss De Sapio's hand-picked candidate" and was roundly defeated by Kenneth Keating.

In agriculture, hand-picked (vs. machine-picked) means carefully chosen, resulting in an unbruised fruit or berry or, more commonly, selected by hand from a larger group of the same product for quality. In politics, the opposite has come to be the meaning.

A "hand-picked successor" implies autocratic domination, subverting democratic processes, and is a charge hurled by whatever group refuses to hold still or go along. The vice-presidential candidate is usually hand-picked by the presidential candidate, though Adlai Stevenson in 1956 made a point of permitting an "open convention" that chose Estes Kefauver over John F. Kennedy.

"In 1908," wrote Harry Truman, "William Howard Taft had been hand-picked by [Theodore] Roosevelt as his successor." He did not add that he himself had been hand-picked by another Roosevelt in 1944.

See HEIR APPARENT.

hanger-on. See HACK.

hang tough strike a determined pose; or, remain resolute.

Eugene Landy's *Underground Dictionary* traces the phrase: "It is used to encourage individuals during a stressful situation, such as a period of withdrawal from a drug. Hang tough was commonly used at Synanon Foundation during the foundation's initial stages when addicts were allowed to withdraw after entering Synanon. Synanon's house in Santa Monica, California has a ship's white life preserver upon which is written 'S.S. Hang Tough' hanging on the wall."

The phrase, which has variant readings of "hang in there" and "tough it out," was used by Hugh Sidey in *Life* on June 19, 1970: "In sum, they agree that the emergence of Patton as a major figure in the Nixon Pantheon is a good sign, meaning that he will continue to hang tough in the crunches."

During the sixteen months of Watergate siege, President Nixon was urged by some to "hang tough," and the phrase has been used in reference to Presidential resolution or irresolution ever since. Ross Baker, a Rutgers University political analyst, commented in February 1993 to *USA Today* on President Clinton's performance early in his Administration: "Whether he has the capacity to hang tough is still an open question. He seems to fold at the slightest sign of disaffection by some interest groups."

"Hang loose" is an older locution, from "hang it easy," a teenage phrase from the early fifties. Some slang authorities speculate that both "hang loose" and "hang tough" are sexual in origin, referring to the relaxed or tense condition of the genitals. Steven Weisman defined "hang loose" in the *New York Times* in 1976 as "the period when a legislator has not made up his mind."

New York Times columnist Tom Wicker speculated in a 1973 note to the author: "I believe 'hang in there' will be found to be a prize-fight term meaning that someone momentarily rocked by the other guy should 'hang in there,' maybe even literally hanging on to the ropes or hanging on to the other guy in a clinch."

"Tough it out" has a longer lineage in slang. R. H. Thornton has six citations in his *American Glossary,* beginning with an 1824 memoir: "We little fellows had to tuff it out as well as we could."

happy camper   satisfied person; team player pleased with the status quo.

Print citations for the term date back at least to 1981, when David Bird wrote in the *New York Times* about homeless people: "It is not a group of happy campers that gets off the bus after its 70-mile journey." A year later, the columnist Mary McGrory applied the term to politics; observing a Republican television ad about prosperity in a region of high unemployment, she wrote, "The happy campers of the commercial have few counterparts in the Peoria area today."

The phrase in its literal sense probably predates 1981 in its use at summer camps. Its reverse, *unhappy camper,* has long described the homesick city child.

By 1985, the two types of *camper* were part of political jargon. Representative Thomas J. Tauke of Iowa commented in 1985 about a toxic-cleanup proposal: "I want the authors of the bill to know that I am not a happy camper." Representative Billy Tauvin of Louisiana responded, "This is the most unhappy campsite in America."

Since then, these terms have rocketed to popularity among slang expressions for satisfaction or discontent. In 1988, when the *Discovery* space shuttle successfully followed the *Challenger* disaster, the flight commander Frederick Hauck signaled the crew's jubilation to Mission Control: "You got a bunch of happy campers up here."

Happy Days Are Here Again   campaign song of FDR in 1932.

Hit songs during the Depression ranged from "Brother, Can You Spare a Dime?" to "Happy Days Are Here Again." Bronx Democratic boss Edward J. Flynn felt that the music to be played when FDR was nominated should be gay and optimistic.

Flynn and FDR-confidant Louis Howe were lying on the floor of Howe's hotel suite in Chicago listening to the nomination on the radio. Roosevelt, a former Navy man, had suggested that at the moment of nomination the convention band should play "Anchors Aweigh." When the musicians began to play the Navy song slowly, Flynn groaned to Howe: "That sounds like a funeral march. Why don't we get them to play something peppy, like 'Happy Days Are Here Again'?" Howe agreed, and Flynn telephoned the convention floor manager to suggest that the band switch to a lively rendition of "Happy Days." Flynn wrote later: "In a moment it began to come over the air. To me, it certainly sounded more cheerful and appropriate to the occasion."

The song soon came to mean for Roosevelt what "Sidewalks of New York" meant to Al Smith. Nobody bothered to point out that the song was written just before the crash of 1929 by Jack Yellen/Milton Agar for use in an MGM movie entitled *Chasing Rainbows.*

At the 1976 Democratic convention, the song was played to recall past Democratic glories for candidate Jimmy Carter. In the 1992 convention, it was replaced by "Don't Stop Thinking About Tomorrow."

The phrase "Happy Days," which is also a toast, was used as the title of a kids' television program in the mid-seventies that was the disseminator of many nonce words.

Happy Warrior   the sobriquet of Al Smith.

At the Democratic National Convention of June 26, 1924, Franklin D. Roosevelt used the nickname in nominating Al Smith: "He is the Happy Warrior of the political battlefield." The Governor of New York and the first Roman Catholic to seek the Presidency, Smith—"the Brown Derby"—became the party's choice four years later, and FDR's label for cheerful combativeness struck. (For another "happy" term, see HAPPY CAMPER; for a less happy facet of the Smith effort, see WHISPERING CAMPAIGN.)

The phrase was a Rooseveltian poetic allusion. In 1807, William Wordsworth titled a poem "Character of the Happy Warrior," asking, "Who is the happy Warrior? Who is he/That every man in arms should wish to be?"

The image of the warrior in politics remains prevalent. Arthur M. Schlesinger, Jr., in *A Thousand Days* quoted John F. Kennedy using the image: "War will exist until that distant day when the conscientious objector enjoys the same reputation and prestige that the warrior does today."

Nowadays the sobriquet of Al Smith may be inverted when used for other politicians. A *Newsweek* profile of George Bush after his unsuccessful campaign for reelection in 1992 was headlined "Unhappy Warrior" and stated, "Bush had never been a very happy warrior, and his appetite had been further dulled by the pasting he had taken for the nastiness of his 1988 campaign."

hardball   rough   political   tactics; stronger than "practical politics" or "pranks," milder than DIRTY TRICKS.

In hearings on September 26, 1973, before the Senate Watergate Committee, Nixon speechwriter Patrick J. Buchanan gave a declension of roughness in politics: "My own view is that there are four gradations. There are things that are certainly utterly outrageous and I would put that in with the kind of demonstrations against Vice President Humphrey in 1968 which denied

him an opportunity to speak for almost a month. Then, there is 'dirty tricks.' Then, there is political hardball. Then there is pranks."

The author first heard the word used on December 20, 1972, by attorney (later Secretary of HEW) Joseph Califano, complaining of Republican tactics during the campaign against Senator George McGovern: "Nobody ever played hardball like you guys." (He was unaware at the time that previous Presidents had used the FBI and CIA for campaign intelligence purposes.)

In trying to show that hardball, as practiced in the 1972 campaign by the Nixon forces, was not necessarily immoral or illegal, the author in his *New York Times* column used the expression "not every hardball is a beanball." *Times* sportswriter Walter "Red" Smith promptly corrected the mixed metaphor: "In sports terminology there is no such thing as 'a hardball.' When the word is used, which is seldom, 'hardball' means the game of baseball as distinct from softball. It does not mean a high, fast pitch. Probably Mr. Safire should be excused, for this was a column applauding Richard Nixon's forthright behavior in the Watergate case. It had an understandably agitated tone."

In political journalism a "softball" or "fat pitch" is a question designed to give an interviewee a rest.

For an earlier use of a game metaphor, see BEANBAG, FULL-COURT PRESS, and GAME PLAN; also SPORTS METAPHORS.

hard line   a firm stand; recently, strong support of the CONTAINMENT of Communism; called "rigid" by soft-liners, who favor ACCOMMODATION.

The "line" appears to have come from PARTY LINE, a Communist phrase. Historian Samuel Eliot Morison wrote: "Thus the cold war began as soon as the hot war was over. Earl Browder, head of the Communist party in the United States, was the first victim of the 'hard line.' For his continuing to preach friendly collaboration between the United States and Russia, which he had been ordered to do in 1941, he was contemptuously deposed in May 1945, by orders from Moscow."

Western powers, led by the U.S., took note of the new Russian line and of Winston Churchill's IRON CURTAIN warning in 1946; NATO was formed, and the policy of containment followed. See CONTAINMENT; MR. X. The "hard line" was pursued in the Korean War, and was subsequently identified with Secretary of State John Foster Dulles throughout the Eisenhower years. At the onset of the war in Vietnam, however, the wisdom of the "hard line" came under increasing attack in the U.S. and abroad.

The *Wall Street Journal* wrote in 1967:

> Such hard-liners as Sens. Bourke Hickenlooper (R.-Iowa) and Frank Lausche (D.-Ohio) can't shake the fear that the various national Communist parties around the world still want to seize political and social control everywhere, that they still have the common goal of toppling capitals. Former Ambassador Kennan, a hard-liner himself during Stalin's day, contends this economic goal is becoming increasingly theoretical. Eastern Europe policy-shapers may continue to make mischief for the West, but for reasons that are uniquely Russian, or Polish, or Rumanian, and not because they're "Communist."

The "Hards" and the "Softs" date back more than a century in U.S. history. New York State sent two warring factions to the 1848 Democratic convention in Baltimore: the *Hunkers,* known as the *Hard Shells* or *Hards,* and the *Barnburners,* known as the *Soft Shells* or *Softs.* The Hards supported the Polk Administration's policy opposing the Wilmot Proviso prohibiting slavery in California and the rest of the Mexican cession; the Softs were against the Democratic Administration's opposition, and fought to limit the extension of slavery. Efforts at a compromise failed, and neither faction took part in the convention.

Digging back, Charles Ledyard Norton in 1890 traced the hard and soft "shells" to sects of the Baptist denomination, so called by their critics because of their supposed similarity to crabs in different stages of development.

Hard-liners are often described as "hard-nosed"; for some reason, soft-liners are never described as "soft-nosed." According to lexicographer Kenneth Hudson, "hard-nosed" was originally applied to bulls: "A hard-nosed bull is one who does not respond when the ring through the cartilage of his nose is twitched by the person leading him on a pole or rope."

The term came in handy after the collapse of Communism and the breakup of the Soviet Union. The former Communists, resisting change, were called "conservatives"; this angered U.S. conservatives, who thought of them as the unreconstructed radicals. A compromise of sorts was reached in calling the opponents to Boris Yeltsin's reforms "hard-liners."

hard money   historically, metallic versus paper currency; recently, applied symbolically to anti-inflationists.

One of the great debates of early U.S. history pitted the "hard-money" against the "soft-money" men. In an 1816 debate Daniel Webster formulated the classical defense of gold and silver currencies: "The framers of the Constitution, and those who enacted the early statutes on this subject, were hard-money men; they had felt and therefore duly appreciated the evils of a paper medium."

Andrew Jackson tied the Democratic party to a hard-money policy during his battle with the banks, and they became known as "Perish Credit, Perish Commerce" men. But in 1840 the party split into hard- and soft-money factions.

Nowadays, paper currency is universally accepted, but the hard and soft terms are still applied symbolically. The hard-money men favor a slow, measured expansion of the money supply, generally no more than 2 or 3 percent a year. The soft-money men—often Democrats, Keynesians, or both—approve pumping greater quantities of currency into circulation as a stimulus to employment and consumption.

Leslie Phillips wrote in *USA Today* in March 1993 that "the heart of President Clinton's campaign finance reform is based on a trade-off: converting unlimited 'soft' money, donations used by political parties to help elect candidates, into regulated—and limited—'hard' money."

hatched removed from political activity by virtue of the Hatch Act.

The Hatch Act, bearing the name of Senator Carl Hatch, a Democrat from New Mexico, whose bill was passed in 1939, says: "It shall be unlawful for any person employed in any administrative position by the United States, or by any department, independent agency, or other agency of the United States . . . to use his official authority for the purpose of interfering with, or affecting the election or the nomination of any candidate . . ." Its purpose was to prevent political appointees from unduly influencing government workers.

The phrase "subject to the restrictions of the Hatch Act" was soon shortened to the verb "hatched," which present usage no longer capitalizes.

In 1970 George Shultz, who had been promoted from Secretary of Labor in the Nixon cabinet to Director of the Office of Management and Budget, was routinely asked to make a speech supporting a candidate in his home state. Shultz looked up from his desk as if he had just pecked his way out of an eggshell and replied, "I can't. I've been hatched."

Presidential advisers use this rule of thumb: if you are on the White House payroll, or you are in a job that has called for Senate confirmation—you've not hatched.

In the late seventies, there was agitation to repeal the Hatch Act because it limited some people's rights to political expression; in this way, reformers were calling for reform of reform.

hatchetman the associate of a politician or officeholder who takes on the unpleasant assignment of forcing supporters into line; also a public figure who engages in strong partisan attacks.

Louis Howe was FDR's private hatchetman, Harold Ickes his public hatchetman in political wars (see MAN ON THE WEDDING CAKE; BAREFOOT BOY FROM WALL STREET). Sherman Adams was occasionally Eisenhower's private hatchetman; Richard Nixon was often accused of being Eisenhower's public hatchetman because of the Vice President's willingness to play a partisan role in contrast to Eisenhower's above-politics position.

Robert Kennedy was the one most often accused of being John Kennedy's hatchetman, though Kenneth O'Donnell often had to perform that function. Lyndon Johnson occasionally used Hubert Humphrey as a public hatchetman (in the partisan public-figure sense); privately, White House aide Marvin Watson was accused of doing the necessary hatcheting, although President Johnson—with his Senate Majority experience—occasionally did the job himself. In 1971 the *Wall Street Journal* sunk the appellation in the head of Nixon counsel Charles Colson.

The derivation indicates both the public and private senses of the expression. In the public sense—one who engages in partisan attacks clearing a path for the above-politics leader—derivation is from American colonial military vocabulary. A hatchetman, or axman, was used to chop foliage in advance of a military group operating in woods or jungle. General George Washington wrote to one of his subordinates: "I think it will be advisable to detain both mulattoes and negroes in your company, and employ them as Pioneers or Hatchetmen."

In the private, arm-twisting sense, the derivation is from the Chinese tong wars of the 1880s, where "hatchet-armed killers" were the "enforcers" of their era, murdering enemies of the tongs for pay.

In current political usage, then, a politician differentiates between the public, or openly partisan, hatchetman and the insider who does the dirty work for a public figure. A HENCHMAN is one cut above a *hanger-on* but one cut below a *hatchetman,* though he may be used for hatcheting chores from time to time.

The work performed is called a "hatchet job" as well as "hatcheting." Harry Truman's assessment of the Republican party in the 1948 campaign: "Gluttons of privilege . . . all set to do a hatchet job on the New Deal."

When peace is made the hatchet is buried.

See GUTFIGHTER.

hat in the ring announcement of active candidacy.

Former President Theodore Roosevelt was actively working to get the Republican presidential nomination in 1912, but had not yet announced that he really wanted to run against his protégé, William Howard Taft.

A number of governors signed a petition asking Roosevelt to take hold of the progressive forces in the GOP and make a run for the nomination. With the petition in his pocket Roosevelt couldn't help answering a reporter's question about his possible candidacy one cold night in Cleveland. "My hat's in the ring. The fight is on, and I'm stripped to the buff."

Roosevelt popularized a boxing phrase used on the American frontier. When a Westerner decided he was willing to fight all comers, he threw his hat in the prize ring, similar to "throwing down the gauntlet" in the days of chivalry.

After newspapers had picked up Roosevelt's "hat in the ring" quote, *Harper's Weekly* said of the bitter feud between Roosevelt and Taft: "Hate, not hat, is in the ring." The construction is flexible and current. Harold Ickes derided young Thomas E. Dewey for "throwing his diaper in the ring," and the *New York Times* in 1967 said that congressional candidate Shirley Temple Black "threw her curls in the ring." The *Los Angeles Times* reported in January 1993 a debate among approximately forty candidates for mayor of L.A.; wrote Faye Fiore of that vast field, "But if former Gov. Edmund G. (Jerry) Brown Jr. had thrown his hat in the ring, you can bet they would have found an extra chair."

have and have-not nations phrase used to dramatize the gulf between the nations rich in resources and industry, and those yet undeveloped and dependent.

Miguel de Cervantes coined the phrase. In the second book of *Don Quixote,* chapter XX, Sancho Panza observes that his grandmother always used to say, "There are only two families in the world, the Haves and the Have-Nots." The Spanish *el tener* and *el no tener* is sometimes translated "have-much and have-little." A parallel aphorism is Rabelais' "one half of the world knows not how the other half lives."

The phrase has always filled a need. Lord Bryce used it in *The American Commonwealth:* "In the hostility of rich and poor, or of capital and labour, in the fears of the Haves and the desire of the Have-nots . . ." Theodore Roosevelt wrote in 1918: ". . . to oscillate between the sheer brutal greed of the haves and sheer brutal greed of the have-nots means to plumb the depths of degradation."

The phrase is used in its general sense defining the chasm between economic classes, and in a more specific sense pointing to the difference between rich and poor nations. H. L. Mencken used the general sense in his blast at Democratic candidate John Davis in the 1924 campaign: "Dr. Coolidge is for the Haves and Dr. La Follette is for the Have Nots. But whom is Dr. Davis for? . . . himself."

Talking about foreign affairs in 1948, Harry Truman used the more specific: "The world was undergoing a major readjustment, with revolution stalking most of the 'have-not' nations. Communism was making the most of this opportunity, thriving on misery as it always does."

America's responsibility toward the "have-not" nations has been a running controversy (see HOTTENTOTS, MILK FOR) in domestic politics. Frequently, when the "have-nots" bite the hand of the "haves" that are trying to feed them, there is a reluctance to continue the largesse (or fulfill the social responsibility, depending on the point of view).

In the 1980s, as the East-West super-power competition came to an end, the haves were referred to as the North, the have-nots as the South.

See THIRD WORLD; WEST, THE.

have the tickets.   See TICKET.

hawks.   See WAR HAWKS.

heartbeat away from the Presidency
a reminder to voters to examine the shortcomings of a vice-presidential candidate.

"The Republican Vice Presidential candidate," Adlai Stevenson said in the Cleveland Arena in 1952, "—who asks you to place him a heartbeat from the Presidency—has attacked me for saying in a court deposition that the character of Alger Hiss was good." Stevenson then launched into a blast at Richard Nixon.

Nixon supporters in the 1960 campaign took a leaf from Stevenson's text. They compiled a list of every one of vice-presidential candidate Lyndon Johnson's votes against civil rights legislation as a representative and senator and circulated a flyer entitled "Only a Heartbeat from the Presidency."

McKinley manager Mark Hanna, seeking to block Theodore Roosevelt from the vice-presidential nomination, used the thought but not the phrase in 1900. "It must always be remembered," one report quoted him—"that there is only one life between the Vice President and the Chief Magistracy of the nation." Another report of the same statement: "Don't any of you realize that there's only one life between this madman and the White House?"

U.S. history to date has shown that there are better than two chances in ten that the President's heartbeat will stop during his term in office. Tyler took over for Harrison; Fillmore for Taylor; Johnson for Lincoln; Arthur for Garfield; Roosevelt for McKinley; Coolidge for Harding; Truman for Roosevelt; Johnson for Kennedy.

The scary phrase was used by reporter Jules Witcover as the title of a book about the forced resignation of Spiro Agnew: *A Heartbeat Away*. It was alluded to by Lloyd Bentsen in his 1988 vice-presidential debate with Dan Quayle (see YOU'RE NO JFK): "This debate tonight is not about the qualifications for the Vice Presidency. The debate is whether or not Dan Quayle and Lloyd Bentsen are qualified to be President. . . . That [the death of a President in midterm] has happened too often in the past. And if that tragedy should occur, we have to step in there without any margin for error. . . ."

heartland the strategic central area of a nation or a land mass; in American political usage, those noncoastal sections where spiritual and moral values are said to be most revered.

The geopolitical theory expounded by Sir Halford Mackinder in 1904 held that Eastern Europe's "heartland" could dominate the continent of Eurasia. From the Elbe to the Amur, the idea went, a self-sufficient area existed that could not be challenged by British mastery of the seas, and held the key to world domination. Naturally, this theory was vigorously disputed by exponents of British seapower.

The modern political use of the word stemmed from Dwight Eisenhower's 1945 Guildhall speech in London, where he referred to his boyhood in Abilene, Kan.: "I come from the very heart of America." There was a double meaning to this, geographic and spiritual, which was picked up by Richard Nixon in the Landon Lecture he delivered at Kansas State University, September 16, 1970: "Now, twenty-five years later, as I speak in the heart of America, I can truly say to you here today you are the heart of America—and the heart of America is strong. The

heart of America is good. The heart of America is sound. It will give—you will give us—the sound and responsible leadership that the great promise of America calls for . . ."

Political analyst Kevin Phillips applied the old geopolitical word to modern U.S. politics in his 1969 book, *The Emerging Republican Majority:* "Twenty-one of the twenty-five Heartland states supported Richard Nixon in 1968. . . . Over the remainder of the century, the Heartland should dominate American politics in tandem with suburbia, the South, and Sun Belt-swayed California." See SUNBELT.

Although the word continues to have this geopolitical meaning, it is more commonly used in a less specific context. "I am always pleased to be here in this great heartland of America," President Nixon told a group of Indiana's elderly citizens in 1971. Garnett Horner, writing in the *Washington Star* on June 25, 1971, used the word in its current spiritual-geographic sense: "'It gives me a lift,' President Nixon remarked during an unscheduled sixty-eight-mile sentimental auto journey through a corn growing section of the heartland of America." *New York Times* correspondent Seymour Topping wrote on July 16, 1971: "The willingness of the President to travel to Peking, to the heartland of the Asian Communist world, cannot fail to impress the Chinese . . ."

hearts and minds. See SLOGANS.

heckle to harass a person, usually a speaker, with comments or questions in the hope of embarrassing or silencing him.

Nikita Khrushchev was heckled at a dinner of the Economics Club of New York in 1959, and won the respect of his audience by skillfully handling the heckler: "I am an old sparrow, so to say, and you cannot muddle me by your cries."

The Middle English word "hekele" meant to comb flax, to tease or ruffle hemp. As early as 1808, a Scottish dictionary began carrying a second definition for "heckle"—"to tease with questions."

Few hecklers today stop at teasing. Most try to make the heckled angry. If the heckled loses his temper, the heckler has won his point.

In 1906 the *New York Times* considered the word fit enough to use in that way and ran a headline: "Hearst Is Heckled Into Talking Taxes."

Campaigning politicians are continually heckled. Their retorts, often carefully written ad libs, if clever enough, can quiet the hecklers quickly. During the 1960 campaign John F. Kennedy was often met by determined and loud young Republican hecklers. Whenever he was faced with a "We want Nixon!" chant, he replied with a good-humored, "I don't think you're going to get him." This was not brilliant repartee, but it pleased crowds and eased the tension and embarrassment of a crowd toward the hecklers within it.

In the same campaign Richard Nixon found that all heckling need not be audible, nor even in English. In Chinatown, Los Angeles, courtesy of Democratic prankster Dick Tuck, there was a huge billboard with a smiling picture of Nixon with the words "Welcome Nixon." However, in Chinese characters the sign asked, "What about the Hughes loan?," a Democratic allegation that Nixon had abused the trust of his office to obtain financial aid for his family.

Sometimes a hard answer can turn away a wrathful heckler. 1964 Republican presidential candidate Barry Goldwater was giving a relatively quiet speech at Rutgers University when a young man leapt to his feet and shouted, "You goddam Fascist bastard!" Goldwater won cheers from a generally hostile audience when he replied, "If you call me a bastard again, I'll meet you outside." Some observers found it fascinating to note at which word he took offense.

Most American politicians, accustomed to what they consider the art of heckling, are amazed at the violence of the heckling in England. On the stump, British candidates often have great difficulty in making themselves heard over the shouts and catcalls of groups of men who come equipped with loudspeakers. However, charming heckling is also a British trait. Sir Alec Douglas-Home, when he was a British Foreign Secretary, said he received the following telegram from an irate citizen: "To hell with you. Offensive letter follows."

heft, political gravitas; weight or substance as a candidate, based on experience or intellectual capacity, or the seriousness with which the public treats his candidacy.

This is a word used frequently in discussions of a candidate's potential, with written citations dating back to 1969, when *Business Week* wrote of "twenty-four House Democrats with political heft." "He's got heft," the opposite of "He's a LIGHTWEIGHT," is usually accompanied by a rising and falling motion of the hand, as if the pleasurable weight of a roll of dimes was being hefted.

The term can be used to cast doubts on political staffs as well as on politicians themselves. *Time* magazine wrote of the new Clinton Administration in January 1993: "Several party veterans predict privately that the President-elect will need to be far more decisive. . . . Last week many of the same officials questioned whether Clinton had chosen a staff of sufficient depth and heft to meet the challenge."

An ancient meaning of the word is to raise aloft ("Inflamed with wrath his raging blade he heft"—Spenser), a past tense of "heave"; a colloquial meaning has long been "influence," which is figurative weight, and its usage increased among politicians in the sixties.

hegemony   domination by one state over others.

Hegemony (preferred accent on the "gem") is the dirty word for leadership. In Greek, a *hegemon* is a leader; among the warring Greek city-states, Athens sought hegemony. Among individuals, this sort of leadership is often seen as laudable, but among states it has always been perceived as predatory. In 1860 the *Times* of London wrote: "No doubt it is a glorious ambition which drives Prussia to assert her claim to the leadership, or as that land of professors phrases it, the 'hegemony' of the German Confederation." In the U.S., *Forum* wrote in 1904: "The hegemon of the Western Hemisphere is the United States."

The word was popularized more recently by Mao Tse-tung. "Dig tunnels deep," he counseled, "store grain, and never seek hegemony." As the split developed in the Communist world, the crucial epithet became "hegemony"—secondarily the domination of imperialism, but primarily Mao's denunciation of the attempt by the Soviet Union to dominate China. When Communist parties in Western Europe sought to show their independence from Moscow so as to improve their appeal locally, "hegemony" was their attack word as well. One Italian Communist suggested that the Marxist "dictatorship of the proletariat" be changed to "the hegemony of the working class." See EUROCOMMUNISM.

In his 1977 book, *A Civil Tongue,*

Edwin Newman had some fun with the word:

> The Soviet and Chinese governments have a way of insulting each other that is peculiarly their own. You seek hegemony, the Chinese will tell the Russians. You seek hegemony, the Russians will tell the Chinese. In the 1950's, some of us on the outside thought that the two governments might be seeking hegemony together, but their paths parted. Ever since, according to the Chinese, the Russians have been looking for hegemony high and low and in every nook and cranny, while according to the Russians the Chinese are obsessed with hegemony and think of nothing else except, in lighter moments, inciting a third world war. An unnamed Pakistani has told the *New York Times,* "The Indians have been bitten by the bug of wanting hegemony of the subcontinent." The *Times* found an Indian to deny it. The hegemoniacal debate goes on.

The term resurfaced in early 1993 in charges that the U.S. and Britain were manipulating the world's currency markets. Pierre Beregovoy, the Socialist prime minister of France, wrote in *Le Monde,* according to the *Washington Post,* that "America was engaged in a drive for global economic hegemony, leaving it bound to oppose a single European currency." Jacques Delors, president of the European Commission, said, "I cannot confirm or deny the existence of such a plot, but I do not exclude that others have evidence."

heir apparent   the chosen successor, who does not always succeed in a democratic society.

If the man at the top feels secure enough, he will designate an heir apparent to carry on his policies after his term or life is over. From the boss's viewpoint, the advantage is a cessation of bickering below; the disadvantage is boredom below, or an unexpected bid for power by the second in command. See HAND-PICKED.

Martin Van Buren was Andrew Jackson's heir apparent, and William Howard Taft had been publicly tapped by Theodore Roosevelt. But "Little Van" could not carry the Jacksonian tradition past a single term. Roosevelt turned on Taft and ran as an independent against him, splitting the Republican vote enough to elect Woodrow Wilson.

Splitting heirs, the *heir expectant* is one who is simply in line for some inheritance; the *heir presumptive* is one who will succeed if the top man dies or quits immediately, but who can be replaced by the birth of a closer relative; and the *heir apparent* is the man to stop when the top man lets his power slip.

Hell before breakfast. See RIGHT TO KNOW.

hellbent for election determined to the point of recklessness; evoking an image of a spirited, horn-blowing, flag-flying campaign.

The phrase appears to have its political origin in Maine in 1840, year of the "Tippecanoe and Tyler Too" election. Edward Kent won the gubernatorial election handily, and a ditty ran: "Maine Went Hellbent For Governor Kent."

See FLAT-OUT.

henchman in fact, a member of the staff of a candidate or party; in an attack, a stooge, hatchetman, hanger-on.

This word has deep roots, starting with the Anglo-Saxon *hengest,* or horse; a hengest-man was a groom, squire, or page. In the Scottish Highlands, the henchman became a gillie, or right-hand man, to the clan leader, where the word picked up its political meaning of a loyal supporter and active worker.

The word is only used pejoratively; nobody ever claims to be anybody else's henchman. Typical use was by Alfred Landon in 1936: "Idealists may have been at the front door preaching social justice, but party henchmen have been at the back door handing out jobs."

A rare but colorful synonym is *janissary,* taken from the sultan's guard in Turkey. For differentiation in current usage, see HACK; HATCHETMAN.

hidebound narrow-minded, reactionary, stubborn; an attack word on conservatives.

In a cliché fight, *a hidebound conservative* could square off with a *bleeding-heart liberal.* The *OED* tracks the word back to Cooper's *Thesaurus* of 1559, talking about a "sickenesse of cattall . . . when their skynnes dooe cleve fast to their bodies, hyde bounde."

The term is still in use. *Business Week* wrote in April 1993 about teachers' unions, including a reference to "the larger and more hidebound National Education Association."

See DYED-IN-THE-WOOL; MOSSBACK; ROCK-RIBBED.

highbinder. See SPELLBINDER.

high cost of living perennial political complaint about inflation; standard charge by the party out of power.

The 1972 *OED Supplement* credits American author William Dean Howells with the earliest use of "cost of living" in 1896: "The pay is not only increased in proportion to the cost of living, but it is really greater."

The earliest political use that this lexicographer has spotted is in the 1912 *Republican Campaign Textbook,* where the subject is addressed as "The Advance in the Cost of Living." The Taft Administration was under attack by Democrats on the tariff issue, and the

Republican National Committee defended itself in this way:

"The increasing cost in recent years of the common necessaries and comforts of life has presented a serious problem to the masses of the people, not alone from the practical side of adjusting expenses to earnings, but also as to the political and economic side, as to whether the advance is to conditions peculiar to the system being applied in our government. It has been charged and is being constantly charged that it is due, in some mysterious way, to the protective tariff and to other conditions assumed to be related to the protective system.

"The most striking feature of the situation, however, is that the advance is not confined to this country or to the countries having protective tariffs, but is world wide, and that in every country the same kind of an agitation is going on, with more or less effort to lay the blame upon 'the party in power' . . ."

The Republicans, split by Teddy Roosevelt's "Bull Moose" party, lost in 1912 to Woodrow Wilson. By 1920, after eight Democratic years, the Republican textbook added an adjective and made the issue its own, using "The High Cost of Living" as its chapter heading:

"To the plain citizen of the United States the term 'High Cost of Living' has a clear and definite meaning. It sums up the hardship and suffering that the American people have borne during the past five years, because of the great rise in the prices of the goods and of the services upon which their income is ordinarily spent." The Republicans had the reason: "The prime cause of the 'High Cost of Living' has been, first and foremost, a fifty percent depreciation of the purchasing power of the dollar, due to a gross expansion of our currency and credit." The party also blamed "re-duced production, burdensome taxation, wage advances and the increased demand for goods."

Two generations later the charge and phrase are in current use. The word INFLATION is used when the consumer price index is approaching DOUBLE DIGIT proportions, and the plainer "high cost of living" (no longer capitalized)—with its vague suggestion that the cost can be brought down—is used to express general dissatisfaction when inflation is not so high.

higher law an appeal to moral or spiritual authority to excuse refusal to obey the laws of man.

This was an abolitionist phrase, probably used first by William Ellery Channing in 1842: "On this point the Constitution, and a still higher law, that of nature and God, speak the same language; and we must insist that these high authorities shall be revered." Senator Daniel Webster agreed. The phrase was taken up by William Seward, of New York, in an antislavery speech in the Senate in 1850: "I know there are laws of various kinds, which regulate the conduct of men . . . But there is a higher law than the Constitution, which regulates our authority over the domain."

Democrats and Whigs (including Abraham Lincoln) thought Seward had gone too far; later this phrase, along with Seward's 1858 characterization of the slavery issue as "an irrepressible conflict," led to Seward's defeat and Lincoln's victory at the Republican convention of 1860.

The idea of a "higher law" has usually conflicted with the RULE OF LAW and a GOVERNMENT OF LAWS, NOT OF MEN. It has been used by dissenters from established laws as justification for civil disobedience. In 1968 the *National Observer* wrote: "America must renounce the popular and poisonous philosophies that glorify anarchy as a heroic response to a 'higher law.'"

The phrase, however, has an idealistic or moralistic ring, and is not usually considered anarchic, or—as used against Seward—anticonstitutional.

Fawn Hall, secretary to Lieutenant Colonel Oliver L. North at the National Security Council, echoed the phrase in her testimony at the Iran-contra hearings in 1987. Asked whether she realized that altering official documents was wrong, she replied, "Sometimes you have to go above the written law."

See CIVIL DISOBEDIENCE.

highest authority. See AUTHORITA-TIVE SOURCES; BACKGROUNDER.

highest note in the scale theory. See OVEREXPOSURE.

high muckey-mucks. See MUCKEY-MUCKS.

high road . . . low road rational approach versus emotional appeal; sticking to the issues versus going for the jugular; Marquis of Queensberry rules versus no-holds-barred.

The phrase became popular in the presidential campaign of 1948, when Republican Thomas E. Dewey selected "the high road" and let voters draw their own conclusions as to what road President Harry Truman was trudging. When Truman compared Dewey's mustache to Adolf Hitler's, Dewey wired Republican state chairmen to see if they thought he should take off the gloves and reply in kind (in earlier campaigns, Dewey had gained a reputation as a slashing speaker). "They all agreed," said GOP speechwriter John Franklin Carter, "that the proper thing for Dewey to do was to ignore Truman's personal attack and continue along the high road to the White House."

Politicians do not consider a "low road" charge the worst kind of insult. In 1958's off-year elections, Eisenhower aide Sherman Adams rehashed charges of Democratic catastrophes like losing our atomic secrets, losing China to the Communists, and described the Korean War as the one "they couldn't end." In Adams's memoirs, he admits: "I was loudly (and not quite inaccurately) accused of 'taking the low road' while the President was keeping his campaign oratory on a high and dignified level."

But the low road is not always an effective course. In the Democratic primary contest for Massachusetts senator in 1962 between Attorney General Edward McCormack and Ted Kennedy, McCormack, trailing, decided to attack Kennedy in a televised debate. The political editor of the *Boston Herald* wrote: "[McCormack's] attack on Kennedy, and the latter's refusal to be drawn into an Army base brawl, apparently created unfavorable reaction to the Attorney General among many viewers, especially women. . . . Kennedy took the high road, and, although he was battered and mauled by McCormack, probably won a strategic victory with the huge TV audience."

Ted Kennedy was following John F. Kennedy's strategy at the 1960 Democratic convention, when Lyndon Johnson baited him in a debate before a joint caucus of the Texas and Massachusetts delegations. *Washington Post* publisher Philip Graham urged Johnson to present himself as a man of wide experience in defense and foreign affairs and avoid the kind of comments about Kennedy's health and his father's alleged pro-Nazi record that Johnson supporters were spreading. Pro-Kennedy historian Arthur Schlesinger, Jr., wrote later: "During the debate Johnson opened with Graham's 'high road' but went on to attempt the personal thrusts which Kennedy parried with such ease and mastery."

Derivation: a "high road," or high way, is the easy way in English usage. In London today the "high streets" are the main traffic arteries. However, the takers of low roads can sometimes make better time, as the balladeer in "Loch Lomond" indicates: "O ye'll take the high road and I'll take the low road and I'll be in Scotland afore ye . . ."

Hill, the Capitol Hill; term for the legislative branch of U.S. government, as White House is for the executive branch.

"On the Hill" is frequently used in roundups of news from Washington, D.C.; White House aides for legislative liaison take messages "up to the Hill." (The judiciary has a similar metaphor, with indictments being handed "up"—to the bench—and decisions handed "down"—from the bench.)

The Hill is real as well as figurative. The base of the Capitol sits 88 feet above sea level, as compared with the White House's 55 feet, with lower areas in between. Before November 21, 1800, when Congress moved from Philadelphia and held its first session in the new Capitol, the eminence was known as "Jenkins Hill," presumably from Thomas Jenkins, who rented the land from one Daniel Carroll, who owned it. Both George Washington and Pierre L'Enfant, who laid out the city of Washington, referred to "Jenkins Hill" in letters.

It is by no means the tallest hill in Washington—the hill on which the National Cathedral stands is over 300 feet—but it is the one that dominates the scene.

Although *the Hill* implies power, an unrelated metaphor, *over the hill*, implies the diminution of power, as even legislators become as *old as the hills*.

hippie language. See COUNTERCULTURE.

historic compromise the bid by Italian Communists to accept a share of national power as part of a multiparty coalition.

In the early seventies, as the Italian Communist party grew in voting strength in local elections, the idea was broached that a coalition might be possible with the long-ruling rightist party, the Christian Democrats.

Arrigo Levi, editor of Italy's *La Stampa*, replied to the author's query with this derivation of the phrase:

"As to 'historic compromise': this was coined by [Enrico] Berlinguer himself, in the famous articles which appeared in the pci's [Italian Communist Party] weekly *Rinascita*, also republished in *l'Unità*, after the end of [Chilean President Salvatore] Allende, as a comment on the reasons that had led to his fall. Fundamentally, Berlinguer criticized Allende's policy of trying to split Chilean Christian Democracy, stated that the pci's policy in Italy was to try and achieve a 'historical compromise' with the whole of Democrazia Cristiana, in order to prevent the kind of reaction which happened in Chile. Though later somewhat criticized by the former leader Luigi Longo, who didn't like the word 'compromise' because of its negative connotations, it has remained as the official 'line' of the party. The *Rinascita* articles appeared on September 28, October 5 and 10, 1973."

The term, whose meaning has broadened, was used in February 1993 at a Capitol Hill hearing on the Middle East: "Perhaps most encouraging for the PEACE PROCESS is the evidence that many Israelis and many Arabs are tired of the conflict and are finally ready for a historic compromise."

See EUROCOMMUNISM.

hit list persons or projects targeted for removal.

In underworld lingo, a "hit" is a murder; a "hit man" is a hired assassin. On the analogy of an older phrase, "shit list," it followed that a "hit list" was a group of individuals to be exterminated.

In politics, the phrase is usually used at a time of transition between Administrations, when the new "Ins" are examining rosters to see what plums are available for replacement with the faithful. If those who are selected for removal can claim any civil service protection, they charge that they have been placed on an Administration "hit list," giving a sinister connotation to old-fashioned PATRONAGE.

The term has also been adopted by the religious right. "Conservative evangelicals," reported the September 15, 1982, *U.S. News & World Report*, "also have drawn up a 'Christian hit list' of liberal members of Congress considered vulnerable in this fall's elections."

The opposite of a hit list for projects is a "must list," a term for top-priority legislation. *New York Times* Albany reporter Steven Weisman wrote in 1976: "In the Capitol, where one man's 'must' is another man's 'maybe,' all the leaders circulate their 'must lists' among themselves to make sure that the bills that 'must' be passed are, in fact, passed. Lists are so popular in Albany that some aides keep lists of their lists." (For a list list, see ENEMIES LIST.)

The nonmurderous, but besmearing, use of "hit" appears to be growing. Carter Administration Attorney General Griffin Bell denounced a newspaper story about him as "nothing less than a 'hit job,'" thus being the first to marry "hit" to "hatchet job," and the *New York Times* on November 17, 1977, reported that the writer so accused "resented [the story] being characterized, even without naming her, as a 'hit job.'"

Hizzoner a sobriquet bestowed on all mayors by writers with an instinct for the jocular.

"Hizzoner the Mayor," for "His Honor the Mayor," was a frequent sound in New York during the incumbency of Fiorello H. La Guardia. Since "the Little Flower" was not stuffy, the playful derogation of the honorific title seemed in place, and has become a part of big-city mayoralties, much as "Veep" has loosely attached itself to the vice presidency. A refinement was introduced when Richard Daley of Chicago was known as "Hizzoner duh Mare."

In December 1977, *Time* reported that the West Virginia town of Coalton was having trouble finding a citizen to serve as mayor, for a salary of only $100 a year. The headline: "It's No Honor to Be Hizzoner."

Washingtonian magazine resurrected the Daley usage in 1993: "'Vote early, vote often.' The most famous axiom of machine politics has already been encoded in your Motor Voter bill, which will extend a uniquely Chicago privilege to all corners of America. Hizzoner would be proud."

Hobson's choice a take-it-or-leave it proposition; in politics, a situation in which you vote for one candidate or do not vote at all.

English poet Thomas Ward wrote in 1630: "Where to elect there is but one/'Tis Hobson's choice,—take that or none."

Sir Richard Steele, in *The Spectator*, No. 509, explained the derivation:

> Mr. Tobias Hobson [Thomas Hobson, 1544–1631] from whom we have the expression . . . was a carrier . . . the first in the Island who let out hackney-horses. He lived in Cambridge, and observing that the scholars

rid hard, his manner was to keep a large stable of horses, with boots, bridles, and whips. . . . When a man came for a horse, he was led into the stable, where there was great choice, but he obliged him to take the horse which stood next to the stable-door; so that every customer was alike well served according to his chance, and every horse ridden with the same justice. From whence it became a proverb, when what ought to be your election was forced upon you, to say Hobson's Choice.

Theodore Bernstein, author of *The Careful Writer,* pointed out that it is incorrect to use the phrase as if it meant the kind of choice involved in a dilemma, as in this sentence: "But how long, in Berlin, must we rely on this cruel Hobson's choice between honoring pledges and eviscerating the world?"

The correct use was in this 1910 New Jersey campaign address by Woodrow Wilson, which marked an early use of "new deal" as well: "If it is reorganization, a new deal and a change you are seeking, it is Hobson's choice. I am sorry for you, but it is really vote for me or not vote at all."

A political synonym is CLOTHESPIN VOTE, in which the voter puts a metaphorical clothespin on his nose and votes for a candidate he does not like because he sees no other choice.

hold still . . . go along   the grudging willingness of a politician to accept publicly, or not to fight privately, a proposed project.

Hold still indicates a greater degree of personal objection and an unwillingness to support publicly; *go along* in current political usage means the political leader will remain passive and indicate his support when asked. For example, "We can't get him to go along, but he'll hold still—he'll have to bite the bullet, but he won't bolt."

When Alice Roosevelt Longworth expressed doubts to George Harvey about the selection of Warren Harding as a candidate, Harvey explained that Harding was best because he would "go along."

Wrote John F. Kennedy in *Profiles in Courage:* "The question is how we will compromise and with whom. For it is easy to seize upon unnecessary concessions, not as means of legitimately resolving conflicts but as methods of 'going along.'"

An old saying in the U.S. Senate is: "The way to get along is to go along." In 1958 Arthur Krock wrote a bit of doggerel called "Wisdom of a House Freshman" that sums up the point:

I love Speaker Rayburn,
His heart is so warm,
And if I obey him
He'll do me no harm.
So I shan't sass the Speaker
One least little bitty
And then I'll wind up
On a major committee.

Degrees of "going along" range from "willingly" to "grudgingly" to "kicking and screaming." The last cannot be used with "hold still."

hold the line   government efforts to restrain the economy; anti-inflation moves.

Four months after he became President, Harry Truman issued an Executive Order gradually relaxing controls over prices, wages, and production as the wartime economy made its transition to peace. This became known as the "hold-the-line order."

"Holding the line against inflation" remains a cliché, taken from a football metaphor ("Hold-that-line!") which in turn comes from a military expression (a line of soldiers trying to prevent an enemy breakthrough).

Other inflation bromides include *inflationary spiral* and *runaway inflation* which *erodes the purchasing power of your dollars* and hurts most *those on fixed incomes.* See INFLATION; DOUBLE DIGIT; OVERHEATED ECONOMY.

Columnist Art Buchwald quoted a mythical professor of the Grim Economic Institute as predicting for 1968: "An inflationary spiral followed by a wage and price merry-go-round which will eventually lead to a roller coaster ride ending on a ferris wheel cycle of high interest rates."

holier than thou. See DO-GOODER; RELIGIOUS METAPHORS.

holistic emphasizing the whole rather than the parts; in politics, mystically comprehensive.

This adjective is based on the 1926 noun *holism,* coined by Jan Christiaan Smuts, who first served as Prime Minister of the Union of South Africa from 1919 to 1924. Smuts developed a theory of evolution in his book, *Holism and Evolution,* in which units are continually integrating into systems; he applied the theory in politics to the British Empire and the League of Nations. Smuts wrote, "The whole-making, holistic tendency, or Holism, operating in and through particular wholes, is seen at all stages of existence."

Within a generation, nutritionists were applying the word to unorthodox approaches to medicine and health. Although traditionalists derogated this sense, *holistic* has since been applied to politics in describing ways of thinking that stress the entirety as more than the sum of its parts.

When Mario Cuomo considered entering the 1992 Presidential race, he used the term in describing a "progressive free-enterprise economy." Cuomo said, "I think the key to my plan is that it is holistic." Recognizing the possible derision of traditionalists, he added, "I told the Fortune 500 CEO's, 'Think of it as *holistic*—but don't use that word; they'll think you smoke marijuana.'"

Holocaust, the the systematic murder of six million Jews during the Nazi regime in Germany.

After World War II the murder of the Jews spawned a new word, "genocide," the coinage of U.S. scholar Raphael Lamkin, and the United Nations in 1948 passed a Convention on the Punishment of the Crime of Genocide.

Somehow, "genocide" was too clinical a description of what had happened; the similar "homicide" is a bureaucratic word for "murder." *Holocaust* first appeared in English around 1250, in a song recounting the Biblical story of Abraham's willingness to sacrifice his son, Isaac, as a burnt offering to God. In 1965 Alexander Donat published a book titled *The Holocaust Kingdom* about the Warsaw Ghetto, and two years later N. Cohn, in *Warrant for Genocide,* wrote that "by the end of 1944 the holocaust was nearing its conclusion." In 1968 the *Manchester Guardian* reported: "There is now within modern history a compartment of 'holocaust studies'—dealing with the wholesale destruction by the Nazis of European Jewry."

"Holo" is rooted in "whole" and "caust" in "burn"—a holocaust is a burnt offering, extended to an all-consuming conflagration. In 1977, when Egyptian President Anwar el-Sadat became the first Arab chief of state to visit Israel, Prime Minister Menachem Begin conducted him to the mausoleum of Yad Vashem, the shrine to the six million Jews who died in what—since only the mid-sixties—has come to be known as the Holocaust.

The word has been extended to encompass more than the mass murder of Jews. From casualties in our Civil War (described then as "a holocaust of lives") to modern genocide in Cambodia, the term has not been limited to any single group. Jews seeking a term for their tragedy have used *Shoah,* the Hebrew word for "catastrophe." Claude Lanzmann entitled his 1985 documentary *Shoah*, a powerful nine-hour history of the killing. The word used often in asserting the need to memorialize the murdered population is *remembrance*, popularized in the title of Herman Wouk's 1978 novel, *War and Remembrance*.

The fear that the Holocaust may be forgotten in coming generations, compounded by the advent of historical "revisionists" who deny or devaluate the Holocaust, has engendered the creation of Holocaust memorials in many parts of the world. One of the most impressive buildings was unveiled in Washington, D.C., in 1993. According to James E. Young, the author of a survey of Holocaust memorials, *The Texture of Memory*, published in 1993, "Today, nearly every major American city is home to at least one, and often several memorials commemorating aspects of the Holocaust."

The slogan, popularized by the militant and marginal Jewish Defense League, recalling the Holocaust, is "Never Again." According to John F. Davenport of New York, this slogan was used first in a 1961 Swedish documentary, *Mein Kampf*, directed by Erwin Leiser; the film ends with a view of Auschwitz accompanied by the narrator's words, "It must never happen again—never again."

When the Holocaust Memorial opened in Washington, D.C., in 1993, Bosnians were being subjected to "ethnic cleansing" by Serbs; speakers recalled the "Never Again" pledge and sought to embarrass President Clinton for allowing genocide to happen again.

See ETHNIC CLEANSING; FINAL SOLUTION.

homeland word used by a group seeking an independent state to assert a moral or historic claim to the territory. This incendiary, evocative term was first used in a political context by Theodor Herzl, at the First Zionist Congress in Basel, Switzerland, in 1897. The "Basel Declaration" called for a Jewish homeland: the German word used was *Heimstätte*, which translates more as "homestead" than the more common *Heimatland*, or "homeland." In 1917, in an effort to marshal Jewish support for the Allies in World War I, British Prime Minister Arthur Balfour embraced the idea in a communication to the second Baron Rothschild.

The Balfour Declaration came close to using the word: "His Majesty's Government view with favor the establishment in Palestine of a national home for the Jewish people . . . nothing shall be done which may prejudice the civil and religious rights of existing non-Jewish communities in Palestine . . ." Formally approved at Versailles in 1919, Balfour's pledge of a "national home" became the basis of the League of Nations Mandate for Palestine. After World War II, a combination of guilt felt by the Allied powers at their inability to stop the murder of six million Jews in Europe (see HOLOCAUST), gratitude for Jewish efforts in North Africa in the face of some Arab support of the Axis powers, and a fierce determination by Jews for "eretz Israel" led to the UN resolution creating a state out of the Jewish "homeland."

When Arabs on Israel's borders failed, after four wars, to conquer the new nation, they made demands for the "rights" mentioned in the Balfour Declaration; although the Palestine Liberation Organization interpreted those rights as a return of Israel to Arab rule, other Arabs—and their UN supporters—saw "the legitimate rights of the Palestinian people" as meaning a separate state in the West Bank and in the Gaza Strip. This "moderate" demand took the form, in the mid-seventies, of a call by third parties for a "homeland" for the Palestinian refugees. Israelis pointed out that the Jewish state had absorbed all Jewish refugees from Arab states, while Arab states had refused to absorb the Palestinians, using the festering camps as a weapon against Israel. Jewish leaders took umbrage at the use of "homeland"—their word—against them.

Israel's supporters were dismayed when, on March 21, 1977, President Carter told a Clinton, Mass., audience: "There has to be a homeland provided for the Palestinian refugees who have suffered for many, many years." Later he denied that "homeland" meant a separate state, as most people construed it; the President said he preferred an "entity," of ambiguous nature, tied to Jordan.

Another example of the power of the word (which stirs feelings akin to, though not as aggressive as, LEBENS-RAUM) was in its appropriation in the early seventies by the white leadership of the Union of South Africa. Some tribal Bantustans, occupied by blacks, were made politically independent, though they remained economically dependent upon South Africa. Columnist James J. Kilpatrick wrote in 1978 that "this widely scorned program of creating 'homelands'" rested upon "the fundamental fact of South African life: the political, cultural and social identity of the blacks is not national; it is tribal." Columnist William Raspberry countered: "They will play at 'reform'—removing racial barriers at only the country's most expensive hotels, for instance—because they value world opinion. For the same reason, they will put new names on old policies—'homelands' instead of 'bantustans' or 'native reserves.'"

home rule   the demand that a state government grant more autonomy and local self-government to cities and counties.

"In campaign season," wrote the *New York Sun* in 1905, "politicians of all stripes and kinds howl for 'Home Rule!' Then they flood to Albany and ask the Legislature to tinker up what they consider imperfect in the city government."

Injection of the phrase into big-city politics was probably begun by Tom Loftin Johnson in his campaigns for mayor of Cleveland, Ohio, in the early 1900s. The full slogan of the Democratic ticket was: "Home Rule; Three Cent Fare; and Just Taxation."

Opponents of Frank "I AM THE LAW" Hague, mayor of Jersey City, in 1939 elected five anti-Hague commissioners in Bayonne, N.J., on the slogan "Home Rule—Not Hague Rule."

The argument for home rule has always been, "the best government is that government which is closest to the people." The argument against it is that many localities are hesitant to take unpopular but necessary steps in taxation, school construction, etc. The argument reaches its highest pitch when a major city in a state is controlled by one party and the state government by another.

Origin of the phrase is English, about 1860, in connection with agitation for self-government in Ireland. Benjamin Disraeli, speaking in Manchester in 1872, suggested that with international troubles brewing, England might be wise to have a loyal Ireland to call upon: "Our connection with Ireland will then be brought painfully to our consciousness, and I should not be at all surprised if the visor of Home Rule should fall off some day, and you beheld a very different countenance." The Home Rule movement, led by the Sinn Fein, ultimately founded the Irish Free State; Northern Ireland remained a part of Great Britain, operating under a Home Rule Act. Modern descendants of the Home Rule movement continue to agitate for an end to partition.

See SHORTCHANGE; DEVOLUTION.

honcho as a noun, the one in charge; as a verb, to follow through.

This Japanese word was brought to the White House in the late sixties by Nixon staffers from California; it began as a noun—"Who's the honcho on this project?"—and soon acquired a verb usage: "Honcho this and don't let it get lost in the bureaucracy."

honest graft money made as a result of political power, without doing anything illegal—no longer considered permissible.

New York newspaperman William Riordan took down and reshaped the thoughts of Tammany leader George Washington Plunkitt as he held court on his favorite rostrum, the New York County Court house bootblack stand in 1905:

> Everybody is talkin' these days about Tammany men growin' rich on graft, but nobody thinks of drawin' the distinction between honest graft and dishonest graft. There's all the difference in the world between the two. Yes, many of our men have grown rich in politics. I have myself. I've made a big fortune out of the game, and I'm gettin' richer every day, but I've not gone in for dishonest graft—blackmailin' gamblers, saloonkeepers, disorderly people, etc.—and neither has any of the men who have made big fortunes in politics.
>
> There's an honest graft, and I'm an example of how it works. I might sum up the whole thing by sayin': "I seen my opportunities and took 'em.". . .
>
> I'll tell you of one case. They were goin' to fix up a big park, no matter where. I got on to it, and went lookin' about for land in that neighborhood.
>
> I could get nothin' at a bargain but a big piece of swamp, but I took it fast enough and held on to it. What turned out was just what I counted on. They couldn't make the park complete without Plunkitt's swamp, and they had to pay a good price for it. Anything dishonest in that?

Times have changed, and such graft is no longer considered "honest." Such gains by a politician or any member of his family are now considered ill-gotten; bribery is permissible only to the extent of "something that can be eaten or smoked in a single day."

Today's "honest graft" is more ephemeral: government officials, when they retire, take jobs with private industry. Admirals who have steered government cargo to certain steamship lines, planning commissioners who have pressed certain zoning matters, find themselves paid off in a way that arouses little or no criticism. It is considered "honest." But it is graft. In the late seventies, this practice became known as the "revolving door," and President Carter proposed legislation that would curb the modern version of Plunkitt's technique.

The term, however, continues to be used. The *National Journal* commented in 1990 on Congress and campaign contributions: "The question is whether the system of 'honest graft' . . . is gridlocking legislation and squeezing the competition out of Congressional elections."

See BOODLE; GRAFT.

honeymoon period the short time after first taking office during which a public official is not set upon by the press.

"Kingdoms have their honeymoon," wrote Thomas Fuller in 1655, "when new Princes are married unto them." The political use is among the first *OED* citations of the word.

"The honeymoon is over." This phrase is used as the interval between election and disenchantment is about to end. In this period, the news generated by an administration on any level of government is primarily appointments, announcements of plans, often a quick vacation that the public considers well-deserved. The opposition cannot carp without appearing to be sore losers; the press has little to criticize and many reporters are even willing to give the new man the benefit of the doubt. In historian Charles Beard's phrase, a "golden glow" emanates from the press.

"Every newly elected Governor," wrote Adlai Stevenson's biographer, Kenneth S. Davis, "has his 'honeymoon' period with the press of the State. Stevenson's [in Illinois] was unusually ecstatic and unusually prolonged."

On the other hand, California Governor Ronald Reagan took some controversial steps regarding the University of California soon after assuming office in 1967 and was promptly blasted by many newspapers. After four months in office, he said: "If this has been a honeymoon, then I've been sleeping alone."

The shortest honeymoon on record for any President was recounted by columnist Murray Kempton in the *New York Post* in December 1977. Colonel Robert McCormick, late publisher of the *Chicago Tribune,* was watching the news tickers in his office in March of 1929, as President Herbert Hoover's inaugural address was being dispatched. After the fourth paragraph he fired his response to his Washington bureau: "This man Hoover wont do. McCormick."

The word refers, of course, to the vacation after a marriage and before settling down, and is derived from the thought that the honeymoon, or full moon, begins to wane from the moment it is full.

honkie. See CHARLIE.

hoopla devices and techniques to stimulate enthusiasm.

"Hoo" is the sound of excitement and gaiety. "Hooray" and "Hoohah!" along with "Whoopee" and "Whoop-de-do" all probably derive from the excited squeals of children.

In politics, hoopla is a necessary ingredient to campaigns to give them bounce, youthfulness, and a sense of fun. At the opening of Rockefeller headquarters at the New York Hilton in the 1966 campaign for governor, Gilbert Robinson, the man in charge of hoopla, was discussing budget with the office manager. He pointed out that an opening rally required balloons, buttons, a sound truck with bunting, and hats and sashes for the "Rockyettes." Multicolored confetti, he explained, cost 10 cents a package, but it was cheaper if you bought it by the pound, at 50 cents per pound.

"I can't give you a budget," the rally man explained, "until I know how big a rally you want."

"Figure a thousand people," the office manager said.

"You want a lot of hoopla?"

The man in charge of the budget took out a requisition slip and calculated rapidly. "Give me fifty pounds of hoopla."

See BALLYHOO; BANDWAGON.

Hooverize originally, to behave in a humanitarian way; since the Depression, to pauperize.

The word reflects the extremes of attitudes toward the late President Herbert Hoover. The verb was first used in 1917, after the first regulations of Hoover's Food Administration were published. It was widely and favorably applied after Hoover's postwar feats—providing food for the Belgians and sending aid to Russia and other devastated lands.

During the Depression, the Democrats made the word synonymous with poverty and despair. A whole class of related words came into being: Hoovervilles—the shabby shantytowns occupied by the jobless, also known as Hoover villages; Hoover soup; and Hoover prosperity. The Democrats ridiculed Hoover's originally optimistic attitude toward the Depression. "Prosperity," they said, "is just Hoovering around the corner." Rhetoric warning of economic doom is sometimes still called RUNNING AGAINST HOOVER.

Thomas V. DiBacco, an American University historian, recounts the most popular valentine verse of World War I, when Hoover was food administrator and his name became synonymous with conserving: "I can Hooverize on dinners, / And on lights and fuel, too, / But I'll never learn to Hooverize / When it comes to loving you."

See RUGGED INDIVIDUALISM; CHICKEN IN EVERY POT.

horse-and-buggy hopelessly old-fashioned; out-of-date.

The phrase became political parlance when Franklin Roosevelt denounced the Supreme Court decision in 1935 striking down the National Recovery Act (see NINE OLD MEN). FDR called the decision "horse-and-buggy law."

A generation later, Rev. Martin Luther King, Jr., used the metaphor in his letter from a Birmingham, Alabama, jail: "The nations of Asia and Africa are moving with jetlike speed toward the goal of political independence, and we still creep at horse-and-buggy pace toward the gaining of a cup of coffee at a lunch counter."

horse-trading hard political bargaining to a conclusion of a deal.

Horse-trading implies a more naked display of power than *bargaining* or *negotiating* and has a no-nonsense connotation.

A good example of the technique was outlined by William V. Reichel, Republican national committeeman from California, to the California delegation committed to Earl Warren in 1944: "We have fifty convention delegates and we're going to get something. At the convention, our votes will get us a Western cabinet member, a Western Supreme Court Justice, and a Western man on every high policy-making body in the government. That's what Warren will be bargaining for. We'll get them or they won't get our votes." As it happened, Warren wound up the vice-presidential nominee on the Dewey ticket, but its loss to Truman and Barkley meant that the horse-trading was all for naught.

hot button word or issue that ignites anger, fear, enthusiasm, or other passionate response.

The phrase is often hyphenated and used adjectivally in *hot-button issue*. Such an issue, frequently involving values or morals, serves to lift an audience out of its seats.

Hot button, perhaps related to *panic button*, began as a marketing term. Walter Kiechel 3d wrote in a September 1978 issue of *Fortune:* "The marketers are searching for what they call 'consumer hot buttons'—needs to be satisfied, desires to be slaked—and the means to push those buttons."

Real-estate brokers picked up the term to refer to fine detailing in home sales; saunas or gold-plated fixtures are examples of "hot buttons" to help close a deal. Computer users have "hot buttons" that can split a screen into two windows with a single keystroke, allowing various sets of data to be seen simultaneously.

Since 1981, *hot button* has been used in political jargon. John L. Stevens, then director of the Republican Governors Association, told the *Washington Post* in 1981, "There are a whole lot of *hot buttons* waiting to be pushed; we're still trying to find out what those buttons are."

Politics, in fact, has become the primary area concerned with *hot buttons*.

Newsweek wrote during the 1988 campaign: "What's a *hot button*? It's something a candidate says to instantly show that his values are the voters' values." *Newsweek* listed abortion and guns as Republican *hot buttons*, and Social Security among those of the Democrats.

In the 1992 campaign for the Democratic Presidential nomination, Edmund G. "Jerry" Brown, Jr., was asked if his call to cut foreign aid included a reduction in aid to Israel. The former California Governor replied evasively: "You know, that Israel thing is a hot-button issue."

For earlier versions of *hot-button issue*, see GUT ISSUE, SWITCHER, and STIR UP THE ANIMALS; for a later version, see WEDGE ISSUE.

hot line   direct teletype link between world leaders, designed to prevent "accidental war."

The idea for a direct communications link between the heads of government in Washington and Moscow was proposed by newsman Jess Gorkin, editor of the Sunday supplement *Parade*, in 1960. He tells the author he got the idea from the Strategic Air Command's "red telephone" system; in the October 30, 1960, issue of *Parade*, Gorkin referred to a "hot line" that provided the SAC controller with "instant contact with 70 bases in ten countries on four continents."

President John F. Kennedy wrote Gorkin on April 23, 1963: "It is heartening to me that the Soviet Government has agreed in principle to the United States suggestion for a 'hot line' between our two countries. I remember when you first brought this new and imaginative idea to my attention back in 1960 . . . your advocacy of faster communications between the United States and the Soviet Union was sharply underlined during the Cuban crisis . . ."

Jack Raymond, in *Power at the Pentagon*, wrote: "The proposal was made by the United States in the light of the Cuba experience, during which, at times, the President and his aides were uncertain whether the Soviet leaders fully understood the import of steps that could lead to nuclear war." After negotiations in Geneva, the "hot line" was set up in September 1963.

White House press secretary Pierre Salinger recalls that he had discussed the matter with one of his counterparts, Mikhail Kharlamov, in January 1962. "It is a chilling, but historic, fact," Salinger wrote later, "that the Russians did not agree to 'hot line' negotiations until after the Cuban missile crisis of October 1962. The delay could have been fatal."

The first non-test use of the first hot line (other lines between different capitals have followed the White House-to-Kremlin line) was in the Arab-Israeli war in 1967. The story was in this *New York Daily News* dispatch:

Washington, June 8. . . . President Johnson told Soviet Premier Kosygin on the Washington-Moscow hot line today that an American ship had been attacked in the Mediterranean and planes from the U.S. 6th Fleet were flying to its aid.

The White House said Johnson told the Kremlin about the incident so that it wouldn't misinterpret the scrambling of the American planes.

Press Secretary George Christian announced that Johnson and Kosygin had used the hot line teletype link "a number of times" since Monday, when the Arab-Israeli war erupted.

The first message was from Kosygin to Johnson Monday. Johnson responded the same day. The series of messages was the first time the hot line has been used in an actual crisis situation since it was installed August 30, 1963.

The hot line is a leased teletype circuit from the White House in Washington to the Kremlin in Moscow. Transmissions are in English from Washington and Russian from Moscow, with instantaneous translations at the other end.

hot property   an attractive candidate, as seen through the eyes of his political sponsors; a comer.

Columnist Max Lerner wrote in the sixties about Governor Ronald Reagan: "He is the hottest upcoming property on the horizon, as the politicians put it."

The term probably comes from show business, where agents often refer to clients in terms of inanimate chattels, and "properties" are people whose talents are salable. A play, scenario, book, or script may also be termed a hot property if it shows commercial promise.

In 1967 the *New York Times* combined the show business and political meanings in an editorial objecting to the sponsorship of a television series begun by Mayor John Lindsay: "If the Mayor's program were unsponsored, it would be quite another matter. But lending his name and office to a sponsored program is commercialism. The Mayor of New York should be nobody's hot property."

"Hot" is not used in the sense of "hot potato," an issue to be avoided because of its sensitivity, but rather in the sense of Wall Street's "hot issue," an underwriting that is oversubscribed and highly sought-after. See POLITICAL CAPITAL, TO MAKE. Another corporate phrase turned political is LAME DUCK; another show business phrase used in politics is "waiting in the wings."

The word "upcoming," as used by Lerner (above) is journalese, its meaning fluctuating between "forthcoming" and "up-and-coming." Bernard Kilgore, chairman of the board of Dow Jones, sent this note to a *Wall Street Journal* editor: "If I see 'upcoming' in the WSJ again, I will be downcoming and someone will be outgoing." (This formulation was used in 1977 by novelist Peter De Vries to denigrate the word "downplay": "If I heard a speaker use it I would upget and outwalk.")

Hottentots, milk for   attack on foreign aid to underdeveloped nations.

On May 8, 1942, Vice President Henry Wallace made his "century of the common man" speech (see COMMON MAN, CENTURY OF THE), disputing the point of view of the Luce publications that the coming hundred years would be "the American Century." Wallace had been raising the hackles of conservatives with his demand for full employment ("sixty million jobs") and pressing forward on New Deal legislation that had been eclipsed by the war effort. During his speech, he said that he had told the wife of the Soviet ambassador—half in fun and half seriously: "The object of this war is to make sure that everybody in the world has the privilege of drinking a quart of milk a day."

The statement was used as a weapon against Wallace. The Hottentots, a nomadic southwest African tribe with a catchy name, had been used as a symbol of an undeveloped—and undevelopable—people even before Lord Salisbury's "Hottentot Speech" in Parliament in 1886 opposing Irish Home Rule. Dutch explorers named the African tribe Hottentot, according to a 1670 Dutch lexicographer, because of the "clucking speech" of the aborigines. Edgar Allan Poe, in 1840, had used the tribal name as typical of preposterous-sounding words: "The Hottentots and Kickapoos are very well in their way. The Yankees alone are preposterous." Wallace's statement was stretched by conservatives into a policy of "milk for the Hottentots."

"Many of Wallace's progressive and well-meaning speeches," wrote Samuel Rosenman, "about improving the standards of living in backward areas of the world had been so unfortunately phrased that they were distorted by the isolationist press into a statement of readiness to embark on crackbrained and unrealistic projects of worldwide charity handouts."

The phrase remains a symbol of selfless aid, with a connotation of hopelessly impractical idealism. Herman Kahn, listing typical U.S. foreign policy aims in 1962, chose four for discussion: "RULE OF LAW, JUST AND LASTING PEACE, FOUR FREEDOMS, Milk for the Hottentots."

See HAVE AND HAVE-NOT NATIONS; THIRD WORLD.

house an ideological, business, or political entity or movement.

House, like "covenant," is a Biblical word borrowed for political use. "All the house of Israel," "dwell in the House of the Lord," and reference to a church as a House of Prayer or House of God laid the groundwork for the metaphor.

Lincoln in 1858 took a quotation from Mark 3:25, "If a house be divided against itself, that house cannot stand," shortened it to "A house divided against itself cannot stand," and added, "I believe this government cannot endure permanently half slave and half free."

The houses of Parliament and houses of Congress refer more to the political bodies than to the buildings containing them. European business empires such as Rothschild and Krupp referred to themselves as "houses," and a young American banker or broker still seeks a position in a "fine old Wall Street house."

In May 1937, a strike at the Republic Steel plant in Chicago erupted into violence, where thirty strikers were shot, ten of whom died. This "Memorial Day Massacre," low point of labor relations in the "sit-down strike" era of the thirties, brought a surprising remark from FDR: "A plague on both your houses." Later the President tried to explain away his quotation from Shakespeare as applying only to extremists of both sides, but CIO president John L. Lewis turned Roosevelt's use of "house" into the familiar "House of Labor" and intoned over nationwide radio: "It ill behooves one who has supped at labor's table and who has been sheltered in labor's house to curse with equal fervor and fine impartiality both labor and its adversaries when they become locked in deadly embrace."

Woodrow Wilson used a variation on the theme when he referred to Warren G. Harding as a man with "a bungalow mind." Lyndon Johnson told a group of reporters during a 1964 stroll: "The Democratic party has been the House of Protest since it was born."

When Barry Goldwater in 1960 urged his followers to work within the Republican party, despite their dissatisfaction with the Rockefeller-Nixon COMPACT OF FIFTH AVENUE that ensured a liberal platform, he told the convention: "This great Republican party is our historic house. This is our home." The shelter metaphor (price "ceilings," tariff "walls," "floor" fights, "fireside" chats) is used as often as the anatomical metaphor. See BODY POLITIC.

household word a satiric reference to a political figure's low "recognition factor."

Like RED HERRING, this was a phrase used by a reporter in a question that gained fame when accepted and repeated by the man being interviewed.

Richard Nixon's choice of Spiro T. Agnew to be his running mate came as a shock to newsmen covering the Republican convention in 1968. On August 8, just after his choice had been announced, the VP-to-be held a news conference at the Hilton Hotel in Miami Beach. Mike Wallace of CBS observed, "The name of Spiro Agnew is hardly a household political word across the nation." Agnew replied, "I would certainly agree with that, yes." Wallace then went on to ask, ". . . what political strength do you actually bring to the ticket?" The candidate answered, "I can't analyze any strength I bring, and I agree with you that the name of Spiro Agnew is not a household name. I certainly hope that it will become one within the next couple of months."

It did. Two years later, columnist James J. Kilpatrick used the now-famous phrase as a synonym for the Vice President: "The Household Word said some things about higher education, and especially about the folly of 'black quotas' that needed badly to be said."

In use, "household name" became transmuted to the more familiar "household word." With Agnew's forced resignation in 1973, use of the phrase diminished and is recalled now with irony or distaste; on his leaving office, he popularized the Latin phrase *nolo contendere,* a plea of guilty without an admission of guilt.

housekeeping bill seemingly innocuous legislation.

"A tricky term with two meanings that are the opposite of each other," wrote *New York Times* Albany reporter Steven R. Weisman of "housekeeping bill" in 1976. "One meaning refers to a measure that embodies a minor technical or procedural alteration in a law. But when a Democrat (or a Republican) gets up in one of the chambers to say 'this is just a little housekeeping bill,' it's a signal to Republicans (or Democrats) to scrutinize the measure to make sure something of consequence isn't being slipped through by subterfuge."

In 1992, Virginia State Delegate Vin-

cent F. Callahan, Jr., a Republican, commented to the *Washington Post* on a spate of Democrat-sponsored bills: "Most of these are housekeeping bills that change a comma, and there are hundreds of them, and the Democrats can say they got all of their bills passed when half the stuff is just nonsense and a waste of time."

human element personal quirks or characteristics that must be taken into consideration in a political plan; the one element over which detailed planning has no control.

Railroad-accident reports occasionally give as a reason for a disaster "human error," often a euphemism for "the engineer dozed off." In political planning, on a tight schedule, time must be allotted for the human element: a trip to the men's room, or a short belt of gin, or a quick phone call to an old girl friend in the city visited. Allowances must be made for the distressing fact that not all politicians act logically; a known grafter can upset his enemies' plans with an inexplicable burst of altruism or social responsibility, or the man counted on for an introduction can get laryngitis.

When Arthur Schlesinger, Jr., at the 1960 Democratic convention, urged Robert Kennedy to move quickly to conciliate the disappointed Stevenson supporters, Kennedy replied, "Arthur, human nature requires that you allow us forty-eight hours. Adlai has given us a rough time over the last three days. In forty-eight hours, I will do anything you want, but right now I don't want to hear anything about the Stevensonians. You must allow for human nature."

At the same convention, a classic example of the human element was Robert Kennedy's comment regarding the confusion around the selection of Lyndon Johnson as the vice-presidential nominee: "My God, this wouldn't have happened except that we were all too tired last night."

The human element enters into far less consequential political matters. Ambassador Richard C. Patterson, New York City's official greeter during the Robert Wagner administration, called his speechwriter late one night with a problem. He was to introduce South Korean President Syngman Rhee at a Waldorf-Astoria luncheon the next day; part of the introduction was to be a telegram from General Douglas MacArthur praising Rhee's "courage and his indomitable will."

"So you'll read the telegram," the speechwriter said, "and everybody will clap. What's the problem?"

"You're forgetting the human element," said Patterson. "Nine people out of ten will flub on the word 'indomitable'—including me. I can just hear myself saying 'indominitabubble' and everybody laughing and embarrassing the guest of honor. Go ahead—you try it."

"Easy," said the speechwriter, "Indominitabubble."

"You see? Let's substitute another word. We can release the accurate text in written form."

The speechwriter thought a moment. "I got it. You got a pencil? 'Indefatigable.'" There was a long silence as Patterson considered hiring a new speechwriter. Then they settled on "steadfast," and the human element triumphed again.

human rights the idea that each person is born with the moral claim on some political freedom which ought not to be denied by any government.

"Ignorance, neglect or contempt of human rights," reads a declaration of the first National Assembly of France, "are the sole causes of public misfortunes and corruptions of government."

The phrase in French was *droits de l'homme* ("the rights of man") taken from the concept of "natural rights" espoused by English political philosopher John Locke in the seventeenth century. Locke held that man, in a theoretical state of nature, was born free; after he mixed his labor with the common property of nature's abundance, he had property of his own. Man then traded part of his absolute freedom to government, for protection of his person and his property "rights."

Locke's "natural rights" were also called "inherent" and "imprescriptible"; when Thomas Jefferson referred to them in the Declaration of Independence, they were "inalienable." When people were denied these rights by kings, Locke argued with some discretion, they could "appeal to Heaven"— a euphemism for revolution, since the cautiously couched theory struck at the root of the divine right of kings.

For nearly two centuries after the American and French revolutions, human rights were called "the rights of man." That was the title of Thomas Paine's book on the subject, and in Herman Melville's *Billy Budd*, the name of the ship on which his moral tale took place was *The Rights of Man.*

In his book *Political Theory and the Rights of Man* (1967), Professor D. D. Raphael, of the University of Glasgow, explained why the name was changed:

> The concept of Human Rights, as they are called in the English text of the [UN] Universal Declaration of 1948, is of course a revival of the eighteenth-century concept of the Rights of Man. According to Mrs. Eleanor Roosevelt, who was Chairman of the United Nations Commission on Human Rights, the old phrase was changed because of an interpretation given to it, at an early stage of international discussion, by a delegate from some benighted country. "I assume," he blandly remarked, "that when we speak of the rights of man, we mean what we say. My government, of course, could not agree to extend these

rights to women." The French text of the Universal Declaration retains the traditional *droits de l'homme,* perhaps because the French . . . are familiar with the dictum that, in the language of the law, "the male is presumed to embrace the female."

Throughout the fifties and sixties, however, the movement for "rights" was directed at the *civil* rights of American blacks; having achieved their fundamental "human" right to freedom, blacks demanded the equality in voting, education and housing that belonged to them in civil law. The phrase "human rights" was, in those decades—as it was when Woodrow Wilson used it—a ho-hum expression of idealism.

Although President Harry Truman had told the UN conference at San Francisco in 1945 that "the Charter is dedicated to the achievement and observance of human rights and freedoms," the Charter's article 2, section seven, limits that dedication in this way: "Nothing contained in the present Charter shall authorize the UN to intervene in matters which are essentially within the domestic jurisdiction of any state . . ."

Hubert Humphrey, in a defining moment of his career, used the term in his defense of civil rights, when he spoke to the Democratic National Convention of 1948: "There are those who say to you—we are rushing this issue of civil rights. I say we are 172 years late. There are those who say—this issue of civil rights is an infringement on states' rights. The time has arrived for the Democratic Party to get out of the shadow of states' rights and walk forthrightly into the bright sunshine of human rights." (See DIXIECRAT.)

In the early seventies Amnesty International, based in London, raised the money to expand its research and did much to publicize the extent of limitations on political freedom in many countries. In 1974 the House of Representatives International Relations Subcommittee on International Organizations and Movements, chaired by Donald Fraser (D-Minn.), held hearings and published a report that thrust the subject into American political debate.

Daniel Patrick Moynihan, the most outspoken of the American UN ambassadors, became most closely identified with the articulation of human rights in a world grown more statist. He challenged many other diplomats who had hitherto criticized the U.S. with impunity, while their own countries routinely denied citizens basic human rights.

At that time the policies of Secretary of State Henry Kissinger, promoting DÉTENTE with its QUIET DIPLOMACY and pragmatic acceptance of the differences between societies, were coming under widening attack. By the beginning of the election primaries of 1976, "the human rights issue" began to flower, offering hard-line conservatives and moralistic liberals common ground: the assertion of American values in a world made up of so many totalitarian states.

Among conservatives, Ronald Reagan picked up the issue in his nearly successful attempt to wrest the Republican nomination from President Gerald Ford; during that primary season, Democratic candidate Jimmy Carter also embraced the subject and the phrase in his desire to incorporate a different approach into his foreign policy statements.

In his inaugural, Mr. Carter put forward the idea in ringing terms: "Our commitment to human rights must be absolute." When he corresponded with Soviet dissenter Andrei Sakharov, this displeased the Soviet Union, which responded angrily in its propaganda, identifying the American human rights campaign as a part of the hawkish "anti-détente faction of Senator Henry Jackson." At the urging of many foreign policy professionals, and to the dismay of some of his early supporters, President Carter moderated the tone of his speaking out about human rights by the end of his first year in office.

In current political usage, *human rights* means more liberty for dissenters in totalitarian lands; *civil rights* is associated with equality for blacks; and *civil liberties* connotes grim approval for the free speech of people espousing unpopular causes. In the 1990s, human rights became the basis for advocacy of intervention within national borders by those who have overcome the VIETNAM SYNDROME. The term is now often used in diplomacy; intervention is debated by those who limit involvement to defending national interests versus those who believe the U.S. has a responsibility to lead the world in enforcing human rights.

humor, self-deprecating   a politician's attempt to take the sting out of a charge by kidding about it; acknowledging a disadvantage in such a charming way as to turn it to an advantage.

Abraham Lincoln joked about his height and plain looks. "Here am I and here is Mrs. Lincoln. That's the long and short of it." And "The Lord prefers common-looking people. That's the reason he makes so many of them."

Humor has been used often in politics, especially in ridiculing an opponent (Churchill re MacDonald: "sheep in sheep's clothing," see INVECTIVE, POLITICAL) but not until the 1950s did the Lincolnesque technique of poking fun at oneself come into such universal political vogue.

Adlai Stevenson led the way in defeat, quoting Lincoln's story about the little boy who stubbed his toe and was too big to cry and hurt too much to laugh. A few months later he added, "A funny thing happened to me on the way to the White House," and when his auto was delayed by a military funeral he observed, "Military heroes always seem to be getting in my way."

John F. Kennedy carried self-deprecating humor forward. Criticized for appointing his younger brother Attorney General, he innocently observed, "I see nothing wrong with giving Robert some legal experience before he goes out to practice law." (According to Arthur Schlesinger, Jr., Robert protested that this joke was not funny, and his brother told him to get used to kidding himself, because people liked it. "Yes, but you weren't kidding yourself," Robert responded. "You were kidding *me*.") Robert Kennedy took up the technique, introducing candidate Adlai Stevenson III in Illinois with the remark, "If there's one thing I can't stand, it's a fellow running on his family name." Senator Ted Kennedy, who bore the brunt of a "nepotism" and "dynasty" charge in Massachusetts, said that he wanted to be judged on his own so much that he thought of changing his name—from Teddy Kennedy to Teddy Roosevelt. Defusing the "born with a silver spoon" bomb, Ted Kennedy quoted a factory worker who said to him, "Senator, I hear you never worked a day in your life, and this is what a lot of people have against you. I want to tell you, you haven't missed a thing."

Bill Clinton, at his first Gridiron dinner in 1993, took some of the sting out of criticism of the role of the First Lady by saying, "The views I express here are those of my wife." In the 1992 campaign debates, Ross Perot—who had been caricatured with jug-ears—began an answer with "I'm all ears."

Alan L. Otten, *Wall Street Journal* political analyst, wrote: "This type of humor has obvious advantages. It's usually a quick throwaway line, less likely to bore an audience than the old-fashioned long anecdote. It disarms critics by making their target appear unafraid of the criticism. It makes the listener feel this can't be such a bad fellow after all."

Humpty Dumpty   sure loser; a sacrificial lamb.

This nursery rhyme character who "sat on a wall" and "had a great fall" was popularized by Lewis Carroll as an early example of anything-goes linguistics: a word, to Humpty Dumpty, meant anything he chose it to mean.

In politics, a Humpty Dumpty is selected to take a great fall in a hopeless race against an unbeatable opponent. The appellation is always contemptuous.

The "dump" in the phrase was given a twist in 1967 by Florida Governor Claude Kirk, who predicted that President Lyndon Johnson would replace Hubert Humphrey with a more exciting running mate in 1968, calling the gambit "Humphrey Dumphrey." In this way, the ancient Mother Goose phrase may have come full circle: it is believed that the rhyming compound's first word was originally a pet form of "Humphrey."

The name was subtly revived after Nixon's fall by reporters Bob Woodward and Carl Bernstein, in their title *All the President's Men;* the allusion was to the inability of Nixon's aides to put together the Nixon presidency after the cracks of Watergate appeared.

A related term, opposite in meaning, is *Mickey Mouse,* used when any candidate chosen to run could beat the unpopular opponent (see LAUNDRY TICKET). This phrase is also used to mean "inadequate" in more general terms; Roy Innis, director of the Congress of Racial Equality, told a CBS interviewer on June 30, 1968: "I am disgusted with the Mickey Mouse welfare programs . . ."

For the political use of related characters, see TWEEDLEDUM AND TWEEDLEDEE.

Hundred Days   most often applied to the productive special session of Congress summoned by Franklin D. Roosevelt in 1933 to cope with the Depression.

The historical parallel to FDR's Hundred Days was Napoleon's escape from Elba and his triumphant march across Europe that finally culminated in disaster at Waterloo. The time span between Napoleon's escape and abdication, however, was 116 days; the hundred days was applied to Louis XVIII's absence from Paris beginning March 20, 1815, as Napoleon arrived, to June 28, when the King returned in state after Napoleon's defeat. The Count de Chambord, prefect of Paris, coined the phrase: "A hundred days, sire, have elapsed since the fatal moment when your Majesty was forced to quit your capital in the midst of tears." When used in reference to that period, the phrase has now come to mean the time of Napoleon's return rather than the King's exile.

Roosevelt's Hundred Days were equally eventful. During the period from March 9 to June 16—exactly one hundred days—the 73rd Congress enacted such milestone legislation as vast public works and relief measures, guarantees of bank deposits, and tighter federal regulation of the banks, agricultural subsidies, the Tennessee Valley Authority, and others.

"The legislative record it set," wrote Raymond Moley, one of FDR's brain trusters, "the impression it created on the public, its impact upon the economy of the nation, and the incredible speed with which important legislation was planned, considered, proposed and enacted has no parallel in the earlier history of the Republic. Nor has there been any parallel since, except under the exigencies of the war that began eight years later." Not even Lyndon Johnson's 89th Congress was comparable, said Moley, because much of its program "had been inherited from the Kennedy years" or were traceable to the Roosevelt era.

While John F. Kennedy was working on his inaugural address, Theodore Sorensen wrote in *Kennedy*, the late President at one point said impatiently, "I'm sick of reading how we're planning another 'Hundred Days' of miracles. Let's put in that this won't all be finished in a hundred days or a thousand." His finished speech thus read: "All this will not be finished in the first hundred days. Nor will it be finished in the first thousand days, nor in the life of this Administration, nor even perhaps in our lifetime on this planet. But let us begin." Historian Arthur Schlesinger, Jr., chose *A Thousand Days*—the approximate length of the Kennedy Administration—as the title of his history of the period. See "LET US CONTINUE."

Britain's Harold Wilson was less reluctant to exploit what had become a cliché. "What we are going to need," he said during his successful 1964 campaign to lead Labour to power and himself to the prime ministership, "is something like what President Kennedy had after years of stagnation—a program of a hundred days of dynamic action."

During the 1992 Presidential campaign, Bill Clinton offered a less-than-prescient prediction: "If I'm elected . . . I'll have the bills ready the day after I'm inaugurated, I'll send them to Congress and we'll have a 100-day period. It will be the most productive period in modern history."

hundred flowers a governing doctrine that permits open disagreement within an Administration.

In 1957 Mao Tse-tung made a speech that appeared to embrace sweet reason: "Ideological struggle is not like other forms of struggle. Crude, coercive methods should not be used in this struggle, but only the method of painstaking reasoning." He went on to use a vivid metaphor: "Let a hundred flowers blossom and a hundred schools of thought contend."

However, when the flowers blossomed, they were ruthlessly cut down. Historian Sidney Hook wrote: "The Communist Party loosed another fierce campaign of purge and suppression, branding these flowers of doctrine as poisonous weeds which must be chopped down." Peking's *People's Daily*, four months after Mao's speech, completed the metaphor: "Only by letting poisonous weeds show themselves above ground can they be uprooted." Two decades later, after Mao's death and the fall of the radical "gang of four," a limited amount of debate was permitted, especially in the form of wall posters. This recalled the "hundred flowers" phrase, but Chinese leaders disagreed with great circumspection: they had learned their lesson.

In American political usage, the phrase is employed—usually sardonically—in descriptions of public disagreements by Administration leaders. This is often referred to in the press as a "let-a-hundred-flowers-bloom technique," and is more frequently condemned for its seeming confusion than praised for its acceptance of open debate.

The *Washington Post* quoted an unidentified military officer in November 1982 on Ronald Reagan's leadership: "Reagan, in essence, let a hundred flowers bloom early in his Administration and that has caused many of the problems with the antinuclear movement in Europe and the United States."

hunker. See BARNBURNERS; HARD LINE.

hurting. See CRUNCH.

hustings specifically, any place from which a campaign speech is made; generally, the campaign trail.

The original meaning was an assembly, any deliberative body; before written ballots became the law in England in 1872, the husting was the place from which candidates for Parliament addressed the electorate. The best-known husting was the upper end or platform of the Guildhall, where the mayor held court.

The etymology is interesting. In Scandinavian countries the word *thing* is currently the name of legislative assemblies and courts of law, taken from the Old Norse *husthing*, literally "house meeting." Old English dropped an *h* to form *hūsting*, which is now used only in the plural, construed as singular, as "The hustings is a place . . ."

In a classic English translation of Demosthenes' *Oration on the Crown*, the Greek orator says: "In what spirit was I to mount the hustings? In the spirit of one having unworthy counsel to offer?—I should have deserved to perish!"

In current use, *on the hustings, on the stump,* and *on the campaign trail* are synonymous, though the archaic *hustings* is more often used semi-humorously. Stephen Chapman used the term in a 1993 commentary on the new Administration: "During the Presidential campaign, Bill Clinton had all the answers. He's since learned that a variety of problems—gays in the military, Haitian refugees, middle-class taxes—are a lot easier to solve from the hustings than from the Oval Office."

Hymie's ferryboat an analogy about the COATTAIL effect of a strong candidate.

Hymie Schorenstein, Brooklyn's Democratic district leader in the twenties, received a complaint from one of his candidates for a local elective office.

"Why is it, Hymie, that your whole budget for posters and literature is for Governor Roosevelt, and nothing for the candidates on the local level? I need to become better known, Roosevelt doesn't. How about a few signs for me?"

Hymie did not answer directly. "You ever watch the ferries come in from Staten Island?" The candidate allowed as how he had, and waited for Hymie's point.

"When that big ferry from Staten Island sails into the ferry slip, it never comes in strictly alone. It drags in all the crap from the harbor behind it." Hymie let the message sink in before adding, "FDR is our Staten Island Ferry."

That is the way the story is most frequently recounted as it worked its way into political legend. When political reporter Richard Reeves used the anecdote (with an early edition of this dictionary as a source), he received a letter in 1976 from John Rae of New York City, an eyewitness to its telling: "I was at a party with Jimmy Walker and Hymie Schorenstein. The ferry story concerned Hymie's nonentity nephew running for the Assembly at the time Walker was running for Mayor. Walker assuaged Hymie by saying he would pull Hymie's nephew in—he coined the ferryslip story which Hymie loved to repeat as did Beau James."

Schorenstein, who despite an inability to read operated most effectively as a county clerk, was preceded in the use of this metaphor by the president of Columbia University, Nicholas Murray Butler, who heard it from Boise Penrose, a leader of the Pennsylvania delegation in the Republican convention of 1912. In the midst of a fistfight between supporters of former President Theodore Roosevelt and President William Howard Taft, Butler wondered how men of that type ever were selected for the responsibility of choosing a presidential nominee. Penrose replied, "Oh, those are the corks, bottles and banana peels washed up by the Roosevelt tide."

See BANDWAGON.

hype. See MEDIA EVENT.

hyphenated American identification of an American's racial or ethnic heritage.

African-American (in place of *black*) has become the foremost use of this hyphenation, although other examples of the formulation range from *Irish-American* to *Italian-American*. It allows the designation of a person's racial or ethnic background by using a capitalized modifier linked to *American* with a hyphen.

The phrase was first defined in Farmer and Henley's slang dictionary in 1893 as "a naturalized citizen." In the early 1900s, *hyphenated American* was used contemptuously to question the allegiance of immigrants to their adopted country.

Nowadays, however, that hyphenation results primarily from self-description and is considered a source of pride in the user's heritage. See ETHNICS.

I

I am the law example of the height of political imperiousness.

Mayor Frank Hague of Jersey City, big-city boss and full-time autocrat, received a bum rap from history on this quotation. The episode involved two youths who wanted to change from day school to night school so that they could go to work, but who were denied working papers by the Board of Education's Special Services Director because the law required them to stay in day school. Mayor Hague cut through the red tape and ordered the official to give the boys working papers. As he proudly recounted the matter before the Men's Club of Emory Church in Jersey City on November 10, 1937: when the school official told him, "That's the law," he replied, "Listen, here is the law. I am the law! Those boys go to work!"

Today such an action would be lauded as the action of a public official pushing aside an unresponsive bureaucracy to "meet human needs"; but Hague had a well-deserved reputation for high-handedness, and the phrase soon lost its context and was used against him.

During World War II Charles de Gaulle irritated Churchill and Roosevelt with his insistent remark, "*Je suis la France.*" This phrase reminded them, and others, of Louis XIV's supposed remark to the 1665 Parliament of Paris, "*L'état, c'est moi*" ("I am the state"). In his 1825 Bunker Hill Monument oration, Daniel Webster gave this interpretation, which could also apply to Hague's remark: "When Louis XIV said I am the state, he expressed the essence of the doctrine of unlimited power. These ideas, founded in the love of power, and long supported by the excess and abuse of it, are yielding in our age to other opinions . . ."

The phrase is current. On April 1, 1978, after several former FBI officials were indicted for violating the civil rights of members of a terrorist group, cartoonist Herblock pictured two agents in raincoats carrying a black bag labeled "illegal operations" and asking: "We broke the law? We *are* the law!"

ideas a catchword for a number of political movements that enjoyed some fame in the U.S.

"One-idea parties" was a nineteenth-century label placed first on anti-Masons and then all minority or splinter parties by members of larger parties. However, some of the ideas were worth looking into:

1. *The idea of freedom:* Associated with the abolitionist cause, the phrase was introduced by Theodore Parker at a New England antislavery convention held in Boston on May 29, 1850. Parker's idea was of "a democracy, that is, a government of all the people, by all the people, for all the people; of course, a government after the principles of eternal justice, the unchanging law of god; for shortness' sake, I will call it the idea of freedom." (Part of this statement was later adopted by Lincoln at Gettysburg.)

2. *The Ohio idea:* The Democratic platform of 1868 stressed the redemption of national debts in specie rather than in paper money. Senator George H. Pendleton summed up this "Ohio Idea" in 1881:

> The Ohio idea is the absolute equality of all men before the law; absolute and equal justice to all men by the law; and, in the administration of our State affairs, the administration of the few powers committed to our State affairs, the administration of the few powers committed to our State legislature by the Constitution in such wise that every man may pursue his own avocations and his own scheme of domestic life according to his tastes . . . as is consistent with the order of society and the peace of the community. And in national affairs, the Ohio idea is the absolute performance of every act to which the plighted faith of the nation is given.

3. *The Plattsburg idea:* With World War I under way, those who advocated preparedness for the U.S. introduced the Plattsburg idea in April, 1915—two years before America's entry into the war. Named for the northern New York State site of a training camp, it called for military training for civilians at similar spots.

4. *The Wisconsin idea:* Graduates of the enlightened University of Wisconsin, which encouraged its students to seek wealth, power, and influence for the betterment of society, fostered the idea. They envisioned a progressive, agrarian-democratic commonwealth—and from 1900 to 1914 they went a long way toward making the idea a reality. With Robert La Follette, Sr., as governor, advocates of the Wisconsin idea enacted a direct primary, tax reform, laws controlling the railroads, initiative and referendum provisions, a corrupt-practices act, child- and female-labor laws, workers' compensation, regulatory agencies for utilities and transportation, and laws covering campaign expenditures, civil service, lobbying, safety, public health, conservation, and the schools.

Tommy G. Thompson, who became Governor of Wisconsin in 1987, defined a newer Wisconsin idea: "My philosophy, or the 'New Wisconsin Idea,' . . . was aimed at moving away from intrusive government, and putting responsibility and initiative back in the hands of *people*."

Current campaign oratory tends to discard the word *idea*, on the grounds that it appears too sudden a notion, substituting the less exciting "plan" or "program," or the more pretentious "concept." The way to derogate any idea is to call it a *notion*.

ideology originally, a system of ideas for political or social action; in current political use, a mental straitjacket, or rigid rules for the philosophically narrow-minded.

French philosopher Destutt de Tracy coined the word in 1796, to mean a rationalist "science of ideas" opposed to ancient metaphysics, and made it the title of his 1801 book, *Idéologie*. Napoleon Bonaparte was the first to give the word a bad name: "It is to the doctrine of the ideologues . . . one must attribute all the misfortunes which have befallen our beautiful France." British historian Thomas Carlyle tried to rescue the word in 1839: "Does the

British reader . . . call this unpleasant doctrine of ours ideology?" But when Marx and Engels joined Napoleon in condemning the word in their 1845 attack on German radicals, titling their book *The German Ideology*, the term could never shake its connotation of foolish rigidity. When the Marx book was finally printed in English in 1927, the word gained currency in the U.S.

"I think 'ideology' is a scare word to most Americans," observed Ronald Reagan to columnists Evans and Novak in 1978. "But a basic political philosophy is the reason for a party existing."

The observation, with the counterpoint use of "philosophy," was semantically accurate. In current use, "ideology" carries the connotation of alien theory, and "ideologues" are seen as demagogues hawking extreme points of view. Such TRUE BELIEVERS practice "cannibalism" within a party by seeking to PURGE its minority elements, refusing to accept the formulation attributed to Senator William Borah: "A Republican is anybody who calls himself a Republican." In this attack, the BIG TENT advocates deprecate the divisiveness of "narrow ideology."

In response, principled partisans who believe a party should "stand for something" insist it must offer a CHOICE, NOT AN ECHO to avoid "metooism" (see ME TOO) and TWEEDLEDUM AND TWEEDLEDEE comparisons that show "not a DIME'S WORTH OF DIFFERENCE." The riposte can be typified in this statement by conservative Howard Phillips, who challenged liberal Republican Senator Edward Brooke of Massachusetts in 1978: "When liberals challenge conservative Republicans, they call it 'base-broadening.' But when conservatives oppose liberal GOPers, it is called 'cannibalism.'"

In this big-tent vs. stand-for-something argument, which bothers Republicans more than Democrats, the meeting ground is "philosophy," or "basic philosophy." The safest phraseology for both sides is an assertion that "certain principles" and "values" cannot be compromised, provided they are not defined.

idiot engineer. See BLOOPER.

I'd rather be right Henry Clay's statement that began as an example of his idealism but now has a flavor of sour grapes.

"I would rather be right than be President." Kentucky Senator Clay made this statement several times to his friends, in a letter in 1839, and in a Senate speech in 1850.

"The Great Compromiser" and "The Great Pacificator" achieved major-party presidential nominations twice and was defeated. See CAN'T-WIN TECHNIQUE. Like Senator Robert A. Taft, a century later, he was too strictly a congressional leader to build nationwide coalitions beyond Congress. After losing the presidency, he tired of hearing his immortal words quoted and said dryly that this particular sentiment "had been applauded beyond its merit."

Clay's use of the statement in a Senate speech was in reply to those who said his Missouri Compromise would hurt his chances for the presidency. For years, congressmen quoted the remark until it became a political bromide; House Speaker Thomas B. Reed answered a Clay-quoter with "the gentleman need not be disturbed, he will never be either."

George M. Cohan wrote a Broadway musical entitled *I'd Rather Be Right* in the thirties, kidding the Administration of Franklin Roosevelt. In it, the President would turn to his secretary and say, "Mac, take a law." FDR enjoyed this and often turned to his secretary, Grace Tully, and said, "Grace, take a law."

Variations on Clay's remark can be found before and after he first sounded it. William McKinley, before his 1896 election, told a friend, "If I cannot be President without promising to make Tom Platt Secretary of the Treasury, I will never be President." Marcus Tullius Cicero (106–43 B.C.) said of the Pythagoreans, "I would rather be wrong with Plato than right with such men as these."

if by whiskey . . . a political STRAD-DLE; taking both sides of an issue; equivocating.

These three words, followed by an ellipsis, refer to the classic speech of equivocation on the issue of prohibition. Now used as a compound modifier—"He gave an if-by-whiskey speech"—the expression may be applied to any political position that fails to take a position.

The originator of this speech was Judge Noah S. Sweat, Jr., of Corinth, Mississippi. Judge Sweat, nicknamed Soggy, for "Sorghum Top" (his hair resembling the tassels atop sugarcane), copyrighted his speech in 1952.

The satiric straddling purports to answer the question of a politician's stance on the controversial matter of drinking whiskey.

"If when you say whiskey," the politician begins, "you mean the Devil's brew, the poison scourge, the bloody monster that defiles innocence . . . then certainly I am against it.

"But, if when you say whiskey," the speechmaker continues, "you mean the oil of conversation, the philosophic wine, . . . that drink the sale of which pours into our treasuries untold millions of dollars, which are used to provide tender care for our little crippled children, our blind, our deaf, our dumb, our pitiful aged and infirm;

to build highways and hospitals and schools, then certainly I am for it."

iffy question a hypothetical question; phrase used by Franklin Roosevelt to avoid giving iffy answers.

"If you run next year, who will your Vice President be?" This type of question is designed to elicit not one answer, but two (Who will be the Vice President? Will you run next year?). Many press conference traps of this kind were neatly avoided by FDR, who merely smiled and said, "That's an iffy question."

New York Governor Averell Harriman, campaigning against Nelson Rockefeller in 1958, was asked if he planned to retain Tammany leader Carmine De Sapio as Secretary of State, and replied, "I think that's an iffy question that doesn't—that I needn't deal with today." Since "bossism" was an important thrust of Rockefeller's campaign, and since the "if" in the question was hardly hypothetical but pertinent to post-election plans, the Harriman use of "iffy question" was an ill-advised evasion. The phrase appears to work only when the question is indeed hypothetical, or "iffy."

For example, Robert Kennedy was asked by reporters in 1964 if he would accept a vice-presidential nomination. He answered such obvious speculation with: "The question reminds me of my brother. When he was posed with such a question, he used to say that is like asking a girl if she would marry that man if he proposed."

Other types of questions include: loaded, slanted, planted, tricky, and innocent.

if it ain't broke, don't fix it leave well enough alone; avoid creating unnecessary trouble or controversy.

Bert Lance, former director of the Office of Management and Budget, introduced this down-home Southernism to political usage in Washington early in the Carter Administration. The *National Journal* indicated its widespread use by 1978 in referring to Democrats who "follow the advice of . . . Bert Lance: 'If it ain't broke, don't fix it.'"

A proverbial equivalent of the hoary punch line *don't make waves*, this expression uses the ungrammatical *ain't* but still fits a traditional grammatical pattern. The conditional *if* clause (the protasis) leads into a main clause (the apodosis), *don't fix it*, which is expressed in the imperative (with its subject *you* understood).

In 1977, the *Washington Post* reported a comment by a Virginia Democrat, state delegate Ira M. Lechner, suggesting an earlier origin: "I support reorganization, but not these helter-skelter efforts. As my father used to say, 'If it ain't broke, don't fix it.'"

Democrats have not been alone, however, in using this nonpartisan rephrasing of *let sleeping dogs lie.* Cathy Mickels, a Republican delegate from Washington, speaking on "The Mac-Neil/Lehrer NewsHour" in August 1992, pushed for a continuation of the party's previously winning ways: "The old adage that states, 'If it ain't broke, don't fix it' applies here. I think it would be foolish to change our platform in any way to deviate from the 1988 winning platform that we have."

if you can't lick 'em . . . join 'em. A frequent bit of advice, origin obscure, given in areas dominated by one party.

The phrase, akin to the Scottish proverb "Better bend than break," carries no connotation of surrender; it is used to indicate that the way to take over the opposition's strength is to adopt their positions and platform. See ME TOO; CO-OPT.

President Harry Truman in his 1948 campaign warned farmers about a variation of this technique supposedly practiced by Republicans: "It's an old political trick: 'If you can't convince 'em, confuse 'em.' But this time it won't work."

if you can't stand the heat . . . get out of the kitchen. A motto often attributed to President Harry S. Truman.

President Truman stressed two facets of the presidency with colorful phrases: "The BUCK STOPS HERE" on the need for decisiveness, and "If you can't stand the heat, get out of the kitchen" on the cheerful expectancy of pressure.

As a senator, Lyndon Baines Johnson phrased the same philosophy in this way: "My daddy told me that if I didn't want to get shot at, I should stay off the firing lines. This is politics."

This phrase is as closely associated with Truman as "GIVE 'EM HELL," "DO-NOTHING CONGRESS," and "RED HERRING," and needs no specific attribution to him for identification. Daniel P. Moynihan, then of the Joint Center for Urban Studies, wrote complaining of an attack on him in *Transaction* in 1967: "A better political scientist than I said the final word on government executives either standing the heat or getting out of the kitchen, but there are levels of personal abuse that make one wonder whether it is worth it." (It was; Moynihan went on to become senator from New York.)

In 1984, the Reverend Jesse Jackson used the saying to emphasize the need for toughness in a Presidential candidate; commenting on his opponents' performance in a three-way debate, he said, "If you can't stand the heat, get out of the kitchen."

When Sir Walter Raleigh, nibbling his nails, wrote "Fain would I climb, yet fear to fall," the more direct Queen Elizabeth I is said to have written in reply: "If thy heart fails thee, climb not at all."

"I have a dream" a memorable speech construction by Rev. Martin Luther

King, Jr., at the Lincoln Memorial during the March on Washington, August 28, 1963.

I say to you today, my friends, that in spite of the difficulties and frustrations of the moment I still have a dream. It is a dream deeply rooted in the American dream . . .

I have a dream that one day on the red hills of Georgia the sons of former slaves and the sons of former slave-owners will be able to sit down together at the table of brotherhood . . .

I have a dream that my four little children will one day live in a nation where they will not be judged by the color of their skin but by the content of their character . . .

I have a dream today . . .

For other examples of vision and inspiration in speeches, see "I SEE" CONSTRUCTION; AMERICAN DREAM; VISION OF AMERICA.

illegitimi non carborundum

a pseudo-Latin phrase meaning "Don't let the bastards grind you down."

Small signs and plaques carrying this message have appeared in U.S. business offices and army posts for at least a generation, since General "Vinegar Joe" Stilwell used it as his motto in World War II. *Carborundum* is a trademark for silicon carbide, a leading commercial grinding substance, probably a blend of the words "carbon" or "carbide" and "corundum" (the hardest mineral except for the diamond), also used as an abrasive.

In politics, the motto was popularized by 1964 Republican nominee Senator Barry Goldwater, who hung the sign in his office. It expressed a suitable be-yourself, don't-compromise attitude that fit "Mr. Conservative."

The *New Republic* in 1967 used a ridiculously bowdlerized translation in reporting on its use by a group of senators who had been characterized as doves: "The Administration brought General Westmoreland all the way from Vietnam to overawe its critics, but the Senate's Democratic and Republican dissenters appropriated Barry Goldwater's old dog-Latin motto, 'Illegitimi non Carborundum,' which roughly means, 'Don't let the so-and-so's shut you up.'"

illuminati. See POWER ELITE.

image persona; the impression that is left by the merchandising of reputation.

Political images and image-makers are post–World War II offspring of television and big-league advertising and public relations. All politicians in all times, of course, seek public affection and respect. But turning this search into a constant and major effort is a recent innovation. John Brooks observed that the preoccupation with "image" sprang from an "unholy . . . liaison between promotion and psychology" that "invaded American politics about the time Eisenhower came to the White House." Almost as one, political writers picked up the term and have yet to put it down. Sir Ernest Gowers in Fowler's *Modern English Usage* calls it an overused "vogue word" but still a valid one in an era when "politicians and advertisers and other advocates of themselves or other causes can . . . project their images into our very homes" via TV.

The personal use of the word, to mean more than a reflection in a glass, was begun by psychologists; "father image" is a familiar psychiatric term. The word was picked up by advertising men as "brand image," meaning the conception on the part of the consumer of a manufacturer's trade name or product; this led to "corporate image," a conception that a public (stockholder, financial community, local community, the trade, etc.) has of a corporation. "A brand image is what you say you are," public relations men like to say, "but a corporate image is what you really are."

As image became a sales tool for opinion molders, it became a handy and modern-sounding word to describe the total public posture and impression of a public figure. Many politicians misuse the word to mean something that belongs to them, much as Peter Pan's shadow, and feel lost without it; the fact is that an image belongs to the public.

The activating verb used with *image* goes back to the use of the word as a reflection, or picture. Images are "projected," as one would project a movie on a screen.

The use of the word may be new, but the idea isn't. The seventeenth-century English writer Thomas Fuller lamented that "Fame sometimes has created something of nothing." It has also created political myths. Charles Evans Hughes, the Republican candidate for President in 1916, was the victim of the so-called ice myth that portrayed him as so withdrawn from the common man that he "communed in the Alps with Kant, solid geometry and Lycurgus." Hughes replied, "I'll plead guilty to knowing Kant, but not guilty as to the solid geometry charge. As to Lycurgus . . . do you think it is anything intoxicating?" Hughes lost the election.

News media play their part in image-making, of course. Calvin Coolidge gave reporters so little good copy that they were forced to resort to embroidery to keep editors and readers awake. Henry Suydam, recalling his days as a Washington correspondent, wrote: "Mr. Coolidge would observe, with respect to a certain bill, 'I'm not in favor of this legislation.' The next morning Washington dispatches began as follows: 'President Coolidge, in a fighting mood, today served no-

tice on Congress that he intended to combat, with all the resources at his command . . . '"

Perhaps the ideal example of a politician's attitude toward his image was expressed by Oliver Cromwell in the instructions to the man painting his portrait: "I desire you will use all your skill to paint my picture truly like me, and not to flatter me at all; but remark all those roughnesses, pimples, warts, and everything as you see me: otherwise I will never pay one farthing for it."

See MADISON AVENUE TECHNIQUES; SELLING CANDIDATES LIKE SOAP.

impact, political   effect on public opinion; jargon that has replaced *repercussions* and *ramifications* and even *results* in current usage.

"Impact" is a word that first became a cliché in the advertising business in the fifties, to describe the effect of an ad on a reader. In a classic "house" ad, the Young and Rubicam agency showed a picture of a boxing glove shattering a boxer's jaw—with the word "impact" printed below—to describe the effectiveness of their brand of advertising.

Some pretentious political public relations practitioners use the phrase often, as "We have to assess the political impact of such an unpopular stand"; the pros dismiss it as jargon.

In the seventies, the noun regressed to a verb, as "How does this impact on the grassroots?" It impacted awkwardly at first, but has taken root.

imperial Presidency   a charge that the Executive Branch has gained more power than the Constitution warrants.

At the end of 1973 Arthur Schlesinger, Jr.—historian of the Jackson era and the New Deal who served as a White House aide during the Presidency of John Kennedy—published *The Imperial Presidency*, which was taken to be an attack on the growth of presidential power. Since the book came out in the midst of the fall of Richard Nixon, it provided an intellectual underpinning to those liberals who otherwise were having problems of consistency with their previous enthusiasm for the growth of power under FDR and their fierce disapproval of its growth under Nixon.

"In recent years the imperial Presidency," read the book's inside-cover blurb, "having established itself in foreign affairs, has made bold bid for supremacy at home. Through a diversity of means—through the mystique of the mandate, through the secrecy system, through executive privilege and impoundment, through political and electronic surveillance in the name of national security, through the use of the White House itself as a base for espionage and sabotage against the political opposition—the imperial Presidency has threatened to become the revolutionary Presidency."

Schlesinger, who was then unaware of many of the abuses of civil liberty that a Senate committee in 1975 showed to have taken place in the sixties, was careful in his introduction to disclaim any desire to cripple the powers of the President: "The answer to the runaway Presidency is not the messenger-boy Presidency. The American democracy must discover a middle ground between making the President a czar and making him a puppet." His timely book confronted the dilemma of all those who had long urged an "activist" presidency and who had been dismayed when too much activism had led to Vietnam and Watergate.

As in the POLITICS OF, a Schlesinger book title became the construction for many variations in phrase-making. Laurence Silberman, at the American Enterprise Institute, published a critique of expanding judicial power which he called "the imperial judiciary"; after the War Powers Act and

the forced resignation of Nixon, Congress gained much power and was frequently criticized as "the imperial congress"; and in May 1978 Robert Manning wrote in the *Atlantic* (which had printed some of Schlesinger's original material in its pages): "Americans wanted no part of an Imperial Presidency. Neither will they tolerate an Imperial Press." In a 1993 opinion piece in the *Chicago Tribune*, David Evans wrote of the need to "restore some overdue constraints on the imperial Presidency's war-making powers."

impudent snobs.   See EFFETE SNOBS.

incomes policy   government influence upon or regulation of wages, prices, and profits, ranging from mild JAWBONING to direct controls.

In the late fifties, U.S. economists, who had been using "wage-price policy" to describe this general area, switched to the British usage, "incomes policy." This was because labor economists felt that wages and prices did not cover the subject of dividends and profits.

The new phrase came to public attention in the late sixties, when inflation persisted longer than most economists had expected. Because of its vagueness, it was especially popular as a solution to inflation by those who wanted to go beyond the customary methods of fiscal and monetary policy, without advocating wage and price controls.

The phrase was given a more specific definition, and the policy a strong boost, by Dr. Arthur Burns, who in 1970 became chairman of the Board of the Federal Reserve System. He called for an incomes policy, centering his proposal on a wage-price stabilization board—relying on voluntary compliance, short of mandatory controls.

Burns's espousal of a stabilization board, at a time when the Administration was using a milder form of incomes policy, moved the definition of the phrase in popular usage toward a more activist meaning. When the author pointed out to the Federal Reserve Chairman that this policy was directly in conflict with all he had written in the past, Burns replied, "I am not afflicted with the notion that what I write is chiseled in granite."

Incomes policy is often confused with, but has a totally different meaning from, *incomes strategy*. The latter has to do with providing money, rather than services or food, to those dependent on public support. Proponents of an incomes strategy hold that the least demeaning way to help the needy is to give them the cash to buy their own essentials; opponents point to ignorance about nutrition standards and the danger of misuse of the welfare money by the recipients.

incumbent in office; running against a challenger.

An incumbent, in its original sense, is one who lies down on the job; the word has the same root as "recumbent" and "succumb." The idea of resting is illustrated in the phrase "It is incumbent upon us," which means "It rests with us," and is as stilted as "It behooves us" (better usage is "We should" or "We must").

Based on past performance, the odds are two to one that an incumbent President will be re-elected. Fourteen have succeeded (FDR three times) out of twenty-two attempts. Those who failed were John Adams in 1800, John Quincy Adams in 1828, Martin Van Buren in 1840, Grover Cleveland in 1888, Benjamin Harrison in 1892, William Howard Taft in 1912, Herbert Hoover in 1932, Gerald Ford in 1976, and George Bush in 1992. See SITTING PRESIDENT. Those who failed of later nomination by their own party were John Tyler in 1844, Millard Fillmore in 1852, Franklin Pierce in 1856, Andrew

Johnson in 1868, and Chester Arthur in 1884; of these, only Pierce had already been elected President "in his own right."

In almost every political race, the incumbent has an edge. Incumbent congressmen have a franking privilege that enables them to regularly report to or survey their constituents, showing themselves busily at work without incurring direct-mail advertising costs. Officeholders can also use their title as part of their name in campaign posters. The extreme example of this was the advertising approach of Jack Tinker and Partners in the 1966 New York campaign for governor: "Governor Rockefeller for Governor." Campaign aide Harry O'Donnell, explaining the choice of the slogan to reporters, said, "It was either that or 'Nelson Rockefeller for Nelson.'"

With the same thought in mind, Republicans in 1971 called their citizens' committee "Committee for the Reelection of the President," which Republican National Chairman Bob Dole dubbed CREEP.

independents. See SWING VOTER; SWITCHER.

indispensable man a term that indicates that the U.S. government can get along without anybody, including the sitting President.

FDR repeated this statement of Woodrow Wilson's, who was running against both a sitting President, William Howard Taft, and former President Theodore Roosevelt seeking a comeback as a third-party candidate: "There is no indispensable man. The government will not collapse and go to pieces if any one of the gentlemen seeking to be entrusted with its guidance should be left at home."

Just before President Eisenhower's heart attack in 1955, as Republicans were urging him to announce his intentions of running again in 1956, he told a gathering of Republican state chairmen at the Brown Palace hotel in Denver, "We don't believe for a minute that the Republican party is so lacking in inspiration, high-quality personnel and leadership that we are dependent on one man . . . humans are frail and they are mortal. Finally you never pin your flag so tightly to one mast that if a ship sinks, you cannot rip it off and nail it to another. It is sometimes good to remember." Within two weeks the President suffered a heart attack, and his words sounded suddenly prophetic.

On the other hand, when Eisenhower wrote about General Alfred M. Gruenther, who succeeded him as Allied Commander in Europe, he referred to him as "practically an indispensable individual."

Foreign Affairs wrote in 1987 of the Cuban missile crisis: ". . . in retrospect the single member of the group who claimed familiarity with the Soviet Union is given credit for being the hero, the absolutely indispensable man during the crisis."

The origin of the phrase is in the French proverb: *"Il n'y a point d'homme nécessaire."* However, James Flexner subtitled his one-volume biography of George Washington *The Indispensable Man.*

inflation loss of the purchasing power of money; in politics, an issue of greatest concern to those on fixed incomes.

Two forms of inflation are *demand-pull,* when there are too many dollars chasing too few goods, and *cost-push,* when wage increases sharply exceed productivity increases, pushing prices ever higher.

The first great quarrel in the U.S. over inflation was tied in with the long-running debate between hard- and soft-money men. The hards warned in 1837 that "a bubble will be

inflated more disastrous in its explosion than the present one."

In 1933, after the burst of a particularly great bubble and the onset of the Depression, the government began talking of "reflationary" measures, such as massive deficit spending. As Raymond Moley wrote: "One zealot said to me at the time that the $3.3 billion"—the amount appropriated for the National Industrial Recovery Act's "reflationary" public works program—"would be better used if it were scattered by aircraft over the country in $1 bills. I suggested that $2 bills would be more appropriate because in the resulting inflation a dollar would mean so little."

During his 1952 campaign, Dwight Eisenhower hit hard at Democratic inflation and promised to correct it. In *Mandate for Change,* he wrote:

> To illustrate inflation I had used a length of board (sawed to the breaking point in two places) to represent the buying power of a 1949 dollar. To demonstrate the decline in the dollar between 1945 and 1952, I would break off the first third of the board. To illustrate the decline that was probable with eight more years of Fair Deal policies, I would break off another chunk of the board, ending up with a wooden equivalent of a 33¢ dollar in terms of 1945 values. We expended a large pile of lumber in this lesson, but the point got across.

With John F. Kennedy's Administration the Keynes-oriented "new economists" (see NEW ECONOMICS) made deficit spending and a moderate dose of controlled, continuing inflation official policy.

After inflation gained momentum in the late sixties under pressure of heavy defense spending, the federal government moved to a "full-employment budget" concept—the limit on spending set at the amount that the tax system would produce at full employment.

The word most closely associated with inflation is "spiral"; an "inflationary spiral," like a Vandyke beard, is a phrase that is most often defined by a gesture of the fingers. The pace of inflation ranges from "creeping" to "galloping," and orators denounce the way it "eats away" at the purchasing power of the dollar. Campaigns using the theme often print tiny replicas of dollar bills and call them "Johnson (or whoever the opponent is) dollars."

In the early seventies, "stagflation" came into use, which *Fortune* magazine defined as "continuing inflation under conditions of stagnant output and rising unemployment." Other terms used to characterize this condition were the hybrid *slumpflation* and the descriptive "inflationary recession." This situation was also described, in a paraphrase of Voltaire's Dr. Pangloss, as "the worst of both worlds."

See HOLD THE LINE; HIGH COST OF LIVING; DOUBLE DIGIT; OVERHEATED ECONOMY; RECESSION.

influence peddler one who has, or claims to have, the contacts and "pull" supposedly necessary to get government contracts and favors from public officials, for a fee.

Testifying before a special Senate subcommittee in 1949, one of many of the FIVE PERCENTERS being investigated said, "I have nothing to sell but influence."

The phrase became common during the concluding years of the Truman Administration as Republicans sought to discredit the Democrats (see MESS IN WASHINGTON; GOVERNMENT BY CRONY).

President Truman was never accused of profiting personally by corruption. But testimony showed that his military aide and close friend, Major General Harry Vaughan, had been active on behalf of people interested in getting to France to bring in perfume base at a time when transportation for such activities was not available. General Vaughan had interceded successfully for others wanting structural steel, then in short supply, in order to put up a racetrack in California and, in fact, had helped others get military contracts.

Vaughan denied having kept anything for himself, and President Truman staunchly sustained him, as he did special assistant and fellow Missourian Donald Dawson, who was charged by another committee (headed by Senator J. William Fulbright) with being the man to see if a loan was wanted from the Reconstruction Finance Corporation.

Synonymous with "influence peddler" was "five percenter," a man who claimed to be able to get government contracts for which he wanted, in return, 5 percent of the value. During that period, sixty-six employees of the Bureau of Internal Revenue were purged and nine went to prison.

Nothing, however, had quite the impact as gifts of deep-freeze units made by a former Army officer, Colonel James V. Hunt, at the suggestion of General Vaughan. They were sent to Mr. Truman's Independence, Missouri, home, to Chief Justice Fred Vinson, and to Secretary of the Treasury John Snyder. Their value was much less than other examples of giving or getting things to which one was not entitled but the "deep freeze" gifts gripped the public mind, as did vicuña coats years later.

President Truman's insistence on standing up for old friends, despite his private fury over having been "sold down the river," hurt his party in 1952.

The predecessor of "influence" was "pull," which Charles Ledyard Norton described in 1890 as "what influence, honorable or dishonorable, can he bring to bear to secure his election, or further party interests." The word is a shortening of "wirepulling," and can be found in "The Boss," a poem by James Russell Lowell:

Skilled to pull wires, he baffles Nature's hope
Who sure intended him to stretch a rope.

What influential consultants sell today is *access*. When *Time* magazine put former Reagan image-maker Michael Deaver on its cover as exemplar of "The Age of Access," the consultant's clout began a steep decline. The word *access* was intended to suggest that the lobbying was limited to the ability to get a fair hearing, but it was recognized as a euphemism for *influence*.

infrastructure skeleton; a political entity's internal administrative apparatus.

This word proves that nobody—not even a great world leader and master of language—can kill a really tenacious bit of jargon.

Winston Churchill tried. Emanuel Shinwell, Labour Minister of Defence, reviewed for the House of Commons in 1950 the results of a meeting of the Consultative Council of the Brussels Treaty Western Union, a predecessor of the Common Market. Shinwell explained that the installation of signal communications, preparation of the headquarters, and division of the airfields were activities now known collectively as working on the "infrastructure."

Churchill rose and gave the use of the word fair warning: "As to this new word with which he has dignified our language, but which perhaps was imposed upon him internationally, I can only say that we must have full opportunity to consider it and to consult the dictionary."

Two months later, in a debate on the Schuman plan to pool European coal and steel, the word appeared again and Sir Winston was ready for it: "In this debate we have had the usual jargon about 'the infrastructure of a supranational authority.' The original authorship is obscure; but it may well be that these words 'infra' and 'supra' have been introduced into our current political parlance by the band of intellectual highbrows who are naturally anxious to impress British labour with the fact that they learned Latin at Winchester."

Considering the prestigious source of the ridicule, infrastructure lay dormant. In the American diplomatic community in Vietnam in the sixties, the word reared its head cautiously. In discussing the need for pursuing the OTHER WAR, diplomats and generals briefed correspondents on the need for a "viable indigenous governmental apparat," i.e., a local Vietnamese government that would be accepted by the people, able to continue after U.S. forces left. This became known as the "infrastructure."

The adjective most often used to modify infrastructure is "viable." "That 'viable' phrase drives me mad," Defense Secretary Robert McNamara once said. "I keep trying to comb it out, but it keeps coming back."

With Churchill gone, linguistic defense collapsed and infrastructure triumphed to describe the organization of both the "friendlies" and the Viet Cong. Typical home-front use was in this 1967 *New Republic* article by Andrew Kopkind: "If [Ronald] Reagan had appeased the people, he had also alienated the major economic interests. California's corporatism, perhaps more than any other state's, relies heavily on the production of technicians and intellectuals to support its 'infrastructure.' Huge technological parks go up around every new campus, the better to feed off the state-subsidized resources."

This indicates that the word has also absorbed the pejorative meaning of "superstructure," or excess organization. John Kenneth Galbraith, in *The New Industrial State,* labeled the "organized intelligence" directing modern industrial production as the "technostructure." But in his 1992 campaign, Bill Clinton emphasized "investment in our infrastructure," by which he meant stimulative public-works spending.

"Structure" has recently become a vogue verb, its meaning drifting from "build," "create," "plan," to "organize."

For another word that could not be stopped, see MEDICARE.

initialese. See ACRONYMS, POLITICAL; ALPHABET AGENCIES.

initials, Presidential a contribution made by newspaper-headline writers to American history.

Prior to 1932, the President was referred to in headlines as the President, or by his last name, occasionally by his nickname ("Teddy," "Cal"), once by his initials (T.R. for Theodore Roosevelt). Presidents, in signing brief memos, would often use the initial of their first name (A. Lincoln). Franklin D. Roosevelt initialed memos "FDR" and his staff referred to him that way.

This proved a boon to headline writers, saving six spaces on both "Roosevelt" and "President." Use of initials was terse but not disrespectful, as "Frank" might have been. English newspapers had long followed the practice—Gladstone was headlined as "GOM" (Grand Old Man). Following FDR, HST was immediately adopted as short for Harry S. Truman. Though Eisenhower initialed short notes "DE," his nickname was short and famous enough to take the place of initials; "Ike," however, was considered too familiar for the *New York Times.*

Irreverent headline writers referred to John F. Kennedy as "Jack" before his election, quickly changing to "JFK" afterward. Sorensen wrote: "JFK—as he persuaded the headline writers to call him, not to imitate FDR but to avoid the youthful 'Jack.'"

Dating even before his association with FDR, LBJ was preoccupied with initials: Lady Bird Johnson, Lynda Bird, Luci Baines all carried the same initials, as did his ranch. "All the Way With LBJ" was used as a preconvention slogan in 1960, but achieved no national recognition. Johnson became LBJ outside his own circle only when he became President. In 1964 he used his initials in campaign advertising: "USA for LBJ" and "All the Way With LBJ."

Jimmy Carter avoided using his initials because "J.C." is usually associated with Jesus Christ.

Nixon's last name was short, which meant headline writers did not need "RN"; miffed, the former President used the initials as the title of his 1978 memoirs. Ford's name was even shorter, doing away with the need for a gruff "GRF." Reagan's initials might have been confused with the abbreviation for "railroad"; Bush's GHWB was too long for his monosyllabic last name; and Bill Clinton's initials could stand for "before Christ" or, worse, "bills for collection." Initialese did, however, crop up in the Clinton Administration with FOB—not "freight on board" but "Friends of Bill."

Inner Club a small, informal group which is reported to hold leadership power in both the House of Representatives and the Senate, especially the Senate.

The phrase is attributed to columnist William S. White, who wrote in 1956 of the "Inner Club where emphasis is still put on seniority and skill in negotiation." It is apparently a relative of the much older description of the U.S. Senate as "the most exclusive gentlemen's club in the world." In a 1986 speech on "The Senate Class of 1958," Senator Robert C. Byrd of West Virginia discussed that year's shift to liberalism: "The Class of 1958, joined by other liberal Senators including Joseph Clark and William Proxmire, tended to brand their seniors as the 'Senate Establishment' and the 'inner club.'"

Its members, whatever their political affiliation, have certain things in common: some degree of seniority and a secure seat; a working belief in compromise; the quality and force of their personality; and a willingness to do solid, difficult work in the committees where legislation is forged.

The members of the Inner Club are by no means always the best-known or eventually the best-rewarded. During his senatorial years John F. Kennedy was never considered a member of the Senate's Inner Club, nor did he aspire to be. Neither was his younger brother, Senator Robert Kennedy.

An example of the group's cohesive power occurred in Hubert Humphrey's first term in the Senate. He came to the upper house as an outspoken liberal, proceeded to launch an attack on Virginia's conservative but highly respected Senator Harry Byrd, and was firmly squelched for his presumption. Senator Humphrey's attitude to the Club organization underwent so strong a change that a few years later he was Assistant Majority Leader under the most ardent exponent of Clubmanship of all, Senate Democratic Majority Leader Lyndon B. Johnson.

The phrase goes beyond the Senate. Kennedy-appointed State Department official Roger Hilsman wrote of the time he and two other aides waited until a large group left the President's office. "The three of us trooped into his oval office through the curved side door from the room his private secretary, Mrs. Lincoln, occupied and found the President rocking away in his chair before the fireplace, reading and signing the last of a pile of letters. He looked up and grinned. 'And now,' he said, 'we have the "inner club."'"

More often, the group closest to the President or a candidate is called the "inner circle." (See IRISH MAFIA.)

When general clubbiness is meant, the *inner* is dropped. "Webster Hubbell, confidant of the Clinton family and nominee for Associate Attorney General," wrote a *New York Times* editorialist in 1993, "publicly dropped his country club membership yesterday and was embraced by that other club, the United States Senate."

inoperative the epitome of unrepentant ground-giving; a correction without an apology.

On April 17, 1973, press secretary Ronald Ziegler came before the White House press corps just after President Nixon had announced "new developments" were forthcoming in the Watergate case. When asked about his own previous statements on the case, as well as the President's earlier speeches denying that anyone on the White House staff was involved, the press secretary said—six separate times—that the "operative" statement was the most recent one issued by the President.

Then, in a situation similar to that which ensnared Harry Truman on RED HERRING, a reporter used the word that later became famous and asked the spokesman if he would adopt it. R. W. "Johnny" Apple of the *New York Times* asked, "Ron, could I follow up on your comment on the 'operative' statement? Would it be fair for us to infer, since what the President said today is now considered the operative statement, to quote you, that the other statement is no longer operative, that it is now inoperative?"

Ziegler, as columnist Nick Thimmesch later put it, "dropped his guard and took the sucker punch." After a minute's fencing, the press secretary replied using the word the reporter knew would provide a devastating lead: "The President refers to the fact that there is new material; therefore, this is the operative statement. The others are inoperative."

The bit of jargon, with its mechanistic metaphor, stirred great derision. The *New York Daily News* White House correspondent, Paul Healy, said, "I think he should resign. His credibility has been ruined." The National Press Club professional relations committee denounced the way Ziegler "has misled the public and affronted the professional standards of the Washington Press Corps." Seven weeks later, the battered Ziegler turned over the briefing function to his deputy, Jerry Warren.

"Inoperative," with its Watergate cover-up connotation, continues to carry a burden of coldly brushing off the past; in 1975, in a *New York* magazine competition, "inoperative statement" was defined as "a lie that no longer works." Ziegler, who was never accused of knowingly telling a lie by the Special Prosecution force, was saddled in history by the word he allowed a reporter to lead him into saying.

The word was used first by the poet John Donne, who wrote before his death in 1631 about "a dead faith, as all faith is that is inoperative." It can be found four times in amendments to the U.S. Constitution, and until the Ziegler usage, was best remembered from Abraham Lincoln's statement on September 13, 1862, explaining why he had not issued an Emancipation Proclamation: "What good would a proclamation of emancipation from me do, especially as we are now situated? I do not want to issue a document that the whole world will see must necessarily be inoperative, like the Pope's bull against the comet." (The Proclamation was announced nine days later; Lincoln had deliberately misled his callers. He misled himself about the papal bull: though Pope Calixtus III decreed "several days of prayer for averting the wrath of God" when Halley's Comet appeared in 1456, the story that he excommunicated the comet by papal bull has been disproven and is inoperative.)

in place an informer situated in a position of trust in the enemy camp.

The word is taken from espionage, where to have an "agent in place" is the most productive form of covert operation. Spy novels and movies gave the phrase currency, and the occasional political use of the idea has kept it current. See the sub-entry on "mole" under CIA-ESE.

In most large campaigns, a covert operation existed to put a secretary, office boy, or messenger into the opposition headquarters. This "agent in place" often does nothing more than bring copies of press releases to opposition headquarters as they are delivered to the press, giving the opposing camp time to prepare a counter-release. Post-Watergate, this practice was usually seen to be more trouble than it was worth, since it ran the risk of a DIRTY TRICKS charge.

The phrase had an antecedent political use before it shifted in meaning to become part of the undercover intelligence lexicon. Abolitionist Wendell Phillips, welcoming the crisis caused by Lincoln's election in 1860, told his followers: "Not an abolitionist, hardly an anti-slavery man, Mr. Lincoln consents to represent an anti-slavery idea. . . . He seems to govern; he only reigns. . . . Lincoln is in *place*, Garrison in power." This was echoed in 1993 by Nigel Lawson, after being removed as Chancellor of the Exchequer by British Prime Minister John Major.

He described the buffeted P.M. as "in office, but not in power."

input. See DECISION-MAKING PROCESS.

ins and outs the party in power and the party out of power; used to show basic similarity in political ideology.

Democrats in 1892 sang this song for the return of Grover Cleveland:

> *Grover, Grover, four more years*
> *of Grover—*
> *In we'll go, Out they'll go,*
> *Then we'll be in clover!*

When asked "What is the difference between the Republicans and the Democrats?" a host of political figures have been credited with the remark: "The only difference is—they're in and we're out."

Herbert Hoover, campaigning against Franklin Roosevelt, in 1932, tried to draw a wider distinction: "This election is not a mere shift from the ins to the outs. It means deciding the directions our nation will take over a century to come." Adlai Stevenson in 1952 derided Republicans for "being out of patience, out of sorts, and . . . out of office."

Attorney General Griffin Bell, criticized for replacing Republican U.S. Attorneys with Democrats despite campaign pledges by Jimmy Carter as candidate to keep politics out of such appointments, surprised reporters with his candor in January 1978: "We have two parties in this country. The 'in' party right now happens to be the Democrats."

There are other meanings to the phrase. An experienced politician is one who *knows the ins and outs* of politics. An *in-and-outer,* however, is a "trimmer," one who cannot be trusted. But in the sense of "in power," and usually capitalized, the Ins of today are the Outs of tomorrow.

inside baseball specialized or private knowledge; the minute political details savored by those in-the-know, found boring by most others.

This prepositional phrase began as a synonym for *scientific baseball,* the tactical approach to playing that emphasizes nuances like the steal or the hit-and-run. The Baltimore Orioles of the 1890s were known for this playing style. Red Barber, the radio broadcaster known as the voice of the Brooklyn Dodgers, said of the term, "I've heard *inside baseball* ever since I've been in baseball. The idea of an inner circle, or sanctum sanctorum, goes back all the way to the days of tribal government."

The sports term was transferred to politics as early as 1978. Myra MacPherson wrote in the *Washington Post* that year about Senator Edward M. Kennedy: "He chairs endlessly boring hearings, . . . then cuts through testimony with inside baseball jokes that no visitors understand but laugh at anyway."

Describing an intimate interest in fine details and minutiae, *inside baseball* may be used admiringly. Michael Kramer wrote in *U.S. News & World Report* in 1988, "It is one of those underappreciated, 'inside baseball' moments that ratify politics as the Ultimate Game."

The same phrase, however, can suggest an excess of concern with trivia. Richard Weiner, chairman of Michigan's Democratic Party, commented: "The people in my state are interested in jobs, the economy, and education. The rest is inside baseball."

inside the Beltway geographically, within the Capital Beltway surrounding Washington, D.C.; metaphorically, minutiae of government gossip of interest only to pundits and lobbyists, but a yawner to the Real World Out There.

The details of insiderdom cherished by insiders are derided as *inside-the-Beltway stuff* by those professing to be in touch with the more important feelings of The Great Unwashed.

The phrase first appeared as a hyphenated modifier in a 1977 *Washington Post* headline on a fishing story: "Inside-the-Beltway Trout Fishing Nears." It was based on the 1951 coinage *beltway* for the surrounding road the British call a *ring road* or *orbital road;* the center of Moscow is similarly circled by the *Sadovoye Koltso,* meaning "garden ring." Malcolm Dill, Baltimore County's first planning director, coined the noun to replace "circumferential route," the term then being used for the Baltimore Beltway. (For a related term, see BELTWAY BANDITS.)

By 1983, its political sense overwhelmed its geographical meaning. A *Newsweek* article quoted a Democratic campaign manager who refused to dismiss a possible return by George McGovern: "If he's perceived as a man on a fool's errand, that's still inside the [Washington] Beltway, not the world as a whole." United Press International also used a bracketed explanation in 1985 when the humorist Mark Russell said of Wyoming Senator Alan Simpson, "Simpson epitomizes the Western disdain for 'inside-the-beltway' [Washington know-it-alls]."

As Vice President, George Bush helped popularize the term. On "Meet the Press" in 1984, he discounted the dispute between Treasury Secretary Donald Regan and economist Martin Feldstein, redundantly calling it "an inside-the-Beltway thing that nobody really cares about." Bush urged his interviewers to listen to President Reagan, not to "the who's-up, who's-down, inside-the-Beltway stuff."

Although the term may be used to derogate narrowed interests, some take it to mean "the inside skinny" and give it a positive spin. A column of newsy gossip in the *Washington Times* uses the phrase for its title, and during the 1992 Presidential campaign, the neutral phrase was picked up by the pundit Mark Shields in discussing the candidacy of Bill Clinton: "He won the inside-the-Beltway primary."

The negative connotation of insular thinking, however, remains with the expression. During the 1991 confirmation hearings of Clarence Thomas for the Supreme Court, Senator Charles Grassley of Iowa spoke of "ordinary American people, who look at things differently than [they] are looked at here inside the Beltway."

The phrase should be hyphenated when used as a modifier before a noun (*inside-the-Beltway wisdom*), and *Beltway* should be capitalized as a specific reference to the Capital Beltway. For a similar term on insider interest, see INSIDE BASEBALL.

instant analysis   the reaction of television commentators following a presidential speech.

The phrase was coined by Vice President Spiro Agnew in his first speech castigating much of the media, in Des Moines, Iowa, on November 13, 1969: ". . . a week ago, President Nixon delivered the most important address of his Administration, one of the most important in our decade. His subject was Vietnam. His hope was to rally the American people to see the conflict through to a lasting and just peace in the Pacific. . . . When the President completed his address—an address that he spent weeks in preparing—his words and policies were subjected to instant analysis and querulous criticism. The audience of seventy million Americans—gathered to hear the President of the United States—was inherited by a small band of network commentators and self-appointed analysts . . . "

This speech, which was written by

Nixon aide Patrick Buchanan, was telecast in its entirety on prime time and did much to make the Vice President both a rallying point and a lightning rod.

The phrase grew out of "instant history," a pejorative term for articles and books about current events on recent Administrations, which in turn percolated from "instant coffee." The use of "instant"—similar to the description of a graduate of Officers Candidate School as a "90-day wonder"—plays on the suspicion of any quick assumption of expertise.

Although Agnew's remarks were roundly denounced by most television newsmen as an infringement of freedom of the press, the subsequent character of analyses following presidential addresses changed markedly from rebuttal to wrap-up.

instinct for the jugular ability to ferret out and attack the hidden weakness of the opponent; willingness to launch an attack that will do lasting damage.

To the tough-minded, the phrase is a compliment; to the tender-minded, it is a reference to the cruelty of wolves who slash at the jugular vein of their quarry to guarantee a kill. Most politicians admire an "instinct for the jugular" in other politicians, but do not like it to show publicly in their candidates.

The vivid phrase, still current, is one of the oldest in U.S. politics. It was coined by Massachusetts Senator Rufus Choate (coiner of "glittering generalities"), directed at another Massachusetts man, John Quincy Adams, sixth President of the U.S. "He has peculiar powers as an assailant, and almost always, even when attacked, gets himself into that attitude by making war upon his accuser; and he has, withal, an instinct for the jugular and the carotid artery, as unerring as that of any carnivorous animal."

The metaphor used as the opposite of

this was reported by Eliot Marshall in the *New Republic* (January 29, 1977): "One former [Henry] Kissinger aide told Les Gelb of the *New York Times,* 'Neither Henry nor I in the first years thought [James] Schlesinger was a man to be taken seriously. Given Jim's turn of mind, his interest in the technical rather than policy issues, we thought he had an instinct for the capillaries.'"

And it can be punned upon: humorist Russell Baker was referred to by a colleague as a man with "an instinct for the jocular."

See GUTFIGHTER; HATCHETMAN.

insurgent. See REFORM.

integration. See WITH ALL DELIBERATE SPEED; SEGREGATION; BUSING TO ACHIEVE RACIAL BALANCE.

intellectual-in-residence a presidential adviser set up in the Johnson Administration to bridge the gap between the White House and the "intellectual community."

First to hold the job was Princeton professor Eric Goldman, who resigned after a year with a blast at the President's unwillingness to accept new ideas. He was succeeded by John P. Roche, former chairman of Americans for Democratic Action. "I am not a governess to the intelligentsia," Roche said in describing his duties. "I am not the President's ambassador to the *Partisan Review* or the Metropolitan Opera." His assignment was primarily as a bridge-builder to such outspoken intellectual critics of the Administration as University of Chicago professor Hans Morgenthau, who promptly said: "He conceives his official task to be the HATCHETMAN who will try to ruin the reputation of those intellectuals who dare openly to disagree with his master."

On NBC's *Meet the Press,* December 25, 1966, former Kennedy and Johnson national security aide McGeorge Bundy was asked to compare the two Presidents on their relations with the academic community. "I think we exaggerated the optimism in 1961 and 1962," he replied, "and we exaggerated the disharmony that exists in the last year or two."

President Johnson said in a 1966 Princeton University speech: "Each time my Cabinet meets I can call the roll of former professors—Humphrey and Rusk, McNamara and Wirtz, Katzenbach . . . Gardner and Weaver. The 371 appointments that I have made as President . . . collectively hold 758 advanced degrees." Despite these statements, the academicians remained unconvinced. "When President Johnson named an intellectual-in-residence in 1964," wrote University of Toronto professor Lewis S. Feuer, "he assigned him the job of seeking the ideas and cooperation of the intellectuals. If the philosophers were not kings, they were to be honored advisers to a Democratic President. Yet no President in American history has evoked the animosity of intellectuals as much as Lyndon Johnson has."

The phrase originated with *poet-in-residence* and *writer-in-residence*, a method used by some colleges to provide the upkeep for a well-known poet or author while enhancing the school's reputation. The whatever-in-residence is rarely expected to teach, but is expected to inspire students with his creative presence.

A misunderstood word contributed to intellectual estrangement soon after Roche took office. To an interviewer, he referred to "the West Side [of New York] Jacobins"; most intellectuals would have taken this allusion to the radicals of the French Revolution in stride, but the word was reported in the *Partisan Review* (quoting a "nationally syndicated column") as "jackal bins," which started a mild

furor in the intellectual community reminiscent of Charles E. Wilson's BIRD DOGS . . . KENNEL DOGS.

intellectuals. See EGGHEAD.

interests. See VESTED INTERESTS.

in the loop. See OUT OF THE LOOP.

intransigent unwilling to compromise; obstructionist, especially regarding peace negotiations.

During the Mideast SHUTTLE DIPLOMACY of 1974, a "senior official aboard the Secretary's plane" (the phrase denoting Secretary of State Henry Kissinger speaking on background) complained that the Israelis were being "intransigent" in his attempt to negotiate an agreement with Arab states. Since this was the first overt criticism of Israel by a high U.S. official, and was soon accompanied by a threat of a "reassessment" of U.S. support, the word received much attention.

"Intransigence," although hard to pronounce, is a word deeply rooted in diplomacy. *Transigere* is Latin for "drive through," and its participle is *transactus*, the basis for "transact": thus, "intransigent" means "unwilling to do business." In diplomacy, this has been interpreted as "uncompromising," and has long been used as a criticism of one party in peace negotiations. The antonym in diplospeak is *forthcoming*.

invective, political personal abuse, vituperation, and ridicule of another; usually wistfully referred to as "a dying art," but never quite dead.

John Randolph of Virginia, who coined "doughface" to describe the supporters of the Missouri Compromise, served as a power in the House and Senate from 1799 to 1829, U.S. minister to Russia in 1830, and died insane in 1833. Recognized as the master of American political invective, Randolph said of Edward Livingstone, then a House member and later Secretary of State: "He is a man of splendid abilities, but utterly corrupt. Like rotten mackerel by moonlight, he shines and stinks."

Throughout his life it was rumored that Randolph was impotent. Congressman Tristram Burges of Rhode Island said in the House about Randolph, "I rejoice that the Father of Lies can never become the Father of Liars," to which he replied, "You pride yourself upon an animal faculty, in respect to which the slave is your equal and the jackass infinitely your superior."

Public blows as low as this, unheard-of today, were commonplace in England and America in the eighteenth and nineteenth centuries. John Montagu, fourth Earl of Sandwich, predicted that his former friend John Wilkes "would either die on the gallows or of a loathsome disease." Wilkes, in a reply usually credited to Disraeli, lashed back: "That depends, my lord, on whether I embrace your principles or your mistress."

Modern American invective has often been reduced to simple name-calling, as with John L. Lewis's description of John Nance Garner: "a poker-playing, whisky-drinking, evil old man." In the thirties, name-calling and invective flourished with General Hugh Johnson, Westbrook Pegler, and Harold Ickes (for Ickes's contributions, see CURMUDGEON). Johnson, a New Dealer turned against Roosevelt, called New Dealers "economic pansies," "a cockeyed crew of wand-waving wizards," and selected Senator Sherman Minton to be "the messenger-boy in chief for the White House janissariat." See HAIL OF DEAD CATS.

Hugh Johnson should not be confused with Hiram Johnson, first two-term (of four years) governor of California, who held this opinion of *Los Angeles Times* publisher Harrison

Grey Otis: "He sits there in senile dementia with a gangrene heart and rotting brain, grimacing at every reform, chattering impotently at all things that are decent, frothing, fuming, violently gibbering, going down to his grave in snarling infamy . . . disgraceful, depraved . . . and putrescent."

Westbrook Pegler, whose most frequent target was Eleanor Roosevelt, did much to popularize the phrase "bleeding-heart liberal" (see BLEEDING HEART), hit gossip columnists as "gents-room journalists," hit intellectuals as "double domes," and infuriated the FBI by widely disseminating left-wing Congressman Vito Marcantonio's description of J. Edgar Hoover as "a Stork Club detective."

Winston Churchill is commonly thought to have directed his famous dig "sheep in sheep's clothing" at Clement Attlee. In a review of the first edition of this book, British historian D. W. Brogan set the record straight: "Sir Winston Churchill never said of Clement Attlee that he was a 'sheep in sheep's clothing.' I have this on the excellent authority of Sir Winston himself. The phrase was totally inapplicable to Mr. Attlee. It was applicable, and applied, to J. Ramsay MacDonald, a very different kind of Labour leader." MacDonald was a favorite target of Churchill's, as illustrated in the following classic of invective without rancor, on a low key: "I remember, when I was a child, being taken to the celebrated Barnum's Circus, which contained an exhibition of freaks and monstrosities, but the exhibit on the programme which I most desired to see was the one described as 'The Boneless Wonder.' My parents judged that that spectacle would be too revolting and demoralising for my youthful eyes, and I have waited fifty years to see the Boneless Wonder sitting on the Treasury Bench."

In current use, political invective has

become more decorous; personal attacks are whispered rather than spoken publicly, for fear they will boomerang. Perhaps Francis Bacon's words are being considered: "Anger makes dull men witty, but it keeps them poor." During the 1992 campaign, however, *Newsday* wrote of "the biting sarcasm, that breathtaking invective" from Republican Pat Buchanan, who said, "Bill Clinton's foreign policy experience is pretty much confined to having had breakfast once at the International House of Pancakes."

investigative reporter. See MUCK-RAKER.

invisible government any group accused of creating public policy immune from public criticism or electoral recall.

"The Invisible Government," wrote David Wise and Thomas B. Ross in their 1964 book of that title, "is not a formal body. It is a loose, amorphous grouping of individuals and agencies drawn from many parts of the visible government. It is not limited to the Central Intelligence Agency, although the CIA is at its heart. . . . This shadow government is shaping the lives of 190,000,000 Americans. Major decisions involving peace or war are taking place out of public view."

In 1967 the editors of *Ramparts* magazine disclosed that foundations acting as conduits for CIA funds had secretly subsidized trips abroad of U.S. student groups. The public reacted severely to this disclosure of a covert operation, and President Johnson ordered it ended. A political cartoon showed a scruffy-looking, bearded beatnik trudging along on a campus, observed by a pair of coeds, one of whom says, "Oh, is he CIA? I thought he was FBI."

After *New York Times* reporter Seymour Hersh broke the story of the CIA's illegal activities in 1975, the "agency"—or as it was also known, "the company"—lost much of its clout. With repeated disclosures (see "family jewels" under CIA-ESE), the intelligence organization ceased to be known as an "invisible government," and adopted the benign term "intelligence community."

The term is current but is no longer aimed at the CIA. A 1991 editorial in the *Seattle Times* wrote of a term-limits initiative that the measure would "not limit power, only transfer it to a permanent, invisible government of legislative staffs and special-interest lobbyists, elected by no one."

"Invisible" is a word with deep and mistrusted roots in American history. Albert Beveridge, senator, orator, and Lincoln biographer, used the phrase at the 1912 Progressive Party convention that nominated Theodore Roosevelt: "These special interests, which suck the people's substance, are bipartisan. They use both parties. They are the invisible government behind the visible government . . . it is this invisible government which is the real danger to American institutions." The phrase was used heavily in the three-man Taft-Roosevelt-Wilson campaign; Wilson joined in denouncing the "special interests" and added: ". . . an invisible empire had been set up above the forms of democracy."

In 1923 the *Review of Reviews* reported that "Governor Parker of Louisiana appeared in Washington to consult with President Harding and the Department of Justice regarding an 'invisible government' that was alleged to be interfering with the administration of justice in his own state and in other parts of the South." The reference was to the Ku Klux Klan, known since the Civil War as "the invisible empire of the South."

The Klan became an issue at the 1924

Democratic convention. Liberal, urban forces behind New York Governor Al Smith wanted to denounce the Klan by name in the party platform; agrarian Democrats behind Wilson's son-in-law, W. G. McAdoo, took a more ambivalent attitude toward the extremists, not wishing to alienate the rural vote where the Klan was strongest. As Barry Goldwater did forty years later with EXTREMISM, McAdoo took the key phrase of his opposition, gave it a twist, and flung it back; playing on the "invisible empire" description of the Klan, he spoke of "the sinister, unscrupulous invisible government which has its seat in the citadel of privilege and finance in New York City."

With William Jennings Bryan's support, McAdoo won the battle against naming the Klan in the platform by a single convention vote. But the bitterness of this issue, as well as the League of Nations, brought forth a moderate dark horse, and John W. Davis was selected as the nominee.

"Invisible government," as a phrase, touches a responsive chord in the minds of people already suspicious of faraway federal government. In the early sixties, ardently anti-Communist Dallas newsletter writer Dan Smoot published a book about the Council on Foreign Relations, titled *The Invisible Government*, which preceded the better-selling Wise-Ross book of the same title.

See DIRTY TRICKS.

in your hands a Lincoln construction used by John Kennedy; an oratorical device of involvement.

From Lincoln's first inaugural: "In your hands, my dissatisfied fellow countrymen, and not in mine, is the momentous issue of civil war."

From Kennedy's inaugural: "In your hands, my fellow citizens, more than mine, will rest the final success or failure of our course."

Irish Mafia the Bostonians of Irish descent who were John Kennedy's earliest and closest political aides.

According to Theodore Sorensen, a Nebraskan with no known Irish blood, Irish Mafia was a "newspaper designation bitterly resented by its designees when first published." Stewart Alsop probably printed it first, but by the time the Kennedy Administration took office in January 1961, Irish Mafia was a smart "in" phrase. Among the group's prominent members were Kenneth O'Donnell, who became Kennedy's appointments secretary; Lawrence O'Brien, chief of congressional liaison and later Democratic National Chairman; and David Powers, a general White House factotum.

Another group, drawn primarily from the academic world typified by McGeorge Bundy, Kennedy's assistant for national security affairs, was often contrasted with the practical politicians of the O'Donnell-O'Brien group. Pierre Salinger, who by background belonged to neither camp, said stories of power struggles between the eggheads and the Mafia "would arouse JFK to profane anger."

The inference that the Kennedy clan leaned heavily on power plotters who rarely saw the sun from their SMOKE-FILLED ROOM hardly blended with the idealistic NEW FRONTIER image. Even worse was the connotation of gangsterism. The original Mafia—named after the Sicilian slang word for boldness or swagger—consisted of primitive racketeers. When an Italian-American group objected in the seventies to what it felt was an ethnic slur, the word was avoided by many law officers.

Although the first use in politics of the word was to compare the most useful qualities of a mob hierarchy to those of men surrounding a President, and to salute the loyalty, dedication, common background and toughness common to both, the jocular tone of the phrase was jolted by revelations in 1975 that the "real" Mafia may have been used by the "Irish Mafia"—or at least the CIA, with Kennedy knowledge—to carry out an assassination attempt against Fidel Castro.

In 1964 political writers showed their nonpartisanship by dubbing Barry Goldwater's Republican coterie from home the "Arizona Mafia." A subsequent article in the *New York Herald Tribune* about English governesses in the U.S. was entitled "The Nanny Mafia." By 1978 the "real" Mafia cloud had passed, and the men in the Carter Administration—Georgians Joseph L. "Jody" Powell, Hamilton Jordan, Griffin Bell, Robert Lipshutz, and others—were often called "the Georgia Mafia," or "Magnolia Mafia." Ronald Reagan's entourage included Ed Meese, William Clark, and Martin Anderson, dubbed part of the "California Mafia." George Bush, from both Maine and Texas, had no Mafia, and the Clinton early cadre went by FOB (Friends of Bill) rather than the "Arkansas Mafia."

When a manager of Dow Corning International wrote to *Business Week* in 1981 objecting to its use of the term "California Mafia," as being in poor taste, the magazine's editor replied: "The term 'California mafia' was in no way intended as a slur. It is well-accepted Washington parlance for a President's tight inner circle—as in John Kennedy's 'Irish mafia' and Jimmy Carter's 'Georgia mafia.'"

The phrase has also been used in city politics. The *Chicago Tribune* wrote in 1992 of Avis LaVelle's departure as deputy press secretary in Mayor Richard Daley's office: "Even though she was not part of Daley's tight-knit, white-male 'Irish mafia' when she linked up with him nearly four years ago, she has since become his most available and valuable public voice, a black woman serving a man who ended the string of two black mayors in a racially divided city."

A recent coinage is *ethnic mafia*, for a group of common ethnic background who use bribery, extortion, and other illegal means to conduct business. Serge Schmemann of the *New York Times* wrote from Russia in 1992: "Ethnic 'mafias' buy politicians and officials in the best tradition of 'The Godfather.'"

iron curtain a barrier to communication between peoples, lowered to permit a regime to operate in a society isolated from outside criticism.

This was one of the two great figures of speech in the generation following World War II (for the other, see COLD WAR). It was popularized by Winston Churchill, who had used it several times before deciding to use it strongly in a speech at Fulton, Missouri, on March 5, 1946: "From Stettin in the Baltic to Trieste in the Adriatic, an iron curtain has descended across the continent. Behind that line lie all the capitals of the ancient states of central and eastern Europe. . . . The safety of the world, ladies and gentlemen, requires a new unity in Europe from which no nation should be permanently outcast."

The forum Churchill chose was an odd one. The president of tiny Westminster College at Fulton wrote to alumnus General Harry Vaughan, President Truman's military aide, inviting Churchill to speak at the college during a forthcoming trip to the United States. Truman endorsed the idea, passed it on to Churchill, who replied that he had something he would like to say.

The "iron curtain speech" of Churchill marked the end of a peaceful honeymoon with Soviet Russia that had existed in the minds of many Americans after World War II. It became the symbol of Soviet oppression, and the rallying cry for the Western European military organization that came to be NATO.

Phrase detectives—principally Ignace Feuerlicht, writing in *American Speech* magazine—tracked down a variety of previous uses. It began as a theatrical phrase. A theater in Lyons, France, introduced a curtain in the eighteenth century to prevent the spread of fire, and in 1794 the Drury Lane Theatre in London did the same. Throughout Europe, "iron curtain" was the name for the fireproof curtain in theaters, and the Earl of Munster, writing of travels in India, used it as a metaphor in 1819: "As if an iron curtain had dropped between us and the Avenging Angel, the deaths diminished."

H. G. Wells used it in 1904 in *The Food of the Gods* as a metaphor for enforced privacy; American author George W. Creel in *A Mechanistic View of War and Peace* in 1915 described France as "a nation of 40 millions with a deeprooted grievance and an iron curtain at its frontier."

The London *Times Literary Supplement* recalled a 1920 use by Viscountess Snowden in her account of a visit to Russia after the war, entitled *Through Bolshevik Russia*: "We were behind the 'iron curtain' at last!"

German militarists liked the phrase. Writing in 1923, Walther Nicolai, who served as intelligence chief of the German General Staff during World War I, used the metaphor about a news blockade the wartime allies had planned to impose upon Germany: "It became clear that in case of war, the enemy would shut off Germany from the outside world as with an iron curtain."

The Moscow *Literary Gazette* carried an editorial headlined "Iron Curtain" in January 1930. The writer, Lev Nikulin, suggested that the bourgeoisie was trying to lower an iron curtain between Russia and the West. The theatrical simile was clear here, because Nikulin was showing how the bourgeoisie was attempting to prevent the spread of the fire of communism.

Hitler's minister of finance, Ludwig Schwerin von Krosigk, was credited with the phrase as well; Nazi propaganda minister Joseph Goebbels used it often, as in this Reuters dispatch appearing in the *Manchester Guardian* of February 23, 1945:

"If the German people lay down their arms, the whole of Eastern and Southern Europe, together with the Reich, will come under Russian occupation. Behind an iron curtain mass butcheries of people would begin."

Later that year, on November 15, Senator Arthur Vandenberg used the phrase in a Senate speech. Meanwhile, on May 12, 1945, Churchill had wired Truman: "An iron curtain is drawn down upon their frontier. We do not know what is going on behind." In his memoirs, Churchill called this "the iron curtain telegram." Ten months later, he popularized the term at Fulton, Missouri.

Predecessors to the iron curtain were the *cordon sanitaire*, which was drawn around western Russia at the end of World War I in an early attempt at "containment" of Communism; the "Wall of China" has often been used as a figure of speech saying "Keep out" in international language, later echoed by the Berlin Wall (see WALL, POLITICAL USE OF); and the French military establishment was denounced during World War II for its "Maginot Line thinking."

Derivatives of the iron curtain are fascinating. Probably the longest-lived was "bamboo curtain," describing the outlook of Communist China. Others included: "Jim Crow curtain," coined by Adam Clayton Powell; the "sand curtain" (between the Arabs and Israel); the "marble curtain" (between newsmen and the government), a coinage of Senator Hubert Humphrey; "cobweb curtain" (separating the English press from the royal court); and a "lace curtain" (the closing of New England to Russian tourists) coined by *Pravda*, its unconscious humor noted by some Irish-Americans. A 1993 editorial in the *Washington Post* tried another variation: "The Clinton Administration continues using the Coast Guard and the Navy as an extension of the Haitian navy . . . transforming Haiti into an island prison. . . . Unlike the Iron Curtain, the Caribbean curtain was erected and is maintained by the U.S. government, supposedly under the guise of humanitarianism."

"I see" construction a favorite device of speechwriters, outlining a vision of the future punctuated with "I see."

Orator Robert G. Ingersoll, who coined the "Plumed Knight" title for candidate James Blaine, offered an example of this highly effective technique in 1876:

I see our country filled with happy homes. . . .
I see a world where thrones have crumbled. . . .
I see a world without a slave. . . .
I see a world at peace . . . a world where labor reaps its full reward. . . .
I see a world without the beggar's outstretched palm . . . the piteous wail of want. . . .
. . . and, as I look, life lengthens, joy deepens, love canopies the earth; and over all, in the great dome, shines the eternal star of human hope.

When Samuel Rosenman prepared a speech for FDR's inaugural in 1937, he used the "I see" repetition in a reportorial, rather than visionary, sense: "I see tens of millions of its citizens" denied the "necessities of life"; "I see millions denied education . . ." Rosenman wrote later: "I had written on the original of the second draft a summation of all the 'I sees' with a final 'I see' . . . the President rubbed out all I had written in pencil after that final 'I see' and after a moment's reflection substituted in his own hand his own summation: 'I see one third of a nation ill-housed, ill-clad, ill-nourished.'"

Rosenman and Robert E. Sherwood collaborated on an FDR speech in 1940 that used the "I see" construction in its visionary sense:

I see an America where factory workers are not discarded after they reach their prime. . . .
I see an America whose rivers and valleys and lakes . . . are protected as the rightful heritage of all the people.
I see an America where small business really has a chance to flourish and grow.
I see an America of great cultural and educational opportunity for all its people.
I see an America where the income from the land shall be implemented and protected. . . .
I see an America devoted to our freedom . . . a people confident in strength because their body and their spirit are secure and unafraid.

Toward the close of his 1952 campaign, Adlai Stevenson outlined his own vision and dream:

I see an America where no man fears to think as he pleases, or say what he thinks.
I see an America where slums and tenements have vanished and children are raised in decency and self-respect.
I see an America where men and women have leisure from toil—leisure to cultivate the resources of the spirit.
I see an America where no man is another's master—where no man's mind is dark with fear.
I see an America at peace with the world.
I see an America as the horizon of human hopes.
This is our design for the American cathedral . . .

Variations of this construction include "I look forward to" and "I HAVE A DREAM." Stevenson used the "I look forward" structure in a Los Angeles speech on the American future on September 11, 1952; John Kennedy used it in 1963, a month before his assassination:

I look forward to a great future for America, a future in which our country will match its military strength with our moral restraint, its wealth with our wisdom, its power with our purpose.

I look forward to an America which will not be afraid of grace and beauty. . . .

I look forward to an America which commands respect throughout the world not only for its strength but for its civilization as well. And I look forward to a world which will be safe not only for democracy and diversity but also for personal distinction.

Preparing his acceptance speech at the 1968 Republican convention, Richard Nixon reviewed all the foregoing, and offered his own vision of America in the year 2000:

I see a day when Americans are once again proud of their flag. . . . I see a day when the President of the United States is respected and his office is honored because it is worthy of respect and worthy of honor. . . . I see a day when we will again have freedom from fear in America and freedom from fear in the world. I see a day when our nation is at peace and the world is at peace and everyone on earth—those who hope, those who aspire, those who crave liberty—will look to America as the shining example of hopes realized and dreams achieved.

In what press secretary Joseph L. Powell described as an "ambitious new text," candidate Jimmy Carter incorporated a passage by speechwriter Patrick Anderson in May 1976: "I see an America that has turned its back on scandals and shame . . . I see an America that does not spy on its own citizens . . ." (See VISION OF AMERICA.)

In rhetoric, the Greek-based term for repeated beginnings is *anaphora*.

ism a political, social, or economic belief or system; in its proper form as a suffix, a way of converting names or ordinary descriptive words into broad labels.

In pragmatic America, dogma (whether right or wrong) has always been slightly suspect. Oswald Garrison Villard, summarizing Calvin Coolidge's appeal to businessmen during the 1924 campaign, said, "He is just what the country needs, a quiet, simple, unobtrusive man, with no isms and no desire for reform."

Derived from the Greek -*ismos*, *ism* can be attached to almost anything for the sake of a catchword either to defend or attack. During William McKinley's Administration, Secretary of War Russell Alger became a controversial figure because of the conduct of his department during the Spanish-American War. "Algerism" became a short-lived but lively topic of conversation—and target for political shafts. Senator Joseph McCarthy died in 1957, but MCCARTHYISM remains an oratorical point of departure.

Capitalism, militarism, pacifism, nationalism, AMERICANISM, and scores of other isms are part of common political discourse, although the meaning of any one term varies widely, depending on the ideology of the user and the context of the use. Charles de Gaulle's concept of nationalism, for instance, differed widely from that of a leader of a former French colony in Africa. The British diplomat Sir Andrew Cohen observed in 1958: "To campaign against colonialism is like barking up a tree that has already been cut down."

Quincy Wright noted that social scientists have "long deplored" such terms because they are "highly sentimentalized, ambiguous, controversial and changeable." But, conceded Wright, it is impossible to "give precise definition to these words or to substitute other words with no connotation in the popular vocabulary."

Two of the angriest political epithets today are RACISM and SEXISM.

isolationism the theory that American interests are best served by a minimum of involvement in foreign affairs and alliances.

Isolationism became a major issue in American politics and a fixture in the American political vocabulary in the post–World War I fight over whether the United States should join the League of Nations. Woodrow Wilson, the great pro-League advocate, castigated those who would have the U.S. retreat into "sullen and selfish isolation." Warren Harding responded: "We seek no part in directing the destinies of the world." Harding prevailed and the country entered its last period of separation from international power politics although even during the 1920s it participated in arms-control conferences.

The rise of Nazism in Germany and the Spanish Civil War once again made isolationism versus internationalism a major domestic issue here. Throughout most of the thirties the country's traditional preference for separation from Europe—what Thomas Jefferson called "the exterminating havoc of one-quarter of the globe"—continued at least nominally in force.

Even Franklin Roosevelt, whose name was to become irrevocably linked with internationalism, said in 1936: "We are not isolationists except insofar as we seek to isolate ourselves completely from war. . . . If we face the choice of profits [from munitions exports] or peace, the nation will answer—must answer—'we choose peace.'" But by 1941 the United States

had become the ARSENAL OF DEMOCRACY, and Pearl Harbor ended the isolationists' dream forever. Senator Arthur Vandenberg, one of the many Republican leaders who abandoned isolation, watched German V-rockets assaulting London in 1944 and mused, "How can there be any immunity or isolation when men can devise weapons like that?" Said the *New Republic:* "Hank Jones, American, is sick of isolation."

After World War II, with relatively little dissent at home, successive Administrations kept the U.S. very much in the mainstream of world affairs. But a variation of the old dispute arose when American involvement in Vietnam became bloody and costly. Lyndon Johnson's Administration was accused, in effect, of extending internationalism beyond the bounds of reason and prudence. Many of the critics were liberals who had favored earlier foreign intervention. Defenders of the Vietnam commitment charged the dissenters with "neo-isolationism." To this Henry Steele Commager, the historian, responded that too much U.S. military activity abroad was leading the country into "intellectual and moral isolationism." See ENTANGLING ALLIANCES; GO-IT-ALONE.

Objectively, the antonym is *internationalism;* isolationists prefer to denounce *interventionism* and *adventurism.*

Israel lobby. See CHINA LOBBY.

issues, the important but dull subjects, treated rationally, which most candidates solemnly promise to campaign upon; a promise usually honored in the breach.

"I intend to campaign on the issues," a candidate frequently announces, and that pledge is dutifully reported as "So-and-so pledged an issue-oriented campaign." The candidate who proclaims his fealty to "the issues" usually refuses to ENGAGE IN PERSONALITIES, which is what interests most voters.

Real issues run the gamut from GUT ISSUE to "burning issue" to the more recent "social issue" and the recurring BREAD-AND-BUTTER ISSUE; but spoken in the plural, construed as singular, "the issues" is gaining a do-good, bogus-intellectual connotation.

The phrase was probably popularized by Senator William E. Borah in the campaign of 1928. On March 10 of that year he charged that the Republican National Committee had accepted over a quarter-million dollars from oil magnate Harry Sinclair, adding that "the people are baffled and discouraged because they cannot get the issues squarely and fairly presented." He then delivered a quotable line: "Give the people issues, and you will not have to sell your souls for campaign funds."

In 1972, after presidential candidate George McGovern dropped Senator Thomas Eagleton from the ticket, a *New York Times* editorial adjured the Democratic team to address "itself vigorously to the real issues," which caused *Times* columnist Russell Baker to comment: "The odd thing about Senator McGovern's Vice Presidential entr'acte was the amount of noise from the press urging that the Vice Presidential crisis be disposed of quickly so that the campaign could proceed to deal with the issues—sometimes called 'the real issues.' Reviewing Presidential campaigns back into the nineteen-fifties, we are led to suspect that the press people who wanted to move on to these 'real issues' were trying to cheat us of what will probably be our one opportunity to perceive Mr. McGovern as he might actually behave in the White House."

In 1977, after a campaign in which he had been accused of being "fuzzy on the issues," President Jimmy Carter told reporter John Sherwood of the *Washington Star* that he felt a kinship with successful congressional campaigners: "We're all fuzzy on the issues. That's proven by the fact that we did get elected. The advantage of being a presidential candidate is that you have a much broader range of issues on which to be fuzzy."

"The issues" is becoming an issue in itself. Richard Reeves, speculating about a possible 1980 Democratic primary race between Jimmy Carter and California Governor Jerry Brown, wrote in the *Washington Monthly:* "Since both can afford pollsters, Carter and Brown will not be that far apart on what the *New Republic* calls 'issues.'" Tom Bethell seized on this line in *Harper's* (January 1978): "There at last were the issues—the Issues—being referred to within ironical quotation marks. As indeed they should be, if it is true that candidates' (or incumbents') positions are now determined by the findings of pollsters rather than by the principles of officeholders or -seekers. If this is so, then 'the issues' have in an important sense disappeared and fully deserve their quotation marks, because they are no longer the object of decision on the part of 'decision-makers' in Washington . . . thus the Issues have become mere ornaments, the wearing of which would inevitably attract such a careful student of style as *Women's Wear Daily.*"

See MAGNET ISSUE; WEDGE ISSUE; HOT BUTTON; GUT ISSUE.

itch to run a yearning for elective office, used most often as a "presidential itch"; a symptom of POTOMAC FEVER and PRESIDENTIAL FEVER.

Rutherford B. Hayes in 1871 wrote in his diary: "If I thought there was the slightest danger of so obscure a personage as I being attacked with that wretched mania, an itching for the White House, I would beg for the prayers of your church for my deliverance." Five years later he was off and running, and won.

The expression is common in English politics as well. Alfred Austin, poet laureate of England at the turn of the century, wrote:

> *You want a seat! Then boldly sate your
> itch;*
> *Be very radical, and very rich.*

item veto. See RIDER.

It's the economy, Stupid! formulaic reminder of central issue or goal.

James Carville, Bill Clinton's political strategist in the 1992 election, placed a sign over his desk in the Little Rock headquarters: "It's the economy, Stupid!" For a campaigner fixed on a need for a central theme, the sign encapsulated a pointed response to the question "What is the campaign about?"

By the end of 1992, the formula of noun-plus-"Stupid!" had become the focus for writers of political headlines.

Ethan H. Siegal of Prudential Securities offered the financial-newsletter headline "It's the *Deficit*, Stupid!" The headline above a David Twersky column in *The Forward* was "The Mideast, Stupid!"

From the Latin *stupere*, "to be stunned," *stupid* is capitalized when used in direct address. In 1964, *Kiss Me, Stupid* was the title of a movie directed by Billy Wilder. In the 1970s, advertisers were told to use "the KISS formula," which stood for "keep it simple, Stupid!" Howard Barbanel, an adman, wrote the author in 1993: "The 'stupid' part refers to the one doing either the copywriting or the selling—as a warning to that person not to be tempted to attempt wedging 'War and Peace' into a 2 × 4 ad or a 15-second spot."

The jocular nature of the imperative takes out the sting of insult; the reader of the notice knows he is merely being urged to keep the central issue in focus.

See GUT ISSUE.

J

Jacobins. See INTELLECTUAL-IN-RESI-DENCE.

janissary. See HENCHMAN.

jawboning the use of presidential admonition as a tool of INCOMES POLICY.

"The jawbone method" was the phrase used by Walter Heller, chairman of the Council of Economic Advisers in 1962, to describe GUIDELINES set down to restrain prices and wages. The most vivid example of this technique was the confrontation between President Kennedy and the steel industry (see S.O.B.).

When the guidelines began to break down in 1965, the word "jawboning" gained a connotation of ineffective protest. President Nixon flatly told the Cabinet Committee on Economic Policy in early 1969: "I'm against jawboning." In economic speeches, he said the economy needed more "backbone, not more jawbone." Even after his announcement of a new economic policy on August 15, 1971, the President retained his distaste for the ineffective connotation of the word; in September, describing the phase of policy that would follow the wage-price freeze, he told a press conference, "you cannot have jawboning that is effective without teeth," which was an appropriate extension of the metaphor.

Jimmy Carter, as President, preferred the phrase "moral suasion," and assigned Robert Strauss, a former Democratic National Chairman, to the job of jawboning business and labor in 1978.

Jim Crow laws and customs that discriminate against, segregate, or humiliate blacks.

"I was offered the Ambassadorship of Liberia once," said Ralph Bunche, after becoming Undersecretary of the United Nations in 1960, "when that post was earmarked for a Negro. I told them I wouldn't take a Jim Crow job."

At the Republican convention in San Francisco in 1964, a band of black demonstrators marched in front of the Cow Palace shouting and clapping "Jim Crow [*clap, clap*]—must go!"

A crow is black. A Kentucky plantation song, sung early in the eighteenth century, coined the name for a dance, or jig:

First on the heel tap, den on de toe,
Ebery time I wheel about
I jump Jim Crow.

In 1829, entertainer Thomas Dartmouth Rice blacked his face and "jumped Jim Crow" in a Louisville theater. Soon after, the name became synonymous with Negro, and around 1840 the segregated Negro car on the Boston Railroad became known as the "Jim Crow." In 1841 the abolitionist *Liberator* told of the indignity to black editor and later diplomat Frederick Douglass: "The conductor . . . ordered Douglass to leave, and to take his seat in the forward car; meaning the 'Jim Crow,' though he felt ashamed to call it by that name."

President Truman took a major step in ending Jim Crow by desegregating the armed services. "Experience on the front has proved," he wrote, "that the morale of troops is strengthened where Jim Crow practices are not imposed." With great pride Truman recounted the reaction of Southern Democrats to his insistence on a strong civil rights plank in the 1948 Democratic platform. As South Carolina Governor J. Strom Thurmond walked out of the convention with his followers, a reporter pointed out, "Truman is only following the platform that Roosevelt advocated." "I agree," Thurmond replied, "but Truman really *means* it."

The legality of Jim Crow was crushed by the Supreme Court desegregation decision of 1954 (see WITH ALL DELIBERATE SPEED). The most dramatic challenge to Jim Crow customs as well as laws came with the "freedom rides" of young blacks in the South in 1961 (see FREEDOM RIDERS). With education and transportation desegregated, blacks—many of whom now prefer to be called African-Americans—targeted housing next. Although Lester Maddox won a narrow victory in Georgia in the 1966 race for governor on a slogan of "Your Home Is Your Castle—Protect It," his ardor cooled somewhat after election day.

In a profile of then Senator Strom Thurmond the *Washington Post* commented in 1993: "He always kept the voters of South Carolina first on his agenda; when the Voting Rights Act of 1965 guaranteed blacks the vote, he dumped segregation for egalitarianism faster than you can say 'Jim Crow.'"

For subsequent developments in the lexicon of civil rights, see SEGREGATION; BUSING TO ACHIEVE RACIAL BALANCE; RACISM; BLACK, POLITICAL USE OF.

jingoism   shrill, aggressive superpatriotism (see SUPERPATRIOTS); chauvinism.

In a Venezuelan boundary dispute between Great Britain and the U.S. in 1895, New York Police Board chief Theodore Roosevelt warned: "We will settle the Venezuelan question in Canada. Canada would surely be conquered, and once wrested from England it would never be restored."

To Senator Henry Cabot Lodge, Roosevelt said, "This country needs a war," but added that "the bankers, brokers and Anglomaniacs generally" seemed to favor "PEACE AT ANY PRICE."

Horrified, President Charles William Eliot of Harvard asked whether anything could be more offensive "than this doctrine of Jingoism, this chip-on-the-shoulder attitude of a ruffian and a bully," and added that both Roosevelt and Lodge were "degenerated sons of Harvard." (Roosevelt became calmer in later years, his best-known remark beginning with "Speak softly.")

The doctrine of jingoism Eliot referred to, along with Roosevelt's "peace at any price" remark, came from the English parliamentary battle in 1876, with Gladstone on one side facing Queen Victoria and Disraeli on the other. The issue was intervention in Turkey over alleged persecution of Christians there. Gladstone held that Britain should support the Christian minorities against the Turks, threatening to bundle the Turks out of Europe "bag and baggage." Disraeli and the

Queen felt it was all a plot by the Russians to expand at the expense of Turkey. When Disraeli threatened the Russians with war if they did not halt the flow of "volunteers" into Turkey, this refrain was heard in the music halls of London:

We don't want to fight, but by Jingo, if
we do,
We've got the ships, we've got the men,
We've got the money, too!

"Jingoism" quickly became a synonym for bellicose remarks and national cockiness. Disraeli was initially forced into neutrality, but when Russia invaded Turkey in 1878, he sent in the British fleet and helped arrange what he called a PEACE WITH HONOR.

In recent times, "jingoism" was a charge leveled at U.S. participation in the war in Vietnam. In answer, McGeorge Bundy wrote that the American people "have refused to give support to easy wrong answers at either extreme. Open opposition has flourished. There has been less jingoism than in any previous war in our history." In 1978, opponents of the Panama Canal treaties, who charged GIVEAWAY, were denounced as "jingoes."

The synonym is SUPERPATRIOTS or chauvinists, from the French chauvin, the name of a real Napoleonic veteran in Scribe's play Le Soldat Laboureur.

Winston Churchill wrote in My Early Life: "I have always been against the pacifists during the quarrel, and against the Jingoes at its close."

job seeks the man   a philosophy of office believed in by the fatalistic, the idealistic, or the lazy.

A paradox exists in the mind of the American voter. He expects a candidate for high office to be mildly reluctant at first, as "the office seeks the man"; then, with the possibility implanted, he expects the candidate to hungrily seek the office. The man must not try too hard at first; he must not fail to try his hardest toward the end. Many a man has played "hard to get" a little too long, the possibility of his candidacy does not take root, and he is dismissed with his acquiescence unspoken.

President Harry Truman, in a passage about "luck" in his memoirs, observed:

If a man starts out to make himself President, he hardly ever arrives. Henry Clay is an outstanding example. He was so sure he would be President that he twice refused the vice-presidency, and in both cases he would have succeeded to the highest office because of the death of the President. James G. Blaine was another such man. And I was convinced . . . that Thomas E. Dewey was another whose determined efforts to make himself President would never materialize.

Richard Nixon took the same fatalistic view: "I have a theory," he said in 1958, "that in the United States those who seek the Presidency never win it. Circumstances rather than a man's ambition determine the result. If he is the right man for the right time, he will be chosen."

Adlai Stevenson, subject of a rare genuine draft in 1952, appeared to many to have overplayed reluctance and humility. In his acceptance speech, he reminded the delegates, "I would not seek your nomination for the presidency because the burdens of that office stagger the imagination. . . its potential . . . smothers exultation and converts vanity to prayer." Many politicians felt he made the right speech at the wrong moment.

The concept of "the job seeks the man" applies less to lesser offices than president. In the case of Supreme Court Justice, however, it applies most of all. When Governor Abraham Ribicoff of Connecticut, a strong and early Kennedy supporter, was asked if he had hopes for the high court, he replied, "He who does not seek is often found. The one thing you should never seek is the Supreme Court."

Columnist Clayton Fritchey wrote in 1967 about the way California Governor Ronald Reagan ducked the question of national candidacy: "When asked about White House aspirations, he declined to be drawn out because, as he reminded the reporters, in this country 'The Office seeks the man,' not the other way around." He added: "Like Lola, what The Office wants, The Office gets. Ask Eisenhower. The General fled to Paris in 1952 and tried to hide out in NATO, but it didn't work. . . . It's time somebody seeks The Office instead of vice versa."

In this expression, *job* and *office* are used interchangeably; *job* is more recent usage, and seems to be ascendant.

Joe Smith a fictional stand-in; surprise star of the 1956 Republican convention; a fictitious nominee for Vice President, the name put in by a delegate who wanted to "dump Nixon."

After Harold Stassen's effort to replace Richard Nixon as the Republican nominee for Vice President proved abortive (see KINGMAKER), the nomination was a foregone conclusion. Speaker Joseph Martin, convention chairman, had been tipped off by Interior Secretary Fred Seaton of Nebraska that "a misguided and recalcitrant Nebraska delegate" was going to put Seaton's name in nomination, using that as a wedge to make a nominating speech. In that proposed speech, National Chairman Len Hall suspected some alarming things were to be said about President Eisenhower's health; Hall urged Martin to avoid giving the Nebraska delegate, Terry Carpenter, a chance to speak.

When Nebraska was reached on the roll call, the head of the delegation said that Carpenter wanted the floor. "Who does he desire to nominate?" asked Martin, probably out of order. The Nebraska chairman did not know. Martin explained that the reason he was asking was that he had a note from "a distinguished son of Nebraska" (Seaton) stating he wanted no part of being nominated. This robbed Carpenter of his candidate, but he thought fast.

"Mr. Chairman," he called out, "we are going to nominate Joe Smith."

"Joe who?"

"Joe Smith!" Amid a roar of laughter in an otherwise cut-and-dried convention, newsmen clustered around the Nebraska delegation. Martin thundered the classic order of the day: "Take your Joe Smith and get outa here!"

See CHARLIE REGAN.

John Bull. See UNCLE SAM.

John Q. Public the mythical average man, or MAN IN THE STREET; often cartooned as bespectacled, long-suffering, clad in a barrel, but eternally optimistic.

In the fifteenth century his name was *Everyman,* hero of English and Dutch morality plays; when Death called him, he asked his friends Beauty, Kindred, and Worldly Goods to go along. They turned him down, and only one—Good Deeds—accompanied Everyman to heaven. See EVERY MAN A KING.

In the Progressive movement of the nineteenth century, he was *The Man of Good Will;* William Graham Sumner called him *the forgotten man* (not to be confused with FDR's FORGOTTEN MAN who lived "on the bottom of the economic pyramid"); and Woodrow Wilson idealized him as *the man on the make* from "out of the unknown homes" who was the hope of America.

Wilson's aim was to set up a government "where the average man, the plain man, the common man, the ignorant man, the unaccomplished man, the poor man had a voice equal to the voice of anybody else in the settlement of the common affairs, an ideal never before realized in the history of the world." See COMMON MAN, CENTURY OF THE.

William Allen White, editor of the *Emporia Gazette,* took the side of the consumer in a 1937 speech: "We are all the children of John Q. Public, and our interests as members of the consuming public are after all our chief end and objective as citizens of our democracy. . . . If labor insists," he warned, "upon maintaining its class lines of bitter intransigent hostility to all capital, the American middle class—old John Q. Public and his heirs and assigns—will not support labor."

He signs specimen checks under the name of *John Doe* and *Richard Roe;* his wife, *Jane Doe,* signs specimen subscription orders for women's magazines. To a younger set, he has a glazed expression that asks, "What—me worry?" and answers to *Alfred E. Newman.* In other incarnations, he appears as *Joe Zilch* and *Joe Blow.* In the 1980s, he was sometimes called *Joe Sixpack.* In China he is known as *Old Hundred Names.* Theatergoers know him as *Littlechap,* who cries, "Stop the world—I want to get off!" Only the Devil himself (Satan, Mephisto, Scratch, Old Nick, Lucifer, etc.) has more aliases.

John is the most common first name, with the "Q" added to give a distinctive, humorously dignified fillip; the last name has genuine built-in dignity, its Latin root *pubes,* "adult."

Not every writer pays him respect. Robert Bendiner wrote in 1960 about the political diminutives—"*little man, common man, small businessman, small farmer,* and the like. In an elec-

tion year, we seem to have an enormous population of midgets. The candidate's immediate audience, however, is never made up of these wee folk; it is made up of *the great people of this great state.* That's you. The little people are your relatives and neighbors."

Johnson treatment   in the broad sense, the "LBJ brand," or style of presidency; in a narrow sense, the technique of badgering, dickering, and overpowering that President Johnson was reputed to use in person-to-person persuasion.

The broad sense is less often used. Jack Bell, AP White House correspondent, called his book about the President *The Johnson Treatment,* subtitled "How Lyndon B. Johnson Took Over the Presidency and Made It His Own."

The Treatment, as it was more specifically known, was described by a recipient, Texas Lieutenant Governor Ben Ramsey, in explaining to Governor Allan Shivers in 1956 why he suddenly switched his support on a matter from Shivers to Johnson: "Lyndon got me by the lapels and put his face on top of mine and talked and talked and talked. I figured it was either get drowned or joining."

The Johnson treatment was generally described as an all-stops-out display of pressure, cajolery, threats, promises of *quid pro quo,* and refusal to take no for an answer. Rowland Evans and Robert Novak described this scene of the persuasion of Senator Richard Russell to become a member of the Warren Commission on the assassination of President Kennedy: "In a conversation lasting most of an hour, Johnson unleashed The Treatment, dormant now for three years. Emotionally, he recalled their long, intimate association. He appealed to Russell as his friend, and he appealed as the President of the

United States. 'If you say no,' Johnson said, 'I'll have you drafted.' Russell accepted, and the Commission was complete."

Used in its general sense, the Johnson treatment is synonymous with his presidential style. The word *style* is almost always used admiringly in regard to Kennedy, derisively regarding Johnson; those who like his style use the Western metaphor, *brand*. Harvard professor Theodore Levitt made the case in favor of The Treatment in the *Harvard Business Review:*

> At best Johnson gets pejorative praise, summarized in tasteless references to the "Johnson Treatment"—the endless telephone calls, implied threats, stubborn push, pleading entreaties, backroom quid pro quos . . .
>
> The Johnson Treatment is nothing more or less than his practice of taking business and other opponents, or potential opponents, into his private and genuine confidence, to talk comfortably about the problems of our people, not intellectually about the issues of our times.

journalese   At the BACKGROUNDERS held by AUTHORITATIVE SOURCES, which can be MEDIA EVENTS in themselves, members of the FOURTH ESTATE—evoking the public's RIGHT TO KNOW—refuse to settle for NO COMMENT or OFF THE RECORD. Instead, reporters protected by a LID and on a NOT FOR ATTRIBUTION basis probe the SOURCES for material for their TICKTOCKS and KEEPERS, sometimes seeking SOUND BITES during their WALTER TIME to enliven MEGOS with the technique of RULE OUT.

Meanwhile, some PUNDITS—anxious for LEAKS but suspicious of PLANTS and scornful of HANDOUTS—reportedly write such infuriating DOPE STORIES, THINK PIECES, and THUMBSUCKERS that they wind up on the ZOO PLANE.

All of the above have separate entries

herein, explicating the murmuring of the media biggies.

juice   political power.

Among the many slang meanings of "juice" (liquor, gasoline, hot money) is "electrical current," which is the metaphoric base of this 1970s political term. To be able to apply "juice" is to be able to flip the switch that generates great political power.

Reporter Nicholas Horrock wrote in the *New York Times* of August 7, 1977, of a plan proposed by the Director of Central Intelligence, Admiral Stansfield Turner, to take over "line authority" of intelligence agencies currently under the Defense Department: "But reportedly, Vice President Mondale . . . opposed the plan on the ground that it would have placed too much of what in Washington is called 'juice' at the admiral's fingertips."

When a surprise roll-call vote overturned an expected voice-vote approval of cargo-preference legislation on October 19, 1977, the *Washington Post* reported the bitter comment of an aide to House Merchant Marine Chairman John Murphy: "We got juiced."

The word is not squeezing out CLOUT.

junket.   See NONPOLITICAL TRIP; FACT-FINDING TRIP.

junketeering gumshoes   derisive description of a European fact-finding tour taken by two members of Senator Joseph McCarthy's subcommittee staff.

Roy M. Cohn and G. David Schine visited U.S. Information Service libraries in Europe during 1954, and recommended that certain books be removed from the shelves. Mr. Cohn informed the author it was Theodore Kaghan, at the U.S. High Commissioner's office in Germany, who coined the phrase.

"It turned out to be one of the most publicized journeys of the decade," wrote Cohn in 1968, characterizing the trip as a "colossal mistake."

"What we failed to foresee was the propaganda uses to which our critics would put the journey. David Schine and I unwittingly handed Joe McCarthy's enemies a perfect opportunity to spread the tale that a couple of young, inexperienced clowns were bustling about Europe, ordering State Department officials around, burning books, creating chaos wherever they went, and disrupting foreign relations."

"Junket" and "junketeer" carry connotations of joyride, a vacation at public (or anyone else's) expense. Congressmen called these NONPOLITICAL TRIPS, inspection tours, or FACT-FINDING TRIPS; critics call them junkets. When a business firm or tourist board invites newsmen on a junket, it is so labeled; some newspapers insist on paying the equivalent air fare to the destination.

"Gumshoe" has a long history. Present word for the item it originally identified is "sneaker"—a canvas shoe with rubber sole and heel used most often in sports. Because the wearer can move most quietly, the gumshoe became synonymous with stealth. See PUSSYFOOTING. Martin Van Buren, who had acquired a certain reputation for wiliness, was accused of "rowing to his object with muffled oars," and "making his way to the White House in gumshoes." A "gumshoe campaign" was used at the turn of the century, especially in the Midwest, to describe a quiet campaign; currently the word is slang for "detective," used often as a verb.

Kaghan's skillful combination of the two words made it an effective derogation of McCarthy's investigators, and

led to the BOOKBURNER speech by Eisenhower.

junta a small group, usually military, that rules a country after a coup d'état.

This Spanish word, meaning "council" or "meeting," was popularized by its 1808 use to describe the groups formed in Spain during the Peninsular War against Napoleon. In Latin America, the noun has been used frequently; it usually denotes a council coming into power as the result of force or revolution and often includes military leaders.

The word comes from the Latin *juncta*, a form of the verb *jungere*, "to join." (In the sense of a self-appointed ruling committee after a coup, the spelling *junto* may also be used, although *junta* is the earlier spelling.) When a group that seizes power is not predominantly military, it is called a CABAL.

Junta is almost always used pejoratively, as the group has by definition come to power through undemocratic means. *Junta* is pronounced HOONta in the United States, after the Spanish pronunciation, and Anglicized as JUN-ta in Britain.

just and lasting peace a Lincoln coinage about the Civil War, used in regard to the settlement of every war since then.

The phrase comes from Lincoln's second inaugural address, along with "bind up the nation's wounds" and "with malice toward none": ". . . to do all which may achieve and cherish a just and lasting peace among ourselves, and with all nations."

President Eisenhower, in his statement at Geneva in 1955, departed slightly from the text to refer to "a just and durable peace," but returned to report to the American people that "we will make constantly brighter the lamp that will one day guide us to our goal—a just and lasting peace."

"Bad" peaces are usually described as *uneasy* or *shaky;* "good" peaces are referred to as *peace with justice* or PEACE WITH HONOR. The overriding ideal, however, appears to be permanence; the Chartist petition of 1828 in England called for the universal suffrage that would bring "true and lasting peace." See FULL GENERATION OF PEACE.

just war. See WAR OF NATIONAL LIBERATION.

K

K_1C_2 a 1952 Republican campaign symbol, combining the three key charges: Korea (and the Democrats' inability to end the war), Communism (SOFT ON), and Corruption (the MESS IN WASHINGTON).

Combinations of numbers and letters resembling chemical or mathematical formulas are sometimes appropriate political devices. For use in the 1964 Goldwater campaign, see AuH_2O = 1964. In Great Britain, "C three C 3" referred to a population classification of the mentally and physically deficient, and came to be a colloquialism for "unfit," similar to the U.S. "4-F."

kangaroo ticket one in which the vice-presidential candidate has greater political appeal than the presidential candidate.

Unnamed friends of Treasury Secretary John F. Connally were described by R. W. Apple in the *New York Times* of October 23, 1971, as saying he would run for Vice President in 1972 if asked by President Nixon, but one condition was "he would insist that the Nixon-Connally partnership be advertised as a 'kangaroo ticket.'"

The phrase may have originated in 1932, when some thought that John Nance Garner, the Democratic vice-presidential nominee (the hindquarters in this analogy), had more spring than Franklin D. Roosevelt (the forequarters). In 1992, Paul Greenberg of the *Arkansas Democrat-Gazette* wrote, "Clinton-Gore may yet turn out to be a kangaroo ticket a la Dukakis-Bentsen: stronger in the hind legs." When Vice President Dan Quayle performed more effectively than George Bush in television debating during that campaign, some pundit suggested the Republicans had fielded a kangaroo ticket.

The kangaroo, a herbivorous, leaping marsupial mammal native to Australia, has made other contributions to American slang. A *kangaroo court* is an irregular tribunal, such as a trial by prisoners in a jail, or a minor court in a frontier jurisdiction. *Kangaroo closure* occurs when a chairman or speaker selects only those amendments of a bill he is interested in as subject to debate. In underworld lingo, a *kangaroo* is a shoplifter with capacious pockets.

keeper a news story held for use at a more newsworthy time.

This journalistic term can be used to

describe an innocent delay of a story until a more propitious moment, or a manipulative delay of a story until it can do the most damage.

"It is largely in the executive offices of the printed press and the networks that slanting the news and its editorial evaluation is to be found," wrote Arthur Krock, former Washington correspondent of the *New York Times*, in a 1975 book. "Important in the process are: the placement of the news by which it can be minimized or magnified; and holding back news stories called 'keepers' for publication on a date when they will have the stronger impact in forming public opinion aligned with the editorial policy of the newspaper concerned."

keister the buttocks.

Keister, which is pronounced KEE-ster and has the variant spelling *keester*, is of uncertain origin, but may have come from the German *Kiste*, "chest." Its earliest English meaning is "suitcase, satchel," particularly in criminal slang for "burglar's toolbag"; in the *National Police Gazette* of 1881 was a listing of New York con artists including "Keister Bob."

The journal *American Speech*, listing in a 1931 glossary the current sense, reported two meanings for the word: "*Keister*, a satchel; also what one sits on."

By 1983, the term "ass" no longer needed a euphemism, except in the *New York Times*, though it is still often avoided as a vulgarism by the jocular use of "rear end," "fanny," and "posterior." President Ronald Reagan in 1983 popularized the old euphemism, expressing his ire at the disclosure of his private conversations by saying, "I've had it up to my keister."

See C.Y.A.

Kennedy Round a series of negotiations begun in 1964 and concluded in

1967 between the U.S. and European nations that succeeded in reducing tariff barriers.

Economists in the Kennedy Administration felt that the General Agreement on Tariffs and Trade—GATT—could be supplemented by U.S. entry into the complex discussions on the reduction of tariffs, with the aim of "freer trade." The Kennedy Administration's Trade Expansion Act of 1962 enabled the U.S. to begin the discussions; though the President was assassinated before the negotiations began, they continued to bear his name.

"Once the Kennedy Round is over," wrote the *New York Times* in 1967, "there will be need for a Johnson Round. . . . If the negotiations produce a package containing reduction in both industrial and agricultural tariffs, the President would have little difficulty convincing Congress and the nation that executive authority for concluding new bargains is essential."

The "Kennedy Round" is a seldom understood phrase. Soon after Lyndon Johnson became President, he turned to Bromley Smith, a member of the National Security Agency staff, and asked plaintively, "Can you tell me in one clear sentence what the Kennedy Round is?"

The Kennedy Round was followed by the Tokyo Round in 1973, as well as by the Uruguay Round. Future rounds are likely to continue to be named after nations or cities rather than individuals.

See WALL, POLITICAL USE OF; SNAKE IN THE TUNNEL.

key aide. See STAFFER.

keynoter one who delivers the keynote, or theme-setting, address at a convention.

In recent years the advent of television has changed the keynote speech, the last refuge of full-blown oratory, into a showcase for young political talent. Each party, anxious to put its best foot forward to the home viewers as well as to the delegates in the hall, has been choosing young, good-looking, articulate keynoters.

The term *keynoter* dates back to the 1920s. Writing of the old-style keynoter, Walter Lippmann said: "A keynoter must never say that two and two make four. It is also the rule that the orator must never use one adjective if he can think of three adjectives, or make one statement except in superlative terms."

Senator Alben Barkley, keynoting the 1932 convention that nominated Franklin Roosevelt, roused the troops in this manner: "Two weeks ago in this place, the Republican party promulgated what it called a plank on the Eighteenth Amendment. It is not a plank. It is a promiscuous agglomeration of scrap-lumber!" See PLATFORM.

After Barkley's STEMWINDER, Will Rogers wrote: "This was no note . . . this was in three volumes . . . but it had to be a long speech for when you start enumerating the things the Republicans have got away with in the last twelve years you have cut yourself out a job."

Less kind was Michael Barone's critique in the April 2, 1990, *U.S. News & World Report:* "As for [Texas Governor Ann] Richards, the Democrats' 1988 national keynoter, she seems afraid to say what she believes."

kinder and gentler nation   the Bush wish for the nation's future; his vision of a peaceful America.

George Bush used the modifiers *kinder* and *gentler* in his acceptance speech at the 1988 Republican National Convention in New Orleans: "But where is it written that we must act as if we do not care, as if we're not moved? Well, I am moved. I want a kinder and gentler nation." (See THOUSAND POINTS OF LIGHT.) The adjectives were chosen by the speechwriter Peggy Noonan to express Bush's vision for the post-Reagan era in America.

Bush repeated the phrase in his Inaugural Address, and the words have become identified with him.

Readers, however, have sought literary sources of the phrase from Tolstoy to Thomas Mann, as well as collocations of the adjectives that predate the Bush usage. Bruno Stein, director of the Institute of Labor Relations at New York University, found this comment made by the defense attorney Clarence Darrow about the labor leader Eugene V. Debs: "There may have lived somewhere a kindlier, gentler, more generous man than Eugene Debs, but I have not known him."

Kingfish   self-proclaimed nickname of Huey Long, governor and later senator from Louisiana, assassinated in 1935.

The nickname was drawn from "Kingfish of the Lodge," a black character on the popular *Amos 'n Andy* radio program. Long's choice of the name showed a good instinct for self-deprecating humor that was to become fashionable a generation later. His son, Russell Long, managed to live down the nickname "Princefish," and became one of the powers of the Senate.

"Share the Wealth" and "EVERY MAN A KING" were two of Long's short slogans. Robert Penn Warren's 1945 novel, *All the King's Men* (its title taken from the Humpty-Dumpty nursery rhyme), was based on Huey Long's life.

kingmaker   one who places another in a position of power when, for reasons of personality, circumstance, or preference, he cannot or will not place himself there.

"In elective governments," wrote

English royalist Roger L'Estrange in the time of Cromwell, "there is a tacit covenant that the king of their own making shall make his makers princes." In 1595 an English writer described a manipulative earl as "that great Kingmaker Warwick."

Rarely do kingmakers serve their sovereigns without expectation of reward. Theodore Roosevelt passed the mantle of the presidency to his personal choice, William Howard Taft, and was convinced he acted with the purest altruism. But when Taft wrote Roosevelt immediately after the election that "you and my brother Charlie" made him President, the estrangement began. Roosevelt wondered to a friend what "brother Charlie" had to do with it, and soon was taking umbrage at what he felt were slights by the new President.

More famous American kingmakers were Henry Clay, who delivered the swing vote necessary to elect John Quincy Adams and received the post of Secretary of State in return, enraging the Jackson men ("Bargain and Corruption" was their slogan); Mark Hanna, Cleveland industrialist who masterminded William McKinley's election; and Harry Daugherty, who spotted Warren Harding, a handsome, small-town newspaper editor in Ohio, and helped him up the ladder through the SMOKE-FILLED ROOM (in which Daugherty was not present) to the White House. Years later Daugherty said of Harding: "I found him sunning himself like a turtle on a log, and I pushed him into the water."

However he exaggerates his own importance, the manipulative politician knows that he is dispensable after power is achieved by his candidate. Since kings tend to resent Pygmalions, the wise counselor admits only to having "helped."

Most recently, television advisers have been given Warwick's sobriquet.

In a *New York Times Magazine* article on advisers Jerry Rafshoon and David Garth, opposed in the 1977 New York mayoral campaign, reporter Joseph Lelyveld described Rafshoon's national reputation as the man who helped "create" Jimmy Carter: "When the votes were in, [Carter] sent his media man a lightly ironic note that hangs now above the fancy new desk in Rafshoon's fancy new office, a block from the White House. 'I'll always be grateful,' the note says, 'that I was able to contribute in a small way to the victory of [the] Rafshoon agency.'"

Mr. Garth, who was Mayor John Lindsay's media adviser, has this quotation on his wall, from Niccolò Machiavelli: "Whoever causes another to become powerful is ruined, because he creates such power either with skill or with force; both these factors are viewed with suspicion by the one who has become powerful."

Currently the term is applied to foreign political figures as well as to Americans. According to the December 3, 1990, *New Republic*, "[Lech Walesa] happily played kingmaker, choosing Mazowiecki, his longtime adviser, as prime minister."

See GRAY EMINENCE; POWER BEHIND THE THRONE; POWER BROKERS.

kiss of death unwelcome support from an unpopular source, occasionally engineered by the opposition.

Occasionally, unpopular organizations move in Machiavellian ways, publicly supporting the candidate they most want to defeat. More often, they will quietly "pass the word" to their members to support a candidate they would like to see elected and then scrupulously avoid making any public statements in his support that might embarrass him.

Governor Al Smith of New York popularized the phrase in its political context in 1926, when he called William Randolph Hearst's support of his opponent, Ogden Mills, "the kiss of death."

Walter Lippmann discussed the technique in 1936: "Thus it has recently been said that Senator Borah received 'the kiss of death' when Dr. Townsend gave him his blessing. Governor Landon has received the kiss of death because Mr. Hearst is for him. Senator Vandenberg has received the kiss of death because someone took it into his head to say that Mr. Hoover is for him. . . . Colonel Knox has been repeatedly kissed to death because certain not too savory Illinois machine politicians are for him . . ."

The phrase is derived from the kiss of Judas and the betrayal of Christ. It is also described as coming from a gangland custom called *omerta*, said to have begun in Sicily. "In the mobs," wrote Russell Baker, "a kiss from the boss is tantamount to arriving at the office one morning and finding your rug gone. When [Joseph] Valachi got the kiss and noted that Johnny Dio was oddly anxious to have him step into the privacy of the showers, Valachi concluded that he was a 'dead duck' and defected."

kitchen cabinet   informal advisers to the President who, while holding only minor offices themselves—or none at all—exert more influence on policy than the real cabinet because of their close personal relations with the Chief Executive.

Early in his first Administration, Andrew Jackson for a time suspended formal cabinet deliberations. His enemies accused him of substituting the judgment of five of his friends—two editors and three minor Treasury Department officials—for that of the regular department heads, especially in directing the attack against the United States Bank. Despite their presumed influence, it was no compliment to be called a member of the kitchen cabinet. Said Davy Crockett in 1834: "I might easily have been mistaken for one of the Kitchen Cabinet, I looked so much like a ghost."

Presidents before and after Jackson were similarly charged. Thomas Jefferson was accused of forming "an invisible, inscrutable, unconstitutional cabinet" that dealt in "back-stairs influence." Jackson's frontier coterie was the first designated as the "kitchen" cabinet, presumably because of his and their reputation for unpolished manners. But the kitchenites had their defenders. The *Washington Globe* described them as "men fresh from the ranks of the people, acquainted with their wants and understanding the current of their opinions."

The term began to lose its sting after Jackson's time. But because most Presidents do have circles of personal friends, the idea remains. Theodore Roosevelt had his "tennis cabinet." Jonathan Daniels refers to Warren Harding's "poker cabinet." Herbert Hoover had an exercise-loving "medicine ball cabinet." Even governors can play the game. In writing of New York's Alfred Smith, Ed Flynn mentions the "golfing cabinet."

Harry Truman facetiously organized what he termed his "kitchen cabinet," consisting of a Secretary for Inflation, Secretary of Reaction, Secretary for Columnists, and Secretary of Semantics ("to furnish me with 40- to 50-dollar words"). See SHADOW CABINET.

More than most modern Presidents, Truman was accused of relying too much on the advice of buddies (see GOVERNMENT BY CRONY). John F. Kennedy later observed: "Congressmen are always advising Presidents to get rid of presidential advisers. That's one of the most constant threads that run through American history, and Presidents ordinarily do not pay attention."

When it became known in 1977 that President Carter's Special Trade Representative, Robert Strauss, was becoming the most listened-to adviser in the President's cabinet, the Texan was asked when he expected to move his office into the White House. "You don't have to be inside the kitchen," he replied, "to be a member of the kitchen cabinet." He went on to become a member of his fellow Texan George Bush's kitchen cabinet—without losing his Democratic connections.

The term is current. *The New Republic* of May 21, 1990, used the phrase in reporting that "the momentous decision to retain General Ortega [the former Sandinista President] as army chief was reached by [President] Chamorro's kitchen cabinet."

kitchen debate the conference between Vice President Nixon and Soviet Chairman Nikita Khrushchev in the "typical American home" at the U.S. exhibition in Moscow in 1959.

There were two debates that day. At the color television exhibit, Khrushchev unexpectedly attacked U.S. policy before the cameras, with the Vice President parrying the remarks, trying to be the good American-exhibition host. By the time the Russian leader strolled out of the studio, however, it was clear that this was only the opening round; the main bout would be elsewhere.

The author, then a press agent publicizing the "typical American home" exhibit, arranged for a mixup in the flow of the crowd, trapping the leaders in their exhibit. Nixon felt that an American kitchen was a suitable forum for a discussion of standards of living and the variety of choice available to American working people. In *Six Crises,* Nixon wrote:

The conversation began innocently enough. We discussed the relative merits of washing machines. Then I decided that this was as good a place as any to answer the charges that had been made in the Soviet press, that only "the rich" in the United States could afford such a house as this.

I made the point that this was a typical house in the United States, costing $14,000, which could be paid over twenty-five or thirty years. Most U.S. veterans of World War II have bought houses like this, in the $10,000 to $15,000 range, I told him, adding that most any steelworker could buy one.

Khrushchev retorted, "We too can find steelworkers and peasants who can pay $14,000 for a flat." He accused American builders of planning obsolescence—building a house to last twenty years, while Soviets build for generations. "If an American citizen does not have dollars," he pointed out, "he has the right to buy this house or sleep on the pavement at night."

The debate was sharp, accompanied by jabbing fingers and lapel-grabbings. Nixon tried to end it with a light touch: "Isn't it better to be talking about the relative merits of our washing machines than the relative strength of our rockets?" But Khrushchev stayed angry: "Yes, that's the kind of competition we want, but your generals say we must compete in rockets. . . . We are strong, we can beat you." Nixon came back hard behind a pointed finger: "You are strong and we are strong. . . . For us to argue who is the stronger misses the point. If war comes, we both lose."

To the observers in the kitchen, the two leaders appeared to be using, rather than losing, their tempers. After a discussion about threats and ultimatums, Nixon broke off the debate with a light remark and Khrushchev picked up the cue, thanking the refrigerator demonstrator "for letting us use her kitchen for our argument."

The event was initially dubbed the

"Sokolniki Summit" (after Sokolniki Park, in which the exhibition was held) by Harrison Salisbury of the *New York Times*. However, Salisbury was accompanied in the kitchen by the author, who assured the Russian guards the reporter was a "refrigerator demonstrator." Eager to publicize the house and kitchen rather than the Russian park, I told other reporters about the "kitchen conference." Salisbury adopted the phrase in briefing other reporters, and it is still recalled as the "kitchen debate" or "kitchen conference."

klong a reaction of dismay at a crisis caused by one's own thoughtlessness.

Senator George McGovern's 1972 campaign manager, Frank Mankiewicz, who coined the term, defined it as "a sudden rush of shit to the heart."

Klongs are divided into the *petit klong,* which can be the horrified realization that you have invited a dozen people to dinner for one hour ago and you are still in the office, and the *grand klong,* which comes to a prosecutor who carefully prepares a case and brings it to fruition one day after the statute of limitations has run out.

knee-jerk liberal an unthinking intellectual; an attack phrase on automatic support of causes favored by the political left.

In current usage, a PROFESSIONAL liberal is the most uncommitted, a FLAMING LIBERAL is the most militant, and a *knee-jerk* liberal the most dull-witted. For answering charges, see HIDEBOUND; ROCK-RIBBED; MOSSBACK.

Knee-jerk is among the most descriptive and least pedantic medical words coined in the past century. Sir Ernest Gowers, a giant of linguistics who edited the second edition of Fowler's *Modern English Usage*, told of its origin in *Plain Words* (1948): "Some seventy years ago a promising young neu-

rologist made a discovery that necessitated the addition of a new word to the English vocabulary. He insisted that this should be *knee-jerk,* and *knee-jerk* it has remained, in spite of the efforts of *patellar reflex* to dislodge it. He was my father; so perhaps I have inherited a prejudice in favor of homemade words."

Knee-jerk has also been applied to conservatives and other shades in the political spectrum. C. W. Smith, writing in the April 1981 *Texas Monthly,* describes "a lukewarm liberal who . . . turns knee-jerk reactionary on learning that his bride is not a virgin."

knock on the door. See RAP IN THE NIGHT.

Know-Nothing a derisive term for a member of the nativist political faction, active during the 1850s, which opposed immigration and sought anti-Catholic measures; hence, a bigot or reactionary.

The Know-Nothings sprang from a number of splinter groups that today would be called part of the radical right. They had several names, such as the Order of the Star-Spangled Banner, the American Party, and the Native American Party (leading to a nickname, "Sams," after Uncle Sam). They were widely described as Know-Nothings because they refused to tell outsiders of their activities. Explained the *Cleveland Plain Dealer* in 1854: "When one Know Nothing wishes to recognize another, he closes one eye, makes an O with his thumb and forefinger and places his nose through it, which, interpreted, reads eye-nose-O—I know nothing." One of the party's key publicists was Anna Ella Carroll, who helped the candidacy of Millard Fillmore.

Although the party had some successes in the 1854 elections, it soon broke up because of internal disputes. Its members joined other parties, but to be accused of having been associated with the Know-Nothings was a political liability. This led Abraham Lincoln to say in 1855: "I am not a Know-Nothing. How could I be? How can anyone who abhors the oppression of negroes, be in favor of degrading classes of white people?" (Note: *Negro* was not at that time capitalized.)

Although the Know-Nothings disintegrated, their spirit lived on in such organizations as the American Protective Association and the Ku Klux Klan. The phrase is still used occasionally to describe reactionaries, SUPERPATRIOTS, and other residents of the far right, as when *Time* magazine described George Wallace as seeking to run for President in 1968 "under a neo-Know Nothing banner."

In 1969 historian Eric Goldman, who as a Johnson aide tried and failed to bring together the White House and the intellectual community, passed this judgment on the conduct of both camps at an ill-fated arts festival, in *The Tragedy of Lyndon Johnson*: "I had seen a President reacting with arrogant know-nothingism, and influential figures in the cultural world reacting with an equally arrogant know-it-allness."

See THIRD-PARTY MOVEMENT; UN-AMERICAN; YAHOO.

kooks, nuts and   extremists; far-right- or left-wingers; distinguished by hate campaigns, occasional scruffiness, and unconventional political behavior.

Gook was a slur used by American soldiers to describe any Asian, friend or foe; *kook* made its appearance in the late fifties as teen-age slang to replace *drip* or *jerk*. *Kooky* described far-out behavior, changing to *kicky* in 1966 regarding mini-skirted clothes with op-art and pop-art patterns, and to *kinky*

in the seventies as a description of taboo sex habits.

Politically, the "nuts and kooks" came into popularity to describe some of the more extreme supporters of Senator Barry Goldwater before his nomination in 1964. Goldwater himself used the word, according to publisher John S. Knight in a post-convention interview: "He [Goldwater] remarked with a wry smile that some of the 'kooks' supporting him are convinced that the concept of metropolitan government is the handiwork of the Communist Party."

The Goldwater managers did what they could to discourage demonstrations of the "kooks," since they were a source of embarrassment easily exploited by the Democrats. Reported Theodore White at the 1964 convention:

> The floor itself was comparatively quiet, Goldwater discipline holding firm; and here one had the full contrast that plagued all reporters throughout the year—the contrast between the Goldwater movement and the Goldwater organization. There is not, and was not, anywhere in the entire high command, in the brains trust or in the organizational structure of the Goldwater campaign, anyone who remotely qualified for the title "kook." Nor was there evident any "kook" on the floor. But the "kooks" dominated the galleries, hating and screaming and reveling in their own frenzy.

Governor Nelson Rockefeller, subjected to the fury of the "kooks" in the galleries, had his finest political moment as he exchanged barbed comments with them.

In 1965 the word "kook" was applied less to right-wingers and more to members of the New Left, especially those who burned draft cards and participated in antiwar demonstrations. "The Movement attracts some of the best young people in the country," wrote Jacobs and Landau in *The New Radicals*, "contrary to the vulgar popular notion that those who are involved are only 'beats,' 'kooks,' and 'potheads.'"

According to historian William Manchester (who presumably heard it from either Jacqueline Kennedy or Kenneth O'Donnell), President Kennedy, on his way to Dallas in 1963, looked at a violently anti-Kennedy advertisement in the *Dallas News*, and commented, "We're heading into nut country today."

A different meaning of "nut" is found in campaign financing: "the nut" is the basic amount needed to get a campaign started. In New York it specifically denotes the two years' salary which candidates for judgeships are expected to contribute before getting the nomination.

One cannot use the word "nut" with impunity. In 1977, when the author described some of the threatening mail that had been in the private files of J. Edgar Hoover as having come from "nuts and kooks," a man who called himself a member of the "Mental Patients Liberation Front" wrote the *New York Times* in protest: "This is offensive . . . he is lumping together all people who act differently, in ignorance of the issues . . . as one of those kooks, who knows a great number of other kooks, I have been in an organization struggling for our liberty, a liberty which has been denied by 300 years of psychiatric abuse."

As can be seen, even admitted nuts and kooks defend themselves from linguistic slurs. Thus, to be quite fair, in current usage a "nut" or "kook" is considered by the speaker to be crazy—hence the synonym "crazies"—but this ought not to be taken for a lack of intelligence. A punch line of an old joke, wherein an asylum inmate helps a confused visitor, is illustrative: "I may be crazy, but I'm not stupid."

Koreagate. See -GATE CONSTRUCTION.

Kremlinologist a Western observer who interpreted the intricate workings of the former Soviet government.

Former Syracuse University professor Harry Schwartz, who was a *New York Times* expert on Soviet affairs, wrote in 1967: "The recent shift in the leadership of the Soviet secret police, perhaps the most sensitive single post in the Moscow bureaucracy, has given Kremlinologists around the world a shot in the arm. From Washington to Peking the effort to analyze the meaning of the change and its impact on the future of Soviet leadership is now in high gear."

Before the breakup of the Soviet Union, Kremlinologists, sometimes called Sovietologists—specialists in Russian affairs—studied the play of news in *Pravda* and *Izvestia*, examined photographs of Red leaders at Lenin's Tomb reviewing troops on May Day to see who stood closest to the top man, and sifted reports of travelers to the Soviet Union. According to *Time* magazine, "in an office of the U.S. embassy in Bonn, a rotund Sovietologist digests a stack of reports that may originate from any one of a thousand sources—a barber in East Berlin, a whorehouse madam in Vienna . . ."

The counterpart term for Chinese Communists is "Pekingologist." See CHINA WATCHERS. In a kind of back-formation, Soviet analyst of U.S. affairs Georgi Arbatov was described in 1978 as an "Americanologist."

Soviet leaders treated the interpretations of foreign pundits with much the same disdain as U.S. officials look askance at predictions by specialists on Washington matters. Said Khrushchev in 1955 of the press interpretation of Soviet attitudes: "They pay little attention to what we say and prefer to read tea leaves."

After the onset of Gorbachev's GLASNOST, Kremlinology was never the same; it had to deal with a torrent of information rather than a few arcane details. The field suffered further under Yeltsin's democratic reforms, but the Kremlin still sits in the heart of Moscow, and Russian intentions are likely to become murkier in future years—or so hope would-be Kremlinologists.

Ku Klux Klan. See INVISIBLE GOVERNMENT.

L

labels oversimplified identification of ideological position; widely used and universally deplored by politicians unwilling to be pigeon-holed.

FDR positioned himself "a little left of center" (see LEFT WING, RIGHT WING; LIBERAL) but once told a press conference about appointees: "If we have the right kind of people, the party label does not mean so much."

Party labels are readily accepted by political figures in those areas where that party's registration dominates, but it has become popular in recent years to denounce ideological labels. In his 1960 State of the Union message, Dwight Eisenhower said: "We live, moreover, in a storm of semantic disorder in which old labels no longer faithfully describe. Police states are called 'people's democracies.' Armed conquest of free people is called 'liberation.' Such slippery slogans make difficult the problem of communicating true faiths, facts and beliefs . . ."

Six years earlier, however, President Eisenhower had tried to come to grips with ideological labels in a well-known statement: "When it comes down to dealing with the relationships between the human in this country and his government, the people in this administration believe in being what I think we would normally call liberal, and when we deal with the economic affairs of this country, we believe in being conservative." (See Adlai Stevenson's riposte in DYNAMIC CONSERVATISM.)

Judging by his popularity, Eisenhower was able to solve a dilemma that had long been plaguing Republicans. More Americans considered themselves "liberal" than "conservative," and the Republicans are more closely identified with conservatism, often placing them in an electoral bind. Thomas E. Dewey was frank to admit it: "One of the standard weapons of party conflict both between conventions and during campaigns is the effort to pin labels on individuals or movements, attractive or sinister, depending upon the point of view. On the whole, the Democratic party in recent years has been the more successful in this use of semantics."

Lyndon Johnson adopted a few labels and rejected labeling in a 1958 statement of his political philosophy:

I am a free man, an American, a United States Senator, and a Democrat, in that order.

I am also a liberal, a conservative, a Texan, a taxpayer, a rancher, a businessman, a consumer, a parent, a voter, and not as young as I used to be nor as old as I expect to be—and I am all these things in no fixed order.

I am unaware of any descriptive word in the second paragraph which qualifies, modifies, amends, or is related by hyphenation to the terms listed in the first paragraph. In consequence, I am not able—nor even the least interested in trying—to define my political philosophy by the choice of a one-word or two-word label.

Sometimes a label is useful: Bill Clinton in 1992 wanted to be known as a "new Democrat," to differentiate himself from the liberal, losing Democrats. But the reasons for political squirming when it comes to ideological labeling are these: (1) A label excludes more voters than it includes, and no politician wants to say "I am not one of you" to a large portion of the electorate. (2) Although in one area one label may predominate, politicians are ambitious; acceptance of a label may preclude advancement. See PRESIDENT OF ALL THE PEOPLE. (3) A label is simplistic, and thoughtful people reject its rigidity.

ladies in tennis shoes. See LITTLE OLD LADIES IN TENNIS SHOES.

Laffer curve. See SUPPLY-SIDE.

lame duck an officeholder whose power is diminished because he is soon to leave office, as a result of defeat or statutory limitation. See EUNUCH RULE.

During the 1920s this venerable phrase was modernized and widely publicized by the campaign for the "lame-duck amendment" which in 1933 was finally ratified as the Twentieth Amendment to the Constitution. Previously the incoming President was forced to wait until March to assume office while the old Congress—some of whose members had been retired at the last election—met in December and held nominal legislative powers until March.

The new system brings November's winners into office in January, thus halving the difficult lame-duck period for the outgoing Administration and, in the absence of an emergency, eliminating the lame-duck session of Congress. Franklin D. Roosevelt's New Deal was the first beneficiary of the change, but not until after the historic HUNDRED DAYS had to be deferred by the last application of the old schedule. Said Rexford Tugwell: "The old stretch of four months, devised for a country without rapid transportation, was a dangerous hiatus in the [Depression] circumstances of 1932–33."

"Lame duck" was originally an eighteenth-century import from Britain meaning a bankrupt businessman; by the 1830s the phrase was used to label politically bankrupt politicians. In 1910 *The Nation* described Election Day casualties hoping for better days as "lame ducks in the sense that they have been winged, but hope to preen their plumage again." Today it is often used snidely, as when a mayor, governor, or President makes "lame-duck appointments" by rewarding friends with judicial posts during his last days in office.

A *Washington Post* piece on Middle East talks in December 1992 commented, "The Arab participants in particular have given up on the lame-duck Bush Administration's ability to affect the outcome and are waiting to see what approach Clinton's still-unnamed foreign policy team will adopt in dealing with the region."

This particular fowl has an honored position in American slang. In addition to lame duck, there is a "sitting duck" (vulnerable), "queer duck" (odd), "dead duck" (finished), and "ducky" (great, unless used scornfully). See Walter Reuther's use of "If it quacks like a duck" in PROVERBS, POLITICAL.

landslide   a resounding victory; one in which the opposition is "buried." ("Snowed under" is better suited for an AVALANCHE.)

In its natural-disaster sense, the word made its appearance about 1838, and headline writers began applying it politically a few years later. (For usage differentiation from "tidal wave," "prairie fire," etc., see DISASTER META- PHORS.)

Alfred M. Landon, "the Coolidge of the West," sported an optimistic slogan in 1936: "Land Landon with a Landslide!" A landslide it was—Roosevelt carried 46 states with 523 electoral votes, Landon 2 states with 8.

The electoral college system makes landslides look more severe than they are. Landon managed to get 16 million votes to Roosevelt's 27 million—37 percent of the popular vote looks a little better than 1.5 percent of the electoral vote.

When Lyndon Johnson squeaked through a senatorial election in Texas— a post-Election Day correction gave him a majority of 87 votes out of almost a million cast—he was dubbed "Landslide Lyndon." The phrase was used again, minus the sarcasm, in 1964— Johnson carried 61 percent of the popular vote. This was not quite as high as Roosevelt's 63 percent in 1936 or Harding's 64 percent in 1920, but it was enough to qualify as a genuine landslide. Before those, the great landslides were Andrew Jackson in 1828 and 1832; U.S. Grant in 1872; Theodore Roosevelt in 1904.

Senator Henry Jackson made a unique use of the word after his New York State Democratic primary victory in April 1976. Against a sizable field, including Jimmy Carter, Senator Jackson won a plurality but fell short of his hoped-for 50 percent of the total vote. Reminded that he had predicted a landslide, he replied, "We got a landslide, but we missed a majority."

After the resounding election defeat of George McGovern in 1972, Senator Thomas Eagleton—who was forced to quit the Democratic ticket when it was revealed he had a history of mental illness—dismissed the episode involving him as merely "one rock in a landslide." Five years later Senator McGovern wrote: "Perhaps that is true, but landslides begin with a single rock."

land war in Asia.   See WRONG WAR; LET ASIANS FIGHT ASIANS.

last hurrah   exit of a politician, especially one who has had a boisterous career; more generally, the final, losing campaign.

The phrase was coined by Edwin O'Connor, who used it as the title for his 1956 novel, *The Last Hurrah*, loosely based on the life of Boston Mayor James Curley, showing the calculations and compromises—as well as the rapport with the people—of an Irish politician in Massachusetts in the first third of the twentieth century.

The title was based on the "hurrah boys," name of the Andrew Jackson enthusiasts in 1828 and 1832, which then became the phrase for any noisy supporter in a campaign filled with HOOPLA. "When General Jackson was first brought before the public," wrote the *Ohio State Journal* in 1828, "his admirers . . . earned for the pains, the appropriate name of 'hurra boys.'"

George William Curtis, editor of *Harper's Magazine*, told this story in a collection of speeches published in 1894:

An anti-Jackson partisan fell into the water, and, when nearly drowned, was seized by the hand and drawn to the surface, while his excited rescuer, delighted to save him, expressed his joy in the familiar phrase, "Hurrah for Jackson!" "What d'you say?" asked the drowning man thickly, but not so far gone that he could not hear the obnoxious name . . ."Hurrah for Jackson!" replied the other. "No, I'll be darned if I'll be saved by a hurrah-for-Jackson man" said the first, shaking off his hand and sinking back into the water.

The word "hurrah" is a seventeenth-century derivation from "huzza," an imitative sound expressing joy and enthusiasm.

In current use the phrase—while usually connoting farewell—can refer to a final win as well. The *National Observer*, after the 1966 New York gubernatorial election, titled an article "The Almost Perfect Political Campaign," with the subtitle "Nelson Rockefeller's Last Hurrah." It was not. And columnists Evans and Novak wrote in the spring of 1977: "Although even staunch Reaganites believe he is too old for anything other than a KINGMAKER's role in 1980, he has by no means ruled out a last hurrah." The hurrahs lasted through his Presidential reelection campaign in 1984.

late unpleasantness. See EUPHEMISMS, POLITICAL.

laundered money funds passed through a foreign account to conceal illegitimate origins.

The corrupt connotation to "launder" was popularized in the 1973 Watergate hearings, as $200,000 in contributions was sent to Mexico and later used to finance illegal Nixon campaign operations of dubious merit.

The word had previously been used in this sense to describe the way "hot money"—that is, gambling profits or undeclared funds from foreign sources—was legitimized before re-entering the country. Metaphorically, the money laundry was used to "cool" rather than "clean" the money, as in this citation supplied the author by lexicographer Peter Tamony in the *San Francisco Call-Bulletin* of June 3, 1935: "There is not a hot money passer in America who will 'wash' this money exchanging it for 'cool' currency—unless it is offered him at such a tremendous discount that he can afford to hold it for years, if necessary, before attempting to pass it."

Mr. Tamony speculates: "As the mob/syndicate took over in Cuba in the decades preceding Fidel Castro, circa 1959, it is probable the *washing/laundering* was done there until Mexico became handy again fifteen years ago."

The locution was used in 1977 to describe the contributions of Korean lobbyist Tongsun Park, who was said to use various cultural foundations as means of "laundering" funds for passage to U.S. congressmen, and in the 1990 prosecution of Panamanian strongman Manuel Noriega.

laundry ticket jocular symbol of the popularity of an individual candidate who does not need organization support to win.

Franklin Roosevelt, running for President in 1932, wanted the strongest possible Democratic candidate to succeed him as governor of New York, helping him to carry the state. Former Governor and presidential nominee Al Smith, although by now a bitter enemy of FDR, united with him in supporting Herbert Lehman, then Lieutenant Governor, but Tammany leader John Curry opposed Lehman.

At the state convention, just an hour before the balloting, both Smith and Roosevelt threatened to denounce Curry on the floor if Lehman was not nominated. What's more, added Smith, he personally would run for mayor and "take the town away" from Curry and Tammany.

"On what ticket?" Curry sneered, with some logic.

"Hell," replied Smith, supremely confident of his power with New York voters, "on a Chinese-laundry ticket."

A related phrase, "laundry list," has a different meaning: a long, soporific list of items in a speech, or a series of patronage requests by a political supporter after a successful campaign.

law and order   stress on repression of violence; regarded by some civil rights supporters since 1964 as the "code words" for repression of blacks.

Some candidates, while not going so far as to oppose integration and civil rights legislation, sought to appeal to the anti-black BACKLASH by stressing law and order and urging control of "crime in the streets." Civil rights advocates, who could not argue against law and order, instead concentrated their fire on the CODE WORD concept, charging this was part of Senator Goldwater's 1964 SOUTHERN STRATEGY aimed at winning anti-integration votes in the South without blatantly appealing to racist feelings.

An editorial in *The Insurgent*, a publication of the W. E. B. DuBois Clubs (a far-left group) said: ". . . the law is built to defend the white power structure. 'Order' means keeping people 'in their place.'"

On the other hand, many "moderates," who in no way intended to attack what they considered legitimate aspirations by blacks, did feel strongly about violence in the streets, which reached a peak during riots in Detroit and Newark in the LONG HOT SUMMER of 1967. But they found it difficult to stress "law and order" without being attacked in turn for using the same phraseology as the subtle racists.

With the mood of the nation turning against violent demonstrations and riots in the mid-sixties, the "code word" counterattack generally failed, and those espousing "law and order"—

for whatever motives, sincere or not— found the issue effective.

The ability to cope with a breakdown in "law and order" was the quality that projected Calvin Coolidge on the scene of U.S. politics. Massachusetts Governor Calvin Coolidge met the crisis of the Boston police strike of 1919 with the statement "There is no right to strike against the public safety by anybody, anywhere, anytime." He was nominated in 1920 for Vice President on the Harding ticket after a convention demonstration with "Law and Order" banners waving.

Wrote Donald R. McCoy, his biographer, in 1966:

> Thus Coolidge, who was no rabble-rouser, had become the uncrowned king of the rabble-rousers and the Saint George of the innocently frightened. He who had given little thought to Marxism had become the champion of the anti-Marxists. He who had often been labor's friend had become a hero of antilabor forces. He who had not wanted to become involved had become deeply involved. He who had been the last in acting had become the first in receiving credit.

The phrase reaches far back into American political history. In the first half of the nineteenth century, Rhode Island was governed under a Colonial charter with a property qualification so high that less than one third of its citizens could vote. A Suffrage Party was formed by Thomas Dorr, which led to "Dorr's Rebellion" in 1842. The political group opposing suffrage called itself the "Law and Order Party."

By the 1990s, the phrase had lost much of its sting. A popular weekly television show called "Law and Order" dealt with the cooperative efforts of police officers and district attorneys to fight crime.

See CRIME IN THE STREETS.

laws, facetious   rules of thumbsucking.

Following are several named laws, drawn mainly from Paul Dickson's compilation, *The Official Rules*:

Brown's Law, from Sam Brown, when a student activist: "Never offend people with style when you can offend them with substance."

Colson's Law, from a poster hanging in Nixon aide Charles Colson's office: "If you've got them by the balls, their hearts and minds will follow."

Dirksen's Law, a version of an old saw promulgated frequently by Senate Minority Leader Everett Dirksen: "The oil can is mightier than the sword."

Hagerty's Law, from James C. Hagerty, press secretary to Dwight Eisenhower, after losing his temper at Art Buchwald: "If you lose your temper at a newspaper columnist, he'll get rich or famous or both."

Parkinson's First Law, from C. Northcote Parkinson: "Work expands so as to fill the time available for its completion."

Peter Principle, from Laurence J. Peter: "In a hierarchy every employee tends to rise to his level of incompetence."

Rayburn's Rule, from Speaker of the House Sam Rayburn: "If you want to get along, go along."

The most famous of these laws, perhaps the original, is *Murphy's Law*, a version of which is familiar to all political rally planners: "If anything can go wrong, it will, and at the worst possible moment."

leader.   See BOSS, BOSSISM; SACHEM; SATRAP; BIGWIG; MUCKEY-MUCKS; MOVERS AND SHAKERS.

leak   disclosure of information, usually concerning government or political activity, through unofficial channels or what some consider improper means.

Lexicographers in the U.S. have had their eye on this term for a long time. In 1832 Noah Webster defined "to leak out" as "to escape privately from confinement or secresy; as a fact or report," and G. W. Matsell in his 1859 *Vocabulum* defined "to leak" as "to impart a secret."

One of the earliest sensational leaks on record occurred in 1844, when Senator Benjamin Tappan of Ohio gave a copy of the still-secret treaty of annexation with Texas to the *New York Evening Post*. The *Post* printed it, an uproar ensued, Tappan admitted his part in it and was censured.

The commonest leaks are those sprung by middle-echelon officials in order to get publicity for themselves or their agencies: an official tips off one reporter or a small group in advance of a general announcement in the hope that the exclusivity will get the story better coverage than it would otherwise enjoy.

Franklin Roosevelt complained bitterly about a number of leaks, including one about Henry Morgenthau's controversial plan (later shelved) to strip Germany of all industry after World War II. In 1955 Dwight Eisenhower said: "I have been plagued by inexplicable, undiscovered leaks in this government." President Johnson was accused of corking leaks by changing his plans once information had come out prematurely.

The *courtesy leak* is used when an official owes a reporter a favor—or would like the reporter to owe him a favor—and uses information as currency. A favorite type of story for use in this transaction is advance word about presidential appointments. Thus a handful of reporters got a scoop on Earl Warren's appointment as Chief Justice. However, while a courtesy leak makes the scoopers happy, the scooped segment of the press thinks morosely of revenge.

There are also *authorized leaks*—disclosures given with euphemistic attribution such as "informed sources" and "government officials." In this case the government wishes to see something in print but would rather not be on the record as formally committed to a particular policy or view. See TRIAL BALLOON; NOT FOR ATTRIBUTION. Some argue that the press should not allow itself to be used in this way. Others justify the practice by pointing out that news BACKGROUNDERS—the sessions at which such information is conveyed—are better than news blackouts.

Authorized leaks have been known to backfire. In one of his first informal meetings with the press, Defense Secretary Robert McNamara disclosed that there really was no MISSILE GAP. This flatly contradicted an important point made during the Kennedy campaign, much to the embarrassment of the new Kennedy Administration.

The most massive leak in U.S. history was "the Pentagon Papers," given by former national security consultant Daniel Ellsberg to the *New York Times*, which caused the Nixon Administration to go to court seeking to enjoin publication. The suppression effort failed.

Director of Central Intelligence Stansfield Turner wrote in the *Washington Post* in 1977 that no nation should countenance the free-wheeling disclosure of its military secrets, and that our society should "trust the judgment of its public servants regarding what should and should not be withheld from the public."

Daniel Schorr, a journalist who had handled more than his share of leaks, wrote in reply: "The awareness that 'secrets' may leak tends to have a healthful, ombudsman effect in government, making covert operators ask themselves how their plans would look if they were exposed. In balance,

this nation has probably been harmed much less by undue exposure than by undue secrecy."

Richard Neustadt, professor of government at Harvard, agreed: "The class of confidential communication commonly called 'leaks' play, in my opinion, a vital role in the functioning of our democracy. A leak is, in essence, an appeal to public opinion. Leaks generally do not occur in dictatorships."

Schorr, in recent years a commentator for National Public Radio, has further observed: "Originally, when information 'leaked,' it was thought of as an accidental seepage—a lost document, a chauffeur's unwary anecdote, loose lips in the Pentagon. Today, when information 'is leaked,' it is a witting (if sometimes witless) action. One leaks (active) to float or sink an idea, aggrandize self . . . or derogate an opponent."

An overreaction to leaks led to Richard Nixon's downfall. In May of 1969 Nixon, Attorney General John Mitchell, and National Security Adviser Henry Kissinger determined to crack down on "national security leaks," using a series of wiretaps by the FBI; when J. Edgar Hoover was reluctant to pursue this technique, a Kissinger aide—David Young—was assigned to a leak-plugging unit that he later dubbed the PLUMBERS.

See PLANT; BACKGROUNDER; WHISTLE-BLOWER.

lebensraum literally, "living space"; an excuse for territorial expansion.

The word was coined by Swedish scientist Rudolf Kjellén and appropriated by a German geographer, Dr. Karl Haushofer, to describe what he considered to be Germany's needs and, therefore, rights.

An English phrase, "land-hunger," had been used earlier to describe the state of a nation whose population is expanding too rapidly for its territory to support.

The Nazis used *Lebensraum* to mean that Germany was crowded, that the fertile portions of Russia were occupied by inferior beings, thus Germany, as the home of the "master race," had the right to take the geographical areas she wanted by war.

Haushofer's views on geography as related to politics, which he called *Weltpolitik* and "geopolitics," were considered gospel by the Nazis, whom he supported enthusiastically.

In 1942, during a visit to Washington by Winston Churchill, Franklin Roosevelt made a speech that greatly impressed the British Prime Minister, especially the line "The world is too small to provide adequate 'living room' for both Hitler and God." "Whoever wrote that sentence," Churchill told FDR, "I'd like to take with me to England." The President did not reply; dramatist Robert E. Sherwood was too valuable to him.

After World War II a German novelist told reporter John Gunther what impressed him most about the U.S.: "Space. *Lebensraum.* The impression that no crisis can be really severe or permanent in this country because people are free to move around so much."

Recent uses of the word no longer refer or even allude to Nazi Germany. Some writers, for example, have characterized the ethnic conflict in the former Yugoslavia as a three-way struggle for Lebensraum. It has been applied even to China, as in the *National Journal* of September 19, 1992: "China's recent assertion of sovereignty over the Spratly Islands in the South China Sea may be one sign of this lebensraum influence." (Notice the lowercase initial, a sure sign of Anglicization.)

The word has also been used by ENVIRONMENTALISTS to project some of the troubles of the world of the future.

In the June 1955 *Fortune* magazine, John von Neumann wrote:

> In the first half of this century the accelerating industrial revolution encountered an absolute limitation—not on technological progress as such, but on an essential safety factor. This safety factor . . . was essentially a matter of geographical and political *Lebensraum:* an ever broader geographical scope for technological activities, combined with an ever broader political integration of the world. Within this expanding framework it was possible to accommodate the major tensions created by technological progress.
>
> Now this safety mechanism is being sharply inhibited; literally and figuratively, we are running out of room. At long last, we begin to feel the effects of the finite, actual size of the earth in a critical way.

The term is current in politics. The *Los Angeles Times* reported in 1993 on Hungary's right-wing leader Istvan Csurka: "Despite the political uproar that has ensued since publication of an August essay replete with anti-Semitic overtones, Csurka insists he speaks for many Hungarians and has no regrets about anything he has said, including his use of the Nazi term *lebensraum*— living space—in his call for expanding the borders."

See PLACE IN THE SUN.

left field   a figurative location slightly less remote than Siberia; out of the ordinary; out of touch; far out.

When used as a place of origin, as in *out of left field*, the phrase has been picked up by politicians and meteorologists as a slang equivalent of *off the wall.* When a professor of atmospheric science predicted a dry spell in the Northeast, Robert Harnack, a meteorologist at Rutgers, ridiculed that forecast as being "completely out of left field."

Baseball's *left field* had become the place of far-outedness by the late

1950s. The phrase *be out in left field* came to have two meanings: "removed from the ordinary; unconventional" and "out of contact with reality; out of touch." A 1960 *New York Times* report on the state of U.S. scientific research uses the phrase in the first sense: ". . . if this country is to compete with Europe and Japan, engineers and scientists must start taking risks 'way out in left field.' " The second meaning is illustrated in a 1959 *Time* magazine article, also in a science context: "The virus theory of cancer causation long seemed to be far out in left field, but growing knowledge tends to link it with other anti-cancer plays." The phrase has no connection to the political left.

Sports fans differ on the reasoning behind the metaphor. Some suggest that left fielders play farther out to get the power balls hit by right-handed players. Others argue that the less desirable seats for spectators are beside the left field.

left wing, right wing   the ideological spectrum; reading from left to right, radical, liberal, centrist or moderate, conservative, reactionary.

The presiding officers of the French National Assembly seated the radicals at the *côté gauche* (left side), the moderates in the center directly in front, and the conservative nobles on the right. Like so many political terms, the "wings" derived from military use, with the use of "left wing" of an army traceable to 1707.

The left-wing–right-wing spectrum is not a straight bar; the relationships are better explained by considering it as a kind of horseshoe. An extreme leftist, or radical, or Communist, has more in common with an extreme reactionary, or fascist, than either has with the moderate.

Franklin Roosevelt established his position in a 1944 press conference

when reporter May Craig asked him if he was going "left or right politically." He replied, "I am going down the whole line a little left of center." See LABELS. Another reporter asked about recent appointments of conservatives. He said, "I have got a lot of people in the Administration—oh, I know some of them are extreme right and extreme left, and everything else. . . . Just think, the crowd here in this room—my gracious, you will find every opinion between left and extreme right."

Sociologist C. Wright Mills, who coined NEW LEFT, defined the "right" as "celebrating society as it is: a going concern," and "to be left" as meaning to "connect up with cultural and political criticism."

One on the left is called RED, pink, PINKO (PARLOR PINK is radical in theory only), commie, bomb-thrower, COMSYMP, FELLOW TRAVELER, and ultraleft.

One on the right is called RADICAL RIGHT, DIEHARD, MOSSBACK, Bourbon, bitterender, ultrarightist, OLD FOGY, standpatter (see STAND PAT), LITTLE OLD LADIES IN TENNIS SHOES, and TROGLODYTIC.

CENTRISTS and MODERATES are ON THE FENCE, STRADDLERS, MIDDLE OF THE ROADERS, OPPORTUNISTS, and ALL THINGS TO ALL MEN, though they claim to be the MAINSTREAM.

Winging nuance: those on the left resent being called "left-wingers" more than those on the right resent being called "right-wingers."

legislative veto.   See ONE-HOUSE VETO.

let Asians fight Asians   a recurrent proposal to replace American troops with allied Asian troops in warfare in the Far East.

In the 1952 presidential campaign, Dwight Eisenhower held that the U.S. commitment of ground troops might be curtailed, the men replaced by

South Korean troops. "If there must be a war there," he is reported to have said, "let it be Asians against Asians."

A few days before the election, as Stevenson realized the power of Eisenhower's "I shall go to Korea" promise, the Democratic candidate attacked the General's Asian suggestion:

"'Let Asians fight Asians' is the authentic voice of a resurgent isolationist. In 1939 the Republican Old Guard, faced with the menace of the Nazi world, was content to say 'Let Europeans fight Europeans', ignoring completely the fact that the menace of Nazism was a menace to Americans . . .'"

The thought has a genuine appeal, similar to the fervent desire to avoid a "land war in Asia." In 1964, President Lyndon Johnson said: "We are not about to send American boys nine or ten thousand miles away from home to do what Asian boys should be doing for themselves."

See VIETNAMIZATION. For a similar word pattern, see LET [WHOMEVER] BE [WHOMEVER].

l'état, c'est moi. See I AM THE LAW.

let 'em eat cake the height of political patronization; an attack phrase against economic suggestions that do not directly benefit the poor.

This is supposed to be one of the examples of hauteur by Marie Antoinette that helped bring about the French Revolution. She never said it.

The reference appears in the sixth book of Jean-Jacques Rousseau's *Confessions*, written about 1767, two or three years before Marie Antoinette's arrival in France: "At length I recollected the thoughtless saying of a great princess, who, on being informed that the country people had no bread, replied, 'Let them eat cake.'"

The remark (in French, *"qu'ils mangent de la brioche"*) is still used to signify unconcern with the needs of the people. When Vice President Agnew delivered a keynote address at a National Governors' Conference in 1971 that included a defense of the profit motive, it was denounced by an anonymous Democratic spokesman as "Marie Antoinette economics."

In 1991, the Senate fell one vote short of overriding George Bush's veto of extending unemployment benefits. The *Seattle Times*, identifying Washington's Senator Slade Gordon as the only Northwest Senator to vote with the President, headlined the article "Let Them Eat Cake."

let me make one thing perfectly clear. See POINTER PHRASES.

let sleeping dogmas lie. See UNLEASH CHIANG.

let's look at the record a rousing appeal to reason by presidential candidate Alfred E. Smith.

The New York governor began using "Let's look at the record" in his campaign against Herbert Hoover. See WHISPERING CAMPAIGN.

The phrase was used both as a defense and an attack phrase in its early days, though in recent years it has become a bromide mainly used in attacks on the opposition record. "As Al Smith used to say, 'Let's look at the record,'" has been used so often that it elicits yawns. For more aggressive attacks on past performance, see TWENTY YEARS OF TREASON.

For other Smith coinages, see BALONEY; DOVES; LAUNDRY TICKET; KISS OF DEATH; LULU; and SANTA CLAUS, NOBODY SHOOTS AT.

let's talk sense. See DIALOGUE.

let the dust settle. See WATCHFUL WAITING.

"let us continue" Lyndon Johnson's exhortation as he stepped into the presidency after the death of John F. Kennedy.

Five days after the Kennedy assassination, President Johnson told a joint session of Congress:

> On the twentieth day of January in 1961, John F. Kennedy told his countrymen that our national work would not be finished "in the first thousand days, nor in the life of this Administration, nor even perhaps in our lifetime on this planet. But," he said, "let us begin."
>
> Today, in this moment of new resolve, I would say to all my fellow Americans, let us continue.
>
> This is our challenge—not to hesitate, not to pause, not to turn about and linger over this evil moment, but to continue on our course . . .

The words were crafted by Kennedy speechwriter Ted Sorensen, but the President's Texas accent grated on the nerves of some of the former President's greatest admirers—the pronunciation of "continya" was later mocked. (Kennedy and Johnson were the only two Presidents up to that point in the twentieth century to have strongly regional accents.)

But the choice of the phrase was apt, recalling the early phrase of Kennedy's and updating it, thereby gracefully acknowledging another's leadership while asserting a leadership of one's own.

Author John Dos Passos wrote of the need for this kind of reaching back and establishing the sense of continuity: "In times of change and danger when there is a quicksand of fear under man's reasoning, a sense of continuity with generations gone before can stretch like a lifeline across the scary president."

By 1967 the context of solemnity in which Johnson had used the phrase was long forgotten, and columnist Russell Baker wrote:

It is curious that we let beloved old phrases expire and trundle off the Old Phrases' Burying Ground without even noticing that they have left us . . . what about "Let Us Continue!"? Gone, simply gone, and all unnoticed. Can it mean that somewhere back there, without noticing it, we stopped continuing? If so, when? If we could pinpoint the moment when we stopped hearing "Let us continue!" we could probably tell to the second when the Vietnam war really started.

let [whomever] be [whomever] a call for a return to basic character or central ideology; a slogan urging the removal of soothing overlays or excessive handling from a political leader.

The phrase, now most often identified with Ronald Reagan, was not new with that President.

In 1648, Sir Francis Nethersole wrote, "Let bygans be bygans." (Wordplay on this cliche about *bygones* came from Meg Greenfield, the *Washington Post* editorialist; when Bhagwan Shree Rajneesh was arrested for wrongdoing, she suggested, "Let Bhagwans be Bhagwans.") The formulaic usage on national character, however, comes from a 1938 poem by Langston Hughes titled "Let America Be America Again," which says, "O, let America be America again—/The land that never has been yet—/And yet must be—/The land where *every* man is free."

Other nations have been inserted into the phrase. In January 1982, a broadcast of the United States Information Agency being aimed at Soviet imperialists took the theme of "let Poland be Poland." A *New York Times* op-ed headline in 1991 urged, "Let Cuba Be Cuba."

Jack Kemp is usually credited with *let Reagan be Reagan*, but he disclaims coinage. Then-Representative Kemp, however, did popularize the phrase by urging the President's HANDLERS to allow Reagan to express his true self. The *New York Times* described in 1982 "a process that has found favor with die-hard conservatives who . . . say it is time to 'Let Reagan Be Reagan.'"

The expression probably reached its heights during Reagan's Presidency. At a final White House briefing of the Reagan Administration, Marlin Fitzwater was asked whether the staff knew of any plans for a final Presidential speech, and he responded, "Let the staff be staff, and let Reagan be Reagan." Because George Bush was more centrist than ideologue, the phrase was not applied to him.

It returned, however, in 1993. Senator David L. Boren, Democrat of Oklahoma, convened a meeting of conservative Democrats to balance the left wing of the Party in negotiations with the new President. Said Senator Boren, "We want to let Clinton be Clinton."

level playing field equity in competition; equality of opportunity.

The American Banker used the phrase in a 1979 article about the Oregon Bankers Association: "Mr. Brawner said the Oregon B.A. welcomed 'any and all competition, on a level playing field,' a metaphor the association has used frequently in arguments for 'competitive equality.'" In 1986, the same magazine elaborated: "When bankers talk about a 'level playing field,' they usually mean that similar financial services firms should be subject to the same 'game rules.'"

Ronald Reagan picked up the term in a 1986 speech against tariffs: "If the United States can trade with other nations on a level playing field, we can outproduce, outcompete, and outsell anybody, anywhere in the world."

Speaking out against protectionists in 1986, Republican Senator Bob Packwood of Oregon added, "That's

their idea of a level playing field—a legislative advantage."

The origin of the phrase is uncertain, perhaps from the playing fields of Eton, and the variations include *level benches.*

The image of a flat surface for equality in battle, however, has roots as old as the Bible. As the servants of Benhadad, King of Syria, tell their leader about the army of Israel: "Their gods are gods of the hills; therefore they were stronger than we; but let us fight against them in the plain, and surely we shall be stronger than they" (1 Kings 20:23).

levels. See GOBBLEDYGOOK.

leverage indirect pressure that can be brought to bear on politicians, particularly delegates at conventions.

The "delegate book" that each serious presidential candidate brings to an open convention includes data on each man's social and business background, as well as his political leanings. This book is for the purpose of "getting to him"—finding some Achilles heel that makes him receptive to the candidate.

Typical question before the convention, while the delegate book is leafed through, is "What kind of leverage do we have there?" In other words, is the delegate's best friend, wife, employer, most important customer, school chum, banker, country club president—anyone in a position to exert pressure—a crowbar to pry that delegate's support away from another candidate?

The process is as old as balloting. Daniel Manning, Grover Cleveland's manager in the 1884 MUGWUMP campaign, gave these instructions to William C. Hudson, who was to open the Cleveland headquarters at Chicago for the convention: "Now, I want you to devote yourself to these doubtful men. Find out the conditions surrounding them, the influences political, commercial and moral. . . . We must subject them to pressure, but first we must learn the sort of pressure that should be applied."

Financial leverage is the use of borrowing power; political leverage is the use of financial or personal pressure.

See FEET TO THE FIRE.

liberal currently, one who believes in more government action to meet individual needs; originally, one who resisted government encroachment on individual liberties.

In the original sense the word described those of the emerging middle classes in France and Great Britain who wanted to throw off the rules the dominant aristocracy had made to cement its own control.

During the 1920s the meaning of the word changed to describe those who believed a certain amount of governmental action was necessary to protect the people's "real" freedoms as opposed to their purely legal—and not necessarily existent—freedoms.

This philosophical about-face led former New York Governor Thomas Dewey to say, after using the original definition, "Two hundred years later, the transmutation of the word, as the alchemist would say, has become one of the wonders of our time."

In U.S. politics the word was used by George Washington to indicate a person of generosity or broad-mindedness, as he expressed distaste for those who would deprive Catholics and Jews of their rights.

The word became part of the American vocabulary in its earlier meaning during a rump convention of Republicans dissatisfied with the presidency of Ulysses S. Grant, at Cincinnati in 1872. German-born Carl Schurz, who chaired the convention, used the word often. So did the leading journalist-thinker of the rebellion, Edwin L. Godkin of *The Nation,* who began his career in England. The short-lived party born of the convention was called "The Liberal Republican" party.

In its present usage, the word acquired significance during the presidency of Franklin D. Roosevelt, who defined it this way during the campaign for his first term: ". . . say that civilization is a tree which, as it grows, continually produces rot and dead wood. The radical says: 'Cut it down.' The conservative says: 'Don't touch it.' The liberal compromises: 'Let's prune, so that we lose neither the old trunk nor the new branches.'"

Liberalism takes criticism from both right and left, leading to various terms of opprobrium. See LEFT WING, RIGHT WING; BLEEDING HEARTS. Herbert Hoover in a magazine article referred to ". . . fuzzy-minded totalitarian liberals who believe that their creeping collectivism can be adopted without destroying personal liberty and representative government."

To its opponents, liberalism and liberals seem to call out for qualifying adjectives expressing contempt. Barry Goldwater, trying to combat the popularity of President Johnson with businessmen, told a U.S. Chamber of Commerce conference, "If you think President Johnson is going to give you any better attention than you have got, you're very, very mistaken. If he's a conservative," said the senator, "I'm a screaming liberal."

Sometimes even liberals cannot avoid the temptation to assault the term. Adlai Stevenson, quoting an uncertain source, once described a liberal as "one who has both feet firmly planted in the air." And columnist Heywood Broun, who came to consider himself a radical, wrote: "A liberal is a man who leaves a room when a fight begins," a definition adopted by militant Saul Alinsky.

The word has fallen on hard times. In the 1976 presidential primaries, Representative Morris Udall told columnist David Broder: "When a word takes on connotations you don't like, it's time to change the label." Henceforth, Udall said—though he would think of himself as a liberal—he would use the word "progressive" instead because the word "liberal" was "associated with abortion, drugs, busing and big-spending wasteful government."

Liberals are variously described as LIMOUSINE, double-domed, scream-ing, KNEE-JERK, professional, BLEED-ING HEART; also see PINKO; PARLOR PINK; COMMITTED; EGGHEAD.

liberation of captive peoples the promise of the Republican platform of 1952 and subsequently of the Eisen-hower Administration that the U.S. would help the people of the countries then under Communist rule gain their freedom.

The 1952 platform was meant to cast aspersions on any "secret agreements" made at Yalta by Roosevelt, Stalin, and Churchill. Russian power, combined with the vague wording of the Yalta agreement, had led to the seizure of most of Eastern and Central Europe by Communist factions, dominated by the Soviet Union.

In the Republican platform, Yalta was condemned as aiding "Commu-nist enslavements." The plank went on: "It will be made clear, on the high-est authority of the President and the Congress, that United States policy, as one of its peaceful purposes, looks happily forward to the genuine inde-pendence of those captive peoples."

General Eisenhower amplified this in an address during the campaign to the American Legion in which, after recit-ing the litany of Communist-domi-nated nations, he said: "We can never rest—and we must so inform all the world, including the Kremlin—that until the enslaved nations of the world have in the fullness of freedom the

right to choose their own path, that then, and then only, can we say that there is a possible way of living peace-fully and permanently with Commu-nism in the world."

In reply, Democratic candidate Adlai Stevenson warned of the dangers such words created. He said to a predomi-nantly Polish audience on Labor Day of 1952: ". . . the cruel grip of Soviet tyranny upon your friends and rela-tives cannot be loosened by loose talk or idle threats. It cannot be loosened by awakening false hopes which might stimulate intemperate action that would only lead your brothers to the execution squads . . ."

President Eisenhower's biographer, Robert J. Donovan, and the longtime State Department trouble-shooter, Robert Murphy, both insisted that the liberation referred to was to come only by peaceful means; John Foster Dulles told a Senate committee that "libera-tion does not mean a war of libera-tion."

This was not quite clear to restive ele-ments in Communist-dominated ("en-slaved") countries, many of whom were convinced that American troops would come to the aid of the Hungar-ian people when they staged their up-rising in 1956. In the U.S., the abortive Hungarian revolt marked the begin-ning of the end of the "liberation of captive peoples" as a political phrase, and it soon went the way of UNLEASH CHIANG.

In a 1976 televised debate with Jimmy Carter, President Ford refused to recognize the dominance of East European nations by the Soviet Union, which was widely interpreted as a foreign-policy political gaffe.

Liberation, a noble World War II word that came to mean the acquisi-tion of booty (as in "liberating" a wine cellar), was frequently used in Com-munist terminology during the Cold War. See WAR OF NATIONAL LIBERA-

TION. It was also adopted by small terrorist groups in the U.S. (the "Symbionese Liberation Army," which kidnapped Patricia Hearst) and large groups abroad (the Palestine Liberation Organization).

lid an assurance of inactivity.

Political reporters need to know not only when news is breaking, but when news is not breaking—so they can plan their lives accordingly. This need to know when there is nothing to know has led to the invention of the pressroom "lid," the assurance to reporters that no news is scheduled for distribution, or press conference planned, until an announced time when the "lid" ends. Reporters can use this promise of suspended animation to protect themselves while they cover other stories, or sun themselves in nearby spas, secure that they will not be caught napping—unless an emergency arises, at which point all lids are off.

The word is taken from "The lid's off," a turn-of-the-century expression for no-holds-barred activity. "Commissioner of Police McAdoo," wrote the *Philadelphia Public Ledger* in 1904, ". . . has taken frequent occasions to deny that the 'lid' was off, to use the slang definition of a lax police administration."

In modern political-press parlance, a lid may be "soft" ("Probably nothing happening, but stick around") to "hard" ("I'm going to the beach, too").

For examples of other forms of "masterly inactivity," see WATCHFUL WAITING.

life is unfair the apology for economic or social inequity; a gentle shrugging off of egalitarian demands.

In a press conference on March 21, 1962, President John F. Kennedy was asked about demonstrations by army reservists who—having "done their time" in the armed forces—resented being mobilized to fight in the Vietnam War. After observing that the calling up of the reservists had "strengthened the foreign policy of the United States," he extemporized in a more philosophical vein:

"There is always inequity in life. Some men are killed in a war and some men are wounded, and some men never leave the country, and some men are stationed in the Antarctic and some are stationed in San Francisco. It's very hard in military or in personal life to assure complete equality. Life is unfair . . ."

The phrase did not at first appear to fit in the ringing, high-minded Kennedy rhetoric; as years went by, it was remembered more than the more carefully crafted utterances in his speeches, and gained an added overtone of fatalism after his assassination.

President Carter, in a press conference on July 12, 1977, used the same argument (with a rough approximation of the phrase) in handling a question about the Supreme Court decision that the federal government was not obligated to provide money for abortions for women who cannot afford them. "There are many things in life that are not fair," the President replied, "that wealthy people can afford and poor people can't. But I don't believe that the federal government should take action to try to make these opportunities exactly equal, particularly when there is a moral factor involved."

The unintended evocation of John Kennedy's remark was widely noted, and reinforced journalistic usage of the phrase. *Washington Post* columnist George F. Will, writing about the Panama Canal treaty negotiated by Ambassador Sol Linowitz, observed: "Carter inherited the negotiations, and the general shape of the outcome. The fight for ratification will diminish his popularity, and defeat—a real possibility—would diminish his stature. It isn't fair, but as has been said, life is unfair."

The term continues to be used in labeling inequities or unfairness. The *Cook Political Report* wrote in 1991: "In the 'life is unfair' category, the population loss in New Jersey has clearly been in the heavily Democratic city of Newark, but it appears that the state's lost seat will be a Republican one."

lift of a driving dream Nixon's description of idealism.

At the Highway Hotel in Concord, New Hampshire, on February 3, 1968, Richard Nixon made the first speech of his second presidential campaign, beginning with "The finest hours in our nation's history have been triumphs of the American spirit. We now are engaged in a great test of that spirit."

The use of a Churchill phrase—"finest hours"—and the use of the Lincolnian construction "We are now engaged"—reflected the candidate's dual purposes: to rally and to heal. The centerpiece of the speech, written by Ray Price, was this line: "What America needs most today is what it once had, but has lost: the lift of a driving dream."

Correspondent Nancy Dickerson, interviewing the President with other network commentators on January 4, 1971, brought up the earliest use of the phrase and observed "many people have failed to perceive the lift of a driving dream." The President replied in part: "Before we can really get the lift of a driving dream, we have to get rid of some of the nightmares we inherited . . ."

After the Watergate revelations had driven Nixon to resignation, his successor, Gerald Ford, evoked the same image in his first speech and most memorable line: "Our long national nightmare is over."

One would think that this phrase would disappear from the political language as the Nixon presidency recedes in memory, but Ray Price's phrase may have staying power independent of memories of its speaker. "It is unclear whether Carter, the problem-solver," wrote Hedrick Smith in the *New York Times Magazine* on January 8, 1978, "understands that his greatest shortcoming so far has been his failure to rouse the nation with the lift of a driving dream . . . he has not used the White House effectively as a BULLY PULPIT."

Others keep it going only in ridicule. The *Chicago Tribune* of October 25, 1992: "If a candidate today talked about 'the lift of a driving dream,' Wayne and Garth would probably repeat the phrase, pause for a moment, then shout 'NOT!'"

lightning may strike the wish of the dark-horse or long-shot candidate; the possibility of a sudden shift in fortune that may nominate a man for major office.

In the California primary before the 1964 Republican nomination, Rockefeller supporters looked in vain for help from other liberals and middle-of-the-roaders in the campaign against Barry Goldwater. "It's understandable," said Nelson Rockefeller, tongue in cheek, four days before Goldwater's narrow victory. "All of them are available for the nomination and hoping that lightning will strike. What other position could they take?" Obviously, if Rockefeller had stopped Goldwater in California, the other Republican leaders who helped him would not be the compromise choice—lightning could only strike someone acceptable to both camps.

The phrase has been in use, in its precise meaning today, for at least a century. R. H. Thornton's *American Glossary* has this definition: "The lightning is said to strike, when a person or a place gains sudden and unexpected fame, notoriety, or good fortune. Not in the dictionaries." He offers this example from the *Congressional Record* of 1879:

"Mr. Sparks: I wish to suggest to the gentleman from Iowa that in districts near his own the lightning has been striking . . .

"Mr. Price: Oh, no . . . no danger of that kind of lightning in my district."

A vivid use of the phrase was made by magazine publisher and parachutist Bernarr Macfadden in 1936. Alva Johnson reported that Macfadden was bilked of a quarter of a million dollars by a group that convinced him he had a chance for the presidency against FDR. "If lightning strikes," the eccentric publisher announced, "it will find me a willing victim."

lightweight   a shallow public figure behind an impressive façade; a politician lacking either intellect, grasp of administrative detail, or guts.

"Lightweight" is an attack word, often as cruel and hard to shake as "loser," usually accompanied with "he just doesn't have it." See STRAW MAN.

A political aide useful for minor roles, but not one to be delegated major responsibility, is also tagged as a lightweight. The opposite—"heavyweight"—is rarely used in the first sense applied to public figures; more often, it refers to political aides who carry prestige and authority. "We need a heavyweight to operate on the top level."

Classic definition of a lightweight, attributed in 1960 to Brooklyn Republican leader John Crews about New York Mayor Robert Wagner: "He's light enough to do a tap dance on a charlotte russe." (Another pastry

metaphor was used by newswoman Louise Lamprey in 1897, in a remark later attributed to Theodore Roosevelt: "President McKinley has no more backbone than a chocolate eclair.")

The word, revived recently and now in frequent political use, can be traced back to 1809 and an allusion to "lightweight princes." In 1882 New York Congressman S. S. Cox said on the House floor, "I never took my friend from New Jersey [George Robeson] to be a lightweight in any regard."

In boxing, a lightweight can be an excellent fighter, even a champion; not so in politics. In the political arena, weight categories do not exist to protect the light from the heavy, and the fastest lightweight is easily taken by the slowest heavyweight.

Other boxing terms used in politics include ARENA, HAT IN THE RING, "throw in the towel," "take off the gloves," "hit below the belt," "on the ropes." Wrestling terms include "eye-gouging" and "no holds barred."

A 1980s synonym was *airhead*, although that locution imputed stupidity rather than lack of seriousness.

See HEFT, POLITICAL.

like ugly on an ape   thoroughly; inescapably; without moderation.

George Bush popularized this dialect term during the 1988 Presidential campaign. He commented to Maureen Dowd of the *New York Times*: "I knew the minute I said 'card-carrying member of the A.C.L.U.' a couple of your best columnists would jump all over me like ugly on an ape."

Seven years earlier, Bush used the phrase in a Vice Presidential statement reported by United Press International: "The Vice President said Russia pounced on the neutron-bomb decision 'like ugly on [an] ape,' but the Soviet Union's reaction was 'thoroughly expected.'"

Variations of the phrase have ranged from *like white on rice* to Jimmy Carter's *like a duck on a June bug*. Perhaps related is the simile *ugly as a hairless monkey*, used in Margaret Mitchell's novel, *Gone With the Wind*. The equating of primates with ugliness can be tracked back as far as William Dampier's report in his 1699 *Voyages and Descriptions*: "The Monkies that are in these Parts are the ugliest I ever saw."

Ugly as an absolute (an adjective used as a noun) dates back to the early nineteenth century: In 1835 the American humorist Augustus Longstreet wrote in *Georgia Scenes, Characters, and Incidents*: "I want to get in the breed of them sort o' men to drive ugly out of my kin folks."

The phrase *like ugly on ape*, without the article *an*, was a favorite saying of the character Festus Haggen, played by Ken Curtis, on the TV western "Gunsmoke" in the mid-1960s.

Bush, however, told David Frost of an earlier source in Texas for *like ugly on an ape*: "That's all over the oil fields. I got it in Odessa in 1948—that's when it started, I guess."

limited modified hangout. See WATERGATE WORDS.

limited war a military conflict in which the goal is defined as something short of total victory and in which one or both combatants may use less than full military resources.

"Limited war," an antonym of TOTAL WAR, became a common phrase—and a politically contentious one—during the Korean conflict. The Truman Administration called its intervention to save South Korea a POLICE ACTION rather than actual war and described its strategy as "limited warfare." The diplomatic rationale for circumlocution was clear: Washington wanted to keep Peking and Moscow out of the fighting and did not want to intensify the battle either rhetorically or militarily. General Douglas MacArthur could not live with the restrictions and Truman finally dismissed him as commander. See NO SUBSTITUTE FOR VICTORY; NO-WIN POLICY.

The Truman-MacArthur showdown and the frustrations of fighting an indecisive war under unusual conditions in a remote land set the issue. The goal of total victory and unconditional surrender in World War II was so fresh in the national consciousness that many forgot, as historian Samuel Eliot Morison pointed out, that "limited war is also in the American tradition." We had fought such wars with Great Britain, Spain, and Mexico. Nonetheless, when the Eisenhower Administration took office, Defense Secretary Charles Wilson said: "We can't afford to fight limited wars. We can only afford to fight a big war, and if there is one, that is the kind it will be."

As a result of this policy decision, the American military establishment during the 1950s emphasized strategic nuclear weapons at what critics said was the expense of conventional forces. But the change was temporary. Secretary of State John Foster Dulles acknowledged that the country had to be flexible enough in its arsenal to inflict less than MASSIVE RETALIATION.

While still a senator, John Kennedy insisted that "limited brushfire war," rather than all-out nuclear conflict, was the more likely threat. As President, Kennedy favored "balanced forces" and "flexible response" and had the military reorganized along these lines.

In 1993, Pentagon planners recommended a "win-hold-win strategy" to reflect budget trims; the idea was to be able to manage two simultaneous conflicts by winning one at a time.

See PEACE WITHOUT VICTORY; MEASURED RESPONSE.

limits to growth. See ENVIRONMEN-
TALIST.

limousine liberal one who takes up
hunger as a cause but has never felt a
pang; who will talk at length about the
public school system but sends his
children to private schools.

Mario Procaccino used this scornful
phrase in New York City's mayoral
campaign of 1969, casting aspersions
of hypocrisy at John Lindsay's followers on the Upper East Side of Manhattan. "Proc" was disdained by opponents who passed along bloopers like
"I want every kid in New York to have
the same chance I did—to come up the
hard way."

But "limousine liberal" was a phrase
that stung, alliteratively caricaturing
people of relative wealth who felt that
the downtrodden should have more at
the expense of the lower middle class.
Race was of course a factor here—
some aristocratic liberals who spoke
out for open housing had no fear of
blacks moving into the expensive
apartment next to them.

Of course, there has never been a
need for a man to be poor to be liberal,
and some aristocrats—FDR, for example—did more for the indigent "one-
third of a nation" than did any member of that third. Thus, in its broadest
sense, the application was unfair. In a
narrower sense, however, it had substance as brought out by Tom Wolfe in
New York magazine, who dissected
"radical chic"—the sponsorship of
groups like the Black Panthers by
some of New York's cultural elite.

Both terms had a sobering effect on
many old-line liberals who had to take
into consideration the needs and votes
of hardhats, homeowners, and people
not poor enough for welfare.

When Bill and Hillary Clinton en-
rolled their daughter Chelsea in the exclusive Sidwell Friends School in
Washington, D.C., the *Sacramento*

Bee of January 12, 1993, told its readers that "to millions of Americans, the
decision will signal that the president-
elect is simply another limousine liberal, a say-one-thing-and-do-another
Democrat, a favorite son of the party
that can't wait to legislate other
people's morality or bus other people's
children across town."

See PARLOR PINK.

Lindley Rule. See NOT FOR ATTRIBU-
TION.

line in the sand. See DRAW A LINE IN
THE SAND.

line-item veto. See RIDER.

linkage a global negotiating strategy
holding that progress on one front is
necessary to, or helpful to, progress on
other fronts.

The word was used by Dr. Henry
Kissinger, President Nixon's national
security adviser, in a background briefing on February 6, 1969, explaining
what the President had said in a press
conference about not wanting to dissociate arms control from political issues.
"To take the question of linkage between the political and the strategic environment," said Kissinger, ". . . the
President would like to deal with the
problem of peace on the entire front in
which peace is challenged and not only
on the military one."

Linkage was intended to describe a
tie between nuclear-arms talks and discussions of political tensions; in the
public mind, however, it has come to
mean a "package deal" in geographic
terms—that is, the U.S. would agree to
reduce tensions in an area where the
Soviets wanted such reduction, in return for détente in another part of the
world where superpower interests
were in conflict.

Ironically, the word was used by U.S.
diplomats in the mid-sixties to object

to the Soviets' connection of U.S. bombing of North Vietnam to détente elsewhere. The popularizer of the term—originally, in the sense of tying foreign affairs to domestic concerns— was James Rosenau, then professor of international relations at Rutgers, who titled a 1968 collection of essays *Linkage Politics*.

The word surfaced again in the Carter Administration, as National Security Adviser Zbigniew Brzezinski sought to establish a linkage between Soviet desire for arms control with Soviet support of Cuban troops in Africa.

See DECOUPLE.

lion and the fox combination of strength and craftiness.

Niccolò Machiavelli wrote in *The Prince*:

> A prince must imitate the fox and the lion, for the lion cannot protect himself from traps, and the fox cannot defend himself from wolves. . . . a prudent ruler ought not to keep faith when by so doing it would be against his interest.

This view of morality is the essence of "Machiavellianism." James MacGregor Burns, in *Roosevelt: The Lion and the Fox*, wrote: "To the idealists who cautioned him he responded again and again that gaining power— winning elections—was the first, indispensable task. He would use the tricks of the fox to serve the purposes of the lion."

The phrase crops up fairly frequently in political columns. On the death of former German Chancellor Konrad Adenauer in 1967, columnist Max Lerner wrote: "Konrad Adenauer had considerable of the lion in him, and even more of the fox—a combination, as Machiavelli was one of the first to see, that gives a man a galloping advantage in politics."

liquidity crisis. See ECONOMIC JARGON.

litmus-test issue a subject used as an indicator of a candidate's ideological purity.

This phrase made its appearance in the mid-seventies to fill the need for a description of topics that separated the COMMITTED from the CENTRISTS, or the TRUE BELIEVERS from the OPPORTUNISTS.

The most frequently discussed "litmus test" was a Republican's position on the Panama Canal treaties of 1977, which supporters of Ronald Reagan said would determine whether any candidate could get the 1980 presidential nomination. A Democratic litmus test was the Humphrey-Hawkins bill to reduce unemployment, and a Republican litmus test was the campaign for an Equal Rights Amendment for women.

In discussing the sale of war planes to Saudi Arabia in 1978, Mr. Reagan told this writer: "It isn't a litmus-test issue"—that is, conservatives could differ without having it considered a test of ideological virtue.

Professional politicians, to whom winning is the paramount issue, like to avoid the litmus. "Whatever Republican disunity may develop," wrote *New York Times* reporter Adam Clymer on June 25, 1978, "the party is doing one thing right, and that is not squabbling much in 1978. The party's right and middle (it has no real left) distrust each other, but they are working hard at electing Republicans without resorting to litmus-test issues . . ."

In the 1980s, the phrase was most often applied to the selection of Supreme Court Justices. That litmus test was their attitude toward abortion.

The phrase comes from the organic dye that turns blue in alkaline solutions, red in acid.

See SWITCHER.

little group of wilful men a small, powerful clique disposed (in its opponent's view) to put its own interests above the public's.

During the post–World War I fight over U.S. entry into the League of Nations, Woodrow Wilson characterized the opposition—centered in the Republican Senate leadership—as stubborn obstructionists. Later writers attributed "little group of wilful men" to Wilson as his theme during the League dispute. In fact, Wilson coined it just before rather than after the war in a speech attacking roughly the same group of Senate isolationists after their successful filibuster killing his bill to allow the arming of merchant vessels. "A little group of wilful men," Wilson said on March 4, 1917, "representing no opinion but their own, has rendered the great government of the United States helpless and contemptible." Perhaps because the same issues and personalities dominated the 1919–20 League campaign, the phrase has been applied indiscriminately.

Wilson's "little group" is often misquoted as a "little band," as that phrase has often been applied to valiant fighters against superior forces. It dates from a group of three hundred Thebans who fought in the fourth century B.C., were annihilated at Chaeronea, and became known to history as "the Sacred Band."

Despite the rather specialized Wilsonian use of "little group," later Presidents borrowed the idea in fights of their own. It became a favorite political gambit to portray oneself as the public's defender against predatory oligarchs and power brokers. Franklin D. Roosevelt answered conservative critics of his economic policy in 1941 by saying: "Beware of that small group of selfish men who would clip the wings of the American eagle in order to feather their own nests."

Harry Truman, faced with labor crises early in his Administration,

summed up: "This is no contest between labor and management. This is a contest between a small group of men and their government." And John F. Kennedy, in his 1962 confrontation with the steel industry over prices, attacked "a tiny handful of steel executives whose pursuit of private power and profit exceeds their sense of public responsibility."

Vice President Spiro Agnew, in his campaign supporting Republican congressional candidates in 1970, chose "band" over "group," but deliberately used the rhythm of the Wilson sentence to recall Senatorial obstructionism: "Will a little band of radical-liberals, with no constituency but each other, succeed in frustrating the will of the new majority of the American people?"

little man.   See JOHN Q. PUBLIC.

little old ladies in tennis shoes   characterization of feminine right-wing extremists.

Columnist Robert Novak informed the author that the phrase was coined in 1961 by Stanley Mosk, then Attorney General of California, in a report on right-wing activity.

The expression was one of many attacking Senator Barry Goldwater's campaign for the Republican nomination in 1963 and 1964. Republican liberals, members of what Goldwater supporters called the Eastern Establishment (Goldwater: "We ought to saw off the Eastern seaboard and float it out to sea") denounced the conservative champion as the captive of the John Birch Society and other extremist groups, which included "nuts and kooks" (see KOOKS, NUTS AND). Among these were a resolute, intensely dedicated women's group—Western (or at least not Eastern urban), unsophisticated, white-haired, and wearing rimless eyeglasses. They were called "the little old ladies in tennis shoes" with considerable disdain. However, their doorbell-ringing helped upset the Rockefeller forces in the crucial California primary.

The tennis-shoes metaphor can be contrasted with the SILK STOCKING metaphor; other political uses of foot coverings include "the heel of a dictator" and Adlai Stevenson's "hole in the shoe" symbol, as well as "gumshoe campaign."

Ronald Reagan, campaigning for governor of California in 1966, joked about the charge of ultraconservative support by addressing audiences occasionally as "Gentlemen—and little ladies in tennis shoes . . ."

As used on the attack, however, the phrase can flash on the edge of viciousness: "It is not little old ladies in tennis shoes who are the hate merchants of the '70s," said AFL-CIO leader George Meany in 1977. "It is slick Madison Avenue types . . ."

The current use remains disdainful. When in 1992 the Smithsonian Institution decided to license four antique American quilts for reproduction in China, members of the national quilt community lashed back. "We are not little old ladies in tennis shoes," said their spokeswoman. "This is a billion-dollar-a-year industry and this institution . . . is cutting our throats having these quilts made offshore for rock-bottom prices."

Editors of *The New Yorker* magazine have frequently pointed out that they were not editing their publication for "the old ladies in Dubuque." In *Here at The New Yorker*, Brendan Gill wrote that the founder-editor, Harold Ross, launched the publication "with the stipulation that it was *not* to be edited for the old lady in Dubuque." The phrase came to mean a low common denominator of taste, and is almost always used patronizingly. There may be a relationship between the ladies in Dubuque (Iowa) and those in tennis shoes (anywhere).

little tin box   symbol of graft; a hiding place for money.

Thomas M. Farley (no relation to James A.) was sheriff of New York County in the early thirties, and a Tammany SACHEM. In his investigation of corruption that led to the resignation of Mayor James Walker, Judge Samuel Seabury discovered that Farley had deposited $396,000 in his bank account over a six-year period. In that time, his total salary had been $90,000. Seabury's interrogation of Farley led to the coinage of the phrase.

"Where did you keep these moneys that you had saved?"
"In a safe deposit box at home in the house."
"Whereabouts at home in the house?"
"In a big safe."
"In a little box in a big safe?"
"In a big box in a big safe."
"And, Sheriff, was this big box that was safely kept in the big safe a tin box or a wooden box?"
"A tin box." [It turned out that Farley's bank deposits, year after year, came from this tin box, which seemed to generate cash all by itself.]
"Kind of a magic box, wasn't it, Sheriff?"
"It was a wonderful box."

In 1959 a musical based on Mayor La Guardia's life called *Fiorello!* was produced by Harold Prince. One of the hit songs was "A Little Tin Box" by Jerry Bock and Sheldon Harnick:

Mister X, May we ask you a question?
It's amazing, is it not?
That the City pays you slightly less
*   than fifty bucks a week*
Yet you've purchased a private yacht.
I am positive Your Honor must be
*   joking*
Any working man could do what I
have done.

*For a month or two I simply gave up
 smoking.
And I put my extra pennies one by
 one
Into a little tin box, a little tin box
There's a cushion for life's rude
 shocks.
There is faith, hope and charity,
Hard won prosperity,
In a little tin box.**

The word's meaning was inverted by Abraham Beame, controller of the City of New York, who used it to refer to the container for sealed bids by banks for city financing. The *New York Times* reported on July 8, 1971: "The ritual of unlocking the city's 'little tin box' and then unsealing the bids got under way at 11:03 A.M. yesterday . . ." In this sense, the box is a symbol of financial fairness and rectitude.

The original sense, however, continues. In 1989, the *Washington Post* reported on Oliver North's testimony in Iran-contra: "North's account of a little tin box, containing $15,000 and stapled to his closet floor, 'echoed,' as the prosecutor noted in his sentencing recommendations, 'the flimsy lies offered by corrupt municipal officials in the days of Tammany Hall.'"

There is no connection between the "little tin box" and the "loose box" of British usage, which refers to the seats set aside for Edward VII's mistresses at his coronation, in turn taken from an enclosure for horses that permits them to move about without tethering.

living wage   enough earnings to pay for necessities and a little more; a frequent promise of politicians seeking labor votes.

This has its roots in a "living price," or the price at which a businessman can make a profit and thereby earn his

living. Congressman John Lind of Minnesota said in the House in 1890: "Things are at a standstill. We have plenty to sell but no buyers at 'living' prices."

Father Coughlin, "the radio priest," who later became a bitter isolationist and anti-Semite, was an ardent supporter of Roosevelt in the early New Deal days, calling for currency inflation, nationalization of the banks, and "a living annual wage."

"Living" wages were contrasted with "starvation wages"; both terms are falling into disuse with the accent on "fringe benefits" and a "guaranteed annual wage." For a related usage, see HIGH COST OF LIVING.

lobby   as a verb, to attempt, as a private citizen or group, to influence governmental decisions and particularly legislative votes; as a noun, a group organized for this purpose.

The practice of lobbying is doubtless as old as the practice of legislating, but the term did not come into vogue until the mid-seventeenth century, when the large anteroom near the English House of Commons floor became known as the lobby. The word is akin to the Old High German *lauba*, meaning a shelter of foliage; when adopted into English, it came to mean a covered walk or passageway. The lobby was a public room, and thus one in which Members of Parliament could be approached by special pleaders, with or without protective foliage.

In the early nineteenth century those who lobbied were called "lobbiers" in the U.S., later "lobbyists." In England a "lobbyist" came to mean a reporter covering Commons, while a "lobbyagent" meant one who urged particular measures.

But in the U.S. during the politically venal 1800s, lobbying and lobbyists earned a bad name from which their professional descendants today, no matter how pure in motive and deed, have yet to clear themselves completely. To Walt Whitman, "lobbiers" were among the "lousy combings and born freedom sellers of the earth." Dennis Tilden Lynch, writing of New York State politics circa 1820, said that "corruption has erected her court. . . . Her throne is the lobby."

In such low repute were lobbyists—universally considered buyers-up of votes and sellers-out of the public welfare—that to be branded one was an almost automatic disqualification for public office. Mark Hanna was William McKinley's political strongman and an intimate as well. But it is said that when Hanna pressed a particular appointment on McKinley, the President replied, "Mark, I would do anything in the world for you, but I cannot put a man in my cabinet who is known as a lobbyist." By this time lobbyists were considered so numerous and powerful that they were sometimes referred to collectively as the Third House of Congress.

Lobbying has grown more diverse. The federal government and some of the states have imposed legislative restrictions in an attempt to end the more blatant abuses. Most lobbyists now operate openly as registered advocates for their employers and clients, appearing before legislative committees and regulatory agency proceedings, where they are often useful in supplying information on complex issues.

At the same time, government has grown so large and complicated that executive agencies sometimes are cast in the role of lobbyists before Congress in competing with other departments for appropriations. Jack Raymond wrote in 1964: "The military services' own public relations and lobbying apparatus has disturbed some observers. The question has been posed whether the total effect of the military pleadings is contrary to the national interest."

When a reporter asked President Harry Truman in 1948, "Would you be against lobbyists who are working for your program?," the President replied, "We probably wouldn't call those people lobbyists. We would call them citizens appearing in the public interest."

For a derogation of pressure groups in international affairs, see CHINA LOBBY; for a disparaging view of lobbyists, see INFLUENCE PEDDLER, FIVE PERCENTER; for a melancholy view, see POCATELLO, YOU CAN'T GO BACK TO.

lobby terms. See NOT FOR ATTRIBUTION.

log cabin humble origins which, when part of a candidate's personal history, are presumed to be worth many votes (now used mostly in a humorous vein).

When the Whigs nominated William Henry Harrison for President in 1840, one of his detractors observed that if someone gave Harrison a supply of hard cider, a small pension, and his choice of how to spend his time, the old hero of Indian fighting would sit contentedly by his log cabin the rest of his days. At that point Harrison owned some 2,000 acres of farmland and a mansion built around the old cabin, but his friends seized on the cider-cabin remark after it was printed in the *Baltimore Republic* as a way of emphasizing their man's plebeian past. Harrison himself campaigned from a log cabin built on a wagon bed that had a seemingly bottomless cider barrel attached. The crowds loved it.

Complained a Democrat: "We defend the policy of the administration; the Whigs answer 'log cabin.' We urge the honesty, sagacity, statesmanship of Van Buren; the Whigs answer that Harrison is a poor man." Harrison won in what became known as the

"Log Cabin and Hard Cider" campaign. See BANNER DISTRICT.

As a specific prop, the log cabin remained a Harrison monopoly, but rare is the candidate or incumbent who fails to point out his close relations with the common man, to the public's apparent approval. From Lincoln's log cabin to Harry Truman's haberdashery store, the lean yesterdays of Presidents are milestones of political folklore—all the more so, it appears, in this era when personal wealth and political success are hardly unrelated. John Nance Garner, a two-term Vice President under Franklin D. Roosevelt, said in 1959, "That log house [in which he was born] did me more good in politics than anything I ever said."

logorrhea.   See FOOT-IN-MOUTH DISEASE.

logrolling   mutual aid among politicians, especially legislators who must vote on many items of economic importance in individual states and districts.

H. L. Mencken traced the use of logrolling back to 1820. Hans Sperber and Travis Trittschuh tracked down derisive newspaper comments of "great log rolling captains" in politics to 1809.

In the *Apocolocyntosis*, written early in the first century A.D. and attributed to Seneca, Hercules urges the gods to deify the Emperor Claudius. The Latin (*Deinde tu si quid volueris, in vicem faciam*) translates: "And then if you may desire something, I would reciprocate."

Among settlers in the wilderness, co-operation in handling logs for land clearing and construction was a force overriding any differences among neighbors. So too in politics. "If you will vote for my interest," said Congressman B. F. Butler in 1870, "I will vote for yours. That is how these tariffs are log-rolled through."

Reformers have inveighed against the practice as assiduously as the practitioners have pursued it. In 1871 the *New York Times* complained of Republicans who established "corrupt alliances with the enemy in the way of log rolling legislation." And in 1967 *Time*, cataloging the problems of the Post Office—then an institution as afflicted by bad politics as any in the country—noted "construction programs pressured on the one side by budget vagaries and on the other by congressional log rolling." *Time* still prefers the two-word usage; most current writers join the two words.

The classic description of the theory of logrolling is attributed to Simon Cameron, Pennsylvania politician who served as Lincoln's first Secretary of War: "You scratch my back and I'll scratch yours."

loneliest job in the world   description of the presidency, emphasizing its "awesome burdens."

It is a wonder that there are any applicants.

Thomas Jefferson, who served first as Vice President, said: "The second office of this government is honorable and easy, the first is a splendid misery." Andrew Jackson called the presidency "a situation of dignified slavery." The term of office has been likened to a term in jail by George Washington, who felt like "a culprit, going to the place of his execution." Warren Harding said, "This White House is a prison. I can't get away from the men who dog my footsteps. I am in jail." Harry Truman agreed; returning from a pre-breakfast stroll, he sighed and told a reporter, "There is the big white jail." He wrote in his memoirs: "To be President of the United States is to be lonely, very lonely at times of great decisions."

"My God," said James Garfield two months after taking office, "what is there in this place that a man should ever want to get into it?" James Buchanan called it "a crown of thorns."

Several Presidents thought it a ruiner of friendships. Grover Cleveland wrote: "Henceforth, I can have no friends . . . I must face the difficulties of a new official life almost alone." John F. Kennedy, who enjoyed the presidency, agreed that it "is not a very good place to make new friends."

Old friendships are often strained. General Omar Bradley had called Dwight Eisenhower "Ike" for forty years; when he properly addressed him as "Mr. President," Eisenhower felt a twinge of isolation. He wrote: "His salutation put me on notice: from then onward, for as long as I held the office, I would . . . be separated from all others, including my oldest and best friends. I would be far more alone now than when commanding the Allied Forces . . ."

Wendell Willkie asked FDR why he kept Harry Hopkins so close to him. FDR replied, "Someday you may well be sitting here where I am now as President of the United States. And when you are, you'll be looking at that door over there and knowing that practically everybody who walks through it wants something out of you. You'll learn what a lonely job this is, and you'll discover the need for somebody like Harry Hopkins who asks for nothing except to serve you."

Of all the burdens of the presidency, loneliness is the one complaint that threads through the writings of the occupants, or inmates, of the White House. William Howard Taft summed it up to Woodrow Wilson on the latter's inauguration day: "I'm glad to be going—this is the loneliest place in the world."

In 1977, the *National Journal* overturned the oxymoron of *splendid misery* (which may have been Jefferson's reworking of Goethe's phrase *radiant misery*): "We can thank Carter for exposing the myth of the 'splendid misery' of the Presidency. He recently told a group of editors that he enjoys being President. 'It is a fairly pleasant life,' he said."

The columnist Mary McGrory further contested the validity of this phrase; in 1990 she wrote, "The term 'splendid misery' underwent considerable erosion during the Reagan years. Ronald Reagan seemed to enjoy himself most of the time. But Reagan was St. Sebastian compared to George Bush, for whom every day in the Oval Office is Christmas. The President's palpable delight in being where he always wanted to be has not waned in the 15 months since he took office."

loner politician who "goes his own way," "keeps his own counsel"; used pejoratively, as one who will not mix or take good advice.

Probably derived from "lone wolf" or "Lone Ranger," the word is applied to those who reject the camaraderie of political life, and on the policy level, who know enough (or think they do) to arrive at conclusions on issues independent of advisers. A loner is not necessarily a maverick; he may not oppose the organization but he does not give the organization a sense of participation in his decisions and his future.

Chicago Democratic Boss Jake Arvey assessed Senator Paul Douglas's beginnings in politics this way: "Paul was a 'loner' in Chicago politics. He was an alderman and somewhat of a stormy petrel. . . . I knew Paul Douglas was thinking about maybe running for Mayor. The indications were that if he did run, he would make the race as an independent Democrat. This was in line with Douglas' history of being a 'loner.'" Arvey talked Douglas out of running for mayor and into running for senator, with Adlai Stevenson running on the same ticket for governor. "In neither case," Arvey continued, "were these men 'developed' in the sense that they came out of the organization. Stevenson was a political unknown about to break on the public consciousness; Douglas had made himself in politics by bucking the organization on many important issues."

Though each man was, in a different way, a "loner," the organization used and was used by them.

Although Henry Kissinger once described himself to Italian interviewer Oriana Fallaci as a kind of lonely cowboy on the international scene—evoking the "Lone Ranger" image, which was followed by some derisive hooting from critics—a "loner" is not a reputation political figures usually seek. Joan Mondale, wife of the former Vice President, used the word and its antonym, "team player"—which, during the Watergate hearings, temporarily gained a negative connotation—in a comment about her husband to reporter Brock Brower in 1977: "He is very much a team player, not a loner."

See MAVERICK.

long hot summer   a threat of violence in black ghettos, when summer heat shortens tempers and crowds gather out of doors.

The phrase began as the title of a 1958 movie based on a number of works by William Faulkner; a television series based on the characters, also called *The Long Hot Summer*, ran on the ABC-TV network in 1965.

"It's going to be a long, hot summer" was a frequent prediction by black leaders in the spring of 1966; the author has not been able to trace the first political use of it, though it probably was used in this sense in 1964. The reference was to the likelihood of violence, from crime in the streets to full-scale rioting.

In June 1967, before the riots of Newark and Detroit, Martin Luther King, Jr., said, "Everyone is worrying about the long hot summer with its threat of riots. We had a long cold winter when little was done about the conditions that create riots." The phrase used to try to calm troubled neighborhoods was usually "Cool it."

Michigan Governor George Romney, who was to face a riot in Detroit that required federal troops to quell, said in April 1967 that the U.S. faced not only long hot summers at home but "the equally forbidding prospect of a long, hot century" throughout the world.

Faulkner's phrase was an apt turnaround of an earlier image that connected unrest with winter. *The Winter of Our Discontent* was a 1961 book by John Steinbeck, its title taken from Shakespeare's *King Richard III*: "Now is the winter of our discontent/Made glorious summer by this sun of York."

John F. Kennedy used that earlier season image in a remark at the conclusion of the frigid 1961 Vienna meeting with Khrushchev: "It's going to be a cold winter."

loop.   See OUT OF THE LOOP.

loose box.   See LITTLE TIN BOX.

loser.   See CAN'T-WIN TECHNIQUE.

loved for the enemies he made
a campaign cry of Grover Cleveland supporters in 1884; innocence by dissociation.

Grover Cleveland, mayor of Buffalo and later governor of New York, did not work well with the SACHEMS of Tammany Hall. While this caused him some difficulty in his home state, the opposition of Tammany leaders was an asset in the campaign for the Democratic nomination. With Samuel Tilden ill and declaring himself out of the running, Cleveland was the leading candidate. In a seconding speech Governor Edward S. Bragg of Wisconsin electrified the delegates with: "They love him most for the enemies he has made." (Senator Joseph McCarthy used the same slogan in a full-page ad in the *Milwaukee Journal* in 1952, as he ran for a second term; New York Mayor Robert F. Wagner was to make substantially the same turning-on-Tammany appeal running for his third term in 1961.)

Franklin D. Roosevelt knew how to exploit the appeal of enmity from an unpopular source. In a Madison Square Garden speech bringing his 1936 campaign to a climax, he zeroed in on the enemy: ". . . financial monopoly, speculation, reckless banking, class antagonism, sectionalism, war profiteering." In a hard voice he said: "Never before in all our history have these forces been so united against one candidate as they stand today. They are unanimous in their *hate* for me—*and I welcome their hatred.*"

Presidents have taken private reassurance from the source of attacks as well. When Harry Truman fired Secretary of Commerce Henry Wallace, he incurred the wrath of the far-left wing. Writing to his mother, the President observed: "Well, now he's out, and the crackpots are having conniption fits. I'm glad they are. It convinces me I'm right."

IBM president Thomas J. Watson, Jr., observed: "Make no little enemies—people with whom you differ for some petty, insignificant reason . . . cultivate 'mighty opposites'—people with whom you disagree on big issues, with whom you will fight to the end over fundamental convictions."

love feast humorous exaggeration of a friendly meeting, especially one that could have revealed tensions and bitterness but ends amicably.

The phrase was originally religious, to describe the "agape," or love feast, among early Christians—an informal dinner, with songs and prayers, prevalent in the first two centuries of Christianity. Suspicions of bacchanalian zeal were voiced early, as the Book of Jude warned of "blemishes on your love feasts"; Pope Paul in 1967 disapproved of changes in the celebration of the Eucharist, following reports of experiments in the liturgy that included mass at home accompanied by modern music, with non-Catholics participating. "Such masses," reported the *New York Times* "are frequently thought of as imitations of the 'agape,' or love feast, common in the early church, and the emphasis is on the close fellowship of small numbers of believers."

Colonel Edward House set up a luncheon for Franklin Roosevelt and Massachusetts Democratic leaders in 1932 to discourage Al Smith. Ralph Martin wrote in *Ballots and Bandwagons:* "Uninvited to this 'love feast', promoted by Colonel House, [former Boston Mayor James] Curley not only showed up with Roosevelt, but invited his own press and newsreel people . . ."

The religious phrase was probably introduced into politics by Mark Twain and Charles Dudley Warner in 1873, in the novel *The Gilded Age*, a story about the politics of Reconstruction. The newspaper in their fictional Washington, D.C., is so much the supporter of the corrupt status quo that it is called the *Daily Love-Feast*.

In 1901 William Jennings Bryan wrote a Republican friend about the revolt of the Western progressives: "Your party is entering upon a struggle by the side of which our contest will seem a love-feast." A more restrained form is "mutual admiration society."

Humorist Art Buchwald used the term in describing the hangover mood among Democrats following Clinton's Inauguration Day: "The love feast is over, and people are snapping at each other's ankles." The headline of the piece was "Victory Takes Fun Out of Politics."

low profile self-denigration to reduce vulnerability; abhorrence of the vivid or dramatic in public posture.

A low profile is one step short of a PASSION FOR ANONYMITY; one who maintains a low profile gets some public exposure, but does not invite attack. It is normally used to describe the low-keyed approach of an individual, but can also be used to characterize an Administration.

Presidential assistant Leonard Garment told an associate in early 1970, "I've kept my profile so low for so long, I've got a permanent backache." The meaning of the expression was best captured in John F. Kennedy's advice to his speechwriter, Ted Sorensen: "Stay out of sight and you stay out of trouble."

The phrase has achieved a certain linguistic universality. "In last year's election campaign," wrote the *Wall Street Journal* on November 15, 1977, in a story about Canadian separatists, "unlike previous contests, the Parti Québécois kept what its strategists called 'le low profile' on the independence issue."

The phrase may have originated in the military: tanks and other armored vehicles were less vulnerable when they presented a low profile. The *Third Barnhart Dictionary of New English* dates the term back to 1964 as a translation of the Japanese *teishisei*, from *tei*, "low," and *shisei*, "posture," which was the motto for the Hayato Ikeda cabinet of 1960–64.

low road. See HIGH ROAD . . . LOW ROAD.

loyal opposition the role of the political opposition in a republican form of government, implying the responsibility to oppose with patriotic motives.

In eighteenth-century Britain when political parties were first being formed, the term was meant to indicate that the party in opposition, like the party in power, was true to the Crown—in fact, loyal—but felt that the best interests of the nation would be served by different policies. It is officially used to describe the party out of power in Great Britain, as "His (Her) Majesty's Loyal Opposition."

In the U.S. it was popularized by Wendell Willkie in a radio speech delivered several days after he and the Republican party had been defeated by President Roosevelt in November 1940.

Willkie spoke of the war already under way in Europe, and of the calls by some for a coalition cabinet of Democrats and Republicans. He rejected such a cabinet (though FDR had already enlisted Republicans Frank Knox and Henry Stimson) and described what he considered to be the role of the Republican party: "A vital element in the balanced operation of democracy is a strong, alert and watchful opposition . . . I say: 'Your function during the next four years is that of the loyal opposition.' . . . Let us not, therefore, fall into the partisan error of opposing things just for the sake of opposition. Ours must not be an opposition against—it must be an opposition for—an opposition for a strong America . . ."

Commented Republican leader Joe Martin: "Willkie got off on the right foot with the whole country, Republicans included, with his Loyal Opposition speech." It was not easy, for the "duty" of the opposition was still felt by many to oppose, and not to cooperate.

That principle had long been articulated. Winston Churchill told of his father, Lord Randolph Churchill, quoting an early-nineteenth-century politician as saying bluntly: "The duty of an Opposition is to oppose."

This might have been a simplification of a statement attributed to a Whig leader named Tierney by Edward Stanley, Earl of Derby. Tierney is quoted as having said: ". . . the duty of an opposition was very simple—it was, to oppose everything, and propose nothing."

In his years as Senate Majority Leader, Lyndon Johnson established himself as a Democratic leader who was frequently prepared to support legislation desired by the Republican Administration of Dwight D. Eisenhower. He expressed his philosophy to fellow Democrats at a Senate conference early in 1953: "I have never agreed with the statement that it is 'the business of the opposition to oppose.' I do not believe that the American people have sent us here merely to obstruct."

But there are those who still subscribe to the Tierney theory. Fred Vinson, Supreme Court Chief Justice from 1946 to 1953, told the story of a Kentucky politician who was asked whom he was going to support in a primary election. The politician's answer: "I don't know yet. I'm waiting to see what the opposition does, so I can take the other side."

"Loyal opposition" is an oxymoron (a phrase made memorable by the jarring juxtaposition of contradictory words); more recent oxymorons are *profitless prosperity*, UNTHINKABLE THOUGHTS, and WAGING PEACE.

As a member of the loyal opposition, Churchill in 1936 flung a handful of oxymorons at the government of Stanley Baldwin: "So they go on in strange paradox, decided only to be undecided, resolved to be irresolute, adamant for drift, solid for fluidity, all-powerful to be impotent."

loyalty oath a pledge of fealty to a government; more specifically in recent years, a promise of abstinence from subversive activities and causes.

The latest concern with loyalty oaths started soon after World War II. Charges of Communist infiltration of the American government became the biggest domestic issue of the late forties and early fifties. Although President Harry Truman sometimes scoffed at it (see RED HERRING), he also issued an Executive Order in 1947—called the "loyalty order"—which prescribed security procedures for the executive branch.

The issue seems to be one that arises periodically after great wars and upheavals. The "red menace" after World War I also made the country security-conscious, and loyalty oaths had a brief vogue.

Another form of loyalty oath is often required by a political party of its convention delegates; it is a pledge to abide by the decision of the convention and not to bolt if dissatisfied. Columnist Arthur Krock wrote: "Without the discipline which was enforced by the 'loyalty' requirement at the Democratic Convention of 1964, a political party as such loses its identity as a responsible group accountable to the people."

During the Civil War, Congress enacted legislation that required Confederate sympathizers to take the *ironclad oath* if they wished to regain their civil rights. No former rebel could hold important public office, for instance, without swearing his opposition to the Confederate cause. Sometimes called the *amnesty oath* in the North, it was more often termed the *damn nasty oath* in the South.

In *Andrew Johnson and Reconstruction*, Eric McKitrick wrote of the

Southern girl who was brought before a Union captain and told she had to swear an oath of loyalty to the Union. "The girl refused on the grounds that it was wrong to swear an oath—her church forbade it, her mother told her that no lady ever swore. The captain insisted that she swear the oath and the girl finally agreed, saying: 'I will swear an oath, but it will be forever on your conscience. Damn all you Yankees to hell! There, Captain, I swore my oath!'"

lulu   payment made to legislators "in lieu of" expenses.

Instead of requiring a detailed accounting of expenditures from its legislators, New York State sets a fixed fee to be paid them in lieu of expenses; if the legislators can skimp on the outlay, they can keep the extra money. Governor Al Smith named them "lulus," a play on the word "lieu" and the meaning of the girl's name in current slang as a whopping mistake, or a "beaut." (Fiorello La Guardia: "When I make a mistake, it's a beaut.")

"Lulu" is in current, if regional, use; attacks on the expense system are made periodically.

See POLITICAL MILEAGE, TO MAKE; PERKS.

lumpenproletariat.   See PROLETARIAT.

lunatic fringe   persons or groups with extreme political views.

The emergence of militant right-wingers and professional anti-Communists since the 1940s revived "lunatic fringe." Since then it has usually been used to denote the far-out right. In one of his last campaign speeches, Franklin Roosevelt in 1944 attacked "labor baiters, bigots and some politicians who use the term Communism

loosely." This "fear propaganda," he said, had been used by fascist blackshirts, Nazi brownshirts, and "in this country by the silver shirts and those on the lunatic fringe." Since then the term has been most frequently applied to "extremism" or the RADICAL RIGHT.

It was not always so. Theodore Roosevelt is generally credited with first using the phrase, or at least giving it currency, in 1913, when he wrote: "Every reform movement has a lunatic fringe." Although himself a progressive and a reformer, Roosevelt said he was talking about "the votaries of any forward movement." The left connotation was clear as TR wrote: "I am always having to fight the silly reactionaries and the inert, fatuous creatures who will not think seriously; and on the other hand to try to exercise some control over the lunatic fringe among the reformers."

Thus, left-leaning radicals were targets of the lunatic label before their rightist cousins. The Republicans in the 1948 election accused the Democrats of being hospitable to a "lunatic fringe" and the Republicans were so charged in 1964.

A Calgary correspondent wrote to advice columnist Ann Landers in 1992: "Every minority has its lunatic fringe, extremists and nut cases who impede progress, block acceptance and make life hard for everybody."

In current usage, labeling from near right to far right goes "rightist," "far rightist," "reactionary," "ultrarightist," MOSSBACK, "dinosaur wing," "troglodyte," and "lunatic fringe."

See LITTLE OLD LADIES IN TENNIS SHOES; KOOKS, NUTS AND; TROGLODYTIC.

lunching him out.   See ADVANCE MAN.

M

machine politics the election of officials and the passage of legislation through the power of an organization created for political action.

The phrase is derogatory because it suggests that the interests of the organization are placed before those of the general public.

Machine politics in the United States is closely linked with New York's Tammany Hall and with urban politics. The Vare organization in Philadelphia (Republican), the Kelly-Nash machine in Chicago (Democratic), and the more recent Democratic organization of Richard Daley, are all examples of machine politics in the classic sense.

The beginnings of big-city organization politics can be tracked back to Tammany (see TAMMANY TIGER). Theodore Roosevelt, himself a politician of substantial skill, wrote that "Van Buren was the first product of what are now called 'machine politics' put into the Presidential chair. The people at large would never have thought of him for President of their own accord; but he had become Jackson's political legatee."

The creation of the first political machine in the U.S. at the end of the eighteenth century in New York has often been credited to Aaron Burr, though recent scholarship downgrades his importance. His political acumen was praised by those who won the right to vote through his political manipulations, and damned by those, led by Alexander Hamilton, whose possession of property had previously held control of the franchise.

The word "machine" is believed by Mencken to have been Burr's invention, though it did not come into general use until after the Civil War. It generally means strict organization, with rewards of one kind or another going to those who work for the organization and observe its disciplines. Discipline is important. As Edward Flynn, the Bronx County Democratic leader who was a national figure in the Roosevelt era, wrote: ". . . the so-called 'independent' voter is foolish to assume that a political machine is run solely on good will, or patronage. For it is not only a machine; it is an army. And in any organization as in any army, there must be discipline."

The charge against machines is that they are undemocratic and invariably encourage corruption. One answer is the primary elections whereby candidates for office may be selected directly by the voters who register for one political party or the other. But the primary system often means selection of the best-known candidate, or the one supported by the organization leadership who can use "troops" to turn out the vote.

To the reformer, the machine is dominated by a BOSS and consists of his HENCHMEN and "dupes"; to a regular, the organization is headed by a "leader" and consists of ACTIVISTS and "public-spirited citizens."

In Japan, the word for political machine is *jiban*, literal translation "base" or "foundation," which is one view of the function of the machine in the party system.

machinery of government metaphor to show complexity of interrelationships within public administration.

"I think we have more machinery of government than is necessary," wrote Thomas Jefferson in 1824. He might have seen the phrase in Edward Gibbon's *Decline and Fall of the Roman Empire*, written between 1776 and 1788: "The nice and artificial machinery of government was out of joint."

Geared to press the *panic button* at the first *feedback* from *machine* politicos, government planners *mesh* their thinking to get *traction* for their programs to *spark* action, *engineering* their budgets so as to ignore *start-up* costs, and *mechanically* warn those *automatons* and *cogs* whose *machinations* might throw *monkey wrenches* into the *works* that *counterproductive* people usually get the *shaft*. See INOPERATIVE; WHEELS WITHIN WHEELS.

President William Howard Taft listened in wonderment to an adviser who spoke of "the machinery of government" and said later to a friend, "You know . . . he really thinks it *is* machinery."

In 1969 a White House aide told President Nixon he would relay a request "to the appropriate mechanism." The President proceeded to reminisce to the author about a visit he had made to Poland in 1959: "There was a steel mill on the itinerary. The Polish diplomat who was my escort officer—a brilliant fellow—turned me over to the plant manager for the usual guided tour. The manager was especially proud of the new machinery in the plant, and he told me all about what it cost and how it speeded up the process. He got a little impatient when I stopped to shake hands with the workers around whatever machine he was showing off. In the car on the way back from the mill, the diplomat said something I've always remembered. 'It's not hard to find men who understand machinery,' he said. 'Our trouble is we don't have enough men who understand men.'"

In 1978 the metaphor was cranking along as merrily as ever. "Carter's an engineering officer, a protégé of Admiral [Hyman] Rickover," said the President's Energy Secretary, James Schlesinger, to Hedrick Smith of the *New York Times*. "Rickover has to know how every single engine or pump works. Carter is that way. He looks upon government as machinery to be improved, to be lubricated."

machismo condescension of the swaggering male; the trappings of manliness used to dominate women and keep them "in their place."

Pronounced ma-*chees*-mo, the word is a favorite of feminists. In the first issue of the magazine *Ms.* in December 1971, the political "machismo factor" (or anti-machismo stand) was defined as "personal rejection of the traditional 'masculine' role . . . and opposition to militarism and violence." A Mexican term, *machismo* is based on the Spanish *macho*, "manly." In March 1967, sociologist David Riesman wrote: "In Spanish-America the term *machismo* designates efforts of a man to appear manly in the approved way, often caricaturing himself in the process."

Politically the word (often as *macho*, or as "manhood") is used as a criticism of intervention. When President Ford in 1975 reacted sharply to the attack on the merchant ship *Mayagüez*, Secretary of State Henry Kissinger explained, "We are not going around looking for opportunities to prove our manhood." Lucy Komisar responded in a *New York Times* Op-Ed article: "It was a curious comment for the question had never been asked, and it made it clear that at a level very close to his consciousness, Secretary Kissinger knew that this was precisely what America's reaction had been all about."

Madison Avenue techniques the other side's gimmicky, slick use of the communications media to play on emotions, contrasted with your own forthright use of modern advertising methods to "get the message to the people."

The phrase "Madison Avenue," in its present sense descriptive of the advertising community, was born in 1944, when an article in the *New Republic* describing advertising's contribution to the war effort was signed "Madison Avenue." "The avenue," as columnists soon called it, covered agencies on Park, Third, and Fifth avenues as well.

"Madison Avenue techniques" is a phrase used to derogate "the Hidden Persuaders" (author Vance Packard's term) who are "SELLING CANDIDATES LIKE SOAP"—neatly packaged, making popular appeals in catchy phrases, always new, ever-improved.

Madison Avenue techniques can be startlingly successful in politics. In Picoaza, a town of 4,000 in Ecuador, the producer of "Pulvapies," a foot powder, tied in to the local campaign for mayor in 1967 with the following slogan: "Vote for any candidate, but if you want well-being and hygiene, vote for Pulvapies." Well-being and hygiene turned out to be GUT ISSUES in Picoaza, and the human candidates were chagrined when the voters chose Pulvapies, the foot powder, over the human candidates for mayor. "Cynics may feel," editorialized the *Wall Street Journal*, "the ensuing result reflects on the literacy of Ecuadorans, but we're not so sure. There are times in this enlightened land when the citizenry would welcome a chance to vote for a ticket that promised, not PIE IN THE SKY, but something down to earth and believable."

See MEDIA EVENT; ON THE MESSAGE; DAISY SPOT; MORNING IN AMERICA.

Mafia. See IRISH MAFIA.

magic time. See WALTER TIME.

magnet issue shared political stance; issue to create coalition or unification.

The ability of a *magnet* (rooted in a stone from Magnesia, an ancient city of Asia Minor) to attract iron led to the political use for attracting voters.

"A 'magnet' issue," explained John J. Pitney, Jr., assistant professor of government at Claremont McKenna College in California, in 1993, "is a positive policy stand that attracts voter support and inspires people to take part in politics." Examples include some of FDR's vote-attracting issues of the Democratic party in the 1930s, including Social Security, workers' rights, and the creation of jobs.

The antonym of *magnet issue* is WEDGE ISSUE. "Wedge issues make powerful weapons," Pitney comments, "but they cannot alone sustain a realignment of the electorate. Disrupting and discrediting the opposition is not the same as creating loyalty to one's own side. That task requires 'magnet' issues."

The metaphor is strong. Francis Bacon wrote in his 1620 Latin work, *Novum Organum,* about three major discoveries, "namely, printing, gunpowder, and the magnet [Mariner's Needle]. For these three have changed the whole face and state of things throughout the world."

See also BREAD-AND-BUTTER ISSUE; GUT ISSUE; HOT BUTTON; ISSUES, THE; PARAMOUNT ISSUE; POCKETBOOK ISSUE.

Magnolia Mafia.   See IRISH MAFIA; SMELL OF MAGNOLIAS.

maiden speech   a first speech, usually in a legislative body.

Probably the best-known example was a fiasco. Benjamin Disraeli, destined to be Prime Minister of Great Britain twice and to enter the House of Lords as the Earl of Beaconsfield, was at the time he first secured a seat in the House of Commons merely an ambitious young man of thirty-two. His maiden speech to that body was badly received; in fact, so raucous was the laughter of the members that Disraeli was forced to take his seat, his speech unfinished. His parting words were: "The time will come when you shall hear me."

The Senate of the United States, which likes to think of itself as the world's greatest deliberative body, long had a tradition that new senators did not deliver their virgin speech-making efforts until they had sat through a congressional session in silence. This rule has been discarded in recent years with the election of men already nationally prominent to that body; for example, the maiden speeches of men like Robert Kennedy of New York and Edward Brooke of Massachusetts, delivered shortly after having taken their places in the Senate, were given careful attention all over the nation. In Great Britain, however, the tradition is current; Winston Churchill called Sir Alan Herbert's maiden effort "a brazen hussy of a speech."

mainstream   the central current, as in philosophy or political doctrine.

"Mainstream"—or variations thereof—has long appealed to writers and statesmen as a symbol of the broad MIDDLE OF THE ROAD. A Japanese proverb notes that "one man can stand still in a flowing stream, but not in a world of men." In 1792 Mary Wollstonecraft wrote in *A Vindication of the Rights of Women*: "In every age there has been a stream of popular opinion that has carried all before it, and given a family character, as it were, to the century."

John F. Kennedy often used the mainstream image, or byplays on it. He told James MacGregor Burns: "Some people have their liberalism 'made' by the time they reach their late 20's. I didn't. I was caught in crosscurrents and eddies. It was only later that I got into the stream of things." Addressing the Irish Parliament in Dublin on June 28, 1963, he returned to the image: "Ireland is moving in the mainstream of current world events. Your destiny lies not as a peaceful island in a sea of trouble but as a maker and shaper of world peace."

No modern politician used the word more often, however, than New York's Governor Nelson Rockefeller. "The mainstream of American political thought and action" was one of his favorite phrases. Speechwriter Hugh Morrow recalled that Rockefeller's first use of the term was in a statement released July 14, 1963:

. . . it has now become crystal clear that the vociferous and well-drilled extremist elements boring within the Party utterly reject these fundamental principles of our heritage. They are, in fact, embarked on a determined and ruthless effort to take over the Party, its platform and its candidates on their own terms—terms that are wholly alien to the sound and honest conservatism that has firmly based the Republican Party in the best of a century's traditions, wholly alien to the sound and honest Republican liberalism that has kept the Party abreast of human needs in a changing world, wholly alien to the broad middle course that accommodates *the mainstream of Republican principle*. This cannot be allowed to happen.

During the 1964 Republican presidential convention, the author and a few other diehard Rockefeller supporters, in a futile effort to halt Barry Goldwater's drive for the nomination, unfurled a 30-foot canvas banner urging Republicans: "Stay in the Mainstream." But the votes were not there; as the old English proverb states, "The stream cannot rise above its source."

In politics, there are streams within streams. While the banner at the 1964 convention referred to the mainstream of political thought, eschewing extremism, the mainstream of thinking within the Republican party shifted to the right in the seventies; the *Washington Star* editorialized in 1977 that a liberal nominee to the Federal Elections Commission "is not what could be considered a 'mainstream' Republican."

George F. Will used the term in a 1986 column: "Senators Howard Metzenbaum and Edward Kennedy, whose liberalism is even more pronounced than the liberalism rejected by 93 states in the last two elections, are not exactly a Lewis and Clark team you would send exploring to locate the American mainstream."

A related meaning can be found in the use of the word as a verb. In *Time* (January 2, 1978), Stefan Kanfer wrote: "'Mainstreaming' is the short form of a long process: the education of disabled children alongside the normal."

See DON'T CHANGE HORSES; EXTREMISM.

majority rule. See ONE MAN, ONE VOTE.

make my day a dare; anticipated delight at an action that will permit a powerful reaction.

In *Sudden Impact*, a 1983 movie starring Clint Eastwood as "Dirty Harry," a violent vigilante cop, the law officer aims his gun at a criminal attempting to reach for his own weapon and snarls, "Go ahead, make my day." The phrase was a challenge to the felon to resist arrest, providing the officer with the chance to kill him, an act that would presumably give the cop pleasure.

Speaking to a conference of business executives in Washington on March 13, 1985, President Ronald Reagan used the imperative phrase in a jocular fashion: "I have my veto pen drawn and ready for any tax increase that Congress might even think of sending up. And I have only one thing to say to the tax increasers: Go ahead, make my day."

Washington Post columnist Mary McGrory wrote: "At last a slogan for the second term of Ronald Reagan . . . a shade more genteel than 'Drop dead,' which is what it really means." More accurately, in political parlance, it means "give me the chance to respond devastatingly."

At the 1988 Republican National Convention, George Bush used a self-mocking variation of the phrase in accepting the Presidential nomination: "There are actually those who claim that I don't always communicate in the clearest, most concise way. But I dare them to keep it up. Go ahead, make my 24-hour time period."

make the world safe for democracy a rallying phrase as America entered World War I which acquired a hollow sound after the war and is currently used as an example of foolishly idealistic intervention.

President Woodrow Wilson's phrase was: "The world must be made safe for democracy." His speech, delivered before Congress on April 2, 1917, went on to disclaim any "selfish ends" on the part of the U.S.

Had it not been for one man, however, Wilson's phrase might never have caught on. Senator John Sharp Williams of Mississippi, a good orator himself, but at this time aged and almost deaf, was leaning forward, concentrating intently on the speech. When Wilson said, "The world must be made safe for democracy," he began slowly—and alone—to clap, continuing until others joined him. This underlined for the reporters in the press gallery that a phrase had been turned.

In the fall of 1941 Adlai Stevenson, at that time representing the Committee to Defend America by Aiding the Allies, said in debate that the U.S. must provide aid for Great Britain because "I do not think that with tyranny in four-fifths of the world, freedom can endure in one-fifth." Caly Judson of the America First Committee replied, "The question we must answer before it is too late is: 'Is this our war?' If it is our war, then we should be in it without delay, even though it will not be the comparatively simple job it was the first time we saved the world for democracy."

The construction was used in that sarcastic manner in this official statement by Kenya's ruling party, the African National Union: "America's presence [in Vietnam] is not in the interests of the people. It is there to make the Far East safe for Coca-Cola."

President Nixon, a Wilson fan, in 1971 varied the phrase: "By his example, Woodrow Wilson helped make the world safe for idealism." But the phrase is still mainly used with sarcasm. In a 1992 commentary on American foreign policy, the *San Francisco Chronicle* asked, "Should America be the world's policeman, intervening in hot spots to make the world safe for democracy?"

See WAR TO END WARS; POLICEMAN OF THE WORLD.

malefactors of great wealth the irresponsible rich; an early attack phrase on Big Business.

Annoyed by continued attacks on him as the destroyer of business and the author of the Panic of 1907, Theodore Roosevelt declared in a speech at Provincetown, Mass., on August 20, 1907, that the trouble had been caused, at least in part, by "ruthless and determined men" hiding "behind the breastworks of corporate organization." He added: "It may well be that the determination of the government to punish certain malefactors of great wealth has been responsible for something of the trouble, at least to the extent of having caused these men to bring about as much financial stress as they can in order to discredit the policy of the government."

For Franklin D. Roosevelt, "ECONOMIC ROYALISTS" and "plutocrats" were latter-day equivalents of his cousin's famous "malefactors."

Words like "malefactor" and "infamy," rarely used but immediately understood, give solemnity and significance to a phrase. "Malefactor" (directly from the Latin *evil-doer*) is used less frequently than its opposite, "benefactor" (*good-doer*) and made TR's phrase successful.

ma, ma, where's pa? See SMEAR.

managed news information generated and distributed by the government in such a way as to give government interest priority over candor.

News management surfaced in October and November 1962 along with the Russian offensive missiles in Cuba to give a name to one of the oldest truisms in the relations of government officials and journalists. Long before he was President, John F. Kennedy warned an aide about the press: "Always remember that their interests and ours ultimately conflict." To the reporter, news is the publication of information that will interest and enlighten his reader. To the official, it is what may affect his own political future.

Newspapers, magazines, and broadcasters harped on news management as soon as the worst of the missile crisis was over, with much justification. There had been some fibbing in high places. Assistant Defense Secretary Arthur Sylvester later talked about the "government's right, if necessary, to lie" and of news as "weaponry." Reporters were barred from ships on blockade duty around Cuba. The White House made requests about self-censorship but refused to impose official censorship. Sylvester in the Pentagon and his counterpart Robert Manning in the State Department imposed requirements irksome to reporters that all interviews be either monitored or reported to an official's superior.

But the missile crisis was unique in the grayness of its status between war and peace. The government was groping for solution by trying to keep all factors—including information—in fine balance. Douglass Cater later wrote: "Certainly news is bound to be regarded as a weapon by officials who are involved in struggles of statecraft. But they are foolish if they expect to say so out loud and get away with it."

Some critics of these policies recalled Nazi propaganda minister Joseph Goebbels' statement: "During a war, news should be given out for instruction rather than for information."

However, the policies were not new. Pierre Salinger, who as Kennedy's press secretary had to take much criticism for news management, pointed out that the very phrase was invented to describe not his activities but those of his predecessor under Dwight Eisenhower, James Hagerty. The author was James Reston of the *New York Times*, who discussed Hagerty's "management of the news." Charles Hurd recalled that Franklin D. Roosevelt was frequently accused of "using the press." Lyndon Johnson was chided for holding too few formal press conferences, too many informal press conferences, for talking too much and saying too little and for having created a CREDIBILITY GAP.

It was ironic that the issue of "news management" should have reached such a peak in the Kennedy Administration. Kennedy himself had usually seemed adept at his press relations and had enjoyed generally favorable coverage. Yet he had his share of scrapes, as when he banned the *New York Herald Tribune* from the White House for its too-vigorous coverage of the Billy Sol Estes case. Robert Kennedy, then Attorney General, was accused of pressuring hostile reporters. The President quipped in the spring of 1962, when asked how he liked the press: "Well, I'm reading it more and enjoying it less."

"Managed" does not always have a manipulative connotation. In the 1990s, "managed competition" was a description of a health care system and "managed trade" was a euphemism for "industrial policy," or more government control of trade.

See MEDIA EVENT; PROPAGANDA.

mandarins.   See OLD CHINA HANDS.

mandate   the authority to carry out a program conferred on an elected official; especially strong after a LAND-SLIDE victory.

Before the midterm elections in 1918, Woodrow Wilson appealed to the nation for a "mandate" to carry out his policies in the form of a Democratic Congress. He did not get one, and later he hit on the idea of a "Senatorial mandate." Wilson's unusual idea was to have those senators who opposed him on such issues as the League of Nations resign, then run in a special election. If they won a clear mandate, Wilson said, he would appoint one of the opposition leaders—perhaps Henry Cabot Lodge—as Secretary of State. Then he and his Vice President would resign, automatically making the Republican Secretary of State the new President—under the Succession Act as it then worked.

In the U.S., the TWO-PARTY SYSTEM has helped ensure the transfer of mandates at frequent intervals. Thus, in 1936, Franklin Roosevelt noted that "it will never be possible for any length of time for any group of the American people, either by reason of wealth or learning or inheritance or economic power, to retain any mandate, any permanent authority to arrogate to itself the political control of American public life."

Significantly, Dwight Eisenhower, who was elected after twenty years of Democratic control of the White House, titled the first volume of his memoirs *Mandate for Change.*

How many votes constitute a mandate for the winner? He must receive at least one vote more than the loser. In his first inaugural address, FDR interpreted his sizable victory as "a mandate [for] direct, vigorous action." John F. Kennedy, on the other hand, won narrowly, yet did not shrink from acting for that reason. "The fact remains that he won," wrote Theodore Sorensen in *Kennedy,* "and on the day after election, and every day thereafter,

he rejected the argument that the country had given him no mandate. Every election has a winner and a loser, he said in effect. The margin is narrow, but the responsibility is clear. There may be difficulties with the Congress, but a margin of only one vote would still be a mandate."

Nonetheless, the closeness of his victory often acted as a brake. "Kennedy had very little leverage," wrote Arthur Schlesinger, Jr. He had been elected "by the slimmest of margins; no one could possibly claim his victory as a mandate for radical change."

In 1955 Walter Lippmann described how a mandate may be achieved by means other than electoral. "Political ideas acquire operative force in human affairs when . . . they acquire legitimacy, when they have the title of being right which binds men's consciences. Then they possess, as the Confucian doctrine has it, 'the mandate of heaven.'"

An interesting use of the word occurred during the British general election in the midst of the worldwide depression of the 1930s. A coalition government was then in power, and it asked voters for a "doctor's mandate"—one that would prescribe the proper treatment for the country's ills.

manifest destiny   the doctrine that it was the duty and fate of the U.S. to expand to the Pacific coast—and beyond.

One of the earliest uses of the phrase is attributed to Andrew Jackson. In 1824, according to biographer John Ward, Jackson described the U.S. as "a country manifestly called by the Almighty to a destiny which Greece and Rome, in the days of their pride, might have envied."

An enthusiastic promoter of the concept was John O'Sullivan, an American diplomat and journalist. In 1839 O'Sullivan wrote: "In its magnificent domain of space and time, the nation of many nations is destined to manifest to mankind the excellence of divine principles." Six years later an unsigned editorial in the expansionist journal *The United States Magazine and Democratic Review* noted that certain foreign governments were trying to prevent the U.S. annexation of Texas and spoke of "our manifest destiny to overspread the continent allotted by Providence for the free development of our yearly multiplying millions." O'Sullivan, it was later learned, was the author of the editorial.

His views were echoed elsewhere. In a congressional debate on the U.S. treaty with Great Britain settling the borders of Oregon in January 1846, Massachusetts' Representative Robert C. Winthrop declared that it was "the right of our manifest destiny to spread over this whole continent." Through the century the phrase echoed and reechoed. James Gordon Bennett wrote in a *New York Herald* editorial on April 3, 1865: "It is our manifest destiny to lead and rule all other nations." The doctrine, to be sure, disturbed many Americans. In his *Journals*, Emerson wrote in 1865: "That word, 'manifest destiny,' which is profanely used, signifies the sense all men have of the prodigious energy and opportunity lying idle here."

It did not lie idle for long. In 1898 President William McKinley told George Cortelyou, an aide, "We need Hawaii just as much and a good deal more than we did California. It is manifest destiny." McKinley's critics saw in this attitude an imperialistic "greed of conquest," but Hawaii was annexed in July 1898. Former President Grover Cleveland, who never cared much for the idea, wrote to a friend at the time: "Hawaii is ours. As I look back upon the first steps in this miserable business and as I contemplate the means used to complete the outrage, I am ashamed of the whole affair."

man in the street the average man; JOHN Q. PUBLIC; the voter of ordinary intelligence.

The phrase was popularized by Ralph Waldo Emerson, in his 1841 essay "On Self-Reliance," regarding the spiritually debilitating effect of civilization on man: "A Greenwich nautical almanac he has, and so being sure of the information when he wants it, the man in the street does not know a star in the sky."

The phrase had been traced by the *OED* to 1831, and Theodore Roosevelt used it in a 1900 letter: "But the man in the street naturally does not look as far ahead as this." Lord Bryce, in *The American Commonwealth*, used "man in the cars" in 1888 in a sense that holds up well today as a condemnation of how too many men in the street form their opinions:

> . . . one need only try the experiment of talking to that representative of public opinion whom the Americans call "the man in the cars" to realize how uniform opinion is among all classes of people, how little there is of that individuality in the ideas of each individual which they would have if he had formed them for himself, how little solidity and substance there is in the political or social ideas of nineteen persons out of every twenty. These ideas, when examined, mostly resolve themselves into two or three prejudices and aversions, two or three prepossessions for a particular leader or section of a party, two or three phrases or catchwords suggesting or embodying arguments which the man who repeats them has not analyzed.

The campaign to eradicate sexism in language has driven the phrase into disuse among politicians. "Person in the street" is acceptable but has not caught on. See MIDDLE AMERICA.

man of the people public figure identified with humble origins and usually a POPULIST philosophy.

"The President will not be a man of the people," warned Founding Father James Wilson in 1787, "but the minion of the Senate." Wilson held that the senatorial veto of presidential appointments would cripple the office of Chief Executive, but the Constitutional Convention disagreed. See ADVICE AND CONSENT.

The meaning of the phrase was narrowed to nonaristocrats with the emergence of Andrew Jackson, whose background and manner were far more plebeian than Washington, the Adamses, Jefferson, Madison, or Monroe. As Harry Truman assessed him: "Jackson was recognized as the 'man of the people'—an advocate of the liberal interpretation of democracy as practised by Jefferson."

In current use, the phrase has dropped most of the "humble origin" connotation and is concerned more with a man who identifies himself with the needs and aspirations of the common man. Thus, a man of wealth—Franklin Roosevelt, for example—could be classed "a man of the people" even to the extent of being a TRAITOR TO HIS CLASS. Evita Perón was seen as a "woman of the people."

Wealthy candidates still seem to feel a need, however, to prove that even if they are rich, they are still "regular guys"—witness Nelson Rockefeller munching a hot dog, Averell Harriman a knish, and supporters of Adlai Stevenson making much of a hole in his shoe. When Wendell Willkie pointed out his Hoosier origins, Harold Ickes nailed him with BAREFOOT BOY FROM WALL STREET.

man on horseback a military figure with political potential; or a would-be dictator; or any strong, authoritarian leader.

The idea, though not the phrase, appeared in a scaffold statement by English rebel Richard Rumbold, hanged in 1685: "I never would believe that Providence had sent a few men into the world, ready booted and spurred to ride, and millions ready saddled and bridled to be ridden."

The phrase was introduced to American politics by General Caleb Cushing, who described to a group of Maine Democrats assembled in Bangor on January 11, 1860, what the impending civil strife would mean to the nation: ". . . cruel war, war at home; and in the perspective distance, a man on horseback with a drawn sword in his hand, some Atlantic Caesar, or Cromwell, or Napoleon."

The predecessor phrase, with the same metaphor, is "on a high horse." Shakespeare had Mark Antony say of Julius Caesar that he "sits high on all people's hearts," and the Reverend John Brown, in a letter to David Garrick dated October 27, 1765, complained of Dr. Samuel Johnson's criticism of Shakespeare: "Altogether upon the high horse, and blustering about Imperial Tragedy!"

Hans Sperber concluded that the phrase was drawn from the "solitary horseman" appearing in six books by a popular novelist of the period, G. P. R. James.

Lincoln professed not to be concerned about the chances of a military dictatorship. In a letter to General Joseph Hooker, who had said the nation needed a dictator, Lincoln wrote: "Only those Generals who gain successes can set up dictators. What I now ask of you is military success, and I will risk the dictatorship."

General George B. McClellan, true to Cushing's prophecy, did turn out to be the Democratic nominee of 1864, losing to Lincoln by 400,000 votes out of 4,000,000. But the "man on horseback" phrase was first applied to a presidential candidate in Ulysses S. Grant's 1868 campaign, and "Vote as You Shot" was a slogan of veterans' groups for many years after the Civil War.

Military men who made it to the top in U.S. history include George Washington, Andrew Jackson, William Henry Harrison, Zachary Taylor, U.S. Grant, Theodore Roosevelt (as a "Rough Rider," he is on the edge of this category), and Dwight D. Eisenhower. Generals who lost presidential bids were Lewis Cass in 1848, Winfield Scott in 1852, McClellan in 1864, and Winfield Scott Hancock in 1880. In addition, Admiral George Dewey and General Douglas MacArthur awaited lightning that never struck. Of the forty-two Americans who have served as President, twenty-two—more than half—had some armed-service background.

Eisenhower, for one, was disturbed by the "man on horseback" image. Sought by both parties for the 1948 nomination, he declared: "The necessary and wise subordination of the military to civil power will be best sustained . . . when lifelong professional soldiers, in the absence of some obvious and overriding reasons, abstain from seeking high political office."

In 1961 E. M. Dealey, chairman of the board of the *Dallas Morning News*, said in an angry letter to President John Kennedy that "we need a man on horseback to lead this nation, and many people in Texas and the Southwest think that you are riding Caroline's bicycle."

Kennedy replied indirectly in a Los Angeles speech, referring to those "voices of extremism" who "look suspiciously at their neighbors and their leaders. They call for a 'man on horseback' because they do not trust the people . . . they object quite rightly to politics intruding on the mil-

itary—but they are very anxious for the military to engage in their kind of politics . . ."

man on the wedding cake   characterization of Republican Presidential candidate Thomas E. Dewey in 1944.

Coinage is in vociferous dispute. In the first edition of this book, the author tentatively wrote: "Though columnist Walter Winchell was often credited with the coinage . . . Harold Ickes, FDR's Secretary of the Interior, was possibly the author."

Winchell promptly took issue: "From page 250 of a new book about the new language of politics: '"Man on the wedding cake" (a characterization of Republican candidate Thomas E. Dewey in 1944) was often credited to Walter Winchell, but Harold Ickes, FDR's Secretary of the Interior, was possibly the author.' But Mr. Ickes wasn't. Alice Longworth and many others were credited with its coinage. 'Dewey, the Little Man On The Wedding Cake' was auth'd by 'Paul Revere, II' in *P.M.*, a New York pro-Democrat newspaper. . . . Mr. Paul Revere, II was not the name-de-ploom of Harold Ickes, but of WW, then under contract to the *New York Mirror*, which was pro-Dewey. (Catch on?)"

Columnist Leonard Lyons took a different position: "The fact is Ethel Barrymore created the line. I printed the story November 3, 1944, quoting Mrs. Longworth: 'Ethel Barrymore said that, and she's mad as hell because I've been getting credit for it.'"

As recently as the 1988 Presidential campaign, the *Los Angeles Times* offered another possible coiner of the expression: "If playwright Clare Boothe Luce called Dewey 'the little man on the wedding cake,' Dukakis is the little man on the Massachusetts regional development brochure."

Since Mrs. Alice Roosevelt Longworth, daughter of Theodore Roosevelt and grande dame of Washington society, was obviously a central figure in the case, the author sent her a query in the last years of her life and received this reply:

"Thanks for your letter. I did *not* coin the phrase 'little man on the wedding cake.' The first time I heard it Mrs. Flandrau remarked 'Dewey looks like the bridegroom on the wedding cake.' I thought it frightfully funny and quoted it to everyone. Then it began to be attributed to me. To everyone who asked if I originated it, I said no and told just what I have written here, though I did admit that 'I gave it currency.'"

Thus, it can be stated with some assurance that the phrase was coined in 1944 by either Walter Winchell, Ethel Barrymore, or author Grace Hodgson Flandrau, probably not Harold Ickes, and was given currency by Mrs. Longworth. Additional claims will be met with suspicion.

Four years later Mrs. Longworth peppered candidate Dewey with "You can't make a soufflé rise twice," and "You have to know Dewey really well to dislike him thoroughly." (She is also credited with the "weaned on a pickle" characterization of President Coolidge, which she attributed to her doctor in her 1933 autobiography. None of her victims fired back, because she was a distinguished lady, old and frail, and she could kill you.)

Dewey was short, mustachioed, formal-looking; calling him "the little man on top of the wedding cake" was as inspired as it was cruel. Walter Winchell added insult to this injury with "He's the only man able to walk under a bed without hitting his head."

Dewey was also young for a Presidential candidate, which was not implied in the wedding-cake reference; Ickes completed the description when the New York governor formally announced his candidacy by commenting, "Dewey has thrown his diaper in the ring."

The phrase returned during the 1992 Presidential campaign. The *National Journal* commented in September 1992, "Though in many ways Clinton is a much more formidable candidate personally than was Dewey, who was often derided as 'the little man on the wedding cake,' vulnerabilities that surfaced during the primaries could jeopardize his prospects. . . ."

Maoism the militant philosophy of Mao Tse-tung, especially as redefined by the split in the Chinese Communist hierarchy in the mid-sixties.

Probably the best-selling book in the world in 1966 was "the little red book," containing quotations from the speeches and writings of Mao, read as scripture by his followers and brandished at demonstrations.

Traditionally, after the revolutionaries come the pragmatists—men with a zeal to administer rather than overthrow. In China this evolution was interrupted by the desire of the architect of the Communist revolution to recapture its revolutionary, doctrinaire spirit. Mao tried to rekindle the spirit of the generation of the Long March in his Red Guards, young men who formed the cadres that launched the CULTURAL REVOLUTION.

Maoism's book of quotations, like most scripture, was written to permit widely varying interpretations. "The Maoists," wrote Columbia professor Doak Barnett, "can appeal to certain writings which emphasize the need for revolutionary radicalism and self-sacrifice; while the anti-Maoists can stress others, which prescribe pragmatic realism and the need to adapt policy to reality."

Essentially, Maoism taught "uninterrupted revolution" and the overriding role of the human will in history: "Nothing in the world is difficult for one who sets his mind to it." The indoctrinated revolutionary character of the people was essential. "An army without culture [revolutionary zeal] is a dull-witted army, and a dull-witted army cannot defeat the enemy."

Philosophies or techniques named after statesmen rarely last. Reference is still made to Socratic reasoning and Aristotelian ethics, Jeffersonian democracy and Churchillian prose, but Stalinism, Gaullism, Titoism, and Maoism faded not long after the deaths of their authors. Marxism-Leninism, however, seems assured of a place in the lexicon of political history.

march on Washington a civil rights rally held in Washington, D.C., in August 1963; the largest demonstration to that date in the city's history.

Its purpose, in the words of its initial proposer, black labor leader A. Philip Randolph, was to give voice to "a great moral protest against racial bias."

Mr. Randolph had proposed such a march twenty years earlier to President Franklin D. Roosevelt as a protest against discrimination against blacks in war industries. The President had used a series of protest meetings in several of the larger American cities as an excuse to issue his Executive Order No. 8802, designed to end such discrimination. That 1943 march never was held.

The Democratic President in the White House in 1963, John F. Kennedy, did not look forward at first to the realization of Mr. Randolph's proposal. One reason for Kennedy's early lack of enthusiasm was his fear that a march, ending at the Capitol as originally intended, would make it appear the Congress was being besieged and thus would have a negative effect on the civil rights bill then being considered.

When the plan was changed to a demonstration around the Lincoln Memorial, the President gave it his public support. In a mid-July news conference he said he understood it would be "a peaceful assembly calling for a redress of grievances" and added, "I think that's in the great tradition." He had no other choice.

There were two basic problems. The march had received so much nationwide publicity that it would seriously jeopardize the civil rights legislation (1) if the number of those attending did not exceed the promised one hundred thousand and (2) if there was any violence.

Both these dangers were overcome. The march, as organized by civil rights leader Bayard Rustin, brought almost a quarter of a million people to the rallying point at the Washington Monument.

When the area around the monument was almost completely filled with people, the demonstrators quietly walked down to the Lincoln Memorial, where several civil rights leaders addressed them. See "I HAVE A DREAM."

At nightfall the demonstrators departed for their home cities. It had been a powerfully moving and peaceful event. President Kennedy said the next day, "This nation can properly be proud."

This nonviolent event was a contrast to the Bonus March of 1932, when the participants rioted and terrified the capital. The *March of Time* film documentaries, and the "March of Dimes" campaign against polio, further popularized the metaphor.

The civil rights march turned out about 200,000. The "New Mobe" march in 1969 turned out 600,000, the peak for marches in Washington. A feminist march and a gay rights march in the early 1990s turned out 250,000 to 300,000.

In current use, although a *march* implies military organization and discipline, it has become less "militant" than a *demonstration*. A curious but revealing linguistic attitude toward *demonstration* was shown in a statement made by an FBI agent in a crowd of several hundred lawmen at the arraignment of former FBI officials in April 1978: "This is not a demonstration. This is a show of support."

Martin, Barton and Fish a campaign catch phrase used with devastating effectiveness by Franklin D. Roosevelt in his campaign for a third term.

Working on a speech for FDR in 1940, Judge Samuel I. Rosenman and dramatist Robert E. Sherwood wanted to mention the Republican party's opposition to moves for preparedness. In the first draft they cited GOP Congressmen Bruce Barton and Hamilton Fish of New York and Joseph Martin of Massachusetts, in that order. Rosenman recalled in *Working With Roosevelt*:

> We sat around—I remember we were writing in my apartment in New York City—working on that paragraph. Then as we read those names, we almost simultaneously hit on the more euphonious and rhythmic sequence of Martin, Barton and Fish. We said nothing about it when we handed the draft to the President, wondering whether he would catch it as he read the sentence aloud. He did. The very first time he read it, his eyes twinkled; and he grinned from ear to ear. . . . He repeated it several times and indicated by swinging his finger in cadence how effective it would be with audiences.

In his own memoirs, *My First 50 Years in Politics*, Martin notes that the line followed the meter of "Wynken, Blynken and Nod." Though he wrote that "I felt no particular resentment over it," Martin did tell FDR that it was "a bit unfair" to blame the GOP alone for the sad state of U.S. military preparedness. As for the famous phrase, Martin declares that the three

men cited had always been good friends. "Roosevelt's attack lent a new bond to our friendship," says Martin. "Afterward, whenever we three would meet one another here and there we used to refer to ourselves as 'members of the firm.'"

massive resistance. See TOKENISM.

massive retaliation national strategy that threatens to meet foreign military challenge with nuclear attack.

Secretary of State John Foster Dulles said in a speech on January 12, 1954, to the Council on Foreign Relations: "Local defense must be reinforced by the further deterrent of massive retaliatory power." Immediately and universally, via microphone and printing press, "massive retaliatory power" was edited to "massive retaliation," and American policy had a label.

Actually, there was little new in Dulles's statement. The Eisenhower Administration had been in office for a year when Dulles made the speech and had already begun to de-emphasize "conventional" or nonnuclear strength while stressing the nuclear. Defense Secretary Charles Wilson had already foreclosed post-Korea LIMITED WAR and put the label of "BIGGER BANG FOR A BUCK" on his goal. And five days before Dulles' speech, Eisenhower himself in his State of the Union address had stressed the need for "massive capability to strike back" against any aggression.

Out of the massive retaliation strategy came generations of nuclear bombers and missiles—and seemingly never-ending controversy as well. General Maxwell Taylor, Army Chief of Staff under President Eisenhower, left the service furious that the Army was being reduced and wrote an angry book called *The Uncertain Trumpet*, in which he called massive retaliation a "great fallacy." Other officers, and writers too, chose sides and debated the issue for years.

As soon as the Kennedy Administration took office, General Taylor was recalled from retirement and eventually installed as Chairman of the Joint Chiefs of Staff. Robert McNamara became Defense Secretary. After one week in office McNamara reported: "A strategy of massive nuclear retaliation . . . [is] believed by few of our friends and none of our enemies." Conventional forces were emphasized, and the bywords became "flexible response" and "MEASURED RESPONSE." But the idea of overwhelming response has not been abandoned; visiting the bridge at Panmunjon in July of 1993, President Clinton warned that if North Korea were ever to use nuclear weapons, "it would be the end of their country."

The adjective "massive"—as used in "massive aid to the cities"—became a vogue word in the liberal lexicon, along with "decent," "obscene," "compassion," "unacceptable," "root cause," and "human needs."

maverick one who is unorthodox in his political views and disdainful of party loyalty, who bears no man's brand.

Maverick drifted into the political vocabulary around the turn of the century; *McClure's* magazine mentioned the occasional appearance of a "maverick legislator." The simplicity and aptness of the metaphor made it both durable and universally understood.

This is an eponymous word, taken—like "boycott" and "bloomer," "cardigan" and "sandwich"—from a person's name. Samuel Maverick, son of an Anglican minister in England, settled in Massachusetts about 1624. Contrary to some reports, he does not seem to have been an "eccentric innkeeper," but a man noted for his hospitality; later an inn, Maverick House in Boston, was named after him and became a well-known political hangout.

His direct descendant, Samuel Augustus Maverick, established himself as a Texas rancher in the mid-1800s (see F. C. Chabot, *With the Makers of San Antonio*, San Antonio, 1937). This Maverick became known for his unbranded calves.

J. David Stern, author of *Maverick Publisher*, advises the author of one theory behind this practice: "Old man Maverick, Texas cattleman of the 1840s, refused to brand his cattle because it was cruelty to animals. His neighbors said he was a hypocrite, liar, and thief, because Maverick's policy allowed him to claim all unbranded cattle on the range. Lawsuits were followed by bloody battles, and brought a new word to our language."

Theodore Roosevelt wrote in 1887 for the edification of Eastern tenderfeet: "Unbranded animals are called mavericks, and when found on the round-up are either branded by the owner of the range . . . or else are sold for the benefit of the association."

Ten years later TR was back in New York himself, winning his reputation as a maverick on the political range. When Cousin Franklin ran for Vice President in 1920 on the Democratic ticket, TR's son, Theodore Jr., was tapped by the Republicans to dispel the idea that FDR was son or political heir to the recently deceased former President. "He's a maverick," said young Theodore about FDR. "He doesn't have the brand of our family."

Despite this pejorative use, independence—and hence maverick's status—has traditionally been considered something of a virtue, especially at election time. Many of the nation's most successful politicians, going back to Andrew Jackson, were mavericks at some stage. Russell Baker wrote Estes Kefauver's epitaph: "From Harry Truman in the White House down through the bull-roasting-and-clam-bake crowd, the party professionals despised him. He was a maverick." In American politics, one who wins many enemies among the pros often wins many friends among the more numerous laymen; thus it is often more difficult for a maverick to get nominated than elected.

See LONER; MUGWUMP.

mayoralty. See HIZZONER; DEAD END, POLITICAL.

McCarthyism   the approach with which the late Senator Joseph R. Mc-Carthy won fame as a Communist-hunter, now applied to any invest-igation that flouts the rights of individuals.

McCarthy burst into prominence after a speech in Wheeling, W.V., on February 9, 1950. "While I cannot take the time to name all of the men in the State Department who have been named as members of the Communist Party and members of a spy ring," he said then, "I have here in my hand a list of 205 that were known to the Secre-tary of State as being members of the Communist Party and who neverthe-less are still working and shaping the policy of the State Department."

Over the next four years the free-swinging charges, the well-timed an-nouncements and press releases that caught newspapers right on deadline, the McCarthy manner during hearings (see POINT OF ORDER) became familiar. His many supporters felt that he suc-ceeded in alerting the nation to the danger of internal subversion.

Probably the first to use the term "McCarthyism" was *Washington Post* cartoonist Herblock (Herbert Block), who, in 1950, showed the word crudely lettered on a barrel of mud that rested precariously on a tower made up of buckets of mud. Said Harry Truman: "A powerful group of

men in the Republican Party is now determined to rise to power through a method of conduct as hostile to Amer-ican ideals as anything we have ever seen. This method has come to be known as McCarthyism."

In *The Fourth Branch of Govern-ment*, Douglass Cater noted that "McCarthyism's greatest threat was not to individual liberty or even to the orderly conduct of government. It corrupted the power to communicate, which is indispensable to men living in a civilized society."

McCarthy, a Republican, was a par-ticularly painful problem for the first Republican Administration in twenty years. When a White House aide drafted a strong anti-McCarthy state-ment, President Eisenhower rejected it, saying, "I will not get in the gutter with *that* guy." The President made it clear, nonetheless, how he felt about the senator's tactics. "McCarthyism," he wrote in his memoirs, "took its toll on many individuals and on the na-tion. No one was safe from charges recklessly made from inside the walls of Congressional immunity. Teachers, government employees, and even min-isters became vulnerable . . . The cost was often tragic."

When McCarthy attacked the Prot-estant clergy and the U.S. Army early in 1954, Eisenhower abandoned some of his restraint. He denounced him as one who tried "to set himself above the laws of our land" and "to override or-ders of the President." On December 2, 1954, the Senate condemned Mc-Carthy. The word "censure," for some reason, was avoided. His power faded quickly thereafter; he died in 1957.

The issue of McCarthyism plagued John F. Kennedy during his 1960 cam-paign for the presidency. As a senato-rial candidate in 1952, Kennedy had gone out of his way to avoid antagonizing McCarthy. "Hell," he later explained to historian Arthur

Schlesinger, Jr., "half my voters in Massachusetts look on McCarthy as a hero." McCarthy did not enter Massachusetts to campaign against Kennedy, and as columnist Emmet John Hughes wrote, if JFK's "view of Joe McCarthy had been publicly and candidly more critical, at a time when such courage counted, he almost certainly would not have reached the White House in 1960."

In the 1968 primary campaign, liberal Senator Eugene McCarthy (D-Minn.) labeled the attacks on his patriotism by President Johnson's supporters "McCarthyism."

The original meaning of the word—of misuse of information by a congressional committee—was echoed in 1976, when a suppressed report by the House Select Intelligence Committee chaired by Otis Pike (D-N.Y.) was printed in the *Village Voice*, including this line: "On September 24, 1975 . . . the Deputy Secretary of State raised for the first time an innuendo that the Committee's action [demanding Executive documents] resembled McCarthyism."

The word resurfaced during the 1991 hearings to confirm Clarence Thomas as a Supreme Court Justice. Thomas, who testified in the same Senate room where the Army-McCarthy hearings took place in 1954, denounced "interest groups [and] hate-mongers" for using tactics "far more dangerous than McCarthyism"; he pointed out that, unlike interest groups and staff aides, "At least McCarthy was elected."

After Anita Hill's testimony alleging sexual harassment, a columnist accused Senator Alan K. Simpson of using McCarthy-like tactics at the hearings. Replied Senator Simpson, "Accusing someone of McCarthyism is a McCarthyist tactic itself." The charge was repeated during the 1992 Presidential and Vice Presidential debates, when Bill Clinton and Al Gore criticized the Bush campaign for questioning Clinton's patriotism and his visit to Moscow as a student at Oxford.

See PHILIPPIC; JUNKETEERING GUMSHOES; CHARACTER ASSASSIN; PROFILES IN COURAGE.

meanwhile, back at the ranch

a Western movie and radio cliché *(The Lone Ranger)* used to refer to Temporary White House activities at the LBJ Ranch near Johnson City, Texas.

An economic report by Goldman, Sachs & Co. analyzed a tax-increase decision and concluded with a paragraph titled "Meanwhile, Down at the Ranch" to show what was under consideration by the President.

Western metaphors were common with Johnson: the "LBJ Brand" of leadership "lassos votes" and "corrals support" for key measures before the Congress. An alternate to "the ranch" is "the Pedernales," pronounced "Purd'nalis," a Texas river flowing through the LBJ Ranch. Columnist Russell Baker observed that anyone who knew and used the word Pedernales had "an inner grasp of the Great Society." See COONSKIN ON THE WALL.

measured response the exercise of restraint in response to provocation or even attack, especially in the military sense.

The phrase was frequently used by President Lyndon Johnson, along with the wish for "no wider war," to describe a stepping up of military activity, carrying the implication that the new action was the result of provocation and was carefully controlled.

These were measures short of total war, a step beyond—but similar in tone—to Franklin Roosevelt's 1939 phrase to help allies of the U.S.: "There are many *methods short of war*, but stronger and more effective than mere words, of bringing home to aggressor governments the aggregate sentiments of our own people." The phrase was promptly misquoted as "measures short of war," and is so remembered.

A generation later the measures short of war became measures of war short of annihilation, spawning *measured* response and its cousins, *controlled, flexible,* and *selective* response. See PENTAGONESE.

These were devised as a military philosophy of the nuclear age, describing a response to an act of aggression against this country which would demonstrate the nation's preparedness to react to such an act with a positive counterstroke but would also signal clearly that peace was desired rather than "all-out" war.

"The rhetoric of restraint," as former presidential aide McGeorge Bundy called it, has not always been the prevailing tone of American politics. Still, whether domestic or international matters are involved, it has always had its advocates. Daniel Webster put it this way: "Liberty exists in proportion to wholesome restraint." See LIMITED WAR.

measures, not men   an alternative phrase for GOVERNMENT OF LAWS, NOT OF MEN and RULE OF LAW.

The inbuilt distrust of rulers and the desire to see rights guaranteed in writing underlies the concept of "measures, not men," a phrase coined by Philip Stanhope, Earl of Chesterfield, in a March 6, 1742, letter. Picked up by Oliver Goldsmith ("Measures, not men, have always been my mark") and later by Edmund Burke, it was attacked by George Canning (later a Prime Minister) in the House of Commons in 1801: "Away with the cant of 'Measures, not men!'—the idle supposition that it is the harness and not the horses that draw the chariot along. If the comparison must be made, if the distinction must be taken, men are

everything, measures comparatively nothing."

Canning, who had the courage to blast the fine-sounding phrase, was associated with it not as its denouncer, but as its author; the *New York World* of September 18, 1874, warned: "There is danger in the blind following of Canning's maxim, 'Measures, not men.'" Obviously, there is danger in a politician's head-on attack of a favorite phrase.

In modern times the idea is best remembered in the form given it by John Adams in his preamble to the Massachusetts Constitution in 1778: "In the government of the Commonwealth of Massachusetts the legislature, executive, and judicial power shall be placed in separate departments, to the end that it might be a GOVERNMENT OF LAWS, NOT OF MEN."

media   a slightly sinister or clinical word for "the press," often intended to carry a manipulative or mechanical connotation.

As Dwight Eisenhower discovered in the roar of approval that followed his 1964 comment about "sensation-seeking columnists and commentators," considerable public sentiment is directed against the press. That latent hostility was dramatized by the reaction to a speech objecting to "instant analysis" and other presumed press sins by Vice President Spiro Agnew in Des Moines in 1970.

In the nineteenth century, "mediae" was a term in phonetics to describe an intermediate sound between the tenues and the aspirates, and in biology for a middle membrane of an artery. Of course, it is the plural of "medium," and the first famous use of that word in the sense of communications was by Lord Francis Bacon in 1605: "But yet is not of necessitie that Cognitions bee expressed by the Medium of Wordes." Another sense, that of an intervening substance, was used by Burton in his *Anatomy of Melancholy* (1621): "To the Sight three things are required, the Object, the Organ and the Medium."

"Mass medium" came into the language in a 1923 article by S. M. Fechheimer in N. T. Praigg's *Advertising & Selling*, where he also used the plural: "Class appeal in mass media." In 1927 *American Speech* "finally decided to allot a definite media to each member," and in 1929 E. O. Hughes wrote in an advertising magazine: "The advertising media to which reference will be made . . . are newspapers, journals, magazines and suchlike printed publications."

J. S. Huxley took a benign view of the emerging word and industry in 1946: "The media of mass communication— the somewhat cumbrous title (commonly abbreviated to 'Mass Media') proposed for agencies, such as the radio, the cinema and the popular press, which are capable of the mass dissemination of word or image. . . . The use of the mass media to foster education, science and culture . . . Regarded from this angle, the mass media fall into the same general category as the libraries and museums—that of servicing agencies for man's higher activities."

Political advertising had much to do with the change in attitude toward the word from a neutral conveyor of information to a manipulator of minds. As television and its use rose in importance in politics, so did the "media adviser" (see SELLING CANDIDATES LIKE SOAP). In the sixties, concern for the changing of opinion by television spot increased with its effectiveness, and "media manipulation" became worrisome.

Around 1970 the phrase "news media" began to gain in frequency of use, which married the fear of advertising with some doubts about the credibility of the purveyors of information.

This was exploited by those who believed that too much power was concentrated in "an unelected elite" from too few news organizations.

The press itself extended the use of the word, dividing into "electronic media" and "print media," discussing "media campaigns," "media event" (for PSEUDO-EVENT), and "media hype" (for too much promotion and attention). In May 1973 the *New York Times* "Winners and Sinners" sheet sent to editorial employees complained: "Media . . . there is no need to overwork the word, which we and everybody else have been doing. Twice in one sentence is a little too much: 'It would appear counterproductive for the Administration to continue to attack the media at a time when it has, in effect, accepted media accounts of the Watergate case' (April 24). Try words like 'journalism,' 'the press,' 'broadcasting,' 'news accounts,' 'newspapers.'"

The word is plural, like data, and normally takes a plural verb. "Media" is a word, but the media are thousands of newspapers, television stations, fax machines, and electronic bulletin boards eagerly covering the words of political leaders blasting "the media." Still, when preceded by *the*, the word is widely used as a singular collective noun, as in "The media wields immense power." The media are resisting this.

media adviser.   See KINGMAKER.

media event   an occasion so stage-managed for wide coverage that the coverage becomes more important than the occasion.

For the background to this phrase, see PSEUDO-EVENT. "Pseudo" has been replaced by "media," but the word "media" has acquired the phoniness of "pseudo." People who are concerned about the manipulation of public opinion, including many in the press (a more likable term for news media), tend to derogate any occasion that appears to be arranged for maximum publicity.

A second meaning of "media event" is an occasion that is important not in itself, but in how the media interprets it. On January 30, 1976, the night of Jimmy Carter's victory in the Iowa presidential caucus, CBS News correspondent Roger Mudd told anchorman Walter Cronkite: "The English [meaning 'twist'] that is applied to these results is going to be applied by the media and the politicians themselves. It's not exactly the precise figures that will be important, it's whether the media and the politicians agree that this man won and this man lost."

Joseph Lelyveld of the *New York Times*, who was covering the coverage, wrote: "That was a working definition of a 'media event': an occasion on which the discussion overwhelms and finally obscures the fragile reality that gives rise to it."

That is the sophisticated definition; most references are rooted in "pseudo-event," or touting of an unimportant story. When Carter Attorney General Griffin Bell held a much-heralded briefing of congressmen about the Justice Department's investigation into payoffs by South Korean businessman Tongsun Park, Representative Patricia Schroeder (D-Colo.) said, "This was a big P.R. media event. I feel gypped. I feel like a co-conspirator in a cover-up."

Investing a minor occurrence with false importance is called "hype," or "media hype," from the euphoric kick one gets from an injection of a narcotic with a hypodermic needle.

Medicare a government program of health insurance for the elderly.

The creation of this word shows how

bureaucracy crumbles before a mighty coinage. It is worth a detailed examination.

In his "economic bill of rights," FDR had called for "the right to adequate medical care and the opportunity to achieve and enjoy good health." In 1945 the Wagner-Murray-Dingell bill providing compulsory health insurance was proposed; this, along with some other Truman health proposals, was attacked as "socialized medicine" and defeated.

The word "medicare" cropped up in early 1956. It was the name applied to the Dependents Medical Care Program of the Department of Defense, probably used first by Jerry Gross, editor of the *Washington Report on Medical Sciences*. The original program called for medical care of dependents of armed services personnel.

But the word outgrew this narrow use in the mid-fifties. Defense Department officials were troubled by the term, which newspapers began to apply both to plans for general medical care and for assistance to the elderly, then being discussed as part of the Social Security program. Dr. Frank Berry, senior medical adviser to the Assistant Secretary of Defense for Manpower, wrote to Abraham Ribicoff, President Kennedy's first Secretary of Health, Education and Welfare, about the confusing overlap in the use of the term. On April 27, 1961, Secretary Ribicoff made one of the most short-lived semantic stands of the decade: "This will acknowledge your letter of April 7 concerning the use of the term 'Medicare.' I am sure that we have no intention of using this term in connection with any present or planned programs to be administered by this Department." (Compare this with Churchill's resistance to INFRASTRUCTURE.)

The scene shifts from Defense to HEW. Wallace Kendall, an information officer, informs the author:

In 1964 and early 1965, we in social security were trying as hard as we could to discourage use of the term "medicare" in connection with the limited program of hospital insurance for older people which was under consideration in Congress. HR-1 and earlier Administration bills would have provided only hospital insurance, not medical insurance, and for this reason we thought "medicare" would be a misleading term.

After the medical insurance part was added in Congress and Public Law 89-97 was passed, the law had been called "the medicare law" in so many newspaper articles and radio-TV broadcasts that it was impossible for us to avoid using it. We were still reluctant; we used it in an appositive way for some weeks: 'the program of health insurance for the aged, often called "medicare."' Then we were urged by many people to go ahead and use the term in a more forthright way. At this point, I called Colonel McKenzie to find out whether or not the Department of Defense would object . . .

Kendall, with a good sense of history, kept a record of his August 12, 1965, conversation with Lieutenant Colonel Vernon McKenzie, assistant for special projects and new programs (health and medical) in the office of the Assistant Secretary of Defense, which McKenzie has seen and corroborates:

When the term was first introduced the Dept. of Defense intended to use it as a specific and meaningful term and they went so far as to register use of the term with the copyright office in the Library of Congress. Col. McKenzie told me that this gave them no legal rights to use of the term; it simply established the fact that they were using it in a certain sense at a certain time. Several private insurance companies later tried using the term, and in at least one case the Dept. of Defense wrote to the company and pointed out that the term was a registered one with a specific meaning within the Dept. of Defense. I gather that the companies stopped selling

"Medicare" policies after receiving these letters from the Dept.

After a while, however, Col. McKenzie and other officers in the Dept. of Defense began to realize that the term was causing confusion instead of clearing it up. Some people used it to mean the entire program of medical care within the Dept. of Defense both for active duty military personnel and their dependents and retired people. Others used it to refer to all kinds of medical care for the dependents of people on active duty. A third group used it to mean only the care of dependents in civilian hospitals.

These confusing factors, plus the increasing use of the term "Medicare" not only by reporters and radio and television news people, but also by Members of Congress and by Presidents—these factors all combined to cause Col. McKenzie to stop using the term "Medicare" in his own work about two years ago.

In passing he observed that it seemed to him that the term "Eldercare" would have been a much more accurate term for the social security bill as it finally passed the House. He had also thought about the term "Fedicare" but he said that there was a certain logic of events that seems to be requiring the Social Security Administration to use the term "Medicare" for the bill now under consideration.

Col. McKenzie said that he has never done anything official about halting the use of the term "Medicare" in the Dept. of Defense but he will now give some thought to the idea of recommending that the military bow out and not use the term any further in order to clear the way for its use by the Social Security Administration.

A question arises: Who in the Department of Defense had the foresight to register the use of the word with the copyright office?

Paul I. Robinson, M.D., was the major general in charge of the Dependents Medical Care Program from 1956 to 1958 and was later chief medical director of the Metropolitan Life Insurance Company. He credits the late Jerry Gross with the word's coinage, and points out that Gross's further sponsorship of "Eldercare" was more descriptive. As to the decision to protect the use of the word legally, he recalls: "Soon after the word began being used early in 1956, I received a call from a man who was making a patent medicine for acne, which he called 'Medicare.' He told me to tell the Defense Department to cut it out. I called the Judge Advocate General to tell him of this, and he said not to worry about it." Immediately afterward, the government copyrighted its use of the name.

State governments adopted such versions as *medicaid* and *medi-Cal*, and a tax-credit plan has been called *medicredit*. In the sixties, *medi-* was almost as popular a prefix as *mini-*, but in the generation that followed, the less colorful "health insurance" and "health reform" subsumed the *medi-* prefix.

MEGO rhetorical soporific; the acronym for "My Eyes Glaze Over."

This useful term is newsmagazine lingo. Like "violin piece" and TICK-TOCK, it was introduced to the author in 1969 by Mel Elfin, then Washington bureau chief of *Newsweek*. "A MEGO is something that is both undeniably important and paralyzingly dull," Elfin reports. "Latin American policy is a MEGO. Petrodollars is a MEGO. I'm falling asleep explaining this to you."

The word is gaining in currency. According to the *San Francisco Chronicle* of October 12, 1992, "The Democratic front-runner [Bill Clinton] ran up the MEGO Factor last night with a performance so robotic that [Jim] Lehrer should have checked the back of his suit for a battery pack."

melting pot the process by which immigrants become Americanized; a nation that assimilates all nationalities and cultures.

The phrase originated in *The Melting Pot*, a turn-of-the-century play by Israel Zangwill, and was quickly accepted as expressing a sense of pride in America's tradition of immigration, alongside Emma Lazarus' poem beginning "Give me your tired, your poor . . ." A predecessor phrase was "Asylum of the Oppressed of Every Nation," from the 1856 Democratic platform.

However, the big-city politician who takes the phrase seriously is soon disabused. Nathan Glazer and Daniel P. Moynihan pointed out in their study of ethnic patterns in New York City, *Beyond the Melting Pot*, that the Italian, Irish, Jewish, black, and Puerto Rican communities of New York are more separate than similar. Ticket-balancing and ethnic appeals are still important to the big-city vote-getter. "New York City is not a melting pot," Thomas E. Dewey told reporter John Gunther in 1947, "it's a boiling pot."

Least assimilated, of course, is the nonwhite American. Political leaders in recent years have exhorted all Americans to apply the melting-pot principle to blacks; John F. Kennedy, in a 1963 civil rights message, called the denial of equal access to public accommodations "a daily insult which has no place in a country proud of its heritage—the heritage of the melting pot, of equal rights, of one nation and one people."

According to the melting-pot theory, immigrants would become Americanized and assimilated. "If the 'melting pot' had completed its work," wrote Henry Fairlie in 1974, "there would be no 'ethnics.'" The existence of persistent patterns of social, cultural, and educational life within large cities shows that this theory did not materialize. A more realistic approach, called "cultural pluralism," emerged in the 1970s, treating the American system more as a salad bowl than a melting pot. This developed into *multiculturalism* in the 1990s, which some felt made up for centuries of denial of racial respect and others held was divisive in American society and derogated the traditions of Western civilization. See ETHNICS.

mending fences. See FENCE MENDING.

men of thought livers of the life of the mind; frequently contrasted with "men of action."

The phrase "men of thought and men of action" was popularized by Woodrow Wilson, but the concept of the tension between the two types has a long history. British essayist William Hazlitt, in an essay "On Thought and Action," observed: "Thought depends on the habitual exercise of the speculative facilities; action, on the determination of the will. The one assigns reasons for things, the other puts causes to act." Personally, he disclaimed the ability to act: "I . . . had rather write one of these Essays than have to seal a letter."

Historian Thomas Babington Macaulay, noting the criticism of men of action, explained: "A politician must often talk and act before he has thought and read. He may be very ill-informed respecting a question . . . but speak he must; and if he is a man of talents, tact, and intrepidity, he soon finds that, even under such circumstances, it is possible to speak successfully." Thomas Carlyle was another man of thought who admired action: "The end of man is an action, and not a thought, though it were the noblest."

Although John Galsworthy held that "a man of action, forced into a state of thought, is unhappy until he can get out of it," Theodore Roosevelt, a man with credentials in both areas, disagreed: "Power undirected by high purpose spells calamity; and high purpose by itself is utterly useless if the power to put it into effect is lacking." Men of action also describe men of thought with the same respect. Argentine dictator Juan Perón said in 1950: "The Peronist movement needs men of action, but it also requires preachers of the doctrine."

John F. Kennedy, early in 1960, hoped "to reopen the channels of communication between the world of thought and the seat of power," and did much to activate thinkers. Richard Nixon, in a 1966 speech on academic freedom, pointed out that "Woodrow Wilson's distinction between men of thought and men of action can no longer be made. The man of thought who will not act is ineffective; the man of action who will not think is dangerous."

The phrase is likely to be unsexed to "person of."

For praise of dreamers, see MOVERS AND SHAKERS; for derogation of intellectuals, see EGGHEAD.

men's room of the Kremlin. See SALT.

mentor. See RABBI.

merchants of death armament manufacturers and sellers; war profiteers.

The phrase comes from the title of a 1934 book by H. C. Engelbrecht and F. C. Hanighan, one of many exposés in the twenties and thirties attempting to prove that the causes of war were economic.

Businessmen have often been suspected of being "profiteers," a word based on the "privateers," free-lance pirates in the service of a nation but not officially part of its navy. Thomas Jefferson observed in a letter in 1814 that "merchants have no country." The German House of Krupp was most commonly identified as the "merchants of death." The "captains of industry" celebrated by Thomas Carlyle became the MALEFACTORS OF GREAT WEALTH of Theodore Roosevelt and the ECONOMIC ROYALISTS denounced by Franklin Roosevelt.

Interventionists have often been accused of economic motives. Vermont Senator Redfield Proctor, after the sinking of the battleship *Maine*, made a speech supporting President McKinley's policy of disputing Cuba with Spain. Speaker Thomas B. Reed dismissed the marble king's remarks with: "A war will make a large market for gravestones."

One Swedish explosives manufacturer was particularly sensitive to characterizations that later became phrased as "merchant of death." Alfred B. Nobel, who invented dynamite by combining nitroglycerine with more stable elements, established a will that made his name synonymous with peace rather than death.

After the Kennedy assassination in 1963, attempts were made to limit the sale of firearms through the mail, which was Lee Harvey Oswald's method of purchase of a gun. The efforts were resisted by the National Rifle Association, quoting the Constitution: ". . . the right to bear arms shall not be abridged." A new use of "merchants of death" sprang up to describe sellers of guns to incompetents, minors, and those likely to participate in race riots.

As international arms dealers enabled Iran and Iraq to build their war machines in the 1980s, the resulting scandals of Iran-contra and Iraqgate revived the term in its original sense. This original meaning was strengthened in the post–Cold War period. A new, lucrative market for arms dealers was created as small countries, no longer able to leave their defense to the superpowers, rushed to arm themselves. "With the collapse of the Soviet trading bloc, or Comecon," worried the *Washington Post* of April 24, 1993, "Eastern Europe could be transformed into a new arms bazaar where terrorists and international pariahs would find merchants of death, desperate for a deal."

mess in Washington specifically the 1952 Republican campaign characterization of the state of affairs; generally, the way the "Outs," of whatever party, always see conditions in the capital under the "Ins."

"It was the 'mess in Washington,' that, more than any other single factor, caused President Truman's image to fade as his term drew to a close," wrote Cabell Phillips in *The Truman Presidency*. There was, he added, a "climate in which a handful of cheats, frauds and simple fourflushers in the government managed to spray the tint of corruption across his second Administration," and by 1952 Truman's popularity was down to 26 percent in public opinion polls.

General Harry H. Vaughan, the President's friend and military aide, became the focus of the charges. A Senate investigating subcommittee reported that FIVE PERCENTERS who hung around the Defense Department, the War Assets Administration, and the Reconstruction Finance Corporation relied on Vaughan's friendship to steer contracts and projects their way. Though the subcommittee found no evidence of direct payoffs, it noted that Vaughan became the channel for some generous contributions to the Democratic party and himself received a deep-freeze from the grateful client of a friend. The deep-freeze (see INFLUENCE PEDDLER) came to symbolize the "mess."

Talk of a "mess" irked Truman. In his memoirs he noted that Adlai Stevenson, campaigning in Oregon in 1952 under the Democratic banner, said he would clean up "the mess in Washington." Wrote Truman: "I wondered if he had been taken in by the Republican fraudulent build-up of flyspecks on our Washington windows into a big blot or 'mess.' For several years the Republican opposition had tried to make a case against the Administration, only to find that the Administration was always alert in rooting out corruption or bad practices wherever they existed."

Though President Eisenhower's speechwriter, Emmet John Hughes, said that he wanted to shun the mess phrase as "petty, self-righteous and extravagant," other advisers urged him to use it. He did. As Eisenhower wrote in his memoirs, the furor over Richard Nixon's campaign fund in 1952 was especially welcome to the Democrats "because of the emphasis we had been putting on the 'mess in Washington' . . . so much evidence of woeful negligence and apparent crookedness had turned up . . . that I had again and again talked about the need for an Administration that would renew Americans' faith in the government."

As a phrase, "the mess" is no newcomer to Washington: when Theodore Roosevelt was being urged to seek the presidency again in 1912, he resisted at first, saying, "I'm not in the running and I'm not going to be dragged into it. Taft created the mess and let Taft take his spanking for it."

The White House mess is an eatery in the basement of the Executive Mansion; "mess" is based on the Navy term for food service area. Walter Shapiro of *Esquire* described that area in the Clinton Administration as "a restaurant, not a management philosophy."

me too a general lack of originality; specifically applied by conservatives to Republicans who stand on liberal platforms.

The phrase first became current when Thomas C. Platt of New York resigned as senator in 1881, following the lead set by his colleague, Senator Roscoe Conkling, after a dispute with President Garfield over patronage appointments in the Empire State. A cartoon of the day showed Platt as a small boy sticking out of Conkling's pocket, with a card labeled "Me, too!" tied to one of his hands.

With the New Deal well launched by 1936, Franklin Roosevelt began ridiculing Republicans for "me too" speeches in which they endorsed his goals but attacked his methods. During his campaign for a second term, he said:

> Let me warn you and let me warn the nation against the smooth evasion which says—of course we believe all these things; we believe in social security; we believe in work for the unemployed; we believe in saving homes. Cross our hearts and hope to die, we believe in all these things; but we do not like the way the present Administration is doing them. Just turn them over to us. We will do all of them—we will do more of them—we will do them better; and, most important of all, the doing of them will not cost anybody anything.

In 1940 the *New York Daily News* sneeringly referred to the GOP candidate for President as "Me Too" Willkie, complaining: "Instead of a knockdown and drag-out political fight, this is getting to be a LOVE FEAST." As Socialist Norman Thomas said of Wendell Willkie: "He agreed with Roosevelt's entire program of social reform—and said it was leading to disaster."

The "me too" label has been pinned on liberal Republicans ever since. In 1948, after New York's Governor Thomas E. Dewey won the presidential nomination, the *Chicago Tribune* protested: "For the third time, a Republican convention fell under vicious influences and nominated a 'me-too' candidate who conducted a 'me-too' campaign." Harry Truman had some fun with the theme. Referring to Dewey's promises, during a Pittsburgh speech on October 23, 1948, he noted: "The candidate says, 'Me, too.' But the Republican record still says, 'We're against it.' These two phrases, 'me, too' and 'we're against it,' sum up the whole Republican campaign."

Adlai Stevenson, campaigning in Denver in September 1952, echoed Truman's earlier speech: "The Republican candidates seem to have clasped all of the social gains of the past 20 years to their bosoms with a 'me-too' fervor that is touching to a Democrat, for imitation still remains the sincerest form of flattery."

Defending liberal Republicans pinned with the "me too" label, Dewey noted during a 1950 series of lectures at Princeton: "There are some loud voices in the Republican Party denouncing all the platforms and nominees with the epithet 'me too.' The complaint and the epithet largely originated with those who hold isolationist or extremely conservative views, or both. As for myself, and I believe most of the members of the Republican Party, we refuse to be against the Ten Commandments just because the Democrats say they are for them."

Significantly, Barry Goldwater, the least "me-tooish" GOP candidate in a generation, campaigned in 1964 on the slogan "a CHOICE, NOT AN ECHO," and suffered one of the worst drubbings in the party's history. Goldwater denounced the "dime store New Deal" several years before George Wallace used the phrase "not a dime's worth of difference" (see DIME'S WORTH OF DIFFERENCE, NOT A).

In a column about GOP resistance to the health care proposal submitted by Hillary Rodham Clinton, Evans and Novak wrote in 1993: "After two years in which Republicans either kept silent or said 'Me too,' the White House is determined to win passage this year. . . ."

See ROAD TO DEFEAT; BIG TENT.

Metroamerican. See MIDDLE AMERICA.

Mickey Mouse. See HUMPTY DUMPTY.

Middle America the payers of most of the taxes, the holders of most of the values, the electors of most of the candidates.

Columnist Joseph Kraft coined the term in a piece on June 23, 1968: "For two years before that," he informed the author, "I had been beating around the term, talking about ordinary Americans, middle-class Americans, Americans who were not young or poor or black and that kind of thing. My focus on that group was stimulated in 1967 by a Labor Department study of living costs for people in the $7,000 to $10,000 income bracket in the major cities. It showed that their requirements were outrunning their earnings and I was struck by the fact and have been writing about it ever since."

A variety of phrases have been coined in recent years to replace JOHN Q. PUBLIC and are used interchangeably. However, there are some nuances of difference:

"Un-young, un-poor, and un-black" is a *statistical* concept, according to Richard Scammon, who used it in response to a question in early 1968. Someone who is none of the three is not necessarily conservative; as Scammon puts it, a left-winger who commands high legal fees and is fifty or so is neither poor, young, nor black.

Middle America is primarily an *economic* concept, as Kraft used it, showing the conflict between the middle class and the classes above and below, though the phrase is sometimes used to mean a state of mind.

The SILENT MAJORITY is a *social* concept, referring to those who uphold traditional morality, and who resent the attention given by the media to the demonstrators and noisemakers.

The Real Majority, title of a book by Scammon and Ben Wattenberg, and *The Emerging Republican Majority*, title of a book by Kevin Phillips, are *political* concepts—the former a brief for political centrism, the latter a brief for conservatism.

The FORGOTTEN MAN is the predecessor phrase for *silent majority*, and is interchangeable with it; an antonym for both, coined by historian Eric Goldman in 1969, is *Metroamerican*, one who is youthful, wealthy, educated, public-spirited, ambivalent, and, as the coiner puts it, "liberal but without ideology . . . flexible, pragmatic, and a devotee of the ironic edge."

The GREAT UNWASHED has fallen into disuse, despite the fact that television sets outnumber bathtubs in America.

Middle American, derived from Kraft's phrase, also dates back to 1968. In 1983, *Business Week* used the term to describe reporter Harrison Salisbury as "a quintessential Middle American, born and raised in Minnesota and a registered Republican."

middle of the road the place where most U.S. national political candidates, Democratic and Republican, take their stand; the land equivalent of the MAINSTREAM.

"The objective of a nominating convention," Henry L. Stoddard wrote in his 1938 book, *It Costs to Be President*, "is not a candidate who is strongest in states certain to be carried by his party, but one who is likely to be the strongest in those states in which party prospects are weakest—in other words, a middle-of-the-road man."

At the turn of the century the term characterized Populists who opposed joining the Democratic party. An 1892 Populist campaign song went:

Side tracks are rough, and they're hard to walk,
Keep in the middle of the road:
Though we haven't got time to stop and talk,
We keep in the middle of the road.

To some, though, it seemed a barren place. "I am a middle-of-the-road man," said Populist James Baird Weaver in 1894, "but I don't propose to lie down across it so no one can get over me. Nothing grows in the middle of the road."

German politician August Bebel, speaking to a congress of the German Social-Democratic party in Dresden in 1903, echoed the theme: "The field of politics always presents the same struggle. There are the Right and the Left, and in the middle is the Swamp. The Swamp is made up of the know-nothings, of them who are without ideas, of them who are always with the majority."

Robert Frost, the poet, took note of Dwight Eisenhower's characterization of his government as middle-of-the-road and snorted: "The middle of the road is where the white line is—and that's the worst place to drive."

Nonetheless, a U.S. President who departs from the middle will find himself in dangerous territory. "Missouri friends represented Mr. Truman as a 'middle-of-the-road' man on all current political and economic issues," complained *New York Times* columnist Arthur Krock in September 1945, "but the 'middle of the road' was way off to one side."

Eisenhower firmly planted his feet in the middle in a 1949 Labor Day speech in St. Louis. "The path to America's future," he said, "lies down the middle of the road between the unfettered power of concentrated wealth . . . and the unbridled power of statism or partisan interests." After his inauguration in 1953, he was advised to stay right there by former President Herbert Hoover. "All you can do is to try to turn away gradually from the path leading to paternalism until it takes a central course, and then stick with it. And both sides will dislike you." Ike took his advice, and declared in his first State of the Union message: "There is, in our affairs at home, a middle way between untrammeled freedom of the individual and the demands for the welfare of the whole nation. This way must avoid government by bureaucracy as carefully as it avoids neglect of the helpless."

He never lost that conviction. In October 1963, three years out of office and irritated at LABELS, he wrote: "I despise all adjectives that try to describe people as liberal or conservative, rightist or leftist, as long as they stay in the useful part of the road." Even more, he added, he despised those who "go to the gutter on either the right or the left, and hurl rocks at those in the center." The next month he noted: "People talk about the middle of the road as though it were unacceptable. Actually, all human problems, excepting morals, come into the gray areas. Things are not all black and white. There have to be compromises. The middle of the road is all of the usable surface. The extremes, right and left, are in the gutters."

See CENTRIST; OPPORTUNIST; MAINSTREAM.

midterm election. See OFF YEAR.

military-industrial complex   a combination of forces that, left unchecked, would soon control the U.S. economy and foreign policy.

Dwight Eisenhower, a military man whose best friends were industrialists, startled the nation with his farewell address on January 17, 1961, warning of the danger of military-industrial power. Speechwriters Malcolm Moos and Ralph Williams had drafted the speech for Eisenhower and are credited with having submitted the famous passage: Until World War II, Eisenhower said, the U.S. had no permanent armaments industry.

> But . . . we can no longer risk emergency improvisation of national defense. We have been compelled to create a permanent armaments industry of vast proportions. Added to this, three and a half million men and women are directly engaged in the defense establishment. . . . Now this conjunction of an immense military establishment and a large arms industry is new in the American experience. The total influence—economic, political, even spiritual—is felt in every city, every State House, every office of the Federal Government. . . . Our toil, resources and livelihood are all involved; so is the very structure of our society.
>
> In the councils of Government, we must guard against the acquisition of unwarranted influence, whether sought or unsought, by the military-industrial complex. The potential for the disastrous rise of misplaced power exists and will persist.

Asked about this statement at a farewell press conference a few days afterward, he added that he was thinking not so much of a willful abuse of power, but of "an almost insidious penetration of our own minds that the only thing this country is engaged in is weaponry and missiles—and I'll tell you we can't afford that."

Walter Lippmann, who had grown increasingly critical of Eisenhower, called his farewell address "in the great tradition. Washington made the theme of his farewell address a warning against allowing the influence of foreign governments to invade our political life. That was then the menace to the civilian power. Now Eisenhower, speaking from his experience and looking ahead, is concerned with a contemporary threat to the supremacy of the civilian power."

Political scientist Harold Lasswell had coined a term in 1941 on this subject. In *The Garrison State* he warned: "The military men who dominate a modern technical society will be very different from the officers of history and tradition. It is probable that the specialists on violence will include in their training a large degree of expertness in many of the skills that we have traditionally accepted as part of modern civilian management." See WHIZ KIDS.

The concept of restraining the military is at least as old as Cicero, who said in 60 B.C.: "Let the soldier yield to the civilian." Woodrow Wilson, preparing for war, insisted "one thing that this country never will endure is a system that can be called militarism. . . . Men who are in charge of edged tools and bidden to prepare them for exact and scientific use grow very impatient if they are not permitted to use them . . ."

But the danger pointed out by Eisenhower was more subtle than militarism, or civilian control of the military. He recognized that there was no line of demarcation between "civilian" and "military" in the modern defense establishment, where huge companies depended on defense contracts. These companies, through their economic impact on an area, had political power of their own that contributed to military appropriation decisions, building a vicious circle or "complex."

When Bill Clinton introduced his economic program to Congress in February 1993, *Newsday* echoed the term in commenting on the seating arrangement in which Hillary Rodham Clinton was between Federal Reserve Board chairman Alan Greenspan and John Sculley, chief executive officer of Apple Computer. Wrote *Newsday*, "Sculley's prominence symbolizes a fact of life in Washington: Through personal contacts and lobbying groups large and small, computer-related industries—Big Silicon—now wield the kind of clout once held by Big Steel, Detroit or the military-industrial complex."

military metaphors Soon after the opening gun of the CAMPAIGN, the STANDARD-BEARER was denounced as a HATCHETMAN, an OLD FOGY, and a *flash in the pan* by the LEFT WING, and it appeared to DIEHARDS that the old WAR-HORSE'S BOOM was a *lost cause*; but the MAN ON HORSEBACK turned out to be a GOOD SOLDIER, and the TROOPS— from PALACE GUARD to OLD GUARD to the FIFTH COLUMN in the enemy *camp*—closed ranks, ignored the SMOKE SCREEN, and did not hesitate to *wave* the BLOODY SHIRT; the CALCULATED RISK of the BANNER DISTRICTS was *saluted* at a victory RALLY, with the SPOILS divided by a TASK FORCE at campaign headquarters before the new Administration's first HUNDRED DAYS.

Of the military phrases above so often used in politics, the not-so-obvious are "hatchetman" (who cleared the woods for General Washington's troops), "flash in the pan" (a cannon charge that misfires), "spoils" (originally of war), "left wing" (of a military front), "hundred days" (Napoleon's final campaign), and "old fogy" (from "phogy," seniority pay for officers). The others appear elsewhere under individual entries. Also see FIELD EXPEDIENT; FIGHTING THE PROBLEM; HOLD THE LINE; LOW PROFILE; ON THE POINT.

Military images appear in international diplomacy (ARSENAL OF DEMOCRACY), and words born in hot and cold wars are used in politics ("fifth column," EYEBALL TO EYEBALL); in return, politicians create phrases for warriors (BIGGER BANG FOR A BUCK, "overkill").

The chaos and waste of a political campaign make metaphors of military campaigns particularly applicable; in a more profound sense, poets like Matthew Arnold apply the metaphor to life in general, as in "Dover Beach":

And here we are as on a darkling plain
Swept with confused alarms of struggle
and flight,
Where ignorant armies clash by night.

In the application of metaphor to politics, only sports, and particularly racing, compares to the military. See SPORTS METAPHORS. WAR-GAMING WORDS will direct the reader to those new words created for military-political use, and PENTAGONESE to more current military jargon.

Even SLOGAN comes from a Scottish war cry.

milk for Hottentots. See HOTTENTOTS, MILK FOR.

ministry of all the talents. See HACK.

mink coats. See INFLUENCE PEDDLER.

minority euphemism for "nonwhite," which is usually a euphemism for black and Hispanic.

When a sociologist refers to a minority, it can be any segment of a public which is not a majority. In political usage, however, the term is usually employed to mean black or Hispanic: a promise to include minorities in appointments is taken to mean that blacks and Americans with roots in Puerto Rico and Mexico will get a share of the patronage.

In national life, Jews are a minority, just as white Anglo-Saxon Protestants are a minority in New York City, but the word's literal meaning must not be confused with its political meaning:

"minority" almost always connotes nonwhite, and usually poor.

In a 1974 *Atlantic Monthly* piece on the language of politics, Henry Fairlie pointed out the change in meaning this word had undergone in two generations: "Fifty years ago, when Ortega y Gasset wrote *The Revolt of the Masses,* 'minorities' meant the privileged few at the top: '. . . the masses are today exercising functions which coincide with those hitherto seemed reserved to minorities . . .' The 'minority' was the elite opposed to 'the masses' . . ."

Curiously, the word "minority" is sometimes also applied to women crusading for equal rights, although in 1990 women were 51.3 percent of the U.S. population, outnumbering males by more than 6 million. The word has such an oppressed-underdog connotation that it is preferred by a group even when that "minority" is a majority. The 1990 census, however, does not apply "minority" to women and keeps them separate from blacks, Hispanics, Asians, and American Indians.

Ethnic groups, though certainly demographic minorities, are not meant when a politician speaks of "minority employment"; for a discussion of this related subject, see ETHNICS.

MIRV. See SALT.

miscalculation the danger of war through a mistaken assessment of another power's intentions or capabilities.

"A favorite Kennedy word," wrote Ted Sorensen, "from my earliest association with him was 'miscalculation.' Long before he read Barbara Tuchman's *The Guns of August*—which he recommended to his staff—he had as a student at Harvard taken a course on the origins of World War I . . . he would cite the 1914 conversation between two German leaders on the origins and expansion of that war, a former chancellor asking, 'How did it all happen?' and his successor saying, 'Ah, if only one knew.'"

Recalling the Soviet miscalculation of the U.S. reaction to placing missiles in Cuba, Kennedy told an aide that the sequel to *The Guns of August* could be "the missiles of October." Kennedy had used the word "miscalculation" in his meeting with Khrushchev in 1961, according to Arthur Schlesinger, Jr., and it irritated the Russian leader. "It was a vague term," he said, and it suggested to him "that America wanted the Soviet Union to sit like a schoolboy with hands on the top of the desk . . . the West should put the word 'miscalculation' into cold storage, for its use did not impress the Soviet Union." Kennedy tried to explain that he meant any nation could be prone to misjudgments, as was the U.S. in failing to foresee Chinese intervention in the Korean War.

In that instance, the Indian ambassador in Peking had already relayed to the U.S. a warning that the Chinese Communists would send in "volunteers" if General MacArthur's troops crossed the 38th parallel in his 1951 counterattack. Dean Rusk, then several steps removed from Secretary of State, contributed to the decision to overlook the warning; later he said frankly, "I was wrong."

That was the second miscalculation in Korea. The first was the mistaken belief by the Communists that if North Korea invaded the south, neither the U.S. nor the UN would respond militarily. Fifteen years later, in Vietnam, the same danger existed in trying to outguess "the other side's" motives, capability, and potential backing. "Miscalculation," wrote the *New York Times* in the spring of 1967, "remains an obvious danger—one that

President Johnson himself has often recognized. Last week, in fact, he was disclosed to have told his daughter Luci one night last summer, as the first raids on Hanoi and Haiphong were on the wing, that if a Soviet ship were accidentally bombed it could well lead to World War III."

This was a misuse of the word, which dates back to 1720. Inadvertent or accidental war differs from miscalculation, which is part of the risk taken in consciously playing power politics on the international scene. War by miscalculation could come about by overconfidence in weaponry, by underestimation of the other side's willingness to "take a stand,"—as in Saddam Hussein's miscalculation of George Bush's resolve, which resulted in Iraq's defeat in Desert Storm—or by steady escalation with no settlement along the way.

See ESCALATION; PREVENTIVE WAR; DOOMSDAY MACHINE; FAIL-SAFE; MEASURED RESPONSE; CALCULATED RISK; SALT.

mishmash confusion; meaningless material.

"Mishmash" is an English word in use for five centuries, particularly applicable in politics to describe the intellectual content of a speech.

Mishmash suggests a picture of lumpy, gray porridge, tasteless and not especially nourishing. A perfect use can be shown in the following communication from an attaché of the Soviet embassy in Washington, D.C.

Haydon Burns, a governor of Florida, misaddressed an invitation to Soviet Foreign Minister Andrei Gromyko as "Ambassador to the United Nations," asking him to speak at a lecture series in Florida. By the time an answer was forthcoming, a new governor had replaced Burns; this is the text of the letter sent Governor Claude R. Kirk:

Dear Sir:

Sometime ago, we received a letter signed by the Honorable Haydon Burns with the kind invitation to visit the place and speak before Daytona Beach Open Forum. We apologize for an unfortunate delay in answering the letter since there was some mishmash in it.

Andrei Gromyko whom the letter was applied to as "Ambassador to the United Nations" is the USSR Foreign Minister in the course of the last ten years. . . .

Besides that, any speaker of our Embassy is not able to participate in "the Open Forum program—1967" as this particular place is restricted to travel by Soviet citizens.

Yours sincerely,
Alexander A. Kokorev
Attaché
USSR Embassy

A second communication, published in *The Groucho Letters,* illustrates a common belief that the word mishmash has a Yiddish derivation:

To the Hon. William R. Scranton, Governor of Pennsylvania

February 24, 1964

Dear Sir:

If you contemplate campaigning in any more Jewish neighborhoods, I suggest you learn how to pronounce "mishmash." It is not pronounced "mash" as you said on "Meet the Press," but rather as though it were spelled MOSH.

Sincerely yours,
Groucho Marx

The author wrote the first draft of this entry under the impression that the word did indeed have a Yiddish derivation; one of his editors sent it back with proof from the *OED* that the word was English, and the entry was accordingly revised. However, when the copy editor saw the revision, she penciled a note in the margin paraphrasing the punch line of an old Jewish joke: "Funny, it doesn't *look* English." She backed up her doubts with a copy of the Groucho letter.

Under this usage pressure, the first editor returned the manuscript to the author with the following note: "Here we go again on mishmash. The word is *not* Yiddish. However, the pronunciation of the word, as if *mishmosh*, is probably due to Yiddish influence in certain regions in the U.S. Perhaps it would be a good idea to add a short sentence of explanation: it's not Yiddish but maybe the pronunciation *-mosh* is due to Yiddish influence—though this pronunciation is not that of the majority of Americans."

Note to publisher: *print as is*. This entry is enough of a mishmash (pronounced *mishmosh*) already.

missile gap   a Kennedy charge that U.S. missile production lagged behind Soviet production; a hot issue in the 1960 presidential campaign, it was soon afterward coolly dismissed as nonexistent by the new Administration.

The Eisenhower Administration decided in the late 1950s not to invest heavily in intercontinental ballistic missiles, on the grounds that they were technologically inadequate; Defense Secretary Neil McElroy was charged by Democrats in Congress with planning a "missile gap." General James Gavin resigned from the Army in 1958 with a blast at the "missile lag." The charge became a key point in the 1960 Kennedy campaign (along with "the prestige gap") but was dismissed by the new Defense Secretary, Robert McNamara, soon after his appointment by Kennedy.

Arthur Schlesinger, Jr., later frankly labeled it a "fake issue"; Ted Sorensen, taking the most charitable view, wrote: "Kennedy's error in 1960 on the 'missile gap' had been the result of the public's being informed too little and too late—even after the facts were certain—about a danger which he had in good faith overstated."

When Pentagon leaks in 1966 indicated an authentic missile gap was developing, the *St. Louis Post-Dispatch* remembered that the first gap turned out to be a myth, adding: "Somebody ought to ask whether the intelligence on which these proposals are based is any better than that of the first missile gap. . . . Once bitten, twice shy; that ought to be the motto in Congress."

The term is still often invoked as a symbol of exaggerated and misleading claims. "The economy may turn out for Bill Clinton what the missile gap was for John Kennedy," warned the *Boston Globe* in November 1992.

For other phrases spawned by this phrase, see GAP; CREDIBILITY GAP.

missiles of October.   See MISCALCULATION; EYEBALL TO EYEBALL.

moderate   positioned slightly to the left of center; a word more acceptable to conservatives than *liberal*, more dynamic than *middle-of-the-roader*.

President Eisenhower began using the word "moderation" in cabinet meetings in late 1954, just after the mid-term elections. Robert Donovan, who had access to cabinet-meeting minutes, reported that the President said on November 4, 1954, that the next two years would be extremely critical ones for the Administration's policy of moderation.

A year later Adlai Stevenson told a fund-raising dinner in Chicago: "I agree that moderation is the spirit of the times. But we best take care lest we confuse moderation for mediocrity, or settle for half answers to hard problems. . . . Moderation, yes! Stagnation, no!" At the same dinner New York Governor Averell Harriman, a

potential foe of Stevenson's for the 1956 Democratic nomination, disagreed: "There is no such word as 'moderation' in the Democratic vocabulary."

Senator Lyndon Johnson, however, on December 12, 1955, declared, "I have always thought of myself as one who has been a moderate in approaching problems." He had used "moderation" often, as had Eisenhower; Joseph Rauh, chairman of Americans for Democratic Action, suggested, "It would make sense to try to figure out what Eisenhower moderation is versus Johnson moderation, if indeed there is a difference."

By the late fifties, "moderate" had established a centrist meaning, weighted slightly liberal. The word was relatively quiescent during the Kennedy years, but reappeared strongly in the Rockefeller-Goldwater fight for the Republican nomination of 1964. Rockefeller National Campaign Director John A. Wells, an attorney who had managed Jacob Javits's LANDSLIDE victory for the Senate in 1962, urged that Rockefeller use "moderate" rather than "liberal" in describing his philosophy in the New Hampshire primary, in the hope of capturing mildly conservative voters who might not identify with "Mr. Conservative," Barry Goldwater. "Moderate" and "MAINSTREAM" became the bywords of the stop-Goldwater movement, and "moderate" appears to have become a permanent label. Conservatives see through it. In describing Illinois Senator Charles Percy as "a sort of inbetween Republican," columnist William F. Buckley, Jr., added: "I resist the word 'moderate' because it is a base-stealing word for the benefit of GOP liberals." It was used in 1993 by President Clinton to describe his new communications counselor, David Gergen, when Clinton felt it necessary to assure the public that he had not taken what was being described as "a lurch to the left."

The predecessor word, "moderation," has had a long history in politics. Robert Clive, in a hot parliamentary debate in 1773, exclaimed, "By God, Mr. Chairman, at this moment I stand astonished at my own moderation!" In 1875 Leon Gambetta, who was to become Premier of France, told the Assembly, "Moderation is the reason of politics."

In his essay "Of Faction," written in 1597, Francis Bacon set forth the epitaph for Republican liberals before the 1964 nomination: ". . . it is often seen, that a few that are stiff, do tire out a great number that are more moderate."

See MIDDLE OF THE ROAD.

modern Republicanism a philosophy of government "liberal in human affairs, conservative in fiscal affairs"; an attempt to give a more progressive label to the GOP.

In 1955 Arthur Larson, then Under Secretary of Labor and a former dean of the University of Pittsburgh Law School, wrote *A Republican Looks at His Party*. Sherman Adams and the President's brother, Dr. Milton Eisenhower, had been anxious to focus on some articulation of the Eisenhower philosophy. Adams brought the book to the President in Walter Reed Hospital, where he was recovering from his ileitis operation, and the President subsequently said the book "expressed my philosophy of government as well as I have seen it in a book of that size."

Though Larson wrote mainly of a "new" Republicanism, his liberal approach was dubbed "modern," and he was attacked by conservatives—Republicans and Democrats alike—when he was appointed to head the U.S. Information Agency. Conservative journalist George Sokolsky complained that the Republican party under Ei-

senhower "has gone so modern that it is indistinguishable from the New Deal." Illinois Representative Noah Mason said, "Essentially Ike's New Republicanism is a form of bribery, a program to buy votes with the voter's own money."

As the 1956 Eisenhower LANDSLIDE rolled in on election night, the President told Richard Nixon what he planned to discuss on the air after Stevenson's concession. "I think I'll talk about Modern Republicanism." He formally used the phrase for the first time that night:

"Modern Republicanism, as I have said time and again, is to follow the Lincoln dictum of what government is for, and then to do it within the concept of competitive economy, sound fiscal arrangement and a sound dollar." The President was referring to this comment of Lincoln's: "The legitimate object of government is to do for a community of people whatever they need to have done, but cannot do at all, or cannot so well do, for themselves—in their separate, and individual capacities. In all that the people can individually do as well for themselves, government ought not to interfere."

"As the publicizer of Modern Republicanism," Sherman Adams wrote, "Larson became a marked man." When he was named to head USIA, Democrats and conservative Republicans joined to slash its budget from $144 million to $105 million. "Eisenhower did not need to be told," said Adams, "that Modern Republicanism as well as economy was behind the attack on Larson's budget." Larson died in 1993.

Though Eisenhower's Administration was marked by its breadth of support, the "modern Republican" phrase was curiously divisive. It implicitly labeled the Old Guard as "OLD FOGY." In the sixties it was used only occasionally, with the "moderns" adopting the more conciliatory "moderate Republican," and in the seventies, NEO-CONSERVATIVE.

See MAINSTREAM; MODERATE; ME TOO.

modified limited hangout. See WATERGATE WORDS.

mollycoddle as a verb, to pamper—a charge made by opponents of many social welfare benefits that recipients are being treated with undue solicitude, to the detriment of working taxpayers; as a noun, a weakling.

Said John Jay Chapman, an American writer and critic, in *Practical Agitation* in 1900: "In a martial age the reformer is called a mollycoddle; in a commercial age, an incompetent, a disturber of values; in a fanatical age, a heretic. If an agitator is not reviled, he is a quack."

In politics, the word is most closely associated with Theodore Roosevelt, who espoused "the strenuous life." In his autobiography he referred to those who opposed the building of battleships and the fortification of the Panama Canal as "the large mollycoddle vote, people who are soft physically and morally."

Like MOSSBACK and SNOLLYGOSTER, it was one of President Harry Truman's favorite Americanisms. "I wasn't going to go down in history," he promised toward the end of his term, "like Pierce or Buchanan or Chester Arthur or Benjamin Harrison—he was one of the most mediocre Presidents we ever had. I wasn't going to be one of your arm-rolling cheek-kissing mollycoddles!"

-monger a suffix meaning "peddler of," used to create derogatory phrases.

Ever since the sixteenth century, "monger"—an Anglo-Saxon word for trade—has had a connotation of petty, disreputable trafficking. Ironmongers and fishmongers carry on respectable enough businesses, as once did warmongers—the word for a mercenary soldier. Boroughmongers were wealthy landowners in England who sold representation of the ROTTEN BOROUGHS.

The suffix has been particularly used to describe people who pass along information: gossipmongers, scandalmongers, rumormongers. In politics, one who warns of imminent danger is sometimes attacked as a panicmonger, or more seriously as a warmonger.

As with other phrases using the idea of war (see WAGING PEACE), a turnaround has taken place and those who speak against containment or intervention have been labeled "peacemongers."

Monroe Doctrine. See DOCTRINES; DOLLAR DIPLOMACY.

moonlighting working for a second source of income; in politics, doing private work for pay at night while on the public payroll during the day.

The word originally applied to the nighttime raids of poverty-stricken Irishmen in the 1880s, to punish unpopular tenants or prevent payments of rents. The concept of working for a second employer after putting in a full day elsewhere was called "smooting" in England at that time, and was prohibited by the trade unions, which wanted to spread the work to as many different members as possible.

A political issue is occasionally raised as to whether policemen and firemen should be allowed to supplement their income by taking a second job during their off-hours. Opponents argue that moonlighting drains the worker's stamina for his civic job; and they claim it leads to conflict of interest in the case of white-collar public workers or officials.

See DOUBLE DIPPING.

moral equivalent of war fervor without destructiveness; an acknowledgment of man's psychological need for the martial arts, with a recommendation that the need be satisfied through peaceful challenges.

William James, in an essay entitled "The Moral Equivalent of War," published in the *International Concilium* in February 1910, wrote: "So long as anti-militarists propose no substitute for war's disciplinary function, no *moral equivalent* of war, analogous, as one might say, to the mechanical equivalent of heat, so long they fail to realize the full inwardness of the situation."

Four U.S. wars later, President Jimmy Carter used the James phrase in his address to the nation on the energy problem on April 19, 1977. He pictured the situation as "the greatest challenge that our country will face in our lifetimes," adding: "Our decision about energy will test the character of the American people and the ability of the President and the Congress to govern this nation. This difficult effort will be the 'moral equivalent of war'— except that we will be uniting our efforts to build and not to destroy." His writers felt that the last phrase, although redundant, was necessary to stress that the President was not advocating any kind of "shooting" war.

After the Senate had refused to pass legislation that would have raised fuel taxes and continued the control of all natural-gas prices, as the President had requested, Mr. Carter took the occasion of a press conference on October 13, 1977, to castigate the oil and gas industry in Trumanesque terms: "Back in April when our national energy policy was presented to the Congress and to the people, I said that because of the importance of it that this was 'the moral equivalent of war' . . . as in the case in time of war, there is potential war profiteering in the impending energy crisis. This could develop with the passing months as the biggest ripoff in history."

Columnist Anthony Lewis of the *New York Times* wrote a few days later: "Even by oil company standards there is something staggering in the pretense that 'freeing' the oil companies to produce more will meet a challenge as critical to this country as import dependence over the next decade. That was even more deserving of President Carter's angry rhetoric than the greed that provoked his talk of war profiteering. (Could he please drop the war image, incidentally? Recent examples of its use, starting with the WAR ON POVERTY, are not very happy.)"

As usual, the targets of the attack used the attacking phrase in their counterattack. A committee of economists supporting the oil industry blazed back in a full-page ad: "Congress has been told that it must rush to pass Mr. Carter's current energy plan. 'This is the moral equivalent of war.' And what is that? William James, from whom President Carter borrowed the phrase, defined 'the moral equivalent of war' as nonmartial suffering, something which involves 'discomfort and annoyance, hunger and wet, pain and cold, squalor and filth.' We do not believe that the American people deserve to have 'discomfort, pain, squalor, etc.' imposed upon them by their government."

Charles Krauthammer of the *Washington Post* wrote in February 1993 on President Clinton's call for economic sacrifice: "It shows in the vast disproportion between the size of the threat posed by the deficit and the magnitude of the sacrifice Clinton is asking of the American people to meet it. As usual with these kinds of summons to the moral equivalent of war—Bush on drugs, Carter on energy—a pop-gun is produced to fight it."

The lofty James phrase received its cruelest blow in the Carter years from *New York Times* columnist Russell Baker, who took to using its feline acronym: MEOW.

moratorium an officially declared stoppage or delay; applied to politics, a truce.

This sonorous word, invariably attached to the verb "declare," stems from the Latin for "delay" but has a more majestic connotation. In 1931 Herbert Hoover called for a one-year moratorium on war-debt payments, and this "debt holiday" was called "the Hoover moratorium." When Lyndon Johnson traveled to a conference of Asian leaders just before the off-year elections of 1966, Republican leaders were compelled to declare a moratorium on foreign-policy criticism while he was gone, for fear of appearing to undercut the President abroad on the business of all the people.

When political figures want to tell their friends to shut up while they try to settle a sticky situation, they find it more polite to "request a moratorium." Ted Sorensen wrote that civil rights leaders in 1963 "were angry at the Kennedys for requesting a moratorium on demonstrations while an agreement was worked out . . ."

Early in the 1992 campaign, the term was used by Democratic candidate Paul Tsongas: "This morning, I call for a moratorium, a kind of nonaggression pact between the candidates. Let's start talking about what we stand for. Let's have a positive program, and let's end this negative advertising that in the last analysis does not serve us, our party, or the American people."

In 1993, J. P. Mackley used the word in a *Washington Post* piece on the war in Bosnia: "Even the Russians, whose historical support for Serbia has worried Western negotiators, could not object to an equal opportunity moratorium on artillery fire."

NBC correspondent Herbert Kaplow, chafing at candidate Richard Nixon's moratorium on Vietnam discussions during the 1968 campaign, suggested to this writer: "You ought to hold your next rally in a huge moratorium."

morning in America upbeat political message; or, derision at unfounded or fuzzy optimism about the country's future.

Ronald Reagan's message of newness began in his second Presidential campaign. Commercials for his reelection showed idyllic scenes of America, accompanied by the promising message "It's morning in America."

The 1984 campaign's glowing message was paraphrased by Anthony Lewis of the *New York Times* in his reading of Reagan: "the sense that he feels good and that we should." Within three years, however, the message was being used against the Republicans, voiced in the *Washington Post* in 1987 as a concern that conservatives must "finally realize that it is not 'morning in America' anymore."

By 1992, the phrase was being satirized as an ideal of undue optimism. A review of the film *Bob Roberts*, a political comedy by Tim Robbins, commented that "Candidate Bob takes the cake, his deer-in-the-headlights gaze trained on his own morning in America." Gary Hart wrote in 1993 about the Reagan years: "The orgy was fun, at least for some, while it lasted. But it carried some bitter costs. The champagne has gone flat. It is no longer 'morning in America.'"

See MADISON AVENUE TECHNIQUES.

mossback a reactionary; one who furiously resists progress of any kind.

The word is derived from a sea creature so ancient that it has moss or seaweed growing on its back. During the Civil War it was used to describe those who fled to the swamps and forests to evade the draft; in the 1870s the word was given a political meaning as a Northern counterpart to a Southern Bourbon.

Emporia Gazette editor William Allen White, in his famed "What's the Matter with Kansas?" editorial in 1896, thundered: "We have an old moss-back Jacksonian who snorts and howls because there is a bath tub in the State House; we are running that old jay for Governor . . ."

Pennsylvania Congressman J. C. Sibley drew a typical word picture in 1900: "Primitive man lived in caverns, clothed himself with skins, and ate his meat raw, sitting on his haunches; and there has never occurred a change for the higher and better forms of life without arousing the hostility of some old mossback, conservative hunker[s], who will prate of those fairer and better days of old, when their grandfathers swung by their tails from the limbs of the trees."

Will Rogers told defeated Democratic candidate Al Smith in 1929: ". . . taken out from under the influence of a lot of these old Mossbacks, you are a pretty progressive fellow, Al, and with you and this fellow Roosevelt as a kind of nucleus, I think we can, with the help of some Progressive young Democratic governors and senators and congressmen, make this thing into a Party, instead of a Memory."

The word was relatively dormant during the thirties and early forties, but President Harry Truman gave it new life in the 1948 campaign. In the Far West he charged that the Republican party's domination by "eastern mossbacks" would stifle the economy of the West. Throughout the country, he denounced the Republican chairmen of Senate and House committees as "a bunch of mossbacks."

One of the lines that best describes a mossback was leveled at House Speaker "Uncle Joe" Cannon: "If he had been present at Creation, he would have voted for Chaos."

The word is current. In 1992 George Bush complained that he had extended a "hand of friendship" to Congress at the start of his term "and these old mossbacks bit it off." And *Newsday* of March 10, 1993, reported that "Clinton joined . . . Richard Nixon in toasting [Strom] Thurmond's inspiring 90-year journey from racist Democratic segregationist to mossback Republican obstructionist."

See DO-NOTHING CONGRESS; TROGLODYTIC.

most favored nation   not, as the phrase implies, special treatment in trade, but an assurance that relations will be "equal to that of the most favored nation."

The essence of "MFN" is that "nobody else gets a better deal." The idea, if not the phrase, appears in the commercial treaty Oliver Cromwell of England negotiated with Sweden in 1654 that won recognition of his commonwealth: people of either confederate "shall have and possess in the countries, lands, dominions and kingdoms of the other as full and ample privileges, and as many exemptions, immunities and liberties, as any foreigner doth or shall possess in the dominions and kingdoms of the said confederate." Cromwell got this idea from the Turkish "capitulations": extraterritorial privileges granted in the twelfth century by Byzantium's successors to the Italian city-states. The *OED* does not have the first use (probably in the late seventeenth century) but a typical phrasing can be found in a 1905 British-Rumanian pact: ". . . the commerce, navigation and industry of each country shall be placed, in all respects, on the footing of the most favoured nation."

The underlying idea behind MFN, as it came to be called in the sixties, is a fair field with no favor: any special privileges demanded by one nation, and agreed to by another, then becomes available to all. That is the "unconditional" MFN, guaranteeing equal treatment without any reciprocal strings attached.

The founders of the U.S., however, recognizing that their new nation was a newcomer to world commerce, and faced with English, French, and Spanish attempts to exclude the newcomer from their overseas possessions, came up with a new wrinkle on the hoary clause: the "conditional" MFN. Only if other nations permitted access to their markets would the U.S. permit access to its own.

That conditional principle can be found in the first U.S. trade treaty, concluded with France, in July of 1778. The idea was to make trade reciprocal and dependent upon receipt of equal treatment. Secretary of State John Quincy Adams wrote in 1818 that such reciprocity could not confer special treatment on any one nation: "If any such advantage is granted for an equivalent, other nations can have no right to claim its enjoyment, even though entitled to be treated as the most favored nation, unless by the reciprocal grant of the same equivalent." (Curiously, Adams' sobriquet was "Old Man Eloquent.")

After World War I, however, the U.S.—which originated the conditional most-favored-nation clause— found it no longer useful, since the condition allowed other countries to discriminate against U.S. exports. "By offering complete and nondiscriminatory treatment," reads a 1974 staff study by the Senate Finance Committee, "the United States sought to obtain the same treatment from other countries . . . Authority for the U.S. to offer unconditional MFN was included in the Tariff Act of 1922 . . . The Trade Agreements Act of 1934 included an unconditional MFN provision and made it a requirement of United States domestic law." From this open policy flowed the U.S. participation in the international General

Agreement on Tariffs and Trade (GATT), which puts MFN in its first provision of Article 1.

The Cold War turned U.S. policy around again. In 1951, Congress directed President Truman to withdraw MFN status from Communist countries. He did so, excepting only Tito's Yugoslavia. When, in 1972, détente became the order of the day, another switch in MFN was sought: Nixon Administration trade experts, led by Peter Flanigan, lobbied to remove this barrier. The verbal approach Flanigan used was not to seek to make the Soviet Union "a most favored nation" (implying special favors to Russia, in the untutored mind) but "to end trade discrimination" ("discrimination" was a word most people were accustomed to being against).

However, when the USSR began to levy exit fees on emigrants, Senator Henry Jackson led Congress into forbidding the extension of most-favored-nation status to "non-market economy" nations which deny their citizens the right to emigrate; the Jackson-Vanik amendment to the Trade Act of 1974 enshrined the principle in law. (See QUIET DIPLOMACY.) For decades afterward, this became important in Sino-American relations, as successive Administrations used MFN to goad China into human rights improvements, especially in Tibet, and to refrain from missile sales to irresponsible regimes.

Proof that the 200-year-old phrase had permanently entered the language could be found in a *Newsweek* cover story (February 13, 1978) on the entertainment industry, which defined a Hollywood "Most Favored Nation Clause" as "a contractual promise to a star who signs early that no latecomer will get a better deal."

mountaintop, take him to the   a private promise, made prior to a conven tion, of high appointive office or a place on the ticket, in return for delegate support.

This phrase rarely appears in print but is current usage in spoken negotiations. "Take him to the mountaintop" implies, first, complete privacy in dealing—unbugged, unwitnessed conversation, promises made that would be denied if repeated. Second, the "mountaintop" offers a pulse-quickening view of the vista below, glimpses of far horizons that persuade the man with the delegates to come across and stay across. A typical use:

> "How's Jones in Kansas?"
>
> "Committed the wrong way. I think the other side promised him Secretary of Agriculture."
>
> "They took him to the mountaintop this early in the campaign?"
>
> "It's a busy mountaintop. I know two other guys who think they have that job sewed up."

In December 1967, Drew Pearson and Jack Anderson wrote that Senator Eugene McCarthy entered Democratic primaries opposing Lyndon Johnson because "McCarthy is bitter at the man who, he thinks, took him up on the mountain to the Vice Presidency, then pushed him off into the Atlantic City breakers."

The phrase appears as "take him up the mountain," "take him on the mountaintop," as well as "take him to the mountaintop."

Mountaintop also appears in labor relations, as "now we have to get them down off the mountaintop." In early stages of negotiations, a labor leader often makes unrealistic demands, fully expecting to scale them down for a settlement. However, his rank and file becomes enamored of items like a four-day week and other "asking prices," and the union leader at settlement time has to bring his own men "down off the mountaintop."

The phrase originates in the temp-

tation of Christ (Matthew 4:8-9): ". . . the devil taketh him up into an exceeding high mountain, and sheweth him all the kingdoms of the world and the glory of them; and saith unto him, All these things will I give thee, if thou wilt fall down and worship me." The stern, get-thee-behind-me response of Jesus led later political tempters to be both more specific and more successful.

See WALKING BACK THE CAT.

Movement, the in the nineteenth century, the progressive tradition; in the early twentieth century, organized labor; in the fifties, civil rights; in the sixties, an amalgam of civil rights and the NEW LEFT; in the seventies and eighties, feminism and the abortion-rights campaign; in the nineties, "TRUE BELIEVER conservatives."

Paul Jacobs and Saul Landau, in *The New Radicals* (1966), defined the phrase this way:

> The Movement is a melange of people, mostly young; organizations, mostly new; and ideals, mostly American. . . . Those in The Movement feel that modern American liberals have substituted empty rhetoric for significant content, obscured the principles of justice by administrative bureaucracy, sacrificed human values for efficiency, and hypocritically justified a brutal attempt to establish American hegemony over the world with sterile anti-Communism. . . .
>
> The new movement is also a revolt against the postwar "over-developed society," with its large bureaucracies in government, corporations, trade unions, and universities. To those in The Movement the new technologies of automation and cybernation, with their computers and memory-bank machines, are instruments of alienation, depersonalizing human relations to a frightening degree.

The labor movement and the civil rights movement had more clear-cut goals, and were readier to communicate their needs to the general public. The amorphous Movement of the sixties appeared to many Americans to have adopted the techniques of previous movements (sit-ins, protests, demonstrations, strikes) without their direction or national leadership.

Some leaders of the sixties Movement were anti-leadership. Tom Hayden warned of "maintaining a dependency on fixed leaders, who inevitably develop interests in maintaining the organization (or themselves) and lose touch with the immediate aspirations of the rank and file." Stokely Carmichael of SNCC, trying to avoid the taint of leadership, assumed the title of "field hand." Vocabulary of the Movement leans heavily on "participate," "initiate," "hang-ups," "community," and "people" (never "masses").

Did the Movement of the sixties lose its battle? Not so, *Commentary* magazine editor Norman Podhoretz told television interviewer Ben Wattenberg in June 1978: "The movement with a capital M, as it used to be called, was made up of a kind of a political arm and a cultural arm. The political arm was called The NEW LEFT, the cultural arm was called the COUNTERCULTURE . . . I think it disappeared because it won. Its critique of American society and institutions came to be widely accepted by people who were not themselves members of that movement . . . You see an ominous growth of neo-isolationist sentiment . . . the idea that the United States is not a benevolent force in world affairs but a malevolent force."

The Movement moved in the seventies to the efforts of women to gain equality in U.S. society, centered often on the campaign to ratify the Equal Rights Amendment. Often called the *Women's Movement*, it made great strides in the eighties and nineties in advancing women's careers in the labor force (despite the GLASS CEILING), in filling political positions, in promoting causes such as PRO-CHOICE activism, and in countering sexual harassment. See SEXISM; WOMEN'S LIB.

In the 1990s, Pat Buchanan referred to his right-wing supporters as "Movement conservatives," distinguishing them from "neo-cons."

movers and shakers opinion leaders; influentials, especially those who are political or economic activists.

Mass-communications theorists like Columbia professor Paul I. Lazarsfeld hold that there is a "two-step flow" of most communication: from source, to opinion leader in that idea's category, to the great number of people.

"Movers and shakers" is applied to both the source group and the transmitting opinion leaders; a strict definition would narrow it down to those who decide policy, develop new ideas, and—most important—make it happen.

Clinton Rossiter explained the self-image of Democratic voters: "They delight in the whole sweep of American history, certain that they have been the 'movers and shakers' and their opponents, whether Federalists or Whigs or Republicans, the 'stick-in-the-muds.'"

Walter Heller used the phrase to describe how Lyndon Johnson sought to achieve consensus, using both private meetings and public pronouncements: ". . . this method combines Presidential persuasion and education of hundreds of the country's 'movers and shakers' *in person* in small White House meetings . . . with public persuasion of millions of citizens by performance under the resulting policies and legislation."

The phrase was coined by nineteenth-century English poet Arthur O'Shaughnessy:

We are the music-makers,
And we are the dreamers
   of dreams . . .
Yet we are the movers and shakers of the
   world forever, it seems.

The phrase is often used with a faint note of derision at those who believe themselves to be powerful. See MUCKEY-MUCKS.

moving the goalposts changing the rules in the middle of the game; allowing an unfair advantage.

As an accusation of unfairness, *moving the goalposts* comes from the language of games. Peter Stothard, while United States editor of the *Times* of London, defined the expression: "This term is British and means 'changing the terms of a debate or a conflict after it's been started.' I expect it's more from children's playing, where the sticks marking the goal can be moved, than from organized football. It's a very common term now, both in politics and in social conversation. A child, for instance, who's been told to keep his room clean for an extra 50 pence a week, and then doesn't get the extra money, may say, 'Hey, you've moved the goalposts.'"

The expression was used in 1978 by Albert V. Casey of American Airlines in a statement to the *Washington Post* about deregulation: "'They keep moving the goal posts,' he lamented."

Within a decade, *moving the goalposts* had moved into political usage. In the late 1980s, a British diplomat used the term after the Reykjavik summit meeting to object to the way "the Russians have withdrawn from that understanding. . . . They have moved the goal posts."

Use of the term is always condemnatory. President Bush played with the phrase in a 1990 talk about his criteria for trade with South Africa: "These conditions are clear-cut and are not open to reinterpretation, and I do not believe in moving the goalposts."

Mr. Clean. See BOY SCOUT.

Mr. Dooley. See DOOLEY, MR.; SUPREME COURT FOLLOWS THE ELECTION RETURNS; BEANBAG.

Mr. Nice Guy everybody's friend; a practitioner of the politics of pacification.

"Nice guys finish last" was the dictum of Brooklyn Dodger baseball manager Leo Durocher in the 1940s (though his actual words were "Nice guys finish seventh"—at that time, last place in the National League), and to a degree this has application to modern politics. Writing about Senator Edmund Muskie in October 1971, David Broder of the *Washington Post* pointed out: "Tagged as a cautious, cool Mr. Nice Guy by most observers, the Maine Senator has turned into a deliberately hard-nosed, independent character, often seeming to go out of his way to demonstrate he is his own man."

As used in politics, the appellation connotes scorn; when a man tries too hard not to make enemies, he appears to lack leadership potential. A skillful politician is one who takes positions that seem uncompromising and forthright—and still does not make enemies.

A variation appeared in the seventies: "good guys," usually plural, was used to mean WHITE HATS or heroes, and intended to be ironically simplistic, as in the good-guy–bad-guy Western movies. Jimmy Breslin's 1975 book about Congressman Thomas P. ("Tip") O'Neill was titled *How the Good Guys Finally Won* (over the "bad guys" of the Nixon Administration).

"Nice guy," as in "Mr. Nice Guy," connotes weakness, while "good guy" has an aura of moral strength (see FIGHT THE GOOD FIGHT). On February

7, 1978, the *Washington Post* ran an article by Lynn Darling on local government officials who found the demands of the political life too demanding—the headline was "Good Guys Bow Out"; and the "good guys" were defined as "These are the types who spend a vacation writing a rent control bill and read much of the night on Wednesday to prepare for a hearing on Friday because all of Thursday will be taken up by a work session . . . In high school, these men and those like them might have been the class grinds, the kind who got straight A's, were captain of the debate team, worked two paper routes and won the science fair to boot."

"No more Mr. Nice Guy" is a warning before retaliation, the end of passive acceptance of unfairness or harsh treatment, the opening pitch of HARDBALL.

This gloves-off warning was popularized in the 1970s. Richard Nixon was asked by the *Washington Post* in 1977 about his response to Vietnam War protests: "When was the moment when in effect, you said, 'OK, no more Mr. Nice Guy'?"

It may have originated as the punch line of a macabre joke: A group of neo-Nazis sought out Hitler, alive and hiding in the Argentine, to lead them in their quest for world domination. "OK," he replied, "but this time—no more Mr. Nice Guy."

The political use of this threat-turned-cliché intensified during the late 1980s. A political consultant was quoted in the *Los Angeles Times* as suggesting that "losing opponents might consider the hardball adage 'Nice guys finish last,' and opt for a 'no more Mr. Nice Guy' strategy in the future."

In the middle of 1992, when James Baker took control of George Bush's failing reelection campaign, Jim Hoagland of the *Washington Post* reported on the change in political strategy:

"And this time, no more Mr. Nice Guy. Baker knows he is not facing the mild-mannered Michael Dukakis in this shootout."

A Clinton aide was quoted in a 1993 *Wall Street Journal* story about dealing with Congress: "No More Mr. Nice Guy."

See BOY SCOUT.

Mr. Republican   a sobriquet for the recognized embodiment of party leader; not always helpful in the general election.

Putting "Mr." before a generic word and applying the name to an individual locks up that area—but may also lock a man inside that area. Senator Robert A. Taft of Ohio was "Mr. Republican" in 1952, but it only served to emphasize the "can't win" charge, since Democratic votes are needed for a Republican nominee to win.

Similarly, Barry Goldwater was styled "Mr. Conservative," which focused and dramatized his specific strength, but limited his appeal.

Richard Nixon, in his introduction of Goldwater at the 1964 Republican convention, sought to overcome the problem in a progression of phrases:

> He is the man who earned and proudly carries the title of Mr. Conservative.
> He is the man who, by the action of this Convention, is now Mr. Republican.
> And he is the man who, after the greatest campaign in history, will be Mr. President—Barry Goldwater.

Mr. X   a sinister figure who cannot be named; or, the nom de plume of George Kennan.

Mr. X—sometimes called Mr. Big—occasionally appears as a character in the last few days of an election campaign. In the New York City mayoralty race of 1953, Manhattan Borough President Robert F. Wagner, Jr., choice of the regular Democrats, was being overshadowed in the press by independent Democrat Rudolph Halley, former chief counsel of the Kefauver crime-investigating committee. A Wagner backer was given some antiracketeering information damaging to local Republicans, but with not enough proof to substantiate a charge against a specific individual. He passed the information to the candidate, who alluded to it in a "Who is Mr. X?" broadcast—capturing the headlines and the curiosity of the voters during the final weekend of the campaign. Wagner was elected.

The danger of any "Mr. X" charge is in mistiming; it must come toward the very end of a campaign, or else voters begin demanding that the speaker answer his own question or shut up. Mishandled, it can also appear to be a desperate last-minute ruse, which it sometimes is.

This is an extension of a technique New York Mayor James J. Walker used to infuriate Fiorello La Guardia, whom he defeated decisively in 1929 despite a variety of scandal charges against the Walker administration. "The question I would like to ask Mr. La Guardia," Walker would say solemnly in many of his speeches, "is: What was he doing in Providence on a certain day in 1926?" Of course, Walker had no evidence La Guardia had ever been in Providence, or if he had been, what he was doing there. It succeeded in needling his opponent.

In foreign affairs, "Mr. X" is now a well-known figure. George F. Kennan, a U.S. State Department policy planner in 1947, wrote a long memorandum to his superiors urging a new, tougher policy toward Communist expansionary aims. Part of the memo was printed in *Foreign Affairs* under the title "Sources of Soviet Conduct," signed by "X." (See CONTAINMENT.) Kennan later surfaced as one of the United States' chief planners on Soviet affairs.

muckey-mucks (muck-a-mucks)
big shots; term of derision for party leaders by party workers.

The expression is still often heard as "high muck-a-muck" because of its probable derivation from Chinook jargon, *hiu* (plenty) *muckamuck* (food); hence, one who has plenty to eat, or a man of power, a big wheel.

The *Democratic State Journal* of California in 1856 wrote: "The professors—the high 'Muck-a-Mucks'—tried fusion, and produced confusion." A comic-strip character in the *Chicago Tribune* in 1947 said, "They's a high-mucky-muck in th' radio business vacationin' here, so we gotta be good."

Synonyms are PARTY ELDERS, INNER CLUB, POWER BROKERS, and BOSS.

For other American Indian expressions in politics, see SACHEM; TAMMANY TIGER; GREAT WHITE FATHER; MUGWUMP; RAINMAKER.

muckraker a journalist who searches through the activities of public organizations seeking to expose conduct contrary to the public interest.

The term, while still used to describe some columnists, reached its greatest popularity in the days of the crusading magazines between 1903 and 1909.

Theodore Roosevelt first used it in its present meaning at a time when he was suspected of being antibusiness by the businessmen who formed an important part of his own Republican party. Articles exposing certain activities in business had already shocked the public when President Roosevelt, first in an off-the-record Gridiron Club speech and later in a speech at the laying of the cornerstone for the new House of Representatives Office Building on April 14, 1906, warned that this kind of antibusiness journalism could go too far. Roosevelt said "the men with the muckrakes are often indispensable to the well being of society; but only if they know when to stop raking the muck, and to look upward to the celestial crown above them, to the crown of worthy endeavor. There are beautiful things above and round about them; and if they gradually grow to feel that the whole world is nothing but muck, their power of usefulness is gone."

Roosevelt's reference was to the Man with the Muck Rake in Bunyan's *Pilgrim's Progress*, the man who could never look any way but down; when offered a celestial crown, he refused to gaze upward and continued to rake the filth on the floor.

The President was repeating a phrase he had found successful at the Gridiron Club dinner of March 17, 1906. Then he had used it more strenuously to describe men who attacked those who had acquired means merely because of wealth "but [who] were prepared to condone crimes of great brutality, including murder, if those committing them can obtain the support of powerful labor organizations."

It was not completely new to politics; as early as 1871 it was used to describe the ambitious politician who rakes in muck, hoping to come up with valuable ammunition.

Mr. Roosevelt's version caught on immediately. One of the most famous—though least virulent—of the school, Ray Stannard Baker, was hailed by a friend on the street almost immediately after the speech with the cheery salutation "Hello, Muckraker." Baker said he didn't know what was meant at the moment but was quickly educated.

Lincoln Steffens, whose articles in *McClure's* magazine made him the leader of the school, wrote in his autobiography: "I did not intend to be a muckraker. I did not know that I was one till President Roosevelt picked the name out of Bunyan's *Pilgrim's Progress* and pinned it on us and even then he said that he did not mean me."

He and others such as Baker and Ida Tarbell, did not long resent the word. According to historian Mark Sullivan, "all the writers of exposure accepted the epithet that was meant for some of them, and in the eyes of most of the public, 'muckraker' became a term of approval."

For a short time the pages of *McClure's, Collier's*, the *American Magazine, Cosmopolitan*, and others were rife with stories of misconduct, previously sheltered from public exposure. In its day, when the exposés in the popular magazines came weekly, a favorite muckraker story was of the wealthy Alaskan miner who walked into a magazine office demanding a crusade. Said the editor, "You certainly are a progressive, aren't you?"

"Progressive!" the miner roared. "I'm a full-fledged insurgent. Why, man, I subscribe to thirteen magazines."

Today's muckrakers prefer the term "investigative reporter." The breed was criticized by Bert Lance, President Carter's first Director of the Office of Management and Budget (see IF IT AIN'T BROKE), who had been driven from office by press criticism of his financial affairs by the author. Lance warned the American Society of Newspaper Editors in April 1978 that censorship could follow press irresponsibility:

The press has always had its share of professional cynics, as quite properly it should. But that once healthy dash of cynicism appears to have become a pervasive and destructive cynicism, another sad legacy of Vietnam and Watergate.

Along with this unhealthy climate of suspicion is a change in the standards governing publication of allegation, rumor and gossip, and an intense post-Watergate competition among investigative reporters. There are more muck*rakers* around these days than muck*makers.*

mudslinging   wild, unsubstantiated charges; a word, like "SMEAR," used to turn an attack back on the attacker.

"Calumniate! Calumniate! Some of it will always stick," advised Beaumarchais in *The Barber of Seville* in 1775. This was based on ancient Latin advice, *Fortiter calumniari, aliquia adhaerebit,* or "Throw plenty of dirt and some of it will be sure to stick."

Sometime after the Civil War, *dirt-throwing* picked up some water to become *mud-throwing, mud-gunning* and the word that gained pre-eminence, *mudslinging.* The *New York Tribune* of April 13, 1876, disagreed with the Latin dictum: "Mud doesn't stick to Mr. Blaine any better than it does to Mr. Bristow. The slander peddlers are having a bad season." The word was so well entrenched by 1878 that the *Tribune* could refer to it obliquely, as "the dredging machine was set at work again yesterday, and brought up a small load of sediment from the dirty stream of Louisiana politics."

Bruce Felknor, of the Fair Campaign Practices Committee, in the sixties classified six presidential campaigns as "spectacularly dirty": Jackson's first election, Lincoln's second, the Hayes-Tilden debacle, Cleveland's first election, Theodore Roosevelt's third campaign and the Hoover-Smith clash of 1928. Harry Truman agreed on the last, recalling: "Al Smith was given the nomination, and that set off the most vicious anti-Catholic, anti-Jewish, anti-Negro movement that we have ever had in any political campaign . . . there was more slander and mudslinging going on than at any time I can remember."

"Mudslinging" (from dirt-throwing) and "dirty politics" are obviously from the same source. "I was told repeatedly not to enter politics," said then-Governor Nelson Rockefeller, "that politics is a 'dirty' business. . . . Politics is the lifeblood of democracy. To call politics 'dirty' is to call democracy 'dirty.'"

Adlai Stevenson in 1954 combined a couple of earthy metaphors to put together a Confucianist epigram: "He who slings mud generally loses ground."

mugwump   bolter; MAVERICK.

Anyone who bolted his political party was a mugwump, especially those Republicans who refused to support the presidential candidacy of James Blaine in 1884. The true mugwump went a step further and gave his support to the Democratic nominee, Grover Cleveland of New York.

The first known use of the word was by John Eliot in his *Indian Bible,* published in 1663, from an Algonquian language, in which the word *mugquomp* is used to define a chief or another individual of high rank. See SACHEM.

In June 1884 it was popularized politically by the *New York Sun* and quickly became common parlance. The Republicans had met in convention and picked Blaine as their candidate. Many figures of stature (though not much influence) in the party decided they could not accept a man they felt was so corrupt. They met June 7, 1884, in Boston and decided to support Cleveland. The *Sun* jeeringly referred to them as "Little Mugwumps," meaning little men attempting to be big chiefs. Little they were not: their ranks sparkled with such names as President Eliot of Harvard, Carl Schurz, Charles Francis Adams, and George William Curtis.

The "little," in fact, was soon dropped; the term "mugwump" persisted and, indeed, those so labeled soon accepted and even affected the description after Admiral Horace Porter defined a mugwump as "a person educated beyond his intellect."

"Mugwumpery" or "mugwumpism" has persisted both here and in Great Britain to describe bolters, though most usually the term has been applied to independent Republicans.

Political lexicographers have always felt obligated to report that a mugwump was described by the *Blue Earth* (Minn.) *Post* in the early 1930s as "a sort of bird that sits on a fence with his mug on one side and his wump on the other."

Theodore Roosevelt, who was persuaded to party orthodoxy in 1884 by Henry Cabot Lodge of Massachusetts, called mugwumps "dudes"—they had also been called "pharisees." Roosevelt professed contempt for mugwumps through the years, right up to the time he bolted the Republican party and ran for the presidency as an independent in 1912.

multiculturalism. See MELTING POT.

multipolar world   a world view beyond East/West relations; a global strategic vision recognizing many different centers of power.

The simpler adjective *bipolar* dates back to 1810; its use in twentieth-century politics was to indicate two opposed centers of power, the U.S. and the U.S.S.R. As early as 1859, however, *multipolar* was coined to describe the possibility of "having several poles." In political usage, the newer adjective acknowledged more than two loci of power, as in "a multipolar world."

In 1980, Alexander Haig spoke with the *Washington Post* about the Soviet threat. The newspaper paraphrased parts of General Haig's comments, reporting, "The bipolar world of the early postwar years has given way to a complex multipolar world with three competitive centers of Marxist influence—one in Moscow, one in Peking and one in the revolutionary Third World."

Henry Kissinger helped popularize the expression. In a 1992 column about the possibilities of peaceful coexistence in the Middle East, Dr. Kissinger wrote, "The readiness to run military risks in faraway countries will diminish in a multipolar world in which doctrines of collective security and U.N. actions rule the day."

Political commentators also considered the effect of this phrase on the 1992 Presidential election. A *Newsday* editorial during the campaign suggested that "the demise of the communist threat and the emergence of a multipolar world has left the G.O.P. without one of its central organizing principles."

See WEST, THE.

Munich analogy   symbol of a place of appeasement leading to war.

Cities that are the scene of a great event, when they are not major capitals that are the scene of too many other great occasions, are often identified with the meaning of that event.

Yalta was the scene of the last meeting of Roosevelt, Churchill, and Stalin toward the end of World War II. "Another Yalta" has come to be used as a warning against gullibility in dealings with Communist leaders.

Guernica, a small city in Spain, was bombed by German aircraft in support of the Franco forces in April 1937; its obliteration came to mean ruthless attacks against defenseless cities, until it was superseded by "another Rotterdam."

Sarajevo, the capital of Bosnia and Herzegovina, was the scene on June 28, 1914, of the assassination of the Archduke Ferdinand, which history texts dubbed "one of the immediate (but not underlying) causes of the World War." "Another Sarajevo" means a spark that ignites a major conflict. This was recalled during the city's siege as Serbian forces sought to drive out Muslim Bosnians after the breakup of Yugoslavia in 1992–93. (See ETHNIC CLEANSING.)

Munich was the scene of an agreement between British Prime Minister Neville Chamberlain, French Premier Édouard Daladier, Hitler, and Mussolini on September 30, 1938, granting Germany the Czech territory of the Sudetenland as well as its defense border. The Czechs were not present at their "sellout." Today, "another Munich" means an agreement that appeases an aggressor at the expense of a weak nation and only leads to greater war later.

Writer Bernard Fall, killed in Vietnam in 1967, wrote a year earlier: "If Munich is not a good example of how to settle the Vietnamese conflict, neither is Guernica, or Sarajevo."

See PEACE FOR OUR TIME; VIETNAM SYNDROME.

musical metaphors "For if the trumpet give an uncertain sound, who shall prepare himself to the battle?" (I Corinthians 14:8) This Biblical musical metaphor has occasionally been applied to political leadership; former Army Chief of Staff General Maxwell Taylor used it as the title of a book, *The Uncertain Trumpet*, attacking the downgrading of conventional army units in the fifties.

The Defense Secretary who later worked closely with Taylor, Robert McNamara (see WHIZ KIDS), became the subject of a musical metaphor. "McNamara's Band," the nickname for his organization, was taken from a turn-of-the-century song beginning "My name is McNamara, I'm the leader of the band . . ."

New York Mayor Fiorello La Guar-

dia orchestrated his administration with sirens chasing fire engines and explosions of temper against "tinhorn gamblers and two-bit politicians." One night at Radio City Music Hall, listening to the organist at intermission, "the Little Flower" explained his theory of administration to his City Council president and protégé, Newbold Morris: "Newbold, that's how our city must be run. Like that organist, you must keep both hands on the keyboard and both feet on the pedals—and never let go!"

A celestial harp was used subtly and skillfully by Abraham Lincoln as a metaphor in his first inaugural address, perhaps the best metaphor of any kind used by any U.S. President: "The mystic chords of memory, stretching from every battlefield and every land, will yet swell the chorus of the Union when again touched, as surely they will be, by the better angels of our nature." The composing of this passage, originally suggested by Secretary of State William Seward, is described in the Introduction to this dictionary.

Playing on President Clinton's ability to play a musical instrument, a pundit in 1993 criticized his "uncertain saxophone."

must list. See HIT LIST.

mutual and balanced. See CODE WORDS.

muzzle to censor; to stifle criticism; an attack word on an attempt to present a united front.

Controversy-seeking journalists have applied the word to the requirement by Eisenhower, Kennedy, and Carter Administrations that all policy speeches by military men be approved by the government and changed or suppressed if they differ materially with official policy.

The best-known example occurred during the first week in office of President Kennedy. The Russians, at the time, were holding several American fliers whose reconnaissance plane had been shot down near Russian waters. Negotiations for their return were in progress. The Chief of Naval Operations, Admiral Arleigh Burke, voluntarily submitted a speech which had a strong anti-Soviet tone. When the speech was toned down and the fact became known, the President was accused of "muzzling" the military.

Kennedy replied: "If a well-known, high-ranking military figure makes a speech which affects foreign policy or possibly military policy, I think that the people and the countries abroad have a right to expect that that speech represents the opinion of the national government. . . . The purpose of the review . . . is to make sure that . . . government speaks with one voice."

An investigation by a senatorial committee headed by Senator Strom Thurmond sought to equate the policy with censorship and being SOFT ON COMMUNISM. The committee received encouragement from a statement made by former President Eisenhower, who somewhat deplored a similar policy of speech review required during his two terms, saying that "after mature consideration" he now felt the policy should be dropped.

Columnist Walter Lippmann felt otherwise, writing, "the talkativeness of American military men, most of them reading speeches written by professional speech writers who are paid by the government, is an international scandal."

The word has been used in a purely political context since at least 1880, when *Harper's Weekly* described a "unit rule" (see GAG RULE) as "a muzzle and gag unworthy of honorable men." In the 1952 campaign, Adlai Stevenson, speaking of the original, liberal Republican supporters of General Eisenhower's candidacy, said their voices seemed to have been absent since the convention. "Someone seems to have muzzled them. It may be they sounded too much like Democrats."

Reporters insist the public has a RIGHT TO KNOW the differences of opinion within the military establishment; Administration officials feel that a general's lobbying encroaches on civilian control of the military.

Despite "the word" from the White House, generals and admirals find a way to leak their points of view to friendly correspondents. A muzzle prevents a dog from biting and barking, but not from growling.

my (use of possessive pronoun) used as "my ambassador," either a slip of the tongue leading to an attack for royalist tendencies, or a deliberate presidential effort to undercut the State Department.

In the campaign of 1940, Franklin Roosevelt referred to Joseph P. Kennedy, Ambassador to the Court of St. James's, as "my ambassador," a phrase which the Republicans promptly pounced on as proof of his dictatorial ambitions in their "no-third term" drive. Similarly, in 1966, Lyndon Johnson played into Republican hands with a reference to "my Congress," giving Richard Nixon an opportunity to flay the "do-anything Congress," a play on Harry Truman's DO-NOTHING CONGRESS.

Abraham Lincoln was attacked in 1858 for his use of "I" in speeches. The *Burlington Gazette* said: ". . . he is known all over Suckerdom by the name of 'the Perpendicular pronoun.'" But President Andrew Johnson drew the most fire on the subject—the *Cleveland Press* made a count of personal and possessive pronouns in an 1866 Johnson speech: "This humble individual, one; myself, two; me, nine; my, 28; I, 69. That's not much, only 109 allusions to himself in a 15 minute speech . . . President Johnson is a my-ty man."

Although John F. Kennedy did not refer to "my" ambassadors in any speech, Arthur Schlesinger, Jr., made this point: "He felt this [the State Department] in some particular sense 'his' department . . . in the relationship between the President and the ambassadors, there had been, it is true, a slippage since Roosevelt's day. Roosevelt regarded them correctly as 'my' ambassadors and encouraged them to supplement their reports to the State Department by personal communication with him." Ambassadors like Kenneth Galbraith in India and George Kennan in Yugoslavia often communicated directly with President Kennedy.

Dwight Eisenhower, a team player, consciously avoided the possessive pronoun. "I don't believe," wrote reporter Robert Donovan, "that Eisenhower has ever used the expression 'my administration' or 'my cabinet.' He speaks of *the* Cabinet or *the* administration."

A speech General Eisenhower made in 1945 in New York City at a dinner in his honor as a war hero suggests that his selection or rejection of the personal pronoun had always been deliberate: "You have great hospitals in your city that are filled with wounded men. I call them 'my wounded men'; they came back from my theatre. I don't want to see any more of them there, ever."

my friends FDR's use of a salutation to establish a warm, personal bond between himself and his audience.

Running for the New York State Senate in 1910, Franklin Roosevelt admired the way his fellow campaigner, Richard Connell, running for U.S.

congressman in that area, established quick rapport with his listeners. FDR copied Connell's "My friends" for that and subsequent campaigns, but the phrase became identified with him because of the lilt of his pronunciation and the special requirement for warmth in radio addresses. No longer was the audience "vast" and "out there"; most listeners were in small groups in their own living rooms, and FDR pressed the intimacy with frequent use of "you and I know . . ."

Roosevelt probably did not know of the trouble the phrase caused for one of his predecessors as governor of New York, "Peace Democrat" Horatio Seymour. Trying to calm a group of draft rioters at City Hall in 1863, he opened his remarks with "My friends"; Republicans attacked him for being unduly friendly to those "copperheads" who opposed the Civil War.

Salutations are overlooked as formalities by most speakers, which (as Seymour discovered) is a mistake. Abraham Lincoln chose his salutations with great care: to the citizens of Springfield, Illinois, upon his departure, he used "My friends," because many of them were his lifelong friends; at Gettysburg he used no salutation at all, appropriate in that atmosphere of solemnity; in his inaugural addresses he said "Fellow countrymen," which was traditional and redundant.

In 1781 John Witherspoon, president of Princeton and coiner of AMERICANISM in the sense of a word peculiarly American, unsuccessfully made the case against "fellow countrymen" as a salutation:

Fellow countrymen. This is a word of very frequent use in America. It has been heard in public orations from men of the first character, and may be daily seen in newspaper publications. It is an evident tautology, for the last word expresses fully the meaning of both. If you open any dictionary you will find the word countryman signifies one born in the same country. You may say fellow citizens, fellow soldiers, fellow subjects, fellow Christians, but not fellow countrymen.

Napoleon gave a martial ring to his addresses and messages to his troops: a simple, forceful "Soldiers." By contrast, the Selective Service system bureaucratically addressed its soldiers-to-be with a ludicrous "Greeting" (not "Greetings"), and a draftee became known as one who "got his greetings."

Nicolai Lenin made "Comrades" famous to the point where all communists were called, often derisively, comrades.

Chief Tecumseh addressed General "Tippecanoe" Harrison with a translation of a dignified Indian greeting: "Friend and Brother." Members of the American labor movement address letters to each other as "Dear Sir and Brother," harking back to more fraternal times.

Jefferson chose "Friends and fellow citizens," and both William Howard Taft and John F. Kennedy preferred "Fellow citizens," with Harry Truman and Dwight Eisenhower leaning toward "My fellow Americans." During the 1940 campaign, Republican nominee Wendell Willkie made "fellow Americans" his own, rasping out his hoarse "Feller Amurrricans . . ."

The most effective "example" of the use of a salutation as a weapon is supposed to be the opening of Franklin Roosevelt's speech to the Daughters of the American Revolution following a dispute about the DAR's emphasis on white Anglo-Saxon lineage. FDR did *not* begin his speech, as legend has it, with "Fellow immigrants." The closest he came to this was a line in his speech to the DAR of April 21, 1938: "Remember, remember always, that all of us, and you and I especially, are descended from immigrants and revolutionists."

It is a shame that "Fellow immigrants" is apocryphal—it would have been the most pointed salutation in history.

myth frozen point of view attacked by John Kennedy; later, ironically, used to describe the aura of legend around Kennedy.

"Myths Respecting American Government" was the title of a speech given by President John F. Kennedy at Yale University, June 11, 1962. "Mythology distracts us everywhere—in government as in business, in politics as in economics, in foreign affairs as in domestic policy." In considering the "myth and reality in our national economy," he said that the dialogue between business and government was "clogged by illusion and platitude," adding, "For the great enemy of the truth is very often not the lie—deliberate, contrived and dishonest—but the myth, persistent, persuasive and unrealistic. Too often we hold fast to the clichés of our forebears. We subject all facts to a prefabricated set of interpretations. We enjoy the comfort of opinion without the discomfort of thought."

The Yale speech was a left-handed holding out of an olive branch to business leaders convinced that the Kennedy Administration was souring on them. (See s.o.b.) Historian Richard Hofstadter had used "The Agrarian Myth and Commercial Realities" as a chapter title in a 1955 book.

Senator J. William Fulbright picked up the "myth and reality" theme in a foreign-affairs context two years later: "We are clinging to old myths in the face of new realities, and we are seeking to escape the contradictions by narrowing the permissible bounds of public discussion, by relegating an increasing number of ideas and viewpoints to a growing category of 'UN-THINKABLE THOUGHTS.'" Included among the "old myths" in this speech (which became expanded into a book entitled *Old Myths and New Realities*) were U.S. policy regarding Cuba, Panama, and Vietnam.

Black author James Baldwin also picked up the myth motif. He wrote in *The Fire Next Time*:

> The American Negro has the great advantage of having never believed that collection of myths to which white Americans cling: that their ancestors were all freedom-loving heroes, that they were born in the greatest country the world has ever seen, or that Americans are invincible in battle and wise in peace, that Americans have always dealt honorably with Mexicans and Indians and all other neighbors or inferiors, that American men are the world's most direct and virile, that American women are pure. Negroes know far more about white Americans than that . . .

Critics of Kennedy also liked the myth phraseology. Author Victor Lasky published a scathing attack on Kennedy in 1963 titled *JFK: The Man and the Myth*. The book was climbing on the best-seller lists until November, when it was withdrawn after the assassination, not to be marketed again for nearly fifteen years. With the martyrdom of a youthful President, the Kennedy mystique or image did soon achieve the proportions of an ancient myth. Tom Wicker referred to the myth in the *New York Times*:

> For my part, I reject the myth . . . I refuse to believe that any but a particular light went out . . . Above all, in Kennedy's case or any other, I refuse to deny the harsh reality of death—that life goes on anyway, not unchanged, for the death of any man must diminish the sum of humanity, but undaunted, unabated in all its glory and misery. That is the meaning of the "ghastly futility" at Dallas. That is what the Kennedy myth distorts.

N

nabob. See NATTERING NABOBS OF NEGATIVISM.

name of the game the goal; the quintessence; the heart of the matter.

Talking about U.S. foreign policy goals in Europe, presidential National Security Adviser (later Ford Foundation head) McGeorge Bundy said in 1966: "Settlement is the name of the game." Senator Frank Church added: "If we are going to play the game, we must remember that the ball is labeled 'relations with the Soviet Union.' If we are not going to play, we will discover that the game will go on without us, and we will soon become spectators in Europe rather than participants."

Campaign literature for Governor George Romney, put out by the Romney for President organization in 1967, carried a banner headline: "Winning is the Name of the Game." This slogan emphasized Romney's early strength in public opinion polls against President Johnson, subtly pressing the "Nixon can't win" theme.

Brooding about the decline of the Broadway column after the collapse of a New York newspaper in May 1967, columnist Robert Sylvester told the *New York Times:* "Now Lee Mortimer is dead, Dorothy Kilgallen is dead, Danton Walker is dead, Louis Sobol is retired. Some of these people were the powerhouses. Some of these people were the name of the game."

In the seventies, the locution was often replaced by "what it's all about," as "Settlement is what it's all about"; or "where it's at," as "Winning is where it's at." But the expression *name of the game* continued to be popular. In July 1978 *Newsweek* averred: "The name of the game is to get the U.S. to cut its oil imports." And Desmond Cory, in *The Circe Complex* (1975), wrote: "Ergonomics, baby. That's the name of the game." In the eighties, the name of the game became "the bottom line" or "net net."

See SPORTS METAPHORS.

nation of shopkeepers derisive description of England; meant to imply small-minded, business-dominated, greedy people.

Earliest known use was not in a pejorative sense. Josiah Tucker, Dean of Gloucester Cathedral (1712–68), wrote in 1763: "What is true of a Shopkeeper is true of a Shop-keeping nation."

The phrase was given currency in 1776 by Adam Smith in *Wealth of Nations:* "To found a great empire for the sole purpose of raising up a people of customers may at first sight appear a project fit only for a nation of shopkeepers. It is, however, a project altogether unfit for a nation of shopkeepers; but extremely fit for a nation whose Government is influenced by shopkeepers."

The phrase was probably already in current usage when Smith used it; on August 1, 1776, American revolutionary Samuel Adams reportedly said in Philadelphia: "Men who content themselves with the semblance of truth and a display of words talk much of our obligations to Great Britain for protection. Had she a single eye to our advantage? A nation of shopkeepers are very seldom so disinterested. Let us not be so amused with words; the extension of commerce was her object."

The phrase became secure in the political lexicon when Napoleon Bonaparte applied it in scorn: *"L'Angleterre est une nation des boutiquiers"* ("England is a nation of shopkeepers").

native reserves. See HOMELAND.

nattering nabobs of negativism

a new version of a denunciation of pessimists as "prophets of gloom and doom." (See GLOOM AND DOOM, PROPHETS OF.)

In the congressional campaigns of 1970, alliteration was one device Vice President Spiro T. Agnew used to call attention to his speeches. "Pusillanimous pussyfooters" and "vicars of vacillation" were his targets, and the phrases had a ring that reporters could not ignore. After the first few speeches, the looked-for alliteration was delivered tongue-in-cheek, culminating in a display of oratorical pyrotechnics in San Diego on September 11, 1970. Working with the Vice President on that speech, this writer offered a choice of alliterations to paral-

lel the Stevenson "prophets of gloom and doom" phrase, but the VP chose to go with both: "In the United States today, we have more than our share of the nattering nabobs of negativism. They have formed their own 4-H Club—the 'hopeless, hysterical hypochondriacs of history.'"

As intended, the line got a laugh from the audience; it was taken seriously by James Reston of the *New York Times,* who called it "the worst example of alliteration in American history." (See Harding's "not nostrums but normalcy, not revolution but restoration, not agitation but adjustment . . . not experiment but equipoise . . ." under ALLITERATION.) Columnist William F. Buckley, Jr., picked it up to apply to the British Prime Minister's problems over the sale of arms to South Africa: "Heath's point was that he has not been elected Her Majesty's first minister in order to take orders on matters affecting English security from nattering nabobs of negativism."

In the construction of the phrase, negativism was the basic word. A practitioner, beginning with *n*, was added next; nabob is a Hindi word for governor, and the word in English has come to mean a self-important potentate, carrying a jocular connotation. (See John Adams's 1776 use under SACHEM.) Nattering, the offbeat adjective that made the phrase memorable, was the last to be found, and its meaning of "complaining" was disputed by columnist Stewart Alsop, who insisted that the word was of British origin and meant "chattering."

The reason this entry is written with such dreary authority is that this lexicographer was the coiner, while serving as a speechwriter-on-loan to Mr. Agnew in the fall of 1970. The unwritten Speechwriters' Code, which proscribes writers from claiming their clients' prose as their own, was suspended in this case because the disgraced former Vice President publicly ascribed the phrase to this scribe, requiring him to deny repeatedly authorship of other Agnewisms such as "effete corps of impudent snobs," "When you've seen one slum, you've seen 'em all," and INSTANT ANALYSIS.

The phrase had legs. From the *Washington Star* of December 20, 1977: "Ray Blanton, the Tennessee governor who's constantly being castigated by political rivals as well as those nattering nabobs of negativism, the media . . . says he's not going to answer reporters' questions any longer 'unless you report the positive side.'" And from *USA Today* of August 20, 1992: "Those 'nattering nabobs of negativism' in the media . . . are under fire again, and a review of network and newspaper stories show that Bush's treatment at the hands of 15,000 reporters has been rocky."

The phrase helped repopularize "nabob," and the word—one cut below a "nizam" in Hindi—is now synonymous with SATRAP, PANJAN-DRUM, POOH-BAH, high MUCKEY-MUCKS, and other members of the POWER ELITE. But some writers have to be different: in the *New York Times Magazine* (January 15, 1978), humorist S. J. Perelman used an alternate Hindi spelling—nawab—in a description of the patrons of Manhattan's "21" Club: "Here congregated tycoon and political nawab, screen idol and press overlord, rock star and capo of capos, secure in the knowledge that no losers were present. Here the illuminati rubbed elbows with the cognoscenti, publishers rubbed knees with nascent lady novelists, male dress designers rubbed thighs and spat at each other like cats. The drumfire of epigrams and the bray of egotism were rising to sawmill pitch . . ."

The device of dismissing doomsayers with alliteration is persistent and pervasive: President Clinton in 1993 denounced the "preachers of pessimism."

natural rights freedoms inherent in humanhood; the birthright of autonomous individuals which can be extended to government for purposes of the protection and development of society.

This term from Western philosophy, sometimes expressed as a singular, entered the political vocabulary in a 1689 translation of a treatise by the Dutch philosopher Baruch Spinoza: "In Democratical Government, no man so transfers his own Natural Right to another, as for ever after to be excluded from consultation, but only transfers it upon the major part of the Society, of which he still makes one."

The ancient idea, known to the Greeks, was further developed by John Locke and Jean Jacques Rousseau. It became a central part of Thomas Jefferson's philosophy, expressed in the Declaration of Independence as *unalienable rights* (which some stylists believed should be *inalienable rights*) including "life, liberty and the pursuit of happiness."

Thomas Paine enlarged upon the theme, further enumerating these privileges in his 1791 tract on *The Rights of Man*: "the natural and imprescriptible rights of man; and these rights are liberty, property, security, and resistance of oppression." These were in contradistinction to the "divine right of kings."

Third World countries have asserted *natural rights* as well, often in the sense of entitlement to the earth's resources and the technological wealth of industrialized nations. The *National Journal* stated in a 1977 commentary on nuclear energy: "Many developing countries regard the possession of the world's most advanced technology as their natural right."

Still current in democratic debate, the phrase (both singular and plural) was used by Senator Gordon J. Humphrey, a conservative from New Hampshire, in a 1989 statement on freedom of speech: The Bill of Rights, he said, protects "the natural right to speak one's mind, however offensive that may be to the hearer. . . . It is a precious right, this binding the power of government so it cannot begin to interfere in the natural rights of any human being."

The subject arose during the controversial hearings on the nomination of Clarence Thomas to the Supreme Court. "One of the more curious displays of cultural illiteracy," wrote the *New York Times*, despite its opposition to the Thomas nomination, "has been the consternation and bafflement created by Judge Clarence Thomas's expressions of esteem for 'natural law.' For some of the critics, it was as though the man had let slip a reference to torture by thumbscrews." Harvard Law Professor Laurence Tribe came back with this: "My objection is not necessarily to 'natural law' thinking, which I agree has a venerable history and much to commend it. My concern is with how Judge Thomas deploys natural-law approaches. He lavishes praise on an essay [by Lewis Lehrman] that uses 'natural law' to insist that all abortions must be outlawed as murder because the fetus has 'natural rights.'" In his hearings, Judge Thomas defused the issue by saying, "My interest in exploring natural law and natural rights was purely in the context of political theory."

See HUMAN RIGHTS.

Neanderthal wing. See DINOSAUR WING.

negative advertising. See DAISY SPOT; -BASHING.

neoconservative a political philosophy that rejects the utopianism and egalitarianism espoused by liberals, but departs from conservatism by embracing collective insurance and cash payments to the needy; a temperate philosophy, not sharply ideological, that takes modern democratic capitalism to be the best course in most cases.

Neoconservatism (the word has triumphed over "the new conservatism") was spawned in the pages of a quarterly, the *Public Interest,* edited by Irving Kristol and Daniel Bell, published by Warren Manshel, and frequently contributed to by Daniel Patrick Moynihan and Seymour Martin Lipset. These former liberals were troubled by the failures of Lyndon Johnson's "Great Society" and dismayed at the way political orders throughout the world—especially the social democracies—were becoming statist and simultaneously less stable. When Keynesian economics began to fail to contain inflation, neoconservatives felt the economic basis for social democracy as it has been practiced began to erode. The last straw for many of the lifelong Democrats was the strident discontent of the youthful counterculture of the sixties, which made liberal elders uncomfortable with the culture that produced it. As it became fashionable all along the political spectrum to be alienated by "big government," that cultural chasm between "new" left and "old" left widened: many of the former liberals could not stomach the permissive attitudes toward pornography, homosexuality, and rejection of group responsibility so often espoused by the inheritors of liberalism.

What distinguished neoconservatism from the "old" conservatism? The novel feature of the new conservatism is a relaxed attitude toward collective responsibility: "A welfare state, properly conceived," wrote Irving Kristol in the *American Spectator* in 1977, "can be an integral part of a conservative society." Such a statement is conservative heresy; conservatism teaches that statism leads to a repression of individuality. But Kristol plunged ahead: "It is antisocialist, of course . . . but it is not upset by the fact that in a populous, complex, and affluent society, people may prefer to purchase certain goods and services collectively rather than individually. . . . People will always want security as much as they want liberty, and the 19th-century liberal-individualist notion that life for all of us should be an enterprise at continual risk is doctrinaire fantasy."

Kristol and "the *Public Interest* crowd," as the neoconservatives are frequently called, see liberal institutions such as Social Security to be bulwarks against further socialization. They hope the effect of their movement will be to remove utopian dreams from practical government. To the socialists (who want to center more power in the state), as well as to the "old" conservatives (who want to place more reliance on the individual), the neoconservatives say that the system the U.S. has now evolved "is certainly not the best of all possible worlds—but the evidence of the twentieth century is quite conclusive that it is the best of all available worlds. That makes it very much worth defending."

An early use of the phrase was by James Schall in *Time* (August 23, 1971): "Judaism and Christianity have always placed primacy in man. Now this primacy is attacked by what I call the neoconservative ecological approach to life." Senator Moynihan recalls that it was Michael Harrington, writer on poverty, who popularized the term at about that time in its present context.

Among political journalists, the word is now almost always clipped to "neocon." MOVEMENT conservatives think of neocons much as unabashed liberals think of moderates.

nepotism. See DYNASTY.

Nervous Nellies the easily upset; President Johnson's characterization of some critics of his Vietnam policy.

On May 17, 1966, the President spoke of "some Nervous Nellies and some who will become frustrated and bothered and break ranks under the strain. And some will turn on their own leaders and their own country, and on our own fighting men."

In slang, the word "nervous" has acquired the connotation of cowardly; "nervous in the service," Army slang, means a psychological disorder leading to a medical discharge, as well as a milder impatience or "itchiness." "Nice Nellie" is slang for prude.

Johnson's exact words show that he differentiated between "Nervous Nellies" and other dissenters, but the catch phrase was so strong that many critics of the policy soon used it as though Johnson had labeled all anti-involvement or anti-escalation forces "Nervous Nellies." A year later, the President added fuel to the fire with a remark about "cussers and doubters."

A useful political technique is to seize on a colorful phrase used by the opposition leader about some segment of your own group, and interpret it as though he referred to everyone opposed to him. For example, a Long Island, New York, candidate in 1962 called a bearded heckler a "greasy pig." The opposition promptly distributed banners and stickers with a drawing of a pig and urged voters to join the "greasy pig campaign." The candidate who made the remark, running in a "safe" district, was defeated; many voters had been convinced that he referred to all his opposition as "greasy pigs."

By 1975 the term had been parodied so often that it became part of the Johnson Administration lore, and was included in a satiric song in a Gridiron Club revue. To the tune of "A Wand'ring Minstrel, I," a reporter portraying Henry Kissinger sang:

A wandering merchant, I
Who deals in confrontation,
Détente and consternation
And schemes that mystify.
Bismarck and Metternich
And me and Machiavelli
I'm not a Nervous Nelly!
I've slippery rhetoric—
Yes, slippery rhetoric.

In May 1992, Andrew Rosenthal of the *New York Times* quoted a White House aide on the progress of the Bush reelection campaign: "It's Nervous Nellies that get unnerved this early in the game and depart from the track you're on."

neutralist a nation that refused alignment with either Communist bloc or Western bloc, acting as mediator between, or beneficiary of, both.

Laotian Premier Souvanna Phouma defined the art of being a neutralist in 1961: "I am a good friend to Communists abroad but I do not like them at home." *Neutral*—as for example, applied to Sweden and Switzerland during World War II—differs from *neutralist*, uncommitted, or *nonaligned* nation. In the U.S. a neutral is considered merely a nonbelligerent, but a neutralist (a term having a pejorative connotation from most Americans' point of view) was a nation that did not understand the threat of world Communism, or that cooperated with the U.S. only when it suited its interests and was not a good "ally" in a pinch.

This is a far cry from Woodrow Wilson's explanation of U.S. neutrality in 1915: "The basis of neutrality is not indifference; it is not self-interest. The basis of neutrality is sympathy for mankind. It is fairness, it is good will, at bottom. It is impartiality of spirit and of judgment."

About the same time, Benito Mussolini was saying: "Neutrals never dominate events. They always sink. Blood alone moves the wheels of history."

Secretary of State Dean Rusk tried to take the edge off the antineutralist feeling in the U.S.: "I do not believe that we ourselves should be unduly concerned about what might be called genuine neutralism because if a new nation is internally vigorous, viable, strong, progressive, its orientation in foreign policy is not so important as its health and strength. . . . I do not believe we ought to ask commitments of a sort that would make it difficult for them to lead their own peoples in development." See SCRAP OF PAPER.

Neutralism was frequently called "the Third Way" in 1957, preparing the ground for the adoption of THIRD WORLD as its replacement. When superpower confrontation ended in the early 1990s, the word went into a deep freeze.

neutrality. See SCRAP OF PAPER.

Never Again. See HOLOCAUST.

never lost a war or won a peace
a frequent criticism of peace negotiations by the "out" party.

Will Rogers's assessment of U.S. diplomacy: "The United States has never lost a war or won a peace." See WINNING THE PEACE.

The point of view simultaneously carries a banner of patriotism and a partisan lance leveled at the bungling peacemakers who "sold out" our national interests. Some Republicans bitterly attacked Woodrow Wilson for advocating U.S. entry into the League of Nations. After World War II, Republicans were suspicious of "secret agreements" purportedly made at Yalta by President Roosevelt.

Thomas E. Dewey made the debatable point in 1950:

> During the First World War we said we wanted nothing for ourselves and nothing is what we got. In the Second World War again we said we wanted nothing and again nothing is what we got. At other times in our history we have known what we wanted and got it. Consider the War of 1812. The actual hostilities were indecisive and often humiliating for us. But at the peace conference which produced the Treaty of Ghent, the United States won a very advantageous frontier with Canada and all the other national objects for which we had fought. That was a war we did not win but we won the peace.

There is substance to the observation that the U.S. has been more successful in warmaking than peacemaking. Canadian Prime Minister Lester Pearson, in receiving the Nobel Peace Prize in 1957, gave one reason: "The grim fact is that we prepare for war like precocious giants and for peace like retarded pygmies."

new, political use of in the past century, no word stands out like "new" in the framing of themes for political movements.

Clement Laird Vallandigham, Ohio Democrat, in 1871 stirred his party with his *new departure:* "It is not a New Departure but a Return: the restoration of the Democratic party once more to the ancient platform of Progress and Reform." Despite the disclaimer, the phrase caught on and helped rejuvenate the staggered Democrats.

Theodore Roosevelt, known for the "Square Deal," also pressed his *New Nationalism* in 1912: "This New Nationalism regards the executive power as the steward of the public welfare."

Woodrow Wilson titled the collection of his campaign speeches *The New Freedom,* taken from this line: "And the day is at hand when it shall be realized on this consecrated soil—a New Freedom—a Liberty widened and deepened to match the broadened life of man in America . . ." Theodore Roosevelt knew a good slogan when he heard one, and quickly tried to put it down: "'The New Freedom' is nothing whatever but the right of the strong to prey on the weak."

But the Wilson phrase clicked, and spawned a wide range of others: the New Poetry, the New History, the New Art, the New Democracy, the New Woman—"the new anything," wrote historian Eric Goldman, "so long as it was new and gave an intoxicating sense of freedom."

As Adolf Hitler was talking of a *New Order,* Franklin Roosevelt was expounding the *New Deal;* in the campaign of 1960, John F. Kennedy talked of a *New Frontier* and Edmund Muskie in 1972 called for a *New Beginning.*

Adlai Stevenson captured this theme in a 1956 address: "There is a *New America* every morning when we wake up. . . . The New America is the sum of many small changes—a new subdivision here, a new school there, a new industry where there had been swampland—changes that add up to a broad transformation of our lives . . ."

In President Jimmy Carter's inaugural address, he invoked a *"new spirit"* several times, but the time was evidently not ripe for the phrase. Ronald Reagan called for a *"new beginning."* George Bush had some success with NEW WORLD ORDER, but that was promptly parodied as "new world disorder" as local wars broke out. Bill Clinton, described as a "New Democrat," used *"new covenant"* nine times in his inaugural address, but that phrase died aborning, perhaps because of its religious ring, suggesting the Ark of the Covenant and the New Testament.

See GREAT, POLITICAL USE OF.

New American Revolution. See REVOLUTION OF RISING EXPECTATIONS.

new broom. See SPOILS SYSTEM; CLEAN SWEEP.

new class the technical and managerial elite.

Communist doctrine teaches that with the destruction of capitalism, a classless society will emerge. That did not happen in the Soviet Union; what emerged instead was a bureaucracy of party and government which substituted power and perquisites for money, and enabled an elite to enjoy luxuries that capitalists use money to buy.

The phrase was coined by Yugoslav Communist Milovan Djilas, in his book *The New Class: An Analysis of the Communist System* (1957). Djilas, later harassed and jailed by Marshal Tito, held that "the new class, the bureaucracy, or more accurately the political bureaucracy, has all the characteristics of earlier ones . . . the Party makes the class, but the class grows as a result and uses the Party as a basis. The class grows stronger, while the Party grows weaker; this is the inescapable fate of every Communist party in power."

In the early seventies Professor Irving Kristol and other NEOCONSERVATIVES used the phrase to describe the academic-technical-governmental-foundation elite that sought to represent and to help, but not be a part of, the working class in the U.S.

A related term is TECHNOCRAT, a back-formation from "technocracy," an intellectual movement in the early thirties that argued for the replacement of consumer-dominated capitalism with an economic system that gave its priority to production at capacity. Because of its similarity to "bureaucrat," with the lowering of public regard for that occupation, the word "technocrat" gained a mechanical and bloodless connotation. In the early seventies Zbigniew Brzezinski, who later became Jimmy Carter's National Security Adviser, coined "the technitronic age" to herald the new society ahead, but that phrase never caught on. Well-educated managers and students of the "new class," whether technocrats, social workers or members of "the CHARLES RIVER GANG," are sometimes distrusted by people who are vaguely worried about machines and computers having too much to do with their lives.

new covenant. See NEW, POLITICAL USE OF; OPEN COVENANTS.

New Deal Franklin D. Roosevelt's program, enunciated in his acceptance speech at the 1932 Democratic convention: since divided into First New Deal (1933–35) and Second (1935–37).

"I pledge you," Roosevelt told the convention, "I pledge myself, to a new deal for the American people. Let us all here assembled constitute ourselves prophets of a new order of competence and of courage. This is more than a political campaign; it is a call to arms. Give me your help, not to win votes alone, but to win in this crusade to restore America to its own people."

This brief peroration, perhaps by Samuel Rosenman, offered commentators four possibilities for a slogan: "new order," which became known as Adolf Hitler's program; "crusade," which became Dwight Eisenhower's theme; "call to arms," which was never picked up by anybody; and "new deal."

On the day of the speech, cartoonist Rollin Kirby drew a sketch of a man leaning on a hoe, looking bewildered but hopeful, watching an airplane flying overhead labeled "New Deal." This was an indication to the Roosevelt forces and the Democratic National Committee that they had an exciting catch phrase. (Cartoonists can do much to propagate a phrase; see McCARTHYISM.)

"I had not the slightest idea that it would take hold the way it did," wrote Rosenman later, "nor did the Governor [Roosevelt] when he read and revised what I had written. In fact, he attached no importance to the two monosyllables. . . . Some have said that it was intended to be a combination of the Square Deal of President Theodore Roosevelt and the New Freedom of President Woodrow Wilson. There was no such intention when it was written or when it was delivered . . . when I handed him the scrap of paper on which the few paragraphs had been written he said that he thought they were all right as a peroration. . . . It was simply one of those phrases that catch public fancy and survive—short, concise, and yet comprehensive enough to cover a great many different concepts."

Other versions of the origin exist. Both Judge Rosenman and Professor Raymond Moley reviewed some of the Roosevelt entries in this book, and in this case, these were Professor Moley's comments:

You will find an account of the preparation of the acceptance speech on pages 23–27 inclusive in my "After Seven Years." When Rosenman says that he wrote it he is in error. The expression "new deal" was in the draft which I left at Albany with Roosevelt. What happened at Albany was not the rewriting of the speech but a rearrangement of it in a somewhat shortened version. If you will look at the exhibit opposite page 14 in my book you will see where the expression appeared first. I merely put this in to carry out the rhythm of the sentences at that point.

Of course, I have in my possession the original drafts before Rosenman and Roosevelt worked on them in Albany and some of the original drafts have Roosevelt's notations on them.

I was not aware that this would be the slogan of the campaign. It was a phrase that would have occurred to almost anyone, and it certainly did not come from the book written by Stuart Chase, for I had not seen the book at that time.

The first person who spotted the importance of the phrase was Herbert Bayard Swope, who wrote a letter to me immediately after the speech was delivered, saying that it should be pulled out and made the keynote of the campaign. I don't know about Rollin Kirby's cartoon.

Later Roosevelt allowed the New Deal legend to be embellished by pointing to Mark Twain's Connecticut Yankee, who said that "when six men out of a thousand crack the whip over their fellows' backs, then what the other nine hundred ninety four dupes need is a new deal" [see CARD METAPHORS].

English reporters pointed out that "A New Deal for Everyone" was David Lloyd George's campaign slogan in 1919, one year before FDR ran unsuccessfully for vice president. Other phrase hunters came up with a few lines from a Woodrow Wilson speech on October 24, 1910: "If it is reorganization, a new deal and a change you are seeking, it is Hobson's Choice. I am sorry for you, but it is really vote for me or not vote at all." Robert La Follette had written in his 1912 autobiography that his Committee of 100 "believe that the time has come for a new deal," and Carl Schurz had used it several times in the previous century, as in 1871: "There were the spoils ahead, with the prospect of a 'new deal.'" Petroleum V. Nasby wrote a year after Lincoln's assassination: "Wilkes Booth's ghost came in, and wanted to know what he wuz to hev in the new deal, 'for,' sed he, 'ef't hadn't been for me, where'd yoo all hev bin?'" And Nicholas Biddle, head of the Bank of the U.S., received a letter in Jackson's day calling for "a new bank and a New Deal." Further search seems unrewarding.

Around the time the speech was delivered, Stuart Chase had written an article in the *New Republic* titled "A New Deal for America," which Rosenman does not recall ever having seen. Suffice it to say the phrase was in the air and meant little until it was given the context of the man, the time and place. Indeed, "time and place" without the man meant nothing; on that same day and from that same rostrum, speaking several hours before Roosevelt, John McDuffie of Alabama nominated John Nance Garner for Vice President with the words: "There is a demand for a new deal in the management of the affairs of the American people."

The phrase was promptly parodied as "New Dole," "Raw Deal," and even "Jew Deal"; a generation later, Adlai Stevenson characterized Dwight Eisenhower's cabinet, made up mostly of businessmen, as "The Big Deal," and George Romney called Lyndon Johnson's administration "The Fast Deal." See DEAL.

New York Times columnist Russell Baker wrote the lexicographer about another possible source for the phrase:

The phrase is used several times by Henry James in "The Princess Casamassima" (1886), which I believe is Henry's only political novel. Reading the book, I became conscious of "new deal" recurring in the characters' discussion of the revolutionary political future they anticipate. In Chapter 34, for example, the Princess—an uptown dilettante of revolution—says, "I'm one of those who believe that a great new deal is destined to take place and that it can't make things worse than they are already."
I note your earlier reference from Petroleum Nasby in 1866, but James's

coming up with it in London 20 years later makes me wonder if the phrase was a political commonplace among political malcontents in the late 19th century. James had no first-hand experience of political people when he set out to write "The Princess," so in his thorough manner spent a lot of time eavesdropping in workingmen's hangouts and talking to people who were involved in politics, to familiarize himself with the lingo.

new departure   a recurrent phrase urging a fresh approach, based on a nautical metaphor. See SHIP OF STATE.

Senator John C. Calhoun of South Carolina used "new departure" frequently in the 1830s: "My aim is fixed, to take a fresh start, a new departure on the States Rights Republican tack." "Tack," of course, is a sailing term; Massachusetts Senator Henry Wilson, one of the founders of the Republican party, picked it up in 1871 in an *Atlantic Monthly* article titled "New Departure of the Republican Party," and sailed on further: ". . . the new under-currents in the popular mind . . . have driven and drifted the ship of state from its former course, and rendered necessary new observations, new calculations and a new departure." Clement Laird Vallandigham, a COPPERHEAD briefly banished by Lincoln to the Confederacy during the Civil War, popularized the phrase in seeking a reorientation of the Democratic party in Ohio in 1871.

At the same time, Republican Henry Wilson was selected by Ulysses S. Grant to run as his Vice President in his second term, opposing the Liberal Republican-Democratic coalition headed by Horace Greeley.

Thus both sides in the campaign of 1872 were hammering away at their own "new departure," successfully preventing a fine theme from gaining any real identity.

new economics   political economic thought stemming from the school of

John Maynard Keynes, holding that government fiscal and monetary policy can help end depressions and stimulate orderly economic growth.

Lord Keynes's publication in 1936 of the *General Theory of Employment, Interest and Money,* followed by Alvin Hansen's "translation" into understandable English and application to the U.S. economy, in turn followed by Paul Samuelson's "neoclassical synthesis" combining the Keynes position with some classical economic theory, resulted in a startling approach to managing a nation's business.

Keynes and his followers, dubbed "new economists" in the late fifties, sought new ways to provide full employment and a high annual growth rate at a minimum cost to the stability of prices and the balance of trade. The concept of "pump-priming," used in the thirties, was vastly expanded, and the idea of reducing deficits by reducing, rather than increasing, taxes at certain stages was introduced. In what was probably the last stand of the old-line economists, Treasury Secretary George Humphrey said in 1957 about government spending during business declines, "I don't think you can spend yourself rich."

The increase in revenues after the 1964 tax cut (which stimulated business and thereby increased the amount of tax revenues received) probably provided the breakthrough for "new economics" in the councils of government. A large question remained: If the new thinking could stimulate the economy out of recessions, could it restrain the economy from inflation?

A key word in the new economist's new vocabulary is TRADE-OFF. Former chairman of the Council of Economic Advisers Walter Heller explains:

The political economist typically thinks in terms of *trade-offs*—for example, the trade-off between jobs and inflation, the problem at which we pitch our Phillips Curves (relating the behavior of prices to the behavior of unemployment); the trade-off between international payments equilibrium and internal expansion, for which monetary policy did the twist (pushing short-term interest rates up to discourage the outflow of volatile funds, while holding long-term rates down to encourage capital spending); the trade-off between price-wage stability and unfettered markets, for which we erected the wage-price guideposts (providing guides to noninflationary wage and price behavior).

The new economics marked the entry of "the Respectable Professors of the Dismal Science," in Carlyle's phrase, into the top level of government planning. John R. Commons, whose "progressive individualism" was a controversial economic approach at the turn of the twentieth century, believed that "the place of the economist is that of adviser to the leaders, if they want him, and not that of propagandist to the masses." But which economist to trust was a dilemma agonizingly expressed by Warren G. Harding: "I know somewhere there is an economist who knows the truth, but I don't know where to find him and haven't the sense to know and trust him when I find him. God, what a job!"

John F. Kennedy tried to take some of the controversial sting out of the new economics by making it appear to be simple, good business management: "What is at stake in our economic decisions today is, not some grand warfare of rival ideologies which will sweep the country with passion, but the practical management of a modern economy."

Herbert Stein wrote in the *Wall Street Journal* in 1993:

Now we come to the New Economics of 1993. Of course, it is not entirely new. Even good old President Eisenhower in 1958, before we were all Keynesians, talked about the possible use of "a little needle" to stimulate the economy. Every president since, except Ronald Reagan, has proposed a stimulus package when the economy was slack. The acceptance or rejection of these proposals left no clear mark on economic history. The Clinton deficit reduction plan is in the same vein as earlier plans.

What is new about Mr. Clinton's New Economics is the degree to which it is willing to intervene in the market. This is seen in the talk about managed international trade, in proposals for price controls in the health industry and in numerous plans for "targeting" investment. All of these ideas have precedents in past practice as well as in the writings of economists. But they seem to have a centrality in the 1993 New Economics that they have not had before, either in practice or in American economic thought.

new face a candidate unscarred by previous major contests, unencumbered by known positions, offering politicians and voters a fresh choice.

A striking example of "new faces" on the national scene was the choice offered Republicans at their 1940 convention: Robert A. Taft, elected senator from Ohio just two years before; Thomas E. Dewey, who had recently been defeated in his first race to be governor of New York; and Wendell L. Willkie, a businessman who had never run for public office. That year the newest face (Willkie's) won; in 1944 Dewey's face was no longer new, but won; in 1948 Dewey's face was the "oldest" by virtue of his previous election defeat, and won again. Both lost to the smiling old face of FDR.

The desire for a new face—"untarred by the brush of defeat"—is perennial at national conventions, but is usually at its peak long before the convention meets. The balance sheet of every well-known candidate includes liabilities: enemies made in previous contests, a possible lost election and a "can't-win" aura, perhaps a haunting record

on what has become an embarrassing issue, and often a contempt-breeding familiarity with his voice and his personality. Because the presence of some new and mysterious candidate like a William Jennings Bryan or a Dwight Eisenhower is a thrilling uncertainty, the appeal of a new face in an "out" party is understandable.

As the Brookings Institution pointed out in 1960, "the limitations of well-known candidates are likely to be about as well understood as their potentialities. But both limitations and potentialities of less-known men can only be guessed at—unless the testing process before the convention is sufficient to bring out evidence."

Suspicion about a new face's "trustworthiness"—i.e., willingness to work with a party—increases as convention time approaches, and public demand for specific stands rises. These combined forces lessen the appeal of a new face, reminding delegates of the security of an "old face"—one less likely to blunder on the campaign trail, one who understands their local political problems, and above all, one whose victory will mean victory for themselves.

The phrase itself was popularized in the Broadway theater by Leonard Sillman, who began producing a series of *New Faces* revues in 1934.

See TIME FOR A CHANGE.

New Federalism a political philosophy that seeks to wed the need for national action with the desire for much greater local participation.

The phrase was coined, and the idea expounded, in a speech to the nation by President Nixon on August 8, 1969. "After a third of a century of power flowing from the people and the States to Washington it is time for a New Federalism in which power, funds and responsibility will flow from Washington to the States and to the people."

See CREATIVE FEDERALISM; POWER TO THE PEOPLE.

Revenue sharing (see TAX SHARING) was a step in the direction of decentralization, which the President developed with a much more heavily funded proposal the next year; on the other hand, welfare reform (see WORKFARE) was a step toward centralization. To explain this seeming anomaly, the President encouraged his aides to do some thinking and writing on the subject.

That brought forth memoranda from "Publius" (this writer) and "Cato" (Tom Charles Huston, an outspoken conservative who later gained notoriety as author of a scheme of admittedly illegal counterespionage known as the Huston Plan).

Wrote Publius in January of 1970, in "New Federalist Paper #1":

> We like the blessings of strong central government: a clear direction toward social goals, a willingness to counteract economic freezings and overheatings, a single voice in world affairs. But we are repelled by centralization's side effects: ineffective administration that breeds resentment, inflexible bureaucracy that breeds alienation.
>
> We also like the blessings of decentralization or "home rule," with its respect for diversity, its ready response to local demands, its personality tailored to its constituents. But we are repelled by frequent local unwillingness or inability to meet human needs.
>
> Do we have to choose one way or the other—centralization or decentralization—taking the bitter with whatever we consider the sweet? Many think not, and have spent the past year working out a synthesis of the most desirable in both central government and home rule. It has been called "The New Federalism.". . . The purpose of the New Federalism is not to wrap liberal principles in conservative clothing, or vice versa; the purpose is to come to grips with a paradox: a need for *both* national unity and local diversity; a need to protect *both* individual equality at the na-

tional level and individual uniqueness at the local level; and a need to *both* establish national goals and decentralize government services.

Replied Cato the following month:

> . . . what New Publius is really advocating is not a New Federalism but a NEW NATIONALISM (a phrase which Theodore Roosevelt unfortunately preempted nearly sixty years ago). At the heart of New Publius' contrived synthesis is this simple proposition: while decision-making must be nationalized, administration should be decentralized . . . he simply brushes aside States rights as a constitutional guarantee; he, New Publius, declares (the Constitution of the United States notwithstanding) that States rights have now become rights of first refusal. Perhaps one should give him the benefit of the doubt and assume that in his eagerness to replace the melting pot with the salad bowl he has inadvertently mixed apples with oranges. If, for example, New Publius is simply saying that within the scope of legitimate federal authority Congress may choose to give the States first option on the administration of a federal program, such a statement is unobjectionable. If, however, New Publius is saying that once the Federal Government determines that a problem—any problem—exists and decides that something should be done about it, the States have the first option to take action and if they refuse, the Federal Government may rightly act on its own—if this be his argument, then not only is it objectionable, it is revolutionary.

These two schools of thought contended, on varying levels and in many ways, throughout the next year; in the 1971 State of the Union message, President Nixon espoused much of the philosophy described in the Publius memorandum.

New Freedom the slogan used by Woodrow Wilson in the presidential campaign of 1912.

Wilson believed with Louis Brandeis, who had won fame as a trust buster and whom he would later appoint to the Supreme Court, that the greatest enemies of the American people were the growing trusts and bigness in industry and commerce in general. He felt that the only instrument which could, and should, do something about this was the federal government.

His New Freedom called for government intervention to safeguard the democratic rights of small business against the industrial behemoths. Wilson described it thus: ". . . a revival of the power of the people, the beginning of an age of thoughtful reconstruction, that makes our thought hark back to the great age in which democracy was set up in America." See CURSE OF BIGNESS.

Wilson's belief that bigness was evil brought him into direct conflict with Theodore Roosevelt, also a candidate. Former President Roosevelt, an early believer in defining an Administration's political philosophy with a slogan—"SQUARE DEAL"—had a new slogan of his own, "the NEW NATIONALISM." Bigness, with a certain necessary minimum of regulation, was perfectly natural from Roosevelt's point of view, and late in life he found nothing reprehensible in trusts.

On this subject Wilson drew the issue: "I take my stand absolutely, where every progressive ought to take his stand, on the proposition that private monopoly is indefensible and intolerable."

His writings and speeches of the campaign were gathered in a 1913 book called *The New Freedom*.

New Frontier style adopted by the Kennedy Administration.

"A new frontier had been discovered," a hard-driving presidential candidate told a crowd in West Middlesex,

Pennsylvania, ". . . the frontier of invention and new wants. Under our American way of life, men with courage and imagination were free to occupy this new frontier and develop it. They built a greater America."

The candidate was Alf Landon, the date August 22, 1936. Landon used the phrase several times in his campaign against Roosevelt, but he could not make too much of it, since *New Frontiers* was the title of a book published two years before by Henry A. Wallace.

Senator Arthur Vandenberg of Michigan strung a few clichés together in a speech in South Dakota, October 11, 1938:

Man cannot live by bread alone. What profiteth it a man if he gain the whole world and lose his own soul? Those who try to trade liberty for security usually wind up by losing both. Eternal vigilance is the price of liberty. Every journey to the forbidden land begins with the first step. These new frontiers that are offered to us are anticonstitutional, antidemocratic, antiliberal Frontiers. They are the potential boundaries of the collectivist state.

In 1951 Walter Prescott Webb wrote a pessimistic piece in the *Atlantic Monthly* decrying the boosterism of those who "speak of new frontiers," adding: "The businessman sees a business frontier in the customers he has not yet reached. . . . The social worker sees a human frontier among the suffering people whose woes he has not alleviated. . . . If you watch these peddlers of substitute frontiers, you will find that nearly everyone wants you to buy something, give something, or believe in something . . . They are all fallacies, these new frontiers, and they are pernicious in proportion to their plausibility and respectability."

Of course, "previous usages" can be found of almost any famous phrase in the English language (see NEW DEAL; GREAT SOCIETY); the important usage was by John F. Kennedy, accepting the Democratic nomination in the Los Angeles Coliseum in 1960: ". . . we stand today on the edge of a new frontier—the frontier of the 1960s, a frontier of unknown opportunities and paths, a frontier of unfulfilled hopes and threats. . . . The new frontier of which I speak is not a set of promises—it is a set of challenges. It sums up not what I intend to offer the American people, but what I intend to ask of them."

Who suggested it to Kennedy? Arthur Schlesinger, Jr., points out in *A Thousand Days* that he had given a speech himself a few months before titled "New Frontiers of American Liberalism"; reporter David Wise credited Walt Whitman Rostow, then an MIT economic historian, with suggesting the phrase to Kennedy at a Boston cocktail party a month before the nomination; later both Rostow and Max Freedman, Washington correspondent for the *Manchester Guardian,* are supposed to have submitted separate drafts of the acceptance speech, each containing the "New Frontier" theme. But a Kennedy intimate informs the lexicographer that neither Freedman nor Rostow submitted any material for this particular speech. He adds that rough draft material was solicited from many sources, including Professor Allan Nevins of Columbia, but that the term itself was in none of them.

Rostow himself informs the lexicographer:

> Your puzzlement about the origins of "The New Frontier" leads me to set down the following extremely minor footnote to history, as I remember it.
> Early in the Kennedy Administration, David Wise wrote a piece for the *New York Herald-Tribune* asserting that I had provided J.F.K. with "Let's get this

country moving again" and "The New Frontier." I called and told Wise I had, indeed, given J.F.K. the first of those phrases but not The New Frontier. After I had gone on for some time in this vein, he asked: "Are you finished?" He then said: "First, the President of the United States said the phrase came from you; second, he showed me a speech draft of yours containing the phrase; third, he told me it came from your book 'The Stages of Economic Growth.'" I subsided and, indeed, found three references to the new frontier theme in "The Stages," which I had forgotten.

Then Max Freedman sent a letter to the *Tribune* saying that Ted Sorensen had used the phrase in a draft of his for Kennedy. When the question has been raised with me occasionally, I have responded that it is wholly possible Freedman was correct; the phrase may well have been in the air at the time; and the issue is trivial because the working politician alone deserves whatever credit there may be in such phrases because he alone takes the responsibility and risk of using them.

The origin here was probably similar to "NOTHING TO FEAR BUT FEAR ITSELF," when Louis Howe—probably—picked it up from a newspaper advertisement and suggested it to FDR. The phrase "new frontier" was in the air in early 1960. For example, the U.S. Chamber of Commerce appointed a Committee on New Frontiers in Technology in April of that year, with the name chosen months before that. "The Chamber would not have adopted this name if it had been already used by and identified with Mr. Kennedy," the secretary of that committee writes the author. After Kennedy made the phrase his own, the Chamber ruefully changed the name of its "new frontiers" committee to the more pedestrian "Committee on Science and Technology."

In *Kennedy,* Ted Sorensen, who prepared the acceptance speech for the candidate, takes a defensive stance: ". . . the basic concept of the New Frontier—and the term itself—were new to this speech. I know of no outsider who suggested that expression, although the theme of the Frontier was contained in more than one draft. Kennedy generally shrank from slogans, and would use this one sparingly, but he liked the idea of a successor to the New Deal and Fair Deal."

Thus Kennedy popularized, probably at Sorensen's suggestion, a phrase that was "around."

New Left a movement, deliberately leaderless, begun in England in 1957 by young radicals who rejected the "old" liberal philosophy; joined in the next decade by pacifists and civil rights militants, who oppose the "power structure" that robs them of their freedom and individuality.

Sociologist C. Wright Mills is credited with the coinage of the phrase in the late fifties. In England, two university periodicals merged in 1959 to form the *New Left Review*, staffed largely by disenchanted young Marxists. At that time in the U.S., a group calling itself SLATE was formed at the University of California's Berkeley campus, and a similar student political party was formed in Chicago. The young intellectuals adopted new vocabularies and new forms to contrast with the "liberal establishment" they felt no longer met their needs. See MOVEMENT, THE.

Mills wrote in 1960: "If there is to be a politics of a New Left, what needs to be analyzed is the structure of institutions, the foundation of policies. In this sense, both in its criticisms and in its proposals, our work is necessarily structural—and so, for us, just now— utopian." His followers seized upon this rationale for their emphasis on questions over answers, their apparent negativism and lack of a program.

In recent use, it encompassed the antibureaucracy, alienated groups who dissociated themselves from the liberals of the "old" left.

From the point of view of Democrats and "regular" liberals, the new left represented a splintering of support or an embarrassment; many Republicans considered it a collection of Vietniks and far-out radicals, with whom no communication was possible, overlooking the common ground possible in a mutual distaste for strong centralized government. See COUNTERCULTURE.

new look a change in defense strategy in 1953, as the Korean War ended, deemphasizing "conventional" forces and relying more on nuclear deterrents. See BIGGER BANG FOR A BUCK.

The phrase came from the fashion world, where it was used in 1947 to describe the Paris-inspired change to radically lower hemlines and softer details after the austere fashions of wartime. The phrase fitted a reassessment of the nation's defense attire.

Defense's new look appealed to those who wanted a reduction in total defense spending, and who felt that our preparation for nontotal "brushfire" wars diminished our threat of nuclear retaliation. It was opposed by many Army generals who agreed with retiring Chief of Staff Matthew Ridgway in assailing the "overemphasis" on air power and MASSIVE RETALIATION.

In his memoirs General Eisenhower traced both the coinage and what he felt was an overreaction:

At about the time of the change-over in the Joint Chiefs of Staff, active fighting in Korea ended. This fact, along with the epochal developments which were transpiring in nuclear armaments, occasioned what Admiral [Arthur] Radford described in a talk late in the year as a "New Look" [at the Press Club, Washington, December 14, 1953].

It happened that this term had a definite place in the parlance of the day; it had been coined to describe noticeable changes in the style of women's dresses (not entirely an improvement, some men felt). Thus the tag "New Look" probably suggested to many minds a picture of a far more radical change in the composition of our armed forces than was truly the case.

New Nationalism Theodore Roosevelt's progressive program of 1910, designed to lead the Republican party toward more liberal paths.

The former President was stamping about Africa in 1910, bored and regretting not having sought a third term. His friend Judge Learned Hand sent him a book by Herbert Croly, *The Promise of America*, which differed from the Jeffersonian ideal of the least government being the best government, and restated and extended much of Roosevelt's own thought. On his return, TR invited Croly to tea in Oyster Bay and promptly took over the program; biographer Henry Pringle thinks the phrase "new nationalism" came from Croly as well.

In a speech at Osawotomie, Kansas, the former President said: "The New Nationalism puts the national need before sectional or personal advantage. . . . This New Nationalism regards the executive power as the steward of the public welfare. It demands of the judiciary that it shall be interested primarily in human welfare rather than in property, just as it demands that the representative body shall represent all the people rather than any one class or section of the people."

Elihu Root shrugged it off with "The only real objection I see to it is calling it 'new,'" but many other Republicans considered it heresy. Two years later, in the Wilson-Taft-Roosevelt "Bull Moose" campaign of 1912, Woodrow Wilson adopted most of the principles expressed by the "New Nationalism" with the exception of an attitude toward trusts, which TR felt were good if properly supervised and Wilson felt were the embodiment of evil. Wilson called his own program "the NEW FREEDOM"; President William Howard Taft was the only candidate running with nothing "new."

Ironically, ten years after Roosevelt introduced the term, Warren G. Harding—apostle of "normalcy"—declared Roosevelt's Osawotomie speech the basis of his platform, but he did not later become known as a proponent of a strong central government.

new order program of Hitler's regime in Germany.

The phrase, in English, is from British poet Alfred Lord Tennyson: "The old order changeth, yielding place to new,/And God fulfills himself in many ways,/Lest one good custom should corrupt the world."

Hitler's use of the phrase *die neue Ordnung* was adapted by Prince Konoye, Premier of Japan, in 1938, as he called for "a new order in East Asia." Before both Hitler and Konoye, Franklin Roosevelt had used the phrase. See NEW DEAL; UNITED WE STAND; NEW WORLD ORDER.

In the seventies, the phrase was picked up by leaders of have-not nations demanding a redistribution of wealth under a "new economic order." See THIRD WORLD.

new paradigm. See PARADIGM SHIFT.

new politics the self-description of a grouping on the left that was occasionally successful in attracting new politicians.

Syndicated columnist Milton Viorst described it as of June 30, 1970:

Basically, the New Politics is a movement on the left and insofar as it can be defined at all, is ideological and anti-organizational. It invented Eugene McCarthy and almost made him president, but it neither began nor ended with the 1968 campaign . . .

On the same day, columnist David Broder observed:

> . . . the parties have been weakened plenty in recent years, particularly the 'new politics' reformers expected. Instead of elevating us to a new plane of issue-oriented direct democracy, it may sweep us backwards toward the primitive brutalities of tribal warfare. When voters lose the habit of identifying themselves as Republicans or Democrats, they may not, as the reformers hoped, begin to think of themselves as conservatives or liberals, or even hawks or doves. They may instead view electoral politics as a power struggle between Italians and Irish, Catholics and Yankees, or blacks and whites. And that we could do without.

Another point of view was expressed by the *Wall Street Journal:*

> A GRASS-ROOTS upsurge for Eugene McCarthy in the Democratic Party gets labeled "the new politics," something better than old ways. Yet, as we recall, a grass-roots upsurge for Barry Goldwater in the Republican Party got labeled political atavism, or something like that. . . . It will be horrible, most of the pontificators tell us, if all those who support Mr. McCarthy are left feeling their efforts did not influence either major party. But somehow no one weeps over the far more fundamental alienation felt by the supporters of George Wallace. How healthy our political system is, it seems, depends a good deal on whose political ox is gored. All of which suggests to us there are no old politics and no new politics. Only politics.

The phrase triggers excitement because it appears to sever ties with the entrenched political leadership, and triggers resentment because it appears to fly a false banner—the techniques are not new at all.

"Hypocrisy" and "expediency" were the twin villains of participants of the new politics, but as reformers come to power, terms like "practical politics" and "necessary compromise" come to the fore. Many people who objected to the new politics focused on the fact that the techniques were far from new, which was hardly in dispute—the trouble was that the new participants expected immediate gratification in their quest for the "old" political power.

new world economic order. See NEW ORDER; THIRD WORLD; NEW WORLD ORDER.

new world order an ideal of cooperation and peace among nations.

Alfred Lord Tennyson pointed to this phrase in his 1842 poem "Morte d'Arthur," in which the dying King Arthur says, "The old order changeth, yielding place to new."

George Bush used his adaptation of Tennyson's phrase in an August 1990 news conference: "As I look at the countries that are chipping in here now, I think we do have a chance at a new world order." He repeated it a month later in urging the United Nations General Assembly to work against chemical and biological weapons: "It is in our hands to leave these dark machines behind, in the dark ages where they belong, and to press forward to cap a historic movement toward a new world order, and a long era of peace."

During his 1991 State of the Union message, Bush called upon all nations "to fulfill the long-held promise of a new world order—where brutality will go unrewarded and aggression will meet collective resistance."

Earlier uses of *new world order* have been less supportive of worldwide unity. Malcolm X commented in his 1965 *Autobiography* (written with Alex Haley): "Let us face reality. We can see in the United Nations a new world order being shaped, along color lines—an alliance among the non-white nations."

Various sources for the phrase have been suggested, from the 1970s New World Information and Communications Order, a UNESCO-sponsored plan, to the Latin phrase on the back of dollar bills: *Novus Ordo Seclorum*, "A New Order of the Ages."

Without *world*, the phrase *new order* conjures images of *die neue Ordnung*, Hitler's language to impose a National Socialist regime in Europe. That phrase, however, was also used in that era by Franklin Delano Roosevelt at the 1932 Democratic National Convention: "Let us all here assembled constitute ourselves prophets of a new order of competence and of courage."

In 1993, President Bill Clinton returned the phrase to its poetic origin in his inaugural address: "Today, as the old order passes, the new world is more free but less stable."

See NEW, POLITICAL USE OF.

nickel-and-diming. See BUTTON-HOLE.

nicknames derisive or laudatory sobriquets that familiarize or stigmatize a politician.

Since the earliest days the chief statesmen of this country have been given nicknames, some of them familiar to every schoolchild: "Father of his Country" for Washington; "Honest Abe" for Lincoln; "Old Hickory" for Jackson; "The Little Giant" for Stephen A. Douglas.

Not every schoolchild is informed that Washington, in his lifetime, was often referred to as "The Stepfather of his Country" and "The Old Fox." Lincoln was derided by Confederates and Northern Democrats alike as "The Baboon" and his wife as "The She-Wolf." U. S. Grant, observed Mencken, "because he was always the soldier more than the politician, escaped with nothing worse than 'The Butcher,' but his successors got it hot and heavy."

Hayes was "The Fraud" as well as "The Hero of '77"; Arthur was "The Dude" and "America's First Gentleman"; Cleveland, "The Stuffed Prophet" and "Perpetual Candidate"; Theodore Roosevelt was "Bull Moose," "MAN ON HORSEBACK," and "Teddy the Meddler." Wilson was "The Phrasemaker" and "The Schoolmaster." Coolidge was "Silent Cal."

The two Roosevelts and Wilson probably provoked more invective than any other President. Franklin Roosevelt was known variously as "Boss," FDR, "Houdini in the White House," "Sphinx," "Squire of Hyde Park," and "THAT MAN IN THE WHITE HOUSE."

Nicknames are often borrowed and transferred: "Great Commoner" (Pitt the elder) to Henry Clay and, later, to William Jennings Bryan; "Bald Eagle of Foggy Bottom" (Robert Lovett, Secretary of Defense) from "The Bald Eagle of Rhode Island," Tristram Burges (1770–1853), a member of Congress.

MR. DOOLEY, referring to "Tiddy" (Teddy Roosevelt), was told not to be disrespectful; he retorted that he was not being disrespectful, he was being affectionate.

President Truman enjoyed "Give 'Em Hell Harry" but not "High Tax Harry." President Eisenhower was simply "Ike." Nixon was "Tricky Dick." With Franklin Roosevelt, John Kennedy, and Lyndon Johnson, presidential initials became popular. President Johnson was both LBJ and "Big Daddy." James Earl Carter, Jr., was the first to formally adopt the informal style with "Jimmy." Ronald Reagan was called "the Great Communicator," while George Bush had no sobriquet but did have a nickname: Poppy.

The "nick" in nickname comes not from the variety of characterizations given the Devil (Old Nick) but from the Middle English *eke,* meaning something added, an extension, or (as a verb) to increase or lengthen (still used as "eke out a living") and an *ekename* became a nickname, or an extra surname applied in jest or familiarity.

See INITIALS, PRESIDENTIAL; SOBRIQUETS.

nightmare. See LIFT OF A DRIVING DREAM.

night mayor a city official of whatever rank assigned to remain at City Hall or tour the city on official business during the night hours.

Begun by the administration of John Lindsay of New York in 1966, the program was intended to publicize the wide-awake, round-the-clock officials and give them an opportunity to make surprise inspections that often resulted in newspaper photos.

The practice derived from the military CQ (charge of quarters) and OD (officer of the day, or on duty) who is responsible for any decisions requiring immediate attention when ordinary authority is off duty.

The phrase itself was coined by James J. Walker, who served as a sparkling, beloved mayor of New York and who resigned in 1932 as a result of Samuel Seabury's investigation of municipal corruption: "Some folks call me the 'night mayor' of New York."

night of the long knives a time of purge; a savage, surprise attack by one's supposed friends.

"It was no secret that this time the revolution would have to be bloody,"

Adolf Hitler told the Reichstag meeting at the Kroll Opera House on July 13, 1934, explaining the events of the weekend of June 29 to July 2; "when we spoke of it, we called it 'The Night of the Long Knives' [*die Nacht der langen Messer*]. . . . In every time and place, rebels have been killed . . . I ordered the leaders of the guilty shot. I also ordered the abscesses caused by our internal and external poisons cauterized until the living flesh was burned."

In the summer of 1934 Hitler was Chancellor, his rise to power helped by the Brown Shirts headed by Ernst Röhm. But the leaders of Germany's regular army were worried about Röhm and the private Nazi militia, who were calling for a "second revolution" to overthrow the military and industrial elite in Germany. Hitler made a deal to enhance his power in government while wiping out his undisciplined former comrades, and personally directed Heinrich Himmler and Reinhard Heydrich of the Gestapo, and their boss, Hermann Göring, to arrest and execute eighty-three of the leaders of the storm troopers. After that weekend, Hitler's power was unchallenged.

The "night," then, was originally supposed to be a time of revolution conceived by Hitler, Röhm and the early Nazis; to its planners the phrase denoted an entire weekend of purge and the elimination of an obstacle to complete power. Ironically, the "night" that took place eliminated one of the men who had planned it, and turned the "second revolution" into an internal purge.

Today, the phrase is an example of the use of catastrophic terms to describe far less bloody developments, like "massacre" for extensive firings. In *Newsday*'s October 12, 1992, report of the first debate between President Bush and candidate Bill Clinton,

David Firestone wrote: "It was not a night of the long knives or self-inflicted wounds; the blood on the debating floor could be measured only in droplets."

See PURGE and PUTSCH; for other Nazi-era terms, see FINAL SOLUTION; HOLOCAUST; and MUNICH ANALOGY.

-nik suffix as in the derisive terms *beatnik, peacenik, Vietnik,* and others. Suggests youth, scruffiness, beardedness, and irresponsibility.

A 1963 *New York Times* headline read: "'Beatnik' Troubles Lexicographer." The lead: "Dr. Charles Talbot Onions . . . celebrated his 90th birthday here recently worrying about the word 'beatnik.'"

Those who "knew their Onions" worried as well; was it a neologism that would last, deserving a place in a dictionary—or a "nonce word" that struts and frets and then is heard no more?

The popularization of the suffix *-nik* probably started with Al Capp, creator of the "Li'l Abner" comic strip, who developed a subseries in the country of "Lower Slobbovia," a land of ice, wolves, and miserable people who spoke a combination of English, Russian, and Yiddish. "Leettle Noodnik" (from the Yiddish *nudnik,* "tedious fellow," or "dope") was one of the characters. The suffix is of Russian origin; *-nik* when added to stems of Russian words means "one who."

-nik crashed like a meteorite into the English language with the launching of the Soviet Sputnik (from *iskustvennyi sputnik zemli,* "artificial satellite [literally: fellow traveler] around the earth") on October 4, 1957. When a second satellite, containing a dog, was launched on November 4, several newspapers tagged it a "muttnik," and the fad of the *-nik* construction was launched as well.

There were no-goodniks and faroutniks, beatniks, and sickniks.

Even the typical suburban home shown at the U.S. exhibition in Moscow—not split-level, but with a walkway splitting it—was called the "Splitnik," coined with inordinate pride by the author.

After some flirtation with "folknik," public fancy in 1958 appeared to settle on "beatnik," probably an outgrowth of the "beat generation," novelist Jack Kerouac's switch on Gertrude Stein's "lost generation." Columnist Herb Caen coined the term in the *San Francisco Chronicle* of April 2, 1958: "*Look* Magazine, preparing a picture spread on S.F.'s Beat Generation (oh, no, not AGAIN!) hosted a party in a No. beach house for 50 Beatniks . . ." The term was active as a derogation of young people who let their hair grow and refused to work, to be replaced in the late sixties by "hippie," a somewhat different subculture.

Time and *Newsweek* turned "beatnik" to "Vietnik" in October 1959, and the pejorative connotation of beatnik—lazy and irresponsible—was transferred to the word for war protesters.

In the mid-seventies the suffix was returned to its country of origin, by way of giving an English word a Russian flavor. A headline in the *New York Times* letters section in June 1977 read: "Robert Toth Explains Refuseniks' Role." A "refusenik" was a Soviet citizen, often Jewish, who was refused permission to emigrate. In Israel, supporters of the Likud coalition of the right were called "Likudniks."

The suffix continues to be productive, albeit mostly in nonce words coined for a specific reason or occasion. In 1987 *People* magazine referred to a streetwise person as a "streetnik," and in 1988 the magazine *Omni* described space-travel buffs as "spaceniks." Also during in the 1980s, "freezenik" was widely applied to supporters of a nuclear-arms freeze and "refusenik" enjoyed a revival in the generalized sense of "one who refuses something," as a financial settlement or an invitation to serve in the armed forces.

nimby "not in my back yard"; refusal to allow unpleasant or dangerous projects to be moved into one's own neighborhood.

The five-letter acronym, pronounced NIM-bee, first appeared in print in a 1980 report in the *Christian Science Monitor:* "A secure landfill anywhere near them is anathema to most Americans today. It's an attitude referred to in the trade as NIMBY—'not in my backyard.'"

By 1986, this expression of intolerance was gaining international acceptance. The *Times* of London described a politician who became "a convert to the Nimby . . . principle. A chief whip who thinks that nuclear waste is too dangerous for his constituency will find it hard to persuade other Tory MPs that it is safe for theirs."

Current use of the acronym is primarily as a noun, often attributive, as in *the nimby syndrome,* and the plural form may be *nimbys* or sometimes *nimbies. The Nation* reported in 1991 on "prisons, sanitation works and other 'NIMBYs'"; this noun is also used for any protest against such projects. From the acronym has come the noun *nimbyism,* a 1989 term for the practice of opposing local facilities for disagreeable projects.

Coinage has been attributed to Walton Rodger of the American Nuclear Society, who used the term as early as 1980 to deride protesters who campaigned against nuclear facilities near their homes.

nine old men a description of the nine Justices of the Supreme Court, a majority of whom blocked Franklin Roosevelt's programs in the mid-1930s.

The average age of the Supreme Court members in 1936 was seventy-one (in 1993 it was seventy). Throughout his first term, Roosevelt had no opportunity to make a single appointment. "Chance and the disinclination of the individuals to leave the Supreme Bench," said Roosevelt, "have now given us a Court in which five Justices will be over 75 years of age before next June and one over 70."

FDR came up with a plan to bring the Court out of what he called "the horse and buggy age." He proposed that for every Supreme Court Justice who failed to quit the bench within six months after reaching his seventieth birthday Congress empower the President to appoint a new Justice up to a total of six.

Roosevelt had overreached himself; his plan was denounced as court-packing, and he found himself on the defensive. "If by that phrase 'packing the Court' it is charged," he said, "that I wish to place on the bench spineless puppets who would disregard the law and would decide specific cases as I wished them to be decided, I make this answer: that no President fit for his office would appoint, and no Senate of honorable men fit for their office would confirm, that kind of appointee to the Supreme Court."

Roosevelt's plan died in committee on July 22, 1937; however, the President's purpose was served when the Court began to show its shifting position. Justice Owen Roberts threw the balance of power to the liberals, and the Court soon upheld a minimum-wage law for women, a National Labor Relations Act, and the Social Security Act.

"By the time the Court recessed for the summer," wrote Samuel Rosenman, "it was obvious that the liberal dissenting views of the minority in

1935 and 1936 had in large measure become the majority views of the Court. As a contemporary wag put it: 'A switch in time saved nine.'"

The phrase "nine old men" was coined by Drew Pearson and Robert S. Allen in a 1936 book dealing with the Court, and was further made famous by a characterization of them as a kind of chorus line in the 1937 Rodgers-Hart musical, *I'd Rather Be Right.*

Since that time, attacks on the age of Supreme Court Justices or senators have been rare. The word "senator" is Latin for "old man" and is based on the same root as "senile." Cruel joke, entirely untrue, on the subject in the 1980s: At a dinner with the other eight Supreme Court Justices, Sandra Day O'Connor was asked by a waiter: "Your meat course?" "Roast beef," she responded. "And what about the vegetables?" the waiter continued. Replied Justice O'Connor: "They'll have to order for themselves."

nitty-gritty detail work; difficult minutiae to be handled by staffers after strategy has been decided higher up.

"SNCC's resources for nitty-gritty organizing—" wrote the *New Republic* in 1967, "and perhaps its will to work in a low key over a long period of time—are thin."

This expression of Southern black origin is in common current use, and one can speculate on its derivation: "nit" means the egg of a louse, something tiny and distasteful; "nit-picking," or fault-finding, uses "nit" in a sense of something small or detailed. (Shakespeare's *Taming of the Shrew:* "Thou flea! thou nit, thou Wintercricket, thou!")

"Grit" is rooted in sand, or dust, and later in coarse meal (as "hominy grits"); as a verb, it means to grind in sand, and to "grit one's teeth." Thus, the rhyming words mean to take tiny details (nitty) and grind them carefully (gritty). Speculation aside, somebody probably thought of it in a flash of inspiration, as with other rhyming compounds like "willy-nilly" (willing or not) and "helter-skelter" (from the German *holter-polter*). These are reduplicated or ricochet words; a political FLIP-FLOP is called a gradational compound.

Nixon Doctrine a foreign policy that sought to maintain U.S. involvement in the affairs of the world, in a way that required allies to bear the manpower burden of their own defense.

In his November 3, 1969, SILENT MAJORITY speech, President Nixon first used the phrase publicly: "Let me briefly explain what has been described as the Nixon Doctrine." (Somewhat self-conscious about using the phrase with his name in it, he toned it down with "what has been described as." Needless to say, he wanted it described exactly that way. It had been called the "Guam Doctrine," because it had been enunciated on that island, but nobody elected Guam.) These were the three principles of the doctrine as set forth in that speech:

> *First,* the United States will keep all of its treaty commitments. *Second,* we shall provide a shield if a nuclear power threatens the freedom of a nation allied with us or of a nation whose survival we consider vital to our security. *Third,* in cases involving other types of aggression, we shall furnish military and economic assistance when requested in accordance with our treaty commitments. But we shall look to the nation directly threatened to assume the primary responsibility of providing the manpower for its defense.

The doctrine first presented at Guam was in a BACKGROUNDER not for direct quotation, and Nixon could not correctly say it was "announced" there.

The operative verb, appropriate for DOCTRINES generally, is "enunciated."

noble experiment sarcastic characterization of Prohibition, based on a phrase of Herbert Hoover's.

Hoover wrote Senator William E. Borah on February 28, 1928, of "a great social and economic experiment, noble in motive and far-reaching in purpose." But there were 327 murders in Chicago alone in one Prohibition year, and not a single conviction for murder that year; the "wets" quoted Isaiah (24:11): "There is a crying for wine in the streets; all joy is darkened, the mirth of the land is gone."

Hoover is best remembered for phrases he nearly said, or claimed he did not originate, or denied having said at all. He did not say "CHICKEN IN EVERY POT"; he said he did not originate "RUGGED INDIVIDUALISM," and as seen here, he did not quite say "NOBLE EXPERIMENT." And he certainly did not name the collection of Depression shacks "Hoovervilles."

"Noble experiment" is applied now to hopelessly lost causes. Its predecessor phrase was "Holy Experiment," English Quaker William Penn's term for his 1682 colony of Pennsylvania. That experiment worked.

See RUNNING AGAINST HOOVER.

nobody drowned at Watergate a slogan used by Nixon partisans to express resentment at what they believed was a double standard of political morality.

In the early stages of the Watergate scandal, many of the President's supporters believed that the break-in at Democratic headquarters was little more than had been described by press secretary Ron Ziegler: a "third-rate burglary." To them, the COVER-UP which aroused such widespread indignation was similar to the attempts made by Senator Edward F. Kennedy in 1969 to seal information at an inquest in Edgartown, Mass., following "the Chappaquiddick incident."

At Chappaquiddick, a young woman named Mary Jo Kopechne had died when a car Senator Kennedy was driving plunged into a river. Nixon supporters, claiming that Senator Kennedy was not subjected to the same rigorous examination that a non-Kennedy would have been under similar circumstances, suggested that the loss of life in the Chappaquiddick incident made it far more important and worthy of investigation than the Watergate break-in. Hence the phrase "nobody drowned at Watergate," which was in the air some months before the *Wall Street Journal* quoted Secretary of Agriculture Earl Butz saying it in 1974.

A curious twist on the construction came in 1978 when Georgia supporters of banker Bert Lance believed he was being hounded out of his job as Jimmy Carter's Director of the Office of Management and Budget for minor irregularities committed when he ran a bank in Calhoun, Georgia. The resentment took the form of a bumper sticker that was reported to be on a car in southern Georgia: "Nobody Drowned at the Calhoun Bank."

no comment an outdated, pretentious phrase to ward off a reporter's query, now used by political novices with no skill at fencing.

When the expression was fairly fresh, Winston Churchill used it with zest. After a White House meeting with President Truman in 1946, he evaded questions with: "I think 'No comment' is a splendid expression. I got it from Sumner Welles."

Before making that discovery, Churchill—early in his career—used a form of excruciating euphemism to avoid a position. When asked, in 1906, if the British government was condoning slavery of Chinese laborers in South

Africa, he replied, "It could not, in the opinion of His Majesty's Government, be classified as slavery in the extreme acceptance of the word without some risk of terminological inexactitude."

Before he was a candidate for President, Franklin Roosevelt said he knew the value of "sitting tight, sawing wood and keeping my mouth shut"; his cousin Theodore had once written: ". . . what is needed for me is to follow the advice given by the New Bedford whaling captain to his mate when he told that all he wanted from him was silence and damn little of that."

At press conferences FDR's favorite evasive action was "That's an IFFY QUESTION." Grover Cleveland was much more blunt; once when asked something he preferred not to answer, he glared at the reporter and said, "Young man, that is an issue too big to be brought up in a brief interview that is drawing rapidly to a close."

Best known for his taciturnity was "Silent Cal" Coolidge, who answered critics with a mild "I have noticed that nothing I never said ever did me any harm." President Lyndon Johnson, when pressed, avoided the words "No comment," substituting something like "I don't have anything to say about that at this time." He passed along advice given him by former House Speaker Sam Rayburn: "You don't have to explain what you don't say."

Another riposte is to challenge the basis or the phraseology of the question or to play tricks with language: at his first press conference as head of the Council of Economic Advisers, Walter Heller listened to a reporter object to a lack of cost estimates of the Administration's anti-recession program. "The inference will be drawn," said the reporter, "that you don't care very much about how much they'll cost." Heller snapped back with a smile: "That may be the inference, but not the implication."

Diplomats must say nothing nice to reporters; Harold Macmillan said of the post of Foreign Secretary, "He is forever poised between a cliché and an indiscretion." UN Secretary General Dag Hammarskjöld phrased his "No comment" as "I never discuss discussions."

Political managers often advise their candidates to say nothing. Tammany chieftain Charles Murphy advised young Mayor-to-be James Walker: "Most of the troubles of the world could be avoided if men opened their minds instead of their mouths." A century earlier, banker Nicholas Biddle told party managers to pass the word to "Tippecanoe" Harrison: "Let him say not one single word about his principles, or his creed—let him say nothing—promise nothing. Let no committee, no convention—no town meeting ever extract from him a single word about what he thinks or what he will do hereafter. Let the use of pen and ink be wholly forbidden."

The reason for Biddle's advice was explained by Alexis de Tocqueville in *Democracy in America:* "The general interest of a party frequently demands that members belonging to it should not speak on great questions which they understand imperfectly; that they should speak but little on those minor questions which impede the great ones; lastly, and for the most part, that they should not speak at all. To keep silence is the most useful service that an indifferent spokesman can render to the Commonwealth."

John Selden, who served in Parliament in the seventeenth century, observed: "Wise men say nothing in dangerous times." Three centuries later, physicist Albert Einstein reduced this advice—and that of Tammany boss Murphy—to the following formula: "If *A* equals success, then the formula is A equals X plus Y plus Z. X is work. Y is play. Z is keep your mouth shut."

Charles de Gaulle put it this way in *The Edge of the Sword:* "There can be no power without mystery. There must always be a 'something' which others cannot altogether fathom, which puzzles them, stirs them, and rivets their attention. . . . Nothing more enhances authority than silence. It is the crowning virtue of the strong, the refuge of the weak, the modesty of the proud, the pride of the humble, the prudence of the wise, and the sense of fools . . .'"

But there is such a thing as carrying a zipped lip too far. In an unauthenticated speech made to party and army cadres in Peking in July 30, 1977, Foreign Minister Huang Hua recalled his use of the phrase when he was China's UN ambassador: "While I was in New York, a Swedish reporter once asked me if he could be of service to me. I said: 'No comment.' That reporter then asked me if we Chinese really had nothing to say except 'No comment.' I repeated: 'No comment.' As a socialist country, however, it does not seem right if our responsible comrades have learned only to say 'No comment.' Sometimes we should give out some news."

In 1985, the *Washington Post* reported Reagan Communications Director Pat Buchanan's standard, jocular response when asked a question by the media: "No comment! And that's off the record." (See OFF THE RECORD.)

no-deal. See DEAL.

-nomics the economic policies of or economic theory of.

This combining form first became popular in 1969, with the formation of *Nixonomics* to indicate Nixon's economic policies. Inside the White House, it was propagated by the lexicographer in his role as economic speechwriter to put the Presidential brand on a turgid policy; outside, it was popularized by the columnists Rowland Evans and Robert Novak.

Its ease of formation is based on the final *n* in Nixon's name; the lack of a final *n* in the names of Ford and Carter may well account for the rare usage of *Fordonomics* and *Carternomics*.

More popular was *Reaganomics*, again with the suffix easily combining with the *n* that ends Reagan's name. Two years after the 1980 Presidential campaign, in which George Bush derided Reagan's supply-side theories as "voodoo economics," Urban League president John Jacob said that *Reaganomics* "is giving voodoo a bad name."

The same combining form, which joins with the final *n* without repeating the letter, has produced *Clintonomics*.

no more Mr. Nice Guy. See MR. NICE GUY.

nonpartisan without thought of party politics.

In current usage, *bipartisan* means the cooperative efforts of both parties in an area usually the scene of party disagreement; *nonpartisan* (or, as Senator Arthur Vandenberg preferred, *unpartisan*) means areas of civic or patriotic interest where party or ideological difference never arises. The meaning corresponds to the prefixes: two-party, no-party.

The phrase most closely associated with nonpartisan is ABOVE POLITICS; with bipartisan, WATER'S EDGE.

Pleas for nonpartisanship stem from Washington's farewell address deploring the "baneful effects of the spirit of party," Madison shaking his head at "faction," and Jefferson stating flatly, "If I could not go to Heaven but with a party, I would not go there at all."

When FDR in 1939 called for "cooperation . . . without trace of partisanship," speechwriter Samuel Rosenman properly called it "a plea for nonpartisanship in the form of bipartisanship."

Denunciations of partisanship and of party connection have been prevalent throughout U.S. history, particularly by weaker candidates who felt the need to prove their independence. Zachary Taylor, for example, whose long military COATTAILS helped popularize that expression, took no controversial positions as a Whig in 1848: "If elected, I would not be the mere president of a party. I would endeavor to act independent of party domination. I should feel bound to administer the government untrammeled by party schemes." Taylor won, but the Whigs lost Congress.

Nonpartisanship is also called for by leaders of a party under attack, with some reason, for corruption. Charles Evans Hughes, a tower of integrity in the Harding Administration, said as scandals like Teapot Dome began to be exposed: "Neither political party has a monopoly of virtue or of rascality. Let wrong be exposed and punished, but let no partisan Pecksniffs affect a 'holier-than-thou' attitude. Guilt is personal and knows no party." Adlai Stevenson, fighting off the "mess in Washington" charge in 1952, used Hughes's statement to no avail.

Rarely if ever do public figures stand foursquare in favor of partisanship, though all will speak up for the TWO-PARTY SYSTEM, another way of saying the same thing. Bronx Democratic boss Ed Flynn got to the heart of the matter: "There is no such thing as nonpartisanship. If there were, there would be no need for elections. The phrase 'nonpartisanship' has a high moral tone. It is used by men running for public office to attract votes, but deep down in their hearts these men know that it is only a word without real meaning. There is, and always

must be, honest disagreement. All of us have our likes and dislikes. And that is the genesis of partisanship."

See PARTISAN; PRESIDENT OF ALL THE PEOPLE.

nonpolitical trip   tongue-in-cheek term for a political tour, or "swing around the circle," made to appear "nonpolitical" for strategic or fund-raising reasons.

When an officeholder travels on official business, the public pays his way; on an admittedly politically motivated journey, he must get his party or his supporters to finance him. In the case of Presidents, the very appearance of acting as President is more potent than any purely or frankly "political" act; therefore, presidential press secretaries straight-facedly announce "nonpolitical" trips that must, whether intended or not, have strong political overtones. (For a similar construction, see FACT-FINDING TRIP.)

Washington attorney Clark Clifford, appointed Defense Secretary in 1968 and an adviser to Democratic candidates and Presidents for a generation, wrote a campaign memo to Harry Truman in 1948 that charted one portion of what was to be a stunning upset:

Since he is President, he cannot be conspicuously active politically until well after the convention. So a President who is also a candidate must resort to subterfuge. He cannot sit silent; he must be in the limelight. . . . He must resort to the kind of trip Roosevelt made famous in the 1940 campaign—the inspection tour. . . . No matter how much the opposition and the press pointed out the political overtones of those trips, the people paid little attention, for what they saw was the Head of State performing his duties.

Manchester Guardian correspondent Alistair Cooke wrote of a 1964 campaign tour of Lyndon Johnson's: ". . . on this 'non-political,' two-day

9000-mile trip, somebody saw to it that 10,000 people turned up in Great Falls, Montana, 25,000 in Blaine, Washington, that he paid a swift courtesy call on the Mormon Church in Salt Lake City, and that he touched down at Seattle, Portland, and Sacramento, the political power stations of the West Coast."

It is hard to get passionate about this practice, especially since Thomas Jefferson and James Madison visited New York in 1791 for political reasons, blandly letting it be known they were looking for wild flowers and a rare species of butterfly in the Hudson Valley. John F. Kennedy, early in the 1960 primaries, referred to this excuse and added, "But I'm not looking for butterflies. I'm looking for votes."

nonstarter   a doomed proposal; a diplomatic démarche that fails to develop or to make progress.

In English horse-racing jargon, a horse entered in a race but withdrawn before the start is called a *nonstarter*; the American term is a *scratch*.

From horse racing, the word was extended into business usage. In the 1970s, *nonstarter* was in frequent use by Washington Foreign Service officers, but the word's diplomatic origins are decades older.

Michael Stoil of Arlington, Virginia, provides a British Foreign Office memo dated February 12, 1918. The unprophetic writer of the memo discusses three potential winners in the struggle for control of Russia at the end of World War I: "The Ukrainian Rada was certainly a bad horse to back, Cossack [the Denikin regime] is almost a nonstarter, but Bolshevik would be the worst of the lot on which to lay our money."

nonviolence   a technique of bringing about social change through peaceful but dramatic demonstrations.

The word is most closely associated with Mohandas K. Gandhi as "the first article of my faith." But the Mahatma's method of "passive resistance" was improved upon by leaders of the civil rights movement in the U.S. in the early 1960s.

The Reverend Martin Luther King, Jr., called 1961 "a year of the victory of the nonviolent method; although blood flowed, not one drop was drawn by a Negro from his adversary."

In Birmingham, Alabama, in 1963, King and his followers were criticized by clergymen of that city for provoking violence. In "Letter from a Birmingham Jail" King answered that criticism: "Is not this like condemning the robbed man because his possession of money precipitated the evil act of robbery?" He added: "I have tried to stand between these two forces saying that we need not follow the 'do-nothingism' of the complacent or the hatred and despair of the black nationalist. There is the more excellent way of love and nonviolent protest. I'm grateful to God that, through the Negro church, the dimension of nonviolence entered our struggle. If this philosophy had not emerged I am convinced that by now many streets of the South would be flowing with floods of blood."

By the mid-sixties, however, the word was used to mock black leaders unable to moderate their own extremists. Though the Student Nonviolent Coordinating Committee had nonviolence in its title, it became an anachronism to SNCC leaders like H. "Rap" Brown, who called in 1967 "for less rooting and more shooting."

no problem   1. easy; 2. yes; 3. you're welcome; 4. the situation is being handled.

This expression of approval has joined *O.K.* among the most famous Americanisms in global use.

The Russian equivalent of the term, for instance, is *nyet problema*. A similar Russian term, *normalno* (from the English *normal*), expresses the idea without offering the same degree of assurance.

Print citations for *no problem* date back to the early 1960s. In 1963, the journal *American Speech* used it to gloss another, slangier synonym: "'No sweat' means 'no problem.'" The overuse of the expression, however, has led to its inclusion in the title of Christine Ammer's dictionary of clichés: *Have a Nice Day—No Problem!*

Out of this expression has come another one bordering on a cliché: "to have a problem with (something)," meaning "to find it unacceptable, disagreeable, unwelcome, etc." It is often used positively, as in "I don't have a problem with that." But equally often it serves as an aggressive (or defensive) verbal tactic, assuming an "attitude," as in this passage in a 1992 issue of *People* magazine: "Evander Holyfield, who'll defend his heavyweight title this week, loosens up with ballet exercises. You got a problem with that?"

normalcy period of retrenchment, of stability; the promise of Warren G. Harding.

"Not heroism but healing, not nostrums but normalcy" was the campaign theme of Ohio publisher Warren Harding in 1920, running with Coolidge against Cox and Roosevelt. For the rest of the quotation, see AL-LITERATION; for variations, see CATCH-WORD.

"After a diet of strong occasions," wrote political scientist Harold Laski, "a nation, like an individual, turns naturally to the chance of a quiet time. 'Normalcy' is always certain to be popular after crises." Wrote Eisenhower in his memoirs: "Twice in this century the United States, at the end of a war, had celebrated the victory, brought the troops back home, and

with relief and hope tried to return to 'normalcy.'" Harding's use of the word might have been a mistake; some say the word was written "normality" and fluffed, but if true, the mistake was fortunate: the word caught on to symbolize not only a campaign but an era.

The much-abused Harding (whose talent for alliteration led to his coinage of FOUNDING FATHERS) was defended on the charge of error by no less an authority than H. B. Woolf, editorial director of G. & C. Merriam Company, who wrote *New York Times* reporter Israel Shenker in 1972: "It is true that Harding's use of *normalcy* subjected him to considerable criticism, but he defended himself by pointing out he found it in the dictionary. (See the *Times* for July 21, 1920.) The word dates from at least 1857, and it is an entry in the 1864, 1890, and 1909 editions of the Merriam-Webster Unabridged."

In a less sloganeering way, Harding returned to the theme that elected him in his inaugural address: "Our supreme task is the resumption of our onward, normal way . . . the normal balances have been impaired, the channels of distribution have been clogged, the relations of labor and management have been strained . . . we must strive to normalcy to reach stability."

In 1993, the term was preferred to *normality* by the *Washington Post* in describing a riot in Mogadishu, Somalia: "The fragile calm that gave a semblance of normalcy to this ravaged city burst apart today as rampaging mobs shouted for American troops to leave, pelted U.S. and U.N. forces with rocks and looted the Egyptian and French embassies."

normalization. See VIETNAMIZATION.

nose count informal, often secret, survey of a likely vote within a relatively small group, frequently within Congress.

Drawn from the verb phrase *to count noses*, this noun phrase is sometimes hyphenated; it is turned into a gerund as *nose-counting*.

The phrase began in the 1930s with the sense of a calculation of numerical size. *Life* magazine reported in 1938: "In London peace-yearning Prime Minister Chamberlain again tried to quarantine the Spanish war by proposing a nose-count and withdrawal of foreign troops."

By 1960, the term was being applied to that decade's census. The *Times* of London commented in September 1960 that "there was much talk just then of the coming 'Nose Count' over the U.S.A. which was one way of making their census sound more personal and pointed." A decade later, *Business Week*, printing the phrase as a one-word compound, referred to the census as "the decennial nosecount."

The term's sense has been narrowed in political usage to the estimation of the outcome of a close vote. A *Christian Science Monitor* article on Western voters in 1986 acknowledged that "a nose count along party lines may be meaningless in much of the region, where party ties tend to be weaker than in the East or the South."

In current use, the phrase—more colorful than *head count*—is applied most often to assessments of strength within legislatures or caucuses; an adept estimator is known as a good nose-counter.

See STRAW POLL.

no substitute for victory the rallying cry of General of the Army Douglas MacArthur, in his address to Congress of April 19, 1951, following his removal from command in the Far East by President Truman.

Said MacArthur:

I know war as few other men now living know it, and nothing to me is more revolting. I have long advocated its complete abolition, as its very destructiveness on both friend and foe has rendered it useless as a means of settling international disputes. . . .

But once [war] was forced upon us, there is no other alternative than to apply every available means to bring it to a swift end. War's very object is victory, not prolonged indecision.

In war there can be no substitute for victory.

This statement put him into conflict with another theory of war that had been gradually evolving: that it is possible to wage deliberately controlled, LIMITED WAR for limited objectives.

The statement should be considered in the context of the times. General MacArthur had ruled Japan since World War II as something of a proconsul, neither brooking nor being offered much interference. He had conducted the Korean conflict in much the same spirit. But he had been refused permission to turn the 600,000 Chinese Nationalist troops on Formosa loose against the mainland with American logistical support. He had been denied the large numbers of reinforcements he had demanded and refused permission to send bombers against enemy bases north of the Yalu River, the border between North Korea and China.

The General's pressure led President Truman and his advisers to consider MacArthur's removal. When the General wrote a letter to Republican House Minority Leader Joseph Martin, which he read in the House of Representatives, Truman determined to replace his Far East Commander. The recall came hastily when it became known that the *Chicago Tribune,* a paper friendly to the General's views, was about to break the story.

The immediate result was a furor in which personalities, strategies, and constitutional positions were thoroughly intermixed. A senatorial investigation was begun by those friendly to the General's views, but the course of the investigation ran eventually in the Administration's favor.

The conflicting theses were stated in May 1951 when Senator Leverett Saltonstall quoted from a speech by Dean Rusk, then Assistant Secretary of State, who formulated the core of the limited-war concept: "What we are trying to do is to maintain peace and security without a general war. We are saying to the aggressors, 'You will not be allowed to get away with your crime. You must stop it.' At the same time we are trying to prevent a general conflagration which would consume the very things we are now trying to defend."

General MacArthur totally rejected the new limited-war theory. "I think," he said, "that introduces into the military sphere a political control such as I have not known in my life or have ever studied."

See NO-WIN POLICY; OLD SOLDIERS NEVER DIE.

not for attribution an agreement between journalist and news source to use information without revealing where it came from.

Not for attribution should not be confused with OFF THE RECORD, when the information is given with the understanding that it will not be used, or with *background*, where a source may be indicated—as "an Administration official" or "a Congressional source" —but not named.

Until late 1971 (when the *Washington Post* began to object to "collusion" between government and press) the Washington press corps had generally accepted the Lindley Rule, named after journalist Ernest K. Lindley, enabling the President to discuss affairs of the day with reporters without either being quoted or referred to at all.

In an article in the *Columbia Journalism Review* entitled "The President Nonspeaks," Ben Bagdikian wrote: "Under the Lindley Rules . . . no meeting took place so far as the public is concerned. If reporters want to use something the nonspeaker has said at the nonmeeting, they must paraphrase the nonspeaker and attribute his ideas to their own intuition or some nameless source." See BACKGROUNDER; TRIAL BALLOON; PLANT.

Mr. Lindley, in 1968 a Special Assistant to Secretary of State Dean Rusk, informed the lexicographer (for attribution):

The Lindley Rule was laid down early in the Truman Administration to enable high ranking officials to discuss important matters—especially those involving international and military affairs—without being quoted or referred to in any way. It was, and is, a rule of no attribution—thus differing from the usual "background rule" permitting attribution to "official sources" or "U.S. officials," etc. Thus the paragraph you quote from Bagdikian is not quite correct—attribution to a "nameless source" is not permitted under the Lindley Rule.

The point is a fine one, but there can be no arguing with Hoyle himself: "not for attribution" means the newsman must take responsibility for the statement without hinting where it came from. This is also called "deep background."

The British use "on lobby terms" for the same technique, from "lobby journalist" who picks up his news outside legislative halls. "Under this system," wrote M.P. Anthony Wedgewood Benn in 1964 in the *Manchester Guardian*, "Ministers and M.P.'s can talk 'on lobby terms' to journalists, confident that nothing they say will be attributed to them; and journalists can always find out what is really happening without bothering to dig on their own. . . . One day some political correspondent is going to tumble to the fact that he would do far better to abandon the cosy comfort of 'lobby terms' and set up the sort of private political intelligence unit that every newspaper should have."

The hyphenated phrase *not-for-attribution* is current. In 1992, *Roll Call* wrote of foreign policy discussed "by some advisors to Clinton (in not-for-attribution conversations)." Howard Kurtz wrote in the *Washington Post* in 1993: "And don't forget how James Baker led a charmed media life by feeding not-for-attribution tidbits to key reporters."

nothing to fear but fear itself a classic phrase of Franklin Roosevelt's, from the opening of his first inaugural address, March 4, 1933.

"This is no occasion of soft speaking or for the raising of false hopes." FDR crossed out that line in an early draft, and substituted the more positive statement:

> This is preeminently the time to speak the truth, the whole truth, frankly and boldly. Nor need we shrink from honestly facing conditions in our country today. This great nation will endure as it has endured, will revive and will prosper.
> So, first of all, let me assert my firm belief that the only thing we have to fear is fear itself—nameless, unreasoning, unjustified terror which paralyzes needed efforts to convert retreat into advance.

Who wrote it? Like NEW DEAL, this has been the subject of some heated controversy among Roosevelt intimates. The copy of the first draft of the speech, in Roosevelt's handwriting, and with a cover note from FDR attesting to its composition at Hyde Park, February 27, 1933, from 9 P.M. to 1:30 A.M., does not contain the famous opening. "The final draft," wrote Sam-

uel I. Rosenman, who edited the Roosevelt public papers, "was typed on March 3. . . . In that last draft the . . . 'fear' sentence had been inserted. The way it was changed was typical of what the President could do with a speech—even in the great rush . . ."

Rosenman never asked Roosevelt where the "fear" sentence came from, and did not notice until after FDR's death that it was not in the first draft. He speculated: "It bears a striking resemblance to a statement about fear written by Henry David Thoreau: 'Nothing is so much to be feared as fear.' Eleanor Roosevelt has told me that one of her friends had given the President a copy of some of Thoreau's writings shortly before the day of inauguration, and that it was in his suite at the hotel while this speech was being polished."

In *FDR: The Lion and the Fox*, historian James MacGregor Burns puts that speculation in such a way that the reader can only draw one conclusion: "In his hotel room Roosevelt worked over the speech. Nearby was a copy of Thoreau, with the words, 'Nothing is so much to be feared as fear.'"

Brain truster Raymond Moley dismisses all this. He stated positively in 1966 that Louis Howe wrote the "fear" line, and that Howe got the idea from a newspaper ad that featured the quote a few weeks before. "I was in Roosevelt's Mayflower suite," Moley wrote this lexicographer, ". . . I saw no books there. Nor was I familiar with Thoreau. I had been with Roosevelt more than a year and never heard him mention Thoreau. . . . And Howe, whose reading—which his asthma-provoked insomnia required—was confined exclusively to detective stories and newspapers, may never have heard of Thoreau."

Moley's history marches to the beat of a different drummer: he was with

FDR at Hyde Park on the night of February 27, and submitted a draft of the inaugural to him. "He read over my draft carefully and then said that he had better write out the text himself because if Louis Howe (who was expected the next morning) failed to see a draft in his (Roosevelt's) handwriting, he would 'have a fit.'" Presumably FDR wanted to conceal from Howe the fact that he had a ghostwriter. After Roosevelt copied out the speech, Moley says he tossed his own first draft into the fire. "Then, in the morning, as had been anticipated, Howe got his hand into the composition. He proceeded to redictate the draft, adding . . . a first paragraph. . . . I do clearly remember that the phrase appeared in a department store's newspaper advertisement some time earlier in February. I assume that Howe, an inveterate newspaper reader, saw it too. . . . To Howe's everlasting credit, he realized that the expression fully fitted the occasion."

The who-wrote-it controversy is dwelt on in some length here because it illustrates (1) the difficulty of pinning down the originator of a phrase, and (2) the relative unimportance of the writer as compared to the speaker and the forum. The message was in the ad, assuming Moley's recollection is correct, but who cared? Who even noticed, besides a gnomelike man who had the ear of the President-elect? The phrase did not belong to Howe, nor to the advertising copywriter, nor to all those who had used it previously (including Sir Francis Bacon: "Nothing is to be feared but fear . . ." Epictetus, Cicero, Burke, William James, and others). It was Roosevelt's phrase, and it might have rated only a modest mention in a news story had it not been spoken in a momentous inaugural address.

In current use, "nothing" takes precedence over "the only thing," as in a 1968 cartoon by Mahood in the *Times*

of London showing Dean Rusk reading a newspaper to a worried Lyndon Johnson: "Apart from Kennedy, McCarthy, Nixon, the Viet Nam war, the Senate Foreign Relations Committee and the price of gold, you have nothing to fear but fear itself."

not too much zeal. See GUNG HO.

November Republicans voters who register in one party to participate in its primary but who intend to vote for the other party in the general election.

This is a Texas expression. Since the Democratic party dominates Texas politics on the local level, many voters who wish to have a voice in the selection of a candidate for sheriff will register Democratic. But their voting habits in the general election, especially on the national scene, run to the opposite party—hence, "November Republicans."

See CROSSOVER VOTE.

novus ordo seclorum. See UNITED WE STAND; NEW WORLD ORDER.

no-win policy attack phrase on what is considered an overly cautious military effort, leading not to victory but to stalemate.

The phrase illustrates the exasperation felt by many people at limited warfare. General Douglas MacArthur (see NO SUBSTITUTE FOR VICTORY) told the Republican convention in 1952: "It is fatal to enter any war without the will to win it." When General Mark Clark returned home in 1953 after the truce in the Korean conflict, he reflected the unsatisfied attitude of many Americans: "I return with feelings of misgiving from my third war—I was the first American commander to put his signature to a paper ending a war when we did not win it."

The fact that Eisenhower was a Republican, conservative at least in fiscal affairs, and a former general with an overwhelming reputation for military judgment, muted the ultraconservative attacks on the lack of a "victory plan" against Communism. But when the Democrats returned to power in 1961, and especially after the Bay of Pigs, a typical comment was made by Rear Admiral Chester Ward (Ret.), of the rightwing American Security Council: "Americans are tired of surrenders covered up as 'negotiated settlements.' . . . For the first time in sixteen years of the cold war, a demand for victory is beginning to roll into Washington."

Barry Goldwater's biography was titled *Victory Is His Flight Plan*. Moderates and liberals had difficulty finding phrases that counseled patience and firmness without provocation. "In the face of right-wing attacks," wrote sociologist David Riesman, "the administration denies that it is pursuing a 'no-win' policy; it argues instead that it is just as combative, only more clever or roundabout."

Bayard Rustin, organizer of the March on Washington, made the phrase part of the civil rights lexicon: he charged black radicals who rejected the help of white liberals with having a "no-win" attitude, seeking shock with no legislative or social goal. "My quarrel with the no-win tendency," Rustin wrote in the February 1965 *Commentary*, ". . . parallels my quarrel with the moderates outside the movement. As the latter lack the vision or the will for fundamental change, the former lack a realistic strategy for achieving it. For such a strategy they substitute militancy. But militancy is a matter of posture and volume and not of effect."

The turnaround of the phrase, proving its permanence, took a long time to come. It was not until November 30, 1977, that the *Washington Star* carried a headline: "On the Middle East, Car-ter Lucks into a 'No-Lose' Position." The antonym is *win-win*.

now is the time . . . for all good men to come to the aid of the party. A typewriter exercise and not a political slogan.

Charles E. Weller, a court reporter in Milwaukee in 1867, devised the sentence to cover most of the keys on the typewriter, a new invention by his friend Christopher Latham Sholes. It has about as much political significance as "the quick brown fox jumps over the lazy dog," which is much more useful, since it covers all 26 letters in the alphabet, compared to Weller's 18.

nuclear family. See FAMILY VALUES.

nuclear proliferation the growth in the number of nations that possess atomic or hydrogen bombs.

The phrase is a mouthful, and a constant challenge to speakers. Atomic jargoneers say that when the possession of atomic weapons *diffuses* among many nations, the result of scientific information's *dissemination,* what takes place is nuclear *proliferation*.

"Proliferation" comes from a Latin root meaning "offspring," and was mainly used in biology to denote division of cells or budding of plants.

Adlai Stevenson used it politically, possibly for the first time, in his 1949 inaugural address as governor of Illinois, describing the process by which state departments mushroomed into large bureaucracies. One newsman told the new governor he had looked up the word and as far as he could tell, it had something to do with the way coral spreads. "That's good," laughed Stevenson, "better than I thought."

As the U.S. Ambassador to the UN, Stevenson used the word often, as in a 1964 broadcast about Soviet attitudes: "They, too, want to insure the world against the proliferation of nuclear weapons."

President Kennedy had said much the same thing, using a smaller word: "The struggle against nuclear spread is as much in the Soviet interest as our own." The word "spread" means the same in this case, is far easier to handle and understand, and was often used later by Senator Robert Kennedy. However, the subject is momentous, and the word "proliferate" is properly ominous.

See SALT.

nuclear trigger. See FINGER ON THE BUTTON; TRIGGER-HAPPY; TRIPWIRE.

numbers game the misleading use of statistics in political argument.

"Figures don't lie, but liars do figure" is an expression often applied to those who play the numbers game. An effective attack phrase against those who marshal sound or unsound statistical arguments, "numbers game" connotes gambling ("the numbers racket").

When the White House in 1954 announced that 2,427 SECURITY RISKS had been removed from their jobs since the Eisenhower administration took office, Adlai Stevenson dubbed it a "numbers game," pointing out that this figure included many who had resigned their posts unaware that they had ever been considered "risks."

"Through two political campaigns," wrote Cabell Phillips in *The Truman Administration,* referring to 1954 and 1956, "Republican party spokesmen played an avid 'numbers game' with the monthly statistics of the Loyalty Review Board to demonstrate the GOP's prowess in cleaning out the Communists left behind by the Democrats. The totals were made to look impressive by lumping voluntary resignations with dismissals. When this bit of chicanery was exposed by the press, the 'numbers game' fell into disuse."

A similar expression is "crowdsmanship," the technique of inducing a police official to overestimate to reporters the number of people in a rally crowd. A cooperative cop can turn a meager airport turnout (adding the pilot and crew, innocent bystanders and the reporters and police themselves) into "a few hundred enthusiastic supporters, despite the threatening weather." Some policemen try to be scientific, estimating crowds by figuring two square feet per person; others have been known to straight-facedly explain, "I get down on my haunches, count the feet, and divide by two."

nut-cutting dirty work; a slang allusion to castration, its political meaning is the denial of favors and the removal of power.

To "get down to the nut-cutting" means to abandon broad policy discussion and deal with hard specifics of patronage and pecking order. The phrase was inadvertently used by Richard Nixon publicly at the end of the 1968 campaign in its second meaning of detail work or "brass tacks" (see NITTY-GRITTY). Other taboo expressions with the same metaphoric source used in and out of politics include "ballbuster" (a slave-driving boss, or a particularly difficult problem) and "by the SHORT HAIRS" (to have another in circumstances where control is an easy matter).

When Senator John Tower was being considered for a cabinet position, an unnamed critic was quoted in the *Boston Globe* of November 22, 1988: "This guy's been really cozy with . . . the services, especially the Navy. If the time for serious nut-cutting came, he could be a real foot-dragger."

See HANG TOUGH.

nuts and kooks. See KOOKS, NUTS AND.

obsolete political terms

anxious seat (potential candidate, probable loser)

backstairs influence (manipulation by hidden supporters)

barnacle (hanger-on)

bashaw (high-ranking politician, from Turkish *pasha*)

big bug (replaced by big shot, big wheel)

black-and-tans (pro-black Southern Republicans)

bogus baby (bad legislation)

bottle holder (adviser, from boxing)

buffalo hunt (cover for territorial acquisitions)

bullwhacker (tough political boss)

candle-box returns (phony votes)

come-outer (bolter)

crawfish (back out of a firm position)

cuttlefish (obscure an issue, confuse)

dirt eater (Southerner favoring Union)

doughface (Northerner favoring slavery)

fat-frying (fund solicitation)

fire eaters (Southern secessionists)

floater (swing voter)

forty thieves (politicians in control of finances)

fugleman (henchman)

half-breed (splinter group, anti-regular)

heroite (Jackson supporter)

hewgag (clarion call for action)

hunker (conservative Democrat)

leg treasurer (official who absconds with money)

loaves and fishes (spoils, plums)

Loco Foco (anti-Tammany, hard-money Democrats)

mucker (reformer)

off horse (disgruntled politician)

organ grinder (partisan newspaperman)

pap (government handouts)

persimmon (plum)

rag baby (greenback Democrat)

regulators (vigilantes)

ring (derogatory, political organization)

rooster (Democratic symbol)

Salt River (place of political defeat)

scratcher (split ticket voter)

shreaker (a bolter)

soap (graft)

still hunt (undercover investigation)

straight-outs (Democrats who tend to bolt)

subsoil (secretly laying the groundwork)

Sunday School (civil service reformers)

swing around the circle (tour the country)

taffy (phony promises)

tin pan (a caucus)

trimmer (opportunist)

wide-awakes (independent Republican clubs)

wire worker (small-time political manager)

young scratcher (antimachine Republican)

obstruction of justice. See SMOKING GUN; STONEWALLING; COVER-UP.

-ocracy combining form for "government" or "power."

This suffix is most often seen in *democracy*, a noun first found in English in the 1500s and ultimately derived from the Greek *demos*, "people," and *kratos*, "power." For a follower or advocate of such power, the combining form is *-crat* or *-ocrat*, as in *democrat*.

Many nouns have been formed using the *-cracy* suffix, usually connected to the root word by the vowel *o*:

intellocracy: This term designates the rule by philosophers and great thinkers of Paris in the mid-twentieth century. As the critic John Sturrock wrote in the *New York Times Book Review* in early 1993, "Once Paris had, not common intellectuals, but *intellocrats*, hardened professionals of abstraction whose job it was to direct the thoughts of their fellow citizens, particularly along the sinuous paths of political correctness . . . The old-style French intellocracy died a sumptuous death in 1980 with Jean-Paul Sartre."

kakistocracy: Meaning "government by the worst citizens," this negative term dates back to 1829.

kleptocracy: From the same first root as *kleptomania*, this word means "rule by thieves." It appeared in an 1819 comment on "titular ornaments, common to the Spanish kleptocracy" and was later applied to the Panamanian regime of Manuel Noriega.

meritocracy: A 1958 coinage, this term refers to advancement by merit,

either in government, with leaders selected by intellectual ability, or in schools, with advancement according to achievement.

mobocracy: This 1754 creation means "rule by the mob." (*Mob* itself is a shortening of the Latin *mobile vulgus*, "inconstant crowd.")

monocracy: Meaning "rule by a single person," this word dates back to 1651.

plutocracy: "Government by the wealthy" is the definition of this 1652 noun, a favorite of FDR's, formed from the Greek *ploutos*, "wealth."

punditocracy: This term (coined by Eric Alterman in 1988) uses *pundit*, a Hindi term from the Sanskrit *pandita* for "learned," now applied to scholars and opinion-givers. An October 1992 piece by David Von Drehle in the *Washington Post* was headlined "Punditocracy Faces Dizzying Spin Cycle," and the reporter satirized talkshow political commentary by suggesting, "Normally, the punditocracy needs at least a day or two to calcify spontaneous reactions into Conventional Wisdom (C.W.). But with debates scheduled for Oct. 11, 13, 15 and 19, there may not be enough time for the orderly formation of group think."

technocracy: Dating back to World War I, this term refers to a society managed by technical experts.

theocracy: Using *the-*, a Greek-based prefix for "god," this 1622 formation refers to any system of government based on divine or religious rules, including leaders who are considered to be guided by God.

October surprise last-minute disruption before a November election; unexpected political stunt or revelation that could affect an election's outcome.

The prospect of an *October surprise* by the opposition, planned or not, worries politicians. In 1980, Reagan campaign manager William Casey told

Washington columnists of his suspicion that Democrats, trailing, would pull a fast one at the last minute, and Vice Presidential candidate George Bush promoted the term in a 1980 campaign statement: "All I know is there's a concern, not just with us but I think generally amongst the electorate, well, this Carter's a politically tough fellow, he'll do anything to get reelected, and let's be prepared for some October surprise."

The Iran-contra controversy, however, turned the attack phrase (as well as a variant, *October fix*) back on the Republicans. For a decade afterward, Carter aides charged that Reagan-Bush campaigners influenced the Ayatollah Khomeini's followers to delay releasing American hostages until after the 1980 election. A Congressional investigation found no evidence of such a plot.

By 1991, the phrase *October surprise* was being applied to any controversial or unpleasant event in October. *U.S. News & World Report* commented in October 1991 that "the big investment story currently unfolding is not in stocks, where the financial press is fanning fears that another nasty October surprise could lie in store. It's in the fixed-income markets—bonds."

office seeks the man. See JOB SEEKS THE MAN.

officialese government jargon, intended to impress, conceal, or confuse; often the result of writing with scissors and pastepot.

Probably the first word along these lines was *legalese,* coined by an exasperated layman who could not make sense out of a legal opinion. However, legalese has the virtue of eliminating ambiguity, and should be read more as a mathematical equation than as prose, anything herein to the contrary notwithstanding.

Commercialese is a clean-prose movement aimed at killing ult., inst., per, and enclosed please find.

Proper names ending in -*n* lend themselves to -*ese*-ing, as in *Reaganese* and *Clintonese. Gamalielese* was H. L. Mencken's word for bloviation by Warren G. Harding. See BLOVIATE.

Charles Dickens wrote humorously of "circumlocution"—which he treated as a combination of circumnavigate and elocution—to describe the lofty pretension of *officialese.* Congressman Maury Maverick coined GOBBLEDYGOOK, and Milton Smith coined BAFFLEGAB.

For examples, see PENTAGONESE; COMMUNIST TERMINOLOGY; CIA-ESE.

official family the appointees of a Chief Executive of nation, state, or city, especially those of great importance or who work closely with him.

In listing the Secret Service code names in use November 1963, author William Manchester grouped the *first family* (Lancer, Lace, Lyric, and Lark—the President, wife, daughter, and son), the *vice-presidential group* (Volunteer, Victoria, Velvet, Venus, Vigilant—the Vice President, wife, two daughters, and aide) and the *official family*: the President's personal secretary, press secretary, military aide, Air Force aide, naval aide, and a White House assistant—all with code names beginning with W—the President's physician, and the Secretary of State.

Current usage of official family is loose. It does cover all cabinet officials, the secretary of the cabinet, if there is one, assistants to the President, his legal counsel, speechwriters and ranking White House aides. It often applies to appointees down to Assistant Secretaries, but at that point the line blurs. A regional director of HUD whom the President is never likely to meet and does not know is equivalent to a second cousin once removed: a member of the family in a formal sense, but whose passing is not mourned unless an inheritance is involved.

Walter Lippmann in 1942 considered men in the official family to be those "participating in the action," as in this passage denouncing publicity men and ghostwriters, whose role the columnist considered cosmetic:

> The address of a President should be an event and not a lecture or a public reading, and the decision about when he should speak and what needs saying can be wisely made, not by supposed experts on public opinion, but only by men participating in the action he is going to talk about. There is all the difference in the world between being assisted by his official family and being assisted by GHOSTWRITERS.

President Grover Cleveland, preparing to bolt the Democratic party in 1896 over the issue of "free silver" being drawn by candidate William Jennings Bryan, used the phrase in a letter to his Secretary of the Interior, Hoke Smith: "You know how free my association with my official family has been . . ." Smith had said: "While I shall not accept the platform, I must support the nominees of the Chicago Convention." Cleveland told him: "It seems to me like straining at a gnat and swallowing a camel."

off the record not for publication; for a reporter's private knowledge only, and not to be used in any way.

Although H. L. Mencken attributed the coinage of this heavily used phrase to Al Smith, he probably meant "LET'S LOOK AT THE RECORD"; Mathews in the *Dictionary of Americanisms* traces "on the record" to 1900, but none of the dictionaries pinpoint the origin of "off the record."

It probably stemmed from FDR's press conferences in the thirties, which had these categories of answers: *direct quotation* when specifically permitted;

indirect quotation, but directly attributable to the President, as "The President said that he . . ."; *background information* (see NOT FOR ATTRIBUTION; BACKGROUNDER) that could not reveal the President as a source; and *off-the-record* information that could not be used at all. Wrote Douglass Cater: "Roosevelt played the various categories with tremendous skill, keeping the correspondents informed even when it did not suit his purpose to inform the public."

Charles Hurd, a White House correspondent in the early thirties, wrote: ". . . the press conference reached, prior to 1941, a pre-eminent place in our system of government. It did bring into the language, unfortunately, the phrase 'off the record.' Soon everyone, from the divorcee being interviewed by the society columnist in the Blue Angel to the ward heeler talking to a police reporter, was preceding answers to inquiries with the phrase 'off the record,' thinking thereby to make their words sound more important—and more likely to be printed."

Perhaps FDR took the term from Harold L. Ickes, who became his Secretary of the Interior. In 1933, Ickes wrote, "He met and answered every question, although in some instances his answers were off the record."

The new weapon occasionally backfired; Ambassador to Great Britain Joseph P. Kennedy gave what he claimed was an off-the-record interview to a *Boston Globe* reporter, who promptly printed Kennedy's thoughts about the King's speech impediment, the Queen's housewifely appearance, Churchill's fondness for brandy, and the notes he kept getting from Eleanor Roosevelt asking him "to have some little Susie Glotz to tea at the Embassy." At that point Kennedy's political future in his own right was finished.

"Off the record" can be abused by reporters who break the confidence to the embarrassment of the source; sources who are embarrassed by an on-the-record comment, and while not willing to lie about not having said it, are willing to claim they said it off the record; and the compromising of reporters by giving them information "off the record" that they would soon be able to find out elsewhere, thereby temporarily blocking them from publishing their story.

Political neophytes misuse the term *off the record* to mean "deep background" or "not for attribution."

Used before a noun as a modifier, the phrase should be hyphenated. The *Cook Political Report* wrote in 1990 about "numerous 'off-the-record' conversations with reliable non-party committee sources."

See NO COMMENT.

off the reservation remaining nominally within a party, but refusing to support the party's candidate.

Off the reservation, in current use, is one step short of TAKING A WALK—supporting the other party's candidate—and two steps short of an outright BOLT—switching to the other party permanently.

Former President Harry Truman explained in his memoirs: "The South's opposition to [Democrat] Al Smith gave Hoover many southern states, and he won by a comfortable margin. In the general election two years later, however, almost all the people who were running for office in the south and had supported [Republican] Hoover were defeated. That was the price they had to pay for going 'off the reservation' in 1928."

In Truman's usage, the phrase included those who actively supported the opposition candidate; most politicians consider outright support of the opposition a shade stronger than "off the reservation."

The phrase refers to American Indian reservations in the days when unscrupulous whites would trade "firewater" for goods, and "off the reservation" was a lonely and dangerous place for a red man to be.

off year elections that take place in the middle of a presidential term, where the turnout is always lower than those years that feature a presidential election; or, an odd-numbered year in which local elections are held.

The expression, in use since the 1870s, indicates the fall-off of enthusiasm from its antonym, "the presidential year." Since candidates for President run every four years, and congressional elections are every two years, every other congressional race is in an "off year"; further, candidates for local offices, as well as some governors, run in years between congressional elections, but there is no special expression for these way-off years.

President Eisenhower told a press conference in 1954 that he did not think a President should intervene "too intensively and directly in off-year Congressional elections," but rather create an "umbrella of accomplishment" under which candidates for his party could run. A reluctance to campaign in off years is a characteristic of Presidents; traditionally, the party in control of the White House loses seats in Congress in off years. The "average" fall-off in House seats ranges from twenty to forty, depending on how far back one wishes to start and whether one chooses all midterms or comparable first or second terms.

The expression is in a state of flux. Since "midterm" is a more accurate term for the nonpresidential congressional years, it is gaining in current usage, while "off year" is being applied more to odd-numbered years in which many elections for local offices take place.

Ohio gang. See SMOKE-FILLED ROOM.

Old China Hands Western journalists or diplomats, often the children of missionaries, who spent years in China.

Author Pearl Buck and Time, Inc. founder Henry Luce, both children of missionaries to China, were the best-known "Old China Hands." Authors Edgar Snow and Alice Tinsdale Hobart were included in this category, along with diplomats John Davies and John Service, who were attacked as Communist sympathizers in the fifties.

The term still enjoys currency. *Time* magazine of December 25, 1989, explaining President Bush's indifference to the pro-democracy movement in China, wrote: "Bush, who lived in Beijing as U.S. envoy for 13 months in 1974 and '75, fancies himself an old China hand. He seems to rate preserving the carefully nurtured U.S. strategic relationship with China well above human-rights considerations."

The *Washington Post* of December 8, 1992, had this to say about the pro-democracy stance of British ambassador to China Chris Patten: "Patten horrifies not only the Tiananmen gang. Cries of anguish are also rising in London from the 'Mandarins,' the small group of old China hands in the British civil service who advised successive prime ministers to tread softly with China to protect British rule in Hong Kong."

China Hand differs from CHINA WATCHER: "hand" connotes previous residence, "watcher" (or *Pekingologist*) connotes observation from outside. And the use of "hand," as meaning "one interested or experienced in," is spreading beyond a single nation: after a summit conference in Tokyo in 1993, a *New York Times* editorial was headlined: "Bill Clinton, Emerging Asia Hand."

old fogy reactionary; one burdened with the barnacles of backwardness.

The word may have a military origin. A fogy is an old military officer, or anyone who receives a "phogey"—seniority pay to one who has served three years in wartime or five years in peacetime. The *Dictionary of American English* traces this use back to 1879, and indicates the likelihood of previous use.

Earlier, author William Makepeace Thackeray used it in *The Book of Snobs,* published in *Punch* in 1846–47: ". . . the honest, rosy old fogies, the mouldy old dandies, the waist-belts and glossy wigs and tight cravats of these most raucous and respectable men." *John Donkey,* an imitator of *Punch,* gave it a political twist a year later in an article titled "The Political Old Fogy."

Congressman John C. Breckenridge, later a Vice President and a candidate against Lincoln in 1860, said in 1852: ". . . their principles are denounced in the cant language of the day as 'old fogyism,' and themselves as 'old fogies' . . . wholly incompetent to fathom the ideas or control the policy of this generation."

Current use has not changed at all. In November 1992, the *Washingtonian* quoted the opinions of average citizens on Washington politicians: "'For a lot of men, coming to Washington is the pinnacle of their careers,' says another woman. 'So therefore, you end up with this whole layer of old-fogy men—in their thirties!'" When in 1990 a curfew was imposed on teenagers in Quantico, Virginia, the *Washington Post* reported the reaction of one teenager who had been detained by the police: "They're a bunch of old fogies who want things their way."

As can be seen, there are any number of ways to spell the phrase; currently, fogy and fogys are preferred over phogy, fogey, fogies, or fogeys.

Youthful conservatives are occasionally referred to as "Young Fogys," but elderly insurgents are not called "Old Turks."

Old Guard   hard-core   loyalist; strongly conservative Republican.

Nobody represents himself as being a member of the Old Guard, since it now has the connotation of hidebound and stodgy. It is most often an epithet used by Democrats against conservative Republicans, or by insurgents against regulars. Among Republicans, the party's wings in the 1880s were the Stalwarts vs. the Half-Breeds; in the 1900s the Regulars vs. the Progressives; in recent years, the Old Guard vs. the Modern Republicans, or (as characterized by liberal Republicans) extremists vs. moderates, or (as characterized by conservatives) me-tooers vs. real Republicans and NEOCONS vs. TRUE BELIEVERS.

When the Old Guard is used in its broadest sense—an entrenched conservative faction in either party—its opposing faction is often called the YOUNG TURKS, or ANGRY YOUNG MEN.

Most Old Fogys and Guardsmen are derided as "implacable." Humorist Vic Gold, in his 1969 book *So You Want to Be a Liberal,* defined "implacable" as "*hard-line, old guard, last ditch.* Pertaining to Non-Liberal zealotry, as distinguished from *principled,* the approved description of Liberal implacability."

When the Republican platform in 1944 "accepted the purposes" of the National Labor Relations Act, the Social Security Act, and other New Deal legislation, Franklin Roosevelt solemnly read the Republican plank to a Democratic audience and commented: "The whole purpose of Republican oratory these days seems to be to switch labels. . . . Can the Old Guard pass itself off as the New Deal? I think not."

Adlai Stevenson, just before his first defeat in 1952, said, "It is a tragedy that the Old Guard has succeeded in doing what Hitler's best general could never do: they have captured Eisenhower."

The expression was used politically in the U.S. as early as 1844. "The Old Guard knows how to die," quoted the *Ohio State Journal,* "but the Old Guard does not know how to surrender. So said Napoleon on a celebrated occasion. So will all the Whigs say . . . we have gallant Whig champions and a glorious cause: 'The Old Guard will never surrender!'" (The Whigs' Clay lost to the Democrats' Polk; after one more victory, Zachary Taylor's, the Whigs surrendered.)

The Old Guard became identified with the Republican party in 1880, by advocates of a third term for Ulysses Grant. Author Don Chidsey wrote: "Three hundred and six of them stood on the burning deck when all but them had fled. One, Chauncey I. Filley, went so far as to have 306 Grant medals struck, and he distributed these: they bore not only the much publicized number, but also the words 'The Old Guard,' and thereby gave Republican reactionaries . . . a new title."

Source of the term was Napoleon's Old Guard, his most loyal troops. Count Pierre-Jacques-Étienne Cambronne, who was captured at the Battle of Waterloo, supposedly said about them: "The Guard dies, but never surrenders." According to French writer Edouard Fournier in 1859, the remark was invented by a reporter named Rougemont; Count Cambronne went to his grave denying he ever said it. The count is remembered today by a monument erected to him in Nantes, upon which is inscribed: "The Guard dies, but never surrenders." This story may be counter-apocryphal, but the count's response to a surrender demand was really supposed to have been "*Merde!*," which is known in France as *le mot de Cambronne*.

The Young Americans for Freedom, a conservative group, gave the diehard phrase a fresh fillip in the seventies by naming their magazine *The New Guard*.

The older expression, however, continues to be used, and can be applied to establishmentarians regardless of party: South Carolina Governor Carroll Campbell told the Republican National Convention in Houston in 1992, "George Bush is working hard to keep this country moving by changing the tax-and-spend philosophy of the old guard in Congress."

old pro one richly experienced in politics, regardless of age; the highest accolade among professionals.

"Old pros," not to be confused with PARTY ELDERS, may be found among: (1) officeholders who "know the ropes" and "where the bodies are buried"; (2) self-proclaimed "amateurs," who can be depended upon to run citizens' movements in a sound professional manner every few years; (3) party professionals, who "can count noses" (see NOSE COUNT) and can be distinguished from "hangers-on," "hacks," and "henchmen."

Curiously, old pros on different sides of the political fence know of one another, but seldom know one another well. This contrasts with opposition-party elected officials, who come to know and often like one another because of their daily contact. To them, Shakespeare's words about lawyers apply: "Adversaries . . . in law strive mightily, but eat and drink as friends."

But professional campaign managers often make it a point to honor their respected foes by not socializing with them. Julius C. C. Edelstein, New York Mayor Robert F. Wagner's executive assistant and campaign planner, once explained why he never met John A. Wells, an eminent attorney who often managed major Republican campaigns in New York. Edelstein told a story about a college student in Chicago in the 1920s. "The student had made contact with a gang of mobsters, and asked if he could observe some of their activities for his course in criminology. The mobsters were strangely delighted by the prospect of a 'perfesser' studying their habits, and they took him under their wing," according to Edelstein's recollection. "One day the student inquired why the gang had to import out-of-state torpedoes to kill off rival hoodlums. Didn't the gang have its own able trigger men? The gangsters explained that the local hoodlums, in all the rival gangs, had grown up together in the same neighborhood. When one was assigned to rub out another, he just couldn't pull the trigger—friendship and sentiment stood in the way. So they had to hire guns from out of town to do the job that only a stranger could do.

"Now, I wouldn't say that campaign managers are quite like torpedoes," Edelstein went on. "But a man who manages a political campaign is in the hottest end of politics, and he is often called on to strike hard for his candidate with no thought of personal consideration."

Edelstein added: "That's why Jack Wells and I are not likely to meet." They never did.

old soldiers never die sentimental touch introduced by General Douglas MacArthur at the conclusion of his speech in 1951, after having been relieved by President Truman.

MacArthur, who favored "hot pursuit" of Communist aircraft into China, was relieved by President Truman, who felt he was insubordinate and trying to dictate rather than carry out policy decided by civilians. Upon his return, MacArthur spoke to a joint meeting of Congress (not a joint session; only Presidents address joint sessions):

"I still remember the refrain of one of the most popular barracks ballads of that day which proclaimed most proudly that old soldiers never die; they just fade away. And like the old soldier in that ballad, I now close my military career and just fade away, an old soldier who tried to do his duty as God gave him the sight to see that duty."

The last few words, overlooked in the rush to look up and issue a recording of "Old Soldiers Never Die," were reminiscent of a phrase in Lincoln's second inaugural: ". . . with firmness in the right, as God gives us to see the right . . ." See NO SUBSTITUTE FOR VICTORY.

old-time religion conservative economics.

Herbert Stein, chairman of the Council of Economic Advisers in 1973, frequently referred to "that old-time religion" in discussing economic policies to eliminate or restrain inflation. Dr. Stein liked the phrase because conservative economics, like religious worship, has been honored more with lip service than with church attendance.

The phrase is in current use, usually with a derisive cast, but not always. "Discipline and patience are required," wrote Tilford Gaines in a Manufacturers Hanover Bank newsletter (September 1974), "if the 'old-time religion' is to work, and there is every reason to hope that it will."

The expression was popularized in the forties by bandleader Phil Harris's rendition of "Gimme Dat Old-time Religion."

old wine in new bottles a derogatory characterization of peace proposals presented in a fresh form but holding to the previous position.

At the Paris peace talks on September 17, 1970, the North Vietnamese and Viet Cong delegations presented an eight-point plan for ending the war that U.S. Ambassador David E. K. Bruce promptly labeled "old wine in new bottles."

This vivid figure of speech made the U.S. delegation's point more dramatically than any ordinary diplomatic rejection as "nothing new." The phrase became part of the language of diplomacy, and when Henry Kissinger, President Nixon's national security adviser, was going over the language of an October 7, 1970, U.S. proposal for a standstill cease-fire and immediate prisoner exchange, he remarked to this writer: "It's new wine."

When the Communists presented another proposal on June 30, 1971, Marilyn Berger of the *Washington Post* wrote: "There appeared to be a determined U.S. effort, however, not to dismiss the Communists' seven point plan in the way the chief U.S. negotiator at the Paris peace talks turned aside the last Communist proposal as 'old wine in new bottles.'"

In 1968 the National Advisory Commission on Civil Disorders—the Kerner Commission, its staff headed by Washington attorney David Ginsburg—reported that "What is new about Black Power is phraseology rather than substance . . . the rhetoric is different, but the ideas are remarkably similar." The heading for that section of its report was "Old Wine in New Bottles."

The expression is current in international commentary. Steve Hurst of Cable News Network remarked of Boris Yeltsin's leadership of Russia in 1992: "President Yeltsin has offered a power-sharing compromise that to most smacks of old wine in new bottles."

A much earlier use was remarked by Herman Melville, who noted in a diary during a European tour in 1849 that he had been given a book by Dr. Augustus Gardner entitled *Old Wine in New Bottles, or Spare Hours of a Student in Paris.*

The phrase is a switch on a line in the Gospel according to St. Matthew (9:17), in which Jesus says: "Neither do men put new wine into old bottles; else the bottles break, and the wine runneth out, and the bottles perish: but they put new wine into new bottles, and both are preserved." In that time, bottles were made of leather, and used bottles could not bear the fermentation strain of new wine; the parable means that the old Law of the Hebrew religion could not encompass the new spirit of Christ's gospel.

In the original use, new wine in old bottles was destructive; in current use, old wine in new bottles is deceptive.

No wine is so old that a pun cannot be uncorked: on May 19, 1976, strategist Stanley Hoffmann scoffed at Secretary of State Henry Kissinger's attempt to put a good face on Franco-American relations with a *New York Times* Op-Ed piece titled "Old Whine, New Bottles."

oleaginous lingo. See BUNK; WEASEL WORDS.

ombudsman an official intermediary between citizen and government to counteract the delay, injustice, and impersonality of bureaucracy.

The word comes from the Old Swedish *umbud,* meaning proxy, or power to act for another. In modern Swedish, an ombudsman can be any kind of agent, from commercial representative to member of Parliament (Riksdag), but the world-wide meaning of the term is taken from what the Swedes call the "JO": *Riksdagens Justitie-*

ombudsman, Parliamentary Commissioner for Justice.

The office was started in Sweden in 1809, has been adopted in varying forms by other Scandinavian countries, New Zealand, and the Philippines, and has aroused world-wide interest as the complexity of government administration grows. In 1967 the State of Hawaii adopted an Ombudsman Act: ". . . the Ombudsman may establish procedures for receiving and processing complaints, conducting investigations, and reporting his findings" without regard to "the finality of any administrative act." The crucial point in his powers is the right to look into "unreasonable, unfair, oppressive, or unnecessarily discriminatory" acts by government officials "*even though* in accordance with law*"* (italics in the act).

"A key characteristic of the Ombudsman," writes Professor Stanley Anderson of the University of California, "is his accessibility to the public. Anyone may file a complaint simply by writing a letter. This is especially important to those deprived of their freedom in jails, hospitals, sanitoria, etc."

A similar function is provided by the military in the U.S. in its office of Inspector General, which overlooks "channels" in its investigations. The argument against ombudsmen is that they take over functions that properly should be handled by mayors, district attorneys, and other elected officials. If these officials are not responsive to legitimate citizen complaints, they should be replaced, not circumvented.

To counter Republican Mayor John V. Lindsay's plan for "little City Halls" throughout New York, Democratic City Council President Frank O'Connor put forth an idea in 1967 that had been proposed often by Democrat Paul O'Dwyer—the ombudsman. Wrote the *New York Times* in support:

> An ombudsman for New York City would be the supergrievance committee chairman, a bridge between the people and their complex and scattered government. If New York were a tiny crossroads, it wouldn't need an ombudsman. But the very bigness of modern government and its inevitable remoteness can hurt both the citizen and the officials supposed to serve him. The ombudsman, "a person of distinguished accomplishments in the field of law or administration," would be available to help ameliorate the frictions of urban life.

Neither plan was carried out; the ombudsman in this and similar cases continued to be the media.

omnibus bill. See PACKAGE DEAL.

on all fours. See UP TO SPEED.

One Glass of Water Doctrine. See DOCTRINES.

one-house bill legislation intended for grandstanding only, not for passage into law.

Lobbyists in state capitals often work on one-house bills: getting passage in the state senate or assembly with the tacit assurance that the bill will be killed in the other house. The lobbyist can then show his client proof of some success without disturbing the status quo. (See FETCHER BILL.)

The term is also used in a literal, serious sense. In 1992, Democratic Congressman Les AuCoin of Oregon summed up the problem with this kind of legislation: "If the Senate abortion-rights champions can't move a bill, it makes it very difficult for the House champions to move a one-House bill." But the more common usage was reflected tartly by Maurice Carroll in the *New York Times* of December 11, 1985: "So-called one-house bills do not make law, but they can make for political rhetoric."

Another meaning has to do with divided legislatures, when one house is Democratic and the other Republican, and the passage of the bill is not venal but equally hopeless, unless it can be tied to another "one-house bill" and a deal struck.

one-house veto a provision in laws that enables either the House or the Senate to cancel Executive actions.

When President Carter vetoed the Department of Energy Authorization Act in November 1977, he said: "It limits the constitutional authority of the President through three one-house veto provisions."

Presidents do not like one-house vetoes; they argue that it erodes the separation of powers. Congressmen like the device, since it gives their institution more control over federal expenditures.

On January 9, 1978, the Supreme Court let stand a decision by the U.S. Court of Claims, which—as Morton Mintz wrote in the *Washington Post* the next day—refrained from striking down "the one-house veto, which enables either the House or the Senate to decide unilaterally whether any of a wide range of governmental actions will survive."

The formal phrase is "legislative veto," which may also extend to legislative action required by both parts of a bicameral legislature. In a message to the Congress on June 21, 1978, President Carter said he understood why Congress has been asserting itself in the seventies, but asked that such mistrust not be directed at him: "The desire for the legislative veto stems in part from Congress' mistrust of the Executive, due to the abuses of years past. Congress responded to those abuses by enacting constructive safeguards in such areas as war powers and the budget process. The legislative veto, however, is an overreaction which increases conflict between the branches of government." Attorney General Griffin Bell added his definition: "Legislative veto is a device whereunder . . . the power is transferred to the Congress to do things that ordinarily the executive department would do."

Mr. Carter pointed out that the legislative veto was first used in 1932, in a bill which authorized President Hoover to reorganize the Executive Branch. (Congress had tried earlier, but Woodrow Wilson was having none of that encroachment.)

A turning point took place in 1983, when the Supreme Court struck down Congress's use of the one-house veto to block federal agencies' regulations. The landmark decision, *Chadha* v. *Immigration and Naturalization Service*, invalidated one-house veto provisions enacted by Congress in hundreds of statutes in the 1930s.

An early use, and possible coinage, of the term *legislative veto* was by John Millett and Lindsay Rogers in the Winter 1941 *Public Administration Review:* "The Legislative Veto and the Reorganization Act of 1939." In the article they wrote that "a new device has been invented: a mandate to the executive to act, and, if the result is not liked, a *legislative veto*." To help FDR reorganize the Executive Branch in 1938, Congress gave him a concurrent resolution, which was a two-house veto. When he demanded a joint resolution instead (which he could veto), Republicans accused him of being a dictator, to which the President responded, "I have none of the qualifications which would make me a successful dictator."

one-idea parties. See IDEAS.

one man, one vote   a slogan urging reapportionment of legislatures so that each legislator represents approximately the same number of people.

Peter Straus, owner of New York radio station WMCA, brought the lawsuit that resulted in the Supreme Court decision setting forth the principle of one man, one vote. He told the author in 1968:

> We wanted to do a radio spot campaign to back up our editorials about reapportionment. But how do you get anybody excited about anything sounding as dull as "reapportionment"? Some people thought we were talking about "proportional representation," and most people don't even know what that is. We needed a phrase, a handle, that would make this issue come to life. Digging through the literature on the subject, and the booklets by the League of Women Voters, one of our writers came across "one man, one vote." We used it, and we hit it hard.

The Supreme Court in 1963 picked up the phrase in its decision in *Gray* v. *Sanders* to forbid a state from electing governors or senators by the county unit system, but modified the slogan to include women voters: "The conception of political equality from the Declaration of Independence, to Lincoln's Gettysburg Address, to the Fifteenth, Seventeenth and Nineteenth Amendments can mean only one thing—one-person, one-vote."

In a subsequent decision, the Court held: "While it may not be possible to draw Congressional districts with mathematical precision, that is no excuse for ignoring our Constitution's plain objective of making equal representation for equal numbers of people the fundamental goal for the House of Representatives." On June 15, 1964, the Court capped the series of decisions with an order to apportion both houses of all state legislatures on the basis of population only.

Since the Senate of the United States is not elected on the basis of population, opposition to the Court's decisions could naturally be expected to be articulated there. Senator Everett Dirksen (R-Ill.), then Minority Leader, called attention to some of the points made in dissent by Justice Harlan: "Legislators can represent their electors only by speaking for their interests—economic, social, political—many of which do reflect the place where electors live," and thus geographic area, as well as population, should be represented. ". . . by focusing exclusively on numbers . . . the Court deals in abstractions which will be recognized even by the politically unsophisticated to have little relevance to the realities of political life." Dirksen proposed a constitutional convention—only the second in U.S. history—to set the matter straight.

Politically, the issue was the transfer of power from rural areas to urban areas, and the slogan did much to crystallize the issue that had been hidden in abstract words. Wrote Arthur Krock: "The one-man, one-vote principle on which the Supreme Court ruling is based has the quality of those political slogans which appeal to the strong streak of idealism in the American people."

The phrase was coined in England early in the nineteenth century in a different context: Major John Cartwright (1740–1824), a radical Member of the House of Commons, called "the Father of Reform," led the fight against "plural voting" with the slogan "one man, one vote." At that time it was possible for a man to cast two ballots, one on the basis of his residence and the other a "business" or "university" qualification. The House of Lords rejected bills passed by the House of Commons on this subject for more than a century; in 1948 the Representation of the People Act finally abolished the right to exercise more than one vote in a parliamentary election.

Both slogan and issue resurfaced in the mid-seventies, as international pressure was applied to the white leadership of Rhodesia and South Africa to allow "majority rule," which many blacks saw as the end of intolerable repression by whites, and which many whites took to be revolution by the blacks. A dispatch to the *London Daily Telegraph* from Salisbury, Rhodesia, dated September 26, 1977 read: "The Rhodesian Government will accept the principle of 'one man, one vote' only if there are adequate safeguards written into a new constitution . . ." That newspaper's conservative columnist, Peregrine Worsthorne, held that "this theory can mean nothing less than a whole great continent's return to primitive savagery" and asked: "'One man, one vote.' When Dr. [Foreign Secretary David] Owen continues to talk about this liberal idea (in relation to Africa) is he not really being as shockingly dishonest as those Marxists who insist on pretending that what is happening behind the Iron Curtain has anything to do with 'the withering away of the State' or 'the dictatorship of the proletariat'?"

Vice President Walter Mondale, visiting South Africa in 1977, raised the issue of majority rule using the phrase "one man, one vote"—readily understandable in the U.S. but causing consternation among his hosts.

As sexism in language came under attack in the 1980s, the phrase was edited to "one person, one vote." The original use, however, remains; in 1993, the *Boston Globe* opined about the war in the former Yugoslavia: "As bestial as the Serbs have been, it is too late to bring back the vision of a unitary, one-man, one-vote state that the Bosnian government hoped for."

one-party press an accusation that the news media favors one political party, and as a result denies the opposition equal or fair coverage.

Andrew Jackson's supporters called any newspaper who opposed their man "the kennel press." In that tradition, Harry Truman wrote: "As far as I was concerned, they had sold out to the SPECIAL INTERESTS, and that is why I referred to them in my campaign speeches as the 'kept press and paid radio.'" Truman reminded his staff that in the elections since 1800, the press had played an important role in thirty-six; eighteen times behind the winner, eighteen times behind the loser. "That was the clearest proof I needed that I had nothing to fear regarding the influence of the newspapers . . ."

Although abolitionist Wendell Phillips had been certain "we live under a government of men and morning newspapers," Democratic candidates in more recent times found press opposition did not ensure defeat. In 1936 FDR told Samuel Rosenman: "Wait till October comes around when we really get a chance to tell the people the facts—which they're not getting now from their newspapers." Harold Ickes confided to his diary that "the outstanding thing about the campaign was the lack of influence of the newspapers . . . the very bitterness of the assault upon the President by the newspapers reacted in his favor."

At that same time, in England, Prime Minister Stanley Baldwin was making much the same discovery. The combined attack of Lord Beaverbrook and Lord Rothermere, the press peers, together with the denunciations of Winston Churchill, did not succeed in destroying Baldwin's leadership of the Conservative party. "It disclosed," wrote historian R. J. Minney, "that the influence of the popular press was by no means as wide and effective as had been imagined." Baldwin suffered in silence, then finally lashed back:

"What the proprietorship of these papers is aiming at is power, and power without responsibility: The prerogative of the harlot throughout the ages."

Adlai Stevenson popularized the phrase "one-party press" in 1952 in a speech to newspapermen of Portland, Oregon:

. . . the overwhelming majority of the press is just against Democrats. And it is against Democrats, so far as I can see, not after a sober and considered review of the alternatives, but automatically, as dogs are against cats. As soon as a newspaper—I speak of the great majority, not of the enlightened ten per cent—sees a Democratic candidate it is filled with an unconquerable yen to chase him up an alley. . . . I am in favor of a two-party system in politics. And I think we have a pretty healthy two-party system at this moment. But I am in favor of a two-party system in our press too. And I am, frankly, considerably concerned when I see the extent to which we are developing a one-party press in a two-party country.

Democrats are not the only ones to suffer from what they feel is slanted treatment from the press. Richard M. Nixon, in what he promised would be his "last press conference" after his unsuccessful race for the governorship of California in 1962, bitterly reminded the reporters covering his campaign of the press's responsibility to "put one lonely reporter on the campaign who will report what the candidate says now and then."

one-party rule charge made by candidates of a minority party in areas where the majority is entrenched; a system that often leads to corruption and inefficiency.

Republicans in the South and in big cities, and Democrats in suburbs and rural areas in the North, join in denouncing "one-party rule." Its opposite is the TWO-PARTY SYSTEM, and its predecessor phrase was probably "one-man power," used to attack Andrew Jackson and his followers, who favored a strong executive branch.

Congressman (later Speaker of the House) Thomas B. Reed said in 1880: "The best system is to have one party govern and the other party watch." This was an excellent argument against coalition and in favor of the two-party system—provided the parties changed places from time to time.

See SOLID SOUTH.

one-term President if said about an incumbent, a charge of weakness and vulnerability; if said about a past occupant of an office, a cool and cruelly accurate account.

The first noted use of the phrase was by Jacob Brinkerhoff, a two-term congressman from Ohio, on the House floor January 13, 1845: "The North had been taunted with the fact that it never had any but one-term presidents, democratic or federal."

Dwight Eisenhower used the phrase in 1968 about Richard Nixon, in a way that imputed courage to the one-termer: "I think Dick's going to be elected President but I think he's going to be a one-term President. I think he's really going to fight inflation, and that will kill him politically." Nixon must have remembered the phrase: in a line he added to the speech he made on April 30, 1970, announcing an incursion into Cambodia, he said: "I would rather be a one-term President and do what I believe is right than to be a two-term President at the cost of seeing America become a second-rate power . . ."

In the first half of the twentieth century, the only one-term Presidents—assuming the phrase to cover one full term of four years, not shortened by death—were William Howard Taft and Herbert Hoover. Since that time, using the same criterion, the one-term Presidents have been Carter and Bush.

In the fall of 1977, *New York Times* columnist Tom Wicker used the phrase in a column headed "One Term for Carter": "People who think and talk about politics are beginning to ask each other openly: 'Is Jimmy Carter a one-term President?' The question may seem strange and premature, when the man has been in office less than a year; yet it has a certain validity."

The power of the incumbency used to make any President an odds-on favorite to succeed himself, but as Wicker pointed out: "When television makes everything visible and immediate, defeats and failures are not exceptions; those who are elected by the tube can be defeated by the tube."

Six months later a lead editorial in the *Times* began: "The story is told in Washington of two Senators. Senator A says, 'Carter is beginning to look like a one-term President.' Senator B replies, 'Yes, but when does it begin?'"

The question of a one-term Presidency was posed early in the Administrations of Reagan, Bush, and Clinton, usually after the HONEYMOON PERIOD ended and ratings dropped. One rarely hears the question asked positively: Will he be a two-term President?

one third of a nation FDR's memorable phrase calling attention to poverty in America.

There was probably more revising and rewriting of President Roosevelt's second inaugural address of January 20, 1937, than any other major Roosevelt speech. Thomas Corcoran, Stanley High, Donald Richberg, and Samuel Rosenman submitted drafts and made changes. FDR insisted on a human treatment of the statistics. "I see tens of millions of its citizens" denied the "necessities of life"; "I see millions denied education, recreation, and the opportunity to better their lot and the lot of their children"; and there followed several other examples of what "I see."

Rosenman had written in an early draft a summation of the "I see's" with a final "I see." He recalls: "I do not remember nor is there a record of what that summation of mine was, for the President rubbed out all I had written in pencil after that final I see and after a moment's reflection substituted in his own hand his summation: 'I see one-third of a nation ill-housed, ill-clad, ill-nourished.'" See "I SEE" CONSTRUCTION.

The fraction as a phrasemaking device, particularly in regard to the poor segment of society, had been successful before. Said Winston Churchill in 1950:

I remember in Victorian days anxious talks about "the submerged tenth" (that part of our people who had not shared in the progress of the age) and then later on in the old Liberal period (the grand old Liberal period) we spoke of going back to bring the rearguard in. The main army we said had reached the camping-ground in all its strength and victory, and we should now, in duty and compassion, go back to pick up the stragglers and those who had fallen by the way and bring them in.

In 1957 President Dwight Eisenhower gave the FDR "one third" turn of phrase a more global view: "From the deserts of North Africa to the islands of the South Pacific, one third of all mankind has entered upon an historic struggle for a new freedom: freedom from grinding poverty." At about the same time, Senate Majority Leader Lyndon Johnson upped the ante: "We live in a world where over two-thirds of the people are 'ill-housed, ill-clad, ill-nourished.' When the madness of the nuclear arms race is halted, mankind's creative efforts can be turned to their relief." See WAR ON POVERTY.

one world internationalist, liberal Republican philosophy of Wendell Willkie, expressed after his defeat by FDR in 1940.

After his campaign, Willkie made a 31,000-mile trip to the Soviet Union, the Middle East, Africa, and China. In Chungking, he called on the Allies to recognize that World War II was not "a simple tactical problem for task forces. It is also a war for men's minds."

On his return he reported to Americans that the U.S. had a vast "reservoir of good will" that was being drained because our war aims were not being articulated. "The United States has lost moral force," he said after U.S. dealings with Admiral Darlan upset liberals, "and by it, we may lose the peace . . . I hate this false finagling with expediency . . ."

Willkie put these thoughts and others in a 1941 book titled *One World*. In one chapter Willkie held "the attitude of the white citizens of this country toward the Negroes has undeniably had some of the unlovely characteristics of an alien imperialism—a smug, racial superiority, a willingness to exploit an unprotected people." To Willkie, "one world" meant a peace founded without regard to a nation's size, wealth, power, or the color of its citizens. "Our western world and our presumed supremacy are now on trial. Our boasting and our big talk leave Asia cold. Men and women in Russia and China and in the Middle East are . . . coming to know that many of the decisions about the future of the world lie in their hands."

One World sold two million copies within two years. "Bookleggers" in China overlooked the copyright and published it under a title that translates: *Within Four Seas, All Are Brothers*.

After the explosion in 1945 of the first atomic bomb, a group of scientists put forth a statement headed "One World or None." Radio commentator Elmer Davis asked: "Has it occurred to them that if their one world turned out to be totalitarian and obscurantist, we might better have no world at all?" See BETTER RED THAN DEAD.

only President we've got. See PRESIDENT OF ALL THE PEOPLE.

only thing we have to fear. See NOTHING TO FEAR BUT FEAR ITSELF.

on the message focused on the main selling point.

"In the lingo of today's spin doctors," the lexicographer wrote in the *New York Times* in 1993, "*focus* means to be 'on the message'—concentrating on the one or two simple issues that ignite a campaign. . . . When you stray 'off the message,' support erodes —not because your strategy is wrong, you insist, but because you're putting so many necessary things on the public plate that people, uncomfortable with complexity, cannot digest it all."

On the message is associated with James Carville, chief Clinton political strategist in 1992 (see IT'S THE ECONOMY, STUPID!). The idea is rooted in the "unique selling proposition," a theory of advertising espoused by Ted Bates in the 1960s—to pick out a single theme that sets a product off from others on the shelf and then concentrate on that theme.

A similar phrase is *on the model*. This term points to the "fit" —cultural and ideological, as well as in terms of age, dress, and degree of enthusiasm—of an individual within a campaign organization. It usually is posed as a question by staffers feeling threatened by older or offbeat types who might not fit in a preconceived mold: "Is he on the model?" means "Is he one of us?"

on the point the vulnerable position of being in the lead of a group of candidates; the position of the FRONT RUNNER.

The derivation of the phrase is from military terminology: the member of a squad of soldiers who "takes the point" (often a volunteer, or a more experienced member of the squad) moves out ahead of his comrades and is the man in the greatest danger. He is more frequently called the "scout" than the "point man," but the terms are synonymous. In an ambush, the experienced ambushing force will allow the scout to penetrate, in order to entrap the entire squad; for this reason, the squad is instructed to be spread wide enough so that the last two men of the wedge are far enough back to avert capture or killing, and can warn the main force. The men at the ends of the inverted "V" (farthest from the "point man" in the middle front) are called the "getaway men," a phrase not yet adopted by politics.

The man "on the point" is the object of "Stop (Whoever)" movements by coalitions of other candidates, and the man whose every misstep is given greatest play by the press.

Colorado Governor John A. Love was asked by a reporter what he thought of the attacks being made in 1967 on then Republican front runner George Romney. He replied: "It's a hard place to live, out there on the point."

In 1977 President Carter's Ambassador to the United Nations, Andrew Young, who had stirred controversy when he hinted at a forthcoming improvement of relations with Cuba, and who created a furor when he said Cuban forces in Angola were "a force for stability" in Africa, agreed on a television panel interview to a description of himself as "a point man"—that is, one who goes out in front of events and takes the heat.

A *Washington Post* editorial disagreed: "To toss off personal opinions—or (in Young's words) to play 'point man'—and then be repudiated is to lose a certain part of one's claim on another government's or the public's attention: to lose effectiveness."

The mixing of horse racing and military metaphors is common in politics. A *front runner* (racing) is *on the point* (military); a *campaign* (origin military) can be a *horse race* (turf); there can be a *boom* (military cannon origin) for a *dark horse* (racing); a *TV blitz* (World War II) in the *home stretch* (last two weeks, racing), as the two *camps* (military) come *down to the wire* (racing) with the *standard-bearers* (military) in a *dead heat* (racing), and the *right wing* (military) threatening to *bolt* (racing). See MILITARY METAPHORS.

"Point man" has been used to describe other advance agents of controversy besides Ambassador Young. The *National Journal* of October 1, 1977, titled a piece about California Congressman James Corman "The House Point Man on Welfare."

A synonym is "cutting edge," as in this *New York Times* editorial (1977): "Secretary Califano has become the cutting edge of the Government's affirmative action drive . . ."

In the late 1980s, *on the cusp* overtook *the cutting edge;* a cusp is a point of a crescent moon.

open convention a political convention which begins with no single candidate having a near majority.

"I don't think any one candidate has enough votes to win," said California Governor Earl Warren on the eve of the 1948 Republican convention. "As long as that prevails it's a wide-open convention."

In 1956, former President Harry Truman let it be known that he favored an open Democratic convention, thereby helping block Adlai Stevenson from "locking everything up" before the convention began. New York Governor Averell Harriman announced he was "for Stevenson" but not necessarily "for him for president." ("What does he think I'm running for," asked Stevenson, "county coroner?") Truman supported Harriman, but Stevenson was able to overcome that challenge as well as Senator Estes Kefauver's.

At that point, Stevenson in turn announced that he favored an "open convention" in the choice of a vice-presidential nominee. The delegates, who couldn't remember a previous opportunity to choose a Vice President freely, almost went for Senator John F. Kennedy, but finally chose Kefauver.

At the 1960 convention Harry Truman didn't feel that John Kennedy "was ready" and again called for an "open convention." Kennedy told an aide: "Mr. Truman regards an open convention as one which studies all the candidates, reviews their records and then takes his advice."

Origin of the phrase may be from gambling terminology: a "wide-open" town is one in which gambling, as well as prostitution, is permitted.

As state primaries gained importance, open conventions became a forlorn hope. With networks seeking ratings, the national conventions have now become a form of coronation.

For the usage of open convention compared with "rigged" or "locked up" convention, see BROKERED CONVENTION.

open covenants Woodrow Wilson's call for "open diplomacy" without secret agreements.

The Fourteen Points included: "Open covenants of peace, openly arrived at, after which there shall be no private international understandings of any kind, but diplomacy shall proceed always frankly and in the public view."

Clemenceau, Lloyd George, and others were dismayed at Wilson's apparent naïveté, because "in the public view" seemed to mean "no confidential discussions" without which diplomacy could not operate. To correct this, Wilson sent his closest adviser, Colonel Edward House, to explain to world leaders what he meant before armistice negotiations began. House used a memorandum, approved by Wilson, on this point:

The purpose is clearly to prohibit treaties, sections of treaties or understandings that are secret. The phrase "openly arrived at" need not cause difficulty. In fact, the President explained to the Senate last winter that his intention was not to exclude confidential diplomatic negotiations involving delicate matters, but to insist that nothing which occurs in the course of such confidential negotiations shall be binding unless it appears in the final covenant made public to the world.

In effect, Wilson's high-sounding words—which had an appeal to millions who were curious about what went on behind the scenes at international conferences—had a meaning to Wilson that required confidential explanation. As Walter Lippmann wrote in 1932: ". . . great masses of people cannot negotiate. They can no more negotiate than they can make love or write books or invent. They can approve or disapprove the results, but if they participate in the negotiation itself they merely shout themselves hoarse and fall into a hopeless deadlock."

At the end of World War II, Republicans were able to use "open covenants" against the party of Wilson. In his "Equal Justice Under Law" speech attacking the war-crimes trials, Senator Robert A. Taft clearly set up the line about secret agreements: "The Atlantic Charter professed a belief in liberty and justice for all nations, but at Teheran, at Yalta, at Moscow, we forgot law and justice. Nothing could be further from a RULE OF LAW than the making of secret agreements distributing the territory of the earth in accordance with power and expediency."

"Open covenants" as used today still requires explanation with every use. It means "no secret agreements," but it also means "sensible private discussions" and as much as says "forget that part about 'openly arrived at.'" Lippmann in 1961 made the point: "By open diplomacy, which only too often means loud-mouthed diplomacy, we can do little to assuage, indeed much to exacerbate these crises. For then one side or the other has to back down if there is to be any accommodation. But in quiet diplomacy, there is no loss of face if a country backs away from an extreme position which has proved to be untenable. For this reason, quiet diplomacy is for the time being the hope of the world."

The word "covenant" rather than treaty or agreement appealed to Wilson. The Covenant of the League of Nations was his phrasing, chosen because he liked the Biblical solemnity of the word. It is possible he took the idea from "The Solemn League and Covenant" of 1643, unifying religious practice in England, Scotland, and Ireland.

Abolitionist leader William Lloyd Garrison liked the word too, in 1831 calling a U.S. Constitution that permitted slavery a "Covenant with Death and an Agreement with Hell," which became a slogan for the Massachusetts Anti-Slavery Society.

In his 1993 inaugural address, Bill Clinton used "new covenant" nine times, but it was not picked up as the style of his Administration.

See PITILESS PUBLICITY; QUIET DIPLOMACY.

Open Door Policy the policy at the turn of the twentieth century, that all important trading nations should have equal trading rights with the Chinese government, with all respecting that country's territorial integrity.

McKinley's Secretary of State, John Hay, goaded by the British government, acted at a time when it looked as though every powerful nation was about to fall on the hapless Chinese government and tear away both concessions and territory. This supported neither British nor American interests. Britain already had rich concessions in the Yangtze Valley; the U.S., though it wanted to share the Chinese market, was not prepared to fight for it.

China in these last days of the Manchu Empire had been badly defeated in a short but decisive war waged against her by Japan. Only the combined disapproval of all the Western nations currently involved in China at the time (1895) had prevented the Japanese from slicing off chunks of the prostrate Celestial Empire.

At British insistence, Hay sent a series of notes to the concerned powers, which included Italy, Japan, and France, as well as Britain and the U.S., asking for assurances that existing treaties would be observed with China.

Secretary Hay did not reveal the contents of the replies but announced in September 1899 that all had concurred. A new series of notes followed, asking all to agree to China's territorial and administrative integrity. Again, this time on January 2, 1900, Mr. Hay pronounced common accord, though keeping the notes from the public eye.

However, the Boxer Rebellion and the Russo-Japanese War of 1904–05 resulted in further encroachments on China, largely by Japan.

The U.S. continued to talk of the Open Door and used the $25 million forced from China as reparations after the Boxer Rebellion to educate young Chinese in America. For some time, successive Chinese governments felt friendly to the U.S. as the least voracious of all the nations which were busily involved in taking away the country's wealth.

In current usage, diplomats refuse to "close the door" on negotiations.

open shop. See CLOSED SHOP; RIGHT TO WORK.

open-skies proposal President Eisenhower's suggestion at the 1954 Geneva Convention to permit unlimited aerial photography of the U.S. and the Soviet Union.

President Eisenhower laid the proposal before Premier Bulganin and Communist party chief Khrushchev:

> I propose . . . to give each other a complete blueprint of our military establishments, from beginning to end, from one end of our countries to the other; lay out the establishments and provide the blueprints to each other. Next, to provide within our countries facilities for aerial photography to the other country—we to provide the facilities within our country, ample facilities for aerial reconnaissance, where you can make all the pictures you choose and take them to your own country to study; you to provide exactly the same facilities for us and we to make these examinations, and by this step to convince the world that we are providing as between ourselves against the possibility of great surprise attack, thus lessening danger and relaxing tension.

When the Soviets showed no inclination to accept this proposal, the U.S. proceeded to open up the Russian skies unilaterally and secretly with U-2 flights. When the "U-2 Incident" broke up a summit conference, the U.S. State Department took pains to point out that the flights had begun immediately after the rejection of our "open skies" proposal. Senator Lyndon Johnson, who frequently built phrases on top of other phrases, added in 1957: "We must create a new world policy. Not just of 'open skies'—but of open eyes, ears, and minds, for all peoples of the world."

open society a social order in which the people are granted a RIGHT TO KNOW as opposed to a "closed society" of a totalitarian state, in which secrecy is predominant.

The phrase achieved common political usage in the fifties, especially after the OPEN-SKIES PROPOSAL by President Eisenhower in 1954; there was another flurry of usage after the U-2 incident in 1959 when it was explained that the U.S. was an "open society" and needed to find ways to explain the goings-on in "closed societies."

Dwight Eisenhower coined one of his best metaphors around the subject of an open society in a draft for a speech that was never delivered. Had the President been permitted to visit the Soviet Union, he would have delivered a speech in Leningrad on May 12, 1960, about Soviet-American relations that used these words:

When I was a boy, we put blinders on horses so they would not shy in fright of a scarecrow, a shadow, a rabbit. But today we human beings deliberately put blinders on ourselves, not to avoid the sight of frightful things, but to ignore a central fact of human existence.

I mean that mankind too often blinds itself to the common lot, to the common purposes, to the common aspirations of humanity everywhere. I mean that all of us too much live in ignorance of our neighbors; or, when we take off our blinders, view them through the contortionist spectacles of propaganda.

And we will continue that way—forever fearful, forever suspicious—until we convince ourselves that the only way to peace is through the mutually open society. Then, at long last, seeing our human neighbors as they really are, we

shall come to realize that we need no more fear them than the horse the rabbit.

The phrase is often used in discussions seeking to explain the necessity of (or deploring the actions of) the Central Intelligence Agency. Walter Lippmann wrote in 1967 about covert CIA support of student groups: ". . . black propaganda, secret interventions, intrigue and subornation are incompatible with our open society. They are the methods of a totalitarian state and without a totalitarian environment of secrecy and terror, they are unworkable. This most unpleasant and embarrassing affair is the proof that an open society cannot act successfully like a totalitarian society."

Said President Johnson soon after, about the bad press he was getting: "There is something about our open society that gives the play to what went wrong instead of what went right." Defense Secretary Robert A. Lovett looked at the problem another way: "I cannot escape the feeling that, as a government, we tend to talk too much. To be sure, we are an open society, but we give the impression of being unbuttoned."

After the phrase was in common use, a new meaning was introduced as part of the language of the civil rights movement. "Open" instead of meaning "nonsecret" was defined as "available to all"—as in "open occupancy" or "open housing." *Ebony* magazine quoted Dr. Leo K. Bishop in this context: "In two decades the Jews and the Roman Catholics have moved into the open society of the United States, and the Negroes will make it too."

operation a naming device for a military action or struggle less than a war.

With only the Congress able to declare a *war*, lesser military actions have required different terms. Harry Truman preferred *police action*, and the 1950s witnessed the Korean *conflict*.

When the United States engaged in military activity in Panama in late 1989, George Bush could argue that *invasion* was too harsh a word, because the elected government of Panama had invited the action. The State Department suggested *consented intervention*, but the action became widely known by the name conceived by Pentagon propagandists: *Operation Just Cause*.

Operation is first found in English in 1391, in Chaucer's *Treatise on the Astrolabe*. Based on the Latin *opera*, meaning "work, effort," the word was applied to a surgical procedure by 1425, and it offers a sense of clinical detachment in labeling a military action short of war.

The military sense is predominant. *Operation Overlord* was Churchill's name for the invasion of the Continent in World War II, and many other secret projects in the planning stage received similarly obscure titles to conceal their objectives. In recent years, the word has been used to precede descriptive or selling titles: The American action to stop Iraq from invading Saudi Arabia in 1991 was called *Operation Desert Shield*, with the name changed to *Operation Desert Storm* as the action changed to drive Iraq out of Kuwait. Famine relief in Somalia, requiring military assistance, was dubbed *Operation Restore Hope*.

opiate of the people a metaphor by Karl Marx about religion, used against Marxism and Communism by its critics for more than a century.

"Religion is the sigh of the oppressed creature," wrote Marx in 1844, in his *Critique of the Hegelian Philosophy of Right*, "the feeling of a heartless world, just as it is the spirit of unspiritual conditions. It is the Opium of the People." The German phrase *Opium des Volkes* can be translated "opium of the people," or "opiate of the people"; the latter is now more commonly used.

Although Marx went on to stress the point—"the first requisite for the people's happiness is the abolition of religion"—Communist leaders in countries with strong religious traditions tried to water down the metaphor. "Marx's position is widely misunderstood," wrote the Socialist Labor party's official organ in 1959. ". . . When the essay was written, opium was used in Europe almost exclusively for relieving pain. . . . Marx was using the word 'opium' in this sense and not in the sense that religion is a stupefier deliberately administered to the people by agents of the ruling class."

As president of Columbia University in 1950, Dwight Eisenhower made a typical attack on the "Godlessness" of Communism, using Marx's vivid phrase against him: "Hundreds of millions behind the Iron Curtain are daily drilled in the slogan: 'There is no God, and religion is an opiate.' But not all the people within the Soviet accept this fallacy; and some day they will educate their rulers, or change them."

Clare Boothe Luce played with the phrase in 1955, calling Communism "the opiate of the intellectuals . . . but no cure, except as a guillotine might be called a cure for a case of dandruff."

A more recent play on the phrase appeared in August 1984 in the *Washington Post*: "Television is not the opiate of the people, it is the Valium. The Republicans are putting on a tediously predictable production designed perhaps to lull and soothe, like most TV shows."

But the best turnaround was in a 1967 editorial in the Suffolk (L.I.) *Sun*, about the LSD prophet, Dr. Timothy Leary, "who hopes to make opiates the religion of the people."

opinion leader   a person or organization able because of position, expertise, or facilities to influence the convictions of others.

An obvious influence might be a newspaper. In 1859 John Stuart Mill wrote in obvious regret: "The mass do not now take their opinions from dignitaries in church or state, from ostensible leaders, or from books. Their thinking is done for them by men much like themselves, addressing them or speaking in their name, on the spur of the moment, through the newspapers."

Congressman Robert La Follette, seeking a second term against the opposition of the regular leaders of the Republican party in Wisconsin, devised a technique for reaching those he considered opinion leaders. Before the 1886 elections, he had the voter list broken down into townships. He then sent such a list to a supporter in that particular area, requesting the names of any of the local men considered to be people whose names had local leadership significance. To these people, he regularly sent accounts of his congressional actions and copies of his speeches. The system worked; despite continued party opposition he was renominated and reelected.

Columbia University behavioral scientist Paul Lazarsfeld led the way to the formulation of the "opinion leader" idea. His theory of the " two-step flow of communication" held that the general public did not take its opinions directly from the mass or class media; instead, these messages were filtered through a layer of respected activists. These opinion leaders, however, do not lead in all categories. For example, a sophisticated high-society type may be an opinion leader in matters of fashion, but she may be a follower of a gregarious housewife in marketing matters, and both these leaders may be followers of a League of Women Voters president in political affairs.

The power of television has eroded the opinion-leader concept in recent years, as persuasive candidates have been able to affect mass opinion "over the heads" of the opinion leaders.

Many politicians accumulate a "Kefauver Christmas list," named after Estes Kefauver's extensive list of contacts, contributors, casual acquaintances, and correspondents who received a Christmas card from the Tennessee senator. Presumably, a good portion of these people are opinion leaders.

opinion of mankind.   See WORLD OPINION.

opportunist   one who sacrifices principle to expediency; a frequent attack word used against too obviously ambitious or fast-rising political figures.

The word grew popular in the political lexicon in the fifties, although Arthur Krock accused Senator Robert Taft of playing "obvious or even opportunist politics" in 1946.

One who is attacked as an opportunist is (1) on the way up, (2) in the public eye, and (3) controversial. As an attack word, "ambitious" was losing its sting because ambition pervades politics and in the proper degree is an excellent trait. The predecessor word, now obsolete, was "trimmer," from one who trims his sails to capture the prevailing breeze.

An opportunist, in current usage, is one who changes his position to comply with what is presently popular (see ALL THINGS TO ALL MEN). "Theodore Roosevelt," said Robert La Follette, "is the ablest living interpreter of what I would call the superficial public sentiment of a given time, and he is spontaneous in his reactions to it." Britain's Harold Wilson attacked Harold Macmillan: "Cynical opportunism in place of leadership, an appeal to cupidity rather than to the moral purpose of the nation."

On the other hand, one who sticks to a single position can be attacked as "inflexible," "mossbacked," "unwilling to meet new situations with new solutions." The most common defense of one who has radically switched his position (Arthur Vandenberg on isolationism, Lyndon Johnson on civil rights) is that the individual has "matured," or "been man enough to admit a mistake," or has become "pragmatic."

In 404 B.C., a member of the Athenian oligarchy named Theramenes was nicknamed *cothurnus*, which was a sandal that could be worn on either foot, because he was considered an opportunist. From this came the expression "He wears the sandals of Theramenes," i.e., he is not to be trusted. Brewer in his *Dictionary of Phrase and Fable* said: "He blew hot and cold with the same breath."

In 1597 Francis Bacon pointed to an example of opportunism still practiced today: "It is commonly seen, that men once placed, take in with the contrary faction to that by which they enter; thinking, belike, that they have the first sure, and now are ready for a new purchase."

Republicans in 1967 were surprised when Michigan Governor George Romney called fellow Republican, Illinois Senator Charles Percy, an opportunist; he later explained that he meant that Percy understood timing, that he knew how to seize an opportunity. This is a positive sense the word may one day gain, but neither was nor is current usage.

The word is rooted is the Latin *ob*, "before," and *portus*, "the harbor,"

and bears a relation to the man who keeps hoping his ship will come in. According to former Nixon speechwriter Benjamin Stein, writing in *Esquire* in 1977, Henry Kissinger's assessment of Mr. Carter's national security adviser, Zbigniew Brzezinski, carried the wistful tone of one whose office-holding ship had come and gone: "He's a bit of an opportunist."

No publication ever gave the idea more of a metaphoric blast than the *Liberation Army Daily*, published in Peking. After the overthrow of the radical "Gang of Four" (consisting of Chairman Mao Tse-tung's widow, Chiang Ching, and three of her followers), the army paper attacked a group of unnamed opportunists who had not been swept from power by Mao's successor, Hua Kuo-feng: "The main features of those who follow the wind are steering the boat according to which way the wind blows and the advocacy of opportunism. Their color changes when they hear the wind, and they sell their soul at a discount. Speculation has become their habit, and they treat any woman who gives them milk as their mother . . . They are like grass growing atop a wall, bending with the wind. They are as changeable as clouds and rain. Their necks function like ball bearings and their waists like spring bands, and wind gauges are planted on their heads." This dazzling display of anti-opportunistic rhetoric was reprinted in the *People's Daily* on January 6, 1978, in the same space where—only two years before—a similar attack on opportunists had been launched by those later labeled the Gang of Four.

See CENTRIST.

options choices; alternatives.

In a sophisticated political sense, the existence of a number of options offers freedom to maneuver; as options are narrowed, the decision maker loses leverage on his adversaries because his chances for TRADE-OFFS are decreased, and the element of surprise is lessened. See NEW ECONOMICS.

President Lyndon Johnson was often quoted as insistent on "keeping my options open." The word "open," in this sense, is used to mean "not narrowed by elimination." Whenever Franklin Roosevelt asked Congress for discretionary authority in legislation, he called it "room to turn around." See WIGGLE ROOM.

The word became popular in Washington in the sixties, probably from the WAR-GAMING vocabulary. The doctrine of flexible response (see MEASURED RESPONSE) and a decision about which weapons systems to develop depends largely on what—and how many—options are available.

This is a far cry from George Washington's use of the word: "There is an option left to the United States of America, whether they will be respectable and prosperous, or contemptible and miserable, as a nation." More often today, the option is between the lesser of two evils; as entertainer Maurice Chevalier said on reaching seventy-two: "Old age isn't so bad when you consider the alternative."

In the early seventies, as a result of National Security Adviser Henry Kissinger's use of the term in backgrounders, "Option Three" became synonymous with compromise. In a choice of five options, option three is nicely situated between extremes, and is the easiest to choose; an option three philosophy is not conducive to bold leadership.

As a verb, *opt* is in academic vogue, connoting a more impulsive selection than the thoughtful *choose*. Bergen Evans used it precisely in *Comfortable Words:* "Confronted with a choice between *choose* and *opt,* my impulse is to opt for *choose.*"

other body   an arch reference by a member of the Senate to the House, and vice versa.

Both houses in a bicameral legislature are jealous of their prerogatives; in the U.S., the "other body" is a way for a legislator to refer to the Senate or the House of Representatives without appearing to pay it too much respect; in current use, the pronunciation attempts to reproduce the "sound" of quotation marks.

The phrase originated in a rule of the British Houses of Parliament which states that a member of one house may make no reference to the proceedings of the other, a vestige of the days when rivalry between the House of Commons and the House of Lords could have led to a constitutional crisis. To get around the old custom, English politicians call their other body "another place."

out of context.   See QUOTED OUT OF CONTEXT; DEFOLIATE.

out of pocket.   See UP TO SPEED.

out of the loop   not informed; outside the circuit of news or information.

George Bush popularized this phrase by insisting that in 1985 he was not involved in Iran-contra discussions or arms-for-hostages negotiations during the Reagan Administration. On January 1, 1987, then–Vice President Bush said of decisions by the National Security Council: "I'm not trying to jump sideways on this, but I think it is important to have the facts. And the facts are that the Vice President is not in the decision making loop. He does not have to sign off on decisions, is sometimes overlooked, although not on purpose by the NSC bureaucracy."

Use of the phrase, however, has not been limited to Bush. In 1986, a White House aide was quoted as saying about the former chief of staff Donald Regan: "A lot of the people he cut out of the loop are gunning for him."

Possible origins of the *loop* phrase range from electrical circuitry and computer processing to a term for a conference or network (*the Big Ten Loop*), all figurative or extended uses of the literal sense "a circle formed with a rope." The circular *loop* has been used since the turn of the century to refer to the railway built around Chicago's business district by Charles Tyson Yerkes; the area itself became known as *the Loop*.

The antonymic phrase, *in the loop*, means "informed; among those consulted," often implying a tight circle. Hedrick Smith used the phrase as a test of insiderness in his 1988 book, *The Power Game: How Washington Works*, under the heading "Are You in the Loop?"

out party.   See INS AND OUTS.

outside world   a splinter party.

A party is a world of its own. Threats to TAKE A WALK or BOLT lead to an outside world—cold, barren, unexplored, with wild voters roaming the tundra.

Don Oberdorfer of the *Washington Post* on July 23, 1971, wrote about plans being made by supporters of former Senator Eugene McCarthy for a fourth party (assuming Governor George Wallace would be a third-party candidate in 1972). An unnamed McCarthy aide said the independent route might be taken if their candidate should lose the Democratic nomination "unfairly": "If we get beat up in the streets and screwed in the caucuses . . . then the 'outside world' is always fair." Oberdorfer correctly defined "outside world" as "the euphemism for a fourth party."

out to lunch.   See UP TO SPEED.

Oval Office   the formal office of the President of the United States; by extension, the center of Executive power.

A headline on page 16 in the *Washington Post* of July 6, 1934, read: "President's New Oval Office/Carefully Planned for Beauty—FDR" The story predicted that the West Wing of the White House would have "a main floor unchanged except for filling in the clothes yard . . ."

According to the January 1935 issue of *Building Modernization*, the expansion of space from 15,000 to 40,000 feet "was accomplished by filling in the old 'drying yard'—a lattice-inclosed square adjacent to the old laundry once used for drying presidential wash. In its place along the side portico, opening on a rose garden, is the office of the President and his personal staff." The office was described as "oval in shape and besides the fact that it is almost always flooded with southern sun, its chief feature is its large bay made up of a series of steel sash windows of immense proportion."

Although Nixon White House curator Clem Conger found citations of the "oval office" in the thirties, the President's office—one of several oval rooms in the White House, including the Diplomatic Reception Room and the "Yellow Room" on the second floor of the residence—did not become known as such through several Administrations. When Harry Truman gave his farewell address from his office on January 15, 1953, he said: "This is the President's Office in the West Wing of the White House." Dwight Eisenhower used "West Wing" to mean center of action during his Presidency and in his book *Mandate for Change*.

Although "The President's oval office" was heard by White House aides in the Johnson Presidency, the phrase did not come into the general language until Mr. Nixon's term. The author recalls that among White House aides who were his colleagues, "Oval Office"—capitalized, and without "the President's" in front of it—was a phrase used to hint at decision making by the President without using his name.

The phrase was speeded into wide public use as a result of Watergate: an early Merriam-Webster citation is an October 19, 1972, story by Robert Semple, Jr., in the *New York Times:* "At the moment, the White House feels, the alleged conspiracy is perceived by most of the public as a distant and even amateurish intrigue far removed from the Oval Office . . ." J. Anthony Lukas reported in the *New York Times Magazine* on July 22, 1973, that "John Dean says [Egil] Krogh told him that orders for the burglary came 'directly from the Oval Office.'" That notion—of the Presidency being more of a place than a man, and thus less personally accountable—was behind the early internal use of "Oval Office," and later led to its popularization.

Lexicographers report a rush of citations late in 1974 and 1975; the White House Historical Association, which in previous editions of its guide referred to "the President's Office," switched in 1973.

"Oval Office," in initial caps, seems to be the only Watergate-era word that carries no unpleasant connotation into the present. Soon after the election of Jimmy Carter, Leslie Gelb—a *New York Times* reporter destined to serve in the Carter State Department before returning to the *Times*—wrote: "A crisis like another Middle East war, saber-rattling by Moscow, the embrace of the foreign policy bureaucracy and the enormous complexity of issues and pressures when viewed from the Oval Office could consign the most ardently believed campaign rhetoric to oblivion."

The phrase has become a neutral reference to the Presidency; similarly, "the West Wing" refers to the President's senior staff, and the "East Wing" to the First Lady's offices, although Hillary Rodham Clinton chose to locate her office in the West Wing.

overexposure the fear held by public figures that continual publicity leads to public boredom.

Kennedy biographers are fond of quoting a passage from this letter by Franklin Roosevelt to Ray Stannard Baker, dated March 20, 1935, that had earlier been quoted by Richard Neustadt in *Presidential Power:*

> I know . . . you will be sympathetic to the point of view that the public psychology and, for that matter, individual psychology, cannot, because of human weakness, be attuned for long periods of time to a constant repetition of the highest note in the scale. . . . Whereas in this country there is a free and sensational press, people tire of seeing the same name, day after day, in the important headlines of the papers, and the same voice, night after night, over the radio . . . if I had tried [in 1935] to keep up the pace of 1933 and 1934, the inevitable histrionics of the new actors, Long and Coughlin and Johnson, would have turned the eyes of the audience away from the main drama itself . . .

Because it is quoted frequently, the "highest-note-in-the-scale" theory has become a kind of credo of political mass communications. "I do not believe it is possible," wrote Ted Sorensen loyally, "to 'overexpose' a President like Kennedy." Then he became pragmatic, to use a word popular in the Kennedy era: "Nevertheless he could not, with any effectiveness, go on the air to denounce Big Steel, or announce a Cuban quarantine, or deliver some momentous message, every month of the year. . . . As a commander saves his biggest guns for the biggest battles, so Kennedy limited his direct national appeals to situations of sufficient importance to demand it and sufficiently fluid to be helped by it."

Eisenhower press secretary James Hagerty felt sufficiently confident of the magnetism of Eisenhower's presence to permit—for the first time—the filming of presidential press conferences, despite the danger of "overexposure." Kennedy extended this to "live" coverage and more frequent conferences; Lyndon Johnson, early in his Administration, made a great many television appearances to "put his stamp" on the presidency. As Arthur Krock wrote: "He does not share the fear of some friends that he is taking too heavy a toll of his incredible energy, and has already incurred whatever political peril there may be in 'overexposure.'" By 1967, however, Johnson made it a point to say less and appear less.

Krock's successor as the Washington correspondent of the *New York Times,* James Reston, applied the exposure yardstick with a photography metaphor to Senator Robert Kennedy in 1967, after a Kennedy dispute with J. Edgar Hoover over wiretapping, and Kennedy's handling of Manchester's book on the assassination: ". . . publicity is not the same thing as power, and while it is often useful to a rising politician, it can sometimes be the opposite. . . . He is better known now, but he looks a little underdeveloped and overexposed."

overheated economy an economy headed toward uncontrollable inflation, with price and wage rises far outpacing productivity.

A classic example of the unconscious use of jargon is this passage from Walter Heller's *New Dimensions of Political Economy* (1967): "Let us assume that a nation which has accepted the idea of tax cuts to overcome slack, to close a 'deflationary gap,' should undertake tax increases to cool off an overheating economy, to close an 'inflationary gap.'"

In pointing to the metaphoric use of "gaps," Heller overlooked his own use of "overheating economy," a piece of economic jargon. Like FLAT-OUT, it is an automobile metaphor; overheated refers to an engine raced too long or loaded too heavily.

See HOLD THE LINE; INFLATION; BAFFLEGAB; NEW ECONOMICS.

overkill a surfeit of power; more nuclear destruction capable of being inflicted than is needed to kill an enemy's entire population.

"In describing the aftermath of a war," Hudson Institute operations analyst Herman Kahn wrote coolly in 1960, "it is not particularly illuminating to use such words as 'intolerable,' 'catastrophic,' 'total destruction,' 'annihilating retaliation,' and so on. Such words would be useful only if it were really true that in a modern war all possible targets would be overkilled by factors of five or ten, as many people have assumed." After coining the word, he advocated a shelter program that would, he thought, cut U.S. casualties from eighty million down to forty million. See UNTHINKABLE THOUGHTS.

U.S. strategic planners picked up the word in explaining their policy of "limited deterrence," which held that if the U.S. had enough atomic weapons to inflict "unacceptable" damage to an enemy, any further expenditure on weapons would only be for "overkill" and a waste of money.

One of the charms of political language is its ability to absorb colorful words, no matter how shocking or bloody the concept. Writing about the ovation given Robert Kennedy at the 1964 Democratic convention, political columnists Rowland Evans and Robert Novak observed: "It brought second thoughts to the politicians who had accused Johnson of overkill in deploying the powers of the Presidency on The Bobby Problem."

In a 1969 speech, William McChesney Martin, then chairman of the Federal Reserve Board, showed how the word could be used in an economic context as well. He described a conversation he had with President Johnson in 1965, in which he pointed out that increased expenditures required higher taxes to avert inflation. "I remember him saying to me, 'Well, yes, I think so too, but we can't do it now. We'd risk overkill.' That was the first time I'd heard that expression used, but I've heard it plenty over the years since, when all the while the economy—and inflationary pressures as well—were burgeoning."

overreact to respond more strongly than necessary, revealing a tendency to panic; in politics, the mark of an amateur.

When President Harry Truman received reports on June 24, 1950, that North Korean troops had invaded South Korea, he was careful not to overreact. "Don't make it ALARMIST," he told reporters. "It could be dangerous, but I hope it isn't. There has been no formal declaration of war that I know of. I can't answer any more questions until I get all the facts." This illustrates one sense of the word: the comment, or "reaction," from a public figure immediately following an event.

The second sense is to take more action than is necessary to counter an opponent's thrust. When steel companies raised their prices in 1962 (see S.O.B.) President Kennedy marshaled all the strength of the presidency to force them to roll back their increase. Wrote Sorensen: "When it was all over, several Republicans . . . would term

these various administration efforts an example of 'over-reacting,' 'tyranny' and 'executive usurpation.'"

The use of "overreact" as an attack word is evident in this 1967 *Wall Street Journal* editorial: "When the United States has used overwhelming force, as in Eisenhower's intervention in Lebanon or Johnson's dash into the Dominican Republic, the results have been relatively happy despite initial charges of overreaction."

The use of the word has traveled. *The Economist* of London urged in 1967 an end to the "baiting" of Foreign Secretary George Brown: ". . . one of Mr. Brown's faults is that he is inclined to over-react. The more he is hounded by the gossip writers (as he is) the more likely he is to over-react and provide them with additional copy. The more he is made to look politically vulnerable by being forced (unnecessarily) to restate major speeches, as he has had to do twice this week, the more likely he is to over-react with a real resignation."

oversight presumed vigilance of a government operation by a congressional committee.

In a working paper for the House Select Committee on Committees, Walter Oleszek wrote in June 1973: "A result of this expansion [of administrative agencies since the New Deal] has been an enlargement of Congress' oversight function, a traditional legislative function that philosopher John Stuart Mill considered as the most important responsibility of a legislature."

This "oversight function" of the U.S. Congress is relatively new, first formally authorized by Section 136 of the Legislative Reorganization Act of 1946: "To assist the Congress in appraising the administration of the laws and developing such amendments or related legislation as it may deem necessary, each standing committee of the

Senate and the House shall exercise continuous watchfulness of the execution by the administrative agencies concerned of any laws, the subject matter of which is within the jurisdiction of such committee . . .

"Continuous watchfulness," Congressmen felt, was too vague, or too time-consuming; in 1970 this was changed to "legislative review." In practice, the investigative part of "oversight" was largely neglected by the Congress, which was more interested during the fifties and sixties in legislative reach—adding to the laws regulating commerce or creating new agencies.

However, with the CIA revelations of the Senate Select Committee on Intelligence in 1975, it became apparent that Congress had been remiss in its obligation to act as a check on actions of the executive branch, especially in the intelligence area. The word "oversight" became voguish in the mid-seventies, not only as an accusation of lack of previous vigilance but as a means of extending congressional power. A related term, "accountability," has a positive connotation, while "monitoring" often carries an intrusive, pejorative tone.

Ted Sorensen, the Kennedy speechwriter rejected by the Senate in 1977 as nominee for Director of Central Intelligence, once wrote wryly: "The word 'oversight' has two meanings, and they chose the wrong one."

"The oversight function," as the word is sometimes attenuated, is occasionally confused with "overview," a favorite term of social scientists. "Oversight" implies supervision or at least some modicum of control, while "overview" implies either a perspective or a survey conducted with Olympian detachment. "Overview" has good lineage: "Too bitter is thy jest," says the King in *Love's Labour's Lost,* written by Shakespeare in 1588. "Are we betrayed thus to thy overview?"

Oversight is also a good example of what is known among lexicographers as a "Janus word," named after the Roman god who faces both ways. A Janus word is one having contradictory or opposite meanings. One meaning of *oversight* is "careless omission" (as in "Kiting that check at the House bank was strictly an oversight"); the other meaning is "watchful care." Members of Congress who fail to exercise the function of *oversight* should not use *oversight* as an excuse.

For other words with opposite meanings, see "sanction" (under QUARANTINE) and TABLE.

oxymoron. See LOYAL OPPOSITION; UNTHINKABLE THOUGHTS; WAGING PEACE.

P

pacification euphemism for crushing guerrilla resistance in an area, either by extermination or, preferably, by constructing a stable socioeconomic system that will persuade them to change sides.

In the minds of military men, pacification has both of the above meanings. The choice of the word—"to make peaceful"—enables political leaders to concentrate on the positive sense and overlook the "or else" implicit in the program.

In the war in Vietnam, the U.S. government wished to make clear that it was assisting in repelling invaders from the North who were using local Vietcong troops as aides to their invasion, rather than accept the Communist view that it was a civil war between South Vietnamese, with "outsiders" meddling. Accordingly, the "war" was against the North Vietnamese, and "pacification" aimed at Vietcong activities.

"Unlike the direct campaign against major Communist military units," wrote McGeorge Bundy in 1967, "the political effort, in all its forms, can take effect only as it engages the energies and convictions of the Vietnamese people themselves. So we must not be surprised that real pacification is hard to get in the Vietnamese countryside."

Lyndon Johnson, in a Nashville, Tennessee, speech on March 16, 1967, used pacification in its constructive sense, again separating it from military success against troops from the North: ". . . our military success has permitted the ground work to be laid for a pacification program which is the long-run key to an independent South Vietnam."

In American history, the word had been relatively dormant since its use as the nickname for Senator Henry Clay of Kentucky, "The Great Pacificator."

In the Serbia-Bosnia ETHNIC CLEANSING of 1992 and 1993, pacification was eschewed and "peacekeeping," later "peacemaking," substituted.

See INFRASTRUCTURE.

package deal an omnibus bill, often containing something for everybody; a compromise that enables an executive to get legislation he wants in return for agreeing to sign legislation he has opposed.

Running for re-election as governor of California in 1950, Earl Warren stressed his nonpartisan stance, resisting efforts to get him to support any other Republican on the ticket, including Richard Nixon for senator: "I have no present intention of endorsing candidates for other offices in the November 7 election. We are all running independent campaigns. I've never believed in package deals. I believe the public is entitled to make its own selection and I'm just interested in one campaign—my own."

This was and is a merchandising expression, referring to the two-for-the-price-of-one sales appeals, or the inclusion of a tube of toothpaste in the same package with a toothbrush.

In an early Eisenhower cabinet meeting, it was pointed out that conservatives resisted a negotiated peace in Korea because they felt it might lead to recognition of Red China. Defense Secretary Charles E. Wilson, a businessman all his life, popped up with: "Is there any possibility for a package deal? Maybe we could recognize Red China and get the Far East issues settled." As Sherman Adams recalled later, "Eisenhower managed to control himself." Emmett Hughes commented, "Quite a few cabinet meetings were jerked to quivering attention by such remarks." (In retrospect, "Engine Charlie" seems more prescient than his more sophisticated colleagues.)

The President explained that such a quid pro quo was not feasible; the phrase "package deal" was not used again in cabinet meetings. However, in his 1957 message to Congress on mutual security, Eisenhower put together a series of foreign operations recommendations into "one vital parcel which we must not neglect."

In 1978, when Jimmy Carter linked the promised sale of jet fighters to Israel with a similar sale to Egypt and Saudi Arabia, his Secretary of State, Cyrus Vance, presented the plan publicly as "a package," and Congress approved the three items in series.

The older term, *omnibus bill*, dates back to the 1850s and is based on the French term for a public conveyance, *voiture omnibus*, "vehicle for everybody." The omnibus bill sweeps together a little of everything. *Time* magazine in late 1992 cited President-elect Clinton's use of the term: "On legislative strategy, Clinton said he would emulate, of all people, Ronald Reagan and pack 'a whole lot of changes into omnibus bills. . . . The fewer votes [in Congress] you have, the better off you are.'"

Package is, however, the more frequent word. In 1993, a Clinton aide was quoted after the successful Republican filibuster of the Administration's "stimulus package": "I knew it was headed for trouble as soon as I heard it called 'the stimulation package.'"

See CHRISTMAS TREE BILLS; LINKAGE.

packing the galleries placing the supporters of one candidate at a national convention in the galleries to the exclusion of others, in the hope of stampeding the delegates.

"We want Willkie! We want Willkie!" The thunderous demand from the galleries at the 1940 Republican convention heartened many a Willkie supporter among the delegations on the floor, and convinced many waverers that a bandwagon was rolling.

The floor manager for Senator Robert A. Taft, R. B. Creager, stormed up to the platform with a complaint to Chairman Joe Martin: when Taft supporters showed up for their gallery seats, they found them already occupied by Willkie fans who were using counterfeit tickets. (For counterfeiting instructions, see SPONTANEOUS DEMONSTRATION.) "It was an open scandal," Martin admitted later, "that several hundred counterfeit tickets had been printed and given to a Willkie claque who filled the best seats in the gallery to the exclusion of holders of bona fide tickets." Creager wanted to be recognized in order to denounce the tactics, but Martin talked him out of it. "We had no evidence in hand . . . we weren't even sure that we could distinguish the counterfeit tickets from the real ones, so skillfully were the former printed."

As the hollering continued, Martin banged his gavel: "I regret to have to admonish those in the galleries to be quiet, and to remind them that they are the guests of this convention . . ."

"Guests, hell," a voice was heard to shout, "we *are* the convention!"

After Willkie was nominated, Taft men insisted that the packing of the galleries had "put over" Willkie. Roscoe Drummond, then a *Christian Science Monitor* correspondent, disagreed: "Willkie was no more 'put over' on the Republican convention than Babe Ruth was 'put over' on the New York Yankees."

Willkie's gallery-packing was in the grand tradition of the first candidate of the Republican party to be elected. According to historian Carl Sandburg, Lincoln supporter Ward Lamon had been to the printers of tickets for seats to the Republican convention held in Chicago's Wigwam in 1860: "Young men worked nearly a whole night signing the names of convention officers to counterfeit seat tickets so that the next day Lincoln men could jam the hall and leave no seats for the Seward shouters."

paid his dues. See CARD-CARRYING.

pairing an agreement between two legislators, in disagreement about an upcoming vote, that neither will be present at the voting; thus, each is on record without the necessity of appearance.

When supporters of John F. Kennedy explained that their candidate was seriously ill at the time of the McCarthy censure, liberal Democrats refused to accept the excuse because, they argued, "the Senator could have been paired against McCarthy."

The system is a useful device when absence is caused by illness or other important official business; similarly, it is an alibi-ruiner. However, Ralph Waldo Emerson made a case against the idea:

> What a vicious practice is this of our politicians at Washington pairing off! as if one man who votes wrong, going away, could excuse you, who mean to vote right, for going away; or as if your presence did not tell in more ways than in your vote. Suppose the three hundred heroes at Thermopylae had paired off with three hundred Persians: would it have been all the same to Greece, and to history?

palace guard attack word on the leader's inner circle from one who has been excluded; those who protect or "insulate" a President, taking an undue share of power.

"Either make up your minds," Eisenhower chief of staff Sherman Adams said to two department heads in some dispute, "or else tell me and I will do it. We must not bother the President with this. He is trying to keep the world from war." Adams (see ABOMINABLE NO-MAN) was denounced by Senator Joseph McCarthy for heading a "palace guard," usurping power by "insulating" the Chief Executive from decisions properly only his.

From the point of view of one unable to reach the leader's ear, the sin of the palace guard is insulation. F. Clifton White, who organized the Draft Goldwater movement only to find himself frozen out when Goldwater was nominated, said nothing against the candidate but was bitter about what he termed "the tight little coterie that insulated him from all other Republicans."

According to Lyndon Johnson, House Speaker Sam Rayburn told Harry Truman soon after Truman became President: "Harry, they'll try to put you behind a wall down here. There will be people who will surround you and cut you off from any ideas but theirs. They'll try to make you think that the President is the smartest man in the world. And, Harry, you know he ain't and I know he ain't."

James Farley broke with FDR in 1940, when he thought there was a possibility of a presidential nomination for himself. Of those days, he wrote: "Housing Administrator Nathan Straus brought me word that the White House 'palace guard' realized the anti-Catholic campaign against me had failed . . ." Earlier, when Farley was a member of that guard, he explained the political subtlety behind the willingness of Louis Howe, FDR's closest adviser, to permit Farley to be close to Roosevelt: "The reason Louis had faith in me and trusted me was that he knew I didn't want to get between him and Roosevelt. In other words, Louis didn't have anything I wanted, see?"

A good political campaign appears to "stay loose," to avoid the strict lines of authority that discourage influential supporters from reaching the candidate or his manager. If the circle of men around a candidate freezes into a few familiar faces, there is a tendency for those men to identify too closely with the candidate and an understandable reluctance of others to try to "break in."

The idea of the palace guard probably comes from the Praetorian Guard, an imperial bodyguard established by the Emperor Augustus which, under later Roman emperors, assumed considerable power of its own. In 1791 James Madison warned that the "stockjobbers will become the praetorian band of the Government, at once its tool and its tyrant." Around "King

Andrew" Jackson's time, the White House was referred to as "the palace," a usage William Leggett objected to in 1837: "The word 'palace' . . . as applied to the President's house is entirely out of place . . ."

The phrase was applied to the Nixon senior staff by Dan Rather and Gary Paul Gates in a 1971 book of that title; because of the Germanic origin of some of the key aides' names (Haldeman, Ehrlichman, Kissinger, Ziegler) the Nixon palace guard was also known as the "Berlin wall."

In the Carter Administration, the number of Georgians on the staff (Joseph Powell, Hamilton Jordan, Robert Lipshutz, Stuart Eizenstadt) led to the occasional use of the "Magnolia Mafia." Carter cabinet secretary Jack Watson insisted: "The White House staff will not be a palace guard giving commands to the rest of government." Asked why he had placed a stern call to a cabinet member, Watson replied, "He will constantly need a presidential perspective on issues, and the White House staff has to give him that perspective."

As used today, *palace guard* is a mild term of reproof to the circle of advisers that must be near a President or governor; *inner circle* (see INNER CLUB) is a term of respect or awe; KITCHEN CABINET is a group of trusted, unofficial advisers on policy; *coterie* implies congeniality, or circle of cronies; *retinue* is critical of the number of people who travel with the executive; *clique* is definitely pejorative, connoting snobbism; MAFIA imputes fierce loyalty, often used in admiration mixed with a dash of fear; OFFICIAL FAMILY is wide-ranging and imputes no criticism; *set*, as in the "Cliveden Set" in wartime England, or "Georgetown cocktail party set," is snobbish with a sinister overlay; *privy council*, used by Roosevelt, never caught on in the U.S.; BRAIN TRUST connotes professors: "the back door to the White House can only be opened with a Phi Beta Kappa key."

panjandrum mock title for a self-appointed big shot; a more intellectual form of POOH-BAH.

In a 1977 book review by *New York Times* cultural writer John Leonard, the mouth-filling word was used in its intended meaning: "As we might expect from Mr. [Ben] Wattenberg—coauthor of *The Real Majority*, adviser to Senator Henry Jackson, panjandrum of the 'centrist' Coalition for a Democratic Majority and public-television personality—*Against All Enemies* has more on its mind than mere entertainment."

In recent years the word has lost some of its bite and come to mean simply "big shot," with a slight connotation of self-importance or pomposity. *Time* magazine of November 16, 1992, referred to Henry Kissinger as "former panjandrum of foreign affairs." A few days later (November 22), the *Chicago Tribune* wrote: ". . . . he [President-elect Bill Clinton] went to Capitol Hill and courted party leaders and the House's committee panjandrums, Democrats Dan Rostenkowski of Illinois and John Dingell of Michigan."

Panjandrum was a word concocted by playwright Samuel Foote in 1755 to test the memory of a character who claimed to be able to repeat anything after having once heard it: "And there were present the Picninnies, and the Joblillies, and the Garyulies, and the Grand Panjandrum himself, with the little round button at top."

Arthur Schlesinger, Jr., referred to newspaper columnists as "panjandrums of the opinion mafia."

paper the file. See C.Y.A.

paper tiger exaggerated danger; false ferociousness; in diplomacy, a blustering nation with no real strength.

"All reactionaries," Mao Tse-tung told correspondent Anna Louise Strong in 1946, "are paper tigers. In appearance, the reactionaries are terrifying, but in reality they are not so powerful."

On other occasions Mao said of imperialists and feudalists: "Look! were these not living, iron tigers, real tigers? But in the end they changed into paper tigers, dead tigers, bean-curd tigers." And of the threat of nuclear destruction: "The atom bomb is a paper tiger which the U.S. reactionaries use to scare people. It looks terrible, but in fact it isn't."

Paper is a word used to symbolize the name of a thing rather than the thing itself; a picture of a cow drawn on paper cannot be milked, nor can a picture of a tiger on paper harm the viewer. Hence, "paper blockade," declared but not enforced; "paper profits," real but unrealized; and "to paper the house," to distribute free tickets to give the illusion of a sellout crowd.

Tiger metaphors have long stalked politics. "Riding the tiger" is an ancient image, used in 1936 by Winston Churchill: "Dictators ride to and fro upon tigers which they dare not dismount. And the tigers are getting hungry." A Tammany chieftain is said to have mounted a tiger's head on an old fire engine to rally his voters, and Thomas Nast locked in the image of a hungry TAMMANY TIGER in a cartoon.

paradigm shift the idea that a shift in perception causes inventive changes throughout; a call for reinventing and reorganizing government, not enlarging it.

Historian Thomas Kuhn introduced this term in his 1970 book, *The Structure of Scientific Revolutions*, explaining the force of scientific change. He explored how old assumptions have historically been replaced by new paradigms, as in the shift from thinking that the sun revolves around the earth. Kuhn's point—that a new paradigm can lead to drastic change—led to the movement for rethinking, or "reinventing," government.

The key word, *paradigm*, offers such synonyms as *model, example, pattern, archetype*. In 1984, "Paradigm Shift" was the title of a book by Robert L. Humphrey on the teaching of universal values.

In 1992, David Osborne and Ted Gaebler applied the idea of a paradigm shift to politics when they wrote *Reinventing Government*. The verb *reinvent* had been popularized in recent usage by the 1985 book *Re-Inventing the Corporation*, by John Naisbitt and Patricia Aburdene. Specifically, the reinventing of government calls for new ways to help the poor and middle class without the problems created by bureaucracy.

James P. Pinkerton, a Bush aide for policy planning, picked up and popularized Kuhn's term in his "New Paradigm" memoranda in 1990, creating a New Paradigm Society to attract speakers like Osborne. At Pinkerton's urging, President George Bush touched on the subject in an April 1990 speech: "When old centralized bureaucratic systems are crumbling, the time has come for yet another paradigm." This formulation, substituting "yet another paradigm" (acronym: YAP) for "the new paradigm," did not lend itself to clarion calling; critical of the idea, Richard Darman, Bush's budget director, who remembered Depression-era song titles, wryly commented that the concept would be dismissed with "Brother, can you spare a paradigm?"

Undaunted, and with some ideological support from Bush Housing and Urban Development Secretary Jack Kemp, a Darman opponent, Pinkerton pressed his libertarian program on op-ed pages and in think tanks, calling for government to help poor children attend private schools and to help tenants gain ownership of public housing. This new paradigm would emphasize decentralization of government, free-market principles, "empowering" the poor, and allowing individual choice, as in parents' rights to choose their children's schools.

The "reinventing government" and "new paradigm" ideas found a welcome at the Progressive Policy Institute in Washington, where Will Marshall brought them to the attention of Arkansas Governor Bill Clinton. After Clinton's election in 1992, Pinkerton wrote in the *Washington Post*: "Maybe it *will* take a Democrat to 'reinvent' our oxidized, barnacled Ozymandias of a government. But if Clinton fails, a reinvented Republican Party will be waiting in the wings."

paramount issue   the overriding concern on the minds of voters in a campaign.

The phrase was popularized by William Jennings Bryan, in regard to free silver, and has had a steady use since. Michigan Governor George Romney called Vietnam the "paramount issue" of 1967 (see UNTHINKABLE THOUGHTS).

Paramount issue implies importance, for rational discussion; BURNING QUESTION is irrational discussion from entrenched positions, as on the question of slavery; GUT ISSUE is one which is not so much discussed as it is felt, as resentment about black gains or fear of social change; POCKETBOOK ISSUE is economic; HOT BUTTON *issue* is social. In recent years, TOPIC A has been in use to define the subject at the tip of many tongues.

Before an issue can become paramount, it must (1) be drawn so as to show a difference between parties, (2) show voters that the issue-drawing party's side is close to their own, and (3) hit home—be important to the voter.

The word *paramount*—"on top of the heights"—was applied to the Chinese leader Teng Hsiao-ping, after he refused to keep a government title while still retaining power. Western reporters gave him the title "paramount leader."

parity the price at which a farmer maintains his purchasing power.

Parity and "price supports" are used interchangeably, further confusing a farm program that most Americans do not understand.

Parity, like "par" and "peer," is from a Latin root meaning "equal." In agricultural policy, it is the price established by government statisticians that will bring the farmer a return equal to a previously favorable base period. The "parity price" gives the farmer a fair return on his investment in comparison with his costs.

To make sure the farmer was adequately paid for his goods, government price supports were begun, meaning that the federal government promised a farmer to purchase his crop at 90 percent of the parity price—provided the farmer planted only on those acres fixed by the government. As Dwight Eisenhower explained it: "At harvest time, if the market price had fallen below the support price . . . a farmer could get a loan from the government, with his crops as collateral, for the full support price. If the market price then rose above the support price, the farmer paid the government back; if not, he kept the loan, and the government took his crop."

The program had been denounced in the New Deal's early days as "a program of scarcity in a hungry land" and mock tears were shed for "little pigs not born" because of the element of the plan that restrained production. Republicans in the sixties pressed a program of "flexible price supports,"

with farmers compensated at between 75 percent and 90 percent of the parity price, depending on scarcity and timing.

Politically, the issue has often been hot, with both parties attacking the other's position as the one that stimulates overproduction, causes huge surpluses, helps the big farmer but not the small, and does not give the farmer his share of national prosperity. Secretaries of Agriculture from Henry Wallace to Ezra Taft Benson to Earl Butz have been centers of political controversy, with "parity" the incendiary word.

In a different sense, the word is in active use in strategic arms control. As the Soviet Union approached (and in some respects outstripped) the United States in the ability to conduct nuclear war, a word was needed to change the desired American posture from continued "superiority." In 1969, "sufficiency" was discussed, but "parity" persevered. ("Equality" would have been misleading, since each superpower led in certain categories and trailed in others.) Nixon speechwriters, distressed that the President could no longer say "America must remain number one" in strategic arms, found their answer in a ringing but accurate "America must be second to none," a positive way of presenting parity.

New Yorker writer Elizabeth Drew wrote in 1978 that Carter Secretary of State Cyrus Vance "suggested that language about parity in weapons be changed to 'essential equivalence.' In the President's [Wake Forest College] speech, this became 'functional equivalence.' [Zbigniew] Brzezinski says that 'functional equivalence' is a new phrase, and a new concept. He says, 'I thought "essential equivalence" didn't convey the point. The term "functional equivalence" means that our weapons need not be identical or similar.'" See SALT.

park-bench orator a private citizen outspoken about public affairs, especially in places of public assembly.

The picture of a man seated, spouting opinions with no responsibility for their consequences if undertaken, is also expressed by ARMCHAIR STRATEGIST. However, "park-bench orator" has a less pejorative connotation, and is less noisy than "soapbox orator," especially since Bernard Baruch made a park bench his headquarters.

When in Washington, Baruch's favorite bench was located in Lafayette Park near the White House, where he would sit bundled in a heavy overcoat in his later years holding conferences with important government officials and newsmen. "His bench," wrote biographer Margaret Coit, "to which mail was duly addressed and delivered, was just off dead center of the park, near the end of the equestrian statue of Andrew Jackson. It was four feet six inches long, just enough to accommodate Baruch and one average-sized Cabinet officer." The bench sits there today, with a bronze plaque nearby identifying it as "the Bernard M. Baruch Bench of Inspiration," and it has been used by at least one Washington pundit as a place to meet and interview White House aides.

The studious lack of ostentation was ostentatious in itself, but the ELDER STATESMAN's stature was such that he could carry it off. Two generations earlier, Baruch had taken the edge off what had been a dirty word by telling the Pujo Committee that his occupation was "speculator" and then defining the need for speculators in the making of markets; in his old age, Baruch did much the same for "park-bench orator."

Use of the term is illustrated in this 1967 *Wall Street Journal* item: "[defining Communism] . . . A pastime for park-bench orators and intense collegians has rather suddenly blown into an important Congressional debate . . ."

parlor pink socialite socialist; in the past, an attack word on a leftist or FELLOW TRAVELER who limited his political radicalism to cocktail-party discussions.

Theodore Roosevelt was the coiner of the "parlor" end in a Minneapolis speech, September 28, 1917: "The *parlor pacifist*, the white-handed or sissy type of pacifist, represents decadence, represents the rotting out of the virile virtues among people who typify the unlovely, senile side of civilization. The rough-neck pacifist, on the contrary, is a mere belated savage who has not been educated to the virtues of national patriotism."

A year later, in a magazine article, Roosevelt applied the noun-become-adjective to the left as "parlor bolshevism." See PROFESSIONAL.

Since Bolsheviks were "reds," their sympathizers were called pinks, or pinkos, especially from the thirties through the fifties; the alliteration of the Roosevelt adjective and the noun locked up the phrase as "parlor pink."

The phrase outlived the use of the word "parlor" in American speech; with changes in housing, the parlor— a small formal sitting room for guests—became merged into a general living room or den. As the room was designed out of houses and apartments, the word parlor—from the French verb *parler*, "to speak"—atrophied, except for its political use in this phrase, and in invitations from spiders to flies. The phrase was replaced for a time by "radical chic," a coinage of journalist Tom Wolfe. In France, the current term is *la gauche de salon.*

See PINKO; RED; FELLOW TRAVELER; LEFT WING, RIGHT WING; LIMOUSINE LIBERAL.

participatory democracy. See TELL IT LIKE IT IS; COMMITTED.

partisan praised as basic to the TWO-PARTY SYSTEM, the adversary system of arriving at truth in government; attacked as introducing unnecessary strife, placing party advantage above the public interest. (For differentiation between partisans, see BIPARTISAN; NONPARTISAN.)

The dispute about the pros and cons of partisan political activity can be illustrated by the following quotations, only some of which are familiar.

George Washington: "The alternate domination of one faction over another, sharpened by the spirit of revenge natural to party dissension, which in different ages and countries has perpetrated the most horrid enormities, is itself a frightful despotism."

Joseph Addison in *The Spectator:* "There is nothing so bad for the face as party zeal. It gives an ill-natured cast to the eye, and a disagreeable sourness to the look. . . . I never knew a party-woman that kept her beauty for a twelve-month."

On the other hand—

John Stuart Mill: "A party of order or stability, and a party of progress or reform, are both necessary elements of a healthy state of political life."

Graham Wallas (see GREAT SOCIETY): "Something is required simpler and more permanent, something which can be loved and trusted, and which can be recognized at successive elections as being the same thing that was loved and trusted before; and a party is such a thing."

In this century, statesmen like Woodrow Wilson felt free to say, "The trouble with the Republican Party is that it has not had a new idea in thirty years," and Dwight Eisenhower, who was ABOVE POLITICS, was not above referring to Democrats in high office as "too big for their britches and too small for their jobs."

The object of that last crack, Harry Truman, enjoyed the heat of the kitchen: "There never was a non-partisan in politics. A man cannot be a nonpartisan and be effective in a political party. When he's in any party he's partisan—he's got to be. The only way a man can act as a non-partisan is when he is in office, either as President or head of a state or country or city." See IF YOU CAN'T STAND THE HEAT . . .

Truman is regarded by many as the example of HAPPY WARRIOR partisanship in the twentieth century, just as Andrew Jackson came to be the focus of partisan attack and support in the formative years of the American party system. (It is true that Jackson wrote President Monroe in 1818, "Now is the time to exterminate the monster called party spirit," but that can be dismissed as a burst of youthful exuberance and is never quoted at Democratic Jackson Day dinners.)

In his preliminary notes for *Profiles in Courage,* John F. Kennedy wrote of Senator Robert A. Taft: "He was partisan in the sense that Harry Truman was—they both had the happy gift of seeing things in bright shades. It is the politicians who see things in similar shades that have a depressing and worrisome time of it."

In 1971, at the dedication of the Johnson Library, President Nixon applied a phrase of Albert Beveridge's to Lyndon Johnson: "a partisan of principle." In 1993, elder statesman Nixon told the author, "I'm no longer a partisan."

The negative view of partisanship was expressed by President Bill Clinton on May 29, 1993: "I have been very concerned that the cumulative effect of some of the things . . . in the news has given to the Administration a tinge that is too partisan and not connected to the mainstream, pro-change, future-oriented policies that I ran for President to implement. . . . We are going beyond the partisanship that damaged this country so badly in the last several years to search for new ideas, a new common ground, a new national unit."

See NONPARTISAN; BIPARTISAN; FUSION.

party. See TWO-PARTY SYSTEM.

party elders the "Grand Old Men" of a party, venerated for their age, presumed sagacity, party service, and present or past political power.

Party elders are occasionally turned to for mediation because they have no political ambitions of their own. In the deadlock of the 1920 Republican convention, a group of what historian Mark Sullivan called the "party elders" gathered to resolve the impasse between General Leonard Wood and Governor Frank Lowden. See SMOKE-FILLED ROOM. Seven senior senators were in the group, and one of them, Henry Cabot Lodge, put forth the name of Warren G. Harding, a man without enemies, who was chosen. Harry Daugherty, Harding's prime mover who was not present at the meeting, referred to the elders as "the Sanhedrin of the Solemn Senators" (a reference to the supreme council of Jews in ancient Jerusalem).

Party elder is probably derived from "church elder," and from the Council of Elders who "appealed" to Napoleon to take over France after the Revolution. The phrase is more partisan than "ELDER STATESMAN," though in the case of former Presidents Harry Truman and Herbert Hoover, each was both a party elder and elder statesman simultaneously. General Eisenhower, who had remained ABOVE POLITICS, was considered only an elder statesman and not a party elder.

A party elder is not to be confused with an OLD PRO, which refers to political experience and not to age. A man can be referred to as an "old pro" in his forties. White hair has been a requirement for party elders, with the exception of Speaker Sam Rayburn, who was bald.

party emblems identifying symbols at the top of a ballot, originally as a signal to illiterate voters, now used as a kind of trademark.

At the time of the Jackson Administration, the Democratic party emblem was a hickory pole and broom ("a new broom sweeps clean" [see CLEAN SWEEP]) which was replaced in the 1840s by a rooster. The story of how the change came about is probably apocryphal, but legend has it that a Democratic leader named Chapman had a reputation for crowing like a gamecock. When the Democrats won, an expression arose: "Tell Chapman to Crow." In 1842 and 1844, after Democratic victories over the Whigs, the rooster became the usual party emblem.

Republicans in the 1850s and 1860s needed a counterpart. While Democrats were being urged to "vote for the big chick," Republicans were told to "vote for the bird on the dollar," an eagle.

In the 1950s, however, with the "white rooster" closely identified with segregation in the South, Democrats there dropped the emblem and replaced it with a variety of others, most often a star.

Minor parties have used the torch and the scale of justice (mainly Socialist), the Liberty Bell (Liberal party), the arm and hammer (labor parties); the Prohibitionists always featured the fountain.

Party emblems differ from party symbols. See ELEPHANT, REPUBLICAN; DONKEY, DEMOCRATIC. National emblems differ from national symbols (John Bull of England, Marianne of France, UNCLE SAM of the U.S.).

For America's national emblem, see BALD EAGLE. Other national emblems include the lion of England (see TWISTING THE LION'S TAIL); the cock, as well as the fleur de lis, of France; the double-headed eagle of Austria, and the black eagle of Prussia.

party faithful the rank-and-file regulars; the hard-core voters and soft-touch contributors.

The originally militant implication of "faithful," taken from its religious usage, appears now to be used of the long-suffering, often overlooked regulars taken for granted by politicians who spend their time wooing the "swing vote."

There is a wistfulness in today's use of the phrase, as if the faithful's hope for ultimate reward is far in the future. The phrase is a cliché in the reportage of fund-raising functions, where "eight hundred of the party faithful turned out to munch rubber chicken and listen to . . ."

REGULAR, with its military origin, implies militant fidelity; *faithful*, with its religious origin, implies mystic, spiritual fidelity; RANK AND FILE, from military via labor, implies fidelity to orders from above; TROOPS, military, are more disciplined than rank and file, and will go out and ring doorbells.

See RELIGIOUS METAPHORS; TRUE BELIEVER.

party line the official position of a political organization.

There are several political meanings of this phrase: (1) the principles or position set down by an authoritarian political organization, to be adhered to at lower levels without deviation; (2) the line or column on a ballot or voting machine displaying the party's nominees (when the display is horizontal, the word *row* is gaining preference over *line*); and (3) in the plural, the lines of demarcation between parties, which regulars do not cross but issues often do.

"Each Communist is entitled to his opinion," said Nikita Khrushchev in 1963 to the party's central committee, "but when the Party adopts a decision, maps out a general line, then all Party members toe the line and do what has been worked out by the collective thinking and will of the party."

Most Americans think of party line as originating with Communist terminology, and use it sweepingly, as communists use "general line"; thus, the "general line of the transition period" in China was a broad directive to Communist cadres to place themselves in strategic positions "in a state of readiness." Later, more specific lines set more immediate targets for takeover and national indoctrination. In the U.S., specific Communist party lines zigzagged before World War II as the Soviet Union first reached an accommodation with, and later fought, Nazi Germany.

The political phrase, perhaps influenced by the name of early rural telephone exchanges, was then adopted in the U.S. as an ironic description of Democratic and Republican positions on specific issues. When Defense Secretary Robert McNamara insisted on military officers clearing all speeches with his office, there were objections to the establishment of "a military party line." See MUZZLE; HUNDRED FLOWERS.

In the second sense of a position on the ballot, a party with a poor comparative registration in an area likes to play down its Democratic or Republican designation, and urges voters to "Vote Row A All the Way"; individual candidates in that position advertise "the next to the last name on Line C."

The third sense was illustrated by Wendell Willkie's call in his 1940 acceptance speech: "Party lines are down; nothing could make that clearer than the nomination by the Republicans of a liberal Democrat who changed his party affiliation because he found democracy in the Republican party and not in the New Deal."

In discussing the Republican choice of Eisenhower over Taft in 1952, Harry Truman used the phrase in that context: "The Republicans, being a minority party, knew they had to borrow strength from the Democratic and independent vote. Their only hope of gaining such strength was to find a candidate whose appeal to the voters would cut across party lines."

Going back in American history, the lines converge. Thomas Hart Benton, writing in the 1830s, used the phrase in a meaning that covered both "the official position" and "demarcation between parties": "Look at the vote in the Senate . . . as clearly defined by a party line as any party question can ever be expected to be." The phrase "Old Line Whigs" referred to the party principles as well as the party periphery, and was probably drawn from the military skirmish line.

party loyalty the ability to support a candidate of an IDEOLOGY not one's own against another party's candidate who does espouse one's own ideology, in the belief that only by "closing ranks" now can your faction come to party power in the future.

"Sometimes party loyalty asks too much," said John F. Kennedy to a Democratic friend, excusing him for supporting Republican Leverett Saltonstall for senator of Massachusetts. But JFK also hinted that if he was reelected in 1964, he would not be too kindly disposed to those in the Democratic party who had thwarted his programs or had opposed him personally. "We can make loyalty to the ticket the test in 1964," he said in 1962, "and then we can deal with those who failed to support the ticket."

The argument against party loyalty is usually founded on "principle": a liberal Democrat finds it sticks in his craw to support a conservative Democrat against a liberal Republican, and vice versa for both parties. Yet this overlooks the nature of the TWO-PARTY SYSTEM in America; the two parties are not ideologically divided, as in England where Labour faces the Conservatives. The BIG TENT of each American party includes factions of the left and right, struggling for control. When one faction wins, it naturally expects its opposing faction to support the majority choice against the other party. If discipline breaks and the minority faction bolts, it surrenders its right to the loyalty of the opposite faction in the next election. Thus, the bolters see their "principle" temporarily upheld as the other party wins, but they are not likely to ever gain control of a united party that can win.

"Party loyalty among too many Liberal Republicans is not even skin deep," wrote Goldwater organizer Clif White after the 1964 debacle. "You either play it their way, or they play for the other side." Asked Goldwater of George Romney: "Where were you, George, when the going was rough?"

Liberal Republicans answered that in 1964 the conservatives were first to break the rules of party loyalty: Goldwater supporters, after so long out of control of the Republican party, offered no olive branch to the losing liberals at the convention, which is traditional in healing party wounds. See EXTREMISM.

Party loyalty can be attacked as blind and unprincipled, but to those who view politics as a practical route to the position of power that can make principles operative, party loyalty is essential.

That is what Benjamin Disraeli was getting at when he said: "Damn principles! Stick to your party."

party of privilege frequent Democratic characterization of the Republican party.

The Democratic platform of 1908 dispensed with subtleties and the gray areas of party overlapping: "The Democratic party is the champion of equal rights and opportunities to all; the Republican party is the party of privilege and private monopoly." As if this were not a wide enough gulf, the platform went on: "The Democratic party listens to the voice of the whole people and gauges progress by the prosperity and advancement of the average man; the Republican party is subservient to the comparatively few who are the beneficiaries of governmental favoritism."

The Republican nominee in 1908, William Howard Taft, won handily, but the emerging phrase was to plague Republicans for years to come. Calvin Coolidge did his best to knock it down. "The governments of the past," he said in 1924, "could fairly be characterized as devices for maintaining in perpetuity the place and position of certain privileged classes . . . The Government of the United States is a device for maintaining in perpetuity the rights of the people, with the ultimate extinction of all privileged classes."

But not even Coolidge sounding like Lenin could alter the stereotype that was forming in the mind of most of the American electorate. Political scientist Clinton Rossiter put it bluntly: "Most men recognize the Republicans as the party of the upper and upper-middle classes and the Democrats as the party of the lower and lower-middle classes. The short title for the former classes is 'the rich,' for the latter 'the poor.'"

In phraseology applied to parties, the Democrats have been fairly successful in tagging Republicans as the "party of privilege" and styling themselves as the PARTY OF THE PEOPLE. For a partial offset, see WAR PARTY. Also see VESTED INTERESTS; TRICKLE-DOWN THEORY.

party of the people Democratic party's characterization of itself.

"Our party is the party of the people," wrote Democrat Grover Cleveland in 1896, "because in its care for the welfare of all our countrymen it resists dangerous schemes born of discontent . . . reinforced by the insidious aid of private selfishness . . ."

In that year William Jennings Bryan, whose "dangerous scheme" of free silver caused Cleveland to bolt, asked in his "Cross of Gold" speech: "Upon which side will the Democratic party fight: upon the side of 'the idle holders of idle capital' or upon the side of 'the struggling masses'? . . . The sympathies of the Democratic party . . . are on the side of the struggling masses who have ever been the foundation of the Democratic party." See TRICKLE-DOWN THEORY.

Renegade and embittered Republicans helped the Democrats seal their slogan throughout the twentieth century. In the Bull Moose campaign of 1912, the Theodore Roosevelt campaign against President Taft included this challenge: "Let us find out whether the Republican party is the party of the plain people; or whether it is the party of the bosses and the sinister interests of special privilege." Democrat Woodrow Wilson, echoing these sentiments, was able to defeat the divided Republicans. After the Dewey defeat by Truman in 1948, liberal Republican Russell Davenport, a top Willkie campaign aide in 1940, complained: "The theme of the last sixteen years (which must now become twenty years) has been—the Republican party versus the people. And the people have won. . . ."

Truman in 1948, and Adlai Stevenson in both of his campaigns, did not neglect the populist theme which had been absorbed by the Democrats. Said Stevenson: ". . . the Democratic Party is the people's party, not the labor party, not the farmer's party, not the employer's party—it is the party of no one because it is the party of everyone."

Lyndon Johnson, using orthography which would have appealed to Noah Webster and George Bernard Shaw, spelled it out in 1966: "The people . . . P-E-E-P-U-L . . ."

party unity the vital ingredient to winning an election, when dissident factions accept the majority decision and unite behind the nominee, grumbling only in private.

American parties have no monopoly on the desire for party unity. "This democratic method of resolving contradictions among the people," wrote Mao Tse-tung in 1957, "was epitomized in 1942 in the formula 'unity, criticism, unity.' . . . It means starting from the desire for unity, resolving contradictions through criticism or struggle and arriving at a new unity on a new basis."

The argument for national unity can be applied to parties. When Lincoln asked, "The Union, is it a marriage bond or a free-love arrangement?" or when Jefferson ameliorated dissension with "every difference of opinion is not a difference of principle," the point was made that splitting was losing.

The Democratic party prides itself on its ability to split wide apart in primaries and come together in time for elections. "No, sir, th' dimycratic party aint on speakin' terms with itsilf," said Mr. DOOLEY to Mr. Hennessey. "Whin ye see two men with white neckties go into a sthreet car an' set in opposite corners while wan mutthers 'Thraiter' an' th' other hisses 'Miscreent' ye can bet they're two dimmycratic leaders thryin' to reunite th' gran' ol' party."

"Party harmony" is used almost interchangeably with "party unity": James Garfield nominated John Sherman "in the interests of party harmony," and Henry Clay, after a nomination defeat was certain, said, "If my name creates any obstacle to Union and Harmony, away with it, and concentrate upon some individual more acceptable to all branches of the opposition."

However, *party harmony* is milder than *party unity*, which is militant; *party loyalty* is the spirit that results in *party regularity*, which in turn is the key to *party unity*.

passion for anonymity a willingness to submerge one's identity for the benefit of a public figure; a passion that sometimes passes as the price of memoirs rises.

Franklin Roosevelt took the phrase from Louis Brownlow, who was chairman of his Committee on Administrative Management in 1936–37. Brownlow was thinking of men like Harry Hopkins and Felix Frankfurter; the Reorganization Act of 1939 permitted the President to add six assistants to his staff, each with what Brownlow had described as a "passion for anonymity."

Historian Eric Goldman directed the author to the source of the phrase. Brownlow, who entitled his 1958 autobiography *A Passion for Anonymity*, credits it to Welsh politician Tom Jones, who served as private secretary to three British Prime Ministers: David Lloyd George, Ramsay MacDonald, and Stanley Baldwin. Brownlow related Jones's comments in 1939 about the need for one key aide.

Being both a Welshman and a veteran of many parliamentary and ministerial battles, he was inclined to put the emphasis on the man rather than on the institution and, therefore, talked more about Sir Maurice Hankey than he did about the Cabinet secretariat. Then he asked me if I would take a message to President Roosevelt for him, a mission which I gladly undertook. The message was this: "Tell the President that the way to solve his problem is to find that one man who would turn out to be another Maurice Hankey, a man possessed of high competence, great physical vigor, and a passion for anonymity." Later, when we rejected the one-man idea and proposed, among other new aids recommended for the President, six administrative assistants, we used Tom Jones's language to describe their qualifications . . .

During his second term FDR chose assistants less colorful than in his first. "The later careers of Moley, Tugwell and Hugh Johnson," wrote Samuel Rosenman, ". . . indicate that there is something about administrative power along the Potomac that excludes the concept of anonymous helpfulness which was the basis of the success of the original BRAIN TRUST."

President John F. Kennedy, in speaking of assistant Kenneth O'Donnell, sketched the qualities he wanted in a White House aide: "He has good nerves and a good memory. He has a passion for anonymity. He is always optimistic." Ted Sorensen wrote that "while few of us had a 'passion for anonymity,' most of us had a preference in that direction." President Kennedy told him to turn down requests for speeches and magazine profiles: "Every man that's ever held a job like yours—Sherman Adams, Harry Hopkins, House, all the rest—has ended up in the [Sorensen substituted a blank for the next word]. Congress was down on them or the President was hurt by them or somebody was mad at them. The best way to stay out of trouble is to stay out of sight."

The ability to stay out of sight is invaluable, of course, to members of what came to be called the INVISIBLE GOVERNMENT, the Central Intelligence Agency. As might be expected, CIA chief Allen Dulles told Congress of the kind of men he was trying to recruit: "The agency should be directed by a relatively small but elite corps of men with a passion for anonymity . . ." Years later, as angry CIA operatives published books, they were denounced by old hands as having a "passion for notoriety."

paternalism.   See GREAT WHITE FATHER.

patronage   governmental appointments made so as to increase political strength.

Dear Tit:
   The bearer understands addition, division and silence. Appoint him!
               Your friend,
                    Bill

According to Charles Ledyard Norton, writing his *Political Americanisms* in 1890, these "qualifications of a successful lobbyist or unscrupulous political worker" first appeared in the *New York Sun* of March 15, 1872, in a letter alleged to have been written by W. H. Kemble, then State Treasurer of Pennsylvania, to T. J. Coffey of Washington, introducing G. O. Evans. This may be legend; the source of "addition, division and silence" has also been given as New York Boss William Marcy Tweed and Pennsylvania Boss Matthew Quay.

Patronage, a necessary ingredient in political life, has always been described by Presidents as an odious task. Thomas Jefferson said: "No duty the President had to perform was so trying as to put the right man in the right place." Andrew Johnson tried to defend himself: "Congress, factious, domineering, tyrannical Congress has undertaken to poison the minds of the American people, and create a feeling against me in consequence of the manner in which I have distributed the public patronage."

Dwight Eisenhower came out of a cabinet meeting on October 9, 1953, in a bad temper. "Everything seems to have been patronage this morning," he said as he left.

The power of appointment carries with it the stigma of favoritism, nepotism, and dishonesty. "Our present mayor," said a clergyman about John ("Honey Fitz") Fitzgerald in 1906, "has the distinction of appointing more saloon keepers and bartenders to public office than any previous mayor."

Some political figures, like Woodrow Wilson in 1913, took a high-minded view and refused to allow political considerations to dictate appointments. Wilson told Albert S. Burleson, his Postmaster General and dispenser of patronage, "On appointments I am not going to advise with reactionary or standpat Senators or Representatives." Burleson quietly pointed out that this meant: ". . . the defeat of the measures of reform that you have next to your heart. The little offices don't amount to anything. They are inconsequential. It doesn't amount to a damn who is postmaster at Paducah, Kentucky. But these little offices mean a great deal to the Senators and Representatives in Congress. . . . If they are turned down, they will hate you and will not vote for anything you want. It is human nature . . ." Wilson gave in.

Rarely do politicians articulate a defense of patronage. Tammany leader Edward Costikyan, who was forced by his reform associates to rename his "Patronage Committee" the "Government Appointments Committee" wrote: "How does one secure good government with good people, and strengthen a political party through the use of the power to appoint people to government office? This is the basic problem in dealing with 'patronage,' and it is one which our mythology prevents us from dealing with effectively. . . . The basic lesson I quickly learned was that a political leader cannot afford to insult his supporters by rewarding his opponents."

The opprobrium connected with patronage, and its association with phrases like "SPOILS SYSTEM" and the "power of public plunder" did not originate with politics. Originally, patronage meant the protection of the rights of the Church. The *OED* traces the word back to 1412: "He . . . sal noth iniure na disese the place throuch na titil of patronage bot as it is granttit . . . in this indenture." Following its defense-of-religion use, the word became associated with the patronage of authors and artists by the Church and the nobility. "Patron of the arts" stems from this.

The effect of the patronage of either kind on the morale of the receiver was observed by Cardinal Wolsey in Shakespeare's *Henry VIII*: "O, how wretched is that poor man that hangs on princes' favours."

In 1976 the U.S. Supreme Court, in *Elrod, Sheriff et al.* v. *Burns et al.*, held that the practice of patronage dismissals in a sheriff's office violated the First and Fourteenth Amendments. In the majority opinion, Justice William Brennan wrote: "More recent times have witnessed a strong decline in [patronage's] use, particularly with respect to public employment. Indeed, only decades after Andrew Jackson's administration, strong discontent with the corruption and inefficiency of the patronage system of public employment eventuated in the Pendleton Act (1883), the foundation of modern civil service. And on the state and local levels, merit systems have increasingly displaced the practice."

In a footnote the Court cited *To the Victor* (1971), a book by Martin

Tolchin and Susan Tolchin, as expert in modern patronage, and its authors supplied this lexicographer with their current definition: "The traditional view had been that patronage referred only to jobs. We defined patronage—after consultation with scores of politicians who said that they were not pressed for jobs but for many other governmental favors—as the disbursement of the discretionary favors of government in exchange for political support."

The purpose of such disbursement was best described by Chicago boss Jacob Arvey: "Politics is the art of putting people under obligation to you."

pax Americana "American peace"; welcome peacekeeping, or unwelcome one-superpower domination.

This phrase is based on the Latin term *pax Romana,* or "Roman peace," the two centuries of peace in the Roman Empire beginning with the reign of Augustus. The word *pax,* "peace" (personified in Roman myth as Pax, the goddess of peace), derives from the verb *pacisci,* meaning "to make a bargain or pact," and it was applied by Pliny the Elder to the extended period of peaceful rule by the Roman Empire.

From *pax Romana* came *pax Britannica* in the nineteenth century, describing the peace that Britain imposed on hostile nations.

The first use of *pax Americana* in print was by the writer Richard Raine in 1967, with derivation dutifully noted: "The whole Western world . . . is living under . . . a Pax Americana, just as the world once lived in peace under a Pax Britannica."

Michael T. Klare, writing in *The Nation* in 1991 about Operation Desert Storm, described a second phase of this peace: "The cold war era, which ended with the tearing down of the Berlin wall, was characterized by U.S. supremacy in the military, economic and political spheres—Pax Americana I. The gulf conflict inaugurates a new era characterized by continuing U.S. military supremacy accompanied by neither economic nor political strength—Pax Americana II."

In 1990, as fax machines gained popularity, an Art Buchwald column satirized the phrase with the headline "Fax Americana."

Other Latinized adjectives have also been joined to this expression for peaceful rule, from the communications-based *pax aeronautica* to the Japanese *pax Nipponica.*

A note of resentment often accompanies the phrase, with the *pax* taken to emphasize "domination" rather than "peace." George Bush, in a 1992 speech to the United Nations General Assembly, sought to dissociate the U.S. from the exclusive responsibility of global policing as well as from the attendant resentment: "We seek a *Pax Universalis,* built upon shared responsibilities and aspirations."

In 1993, the novelist John le Carré predicted, "With the clamps of the Cold War removed, old feuds are going to flare up everywhere. A Pax Americana of some kind is inevitable."

See POLICEMAN OF THE WORLD.

pay as you go the technique of the withholding tax, in which taxes are deducted as income is received; previously, a balanced budget.

"It is incumbent on every generation," Thomas Jefferson wrote a friend in 1820, "to pay its own debts as it goes—a principle which, if acted on, would save one-half the wars of the world." Jefferson took the phrase from an old proverb, often attributed to Benjamin Franklin—"pay as you go" used along with "never live beyond your means."

The phrase has had a long political application. Thurlow Weed, who later became a power in the Republican party, wrote in 1839 in reference to the Erie Canal: "The Democracy proclaimed itself in favor of the 'pay as you go' policy." John Randolph of Roanoke cried in Congress, "Mr. President! I have found the Philosopher's Stone! It is contained in four words: Pay-as-you-go!" Until the adoption of the withholding tax, espoused by Beardsley Ruml, the phrase continued to mean a policy of balanced budgets. With the adoption of the "estimated tax," tax policy extended "pay as you go" to all income, not just wages.

p.c. See POLITICALLY CORRECT.

peace. See FULL GENERATION OF PEACE; JUST AND LASTING PEACE.

peace at any price a slogan formerly used in earnest, now an attack phrase on those considered appeasers.

The idea of a "price" to be paid for peace probably stemmed from the price for liberty. "Eternal vigilance is the price of liberty" is the "quotation" developed out of Irish Judge John Philpot Curran's "The condition upon which God hath given liberty to man is eternal vigilance . . ."

In 1645, Britain's Lord Digby wrote of "the Kingdom's quiet, at any price to the King, to the Church, and to the faithfulest of his party." English poet Arthur H. Clough attributed the first political use of "peace at any price" to French poet and Minister of Foreign Affairs in 1848, Alphonse de Lamartine, although the historian Thomas Arnold wrote in 1823 in his *History of Rome* of Hannibal's probable intent in "purchasing peace at any price." Lord Avebury, in *The Use of Life*, wrote in 1849: "Though not a 'peace-at-any-price' man, I am not ashamed to say I am a peace-at-almost-any-price man."

In 1856 in the U.S., the phrase was used without sarcasm as the rallying cry of the KNOW-NOTHINGS behind former President Millard Fillmore, who ran behind James Buchanan and John Frémont. "Peace at any price—peace and union" was the slogan of those willing to pay the price of slavery to avoid civil war.

A strangely familiar "quotation of the day" appeared in the *New York Times* on January 31, 1959, attributed to Admiral Arthur W. Radford: "The things that will destroy America are prosperity at any price, peace at any price, safety first instead of duty first, the love of soft living and the get-rich-quick feeling of living." The quotation, with the substitution of "life" for "living" at the end, is from Theodore Roosevelt, who liked to inveigh against the "professional pacifists, the peace-at-any-price, nonresistance, universal arbitration people" who he felt were "seeking to Chinafy this country."

On February 1, 1916, Woodrow Wilson told an Iowa audience: "There is a price which is too great to pay for peace, and that price can be put in one word. One cannot pay the price of self-respect."

Senator William Borah, in 1919, attacked Woodrow Wilson's peace treaty and League of Nations with "Would you purchase peace at the cost of any part of our independence?" In 1937 Harold Macmillan urged England to "settle with Germany now, or coerce her now. But don't let us purchase an uncertain peace at a terrible price to be paid later."

The idea of peace having a high price, worth paying, but not going so far as "any" price remains a current political metaphor. At the height of the Cuban missile crisis, President Kennedy said on television: "The cost of freedom is always high, but Americans have always paid it." Bernard Baruch, urging the United Nations to adopt a plan for atomic weapons control in 1946, gave the phrase an added dimension: "The solution will require apparent sacrifice in pride and in position, but better pain as the price of peace than death as the price of war."

In 1991, George Bush repeated the phrase in remarks about America's stance against Iraq: "Appeasement—peace at any price—was never an answer."

peace bloc. See BLOC.

Peace Corps a 1960 Kennedy campaign phrase and idea appealing to youthful idealism, which was translated into an effective program after the campaign.

Senator Hubert Humphrey, along with Senator Richard Neuberger and Congressman Henry Reuss, had proposed several ideas in the late fifties for sending voluntary technical assistance workers overseas. Senator Humphrey provided the author with this background:

> Congressman Henry S. Reuss of Wisconsin played a very important role in a government-sponsored youth service corps. After a visit to Cambodia in 1957, he created the Point Four Youth Corps which he submitted to the House of Representatives early in 1960, calling for a study on his proposal. The study was eventually assigned to the University of Colorado Research Foundation and put under the general direction of Dr. Maurice Albertson. The Albertson report was completed in May 1961. Much of the concrete planning of the present Peace Corps was based on it.
>
> On June 15, 1960, while I was a Senator, I introduced the "Works for Peace" bill. This bill differed from that of Congressman Reuss' in that instead of asking for a study of the Peace Corps, it asked for the Peace Corps itself. President Kennedy took the Peace Corps idea and continued to call it by that name.

After pointing out its origin in Humphrey's work, Arthur Schlesinger, Jr., adds:

> General James Gavin urged a similar plan on Kennedy. Kennedy himself advanced the idea a little tentatively during the campaign—it was mid-October and two in the morning—to an audience of students at the University of Michigan. The response was unexpectedly warm. . . . Later, in California, Kennedy called for the establishment of a peace corps, broadening it from Humphrey's original conception to include women as well as men and older people as well as young.

Ted Sorensen, however, played down Humphrey's contribution in his recollection of the origin: "The Peace Corps proposal, for example, was based on the Mormon and other voluntary religious service efforts, on an editorial Kennedy had read years earlier, on a speech by General Gavin, on a luncheon I had with a Philadelphia businessman, on the suggestions of his academic advisors, on legislation previously introduced and on the written response to a spontaneous latenight challenge he issued to Michigan students."

General Gavin, in response to the author's query, reports that his idea germinated at an October 18, 1960, meeting of a committee of the U.S. Chamber of Commerce.

> The more I thought about it, the more I became convinced that the country should organize something like a Peace Corps.
>
> I returned to Arthur D. Little, Inc., and discussed it with some of my colleagues. One of them wrote a memo to me recommending the title, "Peace Corps." I personally was a bit reluctant to use the "Corps" because of its military connotation. Several days later I addressed a group of educators in Miami, Florida, on Thursday, October 27, and advanced the idea of a Peace Corps to them. A bit to my surprise

they greeted my idea with great enthusiasm and applause. I was sitting between the Governor of South Carolina and the Governor-Elect of Florida at the time and we were all very worried about the outcome of the presidential election. The Governor-Elect of Florida suggested that I should call John F. Kennedy and urge him to adopt the idea.

I returned to Wellesley on Friday, October 28, and got in touch with Mr. Kennedy by phone. He asked me to send him a brief memo on the subject to San Francisco. I wrote the paper over the weekend and referred to the undertaking as the "Peace Corps." Mr. Kennedy spoke on it in San Francisco the following Wednesday, urging the adoption of such a program.

Who, then, "coined" Peace Corps? Humphrey probably coined the phrase, if you define coinage as "first use." General Gavin and his aide at Arthur D. Little "coined" it, if you define coinage as setting up the concept and suggesting the label. John F. Kennedy "coined" it, if you define coinage as making a phrase famous.

Ideas generated in the heat of a campaign rarely see the light of election day (heat and light metaphors may be mixed). To the surprise of many politicians, this suggestion of Gavin's did.

peace feeler a diplomatic probe, real or imagined, to end hostilities.

A feeler has long been defined as a remark or proposal put forth to ascertain the attitudes of others. Colloquially, "to feel out" means to subtly find out another's opinion or disposition.

"Peace feeler" came strongly into the political terminology during the war in Vietnam, as the U.S. sought some receptivity to negotiations by the North Vietnamese government. In 1966, the Johnson administration was criticized for ignoring peace feelers supposedly extended through the United Nations. When Robert Kennedy traveled abroad in 1967, a controversy arose as to whether a peace feeler was extended to him. A Mauldin cartoon showed Senator Kennedy arriving home with a snakelike vine twitching behind him, which he asked: "Can I help it if a peace feeler followed me home?"

Lyndon Johnson gave the phrase the presidential seal on March 15, 1967, in a speech to the Tennessee legislature. "We have just lived through another flurry of 'peace feelers.'" In the context in which the President used it, the phrase carried a connotation of vain hopes, of illusory approaches.

peace for our time British Prime Minister Neville Chamberlain's optimistic prediction before World War II; now used derisively.

Chamberlain returned from the Munich Conference September 30, 1938, convinced that his concessions to Hitler dismembering Czechoslovakia had paved the way to peace. For a fuller discussion, see MUNICH ANALOGY; SELLOUT.

Paraphrasing a remark of Disraeli's (see PEACE WITH HONOR), Chamberlain said, "My good friends: This is the second time in our history that there has come back from Germany to Downing Street peace with honor. I believe it is peace for our time."

The phrase is often misquoted as "Peace *in* our time," perhaps because it appears in that form in Morning Prayer: "Give peace in our time, O Lord."

peaceful coexistence as seen in the U.S., a proposal for fair competition of ideologies ("live and let live"); as long expressed in the former USSR, a program for evolutionary triumph over capitalism.

On June 30, 1954, President Dwight Eisenhower was asked at a news conference: "Mr. President, what are the possibilities for peaceful coexistence between Soviet Russia and Communist China, on the one hand, and the non-Communist nations on the other?" He replied in part:

> For a long, long time, everybody in the United States had urged that we attempt to reach a proper basis for peaceful coexistence. We had found, though, an aggressive attitude on the part of the other side that had made such an accomplishment or consummation not easy to reach. In other words, there had to be good faith on both sides. Moreover, we had to make certain that peaceful coexistence did not mean APPEASEMENT. . . . We have got to find ways of living together.

The phrase, which became a linguistic artifact at the end of the Cold War, can be traced back to Lenin in 1920, who spoke of "peaceful cohabitation with the peoples, with the workers and peasants of all nations." The Ninth All-Russian Congress of Soviets used the term in January 1922: "peaceful and friendly coexistence."

The phrase had its greatest impact when Nikita Khrushchev made it the subject of a speech on January 6, 1961, just before a new American President—John F. Kennedy—was to be inaugurated. Khrushchev's definition: ". . . the policy of peaceful coexistence, as regards its social content, is a form of intense economic, political, and ideological struggle of the proletariat against the aggressive forces of imperialism in the international arena."

This was in line with Russian policy enunciated by Lenin: "International imperialism disposing of the might of capital cannot coexist with the Soviet Republic. Conflict is unavoidable."

However, in October of 1961 the Communist line appeared to change. In the "Programme of the Communist Party of the Soviet Union" a softer line was evident:

> Peaceful coexistence of the socialist and capitalist countries is an objective

necessity for the development of human society. War cannot and must not serve as a means of settling international disputes. Peaceful coexistence or disastrous war—such is the alternative offered by history. . . . Peaceful coexistence implies renunciation of war as a means of settling international disputes, and their solution by negotiation. . . . Peaceful coexistence serves as a basis for the peaceful competition between socialism and capitalism. . . . The policy of peaceful coexistence is in accord with the vital interests of all mankind, except the big monopolymagnates and the militarists.

The zigzags in the PARTY LINE confused many Americans who were under the impression that "peaceful coexistence" meant "live and let live." Barry Goldwater warned in 1961, "Nor is there such a thing as peaceful coexistence." In 1963 John F. Kennedy urged "peaceful cooperation" at the UN, and a year later UN Ambassador Adlai Stevenson defended coexistence as the alternative to "coextinction."

Thus, the phrase means—in the words of Humpty Dumpty—"whatever I choose it to mean."

In the 1990s, the phrase was used beyond U.S.-Russian relations. The *Washington Post* reported in 1993 on the Pope's visit to Africa: "In Benin and Uganda, John Paul stressed peaceful coexistence between Muslims and Christians. . . . 'The way of those who believe in God and want to serve him is not that of domination; it is the way of peace.'"

peacenik. See -NIK SUFFIX.

peace process negotiations to end armed conflict; talks to promote international peace.

As early as 1977, this alliterative phrase was in use in Middle East coverage. In December 1977, the *Washington Post* paraphrased the words of a Damascus newspaper, *Tishrin*, under the control of the Syrian government, which called for Anwar Sadat's resignation after the Begin-Sadat summit: "The only important result of the summit was that Egypt and Israel succeeded in alienating the Palestine Liberation Organization from the peace process."

The *Washington Post* helped popularize the phrase. A 1979 article asserted that "prospects dimmed for Palestine Liberation Organization contacts with the United States and participation in the U.S.-sponsored peace process." Six years later, the same paper commented on terrorism, "The Achille Lauro affair deals Yasser Arafat out of the Mideast peace process, for his Palestine Liberation Organization was using the talks as a cloak for terror against Israel."

The phrase appeared in 1990, when *Newsday* covered a speech by New York Governor Mario Cuomo supporting Israel. According to *Newsday*, "The governor charged that 'the exigencies of the political moment' had prompted the United States to open a dialogue with the Palestine Liberation Organization and to follow a peace process that he said 'is turning out to be unworkable because it depends on assurances of peace from people still committed to the destruction of Israel.'"

To some, the term connotes a continuing movement or progress toward conflict resolution; to others, a fixation on the business of negotiation without moving to closure. In April 1993, the *Washington Post* reported the warning of Hanan Ashrawi, spokeswoman for the Palestinian delegates to the current round of talks, about a recent rise in violence: "I don't want to be the voice of GLOOM AND DOOM. . . . But certainly if this round fails, it's not that the peace process is dead, but it's that you're unleashing forces that are the opposite of the peace process."

peace scare.   See WAGING PEACE.

peace with honor   a wartime leader's excuse for not concluding a peace; or, an explanation to a leader's people that the peace concluded was a good one; or, an assertion that an end to war would not or does not mean surrender.

The earliest use was negative: in 49 B.C. Cicero wrote *turpi pace*, or "peace with dishonor." Burton Stevenson, in his book of proverbs, maxims and phrases, traced the early uses of "peace with honor": Theobald, Count of Champagne, in a letter to Louis the Great in 1125; Shakespeare's *Coriolanus*, twice ("We have made peace/with no less honour to the Antiates/than shame to the Romans"); Sir Kenelm Digby's letter to Lord Bristol in 1625; and Edmund Burke's *Conciliation with America* in 1775.

"Honor" became closely associated with "peace" over the years, always increasing the difficulty of negotiations. In 1864, "peace with dishonor" was thrown by Republicans against the Democratic platform that claimed the Civil War had been a failure and called for peace talks.

The phrase is best remembered and occasionally quoted today because of its use by Benjamin Disraeli, Lord Beaconsfield, Queen Victoria's Prime Minister in 1878. When the Russians forced the Turks to a "dishonorable" peace in the Treaty of San Stefano, Great Britain intervened and demanded a European Congress; fearing war with England, the Russians agreed, and Disraeli traveled to Berlin to negotiate. He forced Russia to give back Macedonia to the Turks, and came away with Cyprus for England in the bargain. He said on his return: "Lord Salisbury and myself have brought you back peace—but a peace I hope with honor, which may satisfy our sovereign and tend to the welfare of the country."

Disraeli was a hero; but England was soon involved in a war in Afghanistan, another against the Zulus in South Africa, a crop failure led to a recession, and Disraeli was turned out of office eighteen months after his "peace with honor."

Today, the phrase is often used along with "peace without surrender," and "no reward for aggression."

peace without victory a Wilsonian phrase urging a limitation to the objectives of World War I and a peace settlement not so harsh to any side as to bring about a future war.

Coming as it did from a neutral U.S. early in 1917, Woodrow Wilson's proposal did not set well with leaders of France and England who were fighting a war against Germany: ". . . it must be a peace without victory. . . . The world must be made safe for democracy." See MAKE THE WORLD SAFE FOR DEMOCRACY.

Like "TOO PROUD TO FIGHT," Wilson's "peace without victory" was greeted with disdain in America as well. He had just won a close election over Charles Evans Hughes, and Wilson's slogan had been "He Kept Us Out of War," but the nation was closely divided and memories of Theodore Roosevelt's "Big Stick" were still green.

When unrestricted submarine warfare brought the U.S. into the conflict later in 1917, "peace without victory" was forgotten in the enthusiasm and fury of war. The traditional American demand for "unconditional surrender" was recalled (the War of 1812 was always forgotten) and Wilson's Fourteen Points as a basis for a peace treaty were taken with a grain of salt by other Allied leaders.

In World War II, unconditional surrender was again the goal, and Churchill's "V" sign assured the Allies that peace would indeed come with victory. Not until the Korean War did the idea of LIMITED WAR appear, and that was met by a statement that there was "NO SUBSTITUTE FOR VICTORY" and denunciations of a "NO-WIN POLICY."

However, most Americans in the late sixties were ready to accept "peace without victory," as they did in Korea, provided an "honorable solution" could be found. Senator J. William Fulbright touched a sensitive nerve in *The Arrogance of Power:*

> When we talk about the freedom of South Vietnam, we may be thinking about how disagreeable it would be to accept a solution short of victory; we may be thinking about how our pride would be injured if we settled for less than we set out to achieve; we may be thinking about our reputation as a great power, fearing that a compromise settlement would shame us before the world, marking us as a second-rate people with flagging courage and determination.

Wilson's phrase, "peace without victory," was not used by DOVES in their argument, perhaps because the compromise they were willing to accept was more of a peace without defeat.

peaking a campaigning technique that seeks to build to a crescendo in the forty-eight hours before Election Day.

Franklin Roosevelt pointed out the difficulty of maintaining the "highest note on the scale" (see OVEREXPOSURE); a candidate who "peaks" too early rarely regains the momentum of his campaigning. For a discussion of the opposite type of strategy, see FLAT-OUT.

The word was probably first used by pollsters, or those studying the popularity charts submitted by pollsters. Graphically, a line showing a rise and fall in voters' attitudes toward a candidate forms a peak. The term was popularized during the Nixon-Kennedy campaign of 1960, with Nixon strategy calling for a steady rise in activity and intensity "peaking" once about three weeks before Election Day, and then peaking again just before the final decision. Kennedy strategy called for a "flat-out campaign," sometimes called an "all-out scramble," starting from the beginning. The closeness of the contest leaves the question of which strategy is "best" unresolved. Many politicians feel the wisest strategy is the one that best fits the nature and stamina of the individual candidate.

"Peaking" was long identified with Nixon. Democratic congressman Michael J. Kirwan writes that the Nixon-Brown race for governor of California in 1962 "contrasted the so-called 'peaking' campaign techniques followed by Nixon to the 'all-out scramble' technique of Brown." D. E. Butler and Anthony King, in *The British General Election of 1964*, wrote:

> Like Mr. Richard Nixon in America, Mr. Wilson believed in the need to "phase" his campaign carefully in order to avoid "wearying" the electorate. He was haunted by the belief that Mr. Gaitskell had lost in 1959 partly because his campaign had "peaked" too early; Labour had drawn ahead mid-way through the campaign only to fall behind in the closing stages. As the period of intensive electioneering drew near, Mr. Wilson was determined to make a great initial impact on the Wembley rally planned for September 12th, then to ease up for a week or two, and then to hit hard in the final fortnight.

Peaking is regarded as a more sophisticated technique than flat-out campaigning, or scrambling, and is usually given more thought by those who start out slightly ahead. Underdogs are best advised to run HELL-BENT FOR ELECTION. When Republican Norbert Tiemann ran against Val Peterson in a 1966 primary for governor of Nebraska, he put in 600 appearances over 65,000 miles and edged out the favored

Peterson by 15,000 votes. "We paced him just right," said Tiemann's campaign manager, David Pierson. "When election day came, we figured he was just about 14 hours away from total collapse."

When President Nixon announced in 1971 that Henry Kissinger had arranged for his visit to China, an Administration punster, worried about the reaction of U.S. conservatives, asked, "Peking too soon?"

peanut politician attack word on a politician, deriding him as mean and insignificant.

"I know them—a set of peanut agitators," said Representative Mike Walsh of New York on May 19, 1854. An editorialist in the *New York Mail* on May 27, 1887, inveighed: "If the Governor would consent not to play peanut politics . . ."

The word "peanut" has had a long history as a synonym for "insignificant." But politicians are careful not to offend anyone. Another congressman told the House: "It would be gross disrespect to a great commercial product of several States in this Union for me to denounce the course pursued by this Administration . . . as 'peanut politics.'"

The phrase "peanut politics" at one time had a lowdown, dirty connotation, as writers pointed out that a peanut (which is a vegetable and not a nut) grows and ripens underground.

Big spenders habitually refer to small sums as "peanuts"; this is probably the meaning from which the phrase is derived. However, another derivation is suggested in an 1880 book by Al G. Field: "Those from the West Side chewed tobacco. All ate peanuts. Special appropriations were requested by John Ward, city hall janitor, to remove the peanut hulls after each talk fest. And thus it was that peanut politics and peanut politicians came to be known in Columbus [Ohio]. Peanut politics like all infections spread until the whole political system became affected."

In World War II, to show his contempt for Generalissimo Chiang Kai-shek, General Joseph Stilwell gave him the code name "Peanut."

Since President Jimmy Carter was a peanut warehouseman, it was natural to assume the phrase would be thrown at him, although he countered with the use of peanuts in campaign parties and a small package of peanuts in lieu of a button. The most frequent use of the metaphor was by those leaving his Administration, who would say, "I'm tired of working for peanuts."

In 1993, Representative Dick Armey of Texas wrote the lexicographer about a wasteful government program: "Under the Agriculture Department's peanut program, a person needs a license from the government—known as a peanut quota—to grow and sell peanuts inside the United States. This protects a Southern peanut grower monopoly, prevents wide competition and artificially boosts the price of peanuts. As a result, every American family pays more for peanut butter and other basic foods using peanuts. Think of it as a miniature OPEC for peanuts."

peckerwood. See REDNECK.

pecking order unofficial hierarchy; status of aides to a chief executive of city, state, or nation, or within a government department. Emerges when no "table of organization" is provided.

Like a linguistic Inspector Javert, Professor Porter G. Perrin of the University of Washington followed the origin and development of this phrase from its technical inception to its modern political use. His evidence, along with other contributions to *American Speech* magazine, is summarized here.

During and following World War I, a Norwegian zoologist-psychologist named Thorleif Schjelderup-Ebbe made some remarkable studies of the social organization of birds, particularly hens. Due to the nature of his subject, he had to develop a group of compound nouns beginning with *hacka*—to peck—such as *hackkombination*, and *hackordning*, or "peck order." Zoologist W. C. Allee of the University of Chicago explained Schjelderup-Ebbe's findings in the U.S.:

He recognized a so-called peck-order in which the animal highest in the order pecks and is not pecked in return while that at the extreme bottom of the order is pecked without pecking in return. The social order is indicated by the giving and receiving of pecks, or by reaction to threats of pecking; and hence the social hierarchy among birds is frequently referred to as the peck-order.

A minor government official would do well to study this followup comment by Mark A. May in a 1929 psychology text: "It seems that the bird which is despot over only a few shows its annoyance at the pecks to which it itself is exposed by especially furious pecking, while the birds that rank high in the pecking order, and so are seldom pecked, are more reasonable."

Professor Allee saw the political possibilities: "I pass over the possibilities of studying the peck-order in women's clubs, faculty groups, families or churches . . . we may be able to work out an adequate control even for the prestige problems of the international peck-order."

Novelist Aldous Huxley, who liked to turn scientific theory to use in fiction dealing with social experiments, picked up the idea in *Point Counter Point*: "Observing the habitual and almost sacred 'pecking order' which prevails among the hens in his poultry yard . . . the politician will meditate on the Catholic hierarchy and Fascism."

Anthropologist Margaret Mead used the phrase in a 1942 book, *And Keep Your Powder Dry*. That year, poet W. H. Auden used the phrase in its original sense in *Nones*: ". . . the smug hens,/Passing close by in their pecking order . . ."

Then the Alsop brothers, Joseph and Stewart, got hold of it in 1954, using it four times that year, in their syndicated column and magazine articles, from a straightforward "in the Washington officialdom, a secretaryless official is at the very bottom of the pecking order," to a less intelligible "Prediction was the byword, with a number of variables used in multiple regression equations determining the pecking order in the status hierarchy." (Explain that to Schjelderup-Ebbe!)

Professor Perrin concluded:

This brief case history of pecking order illustrates the typical progress of words from specialized to general usage, and in addition suggest: (1) that this particular word is definitely established in English and now runs the full range of usage from gobbledygook to poetry; (2) that, when it is used of human beings, its connotation is generally dyslogistic [unfavorable]; and (3) that once acquired, pecking order tends to be habit forming.

When President Clinton urged reporters to "ignore this who's up, who's down stuff," nobody did.

peerless leader   ironic description of a precinct captain or local boss.

The "Peerless Leader" in American history was William Jennings Bryan, three times nominated by the Democrats. Along with "The Great Commoner," a sobriquet that had been applied to William Pitt the elder and later to Henry Clay and Thaddeus Stevens, Bryan was given the sobriquet of "peerless leader," which later was the title of a 1929 biography by Paxton Hibben. (Opponents termed the ticket of Bryan and Arthur Sewall "Brine and Swill.")

Because of the rhyme, the phrase is often rendered "fearless leader" (a Helen Gray Cone poem called Pickett's men at Gettysburg "peerless, fearless, an army's flower"). The pomposity of the phrase has led to its sarcastic use today.

Pekingologist.   See CHINA WATCHERS; KREMLINOLOGIST.

Pentagonese   military-industrial jargon designed to provide its users with a convenient linguistic shorthand that often serves only to obfuscate the obvious, or to lend a sense of importance to routine communications.

In common with other jargon, Pentagonese—a word that entered the language in 1951—provides an "in group" with the sort of security that children achieve when they share a secret handshake and wear rings with hidden compartments. Pentagonese is used not only within the "Puzzle Palace" but also throughout the U.S. military establishment. A sample: Within the *parameters* of a problem (the range of possibilities, not a perimeter), there exist *options* (alternatives) for *tradeoffs* (trades) that will *maximize* (strengthen) the *software* (thinking) to *escalate* (raise) the *state of the art* (what can be done now).

Had experts at Pentagonese gotten their hands on the Gettysburg Address, *New York Times* columnist Arthur Krock wrote in 1962, they might have changed "We are now engaged in a great civil war" to read: "We have entered upon a period of civil uncertainty involving fairly high mobilization." After the 1962 Cuban missile crisis, he constructed this imaginary statement for Defense Secretary Robert McNamara: "Let's be sure we have plenty of options and be certain there will be no overkill. And then, I think, after these options are mirror clear, and to pursue this further would be counter-productive, we can melt this ball of wax and move the hardware from the shelf."

A kissing cousin of Pentagonese is State Departmentese. As Arthur Schlesinger, Jr., wrote in *A Thousand Days*:

> The intellectual exhaustion of the Foreign Service expressed itself in the poverty of the official rhetoric. In meetings the men from State would talk in a bureaucratic patois borrowed in large part from the Department of Defense. We would be exhorted to "zero in" on "the purpose of the drill" (or of the "exercise" or "operation"), to "crank in" this and "phase out" that, to "pinpoint" a "viable" policy and, behind it, a "fallback position," to ignore the "flak" from competing government bureaus or from the Communists, to refrain from "nit-picking" and never to be "counterproductive." Once we were "seized of the problem," preferably in as "hardnosed" a manner as possible, we would review "options," discuss "overall" objectives, seek "breakthroughs," consider "crash programs," "staff out" policies—doing all these things preferably "meaningfully" and "in depth" until we were ready to "finalize" our deliberations, "sign on to" or "sign off on" a conclusion (I could never discover the distinction, if any, between these two locutions), and "implement" a decision.

As *Newsweek* noted in 1967, nuclear weapons "unleashed a fallout of acronyms, neologisms, euphemisms and technical jargon," and the development of antiballistic missiles "has produced a second generation of Strangelovisms." Among the additions to Pentagonese: *megadeaths*, for millions of deaths; *credible deterrent*, a defense that needn't be effective as long as the enemy thinks it is; *preferential defense*, protecting some areas but not others; *rippled attack*, sending missiles in salvos to trick an enemy into using defensive missiles on the first few waves, leaving no defense for later waves.

The Pentagon has popularized, or in some cases invented, scores of other words, from *cost-efficiency* to *quantification* (a reference to McNamara's reliance on facts and figures) and *spasm* (meaning a reflexive response to an enemy attack, real or imagined). Weapons made obsolete by the end of the Cold War have been *overtaken by events*. Something that goes against common sense is described in Pentagonese as *counterintuitive*.

Malcolm McLean, in the *Foreign Service Journal* in 1968, wrote of a survey made at the National War College by Marine Colonel Ralph Spanjer. Lecturers were clocked as to the number of times they used Pentagonese. These were the most frequently used bits of jargon:

quid pro quo	pragmatic
vis-à-vis	caveat
per se	viable
dialogue	ambivalence
xenophobia	scenario
charisma	academician
thrust	escalate
exacerbate	expertise
dichotomy	low silhouette
hegemony	quantum jump
cost effective	flexible response
proliferation	rapprochement
counterproductive	détente

Less frequently used, but mentioned in the survey, were: boggle, simplistic, in-house, time frame, pluralistic, polycentrisms, infrastructure, real world, bipolar, confrontation.

Not mentioned in the survey, but important expressions of the Vietnam war, were "body count," "protective reaction," "sanctuaries," "captured documents," and "enemy situation deteriorating." See VIETNAMIZATION; VIETNAM SYNDROME.

Herman Melville wrote: "A man of true science uses but few hard words, and those only when none other will answer his purpose; whereas the smatterer in science thinks that by mouthing hard words he proves that he understands hard things."

See OPTIONS; ESCALATION; UNFLAPPABLE; SCENARIO; FALLBACK POSITION; VIETNAM LINGO; WHIZ KIDS; PACIFICATION; FALLOUT; INFRASTRUCTURE; WARGAMING WORDS; SALT.

Pentagon Papers. See RIGHT TO KNOW; LEAK.

people of color   members of all nonwhite racial groups.

In the late eigtheenth century, French-speaking colonies used *gens de couleur libérés*, "free people of color." In the "I have a dream" speech at the Lincoln Memorial in August 1963, the Reverend Martin Luther King, Jr., revived the phrase in speaking of American "citizens of color."

People of color is more inclusive than the term *colored people*, long used in South Africa for "people of racially mixed ancestry." That term was first expressed as "coloured countenances" by the historian John Speed in 1611 and is now considered a slur, while *people of color* is often used as a self-description.

Black replaced the newly pejorative *colored people*, except in the name of the National Association for the Advancement of Colored People. James Williams, an NAACP spokesman, explains, "Times change and terms change. Racial designations go through phases; at one time *Negro* was accepted, at an earlier time *colored* and so on. This organization has been in existence for 80 years, and the initials *N.A.A.C.P.* are part of the American vocabulary, firmly embedded in the national consciousness, and we feel it

would not be to our benefit to change our name."

People of color, when used by whites, generally connotes respect. The term includes all nonwhites, however, and should not be considered a synonym for *blacks* or *African-Americans*. (See HYPHENATED AMERICAN.)

people's democracy   a phrase with a redundant root adopted by Communists to differentiate between "their" democracy and "capitalists'" democracy.

Though the political glorification of the word "people" is best known in the close of the Gettysburg Address, "people's party" and "people's ticket" were familiar phrases throughout the nineteenth century. In China, the Manchu dynasty was overthrown in 1911 by forces whose ideological leader was Dr. Sun Yat-sen; among his "Three Principles of the People" was a "Principle of People's Democracy," a long-range plan to be started by the revolutionary leaders.

Later in the twentieth century, Communist governments adopted the style of "people's republics" and Communist terminology used "people's democracies" as a generic phrase for Communist or Communist-dominated nations.

In a good twist on the phrase, the New York Stock Exchange in the early fifties began publicizing "people's capitalism" to dramatize the high degree of stock ownership in the U.S. The Exchange recognized the Communist capture of the word "people," and by combining it with the word most often attacked by Communists put forth a useful counterphrase to "Wall Street warmongers."

People's Republic of China. See GREAT LEAP FORWARD; MAOISM; HUNDRED FLOWERS; CULTURAL REVOLUTION.

perennial candidate attack phrase on one who has tried and failed before.

Republican Harold Stassen is the man most often identified as a "perennial candidate" in recent times; in the previous century, the honor belonged first to Grover Cleveland (the "perpetual candidate") and then to thrice-defeated William Jennings Bryan.

Said Stassen in 1967: "I suppose there is a lot of misunderstanding about me. People try to understand me as seeking office. Actually it's not the office itself. Not at all. It's the office in relation to what I'm trying to do, what I'm seeking. I want a progressive Republican Party."

A similar attack was launched by President Lyndon Johnson in 1966 on Richard Nixon, labeling him a CHRONIC CAMPAIGNER. The effect was to focus attention on Nixon in the closing weeks of the midterm elections, helping him help Republican candidates win back 47 House seats.

perestroika Russian for "restructuring"; the reconstruction or revision of the Soviet political system.

The Russian term entered the English language in the mid-1980s with Gorbachevian reforms. "If words can define an era," wrote Celestine Bohlen of the *Washington Post* in 1986, "then perestroika is the catchword here before Tuesday's opening of the Communist Party Congress as Soviet leader Mikhail Gorbachev enters a decisive phase of his leadership."

Pronounced per-uh-STROY-kuh, this noun has a literal meaning of "rebuilding" and was popularized as the term for political and economic changes in what was then the Soviet Union. Its prominence was underscored by the title of Gorbachev's 1987 book, *Perestroika: New Thinking for Our Country and Our World.* A *New York Times* feature on that book enumerated elements of that restructur-

ing: "He has slightly opened the emigration spigot, given greater freedom to question the party and the government, and faced up to the severe economic difficulties that restrain Soviet military expenditures and force a new look at Afghanistan."

This buzzword is similar to, but not synonymous with, the Russian *peredyshka*, the "breathing space" or "respite" that marked Lenin's secret policy to strengthen Bolshevism. In 1987, *U.S. News & World Report* quoted John Erickson, a Western authority on Soviet military activity, about the similarity of these terms. "We must be careful," Erickson said, "that *perestroika* doesn't turn out to mean *peredyshka.*" (See COMMUNIST TERMINOLOGY.)

A Russian joke of the 1980s played on terms using the *pere-* prefix, which means "re-," as in *reform*: What follows *perestroika* and *peredyshka*? Answer: *perestrelka*. That term means "cross fire," as in *shootout* or *reshoot*, and was meant to label the violent crackdown that might follow a deceptive call for restructuring.

President Boris Yeltsin did not adopt the term for his more extensive reforms, and *perestroika*, like GLASNOST, became fixed in the brief Gorbachev era like flecks of prehistoric insects preserved in Russian amber.

perks clipped form of perquisites; the delicious trappings of power; the cherry on the cake of public service.

"Perks!" wrote Michael Satchell in the *Washington Star* in January 1977. ". . . hundreds of public servants enjoy the perquisites of power, the freebies, privileges, emoluments and prestige that go along with the job, that make life at the office a little nicer, that stamp the individual as a favored employee. Perks! For politicians, Cabinet officers and ranking career bureaucrats, they mean limousines, government jets and even boats to get you from A to B with a corps of chauffeurs, military aides, escort officers, staff assistants, coat holders and Filipino Navy stewards to make sure the steaks are rare, the martinis cold, the trip smooth and trouble-free."

The word was originally a Briticism, according to Merriam-Webster, but appears to be taking hold firmly in coverage of American officialdom. In the sixties, "with perks" was most frequently a description of "fringe benefits" available to corporate officers. "When the day's work is done," wrote the *Wall Street Journal* on July 15, 1971, "Alexander Farkas and his wife whisk out to balmy Westhampton, Long Island, in the company helicopter. That's called a perquisite, or perk, and it's an increasingly popular kind of reward for the executive who has everything but a favorable tax bracket."

Politicians' perks—especially limousine service—came under attack in the mid-seventies, led by Senator William Proxmire's harassment of Pentagon officials whose salaries were supplemented by extra, untaxed services. President Carter, sensitive to the anti-Washington, anti–big shot feeling of most taxpayers, did away with many of the frills enjoyed previously by the White House staff, but these soon came back. Congressman Vic Fazio, Democrat of California, who oversaw the distribution of privileges to members of the House of Representatives, was derided in the late 1980s as "the prince of perks."

Perks are not inexpensive trappings; a car and driver in effect doubles a government official's salary. The new word, and the new interest in the subject, saves the taxpayer sizable amounts, although it is not so much the money as the principle: if the voter has to pay for his haircut, then why, he wonders, should his congressman get one free? The system that used to permit the local cop on the beat to swipe an apple from the vendor, as a right of his job, now frowns on—and even threatens to tax—some of the extra income that is taken in the form of service. Voter irritation with these perks—exacerbated by a check-kiting scandal in 1991—was exploited by Ross Perot in his Independent campaign the following year.

Perks cover a range of presumed rights, including *freebies*, which are small gifts or costless tickets; *annie oaklies*, which are always tickets or passes; and *junkets*, which are ostensible official trips (see JUNKETEERING GUMSHOES). Perquisite is not related to "perky," which comes from the verb "to perch," but is rooted in the Latin *quaerere*, "to seek"—thus, a "query" about a "perk" digs for its own root.

peroration the stirring conclusion of an address, exhorting or uplifting the audience; in political slang, the ZINGER or *snapper*.

"Perorations usually add nothing to the context of the speech," wrote Samuel Rosenman, who wrote many for FDR, "they are more inspirational than informative. Every oration needs one, however, and a well-written peroration can clinch an argument or inspire confidence or lift morale."

In the peroration of his 1932 acceptance address FDR introduced "New Deal": "I pledge you, I pledge myself, to a new deal for the American people." (For the dispute over who wrote it, see NEW DEAL.) Perhaps the most famous peroration was at the conclusion of Lincoln's second inaugural, beginning "With malice toward none . . ."

A well-prepared, well-delivered speech, without peroration, dribbles off and leaves an audience unsatisfied. Simple, clear English prose, the stuff of good speeches, is difficult to make soar; there cannot be many thrilling moments or high notes in any speech, and if there is to be one, the place the audience will remember it most is at the end. Reminder: a reference to God's help is expected, especially on solemn occasions.

"His enthusiasm kindles as he advances," wrote Edmund Burke of a good orator, "and when he arrives at his peroration it is in full blaze." Here is a peroration (closing of Woodrow Wilson's first inaugural) that includes a disclaimer of pride, an element of suspense, a question, a challenge, a summons to the audience to help, a reference to the Deity, and a promise of success:

> This is not a day of triumph; it is a day of dedication. Here muster, not the forces of party, but the forces of humanity. Men's hearts wait upon us; men's lives hang in the balance; men's hopes call upon us to say what we will do. Who shall live up to the great trust? Who dares fail to try? I summon all honest men, all patriotic, all forward-looking men, to my side. God helping me, I will not fail them, if they will but counsel and sustain me!

The word, in Shakespeare's time, meant an overblown, flowery speech ("What means this passionate discourse? This peroration with such circumstance"); since that time, it has come to mean the conclusion or wrap-up of a speech, where some passion is permitted to flower.

personally obnoxious verbal signal that calls down the wrath of "senatorial courtesy"; the Senate then refuses to confirm an appointment opposed by a senator from the state affected.

Senatorial courtesy, or *courtesy of the Senate*, is the gun; *personally obnoxious*, or *personally objectionable*, is the trigger. The system was explained by *Harper's Weekly* in 1870: "Senator Fowler of Tennessee claimed the right which the courtesy of the Senate affords every member of vetoing the ap-

pointment of any postmaster in the place of his residence who is not agreeable to him." Ten years later the magazine defined the phrase in more political terms: "The courtesy of the Senate is an exceedingly smooth phrase. It means control of patronage."

Woodrow Wilson first attempted to fight this system, then gave way. See PATRONAGE. His closest adviser, Colonel Edward House, and Treasury Secretary William McAdoo, both Democrats from New York, sought to break Tammany's power by dispensing patronage to reformers. Senator James O'Gorman of New York, while not closely allied with Tammany, saw this as an effort to build a New York machine that might be a danger to him. He warned the President that such appointments would be "personally obnoxious" to him, and they were not made.

Dwight Eisenhower ran into the same problem when he started making appointments in 1953. He planned to name Val Peterson, a former Nebraska governor, as ambassador to India, but Nebraska senators Hugh Butler and Dwight Griswold, old political enemies of Peterson's, said no. "They informed me," wrote Eisenhower, "that if I should send his name to the Senate they would find it necessary to state on the Senate floor that he was 'personally objectionable'; the Senate has normally honored such an announcement . . ." The President appointed Peterson to several other jobs not requiring Senate approval, and ultimately—after the two senators were gone—as ambassador to Denmark. But it bothered him. "I believe that the custom of allowing one disgruntled senator to block an appointment by the phrase 'personally objectionable' is unjustified and should be disavowed by the Senate."

There has in recent years been a tendency to replace "obnoxious" with "objectionable," a milder word. This is a shame, as "obnoxious" so well describes the true feeling of the dissenting senator.

See BLUE SLIP.

persons of color. See PEOPLE OF COLOR.

phantom coinage. See BACKLASH; MEDICARE; ESCALATION.

Philippic diatribe; tirade; vitriolic attack.

"Forensic Philippics" was FDR's description of some of the Supreme Court decisions striking down New Deal measures. See NINE OLD MEN. The word comes from the three orations of Demosthenes, rousing his fellow Athenians to resist Philip of Macedon; subsequently, the orations of Cicero against Mark Antony were also called Philippics.

Dwight Eisenhower was urged by many friends to ENGAGE IN PERSONALITIES with Senator Joseph McCarthy, using the prestige of the presidency to condemn his methods. In this unpublished letter to broadcaster John R. ("Tex") McCrary, President Eisenhower wrote on December 4, 1954:

> . . . I would not, under any circumstances, glorify—or at least publicize—such an individual by attempting a Presidential Philippic, with him as the target. . . . If young or old want a President who will indulge in billingsgate—and demean the office as it has been demeaned before—they'll have to find another.

philosophy. See IDEOLOGY.

phony war the quiet period after the fall of Poland in 1939 and the German attack on Norway and Denmark in the spring of 1940; also called a "sitzkrieg."

Sitzkrieg, meaning literally "sitting war," was of course a play on *blitzkrieg*. To some Americans, the desultory warfare in this period showed that Britain and France did not really want to fight, but simply entered the war grudgingly, committed as they were to the defense of Poland; these critics also held that Hitler wanted no war with France and Great Britain.

The *London News-Chronicle* on January 19, 1940, headlined: "This is Not a Phoney War: Paris Envoy." The story explained that "phoney" was "American slang, anglicized about 1920."

French Premier Paul Reynaud used the phrase in a radio speech on April 3, 1940: "*Il faut en finir'; tel fut, dès le debut, le refrain qu'on entendit. Et cela signifie qu'il aura pas de* 'phony peace' *après une guerre qui n'est nullement une* 'phony war.'" ("'It must be finished'; that is the constant theme heard since the beginning. And that means that there will not be any *'phony peace'* after a war which is by no means a *'phony war.'"*)

During this time Neville Chamberlain continued as prime minister of England. When the British fleet was repulsed trying to land troops in Norway, he came under heavy criticism in Parliament. On May 9, 1940, he asked Winston Churchill to join his government; Churchill refused. After the German invasion of Holland and Belgium on May 10, Chamberlain agreed to turn over the reins completely to Churchill. There was no more talk of "phony war" nor of weak leadership in Great Britain.

According to Eric Partridge, the word *phoney* can be traced back to 1781 when "the ring-dropping game, one of the old everlastings for fooling the credulous, was known as the fawney rig, the fawney trick, fawney being an English attempt at the Irish *fáinne*, a finger ring." In Great Britain, the word is spelled *phoney*; in the U.S., *phony*.

In the early 1980s, the *Washington Post* wrote of Poland, under threat of

Soviet occupation, that "there is still an atmosphere of 'phony war.' The weapons remain the old ones of political rhetoric, resolutions, verbal ultimatums and threatening allusions."

photo op.   See SOUND BITE.

phrasemaker   one who captures the essence of an issue in a few highly quotable words.

Sloganeer, which now has acquired a pejorative connotation, is the closest synonym. *Ghostwriters, speechwriters,* and *research assistants* who prepare speeches may be *phrasemakers* or they may not. For a discussion of usage, see GHOSTWRITER and SPEECHWRITER. A phrasemaker is similar to a "play doctor" who is called in to add lines and sharpen the scenes of another playwright.

A phrasemaker should be capable of taking an ordinary speech and adding a news lead in the form of inflammable words or a stunning new thought in quotable form. He should also be anonymous; the public has come to accept the idea of a public figure employing a speechwriter, but a phrase must "belong" to the public man and not be attributable to a man behind the scenes, at least not for the life of an Administration.

President Eisenhower called an early assistant of his, Emmet Hughes, "a writer with a talent for phrasemaking."

Some presidents, notably Abraham Lincoln and Theodore Roosevelt, had a genius for phrasemaking. In politics, however, every talent is attackable; among Woodrow Wilson's nicknames were "schoolmaster in politics," "coiner of weasel-words," "professor"—and equally damning, "phrasemaker."

How is a phrase made? If original inspiration is lacking, a play on a previous phrase is customary: "Johnson's War on Poverty has now become a War on Prosperity." This word-substitution in a familiar phrase is a frequent technique; in the congressional campaign of 1966, the Republican decision was to attack President Johnson on the subject of inflation. Possibilities: "Johnson Inflation," "Johnson Dollars Buy Less." Neither very catchy, and the word "inflation" is rather abstract. The High Cost of Living was a well-known and well-understood phrase, and it needed a tight identification with the President. Hence, "the High Cost of Johnson" was used and served its purpose, although it never became a part of the language; see also NATTERING NABOBS OF NEGATIVISM.

Seminal phrases are rare: for coinages, see MEDICARE; COLD WAR; for emphasis using contrast, see CONTRAPUNTAL PHRASES; for adaptation, see TURNAROUNDS; for poetic imagery, see THOUSAND POINTS OF LIGHT; for the most useful phrasemaking word, see NEW, POLITICAL USE OF.

pie in the sky   scornful characterization of liberal or populist promises.

In the vocabulary of rhetorical counterattack—"empty promises," "cruel demogogery," "callous vote-buying" —none has been more durable than "pie in the sky." In the face of this withering return fire, even the word "promise" has disappeared from campaign oratory, supplanted by the more solemn "pledge."

The origin of "pie in the sky" was supplied the author by laborlore specialist Archie Green, a professor of English at Ohio State University. The phrase was coined around 1910 in "The Preacher and the Slave," a composition by legendary labor hero Joe Hill, which became part of the widely distributed "little red songbooks" of the Industrial Workers of the World (the I.W.W., or "Wobblies").

You will eat, bye and bye,
In that glorious land above the sky;
Work and pray, live on hay
You'll get pie in the sky when you die.

Professor Green rightly calls this phrase "the most significant Wobbly contribution to the American vocabulary." Conservative speakers have been seizing on it for denunciation for three generations.

An example of its currency is in a cartoon by Auth for the *Philadelphia Inquirer* in November 1977: people in line for unemployment benefits are shown looking skyward at a vision of a pie labeled "Humphrey-Hawkins," a bill designed to bring down the rate of unemployment in the U.S. And after Larry Flynt, publisher of the raunchy *Hustler* magazine, announced his spiritual rebirth in 1978 thanks to an airborne conversion by Ruth Carter Stapleton, the *Washington Post's Potomac Magazine* headlined: "Piety in the Sky."

See CAMPAIGN ORATORY; for a don't-you-believe-it lexicon, from BALONEY to FREE LUNCH (food is often associated with the metaphors for disbelief), see SANTA CLAUS, NOBODY SHOOTS AT.

pinko   a smear word for anyone in a spectrum ranging from liberal to Communist, but most often applied to FELLOW TRAVELERS.

Pinko, pink, and the more effete PARLOR PINK were often used against Democratic candidates. Just as Republicans after the Civil War said "Not all Democrats were rebels, but all rebels were Democrats," some conservatives in this century have used "Not all Democrats are pinkos, but all pinkos are Democrats."

Those who found Communism "a god that failed" and those who changed their minds about fellow-traveling were the foremost users of the word. When the CIO purged its membership in 1949 of the United

Electrical Workers Union because of their Communist links, former pinko Michael J. Quill, colorful boss of the Transport Workers Union, lashed out at the "pinks, punks and parasites."

In 1926, when *Time* was popularizing the Homeric adjective ("Berkshire-cradled," "Beethoven-locked," "Yankee-shrewd"), its editors were fond of "pinko-liberal" and "pinko-political." See PUNDIT for other *Time* coinages.

Currently the word is used mainly in historical contexts, such as the period of McCARTHYISM, when, according to a letter in *Newsday* of October 23, 1992, "All that was necessary to ruin someone was to suggest to the right person that 'so-and-so' was an adulterer, commie, pinko, homosexual, lesbian, etc." In an attack on Republican ideology, a piece in the August 21, 1992, *Washington Post* reminisced: ". . . for decades the Republican party traveled on its resentments. So much to grind one's teeth about: That Man Roosevelt, the cookie-pushing State Department pinkos who lost China, nattering nabobs of negativism . . ." See RED.

pipeline, in the   in the process of being developed, but not ready for public disclosure; on its way.

Government officials answer complaints of inaction with the assurance that work is "in the pipeline." The phrase was popular in the White House in the early seventies, sometimes carrying a connotation of inexorability: once some proposal got in the pipeline, it could not be stopped, and any attempts to sidetrack it was met with "That train has left the station."

A subtlety of this phrase is in the understanding that not everything in political affairs is cause-and-effect, and that often an event comes about not by virtue of its apparent cause, but because it had already been "in the pipeline." When a project is cut off, it may continue for years because funds to support it were "in the pipeline."

Another meaning of "pipeline" is "channel of information," as "we have a pipeline into the Joint Chiefs."

pissant one who is a stickler for detail; a derogation of a too-technical minor functionary.

In a 1977 *New Republic* piece on former Defense Secretary James Schlesinger, who had been named by President Carter to be his energy chief, Eliot Marshall wrote: "He began his career in the Nixon administration in 1969 as a second-rung functionary in what was then the gritty Bureau of the Budget. As one departing cabinet aide put it, he began as a mere 'pissant' . . . His worldly skills are sometimes referred to as his 'practical sense,' or his appreciation of detail. It explains why he once was considered a pissant."

The word can be used as an adjective ("every pissant line in the Budget"). The Associated Press opined in 1989, "When is the attorney general going to stop trying to stage-manage every little pissant development in this department that has political advantage, and authorize his people to talk to us candidly if not on background?"

Dating back to the seventeenth century, the word probably comes from the ant known as the pismire. For another derogation of low-level bureaucrats, see ANKLE-BITERS.

pissing post. See POWER BASE.

pit-bull politics dirty politics; low-blow campaigning.

This slur on dogs uses the generic term *pit bull*, which is not a breed but a cross between a bulldog and a terrier. (The United Kennel Club does recognize the American pit bull terrier, but the larger American Kennel Club rec-

ognizes a similar dog called the American Staffordshire terrier.)

The term *pit bull* comes from pit fighting, in which animals are forced into bloody confrontations, a brutal activity that has been around for centuries. During Shakespeare's time, the Globe Theatre faced competition from the Bear Garden, featuring fights between dogs and chained bears; England outlawed those fights in 1835.

Sometimes the name *pit bull* is used admiringly as a label connoting courage: In the 1988 Presidential campaign, George Bush referred to himself and his running mate, Dan Quayle, as "a couple of pit bulls." But more often the compound noun, usually hyphenated when used attributively, is pejorative: *Time* magazine labeled the campaign that year "pit-bull politics."

See BIRD DOG . . . KENNEL DOG.

pitiless publicity as Wilson used it, the purifying power of the public gaze on the operations of government, where secrecy can breed corruption; now also the encroachment on privacy by reporters seeking sensation.

Woodrow Wilson used the phrase often in his New Jersey gubernatorial campaign of 1910, and in the presidential campaign of 1912 against Taft and Roosevelt, taking it from Ralph Waldo Emerson's use in "The Conduct of Life": "As gaslight is found to be the best nocturnal police, so the universe protects itself by pitiless publicity."

In the 1912 campaign, Wilson explained: "Publicity is one of the purifying elements of politics. Nothing checks all the bad practices of politics like public exposure. An Irishman, seen digging around the wall of a house, was asked what he was doing. He answered, 'Faith, I am letting the dark out of the cellar.' Now, that's exactly what we want to do."

True to his pledge of welcoming "pitiless publicity," Wilson inaugurated the regular presidential press conference after he took office. At the first, he told reporters: "A large part of the success of public affairs depends on the newspapermen—not so much the editorial writers, because we can live down what they say, as upon the news writers, because news is the atmosphere of public affairs."

The same concern for shining a beam of publicity in the dark corners of diplomacy led to his expression "OPEN COVENANTS, openly arrived at"; but just as he modified that position to include confidential discussions, in his later years in office he withdrew from the regular press conference routine.

A related phrase, "the white light of publicity"—the same metaphor as "letting the dark out"—was coined a few years later by writer Theodore F. MacManus in a 1915 *Saturday Evening Post* article: "In every field of human endeavor, he that is first must perpetually live in the white light of publicity."

The word *publicity* has a double image today. In the Wilsonian sense, it is regarded as a good thing, calling politicians immediately to account for almost every action. Joseph Pulitzer told his editors at the *New York World* in 1895: "Publicity, PUBLICITY, PUBLICITY, is the greatest moral factor and force on our public life."

On the other hand, the press agent or publicity man is often scorned as he inveigles "free publicity" for his "publicity hound" client, either through "cheap stunts" or the manipulative devices of "hidden persuasion" or imagemaking.

As a result of this bad publicity, people in the field often shy away from the phrase "publicity man" or even the word "publicist," which once meant a person dedicated to the affairs of the public, and adopted "public relations counsel," then "communications consultant," then "public affairs coordina-

tor," then "media aide," and occasionally "outreach adviser." To them, publicity—getting space in the press and time on the air for the client's product or principle—is a single arrow in the large quiver of public relations techniques.

As a result of this double image, "pitiless publicity" in current usage is something the public not only gets the benefit of, but which it is constantly subjected to.

The phrase is also used to express concern with too-zealous reporters and photographers who invade privacy, particularly in the coverage of tragedies.

place in the sun justification for expansion and conquest.

Kaiser Wilhelm II, speaking at Hamburg on August 27, 1911, laid the basis for Germany's claim to territorial growth: "No one can dispute with us the place in the sun that is our due."

"Place in the sun" became a German rallying cry during World War I and during the rise of Hitler; the Nazis, however, preferred LEBENSRAUM, "living space."

The phrase can be found in the *Pensées* of Blaise Pascal (Kennet's translation, 1727): "This Dog's mine, sayd the poor Child: this is my place, in the Sun. From so petty a beginning, we can trace the Tyranny and Usurpation of the whole Earth."

plant as a verb, to induce a reporter to ask a question at a press conference; as a noun, a news story released to a single reporter which benefits the person leaking the story; or, an individual placed in an opposition camp.

Anthony Leviero, a Washington correspondent of the *New York Times*, broke an exclusive story in 1951 about the details of the Truman-MacArthur conference on Wake Island. Following MacArthur's dismissal (see OLD SOL-

DIERS NEVER DIE) it occurred to the reporter that the assumption about total agreement between Truman and MacArthur at Wake might be false, and that the Administration might be ready to release the document to refute MacArthur's charges.

Leviero pointed out how he went after the story in a memo, and added:

> This disposes of the stories about a "plant," although I or any other Washington correspondent would gladly accept a planted authentic document. . . . A final word on the claims of discomfited rivals that this was an Administration "plant." Without conceding the story came from the White House, I can say that never in more than three years of covering the place did a member of the President's staff offer me a story. But I often scored by asking at the right time.

In current political usage, a LEAK is usually deliberate, sometimes inadvertent; a *plant* is always deliberate, and connotes "control" of the reporter's story; an *exclusive* has a more legitimate ring, although reporters left out are envious; a *scoop* or *beat* carries the least stigma of deliberate origination by the source, and usually means the reporter dug out the information by his own enterprise.

Question-planting in the U.S. is always surreptitious, and most press secretaries disclaim any use of the practice. On the other hand, French President Charles de Gaulle practiced it openly, according to former Kennedy press secretary Pierre Salinger: "His aides plant every question in advance with pro-Administration reporters, and *Le Président* carefully rehearses the answers."

platform   ideally, the standards to which the wise and honest voters can repair; in practice, a list of principles and positions designed to attract most and offend least, important mainly in the work it gives a convention to do other than select a candidate.

Francis Bacon, in 1623: "The wisdom of a lawmaker consisteth not only in a platform of justice, but in the application thereof." In most early use in the U.S., the word related to the principles of a church, taken from the French word for ground plan of a building. Since the word also came to mean a raised area from which a person could speak, its metaphoric use in politics married both senses. Like STUMP and HUSTING, a place to stand soon was allied to a place to take a stand.

As early as 1803, the *Massachusetts Spy* was writing about "The Platform of Federalism," but it was William Lloyd Garrison in his antislavery *Liberator* who would help popularize the term; in 1844, the first national party platforms were adopted and by 1848 the word was a political standby.

The word "plank" was a natural derivative: in the 1848 "Bigelow Papers," one line of doggerel read: "They kin' o' slipt the planks frum out th' old platform one by one/An' made it gradooally noo, 'fore folks know'd wut wuz done . . ."

In current use, a party platform is taken with great seriousness at a convention, since it enables many compromises to be made and gives appointment plums to many factional leaders, but is soon forgotten in the campaign. A frequent saying, of obscure origin, is that "A platform is not something to stand on, but something to run on" and is soon followed by "A platform is what you start by running on and end by running from."

playing politics   placing partisan gain above the public interest; more mildly, to adeptly embarrass a political opponent.

While it is proper to *participate in* politics, and stimulating to *talk* politics, it is considered reprehensible to *play* politics.

Notwithstanding Frank R. Kent's book title, *The Great Game of Politics*, when politics is played rather than engaged in, the gambling verb (*to play*) casts suspicion on the otherwise innocent noun (*politics*). Walter Lippmann wrote in 1955 that "a political figure must never in so many words admit that in order to gain votes he sacrificed the public good, that he played 'politics.'"

Warnings about playing politics have been popular with Presidents; Herbert Hoover in 1930 in connection with unemployment relief said, "They are playing politics at the expense of human misery"—a charge that was to be repeated a generation later as "playing politics with poverty." Franklin Roosevelt, in his MARTIN, BARTON AND FISH speech before the election of 1940, cautioned Republicans about "playing politics with national defense," and Dwight Eisenhower in 1954 applied it to White House-Capitol Hill relations: "History shows that when the Executive and Legislative Branches are politically in conflict, politics in Washington runs riot. . . . The public good goes begging while politics is played for politics' sake."

A middle ground between the laudatory "participate in politics" and the accusatory "playing politics" appears to be the turning of the noun "politics" into verb or participle: "to politic," or "politicking" has the neutral connotation of campaigning.

For allusions to political activity as gambling, see CARD METAPHORS; as a sport, see SPORTS METAPHORS.

play in Peoria   to elitists, the criterion of the crass; to antiestablishment-arians, the measurement of acceptability in the heartland.

Some White House aides excuse cornball gestures by a politically savvy President with a shrug and "It'll go over well in the boonies," or—in the Nixon Administration—"It'll play in Peoria."

New York Times columnist Russell Baker disparaged the language of the Nixon men in a June 9, 1973, essay: "If the Administration's critics (Eastern liberal intellectuals, 'establishmentari-ans,' 'elitists') complained that they could not understand the language, much less the name of the game, the Nixon men had a standard rebuttal. 'It will play in Peoria,' they said."

The phrase has a hucksteresque quality (see SELLING CANDIDATES LIKE SOAP) derived from its metaphor of politics as a performance; it probably originated in vaudeville, as entertainers discussed how an act would be received in the hinterland. Its coiner, White House aide John Ehrlichman, informs the author: "'Play in Peoria' appeared in a *Wall Street Journal* story after I'd run the school for advance men in NYC in 1968. I used the expression there. Onomatopoeia was the only reason for Peoria, I suppose. And it personified—exemplified—a place, removed from the media centers on the coasts, where the national verdict is cast, according to Nixon doctrine." (Ehrlichman, who also contributed TWISTING SLOWLY, SLOWLY IN THE WIND, probably meant alliteration, the repeating of initial sounds; onomatopoeia is the coining of words that imitate sounds, like *bang* and *buzz*.)

Everett Dirksen (R-Ill.), the Senate Minority Leader, did not like the faint put-down implicit in the phrase, as if Peoria were not cosmopolitan. In 1969, reminiscing about his youth to the author, he gave the connotation attributed to Peoria a different note: "I was born in Pekin, Illinois. A lovely town, kind of on the quiet side. But for those young rakes who wanted excitement—not too far away were the bright lights of Peoria."

House Speaker Tip O'Neill offered a rhyming variant in his 1986 attack on Reagan White House trade policy with South Africa: "Mr. President, your brand of trade policy may play in Pretoria, but it won't play in Peoria."

ploy an artful device aimed at deception; a maneuver of indirection to achieve an objective without revealing the ultimate goal.

This ancient Scottish derivative of "employ"—meaning "escapade" or "merry mischief" to Highland clans— gained in political usage in the 1960s, stimulated by the popularity of Stephen Potter's frequent use in his "one-upmanship" series.

Another possible derivation of ploy comes from the military "deploy"; in infantry terminology, a "ploy" is a means used to diminish the front exposed to the enemy, or to form a column from a line.

Ted Sorensen referred to a diplomatic ploy in discussing the many "inside" accounts of the Kennedy Administration's handling of the Cuban missile crisis in 1962: "Much information has been written about this series of meetings, about who said what, and about such terms as 'hawks and doves,' 'think tank,' 'Ex Comm' and 'Trollope ploy' which I never heard used at the time."

The "Trollope ploy" derives from the nineteenth-century romantic novels of Anthony Trollope, in which the heroine interprets—or deliberately misinterprets—the squeeze of her hand as a proposal of marriage. In the Cuban missile crisis, it was suggested that the most recent communication from Khruschev be ignored, and the U.S. make its reply to an earlier communication as if the most recent message had not been received. "It was Robert Kennedy," wrote Roger Hilsman in 1967's *To Move a Nation*, "who

conceived a brilliant diplomatic maneuver—later dubbed 'The Trollope Ploy' . . ."

The word has political promise, because of its alliteration with politics (a "political ploy"), the degeneration of "gimmick" into so wide a variety of meanings as to make it useless, and the lack of color in "device" or "maneuver." The word it will have to compete with is "gambit," which comes from an opening chess move sacrificing a pawn to improve position and which became a diplomatic word for a concession to begin discussions. In politics, *gambit* is currently synonymous with *ploy* and *trick*.

plum, political an appointive job, especially a sinecure; PATRONAGE.

"Shaking the plum tree" is attributed to Matthew Stanley Quay, political boss of Pennsylvania in 1885 and later U.S. senator.

The idea of political plums falling from a tree is evident in this reply by presidential candidate William Howard Taft in 1908, to a query by editor William Allen White about how Taft got started so young: "I always had my plate the right side up when offices were falling."

The meaning has remained unchanged. Raymond Moley, writing in *Newsweek* in 1967 about Postmaster General Lawrence O'Brien's plans to remove the "political plum tree" from the U.S. postal system by turning it into a nonprofit corporation, reminisced: "Starry-eyed idealists have long since deplored the use of government jobs, contracts and favors as rewards for political service. But they fail to realize that keeping the plum tree is not a happy lot."

The predecessor word, no longer used in politics, was *persimmon*.

Plum is current. A published list of appointive positions is informally called "the Plum Book." After Bill

Clinton's presidential victory in 1992, the *Washington Post* reported, "Some of the biggest plums to be doled out by the Democrats are the 94 U.S. marshal's jobs around the country."

plumber   one who investigates and seeks to plug up leaks of information; specifically, the inept crew of lawbreakers who undertook that task in the Nixon Administration.

Room 16, in the basement of the Old Executive Office Building across West Executive Avenue from the White House, was assigned to G. Gordon Liddy and David Young in 1970. One of their overt jobs was to track terrorist groups, at home and abroad, and to inform White House staffers of means to avoid letter bombs and other dangers. Another, less spoken about, part of their job was to find out who was leaking what information to the press, an activity that fascinated the President and Henry Kissinger.

Liddy later went on to fame and prison as one of the leaders of the Watergate break-in; Young did not get involved in those illegal matters. His contribution to history, however, was the sign he drew and placed on the door of Room 16: "The Plumbers." After the Watergate break-in was exposed, all eavesdropping operations— from the seventeen FBI wiretaps of newsmen and White House aides to the bungled attempts by agents hired by the Plumbers—were widely publicized, culminating with disclosure of clandestine break-ins and other abridgments of Fourth Amendment protections committed by the FBI and CIA in previous Administrations.

When people spoke of the Plumbers in the late seventies, it was usually applied to the Special Investigation Unit, headed by E. Howard Hunt, Jr., and G. Gordon Liddy, that was pressed into action in 1971, after the publication of the Pentagon Papers. The most famous bungled target of the Plumbers was the office of Daniel Ellsberg's psychiatrist, in a search for material that could be used to discredit the leaker of the secret history of the Vietnam War.

See "black bag jobs" under CIA-ESE; and the word from which "plumbers" sprung, LEAK.

plumed knight.   See THE MAN WHO; STALWART.

plump   to give active support; to strive for the election of another without reservation.

An obscure meaning of the word "plump" is "cluster," or group; voting as a bloc, or using a group's votes in a cumulative manner, was known as "to vote plump."

John Adams used it in that way in 1776: "New Jersey has dethroned Franklin, and in a letter, which is just come to my hand from indisputable authority, I am told that the delegates from that county 'will vote plump.'"

The word "plumping" came to have opposite meanings on the same subject in England and the U.S.: "One of the English election phrases for which there is no equivalent in the United States," wrote the *New York Tribune* in 1880, "is 'plumping.' Whenever [an English] constituency returns two members, each voter can give one vote each to any two candidates but he cannot give his two votes to any one candidate. If he chooses he can give one vote to only one candidate, and this is termed 'plumping.'"

In 1904, in the U.S., *Weber's Weekly* showed how the word came to mean the opposite of the English word: "The practice of casting three votes for one candidate has come to be known as 'plumping.' By 'plumping' the minority may concentrate its votes."

This is the same as cumulative voting, practiced in many publicly owned corporations in the U.S., where a number of votes for a slate of directors can be lumped together to be cast for a single director, encouraging minority representation on the Board.

In current use, *plump* has lost its cluster connotation, and has come to mean to solicit support for a candidate, preferably in large clusters. In its verb form, it is sometimes confused with STUMP.

Pocatello, you can't go back to

a melancholy expression about the loss of hometown roots by those who flower in Washington, D.C.

"This is one case in which you can cite your source with confidence," the popularizer writes the author. "It was invented by Dick [Oregon Senator Richard L.] Neuberger and myself in 1943 or 1944."

Present at the creation was Jonathan Daniels, in 1978 editor emeritus of the *Raleigh News and Observer*, and from 1943 through 1945 administrative assistant and later press secretary to President Roosevelt. He recounted the origin of the phrase in his book *Frontier on the Potomac*, published in 1946:

Neuberger had just come back from Alaska and was telling me about the cold up there and the state of his kidneys.

"There's Worth Clark," he said suddenly.

Neuberger regards the State of Idaho as a part of his personal province as a writer.

The ex-Senator joined a party at a table.

"Is he living here now since he was defeated?" I asked. "He probably doesn't know it, but he's a distant cousin of mine."

"Yes," said Dick. "I think he is practicing with Tommy Corcoran."

He drank from a glass of milk.

"You know," he said suddenly, "somebody ought to write an article, 'You Can't Go Back to Pocatello.'"

"Pocatello?"

"That's his home town. It's a big town for Idaho. Oh, I guess twenty thousand people."

"Why can't he go back?"

"It isn't Clark. They just can't. They come down here to the Senate or something. Then they get beat. It isn't easy to go back and practice local law and live local lives."

"It is not only the little towns it's hard to go back to," I said.

And while we watched, big Jim Watson, of Indiana, walked across the room. Nobody noticed him. He had been Republican majority leader of the Senate under Hoover. He was an old man, eighty, I guessed. He had been defeated, too, but he was in Washington still.

"You can't go back to Pocatello," I said.

It would be a good story. You couldn't tell in the big dining room who hadn't gone back but had stayed as bureaucrats on the other side of the street. The lobby and the government were laughing together. The only difference would be which picked up the check. And suddenly the big, wicked lobbyists seemed, above the noise of people eating and talking on expense accounts that auditors far away would approve and the Bureau of Internal Revenue might pass, less wicked than sad.

In current use, the phrase is an insider's alternative to POTOMAC FEVER and is usually changed to "They never go back to Pocatello." In a 1975 editorial the doomed *Washington Star* referred to the bittersweet line as evidence that the much-condemned Washington atmosphere was not all bad: "Whatever its drawbacks—and we acknowledge some—the number of politicians who come here and 'never go back to Pocatello' would indicate that the Nation's Capital is a pretty good place after all."

pocketbook issue   a voter's concern with what is happening to his income and its buying power.

"The great mass of the people," Boston politician Martin Lomasney discovered, "are interested in only three things—food, clothing and shelter."

In the midst of depression or inflation, pocketbook issues take precedence over more esoteric, philosophical appeals, and can exert a greater influence than personalities.

Republicans in 1966 decided to make pocketbook issues their theme; a piece of literature distributed in several areas of the nation was a long paper in the shape of a supermarket cashier's tape, with comparative food prices on it and a denunciation of "Johnson INFLATION." This could be considered fair play, as "Hoover depression" had been a Democratic approach to pocketbook issues for a generation.

A *pocketbook issue* is synonymous with BREAD-AND-BUTTER ISSUE. AFL-CIO President George Meany said of the 1970 congressional race: "The gut issue is going to be the pocketbook issue." In 1993, the *Cook Political Report* wrote, "Pocketbook issues broadly dominate voters' minds, and they worry about the middle class being squeezed and about the deficit." See PARAMOUNT ISSUE; GUT ISSUE; ISSUES, THE; IT'S THE ECONOMY, STUPID!

pocket veto on bills passed within ten days of congressional adjournment, the ability of the president to effectively veto by withholding his signature.

The President may retain a bill for ten days before either signing or vetoing it. If, during that time, the Congress adjourns, the President will have vetoed it merely by "putting it in his pocket."

In practical terms, this means that the President need not give reasons for vetoing the bill, which is why the term originally applied was "silent veto"; such a veto may not be overridden by

a two-thirds vote of the Congress, which is no longer in session.

Andrew Jackson brought the practice into full flower. "The silent veto," wrote Daniel Webster, "is, I believe, the exclusive adoption of the present administration. . . . In an internal improvement bill of a former session, and in the State interest bill, we have had the silent veto, or refusal without reasons." The *Ohio Statesman* headlined "Pocket Vetoes" in 1842.

Abraham Lincoln, at odds with Thaddeus Stevens about the severity to be shown the South after the Civil War, gave the pocket veto a new twist. He let it be known that he was not going to sign the harsh Wade-Davis bill, and that a "pocket veto" would take effect; however, instead of refusing to give his reasons, he issued a proclamation to show which parts of the legislation he would accept. But the Radicals were in no mood for conciliation. Thaddeus Stevens exploded: "What an infamous proclamation! The idea of pocketing a bill and then issuing a proclamation as to how far he will conform to it . . ."

In effect, the ten-day rule gives the President the power to accept or reject legislation passed in the last ten days of any session; congressional leaders try to get important bills through before the President gets this uncheckable power.

The word "veto" comes from the Latin, meaning "I forbid." Louis XVI and Marie Antoinette were called *Monsieur and Madame Veto* by the Jacobins, because of abuse of the veto power given him in 1791 by the Constituent Assembly.

The origin of "pocket" as a synonym for "suppress" was given the author by Senator Edward Kennedy, who referred to the word in a *Virginia Law Review* article (April 1977). In Shakespeare's *The Tempest*, Antonio asks: "If but one of his pockets could speak, would it not say he lies?" Sebastian replies: "Ay, or very falsely pocket up his report."

For a look at the way the Congress evens the score with the President, see ONE-HOUSE VETO.

Podunk. See SOUTH SUCCOTASH.

pointer phrases speechwriters' term for verbal signals that underscore essential points in a speech.

"Let me make one thing perfectly clear," Richard Nixon used to like to say. He stopped using the phrase, just as John Kennedy stopped using the word "vigor" when it became the target of parody. "Quite clear," "crystal clear," and even plain, unadorned "clear" became taboo words in the lexicon of those working with Nixon on speeches.

A speaker who uses a pointer phrase is consciously trying to help his audience understand his message. A reader of written prose can skip back to catch an important point; the listener cannot. The technique appears an oversimplification when transcribed to text for reading, but is a helpful device for the listener whose attention tends to wander. When this writer included a pointer phrase—"make no mistake about it"—in an early draft for a Nixon speech, the President crossed it out with the comment, "Leave this out of the text—if it comes naturally for me to say it, I will."

Here are some other pointer phrases in frequent use today:

> My point is this:
> Let me be quite blunt:
> It all comes down to this:
> In plain words:
> In a nutshell:
> Let's face it:
> The most important thing to remember is this:

In the use of pointer phrases, the most important thing to remember is

this: when any particular phrase is used to excess, it becomes an object of ridicule. A cartoon by Gardner in the *Washington Star* in 1971, soon after the announcement of President Nixon's plan to travel to China, showed Secretary William Rogers bursting into the State Department's translation division to ask: "How do you say 'Let me make one thing perfectly clear' in Chinese?"

Point Four Program. See CONTAINMENT.

point man. See ON THE POINT.

point of order cry of interruption made famous by Senator Joseph McCarthy in 1954.

"Our counsel, Mr. [Ray] Jenkins," said temporary chairman Karl Mundt of the Senate Subcommittee on Investigations, "will now call the first witness—"

"A point of order, Mr. Chairman," said Senator McCarthy at the televised Army-McCarthy hearings. "May I raise a point of order?"

The senator's insistent use of parliamentary device had schoolchildren repeating a phrase that had been limited to formal debates and congressional hearings.

The hearings marked the high point—and the beginning of the decline—of the senator's "era." See McCARTHYISM. Eric Goldman wrote: "The children stopped saying 'Point of order, point of order.' The housewives went back to 'I Love Lucy.' A different subject was filling conversations."

The phrase became the title of a film documentary and articles on the senator, who was censured by the Senate in 1954 and who died in 1957. Though he did not always use the device for determining a breach of the rules, here is why he was able to get the floor from the chairman whenever he chose, from *Robert's Rules of Order*:

While it is the duty of the presiding officer to enforce the rules, members might differ from the Chair as to whether the rules are being violated or the Chair might have noticed a violation of the rules. In either case, the member who thinks there is breach of the rules has the right to raise the question as to whether they are being violated, and this is called raising a question of order or making a point of order. The point of order must be made at the time the breach of order occurs.

In the House of Commons in 1978, visitors protesting the presence of British troops in Northern Ireland threw three bags of manure at the legislators. One Member responded, "Politics is a dirty business," and another called for "a point of ordure."

point with pride . . . view with alarm clichés associated with national party platforms.

A classic party platform has been said to include these elements:

1. "Pointing with pride" at past accomplishments;
2. "Viewing with alarm" the blundering record of the opposition;
3. Clearcut positions on issues long since resolved;
4. Cautious, ambivalent positions on current issues;
5. One nervously-taken stand on a controversial matter.

In 1878, *The Nation* used the phrase in connection with one Republican platform: "Besides 'pointing with pride,' the remainder of the platform approves of 'temperance among the people' and the navigation laws, and exposes the evil designs of the Democrats . . ."In 1892, the same magazine reported: "The Republican Convention in the Portland (Me.) district . . . adopted a platform which

'points with pride' to the McKinley Law . . ."

The phrases are often used today in the full knowledge that they are clichés, most often with the same irony and quotation marks as used a century ago. Anyone using them seriously is considered a blowhard.

pol short for politician.

Use of this shortened form indicates a spurious familiarity with politics. It is an inexperienced reformer's kind of word, resented by those who do not resent "politician"; the user tries to insinuate himself into the political world by using a word that he does not know is disliked by insiders.

Fletcher Knebel, reporter and novelist, put his finger on it in 1964: "'Pol' is to politician what 'cop' is to policeman."

polarize to accentuate the differences within a party; to drive men ordinarily in agreement on many positions to extremes of disagreement.

In California in 1946, moderate Democrat Will Rogers, Jr., campaigned against strongly liberal former Congressman Ellis Patterson for the Democratic nomination to the Senate. "The battle between Rogers and Patterson," Democratic candidate for Governor Robert Kenny said, "polarized the party. It was the one highly emotional issue and it became a touchstone. Nothing else mattered to the partisans of the two men. . . . They just didn't give a damn."

Polarization in a primary often results in the defection of the losers in the general election, and because of that is resisted by both party leadership and the leaders of the "wings." Such polarization is of course encouraged by the opposite party.

"There are many more areas in which we agree than where we disagree," is the cliché often used to try to smooth

over differences. See ELEVENTH COM-
MANDMENT; SURRENDER ON MORNING-
SIDE HEIGHTS. In 1948 the Democratic
party polarized to the point of dropping off both ends: Dixiecrats followed Strom Thurmond, ultraliberals
followed Henry Wallace, leaving
Harry Truman with just enough of a
center to win. In 1964 the ideological
split between Goldwater and Rockefeller polarized the Republican party,
leaving very little middle at all, and this
kind of polarization—the kind CEN-
TRISTS dread—resulted in a Lyndon
Johnson landslide.

In optics, to *polarize* means to affect
light waves so that they vibrate in a
definite pattern. The general sense of
the word used to be "to set a trend."
But politics changed the general sense
of the verb, and *polarity* has come to
mean the concentration of forces in di-
ametrical opposition.

In foreign policy tracts of the early
seventies, and especially in the writings and interviews of Carter National
Security Adviser Zbigniew Brzezinski, the term *bipolar* was used to
signify a world dominated by the opposition of two superpowers; after the
breakup of the Soviet Union, a diffusion of power centers was labeled *multipolar*, where power centers included
China, the THIRD WORLD, the West European bloc, etc.

See LITMUS-TEST ISSUE.

police action   diplomatic euphemism
for a war conducted under United Nations auspices; specifically, the Korean
War.

When the North Koreans invaded
South Korea in 1950, the Soviet delegate was in the midst of a boycott of
UN Security Council sessions, and the
U.S. was able to get through a resolution providing a UN umbrella for our
decision to intervene. Thus, U.S.
troops could serve with some others as
"United Nations forces" in Korea.

The phrase, like RED HERRING, was
placed in President Harry Truman's
mouth by a reporter. At his first press
conference after the North Korean attack, a reporter asked: ". . . are we or
are we not at war?"

"We are not at war," Truman replied
positively, and gave newsmen the unusual (at the time) permission to quote
him directly, adding that the U.S. was
only trying to suppress a "bandit raid"
on the Republic of Korea.

"Would it be correct," asked another
reporter, "to call this a police action
under the United Nations?" Truman
said yes, that was what the action
amounted to. Headline writers took
this as "Truman Calls Intervention
'Police Action,'" which associated the
President closely with the phrase. (As
a term for police activity, the phrase
dates back to 1885; its diplomatic sense
was first used in 1933.)

Since the President was so definite in
his statement that this was not a war,
and since no declaration of war was
ever made, legislative attorneys drawing up bills to make veterans of the
not-a-war eligible for benefits called it
"the Korean Conflict." Similarly, a
later war's legislative euphemism became "the Vietnam Era."

police brutality.   See CIVILIAN
REVIEW.

policeman of the world   an attack
phrase on America's assumption of responsibility as guardian of human
rights and national borders.

"We Americans," said Benjamin
Harrison in 1888, "have no commission from God to police the world."

Theodore Roosevelt disagreed. In his
message to Congress on December 6,
1904, he claimed the duty of the U.S.
was to exercise an "internal police
power" in the Western Hemisphere
because "chronic wrongdoing, or an
impotence which results in a general

loosening of the ties of civilized society, may . . . ultimately require intervention by some civilized nation."

With the adoption of a policy of CONTAINMENT of Communist expansion early in the fifties, Roosevelt's corollary to the Monroe Doctrine was extended throughout the world. Critics of this policy took the position that the United Nations, not the U.S., was properly charged with the responsibility for keeping world peace; moreover, they held, this policy was escalating wars rather than keeping the peace. Supporters of the "world policeman" idea, while rejecting the phrase as slanted to their opponents' arguments, believed the Soviet veto made the UN ineffective in halting aggression; in the vacuum, the U.S. had to step in on the basis of its own long-range self-interest, as well as the ideal of preserving the self-determination of nations.

Senator J. William Fulbright, after quoting Abraham Lincoln's use of the Biblical phrase "judge not that ye be not judged," said: "The United States must decide which of the two sides of its national character is to predominate—the humanism of Lincoln or the arrogance of those who would make America the world's policeman." In the latter half of his sentence, the Foreign Relations Committee chairman was referring to Theodore Roosevelt, but his sense of new reality kept him from attacking a well-loved old myth.

Speaking in Montreal in May 1966, Defense Secretary Robert McNamara surprised and delighted DOVES with "neither conscience nor sanity, itself, suggests that the United States is, should, or could be the Global Gendarme." Without credit to President Harrison, he added, "The United States has no mandate from on high to police the world, and no inclination to do so . . ."

Secretary of State Dean Rusk felt obliged to say a year later that our efforts to pursue peace "does not mean that we are the world's policeman. It does not mean that we aspire to a *pax Americana.*" This was a play on "pax Britannica," meaning the peace imposed upon the world by the power of the British Empire. (See PAX AMERICANA.)

George Ball, former Undersecretary of State who served Lyndon Johnson as the leading dissenter on the escalation of the Vietnam War, objected to the use of this cliché in *Foreign Affairs* (July 1969): ". . . man is still so bedeviled by greed and passion that force and authority must be ever at hand if he is not to blow the world up. So, unhappy as may be the policeman's lot, if we do not walk his thankless beat, who will?"

Discussing international relations in 1983, Ronald Reagan said: "We have no intention of becoming policeman to the world. But as the most powerful country in the West, we have a responsibility to help our friends." In 1992, David Brinkley of ABC asked George Bush: "Are we going to be, to use the old cliché from the past, the world's policeman? Every time there's an unpleasantness in the world, do we pack up our guns and run there?"

police state. See TOTALITARIAN.

policy wonk a grimly serious scholar of the tedious side of public affairs; stiff staffer steeped in study.

In the 1992 election, both Bill Clinton and Al Gore were known to delight in the minutiae of program development, causing Meg Greenfield of *Newsweek* to refer to them as "tough, ambitious, leadership-minded *policy wonks.*"

Wonk in the sense of an overserious student, synonymous with *nerd,* is of obscure origin. It might be related to the nautical slang word for "cadet." *Sports Illustrated* in 1962 wrote: "A *wonk*, sometimes called a 'turkey' or a 'lunch,' roughly corresponds to the 'meatball' of a decade ago." The suggestion that *wonk* may be *know* spelled backward is folk etymology.

In the 1984 Presidential election, Sidney Blumenthal of *The New Republic* was the first to use the phrase in print, referring to Walter Mondale's "thralldom to the *policy wonks* and wise men of the Washington establishment."

political animal   what man is supposed to be; usually employed with open—or grudging—admiration.

Aristotle said it in his *Politics:* "Man is by nature a political animal." Some have since complained that man is too much the political animal, but George Bernard Shaw, for one, was not among them. "It is very doubtful whether man is enough of a political animal," GBS noted in a speech in New York on April 11, 1933, "to produce a good, sensible, serious and efficient constitution. All the evidence is against it."

In *The Kennedy Circle*, Lester Tanzer noted of John Kennedy's Secretary of Defense: "As a political animal, McNamara defies classification. In 1960 he made four campaign contributions. Three of the candidates he supported were liberal Republicans—Senator Clifford Case of New Jersey and John Sherman Cooper of Kentucky, and Paul Bagwell, the unsuccessful Republican candidate for governor of Michigan. The fourth was a Democrat, John F. Kennedy."

The term was often applied to Lyndon Johnson. Writing on May 24, 1964, *New York Times* columnist Arthur Krock noted: "The most political animal to occupy the White House since Andrew Jackson, if not since the creation of the Federal Government, has just completed the first six months of his presidency."

Winston Churchill in 1942 classified animals as to air, sea, and land, and as-

signed allies their proper roles: "We were sea animals, and the United States are to a large extent ocean animals. The Russians are land animals. Happily, we are all three air animals."

If the accent is placed on the second word—as "political *animal*"—the phrase can become an epithet. Reported *Newsweek* in 1967: "Mrs. Lenore Romney became so upset when the governor [George Romney] angrily denounced the President as a 'political animal' that her eyes filled with tears." In 1978 House Speaker Thomas P. "Tip" O'Neill denounced a Republican prosecutor, David Marston, as "He's nothing but a Republican political animal." The Republican leader, John Rhodes, correctly took offense.

See STIR UP THE ANIMALS; RATTLE THE CAGE. For canine metaphors, see BIRD DOG . . . KENNEL DOG and PIT-BULL POLITICS.

political capital, to make   to take unfair partisan advantage; capital is used in the sense of considering political prestige, notoriety, and influence as "property."

"I tell you," said Senate Majority Leader Lyndon Johnson in the debate on the 1957 civil rights bill, "out of whatever experience I have, that there is no political capital in this issue. Nothing lasting, nothing enduring has ever been born from hatred and prejudice—except more hatred and prejudice." In voting for civil rights legislation for the first time in his life, Senator Johnson was determined to make the civil rights bill his own, and it served to add to his political capital as a national, rather than sectional, leader.

The phrase has been traced as far back as an 1842 issue of the *Ohio Statesman*: ". . . the attempt of the whigs . . . to make 'political capital,' as was avowed by whig members, fizzles out . . ." The use of quotation marks indicates the phrase was used earlier than that, and its frequent current use makes this phrase an important political Americanism.

Adlai Stevenson in 1952 tried to blunt the SOFT ON COMMUNISM issue this way: "It is never necessary to call a man a Communist to make political capital. Those of us who have undertaken to practice the ancient but imperfect art of government will always make enough mistakes to keep our critics well supplied with standard ammunition. There is no need for poison gas."

A year after that election, Eisenhower Attorney General Herbert Brownell charged that Harry Dexter White, a Truman Assistant Secretary of the Treasury, was "a Russian spy." Eisenhower recalled later: "The central point in this case was this shocking FBI evidence, but a host of partisan critics chose to ignore this and to attack the Attorney General for 'trying to make capital' out of incontrovertible evidence."

To expend political capital is considered laudable, as to use Presidential popularity to further policy goals.

Business has not contributed nearly as many metaphors to politics as religion, sports, or the military. "Stock" is occasionally used, as in this 1836 *Scioto Gazette* comment: "The rapid advance of Jackson stock in the political market presented too splendid a speculation to be eluded by such jobbers as the house of Van Buren & Company . . ." and the 1876 *Cleveland Leader*'s headline, "Hayes Stock Is Strong."

LAME DUCK is the best-known borrowing from finance, with "gravy train," "angel," "blue sky laws," and BOOM AND BUST used often. For a commercial borrowing, see HOT PROPERTY.

politically correct conforming to liberal or far-left thought on sexual, racial, cultural and environmental issues.

The adjectival phrase, frequently abbreviated to *p.c.* by conservatives attacking regimentation in language and thought by liberals, became a controversial expression on college campuses in the early 1990s.

Politically correct began in the 1970s as an assertion of liberal or progressive activists. The term was used in a December 1975 statement by Karen DeCrow, then president of the National Organization for Women, who said that NOW was taking the "intellectually and politically correct direction."

By the late 1980s, however, conservative activists (or passivists) had turned *politically correct* into an attack phrase, to be flung at opponents as a condemnation of leftist conformity, especially on college campuses.

The noun equivalent of this phrase is "political correctness" (also abbreviated to "p.c."), and one who is not politically correct (from the p.c. standpoint) is dubbed "politically incorrect" and ostracized by those marching in ideological or multicultural lockstep.

The *correct* or *correctness* soon became jocularly used in other combinations, and *environmental correctness, morally correct, patriotically correct,* and even *nutritionally correct* and *sartorially incorrect* found their way into print.

The origin of the phrase is the Maoist *correct thinking*. Chairman Mao Tsetung titled a 1963 thought "Where Do Correct Ideas Come From?" He answered his own question: "They come from social practice, and from it alone." *Correct thinking,* "the disciplined acceptance of a party line," led to the definition of the adjective *correct* as "reflecting the views of the group."

Attempting to police language by labeling as "objectionable" or "hurtful" terms such as *feminine* and *codger* is one ramification of the movement of those considered *politically correct.*

Lending itself to parody, this term appeared at the 1992 Democratic National Convention in New York in *The Official Politically Correct Dictionary and Handbook.* A handout for this book recommended replacing *ballot-box stuffing* with "nontraditional voting," *cliché* with "previously enjoyed sound bite," and *sore loser* with "equanimity-deprived individual with temporarily unmet career objectives."

See THOUGHT POLICE.

political mileage, to make   to seize an opportunity to take political advantage; to make use of the voter appeal inherent in an issue or position.

The word "mileage" was first used to describe a legislator's allowance for traveling costs. Benjamin Franklin in 1754 wrote of "Member's Pay . . . milage for traveling expenses." The word, with an *e* added, gained political significance when the Whigs in 1850 called for "mileage reform." At the time, "constructive mileage" was paid when an extra session of Congress was called; if legislators happened to have remained in Washington, they were paid the cost of a trip to the capital even though they never took the trip. See LULU.

The new meaning is evidently built on this, but the current use is not in dictionaries. Senator Joseph McCarthy discovered plenty of mileage in the SOFT ON COMMUNISM charge; there was mileage in the frustration of Americans about a stalemate in Korea in 1952. John F. Kennedy made political mileage of an ephemeral missile gap, Lyndon Johnson discovered the mileage in poverty, and George Wallace (and later, Jimmy Carter and Ronald Reagan) made mileage out of a general resentment directed at the federal bureaucracy.

Making political mileage implies less unfairness than making POLITICAL CAPITAL.

A South African government minister warned Bishop Desmond Tutu, a Nobel laureate, against supporting sanctions by the international community, adding: "Clearly the Bishop intends to gain a great deal of political mileage out of his ecclesiastical superstardom."

political miracle   cliché indicating an upset or unexpected development.

"Barring a political miracle," wrote *Time* magazine in 1948 about the Dewey-Warren combination favored to swamp Truman, "it was the kind of ticket that could not fail to sweep the Republican party back into power."

Four years later, a WRITE-IN campaign was begun in Eisenhower's behalf by a citizens' group in Minnesota, just after his New Hampshire primary victory over Robert Taft. Professionals warned Eisenhower against it, feeling its likely failure would slow down the bandwagon. Bradshaw Mintener, state chairman of "Minnesotans for Eisenhower," appealed to the voters for "a political miracle." As the General commented later: "It appeared to have happened: more than one hundred thousand people wrote in varying versions of my name."

The word "political" seems to have a particular affinity for the words *miracle, suicide,* and of late, *cool.* Taking any unpopular stand, or one that used to be unpopular and still gives the illusion of courage in opposing it, is called POLITICAL SUICIDE by tut-tutters; and keeping one's "political cool" means refusing to OVERREACT in adversity or triumph.

political similes.   See LIKE UGLY ON AN APE.

political suicide   an obviously unpopular action, which may result in defeat at the polls.

These suicides, like the report of Mark Twain's death, are usually exaggerations. Actions that are unpopular on their face often redound to a candidate's credit as evidence of courage; it may appear to some commentators as "political suicide" to question or oppose automatic increases in funds for education, but some governors who take this controversial step find they may stay alive by proving they have made a white elephant more efficient, or held the line on taxes, or whatever the other side of the coin enables them to say.

The phrase is in international use. Jean-Marie Le Pen, far-right political leader in France, declared in 1988 that Jacques Chirac and other conservative parties had, by ostracizing his National Front, "organized their own political suicide." A Japanese official gave the *New York Times* in 1990 a list of 80 proposals that President Bush could adopt to improve relations, and asked, "Is this a recipe for political suicide? Maybe it is. But you should see America's ideas for Japan."

The phrase, sometimes expressed as "political hara-kiri" (mispronounced Harry Carey), does not mean taking one's own political life deliberately; it means, rather, taking an action that some other people feel will lead to political oblivion.

In that second sense, the word was used by Woodrow Wilson in a letter to Bernard Baruch in 1916 early in the presidential campaign, and could have been applied to Lyndon Johnson's strategy in the 1964 campaign: "I am inclined to follow the course suggested by a friend, who says that he has always followed the rule never to murder a man who is committing suicide."

politician one who engages in a career either in government or in a political party on a full-time, usually professional, basis.

In most countries the practice of politics is considered a respectable profession, worthy of this 1770 definition by English parliamentarian Thomas Burke: "It is the business of the speculative philosopher to mark the proper ends of government. It is the business of the politician, who is the philosopher in action, to find out proper means towards those ends, and to employ them with effect."

That was a far cry from the derogation in Shakespeare's *Richard III*: "meerly a politician, and studied only his owne ends." In 1879 Sir George Campbell reported to his countrymen that "the word 'politician' is used in a bad sense in America as applied to people who . . . are skilled in the area of 'wirepulling.'" In the U.S. the politician has been looked upon with suspicion from the first, because the Colonists felt themselves misunderstood and mistreated by a government in London (in which they were not represented) that inflicted on them such distasteful regulations as the various Acts of Trade and the Stamp Act.

Thomas Jefferson summed up his feeling as "that government is best which governs least." George Washington expressed the feeling of most of his countrymen when in his Farewell Address he referred to "the mere politicians." Later, Artemus Ward said: "I am not a politician, and my other habits are good."

In more recent times, the practice of politics in this country has become more acceptable, and a growing number of men are prepared even to accept the appellation without wincing. One who bore the badge proudly was former President Harry Truman, who told the Reciprocity Club in 1958: "A politician is a man who understands government, and it takes a politician to run a government. A statesman is a politician who's been dead ten or fifteen years."

A professional politician's image is similar to that of the professional soldier: patronized in peacetime, lionized in wartime. Between campaigns, the politician is an embarrassment and a pest to many government officials; at campaign time, he is leader, guide, and confidant.

In current usage, a *public figure* is a celebrity; a *political figure* is an officeholder or likely candidate; a *professional politician* is usually a technician without ideology; a POL is one of *the boys in the backroom*; a GOFER is the lowest political functionary; a *political expert* or *political observer* is often a reporter's fiction for quoting himself without appearing to do so, and an OLD PRO knows enough ropes to hang himself.

politics of a framework for titles, to suit all purposes.

In the 1949 English edition of his book *The Vital Center*, the title used by Arthur Schlesinger, Jr., was *The Politics of Freedom*. He informs the author that titles like *The Strategy of Terror* by Edmund Taylor might have inspired his frequent use of this construction.

Schlesinger followed this with *The Politics of Upheaval* in 1957, and *The Politics of Hope* in 1962. In the 1968 Presidential campaign, Hubert Humphrey tried out "the politics of joy," and in 1970 Senator Edward Kennedy denounced Vice President Agnew's "politics of fear." In 1992, the call by the "hard right" of the Republican party to launch a "cultural war" against homosexuals and abortion-rights activists was denounced by GOP moderates as the "politics of exclusion."

First Lady Hillary Rodham Clinton spoke in 1993 of "the politics of meaning," a phrase from writer Michael Lerner, which she said had to be "thought through on various planes," adding, "We need a new politics of meaning. We need a new ethos of individual responsibility and caring."

On the politics of anything: the word "politics" is construed as singular, as in "Politics is fun," but when it is used to denote a set of beliefs, the plural takes over, as "My politics are nobody's business."

pollster one who measures public opinion, especially with an eye to predicting election results.

"A pinch of probably is worth a pound of perhaps," wrote James Thurber. The politician's desperation for reassurance combined with a journalist's curiosity led to the rise of public opinion polling, a technique in use in the U.S. since the Adams-Jackson-Clay-Crawford presidential race of 1824.

The word "poll" comes from the Middle English *polle*, meaning "top of the head," the part that showed when heads were being counted. Today, a *poll tax* is a head tax; *the polls* are where the heads are counted; and *a poll* is a counting of a sampling of heads, selected at random or by prearrangement, to reflect the opinion of a given populace. Dr. Elmo Roper and Dr. George Gallup were the leaders in the field for many years, establishing their profession in the thirties, blossoming after the debacle of the *Literary Digest* poll of 1936. See STRAW POLL.

"Pollster" is a relatively new word, popularized in—and especially after—the Truman upset of Dewey in 1948. Wrote *Time*, wrong as any, afterward: "The press . . . had failed to do its own doorbell-ringing and bush-beating, it had delegated its journalist's job to the pollsters." The "-ster" suffix is slightly jazzy (jokester, trickster, hipster) and not at all scientific; the people in the business do not like it.

To the best of my memory, the first time the word "pollster" was ever applied to me [Dr. Roper informed the author] was in the summer of 1944, but again according to my memory it didn't achieve anything like its present currency until the campaign of 1948. Since we have always tried to do something above and beyond a mere nose counting job—seeking always for the reasons *why* people were going to do whatever it was they were about to do—I have always preferred to be called a "public opinion analyst." But the press—in its normal omniscience—apparently needs a shorter phrase and I haven't ever developed what might be called an active resentment against the word "pollster." . . . Our organization has never used the word "poll." When we started the first published "poll," we insisted on calling it "The Fortune Survey."

The word was first used as early as 1939, when *Time* magazine commented on FDR's popularity: "Gallup pollsters reported that 43 percent of the voters want Mr. Roosevelt to run again." It was still popular in the 1992 Presidential election. The *Washington Post* wrote of the three-way race by Bush, Clinton, and Perot: "As a consequence, some pollsters say, election results may be much different than the findings of election-eve weekend polls." President Clinton's pollster, Stanley Greenberg, is officially titled "Pollster to the President."

See DEPTH POLLING; TRIAL HEAT.

pollution.   See ENVIRONMENTALIST.

pooh-bah   big shot; pompous functionary.

The word has a huffing and puffing sound, imitative of the "high MUCKEY-MUCKS" it describes. A favorite of Justus Lawrence, aide to General Dwight Eisenhower at Supreme Headquarters Allied Powers, Europe, the term has been given frequent political usage.

When the "McGovern Victory Special" rolled in June of 1972, Haynes Johnson wrote in the *Washington Post*: "They all climbed aboard that train

today; movie stars, jocks, beautiful people, old politicians, new politicians, erstwhile Kennedy and McCarthy followers, big pooh-bahs of the press and other assorted people on the make."

In January 1977, columnist Joseph Kraft supported the doomed nomination of Theodore Sorensen as Director of Central Intelligence: "He is an avowedly political man, not the kind of antiseptic pooh-bah usually picked to build public confidence."

The word is sometimes thought to be derived from A. A. Milne's *Winnie-the-Pooh*, but Pooh-bear is not the source.

The complete derivation is given in this answer to the author's query by Stuart Berg Flexner, who was co-author of the *Dictionary of American Slang*:

Pooh-Bah was first heard the night of March 14, 1885, when Gilbert & Sullivan's *The Mikado* opened (in London's Savoy Theatre, the one Richard D'Oyly Carte built for their operas). Pooh-Bah was the name of the pompous bureaucrat holding many offices and titles, though his real title was "The Lord High Everything Else."

Pooh-Bah really starts the action of the opera because he's the one who informs the Lord High Executioner Ko-Ko that he must execute someone within a month or lose his office, Ko-Ko eventually reporting that he has executed Nanki-Poo (the son of the Mikado traveling in disguise) who has fallen in love with Yum-Yum.

W. S. Gilbert loved these cute/humorous names, Pooh-Bah, Ko-Ko, Nanki-Poo, Yum-Yum, etc. Since he wrote the book and lyrics, everyone assumes he chose the names, and Pooh-Bah merely comes from his combining the two negative exclamations *pooh*! plus *bah*!, typical put-downs from a typical bureaucrat.

By the 1890s the English were using the name Pooh-Bah in a general way, to mean any pompous person with a lot of bureaucratic offices and titles (the English almost always retain the capital P and B though Americans do not).

In 1968 King Taufa'ahau Tupou IV, the 300-pound monarch of Tonga (an island group between New Zealand and Samoa), presided over the Independence Day of his nation happily, and confided: "I'm a bit of a Pooh-Bah, you know, except that I don't cut off any heads."

popular front name adopted by many radical movements, as that of the combined communist and socialist forces in Europe during the 1930s.

This phrase is often capitalized when referring to the specific movement combining radicals, communists, and socialists; this international alliance began in 1935, spreading from France and Spain to Chile by the late 1930s.

In French, the term is *fronte populaire*; in Spanish, *frente popular*. In English, *popular front* has produced various related forms. The practices of this alliance were known as *popular frontism*. Its supporters were *popular fronters*, involved in *popular fronting*, or political activity for the front.

Although the European movement lost effectiveness after 1938, the phrase has resurfaced in recent political struggles in the Middle East. For example, George Habash has led the Popular Front for the Liberation of Palestine, as well as guerrillas or terrorists of the Rejection Front.

populist attuned to the needs of "the people"; now used with a connotation of old-fashioned radicalism; a liberalism rooted deeply in U.S. history.

Lyndon Johnson was called by friendly writers a political leader "in the old populist tradition." When Jimmy Carter inveighed against favoritism (and the Nixon pardon) in his 1976 acceptance speech with "I see no reason why big-shot crooks should go free, while the poor ones

go to jail"—that, too, was described as "populist."

The word is used today with a small *p* as a reminder of the theories rather than the structure of the Populist or "People's party" (see PARTY OF THE PEOPLE), which was a political party of a radical nature that won substantial backing in the U.S.

A populist economic policy in the 1990s is one that features a call to "soak the rich." That phrase, according to *Newsweek* columnist Joe Klein, dates back to the early 1930s; he cites Thomas Kessner's book *Fiorello H. La Guardia and the Making of Modern New York*, which states that on March 10, 1932, the congressman from New York blasted a tax bill in the House and added his own advice: "I am simply going to say, 'Soak the rich.'" The *New York Times* denounced him for those "wild and whirling words."

Periodic depressions and a conviction that the government was dominated by large money interests inimical to both the farmer and the mechanic led to some informal alliances between these groups and socialists. In 1890 a state party calling itself the People's party was founded in Kansas. In that same year, various Farmer's Alliance groups, founded largely to fight the railroads, scored heavily in the South and the West; there, candidates advocating new economic legislation favored by the Alliances were elected in five senatorial contests, six gubernatorial, and forty-six congressional races.

This led to the organization of a national "Populist" party in 1891. At its convention in Omaha it demanded, among other things, public ownership of the railroads, the telegraph and telephone systems; direct election of U.S. senators; a graduated income tax; and cheaper money. The delegates, coming predominantly from the farmers' organizations and the Knights of Labor, wrote a radical platform calling for "a permanent and perpetual . . . union of the labor forces of the United States. . . . The interests of rural and civic [urban] labor are the same, their enemies are identical. . . . We believe that the time has come when the railroad corporations will either own the people, or the people must own the railroads."

Other planks were no more friendly to capitalists. When the Populist candidate, General James B. Weaver, won 22 electoral-college and 1,029,846 popular votes in the 1892 election, many people, including some considered liberals, were fearful of impending revolution.

Watching Populist congressmen in action, novelist Hamlin Garland foresaw "a great periodic upheaval similar to that of '61. Everywhere as I went through the aisles of the House, I saw and heard it . . . the House is a smouldering volcano." A woman announced she was going to Europe "to spend my money before those crazy people take it."

The party lingered on until 1908, but most of its members had returned to the Democratic fold by then and the word is used now by politicians who want to identify with "the little man," who can be found under JOHN Q. PUBLIC. It is also used internationally, as in Maclean's 1983 assessment of leadership in the Philippines: "Even the Communist Party expressed the belief that Aquino had a unique populist approach."

In 1993, New York magazine's media columnist, Edwin Diamond, described the Clinton use of televised town halls and appearances on TV talk shows as "electronic populism."

pork barrel the state or national treasury, into which politicians and government officials dip for "pork," or funds for local projects.

The classic example of the pork barrel is the Rivers and Harbors bill, a piece of legislation that provides morsels for scores of congressmen in the form of appropriations for dams and piers, highways and bridges.

The phrase probably is derived from the pre–Civil War practice of periodically distributing salt pork to the slaves from huge barrels. C. C. Maxey wrote in the National Municipal Review in 1919:

> Oftentimes the eagerness of the slaves would result in a rush upon the pork barrel, in which each would strive to grab as much as possible for himself. Members of Congress in the stampede to get their local appropriation items into the omnibus river and harbor bills behaved so much like Negro slaves rushing the pork barrel, that these bills were facetiously styled "pork barrel" bills, and the system which originated them has thus become known as the pork-barrel system.

A story by E. E. Hale called "The Children of the Public," which appeared in an 1863 issue of Frank Leslie's Illustrated Newspaper, probably also helped popularize the term. In Chapter I, entitled "The Pork Barrel," Hale wrote: "We find that, when an extraordinary contingency arises in life, as just now in ours, we have only to go to our pork barrel, and the fish rises to our hook or spear." The term was widely used by the early 1900s.

By the 1870s, congressmen were regularly referring to "pork," and the word became part of the U.S. political lexicon. Time magazine noted in 1948 that one Peter J. McGuinness "fished in Tammany's pork barrel for 28 years to bring improvement to 'me people.'" In a Baltimore speech on inflation in 1952, Adlai Stevenson pledged "no pork-barreling while our economy is in its present condition." Four decades later, Bob Dole, Senate Republican leader, succeeded in filibustering an early

Clinton economic-stimulus measure by attacking it as "pure pork."

Getting rid of the practice is next to impossible, as former Senator Paul H. Douglas (D-Ill.) wrote: "As groups win their battle for special expenditures," he said, "they lose the more important war for general economy. . . . They are like drunkards who shout for temperance in the intervals between cocktails." See DELIVER.

Still useful in the 1990s, the term was used in a 1993 "Moneyline" report on Cable News Network: "Members of Congress try to bring home the bacon for their constituents, but a politician's bacon is a taxpayer's pork. One watchdog group wants to take a bite out of pork barrel spending and today introduced a pot-bellied pig to make its point." The expression applies internationally: The *Washington Post* wrote in 1993, "Italy's decades of pork-barrel politics have contributed to a national debt exceeding $1 trillion."

pork-chopper   1. full-time union leader or staffer; 2. holder of a political patronage job.

The use of *pork-chopper* by "labor skates" dates back to the 1930s. A *New York Times* article in 1946 discussed the term's meaning for the United Auto Workers: "The rank and file call those who live by income derived from the union 'pork-choppers.'"

This sense of union leaders working for their own interests or enrichment persists. In 1982, the *Wall Street Journal* explained the term: "Pork-choppers are union staffers who try to keep local officials in line for the leadership. Their name . . . alluded to the fact that workers on the union payroll were often better fed than the rank and file."

By 1960, a second sense of the term was overlapping the first. Harold Wentworth and Stuart Berg Flexner, in their *Dictionary of American Slang*, defined *pork-chopper* as one who engages in a form of featherbedding: "a political appointee, union official, or relative or friend of a politician, union officer, or the like, who receives payment for little or no work; one who is put on a payroll as a favor or as a return for past services."

Union officers, as well as rank-and-file workers, have sometimes taken umbrage at the role of pork-choppers. James Balanoff, a steelworker and union official, told William Serrin of the *New York Times* in 1981: "The job is so important to them they can't afford to lose it. The money. The position. The trips, payoffs, to Europe or Japan. They sit silent. Get along and go along, that's the rule."

The compound, which is usually hyphenated but sometimes solid, has also been used with a favorable connotation in politics. The *Almanac of American Politics* in 1990 elaborated on the union background of Charles Hayes, a black leader elected to Congress in 1983, adding "he has been a union official since the 1940's and had been lobbying Congress for more than 20 years—the quintessential pork-chopper."

For the more widely used sense of *pork*, see PORK BARREL.

position paper   a statement of policy on an issue in a campaign, for guidance of speechwriters and supporting speakers; in diplomacy, an *aide-mémoire* at an international conference.

Before any major campaign begins, bright young lawyers are brought in to work on position papers. They check past speeches by the candidate on the subject to be careful of inconsistency, draft the latest "new ideas" on the subject, farm out extra research to academicians specializing in the area. Papers are then drawn on subjects like urban renewal, agricultural policy, air and water pollution, transportation, crime, and housing; in more local campaigns, on "home rule" and traffic congestion, and in national campaigns, on foreign affairs and broad themes of social welfare.

The position papers are useful in briefing a candidate on areas he knows little about and getting a briefing from the candidate on areas he has definite ideas about. They are usually packaged in a looseleaf folder and made available to the writers and headquarters staff; in abridged form the papers may be sent to canvassers (see CANVASS) to equip them with answers to questions likely to be asked when they ring their doorbells.

A position paper is detailed, including a background statement of position; it should not be confused with a brief. When Adlai Stevenson said in 1952, "each day their statement of position moves in like a new fog bank," he was deriding sweeping Republican policy pronouncements, not detailed papers.

In diplomacy, a WHITE PAPER is a formal report issued by a government to define its policy; a *position paper*, also called an *aide-mémoire*, is a private guide to its diplomats. "A full-scale international conference involves difficult and intricate preparation," wrote Dwight Eisenhower; "'position papers'—documents on all conceivable issues, setting forth the position the government intends to present at the meeting—have to be carefully written and approved." Eisenhower added sharply: "Position papers can be written only after a chief executive has decided precisely what his position is to be."

One-page position papers, prepared as answers to anticipated news-conference questions, make up a President's "black briefing book."

positions of strength   power from which to negotiate; diplomatic muscle.

Secretary of State Dean Acheson started the phrase, in slightly different form, on February 16, 1950: "The only way to deal with the Soviet Union, we have found from hard experience, is to create situations of strength."

By the process of double translation, into and from the Russian, the phrase became "positions of strength."

poster.   See SNIPE.

Potemkin village.   See PUTSCH.

Potomac fever   the proximity to power that turns a PASSION FOR ANONYMITY into a notion for notoriety.

An ordinary human being whose statements have been ignored all his life will, upon taking a job in Washington, D.C., find his statements quoted and his picture appearing in newspapers across the country. The sensation that follows, often linked with the drinking of "heady wine," is euphoric; men who have always decried "personal publicity" find it necessary, after their appointment, to utilize the avenues of mass communication to get across their agency's message.

"The rivalry for the attention and support of Congress," wrote Harry Truman in his memoirs, "was, in part, responsible for many news leaks. 'Potomac fever,' too, creates a great desire on the part of people to see their names in print."

Speaking to the National Newspaper Association in 1966 about his role as Lyndon Johnson's press secretary, Bill Moyers pointed out: "'Potomac Fever' can produce a bloated sensation—particularly in the area of the ego—that causes Press Secretaries to take themselves much too seriously. There are many symptoms of this, including hypervexation over the annoyances any reporter—especially the pathological troublemakers—can generate; myopia, which blurs their vision of things afar; and the tiger-in-the-tank syndrome manifested by super-charged reaction to criticism, justified and unjustified."

A similar disease, contracted before arrival in Washington, or a particularly virulent strain contracted while in Washington on a senatorial level, is PRESIDENTIAL FEVER transmitted by the PRESIDENTIAL BUG.

Named for the river that flows through Washington, *Potomac fever* has several symptoms. In 1988, the *Los Angeles Times* quoted a White House veteran on the sickness: "We called it Potomac fever. Because people treat you like a star if you work in the White House, it's easy to start behaving like one. You're mentioned in talk shows and written about in books. Before long some start to feel as if they actually are a little President." Even the President may be susceptible; early in the Clinton Administration, Representative Dick Armey of Texas said on "Meet the Press": "It strikes me that what I've seen in the President is the first, worst, most definitive case of Potomac fever that I've watched in this town."

Related to this illness is *Hill fever*, which afflicts those in proximity to Congressional power on Capitol Hill.

See POCATELLO, YOU CAN'T GO BACK TO.

power base a politician's foundation of support, usually his home district or state.

A favorite axiom of Democrat Jim Farley was this: "The most important lesson for a politician to learn is that he must always be sure he can carry his own precinct."

De Tocqueville took note of this phenomenon in his *Democracy in America*. In aristocracies, he said, a member of the legislature "is rarely in strict dependence on his constituents." But in the United States,

a representative is never sure of his supporters, and, if they forsake him, he is left without a resource. . . . The seeds of his fortune, therefore, are sown in his own neighborhood; from that nook of earth he must start, to raise himself to command the people and to influence the destinies of the world. Thus it is natural that in democratic countries the members of political assemblies should think more of their constituents than of their party, while in aristocracies they think more of their party than of their constituents.

The importance of preserving this base of power has other effects. "There is nothing quite like a Curley or Hague or Crump or even a De Sapio in other countries that have well-developed party systems," wrote Clinton Rossiter in *Parties and Politics in America*. "To be a real boss, and not just a flunky, a politician must have his own base of power and immunity from external discipline, if not from internal revolt."

Not even Presidents are immune from this requirement. Charles Hurd, in *When the New Deal Was Young and Gay*, notes that "all Presidents have had permanent residences that they maintained during their periods in office, partly out of sentiment and partly in order to maintain political 'roots.'"

The term "pissing post" is occasionally used to refer to one's power base, or home district, or political *pied-à-terre*. The author's attention was drawn to this phrase by Professor Edward Banfield of Harvard, who reported its use in Cook County, Illinois, as a "trivial base."

A surprise loss in his home district in Greenwich Village to Ed Koch (later Mayor of New York) toppled Tammany leader Carmine De Sapio from his position as the most powerful Democrat in New York State. For a method of maintaining communications in one's power base, see FENCE MENDING; BACKER.

power behind the throne unofficial adviser of great influence; used to attack an Administration when the President himself is popular.

William Pitt the Elder coined it in 1770: ". . . there is something behind the throne greater than the King himself." Black leader Frederick Douglass echoed it toward the end of the Civil War, but in a benevolent sense: ". . . we are not to be saved by the captain, at this time, but by the crew. We are not to be saved by Abraham Lincoln, but by the power behind the throne, greater than the throne itself."

Woodrow Wilson had his Colonel Edward House, FDR his Louis Howe and later Harry Hopkins, Eisenhower his Sherman Adams.

During the Reagan Administration, First Lady Nancy Reagan wielded enough clout in the White House to be thought of as the power behind the throne. And to the end of his term, George Bush relied so often on James A. Baker that *New York Times* columnist A. B. Rosenthal dubbed the inseparable pair "Bushbaker."

In modern usage, a GOVERNMENT BY CRONY and KITCHEN CABINET are mildest in terms of extralegal influence; a power behind the throne is more severe, PALACE GUARD and a GRAY EMINENCE more sinister, a RUSTLING BEHIND THE JALOUSIES more feminine, and a *Svengali* or a *Rasputin* imply complete control from behind the scenes.

power brokers those who control a bloc and can DELIVER its support; or, middlemen trusted by disparate forces who can help bring about a coalition.

Though the President of the U.S. may exercise great power, he "is endowed with far greater responsibility than authority," wrote Douglass Cater in *Power in Washington*. "To make his office operable, the President often finds himself serving as broker among the power groups rather than as banker drawing on his own limited reserves of power."

Wilfred Funk traces "broker" to the French *brokiere*, or broacher, one who taps wine casks. The broker eventually turned into a middleman, handling anything from marriages to mutual funds.

Bismarck was known as the "honest broker" at the Berlin Conference of 1878 after the Russo-Turk War because all the powers involved won new territories except Germany. But the German Chancellor had achieved an important objective for Germany— the continued isolation of France. At the turn of the century Senator Nelson Aldrich, the Rhode Island Republican, was known as "Morgan's floor broker in the Senate."

During his mayoral campaign and often after he was elected, former Republican John Lindsay spoke scornfully, and often despairingly, of the "power brokers" (a phrase coined by Theodore White) who ran New York behind the scenes. A less detrimental reference appeared in *Newsweek* magazine in 1967. Discussing how critics of the Vietnam War boycotted a 1965 art festival sponsored by the White House, the magazine quoted a Johnson Administration official as saying: "Presidents deal with power. Power is real. Power is not pretty. And I guess these people don't understand power brokers like they do art brokers."

Such brokerage as does go on takes place in "the corridors of power," evoking images of transactions made while walking to and from the "center of power." British novelist C. P. Snow coined the "corridors" in a novel of that title, while Stewart Alsop popularized "the center" in the title of his nonfiction work.

International use of the term continues, sometimes as a single word. A 1984 obituary in *Time* magazine for

Pierre Gemayel, political leader of Lebanon's Christians, described him as "a key powerbroker in the country's factional political strife."

power corrupts a charge usually made by Outs against Ins to persuade voters that it's time for a change.

In a speech in the House of Lords on January 9, 1770, William Pitt the Elder declared: "Unlimited power is apt to corrupt the minds of those who possess it." Sir John Acton later amended this to: "Power tends to corrupt; absolute power corrupts absolutely." In loose quotation, the Acton qualifiers tend to be removed absolutely, leaving only "power corrupts."

Lord Acton's famous maxim was quoted frequently when Franklin Roosevelt was being chided for trying to pack the Supreme Court. John F. Kennedy also touched on the idea. In a speech at Amherst College in October 1963, honoring Robert Frost, Kennedy said: "When power leads man toward arrogance, poetry reminds him of his limitations. When power narrows the area of man's concern, poetry reminds him of the richness and diversity of existence. When power corrupts, poetry cleanses."

Some see politics as an inevitable sullier of souls. In a 1945 essay on "The Evils of Politics and the Ethics of Evil," Hans Morgenthau wrote:

> Only the greatest dissenters of the age have been clearly aware of this necessary evilness of the political act. A great non-liberal thinker writing in the liberal age, such as Lord Acton, will find that "power corrupts . . . absolute power corrupts absolutely," or he will, like Jacob Burckhardt, see in politics the "absolute evil"; or, like Emerson, in force "a practical lie" and corruption in every state.

Others have been less gloomy. "Power does not corrupt men," George Bernard Shaw wrote. "Fools, however, if they get in a position of power, corrupt power." In *The Short Reign of Pippin IV*, novelist John Steinbeck wrote: "The King said: 'Power does not corrupt. Fear corrupts, perhaps the fear of a loss of power.'"

After Margaret Thatcher was thrust out of Downing Street and into the House of Lords, she attacked the Conservative Party position on ties to Europe. Lord Rawlinson then said of Lady Thatcher: "It is not so much power that corrupts, it is the withdrawal of power that pains."

See ARROGANCE OF POWER.

power curve the ability to maintain influence or leadership.

To be *behind the power curve* is to risk crashing; to be *ahead* (or *in front*) *of the power curve* is to be in control of events.

In early 1977, an aide to Jimmy Carter used the negative phrase to refer to a colleague uninformed about the latest decisions: "He's behind the power curve on this." In 1980, the campaigning George Bush spoke to a *Time* reporter who had asked him about his low ratings. "You're behind the power curve," said the former aviator. "You haven't been to Iowa with me, or across the top of New Hampshire to see the improvement." The Bush use suggests a meaning of "not up to date" or "out of touch"; these lead to a loss of influence.

Although the term was used in the 1960s as a statistics-graph test for alternatives, the *power curve* began in aeronautics with the related 1940s term PUSHING THE ENVELOPE. Curves developed by mathematicians and engineers were used to indicate the performance limits of an aircraft, representing its speed, altitude, and other factors. In 1975, *Aviation Week and Space Technology* reported on "a STOL aircraft's tendency to operate on the back side of the power curve."

Aeronautics still uses the phrase. In 1993, the *Houston Chronicle* quoted Eugene Kranz, director of mission operations for Johnson Space Center: "The hardware is moving from design to development and test. We have to stay ahead of the power curve."

As recently as 1992, the ominous term reappeared in a political context, part of *New York Times* coverage of George Bush's strategy concerning Saddam Hussein. The *Times* derided Bush's advisers as "geopoliticians, still behind history's power curve."

power elite a charge that there exists an interlocking directorate of moneymen, politicians, and military men who shape national policy no matter who is elected.

The phrase was the title of a book (1956) by sociologist C. Wright Mills, who held that "neither professional party politicians, nor professional bureaucrats are now at the centers of decision. These centers are occupied by the political directorate of the power elite." Mills said this elite was composed of "the political directorate," the "corporate rich," and the "ascendent military." Together, they formed "over-lapping cliques [which] share decisions having at least national consequences. Insofar as national events are decided, the power elite are those who decide them."

Journalist, later presidential aide Douglass Cater disagreed, calling Mills's theory "too pat to be convincing." He argued that "it would be difficult to document the thesis that an elite really rules on matters of national consequence . . . the growth of giant organizations has not brought cumulatively greater power to the individuals who head them. . . . The swaggering tycoons of business and labor unions no longer exist to dictate their demands to the subservient politicians. . . . Mills' concept of a sinister

and cynical power elite hardly seems applicable to decision-making in Washington today."

As Mills argued in the fifties that a power elite kept intellectuals and liberals out of the decision-making process, conservative journalist William F. Buckley, Jr., was arguing that an "establishment" of intellectuals and liberal politicians was freezing out the prudent, businesslike conservative who understood the American system best.

Mills's theory received an unexpected boost from Dwight Eisenhower in his farewell address. See MILITARY-INDUSTRIAL COMPLEX.

"Elite," a word used earlier to describe specially trained Swiss troops, came to mean the socially select; in this sense, it was widely popularized by a radio program of the thirties and forties, "Duffy's Tavern," "where de elite meet t'eat." In current political use, "intellectual elite" is a derisive term that appears to be as common now as "power elite." In the sixties, WHITE POWER STRUCTURE was the black leaders' phrase for "power elite," and "power structure" lingered into the seventies as "structure" became a vogue word. In the 1992 campaign, Vice President Dan Quayle attacked the "cultural elite."

Jet set and the *Beautiful People*, also terms from the sixties that lingered into the seventies, were not usually members of the power elite, though the old elite and the new sometimes met on press junkets. Columnist John Roche liked *mandarinate; media elite* is usually used in derogation of the Washington press corps, while *media biggies* is a phrase that waggishly describes the potentates of the press; and *illuminati* is used to give an intellectual cast to the banal "celebrity." "Illuminati" has been in political use since 1800: "We have thrown some useful light upon the Illuminati of Connecticut and Massachusetts," wrote the *Philadelphia Aurora*, "and lately upon a similar propaganda in Delaware State." It originally described the holders of candles at baptisms.

power grab attempt to take over leadership; attack word on insurgents.

This is a curious phrase, since those who denounce a power grab do not call themselves "powerholders." Consequently, it is most often used by supporters once removed from the seat of power, with the implication that the reason the insurgents want power is not for the opportunity to render public service, but to have it for power's sake or to use it for their own selfish ends.

The phrase, along with CARPET-BAG-GER, was used often against Robert Kennedy in his successful campaign against Senator Kenneth B. Keating in 1964. Since both candidates were liberals, there was little ideological argument; Keating, to overcome Kennedy's fame and name, played on his opponent's reputation for ruthlessness. This particular thrust reached its high, or low, point when a small boy appeared at a Kennedy rally carrying a sign: "Don't use *me* in your cynical power grab."

"Grab" is a classic political Americanism. The opponents of the Embargo Act of 1807 spelled the word backwards and called it the "O Grab Me" Act, because they felt it favored the agricultural interests of the South over the shipping and commercial interests of New England.

Railroad tycoons were attacked as "land grabbers" for the way they bought valuable land from the government at low prices, often by laying original track in serpentine patterns to pick up added acreage.

The "salary grab" is the best-known use of the word before "power grab." Congress in 1873 raised the President's salary from \$25,000 to \$50,000, gave raises to many other federal officials and judges, and increased a congressman's own draw from \$5,000 to \$7,500. This might have gone through with mild public criticism had not the raises been made retroactive to the start of the Congress then sitting. The "salary grab" became an issue, and the next Congress cut back all salaries except the President and Supreme Court.

powerhouse place of action.

In New York City, "The Powerhouse" is a nickname of the Catholic Archdiocese of New York, in recognition of the political and economic power inherent in the Church. (Similarly, the thirteen subcommittee chairmen of the House Appropriations Committee are called "the College of Cardinals.")

In an article on the Archdiocese in the *World Journal Tribune* in 1967, just before that newspaper's demise, the Church leadership was described as operating

out of the south wing of the old Whitelaw Reid mansion on the east side of Madison Avenue between 50th and 51st Streets. (The north wing is occupied by Random House, a piddling operation—by Church standards—even after its recent merger with Radio Corporation of America.)

The press and some laymen refer knowingly to the Archdiocesan Chancery offices as *The Powerhouse*. The clergy, and others who have business there, call it simply "Madison Avenue." Interestingly, it is in the heart of the area advertising people also call "Madison Avenue." The same turf, but an entirely different world.

In a more general sense, the word is used to describe a place of action and turbulence. "Originally installed in the predominantly feminine East Wing," wrote the *New York Times Magazine* of the shifting position of the INTELLECTUAL-IN-RESIDENCE at the White House, "[John P.] Roche took just two months to become the first academic in recent White House history to be allowed into the powerhouse setting of the West Wing." In the Clinton Administration, First Lady Hillary Rodham Clinton chose to work in the West Wing's powerhouse setting.

power lunch business meal to press the latest agenda or negotiate terms.

This phrase uses *power* as an attributive noun, as in POWER CURVE, a trend begun by baseball's use of *power hitter*. In 1956, the sociologist C. Wright Mills applied POWER ELITE to social movers and shakers; in the 1960s, the author Theodore H. White coined POWER BROKERS.

John F. Mariani, author of *The Dictionary of American Food and Drink*, points to an October 1979 *Esquire* article by Lee Eisenberg as the source of *power lunch*. Eisenberg's essay was titled "America's Most Powerful Lunch." The headline of a 1980 *Washington Post Magazine* feature by Rudy Maxa was "All You Need to Know About Power Lunches at the New Eateries."

Power lunch led quickly to other power meals. According to Florence Fabricant in a 1980 *New York Times* article, the literary agent Morton Janklow coined *power breakfast* for the early-morning business meal at the Regency Hotel in New York. Brenda Fine and Jane E. Lasky, in their *Women's Travel Guide,* listed Washington's "best bets for early-morning power grabbing" and pointed to *working breakfast* as the source of *power breakfast.*

These terms changed somewhat as they were popularized. Originally, they referred only to "meals of the powerful people"; later they came to represent "the type of meal eaten by the powerful," specifically containing low cholesterol and no fat.

A business article in *Newsweek* magazine pointed beyond power meals: "Goodbye power lunch, hello power tea." In 1989, though, the earlier term continued to be predominant; a *Washington Post* article about a British luncheon for Queen Elizabeth and George and Barbara Bush referred to "that Buckingham Palace power lunch."

Still popular in the 1990s, the original term appeared in a 1992 assessment in the *Boston Globe* of a Washington landmark: "Duke Zeibert's restaurant, home of the political power lunch."

power politics political or diplomatic action guided by the principle that "might makes right."

Professor Hans J. Morgenthau, who became well known in the sixties for his attacks on U.S. policy in Vietnam, wrote in 1950: "The illusion that a nation can escape, if only it wants to, from power politics into a realm where action is guided by moral principles rather than by considerations of power . . . is deeply rooted in the American mind." He made the point that world politics as practiced in 1950 and power politics were synonymous: "The choice is not between moral principles and the national interest, devoid of moral dignity, but between one set of moral principles, divorced from reality, and another set of moral principles, derived from political reality."

"Reality" is the operative word in power politics. "Uncle Joe is a realist," FDR was reported to have said about Joseph Stalin. And REALPOLITIK is now used interchangeably with *power politics*, though the former has a scientifically impersonal connotation, and the latter calls up a picture of a big nation pushing little nations around. PRACTICAL POLITICS has some pejorative connotation, but is usually considered the

ART OF THE POSSIBLE. *Power play* is the art of running roughshod over, or "blowing away," the opposition.

power structure. See WHITE POWER STRUCTURE.

power to tax . . . the power to destroy.

"An unlimited power to tax involves, necessarily, the power to destroy," argued Daniel Webster before the U.S. Supreme Court in 1819. The case was the landmark *McCullough* v. *Maryland,* when the state of Maryland sought to tax a branch of the new Bank of the United States. The issue was federal supremacy of the young nation's monetary system, which sought to curtail the issuance of currency by state banks.

Chief Justice John Marshall, writing the Court's decision, agreed "that the power to tax involves the power to destroy; that the power to destroy may defeat and render useless the power to create . . . [the states] have no power, by taxation or otherwise, to retard, impede, burden or in any manner control the operations of the constitutional laws enacted by Congress."

In another decision in 1930, Justice Oliver Wendell Holmes wrote: "The power to tax is not the power to destroy while this court sits."

The phrase has current usage in attacks on the very institution it originally defended—the federal government and its tax policies. Arguing against a federal tax increase for 1967, economist Pierre Rinfret said: "The power to tax is the power to destroy, and a tax increase at this time would destroy our economic growth." Supply-side economists in the 1980s took the position that tax increases destroyed, or at least debilitated, economic growth. See SUPPLY-SIDE.

power to the people slogan of dissident groups of the sixties, especially the Black Panthers.

"Power to the Soviets!" was a battle cry of the Bolsheviks during the Russian Revolution.

In the 1960s, advocates of "participatory democracy" like Tom Hayden of Students for a Democratic Society were calling for a transfer of power to the "people," whom they were able to identify as themselves. Power became a vogue word of the civil rights movement (see BLACK POWER), later parodied as Irish Power and ultimately, for elderly people, Gray Power, and for homosexuals, Gay Power.

"Power to the People," shouted with clenched fist raised in a mock fascist salute, was publicized as a Black Panther slogan at a meeting under the leadership of Bobby Seale in Oakland, California, on July 19, 1969. Earl Caldwell of the *New York Times* reported: "They came with long hair and in faded old Army field jackets, in bulky sweaters and in worn and ragged levis. Most of them were white; some were youthful hippies. The majority were students, and they came off the campuses fired with what they called revolutionary fervor. 'Power to the people,' they shouted. 'Power to the people.' They made it a chant and they used it again and again. When they did, their arms shot into the air with their fists clenched."

practical politics to some, a euphemism for cynical or dishonest dealing; to others, a coming to grips with the reality of people's prejudices and foibles.

"Practical politics," wrote historian Henry Adams in 1906, "consists in ignoring facts." The phrase was in current use at the time, having been popularized by British Prime Minister Gladstone in his "bag and baggage" speech of 1877, dismissing the Turks as "out of the range of practical politics."

A century before Gladstone, Edmund Burke's letter to the Sheriffs of Bristol made a case for practicality in politics: "I was persuaded that government was a practical thing, made for the happiness of mankind, and not to furnish out a spectacle of uniformity to gratify the schemes of visionary politicians. Our business was to rule, not to wrangle; and it would have been a poor compensation that we had triumphed in a dispute, whilst we lost an empire."

Thomas Jefferson, a student of Burke, surprised his friends with his willingness to occasionally set idealism firmly aside. "What is practicable must often control what is pure theory, and the habits of the governed determine in a great degree what is practicable." He considered his own Louisiana Purchase unconstitutional, but he told Congress the agreement with Napoleon must be ratified, "casting behind them Metaphysical subtleties."

The dual meaning of the phrase was evident in 1890, when Charles Ledyard Norton defined "practical politics" in *Political Americanisms*: "The minor details of party management, including practises that are corrupt and criminal, as well as those that are legitimate and honorable. The phrase in the sense was in common colloquial use in 1875."

Theodore Roosevelt, fighting President William Howard Taft for the Republican nomination in 1912, was offered a deal on delegates that might have won him the nomination, but he turned it down unless all "stolen" delegates were purged. See THOU SHALT NOT STEAL. After Taft had won, *New York Times* Washington correspondent O.K. Davis asked the former President why he had been so rigid. The reply defined a practical politician

as applying to one who might cut a few corners but who would not do anything basically dishonest: "Yes, I am a practical politician," said Roosevelt, "and I have played the game. But that was something different. . . . It had gone far beyond the mere question of expediency or political shrewdness. It was a fundamental question of morality."

Teddy's cousin Franklin Roosevelt was often accused of compromising his ideals and gave this Lincoln example to a group of young people questioning him about it: "Lincoln was one of those unfortunate people called a 'politician' but he was a politician who was practical enough to get a great many things for this country. He was a sad man because he couldn't get it all at once. And nobody can." FDR was also fond of quoting Grover Cleveland's practical remark: "We are faced with a condition and not a theory."

In the Eisenhower years, the word *practical* was used for *cynical*, though it fell short of *dishonest*. In his memoirs, Eisenhower told of the amazement of party leaders when he told them he was determined to redeem every one of the 1952 Republican platform's provisions. "More than once I was to hear this view derided by 'practical politicians' who laughed off platforms as traps to catch voters. But whenever they expressed these cynical conclusions to me, they invariably encountered a rebuff that left them a bit embarrassed."

Correspondent Arthur Krock, after the election of the Kennedy-Johnson ticket in 1960, used the word in the same sense as Eisenhower had used it: "Rarely had there been an instance of more cynical 'practical' politics than the choice of Johnson to run on a platform pledging him to major policies and legislation he has steadfastly opposed."

Ever since the Kennedy years, *pragmatic* has been used by political leaders who thought of themselves as "problem-solvers." Although *pragmatic* is rooted in "affairs of state," its meaning became close to "practical" with a modern flavor, and it is now lodged between *dogmatic* and *principled*.

See REALPOLITIK.

prairie fire. See WHIRLWIND CAMPAIGN; DISASTER METAPHORS.

pranks. See HARDBALL; DIRTY TRICKS; RATFUCKING.

praxis. See REVOLUTIONARY PRAXIS.

precinct captain a local commander of political TROOPS, equivalent to a sergeant in an infantry platoon; one who is called on to DELIVER the vote.

"In the old Tammany days," writes former Tammany leader Ed Costikyan, "a political captaincy was a much-prized honor. . . . Such a captain . . . would build up a following among his voters loyal to both his party, his leader, and to him. Ultimately several hundred people would follow his direction on election day, and vote for whichever candidates he told them to."

While the position still carries some local respect, the function has changed. The captain's job now calls for education and persuasion of voters by precinct leaders and their canvassers (see CANVASS) who might not be well acquainted with their target voters. With the welfare function of the local political organization taken over by the government, the captain's service function has been reduced to steering constituents through the maze of government machinery to get "what you might not realize you're entitled to."

With voters increasingly concerned with the campaigns for major office

that they see, hear, and read about in mass media, the precinct captain's job is to point out the importance of local campaigns for minor offices, using the "top of the ticket" to help the rest of the party's slate.

Many political leaders at the top level recognize the importance of providing COATTAILS for local precinct workers to cling to, in return for turning out the vote for the major candidate on Election Day. That was why Mayor Edward Kelly of Chicago said in 1940: "Roosevelt is the greatest precinct captain I've ever known. He's made the job of our workers easy."

pre-emptive strike. See PREVENTIVE WAR.

preference poll. See TRIAL HEAT.

presence diplomatic word for "showing the flag"; particularly, a United Nations force on the scene to avert or end hostilities.

Traditionally, a great power would send a naval squadron to a trouble spot within its SPHERE OF INFLUENCE to remind the locals of the power the squadron symbolized. This is now considered heavy-handed. Modern diplomacy requires the dispatch of military advisers or an economic mission to establish a "presence" underscoring the power's commitment in the area. A specific "military presence" differs from the old-fashioned "showing the flag" by the continuity of the assignment—an extended stay rather than a brief display.

The word has a United Nations origin. In November of 1958, British troops left Jordan; despite inter-Arab "good neighbor" pledges, King Hussein's country was not expected to remain independent. UN Secretary-General Dag Hammarskjöld sent a thirty-man mission to Jordan headed by Pier Spinelli, Italian chief of the UN

European office in Geneva. Spinelli's mission established what came to be called "UN presence" in Amman, Jordan, providing a steadying effect in the area by virtue of evidence of continuing UN interest.

Wrote Andrew Boyd of *The Economist*: "Hammarskjöld also proposed to appoint a 'high-level' representative at UN headquarters who could visit the various Arab countries as required for 'diplomatic actions.' But this official (at once nicknamed 'the absent presence') was never appointed; the Secretary-General found things going smoothly enough to dispense with the idea."

The UN presence was applied to all UN peacekeeping efforts "in the field" as in the Congo and the Gaza Strip. The idea was to keep the great powers out of small wars that could, with Soviet or U.S. intervention, become world wars. When Secretary-General U Thant quickly acceded to Egyptian demand for the withdrawal of the UN force in 1967, he was sharply criticized in the aftermath of the Arab-Israeli conflict.

By that time the usage had spread to non-UN bodies. The U.S. Sixth Fleet in the Mediterranean was "the U.S. presence" and the British Colony at Hong Kong was called "the threatened Western presence on China's border." But a part of the word's effectiveness is its vagueness—a presence can be a visiting diplomat, an aircraft carrier, a permanent military base, or a force of troops. Hammarskjöld, author of the idea, liked the flexibility of the term and insisted on what he called "a completely pragmatic" view: "There is a UN presence wherever the UN is present."

In 1978, Israelis striking into southern Lebanon to punish Palestinian terrorists announced that they would accept a UN presence in their stead; the presence called itself a "peacekeeping force." By the 1990s, serious consideration was given to arming these peacekeepers so that they could become *peacemakers*. This resulted from the deepening involvement of the UN presence in Bosnia and Herzegovina, following the breakup of Yugoslavia and the breakout of ethnic conflict in the Balkans; and in Somalia, where in 1993 UN troops came into armed conflict with a warlord following the killing of Pakistani members of the UN force.

Presidential bug a mythical insect whose bite results in PRESIDENTIAL FEVER; breeds best where the opposition has been swamped, or in an atmosphere charged with power.

The phrase possibly originated with Abraham Lincoln's "chin fly" story, told to Henry Raymond, editor of the *New York Times*. Lincoln's Treasury Secretary, Salmon P. Chase, was often critical of the President, perhaps because he wanted the top job himself. Raymond quoted Lincoln:

". . . you were brought up on a farm, were you not? Then you know what a chin fly is. My brother and I . . . were once plowing corn on a Kentucky farm, I was driving the horse, and he holding the plough. The horse was lazy but on one occasion rushed across the field so that I, with my long legs, could scarcely keep pace with him. On reaching the end of the furrow, I found an enormous chin fly fastened upon him, and knocked him off. My brother asked me what I did that for. I told him I didn't want the old horse bitten in that way. 'Why,' said my brother, 'that's all that made him go!' Now if Mr. C[hase] has a presidential chin fly biting him. I'm not going to knock him off, if it will only make his department go."

The only trouble with this story is that Lincoln's brother died before he was old enough to plow. Maybe Lincoln was exaggerating.

The term is current. Journalist Victor Gold, who collaborated with then

Vice President George Bush on a book, commented on the process in the *Los Angeles Times* in 1987: "But then, Gold said, 'a funny thing happened on the way to the publisher.' Bush, his longtime supporter and former speechwriter said, 'got the Presidential bug.'" In 1993, the *New York Times* asked about former candidate Eugene McCarthy, "Does he still have the Presidential bug?" He replied, "We McCarthys tend to live a long time. My grandfather made it to 98. That being the case, I've still got time for—let's see—for five more tries."

See POTOMAC FEVER; ITCH TO RUN.

Presidential fever a raging desire for the top job, accompanied by the "sweating out" of delegates' decisions.

New York Governor Al Smith said in 1924: "A plague on all individuals who would like to be president!" This particular plague is called "presidential fever," and was so termed at least as far back as 1858, when abolitionist clergyman Theodore Parker wrote: "The Land Fever is more contagious than the Presidential Fever, and equally fatal to the moral powers."

Leading up to his final SHERMAN STATEMENT, General William Tecumseh Sherman said in 1879: "I am not now, and do not intend to get, infected with the presidential fever." Five years later he phrased it slightly differently, as "infested with the poison of presidential aspiration."

In 1879, in tandem with Sherman, Republican James Garfield of Ohio was making feverish notes in his diary. On February 8: "I have so long and so often seen the evil effect of the Presidential fever upon my associates and friends that I am determined it shall not seize me. In almost every case it impairs if it does not destroy the usefulness of its victim." On April 20, 1880, two months before the convention: "I long ago made the resolution that I would

never permit the Presidential fever to get lodgment in my brain. I think it is the one office a man should not set his heart upon." When Grant and Blaine were deadlocked, Garfield's name came up, the fever rose, and he became the twentieth President.

Presidential initials. See INITIALS, PRESIDENTIAL.

Presidential seal. See BALD EAGLE.

Presidential timber. See TIMBER, PRESIDENTIAL.

President of all the people the desire of every President to represent a unified nation, not limited to any blocs, groups, or partisans that elected him.

Of course the President of the United States, as chief of state, *is* "President of all the people" not just those who voted for him. Yet there is a nagging doubt in the minds of most Presidents that they do indeed lead everybody; this doubt has led each President to urge the concept and many to use the phrase. First was James K. Polk, in his 1845 Inaugural Address: "Although in our country the Chief Magistrate must almost of necessity be chosen by a party and stand pledged to its principles and measures, yet in his official action he should not be the President of a part only, but of the whole people of the United States." Since the idea was not to extend authority over those who did not vote for him, but to recognize and show respect for the right to dissent, Polk added: ". . . he should not be unmindful that our fellow-citizens who have differed with him in opinion are entitled to the full and free exercise of their opinions and judgments, and that the rights of all are entitled to respect and regard."

Publicist Herbert Bayard Swope wrote Franklin Roosevelt in 1936 that his strategy should be: ". . . to be firm without being ferocious; to be kindly rather than cold; to be hopeful instead of pessimistic; to be human rather than to be economic; to be insistent upon every man having a chance, and above all, to make yourself appear to be the President of *all* the people . . ."

Writing in 1963 about the early days of the Roosevelt Administration, historian James MacGregor Burns used the phrase: "Like Jefferson and Wilson before him, Roosevelt was starting his administration off on a high, non-partisan note. He would be President of all the people . . ."

President Harry Truman used "whole people," President Polk's formulation, rather than "all the people": "As the President came to be elected by the whole people, he became responsible to the whole people. I used to say the only lobbyist the whole people had in Washington was the President of the United States." Truman biographer Cabell Phillips adds: "'The representative of all the people,' which he conceived the President to be, was no simple slogan but a deeply felt obligation laid upon him by Providence."

Dwight Eisenhower used the phrase in his memoirs: "The man in the White House, I believe, should think of himself as President of all the people."

Eisenhower succeeded more than most in achieving a recognition of leadership by almost all Americans. Wrote Arthur Schlesinger, Jr., about Eisenhower's successor, John Fitzgerald Kennedy: ". . . it seemed that Kennedy suffered from the illusion so common to new Presidents (even Roosevelt had it till 1935) that he, unlike any of his predecessors, could really be President of all the people and achieve his purpose without pain or trauma . . ."

The President most closely identified with the phrase, because of his often-expressed yearning for CONSENSUS, was Lyndon Baines Johnson. Speaking in Minneapolis on June 27, 1964, he used the phrase publicly for the first time and used it again often: "As long as I am President, this Government will not set one group against another—but will build a creative partnership between business and labor, farm areas and urban centers, consumer and producer. This is what I mean when I choose to be a President of all the people."

As can be seen, the phrase is favored by public figures and by historians. A joke during the 1964 campaign was: "If Johnson loses more than eight states, he will refuse to serve because he wants to be 'President of all the people.'"

In the sixties, as Lyndon Johnson's popularity fell, a related phrase came to the fore: the "only President we've got," taken from a frequent remark along those lines by Mr. Johnson. (In the seventies, when former Director of Central Intelligence Richard Helms said, "I only work for one President at a time," the single-President theme was accentuated, though Helms misplaced his "only.") Evidence that the "only President" phrase is part of the political language came in a July 9, 1978, column by Tom Wicker of the *New York Times*, satirically reviewing the Carter Administration as if it were a baseball team managed by Charles Kirbo, Carter's long-time confidant: "'Remember,' drawls Country Kirbo, who has too many smarts to be a playing manager, particularly in this club, 'Peanuts is the only centerfielder we've got.'"

President John F. Kennedy took the idea a step forward: "For each President, we must remember, is the President not only of all who live, but, in a very real sense, of all who have yet to live. His responsibility is not only to those who elected him but also to those who will elect his successors for decades to come."

pressing the flesh handshaking; any form of physical contact between candidate and voter.

The phrase, possibly originating as part of the rhyming jive talk of the 1940s, was politically popularized by Lyndon Johnson in 1960. "I just want to tell you how happy I am that you would come here and howdy and shake hands with us this morning," the vice-presidential candidate told small crowds at whistlestops. "You make us feel so wonderful to come out here and look us in the eye and give us a chance to press the flesh with you."

In the 1960 presidential campaign, a pickpocket in a Los Angeles crowd was reported to have groped inexpertly for someone's wallet and found himself, instead, shaking the hand of the Democratic candidate. Kennedy's grandfather, "Honey Fitz" Fitzgerald, was supposed to have perfected the art of the "Irish Switch": a technique of shaking one voter's hand while talking to a second voter, simultaneously smiling and winking at a third.

G. Mennen "Soapy" Williams, running for governor of Michigan, felt it was necessary to grasp the hands of at least two thousand voters a day. A *Detroit Free Press* reporter chronicled his method of working an auto plant in Flint at the time of a shift change, with hundreds of men streaming in and out:

Williams was standing in a familiar position, straddling the two stairways the men must take for entering the plant. Perhaps one man in 75 would try to slip by the Governor without shaking his hand. He couldn't get away with it. Williams would quickly spot him veering away and give chase. Two or three quick steps and his long legs would be planted firmly in the man's path. He would reach out, grab the man's hand, pump it once and say: "Nice to see you." Then he would smile proudly and step back in front of the two staircases, one foot blocking each.

Senator William Proxmire of Wisconsin estimated that he shook approximately 300,000 hands a year. He had a formula for avoiding politician's grip: always avoid the possibility of knuckle-crunching by shoving your hand into the voter's hand right up against the thumb.

Harry Truman's receiving-line technique was to use the handshake to pull the greeter along and deposit him with the next person on the line.

Politicians agree that "pressing the flesh" requires concentration on the crowd, even when "Irish Switching." Wendell Willkie broke this rule while campaigning in Rushville, Indiana, in 1940, and absent-mindedly shook hands with his own wife. When she protested, he apologized: "Gosh, Billie. Excuse me, I was thinking."

Senator Robert Kennedy often leaned across a platform and reached out with both hands to touch the outstretched hands, thereby covering more people than individual handshakes; Governor Nelson Rockefeller liked to backslap and squeeze arms with his familiar "Hiya, fella."

In an era of television campaigning, the necessity of physical contact is still with us; white candidates in black areas are especially told by their managers of the need to "press the flesh" and "lay on the hands" so as not to appear unwilling to be in close touch. In the Clinton-Gore Administration, the flesh-pressing escalated to bear-hugging.

Yet a former speechwriter, Jeff Greenfield, had a different view of the value of flesh-pressing. On a May 17, 1993, ABC News interview with Mike Wallace, he pointed out that if President Clinton "really wants to define what he's about, ironically he may have to . . . walk away from what his advisers regard his great strength, that one-to-one laying on of hands and pressing the flesh. He may have to resort to an old-fashioned technique called speeches . . ."

press secretary. See GHOSTWRITER.

pressure group attack phrase on a lobbying organization or bloc advancing its own cause.

Political parties gain broad power over short periods; pressure groups seek narrow power over long periods. As organized labor "punishes its enemies and rewards its friends," pressure groups work inside the political system to promote their causes on a continuing basis no matter who is in power.

James Madison, in the *Federalist* Number 10, defined "faction" as we now use "pressure group": "a number of citizens, whether amounting to a majority or minority of the whole, who are united and actuated by some common impulse of passion, or of interest, adverse to the rights of other citizens, or to the permanent and aggregate interests of the community."

Although in Madison's view factions could operate for good or evil, the phrase "pressure group" has a bad connotation. Dwight Eisenhower, describing Henry Cabot Lodge's plea to him to campaign for President in 1952, said the former senator painted the possibility of "at least a partial reversal of the trend toward centralization in government, irresponsible spending, and catering to pressure groups . . ."

The common denominator in any definition of pressure groups is *interest*; if the interest is *special* or *vested*, the pressure is venal, but if the interest is *public*, the pressure is benevolent. "We call them 'interest groups' when we are feeling clinical," wrote historian Clinton Rossiter, "'pressure groups' when we are feeling critical, and 'lobbies' when we are watching them at work in our fifty-one capitals."

See VESTED INTERESTS; LOBBY; BLOC.

preventive war an attack aimed at destroying a prospective enemy before he can launch an attack of his own.

On November 20, 1948, pacifist Bertrand Russell approached the subject in this way: "Either we must have a war against Russia before she has the atom bomb," he told an audience at the Westminster School, "or we will have to lie down and let them govern us."

Once Moscow acquired nuclear weapons, Lord Russell became more disposed to lying down. See BETTER RED THAN DEAD. But others argued that preventive war was preferable to a devastating sneak attack—presumably from Russia or China—in the future. There was some talk of it when mainland China threatened the offshore islands of Quemoy and Matsu in 1955 and again in 1958. During the Berlin crisis in 1961, John F. Kennedy told an interviewer that "a clear attack on Western Europe" might require the U.S. to use nuclear weapons first. As Theodore Sorensen wrote in *Kennedy*, "others read 'preventive war' or 'preemptive strike' overtones into this, but it was in fact longstanding policy and depended on an initial attack by the Soviets."

In Mario Pei's *Language of the Specialists*, Robert E. Hunter says that a first strike must be directed against enemy nuclear systems or else it will leave the attacker open to terrible retaliation.

A first-strike strategy might be adopted where an attacker has a vulnerable force, and must strike first (i.e. before being struck) if at all; where an attacker wishes to achieve "victory" through surprise attack, particularly against a strategically inferior nation (preventive war); where an attacker wishes to preempt a threatened enemy attack; or where a strategically inferior nation wishes to bring about catalytic war involving other powers.

Herman Kahn, in *Thinking About the Unthinkable*, noted:

> Almost all authorities agree that at present the advantages of striking first are so great that, should there seem to be a high probability that the other side is actually attacking, it might be better to risk the certainty of a relatively small retaliatory strike, rather than the high probability of a much more destructive first blow.

Preventive war is still a phrase looked on with revulsion by most Americans; *pre-emptive strike*, however, lost much of its pejorative connotation when it was used to describe the Israeli thrust against the Arabs following Gamal Abdul Nasser's closing of the Gulf of Aqaba in 1967 and its SURGICAL STRIKE against the Iraqi nuclear reactor at Insirik in 1981.

See SALT.

primary an intraparty election to select candidates for a forthcoming general election.

The *closed primary* is restricted to registered members of a particular party. In an *open primary*, voters may cross lines, regardless of their party affiliation, to vote for candidates of another party. See CROSSOVER VOTE.

Designed to give a party's rank and file a greater voice in the choice of candidates (and of convention delegates as well), the primary began appearing in the early nineteenth century. Mencken traces one to New York City in 1827. In the early twentieth century, the presidential-preference primary was launched by the progressive Republicans of the Middle West who wanted to reduce the influence of state party machines in the nomination of candidates. As governor of Wisconsin in 1901, Robert La Follette promoted a direct-primary bill. By 1916 both Republicans and Democrats chose a majority of their national convention delegates by this method. It lost ground for a time, but since the early seventies more states have seen political and publicity advantages in holding them.

Their importance is hotly disputed. In 1952 Senator Estes Kefauver of Tennessee won most of the preferential primaries he entered, but Adlai Stevenson won the Democratic nomination nonetheless. Stevenson considered the presidential primary "almost a useless institution." In 1958 he described it as confusing and time-consuming, and added, "Finally, it is terribly expensive; it's exhausting physically; you burn up yourself, you burn up your ammunition, you burn up your means. I think that it's a very, very questionable method of selecting Presidential candidates and actually it never does. All it does is destroy some candidates."

But it did get John F. Kennedy on the road to nomination in 1960, it provides a "shakedown cruise" for a campaign staff, and it settles arguments about vote-getting ability with some finality. By 1976 Jimmy Carter proved that the winner of most of the early primaries could gain an unstoppable momentum for nomination. See CATTLE SHOW; "New Hampshire bounce" (under CONVENTION BOUNCE).

priorities. See REORDERING PRIORITIES.

privileged sanctuary a base from which attacks can be made without reprisal to that base.

General Douglas MacArthur transferred the phrase from the religious or bird-refuge sense to the military-political in a communiqué on November 6, 1950, after the Chinese Communist "volunteers" entered the Korean War:

> In the face of this victory of United Nations arms the Communists com-

mitted one of the most offensive acts of international lawlessness of historic record by moving without any notice of belligerency elements of alien Communist forces across the Yalu River into North Korea and massing a great concentration of possible reinforcing divisions with adequate supply behind the privileged sanctuary of the adjacent Manchurian border.

Nine days later President Harry Truman stated: "United Nations forces are now being attacked from the safety of a privileged sanctuary."

Since that time, the phrase has appeared in hawkish statements whenever a nonbelligerent provided airfields or supplies for belligerents, where a nation at war could not permit "hot pursuit" by planes or troops without enlarging the war.

The adjective and noun have been married at least since 1788, when Edward Gibbon wrote *The Decline and Fall of the Roman Empire*: "The ancient privilege of sanctuary was transferred to the Christian temples."

"Right of asylum," almost synonymous in one sense, is considerably different in political usage, meaning the protection granted by one state to an individual citizen of another. Oddly, the "right" of asylum is more of a privilege, and the "privilege" of sanctuary is more of a right.

In 1970 President Nixon ordered U.S. troops into Cambodia to counter a North Vietnamese invasion after a pro-Western government overthrew a neutralist regime. Explaining this move to the American people on television, he said: "For the past five years . . . North Vietnam has occupied military sanctuaries all along the Cambodian frontier with South Vietnam . . . neither the United States nor South Vietnam has moved against those enemy sanctuaries because we did not wish to violate the territory of a neutral nation . . ."

The successful operation, which Nixon carefully labeled an "incursion" rather than an "invasion," caused a sharp protest in the U.S. Anthony Lewis suggested this definition in the *New York Times*: "Privileged sanctuary: Area where the enemy can rest and regroup in safety. See Laos, Cambodia. Do not see Thailand, Hawaii, or other base and recreation areas for American forces."

privy council. See BRAIN TRUST.

probe. See WITCH HUNT.

problem. See NO PROBLEM.

procedural safeguard. See RED TAPE.

process, the the majesty of the machinery; the inexorable procedures of government; more broadly, the American way of self-government.

"I realize that, in our democratic process," said Office of Management and Budget Director Bert Lance in July 1977, "government officials at times come under public and political scrutiny. That is part of the process."

"Process" came into vogue in the mid-seventies, a clipped form of both "the democratic process" and the DECISION-MAKING PROCESS, and as a partial replacement for "the SYSTEM" in its positive sense. A favorite word of the Carter White House, it reflected President Carter's interest in the management of the workings of government. Vice President Walter Mondale, assessing President Carter's first year in office to a group of reporters at the end of 1977, said of the President: "Now he has had a year's experience. He has seen this process work first hand. He is anxious that in succeeding years that what he has learned about that process permits him to better schedule and pace his proposals."

Meanwhile, in the office of the Governor of California, an aide described Democrat Edmund "Jerry" Brown's approach to *Washington Post* columnist David Broder, who had been asking about "a core of policy" in Governor Brown's philosophy: "No, I see a particular kind of process reflected in the way the place operates and in the people who are here. He really does want a lot of dialogue. But no consistent philosophy. It drives a lot of people nuts when he quotes Gandhi: 'the means are the ends in process.' Sometimes it drives me nuts, too."

See MACHINERY OF GOVERNMENT; PEACE PROCESS.

pro-choice   supporting a woman's right to have a legal abortion.

This term surfaced in sloganeering to avoid the harshness of "pro-abortion." The inspired use of *choice*, suggesting freedom, reflected polls that showed more people identifying themselves as being "in favor of a woman's right to choose" than "in favor of legal abortion."

Alan L. Otten of the *Wall Street Journal* first used the term in print. In a March 20, 1975, article, the political analyst wrote: "Both right-to-life and pro-choice forces agree the abortion issue is going to be around for a long time." Anti-abortionists used *right-to-life* as their slogan after the 1973 Supreme Court decision that prohibited states from making abortion illegal during the early stages of pregnancy.

Eager to present themselves as being in favor of something positive, the right-to-lifers then chose the term *pro-life*. The *New York Times* reported on January 18, 1976, about a "pastoral plan for pro-life activities."

As the term *abortion* has taken on negative connotations in public perception, the pro-life forces have been accepting the label of *anti-abortion ac-*tivists. Those who favor the euphemism of *pro-choice*, however, will probably resist attempts to recast the debate in terms of the stark expressions *pro-abortion* and *anti-abortion*.

professional   an experienced, cool political operative; or one who protests too much his allegiance to a cause.

For the definition of the first sense, see OLD PRO. For the second, See LIMOUSINE LIBERAL. In the second sense, the adjective turns completely around: a "professional liberal" or "professional intellectual" is one who poses as a liberal or intellectual but does not accept responsibility for the work of promoting a cause. In the same way, a "professional Irishman" is a politician who cultivates his brogue and acts in such a way as to appear to be the very model of what he thinks other Irish-Americans expect an Irishman to be, in an effort to identify with what may no longer be a voting bloc.

In 1918 Theodore Roosevelt used the word as it is used today: "Prominent, although not always powerful, among the latter are the professional intellectuals, who vary from the soft-handed, noisily self-assertive frequenters of frowsy restaurants to the sissy socialists, the pink tea and parlor Bolshevists . . ."

One prevalent use of the term today is not political: "professional virgin" is a frustrated suitor's epithet.

In the first sense, the antonym is "amateur"; in the second sense, the antonym is "authentic."

profiles in courage   any courageous political act, in a phrase popularized by a 1955 book of that title by Senator John F. Kennedy.

"Richard Nixon etched his profile in political courage," wrote columnist Murray Kempton in 1966, "by mentioning the word 'Rockefeller' in Syracuse." This was a sardonic comment about Nixon's strong support of Rockefeller's gubernatorial candidacy in a conservative Republican area of New York. But the "profiles in courage" phrase is frequently used without irony (evoking memories of the assassinated President) whenever any act that will offend voters is undertaken by a political figure.

That was the point of Kennedy's analysis of the crucial moment in the lives of eight American politicians, mostly senators. "It may take courage to battle one's President, one's party or the overwhelming sentiment of one's nation; but these do not compare, it seems to me, to the courage required of the Senator defying the angry power of the very constituents who control his future."

This particular point was flung back at Kennedy, who had remained silent on McCARTHYISM, by Mrs. Eleanor Roosevelt: "I feel that I would hesitate to place the difficult decisions that the next president will have to make with someone who understands what courage is and admires it, but has not quite the independence to have it." After blasts like these, a friend suggested to Kennedy that he had paid a price for giving his book that title. "Yes," he replied dryly, "but I didn't have a chapter in it on myself."

See POLITICAL SUICIDE.

progressive a movement of social protest and economic reforms; a word now offering an alternative to those who do not wish to be labeled LIBERAL.

The late nineteenth century brought the first great progressive surge to the U.S. Russell B. Nye wrote in *Midwestern Progressive Politics*:

Spreading outward after 1870, diminishing in force as it encountered increased resistance from adjacent and politically different areas, the so-called Midwestern spirit of "progressivism"

(or "insurgency" or "radicalism") became a real force in American political life. The Grangers, the Populists, the "progressives," the "insurgents," the Non-Partisan Leaguers, even the Socialists represented phases of this movement.

Progressivism reached high tide in the first decade of the twentieth century. The "Wisconsin idea," a progressive experiment, bore fruit in Robert La Follette's governorship at the beginning of the century. In 1912 the GOP split into progressive and conservative factions, with Theodore Roosevelt leading the progressives. The split is still reflected in divergent wings of the party.

The word retains its attraction. For a time during and after World War II, it was pre-empted by the far-left followers of Henry Wallace, but its frequent use by Republicans—especially in the Theodore Roosevelt context—has restored its luster. In 1948, in an essay titled "What Is Liberalism?," Earl Warren, then governor of California and later Chief Justice of the Supreme Court, wrote:

I would divide people into three groups—reactionary, progressive and radical. I particularly like the term "progressive," not necessarily as a party label, but as a conception. To me it represents true liberalism and the best attitude that we could possibly have in American life. It is distinguishable from both reaction and radicalism, because neither of these philosophies makes for real progress. The reactionary, concerned only with his own position, and indifferent to the welfare of others, would resist progress regardless of changed conditions or human need. The radical does not want to see progress because he hopes that our democratic institutions will fail and that he will be able to take over with some form of alien tyranny.

Similarly, President Lyndon Johnson, in a March 16, 1964, interview, said, "I want to be progressive without getting both feet off the ground at the same time. . . . If I had to place a label on myself, I would want to be a progressive who is prudent." Housing and Urban Development Secretary George Romney had said on several occasions: "I'm as conservative as the Constitution, as liberal as Lincoln and as progressive as Theodore Roosevelt."

Gary Hart in 1993 described the position of "progressive" as at "a point not on, but above, the liberal-conservative spectrum."

proletariat   the lowest class in society; or, the industrial working class.

From the Latin *proletarius*, a member of the lowest class in Roman society, the word entered the English language in the mid-seventeenth century.

Karl Marx defined "proletariat" in a critique of Hegel's *Philosophy of Right*:

> It is not the naturally arising poor but the artificially impoverished, not the human masses mechanically oppressed by the gravity of society but the masses resulting from the drastic dissolution of society, mainly of the middle estate, that form the proletariat, although, as is easily understood, the naturally arising poor and the Germanic serfs gradually join its ranks.

Marx's solution to proletarian poverty was never more forthrightly stated than as the conclusion of his *Communist Manifesto*: "The proletarians have nothing to lose but their chains. They have a world to win. Workingmen of all countries, unite!" (The last line is often more excitingly translated: "Workers of the world, unite!") More specifically, Friedrich Engels, in a letter to a friend in 1875, spelled out the steps by which the proletariat could gain power: "The organization of the working class as a class by means of the trade unions . . . is the very essential point, for this is the

real class organization of the proletariat, in which it carries on its daily struggle with capital, in which it trains itself."

Communist dogma, of course, holds that "the dictatorship of the proletariat" lies just beyond bourgeois rule. Returning to Russia in 1917 to prepare for the Bolshevik takeover, Lenin wrote:

> The peculiarity of the present moment in Russia consists in the transition from the first stage of the Revolution, which gave power to the bourgeoisie because of the insufficient class-consciousness and organization of the proletariat, to the second stage, which must give power to the proletariat, and the poorer peasantry.

Joseph Stalin described proletarian rule in hard terms: "The dictatorship of the proletariat is the domination of the proletariat over the bourgeoisie, untrammeled by law and based on violence and enjoying the sympathy and support of the toiling and exploited masses."

Walter Lippmann, in a column called "How Liberty is Lost," urged the West in 1938 to avoid creating the conditions for a revolution in the name of the proletariat.

> The greatest evil of the modern world is the reduction of the people to a proletarian level by destroying their savings, by depriving them of private property, by making them the helpless employees of a private monopoly or of government monopoly. Unless the means of independence are widely distributed among the people themselves, no real resistance is possible to the advance of tyranny. The experience of Europe shows clearly that when a nation becomes proletarian, the result is not, as the Communists taught, a dictatorship by the proletariat but a dictatorship over the proletariat.

Lumpenproletariat, a German word dressing the lowest class in rags, is occasionally used for emphasis or out of affectation. *Proletarian* is often clipped to *prole*.

See UNDERCLASS.

promises. See CAMPAIGN ORATORY; PIE IN THE SKY.

propaganda   attack word on an adversary's ideas and publicity techniques.

Your side *disseminates information, deals with the issues, communicates the facts, publicizes the truth, gets the message to the people*; the other side engages in PSEUDO-EVENTS, *puffery, deliberate distortion, the* BIG LIE, SMOKE SCREENS, *media hype* and *propaganda*.

In two centuries, the word has traveled from religion to war to politics. The ninth edition of the *Encyclopaedia Britannica* (1875) has an archbishop covering the subject, pointing out its derivation in Pope Gregory XIII's commission of cardinals *de propaganda fide* in the sixteenth century, and Pope Urban VIII's *collegium de propaganda* set up in 1627 to train missionaries. In *Britannica*'s fourteenth edition (1929), the article is concerned with war propaganda; in the current edition, the essay is contributed by political scientist Harold Lasswell.

Senator Daniel Webster, speaking about a revolution in Greece in 1824, helped the word enter the political vocabulary in its adjectival form, as the "emanation of a crusading or propagandist spirit." President Millard Fillmore said in 1852 that the Founding Fathers knew that "it was not possible for this nation to become a 'propagandist' of free principles without arraying against it the combined powers of Europe."

The religious usage became limited in the nineteenth century, replaced by the political. An English magazine in 1844 wrote that "we did not fight to propagandize monarchical principles," and an 1843 dictionary of science, literature, and art by W. T. Brande gave a definition that is quite current: "Derived from this celebrated society [for the propagation of the faith] the name *propaganda* is applied in modern political language as a term of reproach to secret associations for the spread of opinions and principles which are viewed by most governments with horror and aversion." The transmutation of the word from evangelism to sinister political persuasion is not surprising: the word continues to carry its meaning of persuasion by faith rather than by fact. The sinister connotation was emphasized by books on war propaganda after World War I, with titles like *Falsehood in War-Time, Atrocity Propaganda 1914–1918*, and *Spreading Germs of Hate*.

Nazi Minister of Propaganda Paul Joseph Goebbels, however, raised the word and the art to an instrument of national policy and blackened its name forever. In 1923, he said, "It is the absolute right of the State to supervise the formation of public opinion," and in 1943 wrote in his diary: "Not every item of news should be published: rather must those who control news policies endeavor to make every item of news serve a certain purpose." See MANAGED NEWS.

In the U.S., "white propaganda" meant the selection of favorable items for persuasion, and "black propaganda" (jokingly called "impropaganda") the spreading of lies and false rumors. To dissociate our techniques from those of the Nazis, "psychological warfare" was a useful term. Publicist Leo J. Margolin added "paper bullets" in a book title, a phrase from Shakespeare's *Much Ado About Nothing*. A tried-and-untrue technique of black propaganda is *disinformation*, or misinformation which is deliberately spread. CIA operatives were especially proud of the way disinformation—untrue statements inserted into the text of Nikita Khrushchev's "secret speech" and leaked by U.S. agents—embarrassed Soviet propagandists.

Despite occasional efforts to insist the word is neutral, that there is "good" propaganda, current usage is definitely pejorative. Charges of "Communist propaganda" and "imperialist propaganda" are traded, making this word (because of its Latin root and bad connotation) one of the few that mean the same to both Communists and anti-Communists. Sociologist Erwin W. Fellows wrote in 1959 that some of the wartime sting has come out of the word. "The recent shift to a less unfavorable attitude probably reflects . . . increased public recognition and acceptance of the use of powerful channels of communication by special interest groups . . . an increasing awareness of the techniques used to influence opinion and an indifference toward the content communicated."

While all this has been going on, the Society for the Propagation of the Faith continues its work, and visitors to St. Peter's in Rome continue to stroll up the *via Propaganda*.

prophets of gloom and doom. See GLOOM AND DOOM, PROPHETS OF.

protest vote a ballot cast for a candidate who stands no chance of winning, registering dissatisfaction with the other candidates.

Eugene Debs, who served a term in jail for his opposition to World War I, polled 920,000 votes on the Socialist ticket in 1920. At least half of these were non-Socialists who "threw their vote away" on Debs; they were disillusioned with Wilson but were unwilling to vote Republican. See DON'T WASTE YOUR VOTE.

"Vote 'No' for President" was a button worn during the 1964 and 1972 campaigns. A voter unhappy with the choice in the TWO-PARTY SYSTEM has three choices: to pick the lesser of the two evils, to stay home, or to cast a protest vote. Whenever there is a third candidate in the field, he is likely to rate higher in public-opinion polls than his final vote reflects. This is because most voters talk protest during a campaign, but when it comes to the final moment in the voting booth, revert to party or choose the man with a chance whom they dislike least.

Protest voting reached its apogee in 1992 as third-party candidate Ross Perot, running against two-party GRIDLOCK, won nearly 20 percent of the popular vote.

proverbs and axioms, political

GO FIGHT CITY HALL (resigned version); *You can't fight City Hall* (helpless version).

YOU CAN'T BEAT SOMEBODY WITH NOBODY.

You scratch my back, I'll scratch yours. Attributed to Pennsylvania politician Simon Cameron, Lincoln's first War Secretary.

When the water reaches the upper deck, follow the rats. Attributed to FDR's Secretary of the Navy Claude Swanson.

To the victor belong the spoils of the enemy. William Marcy. See SPOILS SYSTEM.

Few die and none resign. Thomas Jefferson.

ROOT, HOG, OR DIE.

THE JOB SEEKS THE MAN.

In politics a man must learn to rise above principle. No attribution found for this, or its more recent version: *We'll double-cross that bridge when we come to it.*

IF YOU CAN'T STAND THE HEAT, *get out of the kitchen.* A favorite of Harry Truman.

Never murder a man who is committing suicide. Woodrow Wilson. See PO-LITICAL SUICIDE.

Nobody shoots at Santa Claus. Al Smith. See SANTA CLAUS, NOBODY SHOOTS AT.

I don't care what the papers say about me as long as they spell my name right. Attributed to Tammany leader "Big Tim" Sullivan.

If you don't go to other people's funerals, they won't go to yours. (Put positively, this delightful proverb suggests that if you do go to other people's funerals, they will attend yours—as ghosts, presumably. No known attribution—probably some ghostwriter.)

If you have an elephant on a string, and the elephant starts to run—better let him run. Attributed to Lincoln.

Forgive but never forget. Attributed to John F. Kennedy by Ted Sorensen in a 1968 television interview.

If it walks like a duck, and quacks like a duck, then it just may be a duck. (On how to tell a Communist, attributed to labor leader Walter Reuther. Among many variations of this phrase is a 1993 use in *Variety*: "What smells like a skunk and looks like a skunk. . . .")

Any party which takes credit for the rain must not be surprised if its opponents blame it for the drought. Dwight Morrow.

Ticker tape isn't spaghetti. Fiorello La Guardia.

Never hold discussions with the monkey when the organ grinder is in the room. Attributed to Winston Churchill, replying to a query from the British ambassador in Rome as to whether he should raise a question with Mussolini or Count Ciano, his Foreign Minister.

Don't roll up your pants legs before you get to the stream. Congressman Emanuel Celler (D-N.Y.).

You can't make a soufflé rise twice. Alice Roosevelt Longworth, on Thomas E. Dewey's second presidential campaign.

No man ever went broke underestimating the intelligence of the American voter. H. L. Mencken.

How you stand depends on where you sit. Attributed to former Bureau of the Budget employee Rufus E. Miles, by University of Chicago professor Arnold Weber.

When the going gets tough, the tough get going. Attributed to John Mitchell by Jeb Magruder during the Watergate hearings; earlier attribution to Joseph P. Kennedy. This has been satirized on T-shirts by substituting *go shopping* for the final *get going.*

You can get a lot more done with a kind word and a gun, than with a kind word alone. Gangster Al Capone, quoted jocularly by economist Walter Heller, in connection with wage and price controls.

IF IT AIN'T BROKE, DON'T FIX IT.

Every man has his price. From a comment made in the House of Commons in 1734 by Sir Robert Walpole: "I know the price of every man in this House . . ."

Don't just do something, stand there! An objection to government meddling; used in a speech in 1970 by Labor Secretary George Shultz.

Speak softly and always carry a big stick. The saying is always identified with Theodore Roosevelt, but he attributed it in this manner: "I have always been fond of the West African proverb . . ."

Watch what we do, not what we say. Attorney General John Mitchell.

Whenever you have to start explaining—you're in trouble. Barber Conable (R-N.Y.).

The duty of an Opposition is to oppose. Attributed by Lord Derby to a Whig named Tierney. See DISH THE WHIGS.

A fish rots from the head first. Democratic Presidential candidate Michael Dukakis in 1988, quoting an old Greek saying in attacking ethical standards in the Reagan Administration.

Don't get mad. Don't get even. Just get elected. THEN get even. Clinton's political strategist James Carville (for more Carville wisdom, see IT'S THE ECONOMY, STUPID!).

The basic maxim of democracy should always be: Turn the rascals out. Arthur Schlesinger, Jr., attributes this saying to Charles A. Dana in 1872.

If you want a friend in Washington, buy a dog. Attributed (falsely) to Harry Truman.

Show me a good loser, and I'll show you a loser. Attributed to Knute Rockne, the Notre Dame football coach.

The dogs may bark, but the caravan moves on forever. Middle East adage cited by publisher Mortimer Zuckerman.

proxy war great-power hostility expressed through client states.

"The first case of a proxy war between China and the Soviet Union," was the way National Security Adviser Zbigniew Brzezinski described the fighting between Vietnam and Cambodia that resulted in a break of relations on New Year's Eve of 1978. He cautioned that the two nations had a tradition of enmity, "but the larger international dimension of the conflict speaks for itself."

Cambodian Communists had the support of the People's Republic of China, while the Soviet Union supported Vietnam. Tass, the official Soviet news agency, wanted no part of a "proxy war" and charged Mr. Carter's aide with trying to "palm off the desired as reality" and attempting to "whip up animosity between the peoples of China and the Soviet Union."

During the 1980s, the rebel war in Afghanistan against Soviet-based government forces was thought by many to be a proxy war between the United States and the Soviet Union.

The phrase is probably rooted in "proxy fight": attempt to get control of a corporate management through a contest for stockholders' proxy votes. Its first political citations are in 1955, taken to mean "localized conflict," then synonymous with "brush-fire war"—meaning a war that was likely to spread quickly unless put out.

psephology the study of elections and voting behavior.

In their 1970 book, *The Real Majority: An Extraordinary Examination of the American Electorate*, Richard M. Scammon and Ben J. Wattenberg popularized the 1952 word and provided the derivation: "from the Greek *psephos*, or pebble. The derivation comes from the ancient Greek custom of voting by dropping colored pebbles into the equivalent of our ballot box."

The authors had a significant impact on the 1970 congressional elections with their argument that "the social issue" was becoming decisive—that voters were most concerned with unrest, alienation, drugs, crime, and changing morality rather than the traditional bread-and-butter issue. Candidates of both parties made much of the social issue, and not until late in the campaign did Democrats take advantage of the economic issue, which Republicans had feared most all along.

On Cable News Network in 1992, Ben Wattenberg explained further: "The non-economic aspect of our politics has been around in our politics for about 25 years, the so-called social issue. . . . Some of the words associated with it are *drugs, riots, quotas, crime in the street, law and order, draft-dodging, flags, buy America first, patriotism, prayer in the school, capital punishment, gay rights, abortion, Mur-*

phy Brown, out-of-wedlock birth, sexual revolution, et cetera."

The Greek pebble-dropping provides the root for a more familiar political word. The Greek *ballein* means "to throw" and is the origin of both "bullet" and "ballot."

An early use of *psephology* was by writer Michael Demarest in the 1964 election issue of *Time;* an Oxford English Dictionary citation from 1952 credits its coinage to R. B. McCallum, a British pioneer in this field of study.

pseudo-event   contrived news; a happening that is made to take place for the purpose of the coverage it will get, or centered on people famous for being well known.

The phrase is historian Daniel Boorstin's, coined in his 1962 book *The Image; or, What Happened to the American Dream?* Boorstin, who later became Librarian of Congress, held that American life has become unreal, based on illusion and images, with heroes replaced by celebrities. The manufactured "event"—a headquarters opening, a press conference for the dissemination of nothing much, a staged picture of a ribbon-cutting or "topping out" ceremony—have taken the place of much real news, designed to manipulate and promote rather than inform. As Boorstin puts it, a pseudo-event "is not a train wreck or an earthquake, but an interview."

The predecessor phrase was "pseudo-statement" used by I. A. Richards in his 1926 *Science and Poetry*: "A pseudo-statement is a form of words which is justified entirely by its effect in releasing or organizing our impulses and attitudes . . . a statement, on the other hand, is justified by its truth."

Reporter Richard Rovere described Senator Joseph McCarthy's skillful use of the press:

He knew how to get into the news even on those rare occasions when in-

vention failed him and he had no un-facts to give out. For example, he invented the morning press conference called for the purpose of announcing an afternoon press conference. . . . This would gain him a headline in the afternoon papers: "New McCarthy Revelations Awaited in Capital." Afternoon would come, and if McCarthy had something, he would give it out, but often enough he had nothing, he wasn't quite ready, that he was having difficulty in getting some of the "documents" he needed or that a "witness" was proving elusive. Morning headlines: "Delay Seen in McCarthy Case—Mystery Witness Being Sought."

Why are Americans prone to a diet of pseudo-events? Because, wrote Boorstin, "Pseudo-events are more sociable. . . . Their occurrence is planned for our convenience."

Boston University political scientist Murray B. Levin, in an analysis of the Edward Kennedy–Edward McCormack Massachusetts Democratic senatorial primary in 1962, suggested that "Edward Kennedy's rise to power and subsequent political stardom, and that of many other candidates, was based partly on . . . Kennedy's ability to pay for the services of men expert in the business of creating and selling pseudo-events."

The concept of the pseudo-event overdramatizes the degree of successful manipulation in American commercial and political affairs; a surprising and newsworthy position taken in an interview is not rendered counterfeit by the fact that it was arranged for maximum coverage. But the idea and the phrase are helpful in both planning for and watching out for "pseudo-events."

In the 1972 campaign for the Democratic presidential nomination, several candidates announced their intention to formally announce their candidacy at a later time. That ploy qualified as a pseudo-event.

The phrase is being replaced by MEDIA EVENT.

public interest, convenience and necessity phrase binding the broadcasting industry to a degree of public-service programming, as they act as licensees of the public airwaves. The phrase has traveled a long legal road. The Federal Communications Commission informs the author that "Picon's" predecessor can be found in the Interstate Commerce Act of 1887, as "public convenience and necessity." Before that, in 1876, in *Munn* v. *Illinois*, 94 U.S. 113, the Supreme Court permitted regulation of prices in a "business affected with a public interest." A new word was slipped into the phrase in the Radio Act of 1927, Public Law 632: "Public convenience, interest or necessity." In 1934, when the Communications Act was passed, an unknown legislator apparently felt that "public convenience" sounded too much like a toilet, and switched the words around to their present "public interest, convenience and necessity."

Speaking to a group of broadcasters while he was still a senator, John F. Kennedy said:

> Will the politician's desire for reelection—and the broadcaster's desire for rating—cause both to flatter every public whim and prejudice—to seek the lowest common denominator of appeal—to put public opinion at all times ahead of the public interest? For myself, I reject that view of politics, and I urge you to reject that view of broadcasting.

In current usage, "public interest" has become a useful antonym to VESTED INTEREST and "special, selfish interest." Franklin Roosevelt used it in his 1936 annual message to Congress, appealing from "the clamor of many private and selfish interests, yes, an appeal from the clamor of partisan interest, to the ideal of the public interest."

The phrase can be traced back at least two centuries to England's Lord Chief Justice Hale's treatise on private property: when "affected with a public interest, it ceases to be *juris privati* only."

Who determines the public interest? Often the "public" member of a board or commission, who serves with an industry member and perhaps a labor member. But the public, writes sociologist C. Wright Mills, "consists of the unidentified and the nonpartisan in a world of defined and partisan interests. . . . What the 'public' stands for, accordingly, is often a vagueness of policy (called 'open-mindedness'), a lack of involvement in public affairs (known as 'reasonableness') and a professional disinterest (known as 'tolerance')."

public office is a public trust phrase popularized by Grover Cleveland, used today in charges of graft or calls for codes of ethics for public officials.

"When a man assumes a public trust," Thomas Jefferson remarked to Baron von Humboldt in 1807, "he should consider himself as public property."

A variety of public men and writers began to mold this into a useful phrase. Henry Clay in 1829: "Government is a trust, and the officers of the government are trustees; and both the trust and the trustees are created for the benefit of the people."

Senator John C. Calhoun, in 1835, began a paragraph: "So long as offices were considered as public trusts, to be conferred on the honest, the faithful, and capable, for the common good, and not for the benefit or gain of the incumbent or his party . . ." By 1872 Senator Charles Sumner was observing, "The phrase, 'public office is a public trust' has of late become common property."

The Democratic national platform in 1876 muddied up the phrase as follows: "Presidents, vice-presidents, judges, senators, representatives, cabinet officers—these and all others in authority are the people's servants. Their offices are not a private prequisite; they are a public trust."

W. C. Hudson, a newsman working for Grover Cleveland in the campaign of 1884, was looking for a phrase to embody integrity in government. He recalled the 1876 platform statement, and found in previous Cleveland speeches statements like "Public officials are the trustees of the people" and "We are the trustees and agents of our fellow citizens, holding their funds in sacred trust." Hudson felt all this provided the basis for a slogan and wrote later:

> I went at the making of one. . . . Public Office is a Public Trust was the result. . . . It was the dogmatic form of what he had expressed with greater elucidation. . . . I took it to the Governor for his inspection. His eye at once went to the top line and pointing to it, he asked:
>
> "Where the deuce did I say that?"
>
> "You've said it a dozen times publicly, but not in those few words," I replied.
>
> "That's so," he said. "That's what I believe. That's what I've said a little better because more fully."
>
> "But this has the merit of brevity," I persisted, "and that is what is required here. The question is, Will you stand for this form?"
>
> "Oh, yes," replied the Governor. "That's what I believe. I'll stand for it and make it my own."

Hudson later learned that the slogan had predated his coinage but insisted he had never been aware of an earlier use when he showed it to Cleveland. The phrase was accepted and used by everyone except Cleveland; as his biographer, Robert McElroy, pointed out: ". . . throughout the campaign, and throughout the remainder of his life, Grover Cleveland continued to express this, his most cherished conviction, not in the words of Hudson's brilliant slogan, but in ponderous

phrases of his own which he persisted in considering better because longer."

Campaigning against Herbert Hoover in 1932, Franklin D. Roosevelt gave the phrase a twist: "Private economic power . . . is a public trust." Adlai Stevenson, in 1952, extended the idea of public office to those (like his opponent, General Eisenhower) who hold public confidence: "A man who has the confidence of the public has a public trust not to abuse that confidence for any ends, let alone his own."

public trough, feeding at the

the practice of politicians and their hangers-on of fattening themselves on public funds; in current jocular use.

The phrase has Biblical roots, recalling how the Prodigal Son, at his nadir, ate from a trough with the swine. *Emporia Gazette* editor William Allen White referred to the story when, in the 1920s he rejected a friend's suggestion that he write a biography of Warren G. Harding. "It isn't Harding's story," said White of the late President and the scandal that followed his death, "it is the story of his times, the story of the Prodigal Son, our democracy that turned away from the things of the spirit, got its share of the patrimony ruthlessly, and went out and lived riotously and ended it by feeding among the swine."

An article in the *New York Tribune*, in 1881, noted that "the Republican Party is tired of bossism, quarrels about patronage, slavery to the machine, and the statesmanship of the feed trough." The word "troughman" was also used to describe a politician who spoons funds from government treasuries—that is, from the public trough. *The Nation*, in 1904, said grafters included "a number of lesser persons spoken of as 'troughsmen.' These used to be called 'henchmen,' then 'heelers,' but the newer word may be accepted without cavil."

A variation of the trough is the "public crib." In his *Thirty Years' View*, Senator Thomas Hart Benton wrote: "They have no other view than to get one elected who will enable them to eat out of the public crib." Still another variation, though one less redolent of corruption and the spoils system, is "public teat." Here the image is warmer, connoting a more paternalistic—or maternalistic—government.

Today the phrase is used less by critics than by politicians in a spirit of camaraderie. Perhaps this is because the image of a hog hungrily munching his garbage or a piglet rooting at its mother is too strong for criticism, crossing over into an area of mild irony. A politician often greets a friend who has just been elected or reappointed with "Still on the public teat?"

pull-aside a mini-démarche; planned but low-key diplomatic approach.

This snippet of diplolingo does not yet have a printed citation but was drawn to the attention of the author in 1993 by Clifford Wharton, Deputy Secretary of State. When, in conversation, Mr. Wharton said of a contact with a foreign counterpart, "It was just a pull-aside," he then defined the term as "a contact made at a reception or similar informal gathering for a specific diplomatic purpose."

This verb-based noun, coined on the analogy of *drop-by* (a brief appearance by a political figure to show respect but not commitment), is more calculated than a chance meeting, less formal than an approach. A *pull-aside* is usually but not always planned; its utility lies in its apparent spontaneity, requiring no advance notification of the other side, and it is begun with taking the target diplomat's arm and saying something like, "Step over here where we can talk."

pump-priming using federal funds to stimulate the economy, usually during a recession or depression.

In the *OED*, to prime a pump is defined as "to pour water down the tube with the view of saturating the sucker, so causing it to swell, and act effectually in bringing up water." The phrase became popular during Franklin Roosevelt's presidency, when vast expenditures for the Public Works and Works Progress Administrations were characterized as pump-priming. "Most revolutionary of all," wrote Charles Hurd in *When the New Deal Was Young and Gay*, "was the theory that when business slackens, the government should spend money—even if it has to go into debt—to 'prime the pump' of the economy." During the 1937–38 recession, FDR said: "The things we had done, which at that time were largely a monetary and pump-priming policy for two years and a half, had brought the expected result, perfectly definitely." He blamed the recession on a drop in pump-priming caused by congressional economizers and the Supreme Court's nullification of several of his agencies.

Norio Ohga, the president of the Sony Corporation, mixed the term with another metaphor in discussing diminished profits in 1992: "You can call the present slowdown a recession. Without pump-priming measures, the economy might plunge into a negative spiral."

Pump-priming, its critics point out, can be overdone. As a May 1722 edition of the New England *Courant* pointed out: "No covetous person will use more Water to fetch the Pump than he designs to pump out again."

The phrase is punnable. In June 1978 a *New York Times* editorial commenting on the plan of President Carter's media adviser, Gerald Rafshoon, to restore some of the imperial trappings to the presidency, was headlined: "Priming the Pomp."

See TRICKLE-DOWN THEORY.

pundit a political analyst, usually associated with a prestigious newspaper or broadcasting network; a harmless noodge.

A *New York Times* editorial of 1921 admired the writing style of President Warren G. Harding: "[He] is not writing for the superfine weighers of verbs and adjectives, but for the men and women who see in his expressions their own ideas, and are truly happy to meet them . . . [it] is a good style, let the pundits rage about it as they will."

In his column about the press in the *Village Voice*, Alexander Cockburn wrote in June 1976: "The use of the word 'governance,' incidentally, is the sure mark of a pundit; the other favored word is 'polity.'"

Mark Cocker, in his 1993 book, *Loneliness and Time: The Story of British Travel Writing*, wrote of the term's historical usage in espionage:

> From the 1860's onwards British intelligence officers had used another strategy to fill some of the political and geographical blanks on the map of their northern borders. Agents, drawn from the Himalayan communities under Indian control and resembling Tibetans in appearance, crossed the mountains disguised as pilgrims. These Asian spies, known collectively as the Pundits, were able to travel extensively in trans-Himalayan regions, even as far as Mongolia, and brought back an enormous quantity of intelligence. The Pundits' work involved enormous risks.

The word lends itself to spoofing, since its first syllable is about word play. *Time* in the fall of 1977 headed an article about a conservative, pun-loving columnist: "Punder on the Right."

The word comes from the Hindi phrase for "learned man." A group of Yale undergraduates founded a club called the Pundits, sponsored by William Lyon Phelps. When Yaleman Henry R. Luce started *Time*, he recalled the term and began applying it, as a courtesy title, to playwright Thornton Wilder and columnist Walter Lippmann.

Today the term is widely applied to almost any member of the media once encompassed in Eisenhower's "sensation-seeking columnists and commentators." The *Washington Post* wrote in 1992 of "the real heavyweights—the pundits, the network stars, the interpreters and analyzers of political tea leaves." In 1988 Eric Alterman coined *punditocracy*.

Also to the American discourse contributed *Time: tycoon, moppet, socialite, cinemactor,* and *adman,* as well as the weird, backward construction of this sentence.

punt and pray. See SPORTS METAPHORS.

puppet (government) a nation or individual controlled by another; a SATELLITE.

Just before the off-year elections of 1966, Defense Secretary Robert McNamara went to the LBJ Ranch in Texas to appear at a press conference with President Johnson. After he made an optimistic report on the progress of the war in Vietnam, Richard Nixon said he had demeaned his office and called him a "Charlie McCarthy," referring to the dummy created by ventriloquist Edgar Bergen which was popular in the heyday of radio (the late thirties, early forties). When General William Westmoreland visited the U.S. in 1967 to enlist support for a long, hard war, Senator George McGovern (D-S.D.)—in a speech calling for an end to escalation—said the general "is obviously doing both in Vietnam or in New York exactly what he is told to do by his commander in chief, the President." Senator Spessard Holland (D-Fla.) rose to say he did not think that "General Westmoreland is a Charlie McCarthy to come over here and tell the people of this country what someone else wants them to hear."

Puppetry is a deep-rooted political metaphor. Political satire was part of the *Punch and Judy* shows of the seventeenth century in England; *Punch*, a satiric British magazine first published in 1841, got its name from the lead character; and "pleased as Punch" comes from the self-satisfaction Punch received from his mischief.

In 1670 Baruch Spinoza used the metaphor in his *Writings on Political Philosophy*: ". . . the object of government is not to change men from rational beings into beasts or puppets, but to enable them to develop their minds and bodies in security, and to employ their reason unshackled . . ." John Adams, in 1775, warned of American subjugation in which "we should be little better than puppets, danced on the wires of the cabinets of Europe."

"Puppet government" achieved its popularity in World War II, when conquering Nazi forces set up local civilian regimes (see QUISLING); however, when Communist-dominated regimes were set up in Eastern Europe after the war, they were mainly referred to as "satellites" and only rarely as puppets.

During the Cold War, *puppet* was frequently used by Communist speakers to refer to small nations supporting the Western position. However, domination of small states is not so easy as it seems. According to McGeorge Bundy, former Kennedy and Johnson national security aide, "Anyone who thinks that the lines of influence from Washington are like so many strings to so many puppets has never sat at the pulling end."

A synonym for *puppet*, with a more contemptuous connotation, is *stooge*.

purge to forcibly eliminate opposition within a party; to retaliate for party irregularity.

The word entered the political vocabulary early: "Pride's Purge" in 1648 was the ejection of ninety-six Presbyterian Members of Parliament by Colonel Thomas Pride in the Cromwell era. In modern history, the term is most often associated with the bloody crackdowns of the Communists. As Thomas Dewey said in his 1950 lectures at Princeton: "In the Soviet Union and its satellites today the purge is both the instrument of change and the means of securing the leadership in undisputed control."

When leaders get the urge to purge, the NIGHT OF THE LONG KNIVES is recalled: on the weekend of June 29 to July 2, 1934, Adolf Hitler and Heinrich Himmler's Black Shirts pounced on eighty-three followers of Ernst Röhm's Brown Shirts and killed them all, establishing Hitler's complete control of the Nazi movement.

The bloodless purge, however, has also been used as an instrument of party politics in the U.S. In 1870, after the Senate defeated President Grant's attempted annexation of Santo Domingo, a party-wide purge followed. "Grant showed vindictive traits," wrote Matthew Josephson in *The Politicos*, and there was much "cutting off of political heads." One victim was Carl Schurz, the transplanted German liberal who had fled to the U.S. after the abortive 1848 Revolution and later became a U.S. senator from Missouri. After refusing to back Grant on the annexation, Schurz found the White House door closed to him and complained to a friend: "Grant has read me out of the Republican Party." See READ OUT OF THE PARTY.

In the 1938 midterm election, Franklin Roosevelt tried to purge those congressmen who consistently torpedoed his programs—particularly three Democratic senators. All three won reelection.

Dwight Eisenhower on several occasions resisted the urge to purge. When Senator Ralph Flanders of Vermont launched his censure effort against Senator Joseph McCarthy, for example, Republican Majority Leader William Knowland resisted and indirectly warned Ike against trying to punish him for it. As Ike wrote in *Mandate for Change*: "Sensing my sympathy with Senator Flanders' action, he [Knowland] cited President Franklin Roosevelt's efforts to 'purge' Senators he did not like. I told him that I would not be trapped into any purging action . . ."

pushing the envelope reaching beyond boundaries; stretching or exceeding the known limits.

This phrase pushed its way into aeronautical literature in the July 3, 1978, issue of *Aviation Week & Space Technology*. An aircraft designed for sea-level operation was being tested for higher flight: "The aircraft's altitude envelope must be expanded to permit a ferry flight across the nation. NASA pilots were to push the envelope to 10,000 feet."

Tom Wolfe popularized the term in 1979 in *The Right Stuff*, a book about astronauts. Wolfe wrote: "The 'envelope' was a flight-test term referring to the limits of a particular aircraft's performance, how tight a turn it could make at such-and-such a speed, and so on. 'Pushing the outside,' probing the outer limits, of the envelope seemed to be the great challenge and satisfaction of flight test."

In 1988, Tom Wolfe told the lexicographer: "I first heard it in 1972, among test pilots who later became astronauts. They were speaking of the performance capabilities of an airplane as

an envelope, as if there were a boundary. Why they chose *envelope*, I don't know, but if you get outside the envelope, you're in trouble." His conjecture is that the test-pilot use started at the Patuxent River Naval Air Station in Maryland during the 1940s.

Envelope, however, is a much older noun in math and science. Alexander H. Flax of the National Academy of Engineering wrote: "Usage of the term *envelope* in science and engineering goes back at least to the mid-19th century. In mathematics the envelope is the outer boundary of a related family of curves." He enclosed a page from a 1904 textbook on mathematical analysis that uses the term.

As early as 1901, the aeronautical noun *envelope* was in use to mean "the gas or air container of a balloon or airship." *Scientific American* explained in 1901: "The balloon is inflated with hydrogen, and in order to maintain at all times a tension on the envelope—that is to say, perfect inflation—a compensating balloon filled with air is placed in the interior." The *Journal of the Royal Aeronautics Society* in 1944 extended the sense of a balloon's inflation to indicate optimum performance of any aircraft: "Tests at other heights can then be confined to what are termed 'envelope' conditions; that is, the engine conditions which will give the maximum economy at any given speed."

The *Dictionary of Military Terms* stretches the noun's definition further: "The three-dimensional space that is within range, altitude and deflection reach of a weapon, particularly an air defense weapon." This term, related to the French verb *envelopper* ("to wrap completely"), has been Anglicized in pronunciation to EN-ve-lope. The verb *push*, as in "you're pushing it," extends the sense of *envelope conditions* to suggest moving beyond current limits into untested areas.

The full phrase *pushing the envelope* is used widely, describing daring activity from politics to stand-up comedy, but the space use continues. In *U.S. News & World Report* in 1986, William Broyles, Jr., wrote of Christa McAuliffe, of the doomed space shuttle *Challenger* crew, as "pushing out the envelope of the planet."

pussyfooting   sidestepping an issue; being mealy-mouthed; not treading where angels fear to tread.

This was a sobriquet of W. E. "Pussyfoot" Johnson, an ardent advocate of Prohibition, who was so named because of his stealthy, unrelenting, catlike approach to revenue-evaders in the Indian Territory. "Special Agent Johnson," wrote the *Muskogee* (Georgia) *Democrat* in 1907, "he of the 'Panther' tread, has resented the action of the peddlers of bogus beer and had them all indicted by the Grand Jury. It is evidently *lèse majesté* to sue a velvet-shod emissary of Uncle Sam's Booze Department."

The word probably began with a note of sneakiness: earliest noted reference was in *Scribner's* magazine of 1893, about men who "were beginning to walk pussy-footed and shy at shadows"; the *Atlanta Constitution* later spotted Theodore Roosevelt's Vice President, Charles Warren Fairbanks, "pussyfooting it around Washington."

Pussyfooting has lost its stealthy connotation and has acquired a meaning of evasion of hard issues. James Farley wrote in 1932: "We Democrats must meet the issue fairly, without any pussyfooting." Wendell Willkie in 1944: "I'm getting pretty sick of the pussyfooters who try to catch the WPA and the National Association of Manufacturers with the same kind of talk." In a speech written by Pat Buchanan, Vice President Spiro Agnew in 1970 denounced the "pusillanimous pussyfooters."

Pussyfoot today has a more cautious, fearful connotation than *straddle* or *on the fence*, works harder at evasion than *sidestep*, is less blatant than *to carry water on both shoulders*, is less investigative than *gumshoe*, and is not as Machiavellian as being ALL THINGS TO ALL MEN. See CREEP.

putsch   an attempted coup; a minor takeover effort that fails.

A *rebellion* is a *revolution* that failed; a *putsch* is a rebellion that was not considered a serious threat.

Adolf Hitler's Beer Hall Putsch took place on November 8, 1923, as the National Socialists, with General Ludendorff as a front, attempted to force the leaders of Bavaria to form a new government under Hitler. "The putsch," wrote William L. Shirer, "even though it was a fiasco, made Hitler a national figure and, in the eyes of many, a patriot and a hero. Nazi propaganda soon transformed it into one of the great legends of the movement." Hitler, tried for treason, was sentenced to five years, serving nine months during which he dictated *Mein Kampf* to Rudolf Hess.

Because of its Nazi association, *putsch* has often been used as an attack word on insurgents in any political situation. Though the French borrowing *coup* (from *coup d'état*, "sudden overthrow of a government by a small group") is more commonly used in English, *putsch* is the more specific term. Like *coup*, the German word means "blow or thrust"; *putsch*, however, adds a Nazi beer-hall connotation and suggests a failed attempt rather than a quick success.

In August 1991, the plot by Communist apparatchiks to reverse "the Second Russian Revolution" was described by the media as a "failed coup." Hard-liners at the Center for Security Policy reported "speculation that Gorbachev may not have been quite the innocent victim of the putsch," adding, "whether one buys the 'Potemkin coup' theory or not." That *coup* is named for Grigori Potemkin, Catherine II's adviser and lover, who supposedly built fake villages along the Dnieper River to fool the Empress about regional development. *Potemkin village* is still the term used for an imposing but phony facade intended to disguise a shabby condition. Use of *Potemkin* to mean "phony" also appears in "Potemkin coup" to speculate that Mikhail Gorbachev may have orchestrated his own victimization.

Sometimes *putsch* is used interchangeably with *coup*. The *Boston Globe* of April 27, 1993, used both words in one sentence: "The most eloquent example of this [Boris Yeltsin's indecisiveness] was his conduct after the putsch in August 1991, when, bathing in the glory of the coup's defeat, he could have dissolved the Congress and all other figments of the Communist regime—yet did not."

Among the puns to come out of the failed takeover in Moscow—which led to the triumph of Boris Yeltsin—was Leon Wieseltier's headline in *The New Republic*, "When Putsch Comes to Shove," along with the Washington lawyer Leonard Garment's description of the bungling family plotters as "the Coup Klutz Clan."

puzzle palace. See PENTAGONESE.

Quadriad a grouping of four of the President's leading economic advisers: the Chairman of the Council of Economic Advisers, the Secretary of the Treasury, the Director of the Office of Management and Budget, and the Chairman of the Federal Reserve Board.

"We originally called this assemblage 'the Fiscal and Financial Advisory Group,'" Walter Heller, former Chairman of the Council of Economic Advisers, informed the author, "but that was a cumbersome designation. I went to the unabridged Webster's in my office and turned to 'quar.' The word 'quartet' seemed prosaic, but then I came across 'quadriad' and was intrigued by the definition: 'a group of four—*rare*.' I suggested this in a note to President Kennedy, and the next time he saw me he said, 'You're a rare group, all right—we'll call it the Quadriad.'"

When the group meets without the Federal Reserve Chairman, it is called the TROIKA.

The designation is handy. On August 13, 1971, when President Nixon was discussing plans for a new economic policy at Camp David with a dozen advisers, he was able to cut the group down to decision-making size without offending anyone—including the speechwriter—by saying, "Now I want to meet with the Quadriad."

By 1983, additions to the Quadriad in the Reagan Administration increased the group to six members, but no change in name (Sextriad?) was contemplated. Nor was it renamed in 1985, as seen in the September 30 *U.S. News & World Report*: "The selection process begins with the 'Quadriad,' actually five top economic policymakers who meet once a week for breakfast."

In the Clinton Administration, the word went into eclipse as a National Economic Council was formed, which —when some of its members met with the independent Federal Reserve Chairman—performed the function of the Quadriad.

quagmire. See VIETNAM SYNDROME.

quality of life the pursuit of happiness unsullied by the drawbacks of modern life; excellence of environment, idealistically reaching beyond an improved standard of living.

The English novelist J. B. Priestley first used the phrase in print, writing in his 1943 *Daylight on Saturday* of "the plans already . . . maturing that would give all our citizens more security, better opportunities, and a nobler quality of life."

Democratic candidate Adlai Stevenson used the phrases "quality of life" and "quality of living" frequently in the campaign of 1956. His source was probably TV commentator Eric Sevareid, who answered this writer's query: "Long ago, I think in '56, I wrote a radio broadcast for a Sunday series we called 'Newsmakers' about the nature of Adlai Stevenson. I put in the phrase 'the quality of life' to try to describe his approach to the national condition as it differed from the stock New Deal approach which, it seemed to me, was pretty directly concerned with more quantities for every group. He read the script later, on an airplane trip; twice, in notes to me, he expressed gratitude for the phrase. He used it often in his speeches."

Stevenson, however, did not elevate the phrase to slogan status. Arthur Schlesinger, Jr., recognized its potential and did more than anyone to popularize it in the intellectual community. In 1955 he wrote a memorandum comparing the "quantitative liberalism of the thirties" to the necessary "qualitative liberalism" of the future, as the needs of people in a depression change in a time of affluence. This memo was published in the *Reporter* magazine in the spring of 1956.

When conservation and pollution, in the mid-sixties, suddenly became transfigured into "the environment" and a new political cause, the "quality of life" phrase was born again—this time to stress the other-than-material needs of the AFFLUENT SOCIETY.

The phrase is now an unassailable political cliché, indispensable to environmentalists, useful as shorthand for orators appealing to youthful voters turned off by promises of a higher standard of living. New York Traffic Commissioner Samuel I. Schwartz used the phrase as a hyphenated modifier in 1984: "As more and more citizens begin to demand a reduction in quality-of-life infractions—such as running red lights—you'll see a return to the time when police stringently enforced laws."

A related cliché is "life style," sociologese for "way of life." (Vice President Agnew castigated the drug culture as "a lifestyle that has neither life nor style.") That term was coined by psychologist Alfred Adler in 1929.

"Quality of life," so well established as a generalized national goal, is overdue for a turnaround, but proponents of zero population growth have yet to denounce "the quantity of life."

See ENVIRONMENTALIST.

quarantine euphemism for blockade, or one-sided embargo.

The health of the BODY POLITIC has long been a rich vein of metaphor for politicians. Jefferson talked of "the disease of liberty" and Lincoln of "the scourge of war."

In the fall of 1937 Franklin Roosevelt wanted to speak out against Hitler and Mussolini. Norman Davis of the State Department drafted a speech that included the phrase "war is contagion." Harold Ickes told Roosevelt that a neighborhood had a right to "quarantine" itself against threatened infection; according to the Interior Secretary, FDR jotted down the word and said he would use it sometime.

"When an epidemic of physical disease starts to spread," FDR said in Chicago, "the community approves and joins in a quarantine of the patients in order to protect the health of the community against the spread of the disease." How to stop this "epidemic of world lawlessness"? He ended on an ambivalent note: "We are adopting such measures as will minimize our risk of involvement, but we cannot have complete protection in a world of disorder . . ."

The next day, reporters led by Ernest K. Lindley (see "Lindley Rule," under NOT FOR ATTRIBUTION) tried to pin him down. How did a quarantine fit in with a policy of neutrality laid down by act of Congress? "I can't give you any clue to it," the President parried, "you will just have to invent one . . ." How about sanctions? "Sanctions is a terrible word. They are right out the window." Is a quarantine a sanction? "No. I said don't talk about sanctions." A reporter said, "This is no longer neutrality." Roosevelt replied, "On the contrary, it might be a stronger neutrality."

By the time John F. Kennedy was faced with the threat of Russian missiles installed in Cuba, the word "quarantine" was installed in the American political lexicon as a kind of stern but peaceful act risking dangerous involvement in a good cause.

Kennedy, according to Roger Hilsman, "again repeated his preference for a blockade and at this time supplied the word quarantine to describe it. This was a phrase with obvious political advantages both at home, where it was reminiscent of President Roosevelt's 'quarantining the aggressors' speech, and abroad, where it struck a less belligerent note than the word blockade."

Sanction, a word with opposite meanings, like OVERSIGHT and TABLE, is still used. The Washington Post reported in 1992: "In Germany, Chancellor Helmut Kohl told television interviewers that the West should escalate its sanctions against Serbia into a complete blockade to throttle the Serb military campaign in Bosnia."

quick and the dead, the the living contrasted with the dead; phrase used by ELDER STATESMAN Bernard Baruch to dramatically pose the choice of mankind in the atomic age.

"My fellow citizens of the world," said Bernard Baruch on June 14, 1946, to a UN meeting in New York's Hunter College gymnasium, "we are here to make a choice between the quick and the dead. . . . That is our business. Behind the black portent of the new atomic age lies a hope which, seized upon with faith, can work our salvation. . . . We must elect World Peace or World Destruction."

The Baruch Plan for an international authority of atomic inspection "with teeth in it" was bravely proposed, supported strongly by President Truman, but was met coldly by the Soviets and took some criticism from the U.S. Senate. It might, however, have begun some foundation-laying for a nuclear test-ban treaty that took place almost twenty years later.

The Baruch phrase might have been the work of his publicist and friend, Herbert Bayard Swope, who said it was; however, while Baruch freely admitted his "COLD WAR" phrase was Swope's, he would never credit the former World editor with his use of "the quick and the dead."

The phrase occurs twice in the Bible (Acts 10:42, 1 Peter 4:5) in the context of Judgment Day. In Shakespeare's Hamlet, Laertes leaped into Ophelia's grave saying, "Now pile your dust upon the quick and dead . . ."

The phrase is recalled from time to time by columnists writing about disarmament. In 1963 Arthur Krock wrote in the New York Times:

> It has been a long time since Bernard M. Baruch, representing the United States, offered the U.S.S.R. the "choice between the quick and the dead" that he said was presented by our proposal of a nuclear weapons test-ban, effectively supervised. The total absence of this proviso from the Moscow compact demonstrates, not only that time has passed, but also the whole concept that our national security can never be risked on the good faith of the U.S.S.R.

quick fix   a snap solution; the foolhardiness of expecting minor treatment to solve a major problem.

George Bush suggested a drug-lingo origin of this term, perhaps unintentionally, in a 1991 comment on indictments of Libyan terrorists. He said the charges were not "some quick hit, quick fix on trying to find the answer."

Hit, now a slang term for "assassination," has been slang since 1949 for the instant gratification felt by a narcotics user. Since 1867, the term *fix-up* was used for a shot of liquor or, more recently, of dope. The current use of *to get a fix* for drug usage began in the 1930s with *to get a fix-up.*

Many mechanics familiar with field expedients—innovative repairs made on the spot with available materials—dispute the drug origins of the term. The *Oxford English Dictionary Supplement* includes a hyphenated *quick-fix,* an adjective for "quickly put into place," dating back to a 1959 advertisement for electrical supplies including "quick-fix reflectors and diffusers."

By the mid-1970s, the term was being applied in politics. In a Christmas 1976 issue, the *National Observer* reported on conflicting advice for President-elect Jimmy Carter: "On the one hand, he is urged to make quick-fix tax cuts and get the economy moving."

Its connotation is almost always negative. In 1980, when Carter ran unsuccessfully for a second term, he derided Ronald Reagan for "fantasy goals of strength without sacrifice, the irresponsible advocacy of short-cut economics and quick-fix defense policy."

Business Week reported in late 1980 that Bernard M. Fauber, chairman of K-Mart Corporation, predicted a dismal economic picture, adding that 1981 "will be a year of great challenge.

There simply aren't any quick-fix solutions."

Other adjectives are often attached to this term, mainly to indicate disapproval of the quick fix. In 1981, *U.S. News & World Report* indicated Reagan's plan as President to resist "panicky, 'quick fix' moves," and a week later the *Los Angeles Times* quoted an economist's disapproval of "miracle, quick-fix solutions."

James A. Baker 3d, Bush's Secretary of State, was more blunt when he told Russians in late 1991, "There are no quick fixes and there are no simple solutions."

The negative twist of the term, though, does not reflect solely on politics or economics. A 1990 stage review in the *New York Times* describes a Biblical production as "a lightly mocking parable of the shallow quick-fix mentality of so many contemporary religious movements."

quiet diplomacy   behind-the-scenes efforts, held to be more effective in achieving desired ends than attempts to publicly embarrass another nation into acceding to the first nation's wishes.

"Through quiet diplomacy," Secretary of State Henry Kissinger told the Synagogue Council of America on October 19, 1976, "this Administration has brought about the release or parole of hundreds of thousands of prisoners throughout the world and mitigated repressive conditions in numerous countries. But we have seldom publicized our specific successes.

"The most striking example has been the case of Jewish emigration from the Soviet Union," Kissinger went on. "The number of Soviet Jews who were permitted to emigrate in 1968 was four hundred; by 1973 that number had risen to 35,000. The reason for this quantum leap lies largely in persistent but private approaches . . . quiet personal discussions . . . no public announcement or confrontation ever took place . . . When even greater advances were sought by confrontation and legislation, the result was tragic. Today Jewish emigration from the Soviet Union has dropped to 10,000 a year . . . moral ends are often not enough in themselves. The means used also have a moral quality and moral consequences."

Kissinger was attacking the "Jackson-Vanik amendment" to trade legislation that publicly and specifically tied MOST FAVORED NATION treatment to emigration policies.

The argument against "quiet diplomacy" was that without public pressure, neither the U.S. government nor the Soviets, with whom it was seeking détente, would enter into any talks at all to protect human rights; also, the dissidents within Iron Curtain countries wanted not so much specific loosening of their personal repression, but were willing to suffer personal deprivation in order to induce basic changes in the Communist system.

Candidate Jimmy Carter, in 1976, firmly allied himself with the forces in favor of human rights publicly sought; after his election, he tempered his rhetoric. But observers noticed. "The shift in President Carter's human-rights campaign from shrill publicity to quiet diplomacy," wrote columnists Evans and Novak in October 1977, ". . . has cost him a powerful cutting edge for domestic politics, but quiet diplomacy . . . may be having a more productive impact on Moscow than the headlines of early 1977."

The counter to that was expressed by Senator Daniel P. Moynihan (D-N.Y.), one of the earliest spokesmen for the human rights campaign, in a *Commentary* article: "It is entirely correct to say that quiet diplomacy is effective in obtaining concessions from totalitarian regimes with respect to particular individuals who need our help. But the result of proceeding in this fashion is that the democracies accommodate the dictators. The dictators let the occasional prisoner out of jail in return for our silence about those jails."

See HUMAN RIGHTS; SAMIZDAT; MOST FAVORED NATION; OPEN COVENANTS; LINKAGE; SUMMITRY.

quisling a collaborator with the enemy; a traitor; one who cooperates with a foreign country in the overthrow of his own, and especially one who then serves in a PUPPET GOVERNMENT.

Major Vidkun Quisling, head of the Nazi party in Norway and of that country's puppet government during World War II, spawned the word. He was executed for treason in 1945.

On May 11, 1940, the *London Daily Express* turned the name into a word: "Two thousand Quislings had been rounded up by Thursday night." On May 22 the *Manchester Evening News* wrote: "Major Quisling, the betrayer of Norway, has given us one of the first new words of the war." In the U.S., *Time* magazine's issue of May 24 dropped the capitalization: "South America becomes very quisling conscious." The *London Star*, on July 10, explained why the word caught on: "The Norwegian traitor was cursed with a name which by its very sound conveyed all the odious, greasy wickedness of the man." The *Manchester Guardian* wondered on October 19: "So far the most significant and valuable addition in this war has been Quisling. Will there be a verb, to quisle?" There was not.

Quisling is an eponymous word, taken from the name of an individual. Other people whose names have become words include Captain Charles Cunningham Boycott, a land agent in County Mayo, Ireland; Miss Amelia Bloomer, American feminist; British

General Henry S. Shrapnel; and a seventeenth-century English hangman named Derrick.

Like most eponyms, *Quisling* eventually lost its initial capital, thereby losing its allusion to a particular person and joining thousands of other common nouns in the vocabulary. A current use, in the context of Illinois politics, is from the December 17, 1992, *Chicago Tribune*: "'As long as there is a quisling in Downstate Illinois, then Downstate will always get sold out,' said one disgruntled Downstate Democrat.'"

Eponymy in politics includes GERRY-MANDER, SOLON, BORK, SHERMAN STATE-MENT, ROORBACK, HOOVERIZE, and SWARTWOUTING. Best known is MAVER-ICK. Once removed from eponymy are phrases like "to pull a Wallace" (to start a third party, to bolt) and "another Stassen" (a PERENNIAL CANDI-DATE).

quota   the number permitted or required; in civil rights terminology, government-set numerical standards to require admission or employment of blacks, on the grounds that this helps to compensate for two centuries of discrimination.

The Latin *quotus* asks the question "How many?" In the first half of this century, the political use of this word was concerned with immigration policy (how many should be let into the U.S. from which other nations) or with discrimination against Jews and Catholics (how many should be allowed into medical schools, country clubs, corporations).

In the civil rights backlash of the 1970s, the word "quota"—like BUS-ING—became politically sensitive, as many who had been proponents of civil rights for blacks in theory did not like the practice; they believed it abridged civil rights for whites. When black activists sought a form of repara-

tions for past prejudice, on the grounds that special preference was due to enable them to enter the "mainstream" of American life, this was attacked as "reverse discrimination"; the argument was made that the Constitution must remain "color-blind" or the courts would be filled with pleas for preference by every minority and ethnic group, undermining the tradition of the MELTING POT.

The critical words in the issue were "affirmative action," "goals," "quotas," and "reverse discrimination."

Affirmative action, as a phrase, was conceived during the Eisenhower Administration; former Secretary of State George Shultz tells the author he recalls that it was being used in the 1955 White House Conference on Equal Job Opportunity. Evidence that this phrase was bubbling up through the bureaucracy was its first official use, six weeks into the Kennedy Administration, in Executive Order 10925 (March, 1961): "The contractor will take affirmative action to ensure that applicants are employed, and that employees are treated, during employment, without regard to their race, creed, color or national origin." These actions came to mean providing remedial education or compensatory training, making certain that testing did not incorporate forms of discrimination, and aggressive recruiting—in other words, sincerely trying to find, and hire or admit qualified blacks.

Goals are numerical targets, set to put a specific criterion before a school or employer or union, which can be achieved through "affirmative action" on agreed "timetables." If good-faith efforts are made to provide equal opportunity, failure to reach the goal would not trigger a government penalty such as cancellation of contracts.

Quotas do not permit of explanations: if the number set by population percentages is not met, penalties ensue;

this rigidity results in the hiring or admission of minority applicants less qualified than other applicants, primarily on the basis of race, and the charge of *reverse discrimination.*

In *Regents of the University of California* v. *Allan Bakke,* decided on June 28, 1978, Justice Lewis Powell, writing for the Supreme Court, swept aside the differences between "goals" and "quotas"—at least as applied in that case— as "semantic distinction beside the point." The point was that nobody could be denied admission to a college specifically by virtue of his race; Bakke, who was white and had claimed "reverse discrimination," won entry. At the same time, the Court held that "race or ethnic background may be deemed a 'plus' in a particular applicant's file"—in other words, that race could be taken into consideration provided it was not the only element in the admissions decision.

This overrode the contention that the Constitution was "color-blind," made by opponents of affirmative action. Ironically, they took this word from the 1896 opinion of John Marshall Harlan in *Plessy* v. *Ferguson,* dissenting from "the wrong this day done" by a Court that upheld SEPARATE BUT EQUAL facilities: "Our constitution is color-blind and neither knows nor tolerates classes among citizens. In respect of civil rights, all citizens are equal before the law. The humblest is a peer of the most powerful."

When this was used by whites in the seventies to protest "reverse discrimination"—the affirmative action taken to redress past discrimination—four justices in the Bakke case held: "We cannot . . . let color blindness become myopia which masks the reality that many 'created equal' have been treated as inferior."

Quota remains a stigmatizing word. When President Clinton nominated Lani Guinier, a civil rights lawyer who

had advocated use of cumulative voting and proportional representation to increase minority representation, she was attacked as a "quota queen" in the *Wall Street Journal* and he was forced to withdraw her nomination to head the Justice Department's Civil Rights Division.

quoted out of context a defensive charge that one's words have been quoted in such a way as to twist the original meaning of the statement.

During the French Revolution, Jean Paul Marat was arrested and tried by the Convention for alleged outrages against that assembly in 1793. In his successful defense, he said: "I demand a consecutive reading . . . for it is not by garbling and mutilating passages that the ideas of an author are to be learnt, it is by reading the context that their meaning may be judged of."

In the 1944 presidential campaign, Franklin Roosevelt was irritated at Thomas E. Dewey's jabs at FDR's "promise" not to campaign "in the usual sense" when he accepted the Democratic nomination. He planned to use the following passage in a speech:

> In accepting the nomination in this campaign I said: "I will not campaign, in the usual sense, for the office."
> Apparently the Republican campaign orators came to the conclusion that meant that they were free to say anything they wanted without contradiction. . . . But in their habit of tearing sentences from their context, which they seem to do in their campaign speeches with great facility, they decided to overlook what I said in the same paragraph. It was this: "I shall, however, feel free to report to the people the facts about matters of concern to them and especially to correct any misrepresentations."
> So last week, I exposed their misrepresentations . . .

Speechwriter Samuel Rosenman felt this was intemperate and out of character, and FDR agreed not to use it. Instead, he made the point obliquely: "I am quoting history to you. I am going by the record. And I am giving you the whole story and not merely a phrase here and a half a phrase there . . ." There was an outburst of laughter at that point and the master orator promptly scrapped the rest of the line: ". . . picked out of context in such a way that they distort the facts." Instead, he said: "In my reading copy there's another half-sentence. You've got the point and I'm not going to use it."

On November 15, 1954, during the debate on Senate Resolution 301 to censure Wisconsin Senator Joseph McCarthy, Senator Samuel J. Ervin, Jr. (D-N.C.), told the Senate:

I now know that the lifting of statements out of context is a typical McCarthy technique . . . practiced by a preacher in North Carolina about 75 years ago. At that time, the women had a habit of wearing their hair in top knots. This preacher deplored that habit. As a consequence, he preached a ripsnorting sermon one morning on the text "Top Knot Come Down."

At the conclusion of his sermon an irate woman, wearing a very pronounced top knot, told the preacher that no such text could be found in the Bible. The preacher thereupon opened the Scriptures to the 17th verse of the 24th chapter of Matthew and pointed to the words: "Let him which is on the housetop not come down to take anything out of his house." Any practitioner of the McCarthy technique of lifting things out of context can readily find the text "top knot come down" in this verse.

R

rabbi political patron; sage adviser; mentor.

In political usage, as Paul Hoffman pointed out in the January 21, 1969, *New York Post*, this word has no religious or spiritual significance. A rabbi in politics is primarily a sponsor or protector, although there is a second meaning of mentor or teacher. "Who's his rabbi?" is a question often asked by wary hatchetmen before cutting loose at a target.

When a speechwriter escaping the White House in 1973 asked *Newsweek* pundit Stewart Alsop to "be my rabbi" in giving advice about which newspaper offer to accept, Alsop—a self-described "confirmed WASP"—delightedly signed all future correspondence with his colleague "Your rabbi, Stew."

Dating back in this sense to the 1950s in New York police slang, *rabbi* was used in a 1989 Cable News Network commentary on the troubled savings and loan associations: "Ninety percent of the S & L's that are in trouble have no political rabbi."

Rabbi is derived from Hebrew for "my master." Its eponymous synonym *mentor* comes from the ancient Greek name for the adviser of young Telemachus, the son of Odysseus. The more frequently used term for mentor is *guru*, from the Indian "holy man" or "teacher," which began to lose its religious connotation in 1949 when Arthur Koestler used it in *The God That Failed* as "My self-confidence as a *Guru* had gone." In political usage, *guru* is for outsiders, *rabbi* for insiders.

racial balance. See BUSING TO ACHIEVE RACIAL BALANCE.

racism originally, an assumption that an individual's abilities and potential were determined by his biological race, and that some races were inherently superior to others; now, a political-diplomatic accusation of harboring or practicing such theories.

"This word [racism]," wrote Harvard Professor J. Anton De Haas in November 1938, "has come into use the last six months, both in Europe and this country . . . Since so much has been said about conflicting isms, it is only natural that a form was chosen which suggested some kind of undesirable character."

Racism was at first directed against Jews. In the nineteenth century, anti-Semites who foresaw a secular age in which religion would not be such a rallying force against Jews put forward the idea of Jewishness being less a religion than a race. Adolf Hitler, with his "master race" ideology, turned theory into savage practice.

In the late 1970s Anne Soukhanov, then associate editor of Merriam-Webster, and later editor of the *American Heritage Dictionary*, informed the author: "Our citations for *racism* ran very heavy from the late 1930s through the late 1940s; most of them referred to fascism. Then they thinned out until the late 1950s, when references to U.S. (and, in particular, to Southern) racism began to build up. The citations seemed to peak for that sense in the Sixties."

Meg Greenfield, writing in *Newsweek* on November 24, 1975, agreed: "US Ambassador [to the UN] Daniel P. Moynihan observes that the term 'racism' only became a fixture of official General Assembly prose sometime in the mid- to late 1960s. The same is true of official prose in this country. I remember being astonished in 1968 by the abandon with which the Kerner commission, appointed by President Johnson to study the causes of civil disorder in our cities, stigmatized vast segments of the American population with the charge of 'white racism.'"

Curiously, the term which had originally characterized (and derogated) attacks on Jews and then became associated with the black civil rights movement, returned as an attack on Jews when the UN General Assembly, dominated by a Soviet-Arab-African coalition, passed a resolution condemning Zionism as a form of racism.

U.S. Ambassador Daniel Patrick Moynihan, on November 10, 1975, observed in the UN: "The term derives from relatively new doctrines—all of them discredited—concerning the human population of the world, to the effect that there are significant biological differences among clearly identifiable groups, and that these differences establish, in effect, different levels of humanity." Opposing the resolution, he declared that "today we have drained the word 'racism' of its meaning . . . The United States of America declares that it does not acknowledge, it will not abide by, it will never acquiesce in this infamous act."

The anti-Israel UN resolution was finally rescinded in December 1991, at the urging of the Bush Administration.

"Racism" became a favored term of Mr. Moynihan's successor, Andrew Young, who returned to the sixties usage regarding blacks, and in Great Britain told his hosts that England "invented racism." When he observed that even Abraham Lincoln, as well as more recent Presidents, had been racist, defining the word to mean "insensitive to racial aspirations," he took some of the passion out of the word.

Both word and problem are likely to remain in the political discourse. Seymour Martin Lipset, writing in the October 1977 *American Spectator*, was pessimistic: "The racism and ethnic tension that have been potent aspects of human experience from ancient days down to the present continue as strong or stronger than ever . . . the story of people's hatred of each other for reasons of ancestry, culture, religion, race or language is far from over."

In the landmark *Bakke* decision, the Supreme Court held in 1978 that race could be considered as a factor determining admission to a college, provided it was not the only factor. "To get beyond racism," wrote Justice Harry Blackmun, "we must first take account of race. And in order to treat some persons equally, we must first treat them differently."

radical chic. See LIMOUSINE LIBERAL; PARLOR PINK.

radical right   attack phrase on right-wing EXTREMISTS, especially on an angry segment that believes treason motivates many of the government's leaders.

Prince Klemens von Metternich, who put the stamp of reaction on the Congress of Vienna in 1814, coined a predecessor phrase—"white radicals"—to define the activists of the far right, counterbalancing the "red radicals" of the left. And attorney Clarence Darrow, who defended a teacher's right to discuss evolution at the Scopes "monkey trial," liked to refer to the Catholic hierarchy as "the right wing of the right wing."

Telford Taylor, a prosecutor at the Nuremberg war-crimes trials, is credited with the coinage of "radical right" in the foreword to his 1954 book, *Grand Inquest*.

Sociologist Daniel Bell picked up the phrase in a 1955 book, *The New American Right*, which he updated and retitled *The Radical Right* in 1963. Bell defined the group as a melange of

soured patricians . . . whose emotional stake lay in a vanishing image of muscular America defying a decadent Europe . . . the "new rich"—the automobile dealers, real-estate manipulators, oil wildcatters—who needed the psychological assurance that they, like their forebears, had earned their own wealth, rather than accumulated it through government aid, and who feared that "taxes" would rob them of that wealth; the rising middle-class strata of the ethnic groups, the Irish and the Germans, who sought to prove their Americanism, the Germans particularly because of the implied taint of disloyalty during World War II; and finally, unique in American cultural history, a small group of intellectuals, many of them cankered ex-Communists, who, pivoting on McCarthy, opened up an attack on liberalism in general.

Writers who use this attack phrase are unanimous in their denunciation of the far right. Alan Barth, writing in 1961:

They are commonly called "Rightist"—a term which connotes conservatism. But in sober truth there is nothing conservative about them. They are much more in a rage to destroy than a fervor to conserve. . . . Sometimes they are referred to as the "radical Right." But the fact is that there is nothing radical about them. They offer no novel solutions to the problems that plague them; indeed, they offer no solutions at all. . . . They are fundamentally and temperamentally "aginners." And perhaps the commonest characteristic among them is anger.

One step short of radical right is *hard right*, as followers of Pat Buchanan were called in 1992.

Radical Middle was the title of a 1970 book by Renata Adler (whose fiction was later described by *Time* magazine as "middling radical"). Canadian Prime Minister Pierre Trudeau picked it up in 1978: "We are a party of the extreme center, the *radical middle*." Because Ross Perot's supporters in 1992 were both angry and of mixed ideology, they were described as "radical middle."

See BIRCHER; LITTLE OLD LADIES IN TENNIS SHOES; EXTREMISM; KOOKS, NUTS AND.

radic-lib   shortened form of radical liberal; a linkage of the unpopular far left with the left, which at election time must move for support to the center.

"What's a good word to describe radical liberals?" Vice President Spiro Agnew wondered aloud to a group of his writers at the start of the 1970 congressional campaign. "Radillectual" sounded anti-intellectual, which wouldn't do; nobody had a good word to describe radical liberals, so the two words remained as a kind of working title until a better one could be found. However, the use of the two words caused great consternation in the liberal community, whose candidates were then climbing in and out of sheriffs' cars to show their concern for law and order, and the search for an alternative phrase was quickly abandoned. One night, on his own, the Vice President tried out the short form—radic-libs—which caught the fancy of headline writers and incensed liberal opponents, who equated it with "COM-SYMP," a short form of Communist sympathizer popularized by the Birch Society in the sixties.

On November 2, 1970, Max Ways wrote in *Fortune* magazine:

> As he employs the phrase . . . radical liberal seems to be an elastic blanket covering a huge bed, strangely cohabited by "the northeastern Establishment," the more inflamed students and the militant blacks. The term radical liberal is bitterly resented by many as an effort to smear liberalism with the unpopular tar of radicalism. . . . To be fair, Agnew did not invent the guilt-by-verbal-association form of terminological confusion. Some years ago, the phrase "radical conservative" was used in both liberal and radical circles. This horrid hybrid, radical conservative, every bit as monstrous as radical liberal, was supposed to describe activist conservatives, such as members of the John Birch Society, who were inclined to ideologize their principles and who exhibited some stylistic similarities to leftist radicals . . .

In the 1840s a British Whig faction described itself as radical liberal; in 1968 the phrase was the title of a book by UCLA professor Arnold S. Kaufman.

rainmaker a lawyer or public relations man capable of making political manna fall on his client.

This apt term burst into the political lexicon in 1968 when new trans-Pacific airline routes were to be awarded, and a half-dozen of President John-son's former political associates were retained by individual airlines to lobby for their interests. The *Atlanta Journal* printed this dispatch from David Hoffman of the *Washington Post*: "Among airline men, corporate officials and consultants with high political contacts are referred to as 'rainmakers'. Half in jest and half in jealousy, airline men say the so-called rainmakers can precipitate new route awards for companies that employ them."

The next year, columnists Rowland Evans and Robert Novak wrote: "No sooner had President Johnson announced his decision on December 19 [1968] in the malevolently contested trans-Pacific air case, than two major airlines—American and Eastern—began a quick search for Republican rainmakers."

Former Attorney General John Mitchell gave a sophisticated definition of the term during his first trial in April 1974, which resulted in acquittal. Sometimes a lobbyist will claim to have done something for a client but the effort leads nowhere; still, he claims to have made it rain. Mr. Mitchell said that a New Jersey Republican leader approached him on behalf of financier Robert Vesco, and asked him to set up a meeting with SEC chairman William J. Casey. But Casey was on vacation and the meeting was never arranged. According to Mitchell: "Rainmaking is a situation where an individual who is trying to obtain a favor for a client does things for the record that never happened."

The term is quite current. The *New York Times* of February 25, 1993, criticized a lobbying bill in Congress for omitting "any disclosure of lobbyists' role as rainmakers for campaign funds." And a March 12, 1993, *Boston Globe* report on Senator Edward (Ted) Kennedy's negative rating in some polls quotes pollster John Gorman's comment: "It is definitely not a good situation to be in. Any ordinary senator with those numbers should start checking out law firms looking for rainmakers."

The word, in its original sense, is associated with the American Indian. The earliest use of the word in print found so far is in Adair's *The history of the American Indians* in 1775: "When the ground is parched, their rain-makers (as they are commonly termed) are to mediate for the beloved red people, with the bountiful holy Spirit of fire." Two centuries later, cloud-seeding operations proved somewhat more reliable, but in both literal and political senses, the rainmaker often takes the credit for rain that was already on the way.

See FIVE PERCENTER; INFLUENCE PEDDLER; LOBBY.

rally as a noun, an event to stimulate and channel enthusiasm; as a verb, to enlist support.

"Rally round the flag" may or may not have been said by General Andrew Jackson at the Battle of New Orleans, but it illustrates the military use of the word, from the French *rallier*, to really or join again, to reassemble scattered troops to fight again. Poet Robert Burns warned of repercussions, "ere we permit a foreign foe,/On British ground to rally."

As might be expected, the military phrase was given a political interpretation in the campaign for a military hero, William Henry ("Tippecanoe") Harrison. "If Pennsylvania should adopt him as her candidate," wrote the *Scioto Gazette* in 1835, "the west will rally around the Old Pioneer." Abolitionist Wendell Phillips followed an extension of the word in the *Liberator* in 1844: ". . . until slavery be abolished, the watchword, the rallying-cry, the motto on the banner of the American Anti-Slavery Society

shall be 'No Union With Slave Holders!'"

The political rally, as practiced today, can be a *streetcorner rally*, one of many brief appearances by the candidate on a city-wide tour, providing an event for local supporters to organize in a neighborhood; a *headquarters rally* or *kick-off rally* to "open" a headquarters largely for the benefit of cameramen; a *coffee klatsch*, a gathering of supporters in a home but nevertheless a rally of sorts (see COFFEE-KLATSCH CAMPAIGN); and the all-stops-out, ring-a-ding, HOOPLA-filled *"Garden" rally* (after Madison Square Garden in New York) or *major rally*, which is also called the *wind-up rally*, at the end of a national campaign, bringing in celebrities, raising funds by charging admission to a section of the best seats, generating publicity and enthusiasm.

A good rally can be potent. Reluctant candidate Dwight Eisenhower wrote General Lucius Clay from Paris in early 1952: "My attitude has undergone a quite significant change since viewing the movie of the Madison Square Garden show . . ."

A checklist prepared by public relations man Gilbert A. Robinson for a Rockefeller for Governor rally in 1966 provides an indication of preparations for one rally:

I. *Invitations*: (a) telegrams to county chairmen; (b) mail cards to volunteers; (c) bulk invitations to organizations.

II. *Program*: (a) music—rock 'n' roll combo; (b) celebrities; (c) emcee; (d) introductions and speeches; (e) balloon and streamer drop from ledge overhead; (f) decorate upstairs headquarters with bunting and posters.

III. *Equipment*: (a) flatbed truck with mounting steps; (b) police parking permit; (c) platform for TV cameras; (d) sign for front of hotel, U.S. and state flags; (e) sound equipment, two speakers on flat bed, two on station wagons roaming area to bring crowds; (f) 150 hand signs on sticks, 160 hats, 50 sashes, 5000 buttons, 500 balloons, 50 pre-rally signs saying "at noon today" to be posted in AM; (g) "Days to Go" sign with removable numbers placed next to elevator in headquarters; (h) walkie-talkie communications.

IV. *Crowd*: (a) telephone team calling volunteers three days before rally; (b) Young Republicans to guarantee 150; (c) tables in crowd with 3 girls manning each to sign up volunteers; (d) police notified and present.

V. *Press arrangements*: (a) invitations; (b) TV arrangements and power; (c) phone follow-up to invitations.

This was a small, successful headquarters opening rally, which attracted about a thousand people and good press coverage. For a major rally, multiply complexities by fifteen. Good managers always distribute ten times as many tickets as there are seats in the hall. See BALLYHOO; BANDWAGON; SPONTANEOUS DEMONSTRATION.

rank and file   the broad range of party members; the TROOPS, more active than the average voter registered with a party.

Al Smith, making a late effort to get the Democratic nomination in 1932, stated that "it would be wiser . . . not to instruct delegates to the convention in favor of any candidate . . ." This ploy was aimed at eroding delegate strength already pledged to Franklin Roosevelt. FDR immediately objected to "the kind of national convention which became merely a trading post for a handful of powerful leaders, and where the nomination itself had nothing to do with the popular choice of the rank and file of the party itself. . . . The rank and file of the party should be heard." See POWER BROKERS.

The phrase, often used in the labor movement, is from the military, where it means the whole body of enlisted men, including corporals but some-

times excepting sergeants. See MILITARY METAPHORS.

rap in the night   symbol for police state that rules by fear; a frightening sound, preliminary to arrest or search.

The crash of gun butts on the door in the dead of night is a device to strike terror into a populace. Nighttime is chosen because the resident is startled out of sleep, and a fear of the dark is added to the fear of authority. The Gestapo made it a kind of trademark. In some cases, night is chosen to avoid publicity.

"The clearest way to show what the rule of law means to us in everyday life," said Dwight Eisenhower in 1958, "is to recall what has happened when there is no rule of law. The dread knock on the door in the middle of the night . . ."

This became a political issue in the U.S. in 1962 following an increase in the price of steel. President John F. Kennedy put pressure on the steel companies to roll back their increase, because he felt it was unjustified and inflationary. As part of this pressure, Attorney General Robert Kennedy asked the Federal Bureau of Investigation to check into newspaper reports of remarks made by Bethlehem Steel executives at a stockholders meeting. "Unhappily," writes Arthur Schlesinger, Jr., "though the instruction went to the FBI in the afternoon, it was apparently passed on to Philadelphia by Pony Express, for the reporter involved was not called till three the next morning. The FBI's postmidnight rap on the door caused a furor."

The "rap in the night" was used against Robert Kennedy in his 1964 senatorial campaign as an indication of his ruthlessness; it was also phrased as "rap on the door" and "knock in the night." In a way, this explains why political canvassers are told by their leaders not to ring doorbells or knock on doors after 9 P.M.

The expression fell into disuse, perhaps temporarily, when rap music became popular in the late 1980s.

ratfucking secretly, sometimes illegally, disrupting an opponent's campaign.

This odious word has its origin in Southern California campus politics, where fierce struggles to determine class presidencies sometimes featured underhanded tactics to confuse or irritate the opposition. In undergraduate politicking, it was considered harmless pranksterism, similar to the mock fury of much intermural sport, but transmitted to the national scene it was seen to be HARDBALL or DIRTY TRICKS.

Donald Segretti was identified by *Time* and by reporters Robert Woodward and Carl Bernstein of the *Washington Post* in October 1972 as having been hired by the Nixon White House to sabotage the Democratic campaign. "Those who did know of the disruption campaign," reported the *New York Times* on October 16, "referred to it as 'rat——,' an obscene phrase alluding to the Democratic candidate victimized by the program. The phrase is understood to be one commonly used on California campuses when some men linked to the case, including Mr. [Dwight] Chapin and Mr. Segretti, were in college there."

The use of the word "rat" to mean "a politician who deserts his party" (as distinguished from "ratfucking," in which a politician dishonors his party) was traced by glossarian Richard H. Thornton to use by Earl Malmesbury in 1792. In the U.S. it made its first appearance in the saying "like a rat deserting a sinking ship" about 1800, and this metaphor was alluded to by Thomas Jefferson in a letter to James Maury dated April 25, 1812: "I think the old

hulk [England] in which you are is near her wreck, and that, like a prudent rat, you should escape in time."

Jefferson's element of prudence remains in the use of the metaphor today. A political proverb attributed to FDR Navy Secretary Claude Swanson is "When the water reaches the upper level, follow the rats."

See "black advance," under ADVANCE MAN.

rather be right. See I'D RATHER BE RIGHT.

rattle the cage attempt by a political figure to break out of the restraints imposed on him by his staff.

This phrase is an arrogation of importance by political staffers who jokingly speak of themselves as zookeepers of gorillas that must be protected from their own rampages.

When Nixon special counsel Charles Colson arranged a night out at the Kennedy Center for Richard Nixon to conform to a sudden presidential whim, he was dressed down by chief of staff H. R. Haldeman in these terms: "You could have put the President's life in jeopardy. The Secret Service wasn't prepared." Asked what to do when the President expressed a desire for an unscheduled public appearance, Colson writes he was told: "Just tell him he can't go, that's all. He rattles his cage all the time. You can't let him out."

A second meaning, when the keeper rather than the gorilla is doing the rattling, is "to warn," as in this *Wall Street Journal* use on July 5, 1977: "A congressional staffer recalls that a lobbyist for the American Israel Public Affairs Committee, after noting that a friendly congressman wasn't on hand for a key vote, ordered the congressman's aide to 'get up there and rattle his cage and get him down here.'"

The metaphor of center of power as prison is not new: Harry Truman referred to the place he worked as "a big white jail."

A related metaphor is *run the traps*. A hunter will check his traps in the morning to see what animals were caught; a reporter will "run the traps" of his sources to check out a story.

raw meat. See STIR UP THE ANIMALS.

reached bought off; corrupted.

A public official may be *approached* with no implication of wrongdoing on his part; when he has been *spoken to*, the implication is that he is neutralized or partially persuaded pending a final decision; when he is *reached*, however, he has been bought and sold.

California Attorney General Earl Warren, launching a gambling investigation in 1939, used the word in its current meaning:

> It is impossible to open a big, notorious gambling operation without buying off public officials. Every time you see such a place, you can be sure they are paying off someone for the privilege to operate. This does not necessarily mean a sheriff or a District Attorney or a chief of police is being reached. Most often, it is someone higher up . . .

The question "Can he be reached?" or "Is he reachable?" is occasionally answered with another word, taken from Chicago gangland investigations and in turn from the Hindu caste system: "untouchable."

See GRAFT; BOODLE; BAGMAN.

reactionary one who believes in returning to governmental and economic conditions of an earlier time; often an attack word on a conservative.

The origin seems to have been French, applied to the conservative groups who opposed the Revolution's extremists.

H. L. Mencken cites its first use in J. A. Froude's *History of England* in 1858, "in the current sense of a politi-cal conservative reactionary. . . . It is now used to designate any opponent of a new device to save humanity." The word was used earlier as a religious term.

Populists and Democratic supporters of William Jennings Bryan popularized it in this country, but as early as 1868, *Harper's Weekly* used "reaction" to describe the Democrats who met in their party's national convention in Ohio: ". . . the resuscitation of every notorious copperhead to control the government is the beautiful plum which 'the great reaction' offers the country."

In more recent times, President Roosevelt said in a 1939 radio speech: "A reactionary is a somnambulist walking backward." Six years later Herbert Hoover, accustomed to the label, wrote: "If it be 'reactionary' to be for free men then I shall be proud of that title for my remaining days." Communist China's Chairman Mao Tse-tung wrote in *Political Science*: "Reactionaries must be deprived of the right to voice their opinions. Only the people have that right."

Like LIBERAL, MIDDLE OF THE ROADER, CENTRIST, and CONSERVATIVE, reactionary—and its counterpart on the left, radical—is a subjective label shifting in meaning with each labeler. However, left-wingers are more likely to be proud of the title "radical" than extreme right-wingers of the label "reactionary." In the late seventies, some ultraconservatives—picking up on the growing use of NEOCONSERVATIVE— called themselves "neoreactionaries."

Forces of reaction is often used as an alternate to the adjective, and *fossilized thinking* and DINOSAUR WING shore up the antediluvian picture of the word. See MOSSBACK; EXTREMISM; HIDEBOUND; OLD FOGY; OLD GUARD; TROGLODYTIC.

read my lips pay close attention; make no mistake about what I say.

When George Bush was first nominated for the Presidency, he told the 1988 Republican National Convention in New Orleans during his acceptance speech: "Congress will push me to raise taxes, and I'll say no, and they'll push, and I'll say no, and they'll push again. And I'll say to them: 'Read my lips. No new taxes.'"

This imperative phrase comes from rock music. In 1978, the singer Tim Curry used the phrase to title an album (which did not include a 1957 song with that title by Joe Greene). Curry recalls getting the phrase from a recording engineer of Italian-American descent: "I would say to him, 'We got it that time,' and he would say, 'Read my lips—we didn't.' That phrase arrested me." He defines the expression as meaning "listen and listen very hard, because I want you to hear what I've got to say."

Sports figures picked up the phrase. A football coach, Mike (Read My Lips) Ditka of the Chicago Bears, got the nickname by emphasizing spoken orders. The heavyweight boxer Michael Spinks predicted he would retire after fighting Mike Tyson: "I'll say, 'Read my lips. I quit. Bye-bye. Forever. In other words, see ya.'"

In a 1987 issue of *Automotive Marketing*, Rosemarie Kitchin explained the term's two-part purpose: "Read my lips! Has anyone ever said that to you? If so, you were the object of an intense attempt at persuasion. Your conversational partner wanted to emphasize a point or belief. And he or she wanted to be sure that you looked and listened both, for a dual sensory impact."

Political usage began about 1982, when Elisabeth Bumiller of the *Washington Post* reported a tense exchange concerning aircraft for the hostages released by Iran in 1981. Joseph Canzeri, a Reagan aide, was told by a State Department official that the aircraft were unavailable, committed elsewhere. Canzeri replied, "Read my lips—these are English words. Uncommit them."

In 1987, Senator Albert Gore questioned Under Secretary of Defense Fred C. Iklé about the Midgetman missile. Interpreting Iklé's lukewarm response, Gore said, "You're saying, 'Read my lips, cut the money.' Your message is clear."

Its use by George Bush in the speech written by Peggy Noonan led to its use against him after he compromised with the Democratic Congress in 1990 and agreed to a tax increase. At first, it plagued him with conservatives; later, it was taken up by Democrats as evidence of Mr. Bush's willingness to break a promise.

Four years later, the Clinton-Gore campaign issued faxes quoting Bush's 1988 statement of "no new taxes" and his 1992 comment on "no more tax increases," followed by spokesman Marlin Fitzwater's qualification, "It wasn't a pledge, no." George Stephanopoulos, Clinton's communications director, based his response on a proverb attributed to labor leader Walter Reuther on how to tell a Communist (see PROVERBS AND AXIOMS, POLITICAL): "If it walks like a duck, and quacks like a duck, then it just may be a duck." Commented Stephanopoulos, "If it looks like 'read my lips,' sounds like 'read my lips' and reads like 'read my lips,' it's 'read my lips.'"

readout   report to the media; public reciting of information about a meeting.

Marlin Fitzwater, Presidential press secretary to George Bush, popularized this noun. A 1990 transcript of a White House press briefing began, "Welcome to the pre-brief—or readout, excuse me—on the visit of President Ben Ali of Tunisia."

Asked by the lexicographer about the usage, Fitzwater replied, "*Readout*

is a colloquial conjunction of two separate expressions. The first is 'to read
your notes,' which is what we do in reporting to the press about a meeting
we attended. The second part, the *out*
part, may be from 'to speak out,' as in
telling the press about what happened."

Fitzwater dated the term back to the
early Reagan Administration. "I've
heard it since I got here in 1983," he
said, providing a definition: "A readout is a report on what happened at a
meeting."

Its source is computerese. The hyphenated form, which appears in the
*Oxford English Dictionary Supple-
ment,* has a primary sense of "the extraction or transfer of data from a storage medium or device."

Pete Cottrell of the University of
Maryland's computer science department refines the meaning: "*Readout*
refers to instrument panels or video
displays. It's human interface with the
machine conveying information, as
opposed to *printout*, which is the output of the machine that you can carry
away in your hand."

Unlike a *handout*, a *readout* requires
no printed form. Instead, it is a public
recitation of information that allows
reporters not only to take notes but
also to film or record or broadcast live.

read out of the party   declared *persona non grata* by party leaders, usually after a BOLT.

The situation is similar to a dismissed
employee grumbling, "You can't fire
me, I quit." When a party leader or
public figure within the party commits
some unpardonable sin (like supporting the opposition), he has in effect deserted; any metaphoric expunging of
his name from the party rolls simply
vents the spleen of the party leadership
deserted. It makes no difference, except to make it more difficult for the
bolter to return.

Nobody actually "reads" anybody
out of a party; if a man says he is a
Democrat, he's a Democrat, no matter
what Democratic leaders say or how
many Republicans he votes for. The
phrase is merely a way of showing
party disapproval.

Like PARTY ELDERS, the origin is in
the Church. As the *Guidebook* in the
Administration of the Discipline of
the Methodist Episcopal Church
states: "It is made the duty of the 'official minister or preacher' at every
quarterly meeting to read the names of
those who have been excluded from
the Church during the preceding quarter. . . . When persons are thus read
out of the society by the official minister," etc. "Reading out the banns" in
church was the thrice-repeated notice
of intended marriage; it was also a
sovereign's summons to his vassals for
military service.

Political use was evident in 1840,
when the *Logansport* (Indiana) *Herald*
wrote: "If their candidates in expectancy are guilty of the unpardonable
sin of telling the truth . . . they're
immediately read out of the party."

When Republican Frank Knox, Alfred Landon's running mate in 1936,
accepted a post in the Roosevelt Administration, Republican National
Chairman John Hamilton "read him
out" of the party. When Earl Warren,
who had turned down the offer to be
Thomas E. Dewey's running mate in
1944, was asked to run with Dewey in
1948, he felt he had to accept. "If he did
turn Dewey down," wrote Warren biographer Leo Katcher, "he would be
reading himself out of politics."

See PURGE. For another term formed
from the same verb phrase, see READ-
OUT.

realpolitik   POWER POLITICS with a scientific sound; international diplomacy
based on strength rather than appeals
to morality and world opinion.

The coiner was German writer Ludwig von Rochau, in his 1853 *Grundsätze der Realpolitik* (Fundamentals of Realpolitik), attacking what he felt were the unrealistic policies of the German Liberals. "The term was particularly applied to Bismarck's policy during and after the years of German unification," writes Professor Donald Cameron Watt in the *Fontana Dictionary of Modern Thought*, "and is to be distinguished from a policy of selfish self-interest or from a ruthless reliance on naked power."

"Historians may argue for years," wrote *Time* magazine about the brief Israeli-Arab war in 1967 (dubbed the "blintzkrieg"), "over who actually fired the first shot. . . . But the *Realpolitik* of Israel's overwhelming triumph has rendered the question largely academic." The *New York Times* editorially noted on June 8, 1967, that "The Kremlin now is trying to cut its losses without too much damage to its posture as 'friend of the Arabs,'" and described the effort as "Russia's Unrealpolitik."

On a different subject—the need to withdraw U.S. forces from Europe to help stem a gold drain—*Time* had written a month earlier: "For an America caught up in a war in Asia, and a vigorous Europe with no foreign entanglements, the first major withdrawal of 'cold war' troops from the Continent also signaled a belated adjustment to *Realpolitik* in the '60s."

In 1939, after the Soviets had signed a nonaggression pact with the Nazis, American Communists were forced to do a sharp zigzag in their party line, causing *The Nation* magazine to scoff at their dialectics. A clergyman wrote a letter to *The Nation*'s editor patiently explaining that Stalin was only fighting for the life of his regime, adding: "I would suggest that you leave the morals of the situation to us parsons and concentrate yourselves upon the realities in terms of *Realpolitik*."

The German word is pronounced re-*al*-pol-i-*tik*; in Europe, it continues to mean "power politics," but in the U.S. the word is used to mean "the realities of politics," which puts it closer to PRACTICAL POLITICS. A coinage based on this word is *realeconomik*, from a 1992 book by Susan and Martin Tolchin, *Selling Our Security: The Erosion of America's Assets*: "The U.S. needs a new vision, a '*realeconomik*' that addresses its need to regain economic ground; otherwise, its role as a world leader will surely diminish over time." See QUIET DIPLOMACY; WORLD OPINION.

reapportionment. See ONE MAN, ONE VOTE.

recession a decline in economic or business activity.

A recession can be *temporary, deep, nationwide, rolling,* or *regional*. According to some economists, a deep recession can become a depression; according to others, recessions are normal parts of a recurring rise and fall of economic activity. A combined recession and INFLATION, involving both rising unemployment and rising prices, is often called STAGFLATION. A colloquial word for a recession is *slump*; if mild, a *downturn* or DIP, which if repeated becomes a *double dip*.

The first use of *recession* in print is recorded in the *OED* in an article in the *Economist* of November 2, 1929, shortly after the stock market crash of October 1929. "The material prosperity of the United States," declared the *Economist*, "is too firmly based, in our opinion, for a revival in industrial activity—even if we have to face an immediate recession of some magnitude—to be long delayed." The "immediate recession" was of *some* magnitude—it lasted ten years and was called the Great Depression.

The prolonged recession plaguing the Bush Administration after the boom of the 1980s was a leading cause of the Republican defeat in 1992 and the election of Bill Clinton, whose mandate to stimulate the economy was encapsulated in the slogan "IT'S THE ECONOMY, STUPID!"

When Alfred Kahn, Jimmy Carter's economic adviser, was forbidden to use the word *recession* lest he be a source of gloom, he substituted the word "banana."

reclama appeal; objection to a decision or a request for review.

Reclama, a popular term in late 1980s spookspeak, began as a clipped form of the noun *reclamation,* based on the verb *reclaim.* All are rooted in the Latin verb *clamare,* "to cry out," by way of a French verb *réclamer,* meaning "to complain, object."

Aviation Week & Space Technology showed military use of the term in 1975: "Navy and Army officials are now in the process of preparing reclamas on the . . . aerial scout helicopters." The same publication used the word six years later, when an angry defense official protested that there was "zero time available to . . . accept reclamas from the services."

The *Naval Terms Dictionary* in 1978 defined the noun as "a request to superior authority to reconsider its decision or its proposed action."

Diplomats picked up the expression from the military. James R. Schlesinger, formerly Director of Central Intelligence and Secretary of Defense, wrote in *Foreign Affairs* magazine in 1986 that Prime Minister Margaret Thatcher "appeared at Camp David to deliver a reclama on Reykjavik."

By the mid-1980s, political use of the word had appeared. In 1984, Secretary of State George P. Shultz discussed the

difference between business and government: "In business you had to be very careful when you told somebody that's working for you to do something, because the chances were very high that he'd do it. In government you didn't have to worry about that, because if he didn't like it, there'd be a reclama."

The word was used in 1989 when Secretary of Defense Richard B. Cheney requested that Brent Scowcroft, the national security adviser, review a request. Scowcroft was overheard commenting, "Cheney has done a reclama."

Like its synonyms *appeal* and *review, reclama* is now equally acceptable in political lingo as noun or verb. Director of Central Intelligence William Webster used it as a verb during a 1989 meeting with George Bush: "I'd like to reclama that."

red color originally symbolizing radicalism and anarchy, now identified with Communism.

Les républicains rouges, so called for their red caps and occasional willingness to dip their hands in the blood of their victims and then wave them in demonstrations, gave the anarchistic tinge to the color associated till then with magic and the Church.

This did not occur, as popularly assumed, during the Revolution of 1789 and the Reign of Terror that followed; the "red Republicans" earned their nickname in the insurrection of June 1848, which led to the establishment of the short-lived Second Republic. The red flag, however, had been used in the 1789 Revolution and was adopted by the Communists in the twentieth century; it had been used in the Roman Empire as a call to arms.

German revolutionaries in the mid-nineteenth century called themselves *rote Republikaner,* and the *Cleveland Plain Dealer* in 1856 made an interesting comparison: "They call themselves 'Red Republicans,' indicating by that name their bloody and revolutionary purposes. They have found congenial spirits in a party in this country called 'BLACK REPUBLICANS.'"

A character in *Uncle Tom's Cabin*, by Harriet Beecher Stowe, warned that "the masses are to rise, and the under class become the upper one." The answer was, "That's one of your red republican humbugs, Augustine!" At the same time, the specter of Communism was haunting Europe, in the Marx-Engels word picture, and the timing was perfect for the color and the cause to come together.

PINKO and PARLOR PINK are obvious derivatives; BLEEDING HEART might have an association. See COLOR METAPHORS.

redheaded Eskimo bill extremely limited focus in legislation; narrowly targeted bill.

The *Washington Post* provides a 1986 citation for this phrase, found almost as rarely in print as its intended beneficiaries are in life. At that time, the Maryland state legislature was considering a tax credit for gasohol, delivering a tax break for a specific petroleum company. Delegate Mary Boergers of Montgomery County, who was in favor of the bill, commented, "It's a redheaded Eskimo," an image that *Post* writer Tom Kenworthy defined as "legislative parlance for a narrowly constructed bill that applies to only one person or company."

Eskimos, who call themselves *Inuit* (meaning "people"), were given their common name from an Algonquian word for "eaters of raw flesh." Among the distinguishing physical characteristics of Eskimos is their straight black hair, emphasizing the rarity of finding a "redheaded Eskimo."

Kenworthy reported another use of legislature lingo in the use of *snake*, ap-

plied by some Maryland delegates to the same bill. Lawrence LaMotte, a Baltimore County Democrat, defined *snake* as "a 'simple' bill, usually very short, which eliminates vast quantities of existing law." Delegate Gerard F. Devlin, another Maryland Democrat, explained the image of *snake* as "a bill where the hidden meaning is disguised in a forest of verbiage."

For an antonym, see "Christmas Tree Bill" under RIDER.

red herring a side issue that draws attention away from the main issue.

From the expression "neither fish nor flesh nor good red herring" in Dryden's *Duke of Guise*; a herring, cured with saltpeter and slowly smoked, turns red. When it is dragged across a trail, the strong smell irritates the nostrils of tracking dogs.

An early political use was by Alfred E. Smith, Governor of New York, campaigning for president in 1928. To an audience in Oklahoma City, he said:

The cry of Tammany Hall is nothing more nor less than a red herring that is pulled across the trail in order to throw us off the scent.

Now this has happened to me before in my State campaigns but I did not consider it of enough importance to talk about. But it has grown to a proportion that compels me to let the country know that at least I know what's behind it; it's nothing more nor less than my religion. [See WHISPERING CAMPAIGN.]

For a phrase to explode into an issue, it needs both forum and context. President Harry Truman's first use of it had the forum of his acceptance speech to the Democratic convention in July 1948, but the room was not gas-filled when the match was struck:

"I am going to call Congress back and ask them to pass laws to halt rising prices, to meet the housing crisis—which they say they are for in their platform. . . . They are going to try to dodge their responsibility. They are going to drag all the red herrings they can across this campaign . . ."

The phrase made no big impression at the time because there was no double meaning to "red." But during the special session of Congress, the House Un-American Activities Committee found two witnesses who unfolded a spectacular tale of Communist intrigue at high government levels. Elizabeth Bentley and Whittaker Chambers started labeling "spy" and "collaborator" such officials as Lauchlin Currie, ex-White House aide; William T. Remington of the Department of Commerce; and the State Department's Alger Hiss.

On Thursday, August 5, 1948, in this new context, a reporter took Truman's convention-speech red-herring phrase and asked, "Mr. President, do you think that the Capitol Hill spy scare is a 'red herring' to divert public attention from inflation?" Truman replied, "Yes, I do," read a prepared statement saying the hearings "are serving no useful purpose," and ad-libbed at its conclusion: "And they are simply a 'red herring' to keep from doing what they ought to do." The reporter asked for permission to quote him directly on the ad lib, and Truman agreed.

Now the phrase had its context and its second meaning—red Communism. Republicans attacked Truman on it, but the issue had not yet ripened—Hiss had not yet been convicted—and the tone of the Dewey campaign did not permit a slashing attack. But by the time the 1952 campaign was under way, "SOFT ON COMMUNISM" was an issue and "red herring" was its shibboleth. Eisenhower, stung by Stevenson's wit, asked, "Is it funny when evidence was discovered that there are Communists in government and we get the cold comfort of the reply, 'red herring'?"

Thus, Truman's first use of the phrase, which passed unnoticed, gave him confidence to accept a reporter's use of it a few weeks later; in the meantime, however, the context and meaning had changed enough to make the use of the phrase a major blunder that haunted Democratic candidates for years. As Senator Robert Taft's wife Martha summed up: "To err is Truman."

redlining delineating an area as a slum in which mortgage financing is not available, thereby speeding its decline.

"Redlining," wrote U.S. District Court Judge David Porter in 1976, "contributes to the decay of our cities." A *Washington Post* editorialist added: "It is a self-fulfilling prophecy. When the first signs of blight or impending racial or economic change appear, some lending institutions, anticipating a drop in market value, draw an imaginary red line around the endangered neighborhood and make no further investments within it. This usually makes it impossible for responsible and credit-worthy people to buy homes and for landlords to make improvements in the 'redlined' neighborhood."

Since many urban slums are inhabited largely by blacks, the practice has been attacked as RACIST. At the behest of liberal legislators, the Connecticut House of Representatives passed a bill prohibiting banks from refusing mortgages on geographic-decline grounds. The California Association of Realtors defined "redlining" in October 1976 as "the practice of denying the availability of home financing without regard to the credit worthiness of the individual or the soundness of the structure," a definition that implies disapproval.

A conservative writer, Robert Bleiberg in *Barron's* magazine, held that government intervention rather than racism was the cause of much urban blight: "Owing to rent control, which, in an age of inflation inexorably forces property owners to the wall, real estate, water and sewer levies go uncollected and the tax base steadily erodes. Physical deterioration spreads from the bombed-out sectors of Bedford-Stuyvesant and the South Bronx to the increasingly beleaguered borough of Manhattan. Much of the city is redlined—who in his right mind will sink his own or other people's money into a vast slum—and building grinds to a near-halt."

The word crossed into diplomatic usage when Israelis told Syrian leaders in 1976 not to cross a "red line" in Lebanon, close to the Lebanese-Israeli border. This may have been influenced by "deadline," which originated in Civil War prison camps as a limit beyond which a prisoner could not walk.

red meat. See STIR UP THE ANIMALS.

redneck a bigoted rural white, especially Southern; used as an attack word on all Southern conservatives or segregationists.

The *Dictionary of American English* traces the use to 1830, when Mrs. Anne Royall in her *Southern Tour* wrote of "the Red Necks, a name bestowed upon the Presbyterians in Fayetteville [North Carolina]." The word came to mean *poor white* or *white trash* in some usages, the *backwoods vote* in others; throughout, however, there runs the strain of racial prejudice. The word belongs in the political lexicon: Albert Kirwan's book on Mississippi politics from 1876 to 1925 was titled *Revolt of the Rednecks*. In his novel *All the King's Men* (1946), about Southern politics, Robert Penn Warren included a line: "Mason county is red-neck country and they don't like niggers . . ."

Huey Long's appeal to the Louisiana rednecks was a source of his power,

though he was not what would be called today a racist. Civil rights workers and liberal writers in recent years have popularized the regional term nationally, using it to identify members of White Citizens Councils. The noun "redneck" can also be used as an adjective, though copy editors prefer to dress it up as "rednecked."

"Look," Florida Governor Claude R. Kirk told a *Saturday Evening Post* writer in 1967, "I'm not one of these red-necked governors like Lester Maddox . . ."

Red-necked, hyphenated, means angry, contrary to the *Post* transcription of the word Kirk used; it probably derives from the flush of blood to the neck and face in a moment of fury, and is not related to "redneck," though a connection could be made in the anger of a bigot. Some say the origin of *redneck* is in the sunburn on the neck of one doing stoop labor; others suggest the abrasion caused by a looping of leather behind the neck during plowing.

In current usage, *prejudiced* is genteel, more concerned with religion than race; *discriminatory* legalistic; *bigoted* blunt; *biased* mild; *anti-black* intellectual and literary; *hate-peddling* reminiscent of the thirties and now outdated; and *redneck* descriptive of what the speaker thinks is ignorant, rustic, anti-black, and anti-Northerner.

George C. Wallace, campaigning in 1968, described some of his followers as "peapickers," "peckerwoods," and "woolhats." Semanticist Mario Pei suggested that "these are evidently to be taken as complimentary replacements for less flattering terms, such as 'redneck' and 'cracker.'"

In *Redneck Power: The Wit and Wisdom of Billy Carter* (1977), the President's brother was quoted as drawing the distinction between the complimentary "good ole boy" and the derogatory "redneck": "Well, a good ole boy . . . is somebody that rides around in a pick-up truck—which I do—and drinks beer and puts 'em in a litter bag. A redneck's one that rides around in a truck and drinks beer and throws 'em out the window."

See BUBBA FACTOR.

red tape bureaucratic sluggishness; unnecessary paperwork; administrative delay.

"Steel Pipes and Red Tape Don't Mix," advertised the British steel industry in 1964, warning voters that a vote for Labour was a vote for nationalization of their industry, with all the bureaucracy it was expected to entail. This was not a borrowed political Americanism, but a coinage attributed to Charles Dickens and popularized by Thomas Carlyle (red tape as a method for securing legal and official documents is mentioned in Maryland Laws of 1696–1715). The author cannot find Dickens' use of the phrase, but a passage from *Little Dorrit*, written in 1857, illustrates the point: "Whatever was required to be done, the Circumlocution Office was beforehand with all the departments in the art of perceiving how not to do it."

In the 1850s, Carlyle in *Latter Day Pamphlets* described a politician as "little other than a redtape Talking-machine, an unhappy Bag of Parliamentary Eloquence." Official documents in England were tied with a string or tape of a reddish color, and many lawyers followed the practice in packaging their briefs. At the turn of the nineteenth century, Washington Irving used the phrase in the U.S., as "His brain was little better than red tape and parchment."

The phrase, along with BUREAUCRACY, is a convenient weapon for citizens frustrated by what might be the delay of sensible administrative review, or what may be, in Shakespeare's phrase, "the insolence of office and the law's delay." *Washington red tape* and the need to *go through channels* called for the creation of *expediters* in World War II, whose job was to *cut through the red tape* and open up *bottlenecks* in war production.

The result of their paper-pushing depresses the most industrious; the late rocket scientist Wernher von Braun said in 1958: "We can lick gravity, but sometimes the paperwork is overwhelming."

The only known defense of red tape was made in 1977 by Herbert Kaufman of the Brookings Institution: "One person's red tape may be another's treasured procedural safeguard . . . We are ambivalent about the appropriate trade-offs between discretion and constraint, each of us demanding the former for ourselves and the latter for our neighbors . . . Accepting red tape as an ineradicable foe is not to give up the fight, but to join battle on the only terms that offer any hope of success."

Mr. Kaufman enlivened the pages of his iconoclastic tract with a cartoon by Lichty: "Gentlemen, the bad news is the company is in a state of bankruptcy . . . the good news is we have complied with federal rules and regulations."

reform the creation of a temporarily organized opposition to an Administration or party hierarchy based upon its corruption, assumption of privilege, or, in some cases, its refusal to share power.

Reformers, often capable of defeating those in power, are less successful in maintaining themselves on top. This fact was bemoaned by Lincoln Steffens, who wrote: "It is an emotional gratification to go out with the crowd and 'smash something.' This is nothing but revolt, and even monarchies have uprisings to the credit of their subjects. But revolt is not reform and one revolutionary administration is not good government."

Steffens was writing about an attempt by a reform mayor, Seth Low, to win re-election in 1903; the Tammany motto was: "To Hell with reform." Tammany won.

Professional politicians have always had disdain for reform movements and reformers. Tammany Mayor John F. Hyland told the Civil Service Reform Association in 1918: "We have had all the reform that we want in this city for some time to come." Another New York mayor, Jimmy Walker, quipped: "A reformer is a guy who rides through a sewer in a glass-bottomed boat."

Reformers have taken abuse from more distinguished sources. Senator Frank Lausche, when governor of Ohio, fought through a compromise increase in unemployment compensation when liberal and reform elements were demanding a much larger increase. Of them, he said, "There can be such a thing as too much reform, if it takes the wheels off the wagon." Earlier, Speaker of the House Thomas Reed wrote his own sardonic definition of reform: "An indefinable something is to be done, in a way nobody knows how, at a time nobody knows when, that will accomplish nobody knows what . . ."

George Washington Plunkitt, of Tammany Hall, expressed his own conviction that reform will always fail: "The fact is that a reformer can't last in politics. He can make a show for awhile, but he always comes down like a rocket. Politics is as much a regular business as the grocery or the dry-goods or the drug business. You've got to be trained up to it or you're sure to fail."

Enthusiasm, moral fervor, and a conviction that reform will save the city, state, nation, and world is a hallmark of the genuine reformer, but to the philosopher George Santayana, it was all spurious. In *The Life of Reason* he wrote: "A thousand reforms have left the world as corrupt as ever, for each successful reform has founded a new institution, and this institution has bred its new and congenial abuses."

It is easy enough to find disdainful references to reform, but the intermittent movement is a vital part of the political system. Those associated with reform movements need not be stereotyped as "goo-goos," the nickname of New York's Good Government Clubs of the 1890s. Eleanor Roosevelt, retired Senator Herbert Lehman, and former Air Force Secretary Thomas K. Finletter were the tough, politically savvy leaders of the reform movement in New York in the late fifties and early sixties.

Columnist Murray Kempton gave an insight into the steel behind Mrs. Roosevelt's charm in quoting a remark she made to congressional candidate Gore Vidal, who had introduced former Tammany leader Carmine de Sapio at a dinner. "The dear old lady," wrote Kempton, "gazed across those hills ennobled by our history and said sweetly, 'I told Carmine that I would get him after what he did to Franklin [Jr.] at the 1954 state convention.'"

Those who try to upset party leadership always call themselves *reformers*; the entrenched leadership prefers to call them *insurgents*.

The word became a euphemism for any planned revision in law in the sixties and seventies. When the Hatch Act (protecting government employees from political influence from their superiors at election time) was attacked as unfairly limiting the political activity of appointees, the suggested return to the old ways was called "reform reform."

"Mr. Carter wants 'legal and judicial reform,'" wrote columnist James J. Kilpatrick in February 1978. "He wants 'criminal code reform.' He wants 'wiretap reform.' He wants 'mining law reform.' He wants 'a series of reforms' . . . 'long-needed reforms' . . . 'to reform the sewage treatment construction grant program' . . . In times past, Presidents have regularly asked that various programs be enlarged, expanded, strengthened, enhanced, improved or even reorganized, but this is not Mr. Carter's approach. Politically, he is the inheritor of Luther, Calvin and Knox. Reform!

"My own thought," concluded Kilpatrick, "is that reform is like garlic in the dressing: a little bit, as every cook knows, goes a very long way."

American political writers, at a loss to describe the scrambled spectrum of Russian politics after the fall of Communism, called the followers of Boris Yeltsin *reformers*.

refusenik. See -NIK SUFFIX.

regime. See ADMINISTRATION.

regular the party-designated candidate in a primary, as opposed to the insurgent; or a loyal party voter, usually a member of a local organization.

In a primary fight within a party for a specific nomination or for local party leadership, the "ins" proudly display "Regular Democratic [or Republican] Candidate" on their posters and literature; the "outs," who cannot very well call themselves "irregulars," usually choose "Independent Republican Candidate" or "Reform Democratic Candidate." See INS AND OUTS.

Most politicians today use a yardstick of willingness to vote in a primary as a test of "regularity": if a voter registers with a party at a general election, he is a *registered Democrat* (or *Republican*), but if he takes the trouble to turn out at a primary—and about three out of ten do in a contest—he

may be considered a *regular*, if he votes for the "ins."

A *regular* is more active than a *registered voter*, less active than a *party worker*. Though a regular is a PARTISAN, a partisan is not necessarily a regular. The *regular vote* is the hard-core strength of any party on Election Day, which usually needs to be supplemented by the independent or SWING VOTE for victory.

See MILITARY METAPHORS.

reign of terror. See TERRORISM.

reinventing government. See PARADIGM SHIFT.

release. See HANDOUT.

religious issue. See WHISPERING CAMPAIGN; UNPACK; REVERSE BIGOTRY; BAILEY MEMORANDUM; RED HERRING.

religious metaphors
All the following political expressions have religious derivations, some not so obvious, which are covered under their separate entries:

    ALL THINGS TO ALL MEN
    BLEEDING HEARTS
    BORN AGAIN
    BULLY PULPIT
    CRUSADE
    CULT OF PERSONALITY
    GRAY EMINENCE
    HELLBENT FOR ELECTION
    LOVE FEAST
    OPEN COVENANTS
    PARTY ELDERS
    PATRONAGE
    PUBLIC TROUGH, FEEDING AT THE
    QUICK AND THE DEAD, THE
    READ OUT OF THE PARTY
    SANTA CLAUS, NOBODY SHOOTS AT
    SIDE OF THE ANGELS
    WITCH HUNT

Used in politics, but not primarily political phrases, are *Bible belt* (a coinage of H. L. Mencken); *holier than thou* (a coinage of Ezekiel); *sacred cow* (from the Hindus).

rendezvous with destiny   fated to be great.

FDR told the 1936 Democratic convention: "There is a mysterious cycle in human events. To some generations much is given. Of other generations much is expected. This generation of Americans has a rendezvous with destiny."

Historian Frank Freidel credits the phrase to Roosevelt's speechwriter Raymond Moley; others say Roosevelt's aide Thomas Corcoran suggested it to the President. Poetic and effective, it stimulated strong reaction. H. L. Mencken warned soon after the speech that "The Rooseveltian 'rendezvous with destiny' will turn out, in November, to be a rendezvous with a bouncer."

Thomas E. Dewey, seeking the Republican nomination in 1940 that ultimately went to Wendell Willkie, tried a substitution: "The President has said we have a 'rendezvous with destiny.' We seem to be on our way toward a rendezvous with despair."

Why was the word "rendezvous" chosen rather than "date with destiny" or "appointment with destiny"? Perhaps because the previous generation of Americans had a "rendezvous with death," in the phrase of U.S. poet Alan Seeger, killed while fighting with the French army in 1916:

> But I've a rendezvous with Death
> At midnight in some flaming town,
> When spring trips north again this year,
> And I to my pledged word am true,
> I shall not fail that rendezvous.

This poem had an effect on a later President. Arthur Schlesinger, Jr., wrote of John F. Kennedy: "On Cape Cod, in October, 1953, when he returned from his wedding trip, he had read his young wife what he said was his favorite poem. She learned it for

him by heart, and he used to love to have her say it. It was Alan Seeger's *I Have a Rendezvous with Death*."

President Lyndon B. Johnson was intrigued by "this generation of Americans," the beginning of the rendezvous with destiny phrase. In his 1964 campaign he said that Barry Goldwater offered a "doctrine that plays loosely with human destiny, and this generation of Americans will have no part of it." The allusion to FDR's "rendezvous with destiny" was subtle; however, in a Nashville, Tennessee, speech on March 16, 1967, Johnson edited FDR's construction into mediocrity: "This generation of Americans is making its imprint on history."

reordering priorities   putting first things first, though what is first to the reorderer is not always first to the reorderee.

This phrase achieved the status of a thundering cliché in the late sixties, when debate began about limiting the size of U.S. defense and space expenditures and directing those resources to "meet human needs." While not the coiner, John Gardner, first at the National Urban Coalition and later at Common Cause, is identified with the phrase.

"Top priority" was heavily used in World War II, and "high priority" became bureaucratese subsequently. In calling for change, the participle used is never *changing* or *reorganizing*; it is occasionally *resetting* or *reassessing* but most frequently *reordering*. A measure of that frequency is the dropping of the hyphen. The word usually appears near another vogue term, "agenda."

In a calculated fashion, and with the relish experienced by soldiers who capture enemy guns and turn them around, the conservative writer of the 1972 budget message of the President (and author of this dictionary) led the huge document with this brief review:

"To the Congress of the United States: In the 1971 budget, America's priorities were quietly but dramatically reordered: for the first time in twenty years, we spent more to meet human needs than we spent on defense."

reportedly a leading WEASEL WORD in journalism; a modifier that uses the fact of repetition to impute truth.

"Alleged," a word whose roots are linked with "litigate," has long been used to avoid libel litigation; the word has since become such a transparent, albeit ineffective, libel-ducker that newsmen now prefer "charge with" or "accused of."

Less precise than "alleged" is "reported" or "reportedly," which is a form of the gossipy "they say"; it implies "nobody has been sued using this before, so here goes." In Communist terminology, the preferred construction was "as is well known."

When *New Yorker* profilist Geoffrey Hellman died, Alden Whitman of the *New York Times* wrote in an obituary that Hellman "feuded fiercely" with his colleagues on the magazine. "One such feud was with Brendan Gill . . . the two were reportedly not on speaking terms." Mr. Gill blazed back in a letter to the editor: "Certainly he and I never had a feud. Moreover, having adjacent offices at the magazine, we spoke almost daily up to the time he fell ill, and we often lunched together. It is a fact that as an old friend of Geoffrey's I was one of the last of his colleagues to be granted the privilege of visiting him as he lay dying. So much for 'reportedly'—a word that has little to recommend its use in write-ups of the distressed living and the defenseless dying."

President Carter's Attorney General, Griffin Bell, put it this way in 1977, justifying his practice of correcting journalistic errors: "Once information is published, it is likely to be reprinted by journalists yet unborn unless a denial has been posted in neon at Times Square."

For a list of other clichés to be used by journalists yet unborn, see JOURNALESE.

Republican an advocate of a democratic form of government, as a DEMOCRAT is an advocate of a republican form of government.

John Adams worried about the word in 1790: ". . . all good government is and must be republican. But, at the same time, you can or will agree with me, that there is not in lexicography a more fraudulent word. . . . Are we not, my friend, in danger of rendering the word republican unpopular in this country by an indiscreet, indeterminate, and equivocal use of it?"

Thomas Jefferson, who used the word as an antonym for "monarchic" all his life, disagreed in 1816: ". . . of the import of the term republic, instead of saying, as has been said, 'that it may mean anything or nothing,' we may say with truth and meaning, that governments are more or less republican as they have more or less of the element of popular election and control in their composition . . ."

Jefferson's party became known as the Republicans; he preferred it to "anti-Federalists" and referred to his opposition as "the anti-republicans."

Hans Sperber and Travis Trittschuh pointed out in the *Dictionary of American Political Terms*, "since the Constitution guarantees to every state a republican form of government, it would seem that republican from the beginning had every chance of becoming a unifying not a partisan word." The party became known as the Democratic-Republicans, and their opposition as the National Republicans, because of this unifying sense of the word in its form-of-government meaning.

In the Jacksonian era, the word's previous bipartisan use led both parties, beginning to take adversary positions after the Era of Good Feeling, to drop it completely. Democratic-Republicans became "Democrats," National Republicans became "Whigs."

As the Whig party fell apart, the term "Republican" began to be bandied about, probably around 1852. In 1854 A. E. Bovay wrote to *New York Tribune* editor Horace Greeley: "Urge them to forget previous political names and organization, and to band together under the name I suggested to you at Lovejoy's Hotel in 1852, while Scott was being nominated. I mean the name Republican." About the same time, Greeley wrote a friend regarding the formation of an antislavery party: "Call it Republican—no prefix, no suffix, but plain Republican." At Jackson, Michigan, in 1854, the party was organized and chose that name, picking John C. Frémont as its first presidential candidate in 1856 with the slogan "Free Soil, Free Men, Frémont."

Strictly speaking, a *republic* is a form of government in which the people exercise their power through elected representatives, while a *democracy* is a government where the people exercise their powers directly *or* through elected representatives. In current usage, the two terms are interchangeable, which is why the definition at the beginning of this entry is not as flippant as it seems.

revanchism a policy or movement to regain territory lost either in war or through treaties signed under duress.

The word is rooted in the French *revanche*, meaning "revenge," which first appeared in English as an ironic use of the French word. Queen Victoria wrote in an 1858 letter, "She never allows a word to be said against Leopold who in revanche is much kinder to her than he was." Using the derivative word *revanchist*, the *Scots Observer* added a political sense in 1926: "It is France's policy [toward Germany] that the sores be kept open even if they give a handle to Monarchist revanchists."

Following World War II, Soviet writers applied *revanchist* to Germans who sought reunification of their country and *revanchism* to the movement for such a reunification as a means of redressing Germany's defeat in World War II. The *New York Times* commented in 1955, "Far from being an instrument of either 'American aggressors' or 'German revanchists' (as Soviet propaganda would picture it), the North Atlantic alliance is entirely a defensive organization."

In the late 1980s, the Soviet use resumed. "German Nazism marched under the standards of revanchism," Foreign Minister Eduard A. Shevardnadze told the United Nations in 1989. "Now . . . the forces of revanchism are again becoming active and are seeking to revise and destroy the postwar realities in Europe."

Charles Bremner, writing in the *Times* of London, discussed the revived usage: "For decades the Kremlin used revanchism almost as a synonym for West Germany, but Mr. Shevardnadze's words appeared to encompass the nationalist movements erupting across the Baltic region as well as Bonn's policy of welcoming the flood of refugees from East Germany." The use, however, is inexact for the Baltic nations seeking to re-establish their previous independence.

Pronounced with the "vanch" of *revanchism* rhyming with "ranch," the term is never self-applied, because it suggests no higher motive for policy than getting even. A scholarly synonym is *irredentism*, from the Italian word for "unredeemed"; this theological term was used by Italian politicians in the nineteenth century who sought to incorporate regions such as Trieste (*Italia irredenta*) into the mother country. Wags like to urge superpatriots to "see your irredentist twice a year."

revenue sharing. See TAX SHARING.

reverse bigotry the technique of crying "foul" to solidify a racial or religious group behind the candidate supposedly being fouled.

In the 1960 campaign, Republicans who carefully did not raise the "religious issue" felt that John F. Kennedy was raising it at every opportunity in cities with large Catholic populations. His speech to the Houston ministers, pleading for no prejudice in the campaign, was telecast often in major cities where—Republicans said—many regular Republicans who were Catholics were persuaded to switch to one of "their own" who was being unfairly attacked because of his religion. This, they charged, was "reverse bigotry." See BAILEY MEMORANDUM.

Congressman Abraham Ribicoff, running for governor of Connecticut in 1954 against John Davis Lodge, said, "Nowhere except in the Democratic party could a boy named Abe Ribicoff be nominated for governor of this state." In *America's Political Dynasties*, Stephen Hess wrote: "The Republicans charged that this was a form of reverse bigotry: Ribicoff, in reply, justified his statement by citing some stories from New York newspapers as evidence that his opponents were conducting an undercover smear campaign against him."

Obviously, "reverse bigotry" is a charge as hotly denied as "bigotry." It applies to racial as well as religious appeals. When the House of Representatives in 1967 denied a seat to Congressman Adam Clayton Powell of New York because of his contempt of court citations and improprieties with committee funds, he claimed that his skin color was the only reason for the censure. The *Miami Herald* disagreed: "By crying again and again that his misfortunes are owed to his race, Powell has persuaded the Harlem constituency that Congress excluded him only because he is a Negro. This ignores a congressional record of almost incredible tolerance." Black activist James Meredith decided to challenge Powell in an election, then changed his mind under pressure from civil rights leaders. ". . . there won't be any election in the contested sense," observed the *Herald*. "Adam Clayton Powell's appeal to reverse bigotry has seen to that."

When less anger is involved, the practice of favoring nonwhites is called *reverse discrimination*. (See QUOTA.)

revisionism a Communist charge that the accused seeks to alter basic tenets of Marxism-Leninism.

In COMMUNIST TERMINOLOGY, *deviationism* is internal criticism or refusal to recognize the official party line at any given moment; *revisionism* is a far more serious charge, as explained in the *Political Dictionary*, published in Moscow in 1958:

> A tendency in the workers' movement which, to please the bourgeoisie, seeks to debase, emasculate, destroy Marxism by means of revision, that is, reconsideration, distortion, and denial of its fundamental tenets. . . . Contemporary revisionism seeks to defame the teaching of Marxism-Leninism, declares it antiquated, allegedly to have lost, at present, significance for social development. Revisionists seek to undermine the faith of the working class and toiling people in socialism.

Communists recognized revisionism as carrying the seeds of self-destruction (and the source of that cliché can be found in BODY POLITIC). Nikita

Khrushchev said on January 6, 1961: "We must always keep our powder dry and wage implacable war on revisionism which tries to wipe out the revolutionary essence of Marxism-Leninism, whitewash modern capitalism, undermine the solidarity of the Communist movement, and encourage Communist Parties to go their separate national ways."

Those who were charged with deviationism and revisionism replied that their accusers were afflicted with *dogmatism*—a sin that, according to the 1961 party program, hinders "a correct appraisal of the changing situation and the use of new opportunities for the benefit of the working class and all democratic forces." Another defense was a countercharge of *sectarianism* defined by the Moscow *Political Dictionary* as "striving to quit the masses and to enclose oneself in a narrow circle, and throttles down the initiative of the toiling masses."

Thus, *revisionists* and the milder *deviationists* stood on one side, with *dogmatists* and the milder *sectarians* on the other. In 1964, Communists in China began issuing polemics saying that the Soviet Union was led by revisionists: "The revisionists are producing their own opposites and will be buried by them."

The Chinese charge could not be more serious in terms of Communist philosophy. Chairman Mao Tse-tung had said in 1957: "The revisionists deny the differences between socialism and capitalism, between the dictatorship of the proletariat and the dictatorship of the bourgeoisie. What they advocate is in fact not the socialist line but the capitalist line. In present circumstances, revisionism is more pernicious than dogmatism." In the -ISM crossfire, the Chinese in the sixties and seventies added hegemonism to their charge of Soviet revisionism, which meant that the Soviets were not only corrupting the Marx-Engels ideal, but seeking to impose their corruption on China.

The split in the Communist camp, magnified first by Chinese and later by Soviet leaders, calls to mind an observation by anthropologist Ruth Benedict in her classic *Patterns of Culture*: "Even given the freest scope by their institutions, men are never inventive enough to make more than minute changes. From the point of view of an outsider the most radical innovations in any culture amount to no more than a minor revision."

revolutionary praxis   practical activity or action for overthrowing the existing political system.

Praxis, "action based on will," comes from the Greek for "doing, acting, practice" (its plural is *praxes*). Sir Philip Sidney was first to use the term in English, in his 1581 treatise on poetry: "For as Aristotle sayeth, it is not *Gnosis* (knowledge) but *Praxis* (action) must be the fruit." During the eighteenth century, Bishop Robert Lowth used the word to indicate "an example of grammatical resolution," leading modern grammarians to contrast *praxis* (speech as action) with *lexis* (speech as meaning).

Political philosophers and historians defined the term in the nineteenth century as "practical activity." Count August von Cieszkowski used this definition in 1838, and Karl Marx soon followed. In his *Dictionary of Political Thought*, Roger Scruton explains that *revolutionary praxis* "sustains itself without ideology, since it is directed to the essential nature of social reality."

In recent decades, the phrase had been largely limited to discussions of religion and politics in Latin America. Michael Novak wrote in the *New York Times Magazine* in 1984, "Liberation theology says that truth lies in revolutionary praxis." In the *National Re-*

view in 1986, Richard John Neuhaus suggested that a reporter at the 1985 Roman Catholic Synod of Bishops missed its deepest meaning because he "had come to cover hot issues, such as revolutionary praxis and women's ordination."

In 1989, ironically, the Marxist sense was revitalized by students demonstrating for democracy in Tiananmen Square in Beijing. Their call for *revolutionary praxis* merged two antithetical senses: the capitalist "practicality" and the revolutionary "action."

revolution of rising expectations

unrest caused by extravagant promises; or, the constructive desire for change based on an optimistic view of society's future; or, the increased demand for a high standard of living that comes when the communications media bring evidence of affluence into poor people's homes.

"Reflections on the Revolution of Rising Expectations" was the title of a 1949 speech by U.S. diplomat Harlan Cleveland. Fifteen years later, in a speech to the UN, Cleveland said: "The phrase has since been attributed to nearly every literate American of our time, but I think this was the first time that phrase saw the light of day." He titled his UN speech "The Evolution of Rising Responsibilities." For a coinage Cleveland resisted, see SALT.

When Theodore Sorensen was asked to list the qualifications of a USIA director to President-elect John F. Kennedy, one of the key points was: ". . . should comprehend the 'revolution of rising expectations' throughout the world, and its impact on U.S. foreign policy."

In 1968 London's *Economist* titled a review of Gunnar Myrdal's *Asian Drama: An Inquiry into the Poverty of Nations* "The Revolution of Falling Expectation?"

"Revolution," a slashing political word, was somewhat defanged by this phrase, and the process has continued in recent years. When violent protesters preached revolution in the late sixties and early seventies, their word was pre-empted, and thereby softened, by Establishment figures. "The American Revolution is a continuing one," said industrialist David Mahoney, upon taking the chairmanship of the American Revolution Bicentennial Commission in 1970, "a peaceful revolution in a system capable of managing change." In his 1971 State of the Union address, President Nixon labeled his revenue sharing, welfare reform, and government reorganization plans "a New American Revolution." Reagan aides labeled their period of change "the Reagan Revolution"; speechwriter Peggy Noonan titled her 1990 book *What I Saw at the Revolution*.

Semantically, *revolution* is violent change, and *evolution* peaceful change, but the assumption of the word "revolution" by those opposed to violence has taken out a lot of the sting; it is a good example of how a democratic system can counter a threat by absorbing its terminology. In a similar way, President Johnson's use of WE SHALL OVERCOME and President Nixon's use of POWER TO THE PEOPLE (in connection with REVENUE SHARING) deafened the original users of the phrases with the System's echoes.

revolving door. See HONEST GRAFT.

rhetoric originally, the study of persuasive presentation of argument, as in speeches; now, bombast, high-flying oratory.

Several forces combined to give a pejorative cast to a word once honored by Aristotle. "DEEDS NOT WORDS" was a favorite saying of Eisenhower's; "lower our voices" was urged by Nixon in his inaugural; and with the escalation of ESCALATION, the phrase "de-escalate the rhetoric" was aimed at political speakers. Rhetoric was associated with the expansive promises of the Kennedy and Johnson Administrations, and when delivery fell short of promise, emptiness insinuated itself into the definition of rhetoric.

In a 1968 column, Art Buchwald conducted an imaginary interview with a man "manufacturing" political rhetoric as if it were bunting and buttons:

"What item has been moving the best?"

"'Law and Order' has been the biggest seller this year. We can't even keep the law and order rhetoric in stock. The minute it's put out on the counter, it's grabbed up."

"What else is selling?"

"'Peace at Home and Abroad' is a very big item. I don't think there's a politician running for office this year who hasn't bought at least one. 'The Crisis of the Cities' is also moving very well, but the one that really surprised us was 'A Piece of the Action.' We made a few samples, and before we knew it, everybody was using it to describe what the minorities wanted. . . ."

"Another big surprise is our 'Erosion' kit. It comes in a set: 'Erosion of the Cities,' 'Erosion of the Dollar,' 'Erosion of Moral Values,' and 'Erosion of America's Prestige Abroad.' We've also been doing well with 'Rebuilding the Urban and Slum Areas' and 'Facing up to the Challenges and Responsibilities of the Disenfranchised.'"

Rhetoric, as a word, is now most often demeaned by those who admired the effective and inspiring use of language by FDR, Adlai Stevenson, and John F. Kennedy. In denouncing its use, Hubert Humphrey in 1968 used a little himself: "It is time to have done with the language of promise; to have done with the language of excess, of exaggeration. It is time not to carry

more sail by way of rhetoric than the ship of state in fact can carry."

Forceful rhetoric is international in scope. In a 1987 column, Mary McGrory of the *Washington Post* wrote that "the Lincoln Memorial, the Jefferson Memorial, Mount Vernon, all speak to the fact that we are not the running dogs of capitalism of Kremlin rhetoric but a nation founded on ideas and ideals." (For more on "running dogs," see FELLOW TRAVELER.)

See BLOVIATE; TROT OUT THE GHOSTS; VISION OF AMERICA; PERORATION.

rhyme, political use of

The device of rhyme can make phrases memorable, as in the American GLOOM AND DOOM and the British description of a price-and-wage-control policy, "squeeze and freeze."

It may also be used subtly, appearing to be more rhythm than rhyme, as an oratorical device, as in this speech by John F. Kennedy to the UN in 1961: "We prefer world law, in an age of self-determination, to world war in the age of mass extermination." The cadence of Jimmy Carter's "a dis*grace* to the human *race*," about the tax system, was rhetorically effective. See THREE-MARTINI LUNCH.

Or rhyme can be used with a kind of light-hearted determination, as in Churchill's "Better jaw-jaw than war-war," or his message to FDR prior to the Yalta Conference in 1945: "No more let us falter. From Malta to Yalta. Let nobody alter."

For political use of poetic construction, see MARTIN, BARTON AND FISH; for poems that spawned political phrases, see MOVERS AND SHAKERS; STROKE OF A PEN; CRADLE-TO-THE-GRAVE; and TWEEDLEDUM AND TWEEDLEDEE.

rich man's war, poor man's fight

protest against inequities in military conscription; of special concern in past years to civil rights leaders and advocates of student deferments.

The slogan originated in the Confederacy in 1861, as a protest against laws favoring wealthy plantation owners; it was then picked up in the North and used in the New York draft riots of 1863. At the time, it was possible for a wealthy man to put up cash to have a "substitute" serve in his stead.

Resentment about who does the financing and who does the fighting exists between allies as well; some Britons in 1940 said, "America will fight to the last drop of English blood," and isolationist Americans turned the phrase around to use against the British.

Regarding student deferments during the Vietnam War, University of Chicago sociologist Morris Janowitz pointed out in *Trans-action* magazine that "a young man's chances of serving in the armed forces are decreased to the extent that he applies his energies to extending his education beyond four years of college." Obviously, this slanted student deferments toward wealthier students who could afford postgraduate education.

During the Korean conflict, the casualty rate of the lowest income groups was four times higher than that of the highest income groups, and black casualties—considering their proportion to the population—were twice as high as white. The Rev. Martin Luther King, Jr., an opponent of U.S. involvement in Vietnam, spoke out often in 1967 about what some black leaders were calling a "white man's war, a black man's fight." "There are twice as many Negroes in combat in Vietnam," said Dr. King, ". . . and twice as many died in action in proportion to their number in the population as whites." Others answered that black re-enlistments ran three times higher than white, accounting for a higher proportion in military service. This was countered with the point that black re-enlistments were high because career opportunities outside the service were almost nonexistent for blacks.

Black leader Floyd McKissick said in 1966 that the war in Vietnam was "a way of drafting black men to go fight yellow men in order to protect this land that the white men stole from the red men."

rider a provision added to a bill not necessarily germane to the bill's purpose.

A bill passed by a legislative body must be signed by a Chief Executive to become a law; in most cases, an *item veto* (more often called a *line-item veto*) is not permitted, and the President, governor or mayor must accept it all or reject it all. Riders are tacked on to unrelated legislation for two reasons: (1) an objectionable rider, sure to be vetoed, is added so as to force a veto of the portion of the bill the rider-sponsoring legislator is trying to "bring down"; (2) a bill that would likely be vetoed by itself is added to important appropriations legislation so as to "slip past" the Chief Executive.

Said President Roosevelt in 1938: "I want you to know that I completely agree with your criticism of legislative 'riders' on tax and appropriation bills. Regardless of the merits or demerits of any such 'riders'—and I do not enter that phase of the discussion at the moment—the manifest fact remains that this practice robs the Executive of legitimate and essential freedom of action in dealing with legislation."

Charles Ledyard Norton offered a fanciful derivation in 1890: "In common speech, a rider is the top rail of a zig-zag fence. Such a fence is 'staked and ridered' when stakes are driven in the angles and a rider laid across them. A rider is not an essential part of a fence, nor of a bill, but it adds considerably to the effectiveness of both."

In fact, the *OED* traces the expression back in English jurisprudence to 1669: "That which is certified shall be annexed to the Record, and is called a Rider-roll."

Riders, carried to an extreme, result in "Christmas Tree Bills." The *New York Times* in 1967 deplored the attempts by protectionists "to tack a series of riders sought by domestic industry onto the Administration's proposals for higher old-age benefits. Their hope is that Congress will give its approval to the entire 'Christmas tree' package. . . . The only sure way to stop the Christmas-tree bill is to chop it down before it is planted."

Elliot Richardson, then Secretary of Health, Education and Welfare, said in 1970: "Until I became Secretary, I had never heard 'Christmas tree' used as a transitive verb." Explained Alan Otten in the *Wall Street Journal:* "On Capitol Hill, the practice of tagging a host of special-interest amendments to a popular bill is known as 'Christmas-treeing' the bill."

rif   to discharge from a government job; or, to eliminate a job category or slot in such a way as to make it difficult for the employee to stay.

To *rif*—from the initials of Reduction in Force—is a sixties Washington acronym that has spread to state capitals. The term is usually heard during the transition between Administrations, and is a euphemism intended to make coolly impersonal what is usually a personal or political decision.

"I thought you'd be interested in a word that has entered the Albany argot as a result of Governor [Hugh] Carey's budget cutbacks," reporter Paul Hoffman wrote the author in 1977, "—the verb *to rif*, usually used in past tense, as 'I've been riffed,' or 'He

was riffed.' Meaning to lose one's job as the result of a Reduction in Force."

Spelled both RIF and "riff," the verb is in Merriam-Webster's *New International Dictionary* (3rd edition); its first citations were from 1953. After a generation, it is fair to assume the transition from acronym has been made, though its specific origin inclines this lexicographer to prefer one *f*.

See HIT LIST; ACRONYMS, POLITICAL.

rigged convention.   See BROKERED CONVENTION; OPEN CONVENTION.

right to know   the entitlement of enlightenment; a new "right" that journalists say exists, justifying their inquiries, which often conflicts with right to privacy and right to a fair trial.

Arthur Hays Sulzberger, former Publisher of the *New York Times*, stated the case for the "right to know" in 1956: "The crux is not the publisher's 'freedom to print'; it is rather, the citizens' 'right to know.'"

Ten years later, columnist Max Lerner took a different view, in connection with Jacqueline Kennedy's successful effort to edit material she had given in confidence to historian William Manchester:

> Clearly there are limits on such a right. We have no right to know about top-secret documents which have not yet been declassified. . . . Nor have we a right to know private things, even about public officials or their families against their wishes.
>
> Thus the right to know is circumscribed by public policy, by taste, by codes of fairness, by the right of privacy.
>
> More important than the right to know is the right to publish.
>
> This too, is a limited right—limited by the obscenity statutes, by libel laws, by judicial interpretations of both. But the right to publish becomes a precious right when there are unwarranted censorship efforts to prevent publication.

The right to know is a philosophical extension, rather than justification, of freedom of the press. In the 1960s, the controversy grew over the issue called "free press vs. fair trial." The Supreme Court held in 1966 that Dr. Samuel Sheppard had been denied his right to a fair trial—i.e., by a jury unprejudiced by information obtained outside the courtroom—because of the press campaign against him conducted primarily by the *Cleveland Press*.

The new "right" shoulders its way among other established rights and resists enthusiastic support. There is an upright ring to "the right to know." In 1984, the *Los Angeles Times* wrote of "right-to-know laws—state and local rules stipulating that a company must disclose to workers, local officials and emergency squads the names and nature of hazardous materials used or produced at local plants."

But when a newsman accepts a court citation for contempt in refusing to reveal a source, he is in effect denying the public's right to know his source, on the grounds that it will—in the long run—make it impossible for him to keep the public informed, which he maintains is the public's "right."

In 1971 the *New York Times* published selections from a secret 47-volume study of the origins of the Vietnam War, which they labeled "Vietnam Archive" but which promptly became known as the "Pentagon Papers." After the series began, the government moved to enjoin publication; the Supreme Court ultimately upheld the right of the *Times* and other newspapers to publish the documents. Chief Justice Burger, in a dissenting opinion, used the phrase in this way: "The newspapers make a derivative claim under the First Amendment; they denominate this right as the public right-to-know; by implication, the *Times* asserts a sole trusteeship of that right by virtue of its journalist 'scoop.' The right is as-serted as an absolute. Of course, the First Amendment right itself is not an absolute, as Justice Holmes so long ago pointed out in his aphorism concerning the right to shout of fire in a crowded theater."

This decision made clear that under circumstances presenting a clear danger to lives or an overriding national interest, the courts would uphold the public's right *not* to know. Soviet dissident and author Alexander Solzhenitsyn (see GULAG) used that phrase in a cultural rather than legal context at a Harvard commencement address in June of 1978: "People also have a right not to know, and it is a much more valuable one. The right not to have their divine souls stuffed with gossip, nonsense, vain talk. A person who works, who leads a meaningful life, does not need this excessive flow of information." Cartoonist Edward Sorel mocked this authoritarian view in *Esquire* magazine with a drawing of the well-to-do and the flag wavers marching under the banner of "Americans for a Closed Society."

The controversy recalled to some writers George Washington's complaint in 1777: "It is much to be wished that our Printers were more discreet in many of their Publications. We see almost in every Paper, Proclamations or accounts transmitted by the Enemy, of an injurious nature. If some hint or caution could be given them on the subject, it might be of material Service."

General William Tecumseh Sherman went further. He arrested one of Horace Greeley's correspondents covering the Civil War for the *New York Herald*, charged him with spying and would have shot him were it not for President Lincoln's intervention. Upon hearing that three other correspondents were killed by artillery, General Sherman observed, "Good, now we shall have news from Hell before breakfast."

right to work a movement to stop making union membership a requirement for employment.

Management has clearly won the battle of semantics with labor while labor has won the more substantive victories. *Right to work* is a management slogan that has been adopted as the generic term for anti–compulsory-union legislation, which labor refers to as *union-busting laws*. Management's term for a factory that will employ only a union member is CLOSED SHOP, connoting the sinister shutting out of workers who refuse to join a union, while the labor term is *union shop*, connoting a smiling band of collectively organized workers; "closed" is the word accepted by the public.

The Taft-Hartley Act permits the union, or closed, shop, but its Section 14b also permits states to pass laws prohibiting them—"right-to-work legislation." In 1958, this turned out to be a SLEEPER issue that upset two well-known Republicans.

Senate Minority Leader William Knowland, a powerful vote-getter in California, was running for governor in 1958 against Attorney General "Pat" Brown. Sam Brightman, publicity head of the Democratic State Committee, asked Brown where he stood on right-to-work. "Oh, I'm against Right-to-Work," Brown said, "but I don't think it's a big issue in California." Brightman disagreed: "The national platform opposes so-called [see SNEER WORDS] 'Right-to-Work.' Speaking out on the issue will help identify you with the national party and it'll help you with labor." Brown spoke out at a press conference, Knowland took issue and made it the focal point of the campaign, and Brown upset the better-known candidate.

Meanwhile, in Ohio, the issue upset Republican Senator John Bricker, heir to Robert A. Taft as a symbol of conservatism, with labor-supported Ste-

phen M. Young winning by 150,000 votes. The Ohio Republican State Chairman, Ray Bliss, had urged the party to evade the issue, was overruled, and emerged from the debacle a political sage.

Right-to-work laws exist in states anxious to attract industry and with no appreciable labor influence. Though organized labor has not been able to repeal Section 14b of Taft-Hartley on the national level, it has successfully defeated right-to-work in major state contests since the issue broke.

"So the right-to-work movement is pretty much dead, right? Wrong," wrote the *Wall Street Journal* in 1967. "The [National Right To Work] Committee is ambitiously building its field staff in selected states and planning bigger public campaigns. And labor is vowing to spend all that's necessary to beat back the attack."

Popularization of the phrase in a different meaning belongs to Socialist leader Eugene V. Debs: "Every man has the inalienable right to work." Ralph Waldo Emerson, in his essay on politics, said, "Every man has a right to be employed," and in the first half of the nineteenth century, the phrase was The Right to Labor. A German writer in 1808 wrote of *das Recht zu Arbeit*, and French social scientist François Fourier published, in the same year, a theory of four movements that included *le droit du travail*. In Franklin Roosevelt's 1944 campaign, the most vital part of his "economic bill of rights" was, "the right of a useful and remunerative job," though he hastened to add, "I believe that private enterprise can give full employment to our people."

In all those cases, the "right to work" meant, "the opportunity to make a living must be given to all."

Early use of the phrase in its present meaning was in a Bernard Partridge cartoon—"the Right to Work"—in

Punch, April 3, 1912. John Bull is saying to a striker: "I can't make you work if you won't; but if this man wants to, I can make you let him. And I will." The capture of the phrase by management was a master stroke, with its built-in implication that unions prevented some men from making a living.

The same turnaround—taking a negative or defensive position and fashioning it into a positive slogan—was used by opponents of abortion in the seventies, who changed their appellation from "anti-abortion" to "right to life." This was soon countered by the proponents of abortion rights with the "right to choose." (See PRO-CHOICE.)

For another example of slanted generics, see "TRUTH-IN" CONSTRUCTION.

ripper bill action of a legislature to emasculate, or "rip out," power held by a lower body or administrative agency dominated by the opposite party.

"Some of the warmest arguments in the legislature," wrote Al Smith, ex-governor of New York, in 1929, ". . . occurred over what were called 'ripper' bills. The party in power would legislate their opponents out of office."

By "Special Acts," state legislatures would set up municipal charters, grant franchises, transfer powers between state agencies, and restrict or expand the powers of governors. A state legislature controlled by one party can "rip" the charter of a city controlled by the other party, and thus elicit demands for HOME RULE; by this means, party leaders can also punish reform elements in their own party.

When in 1979 the Prince Georges County Council in Maryland empowered itself to take over the County Executive's role in deciding where to run water and sewer lines, the action was characterized by the Republican County Executive, Lawrence Hogan, as a *ripper bill*, aimed against him by the all-Democratic Council. "The result was," reported the *Washington Post*, "inevitably, a public confrontation between Hogan . . . and the Democratic council members." The bill was passed, though Hogan, an elected official, remained County Executive.

rising tide lifts all the boats the idea that general prosperity is best for individual welfare.

John F. Kennedy repeatedly sounded the optimistic note that good times would be beneficial to all. In his June 1963 address in Frankfurt, Kennedy said, "As they say on my own Cape Cod, a rising tide lifts all the boats. And a partnership, by definition, serves both partners, without domination or unfair advantage."

Joan Payne, a researcher at the John F. Kennedy Presidential Library in Boston, found an earlier use. Speaking in Newcastle, Pennsylvania, on October 15, 1960, then-Senator Kennedy said in campaigning that "the country is tied together, and a rising tide lifts all the boats."

In 1993, Theodore C. Sorensen informed the author: "As Legislative Assistant to Senator John F. Kennedy, 1953–1961, I often received material from a regional chamber of commerce–type organization called 'The New England Council.' I was favorably struck by the motto set forth on its letterhead: 'The rising tide lifts all the boats,' and not surprisingly it found its way into J.F.K.'s speeches."

Since the 1960s, however, the expression is often balanced by a second clause that adds a note of caution, lest the optimism seem undue. An economist is quoted in a 1987 issue of the *National Journal* on the economic problems in government after a boom: "In a sense, the rising tide lifts all boats. The falling tide in the Defense Department puts ships in the sand selectively."

Nine years before, Vernon Jordan, then an Urban League official, had used the same rhetorical technique before an audience: "There are those who believe, in John F. Kennedy's phrase, that a rising tide lifts all boats. But we must remind them that a rising tide only lifts those boats in the water, and black people are in the drydock of this economy."

Democrats use the "rising tide" line in a positive sense; they deride a similar idea on economics as TRICKLE-DOWN THEORY when used by Republicans.

road to defeat conservative Republican charge that liberal ME TOO tactics have failed.

Senator Everett Dirksen stood at the rostrum in the Chicago Stockyards at the 1952 Republican convention and waved a finger at twice-defeated New York Governor Thomas E. Dewey, now supporting Dwight Eisenhower against Senator Robert A. Taft.

"We followed you before," Dirksen intoned, "and you took us down the road to defeat." Taft men rose and booed Dewey, who sat stonily; the New York delegation returned the jeers, and hecklers shouted at the speaker and each other. Dirksen, who had brought the latent resentment to a head with his "road to defeat" remark, promptly reversed his field: "This is no place for Republicans to be booing any other Republican."

Dirksen was able to live down the divisive statement and become Senate Minority Leader, but Goldwater supporters frequently recalled the remark in the 1964 primary fight against Nelson Rockefeller.

The political-road metaphor is well traveled. The MIDDLE OF THE ROAD is favored on the *campaign trail*; and HIGH ROAD . . . LOW ROAD is referred to by people with sights set on *Pennsylvania Avenue* who decry GUTTER FLYERS and MADISON AVENUE TECHNIQUES as efforts to confuse the MAN IN THE STREET.

rock and a hard place, between a to be in difficulty; in recent usage, to be faced with either a moral dilemma or a HOBSON'S CHOICE.

John Ehrlichman used this phrase in testifying before the Senate Watergate committee; it was common parlance in the White House in the early seventies and became a vogue phrase in politics in the mid-seventies.

With the emphasis on "hard," the phrase seems to suggest that the choice faced is between a rock and a substance even harder than a rock. The meaning is similar to "between the devil and the deep blue sea."

In the *American Thesaurus of Slang*, Lester Berrey and Melvin Van den Bark place the phrase under the entry for "Bewildered; perplexed; baffled" and include it with "against the wall," "flummoxed," "hot and bothered."

In 1921 B. H. Lehman, writing in *Dialect Notes* about words used in California, gave a different interpretation. "To be between a rock and a hard place" is defined as "to be bankrupt." Professor Lehman reported the verb-phrase was "common in Arizona in recent panics, sporadic in California."

The expression has a Western flavor, and many of the aides in the Nixon White House were Westerners; it is likely that they popularized it in a media center like Washington, much as the Japanese word HONCHO was picked up in California and blossomed in the District of Columbia.

It is also likely that the phrase is a colloquial rendering of the classic phrase *between Scylla and Charybdis*, an allusion to Homer's *Odyssey*, in which Ulysses has to sail between Scylla, a monstrous rock, and Charybdis, a raging whirlpool.

In current use the meaning of "confusion" seems to have atrophied; the phrase is generally used now along with another vogue phrase, "to be in big trouble," and carries a special meaning of being torn or tortured by a moral choice.

In the 1970s, *Washington Post* editorial writer Meg Greenfield toyed with, but decided against, the notion of titling an editorial about Afghanistan "Between Iraq and a Hard Place." In the 1990s, with the problems posed by Iraq's Saddam Hussein, the pun was widely used.

rock-ribbed   inflexible, used by a critic; steadfast, or staunch, used by a friend.

"Rock-ribbed" is an adjective that has become associated with conservative Republicans, much as DYED-IN-THE-WOOL is a Democratic term. Poet William Cullen Bryant, in *Thanatopsis*, wrote of "The hills/Rock-ribbed and ancient as the sun . . ." which Senator Andrew Johnson quoted in a political context in 1861: ". . . we stand immovable upon our basis, as on our own native mountains—presenting their craggy brows, their unexplored caverns, their summits, 'rock-ribbed and ancient as the sun'—we stand speaking peace, association and concert to a distracted Republic."

This hyphenated adjective often has a shifting pronunciation. If the noun does not follow, the emphasis is on the second word, as "He is rock-*ribbed*," but if the noun follows, the emphasis is on the first word, as "He is a *rock*-ribbed Republican."

Los Angeles mayoral candidate Tom Houston was described in the *Los Angeles Times* of March 18, 1993, as "moving from rock-ribbed Republican to die-hard Democrat [see DIE-HARDS] during the Vietnam War

. . . So is Houston serious? Confused? A chameleon? Yes. No. And maybe."

roorback   a fictitious slander, an outrageous lie told to smear a political figure during a campaign.

"A roorback!" declared *New York Times* columnist James Reston to a colleague, denouncing a false story about presidential candidate Jimmy Carter during the 1976 campaign. He was not able to find the word in any of the standard dictionaries.

As election day drew near in 1844, the *Ithaca* (N.Y.) *Chronicle* printed what it claimed was a portion of "A Tour Through the Western and Southern States" by a "Baron Roorback," stating that Democratic candidate James K. Polk had bought forty-three slaves and branded his initials on their shoulders. Other newspapers picked up the story, which later turned out to be a forgery by an Ithaca abolitionist. The name is now applied to any last-minute smear, and is why many newspapers are leery of publishing damaging stories on the day before election.

See SMEAR; GUTTER FLYER; OCTOBER SURPRISE.

root and branch   in the entirety; from bottom to top.

The coinage comes from Supreme Court Justice William J. Brennan, Jr., in the 1968 decision of *Green v. County School Board of New Kent County, Virginia.* Justice Brennan delivered the opinion of the Supreme Court against the segregation policies of that Virginia county's school system.

Justice Brennan told the author:

It's the decision that abandoned the "all deliberate speed" standard which had been adopted in the second *Brown* decision, *Brown v. Board of Education,* decided May 31, 1955. The pertinent quote from that opinion directs the district courts to enter orders "as are necessary and proper to admit to public schools on a racially nondiscriminatory basis with all deliberate speed."

Green discarded this approach, holding that "the burden on a school board today is to come forward with a plan that promises realistically to work, and promises realistically to work *now*."

A search by Fred R. Shapiro of the Yale Law School library yielded the full first use of *root and branch* in the 1968 decision. Justice Brennan wrote: "School boards such as the respondent then operating state-compelled dual systems were nevertheless clearly charged with the affirmative duty to take whatever steps might be necessary to convert to a unitary system in which racial discrimination would be eliminated root and branch."

Richard J. Cattani of the *Christian Science Monitor* recalled in a 1981 piece that "Republicans in 1932 fought the Roosevelt program root and branch, to their peril."

In a July 1992 environmental hearing on Capitol Hill, William K. Reilly, administrator of the Environmental Protection Agency, responded to questions about unethical practices of environmental contractors by saying, "I think we are going after the problem *root and branch*."

Using the same conjunction as *tooth and nail*, the *and* of *root and branch* points to the entire plant or tree, or by metaphorical extension, the complete problem or situation. The metaphor is ancient. A translation of *Ta Hsueh*, a Confucian text, states: "All things have roots and branches. All things have beginnings and ends. To know what is first and what is last will lead one near the way."

root, hog, or die a political proverb meaning "work for your office, or leave it."

In lean years, a hungry hog must learn to root in the ground for his food or starve. This proverb probably had nonpolitical origins, but it was popularized early in the Andrew Jackson era.

The *Calumet and War Club* publication in 1836 spelled out the SPOILS SYSTEM agreement of the Jacksonians: "Root, hog, or die—work for your office, or leave it—support the party, right or wrong—are the terms of the agreement."

The original spoils system connotation has worn off and the current occasional use is now a rough exhortation to get out and campaign.

See PROVERBS AND AXIOMS, POLITICAL.

Rose Garden rubbish supposedly ad-lib remarks made by the President on minor occasions, usually prepared in note form by the most junior of White House speechwriters.

Political leaders are expected to make "appropriate remarks" at informal ceremonies, and often wish to have ideas submitted in advance, around which they can extemporize. Since many of these ceremonies take place in places like the White House Rose Garden, the phrase "Rose Garden rubbish" was coined in the Lyndon Johnson speechwriting staff to derogate the job of preparing the seemingly off-the-cuff appropriatenesses. Peter Benchley, a junior speechwriter who later gained fame as the author of the novel *Jaws*, popularized the term in a *Life* article.

The phrase is too self-critical to be used officially around the White House; in the Nixon era, the unloved task was referred to by the President with a musical metaphor: "Grace notes."

John B. McDonald, one of the junior Nixon speechwriters in 1972, wrote an open letter to the Jimmy Carter speechwriters in the *Washington Post* in 1977, cautioning them that not all presidential prose was earth-shaking or even important:

"You're not yet acutely familiar with Rose Garden Rubbish—but you soon will be. Why is the President delighted that Miss Teenage America is calling on him? What does he say to the head of the American Dental Association? What does he tell someone who is off to deliver two musk oxen to the People's Republic of China? . . . these are all real items and the President can't wing them—somebody has to develop some background suggestions for lines of credible commentary. Don't look around—you're it."

The outdoor area near the Oval Office—a small lawn surrounded by flower beds, with magnolia trees in the corners—is called the Rose Garden, though it contains few rose bushes. White House gardeners rarely put red rose plants in, because they consider dark colors "heavy" for a garden, which is the sort of fact a speechwriter would provide a President who was welcoming a delegation of horticulturists.

Rosie Scenario overly optimistic projections of economic growth and incoming revenues, designed to bring budgets into near-balance.

This phrase borrows the word *scenario* from film jargon for a script outline (the word has also been popularized in war games). The modifier plays on the adjective *rosy*, as in the optimism of the mid-nineteenth-century phrase about "seeing through rose-colored glasses" and the nickname *Rosie*.

A 1985 *Washington Post* piece extended the metaphor, suggesting a possible title for budget director David Stockman's book: "How Rosie Scenario Fell Off Her Trojan Horse When It, Too, Stopped to Feed at the Public Trough."

The full name, *Rosie Scenario*, serves as a personification of hope. One political take on George Bush's election in 1988 was that "it means 'Rosie Scenario' assumptions on economic growth and interest rates."

The term is also used in lowercase as a common noun and is finding its way out of economic jargon into general political use. In 1992, the *Chicago Tribune* used the lowercase phrase in discussing the Democrats' hope that Ross Perot's candidacy would help Bill Clinton to "win, or failing that, throw the election into the Democrat-controlled House of Representatives. Oh, what a rosie scenario, Democrat-style."

A synonym for this phrase is *best-case scenario*. The latter was formed in the 1970s on the model of *worst-case scenario*, whose hyphenated modifier dates back to a 1964 use in the field of broadcast technology.

rotten boroughs districts with unusually large representation for a small population.

In England from the sixteenth through eighteenth centuries, "rotten" or "pocket" boroughs existed with as few as a hundred voters sending a representative to Parliament. These seats were controlled by landowners who either bribed or coerced the voters in their area to vote their way; the seats were often sold by "borough-mongers" (see -MONGER). Reform bills in 1832 and 1867 eliminated the practice.

The phrase is traceable to 1771 in England and to Civil War days in the U.S.; the *Cincinnati Enquirer* in 1874 wrote: "The Republican South is Grant's 'rotten borough.'" States like Nevada and Delaware, with two senators despite their small population, were attacked as rotten boroughs, though the Constitution provided two senators for the express reason of protecting the rights of the smaller states.

In recent years the phrase has been used in the campaign to reapportion voting districts in accordance with the principle of ONE MAN, ONE VOTE. The connotation of seats bought and sold is now gone, the meaning of unfair representation remaining. "Three cases protesting apportionment," wrote the *New Republic* in April 1967, "plus a fourth in Virginia, are now before the Supreme Court testing how far one-man, one-vote shall dissolve rotten boroughs. " See GERRYMANDER.

rubber-chicken circuit the interminable series of public luncheons and dinners which are an inescapable part of campaigning and officeholding.

"Rubber" chicken is tough. So is campaigning. Robert Phelps of the *New York Times* described in 1964 the stamina needed by a presidential candidate: "The candidate must be capable of covering up to 200,000 miles by air, ingesting 600 chicken dinners, delivering 2500 speeches, clasping hands with a million persons and smiling gaily while being smacked with 10 tons of confetti." Another *Times* reporter in 1967 wrote of George Wallace's presidential campaign: ". . . his political advance men soon discovered that the baked chicken and green pea circuit was not only willing, but often eager, to have him as a speaker."

FAT CATS at $500-a-plate affairs get steak or roast beef and rissolé potatoes (why always rissolé potatoes?) but at non-fund-raising affairs, where the purpose is to meet the candidate and $50 covers the cost of the function, chicken is *de rigueur*. Candidates are expected to make appearances sitting on the dais of several functions per evening, many philanthropic or civic, at which they make nonpolitical remarks and make a pass at their plates.

The result is often a combination of mental and physical malnutrition, brought on by a revulsion toward hotel food in general, and chicken in particular.

"When the dinners run out," said candidate John F. Kennedy in 1960, "the luncheons begin, and when the luncheons run out, the breakfasts begin. We may all meet next week to get the campaign out of the red with a midnight brunch at eighty-five dollars a person—and I will be there."

According to restaurateur George Lang, the rubberization of chicken requires (1) a miscalculation of timing by the organizing committee, allowing the juices of the chicken to congeal while the dais is being introduced; (2) a chef whose oven is too hot; and (3) a food buyer with a sharp eye for stringy birds. A practiced rubberizer cooks the chicken hours before the function and reheats it for serving; when this is not possible, a tender roast chicken can be made quite rubbery by exposure to a steam table for a few minutes.

Testimonial dinners came under fire after employees of Connecticut Senator Thomas Dodd leaked the senator's files to columnist Drew Pearson, raising the question of the diversion of campaign funds to the personal use of the senator. This caused the *Washington Post* to editorialize in April 1967: "By and large, the 'testimonial dinner' is a political fraud, a gastronomical affront, an ethical outrage, a colossal bore, an insufferable social disaster and financial shakedown."

A counterpart in England is "function fish." In the U.S., the key to the phrase is "circuit": *baked (or roast) chicken circuit, roast beef circuit, chicken-and-mashed-potatoes circuit* are among the many variations. The phrase derives from vaudeville use, when performers were booked into a circuit, or string of theaters; the word bore a treadmill connotation which has carried over into politics.

See WAXWORKS.

rubber stamp a legislature or political figure taking orders from a political leader, or dominated by the executive branch.

"They centered all their powers in the Executive," Herbert Hoover reported Al Smith as saying in 1936 about the last two Congresses, "and that is the reason why you read in the newspapers reference to Congress as the rubber-stamp Congress."

In 1967, former FDR brain truster Raymond Moley disagreed. "The seventy-third Congress was no 'rubber stamp.' Its leadership was rich in talent and experience. The concept of an assembly line from the White House to the Congress cannot be sustained by the facts."

Theodore Roosevelt's biographer, William Thayer, used the phrase in 1919, as an exhortation William Howard Taft (long dominated by Roosevelt) might have heard: "Be your own President; don't be anybody's man or rubber stamp." Edward Conrad Smith, in his 1924 *Dictionary of American Politics*, wrote: ". . . the term was first used to characterize several members of President Wilson's cabinet who seemed to have practically no influence on the conduct of affairs."

On a television program in 1962, Harvard Law Professor Mark De-Wolfe Howe objected to Ted Kennedy's candidacy for senator from Massachusetts: "Seeking an office in the United States Senate, while his brother is in the White House, seems to me to represent a total misunderstanding of the responsibilities of a United States Senator. To have a rubber stamp Senator is to me an offense against the whole tradition that there should be a separation of powers in our government."

In Huey Long's heyday, the Louisiana state legislature was known as "Huey's trained seals." As senator, Long ran the state through the supremely acquiescent Governor O. K. Allen, about whom Huey's brother Earl once said, "A leaf blew in the window of Allen's office one day and fell on his desk. He signed it."

rugged individualism Herbert Hoover's philosophy of economic freedom, equal opportunity, and personal initiative, as opposed to what he considered paternalistic government.

Toward the close of the 1928 campaign against Democrat Al Smith, Herbert Hoover spoke in New York on October 22, determined, as he recalled years later, to "draw the issue of the American system, as opposed to all forms of collectivism." He sketched the background of the necessary government involvement in the economy in World War I, then posed the peacetime dilemma:

> We are challenged with a peacetime choice between the American system of rugged individualism and a European philosophy of diametrically opposed doctrines—doctrines of paternalism and state socialism. The acceptance of these ideas would have meant the destruction of self-government through centralization of government. It would have meant the undermining of the individual initiative and enterprise through which our people have grown to unparalleled greatness.
> The Republican Party from the beginning resolutely turned its face away from these ideas . . .

Six years after the phrase became a part of the American political lexicon, Hoover disclaimed coinage: "While I can make no claim for having introduced the term 'rugged individualism,' I should be proud to have invented it. It has been used by American leaders for over a half-century in eulogy of those God-fearing men and women of honesty whose stamina and character and fearless assertion of rights led them to make their own way in life."

At the time and for many years afterward, opponents of Hoover used the phrase with a sneer. Socialist Norman Thomas, two weeks after the speech was delivered, used the phrase as his text: "Mr. Hoover calls his capitalism 'rugged individualism' and professes to find some peculiar virtue in the wasteful and chaotic mismanagement of coal, in our frantic real-estate speculation . . ."

In 1936, Franklin Roosevelt was too cagey to tackle individualism head-on at the Democratic convention; his reference was oblique: "I believe in individualism . . . up to the point where the individualist starts to operate at the expense of society."

But the association of Hoover with the phrase itself enabled FDR to make it a target in a campaign speech:

> . . . I know how the knees of all of our *rugged individualists* were trembling four years ago and how their hearts fluttered. They came to Washington in great numbers. Washington did not look like a dangerous bureaucracy to them then. Oh, no! It looked like an emergency hospital. . . . And now most of the patients seem to be doing very nicely. Some of them are even well enough to throw their crutches at the doctor.

As hatred of Hoover cooled, the use of "rugged individualism" lost some of its built-in sarcasm, and came to be regarded by most as a quaint hearkening-back to the simple virtues of America's early days. But President Harry S. Truman chose to RUN AGAINST HOOVER as well as Dewey in 1948:

> Many of you remember 1932. . . . Out here on Eighth Avenue veterans were selling apples. Ragged individ-

ualism, I suppose that's what you would call it.

The phrase is still forceful. Thomas V. DiBacco of American University wrote in the *Christian Science Monitor* in 1985: "It's ironic, but for a nation of rugged individualists who have been all too prone to pad their personal expense account books every now and then, Americans as a whole tend to become particularly zealous when public ledgers are at issue."

rule of law the rubric used to attack the assumption of extralegal authority or "inherent power" by the Executive; the assertion that a nation's leaders must abide by a written constitution or unwritten common law.

Though Tom Paine had said a century before that we stood as a nation "where the law is king," the phrase was popularized by A. V. Dicey, in his 1885 *Introduction to the Law of the Constitution*. In his definition, the "rule of law" in England meant that ordinary courts determined every man's legal rights and liabilities; that executive officers had less arbitrary power and more limited discretion than in other European countries; and that government officials could be brought to court for wrongs done even under the cloak of official authority.

In the U.S., this idea is more frequently expressed as GOVERNMENT OF LAWS, NOT OF MEN. Although the maxim "Necessity knows no law" is sometimes used as a justification for emergency actions, most politicians concede that—when the emergency is over—the extralegal acts are not to be condoned. ("Extralegal" is a forgiving euphemism for "illegal," which in turn is less severe than "unlawful.")

Historian J. G. Randall, in his 1926 classic *Constitutional Problems under Lincoln*, wrote of Civil War repression: "Instead of the 'rule of law' prevailing, as Dicey defined it, men were imprisoned outside the law and independent of the courts; and governmental officers were given a privileged place above the law and made immune from penalties for wrongs committed . . . Legally, the Civil War stands out as an eccentric period, a time when constitutional restraints did not fully operate and when the 'rule of law' largely broke down."

Chris Patten, British Governor of Hong Kong before its reversion to Chinese sovereignty in 1997, told columnist Anthony Lewis: "What's made Hong Kong what it is, is the combination of Chinese entrepreneurialism and the rule of law. And the rule of law is not just about judges in court. It's about a free press and an independent legislature."

See MEASURES, NOT MEN; HIGHER LAW.

rule or ruin. See GAG RULE.

rule out to deny the existence of even a remote possibility.

The use of a question that begins "Are you ruling out . . ." is a sign of journalistic desperation. On dull news days, reporters are forced to ask a question that gives them a weak lead either way it is answered.

The only story more tenuous than "The President today ruled out any chance of [whatever]" is "The President today refused to rule out consideration of [whatever]."

The rule-out question gained popularity in the late sixties, especially at press conferences of White House press secretary Ronald Ziegler. An attempt is made occasionally by the questionee to blunt the surefire either-way story with an odd use of language: "I'm not ruling it out, but that doesn't mean I'm ruling it in."

rump session a gathering of dissidents; or, a legislative body that refuses to disband according to law.

"It is not fit that you should sit here any longer!" shouted Oliver Cromwell to the "Rump Parliament." ". . . You shall now give place to better men." After England's Second Civil War of 1648, Cromwell's Colonel Pride ejected ninety-six Presbyterian members from Parliament who were suspected of dealings with the defeated King Charles ("Pride's Purge"), and the remaining sixty were known as the Rump.

The word "rump" is from the Scandinavian word for the hindquarters of an animal, its meaning crossing over to "remnant" or "tail end."

The word was popularized in the U.S. around the time of our own Civil War. In 1860 Stephen Douglas was called the candidate of a "rump convention," and Congress in Reconstruction days was called a "rump Congress" by Democrats who felt it did not represent all the states and was therefore in unlawful session. The most famous rump convention was Theodore Roosevelt's "Bull Moose" split-off from the Republicans in 1912.

In current use, "rump" is used with *caucus, convention, session,* and *meeting,* usually connoting a sorehead minority that cannot lose gracefully.

run between the raindrops dodge repeated attacks or problems; race to escape trouble.

This vivid word picture suggests the need to keep moving to avoid attacks. The term was popularized during the Supreme Court confirmation hearings for Judge David Souter in 1990.

Senator Arlen Specter (R-Pa.) announced his intentions to confirm the candidate, adding, "During these hearings, Judge Souter really had to run between the raindrops in a veritable hurricane."

The movement in the metaphor is in contrast to the forced lack of movement in a similar but not synonymous phrase about being in trouble, *between a* ROCK AND A HARD PLACE.

running against Hoover   making a theme, rather than an individual, the target or villain in a campaign.

"Every campaign needs a villain," Thomas E. Dewey told the author in 1969. He recommended that President Nixon make inflation his villain, just as FDR did with ECONOMIC ROYALISTS and Truman with SPECIAL INTERESTS. "Roosevelt never ran against me," said the man who had lost to FDR. "He just kept running against Hoover."

"Running against Hoover," in political parlance, has little to do with Herbert Hoover as an individual. Instead, the phrase denotes campaigning against the memory of hard times, the fear of joblessness and depression.

As personal recollections of depression days have faded in the minds of most of the population, another fear—frustration, really—has made itself felt, at first articulated by George Wallace in his SEND THEM A MESSAGE campaign against big government, the Establishment, the "pointy-headed professors." Nixon, too, in 1968 would "run against Washington,"(see RUNNING AGAINST WASHINGTON), but in a more muted way, decrying "more of the same" from Hubert Humphrey, but unable—after his own years as Vice President and in Congress—to credibly adopt an outright anti-Washington stance.

An earlier use of "running against" a theme was for a politician to be "against sin." That comes from a legend in the twenties that Mrs. Calvin Coolidge asked her taciturn husband the subject of a sermon he attended. He replied, "Sin." She asked, "What did the preacher have to say?" The President is said to have answered, "He was against it."

running against Washington   representing oneself as a political outsider; seeking power by making the most of not being in power.

Arguing against government excess and bureaucratic gridlock, politicians who cast themselves deliberately as outsiders are said to be *running against Washington*. The phrase became popular during the 1970s when Jimmy Carter presented himself as a newcomer to INSIDE THE BELTWAY politics, a candidate apparently unbeholden to established interest groups and the existing power structure.

Hubert Humphrey in 1976 took on those who were running against Washington. In March, as Jimmy Carter began winning his first primaries, the warhorse from Minnesota said: "Candidates who make an attack on Washington are making an attack on government programs, on the poor, on blacks, on minorities, on the cities. It's a disguised new form of racism, a disguised new form of conservatism."

Bill Clinton echoed that Democratic defense in 1992, attacking Republicans who "have gotten away with running against Washington, and they are the Washington insiders. They are the people that have to take responsibility for not making this government work."

The center of power that is under attack may change, but the phrase retains its meaning. A Soviet studies specialist commented in 1990 on the possibility that Gorbachev would eventually run for president in a popular election: "He will try to run against Moscow, just as someone else won by running against Washington."

For the origin of the phrase, see RUNNING AGAINST HOOVER.

running dogs.   See FELLOW TRAVELER.

running for the exercise   going through the motions of campaigning in a hopeless cause.

Asked on February 10, 1976, who he thought his most likely Democratic opponent would be, President Ford told reporters he thought it would be Senator Hubert Humphrey "—and I think all the rest of them are running for the exercise." (It turned out that Governor Jimmy Carter was running to win.)

When a candidate enlists in a seemingly impossible campaign, he enters a self-hypnotic experience that soon magnifies a *remote possibility* into an *outside chance* into a probability of *making a good showing* into a *good bet for an upset.* He points out that he is not "running for the exercise"; his friends still think he is.

An American *runs* for election; an Englishman *stands* for election; the French verb is *se battre,* to "struggle," or *se présenter,* to "present oneself," for election. The English metaphor is based on a trial: the candidate stands for election as he would "stand trial." The American metaphor is that of a race.

"Run" has a place in a variety of political expressions, its usage traceable to Alexander Hamilton in 1792. See RUN SCARED; RUNNING MATE; FRONT RUNNER. The *Ohio State Journal* in 1840 pointed out that "General Harrison constantly *runs ahead of his ticket.*" A campaign is most frequently compared to a *race,* and an easy victory is *winning in a walk.* Former Interior Secretary Harold Ickes, referring to a poor speech at the Gridiron Club by Senator John Bricker in 1946, said, "Before his speech . . . Bricker thought he was running for the Republican nomination for President. Now he is not only walking, he is limping . . ."

An antonym is SHOO-IN, also a racing expression.

running like a dry creek   describing a campaigner who is not hitting as hard as some of his supporters would like.

Nineteen newspapers of the Scripps-Howard chain ran a front-page editorial in 1952, six weeks after Eisenhower was nominated, declaring "Ike is running like a dry creek." This was just after he half-heartedly defended General George C. Marshall against criticism by Senator William Jenner of Indiana, concluding, "Maybe he made some mistakes. I don't know about that." The editorial said that the General sounded like "just another ME-TOO candidate" and criticized him for not "coming out swinging." "If Ike doesn't know [about Marshall], he had better find out. For that's one of the big issues of this campaign. Ask any mother, father, or wife of a soldier now in Korea. . . . We still cling to the hope that . . . he will hit hard. If he doesn't, he may as well concede defeat." Campaigns also *never get off the ground* or *never catch fire.*

In Eisenhower's case, of course, the *dry creek* wound up in a *flood* of votes, a *tidal wave* of support, as he received *thunderous* ovations and a *shower* of contributions, *snowing under* his opponent and establishing his *don't-rock-the-boat* position in the *mainstream.* For other watery metaphors, see TRICKLE-DOWN THEORY; PUMP-PRIMING.

running mate   a candidate running on the same ticket, for a lower office; most often used in connection with the vice-presidential nominee.

"Governor Marshall bears the highest reputation," said Woodrow Wilson on July 4, 1912, ". . . and I feel honored by having him as a running mate." This was the first recorded use of the phrase by a presidential nominee, though the racing term had been in use in 1900. "Men of all parties," wrote the *Review of Reviews,* "will admit that Mr. Root's name would add positive strength, and that a better man could hardly be selected as Mr. McKinley's 'running mate.'"

In horse racing, a single stable will often enter two horses in a race, the lesser horse used as a pacesetter and called a running mate. This second horse usually vanishes into obscurity. Vice President Hubert Humphrey, reminiscing in 1966 about the 1964 campaign against the Goldwater-Miller ticket: "To this day I have a great deal of respect for Barry Goldwater and his running mate, what's-his-name." This was soon followed by a satiric song by Tom Lehrer, "I Wonder What Happened to Hubert."

When the running mate is stronger or better-known than the candidate for the top job, the result is called a KANGAROO TICKET.

run scared   an admonition to avoid complacency; to run as if a good chance to lose existed, despite indications of likely victory.

"I expect to win running like a singed cat," said Adlai Stevenson in 1952. Dwight Eisenhower in 1956, who had less reason to campaign aggressively, said, "I believe when you are in any contest you should work like there is—to the very last minute—a chance to lose it. This is battle, this is politics, this is anything."

The candidate whose polls show him behind needs no advice to run scared; he does so automatically. The phrase is directed in particular to the candidate who is in the position of Thomas E. Dewey in 1948, considered a SHOO-IN. Hindsighted politicians now say Dewey should have "run scared"—conducted a more aggressive, fighting campaign—but the fact was that the Dewey managers did run scared, at the behest of party leaders—scared of saying anything that would "rock the boat," afraid of making a mistake that would give Truman an opening. See STIR UP THE ANIMALS.

run the traps.   See RATTLE THE CAGE.

rustling behind the jalousies   intervention in political affairs by the candidate's spouse.

John A. Wells, a New York attorney who managed campaigns for such Republicans as Nelson Rockefeller, Jacob Javits, and Louis Lefkowitz, once agreed to manage a political campaign provided, as he put it to the candidate, "there is no rustling behind the jalousies." His condition was met: the candidate's wife, noted for her outspoken opinions about the scheduling of the candidate's time, was effectively silenced for the duration.

The phrase is not as strong as POWER BEHIND THE THRONE or GRAY EMINENCE; its reference is exclusively feminine. A jalousie is a slatted screen, providing concealment without muffling the sound of a swishing skirt.

S

sachem   a party leader.

"Take me to your leader," a bromide used in dealing with savages, is reflected in the first recorded use of "sachem": "They brought us to their Sachim," the 1622 *Journal of the Plantation at Plymouth* records, ". . . very personable, gentle, courteous, and fayre conditioned." The word is from the Narraganset, an Algonquian language, meaning "sagamore" or "party chief," and was used by Tammany leaders as early as 1876. A political joke based on this construction is the grafter's request: "Lead me to your taker."

John Adams, in 1776, wrote of "The patricians, the sachems, the nabobs . . . [who] sigh, moan and fret." The braves and warriors of Tammany named their leader the Grand Sachem, who presided over meetings held at the "wigwam"; today, political leadership meetings are frequently termed "powwows."

The word is not used currently by politicians, but is frequently used—along with SATRAP—by political columnists and reporters. For other Indian words in politics, see MUCKEY-MUCKS; MUGWUMP; CAUCUS; RAIN-MAKER.

safe   applied to a politician, reliable; applied to a district or constituency, taken for granted.

In James Russell Lowell's *Bigelow Papers* of 1862, a character says, "Long 'z ye sift out 'safe' canderdates thet no one aint afeared on." Lincoln Steffens wrote in a 1905 issue of *McClure's*: "The gubernatorial chair [in Rhode Island] never had amounted to much more than an empty honor for 'safe men.'"

In its political use, "safe" means regular and not likely to bolt. Mencken defined it as "not radical," but a radical can be safe to other radicals if he is not likely to turn conservative. When presidential candidates total up likely delegate support, the categories are "safe," "shaky," and "leaning away."

"They don't concede [Harold] Stassen one chance in a million," wrote John Gunther in 1947, ". . . they know that the better the prospects of Republican victory in 1948, the less are Stassen's own chances for the nomination—since, if victory is certain, there is no temptation to choose any but the 'safest' candidate." In 1952 Eisenhower was not nearly as safe to delegates as Senator Robert A. Taft, but after twenty years out of office they preferred a safe bet for election to a safe candidate.

safety net social welfare programs or assistance to protect the needy.

A favorite catch phrase of the Reagan Administration, this term is built on the circus metaphor of a net to catch falling trapeze artists or high-wire performers.

Reagan and his spokesmen added the adjective *social.* David A. Stockman, his director of the Office of Management and Budget (whose sobriquet was "the blow-dried Grim Reaper"), defined the three-word phrase in early 1981: "A social safety net encompasses the long-range programs of basic income security, most of which were established in the New Deal 50 years ago and are now widely accepted."

Stockman continued: "This includes basic Social Security and Medicare, unemployment compensation, the two components of what we call welfare (Aid for Families with Dependent Children and Supplemental Security Income), and basic veterans' benefits."

This metaphor for welfare started in the U.S. in the 1970s, specifically in editorials by Jude Wanniski for the *Wall Street Journal.* He told the lexicographer: "The safety-net idea that I used applied to the international banking system—that is, there would be an international lender of last resort that would serve as a safety net for Third World loans in the event of international turmoil. I always liked the idea of a safety net. When I got to that chapter in the Kemp book, I held on to that metaphor."

That book by Jack Kemp is *An American Renaissance: A Strategy for the 1980's,* written in 1979. Kemp wrote:

Americans have two complementary desires. They want an open, promising ladder of opportunity. And they want a safety net of social services to catch and comfort those less fortunate than themselves. . . . Yet because people want this safety net in place, it doesn't follow that they therefore want it filled up with sufferers. Least of all do they want their assistance to seduce others into habits of dependency.

The net metaphor, however, predates that usage. Chancellor Helmut Schmidt referred to a *net of social security,* perhaps after its popularization in Germany during a metalworkers' strike in the late 1950s. In the late 1970s, Schmidt was quoted as saying, "We must be careful not to take measures which will make this net too wide-meshed so that people fall through."

The earliest citation was submitted by Leslie Lenkowsky, director of research of the Smith Richardson Foundation, who passed along a passage from a speech by Winston Churchill on October 8, 1951:

The difference between our outlook and the Socialist outlook on life is the difference between the ladder and the queue. . . . We ask: "What happens if anyone slips out of his place in the queue?" "Ah!" say the Socialists. "Our officials—and we have plenty of them—come and put him back in it. . . ." And then they come back at us and say: ". . . What is your answer to what happens if anyone slips off the ladder?" Our reply is: "We shall have a good net. . . ."

salami tactics little by little; gradualism.

This figure of speech was a favorite of the Alsop brothers. Wrote Stewart Alsop in *Newsweek,* April 28, 1969: "It remains to be seen just how far the Russians and their Czech and Slovak stooges will have to go in order to complete the process of rescaring the people. One theory is that press censorship, secret-police pressure, and salami tactics will do the trick. Alexander Dubcek will certainly not be the last of the liberals to fall victim to the salami knife."

Two years later, in his syndicated column, Joseph Alsop denounced "the orgy of public hypocrisy touched off by the *Times'* collection of stolen Pentagon documents," pointing out that the two men whose advice was taken by President Johnson were Dean Rusk and Ambassador Llewellyn Thompson: "Both of them pressed strongly for the salami-slicing approach—for 'gradualism' as they called it."

In *The Harper Dictionary of Modern Thought*, Alan Bullock and Oliver Stallybrass credit the coinage to Matyas Rakosi of the Hungarian Communist party, who in 1945 described how he came to power by getting his opposition to slice off its right wing, then its centrists, until only those collaborating with Communists remained in power.

The term still enjoys currency and is sometimes used in the singular. Under the heading "Antiabortion Group to Bolster Local Efforts," the *Washington Post* of June 15, 1990, cited the advice of a "Right to Life" spokesman that "the movement's best approach is a 'salami' tactic, pushing for restrictions on sex-selection abortions or abortions for minors that most voters find offensive."

SALT   Strategic Arms Limitation Talks, begun in Helsinki in November 1969, between the Soviet Union and the U.S. Most often used redundantly, as "SALT talks." Followed in the early 1980s by START, Strategic Arms Reduction Talks. The talks consisted of negotiations seeking to limit and eventually reduce both offensive and defensive strategic nuclear weapons.

There were two SALT rounds: *SALT I* lasted from 1969 through 1972; *SALT II* lasted from 1973 to 1979. A third round of talks began in 1982 but was suspended a year later.

According to John Newhouse, in his *Cold Dawn: The Story of SALT* (1973), the man who invented the acronym SALT is Robert Martin, who was a low-level staffer in the State Department's Bureau of Political-Military Affairs.

"In the Spring of 1968," wrote Newhouse, "when the prospect of talks suddenly brightened, bureaucrats began having to write cables about limiting strategic arms. Any combination of words labeling the process was inevitably cumbersome. Martin, who was then a member of the political section of the U.S. Nato mission in Brussels, finally gave up and concocted SALT. His ambassador, Harlan Cleveland, resisted the term for a while; so did a number of Washington officials, finding it too cute. ACDA [the Arms Control and Disarmament Agency] disliked it. The issue arose at a meeting of senior officials; the CIA finally insisted on formal adoption of SALT because its filing system was already being organized around the term."

Robert Martin confirmed this. Reached in 1978 at the U.S. embassy in Teheran, where he was counselor for Political-Military Affairs, he responded: "The acronym SALT is one that I developed in order to save . . . some of that precious commodity—time . . . The initial reaction, both in Brussels and Washington, was negative. Harlan Cleveland, my Ambassador at USNATO, kept scratching it out, insisting that the four words be spelled out . . . he did not view the acronym as being sufficiently formal and serious for the exercise that the U.S. proposed to begin."

As often happens, the man who resisted the term got credit for it. A German newspaper reported Cleveland (see REVOLUTION OF RISING EXPECTATIONS) to be the author of the acronym. "He sent me a marvelous letter," writes Martin, "expressing delight at the credit being heaped upon him for something he had so belittled originally; yet further proof, he pointed out, that the Chiefs get all of the credit while the poor blighters in the trenches do all the work."

The vocabulary of nuclear warfare causes some shudders (see UNTHINKABLE THOUGHTS), and in some cases, deliberately mocks itself: the acronym for "Mutual Assured Destruction" is MAD. Despite these trepidations, things must have names, and in 1975 the Arms Control and Disarmament Agency issued its revised "SALT lexicon," selections from which follow:

Arms Stability: A strategic force relationship in which neither side perceives the necessity for undertaking major new arms programs in order to avoid being placed at a disadvantage.

Assured Destruction: The ability to inflict an "unacceptable" degree of damage upon an aggressor after absorbing any first strike. [Mutual assured destruction is a condition in which an assured destruction capability is possessed by opposing sides. See also "Unacceptable Damage."]

Ballistic Missile: Any missile which does not rely upon aerodynamic surfaces to produce lift and consequently follows a ballistic trajectory (i.e., that resulting when the body is acted upon only by gravity and aerodynamic drag) when thrust is terminated.

Intercontinental Ballistic Missile (ICBM): A land based, rocket-propelled vehicle capable of delivering a warhead to intercontinental ranges (ranges in excess of about 3,000 nautical miles).

Circular Error Probable (CEP): A measure of the delivery accuracy of a weapon system used as a factor in determining probable damage to targets. It is the radius of a circle around the target at which a missile is aimed within which the warhead has a .5 probability of falling.

Cold Launch: The technique of ejecting a missile from a silo before full ignition of the main engine, sometimes called "Pop-up."

Collateral Damage: The damage to surrounding human and non-human resources, either military or non-military, as the result of action or strikes directed specifically against enemy forces or military facilities. This term was turned into a euphemism during the Gulf War of 1991.

Counterforce Strike: An attack aimed at an adversary's military capability, especially his strategic military capability. [This means the enemy's missiles.]

Countervalue Strike: An attack aimed at an opponent's cities or industries.

Coupling (strategic): The linking of a lower-level conflict, e.g., Soviet/Warsaw Pact military aggression in Europe, to the use of U.S. strategic deterrent forces such as ICBMs, heavy bombers, and SLBMs.

Cruise Missile: A guided missile which uses aerodynamic lift to offset gravity and propulsion to counteract drag. The major portion of a cruise missile's flight path remains within the earth's atmosphere.

Endoatmosphere: From sea level to about 40 nautical miles altitude.

Exoatmosphere: Higher than about 40 nautical miles above sea level.

First Strike (nuclear): The launching of an initial strategic nuclear attack before the opponent has used any strategic weapons himself.

Forward-Based Systems (FBS): A term introduced by the USSR to refer to those U.S. nuclear systems based in third countries or on aircraft carriers and capable of delivering a nuclear strike against the territory of the USSR.

Fractional Orbital Bombardment System (FOBS): A missile that achieves an orbital trajectory, but fires a set of retrorockets before the completion of one revolution in order to slow down, reenter the atmosphere and release the warhead it carries into a normal ballistic trajectory toward its target.

Hardening of Silos: Protection of a missile site with concrete and earth and other measures so as to withstand blast, heat, or radiation from a nuclear attack.

National Technical Means of Verification: Techniques which are under national control for monitoring compliance with the provisions of an agreement. [Such as spy satellites; this overcame Soviet objections to on-site inspections.]

Payload: The reentry vehicle(s) placed on ballistic trajectories by the main propulsion stages and bus.

There are several general types of payload configurations, such as: (a) single reentry vehicles, (b) multiple reentry vehicles (MRV) and (c) multiple independently targetable reentry vehicles (MIRV). (See Reentry Vehicle.)

Preemptive Strike: A nuclear attack initiated in anticipation of an opponent's decision to resort to nuclear war. [This is also used in non-nuclear warfare; the Israelis called their attack on the massing Arab armies in 1967 a "pre-emptive strike."]

Reentry Vehicle (RV): That portion of a ballistic missile designed to carry a nuclear warhead and to reenter the earth's atmosphere in the terminal portion of the missile trajectory. *Multiple Independently Targetable Reentry Vehicle (MIRV)*: Two or more reentry vehicles carried by a single missile and capable of being independently targeted. [Writer Peter Ognibene called MIRV "separate but equal warheads integrated into a single missile but bused to different targets."]

Second Strike: A term usually used to refer to a retaliatory attack in response to a first strike.

Throw-Weight: Ballistic missile throw-weight is the maximum useful weight which has been flight-tested on the boost stages of the missile. The useful weight includes weight of the reentry vehicles, penetration aids, dispensing and release mechanisms, reentry shrouds, covers, buses and propulsion devices with their propellants (but not the final boost stages) which are present at the end of the boost phase.

TRIAD: The term used in referring to the basic structure of the U.S. strategic deterrent force. It is comprised of land-based ICBMs, the strategic bomber force, and the Polaris/Poseidon submarine fleet.

Unacceptable Damage: Degrees of destruction anticipated from an enemy second strike, which is sufficient to deter a nuclear power from launching a first strike.

Verification: The process of determining the degree to which parties to an agreement are complying with provisions of the agreement.

Warhead: That part of a missile, projectile, or torpedo that contains the explosive intended to inflict damage.

Yield: The force of a nuclear explosion expressed in terms of the number of tons of TNT that would have to be exploded to produce the same energy.

The Arms Control agency cautioned readers and negotiators that "the Lexicon is intended for quick reference only, not as a basis for adjudicating definitional problems that might arise in negotiation or in final treaty or agreement language."

One term not in the lexicon is *fratricide*, the first capital crime in the Bible, which Vice President Walter Mondale used in 1978 first in its strategic and later its political sense: "There is a concept in missilry, where you fire too many missiles too close together and they kill each other off—fratricide." Referring to the possibility that President Carter had overloaded the Congress with legislative initiatives in 1977, he added, "I think it can be fratricide—too many issues landing at the same time."

Saltniks seldom interspersed their jargon with shortened words or pet names, but *nuke* occasionally surfaced: as a verb, to make a nuclear strike, or as a noun, to mean a nuclear device, which is a euphemism for a bomb. Writing about the MX intercontinental missile in the *New York Times* on January 4, 1978, former systems analyst Earl Ravenal livened up his copy with a reference to a remark made by (and used against) Senator Barry Goldwater in 1964: "Mobile or with multiple bases, it [MX] would carry up to fourteen 200-kiloton MIRV warheads to within 100 yards of their targets. That kind of accuracy could finally realize Senator Barry Goldwater's vision of lobbing a nuke right into the men's room of the Kremlin." The writer immediately slipped back into the normal SALT idiom: "But, combined with silo-busting yields, it would also make the MX a highly unnerving first-strike counterforce weapon."

salutations. See MY FRIENDS.

samizdat the underground press that planted the seeds of freedom in the former Soviet Union.

"By *samizdat*," wrote *Time* on September 7, 1970, "Russians endlessly retype and clandestinely circulate the work of such banned writers as Alexander Solzhenitsyn."

John L. Hess, writing in the *New York Times* on June 12, 1971, reported that the latest Solzhenitsyn novel, *August 1914*, had an epilogue to its foreign edition noting that the book could not be published in the USSR "except in samizdat" because of censorship: "Samizdat is the hand-to-hand distribution of manuscripts, typed or photographed, of works rejected by Soviet printing houses."

The word comes from the Russian *sam* (self) *izdat* (the first part of the word for publishing), meaning to publish by one's self, probably coined as a pun on Gosizdat, the State Publishing House in Moscow.

The mid-sixties birth of the word coincided with the beginning of recognition outside the USSR that an organized opposition was operating within the Soviet regime. The word was first used in an official Soviet publication, the weekly magazine *Ogonyok*, in September 1971, in a story about dissident physicist Dmitri Mikheyev, defining the word as "in effect, anti-Soviet."

New York Times Soviet expert Harry Schwartz noted soon afterward that the spread of unofficial publications like *Chronicle of Current Events* raised the question of whether a "zone of tolerance" had been created in the USSR for illegal publication of dissent, providing a safety valve for political malcontents.

Through the seventies, that tolerance waxed and waned; after Solzhenitsyn's departure for the West, Soviet physicist Andrei Sakharov became the best-known dissenter, his positions made known by *samizdat*. In time a similar word—*tamizdat*, "published over there"—came to cover publication abroad, with copies smuggled back into the USSR.

By the late seventies, *samizdat* came to mean the material of dissent as well as its system of distribution. In the eighties, one reason given for the absence of personal computers in Soviet cities was that they might provide dissenters with "instant *samizdat*."

Following the dissolution of the Soviet Union, the term continued to be used only in historical contexts or, occasionally, in a general sense meaning "underground press." The latter use is illustrated in a review by Joseph Coates, in the September 10, 1992, *Chicago Tribune*, of a book, *Promises to Keep: A Call for a New American Revolution*, by Richard N. Goodwin: "The most encouraging sign of real renewal in this . . . election year is that this book . . . has circulated in samizdat among the Democratic candidates for president since last fall, when it surfaced in the campaign of Jerry Brown . . ."

See HUMAN RIGHTS; MOST FAVORED NATION; QUIET DIPLOMACY.

sanctions. See QUARANTINE.

sandbag to attack from behind; treat duplicitously by feigning friendship or weakness.

George Bush helped introduce this usage, an example of what news commentator Daniel Schorr calls the language of political victimization, by the early 1980s. "We feel we were sandbagged," he said after a 1980 primary, repeating the verb used by his New Hampshire campaign manager.

Six years later, Secretary of State George P. Shultz referred to the term during a lunch with Turkish officials who complained about U.S. quotas on Turkish imports: "Do you have a word in your language called *sandbag*? I have been brought here in order to have a nice luncheon and get hit behind the ear." The *Wall Street Journal* explained the usage in card-playing terms: "The word means to entice someone into putting money into a poker pot—either by not betting yourself or by betting only a small amount—and then raising back with a large bet later."

At the turn of the century, Farmer and Henley's slang dictionary referred to *sandbag* as a noun from thieves' argot, defined as "a large sausagelike bag of sand dealing a heavy blow that leaves no mark." The American use of the verb has been specifically limited to the sense of "to hit from behind."

Among other possible sources for the verb is theater slang (from the dropping of canvas sandbags used in flying the scenery). The word is used in chess and gambling, as well as in automobile racing, when participants deliberately hold back early in the game in order to win later by surprise.

San Francisco Democrat attack phrase on a liberal activist who blames society for its own ills; the ultimate naysayer or pessimist.

Jeane Kirkpatrick, the columnist and former United Nations Ambassador, introduced this term in 1984. As the Republican National Convention keynote speaker in Dallas, she emphasized the attack tactics of the Democrats at their earlier convention in San Francisco: "When the Soviet Union walked out of arms control negotiations . . . the San Francisco Democrats did not blame Soviet intransigence. They blamed the United States. But then, they always blame America first."

The phrase *San Francisco Democrats* is sometimes alternated with *blame-America-first Democrats*, painting those activists as weak liberals and subtly impugning their patriotism. The imperative *blame America first* is based on the tourism slogan *see America first* and is bottomed on the America-firsters of the late 1930s who favored isolationism and failed to see the threat posed by Hitler.

Still popular in the 1990s, *San Francisco Democrat* was used by the California delegation to the Republican National Convention in 1992. The chairman of that delegation, quoted in the *San Francisco Chronicle*, spoke out against the opposition party as "San Francisco Democrats now cloaked in respectable Madison Square Garden colors [who] wish for us a collective amnesia."

sanitize of a document, to delete damaging statements; of a person, to make innocent by association.

"The President has moved in seven months," wrote John Osborne about Jimmy Carter in the *New Republic* in 1977, "from thought of opening Cabinet meetings to the press, to maybe releasing edited transcripts of Cabinet discussions, to having a White House press officer attend meetings and afterward give reporters a sanitized account."

In that sense, "to sanitize" is to make palatable, or less embarrassing. The cleanliness metaphor—removing political dirt—is obvious, as in the instruction given to H. R. Haldeman to "clean up the tapes," i.e., to remove the material that might raise doubts or eyebrows.

A less obvious meaning of the term is to remain in place after a scandal affecting one's colleagues, thereby proving one's absence of taint. Many Nixon appointees asked to be kept on in the first year of the Ford Administration in order to be thus "sanitized."

Sometimes the word carries a political sting. Members of the House committee investigating the CIA (the "Pike Committee") objected in 1975 to the lack of cooperation they received from the intelligence agency. In the report, which was published in the *Village Voice* by CBS correspondent Daniel Schorr after the House decided to suppress it, the committee stated: "We were given heavily 'sanitized' pieces of paper. 'Sanitized' was merely a euphemism for blank sheets of paper . . ."

Ordinarily the word is only mildly pejorative, as sanitization is taken to be the customary manner of protecting insiders from publication of their indiscreet or unduly frank observations.

The extreme of sanitizing is "shredding," the product of the electric paper shredder; a more venal or deceptive form of avoiding detection is "laundering" (see LAUNDERED MONEY).

Santa Claus, nobody shoots at political proverb about folly of attacking government benefit programs.

Former Governor Alfred E. Smith, in a press conference in New York late in 1933, said, "No sane local official who has hung up an empty stocking over the municipal fireplace is going to shoot Santa Claus just before a hard Christmas."

In 1936, when Smith, the embittered 1928 Democratic presidential candidate, was campaigning against Roosevelt, he shortened the point to a simple "nobody shoots at Santa Claus."

Barry Goldwater, campaigning for the Republican presidential nomination in 1964, told the Economic Club of New York: "It is my chore to ask you to consider the toughest proposition ever faced by believers in the free-enterprise system: the need for a frontal attack against Santa Claus—not the Santa Claus of the holiday season, of course, but the Santa Claus of the free lunch, the government handout, the Santa Claus of something-for-nothing and something-for-everyone."

Another man to shoot at Santa Claus was Orville Freeman, campaigning for a fourth term as governor of Minnesota. According to economist Walter Heller, Freeman went around the state telling people frankly that the services they wanted could only be paid for with higher taxes—that, in his phrase, "There ain't no Santa Claus." He also lost.

A synonym for Santa Claus is "tooth fairy," after the practice of telling a child that if a recently extracted tooth is placed under the pillow at night, a fairy will come and replace the lost tooth with a coin. "Tooth fairy," to mean "a story told to believing children," is in growing use; it carries the same connotation of suspended-reality as Santa Claus, though Santa retains an exclusive franchise for government largesse. USC economics professor Arthur B. Laffer, who provided the intellectual underpinning for the TAX REVOLT in California in 1978, wrote in the July 1978 American Enterprise Institute *Economist:* "In the absence of the 'tooth fairy' the resources spent by the government are the total tax burden on the economy's productive sector."

In the don't-you-believe-it lexicon, BALONEY is the harshest denunciation; PIE IN THE SKY severe but fondly archaic; FREE LUNCH is usually limited to economic affairs; *tooth fairy* requires the most childlike belief; *Santa Claus* and *Uncle Sugar* are most associated with government handouts.

satellite a state formally independent but in fact subordinate to a large imperialist power; occasionally, an official under the domination of another.

The first part of the above definition, used in the Communist *Political Dictionary* (Moscow, 1958), could be agreed to by those members of the FREE WORLD who considered the Soviet Union "a large imperialist power."

This is a politically subjective word; to diehard Communists, the word refers to nations like some of those in Latin America, and even the British Commonwealth; these "lackeys" are within—to continue the metaphor— the U.S. "orbit." To Americans, satellites included the states of Eastern Europe as well as Cuba, whose economy depended on Soviet largesse. Senator Thruston Morton of Kentucky, urging the adoption of a consular treaty with these countries in 1967, hoped that it would lead to changes in "the so-called satellite countries." However, many Americans with ethnic roots in East European nations preferred the phrase "captive nations."

"Satellite" is of Middle French origin, meaning "attendant" or follower, later applied to those sycophants who fawned on French princes; it is a word popularized by politics, not astronomy. In the original sense, Charles de Gaulle characterized the removal of Western Europe from what he considered American domination as "desatellization." See PUPPET (GOVERNMENT).

With the advent of communications and spy satellites orbiting the earth, the word's primary sense changed, and "satellite diplomacy" came to mean the conduct of global affairs on live television transmitted by satellite. (For related terms, see DIPLOMACY.)

satrap minor party official.

This imperial word has had a rough time in politics. Originally from the Old Persian *xshathrapavan*, protector of the imperium, used by Persian provincial governors, the word "satrap" became associated with the unpopular military governors of the South during Reconstruction.

President Andrew Johnson popularized the word in 1866: "I could have remained at the capital with fifty or sixty millions of appropriations . . . with my satraps and dependents in every township." In the off-year election that followed in 1866, this was used against him in a campaign flyer: "Mr. Johnson said that, with forty or fifty millions of dollars placed at his disposal, under the Freedmen's Bureau bill, with his satraps scattered throughout the land, he could make himself a dictator. . . . Satraps, you know, are Turkish officers who are liable to lose their heads by the scimitar if they do anything to displease the Sultan." In 1876 the *New York World* linked "the miserable scallawag and oppressive black satrap."

The word has continued its use as a minor official inclined to officiousness, although John Gunther in his *Inside U.S.A.* called the older brother of Missouri boss Thomas Pendergast "a satrap of considerable eminence."

In current use, BOSS, SACHEM, *leader* are on the top level, with *satrap*, HENCHMAN, HATCHETMAN, and *functionary* below, and TROOPS, *braves*, FAITHFUL *workers*, RANK AND FILE at the bottom. POOH-BAH, high MUCKEY-MUCK, and PANJANDRUM are spoofs of big shots.

Another word associated with the Turkish sultans occasionally used in politics is *janissary*, Turkish slave-soldiers dating back to the fourteenth century, whose 1826 uprising ended in their massacre. An FDR clique in the forties was called the Janissariat.

Saturday Night Massacre the events of the evening of October 20, 1973, when the two top officials of the Department of Justice refused to fire the Watergate Special Prosecutor, and were swept out along with him, leading to a public-opinion FIRESTORM.

Nixon chief of staff Alexander Haig told Attorney General Elliot Richardson to dismiss Special Prosecutor Archibald Cox, who had been pressing hard for subpoenaed White House tapes. Richardson, with tears in his eyes (as Haig later told the author), demurred; he had promised the Senate, as part of his confirmation, he would not fire the Special Prosecutor for any reason other than malfeasance. Haig then called Deputy AG William Ruckelshaus, replacing Richardson as the nation's top law enforcement officer; when Ruckelshaus declined, he reported Haig to have said: "Your commander-in-chief has given you an order. You have no alternative." Ruckelshaus said he did, and resigned. Haig then reached the Solicitor General, Robert Bork, who believed that

there was a constitutional requirement that somebody in charge of the Justice Department carry out a legal order from the nation's elected leader. Bork intended to fire Cox and then resign, but he was persuaded to stay on.

At 8:25 P.M., press secretary Ron Ziegler told reporters in the White House briefing room that the three officials had been removed and the Special Prosecutor's office "abolished." At 9:05, FBI agents took positions inside the Special Prosecution Force offices at 1425 K Street on orders from Haig, who had heard that members of Cox's staff had been removing files for several days (which Cox aide Richard Ben-Veniste later confirmed as true in his Watergate memoirs).

"There was blood all over the floor," said White House aide Leonard Garment to this writer and others during that weekend, and the blood image—as a "massacre"—quickly took hold. By Monday the "Saturday Night Massacre" had become a phrase locked into Watergate terminology.

"Massacre" has long been a sloganizing word: the "Boston Massacre," on the night of March 5, 1770, led to the celebration of "Massacre Day" in Boston until 1783, when the celebration was switched to the Fourth of July. Fans of gangland movies recall the "St. Valentine's Day Massacre." As with many terms of catastrophe or bloodshed, the word "massacre" has been absorbed into politics to denote bloodless coups, and is used ironically: when Admiral Stansfield Turner began dismissing 800 members of the CIA's clandestine branch in late October 1977, the laid-off agents and operatives called it the "Halloween Massacre."

Saturday night, before nearly everybody's day off, has a festive, sometimes violent connotation. In his book *With Nixon* (1978), speechwriter Ray Price compared the angry television commentaries of that crucial weekend in 1973 to "Saturday-Night Specials, the television equivalent of those cheap but lethal handguns that have given Saturday night a bad name."

scalawag rascal; an old political epithet.

Harper's Monthly in 1868 said that "Southern men who side with the Republican Party are called 'Scalliwags.'" The spelling varies, but the term, by the end of the Civil War, was used by Southerners to describe other whites from their own region who helped the Northern officials get established throughout the former Confederate states and who were answerable primarily to the radical Republican faction then dominant in Congress.

In 1865 the *Washington Morning Chronicle's* correspondent wrote that "Whenever a white man appears to vote [in Alabama] every one of these infuriated devils . . . set up a yell calling him 'white negro,' 'low trash,' 'Scalwag.'" The distinction between "scalawag" and CARPETBAGGER was that the latter was of Northern origin.

The word possibly derives from an old Scottish word, *scallag*, meaning "farm servant, rustic" (possibly blended with *wag*, "joker, prankster"); another theory is that its origin can be traced to the Scallaway district of Scotland famed for dwarf cattle. Its first known usage in the U.S. was in 1848 when the word "scalaway" was common in western New York State to describe a mean person, a scapegrace, but all etymologies on this word are speculative.

Early in the Civil War, the *Kelso Stars and Bars* indicated that it was used as a term of general, not necessarily political, contempt. In 1863 this Southern paper wrote that "companies of armed men, gangs of ruffians, gentlemen and scallwags . . . white trash and black trash, were pouring into town from every quarter."

The Reconstruction word has returned to its earlier meaning. Scalawag now means a rascal, one who is never up to any good, rather than a Southerner intent on grinding down his own kind. A recent use, from the *Los Angeles Times* of March 29, 1992, is typical: "A grass-roots campaign is catching fire among people who see [Ross] Perot as a knight in shining armor, come to rescue them from the scoundrels and scalawags ruining the country."

See COPPERHEAD.

scenario military-diplomatic jargon for a detailed plan or likely course of action.

"He believed in giving good men their head," wrote Arthur Schlesinger, Jr., of Ambassador Averell Harriman. "When long, detailed instructions would come across his desk intended for ambassadors in the field—'scenarios,' in the jargon, designed to deprive envoys abroad of all discretion—Harriman, before clearing the message, liked to add a liberating introductory sentence: 'For your guidance, you may wish to consider the following.'"

"Scenario," a theatrical word derived from the Latin *scēna*, is used in wargaming to mean the manner in which military action is expected to develop. Author Herman Kahn, in a 1967 book review, wrote: "Let me now write a scenario for what might have happened if the United States had not reinforced South Viet Nam." Using a conditional construction, Kahn outlined a sequence of what he considered probabilities—North Vietnam's victory and the unification of the country, the fall of Laos, and the likely Communist domination of Thailand, the reinforcement of guerrillas in Malaysia—and "It is now possible to write, if with difficulty, a scenario in which this turned the balance in Indonesia . . . either turning communist or at least joining China as a firm ally." Kahn added, "While the above scenario is not wildly plausible, it is not wildly implausible."

White House correspondent Max Frankel, who later became executive editor of the *New York Times*, wrote in 1967 of the extrapolation of likelihoods in "peace games" that go on within warring governments: "Both are regularly confronted, it seems, by 'scenarios' to step up the war, to step down the war or, in various ways, to interrupt the war—all presented as the quickest way to conclude the war."

In economics, a ROSIE SCENARIO is an optimistic prediction.

See PENTAGONESE; WAR-GAMING WORDS.

scorched earth a policy of destruction in defeat; destroying one's own supplies and possessions to prevent enriching an invading enemy.

In the spring of 1992, Democratic national chairman Ronald H. Brown denounced what he called candidate Jerry Brown's "scorched earth policy" of attacks on Bill Clinton's character and record.

This figurative use of the phrase is rooted in reports of Joseph Stalin's orders to his armies during World War II to destroy grain or supplies that would have gone to the invading Germans. In his broadcast of July 3, 1941, Stalin announced, "All valuable property including nonferrous metals, grain, and fuel which cannot be withdrawn must without fail be destroyed."

His words were promptly designated a "scorched earth policy" because that vivid phrase had been used in the Sino-Japanese war of the 1930s, in which the Chinese *jiaotu (zhengce)* was used for "scorched earth (policy)." A *Times* of London reporter wrote in 1937: "The populace . . . are still disturbed . . . by wild rumors of a 'scorched earth policy' of burning the city before the Japanese enter."

Modern use of the phrase is primarily figurative. During the Presidential campaign of 1992, the term resurfaced in a description of Ross Perot's "Draconian" economic plan; according to the *Los Angeles Times*, "His own scorched-earth approach . . . is commonly dismissed as beyond the pale of public acceptance." After Bush's defeat, the *Boston Globe* commented in early 1993 that "the President has not undertaken a 'scorched earth' policy by releasing a flood of controversial actions, as some critics had feared."

But the literal meaning of the term has not been extinguished. A Mideast report in the *Washington Post* in 1993 mentioned "the few trees that survived Iraq's scorched-earth policy."

scrap of paper attack phrase on a treaty; cavalier treatment of a written diplomatic agreement.

On August 14, 1914, Germany's Theobald von Bethmann-Hollweg wrote to Great Britain's Sir Edward Goschen: "Just for a word—neutrality, a word which in war-time has so often been disregarded—just for a scrap of paper Great Britain is going to make war." The "scrap of paper" was Britain's treaty with Belgium guaranteeing that nation's neutrality. When Belgium was attacked, the British were true to their written guarantee.

"In and ever since 1914," wrote Eric Partridge in *Usage and Abusage*, "one totalitarian state has sneered at the validity of a *scrap of paper*. Bethmann-Hollweg's famous phrase . . . caused Lord Samuel, in 1937, to say that, 'under stress, treaties may become mere scraps of paper.'"

The phrase has currency in writing about international affairs, especially in connection with the phrase "honoring our commitments." A similar phrase on another subject is "STROKE OF A PEN."

In a March 20, 1993, interview on Cable News Network, nuclear weapons expert Gary Milholin commented on the United Nations nuclear non-proliferation treaty of 1970, from which North Korea had just pulled out: ". . . dropping out is a signal that you're planning to make the bomb. Right now it's up to the world to decide whether the treaty is more than just a scrap of paper or whether it really means something."

seal of the President. See BALD EAGLE.

second-class citizen one deprived of his rights, especially voting rights, and particularly black Americans.

"The Constitution does not provide for first and second class citizens," wrote Wendell Willkie in *An American Program*. A generation later Dwight Eisenhower used the phrase several times, but historian Samuel Eliot Morison commented: "It was all very well for President Eisenhower to declare, 'There must be no second-class citizens in this country'—there were, and still are."

Oddly, before the Civil War there was no definition of the term "citizen of the United States." Each state determined federal citizenship, until the Fourteenth Amendment stated that "all persons born or naturalized in the United States, and subject to the jurisdiction thereof, are citizens of the United States and of the States wherein they reside." The "subject to the jurisdiction thereof" clause was inserted to deny citizenship to children of foreign ambassadors and to Indians.

In the post-bellum reaction against Reconstruction, blacks were denied the right to vote by impossible "literacy tests," poll taxes, and direct intim-

idation. Congress in 1957 passed a civil rights law, the first since 1875, to protect the right of blacks to vote, adding other legislation in later years to strengthen it.

In the sixties, "second-class citizen" lost some of its voting-rights meaning and came to mean those to whom education and economic benefits were denied. To new black voters, Republicans pointed to the enactment of the first civil rights legislation under the Eisenhower Administration, and to the Lincoln Republican tradition. Democrats in the North dissociated themselves from "segregation forever" Southern Democrats, and pointed to social welfare legislation inspired by their party.

"Second-class" became a phrase to be avoided generally; transportation companies with "first-class" accommodations offered "coach," "tourist," "economy", "club," "business," and "executive" (even "royal coach" and "deluxe economy") in an effort to get away from "second-class." The only area where the phrase has a happy sound is in the postal service, as publishers seek "second-class mailing privileges," which are in effect a subsidy of distribution costs.

secret agreements. See OPEN COVENANTS; GRAND DESIGN.

secret plan implied but unannounced intentions; shady suggestion of a political proposal that has been prepared but not released.

This phrase, variously considered artful or sinister, dates back to 1968 and Richard Nixon's first successful Presidential campaign. That spring the candidate promised in a speech about Vietnam to "end the war and win the peace in the Pacific." Governor George Romney's supporters raised Nixon's words to the level of a "plan," and the Governor repeatedly asked throughout the New Hampshire campaign, "Where is your secret plan?" (Romney may have taken the phrase, not in quotation marks, from coverage by United Press International reporter Milt Benjamin.)

Nixon was repeatedly quoted as having said, "I have a secret plan to end the war," which he never said. When Anthony Lewis used this false quotation in the *New York Times* during the Nixon Administration, the lexicographer, then a Nixon speechwriter, offered to buy the columnist a lunch if he could come up with the citation; he could not, and stopped using the line.

The expression resurfaced during Ronald Reagan's second campaign. When Democrats charged in 1984 that Reagan had a "secret plan" to raise taxes after the election, the President said he had "no plans" to raise taxes. *No plans*, however, can mean "plans not ready to be announced," and Walter Mondale's criticism led Reagan to promise that he would raise taxes only as "a last resort."

Mondale himself had suffered the same charge earlier in the campaign. During the primaries, he was under attack by Senator John Glenn, who criticized his undue wariness: "To be so cautious that your platform consists of secret plans to be revealed after the elections—to be that cautious is not leadership, it's politics." A *New York Times* headline over that story caught the catch phrase: "Glenn Says Rival Has 'Secret Plans.'"

The term can also provide humor. Wayne Stayskal, a cartoonist for the *Tampa Tribune*, depicted a housewife responding to a political pollster: "I'm a registered Democrat . . . but I've got a secret plan to vote Republican."

secular humanism philosophy of humanistic values or practice of good behavior independent of religion, a frequent target of the religious right.

Although secular humanists are sometimes equated with "ethical atheists," many humanists are agnostics and others belong to organized religions. The disagreement about definition has led to varied use of the phrase, often as a euphemism for "atheism" or as an attack phrase to impugn an opponent's faith in God.

Michael J. Rosenberg, editor of *Near East Report*, offered this definition in 1985: "*Secular humanist* has become the new label employed to indict anyone who opposes school prayer, believes in education or disagrees with the religious right's views on abortion." The evangelist James Kennedy defines *secular humanism* as a "godless, atheistic, evolutionary, amoral, collectivist, socialistic, communistic religion" that poses a threat to schoolchildren.

Roy R. Torcaso, the atheist plaintiff in the 1961 case that popularized the term, cites the definition by Corliss Lamont in *The Philosophy of Humanism*: "joyous service for the greater good of all humanity in this natural world and advocating the methods of reason, science and democracy."

That 1961 Supreme Court case, *Torcaso* v. *Watkins*, cited the term in a footnote of the decision written by Justice Hugo L. Black, using an amicus brief by Joseph L. Blau, a Columbia University professor of religion. The footnote stated, "Among religions in this country, however, which do not teach what would generally be considered belief in the existence of God are Buddhism, Taoism, Ethical Culture, Secular Humanism and others."

The source of the term, however, may be a 1933 religious work, according to Merriam-Webster's citation files. William G. Peck used the term in *The Social Implications of the Oxford Movement*, commenting, "In face of this secular humanism, the return of the Oxford leaders to Catholic doctrine and practice necessarily signified a criticism of the secular standpoint, and the provision of a positive alternative."

As the usagist Jacques Barzun has pointed out, the label has become "a description turned into a tautology," because "humanism by itself is secular, since it makes man and his concerns primary—man the measure, instead of God."

security risk a person considered likely to commit anything from an indiscretion to an act of espionage harming the safety of the U.S.

The expression was popularized during what is loosely termed "the McCarthy era" (see McCARTHYISM) when the Wisconsin senator charged that the State Department was harboring hundreds of security risks. The phrase broadly covered those who could easily be blackmailed (alcoholics and homosexuals), those who had Communist associations or belonged to groups considered subversive by the Justice Department, and those whose close relatives' associations could compromise them.

Attorney General Herbert Brownell charged in 1954 that the Truman Administration harbored a Treasury Department official, Harry Dexter White, who was "a known traitor." Some 2,427 "security risks" were removed from government service in two years, the White House announced, drawing a charge from Adlai Stevenson that it was participating in a NUMBERS GAME.

America's best-known security risk was atomic scientist J. Robert Oppenheimer. He contested the suspension of his secret "Q" clearance before a board set up by the Atomic Energy Commission, which decided he had "fundamental defects of character" because of his "associations" and his nonconforming attitude toward his sworn official obligations. The criteria were set up in the McMahon Act, the commission's regulations, and a White House directive of April 1953.

Testifying on Oppenheimer's behalf before the board, former High Commissioner for Germany John J. McCloy pointed out that scientists like Oppenheimer were needed, and that if anything was done "to dampen their fervor . . . to that extent the security of the United States is impaired . . . a security risk in reverse." See REVERSE BIGOTRY.

When a reporter labeled two State Department employees as "well-known security risks" in a press-conference question, President Kennedy flared in anger, saying he believed the men could carry out their assignments "without detriment to the interests of the United States, and I hope without detriment to their characters by your question."

See LOYALTY OATH.

segregation attack word on the doctrine of separate but equal facilities; the enforced separation of races in fields such as education, housing, and social and economic affairs.

Proponents of what is now accepted as segregation preferred the word "separation," as used in the Supreme Court decision in *Plessy* v. *Ferguson* in 1896: "Laws permitting, and even requiring, their separation in places where they are liable to be brought into contact do not necessarily imply the inferiority of one race to the other . . ." Some proponents accepted the word and defended the practice, as did Judge Thomas P. Brady before the Commonwealth Club of California in 1957: "Segregation in the South is a way of life. It is a precious and sacred custom. It is one of our dearest and most treasured possessions. It is the means whereby we live in social peace, order and security."

Opponents of separation adopted the words "segregation" and "integration," making them a part of the vocabulary as abrasive confrontation terms, joining the issue that was resolved in their favor by the Supreme Court in 1954.

A new word for extreme segregation, popularized by South African Prime Minister Daniel F. Malan, appeared in 1949: *apartheid*. It was derived from the Dutch *apart* (same meaning as English) and *heid* (-hood), or "apartness," the state of being totally segregated. It was not adopted in the U.S.

Wrote South African author Alan Paton in 1960: "'Segregation' is such an active word that it suggests someone is trying to segregate somebody else. So the word 'apartheid' was introduced. Now it has such a stench in the nostrils of the world, they are referring to 'autogenuous development.'"

In its slang form, the word is "segged"—with a hard *g*—for segregated, "de-segged" for desegregated, which became preferred over "integrated." In an Alabama primary early in his career, George Wallace said he had been "out-segged" by a more extreme opponent.

The sale of houses to blacks in formerly all-white neighborhoods is attacked as "blockbusting," taken from the World War II bombing term.

See BUSING TO ACHIEVE RACIAL BALANCE; CIVIL RIGHTS; JIM CROW; FREEDOM RIDERS; RACISM; SEPARATE BUT EQUAL; SIT-IN; WITH ALL DELIBERATE SPEED; QUOTA.

self-appointed. See SNEER WORDS.

self-determination the right of a people to choose its own form of government.

The phrase "national self-determination" is associated with President Woodrow Wilson, and is generally considered to be one of the most important of his Fourteen Points, although it was not one of them at all. Wilson called later for a fairly traditional nationalism based largely on language and common cultural heritage, with boundaries drawn on that basis and the people within them free to choose their own leadership.

The idea had wide appeal for propaganda purposes at the close of World War I; the Versailles settlement, to the surprise of cynics, largely succeeded in achieving Wilson's self-determination aim. Winston Churchill, in 1929, wrote: "Probably less than 3 per cent of the European population are now living under Governments whose nationality they repudiate . . ."

Churchill and Franklin Roosevelt included "self-determination" in the 1941 Atlantic Charter. Three years before, in a speech at the Sportpalast in Berlin, Adolf Hitler made Czechoslovakia his "last territorial demand" and said: "In 1918 Central Europe was torn up and reshaped by some foolish or crazy so-called statesmen under the slogan 'self-determination and the right of nations.' . . . To this, Czechoslovakia owed its existence." Hitler spoke of the oppression of the German-speaking people of that state and sharply reversed his field: ". . . at last, nearly twenty years after, Mr. Wilson's right of self-determination for the 3,500,000 [Germans] must be enforced and we shall not just look on any longer."

The issue of self-determination surfaced strongly, often violently, after the breakup of the Soviet Union; critics of the desire of ethnic groups to secede from established states called their actions "dismemberment."

selling candidates like soap   a charge that MADISON AVENUE TECHNIQUES are being used in a campaign, appealing to emotion rather than reason.

The company that advertises most is Procter & Gamble, manufacturer, among many other things, of Ivory Soap. Successful soap-selling is thus a hallmark of excellence in the advertising fraternity.

Admen have long been active in politics. Bruce Barton, of Batten, Barton, Durstine & Osborn, was the congressman immortalized by FDR's MARTIN, BARTON AND FISH; Chester Bowles, of Benton & Bowles, served as a Kennedy State Department official; his partner, William Benton, was senator from Connecticut. But it is the adman behind the scenes in every political campaign that is most often criticized, with the gibes sometimes written by the admen on the other side. See KING-MAKER.

Since an attack on the Eisenhower spot television campaign was part of Adlai Stevenson's message in 1952, the phrase was used often in that campaign. A typical Stevenson use:

> Man does not live by words alone, despite the fact that sometimes he has to eat them. Alas, in this world he sometimes, or perhaps too often, lives by CATCHWORDS. SLOGANS are normally designed to get action without reflection. This one, "TIME FOR A CHANGE," fits these specifications admirably. This may not be too serious when all that is at stake is whether to buy one cake of soap or another, but I don't think it furnishes a sound basis for deciding a national election.

"Soap" has many uses in politics. In the 1880 Republican campaign it was used as a code word for money in dispatches, was deciphered, and for many years meant funny money, or graft; it is now obsolete. "Soft soap" is a soothing, ingratiating string of platitudes, and a "soapbox" has an origin similar to STUMP: a makeshift platform used by street-corner speakers, with a connotation of use by blowhards or extremists.

sellout betrayal; attack word on a political compromise.

A weak political party that supports an opposition party's candidate in return for patronage is said to sell out; in its simplest sense, a politician who takes graft sells out his constituents.

The phrase has been traced to 1857, when the *Lawrence* (Kansas) *Republican* wrote: "If the *Times* has not been 'sold out' to the Border Ruffian party, it looks very much as if it had been 'chartered.'" In O. Henry's *Trimmed Lamp* (1906), a cynical character said, "When I sell out it's not going to be on any bargain day."

Soon after he became President, Harry Truman demanded that the Russians invite anti-Communist Poles into the Polish government as his price for admission of Poland into the United Nations. The Russians made a small gesture in this direction in 1945 and agreed to drop their objection to the admission of Argentina. When the U.S. agreed to the deal, anti-Communist Poles charged this was "the great sellout."

Previously the best-known diplomatic use of the phrase occurred after the Munich conference of 1938, when British Prime Minister Neville Chamberlain was charged with "selling Czechoslovakia down the river," a phrase with its origins in slavery. The charge was raised again as Serbians took over Bosnia in 1993.

The word is the most popular attack of TRUE BELIEVERS.

sell us the rope. See USEFUL IDIOTS OF THE WEST.

senatorial courtesy. See PERSONALLY OBNOXIOUS.

send them a message a plea to vote symbolically for a candidate who is given little chance to win but whose votes will be seen as endorsement for a different point of view; a way for voters to object to policies of the party in power.

"The average voter," wrote *Washington Post* analyst David Broder in 1972, "sees a great gulf between himself—struggling with the family budget, problems in his kids' schools, the uncertainties of his job and the threats to his neighborhood—and the politicians in power, who act as if they have it made, which they probably do.

"It is that sense of distance—and of indifference from the top—that George Wallace exploited with his brilliant slogan, 'Send Them a Message.'

"That slogan came closer to capturing the mood of the American voters this year than anything else—a mood of distrust for the self-satisfied power possessors . . ."

That was the mood presidential candidate Jimmy Carter sought to catch in his long campaign for the Democratic nomination, which began in earnest in 1974. Like Wallace, he talked the "little man's" language, even spoke in the same accent, but was able to dissociate himself from the Wallace "segregation forever" stigma. Carter avoided the RACIST "message," but ran against Washington (see RUNNING AGAINST WASHINGTON)—exploiting the resentment at unfeeling bureaucrats, or muscle-bound government.

The phrase is current, though the Wallace origin is becoming obscured. Deploring the "instant sociology" that analyzed the thievery during a New York City power blackout in 1977, a *Washington Star* editorialist wrote: "In the book of instant sociology, human behavior is invariably conditioned behavior. People never do anything for the hell of it, or because they're bored, let alone for lack of the disciplines of civility. No, the looters must be trying to send us a Message."

In that usage, "message" was capitalized and given an added meaning, of social significance, as in the propagandistic "message movies." Looking toward the elections of 1978, however, House Minority Leader John Rhodes used the phrase in its traditional form: "I think the watchword should be, 'Send Jimmy Carter a message. Give him a Republican Congress.'"

The frequent form of the phrase today is *send the President a message*. In 1992, the *Chicago Tribune* wrote of Pat Buchanan's strong finish against President Bush in the New Hampshire primary as an "appeal to conservatives who want to send the President a message."

See DIME'S WORTH OF DIFFERENCE, NOT A.

senior citizen. See EUPHEMISMS, POLITICAL.

separate but equal the phrase at the heart of the civil rights dispute, posing the question: Can separate facilities ever be equal?

Justice Henry B. Brown, speaking for the majority of the Supreme Court in the 1896 case of *Plessy* v. *Ferguson*, found that "separate but equal accommodations" satisfied the demands of the Fourteenth Amendment, adding: "We consider the underlying fallacy of the plaintiff's argument to consist in the assumption that the enforced separation of the two races stamps the colored race with a badge of inferiority. If this be so, it is not by reason of anything found in the act, but solely because the colored race chooses to put that construction upon it."

John Marshall Harlan, in dissent, wrote: "If evils will result from the commingling of the two races upon public highways established for the benefit of all, they will be infinitely less than those that will surely come from state legislation regulating the enjoyment of civil rights upon the basis of race. The thin disguise of 'equal' accommodations for passengers in railroad coaches will not mislead any one, nor atone for the wrong this day done . . ."

The doctrine was reversed in a series of decisions of the "Warren Court" in 1954, the most famous of which was handed down on May 11: "We conclude that in the field of public education the doctrine of 'separate but equal' has no place. Separate educational facilities are inherently unequal." And on May 17: "Does segregation of children in public schools solely on the basis of race, even though the physical facilities and other 'tangible' factors may be equal, deprive the children of the minority group of equal education opportunities? We believe that it does. . . . We conclude that in the field of public education the doctrine of 'separate but equal' has no place."

The phrase has its American political origin in the Declaration of Independence, where this nation dissolved its bonds with Great Britain "to assume among the powers of the earth, the separate and equal station to which the Laws of Nature and of Nature's God entitle them." For cross references to other civil rights phrases, see SEGREGATION.

separatism. See DEVOLUTION.

set. See COMMUNITY.

sexism gender-engendered bias; a condemnation, usually made by women, of discrimination on account of sex.

The above definition gingerly avoids sexism. Alma Trinor, a feminist and lexicographer with the *American Heritage Dictionary* in 1973, noted the difference in a Merriam-Webster definition ("prejudice or discrimination against women") and the *American Heritage* definition of the same term: "Discrimination by members of

one sex against the other, especially by males against females, based on the assumption that one sex is superior." Another example of sex in lex, she charged, was the definition of "spokeswoman," which a rival lexicographer called "a female spokesman" and she defined as "a woman who speaks on behalf of another or others."

"Sexism" was popularized on the analogy of RACISM, as sex followed race in the fight against discrimination. The campaign to pass the Equal Rights Amendment beginning in the late sixties focused attention on the charge of "sexism," which covered everything from unintentional slights to serious bias in employment or pay scales.

In a letter to this lexicographer, Ms. Trinor wrote: "*The New Language of Politics* includes: the average man; the common man; the man in the street; the man of the people; the man who; one man, one vote. At this rate, how will women ever get into politics?" Her point: "I find that the word 'man' in its extended senses is the most overworked noun in the language, and it is a word that most definitely excludes women, no matter what dictionaries say to the contrary." Her complaint was prescient; by the nineties, *man* and *mankind* were being replaced in phrases by *person* and *humankind*.

As job discrimination because of age is attacked, a continuation of the racism-sexism pattern can be expected; in mid-1977, Representative Claude Pepper (D-Fla.) sponsored legislation to end "age-ism," which President Carter signed in 1978.

See CONSCIOUSNESS-RAISING; WOMEN'S LIB.

shadow cabinet (government) a formal organization of leaders of the party out of power, to take issue with their counterparts in government.

The system is British, and is drawn from the rarely used meaning of shadow as image or reflection. Whenever a party loses power and becomes the LOYAL OPPOSITION, the specialists in the various departments—who have often served as ministers in the previous government—form a cabinet-out-of-power and sit on the "front bench" of their party in Parliament. "The 'front bench' is more closely in touch with the members on the back benches when the party is in Opposition," writes Sir Ivor Jennings, "than when it is in office."

See BACKBENCHER.

Each member of the shadow cabinet contributes his expert knowledge to the prompt criticism of the government ministry he observes; the public understands that he is the man chosen in advance by the opposition as likely to head that ministry if the party wins the forthcoming election.

Advantages of the shadow cabinet system are that it provides quick, expert rebuttals to government decisions; a certain order to the party position; a coherence to the overall party program, often with a series of specific alternatives. Disadvantages are that too much party discipline leads to rigidity and that young men find it difficult to advance through party hierarchy.

Why hasn't it been adopted in the U.S.? Probably because the TWO-PARTY SYSTEM in America differs sharply from the mainly two-party system in England. There, the parties differ on ideology; here, the parties are much closer in ideology, with a conservative-liberal split within each party. It is difficult to reach a party consensus in the U.S., as convention platform fights indicate, and the TITULAR LEADER of the party out of power in the U.S. has no real authority to speak for the party or to appoint "shadow" ministers.

The closest Americans came to having a "shadow cabinet" was in 1948,

when Thomas E. Dewey, considered the likely winner over Truman, chose several advisers who were widely understood to be his cabinet appointees after his victory; John Foster Dulles, when he spoke on foreign affairs, was referred to as "Dewey's likely Secretary of State." Since that time, candidates running against SITTING PRESIDENTS have avoided picking cabinets in advance, lest it look presumptuous.

During the Vietnam War the phrase was given a new meaning, playing on the sinister connotation of "shadow." The Viet Cong controlled a large portion of South Vietnam by night, slipping into villages to collect "taxes" from people ostensibly under the authority of the anti-Communist regime. After an 83 percent turnout of voters in the 1967 elections, columnist Max Lerner wrote: ". . . with the Cong 'shadow government' which operates at night in the unpacified villages, it took some courage to make this affirmation."

Jesse Jackson in 1990 ran for and won the symbolic office of *shadow Senator* from the District of Columbia, which hopes for statehood.

sharp elbows pushiness or assertiveness; the ability to protect political turf or to encroach on that of others.

Thomas Carlyle paved the way for this noun phrase. The British essayist wrote in 1838: "No man lives without jostling and being jostled. In all ways he has to elbow himself through the world, giving and receiving offense."

In slang, *to bend the elbow* has long been used as an idiom meaning "to drink alcoholic liquor." Francis Grose's 1785 *Dictionary of the Vulgar Tongue* defined *elbow shaker* as "a gamester, one who rattles Sir Hugh's bones—i.e., the dice"; the same reference work included *elbow grease* as "labor" and *elbow room* as "sufficient space to act in." In more recent slang, a cop is known as an *elbow*, synecdoche for the body part used to clear the way quickly through a crowd during a chase.

International politics had picked up the sharpened image by 1980. A Bonn politician was censured that year for describing a German candidate as an ally of "usurers and wheeler-dealers and is a man with razor blades on his elbows."

In American politics, the noun *elbows* has been prominent since the 1984 Presidential campaign. Michael Barone of the *Washington Post* wrote, "This campaign shows that Mondale, far from being a patsy, is a politician with elbows."

The term's connotation, however, has changed. At one time, having sharp elbows was not a compliment, as the German usage shows. Nowadays, though, some display of sharp elbows is needed to show a candidate's *macho* (see MACHISMO) or aggressive side.

sheep in sheep's clothing   Churchillian characterization of Ramsay MacDonald (which Churchill also later used in the House of Commons to derogate Clement Attlee).

Churchill's play on "wolf in sheep's clothing" is sometimes quoted as "sheep in wolf's clothing," but this can slip by unnoticed; "sheep in sheep's clothing" cannot be missed as a jab at mediocrity.

It is the best insult of its kind, aimed at showing a smallness of spirit. Theodore Roosevelt called William Howard Taft a man who "means well but means feebly," and Horace Greeley said of agitator Wendell Phillips that "he cannot conceive of a tempest outside of a teapot."

The term is current. During the Presidential campaign of 1992, Jack Kemp commented: "I'm reminded of what Churchill said about Clement Attlee in the 1940s—he's a sheep in sheep's

clothing. I think the Clinton campaign is sheepish and in sheep clothing."

See INVECTIVE, POLITICAL.

Sherman statement   final and irrevocable declaration of non-candidacy; frequently used term, rarely taken action.

Conservative Republican leader Charles Halleck was disconsolate after a talk with Senator Barry Goldwater in early 1963 about the possibility of a Goldwater candidacy. "He was throwing cold water on the whole idea," Halleck told F. Clifton White, who was to organize the draft-Goldwater movement, "and he was throwing it by the bucketful—with ice cubes in it."

"At least," replied White, "he didn't pull a Sherman on us."

Issuing a Sherman statement—"pulling a Sherman"—is the extreme of nonavailability. General William Tecumseh Sherman, Civil War hero second only to U. S. Grant, wired John B. Henderson, chairman of the Republican National Convention in Chicago on June 5, 1884: "I will not accept if nominated, and will not serve if elected." The directness of this statement has been corrupted by history books into a more pretentious "If nominated I will not accept; if elected I will not serve."

This early twisting of Sherman's statement was prophetic; hopeful supporters of genuinely reluctant public figures always seek to find loopholes in declarations of no interest.

The general's reluctance was no surprise. Twenty years earlier, he had written a friend: "If forced to choose between the penitentiary and the White House for four years, I would say the penitentiary, thank you." In 1868 Governor Horatio Seymour of New York told the Democratic convention: "I must not be nominated by this convention. I could not accept the nomination if tendered, which"—he hurriedly closed a loophole—"I do not expect."

When President Harry Truman was considered a sure loser in 1948, some Democrats turned to Justice William O. Douglas, who affected a horse-wrangler's drawl in reply, "I never was a-running'. I ain't a-runnin', and I ain't goin' tuh."

In that year, Dwight Eisenhower issued a whole series of Sherman statements. To Democratic Senator Claude Pepper: "No matter under what terms, conditions, or premises a proposal might be couched, I would refuse to accept the nomination." To Republican publisher Leonard W. Finder: "I am not available for and could not accept nomination for high public office. My decision is definite and positive. The necessary and wise subordination of the military to civilian power will be best sustained when lifelong professional soldiers abstain from seeking high political office." And to a young reporter at a Pentagon press conference: "Look, son, I cannot conceive of any circumstance that could draw out of me permission to consider me for any political post from dogcatcher to Grand High Supreme King of the Universe."

Can a Sherman statement be taken literally—would any man turn down a firm nomination? There is vice-presidential precedent: one man did say no after formal nomination. Silas Wright, senator and later governor of New York, was nominated as James W. Polk's running mate in 1844 by the Democrats. Angry at Martin Van Buren's defeat, he telegraphed the convention: "I am not and cannot under any circumstances be a candidate before your convention for that office," and he was hastily replaced.

While politicians will take a Sherman statement as evidence of a genuine "no," nobody takes it literally; the man might not campaign, but he would serve. Consider the dialogue between James Farley and FDR in 1940, when Farley—who wanted the nomination himself—tried to persuade the President not to run for a third term.

"What would you do in my place?" the President asked, according to Farley.

"Exactly what General Sherman did many years ago," Farley replied; "issue a statement saying I would refuse to run if nominated and would not serve if elected."

"Jim, if nominated and elected, I could not in these times refuse to take the inaugural oath, even if I knew I would be dead within thirty days."

The cadence of the Sherman phrase is so familiar that it can be used as the basis for parody. When it was important in 1969 for Henry Kissinger to gain a reputation as a "secret swinger" to create a "Dr. Strangelove" reputation and to provide cover for secret trips, he would appeal to White House wags and their friends (Richard Moore, this writer, and television producer Paul Keyes) for lines making that point. An opportunity arose when a picture appeared in many newspapers of Dr. Kissinger at a cocktail party with feminist leader Gloria Steinem, who scotched gossip rumors with an icy mock statement: "I am not now, and have never been, a friend of Henry Kissinger's." The writers huddled, and Kissinger went before a Washington Press Club dinner to recall that rejection, and to add: "But she did not say that if nominated, she would not run"—long pause—"or if elected, she would not serve."

sherpa skilled Himalayan guide; diplomat who assists in preparing for summit meetings.

This word entered diplomatic lingo in the early 1980s, extending the mountain metaphor of *summit*. The earlier *summit meeting* of leaders (see SUMMITRY) led to *sherpa meeting* for the assembly of diplomats who prepare documents for their leaders to sign.

The name *Sherpa*, capitalized, refers to a member of a Tibetan people who live on the southern slopes of the Himalayas in Nepal. A Sherpa is famed for mountain-climbing abilities and guiding others through the dangerous ascents; Sherpa Tenzing became famous in 1953 for assisting Sir Edmund Hillary's team in the first conquest of Mount Everest.

Its first use in diplomatese occurred in a *New York Times* account of a Khrushchev-Eisenhower meeting in July 1955: "There was an array of experts—Sherpa guides, as one British wit put it—behind the mountaineers at the summit."

ship of state   a nation, particularly in regard to its diplomacy.

Sailors always refer to ships as "she"; this expression might be the cause of the use of the feminine reference to nations, as "America will defend her national interests." The description of a nation as a vessel on a course can be traced in English to 1675 and can be found in ancient Greek poetry.

Lincoln liked the metaphor. "If we do not make common cause," he said in 1861, "to save the good old ship of the Union on this voyage, nobody will have the chance to pilot her on another voyage." Grover Cleveland in 1894 wrote much the same thing: "The Ship of Democracy, which has weathered all storms, may sink through the mutiny of those on board." In more recent times, when candidate Thomas E. Dewey in 1948 said, "We need a rudder to our ship of state and a firm hand on the tiller," Republican Joe Martin shrugged, "Sounds good and brings the applause. But promises nothing."

The metaphor offers a tool for criticism; an 1883 reference in the *Congressional Record* says "Twenty percent of the employees in all Departments in the City of Washington . . . are really barnacles upon the ship of state."

Most dramatic use of the phrase was in a message from President Franklin Roosevelt, given to defeated Republican candidate Wendell Willkie in 1941 to take to Winston Churchill, quoting an 1849 poem by Henry Wadsworth Longfellow:

Thou, too, sail on, O Ship of State!
Sail on, O Union, strong and great!
Humanity with all its fears,
With all the hopes of future years,
Is hanging breathless on thy fate!

Other nautical metaphors in politics include Sir Walter Scott's "sea of upturned faces" and Lord Acton's maxim, "The ship exists for the sake of the passengers." *Groundswells* lead to *tides of support*.

George Shultz, former Director of the Office of Management and Budget, concluded a 1971 economic speech with the nautical reference: "Those of you familiar with sailing know what a telltale is—a strip of cloth tied to a mast to show which way the wind is blowing. A captain has the choice of steering his ship by the telltale, following the prevailing winds, or to steer by the compass. In a democracy, you must keep your eye on the telltale, but you must set your course by the compass. That is exactly what the President of the United States is doing. The voice from the bridge says, 'Steady as you go.'"

In 1989, Deputy Secretary of State Lawrence S. Eagleburger made jocular use of the extended metaphor: "Just a few months after Shirley Temple Black was sent to Czechoslovakia, four decades of communism came tumbling down. At that rate it will mean the end of the ship of state and the beginning of the Good Ship Lollipop. And I will have to walk the plank, because I don't sing, act or compose, and I certainly don't dance."

On March 20, 1969, Senator Everett Dirksen delivered a speech drafted by this writer, who vaguely recalled the Dewey usage, and included the line: "Around the world there is the feeling that there is a firm hand on the rudder of our ship of state." One reader of the *Washington Post*, Karl G. Sorg, wrote a letter to the editor observing: "When I am on the high seas, I would like my skipper to keep a firm hand on the tiller, and to leave that rudder alone. Any skipper with a firm hand on the rudder is likely to be in water way over his head." This convinced one speechwriter that ship metaphors are better left to sailors.

See NEW DEPARTURE.

shirtsleeve diplomacy informal, plain-speaking international relations, contrasted with the diplomatic niceties of "striped-pants" diplomacy.

The phrase has a pleasantly hard-working connotation to Americans in current usage, from the expression "roll up one's sleeves" (to get to work). Earlier use of the phrase suggested that American ambassadors were chosen as a result of political contributions; and their demeanor was boorish compared to the conservative mannerisms of diplomats of nations steeped in international affairs.

London's *Pall Mall Gazette*, reporting in 1908 on American customs, wrote: "The Congressmen have a preference for what they picturesquely describe as 'Shirt-sleeve Ambassadors'— men who they think will labor for their country's interests and scorn social fascinations."

John Hay, Theodore Roosevelt's Secretary of State, was probably the first diplomat associated with the phrase. Wrote the *Cyclopaedia of American*

Government in 1914: "Shirt Sleeve Diplomacy. A title which has been given to some of the diplomacy of recent years which has disregarded much of the circumlocution and indirectness of earlier practice and has stated clearly the purpose of the negotiation and the methods by which a state proposed to attain the purpose. This term has been particularly applied to the diplomacy of the United States from the late years of the nineteenth century."

Wealth and social standing are supposed to inhibit the willingness to work in shirtsleeves (to deal informally, directly, often harshly). Columbia University president Nicholas Murray Butler referred to "a society like ours of which it is truly said to be often but three generations 'from shirtsleeves to shirtsleeves.'"

For a different type of diplomat, see COOKIE PUSHER.

shoo-in a certain winner; a candidate who can only be defeated by a POLITICAL MIRACLE.

Like FRONT RUNNER, BOLT, DARK HORSE, and many others, the metaphor is taken from racing, but this one has a fraudulent background. When jockeys form a "ring" and bet on a single horse, they hold back their own mounts and "chase in" or "shoo in" the horse selected to be the winner. *Racing Maxims and Methods of 'Pittsburgh Phil,'* published in 1908, points out: "There were many times presumably that 'Tod' would win through such manipulations, being 'shooed in,' as it were." In *The Underworld Speaks* (1935), A. J. Pollack defines shoo-in as "a horse race in which the winner is the only horse trying."

"To shoo" is a colloquialism meaning to urge gently a person or animal to go in a desired direction. It made its first recorded appearance around the turn of the twentieth century. "Shoo-in"— minus its crooked connotation, now only meaning "sure thing"—began to be used politically in the forties. "Taft Appears to Be Shoo-In for Top Senate G.O.P. Job" headlined the *San Francisco News* in 1948, and *Life* predicted, "Dewey looks like a shoo-in for the presidency."

The word was sufficiently secured in the political lexicon in 1967 to rate a turnaround. The *Wall Street Journal* called the candidate hopelessly running against popular Congressman Adam Clayton Powell in New York's Harlem "a shoo-out."

shoot from the hip. See TRIGGER-HAPPY.

shooting war. See COLD WAR.

shortchange to deny to a city those state services which it considers its due because of taxes paid to the state by residents of the city.

The shortchange charge is made when the different levels of government are controlled by opposing parties. For example, Mayor Robert F. Wagner of New York City, a Democrat, charged that New York State had been shortchanging the city when Thomas E. Dewey, a Republican, was governor. When Averell Harriman, a Democrat, became governor in 1954, the charge was muted, until Republican Nelson Rockefeller became governor in 1958; at that point Mayor Wagner returned to the familiar shortchange theme. When Republican John V. Lindsay became mayor in 1965, he could not make shortchanging an important charge against Rockefeller, whom he supported; instead, he charged Democratic President Lyndon Johnson with shortchanging cities in federal aid.

The shortchange charge is usually made something like this: "The taxpayers of this city pay ten million dollars in taxes to the state, and receive back in services only six million dollars. Yet the farmers in the rural areas pay four million in taxes and get back four million in services." The defense by the higher body is usually: "When this Administration took office, services to localities totaled only four million. Now it is six." A more sophisticated argument, citing the need for state hospitals that can be used by city residents, is seldom made. The shortchange charge is usually not stressed between candidates for the same office, since one group of voters usually benefits from the apparently higher rate paid by other voters, and neither candidate wants to offend an entire bloc; however, the more local candidate has no such restriction on attacking the higher body, provided it is of the opposite party.

Another use of shortchange is made in PORK BARREL legislation, when congressmen feel their district is being overlooked in the dispensing of federal projects. Typical comment was made in 1961 by Representative Ken Hechler of West Virginia: "I am firmly against the kind of LOGROLLING which would subject our defense program to narrowly sectional or selfish pulling and hauling. But I am getting pretty hot under the collar about the way my state of West Virginia is shortchanged in Army, Navy, and Air Force installations. . . . I am going to stand up on my hind legs and roar until West Virginia gets the fair treatment she deserves."

short hairs sensitive point by which a person or faction can be controlled.

In current slang, "to have someone by the short hairs" means to have the other in a totally controllable position; its pubic-hair connotation inhibits its use in polite society. It is not known when "short hairs" acquired this connotation, since the "Short-Hairs"—crew cut workingmen and pugilists—

were members of John Kelly's administration of Tammany Hall in the 1870s. Opposing the Short-Hairs were the wealthy supporters of Samuel Tilden, the "Swallow-Tails" (after their formal clothes), who attempted to seize control of the Democratic party in the state. Tammany continued to fight New York Governor Tilden on the national scene, and the *Cincinnati Democratic Gazette* reported in 1876: "The anti-Tilden New Yorkers began to realize the fact last night that the rowdy or *short hair* element of their forces was disgusting the country delegates and reacting in Tilden's favor."

According to Charles Ledyard Norton in 1890, the Short-Hairs gained their nickname "in deference either to their 'fighting cut' or the supposed recent release from prison." Tammany leader John Morrissey, a retired prizefighter, spoofed the "Swallow-Tail" faction one morning by dressing up in full evening dress and carrying a French dictionary under one arm. He explained that "this sort of thing was necessary in order to retain one's influence."

Throughout the sixties, the wearing of long hair by men was a sign of rebellion; those young men who wore their hair short were considered "jocks," insensitive to political affairs. Some idea of how fast and far the pendulum swings was felt in 1978 when a military honor guard suspended two of its members for "too-short hair."

See NUT-CUTTING.

short list   finalists under consideration; narrowed group of contenders for appointed office.

Short list, from British English, first appeared in print in *Contemporary English: A Personal Speech Record*, a 1927 book by William E. Collinson. His comment that "selection committees to University posts first familiarized me with the meaning of the short list" suggested earlier use of the phrase. *The Economist*, a London weekly, transatlanticized the expression.

Nowadays the term is hyphenated in verb form ("she's been short-listed"), and some dictionaries are making the open compound a solid word on the analogy of *blacklist*. The two-word phrase, however, parallels WATCH LIST, *wait list*, a politician's *wish list*, or a *laundry list* of desired goals.

Synonyms for somebody who's short-listed are not exact: *contender* suggests active soliciting of an office, *competitor* is even more active, and *finalist* carries a beauty-contest connotation. The antonym of *short list* is not "long list," but "everybody else remotely available."

American political usage of the phrase became popular during the 1988 Presidential campaign. At the Republican National Convention, Alexander M. Haig, Jr., described the Democratic ticket as "blind as a bat . . . hanging upside down in dark, damp caves up to its navel in guano," prompting convention chairman Robert H. Michel to remark about the tough language, "That's probably why Al Haig is not on the short list for Vice President." That same year the Associated Press identified Senator Charles S. Robb, Democrat of Virginia, as being "on most short lists of potential Presidential candidates in 1992 or 1996."

The term offers itself for spoofing. A *New Yorker* cartoon by James Stevenson depicts a woman asking her husband, "How come you're never on anybody's short list?"

See ENEMIES LIST.

showing the flag.   See PRESENCE.

shredding.   See SANITIZE.

shrimps whistle   a Russian figure of speech indicating a day never to come.

When Russian Premier Nikita Khrushchev heard a Western suggestion in 1955 that the Soviet Union's fidelity to Communism might fade with the years, he replied, "Those who wait for that must wait until a shrimp learns to whistle."

The image became a favorite of editorial writers doing pieces on PEACEFUL COEXISTENCE. The *New York Times*, suggesting in 1967 that Rhodesian Prime Minister Ian Smith surprise the world by making progress toward majority rule, wrote: "A move so contrary to Mr. Smith's every act since entering public life would confound African experts around the world. Shrimps, in Mr. Khrushchev's colorful expression, would surely whistle."

The nearest American expressions are "until the cows come home" or "until hell freezes over."

shuttle diplomacy negotiations assisted by a middleman hurrying between capitals by jet plane; in particular, the Kissinger peace attempts after the 1973 Arab-Israeli war.

"At week's end," wrote *Time* on March 4, 1974, "Kissinger was to return . . . to the Middle East for another round of 'shuttle diplomacy'— this time to Damascus, Jerusalem and Cairo . . ." By June 24 the magazine had dropped quotation marks and extended the metaphor: "The only possible accomplishment left for Henry Hercules is for him to become an astronaut, and then maybe he could be the first space-shuttle diplomat."

The word "shuttle" might have been introduced to diplomacy by talk of NASA's "space shuttle," which in turn came into the language from the Eastern Airlines Boston–New York–Washington "shuttle," which probably had its origin in New York's Pennsylvania Station–Times Square subway shuttle. All these transportation metaphors are extensions of the weaving shuttle that shoots the thread of the woof between the threads of the warp.

"Diplomacy" has long been a convenient word with which to conclude a new phrase. From DOLLAR DIPLOMACY to GUNBOAT DIPLOMACY, the phrasemaking progressed to the more recent "ping-pong diplomacy" regarding the Chinese, QUIET DIPLOMACY and "media diplomacy," which, for a time, replaced "shuttle diplomacy."

See STEP BY STEP.

sick man of Europe originally Turkey; applied in modern times to whatever European nation is in political or economic trouble.

"To make an alliance with Turkey," writer François Chateaubriand quoted a diplomat in 1807, "is the same as putting your arms around a corpse to make it stand up." This echoed the judgment of Sir Thomas Roe, British ambassador in Constantinople two centuries earlier, who said the Ottoman Empire had "the body of a sick old man who tried to appear healthy, although his end was near." In 1853 Russian Czar Nicholas I told British Ambassador Sir George Seymore, "We have on our hands a sick man—a very sick man," and Turkey was tagged throughout the remainder of the nineteenth century "the sick man of Europe."

The patient changes, but the phrase lingers on. Australian editor Colin Bingham wrote in 1967: "For years after the Second World War, France was frequently described as 'the sick man of Europe,' but by 1966 the United Kingdom's economic difficulties prompted a transient application of the epithet to Britain."

side of the angels the right or acceptable viewpoint; purity of motive.

John Carmody, a *Washington Post* television critic, wrote in 1977 about an anti-McCarthyism program that "there is a certain hand-wringing quality to some of the narration Sunday night (scriptwriters long to be on the side of the angels, too)." In 1989, an economist told the Federal News Service about a budget fight: "Neither side is on the side of the angels; neither side is pure in the sense of what they want to do."

Newsday continued the term's popularization in 1992. Reporting on a Republican judge in Texas, *Newsday* wrote that his battle with extremist party members placed him "on the side of the angels, from the national party's viewpoint."

A variant of the phrase was suggested by New York Governor Mario Cuomo, appearing on "This Week with David Brinkley" in late 1991. Asked about his plan for "an investment-led recovery," Cuomo responded, "I'm trying to stay with the angels."

The source of these phrases is Benjamin Disraeli. In 1864 at the Oxford Diocesan Conference, concerned about Charles Darwin's evolutionary theory, Disraeli asked rhetorically, "Is man an ape or an angel? I, my lord, I am on the side of the angels. I repudiate with indignation and abhorrence those newfangled theories."

sign off on approve; specifically, to initial one's endorsement.

"If you want to make sure the President will sign off on something," Carter White House aide Stuart Eizenstadt told *New Times* writer Robert Shrum in July, 1977, "the best way is to get Bert [Lance] to agree."

This off-again, on-again locution became popular in government in the sixties. (See the Arthur Schlesinger, Jr., puzzlement in PENTAGONESE.) Seeking approval is "running it past" an official, but getting that approval is inducing him to "sign off on" it. In radio parlance, "to sign off" is to go off the air; the noun "signoff" is the conclusion of a broadcast day with an announcement including the call letters, or sign, of the station.

From this, one can extrapolate to the meaning of "sign off" as termination, or final approval—in the sense that the BUCK STOPS HERE, at the top executive's desk. But why the "on"? One may speculate that if "to sign off" is taken to mean "to approve," then the "on" refers to the placement of initials on a document.

The awkward phrase is in rampant Washington use. At the end of 1977 President Carter proudly announced: "I've signed off on the budget." Similar to the military "endorse," the phrase has replaced "clear with" as a verb that helps a bureaucrat share responsibility. See C.Y.A.; CLEAR IT WITH SIDNEY.

An element of "accountability," a favored Washington term in the mid-seventies, is connected with the phrase. Elizabeth Drew, writing in *The New Yorker* (May 1, 1978) about National Security Adviser Zbigniew Brzezinski, pointed to a debate within the Carter Administration about accountability in the President's executive order on intelligence oversight: "The executive order requires that the President must 'sign off' on any activity of any importance. Brzezinski is known to believe that the President should have broad flexibility, including 'deniability'—that is, it should be possible to carry out operations in a way that would enable the President to deny he knew about them."

The vogue use of "on"—as in "add on," or even the Americanization of the British "early on"—is ongoing.

silent majority the remarkable legion of the unremarked, whose individual opinions are not colorful or different enough to make news, but whose collective opinion, when crystallized, can make history.

The voices of the Vietnam dissenters were relatively muted during the first nine months of the Nixon presidency; in October, 1969 a moratorium was organized, featuring a march on Washington, D.C., with more strident demonstrations planned the following month.

In the midst of this rebirth of demonstrations, President Nixon made a televised address, in prime time, that effectively countered the mounting dissent. The November 3 "silent majority" speech might well have had more of an effect on public opinion than any since the FDR acceptance in 1932, buying time for the Vietnamization program. The anti-war demonstrations did not make important news again until the Cambodian incursion six months later.

"If a vocal minority," the President warned, "however fervent its cause, prevails over reason and the will of the majority, this Nation has no future as a free society. Let historians not record that when America was the most powerful nation in the world we passed on the other side of the road and allowed the last hopes for peace and freedom of millions of people to be suffocated by the forces of totalitarianism. And so tonight—to you, the great silent majority of my fellow Americans—I ask for your support."

Nixon, who wrote this speech with no help from his speechwriters, was not consciously "making a phrase." The words in the phrase were not capitalized, nor was the phrase repeated, but it did fill a need for a description of all the people who were not demonstrating, and was promptly taken up by the media.

Though the phrase officially came into the political language on November 3, 1969, it had of course been used previously, and Nixon had used the thought many times.

In a radio speech during the primary campaign, on May 16, 1968, he referred to "the silent center, the millions of people in the middle of the American political spectrum who do not demonstrate, who do not picket or protest loudly. . . . We must remember that all the center is not silent, and all who are silent are not center. But a great many 'quiet Americans' have become committed to answers to social problems that preserve personal freedom."

Throughout the campaign he came back to those "quiet Americans" and "forgotten Americans," and occasionally used "quiet majority."

John F. Kennedy wrote in *Profiles in Courage* (1956): "They were not all right or all conservatives or all liberals. Some of them may have been representing the actual sentiments of the silent majority of their constituents in opposition to the screams of a vocal minority, but most of them were not."

The phrase "silent center" had been used by Senator Paul Douglas in a speech in 1967. Much earlier, Alexis de Tocqueville warned of "the excessive love of the whole community for quiet" leading Americans to ignore military problems until they became acute, and Bulwer-Lytton in 1848 described "the universal noiseless impression through all England" that Harold, last of the Saxon kings, "was now the sole man on whom rested the state—which, whenever it so favors one individual, is irresistible."

Previous usage of any famous phrase can be found. The September 1874 issue of *Harper's New Monthly Magazine* had an article entitled "The Silent Majority"; it was about burial customs around the world, the phrase taken from ancient Greek references to the dead. In Plautus' *Trinummus, ad plures penetrare*—"to join the great majority"—is used as a euphemism for dying.

Vice President Agnew used the phrase in its non-lugubrious sense on

May 9, 1969: "It is time for America's silent majority to stand up for its rights, and let us remember the American majority includes every minority. America's silent majority is bewildered by irrational protest . . ."

During that spring of 1969, David Broder of the *Washington Post* asked historian Theodore White to reflect on the paradoxes that marked the previous election year. Said White: "Never have America's leading cultural media, its university thinkers, its influence makers been more intrigued by experiment and change; but in no election have the mute masses more completely separated themselves from such leadership and thinking. Mr. Nixon's problem is to interpret what the silent people think, and govern the country against the grain of what its more important thinkers think."

Six months later, as White predicted, Nixon rallied "the silent majority." In the late seventies the phrase carried the opprobrium generally accorded Nixon-Agnew utterances, but its users were careful to deride the INSIDE THE BELTWAY phrasemakers rather than the group described. In 1993, Frank Luntz, a Republican pollster, commented to the *Boston Globe* on the Clinton Administration's tax plans: "Now that silent majority is about to scream and reject the tax increases. These people think they've already sacrificed and can't do it anymore." See MIDDLE AMERICA; GREAT UNWASHED.

silent vote   the unmeasurables, who may or may not turn out.

Different meanings: (1) a sector of the public unhappy with the sameness of both parties, which can be turned out only by offering a CHOICE, NOT AN ECHO; (2) a sector that remains "undecided" to pollsters, for such reasons as religious preference, bigotry, or BACKLASH, and remains an unknown quantity until Election Day; (3) the wistfully hoped-for vote that was simply never cast. See STAY-AT-HOMES; TURNOUT.

"In the next election," the *Cincinnati Campaigner* predicted in 1848, "the silent vote for Van Buren will be immense." The former President, running on a third party ticket, picked up one tenth of the vote cast. "The silent vote, as it is called," wrote the *New York Times* in 1880, "is what will tell in November." This is usually a fairly safe prediction. In that case, James Garfield squeaked past Democrat Winfield Scott Hancock with 10,000 votes out of 10 million cast, with a "silent vote"—possibly costing Hancock the election—going to the Greenback splinter party.

The phrase is most often used today by apologists for candidates who are far behind in the public opinion polls; workers for Goldwater in 1964 cheered themselves up with the assurance that an enormous "silent vote" would appear on Election Day.

Of those people old enough to vote for President, almost half do not. Conservatives have long claimed this vote is essentially conservative; others say these potential voters are simply apathetic, illiterate, ill or infirm, or have moved too recently to qualify, and are of all political persuasions.

silk stocking   wealthy; originally used to derogate the upper class, now only as descriptive of a high-income area.

The phrase can be found in the writings of Jefferson ("the Gores and the Pickerings will find their levees crowded with silk stocking gentry, but no yeomanry; an army of officers without soldiers") and Lincoln ("They came not like 'the silk stocking gentry' as they are called by their opponents; but as farmers, mechanics, etc.").

In the era of knee britches and silk hose, only the wealthy could afford silk stockings. The term was used by Jeffersonian Republicans against the well-to-do Federalists. The meaning changed only slightly later, as described by the *Cyclopaedia of American Government* in 1914: "a derisive appellation bestowed by the 'PRACTICAL POLITICIANS' upon those citizens of wealth and high social position who occasionally interfere in politics in support of some reform measure or candidate."

Over the years, *kid glove politics, swallow-tail politician,* and *ruffled shirt* appeared as synonyms, but silk stocking outlived them all, and is similar to "lace curtain" (as opposed to "shanty") used to describe the social classes of Irish-Americans. Louis Howe said he had originally sized up Franklin Roosevelt as a "spoiled, silk-pants sort of guy."

The best-known use of the phrase in its current sense was popularized by Theodore Roosevelt: "I was a Republican from the 'silk stocking' district, the wealthiest district in New York." The *New York Post* wrote in 1903 of "the 'silk stocking' quarter—the middle reaches of Manhattan, between 14th and 96th Street." But it is used generically as well. "In as chairman," wrote *Time* magazine in 1948, "went 47-year-old Hugh Scott, Jr., a three-term congressman from a suburban Philadelphia 'silk stocking' district."

similes, political. See LIKE UGLY ON AN APE.

single-issue politics reduction of a campaign or election to one question.

This approach to politics attempts to project a single issue such as abortion as the determining factor in an election, excluding all other considerations. Such a narrowing of focus, however, draws the criticism that single-issue politics is capable of limit-

ing a general election to a referendum on a specific issue.

Timothy B. Clark wrote in the *National Journal* in 1978, "In an era of single-issue politics and highly organized lobbying, it will be difficult for Congress to restrain itself to the degree necessary to meet Carter's goal." That same year, T. R. Reid of the *Washington Post* commented, "The rampant apathy towards the primary may also stem from the voters' concentration on single-issue politics."

A decade later, the term was applied to political events other than campaigns or elections. After the Senate rejected Robert H. Bork as a Supreme Court nominee in 1987, Ronald Reagan derogated the confirmation process as "a spectacle of misrepresentation and single-issue politics."

R. W. Apple, Jr., of the *New York Times* revived the charge in a 1992 commentary on George Bush's Presidency: "Less welcome is the harsh political fact that pragmatists have trouble building constituencies, especially in this era of single-issue politics."

sit-in a technique of demonstration launched by civil rights activists in 1960 to dramatize segregation in the South.

Four black youths from North Carolina Agricultural and Technical College entered the F. W. Woolworth store in Greensboro, North Carolina, on February 1, 1960, and sat down at the "white" lunch counter. "It is regrettable," said Mayor William G. Enloe of Raleigh as the sit-ins spread throughout the state, "that some of our young Negro students would risk endangering Raleigh's friendly and cooperative race relations by seeking to change a long-standing custom in a manner that is all but destined to fail."

The sit-ins, at first dismissed as a college fad, were destined to bring into prominence the Congress of Racial

Equality (CORE) and to change the pattern of segregation throughout the South.

The "-in" construction quickly caught on, leading to *kneel-ins* and *pray-ins* in the early sixties, *teach-ins* in 1965 (first organized in Michigan by Students for a Democratic Society), and subsequently *love-ins, be-ins, eat-ins,* etc.

John Kennedy, campaigning for President in September 1960, caught the significance of the sit-ins and turned a phrase about them: "He [the President] must exert the great moral and educational force of his office to bring about equal access to public facilities, from churches to lunch-counters, and support the rights of every American to stand up for his rights, even if he must sit down for them."

As the "-in's" proliferated in the sixties, and the original civil rights connotation was diluted by the "hippies," Clark Kerr, ousted president of the University of California, predicted in 1967: "The sit-in will gradually join the coonskin coat as an interesting symbol of a student age retreating into history."

The former meaning of the phrase "to sit in" was "to have a place as a player of a game," especially of cards, and although it remains a colloquialism, it has been traced by the *OED* to 1599.

See FREEDOM RIDERS.

sit room   the White House situation room.

The basement conference room in the White House isn't called "the Crisis Center," because the Administration does not want to cause too much excitement whenever the room is used. A crisis-management team, however, does meet in this communications center, usually chaired by the Vice President.

McGeorge Bundy was John F. Kennedy's national security adviser in 1961, when the situation room was named, later shortened to *sit room.* "I don't think we met down there during the Cuban missile crisis," Bundy told the lexicographer in 1992; neither he nor Ted Sorensen recalls why the room received the name, presumably given for the type of situation (a euphemism for *crisis*) to be handled from that basement room.

George M. Elsey, a speechwriter for Harry Truman, offers this background on precedessor phrases:

The first such was William McKinley's War Room, a small chamber on the southeast corner of the second floor of the Executive Mansion. When I was first assigned to the White House as a young Naval Reserve officer in April 1942, the Executive Clerk was Rudolph Forster, who had been in Presidential service since McKinley's day. He had lively tales of the maps and the telegraph equipment emplaced there, bringing McKinley flash news on the Spanish-American war.

I never heard Forster or any of the other World War I staff report that Wilson had any such room, which was surprising since the War and Navy Departments were even less available to Wilson than they had been to McKinley, having moved to "temporaries" on Constitution Avenue and no longer just steps across West Executive Avenue.

FDR fell in love with Winston Churchill's Map Room installed on the second floor of the White House during Churchill's December 1941 visit. After his guest's departure, FDR ordered a Map Room of his own, to be placed on the ground floor, easily accessible to him as it was directly across the corridor from the elevator. The room is still, 50 years later, known as the Map Room and is so designated on all descriptive material about the White House.

When we closed the Map Room in early 1946, the Army Signal Corps moved in to use the space for equipment required when the President traveled.

The Truman reconstruction forced the Corps' evacuation from the House proper, and neither Intelligence nor Communications functions returned to the mansion.

The cramped basement space is almost always a disappointment to first-time visitors, many of whom expect to see the giant television screens depicted in doomsday movies.

The meeting room's shortened form, *sit room*, is now prevalent. When George Bush visited Maine in 1991, a reporter asked him about a possible release of hostages in the Mideast: "Any hopeful signs on the situation?" Bush replied, "Just talked to the sit room and . . . no new developments overnight at all."

sitting on the fence. See FENCE, ON THE.

sitting President a President in office; the power of incumbency in achieving renomination or reelection.

The phrase derives from a sitting monarch, whose throne is a seat of power, and from a sitting hen, whose inactivity conceals a procreative purpose. A judge is sitting when court is in session, and sitting judges (those holding judicial office, whether court is in or out of session) are rarely considered as candidates (Alton B. Parker was the only one to run for President).

Harry Truman put it this way: "When the President is sitting in the White House, the National Convention of his party has never gone against his recommendations in the choice of a candidate or in the formation of a platform on which that convention is to operate." In his memoirs, the former President pointed out how sitting President Theodore Roosevelt in 1908 could dictate the choice of his successor, William Howard Taft; but in 1912, with all his popularity, Roosevelt could not take the nomination away from the incumbent Taft. He did not add that he, Truman, as a sitting President, found it simple to designate Adlai Stevenson as his choice in 1952, but in 1956 he was unable to deliver for Averell Harriman.

For a time in the mid-sixties, there was talk of Senator Robert Kennedy challenging President Lyndon B. Johnson for the 1968 presidential nomination, which was dismissed by Kennedy associates as "impossible against a sitting President." After a strong showing by Senator Eugene McCarthy in the New Hampshire primary, Kennedy changed his mind and made his move. Similarly, Ronald Reagan's 1976 challenge to President Gerald Ford made the presidential seat more insecure; in 1978, as Jimmy Carter slipped in polls, pundits fanned talk of a challenge to him in the 1980 primaries by California Governor Edmund "Jerry" Brown.

Florida Governor Claude Kirk, warning Republicans against overconfidence when Lyndon Johnson was thought likely to seek reelection, told a press conference: "A sitting president is never a sitting duck."

See INCUMBENT.

sitzkrieg. See PHONY WAR.

sixty million jobs. See HOTTENTOTS, MILK FOR.

skunk at the garden party a hyperethical stiff, seen as undesirable in a gathering of broad-minded pragmatists; a single problem that has the potential to vex or annoy.

More vivid than the clichéd *fly in the ointment*, the folksy *skunk at the garden party* provides a colorful word-picture. Into the midst of a group of elegantly dressed partygoers strolls a small animal capable of causing an enormous stink; after a horrified silence comes a panic that leads to havoc.

This anti-elitist trope appears usually in the negative: "I don't want to be the skunk at the garden party, but . . ." *Skunk* comes from the Algonquian name of the animal and was used figuratively by 1840, along with *polecat*, to label a low or contemptible person. (This animal's use in invective has been popular in American rhetoric. Senator Charles Sumner, an abolitionist in the "bloody Kansas" debate of 1856, was violently beaten after euphemistically referring to another Senator as "the noisome, squat and nameless animal." In recent positive usage, a secret laboratory or experimental division is known as a *skunk works*, based on cartoonist Al Capp's "Skonk Works" in "Li'l Abner.") The term *garden party* is first found in print in Anthony Trollope's 1869 novel *Phineas Finn*: "The Duke's garden party was becoming a mere ball."

Skunk at the garden party, however, is much more recent. A staff member at the *Dictionary of American Regional English* reports that the *skunk at the garden party* image was Wisconsin usage in the early 1970s, with printed references beginning in politics during the 1980s. Representative Pat Schroeder of Colorado said in 1987, "In 1984, I was the skunk in the garden party who said we women have to run like men do," adding, "May your words be tender and juicy, for people often serve them back to you." In the 1988 Presidential primary, former Arizona Governor Bruce Babbitt withdrew from the race and commented that Gary Hart, Jesse Jackson, and he "were sort of skunks at the garden party, always saying, 'This debate is supposed to be about something' and raking our fingers down the chalkboard."

When not self-applied, the expression can be an attack phrase. In 1989, Nicaraguan President Daniel Ortega

Saavedra attended Costa Rica's peace talks for Central America and announced his plan to end the cease-fire in his country; he was soon called this animal expression by an American reporter. George Bush agreed at a news conference: "That's exactly what happened. Mr. Ortega looks like that unwanted animal at a garden party. . . . We're not going to let this one little man who is out of whack with the rest of the hemisphere ruin a very good meeting."

Pulling the punch of using *skunk*, Bush's euphemism forced Ortega to attack the rest of the saying in an op-ed piece for the *New York Times*: "President Bush reacted with a torrent of personal invective. He accused me of spoiling the 'garden party' in Costa Rica. Well, life in my country is no 'garden party.'"

slate   a list of candidates, presented as a "package"; hopefully, take-one-take-all.

TAMMANY boss Charles Murphy reelected his candidate for mayor, George B. McClellan, Jr., in 1906 and promptly submitted a list of names for patronage. McClellan, backed up by New York Governor Charles Evans Hughes, proceeded to fire some Tammany men who already had jobs and turned down most of Murphy's suggestions. When asked by McClellan to supply some more acceptable alternatives, Murphy snapped: "That's my slate. Take it or leave it. I got no other candidates." Ultimately, the Tammany boss won.

The name is taken from the material used in school blackboards; a slate on which students write offers the convenience of easy erasure, something often needed in assembling political teams. Its use can be found as early as 1842.

The word acquired a special meaning for the New Left in the late fifties, when a group of students at the University of California at Berkeley submitted a "Slate of Candidates" to run the student government. As they became involved in a wider field, organizing demonstrations against the House Un-American Activities Committee, the group continued to be known as SLATE.

See TICKET.

sleaze factor sustained ethical trimming; a pattern of alleged petty corruption among one's colleagues or aides.

This base phrase surfaced during the 1980s. A reporter commented to Ronald Reagan at a Presidential press conference in early 1984, "More than a dozen members of your Administration have left under some sort of a cloud, and this is what the Democrats are calling the sleaze factor." Reagan responded, "I reject the use of the word *sleaze.*"

Sleaze, a noun attested since the early 1950s, is a back-formation from *sleazy*, an adjective of unknown origin, though it has often been connected with Silesia, a region in Central Europe. A flimsy cloth woven there was named Sleasie-holland, but the word *sleazy* in the sense of flimsy and unsubstantial is found earlier than the name of the cloth.

A *New York Times* column in 1980, derogating unethical behavior by friends and relatives of Jimmy Carter, was titled "The Politics of Sleaze." (Bert Lance wryly responded, "There's more muck*rakin'* than there is muck*makin'*.")

Laurence Barrett of *Time* magazine introduced *sleaze factor* as a chapter title in his 1983 book, *Gambling with History*. Democrats seized upon that term in 1984 to characterize a pattern of small scandals during the Reagan Administration. In the *Christian Science Monitor* on March 21, 1984, the term was used in quotation marks:

"Asked about the 'sleaze factor' in the campaign, Senator George McGovern told reporters . . . that he expected to see more mention of it." A day later, Walter Mondale said at a news conference that the factor to unite the Democrats in the 1984 campaign "will be the 'sleaze factor' in this Administration," because almost every week "another rotten apple falls from the tree."

Reagan's ability to deflect the *sleaze factor* was nicknamed the *Teflon factor*. (See TEFLON-COATED PRESIDENCY.) For a predecessor phrase, see HONEST GRAFT.

sleeper an amendment slipped into a bill to nullify or alter its intent; or, a piece of legislation whose significance is not realized until after it has been passed.

The political derivation is from both horse racing and cards. In racing, a sleeper is a horse that had been held back in previous races to build up its odds, and then allowed to go full speed in a race on which its owner had bet heavily. (For another fraudulent racing scheme turned into a political expression, see SHOO-IN.) In cards, the 1866 *American Hoyle* states: "A bet (in faro) is said to be a sleeper, when the owner has forgotten it, when it becomes public property, any one having a right to take it." See CARD METAPHORS.

The denunciation of "sleeper amendments" is difficult and embarrassing, since it usually includes an admission that the denouncer was not awake enough to catch the legislation when originally offered. Sleeper has generally replaced the previous slang word—"joker." For a "sleeper issue," one which assumes surprising importance in a campaign, see RIGHT TO WORK.

In spookspeak, it means "an agent long in place but not yet activated." (For more spookspeak, see CIA-ESE.)

sleeping giant unrealized source of great power; untapped or potential force.

This term is perhaps derived from the plight of the title character in Jonathan Swift's 1726 novel, *Gulliver's Travels*. Readers of this classic well remember the part in which Gulliver visits the land of Lilliput, where the tiny inhabitants tie down the giant while he is asleep.

The term itself may have appeared after the attack on Pearl Harbor. *Respectfully Quoted*, a collection of quotations by the Library of Congress, tracks the term to a 1970 motion picture, *Tora, Tora, Tora*. In the film Isoroku Yamamoto, a Japanese admiral in World War II, says, "I fear all we have done is to awaken a sleeping giant and fill him with a terrible resolve." The attributed remark, however, has no printed evidence to support Yamamoto's use. In 1978, Vermont Royster offered another possible source in the *Wall Street Journal*: "'China is a sickly, sleeping giant. But when she awakes the world will tremble.' For over a century and a half that prophecy—attributed to Napoleon by Lord Amherst who visited him at St. Helena on his way back from China in 1816—has remained unfulfilled."

By the 1970s, the term was applied metaphorically to any potential powerhouse of political force. In 1977, a *Washington Post* article referred to the ethnic diversity of voters in the District of Columbia; a District candidate commented that the city's Hispanic community "is a sleeping giant no more."

Implicit in this expression is the notion that the sleeping giant will soon assert a previously unused power. In 1992, the *Los Angeles Times* quoted Oscar Gonzales, a California activist, as saying, "There is the realization that this could be a watershed year, the awakening of the sleeping giant," adding, "The sleeping giant is the vast potential Chicano bloc in Ventura County."

Ronald Reagan applied the term to the United States in 1980, perhaps unconsciously pairing it with the movie Yamamoto's "resolve." On the eve of his election to the Presidency, Reagan sent America's allies a message: "At last the sleeping giant stirs and is filled with a resolve—a resolve that we will win together a struggle for world peace, our struggle for the human spirit."

More recently, the image has been picked up as an expression of untapped personal power. Anthony Robbins, the self-help entrepreneur, entitled a 1991 book on personal empowerment *Awaken the Giant Within*.

slogan rallying cry; catch phrase (see CATCHWORD); a brief message that crystallizes an idea, defines an issue, the best of which thrill, exhort, and inspire.

Good slogans have rhyme, rhythm, or alliteration to make them memorable; great slogans may have none of these, but touch a chord of memory, release pent-up hatreds, or stir men's better natures.

It is in the nature of slogans to appeal to emotions, slipping past rational argument. "Men suppose that reason has command over their words," wrote Lord Bacon in the sixteenth century, "still it happens that words in return exercise authority on reason."

Themes recur in sloganeering. Many of the following have separate entries in this book, but this is an attempt to show some common denominator.

There are slogans that are essentially *promissory*: Reconstruction's Forty Acres and a Mule (which dwindled to Three Acres and A Cow, taken from British radical agrarian Jesse Collings by American populists); The Full Dinner Pail; Every Man a King; $2 a Day and Roast Beef; I Shall Go to Korea; He Can Do More for Massachusetts; Peace and Prosperity.

Other slogans are primarily *warnings*: Don't Let Them Take It Away; Coolidge or Chaos; Hoover and Happiness, or Smith and Soup Houses; You Never Had It So Good; Save the American Way of Life; No Third Term; Let's Keep What We've Got; Your Home Is Your Castle—Protect It.

A call for *change* has been quite effective: Had enough?; Turn the Rascals Out; Time for a Change; Let's Get America Moving Again.

Overtly *rational* slogans have failed: Let's Look at the Record; Let's Talk Sense to the American People; Experience Counts; as has one overtly *antirational*: In Your Heart You Know He's Right.

Challenging is a good slogan technique: Fifty-Four Forty or Fight; Freedom Now.

Appeals to *gratitude* seem weak, but have worked: One Good Term Deserves Another; Keep Him on the Job; He Kept Us Out of War.

There has been a time for *evocative* slogans: A Country Fit for Heroes; General Taylor Never Surrenders; Vote as You Shot.

Alliterative slogans abound: Ban the Bomb; Beat the Bosses; Love That Lyndon; Rum, Romanism, and Rebellion; Tippecanoe and Tyler Too; Wilson's Wisdom Wins Without War; Win with Willkie.

So do *rhyming* slogans: I Like Ike; Jim Crow Must Go; All the Way with LBJ; In Hoover We Trusted, Now We Are Busted; the Grin Will Win.

There are occasional *symbolic* slogans: Log Cabin and Hard Cider; I Am As Strong As a Bull Moose.

And *punning* slogans: Keep Cool with Coolidge; Land a Job with Landon; (and Franklin Pierce won despite) We Polked You in 1844, We'll Pierce You in 1852.

Slogans have been *frantic* (Anything to Beat Grant); *sardonic* (Make Love, Not War; Draft Beer, Not Students); *vicious* (Elect a Leader Not a Lover; Twenty Years of Treason); *meaningless* (Nixon's the One) and *questioning* (Why Not the Best?).

In his 1960 campaign John F. Kennedy gave a general review of slogans, including the names of programs as slogans: "The Democratic party's candidates in this century never ran on slogans like 'Stand Pat with McKinley,' 'Return to Normalcy with Harding,' 'Keep Cool with Coolidge,' and 'Two Chickens in Every Pot with Hoover.' I don't know what Dewey's slogan was because he never worked it out. . . . Our slogans have meaning. Woodrow Wilson's New Freedom, Franklin Roosevelt's New Deal, Harry Truman's Fair Deal, and today, we stand on the threshold of a New Frontier."

The knack of turning a phrase was explained by Theodore Roosevelt to his young aide, Lieutenant Douglas MacArthur, in 1906. MacArthur had asked the President to what he attributed his popularity, and Roosevelt replied, "To put into words what is in their hearts and minds but not in their mouths." ("Hearts and minds" later became a slogan of sorts, as what had to be won in Vietnam. It was still current in 1992, when Harvard law professor Kathleen M. Sullivan wrote in *The New Republic:* "Free speech materialism holds that speech is privileged above conduct. Government may regulate bodies, but not hearts and minds.")

There are those who think sloganeering is a danger. "Slogans are both exciting and comforting," said educator James Bryant Conant in 1934, "but they are also powerful opiates for the conscience: some of mankind's most terrible misdeeds have been committed under the spell of certain magic words or phrases." Examples of this category include: Workers of the World, Unite; Mare Nostrum; Tomorrow the World.

Fowler's *Modern English Usage* defines slogans as "those catchwords with which in the modern world politicians, ideologists, and advertisers try to excite our emotions and atrophy our minds." The word itself comes from the Gaelic *slaugh-gairm*, from *slaugh* (army) and *gairm* (yell), the army-shout or war cry of the Scottish Highlanders, and has been in use, according to the *OED*, since 1513. An early American political use occurs in *Harper's Weekly* in 1854: "As party bitterness has died away . . . let us take up the old slogan: Hurrah for Jackson!"

Good sloganeering advice was provided by University of Wisconsin professor Robert T. Oliver in the February 1937 issue of *American Speech*: "The party out of power would do well to mass its attack behind one or two key phrases. Thus it will gain the same concentration that advertisers seek with their reiteration of They satisfy! Not a cough in a carload! Ask the man who owns one! In the use of slogans, it would appear, the chief poverty is riches. The force of vivid impression through which slogans operate is vitiated when there are too many."

In the seventies there was a trend toward facetious slogans. "Support Mental Health or I'll Kill You" appeared on buttons, but a candidate for local office in Washington won on "Dog Litter—An Issue You Can't Sidestep."

sloganeer. See GHOSTWRITER.

slumlord a landlord who realizes unconscionable profits on crowded slum dwellings, packing in tenants and withholding money for maintenance.

In cities, crusades against slumlords are frequent in local political campaigns, since there are relatively few voters who own real estate and a great many in ghetto areas who resent absentee landlords.

The word appeared in the mid-fifties; an early citation is from a 1957 *New York Times Magazine* article: "The landlord had bitterly protested to the Buildings Commissioner that he was not a 'slumlord' and avowed that he was ready to put the building in condition if he could get a guarantee that it would stay that way; otherwise he had no alternative but to demolish it." Added *Barron's* magazine in 1960: "To prevent the enrichment of slumlords, for example, the General Accounting Office, in fixing property values, would rule out all income earned in defiance of local ordinances."

Slumlords defend themselves by claiming that tenants overcrowd their facilities without their permission, and that vandalism is the cause of most of the complaints. This cuts no ice with campaigning candidates; a typical picture in this genre was Mayor Robert F. Wagner of New York touring a slum dwelling and coming face to face with a large rat.

There is a long tradition against landlords, particularly absentee. Dean Jonathan Swift inveighed against the English landlords of Ireland in the early eighteenth century, and this comment by Richard Hildreth in *Memoirs of a Fugitive* was typical of complaints against Southern plantation owners before the Civil War: "The absentee aristocracy congregates in Charleston, or dapples and astonishes the cities and watering places of the North by its profuse extravagance and reckless dissipation. The plantations are left to the sole management of overseers."

"Slumlord" is a word born with its time out of joint. The word was created by the substitution of the "land" in "landlord" with "slum," which was slang for "room" (possibly from "slumber") in the early nineteenth century, later coming to mean "poverty-stricken neighborhood." But as *slumlord* was being coined, so were euphemisms for *slum;* linguistic urban renewal replaced it with *culturally deprived environment* or *urban ghetto* or *inner city*, making *slumlord* a word in dire need of relocation.

slumpflation. See ECONOMIC JARGON.

slush fund a collection of money for payoffs or for personal use without proper accounting; an attack word on any collection of political contributions.

"Is Dodd Dead?" went the political question early in 1967, a play on the theological argument "Is God Dead?" As a result of an exposé by columnists Drew Pearson and Jack Anderson, Connecticut Senator Thomas Dodd was censured by the Senate for personal use of funds collected ostensibly for campaigning purposes.

Though "slush fund" was used often in Dodd's hearings, the meaning of the phrase is usually narrowed to a specific fund. Richard Nixon was accused by Democrats of having a slush fund in 1952, which he defended in the CHECKERS SPEECH, concurrently releasing contributors, amounts, and purposes. Soon afterward Adlai Stevenson was discovered by Republicans to have a fund as Illinois governor for supplementing the salaries of state employees. Since neither fund had a nefarious purpose, the furor soon died down.

The word is probably derived from the Swedish *slask*, meaning wet, or filth. Naval vessels would sell the slush and other refuse on board; the proceeds went into a fund to purchase sundries for the crew. Later this practice was extended to war-damaged equipment as well, and to military as well as naval refuse and equipment. "The polite Commissary informed us," wrote the *Rio Abajo Press* in 1864, "that they received twelve dollars a barrel for the [coffee] grounds, and thus added materially to the 'slush fund.'"

The first political use found was in 1874. Connecticut Congressman S. W. Kellogg, referring to a $5 million appropriation administered by the Treasury Secretary, said:

It was a matter of economy and good judgment . . . to consolidate all these offices into one bill, and dispense with what has been received out of . . . the "slush fund.". . . We have had this "slush fund" since 1866. It is the fund which my friend from Indiana (Mr. Holman) and my friend from Kentucky (Mr. Beck) talk so much about, although during Andrew Johnson's administration that "slush fund" was five or six times larger than it ever has been since.

Congressman Champ Clark used the term in 1894 in the sense of a campaign fund gathered for propaganda purposes, as he defended President Grover Cleveland, who "was not elected in 1888 because you had got the 'fat fried' out of your manufacturers; because of pious John Wanamaker and $400,000 of campaign slush funds. . . ." See FAT CAT.

What gives a slush fund its sinister current meaning is its inherent lack of accountability—the money goes into a pot and is ladled out without public scrutiny. From the original "fringe benefit" connotation in naval vessels, the phrase has gained a thieving image, as in this 1924 comparison of chicanery by Will Rogers: "If I was running for office I would rather have two friends in the counting room than a Republican slush fund behind me."

smart politics. See PRACTICAL
POLITICS.

smear as a verb, to slander, or to bribe,
or to devastate; as a noun, a malicious
lie, or a payment.

"I know this will not be the last of the
smears," said vice-presidential candidate Richard Nixon in 1952, at the
conclusion of his television defense of
the "Nixon fund." See CHECKERS
SPEECH. "In spite of my explanation
tonight, other smears will be
made. . . . And the purpose of the
smears, I know, is this: to silence me, to
make me let up."

Both the word and the political device are ancient. The word appears in a
variety of languages: the Greek *smyris*,
unguent; the Old Norse *smör*, fat or
butter; the Old English *smeoru*, grease;
Middle English *smere;* modern English *smear*. As a verb, one of its meanings is to besmirch, or pollute, and that
sense—of tainting a reputation—is its
most common political meaning.

A second political meaning—to
bribe—comes from the political use of
GREASE as graft money; a related idea is
to "know which side your bread is
buttered on." This is usually pronounced *schmear*, or *schmier*, from the
German verb "to spread."

"Be thou as pure as snow," Hamlet
told Ophelia, "as chaste as ice, thou
shalt not escape calumny." An attack
on a reputation can be labeled preten-
tiously as *"impugning integrity."* A
more legalistic mind uses *slander* (spoken) or *libel* (written). A later label,
implying systematic smearing, is *character assassination* (see CHARACTER AS-
SASSIN).

Peggy Eaton, wife of Andrew
Jackson's Secretary of War, was ostracized by Washington society for supposedly living with her husband-to-be
before her first husband committed
suicide, and the President accurately
diagnosed the attack on the young
woman as "a plot by Clay and Calhoun to separate Eaton and me." The
lady herself put it quaintly: "It was the
designs of politics that led to the slander of my fair frame . . ." Fathering a
bastard, one of the dirtiest of smears,
was used unsuccessfully against Grover Cleveland, who admitted he supported an illegitimate child; a campaign song was "Ma, Ma, where's Pa?"

A third, and less frequent, meaning
of smear is to devastate, or "to cream,"
from the football use of the word for a
crunching tackle, or the baseball use as
an overwhelming victory. There is an
overlap here, as a person who has been
effectively slandered can be pictured as
left lying on the ground.

Smear was popularized during the
latter part of the Hoover Administration, when Democrats blamed Herbert Hoover for breadlines; the President said that Charlie Michelson, a
former *New York World* reporter acting as head of the Democratic National Committee's publicity department, "came out of the smear
department of yellow journalism."

John J. Raskob, Chairman of the
Democratic National Committee in
1932, taunted the Republicans on their
"smear" charge. "Upon consulting the
dictionary," he told the national convention, "we found a definition of the
word 'smear' to mean, 'to prepare a
dead body with sacred oils before
burial.'"

The Republicans in 1936 continued
to complain about the "Smear Department of the New Deal," but in the next
decade the use of the word became bipartisan. In political terminology, it
was a useful antonym to "whitewash":
Harry Truman wrote that his senatorial investigating committee "was not
going to be used for either a whitewash
or a smear in any matter before it but
was to be used to obtain facts . . ."
Senator Margaret Chase Smith, in her
1950 "Declaration of Conscience"

aimed at Senator Joseph McCarthy, said: "The American people are sick and tired of being afraid to speak their minds lest they be politically smeared as 'Communist' or 'Fascist.' The American people are sick and tired of seeing innocent people smeared and guilty people WHITEWASHED . . ."

The spring and summer of 1960 was a high point of smearing. John F. Kennedy's West Virginia primary campaign featured a smear by Kennedy supporter Franklin D. Roosevelt, Jr., to the effect that Senator Hubert Humphrey had been a draft dodger; the Lyndon Johnson forces, led by Texas Governor John Connally (injured when Kennedy was assassinated, three years later), accused Kennedy's father of harboring anti-Semitic sentiments during World War II.

A question arises: Can the truth be a smear? The Johnson supporters claimed that John Kennedy was a victim of Addison's disease, requiring regular cortisone treatment. The Kennedy forces admitted only "a mild adrenal deficiency," but an article in the *Journal of the American Medical Association* in 1967 substantiated the original charge. Nevertheless, most politicians consider the original attack a smear; while truth may be a legal defense against libel, the spreading of a damaging story about a candidate—even if true—can be considered a smear. Journalists do not agree.

Smear is current. A *Chicago Tribune* editorial at the end of 1992 lectured Republicans about appointments by President-elect Clinton: "What we ought not to have is an obfuscating cloud of smear and slander and distortion."

The predecessor word was ROORBACK; also see GUTTER FLYER and DIRTY TRICKS.

smell of magnolias the difficulty of being a Southerner in a national cam-

paign; or, Southern charm exercised with great political finesse in the South.

"Johnson the candidate," wrote *Life* magazine in 1956 about the candidacy of Senator Lyndon Johnson of Texas, "has grave and probably decisive drawbacks as he, despite the hopes of his supporters, well knows. He has little support in organized labor. He 'smells of magnolias,' *i.e.*, is a Southerner."

Though the phrase seldom appears in print, it has a lively political usage as "magnolia talk"—an intimate, richly accented, we-have-the-same-roots seduction—and as "smell of magnolias," the odor that causes Southern conservatives to sigh and Northern liberals to sniff.

When Richard Nixon impressed the Republican platform committee in 1960 with the need to adopt a strong civil rights plank, a Southern lady from Louisiana told reporter Theodore White, "I know what you Northerners think. But we've lost Louisiana, I tell you, we've lost Louisiana. Lyndon Johnson's going to come across the border now and talk 'magnolia' to them and they'll vote Democratic and we could have had Louisiana, we could have had it." See CORN PONE.

In the presidential campaign of 1976, the presence of a Southerner, Jimmy Carter, at the top of the Democratic ticket led to a new use of the magnolia metaphor: unfriendly writers referred to his wife, Rosalynn Carter, as "the steel magnolia." In April 1978, *Time* magazine referred to the group of Georgians working in the White House as the "magnolia mafia."

smoke and mirrors illusion; use of deception for manipulation.

Jimmy Breslin coined the term in a 1975 book, *How the Good Guys Finally Won*, about House Speaker Tip O'Neill's involvement in the removal of Richard Nixon from the Presidency. Quoting Thomas Hobbes's "The reputation of power is power," Breslin opined that political power is primarily an illusion:

> Mirrors and blue smoke, beautiful blue smoke rolling over the surface of highly polished mirrors, first a thin veil of blue smoke, then a thick cloud that suddenly dissolves into wisps of blue smoke, the mirrors catching it all, bouncing it back and forth. If somebody tells you how to look, there can be seen in the smoke great, magnificent shapes, castles and kingdoms, and maybe they can be yours.

Breslin added that the operator of an illusion begins to believe in it himself, "at the same time knowing that what he is believing in is mirrors and blue smoke."

In usage, Breslin's phrase was inverted as *blue smoke and mirrors*, with the color often clipped. Using the stage metaphor of a magician's act, in which a rabbit is pulled from a hat accompanied by a puff of smoke and sometimes by deceptive mirrors, it had become political jargon by the late 1970s. Bill Peterson wrote in the *Washington Post* on November 13, 1979, about a STRAW POLL showing George Bush as the winner of the Republican nomination for President: "The victory was fleeting, meaningless except in the blue smoke and mirror world of politics."

Jack W. Germond and Jules Witcover used the phrase to title their 1981 book, *Blue Smoke and Mirrors: How Reagan Won and Why Carter Lost the Election of 1980.* Reagan himself used the term, with its extended magician metaphor, to describe the budget process: "Wink and blink and smoke and mirrors, and pulling rabbits out of hats."

During the Iran-contra hearings, Senate counsel Arthur L. Liman asked former National Security Adviser Robert C. McFarlane about support given the Nicaraguan resistance after Congress had cut off aid. Replied McFarlane, "Basically it was smoke and mirrors."

smoke-filled room a place of political intrigue and chicanery, where candidates are selected by party bosses in cigar-chewing sessions.

This sinister phrase is usually attributed to Harry Daugherty, an Ohio Republican who supported Senator Warren Harding for the party's presidential candidacy. Daugherty sensed that the two best-known candidates, General Leonard Wood and Governor Frank Lowden of Illinois, would start off with almost equal support. "The convention will be deadlocked," Daugherty is quoted as having said, "and after the other candidates have gone their limit, some twelve or fifteen men, worn out and bleary-eyed for lack of sleep, will sit down about two o'clock in the morning, around a table in a smoke-filled room in some hotel and decide the nomination. When that time comes, Harding will be selected."

Daugherty later denied having said any such thing, calling "The Fable of the Senatorial Clique" an "amazing yarn." But William Allen White, editor of the *Emporia Gazette* and a respected Republican figure, corroborated the Daugherty prediction. A story filed at 5 A.M. on June 12, 1920, by Associated Press reporter Kirke Simpson, led off with the words "Harding of Ohio was chosen by a group of men in a smoke-filled room early today as Republican candidate for President." Newsmen call this "putting the story in the lead."

Present in Colonel George Harvey's room at the Blackstone Hotel that night were some of the most respected political figures in the U.S.: Senators Wadsworth, Calder, Smoot, Watson, McCormick, and Lodge, along with

Joe Grundy, a political boss who later became a senator. Not present were most of those later to become known as "the Ohio gang."

Historian Mark Sullivan, curious about the birth of a famous saying, elicited a letter from New Yorker Charles E. Hilles, who (Sullivan wrote) "was present at, so to speak, the obstetrical bedside of this verbal birth." The firsthand Hilles account:

"Daugherty was hastily packing his bag in a Waldorf Astoria Hotel room when two reporters called. He expressed regret that he had not time for an interview. One of the reporters persisted . . . he said that he presumed that as Daugherty could not support by an authentic table of delegates his boast that Harding would be the nominee, it followed that Daugherty must expect to win by manipulation—probably in some back room of a hotel with a small group of political managers reduced to pulp by the inevitable vigil and travail.

"The reporter went on to say to Daugherty," Hilles recounted, "that he presumed the conferees would be expected to surrender at 2 A.M. in a smoke-filled room. Daugherty, unaffected by the taunt, retorted carelessly, 'Make it 2:11.'"

(For similar tales of phrases planted by reporters, see RED HERRING and INOPERATIVE.)

As Harry Truman pointed out, "the 'smoke-filled room' was nothing new but Harding's nomination dramatized the tag and made it stick." That kind of session was bound to happen, wrote Thomas E. Dewey, "where there are enough strong candidates to prevent anyone from getting a majority and there is a stalemate."

The era of air-conditioned hotel rooms has blown away most of the literal meaning, but the symbolism makes the phrase current and useful.

Carmine de Sapio, Tammany leader in the fifties, had an eye ailment that made it impossible for him to endure cigarette smoke. In tagging him with a "bossism" charge, his opponents continued to charge him with "operating in a smoke-filled room."

smoke screen disguising intentions or evading issues by creating a diversion or giving a deliberately false impression.

British Prime Minister Harold Wilson attacked a London newspaper, the *Daily Express*, for revealing government secrets in 1967, despite a special commission's findings that the paper was innocent of the charges. Speaking in the House of Commons, a Conservative leader, Reginald Maudling, said of Mr. Wilson, "It is one of his most unlovable characteristics that he is never prepared to admit he is wrong. On the frequent occasions when he is, he tries to escape by throwing up a smokescreen."

The term is in active use in American politics as well. A 1940 cartoon in the *Rochester* (N.Y.) *Times-Union* shows a Democratic donkey flying an airplane which is putting down a smoke screen around various articles labeled "Taxes," "Extravagance," "Third term," "Public debt." At that time Republicans were charging the Roosevelt Administration with trying to hide its domestic errors behind the dangers of this country becoming involved in World War II. The cartoon is captioned "War Issue."

A linguistic spin-off is the word "spoofing," nuclear jargon for creating false alarms or making diversions. This is designed to swamp or confuse an enemy's thermonuclear defense so that it is unable to identify a genuine attack when launched.

In 1993, Bill Clinton urged Americans to ignore polls showing "somebody's up and somebody's down." Said President Clinton: "It's very important that you sort of clear away the political smoke screen and ask yourself, 'What's really at stake here?'"

The derivation of "smoke screen" is naval, from the days when destroyers would dash at high speeds between an enemy fleet and their own, laying down large quantities of black smoke to conceal the movements and intentions of their own vessels. Later, airplanes were sometimes used to accomplish the same aims on the battlefield.

In Japanese politics, a more poetic phrase is used to describe the effort to evade an issue by creating a diversion. Translated literally, it is "throwing up cherry blossoms."

smoking gun   incontrovertible evidence: the proof of guilt that precipitates resignations.

"The chaplain stood with a smoking pistol in his hand," wrote A. Conan Doyle in a Sherlock Holmes story (1894). Such a stance is generally considered suggestive of obvious (sometimes too obvious) guilt.

During the Watergate investigation, Nixon defenders insisted that while much impropriety could be observed, no proof of presidential obstruction of justice—no "smoking gun"—had been found. Then, on the release of the June 23, 1972, tape, H. R. Haldeman was shown to have said to the President that "the FBI is not under control" and that the CIA could be used to block the FBI investigation. When Haldeman said, "And you seem to think the thing to do is to get them the FBI to stop?," the President replied, "Right, fine."

Representative Barber Conable, a conservative Republican, said that the evidence on the June 23 tape "looked like a smoking gun." The term, which had been "in the air" for months, was widely quoted. Within days the President resigned, and the simile's incontrovertible-evidence meaning was reinforced.

The term did not die with Watergate. Covering the Marvin Mandel corruption trial in Maryland, reporter Jerry Oppenheimer wrote in the *Washington Star* in 1977: "While no 'smoking gun' of new damaging evidence is expected to be introduced by the government, knowledgeable observers of the case believe that the 'morality of Maryland politics' in general will stand trial."

In 1992, the term resurfaced when David Shaw of the *Los Angeles Times* was quoted by the *Boston Globe* on the campaign style of Ross Perot: "Unless there's a real smoking gun that the press comes up with, I think that he might be able to manipulate anti-press feelings in the public and turn attacks on him to his advantage."

See WATERGATE WORDS.

snake in the tunnel   an agreement that one nation's exchange rates will fluctuate within a narrower band than other nations' rates; an attempt to give some limited flexibility to fixed exchange rates, opposed by free-marketers who want an unrestricted "float."

This is as good a metaphor as the invisible hand of the "dismal science" of economics has ever crafted, and is remembered more for the vividness of its image than the longevity of its practice. The word-picture combines the evil lurking in "snake in the grass" with the hope implicit in "light at the end of the tunnel." When this lexicographer went to Professor Herbert Stein, who served as a member, and later Chairman, of the Council of Economic Advisers during the early seventies when the snake was in the tunnel, the answer received went more to the way all catch phrases are born than to the serious business of politico-economic etymology.

"It seems that one day in 1972," recounted the droll Dr. Stein, "at a reception following a meeting of the Group of 10 in Paris, Dr. Karl Schiller, German Minister of Economics and Finance, found that the cream cheese had been spread on the lox, instead of vice versa. *'Diese snack ist im eine tummul!'* he exclaimed, meaning, of course, that the snack was mixed up.

"The information director of the Group of 10, who was British, thought Schiller had said that the snack is in the *tunnel*, the underground passage connecting the Château de la Muette with the OECD office building. At a press briefing later, when asked what Dr. Schiller's opinion was, he quoted Schiller as saying that the snack is in the tunnel.

"A stringer for the *Wall Street Journal*," Dr. Stein continued, "misunderstood and cabled to New York that Schiller had said, 'The *snake* is in the tunnel.' And so it all began.

"This story," concluded the eminent economist, "while uninteresting, is also unauthenticated." Coming finally to the object of the author's query, he added: "However, I do have it on good authority that the expression was coined by Dr. Schiller."

Reached in West Germany, and responding in all seriousness, Dr. Schiller recalled the birth of the expression in Brussels at the end of 1970. "The meaning was quite simple," he wrote in March 1978. "At the time, we still had a fixed par value system and it was decided to agree on a narrower margin in the actual exchange rates between EEC countries as a preparatory step towards an economic and monetary union in Europe (Werner Plan) . . . this situation created the so-called 'Tunnel' within which the European exchange rates, i.e., the 'snake,' moved.

"Now that we have a joint floating of the currencies of some European countries against the dollar," Dr. Schiller explained, "we speak of the Snake only as a group consisting of some EEC member and some non-member countries. The Tunnel has, so to speak, disappeared."

Thus, for the reader who wants a straight-faced explanation of the expression, what economists needed was a metaphor for a long, narrow band in which Common Market countries' currencies could go up or down by 1⅛ percent (the snake) while they could vary twice that much up or down against the U.S. dollar (the tunnel). Like a nervous arm in a sleeve, or a wriggling snake in a tunnel.

More important, however, is an understanding of Dr. Stein's points: that folk etymology is easily born, even in economics, and that in multilingual international conferences, much flavor is gained, rather than lost, in translation and transmission.

The metaphor is now primarily used in historical contexts. *Institutional Investor* wrote in 1992: "The so-called 'snake in the tunnel' concept didn't last long, and market pressures caused Europe in 1973 to abandon efforts to keep any limits against the highly volatile dollar."

sneer words adjectives that cast aspersions on high-sounding nouns, or are used as a defense against entrapment by loaded phrases.

"Self-appointed" is probably the most frequently used sneer word, used to modify "guardian," "protector," and "watchdog" of the public interest. Also in this category is "self-proclaimed," "self-styled," and "self-annointed."

"So-called" is often used as a defensive adjective, when a shining phrase has been adopted generically by the opposition. Western diplomats use "so-called 'People's republic'" to show they don't really believe that the people run the republic; enclosing the sneer word and the noun it modifies within quotation marks completes the dissociation. Union leaders opposing "right-to-work" laws acknowledge that the slanted phrase has become generic, and refers to "so-called 'right-to-work' laws, which are really union busting laws . . ."

"Called," "purported," or "said to be" is not limited to English in its aspersion-casting sense; Charles de Gaulle scornfully referred to the United Nations as "*Les nations dites unies.*"

A curled lip can be used in spoken English to show derision, but the use of quotation marks creates the same effect in written prose, as "My opponent 'forgot' to say" or "This entry 'neglects' to mention . . ."

snipe   as a noun, a candidate's poster slapped up on "free space" such as fences, walls, telephone poles; as a verb, to post such advertising clandestinely.

This is a splendid little word long overlooked in political etymology. A "snipe" is a small bird with a long bill, akin to a woodcock; a "snipe hunt" is an elaborate practical joke in which the victim is left in a lonely field at night holding a sack and a tennis racket, one origin of the phrase "left holding the bag"; a snipe is also a fool, or a contemptible person, as in Churchill's "bloodthirsty guttersnipe" reference to Hitler; and it has been used to mean cigarette or cigar butt, as well as a member of a railroad section gang. Somewhere there must be a link that brings all these meanings together.

In its current political use, a snipe is a poster. An explanation is given in *The Relations Explosion*, a 1963 book by this writer:

> Perhaps you have been surprised one morning to see a candidate's "snipes" posted on fences and walls all over town, despite "Post No Bills" warnings. In almost every city, there is an organization well acquainted with building

superintendents and construction crews, which will put up a candidate's snipes for a fee. The plastering-up is done in the dead of night, with no questions asked, but never covers up the snipes of the opposing candidate, for whom the same snipers also work. Amateur snipers soon see their posters covered or disfigured with beards and mustaches.

> An effective political poster should be in glaring color, and should have the candidate's name filling at least a quarter of the poster, visible across streets, with few words of copy.

> We have been speaking here of the "free" poster space, not the normal outdoor billboard advertising. A larger portion of the campaign budget should go to billboards and snipes if the candidate is well-known. Billboards and posters are "reminder" media—they cannot carry much of a message.

In New York City, the sniping business, or racket, or profession, was for many years headed by the night manager of the Waldorf-Astoria.

In China, *dazibao*, or big-character posters, are an effective propaganda tool, sometimes posted on walls by angry students or supporters of disgraced officials. This form of communication occasionally reflects the genuine feelings of a minority.

In Japan, the word for reputation or prestige is *kamban;* its literal translation is poster, signboard, or "snipe."

snollygoster   an unprincipled politician; according to Harry Truman, "a man born out of wedlock."

President Truman revived this obsolete Americanism in a 1952 Labor Day speech at Parkersburg, W. Va., twitting politicians who pray in public to win votes.

The replating of a fanciful term coined during or prior to the Civil War sent reporters to the *Dictionary of American English*, where an entry from the *Columbus Dispatch* in 1895 quoted a Georgia editor's definition: "A snollygoster is a fellow who wants office, regardless of party, platform or principles, and who, whenever he wins, gets there by the sheer force of monumental talknophical assumnancy [sic]."

On September 3, 1952, the *Baltimore Sun* ran an editorial headed "Snolly and Snally" suggesting that the word came from the German *schnelle Geister*, or "Wild Host," which it defined as "birds of prey that terrorize man" and compared such a bird to an "ostentatious, vociferous politico."

Senator Charles Mathias (R-Md.) supplied the author with "information about the Maryland Snallygaster which is apparently a different species from the Missouri Snollygoster mentioned in your *Language of Politics* . . . as you will see, the Maryland Snallygaster was a crude and cruel beast employed against black voters." Senator Mathias enclosed a copy of an article that appeared in the *Valley Register* on March 5, 1909, intended to frighten black voters who intended to go to the polls. The headline was: "Emmitsburg Saw the Great Snallygaster/It Ate a Coal Bin Empty and Then Spit Fire/Looked Like a 'Coonscooper.'"

Webster's New International Dictionary (3rd edition) uses the Maryland "a" spelling and defines: "[perhaps a modification of . . . *schnelle geeschte*, literally quick spirits] a mythical nocturnal creature that is reported chiefly from rural Maryland, is reputed to be part reptile and part bird, and is said to prey on poultry and children."

Presidential use of an obscure political term gives it currency and enriches the vocabulary; for other once-obsolete terms that made it back, see CARPETBAGGER and MERCHANTS OF DEATH; for ones that did not, see OBSOLETE POLITICAL TERMS.

soak the rich. See POPULIST.

s.o.b. abbreviation for "son of a bitch," an appellation which creates a furor whenever the public learns that a President of the United States has used it.

President Harry Truman's military aide, Major General Harry Vaughan, was criticized by columnist Drew Pearson for accepting a medal from Argentine dictator Juan Perón. On February 22, 1949, in Arlington, Va., where Vaughan was being given another award by the Reserve Officers Association, President Truman expressed his feelings:

"I am just as fond of and just as loyal to my military aide as I am to the high brass, and want you to distinctly understand that any s.o.b. who thinks he can cause any one of these people to be discharged by me by some smart aleck statement over the air or in the paper has got another think coming."

White House stenographer Jack Romagna changed s.o.b. to "anyone" in the official transcript, but most newspapers quoted Truman verbatim. The *Christian Science Monitor* simply said "He used a vulgar abbreviation" but the *Chicago Tribune* felt it necessary to explain that "s.o.b. is an abbreviation for a vulgar expression casting reflection on a person's parentage." The *Indianapolis Star* added, "The phrase, freely translated, means male offspring of a female canine." Although Michigan Republican Clare Hoffman declared that "a man who feels impelled to use that sort of language" is not "the kind of man who should hold the office honored by Washington and Lincoln," a few editorial writers applauded the President. Wrote the *St. Louis Post-Dispatch*: "We can well understand the President's use of the term s.o.b. as applied to a certain showman and think that, considering all the circumstances, it was very well applied." Drew Pearson himself capitalized on the attack by urging his listeners and readers to become "Sons of Brotherhood."

Senator William Jenner of Indiana harkened back to the "tall-talk" construction of the mid-nineteenth century in describing columnist Pearson in 1950. "This Drew Pearson," he fulminated carefully, "is a self-appointed, self-made, cross *t*'d, dotted *i*'d, double-documented, super-superlative, revolving s.o.b."

In 1951 Senator Joseph McCarthy denounced Truman as "an s.o.b. who decided to remove MacArthur when drunk."

During the Eisenhower years the use of the epithet and its abbreviation appeared to subside in politics. The Truman-Pearson outburst took a mildly disapproved phrase and made a public issue out of it. In 1946, gentlemanly Senator Leverett Saltonstall of Massachusetts had made light of the fact that like all residents of the Senate Office Building, he received mail addressed "Leverett Saltonstall, S.O.B., Washington, D.C." No eyebrows were raised. The phrase had even had a heroic connotation, when Marine Sergeant Daniel Daly coined a World War I battle cry at Belleau Wood: "Come on, you sons of bitches! Do you want to live forever?" Frederick the Great made a similar statement at Koslin, June 18, 1757.

The phrase made a political comeback in connection with the steel-price rise and rollback in 1962. After U.S. Steel chairman Roger Blough had left the President's office, John F. Kennedy was widely reported to have said: "My father always told me that all businessmen were sons of bitches." This time, however, the furor was not over the President's choice of language (it was in private conversation) but on whether he actually said "all businessmen." Asked about his "rather harsh statement" at a press conference, Kennedy replied, ". . . the statement which I have seen repeated is inaccurate. It quotes my father as having expressed himself strongly to me, and . . . I quoted what he said and indicated that he had not been . . . wholly wrong . . . as it appeared in a daily paper . . . I think the phrase was 'all businessmen.' That's obviously in error, because he was a businessman himself. He was critical of the steel men. But he confined it, and I would confine it. . . . I felt at that time that we had not been treated altogether with frankness, and therefore I felt his view had merit. But that's past."

In May 1961 Kennedy had inadvertently left behind a staff paper at a meeting held with Canadian Prime Minister John Diefenbaker that supposedly referred to the Canadian as an s.o.b. This Kennedy denied. "I couldn't have called him an s.o.b.," Kennedy told Sorensen later. "I didn't know he was one—at that time."

Thus, current use indicates that the phrase is politically acceptable when used by anyone in private conversation; it is considered tasteless when used by public officials in public; and it shocks and horrifies when used publicly by a President.

sobriquets terms of affection or derision used interchangeably with the names of famous men. More grandiose than a nickname.

Tracing the line of American Presidents: *The Father of His Country*, or the *American Fabius*, was succeeded by the *Colossus of Independence*, sometimes called the *Machiavelli of Massachusetts*, and followed by the *Sage of Monticello*, or *Long Tom*. The *Father of the Constitution* was next, and then the *Last of the Cocked Hats*, author of the famous Doctrine; *Old Man Eloquent* (son of *Colossus*) gave way to *Old Hickory* (*King Andrew* to his enemies), and then his protégé, *The Little Magician*, or *Wizard of Kinderhook. Tippecanoe* died in office, making way for the *Accidental President*, then *Young Hickory* (we're up to Polk now) and *Old Rough and Ready*. The *American Louis Philippe* succeeded him, followed by *Purse*—just a play on the name Pierce—and then the *Old Public Functionary*, or *Bachelor President. Father Abraham* came next (called by some the *Illinois Baboon*), with *Sir Veto, Unconditional Surrender, President de Facto* (Tilden supporters wouldn't concede that Hayes was *de jure*), the *Dark Horse*, and the *First Gentleman of this Land*, taking us up to Cleveland, the *Man of Destiny* or *Stuffed Prophet. Grandpa's Grandson* (Tippecanoe was the Grandfather) ushered in *Prosperity's Advance Agent*, succeeded by his Vice President, the *Rough Rider*, and then by William Howard Taft, who was not blessed with an outstanding sobriquet. *The Phrasemaker*, or *Professor*, was followed by Harding (no sobriquet), then *Silent Cal, The Chief, That Man in the White House*, and *Give 'Em Hell Harry*. Sobriquets have paled in recent years—Ike, JFK, LBJ—but Ronald Reagan was called the *Great Communicator* and Bill Clinton has styled himself the *Comeback Kid.*

Tom Braden, in a 1971 column, bemoaned the disappearance of the sobriquet:

> . . . our people have gradually and unconsciously deprived themselves of the romance which once accompanied the nation's business. Suppose today that instead of discussing the relative showing in the polls of Richard Nixon and Edmund Muskie we could speak of the rivalry between Silver Dick and the Boy Orator of the Platte. How much more fun, how much more romantic. . . . Imagine a candidate for President whom people referred to as 'The Plumed Knight,'—which was the way the followers of James C. Blaine talked

about their leader. And after Bryan, Czar Reed was speaker of the House, Blackjack Pershing was leader of American forces in World War I, Fighting Bob La Follette was to run for President on the Progressive ticket and silent Cal Coolidge was to win. . . . But why has the sobriquet gone? Was Eugene McCarthy getting close to the national mood when he wrote a poem about the disappearance of "Kilroy," that sobriquet for the American soldier who—in every battleground and staging area of World War II—"was here"? McCarthy hinted that the disappearance of Kilroy meant the disappearance of pride, and maybe we are lacking in that pride in being American, which caused us to sprinkle our politics with characters like Old Rough and Ready, Tippecanoe, Fuss and Feathers, and the Little Giant. Or for that matter, Honest Abe? The new standard is cool and polite, and correct, and not much fun.

so-called.   See SNEER WORDS.

social issue.   See PSEPHOLOGY.

soft landing   economic slowdown without a full recession; slowed growth of the economy that succeeds in averting inflation.

Astronautics provided this term in the 1950s. In an article on lunar exploration, the *Times* of London reported on March 28, 1958, that "Next [in difficulty] would be a 'soft' (controlled) landing by an unmanned vehicle." That year's Proceedings of the Lunar and Planetary Exploration Colloquium repeated the phrase: "With a soft landing on the moon, one might put down a payload of 225 to 800 pounds."

In the 1970s, the phrase transferred from space use to economic jargon. *Newsweek* reported in September 1973, "Even if the President succeeds in pulling in the rampaging economy for a soft landing, of course, the arrival will be nonetheless bumpy for many."

By the late 1980s, this economic usage was a favorite expression of the Federal Reserve. Robert T. Parry, president of the Federal Reserve Bank of San Francisco, commented in the summer of 1989 that balanced growth "enhances the prospect that we can achieve a soft landing," defining that phrase as "a needed slowdown without a recession. . . . The goal is to have the economy grow at a slow rate relative to its potential to cause the rate of inflation to come down." A 1989 newsletter from the Federal Reserve Bank of Cleveland offered the headline "How Soft a Landing?"

Caroline A. Baum, a Treasury market commentator for Telerate Systems of Jersey City, explained, "Economists turned to a nonsocial science like aeronautics for a term that would adequately describe a maneuver designed to land the economy softly without inflicting damage on itself or its payload." *Soft landing* is used in contrast to the stark *crash landing*.

Other fields have been lifting the same space term. In 1985, a commodities dealer hoped "to organize a soft landing for tin." In 1989, an Israeli scientist said, "We have provided a soft landing for a certain number of immigrants," and a *Financial Times* wine critic complained about some sparkling wines, wishing "to arrange a soft landing back into real wine at some point."

soft money.   See HARD MONEY.

soft on Communism attack phrase formerly used by those convinced that the United States was in danger from internal Communist subversion, or at those who refused to accept a HARD LINE posture abroad.

The charge was most often heard during the peak of Senator Joseph McCarthy's influence. The Soviet Union had acquired nuclear weapons

and increasingly efficient rockets, a legitimate cause for American concern. In a series of trials and hearings, seemingly respectable and in several cases comparatively high-ranking government officials were accused of having been involved in espionage on behalf of Russia. Truman's peremptory defense of RED HERRING made the charge more potent.

The case which gave most ammunition to those making the "soft on Communism" charge was that of Alger Hiss, who had held a series of high governmental posts, including working with the U.S. delegation to the Yalta conference. Hiss was later convicted for perjury. (His family claimed he was cleared retroactively in 1992 by a retired Russian general, but that officer later backtracked.)

Democratic presidential candidate Adlai Stevenson was attacked by Republicans for having made a deposition saying that Alger Hiss's reputation was good. Stevenson said that in the deposition he had testified as a lawyer should, saying what he knew—no more, no less. He went on, "My testimony in the Hiss case no more shows softness towards Communism than the testimony of these Republican leaders (Taft, Bricker, and Joe Martin) shows softness towards corruption."

In the same campaign, retiring President Harry Truman, belatedly recognizing the public appeal of the attack, said, "The most brazen lie of the century has been fabricated by reckless demagogues among the Republicans to the effect that Democrats were soft on Communism."

Mr. Truman, in whose Administration those attacked had held office, also said that the Stevenson forces had made a serious tactical error in allowing themselves to be put on the defensive in the campaign by the "soft on Communism" charges.

The complete phrase is now only in historical use but survives in other "soft on" usages; opponents in 1991 of an attack on Saddam Hussein were called "soft on Saddam."

See MESS IN WASHINGTON; K₁C₂; McCARTHYISM.

soft-pedal a political decision to de-emphasize an issue or topic, without ignoring it completely.

In the 1964 presidential campaign, on the subject of President Johnson's choice of close personal aides, Republicans proceeded to "bear down on" Bobby Baker, but to "soft-pedal" Walter Jenkins because of the personal tragedy involved in his arrest on a morals charge. Because of the distasteful nature of the charges, a sharp attack on Jenkins might have backfired; hence the decision to "soft-pedal" by oblique references to the need for high moral standards in high places, to the great pressures put on aides by an overly demanding President, etc.

Editor Henry Stoddard wrote in 1938: "The weakness of the Hoover Administration was . . . in handling Prohibition. . . . When the campaign [of 1932] opened, [Hoover] handed over to Walter Brown, his Postmaster-General, the task of soft-pedaling Prohibition through the contest. Brought up in Ohio politics Brown knew how to gumshoe so that you have to listen intently to hear the fall of his foot, or to know whether he was coming or going. He handled the issue that way for Hoover, until both realized its futility. It was then too late to change."

While cautious politicians shy from hot issues, GUTFIGHTERS revel in them. "Since political campaigns are played for keeps," wrote reporter Robert Donovan in 1956 about Democratic charges that Stevenson had been hit below the belt, "a campaigner does not soft-pedal a good issue just because it offends the opposition."

The phrase is used in auto racing (to tread lightly on the accelerator pedal) and probably originated in piano playing (the soft pedal cuts down the reverberations of the strings).

Solid South the supposedly monolithic vote of the Southern states for the Democratic party, used now more in the breach than in the observance.

Southerners knew after the Civil War that (1) Lincoln and his BLACK REPUBLICANS freed the slaves, and (2) the CARPETBAGGERS and SCALAWAGS descended on them during Reconstruction under a Republican regime. Not surprisingly, the Democratic party had an appeal for white Southerners.

The phrase "solid South" was popularized by General John Singleton Mosby, a cavalry leader (Mosby's Rangers) on the staff of Confederate General J. E. B. Stuart. Mosby, with his impeccable Southern credentials, startled his Southern friends by coming out in 1876 for Republican Rutherford B. Hayes against Democrat Samuel Tilden. In a letter that was widely publicized at the time, he wrote: "Suppose Hayes is elected with a solid South against him—what are you going to do then?"

Though this phrase has been used by House Speaker Schuyler Colfax in 1858, Mosby's use—in the context of a Southerner fighting against the solidity of the South—gave it political excitement. "The Solid South," reported *Harper's Weekly* immediately afterward, "is the Southern Democracy seeking domination of the United States through the machinery of the Democratic party."

The phrase delighted Republicans; coined by a renegade Democrat, it helped Republicans slightly in the South and strongly in the North. The *New York Tribune* got the origin wrong, but the end result right: "The claim of a 'solid South' is likely to do the Democrats fully as much harm as good. They originated the expression, and the Republicans are using it with great force against them . . ."

In an article titled "The Solid South" in *Century* magazine, Edward Clark wrote:

> The Solid South . . . came into vogue during the Hayes-Tilden canvass of 1876. The Democratic tidal wave in the elections of 1874 had shown a powerful, if not irresistible, drift toward Democracy in all the then lately reconstructed States, as well as in their sisters on the old borderline which had also maintained slavery, but which had not gone into the rebellion. The alliterative term commended itself to the Republican stump speakers and newspaper organs as a happy catch-word, and the idea which underlay it was impressive enough to arrest the attention of the whole country.

Thomas E. Dewey made the same point in 1950: "The only danger nationally has been that one party might become too strong, or able to use the enormous new powers of government to perpetuate itself in office, as is the case in politically lop-sided, machine-dominated cities or in the 'Solid South.'"

Through the years, the South remained solid for the Democratic party; in 1928, when Democrat Al Smith was the candidate, his Catholicism and support of Prohibition repeal defeated him in Texas, Florida, Tennessee, and Virginia; all four of those states went for Republican Dwight Eisenhower in 1952 and 1956, and all but Texas for Nixon in 1960. In 1964 the South was almost solid again, but this time for Republican Barry Goldwater in a vote attributed to the BACKLASH over black civil rights gains.

The tension between Northern Democratic liberals and Southern Democratic conservatives led to an open break in 1948. Governor Strom Thurmond of South Carolina led a delegation of six Democratic governors to a tense meeting at Democratic National Headquarters in Washington, demanding "the highly controversial civil rights legislation" be "withdrawn." Turned down, they issued a joint statement: "The present leadership of the Democratic party will soon realize that the South is no longer 'in the bag.'" Thurmond ran as a third-party candidate to punish Truman (see DIXIECRAT) and later became a Republican.

The South today is still Democratic in local elections, though not nearly as much as before; in national politics, the bloc was busted by Republicans, notably in 1964 by Goldwater, but solidified again for the candidacy of Southerner Jimmy Carter in 1976. But the political tradition of the "new South" is a far cry from the situation described in an anecdote used by Harry Dent in his book *The Prodigal South Returns to Power* (1978):

"In 1924 Senator Coleman L. Blease, Democrat of South Carolina, was alarmed to learn that Republican Calvin Coolidge had won 1123 of 50,131 votes cast in South Carolina in the presidential race.

"'I do not know where he got them,' Blease supposedly said. 'I was astonished to know they were cast and shocked to know they were counted.'"

Today the phrase is used mainly by commentators showing that the "solid" South has turned fluid. See SOUTHERN STRATEGY; SUNBELT.

solon headlinese for legislator; originally meant "wise statesman," now used ironically.

A headline writer who uses "Solons Probe" rather than "Legislators Investigate" saves eleven letters, providing space for two more clichés. Neither solon nor probe is used in the spoken political language.

Solon, an aristocratic Athenian born about 640 B.C., was referred to by Plato in the *Symposium* as "the revered father of Athenian laws," and was also an economist and the first Attic poet.

For other eponymous words in politics, see QUISLING; MAVERICK; PHILIPPIC; GERRYMANDER.

sons of the wild jackass political irregulars inclined to vote against the party line, especially liberal Republicans; also, reformers in general.

John Hay, later Secretary of State, used "wild ass" in the sense of "unreasonable reformer" in an 1890 letter to Theodore Roosevelt: "You have already shown that a man may be absolutely honest and yet practical; a reformer by instinct and a wise politician; brave, bold, and uncompromising, and yet not a wild ass of the desert."

William Jennings Bryan suggested in 1896 that reforming asses occasionally kicked each other's heads in:

> I remember that a few years ago a Populist in Congress stated that the small burros that run wild upon the prairies of South America form a group, when attacked by a ferocious animal, and, putting their heads together and their feet on the outside of the circle, protect themselves from the enemy. But he added that the advocates of reforms sometimes showed less discretion, and turning their heads toward the enemy, kicked each other.

The reference, Hans Sperber and Travis Trittschuh suggest, comes from the "wild asses in the desert" in the Book of Job, 24:5. The wild asses of reform or independence were popularized a generation later. In 1929 Republicans included a number of Westerners who were indifferent to party discipline. Since they were politically akin to the Populists of an earlier generation, the liberal Westerners tended to look upon the more conservative Eastern portion of the party with suspicion as "lackeys of Wall Street." Senator George H. Moses of New Hampshire, lamenting the alliance between these Republicans and liberal Democrats, which blocked the higher tariffs the GOP leadership wanted, said on the Senate floor in 1924: "Mournfully, I prophesy that the program of these sons of the wild jackass who now control the Senate will probably go forward to complete consummation."

Senator Moses later said his inspiration came from the Old Testament, Jeremiah 14:6: "And the wild asses did stand in the high places, they snuffed up the wind like dragons."

The Western liberal Republicans of whom Senator Moses complained were men like Senators Johnson of California, Norris of Nebraska, La Follette of Wisconsin, and Shipstead of Minnesota. In recent times, Eastern and Western Republicans are—or have been—again divided, but lately it has been the conservative Republicans of the West looking with suspicion upon the more liberal Republicans of the East.

soreheads. See TAKE A WALK.

soul deep understanding and sympathy for a cause; a civil rights word of the mid-sixties.

"Soul food" is a term for chitterlings (chit'lins) and other food items popular in black communities; indigenous music is called "soul music." In 1965, "soul brother" began to become popular to describe one sympathetic to black militancy.

During the Newark riots of 1967, black shopowners scrawled "Soul Brother" in soap across their windows, in hopes of deterring looters.

In recent usage, "to have soul" politically is to identify with black unrest and dissatisfaction.

sound bite   snappy snippet of taped comment or news.

The Presidential campaign of 1988 was characterized by the headline over a David R. Gergen essay in *U.S. News & World Report*: "The Politics of Sound Bites."

The phrase *sound bite* refers to clips of quick quotations or memorable words on news broadcasts. The earliest print citation is a piece by Sandy Kyle Bain in the *Washington Post* on June 22, 1980. That article described the coaching of candidates for television by William F. Rhatican: "Remember that any editor watching needs a concise, 30-second sound bite. Anything more than that, you're losing them."

Bill Rhatican, now working in public affairs for the Advertising Council, tells the lexicographer that "the phrase was in the air. I used it in a lecture I gave in the mid-70s advising political candidates on the use of television: if you wander all over the place in your statements, you won't provide pithy sound bites for TV."

Daniel Schorr, senior news analyst for National Public Radio, dates its use back to the early 1960s, when he worked at CBS News. "It came out of the editing room, in the days before videotape," he recalls. "When the producer saw the excerpt he wanted, he'd tell the film editor, 'Take that bite'; out of longer interviews, the bite would be 30 to 45 seconds."

Often the phrase is used to derogate the superficiality of the quick takes—down to an average of eight seconds in the early 1990s—of TV and radio news. Reporter Roger Mudd denounced the Presidential campaign of 1984 as a mixture of "sound bites and photo opportunities." (The latter term, since shortened to *photo op*, meaning "an event staged for photographs," was a Ron Ziegler coinage during the Nixon Admininstration.)

Both of these media-politics phrases, however, may also be used without a pejorative connotation. After the Vice Presidential debate in 1988 when Senator Lloyd Bentsen stunned Dan Quayle with "you're no Jack Kennedy" (see YOU'RE NO JFK), Jeff Greenfield of ABC called that riposte "the biggest sound bite of the night."

sources   a word used by reporters who want to show they are not originating some information to identify people who are passing on the information but do not want their identity known.

During "impeachment summer" of 1974, *New York Times* Washington bureau chief Clifton Daniel, concerned about the overuse of anonymous tips in the news columns, posted a memo to his staff:

> "Sources" has become a discredited word in our business. Let's stop using it.
>
> Sources are people (or pieces of paper). We should identify them whenever possible. When we cannot identify them, we should describe them as fully and accurately as circumstances permit. We should never misrepresent them—as, for example, by pluralizing a single source.
>
> If we cannot identify or describe a source but have absolute confidence in it, we can use information from that source without attribution. A phrase such as "reliably reported" is better than "sources said." If we don't have confidence in a source, we should not use the information, whether attributable or not.

Sources are usually described as "reliable," sometimes as "usually reliable," never as "an unreliable source." Since the Daniel memo, the phrase "who asked that his name not be used" has been used more frequently; "who insisted on anonymity" carries the disapprobation a step further. Reporters at the *Times* were also urged to locate sources, as in "an FBI source" or "an Administration source," which sometimes indicates the possible bias at the point of origin. "Sources close to the investigation" usually mean police or prosecution.

The noun has been turned into a verb as well: a story that is not "sourced" is considered "unsourced."

See AUTHORITATIVE SOURCES; NOT FOR ATTRIBUTION.

Southern strategy an attack phrase attributing racist or at least political motives toward any position taken on desegregation or busing that would be well received by most Southern whites.

In the summer of 1963, the conservative weekly *National Review* published a map showing how Senator Barry Goldwater could win the 1964 election, which included a sweep of the Deep South. In answer to the author's query in 1971, *National Review* publisher William Rusher disclaimed coinage of the phrase itself and added: "I would guess that it goes back to some point in the early 1960s at which the liberals finally became aware of the strategy by which the Goldwater forces proposed to win the nomination and the election of 1964. It seems to me much more likely that the term 'Southern strategy' was invented by the liberals and fastened by them upon the strategy, since the pejorative implication was that the Goldwater forces were preparing to turn their backs upon the blacks and sell out to southern bigotry. (From our standpoint, of course, the correct term would have been 'Southern-Midwestern-Western strategy,' since that was what we really had in mind—a coalition of these three against the dominant Northeast; but obviously such a term would have been too cumbersome.)" See SUNBELT.

Somewhat testily, Senator Goldwater nailed down the coinage in a letter to *Business Week* October 1971:

> The first writer to use the term "southern strategy" was Joe Alsop,

after his visit to my office back in the 1950s. At that time I was chairman of the Senate Campaign Committee and had conducted a very in-depth survey of voting trends in the U.S. for President Eisenhower. This survey showed that the only areas in the whole United States where the Republican Party had been making gains were in the Southwest. For that reason we decided to put more emphasis on that part of the nation, where Republicans historically had not done well.

> That is the so-called "Southern strategy." It has nothing to do with busing, integration, or any other of the so-called closely held concepts of the Southerner. The South began to move into Republican ranks because of the influx of new and younger businessmen from the North who were basically Republican. And they were aided by young Southern Democrats who were sick and tired of the Democratic stranglehold on the South and switched over to the Republican Party. Nowhere in any platform adopted by the Republican Party since I can remember can there be found any thing aimed directly at the South which could be indicative of some strategy employed by the Republican party that the Republican Party does not employ elsewhere."

Goldwater did carry the Deep South in the Johnson landslide, giving the phrase a "losing" connotation, as not only a racist strategy, but a politically mistaken one. In the 1968 presidential campaign, when Nixon's Southern manager, Howard "Bo" Callaway, called for support from voters leaning toward George Wallace, Ward Just wrote in the *Washington Post* that some Republicans "are worried lest Nixon pursue a 'Southern strategy' in his election campaign that would compromise potential support among minority groups and moderates in the North."

Nixon managers let it be known that the 1968 strategy centered on the "battleground" states: California,

New Jersey, Pennsylvania, Ohio, Illinois, Michigan, and Texas, only one of which—Texas—was below the Mason-Dixon line. Wrote Don Irwin in the *Los Angeles Times* on July 14, 1968: "Richard M. Nixon's avowed determination to concentrate on voters in large industrial states if he wins the Republican presidential nomination tells much about the election campaign he has in mind. It appears to bar revival of the all-out 'Southern strategy' that proved so disastrous for the GOP in 1964."

At the Gridiron Dinner spoofing the Nixon Administration in 1970, the hit song of the evening was sung to the tune of "A Dixie Melody":

Rock-a-bye the voters with a Southern
* strategy;*
Don't you fuss; we won't bus children in
* ol' Dixie!*
We'll put George Wallace in decline
Below the Mason-Dixon line
We'll help you save the nation
From things like civil rights and integra-
* tion!*
Weep no more, John Stennis!
We'll pack that court for sure.
We will fight for voting rights—
To keep them white and pure!
A zillion Southern votes we will deliver;
Move Washington down on the Swanee
* River!*
Rockabye with Ol' Massa Nixon and his
* Dixie strategy!*

To practical politicians, any strategy that wins one region at the expense of all others is nonsensical; however, any national election strategy that seeks to include Southern support is attacked as a "Southern strategy" because it helps the attacker disaffect the opposition's support elsewhere.

Although Georgian Jimmy Carter swept the South in 1976 (excepting Virginia), his strategy was never considered to be "Southern"; he won that region because that was where he came from. In a 1989 op-ed piece in the *New York Times,* Jason Berry wrote about politics and civil rights in Louisiana: "The chickens are coming home to roost for the Republican Party. Just at the time when the G.O.P. is trying to attract blacks at the national level, its 20-year-old Southern strategy of playing to racist fears has produced a major embarrassment—David Duke."

The phrase is firmly fixed in the political lexicon not as a strategy, but as a charge of deviousness and discrimination. See SOLID SOUTH.

South Succotash   put-down of a rural area; indication of a place's remoteness.

Ronald Reagan introduced this Americanism into political usage. In 1982, President Reagan questioned media coverage of unemployment: "Is it news that some fellow in South Succotash someplace has just been laid off—that he should be interviewed nationwide?"

The alliterative phrase uses a direction (South) to modify the place name, further suggesting remoteness from a center of activity. The name itself comes from the Narraganset *misickquatash*, meaning "ear of corn," and refers to a dish originally made of corn and beans (sometimes with meat), now usually a mixture of corn and lima beans.

In 1991, a Democratic Policy Committee report offered a partisan comparison of the approaches of Democrats and Republicans in helping the unemployed; the report's title was "South Succotash Revisited."

Although there is a Succotash Point in Rhode Island, Reagan's "South Succotash" uses a fictional name for his derogation of remote areas. Earlier uses of this technique include *Podunk,* or *East Jesus,* or as LBJ aide Liz Carpenter preferred, "Resume Speed, Texas."

special interests.   See VESTED INTERESTS.

special relationship ties between two countries for common self-interests; atypical or exclusionary connection that causes special treatment of one country by another.

Special relationship was first used for the ties between Britain and the United States at the time of World War II. Winston Churchill told the House of Commons on November 7, 1945, "We should not abandon our special relationship with the United States and Canada about the atomic bomb."

The next March, when Churchill delivered the "Iron Curtain speech" at Westminster College in Fulton, Missouri, he repeated the phrase: "Neither the sure prevention of war nor the continuous rise of world organization will be gained without what I have called the fraternal association of the English-speaking peoples. This means a special relationship between the British Commonwealth and Empire and the United States of America."

In Washington, the adjective *special* is more often attached to the noun *interests* than to *relationship*. Other adjectives, however, have long been wedded to that noun; Martin Luther used three modifiers for the noun when he wrote in 1569 that "there is no more lovely, friendly and charming relationship . . . than a good marriage."

The pairing with *special* has been noted as a point of contention for countries not part of this relationship. In *The New Yorker* in 1991, John Newhouse wrote of France's "view of Britain as unwilling to put its role in Europe ahead of a special relationship with Washington."

The term has also been applied to other pairings, some of which include the United States. *Time* magazine reported in 1991 about the fraying of an American-Israeli connection: "If he means what he says, Bush has initiated a fundamental change in America's 'special relationship' with Israel."

Other connections may bypass the United States. Abdul Hamid Sharif, Jordan's envoy to the U.S., commented in 1977, "Gaza used to be under Egyptian administration, and there is a special relationship between all the Arab countries and the Palestinians."

The primary usage of the phrase, though, still refers to the British-American connection. Henry Brandon, the journalist for London's *Sunday Times* who died in 1993, used the term as the title of his memoirs in 1988 (see COST-BENEFIT ANALYSIS for another Brandon usage).

Not everybody agrees that the U.K.-U.S. special relationship is necessarily positive. As early as 1981, in fact, a *Washington Post* column by Philip Geyelin questioned the connection:

> This supposedly "special relationship" is not so much a tradition as it is a sometime thing, evoked for particular purposes at particularly propitious times. One thinks of the pen-pal relationship between Winston Churchill and Franklin Roosevelt; one forgets Suez, or John F. Kennedy being taken neatly to the cleaners in the matter of the Skybolt missile at Nassau by his good friend Harold Macmillan, or Lyndon Johnson upbraiding the British over the sale of buses to Cuba.

On the other side of the Atlantic, a 1992 editorial in Britain's *Independent* stated, "The special relationship between this country and the United States is at its worst when the American authorities demonstrate arrogance and insensitivity and their British counterparts are supine."

speechwriter one who writes speeches on assignment; for differentiation between *ghost, wordsmith, research assistant,* and *press secretary,* see GHOSTWRITER.

Robert Smith, who had done a creditable job as Secretary of the Navy under Thomas Jefferson, faced a problem when he was promoted to Secretary of State by the new President, James Madison. Smith was no writer. Wisely, he accepted the ghostwriting services of the best writer in the federal employ at the time: President Madison.

The President did not consider it menial work; Jefferson and Hamilton and he had helped Washington in the preparation of his Farewell Address, which stands out over most of the first President's turgid prose. Washington had asked them to look over his version, which he asked be "curtailed, if too verbose; and relieve of all tautology, not necessary to enforce the ideas in the original or quoted part. My wish is that the whole may appear in a plain stile; and be handed to the public in an honest; unaffected; simple garb."

Judge Samuel Rosenman, who worked on speeches with FDR, justified a presidential speechwriter's existence on the basis that "there just is not enough time in a President's day" to handle the chore. Some point out that Abraham Lincoln served in a busy era, wrote his own speeches, and turned out some of the best in the English language. But Lincoln, it is argued, had a knack for it; the presidency has grown in complexity; Chief Executives—even senators and congressmen—should not take time from their busy schedules to labor over a speech, certainly not its first draft. And since presidential words carry such import, why not get a great writer to put them down in the clearest, most inspirational way?

Walter Lippmann in 1942 was having none of this. In a column entitled "Something Off My Chest," he wrote:

A public man can and needs to be supplied with material and advice and criticism in preparing an important address. But no one can write an authentic speech for another man; it is as impossible as writing his love letters for him or saying his prayers for him. When he speaks to the people, he and not someone else must speak. For it is much more important that he could be genuine, and it is infinitely more persuasive, than that he be bright, clever, ingenious, entertaining, eloquent, or even grammatical. It is, moreover, a delusion, fostered into an inferiority complex among executives by professional writers, that in an age of specialists some are called to act and some are called to find the right words for men of action to use. The truth is that anyone who knows what he is doing can say what he is doing, and anyone who knows what he thinks can say what he thinks. Those who cannot speak for themselves are, with very rare exceptions, not very sure of what they are doing and of what they mean. The sooner they are found out the better.

Lippmann's view did not prevail; the public does not frown on a President having speechwriters, indeed has come to expect a President to work from others' drafts. The idea of a speechwriter's assignment, in most people's minds, is one gently sold by every top-level speechwriter: to discuss the speech ideas with the public figure, reflect his point of view clearly and in organized fashion, to submit extra phrases and slogans for the top man's consideration, and to rewrite according to the speaker's wishes. This is sometimes exactly what happens.

Who were the modern speechwriters for Presidents? FDR's became well-known: Professor Raymond Moley, Judge Samuel Rosenman, editor Stanley High, dramatist Robert E. Sherwood, lawyer Donald Richberg were among them. Truman's writers were almost totally anonymous: Clark Clifford, George Elsey, Ken Hechler, Charles J. Murphy, and William Hillman would occasionally surface, and Rosenman contributed from time to time. Dwight Eisenhower used Malcolm Moos, Bryce Harlow, William Ewald, Stephen Hess, Arthur Larson, college president Kevin McCann, banker Gabriel Hauge, and journalist Emmet Hughes, among others. With Kennedy, writers became famous again: Ted Sorensen, Arthur Schlesinger, Jr., John Galbraith, and Richard Goodwin were already well known or became so. Lyndon Johnson began with Kennedy holdovers, and soon found journalist Douglass Cater, Horace Busby, Joseph Califano, Harry McPherson, Bill Moyers, Ervin Duggan, and Ben Wattenberg, with Jack Valenti both writing and editing.

The Nixon writing and research operation was headed by James Keogh for two years, with Raymond K. Price replacing him. The senior writers, along with Price, were Patrick Buchanan and the author. Other writers included Lee Huebner, Noel Koch, John Andrews, John McLaughlin, Tex Lezar, William Gavin, and David Gergen, with researchers Ceil Bellinger and Anne Morgan.

Gerald Ford's speechwriters were Robert Hartman, Aram Bakshian, Milton Friedman, Patrick Butler, Paul Theis, and Bob Orben. Jimmy Carter employed the services of James Fallows, Jerome Doolittle, Hendrik Hertzberg, Achsah Nesmith, Griffin Smith, Bernard Aronson, Chris Matthews, Gordon Stewart, and Walter Shapiro.

The Reagan writers were Anthony Dolan, Bentley Elliott, Joshua Gilder, Clark Judge, Peggy Noonan, Landon Parvin, and Dana Rohrabacher. The Bush writers were Mary Kate Cary, Dan McGroarty, Ed McNally, Curt Smith, and Anthony Snow. Chief speechwriter for Bill Clinton is David Kusnet.

All those named above who are still living are members of the Judson Welliver Society, a Washington-based association of former White House speechwriters named after the "literary clerk" for Presidents Harding and Coolidge; Mr. Welliver was the first full-time White House speechwriter.

William Gavin wrote a commentary for the *Baltimore Sun* in 1990 after Maryland Governor William Donald Schaefer's office advertised for a speechwriter in the "Help Wanted" section of the newspaper. The job would entail, according to the ad, "responsibilities for preparing Governor's major speeches, remarks, talking points and other editorial material and publications. Secondary duties include media liaison and special events production. Knowledge of state government issues and excellent writing skills required. General public relations skills and experience preferred."

One question nags public figures employing speechwriters: writers are dangerous, because they publish—will this or that speechwriter kiss and tell? Emmet Hughes, who enjoyed Eisenhower's confidence and did some of his best campaign speechwriting, infuriated Republicans later with what they considered a too-revealing book, *The Ordeal of Power;* Ted Sorensen, John Kennedy's alter ego of the written word, respected many confidences in his memoirs and was criticized for writing a memoir too discreet and defensive. At the first meeting of the Nixon campaign team for the 1968 race, the author was introduced by Nixon, only half in jest, with ". . . and watch what you say—he's a writer."

spellbinder an orator capable of fascinating and persuading an audience, at least temporarily; also, a speech of that type.

This is based on *spellbound*, which means fascinated in the way a cobra is spellbound by a fakir's flute. Its political debut occurred in the 1888 presidential campaign. The *New York Tribune* wrote: "A big and successful dinner was given at Delmonico's by the

Republican Orators—'Spellbinders'—who worked during the recent campaign." The Republican stump speakers were widely publicized during that race between Cleveland and Harrison (which Republican Harrison narrowly won); William Cassius Goodloe was quoted in 1888 as pointing to one and remarking, "Here comes another of the spellbinders!"

Historian Eric Goldman termed General Omar Bradley as "the last man anyone would pick for a spellbinder" in Bradley's surprisingly effective attack on General MacArthur's Korean strategy in 1951. See WRONG WAR.

Of the words that bind: A fascinating speech is a *spellbinder;* a rousing speech is a STEMWINDER; a low blow, or a bodyguard, is a *sidewinder;* an influential but crude or dishonest politician is a *highbinder,* as in this 1920 use by *Emporia Gazette* editor William A. White: ". . . a lot of old high-binder standpatters who haven't had an idea since the fall of Babylon . . ."

spend and spend . . . a New Deal philosophy, attributed to Harry Hopkins, emphasizing the vote-getting potential of federal projects.

Harry Hopkins, who had replaced the late Louis Howe as FDR's closest aide, is supposed to have said to theatrical producer Max Gordon at the Empire Race Track in New York in August 1938: "We will spend and spend, and tax and tax, and elect and elect."

Others in Gordon's box that day denied having heard any such thing; Hopkins denied it; that left Gordon, who had passed the remark to a columnist, out on a limb. He had not realized how the phrase could be used against his friend Hopkins, but he could not call it back. The theatrical producer had been in this dilemma for forty years, and it bothered him. When reached on the telephone by the author, in 1967, he said—as if reading from a small card in his desk blotter—"I have absolutely nothing whatsoever to say about the incident, thank you and goodbye."

Whether or not Hopkins said it, the phrase has been used to attack BIG GOVERNMENT as having raised the PORK BARREL to national policy.

Jonathan Daniels wrote in 1966 of the Tennessee Valley Authority: "As the most damned New Dealer, Harry Hopkins had little to do with its building, yet . . . it loomed as the embodiment of his supposed philosophy 'spend and spend, tax and tax, elect and elect.'"

The phrase is often remembered in this form: tax, tax, tax—spend, spend, spend—elect, elect, elect. A 1967 cartoon by Hesse of the *St. Louis Globe-Democrat* showed President Johnson groping in an empty bag for dollars saying, "Like I say—tax, tax—spend, spe . . ."

As a current Republican attack phrase, its form is usually "tax and spend."

spending cap limit on spending; maximum allowance for expenses.

This term for a ceiling on expenditures dates back at least to the 1970s. John K. Inglehart reported in the *National Journal* in 1977 that "a little-noticed aspect of the [Carter] Administration's proposal would impose an annual spending cap of $2.5 billion on hospital facilities."

Such a limitation may be expressed either as an actual amount ("$2.5 billion") or as a percentage ("a 2 percent spending cap").

The phrase, using a metaphorical sense of *cap* as a cover or top, comes from the image of capping an oil well. Fred Mish of Merriam-Webster reports on its first usage: "We have a somewhat ambiguous citation from The Wall Street Journal of May 22,

1972, applying the term to a 'rule' (perhaps a Federal regulation) which limited the extent to which certain companies could raise their prices at that time."

The term became part of George Bush's campaign pledge during his unsuccessful reelection bid. A *New York Times* report in August 1992 stated, "Mr. Bush favors a Constitutional amendment requiring a balanced budget and says he would put a spending cap on 'mandatory programs.'"

Bill Clinton has also helped popularize the term. In an April 1993 news conference, President Clinton said, "We stayed below the spending caps approved by this Congress, including the Republicans."

Not only *spending* is subject to the imposition of these limits. A recent headline in the *Washington Post* asserted the possibility of medical-cost controls: "Health Care Price Caps Considered."

sphere of influence an economically undeveloped or militarily weak area under the domination of a great power, usually with the agreement or tacit acceptance of other great powers.

Secretary of State Cordell Hull in 1943 predicted that in the postwar world "there will no longer be any need for spheres of influence . . . by which in the unhappy past the nations strove to safeguard their security. . . ."

But Winston Churchill could remember the Anglo-Russian agreement of 1907 dividing Persia into separate spheres of influence—the North for Russia, the South for England; the phrase came naturally to him in 1946, in his IRON CURTAIN speech at Fulton, Mo.: "Warsaw, Berlin, Prague, Vienna, Budapest, Belgrade, Bucharest and Sofia, all these famous cities and the populations around them lie in what I might call the Soviet sphere,

and all are subject, in one form or another, not only to Soviet influence but to a very high and in some cases increasing measure of control from Moscow."

The diplomatic phrase, defined in *Webster's New International Dictionary* as "a region more or less under the control of a nation, but not constituting a formally recognized protectorate," has been used along with *sphere of interest, sphere of action, field of operations*, and *zone of influence* for more than a century. In 1993, former Prime Minister Margaret Thatcher commented that the war in Bosnia may be beyond our "sphere of interest" but is within our "sphere of conscience."

spin deliberate shading of news perception; attempted control of political reaction.

As a verb meaning "to whirl," *spin* dates back to Old English; by the 1950s, the verb also meant "to deceive," perhaps based on "to spin a yarn." Functional shift occurred in the nineteenth century, turning the verb into the noun *spin,* used for the curve or twist put upon a ball in cricket (in billiards, that spin is known as *English*), just as pitchers nowadays "put a spin on" baseballs. As a current noun, *spin* means "twist" or "interpretation," from the combined senses of twisting fiber and telling tales.

During the 1984 Presidential campaign, *spin* entered the political lexicon with the phrase *spin doctor.* A *New York Times* editorial on October 21, 1984, commented on the televising of Presidential debates:

Tonight at about 9:30, seconds after the Reagan-Mondale debate ends, a bazaar will suddenly materialize in the press room. . . . A dozen men in good suits and women in silk dresses will circulate smoothly among the reporters, spouting confident opinions. They won't be just press agents trying to impart a favorable spin to a routine release. They'll be the Spin Doctors, senior advisers to the candidates.

Four days after its first print appearance, *spin doctor* was lowercased and defined by Elisabeth Bumiller in the *Washington Post*: "the advisers who talk to reporters and try to put their own spin, or analysis, on the story."

Spin doctor may be based on the slang sense of the verb *doctor*, as in illegally "doctoring records"; the noun phrase was perhaps built on the analogy of *play doctor*, a writer who fixes an ailing script. An earlier German term that may have led to the political *spin doctor* is *Kopfverdreher*, which literally means "head turner" and figuratively suggests "mind bender."

Spin terms have spun several derivatives, from *spin control* by *spin doctors* or *spinmeisters* who have formed a *spin patrol* operating in an area called *spin valley*.

spirit of   the aura of hope surrounding summit meetings, born of the chance that reasonable men can lessen the threat of war.

"The Spirit of '76" was a favorite name for newspapers just after the American Revolution. On September 13, 1808, a Richmond, Virginia, journal was issued under that name; in Goshen, New York, the *Orange County Patriot; or, The Spirit of Seventy-Six* started five months later. The phrase was frequently used as a colorful masthead for political campaign newspapers, but made its greatest impact as the title of a painting of a boy, an old man, and a Continental Army soldier by Archibald Willard in 1876 shown at the Philadelphia Centennial Exhibition. (The painting now hangs in the Marblehead, Mass., town hall.)

In its international relations sense, "spirit of" was originated by President Eisenhower at the Geneva Conference of 1955. On July 15, before he left for Geneva, Eisenhower warned "as long as this spirit that has prevailed up to now continues to prevail in the world, we cannot expose our rights, our privileges, our homes, our wives, our children to the risk which would come to an unarmed country." Three days later, at the conference, he said, "We are here in response to the peaceful aspirations of mankind to start the kind of discussions which will inject a new spirit into our diplomacy . . ." On his return, he continued to summon that spirit in a July 25 speech: ". . . if we can change the spirit in which these conferences are conducted we will have taken the greatest step toward peace . . ."

By August 25 the word had caught on enough for him to title a speech to the American Bar Association "The Spirit of Geneva," making this point:

> Whether or not such a spirit as this will thrive through the combined intelligence and understanding of men, or will shrivel in the greed and ruthlessness of some, is for the future to tell. But one thing is certain. This spirit and the goals we seek could never have been achieved by violence or when men and nations confronted each other with hearts filled with fear and hatred. At Geneva we strove to help establish this spirit.

British Prime Minister Anthony Eden returned home with what he called "this simple message to the world: it has reduced the danger of war." Foreign Minister Harold Macmillan, who had gleefully said, "there ain't gonna be any war," discovered at a Foreign Ministers conference three months later that the Soviet attitude had hardened; "once more we are back in the strange nightmare where men use the same words to mean different things." But Macmillan remained optimistic: "The Geneva spirit if it is anything is an inward spirit. Its light is not bright today. It burns low. But it burns."

What Eisenhower had heralded as "evidence of a new friendliness in the world" proved illusory. Soviet activity in the Middle East late in 1955 added to the disenchantment.

The next spirit to be conjured was "The Spirit of Camp David," scene of another Khrushchev-Eisenhower meeting in 1959. Camp David is a presidential mountain retreat, called "Shangri-La" by FDR. (That name was taken from FDR's evasive reply when asked where U.S. aircraft that attacked Tokyo early in World War II were based. FDR took the mythical name from a James Hilton novel; Eisenhower renamed the camp after his grandson.) Pictures of the two world leaders strolling through the rustic setting raised hopes once more, quickly dashed by the abortive Paris summit conference and the incident of the downed U-2 reconnaissance plane.

Sherman Adams asked Eisenhower if he noticed at Camp David any hint of the hostility later shown in Paris. "None at all," Eisenhower replied. "At Camp David, they never showed the slightest intimation of any unfriendly intentions. As a matter of fact, when Khrushchev and I were alone together at Camp David he was very convivial with me, especially eager to be friendly. He kept belittling most of our differences and gave every indication of wanting to find ways to straighten them out through peaceful compromise."

A spirit-haunted President Kennedy met Khrushchev in Vienna in 1961. The new President, wrote Ted Sorensen, "wanted no one to think that the surface cordiality in Vienna justified any notion of a new 'Spirit of Geneva, 1955,' or 'Spirit of Camp David, 1959.' But he may have 'overmanaged' the news. His private briefings of the press were so grim, while Khrushchev in public appeared so cheerful, that a legend soon arose that

Vienna had been a traumatic, shattering experience, that Khrushchev had bullied and browbeaten the President and that Kennedy was depressed and disheartened."

Meeting in a place called Hollybush, in Glassboro, New Jersey, in the aftermath of the Arab-Israeli war of 1967, President Johnson and Soviet Premier Alexei Kosygin met in a world atmosphere that no longer took its spirits straight. Wrote the *Times* of London: "Atmospherics, of course, tend to be transient. The spirit of Geneva and the spirit of Camp David were short-lived."

Thus the use of "spirit of" changed from hope to derision, or at least suspicion and more recently back toward hope. Spokesmen for the Soviet Union, in the late seventies, often complained that the Carter campaign for HUMAN RIGHTS endangered the "spirit of DÉTENTE." For Reagan and Gorbachev at Reykjavik, the spirit turned icy.

The skeptical attitude is that of Hotspur's, in Shakespeare's *Henry IV*, Part I, who replied to Glendower's boast that he could "call spirits from the vasty deep" with "Why, so can I, or so can any man; But will they come when you do call for them?"

See SUMMITRY.

splendid misery.   See LONELIEST JOB IN THE WORLD.

splinter group   a dissident faction that splits away from a larger group; if it forms a party, it becomes a splinter party.

"When you get too big a majority," House Speaker Sam Rayburn used to say, "you're immediately in trouble." This became known as "Rayburn's Law," growing out of the Speaker's difficulty in keeping his party in line during FDR's second Administration. "Mr. Sam" felt that lopsided majorities had a way of producing splinter parties and factions along regional, ethnic, or economic lines.

Wooden metaphors abound in politics: PRESIDENTIAL TIMBER, PLATFORM, *plank*, and *splinter*, the least significant of them all.

A great many splinter groups or parties—called the multiparty system, as against the TWO-PARTY SYSTEM—often produce a weak government; the expression "always falling, never fallen" referred to the tendency of French governments to fall as factions bickered, though the French Republic went on. In postwar France, the political return of Charles de Gaulle fused many of the parties of the center and the right; the General himself called one of the smaller splinter groups "that party with six members and seven tendencies!"

In the 1972 presidential campaign, McGovern manager Frank Mankiewicz went to a Reform Democratic club on the West Side of Manhattan to instill enthusiasm for his candidate. After several hours with the articulate, highly splintered group, he came out and said, "Every little meaning has a movement all its own."

See BOLT; THIRD-PARTY MOVEMENT.

split ticket   a ballot cast by a voter without regard for party slates.

A party regular will vote a *straight ticket;* an independent is more likely to vote a *split ticket,* choosing a candidate for governor from one party, a senator from another, an assemblyman possibly from a third.

The man at the top of the ticket is expected to discourage ticket splitting (see COATTAILS); a candidate's strength is sometimes measured in terms of how many of the opposing party regulars he can get to split their tickets and vote for him. However, it is considered disloyal to appeal to voters to vote a split ticket—in effect, this urges

voters to cast their ballots against a candidate's running mates. For this reason, separate committees are formed, called "Democrats for [some Republican]" and vice versa, or "Independents for—."

The expression is found in an 1846 biography of Martin Van Buren: "I was reproached by you for having voted a 'split ticket.'" In 1904 the *New York Post* patiently explained to voters: "To vote a split ticket, which is one for candidates of different parties, the voter should make a cross mark before the name of every candidate for whom he wishes to vote."

Political scientist Clinton Rossiter pointed out in 1960 that the American electorate was tending toward greater reliance on issues and personalities, less on party affiliation.

Thanks to the looseness of legal definitions of party affiliation, to the fact that most of us are called upon to vote several times a year, and to the multiplicity of choices to be made in any one election, we enjoy unusual opportunities to be inconstant and even wayward; and every study made of this subject in recent years confirms the suspicion, with which our politicians must live bravely, that we seize these opportunities gaily. If ticket splitting is our privilege, ticket splitting is our delight.

For other types of tickets, see LAUNDRY TICKET and BALANCED TICKET; for a look at those most likely to split, see SWING VOTER; for the most selective of all, see BULLET VOTE.

spoiler   a candidate with no hope of winning himself, but who is capable of splitting another's vote, thereby spoiling his chances.

Rarely is a candidate defeated for a nomination so vindictive as to run in the general election solely to spoil the chances of the nominee who defeated him. It is not smart politics, as it throws away the chance of toppling the chosen nominee another day. More often, a third party motive is (1) to provide a place for a PROTEST VOTE on a matter of principle, (2) to build a third party into a balance-of-power situation, (3) a long-shot chance of winning.

National Review editor William Buckley ran for mayor of New York in 1965 on the Conservative ticket against Republican-Liberal John Lindsay and Democrat Abraham Beame. His purpose was not to win (when asked what he would do in that eventuality, Buckley replied, "Demand a recount") but to build the Conservative party in New York State and build in a threat to Republicans not to nominate too-liberal candidates. Lindsay supporters dubbed him a "spoiler."

In *Tigers of Tammany*, Alfred Connable and Edward Silverfarb wrote in 1967 of the fight between the "Barnburners" and the "Hunkers" in 1848; when the conservative Hunkers won, nominating Michigan Democrat Senator Lewis Cass, the antislavery Barnburners bolted and joined the Free Soilers to nominate Martin Van Buren. "Martin Van Buren's last political act was to run on principle and thereby doom to defeat the party which he had once unified . . . Tammany's allegiance was split . . . Van Buren was the 'spoiler' in a three-way race."

Conservative Republicans after Goldwater's defeat in 1964 placed a portion of the blame on Governor Nelson Rockefeller, whose primary battles had placed the TRIGGER-HAPPY tag on Goldwater. Conservative Congressman John M. Ashbrook of Ohio said of Rockefeller in *Fortune* magazine in 1967: ". . . he's a great administrator and has a fine personality. But the heart of the problem is his party posture—he's a spoiler." Ashbrook went on to challenge President Nixon in the 1972 primaries. Twenty years later, supporters of President Bush used the same word to describe Pat Buchanan's primary challenge.

spoils system the fruits of party victory to loyal partisans; opposite of "merit system."

Senator William Marcy of New York, defending President Andrew Jackson's appointment of Martin Van Buren as ambassador to Great Britain from an attack by Senator Henry Clay, said in 1832:

> It may be, sir, that the politicians of New York are not as fastidious as some gentlemen are as to disclosing the principles on which they act. They boldly preach what they practice. When they are not contending for victory, they avow their intention of enjoying the fruits of it. . . . If they are successful, they claim, as a matter of right, the advantages of success. They see nothing wrong in the rule, that to the victor belong the spoils of the enemy.

Clay turned the phrase into a weapon against the Democrats in his 1840 statement: "If we acted on the avowed and acknowledged principle of our opponents, 'that the spoils belong to the victors,' we should indeed be unworthy of the support of the people."

William Marcy, who served later as governor of New York, Secretary of War, and Secretary of State, is remembered mainly with scorn because of the coinage of the phrase; his reputation was further besmirched when a Tammany politician named Richard Tweed was said to have named his son after the distinguished American statesman, and William Marcy Tweed—and his "ring"—became the essence of bossism. But the naming was probably a canard: in his 1977 book, *Tweed's New York*, Leo Hershkowitz held that William Marcy was not well known when Tweed was born—that his middle name was

"Magear," which was his mother's maiden name, and the "Marcy" was inserted by newsmen who wanted to associate the New York boss with the father of the "spoils system."

The word "spoils," in its sense of Roman plunder, was used in the King James Version of the Bible as the Israelites were told, "Ye shall spoil the Egyptians," an instruction carried out in 1967, and in Shakespeare: "Are all thy conquests, glories, triumphs, spoils, shrunk to this small measure?" The first political use found so far in the U.S. was in 1812, in the Massachusetts House of Representatives: "The weaker members of the party would be overlooked . . . whilst the more powerful would disagree in the division of the spoils." Two years before Marcy made it famous, Congressman J. S. Johnson said: "The country is treated as a conquered province, and the offices distributed among the victors, as the spoils of the war."

Jackson's Administration increased the use of patronage started by Jefferson, and historians like to quote an 1818 letter from Jackson to President Monroe: "By selecting characters most conspicuous for their probity, virtue, capacity and firmness without regard to party . . . you will acquire for yourself a name as imperishable as monumental marble."

When Jackson was queried later about this letter by one of his private secretaries, he replied, "We are never too old to learn."

Actually, Jackson was not the spoilsman he was made out to be; despite the "new broom" and the CLEAN SWEEP, only about 9 percent of federal officeholders were removed in his first year of office, and less than 20 percent of all previously appointed officeholders were removed on political grounds during his entire two terms. (On the other hand, Benjamin Harrison changed 31,000 out of 55,000 local postmasters within one year.)

The spoils system became the target of civil service reformers, aided by statements like this made by Tammany boss Richard Croker after the election of Thomas Gilroy as mayor of New York in 1893: "You may say for me that offices will be held by politicians." Carl Schurz ripped into the system in 1894: "The spoils system, that practice which turns public offices, high and low, from public trusts into objects of prey and booty for the victorious party, may without extravagance of language be called one of the greatest criminals in our history, if not the greatest."

In modern usage, spoils as a word is used mainly for historical purposes, the slightly less pejorative PATRONAGE having replaced it in regard to appointments. The nature of spoils has changed as well; today, favoritism toward certain aerospace companies, franchises granted large contributors, discretion shown in the prosecution of possible antitrust cases, the placement of bond issues and insurance policies through FAT CAT supporters, and postgovernment employment to friendly officials add up to a much more lucrative version of spoils than the primitive fruits of an earlier day. See HONEST GRAFT.

Political leaders now meet to *slice the pie* rather than *divide the spoils;* RIPPER BILLS are a help in placing power in party hands, and DESERVING DEMOCRATS is a phrase now only used by Republicans.

In *The Beautiful and the Damned,* novelist F. Scott Fitzgerald coined an unusually apt turnaround: "The victor belongs to the spoils."

spokesman. See BACKGROUNDER.

spontaneous demonstration a carefully planned, organized, and routed march around a convention hall by delegates in support of a candidacy.

At the Bull Moose convention in 1912, historian George E. Mowry reports:

Fifteen thousand people roared their welcome [to Theodore Roosevelt]. For 52 minutes, wildly waving red bandanas, they cheered him as they had never cheered anyone else. Here were no claques, no artificial demonstration sustained by artificial devices. None were needed. Men and women simply stood on their feet for an hour because they liked him and believed in him. When Roosevelt himself finally sought to stop the demonstration, the crowd once more broke into song.

In the 1940 Republican convention, the balconies were "packed" with Willkie supporters; their overpowering "We Want Willkie" chant, cued by the candidate's campaign managers, helped sway the convention delegates away from Taft. Ever since, tickets have been carefully allocated to prevent a recurrence. See PACKING THE GALLERIES.

In the 1964 Republican convention at San Francisco's Cow Palace, these were the ground rules laid down by the Republican National Committee for spontaneous demonstrations:

1. Goldwater and Scranton demonstrations to last 22 minutes before gaveling; Rockefeller 11 minutes; all others as long as they like up to 11 minutes.

2. No more than 200 outside demonstrators permitted inside the hall, inclusive of candidate's band, and they must exit at end of demonstration. Twelve-piece National Committee band available for all demonstrations.

3. Only those signs and banners carried by 200 demonstrators permitted; no "stashing" inside hall beforehand; delegates could also carry in signs.

4. Parade route carefully delineated, not to obscure television cameras inside hall.

5. No "drops" of balloons from ceiling.

In practice, each of these rules was deliberately broken by each candidate. Tickets were counterfeited by Goldwater and Scranton forces; Rockefeller had lent most of his convention staff to Scranton, and his skeleton crew had to purchase the counterfeit tickets for an extra hundred demonstrators from the other two camps (from the Goldwater group at $3 each, from Scranton managers at $5 each). Ticket takers at the gate would collect tickets from incoming demonstrators, sell them to floor managers, who would toss them over the fence to more demonstrators.

Each group had a secret cache of signs, banners, and noisemakers inside the hall; the Goldwater managers infuriated the Scranton men by springing a "drop" of gold confetti instead of balloons, staying within the letter of the rules.

The only truly "spontaneous" demonstration was for Senator Hiram Fong of Hawaii, whose small demonstration was joined by many delegates who felt like a walk around the hall and could hardly be criticized for paying tribute to the first non-white placed in nomination.

After Scranton's demonstration, the floor manager (this writer) was given the supreme accolade by the campaign manager, Jack Wells: "I watched it on television, and you couldn't tell it from the real thing."

"A convention feels about demonstrations somewhat like the big man who had a small wife who was in the habit of beating him," wrote William Jennings Bryan. "When asked why he permitted it, he replied that it seemed to please her and did not hurt him."

See VOICE FROM THE SEWER.

spook a ghostwriter; or, a professional spy.

Speechwriters occasionally refer to themselves as "spooks"; derivation from a synonym for ghost. Also used as a verb, "to spook a book."

From the phantomlike operations of its covert agents, "spook" is a friendly, bantering name for spy. In a 1967 story on the Director of the Central Intelligence Agency, *Time* magazine wrote: "Dick Helms has been, in Washington parlance, a 'spook' for nearly 25 years."

After *New York Times* reporter Seymour Hersh in 1975 revealed spying on American citizens by the CIA, and a Senate select committee chaired by Frank Church reported on its investigation, the term lost its madcap, likable, breezy quality and absorbed much of the disapproval directed at the intelligence agency. A controversy arose in 1977 over the use of journalists as "cover" by the CIA, which the *Times* denounced: "American readers have a right to assurance that the journalists they trust for information are not in any sense accountable to unseen paymasters." However, in an editorial entitled "The Spooks and the Press," the *Washington Star* approvingly quoted former columnist Joseph Alsop: "I've done things for [the CIA] when I thought they were the right thing to do. I call it doing my duty as a citizen."

spookspeak. See CIA-ESE.

sports metaphors Shakespeare recognized the value of a sports metaphor in politics; King Henry V exhorted his troops before Harfleur: "I see you stand like greyhounds in the slips, straining upon the start. The game's afoot . . ."

It has been afoot ever since, given an impetus by the Duke of Wellington's "The battle of Waterloo was won on the playing fields of Eton." Football is especially well represented: "Politics is

like football," John F. Kennedy told Pierre Salinger. "If you see daylight, go through the hole." Woodrow Wilson put it more formally: "I have always in my own thought summed up individual liberty, and business liberty, and every other kind of liberty, in the phrase that is common in the sporting world, 'A free field and no favor.'" Soon after taking office in 1933, FDR claimed his Administration had made some "ten-yard gains," adding, "but it is a long field." Truman-campaign strategist Clark Clifford said after the 1948 victory, "We were on our own 20-yard line. We had to be bold. If we kept plugging away in moderate terms, the best we could have done would have been to reach midfield when the gun went off. So we had to throw long passes . . ."

Truman, during the campaign, used a horse to rally his dispirited troops. Citation, one of the great racing thoroughbreds, would lay back at the start of a race and come on with a rush at the end. "I am trying to do in politics what Citation has done in the horse races. I propose at the finish-line on November 2 to come out ahead . . ."

FDR brushed off occasional failures with "I have no expectation of making a hit every time I come to bat," and Sherman Adams dismissed the first Russian Sputnik with a refusal to become engaged in "an outerspace basketball game."

Winston Churchill, defending the Speaker of the House of Commons in 1951, observed: "In these hard party fights under democratic conditions, as in football matches and the like, there are moments when the umpire gets a very rough time."

Political commentators use sports metaphors as well, occasionally mixing them: Theodore White, in *The Making of the President 1964*, wrote: "Like aging prize-fighters, short of wind and stiffening of muscle, the

Southerners were left with no resource but cunning; and cunning told them to delay, day by day, hour by hour, until somewhere, somehow, there might be a turning of national sentiment. It was the strategy, said someone, of 'punt and pray.'"

For boxing metaphors, see HAT IN THE RING and ARENA; for racing metaphors, see DARK HORSE. For football, see FOOTBALL, POLITICAL and GAME PLAN; for baseball, see HARDBALL; for basketball, FULL-COURT PRESS.

Sports metaphors relate closely to many people, which is why politicians spend the time to create them; at other times, they are tossed off without thinking because they are already a part of the language. After a Kennedy aide appeared on Lawrence Spivak's television panel show *Meet the Press*, the President called to say, "They never laid a glove on you." It is the classic remark of a trainer to a prizefighter who has been belted all over the ring.

Ron Nessen, President Ford's press secretary, wrote in 1978 that a favorite White House expression in the Ford years was "Welcome to the NFL"—a term used by announcers for the National Football League when a rookie received his first savage tackle. In the 1980s, a favored metaphor was "a LEVEL PLAYING FIELD," the origin of which has not yet been found.

Sputnik. See -NIK SUFFIX.

Square Deal Theodore Roosevelt's campaign slogan, originally directed against the trusts; also, honest dealing (see CARD METAPHORS).

"We demand that big business give people a square deal," said President Roosevelt in 1901, urging government curbs on the new U.S. Steel Corporation. He took the issue to the people in a tour, urging his "square deal"—a phrase Lincoln Steffens claimed to have suggested—adding, "We do not wish to destroy corporations, but we do wish to make them subserve the public good." Campaigning for election he hammered home, "If elected, I shall see to it that every man has a square deal, no more and no less."

He continued to use the phrase, but the emphasis changed with the years. In 1910 he told a conservative Kansas audience:

I stand for the square deal. But when I say that I am for the square deal, I mean not merely that I stand for fair play under the present rules of the game, but that I stand for having those rules changed so as to work for a more substantial equality of opportunity and of reward for equally good service. One word of warning, which, I think, is hardly necessary in Kansas. When I say I want a square deal for the poor man, I do not mean that I want a square deal for the man who remains poor because he has not got the energy to work for himself. If a man who has had a chance will not make good, then he has got to quit.

When he wrote his autobiography in 1913, he came back to his original use of the phrase in modified form: "We demand that big business give the people a square deal; in return we must insist that when any one engaged in big business honestly endeavors to do right he shall himself be given a square deal."

Every man's phrase is used against him. William Howard Taft, under strenuous attack from his former sponsor, said in 1912: "Mr. Roosevelt prides himself in being a true sportsman. . . . The maxim which he has exalted above all others is that every man is entitled to a square deal. . . . Is he giving me a square deal?"

The Square Deal was followed up by the NEW DEAL of Franklin Roosevelt and the FAIR DEAL of Harry Truman; in its square form, it was used by Wendell Willkie against FDR in 1940. When Lynden O. Pindling, first black Prime Minister of the Bahama Islands, wanted to show his closeness to the U.S., he took broadcaster Tex McCrary's advice and called his 1966 program "The Square Deal."

In current use, the phrase has lost most of its Roosevelt association and reverted to mean simply "honest dealing," as it had when Mark Twain used it in *Life on the Mississippi* in 1883: "Thought I had better give him a square deal." In this general form it was used in 1893 by Missouri Congressman Champ Clark ("What I want is a square deal and a 'divy' all around"), and by Huey Long in 1932 thanking columnist Claude Bowers for a friendly piece: "As a rule, I don't care a damn what any crooked newspaperman says about me, because they're mostly goddam liars; but you gave me a square deal and I want to thank you for it."

stab in the back treachery.

"On this 10th day of June, 1940," said Franklin Roosevelt, "the hand that held the dagger has struck it into the back of its neighbor." When Italy attacked France, French Premier Paul Reynaud had cabled FDR asking for help, using the phrase "stab in the back." When a draft of the President's speech was submitted by the State Department, FDR inserted his version of the phrase but was dissuaded from using it by Sumner Welles. Other Democratic political leaders suggested this phrase might alienate the Italian-American vote in the coming election. However, on his way to the University of Virginia at Charlottesville, FDR wrote it in again and used it.

His successor, Harry Truman, used the same word-picture in a more partisan sense. Addressing 75,000 farmers and their families in Dexter, Iowa, in the 1948 campaign, Truman attacked: "The Republican Congress has already stuck a pitchfork in the farmer's back. They have already done their best to keep price supports from working . . . when you have to sell your grain below the support price because you have no place to store it, you can thank this same Republican Congress." Truman's use of the phrase annoyed Earl Warren, campaigning as Dewey's running mate: "Restraint is not easy when the President accuses Republicans of sticking a pitchfork into the backs of our farmers."

A familiar reflex to military disaster is the *Dolchstoss in den Rücken*, or *Dolchstosslegende*, which Prussian officers used to explain their 1918 defeat; Hitler revived the charge in the thirties, blaming the defeat on Jews. Historian Seymour Martin Lipset held in 1955 that the radical right was using this same kind of alibi for the loss of Eastern Europe, China, and Indochina: "The theory that these events occurred because we were 'stabbed in the back' by a 'hidden force' is much more palatable than admitting that the Communists have stronger political assets than we do."

FDR probably did not realize how apt the phrase was, or how sensitive the Germans would be to that figure of speech. In the medieval legend of the *Nibelungenlied* the hero, Siegfried—tired from being pursued, stopping to drink from a spring—was murdered by a man thrusting a spear into his back, spawning the *Dolchstosslegende*, and making Germans culturally aware of the duplicity of a stab in the back. To Americans, a similar episode is the shooting—in the back—of the Western outlaw Jesse James.

staffer a full-time member of a public figure's headquarters group.

In military terminology, there is a distinction between "line" and "staff"—

between combat command and head-quarters command. In government, "line" came to mean executive departments and "staff" the White House staff; though the staff started to grow in the Roosevelt years, the term "staffer" became prevalent in the Eisenhower years.

The PECKING ORDER: *adviser* or *counselor* carries the most prestige, an *assistant* comes next, a *staffer* follows (with a connotation of permanence), and an *aide* usually brings up the rear, though "aide" can be used to refer to all of the above, and journalists often try to unlock secrets by calling staffers "key aides." Copy editors at the *New York Times* still resist "staffer" as too informal and change the word to "aide."

As a verb, "to staff out"—a favorite of H. R. Haldeman in the Nixon Administration—means to solicit a variety of views on a recommendation before submission to the decision maker.

stagflation. See INFLATION; ECONOMIC JARGON.

stalking horse a decoy; a candidate put forward to split a vote or deadlock a convention, concealing another candidate's plan.

In hunting, a stalking horse is used to conceal a sportsman stalking game, allowing the hunter to get close to his quarry; from this the expression, used in print since 1519, has come to mean a person put forward to mislead. "He uses his folly like a stalking horse," wrote Shakespeare in *As You Like It*, "and under the presentation of that he shoots his wit."

Political writers and politicians have used it freely for over a century. *Niles' Register*, in 1846, said: "The 54–40 Doctrine is a mere stalking horse." In 1866 *Harper's Weekly* wrote of President Andrew Johnson: "He must

know that they would willingly use him as a wedge to split the Union party, as a stalking horse to their own purposes, as a springboard to leap into power." In 1872 Hamilton Fish called Horace Greeley "the stalking horse of the secessionists."

In 1971 columnist Marianne Means wrote: "Senator George McGovern is plagued by this problem more than the other candidates. He has been accused of being a Kennedy stalking horse, sent out merely to soften up Muskie and divide the field until an eventual Kennedy blitz occurs."

The *Los Angeles Times* wrote in 1990 about opposition to Nicaraguan President Violeta Barrios de Chamorro: "Sandinista candidates . . . used their economic battles with the United States to wage a nationalist campaign against Chamorro's American-financed coalition, calling her a stalking horse for yanqui imperialism."

See STRAW MAN; SPOILER.

stalwart an unwavering party regular; a staunch supporter.

James G. Blaine ("The Plumed Knight") of Maine, wrote the *Boston Herald* in 1877: ". . . the Boston Press no more represents the stalwart Republican feeling of New England on the pending issues than the same press did when it demanded the enforcement of the Fugitive Slave law in 1851."

Commented *The Nation* four years later: "The epithet 'Stalwart' as applied to a class of politicians was first used by Mr. Blaine in 1877 to designate those Republicans who were unwilling to give up hostility and distrust of the South as a political motive."

Blaine used the adjective as an accolade; more often, it was an epithet. This was because Republicans had divided into two factions: "Stalwarts," regulars who opposed Blaine, and "Half Breeds," independents who supported him. Blaine was in the position of having his own word appropriated by the opposition. The "Stalwarts," led by New York Senator Roscoe Conkling, organized the "Home Guard" behind General Grant at the Democratic convention; the "Half Breeds" pressed for Blaine. In the deadlock, dark horse James Garfield won the nomination and election.

Blaine was an avid reader of Sir Walter Scott, who frequently used "stalwart." The word is of Anglo-Saxon origin, meaning "foundation-worthy," the Old English meaning "serviceable," which stalwarts are to a party.

Current use has dropped the anti-Southern connotation, retaining the loyal-party-worker meaning. Dwight Eisenhower, in his memoirs, wrote of Senator Robert A. Taft: "In some things I found him unexpectedly 'liberal,' specifically in his attitudes on old-age pensions, school aid, and public housing—attitudes, incidentally, which were miles away from those of some self-described 'Taft stalwarts.'"

Stalwart Democrats are DYED-IN-THE-WOOL, BRASS COLLAR, and YELLOW DOG; and stalwart Republicans are ROCK-RIBBED.

stampede as a noun, panic-stricken decision on the part of delegates to jump on a bandwagon as it gathers speed; as a verb, to stimulate such a movement.

President William McKinley, looking over the field of candidates for his second-term running mate, told Senator Joseph B. Foraker, "I hope you will not allow the convention to be stampeded to Roosevelt for Vice-President." That was Foraker's recollection; true or not, the use of the word is unchanged from its early use and present use.

The Mexican-Spanish word is *estampida*, or *stampedo*, meaning a sudden rush of frightened cattle. The *New*

York Times used a political application in 1876: "It is well known that many nominations, both in State and national Conventions, have been made by what is known as stampedes. A candidate runs ahead of all competitors, but while yet far short of the required number of votes, some County or State which has not kept tally supposes the Plurality man to be nominated, and wishing to be on the winning side changes to him."

Though the noun is most closely identified with convention action, the verb has frequent use in relation to movements rather than people. Thomas E. Dewey in 1948 sounded like an incumbent: "Ours is a magnificent land. Every part of it. Don't let anybody frighten you or try to stampede you into believing America is finished." And Dwight Eisenhower wrote: "Stories written with the purpose of damaging the reputation of a candidate have been a sleazy feature of many political campaigns. I resolved not to let such a story stampede me." See BANDWAGON.

standard-bearer the candidate, who carries the nomination of his party as his "standard."

From the French word meaning "banner," a standard is carried by a leader, as on a flagship. George Washington gave it an early use in America by calling on the delegates to the Constitutional Convention in Philadelphia to "raise a standard to which the wise and honest can repair."

The *New York Herald* in 1848 wrote: "It is on the old platform of principles, and for the good old cause, that the new standard-bearer is to be chosen." For a time, the phrase applied to the vice-presidential candidate as well. "The national convention," recorded the *Congressional Record*, ". . . summoned Garret A. Hobart to be standard-bearer with William McKinley."

The President–Vice President team is still referred to as "standard-bearers" but the Vice President individually is *a*, and never *the*, standard-bearer.

At the Democratic convention of 1884, Daniel Lockwood rose to nominate Grover Cleveland, asking the delegates "to go to the independent and Democratic voters of the country, to go to the young men of the country, the new blood of the country, and present the name of Grover Cleveland as your standard bearer."

The word, despite its archaic tone, is in current use. Theodore White on the 1964 campaign: "So many major Republican candidates avoided their standard-bearer whenever he entered their states that it was an act of grace when Charles Percy appeared in the late afternoon of Goldwater's second day in Illinois for three joint whistle-stop appearances."

In a 1975 *New York Times* column, a political hypocrite was denounced as a "double standard bearer." See BANNER DISTRICT; MILITARY METAPHORS.

stand in the doorway   to resist symbolically; to make a dramatic show of opposition.

Governor George C. Wallace promised to "stand in the doorway" to block the admission of two black students into the University of Alabama on June 13, 1963. This phrase became a symbol of Southern resistance to school integration, much as "he should have taken her by the hand" was a much-used criticism of Eisenhower's refusal to make a dramatic personal gesture at Little Rock, Arkansas.

Wallace, making good his pledge, stood in the doorway of the university administration building at Tuscaloosa and blocked the entry of the two students and federal marshals. President Kennedy promptly federalized part of the Alabama National Guard, which

soon arrived on campus. His symbolic show of resistance recorded by cameramen, Wallace retreated and the students were registered.

Both the "take her by the hand" and "stand in the doorway" expressions were used by Ted Sorensen: "There were recurring suggestions that the President should personally appear in Birmingham and take a Negro child by the hand into a school or lunch counter. But that suggestion badly confused the physical presence of the President with the official presence of his powers. It would have demeaned the dignity of the office by relying on the same kind of dramatic stunt and physical contest that was staged by those Southern governors who 'stood in the doorway.'"

Andrew Kopkind reported in the *New Republic* in 1967 that California Governor Ronald Reagan sought early in his administration to cut funds spent on education and then funds allocated for mental hospitals. "First Reagan stood in the school-house door," he quoted an economist as saying, "then he stood in the nut-house door." As pressures built up, Reagan restored the cuts and retreated from the doorways.

stand pat   to adhere to a position; to accept the status quo; has assumed a reactionary connotation.

"We will stand pat!" Senator Mark Hanna, the foremost McKinley supporter, was supposed to have said in 1900; this has led to the assumption that "Stand Pat with McKinley" was a slogan in that election. This appears to be wrong.

Mark Hanna did give a new political meaning to the poker expression but not until 1902. Hans Sperber and Travis Trittschuh dug up the September 28, 1902, *Cleveland Plain Dealer* that reported on a Hanna speech the preceding day at Akron. Said Hanna:

"About a year ago it was my privilege to attend the opening meeting of the Republican party, and after thinking and looking over the situation, I came to the conclusion—'Let well enough alone.' That was the whole chapter: that is all there was in the campaign of interest to you. Now I say stand pat." The *Plain Dealer* went on to explain what Hanna meant:

> The player "stands pat" when he declines to discard from his hand, and draw other cards, and the supposed earning quality of such a hand is superior to that of three aces. According to the rules of the game it is perfectly honest, however, for a player to hold a pat hand when it has little or no value, and if successful in scaring his opponents into laying down their hands he wins the bank or "pot." This is, we are informed, called a "bluff." Thus it will be seen that Dr. Hanna in his Akron speech invented a singularly appropriate figure of political speech.

Obviously the senator was needled after using this expression; politicians were considered too distinguished to be familiar with poker terminology. "When I told the people 'stand pat,'" Hanna told the *Cincinnati Enquirer* on October 3, 1902, "it was merely to use a familiar saying to express the situation. I have been told that this is a phrase used in the game of poker; but everybody understands it just the same . . ."

The *Enquirer* commented: "Senator Hanna probably got the suggestion of his 'stand pat' speech from some fellow who played poker; but the Senator didn't know that, of course."

Although Hanna popularized the expression (apparently in 1902, casting doubt on its use in the 1900 campaign), he was not the first to use it politically. Speaker Joseph G. ("Uncle Joe") Cannon used the expression in the House in 1896 regarding adherence to high tariffs. The *Congressional Record* of February 28, 1896, reported the following exchange:

> Mr. J. G. Cannon:—That proposition was fought bitterly in the House; but the Senate *stood*, if the gentlemen will allow me the expression, *pat;* . . . and they had their own way, because no bill can pass without an agreement between the two houses.
>
> Mr. G. L. Johnson of Calif.:—I understand the explanation made by the gentleman from Illinois, with the single exception of some technical, abstruse term which he used, but which I suppose is well understood in Illinois, though unfamiliar in California. I will ask the gentlemen however why should not the House "stand pat" as the Senate did? Mr. Cannon:—Oh no: It was invented in California and put into the dictionary there.

After being popularized by Hanna, "stand pat" and "standpatter" came to mean REACTIONARY. Progressive Robert La Follette equated the two words in a comment on Calvin Coolidge's first message to Congress: "It was an able, concise and frank presentation of the stand pat reactionary theory of government." This criticism could not have come as a surprise to Coolidge who had given the following advice to political leaders of Massachusetts when he became Governor there ten years before:

> Expect to be called a standpatter, but don't be a standpatter. Expect to be called a demagogue, but don't be a demagogue. Don't hesitate to be as revolutionary as science. Don't hesitate to be as reactionary as the multiplication table. Don't expect to build up the weak by pulling down the strong. Don't hurry to legislate. Give administration a chance to catch up with legislation.

In his 1960 campaign John F. Kennedy scorned "Stand Pat with McKinley" as an example of Republican reaction. Richard Nixon learned in that campaign that a political phrase could have an embarrassing double meaning.

He countered Kennedy's "Let's get America moving again" with his own "America cannot stand pat." When it was pointed out that his wife, Pat Nixon, might take offense, he hurriedly changed that line in subsequent appearances to "America cannot stand still."

On January 17, 1978, Arthur Schlesinger, Jr., turned it into a one-word -ISM with a *Wall Street Journal* piece entitled "Carter's Retreats into Standpattism."

START. See SALT.

star wars space-based defense; positioning of military equipment in orbit around the earth to shoot down attacking missiles.

On March 23, 1983, Ronald Reagan surprised the arms-control establishment—which had always thought in terms of "mutual assured destruction" (MAD), or deterrence only by threat of retaliation—by calling for a new approach "to counter the awesome Soviet missile threat with measures that are defensive." He asked: "What if free people could live secure in the knowledge that their security did not rest upon the threat of instant U.S. retaliation to deter a Soviet attack, that we could intercept and destroy strategic ballistic missiles before they reached our own soil or that of our allies?" That idea, seen by opponents as both expensive and potentially destabilizing to the balance of terror, immediately became identified as Reagan's "star wars" proposal.

That derisive name came from the title of the hit 1977 film by George Lucas, whose science-fiction vision of rebels against the empire contributed another image to Reaganese (see EVIL EMPIRE). The President protested the nicknaming, saying, "I wish whoever coined that expression would take it back again, because it gives a false impression of what it is we're talking about."

Pentagon officials suggested *Strategic Defense Initiative,* abbreviated SDI, and in 1985 Reagan attempted to interject the redundant "security shield" in his second inaugural address. (One Presidential adviser, fearing the shield was less than promised, complained that they were "up the laser river.")

An informal 1986 poll by the author provided such possible replacements as the acronyms SANE (Spacial Anti-Nuclear Effort) and HOPE (High Orbit Protection Echelon), as well as "global shield." Although the derisive nickname *star wars* stuck, the need for an alternative to MAD saw the funding for an anti-missile program, though substantially different from the original Reagan plan, continue into the Clinton Administration. In May 1993, Secretary of Defense Les Aspin announced the end of the name SDI (Strategic Defense Initiative), and the *Washington Post* headlined the story "'Star Wars' Is Declared Dead."

State of the Union annual report to the Congress required of the President.

Like the few extra vertebrae on the end of the human backbone that used to be the start of a tail, this phrase preserves a word that was once of great political import. The word "union," capitalized when it refers to the United States, was first used in an American context in Massachusetts in 1754: "A motion was made that the Commissioners deliver their opinion whether a Union of all the Colonies is not at present absolutely necessary for their security and defense." Jefferson in 1775 wrote: "A Committee of Congress is gone to improve our circumstances, so as to bring the Canadians into our Union."

It is used casually in Article II, Section 3 of the Constitution, directing that the President "shall from time to time give to the Congress information of the state of the union, and recommend to their consideration such measures as he shall judge necessary and expedient . . ."

At the time of the Civil War, "Union" became a dramatic word, meaning something worth fighting to preserve and, as an adjective, describing Northern forces. A word for Northern soldiers was "Unions," as in this use by Mark Twain in 1874: "When de Unions took dat town . . . dey all run away and lef' me all by myse'f."

By the late nineteenth century, "Unionist" and "Union man" ceased to mean a supporter of a federal union against nullification or secession; gradually, it changed to mean a member of a labor union.

State of the Union *messages* (preferred over *speeches, addresses,* or *reports* just as inaugural speeches are always formally called addresses) have inclined to be lengthy statements of legislative intent; they are a method by which a President takes the initiative in shaping a legislative program for his Administration. An exception was FDR's 1941 message, which became known as "the FOUR FREEDOMS speech." In that speech, as in most State of the Union messages, the phrase itself was used: "Therefore, as your President, performing my constitutional duty to 'give to the Congress information of the state of the Union,' I find it unhappily necessary to report that the future and the safety of our country and of our democracy are overwhelmingly involved in events far beyond our borders."

John F. Kennedy gave the traditional usage a twist in 1963: "I can report to you that the State of this old but youthful Union, in the 175th year of its life, is good." Gerald Ford was the first to say "The State of the Union is not good."

States Rights Democrats. See
DIXIECRAT.

statism belief in state supremacy or in economic control by a tightly centralized government.

Statism dates back to the 1600s in an obsolete religious sense of subjugating religion to political expediency. The modern sense first appeared in print in 1880, when *The Echo* commented, "The Nihilists do not believe in Communism, which is as bad as Statism, and equally deserving of suppression." The political term was popularized during World War I, influenced by the French noun *étatisme*.

In a 1977 *Washington Post* article on Brazil, Bruce Handler wrote of the skepticism of businessmen in Rio de Janeiro about proposed reforms: "They see no difference between creeping statism Brazilian-style and the centrally directed economies typical of Communist countries."

The word has also been used in Mexican government. Octavio Paz, the poet and political writer, told the *New York Times* in 1988, "I believe that populism and statism are experiences that we have already tried and which have led to catastrophe."

In a democracy, *statism* is often used as a political attack term. A recent op-ed piece in the *New York Times* warned about Clintonomics: "Stop him, Democrats, before his desire to be different combines with his talent at telemarketing to lead your party into the black hole of statism."

Playing on the term *welfare state,* Dan Balz wrote in the *Washington Post* in August 1992 that Republican National Convention speakers "attacked the Democrats as carriers of an 'insidious plague' of welfare statism."

stay-at-homes those eligible to vote who do not.

"They are not radical," wrote sociologist C. Wright Mills, "not liberal, not reactionary. They are inactionary. They are out of it. If we accept the Greek's definition of the idiot as an altogether private man, then we must conclude that many American citizens are now idiots."

Political pollsters call them the "politically inert." Politicians call them the SILENT VOTE.

When a person who usually votes stays away from the polls because he is dissatisfied with both candidates, he "goes fishing" (see FISHING EXPEDITION). The great majority of stay-at-homes, however, are apathetic. Political scientist Clinton Rossiter made a breakdown of the stay-at-homes in the 1956 presidential election: 62 million people voted out of 100 million eligible. Of the 38 million who did not, 6 million were "trapped in the political morass of the South"—kept from voting by intimidation and unfair local voting laws. Five million were transient—unable to meet local residence requirements. Another 5 million were ill on Election Day. Two and a half million were away from home and did not cast absentee ballots; another 2.5 million were illiterate. Six hundred thousand were in prisons, homes for the aged, and other institutions, and a like number were residents of the nonvoting District of Columbia.

"This leaves a total of 15.5 million Americans," wrote Rossiter, "who simply found it inconvenient . . . a staggering number of Americans who thought it quite unimportant to act the parts of responsible citizens of a great democracy." Since that time, the percentage of stay-at-homes has increased.

In 1948 President Harry Truman castigated those Democrats he considered responsible for the DO-NOTHING CONGRESS who, "because they stayed at home and did not vote last year, got just the kind of Congress they deserve."

Political scientist Sam Lubell, analyzing the 1948 Truman-Dewey election, came up with a surprising observation: "Far from costing Dewey the election, the [Democratic] stay-at-homes may have saved him almost as crushing a defeat as Landon suffered in 1936."

An elaborate campaign plan was drawn up by the GOP in the 1952 Eisenhower campaign; it claimed that the greatest potential GOP strength was among 45 million "stay-at-homes" and recommended a style of campaign "which could inspire a crusading zeal that is impossible to engender by the 'ME TOO' approach, or anything which promises only to better what the present Administration is doing . . . the recommended strategy is: 'Attack! Attack! Attack!'"

Overcoming the ennui of stay-at-homes is likely to remain an unreached goal of campaigners. A more subtle approach, playing on their guilt, was made by poet Ogden Nash:

> They have such refined and delicate palates
> That they can discover no one worthy of their ballots,
> And then when someone terrible gets elected
> They say, There, that's just what I expected!

The problem of stay-at-homes plagues both parties and is not limited to this country or this time. The French have a saying: "*Qui s'excuse, s'accuse.*"

To the question, "Which is worse—ignorance or apathy?" comes the reply: "I don't know and I don't care." See TURNOUT.

staying bought constancy in corruption.

Simon Cameron, Lincoln's first Secretary of War, who was later censured by Congress for remarkably lax administration, defined "an honest politician" as "a man who, when he's bought, stays bought."

The phrase reappeared and was made part of the political language after the campaign of 1904. Although the Democrats put up Judge Alton B. Parker, a gilt-edged conservative, Republican Theodore Roosevelt was able to attract financial support from Morgan, Rockefeller, Depew, Frick, Harriman, and other industrial and financial titans. Judge Parker accused Roosevelt of having blackmailed the financial giants, promising them immunity from trustbusting if they contributed heavily. At least one, Henry Clay Frick—Andrew Carnegie's man for many years—felt he had been given commitments in return for his donation to Roosevelt.

"He got down on his knees before us," Frick angrily claimed. "We bought the son of a bitch and then he did not stay bought!"

stay the course persist in an action or policy; remain with a plan despite criticism or setbacks.

This phrase, perhaps based on a sailing metaphor of keeping an unchanged course in navigation, was popularized during the 1980 Presidential campaign. The *National Journal* reported before the New Hampshire primary on Ted Kennedy's challenge to the incumbent Jimmy Carter: "While it is obvious that Kennedy intends to stay the course at this point in the campaign, he does so as a challenger to a sitting President and not as the recognized heir apparent."

That same year, the *Washington Post* used the expression in an article on Gary Hart's Senate race in Colorado: "Democrats—and some neutral observers—contend that Hart's appeal is solid enough to stay the course." Later in 1980, the *Post* also reported Carter's use of the term; in discussing the Camp David peace process, the President "predicted that the process will succeed 'if we stay the course.'"

Republicans have helped to popularize the expression. During 1982, according to the *Washington Post,* Ronald Reagan "visited 14 states in 10 days of campaigning since Labor Day, carrying his 'stay the course' message."

A decade later, Timothy J. McNulty of the *Chicago Tribune* repeated the term in his 1992 assessment of George Bush's acceptance speech at the Republican National Convention: "Rejecting talk of any sweeping change in policy or in his administration, Bush decided to stay the course, blame the Democrats and ridicule Bill Clinton."

steamroller rough tactics used by those in control of a political party to overpower those who disagree with them.

The steamroller began to roll at the Republican convention in June 1908. The word was probably first used in this country by a newsman in Chicago, Oswald F. Schuette of the *Inter-Ocean,* about the Roosevelt-Taft supporters within the Republican National Committee disposing of those who protested against the seating at the convention of slates of Taft delegates from Alabama and Arkansas.

Turnabout was called unfair play in 1912 when the Roosevelt supporters at the Republican convention complained that their Southern slates were being steamrollered by a Taft-dominated Republican National Committee.

The word had already been used in international politics some years earlier. In 1902 *Munsey's Magazine* said of Russia: "She sought to achieve her end by means of the 'steam roller' of the concert of Europe."

In 1932 Roosevelt forces surrendered their plan to get the Democratic convention to give up the hoary two-thirds rule on the selection of candidates; it had become obvious they could not win the fight. Candidate Roosevelt wrote the convention acknowledging that asking for revision at that time might be considered unfair by some and saying: ". . . I decline to permit either myself or my friends to be open to the accusation of poor sportsmanship, or to use the methods which could be called, even falsely, those of a steamroller . . ."

In 1956, knowing his nomination was a certainty, President Eisenhower, wired his aide, Sherman Adams, that he must "guard against steamrollering, no matter what the proposition is." He remembered 1952, and the charge made by Ike's supporters against Robert Taft.

Steamrollering is often defined as using overwhelming strength unfairly, or even illegally, mainly by those who have been defeated. As Senator Robert La Follette said in his autobiography: "Whether one is on top of or under the steamroller influences somewhat one's point of view."

stemwinder an orator, or a speech, capable of rousing a crowd.

A stemwinding speech, like a good stump speech, is intended for delivery at large rallies, where roars of approval add to its effectiveness; the whirling image of the word pictures the orator "winding up" and flinging stimulating words and phrases. In current political usage, the word is used to describe a loud, partisan speech, either approvingly or mockingly. Its opposite is a low-key, reasonable-sounding, "sincere" speech, best used on television to reach people at home.

The word is derived from the stemwinding watch or clock, which was a major advance in timepieces pat-

ented in 1866. It soon became the word for modernity and excellence—"Ain't he a stem-winder" can be traced to 1892, and short-story writer O. Henry used it in 1902 in that sense: "There's a new bank examiner over at the First, and he's a stem-winder." Dictionaries of slang at the turn of the century included the word as "the best of its kind; a keyless watch, at the time a new and exquisite improvement."

Though its usage as "excellent" is archaic (some battery-powered watches have no stems at all), the word is actively used in politics. Often one quality of a vice-presidential candidate is his ability to deliver stemwinders, while the presidential candidate delivers less partisan speeches. For comparative usage, see SPELLBINDER.

step by step diplomacy that proceeds cautiously, seeking bilateral agreements rather than a comprehensive solution.

Garry Wills, in the *New York Review of Books* (July 12, 1975), covered much of the vocabulary of Mideast diplomacy in a sentence: "For a country with scholar-rulers, Israel's debates live to an extraordinary degree on slogans: one side's 'step by step' is the other's 'SALAMI TACTICS,' just as a friend's 'piece of peace' is a foe's 'intangible for tangibles.'"

The phrase was associated in 1974 with Secretary of State Henry Kissinger's SHUTTLE DIPLOMACY; coinage was claimed by writer Edward Sheehan in an article in *Foreign Policy* magazine, but reporter David Zuckerman found a quotation dated June 1, 1953, by Secretary of State John Foster Dulles, pledging that the U.S. would help bring about "a step-by-step reduction of tensions in the area and the conclusion of an ultimate peace."

On September 20, 1977, Moshe Dayan, Israeli Foreign Minister in Menachem Begin's government, told a group of Washington reporters that "step by step is dead," and defined the phrase as "a piece of land for a piece of peace." However, Israel soon became uncomfortable with President Carter's plans for a comprehensive settlement at a Geneva conference, fearing a veto over Arab moderation by Arab radicals and the Soviet Union. When Egyptian President Anwar el-Sadat made his dramatic visit to Jerusalem in 1977, talk of direct dealings between Israel and Egypt dominated the Mideast, and "step-by-step"—though never generating the same enthusiasm as when it was first expressed—did not seem such a bad approach to a solution.

Step-by-step (usually hyphenated when used without the "diplomacy") was at first totally identified with Kissinger, although it was originally an Israeli idea, adopted—as Kissinger said on September 16, 1975—after "every attempt to discuss a comprehensive solution failed." The phrase was the subject of a George Ball critique in 1975 in *Newsweek*, and was part of the title of a book about Kissinger by Israeli Matti Golan: *The Secret Conversations of Henry Kissinger: Step by Step in the Middle East*. To dissociate himself from the author of the previous policy, Carter's National Security Adviser Zbigniew Brzezinski referred to an approach of "concentric circles."

steppingstone springboard to higher office; used to show ambition, demeaning the office held at the time or currently aspired to.

Harry Truman offered the vice-presidential nomination in 1948 to Supreme Court Justice William O. Douglas. He considered the offer for a weekend, and then called the President: "I am very sorry, but I have decided not to get into politics. I do not think I should use the Court as a steppingstone."

The only judges to run for President were Alton B. Parker in 1904 and Charles Evans Hughes in 1916; John F. Kennedy once jotted in a notebook: "No congressional leader of the very first rank save James Madison has been elected Pres.,—and apart from Polk, Garfield, McKinley and Truman no parliamentarians of the 2nd rank."

Certainly, House Speakers had tried. Henry Clay in 1824, James Blaine in 1876, Champ Clark in 1912, John Garner in 1932, all tried and failed; only James Polk succeeded. Thirteen men who had served as senators made it, but only one—Harding—made it directly from the Senate in the twentieth century, before the election of 1960, when for the first time two senators (Kennedy and Johnson) ran on the same ticket, against two former senators (Nixon and Lodge).

This was not what Thomas Jefferson had foreseen. "Congress is the great commanding theatre of this nation," he wrote William Wirt in 1808, "and the threshold to whatever department of office a man is qualified to enter." But the best steppingstone to the presidency has been the governor's chair— thirteen governors became President—and the vice presidency, where eleven became President, eight by succession at the President's death. Senator Henry Cabot Lodge at the turn of the century said that the vice presidency should not be looked on with disdain by great men, but should be desired by "our most ambitious men . . . as a stepping stone to higher office." Theodore Roosevelt, on the other hand, called it "a steppingstone . . . to oblivion."

The cabinet, especially in our early history, was an excellent steppingstone (nine made it), and the man to be was Secretary of State; in the twentieth century, Taft of the War Department and Hoover of the Commerce Department became Chief Executive.

In current usage the word is often employed to attack a candidate for having his sights set on greater things than the office he is currently running for. This attack was potent in California, as William Knowland discovered, but New Yorkers were delighted to vote for a governor who could be presidential material.

The term is sometimes suggested as an afterthought. The *Seattle Times* wrote in 1992 about an election for the state of Washington's Attorney General: "At stake is a statewide post that many political observers and candidates believe could play an important role on 1990 issues: child abuse, the environment, growth management, crime and abortion. Besides, it can be a steppingstone to higher office."

Critics of Michigan Governor George Romney, and later of candidate Jimmy Carter, seizing on what they considered an overly devout, evangelical nature, spread a joke that their target was "only seeking the White House as a steppingstone."

stir up the animals start an unwanted controversy; take a position that could needlessly incur criticism.

Reviewing the 1948 campaign strategy, Dewey's (later Eisenhower's) press secretary James Hagerty said: "The main campaign worry was not to rock the boat. While Governor Dewey set the strategy, he was greatly influenced by the state chairmen and local leaders. They kept saying, telegraphing, and writing that the campaign had to be kept on a low [quiet] level, that there was no need to stir up the animals."

Obviously, this is a zoo or circus metaphor, referring to the commotion caused by sleeping denizens when wakened. For an early use of a similar metaphor, see POLITICAL ANIMAL.

"The animals" is a half-jocular, half-derisive reference to a lower order of life; news reporters frequently call broadcasting technicians by that name, which is never appreciated. (See ZOO PLANE.) "Animals" alone is also a derogation of criminals, with overtones of up-from-the-jungle racism. When an outbreak of looting followed a power outage in New York City in July 1977, the blacks and Hispanic citizens who were pictured carting away merchandise were castigated as "animals" by black businessmen. The accusation by blacks of other blacks made possible the television use of a word that would ordinarily be taboo because of its African-jungle connotation.

A closely related expression is "raw meat," or "red meat," which means material in a speech designed to elicit a strong reaction from the audience. This has to do with controversial subject matter more than style; in current usage, "Let's give 'em some raw meat" is defined as an instruction to deal with matters that will make an audience, like a lion, roar its approval. See RATTLE THE CAGE; FEEDING FRENZY.

stonewalling saying "NO COMMENT"; HANGING TOUGH; a policy based on resistance to revelation.

The word was popularized during the Watergate investigation. As transcribed from the Nixon tapes, White House counsel John Dean assured the President on February 28, 1973: "We are stonewalling totally." Mr. Nixon picked up the word, which was in widening use, and on March 22 directed: "I want you to stonewall it, let them plead the Fifth Amendment, cover up or anything else . . ."

Several witnesses before the Senate Watergate Committee attributed the word to John Mitchell. During an interrogation in which the former Attorney General volunteered nothing, Senator Lowell Weicker (R-Conn.) asked if his testimony was "an exercise in stonewalling." Mitchell replied, "I don't know that term. Is that a Yankee term from Connecticut?"

In his 1976 campaign, candidate Jimmy Carter castigated President Ford's "inaccessibility" by charging: "In this Administration a stonewall seems to mean not letting American people have a right to know what's our own business."

The word's roots had heroic, if defensive, connotations. On July 21, 1861, at the First Battle of Bull Run, Confederate General Thomas Jonathan Jackson held his position and earned his sobriquet when a Southern officer was said to have cried, "There stands Jackson like a stone wall—rally behind the Virginians!"

As a verb, it comes from Australian cricket slang, meaning to block balls persistently, playing only on the defensive. In the sense of obstruction as a strategy, the word was transferred to the business and political worlds in that region; the *Victorian Hansard* in 1876 asked "whether the six members constituted 'the stone wall' which was to oppose all progress?"

A related second meaning is to delay, filibuster, or stall. James Reston wrote in the *New York Times* in 1961 that the Kennedy Administration was "stonewalling for time in order to close the missile gap . . ." "To stonewall" is to impede an inquiry, usually through silence, sometimes through delay, and is not as pejorative as COVER UP, which is a more sinister form of obstruction of justice.

The word now appears to be firmly fixed in the political lexicon; in a letter to the author from federal prison dated July 23, 1977, former Attorney General John Mitchell wrote: "Please keep after the establishment and make them account. You should continue to have a field day with Koreagate. Sooner or later they will have to quit stonewalling and get on with the fireworks."

Richard L. Berke of the *New York Times* used the term in a 1993 article on campaign reform: "Though President Clinton has vowed to change how candidates get elected by pushing through a campaign finance reform package, the passage of a serious bill anytime soon is far from assured. Congress has its reasons for stonewalling. And so, after all, may the President."

stopping the clock avoiding a legislative deadline by pretending time is not marching on; halting time or allowing time out; or, attempting to ignore progress.

Stopping the clock comes from sports, specifically the time clock for a football or basketball game. Just as calling a timeout *stops the clock*, this phrase is applied to any attempt to take time out for thought or reflection.

Usually used with a negative twist, the phrase appeared in a *Washington Post* report in 1978. A *Post* headline encapsulated the inevitability of nuclear power as "No Stopping the Clock." When applied in a more urgent context to the imminence of a nuclear war, the phrase usually alludes to the famous Doomsday Clock on the cover of the *Bulletin of the Atomic Scientists* (see DOOMSDAY MACHINE).

A *Los Angeles Times* commentary on George Bush's leadership stated, "In the American Presidency, once the votes are counted, there are no timeouts for the winner, there is no stopping the clock or turning off the tape. Everything counts."

Occasionally, though, the expression can take a positive form. Margaret Tutwiler of the State Department used the plural *clocks* during a Bush Administration media briefing. Discussing fast-changing situations in the Soviet Republics in 1991, Tutwiler said, "I'm going to try to do the best that I can to give you an update, but I'm stopping the clocks while we're sitting here; in freezing time, things could be going on this moment while I'm speaking."

A related metaphor, *turning back the clock* or *setting back the clock*, dates back to the 1600s. Usually used in the negative, this expression suggests irreversibility in not being able to turn back the clock.

straddle. See FENCE, ON THE.

straight arrow a person beyond moral reproach; a model of uprightness or, when used derisively, uptightness.

A noun phrase to label somebody who is without vice, *straight arrow* uses a sixteenth-century sense of the adjective *straight*: "honest." The simile "straight as a shingle" led to the variant "straight as an arrow," now shortened to *straight arrow*.

A popular radio drama of the late 1940s took the eponymous title "Straight Arrow," its hero named for his skill in archery as well as for his moral outlook. In 1967, Jann Wenner of *Rolling Stone* magazine selected Straight Arrow as the name of his publishing house, explaining that his choice was a term for "square dealing." The counterculture use in the 1960s led to a connotation of Boy Scout probity, sometimes disparaged as rigidity. (See BOY SCOUT, which also covers the use of "Mr. Clean," the name of a household detergent also applied to straight arrows.)

The *New York Times* pointed to the political use of the term, both as a two-word noun phrase and as a hyphenated modifier, in 1979. "A 'Straight Arrow' Quits the Pentagon" headlined an article about Stanley Resor, who was described as a "'straight-arrow' public servant who simply got 'frozen out' by a bureaucracy whose power games he had no taste for."

straight ticket. See TICKET; SPLIT TICKET.

strange bedfellows enemies forced by circumstances to work together; members of an unlikely alliance, often attacked as an UNHOLY ALLIANCE.

"True it is," wrote Charles Dudley Warner in 1850, "that politics makes strange bedfellows." Warner, editor of the *Hartford* (Conn.) *Courant*, was co-author with Mark Twain of *The Gilded Age;* he might have taken the expression from Edward George Bulwer-Lytton's novel *The Caxtons*, published in 1849, which contained the phrase "Poverty has strange bedfellows."

More likely, the source for both was Act II, scene 2 of Shakespeare's *The Tempest*, when a storm drives Trinculo to seek shelter under a gabardine sheet with Caliban, whom he regards as a monster: "There is no other shelter hereabout: misery acquaints a man with strange bedfellows. I will here shroud until the dregs of the storm be past."

In current usage, both misery and poverty have given way to politics as the excuse for strange bedfellows. Historian Mark Sullivan titled a chapter "Strange Bedfellows" when he wrote in *Our Times* (1930) about the cooperation between Senator "Pitchfork Ben" Tillman and his arch-enemy, Theodore Roosevelt, on a bill to end rate preferences on railroads.

The most dramatic strange bedfellow in modern times was Joseph Stalin. When the Soviet Union signed a non-aggression pact with anti-Communist Germany in 1939, later following Hitler's invasion of Poland with an invasion of their own from the east, British cartoonist David Low presented the paradox in all its absurdity: the two leaders bowing to each other over the smoking ruins of Poland, Hitler saying to Stalin, "The scum of the earth, I believe?" and Stalin courteously replying, "The bloody assassin of the workers, I presume?"

After Russia was attacked by Germany, Stalin became Churchill's strange bedfellow. When the British Prime Minister was asked how he could say anything good about the Communist dictator, he replied, "If Hitler invaded Hell, I would make at least a favourable reference to the Devil in the House of Commons."

In recent years the phrase has been heard more frequently, perhaps because odd alliances for expediency's sake are growing more common. Editorialized the short-lived *New York World Journal Tribune* in February 1967: "Everybody knows that politics makes strange bedfellows. It doubtless would surprise Robert Kennedy to wake up any morning now in the same bed with Arkansas' Sen. J. William Fulbright. At least they would have conversational rapport over crumpets and coffee as dissenters in foreign policy."

When columnists decided to speculate about a Rockefeller-Reagan Republican ticket for 1968, the phrase came naturally. James Reston in the *New York Times*: "No candidate has ever lost New York and California and won the Presidency. This is the beginning of the strange bedfellows story." Max Lerner in the *New York Post*: ". . . a good Presidential ticket, like a good marriage, does not have to be logically consistent, nor one of sweet harmony. Sometimes it is the neurotic interactions in marriage that make it hold together—which may be true of political bedfellows as well. In fact, the very daring of matching this particular pair of partners might enable them to get away with the absurdity of it."

The latent double meaning of the phrase surfaced in the House of Representatives in the thirties. Former House Speaker Joe Martin recalled a member shouting, "I say to you, Mr. Speaker, that politics makes strange bedfellows. Especially since women got into 'em."

Strategic Defense Initiative.   See STAR WARS.

straw man (man of straw)   a weakling; one who is all façade, no substance; also, a false issue or phony candidate set up to be easily knocked down.

"Condemn me if you will," said President William Howard Taft in 1912, under savage attack from the man who made him President and who now wanted the job back, "but condemn me by other witnesses than Theodore Roosevelt. I was a man of straw; but I have been a man of straw long enough. Every man who has blood in his body, and who has been misrepresented as I have . . . is forced to fight."

A man of straw—one who looks like a man but is stuffed with straw—comes from the farmer's scarecrow, and from its military use as a false target set up to draw enemy fire. The phrase was used by Taft in the sense of LIGHTWEIGHT; in the following use, the synonym would be STALKING HORSE.

Columnist Clayton Fritchey wrote with some sarcasm in 1967 that "The Fearless Ninetieth [Congress] . . . has shown once more that it wears no strawman's collar" by enacting a bill against race riots "which is aimed at the strawman of the mythical 'outside agitator.'"

A more profound term, very similar, is *hollow man*. The quality of bloodlessness equates *straw* and *hollow*, as in this use by Jersey City Democratic leader Frank Hague about Governor Franklin Roosevelt: ". . . a weather vane, beautiful against the sky, shining and resplendent, built of hollow brass." *The Hollow Men* is a poem by

T. S. Eliot, the title of which is said by some analysts to characterize the post-war politicians of the Western world. The poem concludes: "This is the way the world ends/Not with a bang but a whimper." Historian Samuel Eliot Morison wrote: "Congress, too, was full of hollow men. William E. Borah, perpetual senator from Idaho, was the most pretentious and the emptiest, although he looked more like a statesman than any senator since Daniel Webster. Borah would support any liberal bill with great rumbling oratory, yet in the end vote with the regular Republicans. Senator Norris said of him, 'He fights until he sees the whites of their eyes.'" See TURNAROUNDS.

The danger of the emptiness of the straw or hollow man, stressing the nonhuman quality, was shown by Barbara Garson in 1965 in *MacBird*, a play in Shakespearean verse suggesting that Lyndon Johnson was responsible for the death of John Kennedy. A character most readily identified as Robert Kennedy, called Robert Ken O'Dunc, says at the end in the accents of Macduff:

To free his sons from paralyzing scruples
And temper us for roles of world author-
ity
Our pulpy human hearts were cut away.
And in their place, precision apparatus
Of steel and plastic tubing was inserted.
The sticky, humid blood was drained
and then
A tepid antiseptic brine injected.

Not all writers attack the emptiness of politicians; many members of the NEW LEFT identified with the feeling, and "hollow" is often used to articulate ALIENATION: "The sense of the body growing empty within," as novelist Norman Mailer explained it to a Berkeley crowd, "of the psyche pierced by a wound whose dimensions keep opening, that unendurable conviction that one is hollow, displaced, without a single identity at one's center."

"The key word here again is responsibility," said a *Washington Post* editorial in 1993, using the term in discussing broadcast practices. "When Howard Stern and his supporters whine about First Amendment rights, they set up their straw man."

An African affairs scholar, Sue Cott Wunderman, informed the author that the phrase has an independent West African root. Tribes were reluctant to have their real chiefs deal with French colonial officials. William Foltz points out in *From French West Africa to the Mali Federation:* "Usually a younger man or an elder of inferior caste or status was put up by the people themselves as a 'straw chief' to deal with the conqueror, but beneath the dignity of the tribesman really in charge."

See CHARLIE REGAN.

straw poll (straw vote) originally an informal survey of a small group to determine opinion; now becoming a term for a scientific, large-scale poll based on the theory of a random sample.

"Ballads, bon mots, anecdotes, give us better insight into the depths of past centuries than grave and voluminous chronicles," wrote Ralph Waldo Emerson in his *Journals*. "'A Straw,' says Selden, 'thrown up into the air will show how the wind sits, which cannot be learned by casting up a stone.'"

Emerson was right in the point he was making, though he took some liberties with the quotation from John Selden (1584–1654), who wrote, "Take a straw and throw it up into the Air—you may see by that which way the Wind is," adding, "More solid things do not show the Complexion of the times so well, as Ballads and Libels." However, an earlier use of a similar phrase can be found in Shakespeare's *Merchant of Venice*, Act I, scene 1: "I should be still/Plucking the grass to know where sits the wind."

A straw is metaphorically *powerful* (the *last straw* can break a camel's back), *necessary* (you can't *make bricks* without it), empty (STRAW MAN), and *not so powerful* (a *straw boss* is a foreman who can give orders but carries no executive responsibility).

A *straw in the wind*, probably derived from Selden's usage, is a rough indication or portent, similar to a *cloud no bigger than a man's hand* on the horizon. (Philip Davidson in *Propaganda and the American Revolution 1763–1783* quotes Josiah Quincy the younger, writing about colonial agitation against Britain in 1773: "Our hemisphere is calm, but the diviners of our political sky see a cloud at the horizon, though not bigger than a hand." The source is biblical; 1 Kings 18:44 states, "Behold, there ariseth a little cloud out of the sea, like a man's hand.")

The term *straw vote* is traced to the *Cleveland Leader* in 1866, with indications that it had been used long before: "A straw vote taken on a Toledo train yesterday resulted as follows: [Andrew] Johnson 12, Congress, 47." Surveys had often been taken on river steamboats, and *steamboat vote* was a predecessor phrase that was considered "a straw," as in this item in *Old Zack*, an 1848 publication about Zachary Taylor: "Straws.—For a while the Locofoco papers ventured to publish steamboat votes . . . A vote was taken on the Steamer Fairmount on her trip to Pittsburgh.—This is the vote: Taylor 75, Cass 37, Van Buren 4."

Most modern public-opinion surveys create a panel of voters, based on age, previous voting record, location, socioeconomic background, ethnic group, and so on, hoping to build a cross-section of the actual population make-up. However, straw polls—if they gather enough straws, or votes— can reflect the attitudes of the population of an area if they adhere rigidly to a "random sample" of, say, every hundredth person in a telephone book, and not just those easiest to reach or passing by a certain corner.

Best-known of these wide-scale straw polls is the one conducted at election time in New York City by the *Daily News*, which has called elections correctly on all but two occasions in almost forty years. The first error was when the poll was just getting started, and the second in 1965, when it predicted Abraham Beame over John Lindsay for mayor. When the *News* poll technicians select a name out of phone books or voter registration lists, an interviewer is sent to that apartment; if the resident is not home, he keeps returning, because going next door for a substitute would throw the random sample out of kilter. If he is unable to get his target straw, the interviewer gets another name from the statistician.

Strength of a big straw poll is in the size of its sample, and the fact that most people do *not* change their vote in the final two weeks; weakness of such polling is that some people *do* change their minds, which can be decisive in a "squeaker," and the pollsters are stuck with straws carefully gathered in a final go-around that begins several weeks before Election Day.

When the poll shows a candidate behind, his supporters say with O. Henry in a 1913 story: "A straw vote only shows which way the hot air blows."

See POLLSTER; DEPTH POLLING; TRIAL HEAT.

street money.   See WALKING-AROUND MONEY.

street smarts   savvy; cunning; intuitive understanding of the way the urban voter will react.

"To have the smarts" is to be mentally sharp; the specific "street smarts" is a political insider's term, rarely in print, meaning sensitivity to opinions at the grassroots, gained by experience, without benefit of polls.

In 1972, reporter Paul Hoffman wrote: "Street smarts—in New York City, Wagner, Lefkowitz and Javits have it, Rockefeller and Lindsay do not."

Beyond politics, the phrase is used to mean an understanding of the ways of the real world. In a 1972 article on the rock group the Rolling Stones, *Time* reported: ". . . the Stones from the start based their appeal partly on their reputation as delinquents. They were always too shaggy, too street smart . . ."

In the Southern U.S., new-products marketer Phyllis Y. Bishop reported in 1977 that a variant phrase with the same meaning is "street sense."

strict constructionist in law, one who tends to interpret the Constitution literally, as meaning exactly what it says and no more, much as a fundamentalist interprets the Bible; in politics, one who feels that judges in their broad interpretation of the law have been encroaching on the lawmaking function of the legislative branch.

The *Congressional Globe*, in 1841, defined a "strict constructionist" as "a Pharisee's Pharisee." In 1850 a Pennsylvania congressman named Chandler explained the breed to his House colleagues in this way: "You remember the anecdote of the youngster who received an admonition from his father that it was time to be steady, make some money and take a wife. 'Why, sir,' said he, 'I like the money-making, but whose wife shall I take?' He was a strict constructionist."

"We need more strict constructionists on the highest court of the United States," said Richard Nixon in a law-and-order speech on October 22, 1968, reprising a theme he had made

frequently during the campaign. The emphasis was on the "strict."

The phrase connoted hard-line judges, who would not hamstring law enforcement officials with pettifogging procedural complaints. It connoted something else as well—judges who would not let their own social beliefs carry them into the lawmaking region reserved to Congress.

That is the general understanding of the term today, which distresses many lawyers who believe that such usage confusingly encompasses two different doctrines—one of *strict construction*, and the other of *judicial restraint*.

In law, according to Bouvier's *Law Dictionary*, "A *strict* construction is one which limits the application of the provisions of the instrument or agreement to cases clearly described by the words used. It is called, also, literal.

"A *liberal* construction is one by which the letter is enlarged or restrained so as more effectually to accomplish the end in view. It is called, also, equitable."

Judicial restraint, or self-limitation, deals with a related but different matter: the extent to which judicial decisions on cases "make" law. Justice Frankfurter in 1937 put the case for judicial restraint in these words: "Such self-limitation is not abnegation; it is the expression of an energizing philosophy of the distribution of governmental powers. For a court to hold that decision does not belong to it, is merely to recognize that a problem calls for the exercise of initiative and experimentation possessed only by political processes, and should not be subjected to the confined procedure of a lawsuit and the uncreative resources of judicial review."

President Nixon did not put a strict construction on his use of the term "strict construction"; he interpreted it broadly, to include judicial restraint. Explaining his appointment of Warren

Burger to be Chief Justice, he said: "I happen to believe that the Constitution should be strictly interpreted, and I believe, as did Mr. Justice Frankfurter . . . [who] felt it was his responsibility to interpret the Constitution, and it was the right of the Congress to write the laws and have great leeway to write those laws, and he should be very conservative in overthrowing a law passed by the elected representatives at the state or Federal level . . ."

While most strict constructionists are also believers in judicial restraint, it would be possible to abandon judicial restraint in pursuit of strict construction.

Historically, the "construction," or interpretation, of the Constitution is our longest-lived controversy. Soon after the document was written, public opinion was divided between the "strict constructionists" (the Democrat-Republicans behind Thomas Jefferson) and the "loose constructionists" (the Federalists, favoring a strong central government, behind Hamilton).

Chief Justice John Marshall made a case for loose construction in *Maryland* v. *McCulloch*: "Let the end be legitimate, let it be within the scope of the Constitution, and all means which are appropriate, which are plainly adapted to that end, which are not prohibited, but consist with the letter and spirit of the Constitution, are constitutional." In modern times, Justice Hugo Black, whose liberal opinions often made him the target of many who considered themselves strict constructionists, used this language in dissenting from a decision that extended the Due Process clause to include the need to prove guilt "beyond a reasonable doubt": "In two places the Constitution provides for trial by jury, but nowhere in that document is there any statement that conviction of crime re-

quires proof of guilt beyond a reasonable doubt. The Constitution thus goes into some detail to spell out what kind of trial a defendant charged with crime should have, and I believe the Court has no power to add to or subtract from the procedures set forth by the Founders." Justice Black was also fond of pointing to the words in the First Amendment that read "Congress shall make no law . . ." and commenting, "'No law' means *no law*."

strike a blow for freedom a pleasant drink in a politician's office, accompanied by informal political discussion; a legislative code phrase.

"On a hot afternoon in 1958," wrote Rowland Evans and Robert Novak in 1966, "Speaker Sam Rayburn's 'BOARD OF EDUCATION' met in his offices, as it did almost every day after work to 'strike a blow for freedom'—good political talk accompanied by good whiskey." The phrase is especially used among Texans and effectively confuses outsiders; when Texas Congressman Olin E. Teague invited the author to "strike a blow for freedom" one evening in 1963, about the last thing expected was a glass of Early Times bourbon along with a general discussion of the political scene.

New York Daily News columnist Ted Lewis, who covered Washington for United Press in the early thirties, attributes coinage to Vice President John Garner. He informs the author: "Garner called it striking a blow for liberty. He was a stingy man with the liquor, though—he could strike a blow with a thimbleful."

A similar phrase has long existed in England. To a tavernkeeper, an "Act of Parliament" is a small (which means weak) beer, stemming from an ancient requirement that landlords billeting soldiers had to provide five pints of small beer free to each—"by Act of Parliament."

The "strike a blow for freedom" phrase is sufficiently pretentious to make it useful for an ironic twist, even to the extent of giving it a meaning of enjoying a straight shot of whiskey. However, some political leaders still use the phrase in the original context. Said Rhodesian Prime Minister Ian Smith in 1965 as he broke from Great Britain: "We have struck a blow for the preservation of justice, civilization, and Christianity; and in the spirit of this belief we have this day assumed our sovereign independence." Thirteen years later he acquiesced in majority rule by blacks, which many felt was more of a "blow for freedom."

strike force. See TASK FORCE.

striped-pants diplomacy. See SHIRTSLEEVE DIPLOMACY.

stroke as a verb, to persuade soothingly, or to hold in line with murmured reassurances; as a noun, influence.

When the White House is concerned with a legislator's possible defection on a vote, instructions are passed to the congressman's colleagues or to lobbyists to "stroke" him (from the image of the raised hackles of an angry or frightened animal).

The noun form is less frequently used, and has a different meaning: a person with "stroke" is one with CLOUT; the metaphor is possibly from golf or tennis.

When the author used this definition in a *New York Times* article in 1975, Meridyth Senes of Wynnewood, Pa., wrote: "If anything, 'stroke' . . . would have derived more from the street phrase 'different strokes for different folks,' with its obvious sexual connotation." The suggestion that "stroke" as a verb has to do with the rhythm of intercourse is not far-fetched: in Navy slang, "to stroke

around" is to wander about, looking for company, similar to the Air Force term "strafing the *Strasse*." Significantly, "to stroke" in auto-racing argot means to mill the crankshaft for a longer plunge.

Russell Baker of the *New York Times*, on April 4, 1978, compared stroking to another form of presidential persuasion, JAWBONING: "President Nixon, revolted by such direct methods, preferred what he called 'stroking,' a process of jawboning so sweet to the strokee's earbones that the victim fell into a hypnotic state in which he could be deboned without realizing it."

stroke of a pen by executive order; action that can be taken by a Chief Executive without legislative action.

Candidate John F. Kennedy said in 1960 that the President could end discrimination in federally financed housing with a "stroke of the pen," a phrase that was then current with civil rights leaders impatient with Eisenhower. When Kennedy, as President, delayed taking such action himself, Martin Luther King, Jr., called on him to "give segregation its death blow through a stroke of the pen," and disenchanted civil rights advocates began sending pens to the White House as a not-so-subtle reminder.

Typical prose use was in this passage from a 1966 book by Raymond Moley: "The closing of the banks was the anesthetic before the major operation. A proclamation that had been considered for weeks, assured of authority under the law, required merely the stroke of a White House pen. The hard part lay ahead."

In 1971 Leonard Woodcock, president of the United Automobile Workers, objected to a wage-price freeze in these words: "If this Administration thinks that just by issuing an edict, by the stroke of a pen, they can tear up contracts, they are saying to us they want war. If they want war, they can have war."

The political coinage was by stockbroker-poet Edmund Clarence Stedman (1833–1908) in a poem titled "Wanted—A Man":

Give us a man of God's own mould,
Born to marshal his fellow-men;
One whose fame is not bought and sold
At the stroke of a politician's pen.

stump as a noun, the campaign trail; as a verb, to exhort informally, usually outdoors, in a campaign.

To achieve a dominating posture, a frontier speechmaker would use a convenient tree stump as a platform. The earliest reference clearly shows the origin; Ann Maury, in her 1716 *Memoirs of a Huguenot Family*, wrote, "I went down to the Saponey Indian town. There is in the center of the circle a great stump of a tree. I asked the reason they left it standing, and they informed me that it was for one of their head men to stand upon when he had anything of consequence to relate to them, so that being raised, he might the better be heard."

By 1838 it was part of the American political vocabulary. The *New York Herald* tells of the Speaker of the House, James K. Polk, "Stumping it about the State of Tennessee." And the *Hamilton* (Ohio) *Intelligencer* was editorializing sniffily about this innovation which it was quite certain would not last: "'Stumping it' is a new game for candidates for Governor in Ohio, and we very much doubt whether the 'Experiment' will be sanctioned by a dignified people."

Congressman Isaac N. Arnold of Illinois, reminiscing in an address before the House of Representatives about the career of Abraham Lincoln, recounted how, a few years earlier, "The friends of Lincoln were not without anxiety when the challenge was given,

and accepted, for a campaign on the stump" (with Stephen A. Douglas as the opposition).

As with other apt phrases, this one was picked up across the ocean, sometimes in exalted circles. Prime Minister Gladstone displeased Queen Victoria by campaigning for a broadening of the eligible electorate in a tour through Scotland while she was staying at her Balmoral residence in the same area. Her Majesty's secretary, General Ponsonby, noted "his constant speeches at every station. . . . The Queen is utterly disgusted with his stump oratory—so unworthy of his position—almost under her very nose."

Others have defined stump oratory in the same vein, as bombastic, even inflammatory; generally the word is accepted today in its original sense, and no candidate can afford to let a campaign go by without taking to the stump. See HUSTINGS; STEMWINDER.

Another meaning of stump, as a verb, is to pose a question that the person asked cannot answer. It is possible that this is connected with embarrassed stump speakers.

After listening to a speech by President Harding in 1921, H. L. Mencken wrote: "The stump speech, put into cold type, maketh the judicious to grieve. But roared from an actual stump, with arms flying and eyes flashing and the old flag overhead, it is certainly and brilliantly effective."

The word is current. During the Presidential campaign of 1992, the *Boston Globe* wrote of Hillary Rodham Clinton: "To observe her up close during a full (very full) day on the stump is to understand why Arkansas folks are called 'razorbacks.'"

See THE SPEECH.

suaviter in modo. See EGGHEAD.

sufficiency. See PARITY.

summitry the art of dealing at the top level; the notion that diplomacy can best be practiced by face-to-face meeting of world leaders.

Winston Churchill, unhappy with the international impasse in 1950 that his friend Bernard Baruch had described as the COLD WAR, recalled the wartime meetings with Stalin and Roosevelt and issued a call for a "parley at the summit."

Immediately, diplomats around the world pointed out that such a meeting would bring about little of substance, that the hopes of the world would be raised and dashed, and that many months of intricate preplanning on lower levels would be necessary before any decisions could be made as to what would be discussed.

Churchill dismissed all this. "This conference should not be overhung by a ponderous or rigid agenda or led into mazes of technical details, zealously contested by hordes of experts and officials drawn up in a vast cumbrous array."

As a rule, foreign ministers resist summit conferences, on the theory that world problems are too complex to be left to world leaders and the world is led to expect too much; what's more, the second echelon is left to fight over what was said, meant, and not meant. "Conferences at the top level are always courteous," career diplomat Averell Harriman said in 1955. "Name-calling is left to the foreign ministers."

After his first conference with Nikita Khrushchev (see SPIRIT OF), Dwight Eisenhower found that conferences at the top level can be disastrous. The 1959 summit conference in Paris was aborted by Khrushchev over the U-2 incident. On his way home, the disappointed President spoke to the staff of the U.S. embassy in Lisbon: "Did you see that cartoon not long ago where it says, 'The next speaker needs all the introduction he can get'? Well, I rather feel that way, after coming from this last meeting in Paris."

Turning a careful phrase in 1959, Senator John Kennedy said, "It is far better that we meet at the summit than at the brink." As President, he had a rough session at the summit with Khrushchev in 1961. But, wrote Sorensen, "The Soviet leader also made clear his belief in summitry. If the heads of state cannot resolve problems, how can officials at a lower level? He liked as much personal contact as possible, he said, no matter how able one's ambassadors might be—just as natural love is better than love through interpreters."

An unexpected defense of summitry came from Indian diplomat Arthur Lall in *Modern International Negotiation* in 1967: "The public exhortations, the invitations to Washington and Moscow, the wooing by important powers, praise for the acumen and wisdom of its statesmen, appeals in the interest of world harmony, and the spotlight and the publicity of international conferences, go to make up a much more acceptable political context for action by most governments than a courtroom or than wholly QUIET DIPLOMACY."

A question that always arises in debating the use of summitry is: How much freedom of action does a world leader have? How bound is he by past policy, and how much leeway does his Politburo or Congress or public opinion at home give him? The quiet style of Alexei Kosygin led this question to be asked in 1967 before the summit conference with Lyndon Johnson at Glassboro, New Jersey. This meeting was arranged hurriedly, during a trip to the UN to debate the Arab-Israeli war, proving that the need for extended advance preparation was not as overwhelming as it seemed. Though the conference was fringed with warnings not to expect much, and indeed did not produce much, President Johnson expressed this attitude afterward: "It does help a lot to sit down and look at a man right in the eye and try to reason with him, particularly if he is trying to reason with you." See COME NOW, AND LET US REASON TOGETHER.

In late 1971, on the eve of several international conferences, Peter Lisagor of the *Chicago Daily News* wrote: "On the face of things, the President would seem to have another spectacular in the works, designed to reduce the terror on earth even as it enhances his own fortunes. The mixture is hard to deplore. Yet summit diplomacy is risky business, consuming presidential prestige and power in enterprises that may produce a small return. It often is an act of self-exaltation, an ego trip."

In *Present at the Creation*, Dean Acheson wrote in 1970 that summitry traced back to the early sixteenth century, and that in only two cases was it clearly successful: the meetings at Münster and Osnabrück in 1648 that ended the Thirty Years' War with the Peace of Westphalia, and the Congress of Vienna in 1814.

Summits have "all too often been a gamble, the experience nerve-wracking and the results unsatisfactory," wrote the former Secretary of State, quoting advice given to Woodrow Wilson's aide, Colonel Edward House, on the eve of Wilson's journey to Europe. "The moment President Wilson sits at the council table with these prime ministers and foreign secretaries," the adviser said, "he has lost all the power that comes from distance and detachment . . . he becomes merely a negotiator dealing with other negotiators."

Acheson added: "When a chief of state or head of government makes a fumble, the goal line is open behind him."

The term has been extended in recent usage to include a wide variety of meetings: "earth summit," "economic summit," "housing summit," "conservation summit," "farm summit," "smog summit," and "fashion summit" suggest the word's overuse.

In a nondiplomatic context, the best-known uses of the word *summit* were Napoleon's ("Soldiers, from the summits of the pyramids, forty centuries look down upon you") and Edmund Burke's eulogy of Charles James Fox, quoted by John Kennedy as the keynote in *Profiles in Courage*, and recalled after the Cuban missile crisis of 1962: "He may live long, he may do much. But here is the summit. He never can exceed what he does this day."

sunbelt that string of states across the South, Southwest, and Western U.S. which—by virtue of attractive climate and economic opportunity—have seen their populations grow dramatically, thereby becoming important (and often conservative) political forces.

Kevin Phillips, dubbed by *Newsweek* columnist Meg Greenfield "the prophet-geographer of the New Right," coined the phrase while writing his book *The Emerging Republican Majority* in 1967. That work, however, was not published until 1969; in the meantime, writer Garry Wills used it in a magazine article, quoting Phillips as the source, just before the Nixon Administration took office. In his book, Phillips held that a new political cycle was coming, its trend conservative and anti-Establishment. He rested a portion of his argument "on the post-1945 migration of many white Americans (including many of the traditionally Democratic white ethnic groups) to suburbia and the Sun Belt states of Florida, Texas, Arizona and California."

After its coinage in that political context, and its subsequent denunciation as part of a SOUTHERN STRATEGY, writers of demographic and economic stories found "sunbelt" useful. In the first half of the seventies, while the population of the twenty-one Northeastern and North Central states remained static, the population of the "sunbelt" states (using the phrase to include all the South and West) increased by about 2 percent per year. Advertising executive Mary Wells Lawrence called the growth area "the golden horseshoe": its U-shape stretched from Washington, D.C., around to Southern California and up the West Coast to Washington State. She pointed to the social impact of the new dominance of these areas: increased mobility, indoor-outdoor living, and a divorce rate double that of the Northeast.

In most current use, Phillips's two-word phrase is compressed to one word: A *New York Times* headline of January 25, 1978, read: "Census Data Show Growth Slowing in Part of Sunbelt." The absence of quotation marks illustrated the wide acceptance of the phrase.

The parent of the phrase was "Bible belt," a coinage of H. L. Mencken. An offspring is "rust belt," the strip of industrial states in the Northeast and Midwest.

sunset law a provision in a bill shutting off a program on a specific date, requiring re-examination and a fresh authorization in the future; a device to worry bureaucrats.

The technique, and the phrase, began in Colorado. Answering the author's query, Rosalie Schiff of Colorado Common Cause states: "The phrase 'sunset law' was coined by Mr. Craig Barnes, a member of our Board of Directors, at an Issues committee meeting in May 1975 . . . To our knowledge the term had not been used or suggested elsewhere. Mr. Barnes

coined the term to describe a process whereby agencies would terminate periodically unless they could justify their continued existence. Since affirmative legislative action would be required for continued life, should an agency fail to prove a public need for its existence, the 'sun would set' on said agency.

"The two-fold purpose of Sunset is to require more public accountability from these agencies and to reduce the proliferation and growth of bureaucracy."

The idea behind the mechanism was expressed in *Go East, Young Man* by Supreme Court Justice William O. Douglas: "The great creative work of a federal agency must be done in the first decade of its existence if it is to be done at all. After that it is likely to become a prison of bureaucracy and of the inertia demanded by the Establishment of any respected agency. That is why I told FDR over and over again that every agency he created should be abolished in ten years. And since he might not be around to dissolve it, he should insert in the basic charter of the agency a provision for its termination. Roosevelt would always roar with delight at that suggestion, and of course never did do anything about it."

Because administrative agencies tend, after a while, to identify with the interests they are supposed to administer or regulate, the idea of incorporating a termination date appealed to many Colorado liberals; conservatives could be expected to be for any anti-bureaucratic measure. As a result of this broad appeal, sunset provisions passed handily in that state, later in Florida (perhaps due to an interest in SUNSHINE LAWS) and—with the sponsorship of Senator Edmund Muskie—nationally. Said Senator Muskie in proposing a "spending reform" act in 1976, the sunset plan was "a sensible plan for making certain that the programs we approve are working, and for ending those programs which are no longer needed."

The cut-off idea was embraced by candidate Jimmy Carter in his 1976 campaign, as the legislative counterpart of his administrative ZERO-BASE BUDGETING. "Sunset is the congressional complement to zero base budgeting in the Executive Branch," wrote Senator Muskie. "Sunset, too, is considerably more than program evaluation." However, the sun sometimes sets on a good coinage: the bill he put forward to require new budget authority every five years was titled "The Program Evaluation Act of 1977."

Colorado's new law caused some of its proponents to glow with pride. "We kayoed the athletic commission, flushed the sanitary engineers, and clipped the barbers," claimed Senate president Fred Anderson in 1977. The triple metaphor attracted the attention of *Rocky Mountain News* reporter Peter Blake, writing in *Inquiry* magazine: "The athletic commission never did much anyway, since there is virtually no professional boxing in Colorado. The main function of the board for professional sanitarians was to bestow honorary appendages on certain government employees, like 'Esq' for a lawyer. And as for the barber board, it was not clipped at all; it was merely combined with the cosmetology board (which controls hairdressers) and it is stronger than ever. In short, all the Colorado legislature has done so far is put a few dying animals out of their misery. Most regulatory agencies continue to bask in the noonday sun."

sunshine laws measures to force the conduct of public business in public.

"Publicity is justly commended," wrote Supreme Court Justice Louis D. Brandeis, "as a remedy for social and industrial disease. Sunlight is said to be the best disinfectant and electric light the most efficient policeman."

The Florida Sunshine Act was first proposed in 1961; while it was being debated for six years, five other states—Arkansas, Indiana, Nebraska, New Jersey, and New Mexico—enacted open-meeting laws. The Florida act directed "All meetings . . . at which official acts are to be taken are declared to be public meetings open to the public at all times, and no resolution, rule, regulation or formal action shall be considered binding except as taken or made at such meeting."

In proposing similar legislation on the national level, Florida Senator Lawton Chiles wrote in 1974: "Experience under the sunshine law has shown that the open meeting principle does not hamper public business operations, but rather increases public confidence in government . . . Closed doors are not necessary to sound resolution of conflicting views and interests."

Many legislators who do not like to derogate open meetings publicly disagree privately: in the horse trading that goes on in closed committee sessions, they hold, sensible compromises are reached that could not be struck in the harsh light of PITILESS PUBLICITY. Although the Freedom of Information Act has made much material in the executive branch available to citizens, Congress has been unwilling to provide such access to its own files and deliberations. In states with sunshine laws, it is charged, much of the public business is done in advance of open meetings—in secret, making the "open" meeting a charade.

Despite the criticism of impracticality, and the derision leveled at OPEN COVENANTS, OPENLY ARRIVED AT, the pressure toward "government in the sunshine" has helped the trend toward more public disclosure of the governmental activities. For example, the author received a notice from the U.S. Commission on Civil Rights: "In accordance with the Government in the Sunshine Act, we are providing you notice of a change in the Dec. 8, 1977 activities of the Commission." The notice listed a new time and place of meeting, adding: "Agenda: a discussion of the Sunshine Act."

superpatriots flag-waving extremists; attack phrase on those who protest too much their love of country.

"I don't think the United States needs super-patriots," wrote President Eisenhower in 1962. "We need patriotism, honestly practiced by all of us, and we don't need these people that are more patriotic than you or anybody else."

Carl Schurz defined "mock patriotism" as "the kind of sentiment which leads a man to say with Decatur 'Our country, right or wrong.'" During the Spanish-American War, William McKinley warned the hotheads: "Impatience is not patriotism."

Time wrote in 1939 of a type called the "patrioteer," harshly defined as "the professional patriot, the kind of refuge-seeking scoundrel who waves a red-white-and-blue handkerchief when he should be wiping his own nose."

Dr. Samuel Johnson found plain—not even super—patriotism "the last refuge of a scoundrel." Some are more charitable. Adlai Stevenson, writing of the McCarthy era: "We have survived it. We shall survive John Birchism and all the rest of the super patriots—but only at the price of perpetual and truly patriotic vigilance."

The fashion in "super" words—from supercolossal to superduper and superpower—was set by George Bernard Shaw. Nietzsche's *Übermensch* had been translated as "Overman" or "Beyondman"; Shaw coined "Superman," who later left politics to become

a comic strip "man of steel." "Superstar" became a familiar word of the sixties in both show business and sports, and "superpower" and appellation in world politics. "We will never become a superpower," Chinese Premier Chou En-lai told the Canadian Broadcasting Company in July of 1971; "we are opposed to the POWER POLITICS of the big powers." Though Chou used the term pejoratively, as leaders of nonsuperpowers occasionally do, the word is more generally used neutrally in reference to the U.S. and the Soviet Union.

A synonymous prefix, "ultra," is also used politically. There are ultraconservatives and ultraliberals; though there are superpatriots, there are no supertraitors.

Conservative satirist Vic Gold spoofed the fashion of denigrating patriotic fervor as "superpatriotism" by titling a fictitious work "Paul Revere and the Superpatriotic Tradition in American History."

See KOOKS, NUTS AND; LITTLE OLD LADIES IN TENNIS SHOES; TURNAROUNDS.

supply-side economic theory emphasizing the use of tax cuts to stimulate production and growth.

This emphasis on *supply*, or potential output, counters the traditional theory, expounded by the British economist John Maynard Keynes, of the need to stimulate *demand* by consumers. The Keynesian view, emphasizing consumption over production, calls for increased government involvement in the economy.

According to supply-side theory, however, less government intervention is preferred. This theory holds that lower tax rates create incentives for more work and investment, producing long-term growth without inflation and shrinking the budget deficit. Liberal politicians lean toward demand-side economics, with its government activism; conservative politicians lean toward supply-side economics, which is closer to *laissez-faire*.

Economist Herbert Stein coined *supply-side fiscalism*, first used in the *Wall Street Journal* in 1976: "Supply-side fiscalists . . . agree that tax changes do not affect total demand, but they emphasize the effects on supply." Although he provided the name for the movement, Stein (see OLD-TIME RELIGION) was often a critic of it. The foremost supply-side economist was Arthur Laffer, whose "Laffer curve," originally drawn on a cocktail napkin, was a parabola showing the correlation between tax rates and economic activity; the higher the tax rate, the lower the tax revenues generated. The leading publicist of what he termed "supply-side economics" was the economics writer and editorialist Jude Wanniski.

In the 1980s, Ronald Reagan's support of the theory made the term synonymous with *Reaganomics* (see -NOMICS). Although George Bush had once denounced this economic policy (see VOODOO ECONOMICS), the *Chicago Tribune* reported during the 1992 campaign that "President Bush is returning to the supply-side economic program of Ronald Reagan in promising across-the-board tax cuts and spending reductions to lift the economy out of the most prolonged economic slump since the 1930's."

Orthodox economists have remained dubious of the theory, while Democrats in the 1990s denounced it as the source of deficits (see TRICKLE-DOWN THEORY); Republicans responded that increased spending, not tax cuts, raised the national debt (see SOAK THE RICH).

The political leader most closely associated with supply-side was Representative Jack Kemp, who embodied the theory in the Kemp-Roth tax-reducing bill in 1984, and espoused it during his primary campaign for President in 1988. Asked for a definition of this economic theory, he said it was

> based on the classical economic philosophy of Adam Smith, David Ricardo and Jean Baptiste Say. It rests on the idea that people respond to rewards and incentives for output, production and work, i.e. the supply side of the economy. It stresses incentive-driven economic policies, most importantly, low tax rates on labor, capital and risk-taking entrepreneurs, free trade, less government regulation and spending restraint.

Supreme Court follows the election returns a view that the supposedly dispassionate and disinterested Supreme Court bench usually reflects the current political scene.

This bit of irreverence was the work of Finley Peter Dunne's "Mr. Dooley."

America's war against Spain had just been concluded. The majority of Congress, swept up by a new feeling of America's MANIFEST DESTINY had approved the taking of the Philippines and of Puerto Rico from Spain. Puerto Rico was not part of the U.S.; yet our government claimed the right to collect taxes and to levy tariffs among its people. The Democratic party, in convention in 1900, had contended that wherever U.S. sovereignty extended, the people of that area gained the rights and protection of the U.S. Constitution; in the phrase of the day, "We hold that the Constitution follows the flag." The Democrats lost.

The Court labored until it came up with a fuzzy doctrine: territories like Puerto Rico weren't exactly foreign, since the U.S. had acquired them; on the other hand, they weren't really domestic, either, so the U.S. government did have the right to levy taxes on these unrepresented people. This, more or less, agreed with the position of the winning Republicans.

All of which drew from Mr. Dooley the caustic comment, "No matter whether th' Constitution follows th' flag or not, the Supreme Coort follows the iliction returns."

Chief Justice Hughes once said, "We are under a Constitution, but the Constitution is what the judges say it is." By and large, the members of the Court reflect their time and the judgments of the populace, giving support to Dunne's gibe.

See NINE OLD MEN; DOOLEY, MR.

surface to allow to become known; to bring a secret supporter into public view.

In many campaigns, there are those who are willing to provide ideas, solicitation efforts, and money on an "off-the-record" basis. In addition, there are those whom the candidate may not wish to have publicly support him.

When these supporters decide to switch from covert to overt, they are said to "surface"; often they are forced to surface by inquisitive newsmen.

Politics adopted the word from espionage, where the word is used in the same way. "CIA Director Richard Helms's public record for the next five years is a total blank," wrote *Time* magazine. "When he surfaced in 1952, it was as deputy to the chief of the plans division, the so-called 'dirty tricks' department . . ."

Apparently the word, as a verb and in its present sense, comes from the action of a submerged submarine coming to the surface of the water.

surgical strike attack designed to destroy a military facility with a minimum of civilian deaths; a narrowly focused action executed quickly and precisely.

The phrase was popularized in 1981, when Israeli bombers obliterated a plant near Baghdad where the Iraqi dictator Saddam Hussein was building a nuclear weapon; *surgical strike* reappeared during the spring of 1986, when the United States mounted a bombing raid on Qaddafi forces in Libya.

Its origins, however, were at least two decades earlier. "Following a conversation with President Kennedy," Murray Marder wrote in a 1981 *Washington Post* article, "the late Stewart Alsop wrote in the *Saturday Evening Post* that 'a surgical strike' against China's gaseous diffusion plant at Lop Nor was under serious consideration."

Martin Nolan of the *Boston Globe* offered a more precise citation. Nolan found that Theodore Sorensen wrote in his 1964 memoir, *Kennedy,* about White House discussions of an attack on Cuba: "The idea of American planes suddenly and swiftly eliminating the missile complex with conventional bombs in a matter of minutes—a so-called 'surgical' strike—had appeal to almost everyone first considering the matter."

Arthur M. Schlesinger, Jr., used a similar term in an April 5, 1961, memo to John F. Kennedy on overthrowing Castro: "If we could achieve this by a swift, surgical stroke, I would be for it." Schlesinger told the lexicographer recently, "I don't know when *stroke* evolved into *strike,* but the escalation seems natural enough." (The Middle English *striken* and Old English *strican,* roots of *strike,* meant "to stroke.") The historian hastened to explain: "The memorandum went on to say that I doubted that Castro's regime could be removed surgically and that I was therefore opposed to the Bay of Pigs," adding, "You might have added to your definition of *surgical* as a military modifier that the impression conveyed of precision, quickness, cleanness and incisiveness is entirely spurious. War, as the late W. T. Sherman pointed out, is not surgical."

surrender on Morningside Heights
a party-unity conference between Eisenhower and Taft after the bruising
fight for the 1952 nomination, which
Democrats tried to exploit.

Like the Nixon-Rockefeller COM-
PACT OF FIFTH AVENUE in 1960, the
meeting between Dwight Eisenhower
and Robert A. Taft in 1952 was an attempt at unifying a party that was immediately characterized as a SELL-OUT
by the opposition party, as well as by
some disgruntled Republican liberals.

The meeting took place on September 12, 1952, at 60 Morningside Drive
in New York City, Eisenhower's residence as president of Columbia University. Earlier, Taft had let it be
known from his post-convention vacation retreat in Murray Bay, Canada,
that his price for active support of the
ticket would be some written assurances on policy. This Democrats called
"the ultimatum of Murray Bay," but it
did not catch on; Adlai Stevenson's
characterization of the meeting as "the
surrender on Morningside Heights"
had greater appeal.

A statement issued after the meeting
had a strong Taft flavor. They had
agreed that an issue at home was "liberty against creeping socialization"
and Taft added, "General Eisenhower
emphatically agrees with me in the
proposal to reduce drastically over-all
expenses. . . . General Eisenhower
has also told me that he believes
strongly in our system of Constitutional limitations on Government
power and that he abhors the left-wing
theory that the Executive had unlimited powers. . . . General Eisenhower has also told me that he believes
in the basic principles of the Taft-
Hartley Law, its protection of the people and the freedom of the union members themselves against the arbitrary
use of power by big business or big
labor, and is opposed to its repeal . . ." He concluded, "It is fair to

say that our differences are differences
of degree."

Stevenson slammed away at the
meeting throughout the campaign: "I
wonder what happened to all those
declarations of undying principle we
heard from both sides while they were
calling each other nasty names in Chicago. . . . It looks as if Taft lost the
nomination but won the nomi-
nee . . . when he walked out of the
General's house in New York with the
surrender in writing I have never seen
such a contented smile since the cat
swallowed the canary . . . part of the
price of the embrace on Morningside
Heights has been to lay no affirmative
program before this nation for its approval."

Eisenhower recalled:

Some journalists and the Democratic
nominee, however, seemed to think that
here was raw drama. The opposition
saw in this meeting a great "surrender
on Morningside Heights." The fact was
that Senator Taft and I had agreed emphatically on the need for fiscal sanity in
the government, as on most other issues, long before the breakfast talk. In
the succeeding weeks he evidenced his
enthusiasm for our common cause by a
rugged round of campaigning which included more than thirty speeches in
nineteen states.

This is one of the classic minuets of
politics. A savage primary is followed
by a sullen requirement for assurances;
these are then given at a sweetness-
and-light unity meeting or LOVE FEAST;
this is then attacked and derided by the
opposition which tries to keep the primary split from healing; that attack is
then pooh-poohed by the unifying
candidates. The French analysis of this
type of activity was given by Alphonse
Karr in 1849: "*Plus ça change, plus c'est
la même chose*"—the more things
change, the more they stay the same.

surrogates. See ADVANCE MAN.

swap horses. See DON'T CHANGE
HORSES.

Swartwouting absconding with public funds; embezzling.

An example of eponymy (using
proper names to create words) like
boycott and *sandwich,* this word is
based on the name of Samuel
Swartwout, a nineteenth-century collector for the port of New York. During Andrew Jackson's Presidency,
Swartwout absconded to England
with more than a million dollars of
public money.

This older Americanism was in use
by the 1830s in the form of a noun
meaning "embezzler." Soon the name
was turned into a verb meaning "to ab-
scond"; in 1839, the *Kentucky Observer* reported on fiscal trouble:
"That the Bank, at some time, would
fall into the hands of scoundrels, who
would Swartwout its funds, is altogether probable."

Other forms of the name are also
capitalized and include the gerund
Swartwouting for "embezzlement"
(or "official peculation," as it was referred to in 1876) and the agent noun
Swartwouter for "one who absconds."

The name is still alluded to in coverage of scandals and graft. In 1978,
Haynes Johnson of the *Washington
Post* wrote of allegations about theft in
the General Services Administration,
including "bribery, kickbacks, padded
costs for equipment. Shades of
Swartwout . . . and right here in
Jimmy Carter's Washington."

The illegal maneuverings of Samuel
Swartwout also provided readers of
the *Georgia Journal* in 1841 with a lesson in synonymy: "What will Webster
do now with his dictionary? He
[Swartwout] has made a new verb,
thus, To Swartwout . . . to absquat-
ulate, run away, evaporate, back out,
mosey, cut stick, mizle, slope, slant,

cut dirt, make tracks, take the sabine
slide, and disappear."

sweetheart shorter than arm's length;
collusive.

In labor terminology, a "sweetheart
contract" is one in which a union
leader makes an unfavorable settlement for his fellow employees and
then takes an emolument from management on the side.

The adjective has crossed into political parlance without the specifically illegal meaning, but with a connotation
of favoritism. In 1977 President
Carter's Director of the Office of
Management and Budget, Bert Lance,
was accused by this author of arranging for a "sweetheart loan"; that is, one
on abnormally favorable terms. *New
York Times* columnist Tom Wicker
used the word in July 1977 in its most
modestly pejorative sense: "The
Administration's broader anti-inflation policy is based on a vague, soft,
sweetheart reliance on business volun-
tarism . . ."

In business, a "sweetener" is an acceptable extra incentive to close a deal;
in politics, such sweetness strikes a
sour note.

swing around the circle. See NON-
POLITICAL TRIP.

swing voter one who votes for the
man, not the party; the independent
vote that often "swings" elections one
way or the other.

Several political scientists have estimated that not more than 60 percent of
the American electorate is partisan and
regular in its voting habits. As personalities and issues have become more
significant than party affiliation, the
size of the swing vote has grown. Pollster Samuel Lubell noted in 1959 that
the electorate "seems to have undergone a curious quickening of its voting
reflexes" in elections since 1948, mak-

ing it "easier to shift the party allegiance of the American voter."

"Swing vote" and "swing voter" are not used to any extent in England; instead, an obsolete American expression, "floater," defines the independent group. In the U.S., floater enjoyed its greatest popularity in 1888, when the Treasurer of the Republican National Committee, W. W. Dudley, was charged with recommending to the Indiana state committee that they secure "floaters in blocks of five." This was construed to mean the purchase of votes wholesale; politicians in ancient Greece dealt out bribes to voters in "blocks of ten."

The slang term for public is rooted in fickleness; the word "mob," considered slang but in use in the English language since the sixteenth century, is traced to Claudius, a Latin poet of the third century B.C., who wrote of *mobile . . . vulgus* (the fickle crowd). Johann Wolfgang von Goethe came up with a simile that explains one reason for the growth of the swing vote: "In politics, as on the sickbed, people toss from one side to the other, thinking they will be more comfortable."

switcher registered voter in one party likely to "split his ticket" (see SPLIT TICKET) on the basis of having done so before.

Pollster Oliver Quayle included a "switcher analysis" in most of his surveys of the voting complexion of an area. These are voters who have crossed party lines in previous elections, indicating a lack of deep party commitment and a likely source of votes for an attractive opposition candidate.

Independents and SWING VOTERS have no party alliances; *switchers* do, if only nominal.

Adlai Stevenson told a story in 1952 about "the little boy who asked his father what a convert was, and the fa-

ther—evidently a politically minded father—said, 'Well, son, if a Republican becomes a Democrat, he is a convert.' And what, asked the boy, is a Democrat who becomes a Republican? With a scowl his father said, 'Why, he's a traitor, of course.'"

A "switcher issue" is one that causes a fiercely committed voter to abandon all other patterns and preferences: in the seventies, abortion and gun control were switcher issues.

syntax, Presidential. See EISEN-HOWER SYNTAX.

system, the the political structure, not to be despised when it works for you.

Originally "the system" was a phrase accompanied by a sneer, synonymous with "City Hall" or "the Establishment" or "the bureaucracy." In 1974, however, as the forces of government joined the anti-Nixon protestors, the phrase "The System Works" came into wide use, and the system took on a rosy glow as a protector of individual rights.

The nonpejorative use of the system was, in turn, parodied. In the *American Spectator* (January 1977), editor R. Emmet Tyrrell disparaged the Carter election victory as having been the result of a bored electorate: "The voice was faint: 27.5 percent of the people said Jimmy, 26 percent said Jerry, and a whopping 46.5 percent said yecch. The system works!"

Although the phrase was used in a positive sense, it had not lost its overtone of entrenched-authority-to-be-opposed. In 1978, when Philadelphia U.S. Attorney David Marston, a Republican, was fired with an explanation from Democratic Attorney General Griffin Bell that "we have a system" (see INS AND OUTS), Marston retorted, "I don't agree with that. They had a system too in Philadelphia before I got there and I didn't accept that system." In the sense used by Marston, "the system" was a matrix of official corruption and mob influence.

As "the system" has replaced "the Establishment," it has been overtaken in some ways by the "PROCESS"; see that entry for differences, and AMERICAN SYSTEM for origins.

T

table 1. propose for discussion; 2. postpone discussion.

Like *sanction* and *cleave*, the verb *table* is an example of antilogy, a word that holds opposite meanings.

This verb began in British English in the eighteenth century with the sense of "to bring up for consideration or discussion." According to the *Oxford English Dictionary*, the earliest citation for this legislative sense is in the 1718 correspondence of the Scottish theologian Robert Wodrow: "Another act was passed . . . that all appeals should be brought up and tabled before the Bills, within three days after the Assembly sit down." Its source is the 1646 phrase *upon the table*, meaning "under consideration."

In American usage, however, the verb *table* took the opposite meaning in the mid-1800s of "to put away or postpone discussion," a synonym of the verb *shelve*. This sense of delay was commented on by London's *Daily Telegraph* in 1866: "To table a resolution has nearly the same effect in America as the order to read a bill 'this day six months' has in England."

Leaving a proposal *to lie on the table* led to this sense of postponing indefinitely. The Archives of New Jersey show this political delaying tactic as early as 1744: "The House of Representatives . . . would not commit it [a bill] but ordered it to be on the table."

Confusion still exists about the dual meanings, particularly when an American politician uses the primarily British sense. On "The MacNeil/Lehrer NewsHour" in 1985, Senator Sam Nunn said of a U.S.-Soviet summit, "The good news from the Soviets is that at last they are tabling something."

For another word with opposite meanings, see OVERSIGHT.

take a walk leave the party after a dispute.

The phrase entered the political language with Al Smith's comment after the renomination of FDR in 1936: "I guess I'll have to take a walk." Democrats lashed back at him with his own symbol: "The Brown Derby has gone high hat."

Those who BOLT—a racing term—are called MUGWUMPS—an Indian term—and *soreheads,* from the expression "mad as a bear with a sore head." An *Albany* (N.Y.) *Weekly Argus* correspondent wrote in 1848: "I have just returned from a ringed, striped, and speckled 'sore-head' demonstration at

Sharon Springs," in regard to the formation of the Free Soil party.

Bolters have been denounced by party regulars as "shreakers" (now obsolete) determined to "rule or ruin" (still in use). To *bolt* and to *take a walk* and to *change stripes* is to make an (almost) irrevocable decision to *cross the street* to the other party; to *sit it out* or to *go fishing* means to remain within the party without supporting—but not publicly rejecting—its candidate in a particular election. To go OFF THE RESERVATION is to take a short, temporary walk, opposing a candidate of one's own party with the intention of returning to the fold after the election.

take her by the hand. See STAND IN THE DOORWAY.

Tammany tiger symbol of big-city machines.

The Society of Tammany was a fraternal organization which controlled the New York Democratic party from the middle of the nineteenth century to the middle of the twentieth: often corrupt, sometimes effective, it was the prototype of all urban political machines in the U.S. and remains the best known today.

At its height, the motto of its leadership might well have been the remark made by Tammany leader George Washington Plunkitt: "I seen my opportunities and I took 'em."

The organization was founded in 1789 by New Yorkers who thought they saw a dangerous drift toward aristocracy in the popularity among the wealthier and wellborn of such societies as St. Andrew's. The Society, named after a Delaware chief famed for his sagacity—Chief Tamany, or more likely, Tamanend—dedicated itself to the defense of democracy. At the beginning of the nineteenth century, with Aaron Burr's help, it became the most efficient political organization of the day.

Legend has it that the tiger symbol came from a stuffed tiger's head on the front of a fire engine used by Tammany in parades; cartoonist Thomas Nast popularized the tiger symbol in his attacks on the Tweed Ring, which is believed to have stolen anywhere from $200 to $300 million in its heyday.

Those who thought Nast's attacks and the subsequent exposures meant the end of Tammany were mistaken. "Honest John" Kelly took over, creating the classic structure of absolute, unquestioning autocracy which was inherited by Richard Croker and later by Charles Murphy.

Reformers were in continual battle with Tammany; nearby boroughs were determined to keep their minions out. In 1876 R. G. Ingersoll said, "Tammany Hall bears the same relation to a penitentiary as a Sunday-school to the church." And in Brooklyn, the motto was: "The Tiger shall not cross the Bridge."

In modern times, Carmine De Sapio did much to reform the autocratic system—and cause his own downfall—by bringing about the direct election of district leaders by the RANK AND FILE. His successors have tried to stress the name "New York County Democratic Organization," as if Tammany were not the name of the club. Cartoonists, however, have too much invested in the tiger to let it die. But now the tiger, as drawn on most editorial pages, has lost much of its ferocity and usually appears battered and bandaged, but still alive.

See SACHEM; PAPER TIGER.

tantamount to election as much as elected.

There must be an unwritten law prohibiting the use of the following: "Nomination in that solidly partisan district is the *equivalent* of election," or "being nominated there is as much as being elected." Equivalent to, as much as, the same as, equal to, amounts to— all are crushed under the heel of the overwhelming political cliché, "tantamount to election."

In February 1993, the *Chicago Tribune* wrote of local primaries: "In both elections, victory in the primary is tantamount to election in April."

Once the tanta is mounted, Election Day is a formality; the political pundit's favorite bromide rides triumphantly into the jungle of jargon. An amusing election-night parlor game is to count the number of times "tantamount to election" is used on television, a competition more rewarding to the viewer than seeing who calls the winners first on the basis of the fewest returns.

Only ridicule can break up such a rigidly stereotyped phrase; for the foreseeable future, "tantamount" will remain as close to "election" as "unmitigated" remains wedded to "gall."

taps and bugs electronic eavesdropping equipment.

A "tap," short for "wiretap," means an intercept placed on a telephone; a "bug" is a tiny transmitter designed to send conversations to a receiver elsewhere. To be "wired" means to be outfitted with a "bug" so as to transmit a conversation to a receiver out of sight. Confusion is caused when a "bug" is used in a "tap"—by placing a transmitter in a telephone, the conversation is effectively tapped, though no wire intercept is made.

"To have a tap in" does not necessarily mean to have a wiretap monitoring somebody; frequently the phrase means to have nonelectronic access to a leaker, the meaning taken from the way sap is tapped from a tree.

Lexicographer Peter Tamony found an early use of the word in Civil War literature, referring to a telegraph wire.

"Tapping the wires at Lebanon Junction," ran an account of Morgan's raid of 1863, "we learned from intercepted despatches that the garrison at Louisville was much alarmed, and in expectation of immediate attack."

In 1878, two years after Alexander Graham Bell invented the telephone, George B. Preston warned: "The observations made in the course of these experiments convinced those present that the telephone presents facilities for the dangerous practice of tapping the wire, which may make it useful or dangerous, according as it is used for proper or dangerous purposes."

Mr. Tamony wrote the author: "Telephone wiretapping, according to the New York police, dates from 1895 when a former employee of the N.Y. Telephone company walked into headquarters to suggest the possibilities of such information gathering and surveillance. However, another story bases such methods from a chance discovery of the 'Extension telephone' in a home by a telephone company employee in 1909, this man becoming the 'King of the Wiretappers' in the service of the U.S. government from 1920 to 1949. During World War I, eavesdropping was widely encouraged, the government tapping thousands of lines from a central office switchboard set up in the N.Y. Customs House. Whenever a suspected alien lifted his receiver a light flashed, and a stenographer recorded the conversation."

The author, whose home telephone was tapped on White House orders by the FBI in 1969, later obtained the order from one agent to another for "technical surveillance," which was the government euphemism for wiretapping. Searching for earlier political use, the author was directed to William Roscoe Thayer's biography of Theodore Roosevelt, written in 1919, in the section about the Republican convention in Chicago in 1912: "Roosevelt had not intended to appear at the Convention, but when he discovered that the long-distance telephone from Chicago to Oyster Bay, by which his managers conferred with him, was being tapped, he changed his mind."

The term "bugged," in the sense of "electronically overheard," came into use in the twenties. In A. J. Pollock's *The Underworld Speaks* (San Francisco, 1935) an entry reads: "Bugged, a room in which a dictaphone has been installed by the police." Speculated Mr. Tamony: "As anything that impeded a criminal process was a nuisance, a *bugbear*, calculated to drive a burglar crazy, or bugs, these perhaps are the basis of the allusion to sound detection and wiring."

For a different etymology of BUG, see that entry.

tariffs. See KENNEDY ROUND.

task force committee given a military name to make it sound vigorous.

The appointment of a committee has long been an effective political gambit to avoid direct action, but many people began to bridle at the word—"another committee" became a derisive term implying delay, unfiled reports, and meandering discussion leading up blind alleys.

Television commentator Richard Harkness took note of this prevalent attitude in 1960. "When it comes to facing up to serious problems," he wrote, "each candidate will pledge to appoint a committee. And what is a committee? A group of the unwilling, picked from the unfit, to do the unnecessary. But it all sounds great in a campaign speech." See BLUE RIBBON PANEL.

John F. Kennedy fulfilled the promises to appoint committees, but he avoided the static word. Within two weeks after his election, the former naval officer dictated a memorandum to his aides on Latin America ("Who should chair the task force—what about Berle?") and Africa ("We should set up a similar task force . . .") and foreign aid ("We should set up a task force on the distribution of our agricultural surpluses abroad . . .").

In 1960, as "task force" reached full flower, two linguistics professors discussed the matter in an issue of *American Speech.* Acheson L. Hench of the University of Virginia revealed a usage that he had cherished for eleven years waiting for the phrase to mature: a clipping from the March 1, 1949, *Richmond* (Va.) *Times Dispatch:* "The work stoppage [the strike of garbage and trash collectors] resulted from an attempt by the city to try out a 'task force' system of collections. Under this plan, workers are assigned a certain route to be covered each day. When they complete their route, they can go home, regardless of how long it has taken . . . if they fail to get over the entire route in one regular work day, they must catch up the next day. The 'task force' system was to have been tried by 21 collectors in South Richmond . . ."

Professor Thomas Pyles of Northwestern University performed a linguistic feat by using twelve space-age clichés in a single intelligible sentence: "*Task force* and *breakthrough* are attractive additions to the vocabulary of those who are geared to the space age, who spearhead drives, set target dates, make spot checks, give rundowns and fill-ins—in short, of those who take an overall view instead of merely a comprehensive one, and who give the rest of us the advantage of their thinking on whatever is truly meaningful in the American way of life."

In the Justice Department, a committee of lawyers set up in a region to combat organized crime is called a "strike force"—like "task force," a naval term.

In the Clinton White House, the preferred term became WORKING GROUP.

tax and spend. See SPEND AND SPEND . . .

tax and tax. See SPEND AND SPEND . . .

tax revolt a movement to roll back rapidly increasing property taxes; more generally, an uprising of middle-class taxpayers against the rise in the cost of government.

Who shall be taxed how much has always been a most sensitive political subject. Liberals, sensing voter discontent about the rise in taxes in the seventies, concentrated on the unfairness of the tax system: "tax inequities." In this way, they sought to channel the resentment along populist lines: the reason our tax system is "a disgrace to the human race," as candidate Jimmy Carter put it, was that rich people were getting through the tax "loopholes" and the average man had to pay the rich man's share.

The phrase "taxpayer's revolt" was originally popularized around this unfairness idea. In 1968 Joseph Barr—longtime Undersecretary of the Treasury, appointed to the top job in President Johnson's final months in office—created a stir by testifying to Congress that more than 240 people who earned over a quarter-million dollars were paying no taxes, thanks to the "loopholes" (otherwise called incentives) in the tax system. He predicted that resentment at this kind of inequity would cause a "taxpayer's revolt."

The Nixon Administration, in its 1969 tax-reform act, worked out a "minimum tax" schedule that made it difficult for anyone to completely avoid tax payments, but the stress on unfairness was continued by Democratic candidates George McGovern in 1972 and Jimmy Carter in 1976 (see THREE-MARTINI LUNCH).

However, what ultimately caused the "tax revolt" of 1978 was not resentment at unfairness so much as anger by middle-class taxpayers at the rising level of taxation. Many felt their taxes provided too much welfare for the nonworking, and too much work for "bureaucrats."

"Tax-bracket creep" was one element: with a DOUBLE DIGIT inflation, these middle-income taxpayers found themselves pushed into higher tax brackets on the same purchasing power. In the state of California, soaring property taxes were the trigger: as property assessments rose, many retired homeowners—whose income was fixed, or who were living on savings, the value of which was eroding—were forced to move to cheaper neighborhoods, which seemed to them the antithesis of the American dream.

A movement to lower the tax rates substantially and permanently had been brewing in the mid-seventies. Arthur Laffer, a USC economist, interested Congressman Jack Kemp (R-N.Y.) and others in the "Laffer curve," a chart showing the relationship between tax rates and revenue production: it was his idea that the current high tax rates depressed incentive and growth, and lowered revenues—defeating its own purpose. This approach provided the philosophical framework to a drive to cut tax rates that would otherwise be suspect as "irresponsible."

In June of 1978, despite the united opposition of California Governor Edmund G. Brown and most of the press and political leadership in that state, "Proposition 13"—the Jarvis-Gann initiative to reduce property taxes to 1 percent of market value—passed by a 2-to-1 landslide. Howard Jarvis, a veteran tax lobbyist, appeared on the cover of *Time,* and both *Time* and *Newsweek* featured the same phrase on their covers: "Tax Revolt!"

"The cry of pain from voters," grumbled the *New York Times* editorially, "has made tax cutting a new political credo. And the theory offered by the Laffer Curve makes the idea even more seductive . . . unfortunately, with inflation running close to 10 percent, the Federal Government cannot afford to cut taxes . . ."

Which was the way of FISCAL INTEGRITY: holding down the deficits by maintaining tax rates? Or cutting taxes on the theory that this would ultimately increase revenues, an anomaly that had taken place in the early sixties? In the "tax revolt" (the preferred shortening of "taxpayer's revolt"), liberals, worried about a cut in services to the poor, were surprised to find some NEW CONSERVATIVES willing to take the chance of high short-term deficits. They suspected rightly that the conservatives would call for a cut in government spending if the deficit stayed too high too long.

Thus the original "revolt" over tax *unfairness* never took place; instead, the voters in California rebelled against the *levels* of taxation. Many political leaders saw this as evidence that voters wanted to SEND THEM A MESSAGE: more than tax reform, what was wanted was tax reduction, which was given the votes during the Reagan Administration. The "revolt" was put down somewhat during the Bush Administration (see READ MY LIPS) and subdued, for a time at least, during the Clinton years.

tax sharing collection of revenues by the federal government, returned directly to the state governments without federal control of state expenditures.

Grants-in-aid from the federal government to the states include close supervision of spending. The special attraction to states of *tax sharing* is that it eliminates federal control of the way federally collected money is spent, while removing from states the political stigma of tax collection.

Walter Heller, first Kennedy's and then Johnson's chairman of the Council of Economic Advisers, began to promote the plan in 1964. As the economy produced greater tax revenues, he reasoned, the extra money could be used for increased federal spending (and further undesirable centralization) *or* tax reduction (not likely) *or* reduction of the national debt (deflationary and least likely of all). A fourth alternative could be the return of a portion of the federal tax revenues to the states for expenditures as they saw fit.

Heller took as his text a White House press release promising exploration of new "methods of channeling federal revenues to states and localities which will reinforce their independence while enlarging their capacity to serve their citizens."

Expanding on this theme, Heller held: "Federal grants to serve highly specialized objectives have proliferated in recent years. And once established, they do not yield gracefully to change or abolition. Unless this trend is reversed, federal aids may weave a web of particularism, complexity, and federal direction which will significantly inhibit a state's freedom of movement. The picture of Gulliver and the Lilliputians comes to mind."

After flirting with the idea as part of his CREATIVE FEDERALISM, President Johnson backed away from tax sharing, partly because of the growing needs of the war in Vietnam, partly because Heller's TRIAL BALLOON had drawn fire from some liberals. Leon Keyserling (like most economists, he called the plan *revenue sharing*) pointed out: "The more we become *one* nation rather than *fifty* states, the more our economic and social problems require national treatment."

Republicans in Congress and in the state capitols loved the idea and took it to heart. They pointed to the cost efficiency of collection, and more important to the renewal of supervision of spending by "government closest to the people"—i.e., the states and localities, where Republicans traditionally fared better than on the national level.

Richard Nixon preferred the term "revenue sharing" and made it the keystone of his "New American Revolution"—the method by which he proposed to "reverse the flow of power in this country."

In his 1973 budget message, he wrote: "Revenue sharing has been debated at length. . . . The states and cities urgently require this aid; individual Americans need it for everything from improved law enforcement to tax relief." Democrats in Congress, seeing this as a diminution of their power, refused to share the President's enthusiasm, and passed a bill for a limited amount of string-free aid to states.

Twenty years later, when Bill Clinton proposed a form of revenue sharing in an economic stimulus bill, Republicans behind Minority Leader Bob Dole described it as "pork" (see PORK BARREL) and successfully blocked it.

teach-in. See SIT-IN.

technocrat a scientist or engineer in a position of power, making policy in areas that appear too difficult for the laymen to judge.

"How unlike Stalin and Khrushchev," wrote the *Saturday Evening Post* during Alexei Kosygin's first visit to the U.S. in 1967, "is the quiet, rather dour technocrat Kosygin."

Technocracy was a movement that enjoyed a brief vogue in California early in the Depression. Coined in 1919 by William Henry Smythe in a call for a rule by technicians, it was popularized by disciples of Thorstein Veblen, using his 1921 book, *The Engineers and the Price System,* as their guide. The movement urged that government be placed in the hands of scientists and engineers ("But Hoover was an engineer" was one criticism); the end of the profit system; the application of all modern techniques and discoveries to the alleviation of human want; a working-age span from twenty-five years to forty-five years; and a work year of 132 hours.

Historian Robert Glass Cleland described technocracy as "a strange mixture, so far as the layman is qualified to judge, of scientific principles, mumbo jumbo, and skillful publicity." Its immediate successor was "Utopianism," which Cleland called "a goulash of technocracy, State Socialism, the Ku Klux Klan, Populism, Pacifism, Evangelism and Voodoo." (Slogans for these kinds of goulash were "End Poverty in California" and "Thirty Dollars Every Thursday.")

After a period of disuse, "technocrat" came back into use in the fifties to describe members of the MILITARY-INDUSTRIAL COMPLEX who deal with the expenditures of huge sums for weapons systems. The newer use of the word is simply a shortening of "technical bureaucrat," or administrator of scientific programs for industry and government. As with most words ending in -crat, it is mildly pejorative: though *democrat* is good, *autocrat, aristocrat, bureaucrat* (see BUREAUCRACY), and *technocrat* are suspect.

The underlying suspicion of technocrats was expressed by Harold Macmillan in 1950: "Fearing the weakness of democracy men have often sought safety in technocrats. There is nothing new in this. It is as old as Plato. But frankly the idea is not attractive to the British. . . . We have not overthrown the divine right of kings to fall down before the divine right of experts."

See NEW CLASS.

Teflon-coated Presidency

a President's ability to deflect charges of sleaze or corruption aimed at his Administration.

Representative Patricia Schroeder, Democrat of Colorado, first used the phrase *the Teflon-coated Presidency* in the summer of 1983 to refer to Ronald Reagan's ability to overcome charges of corruption in his Administration (see SLEAZE FACTOR).

Noting that Teflon allows eggs to slide easily out of a frying pan, Representative Schroeder told the House: "Mr. Speaker, after carefully watching Ronald Reagan, he is attempting a great breakthrough in political technology—he has been perfecting the Teflon-coated Presidency." (The Du Pont trade name *Teflon* comes from poly*tetrafl*uorethylene, a coating bonded to metal pans to keep food from sticking.)

Influenced by *sleaze factor*, the Teflon phrase took on the parallel form of *Teflon factor*. Tim Carrington wrote in the *Wall Street Journal* in April 1984 about "the Teflon factor, which refers to the President's apparent political immunity to most of his aides' mistakes or misdeeds . . . . Ronald Reagan's ability to deflect embarrassment seems nothing short of uncanny."

The antonym of this term uses another product name, in *Velcro Presidency*. That phrase, from the trademarked *Velcro* for a fabric tape with adhesive qualities, provided the label for criticism that stuck to the Bush Administration.

tell it like it is an exhortation by student demonstrators and crowds to their leaders, demanding an articulation of the audience's own feelings.

Evidence of the New Left's faith in "participatory democracy" (or fetish of leadership-rejection) was that its most popular battle cry was directed not from speaker to crowd, but from crowd to speaker. Though this was hardly new—"GIVE 'EM HELL, HARRY!" was one precursor—it indicated a rare and powerful two-way communication between spokesman and group. In Arab countries, demonstrations have long been conducted in a singsong, speaker-shouts, crowd-shouts-back fashion. In his MARTIN, BARTON AND FISH speech, FDR encouraged the crowd to anticipate repetition of the slogan and join in. But rarely in U.S. politics has the rank and file been so much an organized, disciplined, practiced part of a demonstration as in the civil rights and commingled New Left movement, with its chanting, clapping, "Jim, Crow, [*clap, clap*] Must, Go!" This participation has extended to speech-listening, where the listener encourages the speaker with approving shouts.

Alert cartoonists and writers in 1967 picked up the expression and used or parodied it. A cartoon in the *New York Times Book Review* showed a long-haired, "with-it" teenager calling to his balding, bespectacled father sitting at a typewriter: "Write it like it is, Pop!"

Profilist Thomas B. Morgan, writing in *Life* about playwright Edward Albee, concluded: "One can only hope that one day—perhaps even next season—he will find a new spark that will enable him once again to tell it like it is."

Grammarians would render the slogan "Tell it the way it is," or "Tell it as it is," but standard usage was dealt a near-fatal blow in the U.S. by the R. J. Reynolds Tobacco Company's slogan, "Winston Tastes Good Like a Cigarette Should."

The expression began to fade in the late sixties, to be replaced by "Right on!"

tennis shoes. See LITTLE OLD LADIES IN TENNIS SHOES.

terrorism   persuasion by fear; the intimidation of society by a small group, using as its weapon that society's repugnance at the murder of innocents.

Terrorisme may have originated with the Jacobins of the French Revolution. *Le Néologiste Français* (published in 1796) claimed that the extremists had coined the term about themselves and used it proudly, but soon after the "reign of terror," the word was a term of abuse with a connotation of criminality. In 1795 British statesman Edmund Burke wrote of "thousands of those hell hounds called terrorists" that afflicted the French people.

Although it temporarily had a secondary meaning of ALARMIST, the word "terrorist" traveled from the particular Jacobins to a system using fear of sudden and unexpectable violence to coerce others into obedience, or—in modern times—to trigger such official repression as to encourage revolution.

The names of sects employing terrorism have become synonyms for violence or irrationality. In A.D. 70, the *zealots* in Palestine had a group called the "sicarii" who attacked crowds on holidays; in the eleventh century, the *assassins* roamed Persia and Syria, killing political leaders systematically, always with a dagger as a part of a sacramental act; in the nineteenth century, the *thugs* in India always strangled their political victims with a silk tie.

In his book *Terrorism* (1977), Walter Laqueur focused on the dilemma that faces the targets of political fear: "The debate on whether or not one should compromise with terrorists has lasted a long time. Concessions may be advisable in some exceptional cases; consistent conciliation of terrorism on the other hand is bound to claim a higher toll in human life in the long run than resisting it . . . societies facing a determined terrorist onslaught will opt for a hard-line policy in any case." The unanswerable question that faces all students of terrorism: What to do when a terrorist group builds or acquires a nuclear weapon, and the means of its delivery?

The American use of the word was traced by Sperber and Trittschuh to an issue of *Atlantic Monthly* in 1858: "Every form of terrorism [in Kansas], to which tyrants all alike instinctively resort to disarm resistance to their will, was launched at the property, the lives, and the happiness of the defenseless settlers." In 1868 *Harper's Weekly* headed an article about Democratic tactics to win Southern elections as "Political terrorism."

The words that describe terrorists reflect the bias of the describer. A *bomb thrower*, once a description of the bearded, wild-eyed anarchists of the 1890s, is now a term of amused contempt; a *partisan* connotes an irregular army unit, with a positive connotation lingering from the anti-Nazi partisans of Yugoslavia; a *guerrilla* is also positive, a hit-and-run defender of land against an invader, with the word used in Wellington's dispatches from the Peninsula campaign; *commando* is usually a self-description by a force striking in secret, and though it dates to the eighteenth century, is colored by its use for shock troops in Great Britain in World War II; *skyjacker* is an American neologism based on "hijacker," and is usually taken to mean a single deranged person unless further modified; *freedom fighter* is the most laudatory of descriptions, with a value judgment clear in the name, coined in a John Lehmann poem of 1942: "Their freedom-fighters staining red the snow."

Only the appellation *terrorist* is rejected by users of terror; the word is unqualifiedly negative, even though the philosophy can be construed to be—in the words of Wilhelm Weitling, the first German Communist—"founding the kingdom of heaven by unleashing the forces of hell."

testimonial dinners. See RUBBER-CHICKEN CIRCUIT.

that dog won't hunt the action or approach won't work; a contemptuous dismissal of an idea's viability.

This Southernism is taken from the image of an ineffectual hound (though some say it can refer to a wise hunting dog that refuses to follow a false trail). The term is defined by Robert Hendrickson in *Whistlin' Dixie: A Dictionary of Southern Expressions* as "that idea or theory isn't logical, doesn't wash."

The phrase was popularized by, and is still associated with, Lyndon Johnson, especially in the reminiscences of his aide, Jack Valenti. The idiomatic expression was used in print by the *Washington Post* in 1984: *Post* staff writer Bill Peterson quoted Jefferson County Judge Mitch McConnell, a Kentucky Republican, who dismissed speculation that rural voters would prefer the Democrats because of the religion issue: "That dog don't hunt in Kentucky."

More recent speakers have attempted to fix the grammar of the Southern saying. New York State Senator John Marchi used the dismissive words in 1985, saying of a Reagan tax-revision plan, "This dog won't hunt." (The rhyming contraction *won't* replaces the ungrammatical use of *don't*.)

After his unsuccessful run for Vice President, Senator Lloyd Bentsen of Texas criticized George Bush in 1989 for attempting to blame the Democratic Congress for problems with the economy. Said Bentsen, "From one Texan to another, Mr. President, this message should be clear to you: That old dog won't hunt."

Always expressed negatively, the saying is sometimes couched in uncertainty, with the dialectal flavor drained out. During a 1992 District of Columbia election, Joslyn Williams, president of a District union group, criticized a campaign strategy: "As they say in Southern politics, I don't think that dog will hunt."

That Man in the White House

a denunciation of Franklin Roosevelt by those too furious with him to even mention his name; now, an exasperated reference to any President.

FDR, hailed by Democrats in 1936 as "The Gallant Leader" and "The Gideon of Democracy," was called by Republicans "The New Deal Caesar," "The Raw Dealocrat," "The American Dictator," "The Feather-Duster of Dutchess County," "Kangaroosevelt," "Franklin Deficit Roosevelt," and most often "That Man in the White House."

Frank Sullivan, collecting clichés for *The New Yorker* in the early days of the New Deal, headed his list with "That Madman in the White House" and "That Fellow Down in Washington," who was admonished "You can't spend your way out of a Depression" and "Our children's children will be paying." Jokes of the time were "There's only six Dwarfs now . . . Dopey's in the White House" and "Why is a WPA worker like King Solomon? . . . He takes his pick and goes to bed."

Many commuter lines had what some of their riders called "Assassination Specials"; Robert Bendiner reported: ". . . the President of the United States was referred to by the kindlier passengers as 'That Man,' a designation useful for those who didn't want to be nasty in front of children and who couldn't bear to pronounce the dread name." When Elsa Maxwell threw a "Pet Hates Ball," guests were warned not to come dressed as "that man" with a cigarette holder because the ball would be jammed with imitation Roosevelts.

Like many epithets, it was soon adopted in an affectionate manner by the target's supporters. When Bronx Democratic leader Ed Flynn accepted the post of national chairman, he went home to break the news to his wife that they would have to move to Washington. "That silly grin on your face," Mrs. Flynn said to him before he said anything, "tells me 'that man' has talked you into it."

The phrase did not vanish with Roosevelt. It is now used occasionally to refer to any President who must accept criticism with the job. Political scientist Richard Neustadt wrote in 1960 that the public's "unreality" was an unseen enemy of the prestige and power of any President: "the groundless hopes, the unexpected happenings, the unaccepted outcomes that members of their public feel in daily life and relate, somehow, anyhow, to That Man in the White House."

See TRAITOR TO HIS CLASS.

the man who the nominee; the person proposed for a nomination.

Speculation about a party designee usually includes the phrase "Who will be 'the man who'?" The phrase is taken from bombastic nomination speeches; since the speaker knows that the signal for a demonstration will be mention of the name of the man he is proposing, he usually refrains from giving the signal until the end of his speech. Throughout the nominating speech, of course, the audience knows who "the man who" is.

Until 1876, nominations at national political conventions were mercifully brief: in the 1860 Republican convention, Abraham Lincoln was put in nomination by Norman B. Judd of Illinois with a single sentence.

The oratorical dam burst in 1876 with the nomination of James G. Blaine by the Republicans. Robert G. Ingersoll of Illinois gave Blaine the title of "The Plumed Knight" in this classic "man-who":

> Our country . . . asks for a man who has the audacity of genius; asks for a man who is the grandest combination of heart, conscience and brain beneath her flag. . . .
> Like an armed warrior, like a plumed knight, James G. Blaine marched down the halls of the American Congress and threw his shining lance full and fair against the brazen foreheads of the defamers of our country and the maligners of his honor. . . .
> Gentlemen of the convention . . . Illinois nominates for the next president of the United States that prince of parliamentarians, that leader of leaders, James G. Blaine.

"The Man" (without the who) is a reference of blacks to white men; of staffers to their leader; and in Washington, D.C., of politicians to the President.

themeless pudding   unfocused discussion; argument lacking punch or clear purpose.

Winston Churchill is credited with introducing this metaphor in response to an unpalatable dish set before him. Lord Home's 1976 *The Way the Wind Blows,* according to the *Oxford Dictionary of Quotations*, relates Churchill's comment: "Take away that pudding—it has no theme."

In covering one of Ronald Reagan's major speeches of 1983, this columnist turned Churchill's clauses into a compact noun phrase: "The themeless pudding called this year's State of the Union address was a series of banalities intended to ingratiate the President with his political opposition."

Richard Cohen of the *Washington Post* echoed the expression in an editorial comment on the 1988 election: "The current campaign is a themeless pudding."

By 1992, this tasty trope was part of the vocabulary of political pointlessness. Helen Dewar of the *Washington Post* proposed a recipe for policy proposals: "Democrats have always had more of a domestic agenda than Bush. But it tended to resemble a themeless pudding—a dash of transportation, a pinch of energy and a big dollop from the pork barrel."

there you go again "you're wrong again"; a dismissal that suggests one's opponent repeatedly presents misleading or erroneous information.

Ronald Reagan popularized this apparently friendly dismissal in his October debate with Jimmy Carter during the 1980 Presidential campaign. When Carter tried to paint Reagan as a warmonger—likely to be trigger-happy in the event of a nuclear confrontation—Reagan began his denial of the charge by saying, "Now there you go again, Mr. President."

At the time, the *Washington Post* offered a baseball analogy:

> Softballer Jimmy Carter served up a fat pitch that gave Reagan a chance to knock it out of the ballpark and then plaster an engaging Irish grin on his face and hold it determinedly in place until the TV cameras had made a "freeze frame" of it . . . . He was just a nice, good-humored, friendly, peace-loving fellow who kept saying, patiently and politely, "Now there you go again, Mr. President."

The term has remained current. When Republican Minority Leader Bob Dole did not support the Bush campaign's anti-Perot attacks during the 1992 campaign, Michael Kramer of *Time* magazine wrote: "While Dole's stance was unwelcome, there was only the slightest there-he-goes-again head-shaking at the White House, for everyone knows that Dole is a special case."

The power of the folksily dismissive phrase should not be underestimated. The pollster Louis Harris recalled the 1980 election for the *Boston Globe* in 1992: "Reagan was behind until October 10 and the debate, when he said to Carter, 'There you go again.'"

***the* speech** the standard stump speech developed during a campaign, compressing all the best issues and punch lines into a single adaptable package.

When *the* speech begins, reporters roll up their eyes and put away their pencils; they have heard it a hundred times. It contains the applause-pulling and laugh-getting lines of a dozen other speeches made in the same campaign by the same candidate. The difference is that it is not a television speech, with the necessity for new material; it is this particular candidate's particular gospel, refined to a rhythm comfortable for him, edited by practice and crowd reaction, punching away at the issues with pet phrases ("that do-nothing Eightieth Congress . . . I think we have to get America moving again . . . that's your money he's spending, not his . . . the brotherhood of Man and the Fatherhood of God . . .").

A half-dozen writers may write speeches, but nobody, not even the candidate, writes what politicians call *the* speech. It seems to evolve by itself, and is carried around like sourdough to mix in with local jokes, timely references to newsbreaks and deferences to local party politicians.

When a candidate does not have his own *the* speech by the end of a campaign, he has not figured out in his own mind what the campaign was really all about.

In 1993, a *Washington Post* editorial stated: "If President Clinton continues to encounter difficulties in his fight over the budget, you can count on hearing more about welfare reform. That's because Mr. Clinton, first as a candidate and then as President, has always trotted out his excellent talk about welfare whenever he's run into political trouble. That's fine, but the next time he gives 'the speech,' he ought to be closer to achieving something real."

thinking about the unthinkable.
See UNTHINKABLE THOUGHTS.

think piece. See BACKGROUNDER; DOPE STORY; THUMBSUCKER.

think tank the brain; or a group of advisers; or, specifically, a research organization developing plans and projects for government and defense-connected industries.

Harry Truman, on his eightieth birthday, in 1964, used the phrase in its original sense of "brain," hoping to live until ninety, but only "if the old think tank is working."

The phrase enjoyed a brief period as substitute for BRAIN TRUST as politicians turned to colleges for TASK FORCES of academicians to provide new approaches to solving new and old problems. This meaning was superseded with the emergence of the RAND Corporation, the Hudson Institute, and similar institutions, where physical and social scientists can exercise and socialize in pleasant surroundings while doing profound research and planning on government or commercial assignments.

RAND, an acronym for "Research and Development," was set up in 1946 by Air Force General "Hap" Arnold. (Some say the name came from "random sample," which the firm used in its early research days.) He recognized the need for scientists to work in civilian surroundings, but wanted to keep their brainpower available to the military establishment. "Observers impressed with the high-level intellectual atmosphere at RAND," *Ramparts* magazine editor Sol Stern wrote, "have often referred to the Corporation as 'a university without students.' It would be more accurate to say that RAND, like other think tanks, has become a kind of halfway house between the university and the Department of Defense."

In a week-long series of articles on "U.S. Think Tanks: A $2 Billion Industry," *New York Times* reporter Richard Reeves wrote in 1967:

The work of think tanks is often similar to work done by universities, industrial research-and-development departments and management consultants. Although the term is used arbitrarily, the think tanks have one thing in common: all are groups of men with impressive credentials who conduct interdisciplinary research.

In politics as well as science, the necessity for solitude and time to figure out plans and programs in the midst of hectic campaigns is always a problem, and many politicians envy the scientists at "think tanks" their reflective opportunity. When Senator David Hill of New York was told that Democratic candidate William Jennings Bryan was making up to sixteen campaign speeches a day, he wondered pointedly: "When does he think?"

The term's popularity is underscored by a computerized Nexis search revealing more than a thousand uses in print. How old is the term? A dictionary of ancient Greek phrases includes a term translated as "a think shop," attributed to the Greek playwright Aristophanes.

See SCENARIO.

third-party movement a bolter's extreme.

Third parties engender no warmth in the hearts of most professional politicians. Thomas E. Dewey, who had his troubles first with the American Labor party and then with the Liberal party, both exclusively New York organizations, said that such sectional parties "have proved to be a menace to responsible government elsewhere." On the national scene, however, Dewey found occasional justification for third parties. Historian Richard Hofstadter noted that their principal role is to provide ideas when the two major parties have stagnated. "Third parties," he wrote, "are like bees: Once they have stung, they die."

The POPULISTS, most successful of the third parties, expressed a radical, primarily rural, revolt against the uncontrolled power of industry in general and the railroad in particular. They won twenty-two electoral votes in 1892 but they, together with such parts of their platform as unlimited coinage of silver (cheap money) and avowed enmity to unfeeling business interests, were ultimately absorbed by the Democrats.

The income tax and the direct election of senators were Populist ideas; each came to pass a generation after the party died. Their influence in the West lingered among the Republicans as well, leading to the Progressive revolt against Eastern-dominated, Republican conservatism. The break came in the Progressive "Bull Moose" campaign of 1912: Theodore Roosevelt's stand at ARMAGEDDON divided Republicans and elected Woodrow Wilson.

Progressivism was the watchword again when liberals, disgusted with a contest in which both major parties seemed to vie as to which was the more conservative, scored some minimal success with Senator Robert La Follette of Wisconsin as their candidate. See DON'T WASTE YOUR VOTE.

In 1948 a potpourri of liberals, radicals, and disguised Communists again went to the people, headed by former Vice President Henry Wallace, who told his followers, "When the old parties rot, the people have a right to be heard through a new party."

In that same campaign there was still another party, the States Rights Democrats. They hoped that Governor Strom Thurmond of South Carolina, calling for racial segregation and political conservatism, could win enough support to throw the final presidential selection into the House of Representatives where, on a state-by-state count, the South might make its views dominate. This happened in 1824, denying Andrew Jackson the White House despite his plurality; the idea occurred in 1968 to George Wallace as well.

There is always a core around which a third-party movement can gather support. Those fearful of change or dissatisfied with its pace often agree with cockroach critic archy, of Don Marquis' *archy and mehitabel*, who answered the Announcer's question "Do you think the time is ripe for launching a third national political party in America?" with "It is more than ripe it is rotten."

In 1968, Alabama's George Wallace achieved 9 percent of the vote, making his 1972 plans a concern to both parties. (See SEND THEM A MESSAGE.) Such was the likelihood of his third-party campaign continuing, before an assassination attempt crippled him, that other splinter movements in the early seventies were automatically called "fourth parties." In 1992, Ross Perot's third party achieved nearly 20 percent of the vote cast, the highest percentage since Bull Moose days.

See BOLT; SPLINTER GROUP.

third-rate burglary. See NOBODY DROWNED AT WATERGATE.

third term. See VOICE FROM THE
SEWER; SMOKE SCREEN.

third world originally, nations—usu-
ally underdeveloped—that were not
aligned diplomatically with the FREE
WORLD of Western democracies or the
"Communist world"; later, the Arab-
African-Latin American-Indian bloc,
with which the People's Republic of
China often identifies.

The phrase was originally French
(tiers monde), in use to describe the
neutralists (see NEUTRALIST) in the
Cold War since the late forties. Alfred
Sauvy, the French sociologist who
died in 1990, was credited with coining
the phrase in 1952. As the *Barnhart
Dictionary of New English Since 1963*
points out, the reason for the archaic
tiers, rather than the modern French
troisième, is that the phrase is patterned after *tiers état,* or "Third Estate" (the commoners, who often
fought the first and second estates, the
king and clergy). See FOURTH ESTATE.
The idea behind "third world" was
that it would represent the common
man, standing independent of the first
and second worlds of established
power.

The phrase came into U.S. use in the
sixties. "The students, following the
gospel of Marcuse, look to the Third
World," wrote Philip Shabecoff in the
New York Times Magazine in a typical
late-sixties usage, "to Fidel Castro and
Ho Chi Minh, for salvation." "Third
Worlders" were Africans, Asians, or
Arabs.

However, with the oil-price increases
of the mid-seventies, some third-
world countries—Nigeria, Venezuela,
Saudi Arabia—became far more
wealthy, and lost some popular support among liberals in the U.S. In addition, when the "Group of 77" (as 126
nations in the UN called themselves)
demanded a "new world economic
order"—in effect, a redistribution of

wealth from "have" to "have-not" nations—and topped that with a UN
vote equating Zionism with RACISM,
the third world became a more pejorative label in the U.S.

With the end of the bipolar geopolitical world in 1990, a MULTIPOLAR
WORLD was spawned; the third world
became the South in a North-South relationship.

"The 'Third World' urgently needs
to be renamed," wrote Henry Grunwald in the Summer 1993 issue of *Foreign Affairs,* "and not only because the
'Second World' has collapsed. The inadequacy of a label covering everything from dysfunctional non-coun-
tries in Africa to emerging industrial
powers in South America indicates a
lack of press understanding and attention."

those who the amorphous armies of
the vaguely venal; a rhetorical device
that enables an attacker to ostenta-
tiously avoid naming names.

"There are those who say . . ." This
frequently employed technique in political discourse enables a speaker to
lump together moderate adversaries
with extremists, thereby discrediting
the moderates; and to characterize an
opposing position in its most easily
attackable terms.

"Those who" are never right; they
are often dangerous, if unwitting, tools
of sinister forces; and they are always
triumphed over. Their only supporters
are "some," as in "Some say . . ."
See STRAW MAN.

thought police hypersensitive censors; an attack phrase on intrusive attempts to enforce conformity to
POLITICALLY CORRECT ideas.

Newsweek used the term *thought police* as the headline of its December 24,
1990, issue, the cover story of which
was about political correctness on
campus. "After the *Newsweek* story

came out," Lynne Cheney, chairman of the National Endowment for the Humanities, told the television interviewer Jim Lehrer, "I was called by more than one representative of the media saying we're doing a story about PC; we want you to represent the thought police."

In 1993, a University of Pennsylvania student, trying to study late one evening, called a noisy group of fellow students "water buffalo" who belonged in a zoo. The university threatened him with expulsion for what some claimed was an ethnic slur; after the noisemaking group withdrew its complaint, the student's attorney suggested "the university do some serious soul searching about its politicizing of normal student interactions, about its speech and thought police . . . ."

In his book *Kindly Inquisitors: The New Attacks on Free Thought*, Jonathan Rauch extended the metaphor to *thought vigilantes*, stressing the unofficial nature of the "police."

The phrase originated as a colloquial name for the Special Higher Police (*Tokubetsu Koto Keisatsu*) of pre-World War II Japan, whose mission was to imprison political dissenters. After the war, in 1945, the *Baltimore Sun* wrote of "an order imposing freedom of speech, thought, religion and assembly on the Japanese people, and requiring the immediate liberation of those imprisoned for political offenses by the so-called 'thought police.'"

It was George Orwell's novel *Nineteen Eighty-Four*, which appeared in 1949, that popularized the phrase as the name (capitalized) of the dreaded police force in the fictional totalitarian state, whose function was to suppress freedom of thought. The term was applied during the Cold War to the Soviet secret police. Its current use as an attack phrase is intended to evoke an image of mindless suppressors of free speech.

thousand days phrase associated with the length of the Kennedy Administration, from January 20, 1961, to November 22, 1963, or 1,037 days.

The phrase, taken from Kennedy's inaugural address, was quoted five days after his assassination by President Johnson before a joint session of Congress:

> On the twentieth day of January in 1961, John F. Kennedy told his countrymen that our national work would not be finished "in the first thousand days, nor in the life of this Administration, nor even perhaps in our lifetime on this planet. But," he said, "let us begin."
>
> Today, in this moment of new resolve, I would say to all my fellow Americans, let us continue.

Johnson dropped a "one" in quoting Kennedy, probably for rhetorical cause. Kennedy used "one thousand days" to compare with "one hundred days" as follows:

"All this will not be finished in the first one hundred days. Nor will it be finished in the first one thousand days . . ."

Arthur Schlesinger, Jr., chose *A Thousand Days* for the title of his book on the Kennedy Administration.

See HUNDRED DAYS; "LET US CONTINUE."

thousand percent less than total support; fulsome verbal backing as abandonment is being planned.

As Senator George McGovern's 1972 presidential campaign got under way, the secret mental health record of his running mate, Senator Thomas Eagleton, was revealed: three hospital stays for exhaustion and depression, complete with shock therapy. Senator McGovern at first backed his colleague, who had not told him of this vulnerability, but then—while professing "a thousand percent" support—was accused of undercutting him with hints to the press that he wished Senator

Eagleton would voluntarily remove himself from the ticket.

In *Grassroots,* his memoirs that appeared in early 1978, Senator McGovern gave his account of the key phrase of the episode: "Carl Leubsdorf of the Associated Press tracked me down on a tennis court and asked me what I thought the public reaction to Eagleton's disclosure would be. I answered truthfully, and I thought, harmlessly, by saying, 'We'll have to wait and see.' The Leubsdorf story was filed accurately enough, but the headline on the story in some papers was typified by this one: McGOVERN RECONSIDERING EAGLETON DECISION. "Gary Hart [then McGovern's campaign manager, later a senator] called me from Washington in distress about what appeared to be a weakening of our public position. . . . I angrily called [press secretary] Dick Dougherty and ordered him to tell the press that the Leubsdorf story was false and that I was backing Eagleton 'a thousand percent.'"

The Democratic nominee reported that he privately cautioned Senator Eagleton on the phone that he might have to reconsider, but "to my amazement, I was to learn that almost as soon as our conversation ended, Tom went out of his San Francisco motel and told the press corps, 'McGovern still backs Eagleton one thousand percent.'"

McGovern told the press corps traveling with him at the Sylvan Lake Lodge in the Black Hills of South Dakota a story different from Eagleton's: ". . . as calmly as I could, [I] let the journalists traveling with me know that I was reviewing the situation. . . . The press reaction astounded me. The reporters saw my forewarning as a stab in Tom Eagleton's back. They concluded that while having stated publicly a few days earlier that I was 1,000 percent for Eagleton, I was using

them to force Eagleton off the ticket without confronting him face to face . . . they were unaware of my effort to reach Eagleton that evening . . ."

Since that time, the expression "one thousand percent"—a tenfold emphasis of Theodore Roosevelt's "one hundred percent American"—has been treated with skepticism and used only in irony, accompanied by comments like "With friends like these, who needs enemies?"

See LANDSLIDE.

thousand points of light   metaphor for volunteerism; community service that costs the taxpayer nothing.

George Bush introduced the phrase into political discourse during the 1988 campaign. In his acceptance speech at the Republican National Convention in New Orleans that year, he depicted America as a vast network of service organizations: "We are a nation of communities, of thousands and tens of thousands of ethnic, religious, social, business, labor union, neighborhood, regional and other organizations, all of them varied, voluntary and unique. This is America . . . a brilliant diversity spread like stars, like a thousand points of light in a broad and peaceful sky."

Bush echoed the theme in his Inaugural Address in January 1989: "And I am speaking of a new engagement in the lives of others—a new activism, hands-on and involved, that gets the job done. I've spoken of a thousand points of light—of all the community organizations that are spread like stars throughout the nation doing good."

The concept was further popularized in a top-40 country hit by Randy Travis. In that 1991 song about volunteerism, titled "Point of Light," Travis sings: "When you take what's wrong and you try to make it right, you can be a point of light."

Peggy Noonan, Bush's speechwriter who supplied him with the luminescent phrase, discussed the term in her 1990 book, *What I Saw at the Revolution*:

It was my favorite phrase in the speech because its power is born of the fact that it sounds like what it is describing: an expanse of separate yet connected entities sprinkled across a broad and peaceful sky, which is America, the stretched continent. Why stars for communities? I don't know, it was right. Separate, bright and shining, each part of a whole and yet discrete. Why a thousand? I don't know. A thousand clowns, a thousand days—a hundred wasn't enough and a million is too many.

Noonan chronicles the results of searching for the phrase's origins. Suggestions ranged from a Nazi hymnbook to citations from C. S. Lewis and a letter by Vincent Van Gogh. An engineer gave a speech in Venice at the turn of the century urging the city managers to add electricity and fill the city with "a thousand points of light." Of the various possibilities, Noonan suggests that the most likely source was her earlier reading of Thomas Wolfe's novel *The Web and the Rock*, which contains the phrase "a thousand points of friendly light."

Democrats later used the phrase to attack Bush's economic strategy. The *Los Angeles Times* reported in November 1991 about the words of one Democratic candidate at a meeting of the political party in New Hampshire: "If you are on welfare and food stamps, you can't hardly pay your light bill and be one of the thousand points of light . . . let alone buy a house or a car." And former Senator Gary Hart wrote in 1993: "Like a prim Anglican bishop delicately stepping over the bodies of the hungry and the homeless, Reagan's successor cynically put forward the homily of something called a thousand points of light.

Presumably, this was meant to suggest that the human detritus of rampant laissez-faire could be accounted for if only each buccaneer would put just a farthing more in the Sabbath collection box."

Still, in an unusual gesture of nonpartisanship, the Points of Light Foundation, a national community service organization founded in 1990, continued to be financed in 1993 as a part of President Bill Clinton's own national service initiative.

thou shalt not steal convention battle cry of 1912 and 1952, directed at candidates named Taft.

"From the outset," said Theodore Roosevelt's campaign manager, Senator Joseph Dixon of Montana, "the scheme to renominate Taft was a scheme to steal the nomination." As most state conventions in 1912 went for President William Howard Taft over former President Roosevelt, Dixon cried foul. "You will become a deliberate receiver of stolen goods," he charged in an open letter. At the convention, the national committee leaned hard toward Taft whenever there was a contested delegation: 164 Taft delegates were seated to 19 for Roosevelt in contests. "A fraud," said Roosevelt, "as vulgar, as brazen and as cynically open as any ever committed by the Tweed regime . . ." He labeled them "stolen delegates" and thundered the Biblical commandment: "Thou shalt not steal!"

It didn't work. Taft got the nomination, Teddy formed a third party to stand at ARMAGEDDON and industrialist Chauncey Depew correctly sized up the situation: "The only question now is which corpse gets the most flowers." Democrat Woodrow Wilson won.

Forty years later, the commandment worked. In the 1952 Eisenhower-Taft clash, the balance of power was held by the Southern delegations whose election was contested. Eisenhower's manager, Henry Cabot Lodge, said: "In the interest of fair play and decency, we will support at the opening session a resolution to amend the rules and to bar these contested delegates from voting to seat themselves or other contested delegations—regardless of whether they are for us or for Senator Taft."

The "fair play" resolution and "Thou shalt not steal" charge gave the Eisenhower forces their moral issue; the General was quoted as growling about "cattle rustlers."

Stephen Hess wrote: "There was a grand irony in charging the two Tafts, William Howard and his son Robert, both with trying to steal presidential nominations. Bob had been called 'Mr. Integrity,' and it was certainly an inherited characteristic. Yet at the 1912 convention and forty years later their opponents contended that the Tafts had secured Southern delegates by foul means."

Politicians are continually on the lookout for slight shadings of immorality by the opposition. Often a public that will shrug off major blunders or serious breaches of morality will become infuriated by a small trick. Winston Churchill, speaking in the House of Commons on the conciliation of South Africa in 1906, put it this way: "In dealing with nationalities, nothing is more fatal than a dodge. Wrongs will be forgiven, sufferings and losses will be forgiven or forgotten, battles will be remembered only as they recall the martial virtues of the combatants; but anything like a trick, will always rankle."

Exodus 20:15 offers *thou shalt not steal* as the eighth of the Ten Commandments. See ELEVENTH COMMANDMENT for a political addition to the Biblical list.

three-eye league a high-status club that can be joined by any politician willing to tour Ireland, Italy, and Israel.

In many big cities, three of the largest—or at least most active—ethnic groups are the Irish, Italians, and Jews. In the fifties, so many urban political figures made the new Grand Tour that it gained the "Three-Eye" label.

In baseball, the Three-Eye League was a decidedly minor league made up of teams in Illinois, Indiana, and Iowa; it came to typify "bush league" and was spoken of as a kind of Siberia for pitchers who could not find the plate. But in urban politics, a man who hits well in the Three-Eye League belongs on the All-Star team.

three-martini lunch symbol of tax unfairness.

In the keynote speech at the Democratic National Convention in Miami Beach on July 11, 1972, Florida Governor Reubin Askew zinged the "system" that has "forgotten the average man or woman in America today. What can we expect them to think," he asked rhetorically, "when the business lunch of steak and martinis is tax-deductible, but the workingman's lunch of salami and cheese is not?" The line by speechwriter Roland Page was little noticed at the time, but was destined for two revivals.

George McGovern, who became the 1972 Democratic nominee, picked up the "martini lunch" in his campaign and improved it: "The rich businessman can deduct his three-martini lunch, but you can't take off the price of a baloney sandwich." The applause-getting line became a part of THE SPEECH, but it was lost in the debacle of his "THOUSAND PERCENT support" for a running mate he was in the process of dropping, in a campaign that was lost before it began.

The line survived the McGovern campaign. The picture of the FAT CAT imbibing while the workingman paid appealed to the populism of Jimmy Carter (see POPULIST). As he began his

21-month trek to the 1976 nomination, Carter took the line as his own, beginning with "expense-account lunch" and then adding the "martini" (a gin-and-vermouth cocktail which derives its name from an Italian vermouth). Candidate Carter called such a tax system "a disgrace to the human race," which had a nice rhyme; after Carter's victory in November, Senator Edward Kennedy of Massachusetts added: "There are few more vivid symbols of the disgrace of our current tax laws than the martini lunch." (The rhyme resurfaced during the 1992 Democratic Presidential primaries, when candidate Jerry Brown proposed a 13-percent flat tax: "The whole idea of the 13-percent flat tax is fairness. Strip away what Jimmy Carter called the disgrace to the human race—the tax code.")

Finally a counterattack began, not from the expected source of wealthy, inebriated martini-lunchers, but from the Hotel and Restaurant Employees and Bartenders Union (AFL-CIO), which issued a press release in 1977 with this lead: "Martini lunches make an appealing villain, but the martinis are made by bartenders and the meals served are served by waiters after being prepared by chefs."

When President Carter floated a trial balloon of tax reform in which only half of a business luncheon or similar entertainment could be deducted, *Newsweek* columnist George F. Will pointed to the irony of the union opposition: "So what is intended as an attack on privilege is opposed by the proletariat." As for himself, the conservative writer argued, "the tax subsidy for the 'Martini lunches' is a defect in the nation's moral system."

NEOCONSERVATIVE Irving Kristol disagreed: in the *Wall Street Journal* on October 18, 1977, he wrote: "Senator McGovern, in the 1972 campaign, tried—and failed—to make an issue out of the 'two-martini lunch' . . . apparently, President Carter is convinced that the Senator underestimated the seriousness of the situation . . . if you spend all your time worrying whether or not a business executive is getting a tax-free martini with his lunch, you might very well fail to pay due attention to the obvious—that is, encouraging businessmen to make profits."

Despite the catchiness of the martini-lunch phrase, it was not tax "reform" that most voters wanted, but tax reduction. Resentment in the late seventies and again in the early nineties, was directed not at the rich businessman, but at the tax-guzzling bureaucracy. See TAX REVOLT.

The use of libations to loosen up a tough customer has another term, coined on the analogy of "hard sell" in the late fifties: "wet sell," defined in the *Polyglot Dictionary* as "a business deal facilitated by alcohol."

The other use of a cocktail in political rhetoric is a standard gibe at the sitting President's economic policy: "Recipe for a [whatever President] cocktail: economy on the rocks." For more on the metaphoric use of delicatessen meats, see BALONEY and SALAMI TACTICS.

Throttlebottom caricature of a bumbling Vice President.

From the 1931 Kaufman-Ryskind-Gershwin musical satire, *Of Thee I Sing,* where Vice President Alexander Throttlebottom, played by Victor Moore, had to join a guided tour to get into the White House. Little-known Charles Curtis was Hoover's Vice President when this show was written.

The Vice Presidency has taken its share of abuse. John Adams said: "My country has in its wisdom contrived for me the most insignificant office that ever the invention of man contrived or his imagination conceived.

. . . Today I am nothing, but tomorrow I may be everything."

He may be sure of being ridiculed. In November of 1977 *New Times* magazine headlined an item about Vice President Walter Mondale with this pun: "Throttlebottoming out." Vice President Dan Quayle was the butt of many jokes, which he did his best to accept good-naturedly. The *Boston Globe* of July 27, 1992, referred to him as "Dan Quayle, who has reaped his share of the indignity heaped upon heirs to Throttlebottom's throne."

For other assessments, see VEEP; DEAD END, POLITICAL; STEPPINGSTONE; HEARTBEAT AWAY FROM THE PRESIDENCY.

throw away your vote. See DON'T WASTE YOUR VOTE.

thumbsucker a political reporter's term for an analytical story; or a think piece devoid of legwork.

From time to time in the early seventies, Don Oberdorfer of the *Washington Post* would call this writer at the White House and begin the conversation with "I'm doing a thumbsucker for tomorrow."

The term is currently limited to journalists' argot, and because of its similarity to an obscene word, may not cross over to general use, as has a related term, DOPE STORY.

Journalist Stewart Alsop, in his 1973 book *Stay of Execution*, used the term: "Walter Lippmann wrote the best straight think-pieces, or thumbsuckers as they are called in the trade, of any journalist of our time." In December 1977 "The Ear," a gossip column in the *Washington Star*, ran this item about *New York Times* reporter James Wooten: "Jim will become a kind of Haynes Johnson, if you get Ear's meaning. (Say Thumb Suckers if you're in the biz . . .)." The meaning was that Wooten might write fewer

hard-news stories and more stories with a sociological bent, which sometimes require more thought and introspection.

Reporters and editors use the term in its second sense with derision, to mean the opposite of "well researched," as in this letter from John Sweet, publisher of *U.S. News & World Report*, in its January 2, 1978, issue, promoting the cover article: "'Life in the 80s'—see page 75—is not one of those 'thumb sucker' articles consisting of opinions from futurists, gathered over THREE-MARTINI LUNCHES . . ."

A 1990 editorial in *Roll Call* echoed the derision: "That public cynicism is a fact of life, but, we feel, it's unjustified. It is the handiwork of a class of professional thumb-suckers (journalists, analysts, lawyers, and other public affairs hangers-on) who seem to believe that to bash the American political system is a mark of keen sophistication."

In current usage, a *background piece* provides general information, not to be confused with the story that results from a BACKGROUNDER, which a reporter calls a *dope story* and a SOURCE calls a *plant;* a *dope story* is an analytical piece that can make news; a *think piece* or *thumbsucker* is an attempt at punditry (see PUNDIT).

thunder on the left liberal objections.

"An end to the Vietnam War would change the situation drastically," wrote Louis Heren in the *Times* of London in 1968. "Much of the thunder from the left would die away, and the right, as represented by Mr. George Wallace, would be more clearly identified as anti-racist."

The phrase harkens to days of fierce liberalism, first in England and then in the U.S.; currently it is used mainly in an ironic sense, as if the rumbling were remote.

The phrase was popularized as the title of a book by Christopher Morley in 1925. Professor Irwin Stark of City College of New York directed the author to its origin in *The Dangers of This Mortall Life,* by Sir Eustace Peachtree, who was said to have flourished about 1640: "Among the notionable dictes of antique Rome was the fancy that when men heard thunder on the left the gods had somewhat of special advertisement to impart. Then did the prudent pause and lay down their affaires to study what omen Jove intended."

One might have thought that such a gentleman as Sir Eustace Peachtree had existed, since the source given was *Bartlett's Familiar Quotations* (11th and 12th editions). However, "Kit" Morley liked an occasional practical joke, and the "quotation" placed in *Bartlett's*—which Morley helped edit—was a hoax. It is no longer in recent editions, which is a pity, since it added a human element to a compilation of quotations.

On the analogy of Morley's title, "thunder on the right" is occasionally used to describe conservative mutterings. When *Time* wrote a piece on this writer in 1977, calling attention to his interest in puns as well as his right-wing espousals, the headline was "Punder on the Right."

ticket the slate of candidates, running as a team.

"The old ticket forever!" wrote Benjamin Franklin's daughter Sarah in 1766, her usage duly noted by Webster in 1879. ". . . its usage in this sense dates back to early colonial times," Charles Ledyard Norton wrote in 1890, "since Mrs. Bache (*née* Franklin) would not have used the word in this sense had not its meaning been popularly recognized."

Tickets discussed elsewhere in this book include BALANCED TICKET, with hopefully broad-based appeal; SPLIT TICKET, a voter selection, as from a Chinese menu, of "one from column A, one from column B." Al Smith joked about being able to win on a LAUNDRY TICKET, while politicians are only half in jest about their imaginary, unbeatable DREAM TICKET. A predecessor to split ticket was *mixed ticket,* now obsolete; *scratched ticket,* where a name was erased on a paper ballot, was made obsolete by the voting machine.

Political regulars prefer the "straight ticket," which in voting-machine times became "vote row A all the way." The practice was being described as "straight" over a century ago. "Old Henry," wrote *Harper's* in January 1860, "generally votes a 'straight ticket' . . ." Lord Bryce, an English observer of American politics, used a variant form in his 1888 *American Commonwealth*: "The electors . . . give little thought to the personal qualifications of the candidates, and vote the 'straight-out ticket.'"

Harry Truman used the word to stretch a historical point: "Lincoln had dropped Hannibal Hamlin of Maine because he wanted a Union ticket. Lincoln was elected in 1864 on the American Union ticket and not on the Republican ticket." (To err is Truman: Lincoln was elected in 1864 on the National Union ticket.)

At one time, *ticket* was synonymous with "ballot"; voters cast their tickets, or written slips of paper. This sense has been preserved in the current political phrase, *to have the tickets,* meaning to have enough votes to win.

tick-tock journalists' argot for a story detailing the chronology leading up to a major announcement or event.

"I'm doing a tick-tock on the new economic policy," Henry Hubbard, White House correspondent for *Newsweek,* told the writer after the President had frozen wages and prices on August 15, 1971.

George Bush misused the onomatopoeic term in 1990 while defending his tour of defense installations during a time of disarmament talk: "I think it was a good trip, and I've read some tick-tock inside here, but it doesn't bother me a bit."

A tick-tock (the metaphor, obviously, of a clock moving toward a fateful hour) is often written with boldface dates indicating significant meetings or preliminary events, and is more reportorial than a "think piece" or THUMBSUCKER.

In 1991, Margaret Tutwiler resisted providing details at a State Department briefing: "We're not going to go through a laundry list or a tick-tock, or here are options that we may or may not pick and choose from."

Another term especially associated with newsmagazines is "violin piece," which is the lead story in the magazine that sets the tone of the week. Usage: "What's the violin this week?" "The economy," or "The isolation of the President." A purple-prose assessment of the national mood once led newsmagazines in the thirties as if to the accompaniment of a violin; this has been modified in recent times to a general story that is intended to capture the significant trend of the week. Though the style is less ornate, the term lingers on.

Another time metaphor is *two minutes to midnight* (see DOOMSDAY MACHINE); for a different clock metaphor, see STOPPING THE CLOCK.

tilt   lean toward, give preferred treatment to.

"Tilt toward Pakistan." Columnist Jack Anderson reported in 1971 that Henry Kissinger had passed on this advice from Richard Nixon at a National Security Council meeting on the India-Pakistan dispute about Bangladesh.

Mr. Nixon wanted to rebuke the neutralist Indian government and help Mohammed Yahya Khan in Pakistan, who was helping him to arrange his trip to China.

"Tilt" was a favorite Nixon locution, referring not to the warning flashed when a pinball machine is tampered with, but to the angle of "slant." ("A few individuals think and speak for themselves," wrote Hiram Haydn in the *American Scholar* in 1946, "a few newspapers refuse to tilt their headlines and news stories to satisfy their advertisers' slanted views . . .")

After the widely noted Anderson quotation, the word gained in favor. "With all its reins on the bureaucrat," wrote Leslie Gelb and Morton Halperin in *Harper's* in June 1972, "the new system did not prevent part of the bureaucracy from tilting the 'wrong way' [meaning against the President, as revealed in the Anderson papers] in the recent India-Pakistan crisis."

In the synonymy of SPIN, *tilt* has a purpose: it is crisper than "lean toward," breezier than "favor," and less pejorative than "slant." Its adoption as part of the diplomatic lingo was evident in this use by Harvard professor Jerome Alan Cohen in a *Foreign Affairs* article in 1976: "Or do the realities of world politics say that the United States should 'lean to one side'—that of Peking? . . . If so, how, and to what extent, should such a de facto tilt be carried out?"

The word is often also used as a noun, meaning slant or bias. A "pro-Soviet tilt" was looked at askance by Washington during the Cold War, as a "pro-Arab tilt" by the State Department is often of concern to Israelis.

Wags refer to any hotel in Pisa, Italy, as "the tiltin' Hilton."

timber, Presidential   a man who could be THE MAN WHO; one who has the background, personality, and voter appeal to "go all the way" to the White House.

The metaphor originated with Sir Francis Bacon, whose "Essay on Goodness," written in 1612, was about men whose nature was the opposite of goodness, in whom there was a "natural malignity." "Such dispositions are the very errors of human nature, and yet they are the fittest timber to make great politics of." He compared these warped men to "knee timber," wood that has grown crooked and has been cut so as to form an angle "that is good for ships that are ordained to be tossed, but not for building houses that shall stand firm."

Political uses of the metaphor in the U.S. go back as far as 1833. The *Cleveland Plain Dealer* grumbled in 1880 that "the situation now so chaotic arises from the fact that there is a superabundance of timber."

Finley Peter Dunne's Mr. Dooley (see DOOLEY, MR.) offered his friend Hennessey this advice: "If ye say about a man that he's good prisidintial timber he'll buy ye a dhrink. If ye say he's good vice-prisidintial timber ye mane that he isn't good enough to be cut up into shingles, an' ye'd better be careful."

The qualities that make a man's timber "Presidential" include the timbre of his voice and the warmth of his smile; courage (his timbers cannot be shivered); either a proven record of vote-getting power or a powerful vote in the opinion polls; age between forty and sixty; a power base in a major state or national renown; nothing in his record that would permanently alienate a major group or region; and AVAILABILITY. The qualities that make a good President—judgment, intelligence, decisiveness, character—are not always the qualities that make good Presidential timber. In that regard, Bacon's point remains a good definition: Presidential timber is that which best resists twists and strain—"ordained to be tossed"—but not necessarily to support weight.

time for a change appeal to unrest and dissatisfaction; Republican slogan in 1944, 1948, and finally—successfully—in 1952.

Thomas E. Dewey said in San Francisco, September 21, 1944: "That's why it's time for a change." In 1946, a better slogan—"HAD ENOUGH?"—came on the Republican scene, and "Time for a Change" became a subsidiary slogan in the campaign of 1948. Dewey's running mate, Earl Warren, modified it further in his own speeches, predicting that the American people would turn to the Republicans "not because they want a change, but because they want a chance."

By 1952 the Democrats had been in power for twenty consecutive years. Long before, Democrat Grover Cleveland had made a similar point about long Republican rule: "Parties may be so long in power, and may become so arrogant and careless of the interests of the people, as to grow heedless of their responsibility to their masters." The *New York Times* editorialized in 1952: "The Republicans have pegged their campaign largely on one theme—that it's time for a change because of the 'top to bottom MESS IN WASHINGTON.'"

Democratic candidate Adlai Stevenson, whose grandfather—Cleveland's running mate—had exploited the desire for new faces, felt the pull of the appeal, and fought directly against the phrase: "As divided, as silent as both wings of the Republican Party are on major objectives, on policies to guide the nation, they have wholeheartedly united on one profound proposition: 'It's time for a change.' . . . They talk of change. These days they do little else but talk of change. But where were the Republicans when the great changes of these twenty years were made? I'll tell you where they were. They were trying to stop the changes."

The desire for a "new face," a "fresh approach," is strong; counterbalancing it is another human feeling, a resistance to making changes in high places, illustrated by phrases like "the Devil we know" and "DON'T CHANGE HORSES." In the *British General Election of 1964,* D. E. Butler and Anthony King wrote: "Yet perhaps the most important issue of all was one that scarcely figured in the manifestos, television broadcasts or speeches—the feeling that it was time for a change. . . . If the feeling did exist, it could not be argued with: it could only be exorcised, or displaced by another, more powerful feeling. 'The issue at this election,' as one Conservative put it privately, 'is time for a change versus fear of change. Who wins will depend on which feeling is stronger.'"

Al Gore, at the 1992 Democratic Convention, tried a variation in addressing the Bush Administration: "It is time for you to go."

See SELLING CANDIDATES LIKE SOAP.

tin box. See LITTLE TIN BOX.

tinhorn politician. See TWO-BIT POLITICIAN.

titular leader the most recently defeated Presidential candidate of the party out of power; leader in name, not necessarily in fact.

Both Thomas E. Dewey and Adlai Stevenson, "titular leaders" of their parties for eight years, felt ambivalent about the phrase. Dewey wrote in 1950: "Who speaks for the party out of power? It has its last nominee for President who is called the 'Titular Head of the Party.' I have held that title in my party now for nearly six years and I still have some doubts about what it means except that I am the last, duly nominated spokesman for my party."

Stevenson said in 1956:

The titular leader has no clear and defined authority within his party. He has no party office, no staff, no funds, nor is there any system of consultation whereby he may be advised of party policy and through which he may help to shape that policy. There are no devices such as the British have developed through which he can communicate directly and responsibly with the leaders of the party in power. Yet he is generally deemed the leading spokesman of his party.

Because there is no "leader of the opposition" in America as in Great Britain, the defeated candidate is often challenged by the wing of the party that felt it could have done better. A year after Willkie's defeat in 1940, Senator Robert A. Taft said that Willkie could not "speak for the Republican party," because there was "no justification in precedent or principle for the view that a defeated candidate for President is the titular leader of the party."

The titular leader, however, does carry a special responsibility to oppose the incumbents. In the late thirties, Republican candidate Alf Landon told Republican Minority Leader Joe Martin that Roosevelt had offered him the post of Secretary of War. "I advised him not to accept," wrote Martin. "He was, after all, the titular head of the Republican Party, and I felt it would be damaging to the Party for him to enter Roosevelt's Cabinet at a time when we were coming up to a convention and a campaign."

Does a titular leader have any special advantage in recapturing a nomination? Probably not. Wendell Willkie, defeated in the primaries of 1944, dropped out of the race. Thomas E. Dewey lost to Harold Stassen in Wisconsin and Nebraska in 1948, but was able to win in Oregon and go into the convention as the favorite. Adlai Stevenson in 1956 started to play the same reluctant role that had been so successful for him in 1952, but soon discovered—after primary losses in New Hampshire and Minnesota—that he needed some victories to capture the nomination. He dropped his reluctance, campaigned in Oregon, Florida, and California, and won those primaries and the nomination.

The role of the titular leader, never really defined, is what the man makes it. William Jennings Bryan, who seemed to be a born titular leader, made much of the position and became Woodrow Wilson's Secretary of State. Alfred E. Smith was an outspoken anti-Republican voice between 1928 and 1932 until he found himself losing the mantle of leadership to Franklin Roosevelt. Dewey was the titular leader most responsible for the choice of his successor, fighting for Eisenhower and defeating his archrival, Robert A. Taft. Richard Nixon was campaigning for governor of California in the midst of his titular leadership and did not really speak for the party; oddly, he assumed that role in the 1966 off-year elections in the midst of Barry Goldwater's titular leadership.

The word has a built-in derogation: titular means "holding the title"—nominal, or "in name only." In *Newsday* of February 1, 1993, columnist Marvin Kitman derogated Pat Buchanan, who had been a Presidential candidate in 1992, as "the titular leader of the brown-shirt wing of the Republican party." It is likely to continue to be applied only to men.

to err is Truman. See RED HERRING.

to hell with the cheese. See FIGHTING THE PROBLEM.

tokenism resistance to change by dint of symbolic acceptance; lip service; yielding to the principle but not the practice.

Newsweek reported in 1963:

> . . . for every Western Electric, Lockheed, or R. J. Reynolds making sincere desegregation efforts, there is another firm—more likely several others—practicing "tokenism." "There are a lot of showcase companies which say 'Look, there's our Negro over there,'" reports Atlanta's Noyes Collinson, an executive of the American Friends Service Committee.
> Negro leaders hurl the tokenism charge at all the steel, auto and textile giants, at the airlines and most banks and utilities, and at the communications industry.

Writing in 1964, Professor Alan Westin pointed out that during 1963 in the eleven Southern states, black school enrollment was 2,840,452; of those, only 12,868 were registered in schools that also had white students, with Texas accounting for more than half the tiny percentage. "It was against this backdrop of wholesale noncompliance and 'tokenism' in the Old South and a seeming halt to the process of integration in the border states that the Negro community looked at school integration as the 1963 school year came to a close."

In the rhetoric of racial resistance, *gradualism* proceeds WITH ALL DELIBERATE SPEED, with emphasis on the deliberate; *massive resistance,* a play on Gandhi's "passive resistance," is outright opposition to any form of desegregation; and *tokenism* tries to preserve the pattern of segregation by pretending to let it win. To civil rights advocates—and to feminists crashing into a "glass ceiling"—gradualism delays, massive resistance denies, and tokenism deceives.

Tomming. See UNCLE TOM.

too little and too late a criticism of unpreparedness and inadequacy.

"Too Late" was the caption of a famous 1885 *Punch* cartoon showing the belatedly dispatched relief column reaching Khartoum two days after the death of General "Chinese" Gordon at the hands of the African Mahdi.

The addition of "too little" to the words made a phrase both balanced and pointed. Professor Allan Nevins of Columbia coined it in an article titled "Germany Disturbs the Peace" in the May 1935 *Current History*: "The former allies have blundered in the past by offering Germany too little, and offering even that too late, until finally Nazi Germany has become a menace to all mankind."

The phrase was sharpened and popularized by David Lloyd George, who had served as Great Britain's Prime Minister during World War I. On the day after the fall of Finland—March 13, 1940—the seventy-seven-year-old statesman told the House of Commons: "It is the old trouble—too late. Too late with Czechoslovakia, too late with Poland, certainly too late with Finland. It is always too late, or too little, or both."

Throughout the early part of World War II, the phrase was used to deride Allied defeats and lack of preparation. Toward the end of the war, "enough and on time" was used to explain the reason for Allied successes.

After the war, the phrase was used by an "out" party to attack policy on the grounds of inadequacy, which is a political attack permitting little counterattack. John F. Kennedy, campaigning in 1960, called an Eisenhower embargo on shipments to Cuba "too little and too late," suggesting that the U.S. also "attempt to strengthen the non-Batista democratic anti-Castro forces in exile. . . ." In his memoirs of the Kennedy Administration, Ted Sorensen used the phrase in its current generic sense: "Kennedy's error in 1960 on the 'MISSILE GAP' had been the result of the public's being informed too little and too late—even after the facts were certain—about a danger which he had in good faith overstated."

The danger of delayed decision was expressed in different words by Defense Secretary Charles E. Wilson early in the Eisenhower Administration. "I have so many people in my department," he said sadly, "who keep putting off decisions until the only thing left to do is the wrong thing."

New York State Controller Arthur Levitt said in 1967 regarding a $2.5 billion transportation bond issue: "Too much, too soon" (the title of a 1957 autobiography by Diana Barrymore). The possibilities of this phrase are not yet exhausted. "Too much, too late" was never tried by opponents of bombing North Vietnam, and a use may even be found for "too little, too soon."

too old to cry.   See CONCESSION SPEECH.

too proud to fight   a high-minded Wilsonian defense of neutrality that helped unite his opposition.

A British ship, the *Lusitania*, was sunk with many Americans aboard on May 7, 1915, by a German submarine. Three days later, clinging to his "mediator nation" philosophy, President Wilson said to a group of newly naturalized citizens: "The example of America must be the example not merely of peace because it will not fight, but of peace because peace is the healing and elevating influence of the world and strife is not. There is such a thing as a man being too proud to fight. There is such a thing as a nation being so right that it does not need to convince others by force that it is right . . ."

The "too proud to fight" phrase was used as a gibe at Wilson until his policy changed and he toured the country urging preparedness for war. Years later, *Nation* editor Oswald Garrison Villard claimed authorship: "I supplied the President through Tumulty with a phrase which brought down upon him a storm of abuse and denunciation. The words 'too proud to fight' were mine."

But neither the phrase nor the criticism of it died. In 1961, former Congresswoman and Ambassador Clare Boothe Luce quoted Wilson's statement as an example of how not to keep the peace:

This was certainly a statement which the embattled French and British heard with dismay and contempt and bitterness. How can a man be proud not to fight while his friends are being killed and even conquered in a war they did not start? America was not too proud to sell guns, make loans, ship supplies to the Allied side, and to heap abuse on Kaiser Bill—a procedure which American morality permitted us nevertheless to call "neutrality," since neutrality also consisted entirely in not joining the fighting until "war came."

The phrase, however, had its defenders later in the decade. Some used it to justify a U.S. withdrawal from Southeast Asia. A quite different use was made of it in 1967 by Florida Governor Claude R. Kirk in giving awards to young blacks who helped "cool" a race riot in Tampa before any lives were lost: "Half a century ago, an American President was vilified for suggesting that there are occasions when courageous men should be 'too proud to fight.'

"Negro leaders in Tampa last week showed they were too proud—too conscious of their real responsibility—to allow the hoodlums to take over, to allow vandals to loot and burn and terrorize their neighbors under a false cover of racial tension."

tooth fairy. See SANTA CLAUS, NOBODY SHOOTS AT.

Topic A the subject at the tip of everybody's tongue; a continuing news story that currently gets top coverage.

The expression appeared in the late fifties and was formalized by the *New York Herald Tribune,* which headed the lead item in its front-page news summary "Topic A."

A politician ignores Topic A at the peril of being ignored himself. In current usage, PARAMOUNT ISSUE is synonymous with—though more sedate than—*burning question:* both must be addressed by both parties in depth. GUT ISSUE is an underlying social phenomenon, like a religious or racial issue, and need never be addressed head-on. *Topic A* is the event or running story that draws attention that day or week, generating arguments, cartoons, and jokes, and requires some attention from a public figure who cannot appear to be out of touch.

torch has been passed an allusion to a new generation, or at least the transfer of responsibility to a more vigorous group.

"Let the word go forth from this time and place," said John F. Kennedy at his inaugural, "to friend and foe alike, that the torch has been passed to a new generation of Americans . . ."

The torch is a favorite political symbol. In 1555, just before being burned at the stake for heresy, English prelate Hugh Latimer said, "Be of good cheer, brother, we shall this day kindle such a torch in England as, I trust in God, shall never be extinguished."

The image of passing the torch probably derived from the passing of a lighted torch by relay runners from Greece to light the Olympic flame at the openings of the Olympic Games. The image was popularized in a sentimental World War I poem by John McCrae:

Take up our quarrel with the foe:
To you from failing hands we throw

The torch; be yours to hold it high.
If ye break faith with us who die
We shall not sleep, though poppies grow
In Flanders fields.

An incendiary speaker is called a *firebrand*; the statue in New York harbor holds the *torch of liberty*; a rejected lover *carries the torch*; and the liberation of North Africa in World War II was *Operation Torch*.

totalitarian highly centralized government, permeating all aspects of the society it controls, repressing internal opposition and promoting a fear and awe of the leadership.

"Police state" is a popular derogatory synonym for totalitarian government, popularized during the era of Nazi Germany and Fascist Italy.

"Totalitarian" is to the free world vocabulary what "imperialist" was to Communist terminology. Walt Whitman Rostow, later an adviser to the Johnson Administration, wrote in 1952:

> A totalitarian regime . . . can be defined as a state in which the potentialities for control over society by governmental authority are exploited to the limit of available modern techniques—where no significant effort is made to achieve the compromise between the sanctity of the individual and the exigencies of efficient communal life; where the moral weakness of men in the administration of concentrated power is ignored; where the aspiration toward a higher degree of democratic quality is not recognized as a good; and where, conversely, the extreme authority of concentrated power is projected as an intrinsic virtue.

Existentialist philosopher Karl Jaspers gave this view in 1961:

> The totalitarian world is weak at home and strong abroad. At home it can maintain its rule only by terror, but abroad, on the soil of the free world, it can utilize the rules of this world to carry on propaganda and to form subversive organizations with immense resources by centrally planned and directed totalitarian methods. The free world can meet this propaganda only with its own spiritual power, with the ethos of its principle, which will eventually let the propaganda machine idle without effect. With subversive organizations—that incipient formation of a totalitarian state within the free state—it must cope by vigilance and police action under law. It must not resort to totalitarian methods, for if it did, it would destroy its own essence.

In 1975, French philosopher-columnist Jean-François Revel wrote *The Totalitarian Temptation*, challenging the argument of EUROCOMMUNISTS that they offered "Communism with a human face." He used the example provided by Alexander Solzhenitsyn (see GULAG) to show that severe repression was part of the essence of Communism.

Friendly dictators are euphemized as *paternalistic*; totalitarian regimes posing no threat of aggression are called *authoritarian*.

total war wars involving a general mobilization, destruction of the opposition's productive capacity; a war carried "home" to the enemy.

The phrase was popularized by a book, *Der totale Krieg*, by Nazi General Erich Ludendorff in 1935. The aging general, who was the chief German strategist in World War I, stressed the need to mobilize the economy of a nation behind a war effort. The German word for this mobilization was *Wehrwirtschaft*, or war economy, based on rearmament that would prepare an economy for the strain of war.

"Total," therefore, did not mean "more ferocious than usual"; it meant the addition of economic and psychological warfare to what had once been a strictly military affair. During World War II, its meaning changed to "all-out effort" and the destruction of civilian population centers.

In current usage, *total war* is sometimes used as a contrast to LIMITED WAR, though it is more often replaced by *all-out* or *nuclear war*, and *World War III*.

Total, however, has become a favorite oratorical word for politicians favoring "total commitment," "total involvement," "bold new total approaches to problems which must be viewed in their totality."

In the seventies the word was turned into a verb to mean "destroy completely"—as: "In the crash, my car was totaled."

tough-minded and tender-minded. See DOVES.

trade-off   compromise; the tension that exists between divergent but mutually necessary elements, such as target date and cost.

The word was a favorite of the NEW ECONOMICS and an explanation by Walter Heller is included in that entry. The delicate-balance meaning is limited to the fields of economy and defense, however. To politicians, the word is used as BARGAINING CHIP, an expendable person or issue that can be used to close a negotiation (or make a distasteful deal more palatable by using it as a "sweetener").

In the sense of political compromise, the word is not new. Republicans in 1940 planned to use the youthful Thomas E. Dewey in a cavalier fashion. A Republican leader was reported to have said that the original plan was to use him as "a STALKING HORSE and trade him off later."

trained seals.   See RUBBER STAMP.

trains ran on time   a defense of the Fascist "corporate state" on the basis of its efficiency; now only used derisively.

Whenever a government or political organization abridges personal liberties—giving as its reason the need for "master planning" or "efficiency"—the mid-thirties expression is recalled: "But you have to admit that Mussolini made the Italian trains run on time."

Writing about Boss Ed Crump of Tennessee in 1947, John Gunther made the point vividly:

> Of course the boss has given Memphis first-class government—in some respects. But almost all the creditable items are the equivalent of Mussolini making the trains in Italy "run on time." Perhaps they did run on time, and a good thing too. But at what sacrifice?—at what cost to things much more important? Mr. Crump has made Memphis a "clean" enough city. But it is a community that has not really functioned as a democracy for more than a quarter of a century; a whole generation has grown up without fulfilling the first and simplest duty of citizenship, that of exercising political choice.

traitor to his class   epithet applied to Franklin Roosevelt.

"His background belied his political philosophy," wrote White House correspondent Charles Hurd. "On several occasions he laughed rather grimly at the comment that he was 'a traitor to his class.'"

Roosevelt's "class" included ancestors dating back two hundred years in America; he was educated at Groton and Harvard, and lived like a country squire in fashionable Hyde Park, New York. In the twenties and early thirties, millionaires and men of high social standing were not identified with liberal positions or considered "men of the people," a situation since rectified. At the time of FDR's election to the presidency, he was probably the wealthiest person ever to hold that office.

Roosevelt's New Deal programs were especially startling to those fellow-patricians who felt he would be "reasonable" once elected; indeed, his pre-election speeches laid heavy stress on budget balancing and efficiency in government. For an idea of the depth of antipathy FDR inspired among members of his "class," see THAT MAN IN THE WHITE HOUSE.

FDR led the way for other men of wealth in politics, particularly in New York State. Herbert Lehman of the banking family, Averell Harriman of the railroad family, Nelson Rockefeller of the oil and banking family, and Robert Kennedy of the Kennedy family have since held high office in New York.

Sir Denis Brogan showed a variation of class distinctions in the U.S. in this way: "There is the famous story of a lively discussion in a smart New York club in which FDR was attacked as being 'a traitor to his class.' A member who was the head of a very old, distinguished and, more important, rich family (he is the father of the present junior Senator from Rhode Island) protested. 'The President is not a traitor to your class; he doesn't belong to it. You are business men. He is a gentleman.'"

trial balloon a testing of public reaction by suggestion of an idea through another person, causing no embarrassment to the author if the reaction is not good.

The idea of placing a political toe in the water—with no commitment to plunge in—by the use of NOT FOR ATTRIBUTION stories to reporters was developed by Theodore Roosevelt. Quincy Howe wrote: "He also originated the 'trial-balloon' technique and gave favored correspondents 'OFF-THE-RECORD' statements that they attributed to 'AUTHORITATIVE SOURCES.' If the statement caught on, Roosevelt would make it his own. If it fell flat, he would drop it."

Pointing out that Teddy Roosevelt had ordered the first White House press room installed (after he noticed a group of rain-soaked newsmen standing disconsolately at the gate), AP correspondent Jack Bell observed: "Roosevelt was a great man for trial balloons. He tried out some of his ideas on the reporters. If they backfired, he denied everything and denounced the newsmen for printing what he had told them."

Another White House correspondent—Charles Hurd—recalled the use made of the technique by Teddy's cousin, Franklin Roosevelt:

> Roosevelt showed himself to be the master of the "trial balloon." A trial balloon is a politician's idea launched for public reaction before he commits himself. By this means, much background, argument, good and bad reaction can be studied.
> . . . The trial balloons and other techniques quickly won Roosevelt a reputation—not bothersome at all to him—of being less consistent than some other political leaders. He would blithely shift any course of action, if the public reacted negatively.

Reporters are not the only medium of the trial balloon. Minor officials, major party spokesmen, even university professors may be used by accomplished ballooners to float out an idea. The balloonee—the spokesman or reporter—always denies that he is being used in that manner, always righteously, often rightly. Walter Heller refused to concede that his plan of TAX SHARING was a Johnson trial balloon. It may not have been so motivated, but the criticism it engendered from liberals, among other things, caused the President to back away from it, making the Heller proposal a trial balloon, intended or not.

"When I made the speech on 'Old Myths and New Realities'" (see GRAND

DESIGN), wrote Senator J. William Fulbright, "many persons immediately assumed that it was a 'trial balloon' inspired by the White House. It was not."

Before Bill Clinton's health-care reform program was unveiled to the public, rumors and reports streamed from the White House. "Some," explained *Time* magazine of May 24, 1993, "apparently were Administration trial balloons . . . Many more, or so White House insiders insist, were leaks from some of the 500-plus members of the Administration's health-care task force."

An alternative to the trial balloon is "putting a ball in the air" which differs in that the ballooner admits to being the source. Dean Acheson (then Truman's Undersecretary of State) made a probing address in 1947 that indicated a direction that led to the Marshall Plan, and carefully got White House clearance. "I wanted everyone to understand," said Acheson some years later, "that I was putting a ball in the air and that we had all better be prepared to field it when it came down, because if it just landed, *plunk!* on the ground, it would be a very bad thing."

The derivation may not be as obvious as it seems. A trial balloon is a balloon put up to test the direction and velocity of the wind in balloon ascensions and kite-flying contests. Both "kites" and "balloons," however, have speculative and fraudulent connotations in their history, and like LAME DUCK might be a political borrowing from business. "Ballooning a stock" meant promoting its rise by spreading false information, a technique now described as "touting"; this was also described at one time as "kite-flying." Issuing a check with no money yet in the bank to cover it is still called "kiting a check." It could be that the speculative meaning was helped into politics by its financial usage.

The phrase may be of French origin. In the *Great Englishmen of the Six-*teenth Century,* S. Lee wrote in 1907: "Bacon set forth these views as mere *balloons d'essai,* as straws to show him which way the wind blew."

For methods of launching trial balloons, see LEAK; BACKGROUNDER; NOT FOR ATTRIBUTION; DOPE STORY; BALLOON GOES UP.

trial heat   a mock election by poll of a limited number of candidates.

This is a poll that asks: "Supposing the election were being held today; of the following candidates, which one would you vote for?" It differs from DEPTH POLLING, and many other more useful "issues" polls.

A trial heat, or *mano a mano* survey (expression taken from the bullfight ring), is the poll most interesting to the public, most gossiped about, and often least useful to professional politicians. It indicates only where one stands on a given day; it does not indicate what to do or in what direction public opinion is likely to go or what issues are growing in importance. However, the trial heat may be devastating in a CAN'T WIN campaign, convincing delegates to switch to another candidate who runs better in a trial heat against an incumbent.

In current use, a *trial heat* is between candidates of opposing parties; a *preference poll* is among candidates of a single party. The candidate leading the preference poll is not necessarily the strongest in the trial heat; Taft was preferred by Republicans in 1952 who were swayed by Eisenhower's power in the trial heats.

In racing and track sports, a trial heat is often an elimination of competitors before a major race; this is not its political meaning, which is why it is confused with preference poll.

See POLLSTER.

trick.   See THOU SHALT NOT STEAL.

trickle-down theory idea that aid to the prosperity of large corporations will "trickle down" to employees and irrigate the economy.

William Jennings Bryan drew the metaphor, if not the phrase, in his "Cross of Gold" speech in 1896: "There are two ideas of government. There are those who believe that, if you will only legislate to make the well-to-do prosperous, their prosperity will leak through on those below. The Democratic idea, however, has been that if you legislate to make the masses prosperous, their prosperity will find its way up through every class which rests upon them."

At the 1975 Gridiron Dinner, a newsman impersonating presidential press secretary Ron Nessen led a group of cheerleaders serenading President Gerald Ford with this spoof of "Buckle Down, Winsocki":

Trickle down, Winsocki, trickle down,
You can win, Winsocki, if you trickle down,
Give a tax rebate
To the highest rate,
Let it gravitate
And trickle down.

In the campaign of 1932, Herbert Hoover argued that public relief measures proposed by some Democrats were "playing politics with human misery" and that his program was aimed at restoring prosperity to corporations and banks which would in turn reinvigorate the economy. The Democrats derided this as a "trickle-down theory" aimed at "feeding the sparrows by feeding the horses."

The opposition theory retained water as the metaphor in the phrase PUMP-PRIMING.

In current use, Republicans—twice stung by the phrase—shy away from it. Robert Donovan reported that in an Eisenhower cabinet meeting in 1954, "this attitude refuted charges that Re-

publicans were bound to the 'trickle down' theory of economics—the theory of helping the few at the top in expectation that the benefits will then seep down to the rest of the people." Reagan pollster Richard Wirthlin told the *Washington Post* in 1988: "It's much harder to make the trickle-down theory work in politics than in economics."

Democrats will not let the phrase evaporate: It was used by Walter Mondale in 1984, Michael Dukakis in 1988, and Bill Clinton in 1992. The Republican riposte is JFK's "a RISING TIDE LIFTS ALL THE BOATS." Yet another watery metaphor is SOAK THE RICH.

See PARTY OF THE PEOPLE.

trigger-happy inclined to a panicky decision on war; bellicose.

Barry Goldwater, tagged as "trigger-happy" early in his primary campaign against Nelson Rockefeller in 1964, heard the identification reiterated by the Scranton forces at the convention, and could not shake it throughout the general election campaign. His use of DEFOLIATE and stress on "victory" were turned into issues that pictured him as an irresponsible candidate who "shot from the hip" and whose election would plunge the country into nuclear war.

The Democratic advertising agency, Doyle Dane Bernbach Inc., produced two commercials so extreme that they were quickly withdrawn. One pictured a hand reaching toward a nuclear button (see FINGER ON THE BUTTON). Another, which became known as the DAISY SPOT, showed a little girl pulling the petals off a daisy, with a voice of doom in the background counting down the firing of a missile with each petal pulled.

"Finally," wrote Theodore White, "there was the hazard of the bomb, the 'trigger issue,' which Goldwater must somehow erase or neutralize, as Kennedy had neutralized the issue of religion in 1960. Yet here again the candidate seemed so stunned, so shocked by the attack on him as a killer, that he could not clear his mind to guide a counter-attack."

Goldwater characterized this as "the warmonger charge" but Democrats did not need to use the word warmonger (see -MONGER); trigger-happy was good enough. Art Buchwald wrote a column long after the election about how happy he was that Goldwater had not been elected, because of all the escalation that would have resulted. He then proceeded to list all Johnson's escalating decisions. In this vein, economist Pierre Rinfret told a group of economists in 1966 of the lady who said, "They told me if I voted for Goldwater, we'd be at war in six months, and by golly, I voted for Goldwater and we were."

The compound adjective made a brief political appearance in the previous campaign. When Richard Nixon made clear he would defend the islands of Quemoy and Matsu off the shore of mainland China—an outpost of the Chiang Kai-shek forces in Taiwan— John F. Kennedy called this position "trigger-happy." Ted Sorensen, in retrospect, called this one of the rare occasions Kennedy "stepped over the borders of fair comment."

It was also used against Ronald Reagan by the Jimmy Carter campaign in 1980, as part of a general imputation of COWBOY irresponsibility.

The Western allusion made its first political appearance in 1904 as "hair-trigger," to describe Teddy Roosevelt's impulsiveness. Roosevelt himself used the phrase in 1908, predicting a "hair-trigger convention." The word submerged for many years until it was reactivated during World War II.

At that time there were a rash of "happy's." The original, *slap-happy*, or dizzy, intoxicated, was closely akin to

punch-drunk. The first variations appeared in 1940 ("I'm *snap-happy* since I discovered Kleenex cleans the . . . lens of my camera"), *power-happy* for power-crazed, *footlight-happy* for stage-struck, etc. Military applications were legion: *stripe-happy, bomb-happy, flak-happy,* and in a *Life* magazine of November 1, 1943: "Cadets are taught here to be 'trigger happy': to shoot at anything any time." As can be seen, the adjective "happy" is like an unstable chemical ready to form a compound with anything. When it joins with a noun, it transforms the noun into a hyphenated adjective, useful information for grammar-happy readers.

tripwire the presence of troops in an area as hostages to peace, an attack on whom would automatically trigger military involvement of the nation from which the token force is drawn.

The expression took on its strategic sense early in the COLD WAR, in connection with the garrison of U.S. troops in Berlin. The troops were placed in that four-power city, an island surrounded by East Germany, not to make a serious defense in case of attack but to provide the "tripwire," or national commitment to come to their rescue or avenge their loss.

Later the word was used in NATO terminology, to justify the presence of 300,000 American armed forces in Europe: not that this force would stop a Soviet offensive to seize Europe, but it would trigger U.S. nuclear response. In PENTAGONESE, this is part of "automaticism," a technique that removes the possibility of a craven response and thus contributes to a DETERRENT. *The Observer* wrote in 1957: "The German electorate are baffled as to whether NATO is meant to defend their soil, or provide the tripwire for a Soviet-American suicide pact."

The term is based on military tactics: a device, strung low along the ground, to be tripped over by an advancing scout which sets off a signal or an explosion.

Still in use, it appeared in a 1993 *Boston Globe* piece on post-Gulf War relations with Iraq: "In a further warning to Iraq, the United States dispatched a battalion of troops to Kuwait to act as a tripwire against any further Iraqi incursions into Kuwait."

troglodytic out of the political Stone Age; traditional to the point of seeming prehistoric; like a caveman.

Pronounced trog-loh-DIH-tik, this adjective comes from *troglodyte*, a term for a primitive cave-dweller, found in English since the mid-1500s. Borrowed from the Greek *troglodytes* (formed from *trogle*, "hole, cave," and *dyein*, "to go into"), the term in the nineteenth century took on a transferred sense, similar to *ape* and *Neanderthal*, of "an uncouth person." Robert Louis Stevenson wrote in his 1886 horror story, *The Strange Case of Dr. Jekyll and Mr. Hyde*, of the transformed title character: "God bless me, the man seems hardly human! Something troglodytic . . . ?"

In the early twentieth century, the adjective described anybody old-fashioned and apathetic to current affairs. *Blackwell's Magazine* wrote in 1910 about "a respectable troglodytic peer." In the 1950s, British slang clipped the noun to *trog*, although American usage continues to favor the full term.

By 1980, the term gained a sense of "reactionary" or "extremely conservative" as it became fixed in political usage. The *National Journal* reported in August 1980 on attempts to modernize public utilities; a House subcommittee staff member, according to the *Journal*, said that this industry has some of "the most troglodytic, traditional utility managers to deal with."

A decade later, the adjective was used as an attack term during a Massachusetts political campaign. The *Boston Globe* quoted a candidate who criticized his opponent's attitude in failing to endorse sex education as "troglodytic." See LEFT WING, RIGHT WING.

troika in diplomacy, an executive committee of three—one from each differing camp, the other neutral; in economics, the President's three leading economic advisers.

At a General Assembly session in New York in the fall of 1960, Nikita S. Khrushchev proposed that the office of Secretary-General of the United Nations be replaced by a trio of Secretaries-General, one each for the Communist, capitalist, and NEUTRALIST states.

The Soviet Premier's proposal followed action by the United Nations in the Congo which angered the Russians. Since all decisions by the troika would have had to be unanimous, it was quite clear that its aim was to make effective action by the international organization unlikely. John F. Kennedy said of the proposal at the time that it would "entrench the COLD WAR in the headquarters of peace."

The proposal was directed against the Secretary-General of the time, Dag Hammarskjöld. Khrushchev called Hammarskjöld a "nice man" but, unfortunately, the representative of "the imperialist nations." At this session Khrushchev took off a shoe and pounded it on his desk.

The word was adopted in the sixties to describe a triad of Administration economic officials: the Chairman of the Council of Economic Advisers, the Director of the Office of Management and Budget, and the Secretary of the Treasury. When joined by the Chairman of the Federal Reserve Board, they become the QUADRIAD.

Early in the Reagan Administration, the White House staff triumvirate of

James Baker, Ed Meese, and Michael Deaver was referred to as a *troika*; it proved unwieldy, and Baker emerged as top man.

The word is Russian; it means a sled pulled by three horses. Since its UN introduction, it has come to mean any political triumvirate.

Trollope ploy.   See PLOY.

troops   party workers, or those volunteers willing to ring doorbells.

Primary *campaigns* are decided by the *regular* organization's ability to "turn out the *troops*"; the opposing *camp* sets up a *cadre* of *volunteers* who are expected to turn out *troops* of their own. The italicized terms are MILITARY METAPHORS; *troops* is a term gaining preference over *workers*, possibly because of Communist use of the latter.

"Troops" is a collective plural noun from *troupe*, used as "The troops are getting restless." Similarly, a *cohort* was originally a group of soldiers, but now means a single ally or crony.

Although "troops" is mainly used to mean low-level workers, it means all supporters in a campaign. David Broder, writing about the political experts gathering around Governor Ronald Reagan in 1967, headlined his column with a military triple metaphor: "Gunning for a Draft: The Reagan Troops."
See PARTY FAITHFUL.

trot out the ghosts   speechwriters' term for reference to the past luminaries of the speaker's party and to the past "failures" of the opposition party.

"I stand in direct succession to Woodrow Wilson and Franklin Roosevelt and Harry Truman," candidate John F. Kennedy said often in a version of THE SPEECH. "Mr. Nixon, the Republican leader, stands in direct succession to McKinley, to Coolidge, to Hoover, to Landon and to Dewey." He did not mention Eisenhower.

Republican reference to "the party of Lincoln" is another example of "trotting out the ghosts," although constant quotation of Lincoln by Adlai Stevenson and John Kennedy has resulted in watering down of Lincoln's Republican identification, an erosion which Republicans combat each year at their Lincoln Day dinners.

A good example of "trotting out the ghosts" was Warren G. Harding's 1912 nomination of William Howard Taft; the future President's speech was, in his words, "glorying in retrospection." He hailed Taft as one "as wise and patient as Abraham Lincoln, as modest and dauntless as Ulysses S. Grant, as temperate and peace-loving as Rutherford B. Hayes, as patriotic and intellectual as James A. Garfield, as courtly and generous as Chester A. Arthur, as learned in the law as Benjamin Harrison, as sympathetic and brave as William McKinley, as progressive as his predecessor."

Harding did not mention the name of "his predecessor" because he was Theodore Roosevelt, who was running against Taft for the nomination. Harding feared that that particular ghost was too lively to trot out.

true believer   used in friendly fashion, a loyalist and comrade in arms; used by a political opponent, a fanatic.

In current political usage, "true believer" is most often applied to conservatives, as one who holds firmly to the articles of faith and considers any compromise of them for political gain to be an abandonment of basic principles. The most frequently used charge by a true believer is SELLOUT.

The term is applied to any hard-line group. "To the pragmatists such as Chou En-lai," editorialized the *New York Times* in October 1971, "the invitation to the American President was an opportunity to advance China's prestige on the world scene and to deter the preventive war advocates in Moscow. But to the true believers in Peking, the invitation must have seemed a sellout of all China's proclaimed revolutionary principles—as reprehensible in the eyes of those fanatics as was Nikita Khrushchev's visit to the United States in 1959 as President Eisenhower's guest."

But the expression need not reflect either fanaticism or tough-mindedness; a certain affection for steadfastness can be seen in the use of the phrase as the title of a 1953 book by longshoreman-philosopher Eric Hoffer, and in the *Wall Street Journal*'s farewell to Hubert Humphrey on January 16, 1978: "Last of the True Believers?"

The phrase is used internationally. Glenn Frankel of the *Washington Post* wrote from Johannesburg, South Africa, in 1992: "For many blacks, routine acts of daily life such as commuting to work have become fraught with danger. Police, once true believers and loyal enforcers of the old order, seem laconic and demoralized."

The origin is in the Koran, written in the seventh century: "O true believers, take your necessary precautions against your enemies, and either go forth to war in separate parties, or go forth all together in a body."

See IDEOLOGY; LITMUS-TEST ISSUE; PARTY FAITHFUL.

Truman Doctrine. See DOCTRINES.

"truth-in" construction a device to build persuasion into the generic name of legislation.

"Truth in Packaging" legislation caused running controversy in the early sixties. Proponents held that the public needed to be protected from misleading claims on packages of goods, especially regarding weight and bulk; opponents felt such restraints were captious, unnecessary, and a step toward government control of all advertising.

"Truth in Lending" followed, with proponents seeking to force banks, loan companies, and all suppliers of credit to show borrowers exactly how much the interest charges would add to costs.

The technique of slipping a message in a name (see RIGHT TO WORK) did not begin with truth in packaging. Early New Deal legislation included an attempted reform of the Wall Street community. "Undiscriminating people," wrote Raymond Moley, "described the securities bill [of 1933] as the 'Truth in Securities Act.' . . . But as the year passed, even Roosevelt realized that the Act in its existing form was unworkable . . ." This led to the Securities Act of 1934, and the Securities and Exchange Commission. This act continued to be called "Truth in Securities" throughout the thirties, though the designation is no longer current.

Columnist Max Lerner wrote in 1939:

> In meeting the propaganda danger, something like the SEC pattern would be the most effective procedure. We have a Truth in Securities Act to make sure that there is no rigging of the stock market . . . are we to have nothing to protect us against the infinitely more dangerous advertising of anti-labor, anti-democratic, anti-Semitic lies?
>
> I know that liberals will immediately say: Why could not a Truth in Opinion Act be used against the left as well as the right? The answer is that it is already in use against the left.

truth squad a team of officials, usually congressmen, organized to harass an opposition candidate by following close on his heels with refutations.

The phrase has a built-in advantage, implying what the opposition leader says is not true. The technique is useful and growing, since it makes the opposition more careful in its charges and gets newspaper space with "the last word" after a candidate has left a city.

John F. Kennedy was dogged by a "truth squad" headed by Republican Senator Hugh Scott of Pennsylvania in the 1960 campaign. Toward the end of the campaign, he used them as a foil: "Now we have five days before this campaign is over. I cannot predict what is going to happen. The 'truth squad' has been ditched. They told the truth once and they don't let them travel around anymore."

The term may have had its origin in the Agriculture Department's so-called Poison Squad at the turn of the century. The department's Chief Chemist, Dr. Harvey W. Wiley, had collected a group of young scientists so dedicated to the fight for good food-and-drug legislation that they won the nickname by actually testing adulterated foods on themselves. Their efforts and the publicity about the adulteration of food—and particularly meat—led to the Pure Food Bill of 1906.

Its early use as a political technique was in 1919, when a group of Republican congressmen dogged Woodrow Wilson's steps as he tried to sell the idea of the League of Nations to the American people.

The best squelch was Adlai Stevenson's, who said of a Republican squad following him around in 1956: "A truth squad bears the same relationship to 'truth' as a Fire Department does to 'fire.'"

Tuesday Lunch. See WEDNESDAY CLUB.

turkey farm a PATRONAGE-packed agency.

In 1992, the *New York Times* ran an editorial about Washington's slow response to the victims of Hurricane Andrew. Blame was primarily directed at the Bush Administration's neglect of the Federal Emergency Management Agency. Staff investigators for the House Appropriations Committee said that FEMA was "widely viewed as a dumping ground" for political appointees, "a turkey farm, if you will."

Rooted in theatrical slang for "flop show," *turkey* became associated in the 1960s with any congenital failure. This fowl derogation (see BIRD META-PHORS) flies in the face of Ben Franklin's suggestion for our national bird; instead of supporting the bald eagle, Franklin preferred the turkey.

turnarounds creating a phrase by reversing the construction of a famous saying; antithesis.

Franklin Roosevelt in 1932 said that the aim of the national economy "should not be the survival of the fittest," but rather "the fitting of as many human beings as possible into the scheme of surviving."

"It has been said of the world's history hitherto," said Abraham Lincoln, "that might makes right. It is for us and for our time to reverse the maxim, and to say that right makes might." He liked that turnaround, using it again in his 1860 Cooper Union speech: "Let us have faith that right makes might, and in that faith let us to the end dare to do our duty as we understand it."

Turnarounds are not to be confused with *parallel constructions*, often created for purposes of ridicule: G. K. Chesterton undermined "my country, right or wrong" with "my mother, drunk or sober" and anti-Goldwater partisans paralleled "In Your Heart You Know He's Right" with "In Your Guts You Know He's Nuts."

President James Buchanan, never noted for his wit, provided a classic turnaround in 1858, after an off-year setback at the polls: "We have met the enemy and we are theirs." (Cartoonist Walt Kelly, in "Pogo," also played with Captain Oliver Perry's line: "We have met the enemy and he is us.")

See Fitzgerald's use under SPOILS SYSTEM, and "shoo-out" under SHOO-IN.

turnip day. See DO-NOTHING CONGRESS.

turnout the number of voters on Election Day; also, the size of a partisan crowd.

Lip service is always given to the advisability of getting everyone to come to the polls. Franklin D. Roosevelt on election eve in 1940 said on the radio: "Last Saturday night, I said that freedom of speech is of no use to the man who has nothing to say and that freedom of worship is of no use to the man who has lost his God. And tonight I should like to add that a free election is of no use to the man who is too indifferent to vote . . ."

But what the working politician really means is the need for his own side to turn out the vote. The importance of doing so may have been illustrated by the rueful remark of Archibald Crossley, one of the many incorrect pollsters in the 1948 Truman-Dewey contest, who said later, "The result clearly showed what happens when one party gets out its vote and the other does not." (For a contrary opinion, see Samuel Lubell's comment under STAY-AT-HOMES.)

Systematic party efforts at turnout probably started with Aaron Burr and his Tammany Hall organization in 1800. Using a card index of the voters, members of the Society of Tammany made sure that all the PARTY FAITHFUL went to the polls.

According to columnist Leonard Lyons, President Johnson was touched by the huge crowd which greeted him at the airport in Seoul, Korea. Johnson said he had asked his host how large

the crowd was and the President of Korea replied, "Two million, two million people"—and then continued earnestly, "I'm sorry, President Johnson, but that's all the people I have."

The word has been exported. In the South Vietnamese election of 1967, civilian candidate Tran Van Huong nodded approvingly at a crowd that had come to hear him speak and told a reporter, "If everywhere we go from now on, the publicity and the turnout are as good, I am satisfied."

Not everyone is impressed by the need to turn out the vote. There was, for instance, the proverbial little old lady, quoted by comedian Jack Paar, who firmly stated, "I never vote. It only encourages them."

turn the rascals out. See PROVERBS AND AXIOMS, POLITICAL.

Tweedledum and Tweedledee literary characters used to attack the similarity of the two parties by those who claim to see not a DIME'S WORTH OF DIFFERENCE.

The twinlike characters popularized by Lewis Carroll in 1869 were injected into American political discourse by cartoonist Thomas Nast throughout the 1870s as he caricatured the characters chosen by "Boss" Tweed of Tammany. Long after Nast, the useful device has been brought into political play.

"There is little doubt," wrote Clinton Rossiter in 1960, "that many voters see nothing to choose between the Tweedledumism of the Democrats and Tweedledeeism of the Republicans. Lacking any third choice, they fail to choose at all."

As a Republican candidate attacked by disappointed conservatives as being a "me-tooer" (see ME TOO), Thomas E. Dewey wrote:

It is only necessary to compare the platforms of both parties in a normal presidential year to find how similar they are. This similarity is highly objectionable to a vociferous few. They rail at both parties, saying they represent nothing but a choice between Tweedledee and Tweedledum . . . . These impractical theorists with a "passion for neatness" demand that our parties be sharply divided, one against the other, in interest, membership, and doctrine. They want to drive all moderates and liberals out of the Republican party and then have the remainder join forces with the conservative groups of the South. Then they would have everything very neatly arranged, indeed. The Democratic party would be the liberal-to-radical party. The Republican party would be the conservative-to-reactionary party. The results would be neatly arranged too. The Republicans would lose every election and the Democrats would win every election.

Tweedledum and Tweedledee are generally assumed to be creations of Lewis Carroll; in his *Through the Looking Glass*, they sing the ditty "The Walrus and the Carpenter." Carroll took them from John Byrom's satire about bickering schools of musicians in the 1750s whose real difference was negligible. The best-known Byrom verse:

Some say compared to Bononcini
That Mynheer Handel's but a ninny;
Others aver that he to Handel
Is scarcely fit to hold a candle.
Strange all this difference should be
'Twixt tweedle-dum and tweedle-dee.

Tweed Ring. See TAMMANY TIGER.

twenty years of treason an extreme version of the SOFT ON COMMUNISM charge, referring to the period (1932–52) in which Democrats occupied the White House.

In early 1954 Senator Joseph McCarthy made a series of speeches arranged by the Republican National Committee in nine cities, giving them the title "Twenty Years of Treason." In Charleston, W.Va., he stated the theme: "The issue between the Republicans and Democrats is clearly drawn. It has been deliberately drawn by those who have been in charge of twenty years of treason."

"Dwight Eisenhower," wrote Robert Donovan, "was quick to proclaim his belief in the loyalty of Democrats in disassociating himself from McCarthy's claim that the Roosevelt and Truman administrations represented 'twenty years of treason.'" As the Senator demanded information from Administration appointees in hearings, the White House bluntly stated that its rights "cannot be usurped by any individual who may seek to set himself above the laws of our land." The use of "individual" rather than "man" or "person" or even "anyone" is pure Eisenhower style, indicating that he personally composed or edited the statement.

Senator McCarthy promptly amended his phrase, referring to "the evidence of treason that has been growing over the past twenty—[*pause*]—twenty-one years." See McCARTHYISM; POINT OF ORDER.

The phrase is used today mainly in recollections of the McCarthy era, though as late as 1960 the Bulletin of the John Birch Society held that the "key" to the advance of world Communism was "treason right within our government and the place to find it is right in Washington."

If this be demagoguery, some made the most of it. The combination of alliteration and neat packaging of the combined Roosevelt-Truman Administrations made "twenty years of treason" a well-turned catch phrase.

The construction, however, predated McCarthy. In Great Britain, Labour party spokesmen since the end of World War II have hammered at the Conservatives for "thirteen wasted years," blaming the nation's ills on thirteen consecutive years of Conservative domination.

This was preceded by a 1936 Republican convention keynote address punctuated with "three long years!" This slogan threatened to become effective until FDR flattened it with his own account of the Harding-Coolidge-Hoover era: "Nine mocking years with the golden calf and three long years of the scourge . . . nine crazy years at the ticker and three long years in the breadline!"

twisting slowly, slowly in the wind

left exposed to political attack; abandoned.

The phrase was made a part of the political vocabulary in 1973 by White House Domestic Council director John Ehrlichman, who reported to this lexicographer on its origin: "'Twisting slowly' is on a recording I made of a phone talk with [John] Dean re [FBI Acting Director] Pat Gray. RN [Richard Nixon] had decided to withdraw his nomination but no one had told Gray, and Pat was going back to the Judiciary Committee and taking punishment day after day. He was a corpse hanging there and RN hadn't yet cut him down for a decent burial. It seemed an apt description."

The nice overkill of the word—treating an undefended aide as a corpse dangling in the breeze—is in the grand tradition of political hyperbole, and has been used frequently since, especially regarding confirmation hearings.

The phrase has an ancient "hanging" connotation: in his 1785 edition of *A Dictionary of the Vulgar Tongue*, Captain Frances Grose lists "twisted" as "executed, hanged" and there is another reference to that lugubrious meaning in the *New Canting Dictionary* (1725). Slang expert Stuart Berg Flexner, in a letter to the author, sug-

gested: "I find that the trap-door scaffold and the hangman's knot weren't accepted before the 19th century, meaning that before this late date victims suffered slow strangulation while out there kicking and twisting at the end of the rope."

The most vivid fictional use of the metaphor (and perhaps Ehrlichman's unconscious source) was in the concluding paragraph of Aldous Huxley's *Brave New World,* written in 1932: "Just under the crown of the arch dangled a pair of feet . . . Slowly, very slowly, like two unhurried compass needles, the feet turned towards the right; north, northeast, east, south-east, south, south-south-west; then paused, and, after a few seconds, turned as unhurriedly back towards the left. South-south-west, south, south-east, east . . ."

The Ehrlichman phrase will probably become fixed in the political lexicon more securely than most other WATERGATE WORDS. In 1976 the British publication *The Economist* explained how Hua Kuo-feng's rise led to the downfall of Chiang Ching, widow of Chairman Mao Tse-tung, and titled the story: "How Hua Left Mrs. Mao Twisting in the Wind."

In 1990, R. W. Apple, Jr., of the *New York Times* wrote: "April C. Glaspie, the American Ambassador to Baghdad, was on leave when Saddam Hussein attacked on Aug. 2. Many believe she is the leading Foreign Service authority on the Arab world, but she remains in Washington, with little role to play except twisting slowly in the wind."

A related, though less horrific, metaphor for a nominee left unsupported is *hung out to dry.*

twisting the lion's tail

speeches originally aimed at nineteenth-century Irish voters; now, any attack on the British government.

Early written references are few, though *Harper's Weekly* in 1872 ran a cartoon showing President Grant with his foot on the British lion's tail. Later, in 1889, Theodore Roosevelt wrote that "just at present our statesmen seem inclined to abandon the tail of the lion and instead we are plucking vigorously at the caudal feathers of that delightful war-fowl, the German eagle—a cousin of our own bald-headed bird of prey" (see BALD EAGLE).

Carl Schurz indicated in 1898 that the phrase was already familiar when he wrote: ". . . for the present attitude of Great Britain will no longer permit the American demagogue to seek popularity by twisting the British Lion's tail."

The expression is sometimes used in the general sense of an attack on traditional institutions. When in 1986 Maryland's Attorney General Stephen Sachs announced his candidacy for the governorship, he declared: "There is an element of twisting the lion's tail in me. I do enjoy the unmasking of hypocrisy . . . challenging bigness when bigness is wrong."

The phrase remains current as the act becomes more frequent.

two-bit politician a cheap politician, often used in conjunction with "tinhorn gambler," with adjectives interchangeable.

"Tinhorn politician" was an epithet coined by William Allen White in an *Emporia* (Kansas) *Gazette* editorial on October 25, 1901. "Tinhorn gambler" has been traced back to an 1885 issue of the *New Mexican Review:* "We have been greatly annoyed of late by a lot of tin horn gamblers and prostitutes."

New York Mayor Fiorello La Guardia lumped both usages together in frequent blasts at the "tinhorn gamblers and two-bit politicians." Former Tammany leader Edward Costikyan

wrote in 1966: "La Guardia fortified the anti-political-leader bias of the good-government tradition. His tirades against 'tinhorn gamblers' and 'two-bit politicians' deepened the public association between politicians and evildoers. In retrospect, his administration became a myth—a myth which equated good government with the absence of political leaders in government . . ."

An obvious derivation might appear to be from a cheap, or tin, noisemaker—hence, noisy politician of a low variety. However, historian George Willison offers a more plausible explanation in discussing gambling ethics of the early West in *Here They Found Gold:* "Chuck-a-luck operators shake their dice in a small churnlike affair of metal—hence the expression 'tinhorn gambler,' for the game is rather looked down on as one for 'chubbers' and chuck-a-luck gamblers are never admitted within the aristocratic circle of faro-dealers."

two cars in every garage. See CHICKEN IN EVERY POT.

two minutes to midnight. See DOOMSDAY MACHINE.

two-party system in American thinking, happy medium between one-party control and a profusion of splinter parties; something most U.S. politicians speak of with reverence.

"I think it is very important that we have a two-party country," President Lyndon Johnson joked at a press conference in 1964. "I am a fellow that likes small parties, and the Republican party is about the size I like."

The two-party system, a practice seldom found outside the U.S. and Great Britain, is a phrase difficult to find in early writings about government, but there are plenty of strong opinions about the general idea. Warnings against parties in general range from George Washington's "The spirit of party serves always to distract the public councils, and enfeeble the public administration" (1796) to Nikita Khrushchev's "After the liquidation of classes we have a monolithic society. Therefore, why found another party? That would be like voluntarily letting someone put a flea in your shirt" (1957).

Most of the comments about the division of political activity by parties, gleefully quoted today by those who plead for more BIPARTISANSHIP in foreign policy and urban affairs, are based on ideological division (as in England and France) rather than administrative division (as in the U.S.). Joseph Addison wrote about a philosophical split in *The Spectator* in 1711: "There can not a greater judgment befall a country than such a dreadful spirit of division as rends a government into two distinct people, and makes them greater strangers and more averse to one another than if they were actually two different nations." The wrench of ideological faction concerned Thomas Jefferson in 1789: "If I could not go to Heaven but with a party I would not go there at all."

The early defenders of the two-party system also spoke mostly of ideological division. "Party divisions," wrote Edmund Burke in 1769, "whether on the whole operating for good or evil, are things inseparable from free government." Horace Walpole wrote in 1760 that "A nation without parties is soon a nation without curiosity," and Disraeli in 1864 held that "Party is organized opinion."

Another reason given for the two-party system was the inherent cleansing process of having INS AND OUTS. Congressman, later autocratic Speaker, Thomas B. Reed put it bluntly in 1880: "The best system is to have one party govern and the other party watch." The "watching," in its active sense, meant keeping it honest and responsive; competition for office bred new programs and advances.

The ideological differences within each major U.S. party are greater than the difference between the parties, despite attempts to delineate fundamental schisms of beliefs. Democratic orators have tried to separate themselves—the PARTY OF THE PEOPLE—from the "party of the SPECIAL INTERESTS"; the Republicans have countered with variations of their platform of 1908: "The trend of Democracy is toward Socialism, while the Republican party stands for a wise and regulated individualism. Socialism would destroy wealth; Republicanism would prevent its abuse."

There is undoubtedly a general difference in the approach, appeal, and personality of the two U.S. parties, but the "two-party system" is more of a means to political power and administration than a means to social revolution. In this sense, the system is much the same as our "adversary system" of criminal justice, in which the truth is expected to win in fair competition.

Coalition is always a danger to the two-party system. FDR's war cabinet brought in Republicans Stimson and Knox; Churchill's deputy was his archrival, Clement Attlee. Wendell Willkie, in his LOYAL OPPOSITION speech, drew the line: "We, who stand ready to serve our country behind our Commander in Chief, nevertheless retain the right, and I will say the duty, to debate the course of our government. Ours is a two-party system. Should we ever permit one party to dominate our lives entirely, democracy would collapse and we would have dictatorship."

To most Americans, the two-party system is a contrasting phrase for *one-party rule* or *single-party domination*. It ranks with FREE ENTERPRISE, the

AMERICAN WAY OF LIFE, CHECKS AND BALANCES, and the AMERICAN DREAM as an unassailable political phrase.

Whenever one party wins a particularly lopsided victory, as in 1936, 1964, 1972, and 1984, fears are expressed about the future of the system. Politicians worry about the U.S. adopting a configuration of power such as that in Japan's Diet in most of the postwar period, which Yale professor Warren M. Tsuneishi called "the one-and-one-half party system" characterized by "a dominant party that monopolizes power and alone knows how to govern while opposed by a permanent minority group that at times seems 'positively afraid of power.'" Somehow, in the U.S., the pendulum has always managed to swing back.

A left-handed but intensely practical reason for attaching oneself to one of two parties was given by George Savile, Marquess of Halifax, in 1690: "If there are two parties a man ought to adhere to that which he disliketh least, though in the whole he doth not approve it; for whilst he doth not list himself in one or the other party, he is looked upon as such a straggler that he is fallen upon by both."

See ME TOO; TWEEDLEDUM AND TWEEDLEDEE; PARTISAN; PARTY LOYALTY; THIRD- PARTY MOVEMENT.

U

ugly Americans   American diplomats and businessmen abroad who undercut foreign policy with their pomposity, high living, and lack of communication with the great majority of natives.

The phrase was taken from Eugene Burdick and William Lederer's *The Ugly American,* a group of related fictional stories about U.S. businessmen and officials in Southeast Asia.

In the book, published in 1958, the "ugly American" was a man who embodied just the opposite of what the phrase has come to mean. He was a hard-working, compassionate American who helped to overcome the ill will caused by other characters in the book. "Ugly" referred to his physical appearance. However, since the novel attacked those Americans who caused resentment by their isolation and greed, the word "ugly" has come to be applied to the villains of the piece.

Graham Greene titled a subsequent book *The Quiet American;* Victor Lasky wrote about blunders in Soviet diplomacy in *The Ugly Russians.*

New York Times correspondent Michael Kaufman wrote from Africa in July 1978: "'The Ugly Nigerian' has become a cliché in parts of Africa . . . as in the case of the stereo-typed American, the newer epithet is the product as much of admiration and envy as of contempt."

ugly on an ape.   See LIKE UGLY ON AN APE.

umbrella symbol   APPEASEMENT, from the umbrella carried by British Prime Minister Neville Chamberlain on his return from the Munich Conference (see MUNICH ANALOGY).

A character of Fred Allen's radio program in the thirties who was afflicted with amnesia and trying—by the slow process of elimination—to figure out who he was, said, "I don't have an umbrella—so I can't be Neville Chamberlain."

The continuing close identification with Chamberlain, appeasement, and umbrellas is illustrated in this passage from historian Eric Goldman's *The Crucial Decade* about Eisenhower's arrival at an airport: "When the President's plane, the Columbine III, neared the Washington airport, a summer shower was spattering the Capital. Vice-President Richard Nixon issued an instruction to the officials going out to the airport. No umbrellas, the Vice-President said, because people might be reminded of Prime Minister Neville

Chamberlain coming back with his umbrella from the Munich appeasement of Hitler."

In the final days before the Democratic nomination in 1960, columnists Rowland Evans and Robert Novak claimed that candidate Lyndon Johnson joined the attack on Joseph P. Kennedy, his rival's father, recalling the former ambassador's reputation for appeasement. "On the very day of the balloting, July 14," they wrote, "Johnson took up the cry: 'I wasn't any Chamberlain umbrella-policy man. I never thought Hitler was right.'"

The umbrella has other political symbolic meanings as well. A presidential program can be an umbrella under which congressional candidates scurry before an election. Not surprisingly, the symbol can be extended from mild protection to military preparedness to pessimism. "The American people," wrote Al Smith in 1931, "never carry an umbrella. They prepare to walk in eternal sunshine."

For other symbols in politics, see CIGARETTE-HOLDER SYMBOL.

un-American not conforming to the ideology or sharing the same values as the particular American using the term.

The word "American," as used in the term "un-American," describes neither one's nationality (a U.S. citizen) nor one's point of origin (the Western Hemisphere). American in this sense is short for AMERICANISM, a creed based on economic opportunity, political freedom, and social mobility.

The Fourth of July is not merely a national holiday hailing the birth of a nation, like Bastille Day in France; it is more of a commemoration of the realization of an ideology, comparable to the Communist May Day.

One who is "un-American" does not, in the accuser's opinion, share that ideology. "This concept of 'un-American activities,' as far as I know, does not have its counterpart in other countries," wrote Berkeley professor Seymour Martin Lipset. "American patriotism is allegiance to values, to a creed, not solely to a nation. An American political leader could not say, as Winston Churchill did in 1940, that the English Communist Party was composed of Englishmen, and he did not fear an Englishman . . . this emphasis on ideological conformity to presumably common political values . . . legitimatizes the hunt for 'un-Americans' in our midst."

The word might have had its origin in the aristocratic point of view of Alexander Hamilton, alluded to in this 1880 letter by President James Garfield: "More than a hundred years ago, a young student of Columbia College was arguing the ideas of the American Revolution and American Union against the un-American loyalty to monarchy of his college president and professors." Printed citations date back to the early nineteenth century.

The word gained political popularity in a reaction against the American, or KNOW-NOTHING, party in the mid-nineteenth century. The anti-Catholic, anti-Semitic, antiforeign philosophy of the "Sams," styled as American, naturally drew a blast as anti-American, or un-American, as in this 1844 pamphlet: "Misguided men assuming the title Native American, but un-American at heart, breathing destruction on those not born here, denouncing a whole religious community and all professing a particular faith, have been joined with the Whigs."

Republican William Seward added a few years later: ". . . every thing is un-American which makes a distinction of whatever kind, in this country, between the native born American and him whose lot is directed to be cast here by an overruling Providence. . ."

In its early use, then, the word meant

"intolerant"; this usage continues today as a second meaning of the word, as intolerant not of religion or race but of dissent or any form of radicalism.

After the collapse of the Know-Nothings, *un-American* took on its antiradical, antinonconformist coloration. The *New York Times* complained in 1870 that the *New York Tribune* "stigmatizes its opponent as false to his party, or as 'un-American'—its two favorite and well-worn labels."

The Democratic platform of 1896 held gold bimetallism to be "not only un-American, but anti-American"; soon afterward editor William Allen White began a generation-long campaign against Bryan's "un-American doctrine of state paternalism." Third-party candidate Robert La Follette in 1924 stressed his movement's moderation: "We are unalterably opposed to any class government, whether it be the existing dictatorship of plutocracy or the dictatorship of the proletariat. Both are essentially undemocratic and un-American."

The word gained its greatest prominence in the late thirties as the name of a congressional committee, nicknamed by its initials in the sixties, HUAC. *The New Yorker* commented in 1948:

> One questionable thing about the House Committee on un-American Activities is its name. . . . The word "un-American," besides beginning with a small letter and gradually working up to a capital, is essentially a foolish, bad word, hardly worth the little hyphen it needs to hold it together. Literally, nothing in this country can be said to be un-American. "Un" means "not," and anything that happens within our borders is American, no matter what its nature, no matter how far off the beam it may be.

The word is used as an epithet casting the person attacked outside the pale of common values; its use, however, carries the built-in boomerang of indicating the user to be intolerant of dissent. An opinion piece in *Newsday* during the 1992 Presidential campaign commented: "Bush at his debate lectern had renewed his innuendo that Bill Clinton's opposition to the Vietnam War and draft avoidance at that time had been un-American, near traitorous."

Conservative Barry M. Goldwater wrote a *Washington Post* essay in 1993 in favor of lifting the ban on homosexuals in the military; the headline was "The Gay Ban: Just Plain Un-American."

uncertain trumpet. See MUSICAL METAPHORS.

Uncle Sam   symbol for the collective citizenry of the U.S.

In the minds of most Americans, Uncle Sam is a stern-looking man on a World War I recruiting poster by James Montgomery Flagg pointing his finger directly at the viewer and saying: "I want YOU for the U.S. Army."

He was created in the War of 1812. The first written record of his appearance is in the *Troy* (N.Y.) *Post*, September 3, 1813: "'Loss upon loss,' and 'no ill luck stir[r]ing but what lights upon Uncle Sam's shoulders,' exclaim the Government editors, in every part of the Country. . . . This cant name for our government has got almost as current as 'John Bull.' The letters U.S. on the government waggons &c are supposed to have given rise to it." (John Bull had a more specific genesis in a 1712 satire by Dr. John Arbuthnot, and is now the cartoonists' symbol—along with a lion—of Great Britain.)

Forst's *Naval History of the United States* relates that a government inspector of provisions in Troy, New York, named Samuel Wilson was the original Uncle Sam. He was supposed to have been given the nickname during the War of 1812 by workmen in the military stores handling casks labeled "E.A.—U.S.," with Elbert Anderson the name of the contractor. The story is not substantiated.

Charles Ledyard Norton wrote in 1890: "Uncle Sam is for Americans what John Bull is for the English, save that he is always pictorially represented in exaggerated and impossible habiliments, such as might be worn on the stage by a burlesque actor, and with a personality to match, while the typical John Bull takes life seriously in sober garb, like a 'fine old English gentleman.'"

There is, however, a tradition of taking advantage of Uncle Sam. In current usage, when Uncle Sam is being described as one unduly taken advantage of, he becomes *Uncle Sugar*. To European debtor nations in the 1920s, U.S. stood for *Uncle Shylock*, demanding his pound of flesh. Individual Americans were known for a time as BROTHER JONATHAN; members of the Know-Nothing party, styled the "American" party, were known as "Sams" after the Uncle Sam symbol.

There may be some Uncle Sam connection with a small boy's demand that another quit a fight by "saying uncle"; at any rate, when a politician talks about *going to Uncle,* he means going to the federal government for aid.

Uncle Tom a subservient black; as an "ism," inadequate militancy on civil rights; verb form, "Tomming."

Time magazine in 1963 defined the then-current usage of "Uncle Tom" as "one who warns against violence in civil rights demonstrations." A subsequent definition by Alex Haley, in the March 1, 1964, *New York Times Magazine,* is broader: "Uncle Tom: A Negro accused by another of comporting himself among white people in a manner which the accuser interprets as servile or cowardly; or a Negro who

other Negroes feel has betrayed, or sullied, in any way, a dignified, militant, forthright Negro image."

The usage in that sense was at least a generation old. In 1943 Roi Ottley wrote in *New World A-Coming:* "These Southern leaders, sometimes called 'Uncle Toms' by the more radical Negroes, apparently have not made up their minds which way to turn in the present crisis."

By the mid-1960s "Uncle Tom" was one of the worst names a black could direct at another, and posed a danger to any black speaking out for moderation (see BLACK POWER). In 1963, when President Kennedy sent the 88th Congress a far-reaching civil rights bill, a "Community Relations Service" was incorporated to work with local communities. In naming this service, Ted Sorensen wrote, "Negro Congressmen had urged that the words 'mediation' and 'conciliation' had an 'Uncle Tom' air about them and should be stricken from the title."

The largest-circulation black magazine, *Ebony,* made this comparison: "Not unlike those Jews who actively helped their exterminators, are the Uncle Toms who collaborate with white racists by playing the roles of apologist and informer. . . . Such duplicity and complacency, coupled with the old custom of adjusting to a position of inferiority rather than insisting upon his constitutional rights, would have led the Negro to his Buchenwald, had he not learned the prudence—and the power—of positive resistance."

Origin of the phrase, obviously, was Harriet Beecher Stowe's 1852 novel *Uncle Tom's Cabin,* which did more than any other book of the period to dramatize the evils of slavery and became an abolitionists' bible. In 1853 the *New York Tribune* reported the European reception of the Stowe book: "Europe has achieved the luxury of a new sensation in the reception and digestion of Mrs. Stowe's great work. . . . Even our Diplomacy stands aghast at the rushing, swelling flood of Uncle Tomism which is now sweeping over the continent."

The original Uncle Tom was said to have been a slave subsequently ordained as the Rev. J. Henson and presented to Queen Victoria in 1876. A variety of usages of the phrase followed: among them Uncle Tomitude, Uncle Tomized, and Uncle Tomific.

It was not until the civil rights movement gained new momentum in this century that the meaning of Uncle Tom changed from "long-suffering but heroic" to "subservient and not militant enough."

Today some blacks feel that the use of "Uncle" and "Aunt" has often been a racial slight by whites reluctant to give older blacks the titles of "Mr." or "Mrs." Some commercial trade names using avuncular titles—like "Aunt Jemima Pancake Mix" and "Uncle Ben's Rice"—have avoided criticism by changing the picture of their characters to appear slimmer and more attractive, less the stereotype of the "Mammy" or "Uncle Tom."

The name Tom has been used as a generic slight throughout the history of the English language. Tom Fool (leading to tomfoolery) and Tom Farthing were early English dunces; a famous midget was named Tom Thumb, and *tommyrot, tomcat,* and *tomboy* are still in use.

During the MARCH ON WASHINGTON in August 1963 a favorite song was "Keep On a-Walkin'" with its final verse:

Ain't gonna let no Uncle Tom,
Lawdy, turn me 'round, turn
me 'round, turn me 'round,
Ain't gonna let no Uncle Tom,
Lawdy, turn me 'round,
Keep on a-walkin' (yea!)
Keep on a-talkin' (yea!)
Marchin' on to Freedom land.

A synonym for Uncle Tom is "Oreo," the trade name of a cookie that is black on the outside and white in the middle. Similarly, "Toms" among American Indians have been called "apple"—red outside, white inside—and Asians call someone who is yellow on the outside and white on the inside a "banana."

As might be expected, feminists refer to women who cater to male chauvinism as "Aunt Toms."

uncommitted nations. See THIRD WORLD; NEUTRALIST.

underclass the permanently poor; the underemployed and unemployable; society's lowest economic grouping.

The term was coined by Harriet Beecher Stowe, who had a character say in her 1852 novel, *Uncle Tom's Cabin*: "The masses are to rise, and the under class become the upper one."

In 1918, this was reported in Hugh MacDiarmid's *The Company I've Kept*: "The whole history of Society has proved that Society moves forward as a consequence of an underclass overcoming the resistance of a class on top of them."

The social significance of this grouping has been reported since the mid-1960s. The *London Observer* stated in 1964 that "the Negro's protest today is but the first rumbling of the 'underclass.'" The *Seattle Times* noted in 1967 the migration of rural workers to the cities to "join the urban 'underclass.'" *Harper's* magazine commented in 1971 on the urban migration: "Combined with the large influx of Southern blacks during the same period, this process was leaving the ghetto more and more the precinct of a depressed underclass."

In 1993, Chandler Amy Rand wrote in *The Recorder* about social services: "Pass through the doors of most nonprofits and you'll find the despair and inspiration of the indigent, the homeless, the disabled, the abused, the runaways, the AIDS victims, the refugees—the underclass."

The preposition *under* provides a connotation of unfair subordination not normally expressed by the 1772 *lower class*; the antonym is not "overclass" but the 1837 *upper-class*. Although sometimes hyphenated, *underclass* has become a solid word.

underground press. See SAMIZDAT.

unfinished business reason usually given, after much public soul-searching, for running again.

No man ever runs again because he likes the job, because he couldn't make as much in private industry, because he enjoys the play of power, because retirement would be boring, or because he owes too many people too many favors.

On the contrary, reassuming the burdens of office is a great personal sacrifice. His neglected family will gamely go along with his decision because the country, state, or assembly district must come first. The crushing demands of the job must be faced again for another term because the party and the nation need him.

Why does he do it? Why does he hang on grimly to the onerous torch rather than pass it on to the next generation of grasping, ambitious, inexperienced Young Turks who are eager to get their hands on it? The standard reason: "unfinished business."

Any number of quotations from Presidents who chose to run again could be used here, but Harry Truman phrased it in its classic form:

> The compelling motive in my decision to run for the Presidency in 1948 was the same as it had been in 1944. There was still "unfinished business" confronting the most successful fifteen years of Democratic administration in the history of the country. . . . I also felt, without undue ego, that this was no

time for a new and inexperienced hand to take over the government and risk the interruption of our domestic program and put a dangerous strain on our delicately balanced foreign policy.

unflappable calm in a crisis; unmoved by furor.

The sobriquet "unflappable Mac" was applied to Harold Macmillan, British Foreign Minister and Prime Minister (1957–63). For a time spanning the Suez crisis to the Profumo affair he retained his reputation for imperturbability in the face of political storms. In 1967 Mayor Jerome Cavanagh of Detroit was described by the *New York Times* in a profile during the racial riots in his city as "unflappable."

The opening lines from Kipling's "If" describe the unflappable man:

> *If you can keep your head*
> *when all about you*
> *Are losing theirs and blaming*
> *it on you . . .*

A commentary on this poem appeared in the form of signs put up in offices by advertising executives in the early sixties: "If you can keep your head when all about you are losing theirs—perhaps you don't understand the gravity of the situation."

Flap, according to H. L. Mencken, originated with British aviators in World War I as a word for air raid. The mental picture of the flapping wings of birds when frightened is apt; a political flap is a minor crisis, with assurances by professionals that "this, too, shall pass." "Flapdoodle," or nonsense, can be traced back to the American Civil War.

A frequently used synonym for "flap," milder than a FEEDING FRENZY or a FIRESTORM, is *brouhaha*, a fifteenth-century French word for "commotion" or "hubbub" which was introduced into English letters by Oliver Wendell Holmes, Sr., in 1890. The probable origin of brouhaha is the Hebrew *baruch habba*, "blessed be he who enters," exclaimed by synagogue worshipers as part of certain festival prayers.

For the causes of flaps, see FLAK and FALLOUT.

ungovernable   what pessimists consider every major U.S. city to be.

"Is New York City ungovernable?" was a question often asked in the late sixties when strikes, smog, congestion, and a general malaise afflicted the city dweller. The word was probably first used by CBS commentator Eric Sevareid.

"Ungovernable" soon became an urban affairs cliché, trotted out in think pieces following each new strike by public employees, along with "crisis of the cities," the title of a series by the *New York Herald Tribune* in the early sixties.

This adjective, which dates back to 1673, is still in use. Frank Clifford wrote in the *Los Angeles Times* about a recent L.A. mayor's race: "Voters made it clear they did not think the city was ungovernable."

"Governance," another word from the same French root, sprouted in academia and became a vogue-word substitute for "government" or "governing."

unholy alliance   attack phrase on any political agreement, especially when disparate elements find themselves in opposition to the same thing.

"Unholy alliance" was Franklin Roosevelt's characterization of the groups backing Wendell Willkie in the 1940 presidential campaign. Both John L. Lewis, head of the United Mine Workers, and the American Communist party opposed Roosevelt for different reasons; he skillfully used their support of Willkie as a KISS OF DEATH. Wrote Samuel Rosenman: "The Presi-

dent, who for years had been called by political enemies a Communist or a tool of the Communists, was now able to turn the tables on his Republican adversary, and attack the alliance of the Communists, the dictatorial labor leader Lewis, and the old-guard reactionary Republican leaders. This opportunity was unique in his political experience, and he cheerfully took full advantage of it." FDR warned:

> There is something very ominous in this combination . . . within the Republican Party between the extreme reactionary and the extreme radical elements of this country. . . . We all know the story of the unfortunate chameleon which turned brown when placed on a brown rug, and turned red when placed on a red rug, but who died a tragic death when they put him on a Scotch plaid. We all know what would happen to Government if it tried to fulfill all the secret understandings and promises made between the conflicting groups which are now backing the Republican Party.

Bernard Schwartz was an energetic counsel for a House subcommittee investigating the Federal Communications Commission in 1958. When he appeared overzealous to members of the subcommittee, he was fired. His subsequent statement illustrates the current usage of the word: "I accuse the majority of this subcommittee, in order to further their own partisan interests, of joining an unholy alliance between business and the White House to obtain a WHITEWASH."

All "unholy" alliances are based on the "Holy Alliance" signed by the kings of Russia, Prussia, and Austria in Paris in 1815.

See STRANGE BEDFELLOWS; COALITION.

unilateralism   going it alone; a foreign policy that disregards the views of allies.

This word started as a variant of the earlier (1844) noun *unilaterality*. The *-ism* variant is first found in print in 1926, when *Public Opinion* printed that "we must . . . surmount national and social unilateralism in the domain of the spirit." The combining form *uni-*, meaning "one" as in the single-wheeled *unicycle*, differentiates this term from *bilateralism's* reciprocity or *multilateralism's* many-sided approach.

The adjective form, *unilateral*, has been primarily used in politics in the phrase *unilateral disarmament*. Referring to a one-sided decision to destroy weaponry, the term first appeared in a 1929 report in the *Times* of London: "Lord Salisbury agreed that unilateral disarmament had probably reached its limits."

Unilateralism entered American political usage in the 1950s. The historian Arthur Schlesinger, Jr., wrote in 1951: "Unilateralism, to coin one more gobbledygook term, has become the new isolationism. Go it alone; meet force with maximum force; there is no substitute for victory; do not worry about consequences: these are the tenets of the new faith." A *Washington Post* article in 1977 quoted Peter Walters, a British shipping magnate, on "the increasing tendency in the United States toward unilateralism and protectionism."

Gaining a specific sense of "foreign policy that ignores the views of allies," the term was used by Henry Kissinger in his 1979 book, *The White House Years*: "From an early hostility to the American alliance with Japan, . . . the Chinese leaders soon came . . . to view it as a guarantee of America's continued interest in the Western Pacific and a rein on Japanese unilateralism."

The position, however, can provoke criticism of extremism. In 1992, a Pentagon planning paper was revised, according to the *Washington Post*, so that American policy would no longer "aim at nothing less than a—benevolent—world domination. While it keeps the United States very much in business as a global military power, it implicitly disavows the muscle-flexing unilateralism."

Asked about the U.S. role in Bosnia in 1993, Bill Clinton replied: "But I also believe it is imperative that we work with our allies on this. The United States is not in a position to move unilaterally, nor should we."

See GO-IT-ALONE; POLICEMAN OF THE WORLD.

uninhibited, robust and wide-open

complete and uncensored; free to debate thoroughly.

This tripartite modifier appeared first in a 1964 Supreme Court ruling on freedom of speech. Associate Justice William J. Brennan, Jr., issued the opinion in the libel case of *New York Times Co. v. Sullivan*: "We consider this case against the background of a profound national commitment to the principle that debate on public issues should be uninhibited, robust and wide-open, and that it may well include vehement, caustic and sometimes unpleasantly sharp attacks on government and public officials."

Somewhat redundant in its call for open debate, the phrase has been repeatedly used in the decades since that decision to justify both spoken and written freedom. It appeared, for example, in a 1984 *Washington Post* editorial about the placement of posters on public transportation. The *Post* quoted the Supreme Court decision for debate that is "'uninhibited, robust and wide-open,'" adding, "Public agencies allocating public space for the expression of political views have a special obligation to protect these rights."

Union. See STATE OF THE UNION.

United Nations international organization of member states; name coined by FDR.

Samuel Rosenman wrote of the bathroom agreement that named the world body:

> He [FDR] was also pleased—and proud—that it was he who had suggested the phrase "United Nations" to Churchill. Churchill, in public utterances, had referred to them as "Allied Nations" and "Associated Nations." The President thought of "United Nations," not as an analogy to "United States," but rather as expressive of the fact that the Allies were united in a common purpose. Having hit upon that phrase one day, he immediately had someone wheel him right into Churchill's room, interrupting the Churchillian bath, and the two agreed then and there upon the name. The same name was used three years later to designate the formal worldwide entity, the United Nations Organization.

The British Prime Minister confirmed this in his war memoirs: "The President has chosen the title 'United Nations' for all the Powers now working together. This is much better than 'Alliance,' which places him in constitutional difficulties, or 'Associated Powers,' which is flat."

Bartlett's Familiar Quotations offers the specific passage from Lord Byron's 1812 poetic work, "Childe Harold's Pilgrimage," that Churchill quoted to FDR in 1941 to support the term *United Nations*:

Thou fatal Waterloo.
Millions of tongues record thee, and anew
Their children's lips shall echo them and say—
"Here, where the sword united nations drew,
Our countrymen were warring on that day!"
And this is much, and all which will not pass away.

Ironically, it was another American President, Woodrow Wilson, who chose "covenant" rather than "agreement" or "treaty" in the "Covenant of the League of Nations"; he felt that the Old Testament word, recalling God's covenant with Abraham, added a necessary solemnity.

United States of America coinage attributed to pamphleteer Thomas Paine.

Claims a biographer, in *Tom Paine, America's Godfather:* "To Paine also belongs the honor of naming our country the 'United States of America.' He was the first to use the name in print, and it was his own creation." Soon after the Declaration of Independence, Paine brandished the title at Lord Howe. "The United States of America," he wrote in the second issue of *The Crisis,* "will sound as pompously in the world or in history as The Kingdom of Great Britain." ("Pompous" then meant "important," rather than the present meaning, "self-important.")

The naming was authoritative. The Articles of Confederation begin: "Article I. The style of this confederacy shall be, 'THE UNITED STATES OF AMERICA.'"

In current usage, it is referred to as the U.S., which is often written as US. The use of all three initials seems corny, as in "the good old U.S.A.," though such corniness is embraced in the expression "U.S. of A." It is known familiarly as UNCLE SAM and Uncle Sugar.

united we stand an early U.S. motto that never quite made it to official status.

John Dickenson wrote "The Patriot's Appeal" in 1776:

Then join hand in hand, brave Americans all—
By uniting we stand, by dividing we fall.

The State of Kentucky sharpened it to "United we stand; divided we fall" and adopted it as its state motto in 1792. But the U.S. had adopted another motto in 1777—"E Pluribus Unum" (From Many, One), first found on the title page of the *Gentleman's Miscellany* in January 1692—and "united we stand" was blocked, though many Americans still think it is the translation for *E Pluribus Unum.*

Salmon P. Chase, Lincoln's Secretary of the Treasury, placed "In God We Trust" on coins to go with "E Pluribus Unum" and "Liberty," crowding the coin so that there was obviously no space left for "United We Stand." The rear of the Great Seal, published on every dollar bill, contains some Latin slogans not known to one American in a million. "Annuit Coeptis" means "He [God] has favored our undertakings" (from Vergil's *Aeneid,* Book IX, verse 625), and "Novus Ordo Seclorum" means "A new order of the ages" (from Vergil's fourth *Eclogue*). Both mottoes were proposed by Charles Thomson, Secretary of Congress, in a report adopted by the Continental Congress on June 20, 1782. Why? Edwin S. Costrell, chief of the Historical Division of the U.S. Department of State, informed the author: "In response to your query 'why they appear on the Seal,' I can only conjecture that Thomson, in proposing the mottoes, and the Congress, in adopting them, considered them to be appropriate."

"United we stand, divided we fall" combines two old concepts. "Union is Strength" is an old English proverb; the idea is expressed in Shakespeare's *King John:* "This union shall do more than battery can/To our fast-closed gates." "Divide and conquer" (in the original, "divide and reign") has a record at least as old as 1633.

In 1992, Ross Perot styled his nascent political organization "United We Stand America," but by 1993 many of his early supporters stood disunited.

"America the Beautiful" is more singable than "The Star-Spangled Banner," which, however, remains the national anthem. Similarly, "United we stand" is stronger and more intelligible than any Latin motto, including the sacrosanct "E Pluribus Unum"; unfortunately, its supporters have been divided.

unleash Chiang Republican promise to remove restraints on Chiang Kaishek's Taiwan forces, which it was felt might intimidate Communist China; promise was kept, but China was not intimidated.

In the late forties and early fifties, there was a strong feeling in the U.S. that the "let the dust settle" policy had caused the free world to "lose" China to Communism. To add insult to injury, the anti-Communist Chinese forces on Formosa were being held back from launching an invasion of their homeland. See "WHO-LOST" CONSTRUCTION.

John Foster Dulles, first Dewey's and then Eisenhower's chief foreign policy adviser, was the American most associated with a promise to "unleash Chiang." When he became President, Eisenhower redeemed the Republican pledge with this statement:

> In June, 1950, following the aggressive attack on the Republic of Korea, the United States Seventh Fleet was instructed both to prevent attack upon Formosa and also to insure that Formosa should not be used as a base of operations against the Chinese Communist mainland. . . . I am . . . issuing instructions that the Seventh Fleet no longer be employed to shield Communist China. Permit me to make crystal clear this order implies no aggressive intent on our part. But we certainly have no obligation to protect a nation fighting us in Korea.

In fact, the Seventh Fleet had been protecting Formosa (now Taiwan) from invasion by China, and not vice versa. The purpose of the removal of the "shield" was to put Communist China on notice that the U.S. might have a surprise in store, and to require deployment of defense forces opposite Formosa on the mainland. But when years slipped by and no action was taken by Chiang's forces—nor was any permitted by the U.S.—the phrase boomeranged, and became a derisive term for foreign policy bluffing.

When the offshore islands of Quemoy and Matsu were bombarded early in 1955, the Administration took a deliberately vague posture, indicating the U.S. would come to their defense if they were considered necessary to the defense of Formosa. At the same time, a promise was extracted from the Nationalists not to invade the mainland without first informing the U.S. Critics called this "re-leashing Chiang." After the 1972 signing of the Shanghai Communiqué between the U.S. and the People's Republic of China, the phrase was used only in ironic recollection.

The phrase was and is associated with Secretary of State Dulles, usually critically. Writing about "journalese" in the *Dictionary of Contemporary American Usage*, Bergen and Cornelia Evans wrote in 1957: "Certain pompous phrases must remain permanently set up in type: *bipartisan foreign policy, act of overt aggression . . . titular head of the party, diplomat without portfolio . . . policy of containment.* But to assume such inflated terminology is confined to newspapers is to be as ignorant as unjust. It was not some petty, pretentious scribbler who invented *massive retaliation* and *agonizing reappraisal* or spoke of *unleashing* Chiang Kai-shek." The Evanses left out LIBERATION OF CAPTIVE PEOPLES and BRINKMANSHIP in the last grouping, and a less colorful successor to Dulles, Dean Rusk, popularized EYEBALL TO EYEBALL.

President George Bush, a competitive tennis player, was famed for his exhortations during a game. When at the net in a doubles game, he habitually called for a power serve by his partner by shouting "Unleash Chiang!"

The "unleash" metaphor was used successfully by British MP, later Prime Minister, Harold Macmillan in 1945: he advocated "the unleashing of production" after the war, playing further on the canine image by urging the Labour party to "let sleeping dogmas lie."

unpack punch line of a religious-racial issue joke.

Threats of rampant popery in the U.S. if Catholic Al Smith were elected in 1928 led to this gag: When Smith lost to Hoover, he was said to have sent a one-word wire to the Pope in the Vatican: "Unpack."

When a Catholic finally was elected, in 1960, he took a strong position against federal aid to parochial schools. John F. Kennedy, proposing an education bill to Congress, knew it would cause some anger in Catholic circles. He turned around the old Smith joke: "As all of you know, some circles invented the myth that after Al Smith's defeat in 1928, he sent a one-word telegram to the Pope: 'Unpack.' After my press conference on the school bill, I received a one-word wire from the Pope: 'Pack.'"

After Kennedy was assassinated, blacks were worried about the Administration of Texan Lyndon Johnson. After his first speech to the joint session of Congress on November 27, 1963, in which he called for civil rights legislation, black comedian Dick Gregory revived the gag: "Twenty million of us unpacked our bags."

un-poor, un-young, un-black. See MIDDLE AMERICA.

unthinkable thoughts proposals too mind-boggling to discuss; phrase used by those who want to advance schemes that shatter shibboleths.

The word became agitated in political parlance by nuclear physicist Herman Kahn, who wrote *On Thermonuclear War* in 1959. James Newman in *Scientific American* magazine attacked Kahn's character as well as style of writing in a vitriolic review calling his book "a moral tract on how to justify mass murder." The reviewer's lead was memorable: "*Is there really a Herman Kahn? It's hard to believe. Doubts cross one's mind almost from the first page of this deplorable book: no one could write like this; no one could think like this. Perhaps the whole thing is a staff hoax in bad taste.*"

Perturbed about the violence of the reviewer's onslaught, Kahn wrote the editor of *Scientific American*, Dennis Flanagan, asking him to consider a rebuttal entitled "Thinking about the Unthinkable." Flanagan replied: "I do not think there is much point in thinking about the unthinkable; surely it is more profitable to think about the thinkable . . . nuclear war is unthinkable. I should prefer to devote my thoughts to how nuclear war can be prevented."

Kahn wrote a 1962 book, entitled, oddly enough, *Thinking about the Unthinkable*. He made his point in this manner:

It is characteristic of our times that many intelligent and sincere people are willing to argue that it is immoral to think and even more immoral to write in detail about having to fight a thermonuclear war. . . . In a sense we are acting like those ancient kings who punished messengers who brought them bad news. . . . In our times,

thermonuclear war may seem unthinkable, immoral, insane, hideous, or highly unlikely, but it is not impossible. To act intelligently we must learn as much as we can about the risks. We may thereby be able better to avoid nuclear war.

Senate Foreign Relations Committee chairman J. William Fulbright further popularized the term in 1964:

It is within our ability, and unquestionably in our interests, to cut loose from established myths and to start thinking some "unthinkable thoughts" —about the cold war and East-West relations, about the underdeveloped countries and particularly those in Latin America, about the changing nature of the Chinese Communist threat in Asia, and about the festering war in Vietnam. . . . The Soviet Union is of course one of the users of the Panama Canal, albeit a minor one, and this fact suggests an "unthinkable thought": the possibility of Soviet participation in a consortium constituted to build and operate a new Central American canal. I am not advocating Soviet participation, but neither do I think it must be ruled out as "unthinkable."

Technically, "unthinkable" should be limited to such metaphysical concepts as infinity and the nature of God, but in current usage it is synonymous with "inconceivable" with a pinch of condemnation added.

A 1978 usage by columnist Meg Greenfield in *Newsweek* brought the phrase closer to the purely political arena. "'Thinking about the unthinkable'—the old nuclear strategist's phrase—has a new meaning in Washington these days," she wrote. "It means thinking about the possibility that the Senate will reject the SALT agreement Jimmy Carter brings home."

upcoming. See HOT PROPERTY.

up to speed familiar with the latest details; *au courant;* briefed and ready to answer questions.

A newly appointed cabinet officer is brought "up to speed" by the permanent bureaucracy before his confirmation hearings; a White House aide who has been on vacation or working on a special assignment must be brought "up to speed" by his colleagues when he returns; a President, preparing for a press conference, needs to be brought "up to speed" on a variety of topics that have not been the focus of recent attention.

This phrase was made part of Washington parlance by White House aides with advertising backgrounds in the sixties. One origin is said to be in radio, referring to the need to bring an electrical transcription up to a certain number of revolutions per minute on a turntable before turning up the sound for broadcast, to avoid jarring listeners with a "wow" sound. In television, it was defined in the *1955 Television Dictionary/Handbook for Sponsors* as "Time when the camera and sound mechanisms are ready for filming and moving at the same speed."

The *National Journal* used the term in a 1993 report on the Clinton Administration: "As the Clinton transition team scrambled to get up to speed on Haiti, it seemed like old home week at the State Department."

The opposite of being "up to speed" is, curiously, *out of pocket,* a phrase that used to mean "unreimbursed," but in the seventies came to mean *out of touch,* or in its most extreme form, *out to lunch.* A related term, from moviemaker's lingo, is *off my screen*— that is, beyond my ken. A synonym for "up to speed," in its sense of being ready to go, with all in agreement, is *on all fours.*

used car salesman symbol of slickness or untrustworthiness.

Nobody trusts a used car salesman, whose job—according to the stereotype—is to cover up defects and make the used look almost new. In politics, the symbol usually appears in the full form of a question, "Would you buy a used car from this man?" Its political usage is sometimes meant to gauge voter confidence in a candidate or elected official, although it is often an attack phrase, designed to elicit the metaphor of any used car that's a "lemon."

The phrase was one of the first used to derogate Richard Nixon early in his California career, and it was resuscitated after his downfall. Dan Aykroyd, the "Saturday Night Live" comedian, used the phrase in his 1970s send-ups of the first man to resign the Presidency. The *Washington Post Magazine* described one of Aykroyd's routines in 1978: "Suddenly, Richard Nixon's voice jerks you awake: 'There used to be a saying in America, "Would you buy a used car from this man?"' he tells you, moving that awkward way he sometimes did during unrehearsed public appearances, his arms all akimbo. 'Well, now you can. At San Clemente Dodge-Chrysler, we're offering a full range. . . .'"

In 1990, the *San Francisco Chronicle* described an advertising campaign for Volkswagen: "Ads that feature the familiar face of Richard Nixon, America's unfunniest past President, with the classic line, 'Would you buy a used car from this man?'

"The answer provided by the ad: 'Depends on the car.'"

See AUTOMOBILE METAPHOR.

useful idiots of the West Communist derogation of liberals, later picked up by Western hard-liners.

During the mid-1980s, the expression became common among geopoliticians. In early 1987, Zbigniew Brzezinski used *useful idiots of the West* in deriding "so-called notables who were convened as props for Gorbachev's speech"; those foreign-affairs experts included former Secretaries of State Cyrus R. Vance and Henry A. Kissinger and former United Nations Ambassador Jeane Kirkpatrick. The historically resonant phrase is more powerful than *unwitting dupe*, but less damaging than the outmoded FELLOW TRAVELER.

In *Business Week* in 1987, West German Chancellor Helmut Kohl derided "fellow travelers who support this [Soviet] propaganda effort in Western Europe. We call them useful idiots." John Vinocur wrote in the *New York Times*: "Maarten van Traa, the Dutch Socialists' international secretary, insists that the party is not playing the role of the useful idiots for the Russians, a phrase used by Lenin to describe left-liberals and Social Democrats." The phrase has also been used about Central American politics, as in the *New York Times* headline, "Lenin's 'Useful Idiots' in Salvador."

The key word, *idiot*, comes from Greek *idiotes*, meaning "ignorant person." The sense of a feeble-minded person, one having an I.Q. lower than 25, is no longer used; instead, the current use is synonymous with *imbecile, fool*, or the slang word *jerk*.

Usually attributed to Lenin, the phrase has not been found in any of his writings. Grant Harris, senior reference librarian at the Library of Congress, said, "We get queries on *useful idiots of the West* all the time. We have not been able to identify this phrase among his published works." Neither Tass, the Russian news agency, nor Communist Party headquarters in New York City can offer the source.

Mr. Harris suggested a source put forth by former Colgate professor Albert Parry, who wrote in the *St. Petersburg Times* about the 1966 book *People and Portraits: A Tragic Cycle*. That book was written by Yuri Annenkov, a painter who was commissioned by the Communist Party in 1921 to do a portrait of Lenin and who had access after Lenin's death to the leader's personal papers at the Lenin Institute in Moscow.

Here are Annenkov's notes, supposedly taken from Lenin's handwriting, with italics as in the original:

> To speak the truth is a *petit-bourgeois* habit. To lie, on the contrary, is often justified by the lie's aim. The whole world's capitalists and their governments, as they pant to win the Soviet market, *will close their eyes* to the above-mentioned reality and will thus transform themselves into men who are *deaf, dumb and blind*. They will give us credits. . . . They will toil to prepare their own suicide.

(That last phrase is perhaps a source of another unsourced Lenin attribution, "The capitalists will sell us the rope with which to hang them.")

Utopianism. See TECHNOCRAT; WAR TO END WARS.

V

vast wasteland a criticism of television programming; a gloomy description about the results of any unfulfilled effort.

Newton Minow, a law partner of Adlai Stevenson's appointed by John F. Kennedy to be chairman of the Federal Communications Commission, astounded a National Association of Broadcasters audience in 1961. He said that if anyone watched television from morning to night, "I can assure you that you will observe a vast wasteland." (After Minow's talk, a broadcaster told him, "That was the worst speech I ever heard in my whole life." LeRoy Collins, the head of NAB, tried to be kind and assured Minow, "That man has no mind of his own. He just repeats everything he hears.")

Minow's use of the phrase was taken up immediately because (1) it was directed to an audience in the communications field; (2) that audience is notorious for self-flagellation on artistic grounds while it increases earnings on mediocre programs; and (3) previous phrases of criticism—"boob tube," "idiot box," and "videot"—were too frivolous or severe. Minow's phrase combined a proper forum with, perhaps, a fitting literary source—poet T. S. Eliot's *The Waste Land*.

Joseph P. Kennedy told Minow that "this was the best speech since January 20 [the inaugural address]—give 'em hell—hit 'em again." President Kennedy let Minow take the lead on the subject of television programming. At a press conference July 24, 1962, Kennedy was asked if the introduction of the Telstar communications satellite meant that "the U.S. networks should make a greater effort to do something about the 'vast wasteland.'" Kennedy evaded the question: "I'm going to leave Mr. Minow to argue the wasteland issue, I think."

In 1952 Minow's associate Adlai Stevenson quoted an unnamed "famous American critic" as saying that "the South was the wasteland of the mind." The phrase continues to be used in this general sense, usually recalling the description of television. Former President Eisenhower called President Kennedy's economic program in 1963 "fiscal recklessness" that would lead not to "a free country with bright opportunities but a vast wasteland of debt and financial chaos."

veep affectionate nickname for the Vice President.

Senate Majority Leader Alben Barkley of Kentucky was a popular choice for Truman's Vice President in 1948, after Justice William O. Douglas turned down the nomination. At that time, more and more corporate Vice Presidents were becoming known as "VPs," and the familiar form "veep"— to describe an informal-minded man—was natural.

Barkley's successor, Richard Nixon, sidestepped the title: "I think *veep* was a term of affection applied to Mr. Barkley and should go out with him." Barkley then appropriated the acronym for a television series, *Meet the Veep*.

Writing about acronyms for *American Speech* magazine in 1955, Temple University's S. V. Baum predicted: "It is a near certainty that *veep* will pass out of general use and will eventually fall into linguistic obsolescence." Its use did decline for a time, but it remains a useful alternative to VP for headline writers and political punsters. *Newsweek*, in a 1967 article on candidates for the Republican vice-presidential nomination, said that Governors Love, Kirk, and Chafee and Senators Tower and Javits were entries in "The Veepstakes." And in 1993, *U.S. News & World Report* referred to Dan Quayle as "the former veep," while the *Washington Post* regularly reported on "Veep Al Gore." The debate between Quayle, Gore, and Ross Perot's VP James Stockdale in 1992 was called the "Veep Debate." So much for predictions on the fate of words.

Asked after the 1992 defeat of the Bush-Quayle ticket if he would go through all the abuse if he had it to do again, Dan Quayle told a small group: "Yes. One out of three makes it to the Presidency." (See HEARTBEAT AWAY FROM THE PRESIDENCY.)

Velcro Presidency. See TEFLON-COATED PRESIDENCY.

vested interests the wealthy; the powerful; the privileged class; the Establishment.

Great Britain's policy in the nineteenth century was reputed to have been that a great power had only interests, never friends. The interests— *vested*, *special*, *predatory*, and *sinister*—have made no new friends since.

Vested (from its meaning of clothed) legally means a consummated right. The term "vested rights" was used in a political sense by English essayist and historian Thomas Babington Macaulay in 1857: "On one side is a statesman preaching patience, respect for vested rights. . . . On the other side is a demagogue ranting about the tyranny of capitalists. . . . Which of the two candidates is likely to be preferred by a working-man who hears his children cry for bread?"

Economists had an affinity for the phrase. American economist and politician Henry George, who died of apoplexy while running for mayor of New York City in 1897, probably coined the term "vested interests" in urging a single tax on landowners. Essayist Agnes Repplier wrote at the turn of the century that "A world of vested interests is not a world which welcomes the disruptive force of candor." British economist John Maynard Keynes wrote in 1947, in his *General Theory:* "I am sure that the power of vested interests is vastly exaggerated compared with the gradual encroachment of ideas . . . it is ideas, not vested interests, which are dangerous for good or evil." Walter Heller, leading Kennedy-Johnson economic adviser, used the phrase in 1966: "As a statesman, a President has a vital, not to say vested, interest on behalf of the nation, in prosperity and rapid growth."

The "interest" half of the phrase is more interesting. English philosopher Jeremy Bentham became suspicious of the "sinister interests" early in the nineteenth century. Prime Minister William Gladstone said, "The interests are always awake while the country often slumbers and sleeps." In 1883 Joseph Chamberlain, defending English radicalism, said that "private interests are like a disciplined regiment while the public good was defended by an unorganized mob."

"The Interests," wrote H. L. Mencken, ". . . were first heard of during the Bryan saturnalia of vituperation at the end of the Nineteenth Century." William Jennings Bryan called them "the predatory interests" in his three campaigns; Robert La Follette attacked "special privilege" at the same time, and the two expressions merged with Theodore Roosevelt's attack on SPECIAL INTERESTS.

Roosevelt, who attacked President Taft as "a tool of the interests," left no group out, hitting equally at "the big special interests and the little special interests." The man who benefited by the Roosevelt-Taft split, Woodrow Wilson, was not above adopting the magic "radical" word: "The business of government is to organize the common interest against the special interests."

Because the word "interest" had a progressive-populist-radical tradition, Republicans as a rule stayed away from it. But Wendell Willkie, campaigning in 1940 first for the nomination and then against FDR, used it in both directions. First, he charged that the Republican Old Guard was "corrupted by vested interests in its own ranks and by reactionary forces. It forgot its own liberal tradition." After he became the nominee, he gave it a new twist in a "petition" to FDR: "Give up this vested interest that you have in the depression, open your eyes to the future, help us to build a New World."

More than anyone else in modern times, Harry Truman revived the battle cry. He declared in several campaigns that the task of the Democratic party was to take government out of the hands of "the special interests" and return it to "the people"; in 1948, he dipped into Robert La Follette's vocabulary to specify a portion of those interests as "gluttons of privilege."

Politicians know that attacking "interests" has become a cliché, but there continues a certain STEMWINDING affection for the word, especially by Democrats. It has been spoofed: Victor Aloysius ("Just Call Me Vic") Meyers, Lieutenant Governor of Washington during World War II, told reporters: "Habitually I go without a vest so that I can't be accused of standing for the vested interests."

veto. See POCKET VETO; ONE-HOUSE VETO.

Vice Presidency. See VEEP; THROTTLEBOTTOM; STEPPINGSTONE; RUNNING MATE; DEAD END, POLITICAL; HEARTBEAT AWAY FROM THE PRESIDENCY.

victory has a thousand fathers
expression made famous by President John F. Kennedy in 1961 as he assumed responsibility for the BAY OF PIGS FIASCO: "Victory has a thousand fathers, but defeat is an orphan."

When Kennedy was asked the source of this expression, he told an aide, "Oh, I don't know; it's just an old saying." *Bartlett's Familiar Quotations* cites a 1942 use by Count Galeazzo Ciano, in *The Ciano Diaries*: "As always, victory finds a hundred fathers but defeat is an orphan."

It had been reported earlier. N.Y.C. Transit Commissioner John J. Gilhooley told the author he heard Philippines Ambassador Carlos Romulo use this expression to describe the Korean conflict to Secretary of State John Foster Dulles on an airplane en route to a CIO convention in 1953.

Phrase watcher Paul Hoffman informed the author that the phrase, in its entirety, and used just as President Kennedy used it, "is spoken by the character portraying Field Marshal von Rundstedt in the film *The Desert Fox* (1951)."

The number of fathers has remained inflated. Representative Stephen J. Solarz of New York used the expression in 1992, but tried a variation on *orphan*: "As you know, victory has a thousand fathers while defeat is an only child."

vicuña coat.   See INFLUENCE PEDDLER; ABOMINABLE NO-MAN.

Vietnamization   a plan for the extrication of U.S. ground forces from Vietnam, with the concurrent build-up of South Vietnamese forces, so as to provide the South Vietnamese people with what President Nixon called "a reasonable chance for survival."

The predecessor word, used in the later stages of the Johnson Administration by both Democrats and Republicans, was the awkward "de-Americanization." In 1968, however, this began to be replaced by reporters and American officials in Saigon with "Vietnamization."

In a dispatch from Saigon to the *Los Angeles Times* by correspondent Robert Elegant on February 16, 1969, a distinction was drawn: "In Washington the fashionable term is 'de-Americanizing' the Vietnam War. In Saigon, men talk of 'Vietnamizing' the allied military machine. The two efforts must obviously go hand-in-hand. The semantic difference is slight, but the actual difference is great. Washington is primarily concerned with reducing the American commitment—with regard to developments on the battlefield and in Paris. For reasons equally apparent, both Americans and Vietnamese in Saigon are primarily concerned with building an effective native military force to cope with Communist forces when the American presence is greatly reduced—and eventually removed."

The word was popularized in the U.S. by Secretary of Defense Melvin Laird. He first used it in verb form on *Meet the Press*, March 23, 1969:

"I believe that we can move toward Vietnamizing the war by the program that I outlined to the Armed Services Committee on Wednesday, by modernizing the forces of the South Vietnamese on a realistic basis."

In his November 3 SILENT MAJORITY speech, President Nixon gave the word the presidential imprimatur: "The Vietnamization Plan was launched following Secretary Laird's visit to Vietnam in March. Under the plan, I ordered first a substantial increase in the training and equipment of South Vietnamese forces." He described "our plan for Vietnamization . . . a plan in which we will withdraw all of our forces from Vietnam on a schedule in accordance with our program, as the South Vietnamese become strong enough to defend their own freedom."

President Thieu did not like the word. On November 15 he publicly urged the Vietnamese media to avoid using the term because he felt it gave credence to North Vietnamese charges that the U.S. was turning the fighting over to "puppet, mercenary troops." But he did not offer an alternative phrase, and Vietnamization had already taken hold.

The "-ization" construction had been used in diplomacy before. "Balkanization" was used to mean the breakup of an empire into small, usually ineffective, states. The West German newspaper *Die Zeit* used it in a modern context in 1968: "After the Second World War, we witnessed the Communization of the Balkans. Today we witness the Balkanization of Communism."

Americanization never before had a diplomatic meaning; it was used to refer to the assimilation of immigrants, and in the sixties the book and motion picture called *The Americanization of Emily* used the word in a more general way. The de-Americanization word was a new formulation of the LET ASIANS FIGHT ASIANS idea, sterilized by the mouth-filling nature of the word.

"Normalization" became popular in the diplomatic lexicon in 1971, popularized by Henry Kissinger and usually referring to relations between the U.S. and mainland China. A bland, unexciting word was required here, and "normalization" is so bland as to be tranquilizing. ("Tranquilize" is a pretentious word for "calm.") The use of the "-ization" suffix (see FINLANDIZATION) can stretch too far: Calling for arming of the Bosnian Muslims in 1993, some used "Bosnia-Herzegovinization."

"-ize" can be used linguistically for good or evil. A word like "modernize" transforms an adjective into a needed verb, but a word like "finalize" is a pretentious substitute for "finish." "In the early stages of finalization" is bureaucratese for "not finished yet."

See WINDING DOWN; VIETNAM LINGO.

Vietnam lingo words and phrases left over from the Vietnam War, now only used bitterly or ironically, usually to derogate political and military hawkishness.

Washington writer Paul Dickson ran down a farrago of these expressions in a *New York Times* Op-Ed piece in 1972: "Many of the words and terms of the war are by now so completely debunked and abused that if they were not so laden with tragedy they would be funny. Among them: 'PACIFICATION,' 'light at the end of the tunnel,' 'body count,' 'free-fire zone,' 'HEARTS AND MINDS of the people' . . . 'kill ration' . . . 'search and destroy' . . ." (See VIETNAMIZATION; HACK IT; WINDING DOWN; VIETNAM SYNDROME.)

In the investigation of the destruction of the village of My Lai, the term "waste" to mean "kill" was used by Lieutenant William Calley. Linguist Mario Pei traced the use of the word in the *Modern Age* quarterly review:

> *To lay waste* goes back to Middle English, and there is an antiquated legal use of *to waste* (to do away with) in the sense of to destroy property (but not human life). From 1689 on we find *to waste* (to do away with) used in connection with such impersonal things as sin and sorrow. Shakespeare comes a shade closer to the modern usage in "Would he were wasted, marrow, bones and all." Wentworth and Flexner's *Dictionary of American Slang* informs us that the verbal use of *waste* originated with teenage gangs, becoming current in the 1950's in the sense of to defeat decisively, to destroy. This is still not the precise counterpart of "We were ordered to waste all the villagers," and it is possible that this ultimate semantic shift originated in Vietnam.

A reprise of these terms by war correspondent Homer Bigart in the *New Republic* in 1977 showed how they were used in bitter hindsight, with an interesting twist to "waste":

> Let us rejoice over the demise of some dreary slogans associated with the Vietnam conflict. For the next imbroglio a whole new set of incantations are needed. Our leaders no longer can tell us to get out there and fight to keep the dominoes from falling. Nobody will profess to see the light at the end of the tunnel. There will be no more crusades to win the hearts and minds of people and save them from aggression. One term—"waste"—is not easily shelved. GIs in Vietnam used it as a synonym for kill. When a man was killed he was wasted. A chillingly appropriate term for the 46,229 Americans who fell in action in the Indochina War.

Vietnam syndrome the belief that foreign military intervention is unwinnable and therefore a "quagmire" to be avoided; the inability to make and follow through with overseas commitments.

Originally the term referred to a mental disorder suffered by Vietnam veterans after returning to the United States. Ralph Blumenthal wrote in the *New York Times* in 1971: "Some officers here said they were afflicted by . . . 'Vietnam syndrome.' The symptoms are those that might be expected in any period of slackness after the kind of tension prevailing in a war zone. . . . There is a vague longing to return to Vietnam." Major David Hoh, a chaplain for the 197th Infantry Brigade, was credited with coining the term in 1970.

By the late 1970s, however, the term was lengthened to *post-Vietnam syndrome* and referred to an unwillingness to commit to an unwinnable conflict. *Newsweek* wrote in 1978 about Senator Sam Nunn's legislation allowing the President to call up reservists without a declaration of an emergency: "He argues that such emergency powers are necessary to counter a 'post-Vietnam syndrome' that might otherwise paralyze Congress in times of crisis."

America's fast victory in the Gulf War in 1991 led George Bush to say, "It is my hope that when this is over, we will have kicked, once and for all, the so-called Vietnam syndrome."

The term is used internationally. Martin Woollacott of Britain's *Manchester Guardian Weekly* wrote in April 1993 about the war in Bosnia:

> President Bush said after the Gulf War, "By God, we have kicked the Vietnam syndrome once and for all!" The fears over Yugoslavia show that to be untrue. Nor should the "syndrome" necessarily be kicked. Military intervention in modern times has been everywhere dangerous and often unsuccessful. It has cost soldiers their lives and politicians their jobs. The goals of intervention are often not easily attainable by the military means that seem to be the only available instruments.

The Vietnam syndrome often clashes with the MUNICH ANALOGY.

Vietnik. See -NIK SUFFIX.

violin piece. See TICK-TOCK.

vision of America the kind of society a leader is required to hope for; once an uplifting and inspiring part of any campaign, now considered a cliché.

Among speechwriters, the "I SEE" CONSTRUCTION has a revered place in political oratory. When candidate Jimmy Carter was asked what his vision of America was, he turned to writer Patrick Anderson in the summer of 1976 to produce the appropriate speech. Mr. Anderson provided a draft with "I see" at the beginning of many sentences of its peroration, in the grand tradition, which Mr. Carter used effectively; when it was pointed out by the author that the technique was time-honored, there was some consternation at Carter headquarters, which wanted its candidate to be antipolitical, and the phraseology was dropped.

In *New York* magazine on October 25, 1976, "Adam Smith" (George Goodman) showed how the phrase had become a cliché by capitalizing it: "In the age of instantaneous transmission, these surveys will have been well-studied by the candidates, who will emphasize right and wrong in the Vision of America."

The following week, columnist Russell Baker wrote in the *New York Times Magazine*: "So I decided to vote for President Ford because he had a vision of America. Then a ghostwriter who specializes in composing vision-of-America speeches for politicians explained that this was baloney because Mr. Ford had never been anywhere in America except Grand Rapids, Capitol Hill and the Burning Tree Golf Club, and what's more, nobody had a vision of America anymore, even the ghostwriters who specialized in vision-of-America speeches."

But even thus lampooned, the phrase lives on: in September 1977 Carter pollster Pat Caddell was reported by *Time* to believe "The President needs to spell out more clearly the vision he has for America . . ."

vision thing a weary acknowledgment that a leader must articulate inspiring goals, usually expressed as a VISION OF AMERICA.

This phrase comes from George Bush. Reporting on political vision in 1987, the *National Journal* added parenthetically, "[Bob] Dole calls it 'the V-word,' while Bush awkwardly refers to 'the vision thing.'"

The term is typical of Bush's reliance on yuppie phrases in which attributive nouns modify *thing* (a habit derided by critics as his "thing thing"). The lawyer Terry Eastland told the *Washington Post* in 1992 that some conservative columnists had become Bush-bashers because "they believe he squandered Ronald Reagan's legacy. Bush is more nearly a 19th-century President, a guy who is not good at giving speeches and has disparaged the 'vision thing.'"

Even before Bush's Presidency, however, the *thing* locution was common in the Oval Office. During the Reagan Administration, a controversy about Michael Deaver, an assistant to the President, was minimized within the White House as "the Deaver thing."

Bush's phrase of foresight is now applied to any political contestant lacking concrete statements of goals or plans. Republican Pete Wilson, for example, was assessed by the *Los Angeles Times* during his successful 1990 campaign to be California's Governor: "In the exacting scrutiny of the Governor's race, Democrats believe Wilson may fall short on what George Bush calls 'the vision thing.'"

vital center. See CENTRIST.

voice from the sewer any anonymous, disembodied voice in a crowd that seeks to stampede or heckle; particularly, the unidentified voice at a hidden microphone that reassured the 1940 Democratic convention.

Senate Majority Leader Alben Barkley electrified the convention audience with a message from President Roosevelt that at first seemed like a warning not to nominate him for a third term: "The President has never had, and has not today, any desire or purpose to continue in the office of President, to be a candidate for that office, or to be nominated by the convention for that office. He wishes in all earnestness and sincerity to make it clear that all of the delegates to this convention are free to vote for any candidate."

Stunned silence followed. Then a voice on the loudspeaker began the chant, "We want Roosevelt!" and the "draft" began. It turned out that the "voice from the sewer," as it was called, was a member of Chicago Mayor Edward J. Kelley's organization, primed to begin the chant immediately after the Barkley bombshell.

The push for a third Presidential term led to the pun of *third termite*. During Ronald Reagan's second term, Bill Curry wrote in the *Los Angeles Times* in 1986: "Unheard of since 1973, when America last had a President serving his second term, the Termite—a usually derogatory reference to a third Presidential term—is again chomping its way into the American political scene."

See SPONTANEOUS DEMONSTRATION.

voice of the people.   See VOX POPULI.

volunteers   unpaid political workers, enthusiastic and vital to a campaign, or a method of committing troops without officially entering a war.

The Eisenhower "volunteers" and CITIZENS COMMITTEE gave pep, sparkle, panache, and a sense of idealistic purpose to the Republican campaign of 1952. See AMATEURS; BANDWAGON. In 1960 the President wondered aloud to Sherman Adams, "What happened to all those fine young people with stars in their eyes who sailed balloons and rang doorbells for us in 1952?"

Adlai Stevenson also attracted a devoted group of volunteers in his 1952 campaign, but by 1956 the ranks of the starry-eyed had dwindled for him as well. Volunteers are attracted mainly by personal CHARISMA and partially by a desire to participate in the fun of a campaign, very little by any expectation of appointive office.

Direct-mail advertising of candidates almost always carries a "volunteer card." (Check one: I will (a) address envelopes, (b) hold a coffee klatsch for the candidate in my home, (c) canvass my building, (d) contribute funds, (e) participate in a telephone solicitation.) The "pull" on these cards indicates to the managers what kind of campaign organization they can expect.

Many volunteers come to a headquarters once, get bored if given an assignment they consider beneath their talents, and disappear; others amaze a campaign staff with a zeal that can never really be purchased. Alexis de Toqueville noted it in *Democracy in America*: "I have often admired the extreme skill with which the inhabitants of the United States succeed in proposing a common object for the exercise of a great many men and inducing them voluntarily to pursue it . . ."

In its international warfare meaning, the word was popularized in the Spanish Civil War. German and Italian troops were dispatched to General Francisco Franco by Hitler and Mussolini under the guise of "volunteers." Foreign nationals supporting Loyalist forces were also called volunteers, but quotation marks did not appear around the word because it was felt in the U.S. that they were genuine idealists, not troops serving the disguised interests of their respective countries.

When the Chinese Communists decided to enter the Korean War, they reused this technique and term, which has since become a standard method of intervention, along with "military advisers."

voodoo economics   derogation of Ronald Reagan's economic policies.

George Bush introduced this phrase during his 1980 campaign for the Republican nomination. Before being chosen Reagan's running mate, he attacked Reagan's supply-side theories as *voodoo economics*, using a term for the religious rites involving sorcery that originated in West Africa (in Ewe, *vodu* means "spirit, demon").

Suggesting witchcraft rather than practicality, *voodoo economics* became linked to *Reaganomics* (see -NOMICS). John Jacob, president of the Urban League, commented in 1982 that Reaganomics "is giving voodoo a bad name."

The derogatory phrase came back to haunt its originator. When George Bush subsequently ran for Vice President on the Reagan ticket in 1980 and 1984, and when he ran on his own in 1988 and 1992, Democratic detractors pointed out that the Reagan economic policies had once been ridiculed by Bush with this expression. (Another charge of "deep voodoo" was a rhyming play on Bush's label of political trouble with the baby-talk reduplication of "in deep doodoo.")

The phrase did not disappear with Reagan and Bush. In 1993, playing on the redundancy line attributed to Yogi Berra ("It's déjà vu all over again"), Raymond DeVoe wrote in a market letter critical of populist economics: "Sounds like 'Deja Voodoo' all over again."

See SUPPLY-SIDE.

vote early and often an election day greeting by politicians.

This is the sort of line that is ordinarily lost in the mists of election time, but historian James Morgan found the originator in his 1926 book of biographies: the jokester was John Van Buren, New York lawyer, who was the son of President Martin Van Buren.

Republican opponents to the "motor-voter" bill in 1993 said that the ability of voters to register at Motor Vehicle Bureaus was an "open invitation to vote early and often."

vote fraud. See BALLOT-BOX STUFFING; CEMETERY VOTE.

vote of confidence legislative reassurance; more generally, any expression of support.

The phrase originated in the British Parliament, where it is a division of the House of Commons in which the government tests its strength. Members of the majority party must vote with their party; if enough defect to lose a vote, the government is expected to call for a general election.

Conversely, if a motion of no confidence is introduced by the opposition in the House of Commons and passes, the result is called a *vote of censure* (although it contains the words "no confidence," the British do not refer to it

as a *vote of no confidence*); in that case, the government is "upset" or "falls," and an election is called. American usage is the opposite. A *Washington Post* headline in 1993 read: "Japan's [Kiichi] Miyazawa Loses Vote of No Confidence."

When criticism of the conduct of the war rose in 1942, Prime Minister Winston Churchill asked for a vote of confidence, calling the procedure "thoroughly normal, constitutional, and democratic"; after three days of debate, the motion was carried 464 to 1. In effect, Churchill brought the criticism to a head and then mustered support for his policies.

In the U.S., there is no such formal method of saying, "There may be sniping, but when the chips are down, we have a majority." As used in this country, the phrase means some voter expression, such as a special local election or a referendum, that is interpreted as a renewed MANDATE; or a reelection, which is called "a vote of confidence for his policies," or any pat on the back from a group of supporters. *Newsweek* reported in 1967 that a group of anti-Reagan voters in California had hopes of forcing a "recall" election: "They want to make him face an embarrassing 'vote of confidence.'"

vox populi . . . vox Dei. "The voice of the people is the voice of God."

The phrase is attributed to Alcuin, in an epistle to Charlemagne, around the year 800. It was used as the text of a sermon by Walter Reynolds, Archbishop of Canterbury, early in the fourteenth century at the coronation of Edward III; the "voice of the people," through the nobles, had dethroned Edward II.

The thought is beautiful and universal; the Japanese language has a parallel proverb: "Heaven has no mouth but it talks through the people." However, the phrase has been used to justify the bending of leadership to the popular will, and in that sense has been attacked, for instance by:

Alexander Hamilton, who said in a speech to the Federal Convention in 1787: "The voice of the people has been said to be the voice of God; and, however generally this maxim has been quoted and believed, it is not true to fact. The people are turbulent and changing; they seldom judge or determine right."

Theodore Roosevelt, who said: "It may be that the voice of the people is the voice of God in fifty-one cases out of a hundred; but in the remaining forty-nine it is quite as likely to be the voice of the devil, or what is still worse, the voice of a fool."

General William Tecumseh Sherman, who wrote in a letter to his wife in 1863: "Vox populi, vox humbug."

Walter Lippmann, who in 1925 gave the phrase a narrower meaning: "I have conceived public opinion to be, not the voice of God, nor the voice of society, but the voice of the interested spectators of action."

Dwight Eisenhower, who, after viewing the film in Paris of Tex McCrary's Madison Square Garden rally of 15,000 people urging him to come home and run in 1952, yelling "We Like Ike!" found the voice unclear: "Even though we agree with the old proverb, 'The voice of the people is the voice of God,' it is not always easy to determine just what that voice is saying. I continue to get letters from certain of my friends who are almost as violent in their urgent recommendations that I do not make an early visit home as those who believe that I should come."

Currently the phrase is used as a fanciful equivalent of "public opinion." According to the *Chicago Tribune* of February 13, 1993, "the call-in shows absolutely do not speak the vox populi."

The phrase has been used as a barb (Abraham Lincoln was called "Fox populi" by *Vanity Fair*), as the title of a radio show ("Vox Pop") and as doggerel in the presidential campaign of 1920:

Cox or Harding, Harding or Cox?
You tell us, populi, you got the vox.

waffle to straddle or refuse to commit; to use WEASEL WORDS.

At the time of the Israeli-Arab war in 1967, U.S. Secretary of State Dean Rusk evaded a question from Senator John Sherman Cooper (R-Ky.) regarding a declaration of intent to keep open the Gulf of Aqaba to all international shipping. Rusk said, "That matter has not been finally decided. There are some plusses and minuses. At the present time, no, I cannot give you a final answer."

A dispatch by Chalmers Roberts of the *Los Angeles Times-Washington Post* syndicate commented, "That sort of response led Senators and Representatives to tell reporters afterwards that Rusk had waffled about supporting Israel. One said, 'They just walked around it.'"

Suddenly the rare verb found new admirers. C. L. Sulzberger of the *New York Times* wrote on June 11, 1967: "The United States can claim no credit for Israel's swift victory, but the fact of that victory was of strategic benefit to us although our role was confined to waffling."

Newsweek's July 19 issue, written a week before, reported that "many Jews felt that Israel had been forced to go to war because of waffling by the Administration. . . ."

In a letter dated June 13 to the *Times* of London, Desmond Donnelly, a Labour Member of Parliament, demanded: "Are the Western powers going to act about the Arab refugees or continue to waffle?"

It seemed as if journalism had been taken over by a chef who had over-ordered waffle mix and told his waiters, "Push waffles." Occasionally when a bellwether reporter uses an out-of-the-ordinary word in a particular context, there follows a brief flurry of usage by other commentators and soon the word returns to limbo.

The word is derived from *waff*, a Scottish word for wave, and its dictionary definition is "to flutter or flap like a clumsy bird." Another possible derivation is from *waff*, to bark and snarl, or to talk foolishly.

The word is also used as a noun, meaning "equivocal or evasive language." After President Clinton told a TV reporter that maybe his plans for a tax increase on the use of waterways should be "reexamined," the *Boston Globe* of May 29, 1993, reported: "The presidential waffle spurred the lobbying campaign and set off a stampede in the Senate [which] passed, by an 88-to-12 vote, a resolution opposing any increase in the tax."

In its political use, to *waffle* is synonymous with the verb to *fudge*, which appears also to be taken from the name of a food—in this case a candy—but actually comes from to *fadge,* to succeed. In Washington, the State Department is called "the fudge factory." Former President Gerald Ford, in a December 1977 breakfast meeting with reporters, was asked about the change in President Carter's position on the Panama Canal, and replied with candor, "I think we both fudged a little on Panama in the campaign." That was a far cry from his charge about Carter in the 1976 campaign: "He wavers, he wanders, he wiggles and he waffles, and he shouldn't be President of the United States."

waging peace   Eisenhower's phrase showing the new nature of foreign relations; it means ideological competition without warfare; no "war" but also no real "peace."

Dwight Eisenhower used the phrase as the title of a volume of his memoirs: he followed *Mandate for Change* with *Waging the Peace.*

The technique of substituting the word "peace" for the word "war" is frequently used, often effectively. When the stock market, booming in a wartime economy, gets news of the likelihood of peace, any market drop is termed a "peace scare"; opponents of the U.S. effort in Vietnam have been called "peacemongers."

In 1946 Ely Culbertson wrote: "God and the politicians willing, the United States can declare peace on the world, and win it." This continued a linguistic tradition popularized by Napoleon in 1802, who said after the signing of the Treaty of Amiens, "What a beautiful fix we are in now: peace has been declared!"

walking-around money   cash payoffs to precinct workers.

Campaign managers searching for a euphemism to gently describe payments to doorbell-ringing volunteers came up with "walking-around money" at a date uncertain; the phrase was popularized in the early sixties. Managers often feel that a precinct captain should have a few dollars in his pocket to pay for a babysitter, or buy a potential voter a drink, or pay a parking fine; thus, the cash is distributed for these "anticipated expenses." In fact, rarely are the expenses used other than as recompense for the captain's time, but the phrase is as common as "miscellaneous" on political expense accounts.

On June 16, 1976, the *Washington Post* editorial wondered "how much of the $40,000 [spent to defeat Democratic Senator Joseph Tydings in 1970] was spent for 'walking-around money' in Baltimore City on election day."

Sometimes the practice is called "street money." The Associated Press reported on August 9, 1976: "The Jimmy Carter campaign gave donations to black ministers who supported him in the California primary and paid out other 'street money' that was not properly accounted for, the *Los Angeles Times* said in its Sunday editions." The *New York Times* correspondent covering the same story, Charles Mohr, wrote: ". . . the use of subcontractors, or neighborhood leaders, who are given 'walking around money' is an established part of political life in some cities."

Michael Kiernan of the *Washington Star* wrote on September 13 of that year—with the street-money issue raised in the post-Watergate morality—that

walking-around money . . . is the phrase used to describe the money political candidates give Baltimore political clubs just prior to a city election for all sorts of purposes—like canvassing, poll-watching, the printing of ballots and getting out the vote. Some purists in Baltimore insist the term only should be applied to money spent by political clubs in showing a candidate around a ward or precinct. It is "mingling money," as one Baltimore politician put it this week. The other expenditures more properly are called "election day expenses."

Whatever the proper definition, Jack Pollack gets the drift. "Oh, I know what you mean. You give a guy a $50 bill before the election and he does a chore for you. So what?"

The phrase is usually hyphenated; in pronunciation, the *g* in "walking" is always clipped.

walking back the cat   retreating from a negotiating position; or, examining what was known in the light of what has been revealed.

Foreign service officers use this diplomatic slang, which is similar to the "down off the mountaintop" expression of labor leaders faced with the need to reduce demands. (See MOUNTAINTOP, TAKE HIM TO THE.)

When President Carter's chief armaments negotiator, Paul Warnke, was criticized for making an unrevealed concession to the Soviets in strategic arms limitation talks, columnists Rowland Evans and Robert Novak wrote on April 29, 1977: "The 600-kilometer mystery, therefore, raises suspicions that Paul Warnke will begin 'walking back the cat' on the Carter SALT package, unless checked by the President himself."

The second sense, as used in spookspeak, is illustrated in this 1986 *Chicago Tribune* opinion piece discussing the investigation into the past of Austrian leader Kurt Waldheim: "Intelligence agencies are now 'walking back the cat'—reconstructing events and decisions in light of Waldheim's Nazi past and who might have known and made use of it."

wall, political use of   the Berlin Wall was erected August 13, 1961, after the rate of refugees arriving in West Berlin had reached 300 per day. The Western powers in Berlin, caught unaware, decided not to react and the Wall became a *de facto* part of the joint occupation of the former German capital. Some propaganda advantage was sought by naming it "The Wall of Shame," and visiting politicians on NONPOLITICAL TRIPS made it a standard part of their itinerary, posing for pictures looking sternly across the barbed wire atop the concrete blocks; it was torn down in 1989.

Walls and similar obstructions (see IRON CURTAIN and for the opposite, BRIDGE BUILDING) have always been a useful political metaphor, often in regard to tariffs. Thomas Jefferson spoke of the need for "a wall of separation between church and state." John F. Kennedy, the day before his assassination, used a wall to draw an excellent word picture: "This nation has tossed its cap over the wall of space—and we have no choice but to follow it . . . With the help of all those who labor in the space endeavor, with the help and support of all Americans, we will climb this wall with safety and with speed—and we shall then explore the wonders on the other side."

In the Nixon presidency, H. R. Haldeman and John Ehrlichman—because of their Germanic names and assignment to restrain access to the President—became known as "The Berlin Wall."

See STONEWALLING.

Walter time   the on-air time guaranteed to a network anchor.

"In the 23 minutes of noncommercial time on an evening network news broadcast," a network anchorperson informs the lexicographer, "many of us have a length of time specified in contracts that we must be on the air.

It's about nine minutes in most cases, and it is called 'Walter time'—named after Walter Cronkite of CBS."

The term, for which there is no printed citation, is used by political media consultants, as in "I know you can't assign a crew for a sound bite on this story, but can't you just cover what he said in Walter time?"

Asked to confirm this usage, Sam Donaldson of ABC said he'd heard both "Walter time" and "magic time," and he recalled that it means about six minutes of airtime.

war clouds metaphor (approaching cliché) about an approaching conflict.

"A cloud hangs over your heads and ours," Richard Henry Lee, of the Continental Congress, told the people of Great Britain in 1775. "Ere this reaches you, it may probably burst upon us . . . let us entreat Heaven to avert our ruin and the destruction that threatens our friends, brethren, and countrymen on the other side of the Atlantic."

"As the war clouds gather, far across the sea," are the opening words of the verse to Irving Berlin's "God Bless America." Dwight Eisenhower used it uncharacteristically in describing the arms race: "Under a cloud of war, it was humanity hanging from a cross of iron."

The metaphor could use a good rest. For too long, clouds of suspicion have led to storms of criticism, and war clouds to mushroom clouds.

ward heeler hack, hanger-on, hangdog politician.

"As the crowd dispersed into the corridor," the *New York Times* wrote in 1876, "a gentleman happened to say that the gang in the room was composed of Tammany 'heelers', when a Tammany retainer taking umbrage at the epithet knocked the gentleman down."

The gentleman deserved it; "heeler" comes from the way a dog is "brought to heel" to follow its master closely. In 1912 Herbert Croly wrote of Mark Hanna: "He used to go to the businessmen of his ward, and try to persuade them . . . that they, the taxpayers, and not the wardheelers, should rule the city."

"Ward" is still used in many cities as a political subdivision; ward heeler was preceded by "ward politician," which can be traced to Washington Irving's *Salmagundi* in 1807: "He, however, maintained as mysterious a countenance as a Seventh Ward politician."

The word still has sting to reformers; to regulars, a ward heeler is a term of fond condescension. The *San Francisco Chronicle* commented in 1993 on Bill Clinton's failed nominations of women: "It wasn't sexism that torpedoed Baird and Wood: It's the fact that they didn't raise buckets of billions for Clinton. Ward heelers can expect Clinton to stand by their past transgressions; competent individuals, without industrial-strength fund-raising in their past, live or die by their press."

Occasionally the ward heeler will have defenders, such as Boss Martin Lomasney of Boston: "I think that there's got to be in every ward somebody that any bloke can come to—no matter what he's done—and get help. Help, none of your law and justice, but help."

war-gaming words. See FAIL-SAFE; INFRASTRUCTURE; MEASURED RESPONSE; OPTIONS; OVERKILL; PACIFICATION; PENTAGONESE; PREVENTIVE WAR; SCENARIO; SALT.

war hawks bellicose statesmen; an early American phrase that was replaced by "jingoist" and later reappeared as "hawk." See DOVES, JINGOISM.

"In a contest between a hawk and dove," wrote Senator J. William Fulbright, "the hawk has a great advantage, not because it is a better bird but because it is a bigger bird with lethal talons and a highly developed will to use them." The senator also wrote: "The agitation of the 'war hawks' of 1812, and of the Committee on the Conduct of the War in the 1860s, and the neutrality legislation of the 1930s are among the more striking instances which may be cited from the past of the Congress either forcing or binding the hands of the executive."

"War hawk" was a coinage of Thomas Jefferson in 1798 ("as for Jefferson," wrote H. L. Mencken, "he produced two of the best bugaboos of all time in his *war hawks* and *monocrats*"). Wrote Jefferson to James Madison on April 26, 1798: "At present, the war hawks talk of septemberizing, deportation, and the examples for quelling sedition set by the French executive." The phrase was originally applied to those Federalists who wished to bring on a war with France. In 1810 the epithet—along with "war dogs"—was revived by Jeffersonian Republican John Randolph against the "war Republicans," who were accused of seeking a renewal of war with England to expand into Canada and take Florida from Spain, Britain's ally. The group included Senators Johnson, Calhoun, Lowndes, Cheves, Grundy, and Porter, led by House Speaker Henry Clay. Clay was "the" War Hawk; later in life he was to become known as the Great Pacificator (see CAN'T-WIN TECHNIQUE). The war hawks succeeded in bringing on the War of 1812. Recent scholarship indicates that patriotism—i.e., resentment at British interference with American rights—rather than expansionism motivated the war hawks.

Some will find comfort in the fact that the American bald eagle is a species of hawk; others will point out that its close relation is the vulture.

Senator Joseph I. Lieberman of Connecticut said in 1993: "It isn't hawks and doves anymore. It's internationalists and isolationists." When interventionists make exceptions, or when isolationists urge intervention, they are called *dawks*.

war horse a veteran campaigner who has had a battle-scarred career in politics.

Samuel Medary, a leading Ohio editor in the mid-nineteenth century, who is credited with the coinage of "Fifty-Four Forty or Fight," was nicknamed "The War Horse of Democracy." Robert E. Lee affectionately called James Longstreet "my old war horse."

This MILITARY METAPHOR comes from the charger used in battle. "[Thou] didst pick up Andrew Jackson," wrote Herman Melville in *Moby Dick,* "[and] didst hurl him upon a warhorse."

In the vote-as-you-shot, BLOODY SHIRT politics of Reconstruction, the war horses had an edge. In time the phrase came to be an affectionate, occasionally contemptuous name for a veteran politician. "There poured into the city by every train," wrote the *Weekly New Mexican Review* in 1885, ". . . democratic 'war horses' from the four corners of New Mexico."

"War horse" is in current use, though it is not as frequent as WHEELHORSE, which has a more reliable and less bellicose connotation.

war of national liberation
Communist terminology for a "just war" against "colonial" powers, started by a faction within the country and possibly assisted by a Communist neighbor.

Nikita Khrushchev, in a January 6, 1961, speech in Moscow, stated: "Liberation wars will continue to exist as long as imperialism exists, as long as colonialism exists. These are revolutionary wars. Such wars are not only admissible but inevitable. . . . The Communists fully support such just wars and march in the front rank with the peoples waging liberation struggles."

The party line did not end with Khrushchev's fall. In 1967 Alexei Kosygin said: "We [the Soviet leaders] believe that national liberation wars are just wars and that they will continue as long as there is national oppression by imperialist powers. Take Southern Rhodesia. There will be a national liberation war there."

The "war of national liberation" is an extension of the FIFTH COLUMN technique in an era where fear of nuclear warfare causes nations to limit their warfare. The phrase does not mean "popular uprising" to Western minds; it means deliberate subversion and attempted takeover of a state with local guerrillas supported from outside.

Obviously the meaning of the phrase depends on who is using it. Abraham Lincoln illustrated this dilemma in 1864: "The shepherd drives the wolf from the sheep's throat, for which the sheep thanks the shepherd as his liberator, while the wolf denounces him for the same act as the destroyer of liberty."

In that manner, a Soviet leader could have substituted "Soviet Union" for "United States" in the following statement by Harry Truman in 1947, and found it perfectly consistent: "I believe it must be the policy of the United States to support free peoples who are resisting attempted subjugation by armed minorities or by outside pressure."

The phrase itself was not born in the cold war. MUGWUMP statesman Carl Schurz, opposing the annexation of Hawaii and the Philippines in 1889, reminded President McKinley that the American people who went to war against Spain over Cuba "were indeed willing to wage a war of liberation, but would not have consented to a war of conquest."

war of nerves in political terms, psychological pressure; in diplomacy, threats, and feints to the point of terrorization.

Adolf Hitler dissected the theory in *Mein Kampf:* "At a given sign it unleashes a veritable barrage of lies and slanders against whatever adversary seems most dangerous, until the nerves of the attacked persons break down. . . . This is a tactic based on precise calculation of all human weaknesses, and its result will lead to success with almost mathematical certainty . . ." See PHONY WAR.

Before Bernard Baruch's use of COLD WAR filled the need for a new phrase, "war of nerves" was used by world leaders to describe the tension building between the Soviet Union and the West. In 1946, upon receipt of George Kennan's CONTAINMENT memorandum (see MR. X), Secretary of State James Byrnes stated that "we must not conduct a war of nerves to achieve strategic ends" and indicated that the Soviets should not conduct one either. Harold Macmillan, worried about what he called the "cordon sanitaire" of satellites in Eastern Europe, in 1947 warned Parliament that the situation was "only a war of nerves, but a war of nerves may be very dangerous."

On a personal level, some reporters said that a war of nerves was conducted against Justice Felix Frankfurter to get him to resign from the Supreme Court bench in 1953. *The Nation* wrote:

Sen. William Knowland is said to have demanded, as his price for accepting the truce in Korea . . . the appointment of Governor Warren to the first Supreme Court vacancy. . . . Recently a curious war of nerves has been launched to induce Justice Frankfurter to resign. It has taken the form of stories that his letter of resignation is on the President's desk, pointed inquiries about his health, a drumbeat insistence in the gossip columns. . . .

Frankfurter sent word to Warren through one of the badgering newsmen, Clint Mosher of the *San Francisco Examiner:* "Tell him I would not want it on my conscience that I had kept him off the Supreme Court." Warren did get the next available seat, but it was not Frankfurter's, who remained on the court for a decade, outlasting five other justices in that time.

A more modern term, with a military ring, is "psywar" or "psychological warfare" (see PROPAGANDA); its practitioners are called "psyops."

The older term is still used, however. In 1993, after the breakup of the Soviet Union, Georgia announced that it had shot down a Russian warplane. Commented the *Washington Post:* "The downing of the Russian air force fighter plane . . . is the most serious incident in a gradually escalating war of nerves between the two former Soviet republics."

war on poverty President Lyndon Johnson's catch phrase for his domestic social welfare program, reminiscent of FDR's ONE THIRD OF A NATION.

England's Edmund Burke foresaw the need and the probable reaction. "Government is a contrivance of human wisdom to provide for human *wants,*" he wrote after the French Revolution. Later, he added, "and having looked to Government for bread, on the very first scarcity they will turn and bite the hand that fed them."

In the U.S., *Progress and Poverty* by economist Henry George (see VESTED INTERESTS), published in 1879, was one of the biggest nonfiction best sellers of the times.

Herbert Hoover, who earned a reputation after World War I as a man concerned with the relief of suffering, said in 1928: "We in America today are nearer to the final triumph over poverty than ever before in the history of any land." The stock-market crash came one year later, and newsman Elmer Davis called 1930 "the Second Year of the Abolition of Poverty."

It was not until the early sixties, however, that governmental action to alleviate poverty found its slogan. Three books paved the way: John Galbraith's *The Affluent Society* (see AFFLUENT SOCIETY) in 1958, with a provocative chapter on "The New Position of Poverty"; a study directed by economist Leon Keyserling in 1962 called "Poverty and Deprivation in the U.S.—The Plight of Two-Fifths of the Nation"; and most important, *The Other America* (1962), a passionate book by Michael Harrington showing how poverty haunts our otherwise affluent society, and translating the statistics into bitter, human terms.

Campaigning in 1960, John F. Kennedy had been impressed by the extent of poverty in West Virginia and elsewhere in Appalachia and used the phrase that was to be the Johnson battle cry: "The war against poverty and degradation is not yet over . . ." A year earlier Dwight Eisenhower in New Delhi had called for "a successful war against hunger—the sort of war that dignifies and exalts human beings."

President Johnson, in his first address to a joint session of Congress five days after the Kennedy assassination, promised to "carry on the fight against poverty." In a meeting of his staff going over the State of the Union message a month later, he said he was worried about the word "poverty." "It's not poverty," he said, "it's wastage of resources and human lives"—but nobody came up with a better word, so the President agreed to call it a "poverty" program.

In that speech, the phrase became his own: "Unfortunately many Americans live on the outskirts of hope, some because of their poverty and some because of their color, and all too many because of both. Our task is to help replace their despair with unconditional war on poverty in America . . ."

By 1966 the phrase was open to attack. Republicans pointed out waste and inefficiency in local programs, and pledged to "take the profit out of poverty." In an economic context, Richard Nixon said the President's unwillingness to cut non-defense spending amounted to "a war on prosperity."

Soon many programs became "wars." Every racketeering crackdown became a "war on crime," even education programs were labeled "wars on ignorance." Richard Nixon declared a "war on cancer," and Ronald Reagan had a "war on drugs." One sloganeer, who refused to let his candidate name a highway safety program a "war on roadhogs," declared he would start a war of his own—"a war to end 'wars'."

war party desperation charge against the Democrats; like DEPRESSION PARTY against Republicans, considered a low blow.

"He kept us out of war" was the proud Democratic slogan in 1916, re-electing Wilson. "I hate war" was a familiar Franklin Roosevelt line in 1939. By the time of the Vietnam War—the fourth in this century entered under Democratic Administrations—Democrats were understandably touchy about the charge of being the "war party."

Not surprising, then, is the emphasis by Democratic candidates on peace, paralleling the emphasis of Republicans on prosperity. Former Eisenhower speechwriter Emmet Hughes

wrote about the 1952 campaign: ". . . the irony was this: each party recognized that its popular strength was plainly greater in the sphere where its public record was plainly weaker. Democrats feared popular distrust of their foreign policies as deeply as Republicans feared popular distrust of their domestic policies. Each was haunted by its own caricature—the Democrats as 'the Party of War,' the Republicans as 'the Party of Depression.'"

war to end wars an idealistic World War I slogan, now used only cynically.

Like MAKE THE WORLD SAFE FOR DEMOCRACY, this phrase is associated with Woodrow Wilson and the disillusionment following World War I.

The phrase was not Wilson's. *The War That Will End War* was the title of a 1914 book by English author H. G. Wells; in *Portraits from Memory,* in 1956, Bertrand Russell recalled that it was Wells who popularized the phrase.

When Neville Chamberlain returned from Munich (see MUNICH ANALOGY) with what he called "PEACE FOR OUR TIME," *The Nation* headlined its issue: "A Peace to End Peace." That phrase had been applied before to the Treaty of Versailles.

The phrase has a steady current use. In 1967, Walter Lippmann described Secretary of State Dean Rusk in *Newsweek* as "one of the few surviving TRUE BELIEVERS among statesmen, in the great Utopian Delusion which has been employed so extensively by propagandists ever since it was fabricated in the first world war. The delusion is that whatever war we are fighting is a war to end war. Anyone with experience and some toughness of mind knows from the history of the past 50 years that these wars which are supposed to end wars have never, in fact, ended wars. The historical record is quite plain: on the contrary, each of the wars to end wars has set the stage for the next war."

Richard Nixon, in the peroration of his November 3, 1969, SILENT MAJORITY speech, recognized the grandiose nature of the promise and set more realistic sights: "Tonight I do not tell you that the war in Vietnam is the war to end wars. But I do say this: I have initiated a plan which will end this war in a way that will bring us closer to that great goal to which Woodrow Wilson and every American President in our history has been dedicated—the goal of a just and lasting peace. . . .'"

The phrase is primarily used in historical context. A 1988 book review in the *Washington Post* commented: "When the war to end war finally came to a halt on the bloodsoaked fields of northeastern France, the principal participants—America excepted—were exhausted."

See FULL GENERATION OF PEACE.

warts and all. See IMAGE.

WASP White Anglo-Saxon Protestant: an ethnic group.

By the time the expression "WASP" came to be used, White Anglo-Saxon Protestants were no longer the majority of Americans. In urban politics, ticket-balancing to attract the votes of minority groups—Catholics, Jews, Irish, Germans, Puerto Ricans, or blacks—has become accepted. In some circles, WASP is used to connote snobbish patrician types, but politicians use it affectionately in the big cities.

Richard Scammon and Ben Wattenberg wrote in 1965:

> Some day someone will write an inspiring piece about one of America's greatest and most colorful minority groups. They came here on crowded ships, were resented by the natives and had to struggle mightily for every ad-

vance they made against a hostile environment. Despite these handicaps, despite even a skin color different from the native Americans, this hardy group prospered and, in prospering, helped build the nation. . . . The only thing different about the group is that it is the one traditionally viewed as the "American majority." For the minority group described is of course the "White Anglo-Saxon Protestant," further qualified today as "native-born of native parentage." The key point is that neither the WASP-NN, nor any solidified ethnic or religious group constitutes an "American majority."

The facts are that about one American in ten is nonwhite; one in six is foreign-born or has a foreign-born parent; one in four is a Catholic; and two out of three are *not* of Anglo-Saxon descent.

Accused of being "waspish" toward the press in 1971, Herbert Stein, newly appointed chairman of the Council of Economic Advisers, retorted, "I'm not waspish, I'm Jewish."

waste. See VIETNAM LINGO.

waste, fraud and abuse catchall derogation of the budget.

The tripartite term first appeared during the Carter Administration. In a story without a byline, the Associated Press reported on April 3, 1978, that the Department of Health, Education and Welfare misspent up to $7.4 billion in the fiscal year 1977 "because of waste, fraud and abuse"; this phrase was a reformulation of a statement by HEW Secretary Joseph Califano, who sought "to reduce fraud, abuse and error."

Califano's formulation was a reworking of the words used in Jimmy Carter's fireside talk of February 2, 1977: "I will support the Congress on its effort to deal with the widespread fraud and waste and abuse in our Medicaid system."

Subsequent Presidents have echoed the phrase. Ronald Reagan picked it up, for instance, in his first Presidential campaign. In September 1980, Reagan told a rally of senior citizens in Philadelphia: "I will not tolerate, and will fight with all my strength, the inexcusable waste, fraud and abuse of government programs—many of which are aimed at older Americans."

George Bush lengthed the phrase in December 1989, when he signed into law new rules for the scandal-ridden Department of Housing and Urban Development. According to Bush, these measures would "improve program management and financial accountability at HUD and make that department's programs less susceptible to waste, fraud, abuse and political influence."

In March 1993, *Newsweek* reported on broken campaign promises by Bill Clinton: "Throughout the campaign, he repeatedly said he could pay for extending health coverage to the 36 million uninsured Americans simply by eliminating waste, fraud and abuse in the system, which he estimated to be more than $200 billion."

In a July 1993 piece in *Newsweek*, columnist Meg Greenfield wrote: "My guess is that so far as expenditure of government time and money go . . . we are in much of this process observing a classic case of the dread big three: waste, fraud and abuse."

wasteland. See VAST WASTELAND.

watchdog committee a committee that "probes" waste in government operations, or overseas expenditures in agencies like the Central Intelligence Agency or the Atomic Energy Commission.

The "watchdogs of the Treasury," a usage traced back to 1827, were originally those trying to hold down government spending; the meaning today

has narrowed to trying to cut waste out of specific areas of spending.

In the earlier sense, Representative William S. Holman of Indiana was given the sobriquet "The Watchdog of the Treasury" in the mid-nineteenth century, along with his earlier nickname "The Great Objector" (to appropriations bills in the House).

In the current sense, Senator Lyndon Johnson headed the Defense Preparedness Subcommittee of the Senate Armed Services Committee in 1951, investigating the conduct of the Korean conflict. The same kind of work made Senator Harry Truman famous during World War II. Economic journalist Eliot Janeway wrote a glowing account of "Johnson of the 'Watchdog Committee'" in the *New York Times Magazine* in 1951, and *Newsweek* put Johnson on its cover with the caption "Watchdog in Chief."

See OVERSIGHT; CANINE METAPHORS.

watchful waiting diplomatic restraint, or a justification for inaction.

President Woodrow Wilson did not want to be drawn into a war with Mexico in 1913. "We shall not," he told Congress, "I believe, be obliged to alter our policy of watchful waiting." President Victoriano Huerta had seized power, murdered the previous president, and provoked an incident by arresting a group of U.S. Marines. Wilson sent in troops that took Veracruz.

The phrase had been used by President Grover Cleveland in a letter in 1893 criticizing the U.S. seizure of Hawaii: "There seemed to arise . . . the precise opportunity for which he was watchfully waiting. . . ."

The "watchful" gives purpose to the "waiting," like a cat on a stakeout in front of a mousehole. The *New York Times* editorialized in 1967: "The United States has an embassy in Port-au-Prince. Its policy is to adopt a 'correct attitude' toward the Duvalier Government. It watches and it waits."

The predecessor phrase was "masterly inactivity" by Sir James Mackintosh (1765–1832), who was also the espouser of "disciplined inaction": "The Commons, faithful to their system, remained in a wise and masterly inactivity."

In opposition to the look-before-you-leap school is the he-who-hesitates-is-lost school, whose favorite derogation has been "Let the dust settle," a 1950s condemnation of U.S. China policy, which, its critics felt, permitted Mao Tse-tung's Communists to take over mainland China.

watch list   notice of possible concern; list of potential problems or dangers.

In 1977, this phrase entered political jargon from the field of finance. Hobart Rowen of the *Washington Post* reported that two of the five largest banks in New York showed danger signals and "were on the Fed's 'watch list' as a result."

Unlike the positive SHORT LIST of promising candidates, *watch list* is applied primarily to negative or potentially troublesome situations. In the *Christian Science Monitor* in 1985, the term was hyphenated and used to introduce a list of "hot spots" for potential Republican losses: "Some political analysts would add a few more G.O.P.-held Senate seats to their watch-list: North Dakota, Nevada and possibly Oklahoma."

A watch list can be composed of people's names as well as state names and financial institutions. The editorial page of the *Washington Post* in 1992 discussed the Justice Department's documenting of Kurt Waldheim's past, including "the acts of Nazi persecution for which Mr. Waldheim was placed on the 'watch list' and barred from entering the country."

Watergate words

"Watergate," like "Teapot Dome," means everything associated with a scandal that became a national trauma.

"Watergate" means a place: the hotel–offices–apartment-house complex in Washington, D.C., facing the Potomac, named after the dockside facility that once occupied the site, into which the "waterbugs" stole to plant a BUG in the offices of the Democratic National Committee.

"Watergate" means a time: the period from June 17, 1972, when the "break-in" was considered merely a madcap "caper," to the near-impeachment, resignation and pardon of President Nixon, and then back in time to the start of eavesdropping in his Administration by the PLUMBERS.

And Watergate means a mood: a time of revulsion against the ENEMIES LISTS and the laundering (see LAUNDERED MONEY) of campaign contributions, of diehards who protested "double standards" and "ex post facto morality," of tips from *"Deep Throat,"* of condemnation of the men of CREEP who "shredded" and DEEP-SIXED evidence in a COVER-UP.

"Watergate" came to mean a drama on the grandest scale: of a search for the SMOKING GUN by the STRAIGHT ARROWS, of the FIRESTORM that followed the SATURDAY NIGHT MASSACRE of the "good guys," of the STONEWALLING about DIRTY TRICKS and "White House horrors" by the BIG ENCHILADA, of plans to "paper the file" by "team players" who had not been brought UP TO SPEED, of the RATFUCKING of the "black advance," of legalese like "misprision of a felony" and EXECUTIVE PRIVILEGE, of a "sinister force" known only as the OVAL OFFICE capable of producing an 18½-minute GAP.

After the "stroking" had failed, after the "hanging tough" (see HANG TOUGH) and the "limited modified hangout route" had led nowhere, the men who had maneuvered themselves between a ROCK AND A HARD PLACE found themselves TWISTING SLOWLY, SLOWLY IN THE WIND. A few instant revisionists with the best anti-Nixonian credentials observed that more than a few "abuses of power" had been perpetrated in the name of civil liberty, and that NOBODY DROWNED AT WATERGATE, but that a perspective on the "long national nightmare" was too soon AT THAT POINT IN TIME.

Watergate words continue to be revived. John D. Ehrlichman's statement about a "modified limited hangout" was reworked by George Bush. According to Rich Jaroslovsky of the *Wall Street Journal*, Bush described a Presidential photo session in 1989 as "a modified limited photo op cum statement sans questions."

See -GATE CONSTRUCTION.

water's edge where partisan politics, in the interests of national foreign policy, supposedly stops.

Democratic Majority Leader Lyndon Johnson viewed the election in 1956 of a Democratic Congress and a Republican President as an affirmation of the principles of the bipartisanship he had been talking about since 1952. According to Arthur Krock, "As defined by Lyndon Johnson, . . . these principles were: Partisan politics stops 'at the water's edge.' The only test of all legislation is whether 'it is good for the country.'"

In 1964, harking back to his Majority Leader's role, President Johnson repeated one of his favorite phrases: "I took the position that politics stopped at the water's edge. We had but one President and Commander-in-Chief."

The phrase is most frequently used in connection with "BIPARTISAN foreign policy." The architect of the policy, Senator Arthur Vandenberg, used it in his own 1950 definition to a constituent: "To me 'bipartisan foreign policy' means a mutual effort under our indispensable two-party system to unite our official voice at the water's edge. . . ."

"What mainly stops at the water's edge," countered historian James MacGregor Burns, "is not party politics in general but congressional party politics in particular. The real 'UNHOLY ALLIANCE' to a good congressional Republican is the historic coalition between the internationalists in both parties."

Describing Harry Truman, Richard Neustadt wrote: "He played 'Chief of State' like a gracious host, 'Chief of Party' like an organization politician, 'Chief of Foreign Policy' like a career official anxious to obey his own injunction that 'politics stops at the water's edge.'"

Describing Woodrow Wilson, Winston Churchill sidestepped the use of a cliché by substituting other words: "He did not truly divine the instinct of the American people. First and foremost, all through and last, he was a party man. The spacious philanthropy which he exhaled upon Europe stopped quite sharply at the coasts of his own country."

watershed election a campaign that decides the course of politics for decades; one that is especially memorable, or that proves to be a dividing line between historical periods.

California Lieutenant Governor Robert Finch said in 1967: "The Nixon-Kennedy campaign of 1960 will prove to be the great watershed election of this century."

And in 1993, William Kristol, former Chief of Staff to Vice President Dan Quayle, said: "Bill Clinton has a strategy . . . to make the 1992 election more than just a routine election where power passes from one party to the other. He would like to make the 1992 election a watershed election, upon which he builds a new governing, liberal Democratic majority."

The literal meaning of "watershed" is a water-storage area making the surrounding region fertile, or providing a city with its water supply. A second meaning is "dividing line" as between drainage areas. The political meaning comes from both the nourishing meaning (of the vital water-holding uplands) and the epochal meaning (a line between two areas, or a moment between two eras).

The political meaning emerges in these examples. Biographer Leo Katcher: "The University of California was one of the great watersheds of experience for Earl Warren." *Times* of London headline, 1965: "Parliament at a Watershed." Treasury Secretary Douglas Dillon, describing 1961–64 as "a watershed in the development of American economic policy." Author Theodore White: "The great revolutionary in the flow of ideas proved to be John Fitzgerald Kennedy. . . . He was the watershed."

The word crested in the late sixties. Here are three examples from the *New York Times* taken from a three-month period in 1967: "The Cuban confrontation," wrote C. L. Sulzberger, "was a historic watershed but the U.S. didn't gain much from it save prestige . . ." A dispatch from Tokyo quoted visiting Richard M. Nixon as praising the new political and economic leadership of Japan and describing that country as "at a watershed." And Henry Steele Commager, Amherst professor of history, wrote: "In the great watershed of the eighteen-nineties we found ourselves, somewhat to our own surprise, a world power."

In 1968 this writer suggested to candidate Richard Nixon that he adopt the word to describe the forthcoming election, which he did in several speeches. However, in 1969, when *Newsweek* described a conference on

Midway Island about Vietnam as "a watershed in the quagmire," editorial writer Meg Greenfield of the *Washington Post* proceeded to blast the shed out of the water: ". . . I have also become an incurable, even obsessive collector of printed watersheds, of which I believe I now have the best collection in town—watersheds perching on escalation ladders, watersheds embedded in arms spirals, watersheds wrapped (like chicken livers, perhaps) in an enigma. It is not, however, an expression that I would dare to use myself. I came to that drainage basin two years ago and paddled left, into the sunset."

Ms. Greenfield's sandbagging of the watershed flood was widely hailed. "In terms of getting things done," she wrote in a follow-up article, "a number of MOVERS AND SHAKERS stepped forward to reveal their sympathy. . . . for instance, a principal presidential speechwriter (who had done invaluable pioneer work on the subject in his political lexicon) sent a letter to say that 'watershed' deserved all the opprobrium we could heap upon it, and he added that the term had long since been dropped from the presidential vocabulary. From the Executive Offices, no less, of Encyclopaedia Britannica came a heartrending executive vow 'never again to drown in a sea of watersheds.' . . . And, finally, it can be reliably reported that the Secretary of State acknowledged having seized upon this frail document in support of his own lonely battle to rid the State Department's prose of its embarrassment of watersheds . . ."

However, two leading political figures—Dr. Henry Kissinger and then Senate Majority Leader Mike Mansfield—had used the word in the interim. "I was still prepared to issue a rather favorable report," continued Ms. Greenfield, "speaking harshly only to these two offenders. I was only dissuaded from doing so by a sharp-eyed colleague, who asked how I would explain exactly whom I spoke for at the *Washington Post,* which had only recently hailed the Apollo moon adventure as—yes—'a watershed' in history in space . . . I would be less than candid if I did not report that, at the present time, there is no light at the end of the watershed."

wave of the future admiring description of totalitarianism; a phrase used today only to be denied or derogated.

In 1940, poet Anne Morrow Lindbergh, influenced by her isolationist husband Charles Lindbergh, wrote a long essay published as a book with the title *The Wave of the Future,* which many readers took to be an apologia for Fascism.

Working on Roosevelt's third inaugural address, speechwriter Robert Sherwood said to the President, "I certainly wish we could use that terrible phrase, 'the wave of the future.'" Samuel Rosenman recollects FDR calmly saying, "Why not?" and dictating the following: "There are men who believe that democracy, as a form of government and a frame of life, is limited or measured by a kind of mystical and artificial fate—that, for some unexplained reason, tyranny and slavery have become the surging wave of the future—and that freedom is an ebbing tide. But we Americans know that this is not true."

A few months later Interior Secretary Harold Ickes castigated what he called "the wavers of the future" at an "I Am an American Day" rally in New York's Central Park:

> For years we have been told that we are beaten, decayed, and that no part of the world belongs to us any longer. Some amongst us have fallen for this carefully pickled tripe . . . this calculated poison. Some amongst us have begun to preach that the "wave of the future" has passed over us and left us a wet, dead fish.
>
> Americans, with the aid of our brave allies—yes, let's call them "allies"—the British, can and will build the only future worth having. I mean a future, not of concentration camps, not of physical torture and mental straitjackets, not of sawdust bread or sawdust Caesars—I mean a future when free men will live free lives in dignity and in security. This tide of the future, the democratic future, is ours.

The same technique of setting up "wave of the future" as a kind of straw man phrase, and then knocking it down, has been used often since. The change in the past generation has been to identify Communism rather than Fascism as the "waver." President John Kennedy, speaking to students at the Berkeley campus of the University of California, said: "No one can doubt that the wave of the future is not the conquest of the world by a single dogmatic creed but the liberation of the diverse energies of free nations and free men."

In the 1968 campaign Richard Nixon found a sure-fire applause line in "the wave of crime must not become the wave of the future."

The word "future" was given a bad name not only by the Lindbergh use, but by a 1920s comment of author Lincoln Steffens about the Soviet Union: "I have been over into the future, and it works."

The undulation of the sea, in use politically as GROUNDSWELL, was best used metaphorically by Ralph Waldo Emerson in his essay "On Self-Reliance": "Society is a wave. The wave moves onward, but the water of which it is composed does not. . . . The persons who make up a nation today, next year die, and their experiences with them."

waxworks dais guests at a political dinner.

"It's a pleasure to be back up here as a member of the waxworks," defeated senatorial candidate Bernard Shanley told a New Jersey political dinner in 1968.

The reference is to Madame (Marie) Tussaud's Exhibition, a wax museum in Paris during the Reign of Terror which moved to London and became a landmark with its lifelike representations of historical figures.

People who sit on daises, even when thoroughly bored, must appear friendly and interested. The resulting expression is a frozen or waxen smile which, when strung out in a line of twenty people, makes "waxworks" an apt description. See RUBBER-CHICKEN CIRCUIT.

weaned on a pickle. See MAN ON THE WEDDING CAKE.

we are all declaration of membership in a group that becomes highly quotable when expressed by an unlikely source.

The first well-known use was unifying rather than surprising. "We have called by different names brethren of the same principle," said Thomas Jefferson in his first inaugural address. "We are all Republicans, we are all Federalists."

When the Prince of Wales (later Edward VII) used it in an 1895 speech in England, it startled the world: "We are all Socialists now-a-days." (Sir Denis Brogan credited this line to Sir William Harcourt.)

And conservative economist Milton Friedman put the NEW ECONOMICS over the top when *Time* magazine put his remark on its cover in 1965: "We are all Keynesians now." Liberal economist Walter Heller commented a year later: "When Milton Friedman, the chief guardian of the laissez-faire tradition in American economics, said not long ago, 'We are all Keynesians now,' the profession said 'Amen.'" Overlooked was the second half of Friedman's remark: "—and there are no longer any Keynesians."

"We are all guilty" was described in 1969 by linguist Mario Pei as "perhaps the most ingenious of all Communistic slogans created to demoralize us by giving us collective and inherited guilt as a substitute for individual responsibility."

weasel words ambiguous speech; deliberately fuzzy phraseology.

"One of our defects as a nation," said Theodore Roosevelt in 1916, "is a tendency to use what have been called weasel words." He had popularized the phrase as President, and gave this example of what he meant: "You can have universal training, or you can have voluntary training, but when you use the word voluntary to qualify the word universal, you are using a weasel word; it has sucked all the meaning out of universal. The words flatly contradict one another." (The origin of that metaphor can be found in Shakespeare's *As You Like It*, Act II, Scene 5, when "the melancholy Jaques" asks Lord Amiens to continue his singing: "I can suck melancholy out of a song, as a weasel sucks eggs.")

Author Stewart Chaplin explained the phrase in an article about political platforms in a 1900 issue of *Century* magazine: ". . . weasel words are words that suck all the life out of the words next to them, just as a weasel sucks an egg and leaves the shell. If you heft the egg afterward it's as light as a feather, and not very filling when you're hungry; but a basketful of them would make quite a show, and would bamboozle the unwary."

President Franklin D. Roosevelt, according to speechwriter Samuel Rosenman, "was extremely impatient with some of the drafts that came over from the State Department during those years, and with some of the suggested corrections in the drafts he had sent over to them for consideration. He felt that they were too apt to use 'weasel words' (a favored phrase he had borrowed from Theodore Roosevelt); that they made too many reservations and were too diplomatically reserved."

Editor William Allen White, writing about the direct quality of Wendell Willkie in 1940, thought the Republican candidate was making headway because "The American people are tired of the smoothy in politics—even if he is honest. They don't like the oleaginous weasel words with which so many politicians grease their way back when they venture upon a dangerous salient of honesty."

The colloquial verb "to weasel" means to renege on a promise, usually for some cowardly reason. The *Dictionary of American Slang* points out that the prison term "weasel" refers to an informer, adding that "applied to small, thin males, the word retains its physical connotation." Why the weasel has acquired a cowardly reputation is not known; it is a bold, vicious little beast that kills more than it can eat; in snowy areas, it acquires a white coat and enters judicial metaphors as "ermine."

President Nixon, in a meeting with Chinese Premier Chou En-lai in Peking in 1972, first used the word in high-level international diplomacy (and, ironically, presaged the use of COVER-UP in the same sentence): "The conventional way to handle a meeting at the summit like this, while the whole world is watching is to have meetings for several days, which we will have, to have discussions and discover differences, which we will do, and then put out a weasel-worded communiqué covering up the problems." Nixon then disclaimed such intention.

In 1992, Presidential candidate Bill Clinton was asked on NBC's *Today* show to clear up his stance on the Gennifer Flowers allegations of marital infidelity. As reported in *Time* magazine of July 13, 1992, his questioner said, "'Just skip any weasel words and give us a direct answer.' Clinton proceeded to repeat his familiar weasel words: Flowers' story . . . was 'not the truth,' the Clinton marriage has 'had some troubles,' . . ."

President Eisenhower wrote to Ambassador to Italy Clare Boothe Luce in 1953: "I assure you first that, so far as I know, we have no intention of weaseling on our October 8th decision on Trieste." In that statement, "so far as I know" are weasel words.

See REPORTEDLY; WAFFLE.

wedge issue a HOT BUTTON subject that splits a coalition or constituency.

Stuart E. Eizenstadt, once an adviser to Jimmy Carter, used the term in 1990 when White House aides fought over the relationship between affirmative action and quotas. He commented that Republicans in the Bush Administration had "a need to give the Reagan Democrats red meat [see STIR UP THE ANIMALS] at a time when the economy is going into the tank, and they see civil rights and quotas as a wedge issue."

"I was looking for a phrase," Eizenstadt told the lexicographer in 1992, "to illustrate the attempt to split the coalition of working-class whites and blacks, the two constituencies Roosevelt unified on economic grounds. The image came to mind of a wedge being driven."

The phrase was in the air at the time. In 1989, Eric Alterman, a senior fellow of the World Policy Institute, wrote of Lee Atwater's campaign strategy for George Bush. Alterman noted the emphasis on Willie Horton, a black man convicted of murder who raped a white woman while on furlough from a Massachusetts prison: "Atwater served notice on two occasions that the Horton furlough would be a central 'wedge' issue for the Republicans." The quotation marks around *wedge* suggest earlier usage.

James Carville, a Clinton strategist, picked up the phrase in 1992. Charging that George Bush's advisers lacked an agenda, Carville said they had to "dust off the Republican manual, which is to go to wedge issues: 'We can't lead the country so maybe we can divide it.'"

Wedge, with Germanic roots, is a forceful verb and noun that improves on the Latin-based POLARIZE and *polarization*. Often used by liberals and moderates, *wedge issue* serves as an attack term aimed at conservatives who bring up sensitive social subjects, such as abortion or homosexual rights, under the rubric of FAMILY VALUES during a campaign. The wedge, though, is not necessarily racial; politicians on the right see free trade as a wedge issue for dividing environmentalists and workers on the left.

The antonym of *wedge issue* is MAGNET ISSUE. See also BREAD-AND-BUTTER ISSUE; GUT ISSUE; ISSUES, THE; PARAMOUNT ISSUE; POCKETBOOK ISSUE.

Wednesday Club   the best-known of the many luncheon groups of legislators in Washington; more of a real club, but far less a center of power than the Senate's INNER CLUB.

The Wednesday Club is a group of Republican moderates; the Marching and Chowder Society is a more conservative group of MOVERS AND SHAKERS in which then Republican House leader Gerald Ford was prominent; similar groups meeting in Washington include the S.O.S. (Save Our Souls), the Sundowners (older members), and A-Corns. In New York, a widely diverse group of leaders in business, the professions, and the arts calls itself "the Wednesday Ten."

The "Tuesday Lunch" was a Johnson Administration addition. "Every week at the White House," wrote the *New York Post* in 1967, "President Johnson and three of his top officials—Robert McNamara, Dean Rusk, Walt Whitman Rostow—get together for a solemn occasion that has come to be known as the Tuesday Lunch."

English slang authorities trace "Blue Monday" to the sadness of children returning to school after a happy weekend, and "Black Friday" to mid-nineteenth century financial panics.

welfare reform.   See WORKFARE.

welfare state   government that provides economic protection for all its citizens; this is done, say its critics, at the price of individual liberty and removes incentives needed for economic growth.

When British politician Edward Hallett Carr said in 1948, "Let us substitute welfare for wealth as our governing purpose," linguistics expert Simeon Potter delightedly pointed out that the word "wealth" had returned to its original meaning: "weal," "well-being," and "welfare."

The welfare state, publicized by *New Republic* editor Herbert Croly at the turn of the twentieth century, had often been applied to the government of Sweden, and after World War II, particularly to Great Britain. Conservatives in England, accepting many social security programs short of nationalization, often reacted bitterly. In 1951 a reader of *Picture Post* urged Prime Minister Clement Attlee to dismiss "everyone who used the term 'welfare state,' because 'nobody is very well, and the state of the fare is rotten.'"

The phrase had a competitor at the start. *The Servile State* was the title of a 1913 book by Hilaire Belloc, which he defined as "that arrangement of society in which so considerable a number of the families and individuals are constrained by positive law to labor for the advantage of other families and individuals as to stamp the whole community with the mark of such labor." But statism was not ripe for an attack phrase so early; the welfare state triumphed as a proud assertion at first, and later became an epithet.

Current use in the U.S. is as an attack phrase. Those who urge more social welfare legislation rarely use the term; those who oppose it use "welfare state" as synonymous with CREEPING SOCIALISM. The use of "state" in the sense of "society" has a totalitarian connotation: "police state," "garrison state," "corporate state," "state socialism." Theologian Michael Novak, writing in *Forbes* magazine in 1993, derogated "the nanny state."

The fire is not only directed at left-wingers. The *Chicago Tribune* said of Eisenhower's 1955 State of the Union message: "Welfare statism and a tender if meddlesome solicitude for every fancied want of a once self-reliant citizenry were pyramided and compounded in this message." See WORKFARE.

Welfare—the word without the "state"—has had a curious history. It began as a cousin of its turnaround "farewell," and was used by Shakespeare politically in *Henry VI*, as Warwick advised "study for the people's welfare." In the U.S. the word first appeared in its aid-to-people sense in a 1904 *Century* magazine article about "the welfare manager . . . is a recognized intermediary between the employers and employees of mercantile houses and manufacturing plants." Lexicographer of Americanisms Mitford Mathews found a citation from a year later in the *Westminster Gazette:* "The home of the 'welfare policy' is the city of Dayton, Ohio." British etymologist Sir Ernest Weekly explained: "*Welfare,* as in 'child welfare,'

'welfare centre,' and so forth, was first used in this special sense in Ohio in 1904."

The name of an island next to Manhattan, in the East River, gives a clue to the fortunes of the word in recent years. Blackwell's Island, the site of a prison, was renamed Welfare Island in the thirties, as some of its facilities were turned to other than penal use. In the seventies, when housing developers wanted to rent out apartments on the island, they insisted on a name change—"welfare" was too evocative of charity and the poor. It is now Roosevelt Island.

Welliver Society.   See SPEECHWRITER.

Weltanschauung   world view.

The use of foreign words for political concepts or practices is usually regarded as pretentious by politicians. News magazines may write of a candidate's "apparat" being concerned with REALPOLITIK but neither of the words is in the spoken tongue of seasoned politicians.

Joseph Alsop, wrote Douglass Cater in *The Fourth Branch of Government,* "can claim to have a reasoned *Weltanschauung.*" Thermonuclear thinker Herman Kahn countered his critics by saying that "often the reluctance to think about these problems is not caused by the advocacy of any particular *Weltanschauung.* Rather it is based on nothing sounder than a supernatural fear of the magical power of words . . ."

Intellectuals do, however, use foreign words in their conversation, and usually unselfconsciously. The *National Journal* of December 12, 1992, quoted Ira Magaziner, a Clinton adviser, as saying, "I think you'll see it [the Kennedy idealism] a little bit in the whole Clinton weltanschauung."

Other German words used tangentially in politics are *Zeitgeist* (spirit of the age), *Schadenfreude* (the guilty pleasure one feels at the sufferings of friends), *Weltschmerz* (world-weariness), and *Fingerspitzengefühl* (a "feel" for nuances).

We Polked You in 1844, We'll Pierce You in 1852. See SLOGAN; DARK HORSE.

We Shall Overcome civil rights chant of the early sixties.

More than any other song, "We Shall Overcome" was the anthem of the civil rights movement led by the "moderates"; it was one of the highlights of the 1963 March on Washington and was sung in front of the Lincoln Memorial.

Arthur Schlesinger, Jr., called the tune "an old Baptist hymn"; John Anthony Scott in *The Ballad of America* called it "an old spiritual," pointing out that it originated among the coal miners of West Virginia in the early New Deal days. Stevenson's *MacMillan Book of Quotations* credits the tune to Mrs. Zilphia Horton, who conducted a folk school in Tennessee in the 1940s, and additional verses to folk singers Pete Seeger, Frank Hamilton, and Guy Carawan in 1962.

The words are familiar to every civil rights marcher:

> We shall end Jim Crow, we shall end Jim
>   Crow,
> We shall end Jim Crow some day, some
>   day;
> Oh, deep in my heart, I know that I do
>   believe
> We shall end Jim Crow some day.
> We shall overcome, we shall overcome,
> We shall overcome some day, some day;
> Oh, deep in my heart, I know that I do
>   believe
> We shall overcome some day.

President Johnson chose it as his text in a speech to a joint session of Congress in 1965, urging them to adopt a voting rights bill: "It is not just Negroes but really it is all of us who must overcome the crippling legacy of bigotry and injustice. And we shall overcome . . . these enemies, too, poverty, disease, and ignorance, we shall overcome."

See JIM CROW.

West, the democratic industrial nations; national powers of Central and Western Europe and North America (sometimes including Japan) no longer in confrontation with what had been the Communist bloc.

In the old East-West relationship, the West was the FREE WORLD; it faced the Communist world, with the confrontation of powers observed by the THIRD WORLD, also called NEUTRALISTs. With the breakup of the Soviet Union, that nomenclature was knocked into a cocked hat.

Modern democracy began in the West—that is, England and its Western Hemisphere colonies, in France, and elsewhere in Western Europe—which led to democratic values, and much of modern civilization, becoming known as "Western." Central European and Russian history was more autocratic as a rule and, from a Western point of view, "Eastern," while Japan and China were "Far Eastern." In the 1970s, that ethnocentric bias in language was noted, and the U.S. State Department changed "Far East" to "Asian" and "Near East" to "Eastern Mediterranean."

In the eyes of many in Islamic nations, the West is the Christian world plus Israel; "Western values" are looked upon as materialistic and insufficiently religious. People in nations with a tradition of democracy, free enterprise, and respect for individual rights consider these to be "Western values," in contrast to the monarchic and fundamentalist traditions prevalent in many Muslim nations. Kishosre Mahbubani entitled an article in the *National Interest* in 1992 about the troubled responses of non-Western civilizations to Western power and values "The West and the Rest"; a goal of the "rest" was to modernize but not to Westernize.

In the eyes of many in the newly created nations that had been the Soviet Union, as well as in that former superpower's SATELLITE countries, "the West" was the world of prosperity, victors in the COLD WAR; the other side of what had been the IRON CURTAIN was seen to be the (sometimes selfish) land of opportunity.

As described in the entry on HAVE AND HAVE-NOT NATIONS, the "haves" were the North, the "have-nots" the South; this neat economic construct was confused by the end of the East-West power metaphor, and the prosperous West became synonymous with the North.

Thus, the West retained a vestigial political meaning as "not the East"—culturally not Russian or Chinese, ideologically not autocratic or hierarchical. The paradoxical inclusion of Japan as part of the West attests to the ability of cultural, economic, and political trends—in this case, Westernization—to overcome geography.

wets a word attacking liberals or believers in accommodation; Britishism for *doves*.

When West German Chancellor Helmut Kohl was criticized for undercutting American policy in 1989, an unidentified American official told London's *Sunday Telegraph*: "We are used to such NATO antics from the alliance's wets like Belgium and the Netherlands, but to experience a STAB IN THE BACK like this from the Germans really does shake my faith in NATO." The paper's headline read "A 'Stab in the Back' by NATO's New Wets."

In British slang, *wet* has been used as an adjective for "ineffectual" or "inept" since World War I; in American slang, *drip* or *nerd* is used to label that type of person. The *Oxford English Dictionary* defines the political use of the noun *wet* as "a politician with liberal or middle-of-the-road views on controversial issues (often applied to members of the Conservative Party opposed to the monetarist policies of Margaret Thatcher)." The *superdoves* in American usage are known in Britain as *wringing wets*.

Wrote *The Observer* in 1981:

> The term "Wet" was originally used by Mrs. Thatcher, who meant it in the old sense of "soppy," as in "What do you mean the unions won't like it, Jim? Don't be so wet." It meant feeble, liable to take the easy option, lacking intellectual and political hardness. Like so many insults, it was gleefully adopted by its victims, and so came by its present meaning of liberal, leftish, anti-ideological.

The antonym for the adjective-turned-noun *wet* is *dry*. (The same words in United States politics once applied to those for or against the prohibition of alcohol.) Melbourne's *The Age* commented in 1983 on British politics: "In contrast to the expansionist, protectionist and welfare-oriented Wets, the Dries stand for small government, economic rationality and individual responsibility."

In spookspeak, a different sense applies: assassinations are called "wet work."

we will bury you an offhand remark by a Russian leader that was blown up into a dire threat by Westerners.

"Whether you like it or not," Nikita Khrushchev told Western diplomats at a Kremlin reception in November 1956, "history is on our side. We will bury you."

He chose the wrong word. In context, he appears to have meant "outstrip," "beat," or "leave you far behind." The reaction to the word he chose, however, was shock and anger: "bury" was a word too close to death. Two years later *Pravda* quoted the Soviet leader in a kind of retraction: "My life would be too short to bury every one of you if this were to occur to me. . . . I said that in the course of historical progress and in the historical sense, capitalism would be buried and communism would come to replace capitalism."

On a trip to the U.S. in 1959, the Russian Premier was angered by Los Angeles Mayor Norris Poulson's hometown grandstanding ("You shall not bury us . . . if challenged, we shall fight to the death") and spelled out the evolutionary character of the burial. "The words 'We will bury capitalism' should not be taken literally as indicating what is done by ordinary gravediggers who carry a spade and dig graves and bury the dead. What I had in mind was the outlook for the development of human society. Socialism will inevitably succeed capitalism."

But Khrushchev was never able to inter the statement. After a while, he took it philosophically. To a group of Westerners in the audience in Yugoslavia, he remarked, "I once said, 'We will bury you,' and I got into trouble with it. Of course we will not bury you with a shovel. Your own working class will bury you."

Six months later, in his first State of the Union message, Lyndon Johnson made a point of it again. "We intend to bury no one—and we do not intend to be buried."

what's good for General Motors

. . . is good for the country. A misquotation used to show the supposed big-business bias of the Eisenhower Administration.

Charles E. Wilson, called "Engine Charlie" to distinguish him from the former head of General Electric, Charles E. ("Electric Charlie") Wilson, gave a fairly innocent answer to a question posed by a senator at the hearing before approval of his nomination for Secretary of Defense: ". . . if a situation did arise where you had to make a decision which was extremely adverse to the interests of your stock and General Motors Corporation, or any of these other companies, or extremely adverse to the company, in the interests of the United States Government, could you make that decision?"

Mr. Wilson: "Yes, sir, I could. I cannot conceive of one because for years I thought what was good for our country was good for General Motors, and vice versa. The difference did not exist. Our country is too big. It goes with the welfare of the country. Our contribution to the nation is considerable."

As Eisenhower put it in his memoirs: "This was interpreted and broadcast—it still is—in the form of 'What is good for General Motors is good for the country,' and of course the breastbeaters had a field day."

The construction has become locked into the political lexicon, taking many forms. In 1970 President Nixon told black leader Whitney Young, Jr., shortly before his death: "To paraphrase a former Defense Secretary, what's good for the Urban League is good for the country."

See BIRD DOG . . . KENNEL DOG.

wheelhorse dependable party man; a regular.

A wheelhorse in a team is one that bears the most weight; hitched between the shafts, he pulls more of a load than the leader. Like WAR HORSE, the phrase has been used politically for over a century; the *Marion* (Ohio) *Eagle* wrote in 1848 about Lewis Cass that he "has been the very wheel horse on which the party has relied to carry through all their great measures."

Historian Eric Goldman, writing about the struggle to find a vice-presidential nominee for Harry Truman in 1948: "Finally a sacrificial victim was found—the faithful party wheelhorse Alben Barkley."

John F. Kennedy used the word in 1960, discussing his early days as a congressman: "We were just worms over in the House—nobody paid much attention to us nationally. And I had come back from the service, not as a Democratic wheelhorse who came up through the ranks. I came in sort of sideways."

wheels within wheels the minutiae of government; the infinitely detailed workings that a leader must not concern himself with, at the peril of wasting the time needed for broad policy.

Wendell L. Willkie, defeated Republican nominee in 1940, gave this phrase political context in a 1943 *Reader's Digest* article titled: "Better Management, Please, Mr. President!" Willkie held that Roosevelt was too "zealous for the accumulation of power and loath to disburse it," and pointed out that the presidency of the United States "is not a small-claims court." His main point:

> The President's desk is cluttered and his mind distracted by his concern with the wheels within wheels, the foremen and the subforemen of our gigantic Federal machine. He is his own supervisor and trouble shooter. Broken parts are brought to him for patching and he undertakes to patch them. Bruised feelings are brought for his treatment and he sets about anointing them.
> No man could do all these things well. No President should try.

The phrase probably comes from the Bible, Ezekiel 1:16: ". . . Their work was as it were a wheel in the middle of a wheel." The expression was used in Shaftesbury's *Characters* in 1709: "Thus we have Wheels within Wheels.

And in some national constitutions . . . we have one Empire within another."

Other uses of the word "wheel" in American slang often applied to politics are *big wheel,* a derogatory term for a man of authority and power, probably derived from "the man at the wheel" or baseball's "sidewheeler," a left-handed sidearm pitcher; and *wheeler-dealer,* one who acts independently, ruthlessly, and often unethically, probably derived from gambling's roulette wheel (wheeler) and card shark (dealer).

whip a party leader, chosen in caucus, who makes certain that members are present for important votes, and vote the way the leadership wants.

The *party whip* must be tough and tactful; he is expected to turn out every member on crucial party-line votes. In recent years in the U.S., the whip's job is considered the best STEPPINGSTONE to party congressional leadership. Mike Mansfield, party whip under Lyndon Johnson, became Majority Leader of the Senate when Johnson was elected Vice President. Robert Byrd, who defeated Edward Kennedy in a struggle for party whip, succeeded Mansfield.

The word comes from "whipper-in," a man assigned to keep the hounds from straying in a fox hunt, and was turned into a political word in England in the eighteenth century. Benjamin Disraeli said the Government Chief Whip's office required "consummate knowledge of human nature, the most amiable flexibility, and complete self-control."

In England, a *documentary whip* is a weekly agenda sent to Members of Parliament, with attendance requirements underlined. Sir Wilfred Lawson explained that a one-line whip meant "you ought to attend"; a two-line whip meant "you should attend"; a three-line whip meant "you must attend"; and a four-line whip "stay away at your peril."

The official name of the party whip in the U.S. is *assistant floor leader*. Its original whipping-in meaning is illustrated in an observation made by General Maxwell Taylor, who explained the relationship of the Chairman of the Joint Chiefs of Staff to the other chiefs of staff: "a sort of party whip, charged with conveying the official line to the chiefs."

whipsaw   to accept money from both sides in a dispute.

In lumbering, a whipsaw—operated by two men—cuts both ways; in poker, two players in collusion bid up the pot to cheat a third; in the business of bribery, a legislator will whipsaw two opposing crooked lobbyists by accepting money for a "fix" from both and then delivering for only one.

Charles Ledyard Norton suggested in 1890 that the term originated in the New York State Legislature (cradle of LULUS). An old Albany joke concerns a grafting boss who called two "fixers" into his office and said, "One of you paid me two thousand dollars to get this bill passed. The other paid me one thousand to get it killed. I want to be fair. How about the second guy paying me another thousand—making two even from each—and we'll debate the bill on its merits?"

whirlwind campaign   a busy campaign, usually of short duration.

This is a DISASTER METAPHOR that began in the Harrison-Van Buren campaign of 1840. A campaign that "spreads like a prairie fire" was already a political expression, and whirlwind—occasionally the result of a prairie fire—was a natural extension. "The prairies are on fire," wrote the *Annals of Cleveland* in 1840, "and the

whirlwind they create will be felt east of the mountains . . ."

In 1896 the *Review of Reviews* reported that William McKinley's FRONT-PORCH CAMPAIGN speeches were carefully prepared in advance, "punctuated with statistics and precise statements of fact which a 'whirlwind campaign' from a platform would not allow."

The phrase is in current use, but is beginning to appear quaint, like "whirlwind courtship," a prelude to obsolescence.

whispering campaign   word of foul mouth; a slander about a candidate's sex life, drinking habits, or possible mental or physical disability.

"Where there is whispering there is lying" is an English proverb traced back to 1678; John Randolph, fighting the WAR HAWKS in 1811, said his opponents' plan was "to assail me by every species of calumny and whisper, but Parthian-like never to show their faces or give battle on fixed ground."

The phrase "whispering campaign" was popularized in the presidential campaign of 1928. In an Edwin Marcus cartoon in the *New York Times*, a bigot with a rifle labeled "whispering campaign" was shown hiding behind a large jug labeled "prohibition issue," taking aim at candidate Al Smith. The anti-Catholic rumors (see UNPACK) undoubtedly harmed his candidacy, though he was beaten more by general prosperity and the prohibition issue. After the campaign, Smith wrote: "I was probably the outstanding victim of the last half-century of a whispering campaign."

Reporter Elliott Bell, later a director of McGraw-Hill, wrote of a similar campaign attacking Franklin Roosevelt as "mentally deranged" in the early New Deal days. "It came out in the course of a Senate investigation that an obscure and misguided publicity man had conceived the idea of undermining the President by a whispering campaign to the effect that his mind was unbalanced."

John F. Kennedy in 1960 suffered from a whispering campaign—in no way connected with his Catholicism—about his back ailment. Before the convention the "Addison's disease" charge was talked about; it turned out to be largely true, but is still classified as a whispering campaign, indicating the meaning comes from the method of dissemination rather than the content. See SMEAR; ROORBACK.

whistleblower a government employee who "goes public" with complaints of mismanagement or corruption in his agency.

On June 13, 1977, the Institute for Policy Studies in Washington called together a "conference on whistleblowing," to focus "on government harassment of workers who publicly disclose mismanagement, illegality and other wrongdoing by agency heads."

In December of that year, *Village Voice* writers James Ridgeway and Alexander Cockburn used the expression in print: "Then there is the case of whistle-blower Dr. J. Anthony Morris. He has long argued against government inoculation programs (including the swine-flu-shot fiasco). Morris recently lost his case in the Civil Service Commission . . ."

The best-known whistleblower (the hyphen was being lost as the word became better known) is Air Force cost expert Ernest Fitzgerald. During the 1976 campaign, candidate Jimmy Carter said "the Fitzgerald case, where a dedicated civil servant was fired from the Defense Department for reporting cost overruns, must never be repeated." Fitzgerald, who did get a job within government, has not since been one of its most trusted insiders.

The activity can be a reason for, or an excuse for, being fired. After widespread firings at the CIA in late 1977, John Kendall of the *Los Angeles Times* wrote on January 2, 1978, of one of those dismissed: "For half his career he says he considered himself a 'whistle blower' who tried to correct perceived faults in the CIA's domestic operations." When the CIA retorted that the man had been fired for insubordination, the ex-employee said, he "became a 'whistleblower' to correct [abuses] with full realization he was harming his career."

"Whistleblower" has a positive connotation (contrary to its predecessor slang term, "whistler," for police informer); the phrase portrays a public servant risking his job by publicly blowing a whistle to call attention to a crime. A related term is "leaker" (see LEAK; PLUMBER), which connotes stealthiness in exposure, and describes an employee not willing to risk dismissal by becoming known as a SOURCE.

whistlestopping going to the people by railroad train with a series of short, ad-lib speeches in small communities.

The *Jackson* (Tennessee) *Sun* gave the background of the word in 1952:

A "whistle-stop," in railroad terms, is a community too small to enjoy a regular scheduled service. Customarily, the passenger trains whiz right by. But if there are passengers to be discharged, shortly before the train approaches the station, the conductor signifies that fact by pulling the signal cord. The engineer responds with two toots of the whistle. Naturally enough, such unscheduled pauses became known as "whistlestops." The communities were "whistle-stop towns," shortened in the course of time to "whistle-stops."

President Harry Truman discovered a gift for ad-libbing speeches in May 1948. "My first formal experience at extemporaneous speaking had come just a few weeks before I opened the whistle-stop tour in June. After reading an address to the American Society of Newspaper Editors in April, I decided to talk 'off the cuff' on American relations with Russia. When I finished my remarks about thirty minutes later, I was surprised to get the most enthusiastic applause . . ."

Truman made an old-fashioned back-of-the-platform railroad tour of the nation, ad-libbing seventy-one out of seventy-six speeches. Senator Robert A. Taft, speaking to the Union League Club in Philadelphia, derided the spectacle of an American President "black-guarding Congress at whistlestops all across the country."

Taft had blundered; "whistlestop" was an insult to a town, nearly as bad as calling its residents "hicks." Railroad men had stopped calling small stations whistlestops years ago, preferring "flag stop" or "flag station" so as not to offend the citizens of small towns. The Democratic National Committee wired the mayors of thirty-five cities through which Truman had passed asking if they agreed with Taft's slur on their civic importance. "Very poor taste," said the mayor of Gary, Indiana; "Must have the wrong city," replied the mayor of Eugene, Oregon.

Truman said later about the word "whistlestop": "You know, that phrase was invented by Senator Taft on October 8, 1948. The Republicans were trying to make fun of my efforts to take the issues in that campaign directly to the people all over the country."

An AP reporter showed how the word had become locked into politics in this 1952 lead: "Whistlestopper Harry S. Truman lent a hand to Adlai Stevenson here Saturday in the biggest 'whistlestop' of them all." The reference was to New York City.

In the 1976 campaign President Gerald Ford hired a riverboat to cruise into the heart of Jimmy Carter strength in the South; it was called "the whistlefloat." Evidently any conveyance used by a candidate to reach small towns, such as the bus chosen by Clinton and Gore in 1992, can be described as a whistle-whatever.

For a blunder that took place while a candidate whistlestopped, see BLOOPER.

white backlash.   See BACKLASH.

white hats   good guys; MR. NICE GUYS. Liberal members of Washington's permanent establishment differentiated between Nixon Administration officials in this Western-movie metaphor, where heroes wear white hats and villains wear black.

White-hat status was given Robert Finch, Leonard Garment, Elliot Richardson, Peter Flanigan, Henry Kissinger, George Shultz, and Peter Peterson, among others; viewed as "black hats" by liberal hostesses were John Mitchell, H. R. Haldeman, Murray Chotiner, Charles Colson, and anyone associated with the Vice President.

The phrase was given currency in the late sixties by TV commentator and hostess Barbara Howar, who once invited this writer to a party with the admonition: "Wear your white hat."

The white hat has an ancient political history. In fourteenth-century Flanders, the badge of the democratic party, led by Ghent brewer Jacob von Artevelde, was the white hat. In England, during the administrations of the Duke of Wellington and Robert Peel, radical protesters wore the white hat as a form of derision.

The metaphor lends itself to cartoon treatment. On the cover of the *National Journal* for December 17, 1977, a group of black-hatted cloak-and-dagger types are shown marching into the office of reform-minded Director of Central Intelligence Stansfield Turner, and then marching out wearing white hats.

In India, as in the U.S., the white hat is a symbol of political purity. "Before the last few shifts of the sands of Indian politics," wrote *New York Times* correspondent William Borders from New Delhi in 1978, "it was possible to identify Congress Party members by their starchy white 'Gandhi caps,' named after Mohandas K. Gandhi, the independence hero. But now the caps are worn on all sides . . ."

See BLACK HATS.

White House the metaphoric center of executive power; or the place where the President of the U.S. is at any moment; or the Executive Mansion in Washington, D.C.

The White House, in its figurative and most often used sense, is the presidency. "A White House spokesman" is a presidential spokesman. The "White House Office" includes staffers who do not have a pass to get into the President's house.

To Americans, it combines the tradition of Buckingham Palace with the working center of power at 10 Downing Street. Its symbolism is evident in this mid-sixties use by *Ebony* magazine: "There is a joke going the rounds about a telephone conversation between Martin Luther King and John F. Kennedy. Says the President: 'Yes, Dr. King. I know, Dr. King. I understand, Dr. King. But Dr. King—it has always been known as the White House!'"

The second sense of the usage, as a dateline, was also described by Eisenhower: "The dateline 'White House' carries a meaning far broader than a mere structure or location; the White House, in newspaper stories, always means the President's headquarters, all

the time, even when dispatches identify it as the 'Summer' or the 'Vacation' [or 'western'] White House."

As a specific house, it was known as the Executive Mansion (which is its formal title) until its destruction by the British in 1814, when it was rebuilt and painted white and became known informally as the White House. Theodore Roosevelt changed the stationery from "Executive Mansion" to "The White House," formalizing the name.

As a place to live, its prisonlike, goldfish-bowl, transient nature gets complaints from its residents. Harry Truman called it "a big white jail"; Theodore Roosevelt said, "You don't live there, you're only Exhibit A to the country." And when a senator joked to Calvin Coolidge, "I wonder who lives there," the President replied, "Nobody. They just come and go."

In calibrating power, the OVAL OFFICE gets the most attention; then the West Wing, and finally the most general, the White House. Carter presidential aide Hamilton Jordan informed the author that when they placed phone calls, there was little of the imperious "The White House is on the line"; in fact, he reported that Attorney General Griffin Bell liked to say, "The White House is a building. Don't tell me 'the White House' is calling—I work for the President."

white man's war. See RICH MAN'S WAR, POOR MAN'S FIGHT.

White Paper a statement of official government policy with background documentation.

In the U.S., a "blue book" is a directory of the social elite; in England, it is an extended explanation of government policy, bound in blue covers. See RED TAPE. "White Paper" was the English terminology for a report too short to be bound as a blue book, and that phrase was adopted in the U.S.

American political usage leans harder on the background than the policy. (Sorensen: "All the economists in government were to pull together a 'Fact Book' or 'White Paper' on steel to be widely distributed.") The *Washington Post* in 1985 requested evidence from the State Department to support Ronald Reagan's assertion that Nicaragua was "a focal point for the world terrorist network"; the newspaper reported what was received: "The unclassified documents included several recent and not-so-recent public 'white papers' and briefing transcripts that outline Administration views . . . ."

"Black book" is a newer variation. *Wall Street Journal*, 1967: "Israel published a 'black book' charging that Soviet propaganda paved the way for justifying an Arab attack on Israel."

In current use, a *White Paper* (usually capitalized) is an official statement with the government rationale; a POSITION PAPER is an unofficial document that can be synonymous with *aide-mémoire* in diplomacy, or may mean a candidate's stand with background; a *blue book* is limited to Great Britain and means a lengthy statement of policy, a *black book* is a documented charge or attacking brief, and the *black briefing book* is the loose-leaf notebook the President of the U.S. studies before news conferences.

white power structure American society, as viewed by the black militant, conspiring to retain "Establishment" control and excluding African-Americans.

The phrase was introduced by black intellectuals early in the more militant phase of the civil rights movement, with or without the word "white." Barbara Brandt of SNCC used it typically in 1965: "In trying to become part of the power structure, he [the Negro] is forced to lose his militancy;

he forgets the people he should be fighting for. He has been taken over by the system."

Theodore White, in *The Making of the President 1964*, gave this definition:

> The term "power structure" when translated down to the level of the street becomes the term "whitey"—and "whitey" in the Negro ghetto is as contemptuous a word as "nigger" is in a Southern village. . . . Translated out to where it reaches juvenile hoodlums in the streets, it lifts from them the responsibility for anything—"whitey" made it this way, so "whitey" has got to fix it. . . . The dogma requires Negro leaders, too, to denounce the entire power structure; it forbids them to recognize its awkward, ponderous but sincere effort to wipe out prejudice. They must stand by and watch rioting and looting—and explain to their children and followers that it is wrongful, yet that the power structure caused it.

white racism. See RACISM.

whitewash. See SMEAR; WITCH HUNT.

whitey. See WHITE POWER STRUCTURE; CHARLIE.

Whiz Kids the relatively young executive team skilled in the most modern management methods, brought to the Defense Department in 1961 by Secretary Robert McNamara.

McNamara, then forty-five, was a member of the original "Whiz Kids" at the Ford Motor Company, one of ten Army Air Force statistical-control experts who came to Ford in a group in 1946 (Arjay Miller, later Ford president, was also a member).

The Ford nickname was picked up by Pentagon officials who resented what they felt was high-handed, ruthless administration by youthful civilians who relied too heavily on "thinking machines."

Meanwhile, back at Ford, *Fortune* magazine reported in 1966: "There's another generation of Whiz Kids at Ford—they're young, unabashedly brainy, boundlessly aggressive, open to new ideas—and they don't want to be called 'Whiz Kids.'"

The McNamara group at the Pentagon often relied on PERT—the Program Evaluation and Review Technique—a computerized decision-indicating method of pointing to the "critical path" that will most efficiently produce a new weapons system. Their espousal of this advanced technique reinforced the "Whiz Kid" image of them held by some military planners.

The word "whiz" came into American slang about 1880 as a short form of "wizard"; the phrase grew out of "The Quiz Kids," a radio program of the forties featuring brilliant youngsters.

"Whiz Kids" was probably first applied to the University of Illinois basketball team in the late 1940s.

who gets what, when, and how

a frequent definition of politics, stressing its less spiritual rewards.

The phrase was coined by political scientist Harold Lasswell in 1936, as *who gets what, when, how*. The *Political Primer for All Americans* (1944) added an introspective word to the definition: "Politics is the science of how who gets what, when and why."

"The structure of coalition politics," wrote James MacGregor Burns in 1963, "is inevitably the structure of 'who gets what, when and how' in American national politics. As the Madisonian system in being, it is also the structure of slowdown and stalemate in American Government."

Burns was using the old definition in the sense of a division of the power of the executive; in most uses, it is a division of the spoils, such as "slicing the pie" or "divvying up the melon."

For a more frequent and more charitable definition of politics, see ART OF THE POSSIBLE. For the less uplifting side, see SPOILS SYSTEM and PATRONAGE.

whole hog.   See DYED-IN-THE-WOOL.

"who-lost" construction   a device to level a charge of failure to foresee and avert foreign-policy disaster.

"The HOT-BUTTON issue in the 1950s was 'Who lost China?,'" said Richard Nixon in 1992. "If Yeltsin goes down, the question 'Who lost Russia?' will be an infinitely more devastating issue in the 1990s."

After Mao Tse-tung's Communists defeated Chiang Kai-shek's Kuomintang forces in China, conservatives in the U.S. criticized the failure of the Truman Administration, with its LET THE DUST SETTLE policy, to adequately support the anti-Communist forces, who were forced to flee to Taiwan. The watchword of the right-wing Sinologists was "Who lost China?"

Although liberals pointed out that China was not "ours" to lose, the attack phrase stung and put Democrats on the defensive. The construction, with its resonance of foreign-policy failure, was used again after the Bay of Pigs disaster, when Kennedy critics asked, "Who lost Cuba?"

Robert Blackwill, the National Security Council specialist on the Soviet Union during the early years of the Bush Administration, was asked by the author about White House refusal to back the Russian reformers who believed that PERESTROIKA was proceeding too slowly and was a mask for the continuance of Communism. He explained the continuance of the Reagan-Bush embrace of the current Moscow leadership with: "there's the who-lost-Gorbachev problem."

Who's Polk? See DARK HORSE.

wiggle room   space to move around; the ability to modify one's position and avoid political embarrassment through flexibility.

Wiggle room began its sinuous movement in the late 1970s. *Business Week* reported on September 11, 1978: "Congress has drafted regulatory legislation in a way that gives agencies . . . as little 'wiggle room' as possible." A week later, *Newsweek* also used the phrase: "When it came to plugging Democratic candidates, Rosalynn Carter was sensitive enough to give each a little wiggle room—to dodge clear of her husband's political liabilities."

The expression is still used. Mike Jendrzejczyk, Washington representative of Asia Watch, a human rights group, commented on Clinton Administration expectations for China in a 1993 strategy: "There's an enormous amount of wiggle room."

This term is based on the verb *wiggle*, akin to the Old English *wegan*, "to move." An alliterative variant, *wriggle room*, is sometimes used; in 1988, a *New York Times* editorial commented on a vague position taken by Michael Dukakis on moving the United States Embassy from Tel Aviv to Jerusalem: "He has thus left himself wriggling room should he be elected." The genteelism of *wriggle room*, however, has not been able to supplant *wiggle room* as a space more confining than *escape hatch* but less so than *crawl space*.

wilderness years   the "down time" of a politician's career; the difficult years between periods of popular acceptance or success.

A 1983 review in the *Washington Post* chronicles a drama about "a stubborn man, Winston Churchill in the 1930's, 'the wilderness years.'"

This term, which expresses trying times for a politician, is a recent metaphor based on a Biblical image. In Numbers 14, God tells Moses of the punishment for his faithless followers who left Egypt for the Promised Land: "And your children shall wander in the wilderness forty years . . . until your carcasses be wasted in the wilderness."

Churchill picked up the term in his early writings; in 1905, he called Gladstone "that strange prophet of Israel who for thirty years had wandered in the wilderness of fiscal heresy"; writing of Moses, Churchill said, "Every prophet has to come from civilization, but every prophet has to go into the wilderness."

Richard Nixon, in the 1960s, often referred to the "wilderness years of de Gaulle and Churchill," comparing them to his own time of wandering in the wastes of public rejection. During difficult times in 1987, according to the *Chicago Tribune*, Ronald Reagan remained in the White House, "staffed largely by relative strangers who, unlike such longtime loyalists and family retainers as Michael Deaver, Ed Meese and Lyn Nofziger, were unknown to him in the wilderness years of his quest for the Presidency."

Jerry Brown used the phrase in 1992 in what the *Los Angeles Times* reported as "his so-called 'wilderness' years from 1983 to 1989, following his second gubernatorial term." Such a period of disfavor, however, can prove beneficial. Brown seemed to experience a Biblical wandering during those wilderness years, commented the newspaper, "that enabled him to discover through travel, studies and writings a way to integrate his Roman Catholic religious values with political action."

According to Ta-kuang Chang, a New York attorney, a similar term can be found in the Chinese language. "The word *ye* ordinarily means 'wilderness,'" he informed the lexicographer, "but is commonly used in opposition to the word *chao* (meaning 'government' or, literally, 'the emperor's court') to refer to not being in government service and being among the people."

windfall profits a sudden financial bonanza to a private firm or individual caused by a change in government policy.

In October 1977 President Jimmy Carter laced into the opponents of his energy program as "war profiteers" whose "windfall profits" constituted the "biggest ripoff in our history."

The word "windfall," in its sense of an unexpected gift, such as a piece of fruit blown off a tree, has been in the language since the mid-sixteenth century. It was applied politically by Franklin Roosevelt in a message to Congress accompanying the 1936 Revenue Bill; the Supreme Court, in January of that year, had held a processing tax provision of the Agricultural Adjustment Act unconstitutional, and FDR's message was drawn to deny to processors a "windfall" from the tax they had already collected: "The first relates to the taxation of what may well be termed a 'windfall' received by certain taxpayers," wrote President Roosevelt on March 3, 1936. Supporting the Administration bill, Representative John McCormack of Massachusetts said on the House floor that "the tax on unjust enrichment" amounted to a "windfall."

An "excess profits tax" was used in World War I; it is still the formal name for the "windfall profits tax," which remains polemical.

Modifiers for profits have turned from "healthy" or "surging" to "swollen" and "obscene." These last two are recognized as judgmental, while "windfall" is taken to be descriptive of something unexpected and unfair.

winding down de-escalating; causing to come to an end gradually.

This was one of the oddest terms to come out of the war in Vietnam, and the author is unable to determine first usage or even the reasons for its use.

The verb "to wind" is most often followed by "up" in the sense of "to conclude"; the noun "windup" means "conclusion." Therefore, the process of VIETNAMIZATION could logically be called "the winding up of the war in Vietnam." But the term that came into use in 1969, and was elevated to cliché status in 1970, was "winding down the war."

The metaphor is that of a clock that is wound up by hand and—in the process of doing its job—runs down, or may be said to "wind down." Unwind has a modern meaning of "relax." The trouble with the metaphor in this case is that "winding down" has a passive connotation—that is, one may permit a clock to wind itself down, but no action is taken to remove the tension in the mainspring. However, the term is used here in an active sense.

William Zinsser, in the May 21, 1971, issue of *Life* magazine, had some fun with the phrase: "I submit that if science tells us anything, it tells us that man can only wind things *up*. Indeed, in the long and restless search of *Homo sapiens* for mastery of his physical environment, one invention that continues to elude him is the downwinder . . ."

Whatever the source, the term has come to mean the deliberate, steady pursuit of a policy to reduce the intensity of a war, in the hopes of an honorable extrication, and is used in defense of that policy, not to attack it.

window of opportunity availability for action or attack.

Space jargon provided the source for the term *launch window* in the mid-1960s. Walter Sullivan used it in quotation marks when he reported in the *New York Times* of October 18, 1967: "The Soviet and American vehicles flew to Venus close together because both were fired during one of the periodic 'windows' for such shots. These are brief periods of time when Venus is overtaking the Earth and relative positions of the two planets are propitious." Through that alignment, an imaginary hole or "window" in the sky allowed rockets to be launched successfully.

Another metaphoric *window* comes from the positioning of bank tellers at one time behind barred windows. The nation's *credit window* referred to the Federal Reserve's willingness to offer credit; the *gold window* named the Treasury's willingness to convert gold into dollars.

From these *windows* came the sense of "small space or short period to get something accomplished." The phrase *window of vulnerability* appeared in the 1970s; John Newhouse, a former arms-control official, noted that the term entered the Senate's SALT II hearings during the summer of 1979. Mr. Newhouse wrote to the lexicographer at that time: "The phrase describes a time just ahead when improved Soviet missile forces will, in theory, be able to destroy most of America's silo-based Minuteman ICBM's in a literal bolt from the blue."

Ronald Reagan picked up the political usage in 1981. Defending a cut in defense spending, he explained on September 24, 1981, "I'll confess, I was reluctant about this, because of the long way we have to go before the dangerous window of vulnerability confronting us will be appreciably narrowed."

Window of opportunity describes the view from the other side of that window, providing the chance to pass through an opening in space or time. *Time* magazine first reported the phrase in its November 12, 1979, issue: "Frank Barnett of the National Strategy Information Center, a hawkish think tank, warned of a 'Soviet window of opportunity' in the 1980s."

The optimism of the 1980s made the phrase popular. In March 1984 *Business Week* wrote: "The success of Reaganomics in spurring growth has opened a unique window of opportunity. Economic expansion is so strong that taxes can be increased and government spending can be cut now without causing a major slowdown." But Reagan's prospects with Congress were not quite so rosy as his second term began. "He has a window of opportunity," observed a Republican senator from a Midwestern state, quoted in the November 26, 1984, issue of *U.S. News & World Report*. "But it's very small. . . ."

winds of change   a fundamental shift in power or policy; an inexorable current not under control of leaders.

The phrase was popularized in its present context by British Prime Minister Harold Macmillan in an address to the South African Parliament, February 4, 1960, speaking about the future of Africa: "The wind of change is blowing through the Continent. Whether we like it or not, this growth of national consciousness is a political fact."

In an editorial, the *Christian Science Monitor* later congratulated Macmillan (see UNFLAPPABLE) on coining an excellent expression, and pointed to *The Libation-bearers*, written by Aeschylus in 458 B.C.: "Zeus at last may cause our ill winds to change."

As with most memorable phrases, a long history can be traced, which does not detract from the ring of originality. Of course nothing is more changeable than the direction of the wind, but the use of the simple metaphor in the turmoil of African affairs was apt.

An early use of changing winds can be found in *Sweet William's Farewell to Black-Eyed Susan* by English poet John Gay (1685–1732):

We only part to meet again.
Change, as ye list, ye winds; my heart shall be
The faithful compass that still points to thee.

Typical use of the wind metaphor in modern times was by Indian Prime Minister Jawaharlal Nehru in 1947: "The masses are awake and they demand their heritage. Strong winds are blowing all over Asia. Let us not be afraid of them but rather welcome them for only with their help can we build the new Asia of our dreams."

And John Gunther wrote of the Mormon community in Utah in 1947: ". . . the astringent winds of a new world, which bewilder the older believers, are beating mercilessly at the pillar they drove into the desert."

Windy, of course, is slang for long-winded, and is related to "full of hot air." *Winds of doctrine* was used by Milton in *Areopagitica* (1644): "Though all the winds of doctrine were let loose to play upon the earth, so Truth be in the field, we do injuriously, by licensing and prohibiting, to misdoubt her strength."

George Santayana used *Winds of Doctrine* as the title of a book in 1913. In 1934 British Prime Minister Stanley Baldwin said: "There is a wind of nationalism and freedom blowing around the world."

When Harold Macmillan came to titling his own memoirs in 1966, he accepted the editing of common usage that changed his "wind of change" to "winds" and called his book *The Winds of Change*.

winnability. See CAN'T-WIN TECHNIQUE.

winning. See CAN'T-WIN TECHNIQUE; NO-WIN POLICY; NO SUBSTITUTE FOR VICTORY; ZERO-SUM GAME; and the saying under PROVERBS AND AXIOMS, POLITICAL that goes "Show me a good loser, and I'll show you a loser."

winning the peace the only promise of victory possible in LIMITED WARS.

When it became apparent in the late sixties that the cost of victory in South Vietnam would be too high, political emphasis in the U.S. shifted to an honorable settlement. Thus, in the 1968 primary campaign, Richard Nixon pledged to "end the war and win the peace," which caused supporters of George Romney to demand that Nixon make public a "SECRET PLAN to end the war."

The use of the word "win" appealed to those who were distressed at a no-win strategy (see NO-WIN POLICY) and disturbed those who feared that military victory was Nixon's objective. As President, Nixon held to the policy, and occasionally the rhetoric, of "winning a peace"—through a withdrawal that would give the South Vietnamese "a reasonable chance of survival as a free people."

The phrase is based on the time-honored device of military terms to describe peace (see WAGING PEACE) and is taken directly from Will Rogers' aphorism: "The United States has never lost a war or won a peace." See NEVER LOST A WAR OR WON A PEACE.

wiretap. See TAPS AND BUGS.

wish list. See ENEMIES LIST.

witch hunt investigation characterized by hysteria.

Woodrow Wilson's Attorney General, A. Mitchell Palmer, led what was called a "Red hunt" just after World War I, finding "Communists under every bed."

The phrase "witch hunt"—an allusion to the Salem, Massachusetts, witch trials in the seventeenth century—is now applied to investigations considered to be motivated by a desire to capitalize on a popular fear. One of Eisenhower's campaign pledges made on the eve of election in 1952 was that we would engage in no "witch hunts or character assassination," adding he would strive to "prevent infiltration of Communists and FELLOW TRAVELERS" into government that straddled the "McCarthy issue."

A *witch hunt*—an attack phrase on an attack—is the opposite of a *whitewash* (see SMEAR), which is an attack on an exoneration. A witch hunt is a FISHING EXPEDITION with a vengeance.

Controller of the Currency John Heimann, in describing the ground rules for a 1977 investigation of Bert Lance by his office, showed a nice understanding of the Scylla and Charybdis of probes when he told his employees: "I want this to be neither a whitewash nor a witch hunt." (See ROCK AND A HARD PLACE, BETWEEN A.)

with all deliberate speed the operative phrase in the U.S. Supreme Court decision striking down segregation in schools. See SEPARATE BUT EQUAL.

On May 17, 1954, in *Brown v. Board of Education*, the Supreme Court directed public schools throughout the U.S. to integrate; a year later, on May 31, 1955, another unanimous Court directed that this be done "with all deliberate speed."

The question was soon raised: How speedy is "deliberate"? The Court obviously chose the phrase so as to give some flexibility to the lower courts in determining compliance, and the phrase became the center of legal controversy for the next decade. In 1964, writing for the majority in a decision ordering reopening of Virginia schools that closed rather than integrate, Hugo

Black stated: "There has been entirely too much deliberation and not enough speed. The time for mere 'deliberate speed' has run out . . ."

The phrase can be found in a poem by Francis Thompson, "The Hound of Heaven," written in 1893: "But with unhurrying chase/And unperturbed pace/Deliberate speed, majestic instancy . . ."

The Supreme Court, however, probably chose the phrase from a 1912 decision by Justice Oliver Wendell Holmes, in the case of *Virginia* v. *West Virginia*: ". . . a State cannot be expected to move with the celerity of a private business man; it is enough it proceeds, in the language of the English Chancery, with all deliberate speed."

Drawing on Holmes, Justice Felix Frankfurter used the phrase five times in cases preceding the desegregation decisions. Although scholars assume Justice Holmes knew what he was talking about in attributing the phrase to English Chancery practice, diligent research has failed to come up with a single quotable instance of its use.

The most fascinating clue was found in a letter to his publisher from George Gordon, Lord Byron, dated April 6, 1819. The poet had often been threatened with Chancery Court action, and in *Don Juan* wrote that his hero was "sole heir to a Chancery suit." Writing to publisher John Murray, he complained of a previous exhaustion that obliged him to "reform my 'way of life' which was conducting me from the 'yellow leaf' to the ground with all deliberate speed." Certainty in phrase detection is rare; it can only be assumed that Byron drew the phrase from his Chancery experience.

Gregg Golden of Washington provides an earlier use, from Sir Walter Scott's 1817 novel *Rob Roy*, in which an evil cousin has carried off valuable papers: "For that portion which he had converted into cash and expended on his own or on political intrigues, there was no mode of recovering it but by a suit at law, which was forthwith commenced, and proceeded, as our law-agents assured us, with all deliberate speed."

The more familiar Chancery phrase was "all convenient speed," which can also be found in Shakespeare's *The Merchant of Venice.* Just before Shylock's trial, Portia sends Balthasar to consult a lawyer and her messenger replies, "Madame, I go with all convenient speed." Robert Browning used this, as did Abraham Lincoln ("with all convenient dispatch"). Lincoln approached this thought from another angle in 1861 when asked if he favored the immediate emancipation of the slaves. "It will do no good," he replied, "to go ahead any faster than the country will follow. . . . You know the old Latin motto, *festina lente.*" That motto, a frequent saying of Augustus Caesar, means "make haste slowly."

For much of the above information the writer is indebted to Justice Potter Stewart and to Professor Alwin Thaler of the University of Tennessee.

The term is current. In 1993, *Newsday* commented on Bill Clinton's campaign promise to gay and lesbian groups to lift the military ban on homosexuals: "Even they . . . must have been surprised by what were almost the first words out of his mouth after his election—that he would proceed with all deliberate speed to lift the restriction."

"Deliberate speed" is almost an oxymoron, a phrase or epigram built on the jarring juxtaposition of opposites, like "thunderous silence" or "cruel kindness." It does not qualify as a full-fledged oxymoron (a word that columnist William Buckley, Jr., uses because it sounds like an insult) for the reason that it is possible to have a "speedy deliberation." See LOYAL OPPOSITION.

Women's Lib a movement promoting equal rights for women, more militant than similar women's rights and women's suffrage movements in the past.

Betty Friedan, whose 1963 book, *The Feminine Mystique,* focused on the emptiness in the lives of suburban women, told the author that the phrase originated with the women of Students for a Democratic Society in the late sixties. Feminist editor Gloria Steinem, in response to the author's query in the mid-1970s, confirmed this:

As far as I know, Women's Liberation is a phrase that sprang from the women of SNCC and the women of SDS . . . I think I first heard it early in 1967. Those women were very active. They went to jail with the men, demonstrated with the men, and earned Ph.D.'s with the men. Yet, when they got back to their organizational meetings they were supposed to make coffee, not revolutionary policy. This made it very clear to them that the revolution they were fighting was not necessarily going to benefit the other half of the human race.

Shortening the phrase to Women's Lib is a bit of ridicule perpetrated by the press. Would you say Black Lib? Puerto Rican Lib? I doubt it. The cavalier shortening is a kind of put-down in itself. Because of this, and because of the vast enlargement of the numbers of women involved, women now tend to say "Women's Movement" rather than Women's Liberation.

In either case, the phrase indicates a large umbrella movement, comprised of hundreds of local or national organizations, plus consciousness-changing among many, many women who belong to no organizations at all. In that sense, I suppose it's comparable to "Civil Rights Movement" as a phrase.

In its unshortened form, Women's Liberation was considered appropriate by many of its leaders. Kate Millet, who wrote *Sexual Politics* in 1970, said, "Women's Liberation is my life."

The attack phrases of the movement (see MOVEMENT, THE) are "male chauvinist" (for origin of chauvinist, see JINGOISM), "sexual harassment," made especially vivid in the charges brought by Anita Hill in the Clarence Thomas Supreme Court confirmation hearings, and SEXISM. *Time* magazine wrote in 1970: "Sexism was the sin of one professor who admitted at a San Francisco meeting of the staid Modern Language Association that, all things considered, he would look at a girl's legs when considering her for a teaching post. 'You bastard, you bastard!' one girl screamed (s.o.b. is out in the best feminist lexicons)." (A generation later, "one young woman" would be substituted for "girl," a word now confined to females in their early teens or younger.)

The phrase is passing out of use, except in historical contexts.

An attack word on feminists, popularized in the early 1990s by Rush Limbaugh, the radio polemicist, was *feminazi*. See MACHISMO; CONSCIOUSNESS-RAISING.

wonk. See POLICY WONK.

woodshed, take him to the to punish briskly but gently.

When President Reagan's Director of the Office of Management and Budget, David Stockman, called Reaganomics "a Trojan horse" in a series of indiscreet interviews to the *Atlantic Monthly* in 1981, the President summoned him to the White House for a meeting. Stockman characterized it as being "taken to the woodshed"—chastised verbally but not threatened with dismissal.

A decade later, another budget director gave an equally revealing interview to a breakfast group of reporters. Leon

Panetta said the free trade treaty with Mexico, supported by President Clinton, was "dead," and that expensive health-care reform legislation being prepared by Hillary Rodham Clinton should be delayed.

Asked about this, Bill Clinton laughed it off by referring to the Stockman metaphor: "I don't need to take him to the woodshed. . . . I need for him to sort of get his spirits up."

The expression, its first printed citation in 1907, comes from taking a misbehaving child out of the presence of others—in rural areas, to a woodshed outside the house—for punishment.

-word combining form used with an initial capital letter to refer euphemistically to something potentially distasteful or politically controversial.

This use of initialese became popular during the mid-1980s, when *-question* was the more frequent combining form after a capitalized initial. When Gary Hart was asked about adultery, for instance, the media labeled that suggestion of impropriety the *A-question*. After Judge Douglas H. Ginsburg was nominated to the Supreme Court, he was forced to admit that he'd smoked marijuana in the early 1970s; Sam Donaldson of ABC called that issue the *M-question*.

In late 1987, *-word* replaced *-question* as the preferred form. A *Washington Post* editorial noted the reluctance of candidates to talk about raising taxes after Walter Mondale's 1984 defeat: "They've been Mondaled. You say the T-word and you die." An editorial in the *New York Times* commented, "These days the mere mention of the U-word—unemployment—sends shivers through the ranks of Moscow's economic reformers."

This *-word* construction may be rooted in baby-talk euphemism. "The Rating Code office told me a mandatory R went to any film using one of 17 words," said Roy E. Disney, producer of the movie *Pacific High*, in a 1980 interview with the Associated Press. "The picture has four of what my mother calls 'that F-word.'"

Nowadays, however, the expression is used in mock-horror to designate plain terms. In print, blanks can be left in supposedly dirty words; as the *Washington Post* reported in 1987, "The only way even to begin to do these things is to raise t___s."

By 1991, the use of *-word* had become so widespread a cliché that the *New York Times* felt compelled to editorialize on the subject. "The Cute Alphabet is filling up fast," commented the editorial page of June 6, 1991. "'R' has fallen, as in 'the R word,' the nervous euphemism for recession. . . . Last week President Bush swept up the 'Q' word, applying it to supposed quotas in employment."

workers.   See TROOPS; VOLUNTEERS.

work ethic   the idea that work in itself is good for a person, molding character and inspiring a quality of thrift and an understanding of values.

In *The Protestant Ethic and the Spirit of Capitalism* (1904), Max Weber pointed to a paradox: although the pursuit of money was once regarded as unworthy of a Christian, and the possession of riches seen long ago as evidence of selfishness, in modern times religion has endowed material success with the aura of godliness. Calvinism's themes of hard work and personal asceticism led to the accumulation of fortunes, which was considered the mark of a good man—thus, went Weber's thesis, "the Puritan stood at the cradle of economic man," providing "good conscience in money making."

At its coinage, then, the Protestant ethic (later Puritan ethic, or work ethic) was intended to be a term of derogation by its author. It has since gained in stature and is now a compliment, politically popularized in a Labor Day speech by Richard Nixon in 1972.

President Nixon was impressed with a memorandum entitled "The Problem of the Blue-Collar Worker," written in 1970 by Assistant Secretary of Labor Jerome Rosow. Inflation and the cost of family education had driven up these workers' cost of living at a time when their income was topping out, the memo showed, and white-collar work had been glamorized while blue-collar jobs were denigrated as menial.

This writer, then a White House speechwriter, was assigned a speech on the "dignity of work" to reassure these lower-middle-class ETHNICS that their work was respectable and respected, and—in retrospect—to exploit a resentment at "the greening of America" that put too great a stress on youth and intellectual endeavors while patronizing the calloused hand.

A speech was drafted on the work ethic; the President removed references to "Protestant" and broadcast the speech on radio with some pride: "As the name implies, the work ethic holds that labor is good in itself; that a man or woman at work not only makes a contribution to his fellow man, but becomes a better person by virtue of the act of working. The work ethic is ingrained in the American character. That is why most of us consider it immoral to be lazy or slothful—even if a person is well off enough not to work." Here the President wrote in: "—or can avoid work by going on welfare."

Columnist Max Lerner, with an eye for sociology in politics, noted: "President Nixon's Labor Day sermonette on the work ethic was addressed not only to the traditional audience of union members but also to the South and Midwest, where the language of the work ethic is politically warming, and to the whole middle class which feels that honest work has gone down the drain."

The phrase is in current use, although it occasions this riposte to politicians who evoke it: "What are you doing about people who have the work ethic but who cannot find jobs?"

workfare conservative label for welfare reform, stressing an intent to "get people off welfare rolls and onto payrolls."

Harper's magazine in July 1968 discussed the goals of civil rights leader James Charles Evers: "One of Evers' programs is what he calls workfare; he has said that everybody ought to work for what he gets."

In the late spring of 1969, the Nixon Administration's plan for the overhaul of the welfare system was at an impasse: counselors Arthur Burns and Daniel P. Moynihan differed on the need for a work requirement. George Shultz, then Labor Secretary, came up with a solution that was not a compromise, but a fresh approach: supplementing the incomes of the working poor, to provide an incentive to move from welfare to work.

Inside the government, the plan was originally called Family Security, but that was too much like Social Security; "Fair Share" was proposed, but that sounded to conservative members of the Administration too much like FAIR DEAL or share-the-wealth. At a cabinet meeting at Camp David, President Nixon directed some of the discussion of the plan to its name, because he had already decided on substance and wanted its opponents to get their licks in somewhere. Family Assistance Plan was decided upon, despite this writer's concern about the acronym of its ini-

tials sounding like an expression of a cartoon character named Major Hoople.

However, in his nationwide television address on August 8, 1969, the President tried out the new word: "In the final analysis, we cannot talk our way out of poverty; we cannot legislate our way out of poverty; but this Nation can work its way out of poverty. What America needs now is not more welfare, but more 'workfare.'" In his message to the Congress three days later, he used the term again: "This would be the effect of the transformation of welfare into 'workfare,' a new work-rewarding program . . ." By 1986, *Time* magazine reported that more than twenty states were experimenting with some form of workfare.

The emphasis on the work requirement—called "the conservative rhetoric"—was said to offend many liberals who ordinarily might be expected to support the program. Whether the rhetoric was the cause, or a resentment that this major social legislation should be credited to a longtime political adversary underlay it, the welfare reform legislation bogged down in a combination of conservative opposition and liberal lack of enthusiasm.

Welfare, as a word, has fallen far from its heights as one of the basic national purposes described in the Constitution: "to promote the general welfare." Today, recipients and taxpayers alike characterize it as "the welfare mess," the "archaic welfare system" and the "welfare quagmire." See WELFARE STATE; ENTITLEMENT.

"Work," on the other hand, is doing better all the time, despite the efforts to change "workers" into "employees" and ultimately to bloodless "personnel." (Richard P. Nathan's 1993 book, *Turning Promises into Performance*, used the term in its subtitle: *The Management Challenge of Implementing Workfare*.) This was a far cry from the sixties, when demonstration organizer Abbie Hoffman called work "the only dirty four-letter word in the English language."

working group TASK FORCE, committee, or group organized for a single cause or project.

Originally the word *committee* was used for political action, but it was replaced by *task force* in the 1960s after *committee* gained a connotation of delay. Replacing *task force* in turn is the noun *group*, taken from British military aviation and later adopted in British business.

By the late 1970s, a gerund was being used attributively to describe the activity of this latest designation: *working group*. Perhaps based on the use of *working lunch* for a business meal or *working vacation* for productive time away from the office, this phrase was being used in the White House in 1979. The committee working on the Strategic Arms Limitation Talks took the name of "the SALT working group." In 1993, Hillary Rodham Clinton and Ira Magaziner of the Clinton Health Care Task Force called many of its subdivisions "working groups." See BLUE RIBBON PANEL.

working the room/fence ingratiating oneself with fellow guests; PRESSING THE FLESH of those who came to greet a candidate.

To *work a room* is to do the political work in a roomful of people—that is, to make an effort to greet each person individually.

Washington Post reporters Nancy Collins and Donnie Radcliffe wrote that at a 1977 Pan American reception in Washington, "Rosalynn Carter . . . instantly began working the room much as she had during the months Jimmy Carter was trying to win the White House."

New York Times reporter Judith Miller wrote in 1982 that "Henry Kissinger, working the room like a politician, embraced Norman Podhoretz. . . ."

At a party given in her Georgetown home by Pamela Harriman in 1992, ABC-TV Washington Bureau chief Tim Russert told Howard Kurtz of the *Washington Post*: "I got five or six tips I'm pursuing. . . . I saw my competition working the room just as vigorously."

A more recent coinage is *working the fence*, the habit of politicians greeting the people lined up behind a fence, usually at an airport. When President Ford was shot at twice during a two-week period in 1975, Howard Flieger wrote in *U.S. News & World Report*:

> The time is past due for the President and those who aspire to his job to stop "working the fence." That is a politician's term to describe the practice of candidates walking along the restraining lines at airports and such public places to shake as many hands and exchange as many greetings as possible. . . . It produced dramatic pictures for the TV news shows. It has come to be regarded by many politicians as the ultimate common touch—the modern-day equivalent of baby-kissing. And it is foolhardy.

But the practice continues as part of campaigning, and not just in America: *U.S. News* in 1987 described Mikhail Gorbachev as "jailing crooks, firing incompetents, attacking drunkenness, freeing the arts and media, working the fences like an American politician."

world opinion the moral force, real or imagined, of the anticipated reaction of uncommitted nations, or of leaders not firmly aligned with any international power group.

The idea is rooted in the Declaration of Independence: ". . . a decent Respect to the Opinions of Mankind requires that they should declare the causes which impel them to the Separation. . . . To prove this, let Facts be submitted to a candid World."

The phrase was probably written by Thomas Jefferson, who used it later: "The good opinion of mankind, like the lever of Archimedes with the given fulcrum, moves the world."

Daniel Webster, speaking to the House of Representatives on January 19, 1823, about the Greek revolution, gave the phrase its moral overtones: "Moral causes come into consideration, in proportion as the progress of knowledge is advanced; and the *public opinion* of the civilized world is rapidly gaining an ascendancy over mere brutal force."

After Jefferson, the phrase was most closely associated with President Woodrow Wilson, who used it in his PEACE WITHOUT VICTORY address early in 1917: "The present war must first be ended; but we owe it to candor and to a just regard for the opinion of mankind to say that, so far as our participation in guarantees of future peace is concerned, it makes a great deal of difference in what way and upon what terms it is ended." In his speech, Wilson used "mankind" as in the Declaration of Independence. Thirteen months earlier, in a letter to Colonel House, he wrote: "If either party to the present war will let us say to the other that they are willing to discuss peace on such terms, it will clearly be our duty to use our utmost *moral* force to oblige the other to parley, and I do not see how they could stand in the *opinion of the world* if they refused."

Dwight Eisenhower, in his SPIRIT OF Geneva speech in 1955, gave a quasi-legal standing to world opinion: "The case of the several leading nations on both sides is on trial before the bar of world opinion."

As can be seen, many political leaders have made obeisances to "the opinion of mankind" and "world opinion" (which is now more frequently used than the Jeffersonian phrase). In practice, however, the requirements of national policy have often led to decisions contrary to the "dictates" of world opinion. Who, after all, forms world opinion? In most cases, the phrase is used to mean its effect on the "uncommitted nations" of the THIRD WORLD and other neutralist forces in Western nations. Not all of these, however, feel bound by world opinion themselves: India's takeover of Portuguese Goa, an enclave on its coast, flew in the face of world opinion—at least in Western eyes—but accomplished what India's leaders felt was an important national goal.

South Carolina Congressman Mendel Rivers, chairman of the House Armed Services Committee, urged in September 1966 that the U.S. "flatten Hanoi if necessary" and "let world opinion go fly a kite." This was generally regarded as a hard-line extreme.

Ralph Waldo Emerson suggested a kind of compromise in 1841: "It is easy in the world to live after the world's opinion; it is easy in solitude to live after our own; but the great man is he who in the midst of the crowd keeps with perfect sweetness the independence of solitude."

world policeman. See POLICEMAN OF THE WORLD.

world view. See WELTANSCHAUUNG.

worst of both worlds. See INFLATION.

wrap-up. See ADVANCE MAN.

write-in a vote requiring the voter's "writing-in" of the candidate's name, rather than marking a ballot or pulling a lever next to a printed name.

Politicians go to great lengths to

make voting easier for the voter. Party symbols (see PARTY EMBLEMS) appear above the line to reassure the nearly illiterate; parties jockey for the first line or column, as if the inside track provides greater speed; "sample ballots" are distributed as literature, with a large arrow pointing to the candidate's name and the rest of the ballot screened with a dull gray overlay. Accordingly, a "write-in"—where the voter has to work, rather than react—is given little chance of winning.

On primaries, however, a successful write-in campaign occasionally comes to pass. In 1964 in New Hampshire, a late-starting, enthusiastic campaign for former Senator Henry Cabot Lodge upset the well-financed campaigns of Barry Goldwater and Nelson Rockefeller.

Dwight Eisenhower recalled the Minnesota primary of 1952, which gave a big boost to his candidacy: "The effort to promote a write-in vote had, as with the Madison Square Garden meeting, been opposed by persons who, while participating in the effort to make me a candidate, believed that any write-in effort was doomed to miserable failure and would have a depressing effect." For the result, see POLITICAL MIRACLE.

wrong war   a criticism of military strategy.

President Harry Truman and General Douglas MacArthur clashed in 1951 over the strategic course to take in Korea. As 200,000 Chinese Communist VOLUNTEERS swarmed across the Yalu River to retake North Korea, MacArthur wanted to strike back at China's PRIVILEGED SANCTUARIES in force, but the President restrained him. General Omar Bradley, Chairman of the Joint Chiefs of Staff, supported Truman's position before Congress, calling the MacArthur strategy "the wrong war, at the wrong place and at the wrong time, and with the wrong enemy." See NO SUBSTITUTE FOR VICTORY.

Critics of a "land war in Asia" often termed this kind of involvement "the wrong war," though no "air war in Asia" was ever posed as "the right war." Benjamin Franklin said, "There never was a good war or a bad peace," and educator Charles Eliot Norton, denouncing the Spanish-American War in 1898, said, "If a war be undertaken for the most righteous end, before the resources of peace have been tried and proved vain to secure it, that war has no defense, it is a national crime." The antonym to "wrong war" is "just war"; see WAR OF NATIONAL LIBERATION.

President Johnson used the Bradley construction in a different way, as he appointed the first black, Thurgood Marshall, to the U.S. Supreme Court in 1967: "I believe it is the right thing to do, the right time to do it, the right man and the right place."

X. See MR. X.

yahoo a political brute.

Senator Herbert Lehman of New York walked down the Senate aisle to confront Senator Joseph McCarthy, who told him, "Go back to your seat, old man." Wrote Stewart Alsop in his 1968 book *The Center*: "Thus old Senator Lehman's back, waddling off in retreat, seemed to symbolize the final defeat of decency and the triumph of the yahoos."

In 1970 a reader of the *Washington Post* wrote the editor: "Justice Douglas makes a perfect target for the KNOW-NOTHINGS overrunning Washington. . . . The Yahoos are on the loose. Who is to stop them?"

In 1978, as Washington social pages reported blunders by "the Georgians" on the staff of President Carter, Meg Greenfield wrote in *Newsweek*: "There are far too many Carter Administration Georgians in town who do not play the bumpkin game to lend credibility to the notion that the principal tension here is between a stuffy, decrepit Establishment and a bunch of bare-chested, peanut-feeding Yahoos."

The word comes from Jonathan Swift's *Gulliver's Travels*, written in 1726, coined by him to describe a race of brutes in the form of men who are slaves to the noble breed of "houyhnhnm," highly intelligent horses. It has also been used as a cheer, similar to "yippee" and "hooray," and the two senses combined in Yates's *The Rock Ahead* (1868), describing "a dam low-bred lot, yahooin' all over the place."

The trend is against capitalization in modern political use, which applies the word almost exclusively to anti-intellectual right wingers (see REDNECK; DINOSAUR WING).

Yalta. See MUNICH ANALOGY; OPEN COVENANTS.

yardsticks. See GUIDELINES.

yellow dog Democrat an unswerving party loyalist; used only as a compliment.

A yellow dog is a cur. In labor terminology, a "yellow dog contract" is an agreement signed by employees not to join a union.

But the yellow dog has taken on a different political coloration as a Southern regionalism. When Senator Tom Heflin of Alabama refused to support fellow Democrat Al Smith in the 1928 election and bolted to Herbert Hoover, other Alabamans who disagreed with Heflin popularized the line "I'd vote for a yellow dog if he ran on the Democratic ticket."

This was hardly complimentary to Smith, but it did illustrate the lengths to which some Southern Democrats would go in supporting the ticket.

The phrase is in active use in the Deep South, as an admiring description of a fellow REGULAR. See BRASS COLLAR DEMOCRAT.

yes, but   one who supports a principle but refuses to support its implementation; more a straggler than a follower.

This was a coinage of Franklin D. Roosevelt's, when he was under fire in 1937 for trying to PURGE the Democratic party of its conservative members. Writes Samuel Rosenman: "He invented a new word to describe the Congressman who publicly approved a progressive objective but who always found something wrong with any specific proposal to gain that objective—'a yes-but' fellow."

In 1952 Adlai Stevenson, a close student of Rooseveltian phrases, blasted his opposition in these terms: "The Republicans have a 'me, too' candidate running on a 'yes, but' platform, advised by a 'has been' staff . . ."

The phrase, while never as popular as ME TOO, remains alive. Columnist Flora Lewis, writing with prescience of possible successors to Charles de Gaulle in 1967: "Emerging from the shadow of de Gaulle is . . . the lean, eager face of Valéry Giscard d'Estaing, who says 'yes, but' to de Gaullism to separate his profile from the crowd."

you can't beat somebody with nobody   proverb used when an "out" party is jubilant over the "in" party's unpopularity, and then is faced with the task of finding a well-known candidate. See INS AND OUTS.

Historian Mark Sullivan wrote in 1930: "When, finally, [Theodore]

Roosevelt put his mind upon selecting his successor . . . he was moved by the axiom of practical politics which says, 'You can't beat somebody with nobody.'" The proverb was current at the turn of the century, and is often attributed to "Uncle Joe" Cannon, House Speaker from 1903 to 1911.

Its origin may be in a Lincoln anecdote, taken from Carl Sandburg's writings, related by Everett McKinley Dirksen on the floor of the Senate:

> When I think of all the comments by persons who seem to think they are better able to do this job in the defense field than is the President of the United States, I think of the Committee on the Conduct of the War, which was established away back in the Civil War days. . . . On that committee there was a man named Benjamin Wade, from Ohio. He started out as a canal driver and as a mule skinner. Then he became a teacher, as I recall, and then a lawyer. That qualified him to conduct a war. He marched down to the White House, shook his finger at Lincoln, and said, "You have to fire General McClellan." Lincoln said, "Well, whom shall I use to replace him?" And Wade said, "Anybody." Lincoln, out of his majestic concepts, said, "I cannot fight a war with anybody; I must have somebody."
>
> Away back in those days we had a little of the same attitude which is now apparent.

The phrase is current. During the 1992 Presidential campaign, the *Chicago Tribune* applied two clichés of CONVENTIONAL WISDOM to George Bush and Bill Clinton: "One cliché is that whenever a President is running for re-election, the campaign is a referendum on the incumbent. That has been the case in the past and makes sense, so it's probably true. And if it is, President Bush has already lost the election. But of course he has not, because this cliché runs up against another—you can't beat somebody with nobody—and a little-known candidate with questions about his past isn't going to get elected President."

See PROVERBS AND AXIOMS, POLITICAL.

you can't fight City Hall. See GO FIGHT CITY HALL.

you never had it so good slogan of "In" party stressing prosperity.

"You Never Had It So Good" was the Democratic party slogan in the 1952 Stevenson campaign against Eisenhower. See $K_1 C_2$. Those "madly for Adlai" were not enthusiastic about the slogan, since it appeared as a weak defense against the MESS IN WASHINGTON. Arthur Schlesinger, Jr., writing in 1965, tried to dissociate Stevenson from it: "In the last days of Truman the party motto had been, 'You never had it so good.' The essence of the party appeal was not to demand exertions but to promise benefits. Stevenson changed all that."

In 1955 the British Conservative party did better with the slogan. The official Tory campaign theme was "Conservative Freedom Works" but the unofficial battle cry was taken from the American campaign three years earlier. British author John Montgomery wrote in his book *The Fifties:* "Mr. Harold Macmillan's statement, that the British people had 'never had it so good,' attracted wide attention. It was, however, only a half-truth. It failed to convince many housewives, struggling against the rising prices of food and other essentials, or brides, or business girls striving to furnish homes, or youngsters attempting to save to get married."

Whenever any political leader asks voters to count their blessings, the criticism heightens, with "You never had it so good" now turned into an attack phrase. Lyndon Johnson in 1967 set forth some of the things that were right about America: "We produce more goods, we transport more goods and we use more goods than anyone in the world. We own almost a third of the world's railroad tracks. We own almost two-thirds of the world's automobiles. We own half the trucks in the world. And although we have only about 6 per cent of the population in the world, we have half its wealth."

Columnist James Reston commented: "This, of course, is the old doctrine of 'you-never-had-it-so-good.' . . . The Johnson theme will probably do all right, especially since the Republicans have renewed their old game of self-destruction. It is the poor voters who are in trouble, for they are about to be overwhelmed by all the accumulated political rubbish of the centuries."

Young Turks insurgents; restive elements within a party seeking control or at least a voice; usually, not always, comparatively young.

The Young Turks were the reformers of the Ottoman Empire, a revolutionary group that seized power in 1908 from the aging sultans; in 1922 the House of Osman gave up and the Young Turks—middle-aged by then—set up a republic.

The name was used to describe a group of Republican senators in 1929 who broke with their leadership over tariff legislation. Wrote *Time* magazine at the time: "Spectators of the Senate tariff war last week gasped with surprise at the sight of a trim new regiment marching briskly and in close order out of the Republican redoubts. These new Republican warriors were called the Young Turks, a band of about 20 who had mutinied against the feeble leadership of the OLD GUARD. For Senators they were young men (average age: 56). As legislative legionnaires they were mostly rookies serving their first Senate enlistment."

Today the phrase is used to describe any faction impatient with delay or defeat, seeking action. Party regulars use it patronizingly, but those so labeled do not resent it. The phrase was eclipsed for a time by ANGRY YOUNG MEN.

During the Bermuda Conference of 1953, Winston Churchill digressed from the agenda to discuss imperialism with Dwight Eisenhower, expressing his doubts about the wisdom of self-government for peoples not yet ready for it. When the American President disagreed with a portion of the Prime Minister's argument, Churchill smiled and said, "You're just like the Young Turks in my government."

you're no JFK attack phrase for "don't overestimate yourself."

In the debates of the 1988 Presidential campaign, the most powerful blow was struck during the facedown of the Vice Presidential candidates, Dan Quayle and Lloyd Bentsen.

When then-Senator Quayle suggested similarities between his qualifications and those of the former Democratic President, Senator Bentsen slammed back with an effective if somewhat unfair rejoinder: "Senator, I served with Jack Kennedy, I knew Jack Kennedy. Jack Kennedy was a friend of mine. Senator, you're no Jack Kennedy."

Since its 1988 introduction, that zinger has been reworked in seemingly endless variations. The uses range from a *New Yorker* art critique of 1991 ("George Moore is no Cézanne") to a 1992 headline of a *New York Times* review for a biography of the Confederacy's President Jefferson Davis ("He Was No Abe Lincoln").

Dan Quayle, in turn, tried the line at the Republican National Convention in 1992. After Bill Clinton compared his experience to an earlier President who'd also had experience only in state government, Quayle announced, "Bill Clinton, you're no Ronald Reagan." Tom Brokaw of NBC News then commented on the line, "They've probably worn that one out."

The most effective recycling of the line, though, came from Ronald Reagan himself at the same convention. Noting the middle name of William Jefferson Clinton, the aging Reagan wryly added, "This fellow they've nominated claims he's the new Thomas Jefferson. Well, let me tell you something. I knew Thomas Jefferson. He was a friend of mine. And, Governor, you're no Thomas Jefferson."

your home is your castle a slogan appealing to whites opposed to residential integration.

George Mahoney, perennial candidate for statewide office in Maryland, used this slogan in his 1966 campaign. It was picked up by Louise Day Hicks, candidate for mayor of Boston in 1967; both campaigns lost.

"Your Home Is Your Castle—Protect It" was regarded as a CODE WORD phrase by most analysts, playing on the prejudices of voters concerned with property values in their neighborhoods if blacks moved in.

The phrase "a man's home is his castle" is taken from a proverb and was codified in English law by Sir Edward Coke in 1604: "For a man's house is his castle, *et domus sua cuique tutissimum refugium.* . . . Resolved: The house of every man is his castle, and if thieves come to a man's house to rob or murder, and the owner or his servants kill any of the thieves in defence of himself and his house, it is no felony and he lose nothing . . ."

In recent usage, the proverb has been more the property of the "gun lobby" than of opponents of desegregation.

Z

zero-base budgeting starting a budget from scratch every year, challenging all assumptions of allocations; a management technique intended to improve efficiency.

Peter A. Pyhrr, manager, Staff Control, of Texas Instruments in Dallas, wrote an article in the *Harvard Business Review* (November-December 1970) coining the phrase and describing the technique. He began by quoting a speech made on December 2, 1969, by Dr. Arthur Burns, then counselor to the President: "Customarily, the officials in charge of an established program have to justify only the increase which they seek above last year's appropriation. In other words, what they are already spending is usually accepted as necessary, without examination. Substantial savings could undoubtedly be realized if every agency . . . made a case for its entire appropriation request every year, just as if its program or programs were entirely new."

Commented Mr. Pyhrr: "Burns was advocating that government agencies start from ground zero, as it were, with each year's budget and present their requests for appropriations in such a fashion that all funds can be allocated on the basis of cost/benefit or some similar kind of evaluative analysis."

The use of the "ground zero" metaphor was in error: "ground zero" refers to that area on the ground directly below an atomic explosion, the epicenter from which the distance from the middle is measured, and does not imply getting to the bottom of things. But the phrase and the article caught the eye of management-conscious Governor Jimmy Carter of Georgia, who hired Mr. Pyhrr to come to Atlanta and try out his ideas.

During the 1976 campaign Mr. Carter used the phrase frequently, as evidence of his managerial know-how. When in office—on April 28, 1977—President Carter described it this way: "We have a means now to put into effect a new budgeting system called zero-base budgeting, that will let us go deep within the government as the 1979 Fiscal year budget is prepared to eliminate unnecessary programs and to re-examine those things that are now accepted as impervious to criticism and scrutiny and analysis, and to bring them to the surface and look them over again and see which ones need to be continued, which ones enhanced, which ones reduced or abolished."

Mr. Carter's Office of Media Liaison defined it in these words: "In zero-base budgeting, the budget process for all federal agencies start from zero—no funding at all. The agencies must build their budget each year from the ground up, insuring that spending is as economical as possible."

The technique has been criticized, more for presuming to be new than for its basic idea; in an article in the *Wall Street Journal* on April 27, 1977, Harvard Business School professor Robert Anthony held: "Under the term 'management by objectives' this idea has been common in industry and in certain parts of the government for years . . . so, even though zero-base budgeting is a fraud, and even though the good parts of it are not new, experienced budget people should not let the phrase make them nauseous [*sic*]. They should disregard the rhetoric and latch on to the term as a way of accomplishing what really needs to be accomplished anyway."

By the 1980s the idea had lost its charm. "We've been MBOed and ZBBed," one Reagan official complained, referring to the concepts of "management by objective" and zero-base budgeting. "Every few years there's a new gimmick. The next one may be the 'Age of Accountability.'"

See SUNSET LAW.

zero-sum game in politics or diplomacy, a confrontation in which a face-saving way out is impossible, and one side wins what the other side loses.

Asked in May 1993 about the Clinton Administration's projected tax increases, C. Clinton Stretch, a former counsel to the Joint Committee on Taxation, replied: "We're playing a zero-sum game. Those who benefit by getting something out of this set of tax increases are going to do so only by harming someone else."

In game theory, pioneered by Professors John von Neumann and Oskar Morgenstern, a game in which the interests of the two players are diametri-

cally opposed is called "zero-sum"—that is, the sum of the winnings is always zero, with one player winning what the other loses. A non-zero-sum game is one in which both sides can both win or lose—for example, in a labor-management negotiation, if no agreement is reached and a disruptive strike ensues, both sides have lost. In a successful peace negotiation, considering the savings of not fighting a war, both sides have won.

Game theory is closely studied by national security strategists, and a confrontation to be avoided at all costs is often referred to as a "zero-sum game," which is a form of NO-WIN POLICY.

zinger a barb; or, a punch line; or, a stirring conclusion to a speech.

"Zing" is a word with many slang meanings, from "punch" to "liveliness." ("It don't mean a thing if you ain't got that zing.") In politics, a "zinger" is a verbal jab at an opponent, often on the light side, well short of a denunciation, or "blast." Common usage in this sense: "Give him a zinger and see how he reacts."

"Zing" also has a verb form. The Spring 1978 catalogue for Arlington House publishers advertised *The Power of the Positive Woman*, by Phyllis Schlafly, with this line: "The nation's leading ERA [Equal Rights Amendment] opponent zings Womens' Lib and the ERA in her first book on women." The verb "to zing" describes criticism less forceful than a related slang verb, "to zap," from a Johnny Hart comic strip, "B.C.," which was usually accompanied by a bolt of lightning.

Speechwriters use zinger in another sense, that of a moment of uplift or poignancy in a speech, or a punch line likely to trigger applause. When a zinger comes at the end of a speech or line of thought, it is called a "snapper"

(from "to snap out of it"). See PERORA-
TION.

zoo plane the least desirable campaign
transportation; airborne home of the
scorned animals of television technology. (See STIR UP THE ANIMALS.)

Late in most presidential campaigns,
the candidate's aircraft has room only
for a press "pool"—that handful of reporters who stay close to "the Man"
while staying in touch with the accompanying press plane, which lands first
at campaign stops to report the arrival
and swell the crowd. Often a second
press plane is needed to accommodate
photographers, television crews, and
reporters from less prestigious publications or from local stations.

Jules Witcover, then a *Washington
Post* reporter, wrote in 1973 about a
Republican observer who was discovered on a Democratic campaign plane:
"Given campaign press credentials as a
representative of the Women's News
Service and a freelance book writer,
she was shunted to the 'zoo plane'—
the No. 2 plane in the McGovern entourage. It was so named by reporters
because it mostly carried TV cameramen and technicians—'the animals' in
the quasi-affectionate, quasi-snobbish
parlance of political campaigns."

The author first heard the expression
in the campaign of 1968, when Republican press aide Ronald Ziegler said
jokingly to a critical "pool" reporter:
"You'll never get off the zoo plane
after this."

In 1987, the *Los Angeles Times* wrote
of the Presidential entourage who "fly
on Air Force One or with the press in
the accompanying 'zoo plane' (which
is paid for by the media who fly in it)."

In 1993, another animalistic metaphor entered political jargon. The
Washington Post reported on press
secretary Dee Dee Myers and the
White House press corps: "She calls
them 'the beasts.'"

Zulu. See BRAVO ZULU.

RESEARCH,
METHODOLOGY,
AND CREDITS

In the beginning are the words.

Which words make up the current political lexicon? To find out, the lexicographer must survey much of the writing and speaking in the field today with an eye and an ear for the current, the clichéd, and the colorful.

The technique is to make the words come to him. A reading plan comes first, to be certain all periods are covered in books on history and biography, weighted to this century, and heavily weighted to the last eight presidential administrations. This chronology is then crosshatched by reading on a subject: books and guides to politics on the precinct level, on foreign policy, on defense, on national conventions. Collections of quotations come next, dictionaries of slang, and the other dictionaries on government and politics that have been written over the years. And all the while, the daily newspapers and weekly news magazines and Sunday afternoon television panel shows must be culled, especially the syndicated political columnists to whom the political language is second nature.

The lexicographer selects a book, magazine, or newspaper in his plan, trains his eye to look for catch phrases, and begins scanning. In a book on the Truman Administration he runs across a phrase—*red herring*, for example—and makes out a 5 × 7 index card for it, noting the title and page of the book that refers to it. After a hundred books and a thousand newspaper columns, he has about 2,000 of those index cards. Reading the *Oxford Book of English Proverbs*, he comes to an 1890 political use of the phrase as well as a sixteenth-century use from John Heywood's proverbs; a bell rings, and a check is made to see if he already has that card. He has; there are three other notations on that entry already, all in current use.

Three hundred books and uncounted columns later, the card file begins to say something. There are not that many more cards—perhaps 2,500 in all—but some have a dozen notations and others only the one that caused the card to be made out. Two possibilities arise: either many of the cards contain words that do not belong in a current dictionary or something is wrong with the reading plan.

This is where political experience is useful. He knows the word *lightweight* is current and active, because he uses it himself and has heard it often; a single notation on the card means more digging is needed. On the other hand, a single notation on *janissary*, which he does not hear or use himself, is a good indication that the word deserves only a passing reference under *henchman* or a mention that *brain trust* was once labeled the "janissariat." Perhaps it's worth a cross reference; perhaps it should be lumped in with an entry on *obsolete political terms* or perhaps forgotten.

There comes a point, though, when the lexicographer no longer has the remotest idea what the little squiggles on the index cards refer to. The bibliography code indicates that *Sor/Dec* is *Decision Making in the White House* by Ted Sorensen, but he does not remember anything about what was in that book on that page that made him write down that notation. Going back to *red herring*, an average entry, this is what the card looks like:

Tru Ad 385,6	Stone 317
Truman 242	Eng Prov 309, 510
Goldman Cru 225	DAPT 363
Hess 324	Cater 4th 37
Phillips 228	Krock 150, 164
Donovan 180	W. Johnson 285
Bart 92a	Dict Origins 291

This means the books that will help with this entry are: Barton J. Bernstein and Allen J. Matusow, *The Truman Administration;* Harry S. Truman, *Years of Trial and Hope;* Eric F. Goldman, *The Crucial Decade—and After;* Stephen Hess, *America's Political Dynasties;* Cabell Phillips, *The Truman Presidency;* Robert J. Donovan, *The Inside Story;* John Bartlett, *Familiar Quotations;* Irving Stone, *They Also Ran;* William George Smith and Janet E. Heseltine, *Oxford Dictionary of English Proverbs;* Sperber and Trittschuh, *American Political Terms: An Historical Dictionary;* Douglass Cater, *The Fourth Branch of Government;* Arthur Krock, *In the Nation: 1932–1966;* Walter Johnson, *1600 Pennsylvania Avenue;* William and Mary Morris, *Dictionary of Word and Phrase Origins.*

With the aid of four paperweights, two heavy rulers, one cracked binding, and by laying some books across portions of others, he can see all the results of the book research on that entry. Meanwhile, back in the filing cabinet, he has a file folder that corresponds to each one of the active index cards, containing the pages torn out of magazines and newspapers and the little notes made from television programs. These are spread out on the floor.

The building of an entry begins. Suddenly a word or phrase takes shape, differences in usage and meaning appear, and a small version of the "great conversation" Mortimer Adler wrote about in his *Syntopicon* can be heard.

And the holes show up. Everything but the actual coinage or the most famous use is there, or the uses in print do not jibe with the use the lexicographer knows (*graveyard*, for example, is a political secret, not just a dead end); or, the sources show meaning, coinage, and development, with a good quotation about the subject—but no usage in the past few years that includes the phrase itself. The lexicographer goes back to the publications a second time to fill the holes.

Among books of quotations, H. L. Mencken's *New Dictionary of Quotations* is by far the most helpful in this area, though many entries were "hidden" under what, for political phrase selection, were the wrong headings. *Bartlett's Familiar Quotations* is weak on contemporary quotations, though its index of first lines is superb for finding derivations; Bergen Evans's *Dictionary of Quotations* has an even better index. George Seldes's *The Great Quotations* leans hard on the unpopular and offbeat thinkers, usefully supplementing *Bartlett's*, and the compiler went to the trouble of contacting many of his sources for clarification. James Simpson's *Contemporary Quotations* is necessary for more recent words of wisdom, and the *Home Book of American Quotations* usefully groups follow-up comments under the original quotation.

All quotation books, however, have a habit of establishing "first use" that is often undercut by the *Dictionary of American English* and Mathews's *Dictionary of Americanisms*, as well as by *American Speech*, a quarterly publication whose sixty-plus years of back issues were made available to me by Random House. These publications take scholarly delight in finding earlier uses of famous phrases and, therefore, most entries in this dictionary speak of "popularized by" rather than "coined by."

Political dictionaries were started by—or perhaps popularized by—Charles Ledyard Norton, whose *Political Americanisms*, published in 1890, is a charming, personal survey of the political language of his day. Since then, political dictionaries have been more descriptive of the terms of government ("amendment," *lobby*, "legislator") and the terms of history (*Monroe Doctrine*, "XYZ Incident," "Marshall Plan") with a few of the classics of political language sprinkled in (*logrolling, pork barrel, caucus*).

The breakthrough in the field of the language of politics was in 1962, with Hans Sperber and Travis Trittschuh's dictionary, *American Political Terms*, the work cited most often herein. There is about a 20 percent overlap in terms covered by that book and this; however, their emphasis is philological and historical, whereas this book stresses current political usage. But this dictionary draws heavily on what they modestly termed their "bagful of seeds."

In the early editions of this dictionary, the lexicographer made a conscious if perverse decision to stay away from the *Oxford English Dictionary*. Too many of us use that treasure house of the written word as a crutch; the author was determined to find his own relatively recent citations and come to his own decisions about the development of the meaning of political terms. Besides, Eric Partridge, author of a vast and seminal dictionary of slang, told a budding lexicographer in the British Library Reading Room one day in the 1960s that leaning on the *OED* was failing to do one's own work.

Two developments changed my mind for this edition. One was Robert Burchfield's authoritative four-volume supplement to the *OED*, up-to-date scholarship that it would be silly to ignore, especially since my older entries have their own "original" citations. Second, the Nexis electronic library—a database of most of the important periodicals and newspapers—gives all researchers near-equal standing in the citation-finding business, except for books. Thus the political lexicographer no longer has to keep a card file on *thought police*, for example; a search by Nexis quickly offers the citations for the past twenty years, as well as the *OED* Supplement's entry on "thought" that tracks the phrase back to Japan before World War II. It is included in this edition with a cross reference to *politically correct*, for which the *thought police* are the enforcers.

Lexicography is a lot easier in the computer era; still, the author is glad to have bottomed this dictionary on books not yet scanned into Nexis, along with his own reporting on phrases in his weekly *New York Times* "On Language" column. And not even a complete search of all the books, magazines, and newspapers fill up all the gaps in the research. One entry in five required a letter to a source; amazingly, out of 250 letters written to people who were "there" at phrase coinages, the author received some 150 useful replies. Some, like *snake in the tunnel*, found the coiner. Sargent Shriver wrote to say he was sorry about not knowing the origin of *Peace Corps*, but Hubert Humphrey and General James Gavin contributed what they knew, and the reader can now watch the phrase develop. Alf Landon, queried about *New Frontier*, had a Kansas University professor look up his use of the phrase in 1936 and passed it along; Mrs. Herbert Bayard Swope, a month before her death, turned over a file of correspondence by her husband detailing the origin of *cold war.*

The earlier the Administration, the more willing were the participants to reply for quotation. Professor Raymond Moley and Judge Samuel Rosenman generously supplied firsthand information on FDR's speeches and coinages. Elizabeth B. Drewry at the Roosevelt Library in Hyde Park offered prompt and thorough help to any historian. The Library of Congress is set up to aid government officials and not the general public, but after a certain amount of badgering, contacts can be made; the entries on *windfall profits; Hill, the;* and *united we stand* are better for them. The Pentagon threw up its hands at the origin of *escalate*, but an official at Health, Education and Welfare opened a fascinating trail to the origin of *Medicare.*

Because the author worked on Eisenhower, Rockefeller, and Nixon campaigns, some speechwriters and aides of those men were available for checking origins and usages by telephone; in some instances, like *kitchen debate, spontaneous demonstration, hoopla, workfare, work ethic, nattering nabobs of negativism, black capitalism,* and *field expedient,* he was present and could write from personal experience. Officials of the Kennedy Administration were understandably more cautious, requesting anonymity in many cases, but were helpful nonetheless. When the lexicographer wrote Dean Rusk for verification of a coinage, he received a reply from the special assistant to the Secretary of State, Ernest K. Lindley; a quick follow-up resulted in a horse's-mouth definition of "Lindley Rule" (see *not for attribution*).

The author also has an advantage known to few lexicographers: in covering the latest locutions, he first makes his mistakes in a *New York Times* newspaper column that is syndicated in hundreds of other newspapers, including the world-girdling *International Herald Tribune.* Any straying from accuracy in etymology or current usage causes readers—called the Gotcha! Gang—to correct and emend assertions and speculations before errors are entered into the dictionary. Some will sneak in, and be corrected in later editions, but not for lack of close surveillance by the legions of "lexicographic irregulars."

The first edition of this dictionary was begun in 1966 with the active encouragement of Robert Loomis, then a young editor at Random House and now a division vice president and executive editor of Random House Adult Books; it was he, ever the optimist, who suggested a new edition in 1993. This time around, however, it could no longer be a one-man operation; Kate Medina, also a division vice president and executive editor, and editor of all my books at Random House, enabled me to draw on the time and talent of Sol Steinmetz, executive editor of the Random House dictionaries, for updating citations to old entries, for sound lexicographic judgments, and for keeping me on deadline. Mr. Steinmetz was ably assisted by Judy Kaplan, Jesse Sheidlower, Carol Braham, Maria Padilla, Karen Osborne, and Wanda Nixon Hernandez.

The general editor for this fourth edition is Jeffrey McQuain, who for the past ten years has been the chief research associate on my "On Language" column in the *New York Times Magazine.* Mr. McQuain wrote the first draft of nearly all the 200 new entries in this edition, from *abolitionist* to *you're no JFK.* He laboriously collated the additional citations from Steinmetz, and the scribbled commentary and sometimes extended revisions of new entries and updatings of old entries from me.

In gathering much of the raw material that began in my *Times* column and found its way into this dictionary, I am indebted to Jeanne Smith at the Library of Congress; Ann Elise Rubin, my *Times* editorial assistant; Barclay Walsh and Monica Borkowski in the *Times* library; *Times Magazine* editors Ed Klein, James Greenfield, Warren Hoge, Harvey Shapiro, Jack Rosenthal, and Michael Molyneux; op-ed copy editors Steve Pickering, Linda Cohn, and Sue Kirby, and typist Rebecca Lawrence. Lexicographers who often help are Fred Mish of Merriam-Webster and Anne Soukhanov of *American Heritage Dictionary.* My late brother, the quotations anthologist Len Safir, contributed many citations over the years.

The political language is certain to keep changing, but no further editions of this work should be expected until the new millennium.

Index

Abourezk, James, 217
Abrams, Creighton, 312
Aburdene, Patricia, 548
Acheson, Dean, 3, 598, 771, 812
Acton, Lord, 601, 702
Adair (historian), 643
Adamic, Louis, 310
Adams, Henry, 605
Adams, John, 212, 248, 293, 356, 443, 582, 627, 800–801
  balance of power, 38
  caucus, 109
  demagogue, 174–75
  Democrat, 176
  Republican, 658
  sachem, 680
Adams, John Quincy, 121, 128, 223, 242, 276, 356, 365, 388, 464
  cabal, 96
  campaign, 98
  card metaphors, 106
  deal, 169
Adams, Paul, 194
Adams, Samuel, 479
Adams, Sherman, 129, 169, 283, 544, 600, 742, 758, 846
  Abominable No-man, 1
  bird dog...kennel dog, 56
  brinkmanship, 85–86
  hatchetman, 319
  high road...low road, 327
  modern Republicanism, 459
  palace guard, 545
Adams, Thomas, 45
Addison, Joseph, 551, 823
Adelson, Herbert, 53–54
Adenauer, Konrad, 414
Adler, Alfred, 632
Aeschylus, 879

Agar, Milton, 316
Agnew, Spiro T., 141, 214, 282, 404, 415, 443, 593, 629, 632
  alliteration, 13–14
  effete snobs, 208
  household word, 339–40
  instant analysis, 364–65
  nattering nabobs of negativism, 479–80
  radic-lib, 641–42
  silent majority, 708–9
Aiken, George, 146, 198
Ailes, Roger, 24
Albee, Edward, 18
Albert, Carl, 68
Albertson, Maurice, 561
Alcuin, 847
Aldrich, Nelson, 600
Algeo, John, 273–74
Alger, Russell, 373
Alinsky, Saul, 407
Allee, W. C., 567
Allen, Fred, 825
Allen, George, 42
Allen, O. K., 674
Allen, Richard V., 4, 71, 139, 185
Allen, Robert S., 500
Allen, Steve, 51
Allende Gossens, Salvador, 178
Alliluyeva, Svetlana, 163
Allsop, Kenneth, 21
Alsop, John, 209
Alsop, Joseph, 191, 285, 568, 747, 866
  salami tactics, 681–82
Alsop, Stewart, 113, 187, 198, 226, 232, 479, 568, 600, 639, 776, 801, 890
  civil disobedience, 127
  Dr. Fell syndrome, 201

  egghead, 208–9
  Irish Mafia, 369
  salami tactics, 681–82
Alterman, Eric, 514, 626, 864
Ames, Mary Clemmer, 252
Amis, Kingsley, 20, 154
Amory, Cleveland, 188
Anderson, Elbert, 828
Anderson, Jack, 465, 718, 803
Anderson, John, 140
Anderson, Martin, 370
Anderson, Patrick, 373, 844
Anderson, Stanley, 522
Andrews, Julie, 97
Annenkov, Yuri, 838
Anthony, Carl Sferrazza, 252
Anthony, Robert, 895
Apple, R. W., Jr. (Johnny), 160, 361, 385, 710, 821
Arbatov, Georgi, 393
Arbuthnot, John, 827
Arias Sanchez, Oscar, 238
Aristophanes, 793
Aristotle, 589, 661–62
Armey, Dick, 567, 599
Armstrong, Louis, 265
Arnold, Henry Harley (Hap), 793
Arnold, Isaac N., 769
Arnold, Matthew, 455
Arnold, Thomas, 560
Artevelde, Jacob von, 873
Arthur, Chester, 43, 356, 496
Arvey, Jacob (Jake), 105, 420–21, 559
Ashbrook, John M., 744
Askew, Reubin, 799
Aspin, Les, 4, 754
Asquith, Herbert Henry, 183
Astor, Vincent, 262
Atherton, C. G., 276
Attlee, Clement, 367, 700, 823, 865

Atwater, Lee, 54, 145, 864–65
AuCoin, Les, 523
Auden, W. H., 568
Augustus, Emperor, 546, 882
Austin, Alfred, 376
Austin, Warren, 66
Avebury, Lord, 560
Aykroyd, Dan, 837

Babbitt, Bruce, 713
Bacon, Francis, 2, 143, 368,
    429, 443, 459, 536, 579,
    715, 804
Bagdikian, Ben, 508
Bagwell, Paul, 589
Bailar, Theresa Hong, 284
Bailey, John, 37
Bain, Sandy Kyle, 733
Baker, Bobby, 730
Baker, Howard, 250
Baker, James A., 3d, 468, 509,
    600, 634, 816
    balloon goes up, 40
    defining moment, 173
Baker, Newton, 175
Baker, Ray Stannard, 470
Baker, Ross, 220, 315
Baker, Russell, 97, 138, 150,
    195, 278, 365, 389, 405,
    440–42, 461, 487, 580,
    768, 844–45
Bakke, Allan, 637
Balanoff, James, 597
Baldwin, James, 114, 303, 305,
    477
Baldwin, Stanley, 424, 526
Balfour, Arthur, 332
Ball, George, 588, 759
Balz, Dan, 755
Bandar bin-Sultan, 22, 40
Banfield, Edward, 599
Barbanel, Howard, 376
Barber, Walter (Red), 70, 363
Baren, Alan, 233
Barère de Vieuzac, Bertrand
    de, 11
Barkley, Alben W., 3, 91, 128,
    283, 387, 840, 845
    caretaker, 107
Barnes, Craig, 772
Barnett, Doak, 437
Barnett, Frank, 879
Barnum, P. T., 42–43
Barone, Michael, 160, 387, 700
Barr, Joseph, 785
Barr, Roseanne, 253
Barr, William, 155
Barrère, Albert, 67
Barrett, Laurence, 714
Barry, Dave, 195
Barrymore, Ethel, 436–37
Barth, Alan, 55, 641
Bartlett, Charles, 198, 212, 232

Barton, Bruce, 439, 696
Baruch, Bernard M., 99, 135,
    212, 560–61, 592, 770, 854
    park-bench orator, 550
    quick and the dead, the, 633
Barzun, Jacques, 234, 694
Bates, Katherine Lee, 17
Bates, Ted, 529
Baum, Caroline A., 729
Baum, S. V., 840
Beall, George, 218
Beame, Abraham, 279, 417,
    765
Beard, Charles, 335
Beaumarchais, Pierre
    Augustin Caron de, 471
Beaverbrook, Lord, 526
Bebel, August, 452
Begin, Menachem, 331
Bell, Daniel, 481, 641
Bell, Elliott, 871
Bell, George, 217
Bell, Griffin, 329, 363, 370,
    445, 524, 658, 779, 874
Bell, Jack, 125, 144, 381
Belloc, Hilaire, 865–66
Benchley, Peter, 671
Bendiner, Robert, 381, 790–91
Benedict, Ruth, 661
Benn, Anthony Wedgewood,
    508–9
Bennett, James Gordon, 213,
    434
Bennett, William J., 216
Bentham, Jeremy, 126, 840–41
Bentley, Elizabeth, 652
Benton, Thomas Hart, 30,
    310, 554, 625
Benton, William, 696
Bentsen, Lloyd, 300, 322, 733,
    790
Ben-Veniste, Richard, 689
Beregovoy, Pierre, 324
Bergen, Edgar, 626
Berger, Marilyn, 521
Berger, Raoul, 230
Berke, Richard L., 761
Berlin, Irving, 100, 852
Berlinguer, Enrico, 228, 328
Bernstein, Carl, 344, 645
Bernstein, Theodore M., 131,
    330
Berra, Yogi, 847
Berrey, Lester, 265, 669
Berry, Frank, 445
Berry, Jason, 735
Betancourt, Ernesto, 12
Bethell, Tom, 375
Bethmann-Hollweg,
    Theobald von, 691
Beveridge, Albert J., 296, 368,
    551
Biddle, Nicholas, 487, 502

Biden, Joe, 308
Bierbauer, Charles, 232
Bigart, Homer, 843
Bilandic, Michael A., 299
Bingham, Colin, 706
Binns, John, 310
Birch, John, 56
Bird, David, 316
Birrell, Augustine, 201
Bishop, Abraham, 260
Bishop, Leo K., 533
Bishop, Phyllis Y., 766
Bismarck, Otto von, 27, 649
Black, Hugo L., 693, 767, 881
Black, Shirley Temple, 320
Blackmun, Harry, 640
Blackstone, William, 302–3
Blackwill, Robert, 876
Blaine, James G., 65, 117, 200,
    242, 246, 379, 759
    ballot-box stuffing, 41
    boodle, 71–72
    cowboy, 156
    mugwump, 471
    stalwart, 750–51
    the man who, 791
Blake, Peter, 773
Blake, William, 313
Blanton, Ray, 480
Blau, Joseph L., 693
Blease, Coleman L., 731
Blieberg, Robert, 652–53
Bliss, Ray, 296, 667
Bloomer, Amelia, 635
Blough, Roger, 727
Blumenthal, Ralph, 844
Blumenthal, Sidney, 589
Bock, Jerry, 416–17
Boergers, Mary, 651
Bohlen, Celestine, 571
Bolinger, Dwight, 273
Boone, Daniel, 150
Boorstin, Daniel, 622
Booth, John Wilkes, 486–87
Borah, William E., 350, 375,
    389, 501, 560, 764
Boren, David L., 406
Bork, Robert H., 8, 76, 689,
    710
Bovay, A. E., 659
Bowles, Chester, 696
Boycott, Charles
    Cunningham, 635
Boyd, Andrew, 608
Boyd, John, 80
Braaten, David, 57, 179
Braden, Tom, 728
Bradford, Gershom, 172
Bradlee, Benjamin, 34
Bradley, Bill, 251
Bradley, Mrs. Omar, 97
Bradley, Omar, 290, 420, 739,
    888

Brady, Dorothy, 264
Brady, Nicolas F., 161
Brady, Thomas P., 694
Braestrup, Peter, 95
Bragg, Edward S., 422
Brande, W. T., 618
Brandeis, Louis D., 52,
     164–65, 773
Brandon, Henry, 153, 736
Brandt, Barbara, 875
Brecht, Bertolt, 10
Breckenridge, John C., 518
Bremner, Charles, 659
Brennan, William J., Jr., 61,
     558, 670–71, 832
   chilling effect, 118
Bresler, Robert, 45
Breslin, Jimmy, 60, 467,
     720–21
Brewer, E. Cobham, 536
Brezhnev, Leonid I., 179,
     189–90
Bricker, John, 102, 170, 667,
     678
Brightman, Sam, 667
Brimmer, Andrew, 206
Brinkerhoff, Jacob, 527
Broder, David, 19–20, 69, 408,
     467, 495, 615, 697, 709,
     816
Brogan, Denis W., 167, 367,
     811, 863
Brokaw, Tom, 893
Bromfield, Louis, 209
Brook, Douglas A., 47
Brooke, Edward, 200–201,
     350, 429
Brooks, Cleanth, 28
Brooks, James, 107
Brooks, John, 353
Brough, John, 82
Brougham, Lord, 264
Broun, Heywood, 407
Browder, Earl, 318
Brower, Brock, 421
Brown, Edmund G. (Pat), 667
Brown, Edmund G. (Jerry),
     Jr., 320, 337, 375, 615,
     686, 691, 712, 785, 800,
     877
Brown, George (politician),
     285, 541
Brown, George (general), 120
Brown, George R., 259
Brown, H. (Rap), 61, 505
Brown, Henry B., 697
Brown, John, 63, 435
Brown, Ronald H., 691
Brown, Sam, 400
Brown, Thomas (Tom), 201
Brown, Walter, 730
Browne, Charles Farrar. See
     Ward, Artemus

Brownell, Herbert, 181, 210,
     229–30, 590, 694
Browning, Robert, 882
Brownlow, Louis, 556–57
Broyles, William, Jr., 629
Bruce, David E. K., 521
Bruhn, Fred, 287
Bryan, Richard, 25
Bryan, William Jennings, 57,
     112, 270–71, 297, 310,
     369, 422, 496, 516, 548,
     646, 746, 793, 827, 841
   arena, 23
   concession speech, 141
   cooling-off period, 150
   demagogue, 175
   deserving Democrats, 178
   Dooley, Mr., 195
   party of the people, 555
   peerless leader, 568
   sons of the wild jackass, 732
   titular leader, 806
   trickle-down theory, 813
Bryant, William Cullen, 670
Bryce, James, 104, 121, 321,
     434, 802
Brzezinski, Zbigniew, 4, 136,
     414, 485, 536, 549, 587,
     707, 759
   proxy war, 621
   useful idiots of the West,
     837–38
Buchanan, James, 70, 305, 818
Buchanan, Patrick J., 151,
     237, 365, 368, 466, 503,
     629, 641, 697, 738
   amen corner, 16
   bubba factor, 87
   effete snobs, 208
   hardball, 317
Buchwald, Art, 67, 192, 195,
     331, 422–23, 559, 663, 814
Buck, Pearl, 518
Buckley, Charles, 78
Buckley, William F., Jr., 78,
     148, 458, 479, 602, 744,
     882
Bulganin, Nikolai, 136, 178
Bull, John, 668
Bullock, Alan, 682
Bulwer-Lytton, Edward
     George, 252, 708, 762
Bumiller, Elisabeth, 647, 741
Bunche, Ralph, 377
Bundy, McGeorge, 11, 366,
     369, 379, 443, 478, 543,
     627, 711
   doves, 198–99
Bunyan, Paul, 470
Burch, Dean, 166
Burdick, Eugene, 825
Burger, Warren, 666, 766–67
Burges, Tristram, 367, 496

Burke, Arleigh, 180, 474473
Burke, Edmund, 144, 157,
     198–99, 212, 218, 303,
     443, 564, 573, 606, 771,
     789, 823
   fourth estate, 264
   war on poverty, 855
Burke, Thomas, 592
Burke, William, 76
Burleson, Albert S., 558
Burleson, Omar, 69
Burns, Arthur, 73, 206,
     355–56, 885, 894
Burns, Haydon, 456
Burns, James MacGregor,
     77–78, 89, 116–17, 132,
     414, 429, 509, 610, 860,
     876
Burns, Robert, 643
Burr, Aaron, 426, 819
Burton, Richard, 97
Burton, Robert, 444
Bush, Barbara, 604
Bush, George, 8, 65, 116, 146,
     184, 214, 237, 265–66,
     269, 300, 308, 317, 370,
     390, 396, 404, 406, 420,
     430, 456, 497–98, 503,
     515, 518, 520, 534, 548,
     559, 561, 592, 600, 604,
     609, 640, 691, 710, 721,
     736, 761, 803, 860,
     864–65, 876, 891
   acronyms, political, 4
   alliteration, 14
   arena, 24
   are you any better off...?, 25
   bracketing, 79
   bubba factor, 87
   cant, 102
   character assassin, 112
   Cloud-Cuckoo-Land, 131
   code words, 134–35
   cold war, 136
   convention bounce, 149
   cost-benefit analysis, 152
   decouple, 171
   defining moment, 173
   demagogue, 175
   don't waste your vote, 195
   draw a line in the sand, 200
   empowerment, 215
   handlers, 314
   inside the Beltway, 364
   kinder and gentler nation,
     387
   like ugly on an ape, 411–12
   mossback, 463
   moving the goalposts, 467
   Mr. Nice Guy, 468
   new world order, 495
   out of the loop, 537
   pit-bull politics, 577

Bush, George *(cont.)*
  power curve, 601–2
  quick fix, 634
  read my lips, 647
  Rosie Scenario, 672
  sandbag, 686
  sit room, 712
  skunk at the garden party,
    713
  speechwriter, 738
  spending cap, 740
  stay the course, 757
  supply-side, 775
  thousand points of light,
    797–98
  unleash Chiang, 835
  Vietnam syndrome, 844
  vision thing, 845
  voodoo economics, 846–47
  waste, fraud and abuse, 858
Butcher, Harry C., 250
Butler, Benjamin F., 175, 419
Butler, D. E., 566, 805
Butler, Hugh, 573
Butler, Nicholas Murray,
    346–47, 703
Butler, Samuel, 171
Butterfield, Fox, 267–68
Butterworth, Benjamin, 41
Butz, Earl, 251, 501
Byrd, Harry, 361
Byrd, Robert, 361, 870
Byrnes, James F., 48, 128, 854
Byrom, John, 820
Byron, Lord (George
    Gordon), 64, 834, 881

Caddell, Pat, 215, 845
Caen, Herb, 498
Caldwell, Earl, 605
Calhoun, John C., 189, 299,
    487, 623
Califano, Joseph, 317, 857
Calixtus III, Pope, 362
Callahan, Vincent F., Jr., 340
Callaway, Howard (Bo), 734
Calley, William, 843
Calloway, Cab, 50
Cambronne, Pierre-Jacques-
    Étienne, 519
Cameron, Simon, 619, 757
Campbell, Carroll, 520
Campbell, George, 592
Canellos, Peter, 272
Canning, George, 145, 443
Cannon, Joseph G. (Uncle
    Joe), 245, 463, 753, 891
Canzeri, Joseph, 647
Capone, Al, 19, 620
Capp, Al, 30, 498, 713
Carawan, Guy, 867
Card, Andrew, 145
Carey, Hugh, 665

Carlson, Evans F., 308
Carlyle, Thomas, 249, 264,
    349–50, 448–49, 488, 654,
    699
Carmichael, Stokely, 27, 113,
    266, 466
  black power, 60–61
Carmody, John, 706–7
Carpenter, Liz, 735
Carpenter, Terry, 380
Carr, Edward Hallett, 865
Carrington, Tim, 788
Carroll, Anna Ella, 391
Carroll, Daniel, 328
Carroll, Lewis, 286, 344,
    819–20
Carroll, Maurice, 523
Carswell, G. Harrold, 8
Carter, Billy, 279, 653–54
Carter, Hodding, III, 291
Carter, Jimmy, 8, 11, 119, 125,
    159, 178, 214, 233, 241,
    251, 254, 270–71, 287,
    300, 316, 334, 370, 375,
    377, 388, 390, 410, 412,
    420, 484, 496–97, 515,
    544, 567, 572, 591, 613,
    671–72, 685, 712, 720,
    731, 735, 754, 759–60,
    773, 779, 785, 814, 836,
    873
  bargaining chip, 44–45
  benign neglect, 49
  bite the bullet, 58
  born again, 76–77
  briefing book, 84
  buck stops here, 88
  buzzword, 94
  cant, 102
  catchword, 108
  code words, 134
  convention bounce, 149
  cost-benefit analysis, 152
  economic royalists, 207
  effect, 207
  ethnic purity, 225
  fallback position, 236
  glitch, 284
  homeland, 333
  human rights, 342–43
  initials, Presidential, 360
  "I see" construction, 373
  life is unfair, 409
  machinery of government,
    427
  moral equivalent of war, 461
  one-house veto, 523–24
  one-term President, 527
  populist, 595
  process, the, 614–15
  quick fix, 634
  quiet diplomacy, 635
  reform, 655

  rhyme, political use of, 663
  running against
    Washington, 677
  sanitize, 687
  send them a message, 697
  sign off on, 707
  spirit of, 742
  stay the course, 757
  stonewalling, 761
  there you go again, 792
  three-martini lunch,
    799–800
  vision of America, 844–45
  walking-around money, 850
  waste, fraud and abuse, 857
  windfall profits, 878
  zero-base budgeting,
    894–95
Carter, John Franklin, 327
Carter, Rosalynn, 720, 877,
    886
Cartwright, John, 525
Carville, James, 310, 376, 529,
    621, 865
Case, Clifford, 589
Casey, Albert V., 467
Casey, Robert, 258
Casey, William J., 514–15, 642
Cass, Lewis, 166–67, 436, 744,
    869
Castro, Fidel, 124, 292, 370,
    398, 776
Cater, Douglass, 89, 234–35,
    300, 432, 441, 516, 600,
    602, 738, 866
Cattani, Richard J., 671
Catton, Bruce, 58
Cavanagh, Jerome, 830
Celler, Emanuel, 253, 620
Cervantes, Miguel de, 320–21
Chabot, F. C., 440
Chamberlain, Joseph, 841
Chamberlain, Neville, 171,
    473, 507, 574, 696, 856
  appeasement, 23
  peace for our time, 562
  umbrella symbol, 825–26
Chamberlin, William Henry,
    146
Chambers, Whittaker, 652
Chambord, Count de, 344
Chamorro, Violeta Barrios
    de, 750
Chance, Paul, 59
Chandler, Raymond, 155
Chandler, Zachary, 82
Channing, William Ellery, 326
Chapin, Dwight, 7, 645
Chaplin, Stewart, 863
Chapman (Democratic
    leader), 552
Chapman, John Jay, 460
Chapman, Stephen, 346

Charles I, King of England, 171
Charles II, King of England, 96
Chase, Salmon P., 608, 834
Chase, Stuart, 486–87
Chateaubriand, François, 706
Chaucer, Geoffrey, 534
Cheney, Lynne, 796
Cheney, Richard B., 650
Chesterfield, Earl of. *See* Stanhope, Philip
Chesterton, G. K., 818
Chevalier, Maurice, 537
Chiang Ching, 536, 821
Chiang Kai-shek, 119, 567, 834–35
Chidsey, Don, 519
Chiles, Lawton, 773
Chirac, Jacques, 46, 592
Choate, Rufus, 265, 365
Chotiner, Murray, 873
Chou En-lai, 774, 864
Christian, George, 337
Christophe, 279
Christopher, George, 214, 254, 256
Christopher, Warren, 34
Church, Frank, 478, 747
Church, George, 208
Churchill, Charles, 13
Churchill, Randolph, 424
Churchill, Winston, 3, 116, 120, 125, 141, 162, 245, 295, 318, 343, 379, 402, 526, 528, 534, 547, 565, 573, 589, 620, 702, 799, 826, 847, 860
  appeasement, 23
  balance of power, 38
  baloney, 42
  bird dog...kennel dog, 57
  blood, sweat, and tears, 64–65
  business as usual, 91
  card metaphors, 106
  full generation of peace, 272
  generation gap, 279
  infrastructure, 359
  invective, political, 367
  iron curtain, 370–71
  loyal opposition, 424
  no comment, 501–2
  phony war, 574
  rhyme, political use of, 663
  safety net, 681
  self-determination, 695
  sheep in sheep's clothing, 700
  special relationship, 736
  sphere of influence, 740
  sports metaphors, 747
  strange bedfellows, 763
  summitry, 770–71
  themeless pudding, 791–92
  United Nations, 833
  wilderness years, 877
  Young Turks, 893
Ciano, Count Galeazzo, 841
Cicero, Marcus Tullius, 143, 351, 454, 564, 574
Cieszkowski, August von, 661
Claerbaut, David, 281
Clark, Champ, 57, 718, 749, 759
Clark, Edward, 731
Clark, Mark, 510
Clark, Timothy B., 710
Clark, William, 370
Claudius, 779
Clay, Henry, 86, 121, 167, 239, 299, 388, 496, 543, 556, 568, 759
  American system, 19
  arena, 23
  can't-win technique, 102
  clean sweep, 128
  concession speech, 141
  deal, 169
  I'd rather be right, 350
  public office is a public trust, 623
  spoils system, 744
  war hawks, 853
Clay, Lucius, 97, 643
Cleaveland, Brad, 35–36
Cleland, Robert Glass, 787
Clemenceau, Georges, 63
Cleveland, Grover, 171, 363, 406, 420, 434, 471, 496, 502, 516, 571, 606, 718–19, 804, 858
  advice and consent, 8
  ballot-box stuffing, 41
  loved for the enemies he made, 421
  mugwump, 471
  party of the people, 555
  public office is a public trust, 623–24
  ship of state, 702
Cleveland, Harlan, 662, 682–83
Clifford, Clark, 20, 106, 193, 504, 737, 747
Clifford, Frank, 831
Clinton, Bill, 38, 116, 125, 220, 224, 227, 237, 246, 253, 255, 269, 271, 279, 285–86, 315, 319, 332, 346, 360, 364, 368, 372, 396, 406, 423, 437, 440, 442, 454, 458–59, 468, 473, 480, 484–85, 489, 496–98, 503, 518, 531, 544, 547–48, 551–52, 568, 581–82, 596–97, 611–12, 631, 637, 647, 672, 720, 728, 738, 755, 787, 813, 827, 832, 852, 866
  alliteration, 14
  Bay of Pigs fiasco, 46
  bean counter, 47–48
  bubba factor, 87
  Camelot, 97
  campaign songs, 100
  cant, 102
  centrist, 111
  containment, 147
  convention bounce, 149
  cost-benefit analysis, 153
  don't waste your vote, 195
  dope story, 197
  dream ticket, 201
  go to Korea, 291
  gridlock, 305
  heft, political, 323–24
  humor, self-deprecating, 343
  Hundred Days, 345
  limousine liberal, 413
  MEGO, 447
  policy wonk, 588
  recession, 650
  running against Washington, 677
  smoke screen, 722–23
  spending cap, 740
  the speech, 793
  waffle, 849
  waste, fraud and abuse, 858
  watershed election, 860–61
  weasel words, 864
  with all deliberate speed, 882
  woodshed, take him to the, 883
  you're no JFK, 893
Clinton, Chelsea, 413
Clinton, Hillary Rodham, 4, 67, 205, 237, 252, 255, 451, 454, 539, 593, 604, 769, 883, 886
  bork, 76
Clive, Robert, 459
Clough, Arthur H., 560
Clymer, Adam, 414
Coates, Joseph, 686
Cobbett, William, 264
Cochran, Negley Dakin, 208
Cockburn, Alexander, 626, 872
Cocker, Mark, 626
Cohan, George M., 350
Cohen, Andrew, 373
Cohen, Ariel, 309
Cohen, David, 267
Cohen, Gerald, 50
Cohen, Jerome Alan, 803

Cohen, Richard, 792
Cohn, N., 331
Cohn, Roy M., 72, 382–83
Coit, Margaret, 550
Coke, Edward, 893
Colby, William, 124, 178
Coleman, William, 290
Colfax, Schuyler, 730
Collings, Jesse, 715
Collins, LeRoy, 839
Collins, Nancy, 886
Collinson, William E., 705
Colson, Charles, 76, 83, 217,
    271, 320, 400, 645, 873
Commager, Henry Steele,
    228, 374, 861
Commons, John R., 488
Conable, Barber, 620, 723
Conant, James Bryant, 716–17
Cone, Helen Gray, 568
Confucius, 139
Conger, Clem, 538
Conkling, Roscoe, 200, 450,
    751
Connable, Alfred, 744
Connally, John F., 54, 191,
    385, 720
Connell, Richard, 475
Connor, Bull, 266
Conrad (cartoonist), 252
Conyers, John, 217
Cooke, Alistair, 162, 504
Coolidge, Calvin, 100, 125,
    216, 321, 354, 373, 399,
    437, 496, 502, 555, 677,
    731, 753, 874
  buck stops here, the, 87–88
  demagogue, 175
Coolidge, Mrs. Calvin, 677
Cooper, John Sherman, 200,
    849
Cooper, Sherman, 589
Coppleson, V. M., 240
Corcoran, Thomas, 52, 527
Corman, James, 530
Cornuelle, Richard, 18
Cortelyou, George, 434
Corwin, Edward, 3
Cory, Desmond, 478
Costikyan, Edward, 38, 274,
    558, 607, 822
Costikyan, Frances, 104–5
Costrell, Edwin S., 834
Cottrell, Pete, 648
Coughlin, Charles E., 417
Cox, Archibald, 251, 293, 689
Cox, James, 188
Cox, S. S., 107, 411
Craig, May, 403
Crain (District Attorney of
    New York), 156
Cramer, William, 92
Crane, Dan, 32

Creager, R. B., 544
Creel, George W., 371
Crews, John, 411
Crockett, Davy, 57, 389
Croker, J. Wilson, 145
Croker, Richard, 745, 782
Croly, Herbert, 494, 852, 865
Cromwell, Oliver, 354, 463,
    676
Cronkite, Walter, 51, 852
Cross, Anna M., 302
Crossley, Archibald, 819
Culbertson, Ely, 105–6, 850
Cuomo, Mario, 126, 237, 279,
    564, 707
  edifice complex, 207
  holistic, 331
Curley, James M., 79, 397,
    422
Curran, John Philpot, 560
Currie, Lauchlin, 652
Curry, Bill, 845–46
Curry, John, 398
Curry, Tim, 647
Curtis, Charles, 800
Curtis, Francis, 213
Curtis, George William,
    397–98
Curtis, Ken, 412
Cushing, Caleb, 435
Czurka, Istvan, 402

Daladier, Édouard, 473
Daley, Richard J., 184, 329,
    426
Daley, Richard M., 370
Daly, Daniel, 727
Dampier, William, 412
Dana, Charles A., 621
Dana, Richard Henry, 104
Daniel, Clifton, 733
Daniels, Jonathan, 14, 125,
    298, 389, 583, 739
Darling, Lynn, 468
Darman, Richard, 84, 548
Darnton, John, 80
Darrow, Clarence, 641
Darwin, Charles, 707
Daugherty, Harry, 388, 552,
    721–22
Davenport, John F., 332
Davenport, Russell, 555
Davidson, Philip, 765
Davies, John, 172, 518
Davis, David, 169
Davis, Elmer, 529, 855
Davis, Forrest, 295
Davis, Jefferson, 62, 297
Davis, John W., 321, 369
Davis, Kenneth S., 149, 335
Davis, Norman, 632
Davis, O. K., 606
Davis, Sharon, 281

Dawson, Donald, 358
Dayan, Moshe, 232, 758
Dealey, E. M., 436
Dean, John, 172, 216–17, 539,
    760, 821
Deaver, Michael, 359, 816, 845
Debs, Eugene V., 387, 619, 667
DeCrow, Karen, 590
Defoe, Daniel, 21
de Gaulle, Charles, 348, 373,
    503, 579, 688, 725, 743,
    891
De Hass, J. Anton, 639
Delors, Jacques, 324
Demarest, Michael, 622
Demosthenes, 346, 574
Dempsey, Jack, 314
DeNardis, Lawrence, 69
Dent, Harry, 731
Depew, Chauncey, 798
Derby, Lord, 187–88, 620
Derrick (hangman), 636
De Sapio, Carmine, 78, 315,
    351, 599, 722
Deschler, Lewis, 68
De Spira, John, 108
Destutt de Tracy, Antoine, 349
De Vere, M. Schele, 104
Devlin, Gerald F., 651
DeVoe, Raymond, Jr., 168, 847
De Vries, Peter, 338
Dewar, Helen, 792
Dewey, George, 2
Dewey, Thomas E., 10, 45,
    116, 164, 244, 271, 320,
    379, 407, 447, 489, 591,
    648, 722, 731, 760, 810
  baloney, 42
  big government, 52–53
  bipartisan, 55
  blooper, 66
  campaign train, 100
  can't-win technique, 102
  deal, 170
  deliver, 174
  Democrat, 176
  Dewey blitz, 181
  don't change horses, 193–94
  high road...low road, 327
  labels, 395
  man on the wedding cake,
      436–37
  me too, 450–51
  never lost a war or won a
      peace, 484
  purge, 627
  rendezvous with destiny,
      657
  road to defeat, 669
  running against Hoover,
      677
  run scared, 679
  ship of state, 702

shoo-in, 704
stampede, 751
stay-at-homes, 756
third-party movement, 794
time for a change, 804
titular leader, 805–6
Tweedledum and
    Tweedledee, 819–20
Diamond, Edwin, 596
DiBacco, Thomas V., 336, 675
Dicey, A. V., 675
Dichter, Ernest, 177
Dickens, Charles, 54, 515, 654
Dickenson, James, 258
Dickenson, John, 833
Dickerson, Nancy, 410
Dickson, Paul, 400, 843
Diefenbaker, John, 727
Diem, Ngo Dinh, 191
Dies, Martin, 164
Digby, Kenelm, 560, 564
Dill, Malcolm, 364
Dillon, Douglas, 861
Dilworth, Richardson, 168
Dingell, John, 547
Dio, Johnny, 389
Dirksen, Everett, 125, 400,
    525, 580, 703, 891
    Alliance for Progress, 13
    road to defeat, 669
Di Salle, Michael, 289–90
Disney, Roy E., 884
Disraeli, Benjamin, 175, 274,
    367, 378, 554, 823
    alliteration, 13
    all things to all men, 14
    Boy Scout, 78
    conservative, 144–45
    dark horse, 167
    home rule, 333
    maiden speech, 429
    peace with honor, 564–65
    side of the angels, 707
    whip, 870
Ditka, Mike, 647
Dixon, Frank, 189
Dixon, Joseph, 162, 798
Dixon, Thomas, 175
Djilas, Milovan, 227, 485
Dobrynin, Anatoly, 33
Dodd, Thomas, 673, 718
Dolan, Anthony R., 228
Dole, Robert, 109, 149, 214,
    305, 356, 596, 792, 845
    CREEP, 158–59
Donaldson, Sam, 852, 883
Donat, Alexander, 331
Donne, John, 64, 362
Donnelly, Desmond, 849
Donnelly, Ignatius, 192
Donovan, Robert J., 253, 307,
    408, 458, 475, 730, 820,
    813

Dorgan, Byron L., 291
Dorr, Thomas, 399
Dos Passos, John, 299, 405
Dougherty, Dick, 797
Douglas, Frederick, 600
Douglas, Paul H., 174,
    420–21, 597, 708
Douglas, Stephen A., 62, 189,
    300, 496
Douglas, William O., 128,
    701, 759, 772, 840, 890
Douglas-Home, Alec, 66, 323
Douglass, Frederick, 378
Dowd, Maureen, 233–34, 411
Downey, Sheridan, 268
Doyle, A. Conan, 723
Draper, Theodore, 27
Drew, Elizabeth, 186, 549, 707
Drummond, Roscoe, 545
Drury, Allen, 7
Dryden, John, 276–77
    red herring, 651
Dubcek, Alexander, 682
DuBois, Arthur E., 39
DuBois, W.E.B., 59
Dudley, W. W., 778
Dukakis, Michael, 79, 257,
    436, 621, 813, 877
    Cloud-Cuckoo-Land,
    131
Dulles, Allen, 557
Dulles, John Foster, 318, 408,
    412, 699, 758, 834–35, 841
    agonizing reappraisal, 10–11
    American boys, 17
    bigger bang for a buck, 52
    brinkmanship, 85
    containment, 146
    empty chair, 216
    massive retaliation, 439
Dunne, Finley Peter, 119,
    775–76, 804
    beanbag, 46–47
    Dooley, Mr., 195
Durham, Earl of, 49
Durkin, Martin, 210
Durocher, Leo, 467
Dyer, John, 156

Eagleburger, Lawrence S.,
    702–3
Eagleton, Thomas, 375, 397,
    796–97
Eastland, James, 67–68
Eastwood, Clint, 430
Eaton, Peggy, 719
Eban, Abba, 180
Edelstein, Julius C. C., 520
Eden, Anthony, 741
Edison, Thomas Alva, 17–18
Edmunds, G. F., 288
Edward II, King of England,
    847

Edward VII, King of Great
    Britain, 167, 183, 417, 863
Ehrlichman, John, 580, 669,
    821, 851, 860
    big enchilada, 51
    deep-six, 172
Einstein, Albert, 502
Eisenberg, Lee, 604
Eisenhower, Dwight D., 8,
    93, 182, 229, 234, 248,
    257–58, 260, 282, 288–89,
    292, 300, 304, 360, 400,
    436, 443, 450, 457,
    475–76, 487–89, 496, 506,
    510–11, 517, 528, 534,
    538, 545, 549, 552, 575,
    602, 662, 702, 731,
    750–51, 756, 825, 852,
    864, 866, 893
    Abominable No-man, 1
    above politics, 2
    advance man, 6
    arena, 24
    baloney, 42
    bandwagon, 43
    big government, 53
    bipartisan, 55
    Bircher, 55
    body politic, 69
    bookburners, 2, 72–73
    cabal, 96
    campaign promises, 99
    campaign songs, 100
    cant, 102
    captive candidate, 105
    character assassin, 111
    Checkers speech, 115
    compact of Fifth Avenue,
    140–41
    consensus, 143–44
    creeping socialism, 159
    crusade, 161–62
    deed not words, 171
    demagogue, 175
    Depression party, 177
    détente, 178–79
    doctrine, 189
    domino theory, 191
    dynamic conservatism, 202
    egghead, 209
    eight millionaires and a
        plumber, 210
    Eisenhower syntax, 210–11
    engage in personalities,
    217–18
    field expedient, 244
    free world, 268
    go to Korea, 290
    hatchetman, 319
    heartland, 322
    high road...low road, 327
    indispensable man, 356–57
    inflation, 357

Eisenhower, Dwight D. (*cont.*)
  just and lasting peace,
    383–84
  labels, 395
  let Asians fight Asians,
    403–4
  liberation of captive
    peoples, 408
  loneliest job in the world,
    420
  McCarthyism, 441
  mandate, 433
  massive retaliation, 439
  middle of the road, 452–53
  military-industrial
    complex, 453–54
  moderate, 458
  modern Republicanism, 459
  new look, 493–94
  one-term President, 527
  open-skies proposal, 532–33
  open society, 533
  peaceful coexistence,
    562–63
  personally obnoxious, 573
  Philippic, 574
  playing politics, 580
  political miracle, 591
  position paper, 598
  practical politics, 606
  President of all the people,
    610
  pressure group, 612
  purge, 628
  rap in the night, 644
  red herring, 652
  running like a dry creek,
    678
  run scared, 679
  safe, 680–81
  second-class citizen, 692
  Sherman statement, 701
  speechwriter, 737–38
  spirit of, 741–42
  stampede, 751
  steamroller, 758
  superpatriots, 774
  surrender on Morningside
    Heights, 777
  thou shalt not steal, 798–99
  twenty years of treason, 820
  unleash Chiang, 834–35
  vast wasteland, 839
  volunteers, 846
  vox populi, 848
  waging peace, 850
  White House, 874
  witch hunt, 881
  world opinion, 887
  write-in, 888
Eisenhower, Milton, 459
Eizenstadt, Stuart, 707
Eizenstat, Stuart E., 864

Elegant, Robert, 842
Elfin, Mel, 447
Eliot, Charles William, 378
Eliot, John, 471
Eliot, T. S., 215, 764, 839
Elizabeth I, Queen of
  England, 352
Elizabeth II, Queen of Great
  Britain, 604
Ellerbee, Linda, 284
Ellsberg, Daniel, 401, 582
Elsberg, N. A., 213
Elsey, George M., 711, 737
Emerson, Ralph Waldo, 154,
  265, 434, 545, 577, 764,
  862, 887
Engelbrecht, H. C., 448
Engels, Friedrich, 139, 350,
  617
Enloe, William G., 710
Ennis, Edward Roland, 81–82
Epstein, Jay, 283
Erickson, John, 571
Ervin, Samuel J., Jr., 638
Estes, Billy Sol, 432
Evans, Bergen, 835
Evans, Cornelia, 835
Evans, David, 355
Evans, G. O., 557
Evans, Rowland, 27, 159, 184,
  381, 398, 451, 503, 541,
  635, 642, 767, 826, 851
  backlash, 35
  born again, 77
  break all the china, 83
  economic jargon, 206
Evarts, William, 194
Everett, Edward, 265
Evers, James Charles, 885
Ewald, William, 737

Fabricant, Florence, 604
Fahy, Charles, 142
Fairbanks, Charles Warren,
  629
Fairlie, Henry, 205, 226, 447
Fall, Bernard, 473
Fallaci, Oriana, 421
Farkas, Alexander, 572
Farley, James, 15, 26–27, 214,
  546, 629, 701
Farley, Thomas M., 416
Farmer (editor), 686
Farmer, James, 61, 266
Farrell, James T., 159
Fauber, Bernard M., 634
Faulkner, William, 28, 421
Fazio, Vic, 572
Fechheimer, S. M., 444
Feiffer, Jules, 59, 187
Feinstein, Dianne, 250
Feldstein, Martin, 364
Felknor, Bruce, 110, 185, 471

Fellows, Erwin W., 619
Ferdinand, Archduke, 472–73
Feuer, Lewis S., 366
Feuerlicht, Ignace, 371
Fialka, John, 251
Field, Al G., 566
Filley, Chauncey I., 519
Fillmore, Millard, 356, 560,
  618
Finch, Robert, 860, 873
Finder, Leonard W., 701
Fine, Brenda, 604
Finletter, Thomas K., 655
Fiore, Faye, 320
Firestone, David, 498
Fischer, Rudolph, 265
Fish, Hamilton, 167, 439
Fitch, George, 80
Fitzgerald, Ernest, 872
Fitzgerald, F. Scott, 745
Fitzgerald, John (Honey
  Fitz), 558, 611
Fitzwater, Marlin, 406, 647–48
Flack, Gene, 255
Flagg, James Montgomery,
  827
Flanagan, Dennis, 836
Flanders, Ralph, 628
Flandrau, Grace Hodgson,
  437
Flanigan, Peter, 464, 873
Flaubert, Gustave, 181
Flax, Alexander H., 628
Flexner, James, 357
Flexner, Stuart Berg, 88, 262,
  267, 594, 597, 821
Flieger, Howard, 886
Flood, Daniel, 279
Flowers, Gennifer, 864
Flynn, Edward J., 9, 15, 78,
  162, 275, 316, 389, 426,
  504, 791
Flynt, Josiah, 294
Flynt, Larry, 576
Folk, Joseph W., 294
Folliard, Edward, 106, 259
Foltz, William, 764
Fong, Hiram, 239, 746
Foote, Samuel, 547
Foraker, Joseph B., 751
Ford, Gerald, 125, 226, 251,
  300, 308, 356, 360, 408,
  410, 428, 712, 755, 761,
  844–45, 850, 865, 873, 886
  big government, 53
  big tent, 54
  bite the bullet, 57
  caretaker, 107
  crossover vote, 160
  détente, 179
  running for the exercise, 678
  speechwriter, 738
Ford, Henry, 16–17

Forster, John P., 238
Forstmann, Theodore J., 216
Fortas, Abe, 155
Fournier, Edouard, 519
Fowler (senator), 573
Fowler, Elizabeth M., 148
Fox, Charles James, 771
Frank, Ceil, 220
Frankel, Glenn, 152, 817
Frankel, Max, 26, 173, 301, 691
Frankfurter, Felix, 27, 121, 178, 195, 304, 766–67, 854–55, 881
Franklin, Benjamin, 559, 591, 818, 888
Franklin, Sarah, 802
Fraser, Donald, 342
Freedman, Max, 492
Freeman, Orville, 687
Freidel, Frank, 657
Frémont, John C., 659
Freud, Sigmund, 214
Frick, Henry Clay, 757
Friedan, Betty, 882
Friedman, Milton, 267, 863
Friedman, Murray, 266
Friedman, Steven, 62
Fritchey, Clayton, 380, 763
Frost, David, 16, 155, 412
Frost, Robert, 243, 452
Froude, J. A., 646
Fulbright, J. William, 236, 303, 358, 565, 588, 763, 812, 853
  arrogance of power, 26–27
  Boy Scout, 78
  bridge building, 83
  domino theory, 191–92
  myth, 476–77
  unthinkable thoughts, 836
Fuller, Thomas, 334, 354
Funk, Wilfred, 41, 600
Furcolo, Foster, 107
Futrell, William, 272

Gaebler, Ted, 548
Gaines, Tilford, 521
Galbraith, John Kenneth, 360, 475, 738, 855
  affluent society, 9
  conventional wisdom, 148
Gall, Peter, 85
Gallup, George, 177, 593
Galsworthy, John, 448
Gambetta, Leon, 459
Gandhi, Mohandas K., 126, 505, 615, 806, 874
Gardner (political cartoonist), 585
Gardner, Augustus, 522
Gardner, John, 186, 657
Garfield, James A., 66, 169,

420, 556, 609, 751, 826
body politic, 69
draft, Presidential, 199–200
Garland, Hamlin, 596
Garment, Leonard, 423, 630, 689, 873
Garner, John Nance, 256, 367, 385, 419, 487, 759, 767
Garrison, William Lloyd, 1, 125, 531, 579
Garson, Barbara, 764
Garth, David, 388
Gasnell, Harold, 132
Gates, Gary Paul, 546
Gavin, James, 457, 561–62
Gavin, William, 738
Gay, John, 880
Gayn, Mark, 163
Gaytan de Ayala, Javier, 244
Gelb, Leslie, 190, 365, 539, 803
Gemayel, Pierre, 601
George, Henry, 840, 855
George V, King of Great Britain, 183
Gephardt, Richard, 257
Gerard, Jean, 238
Gergen, David R., 458–59, 733, 738
Germond, Jack W., 47, 721
Gerry, Elbridge, 279–80
Geyelin, Philip, 736
Gibbon, Edward, 65, 427, 614
Gibson, H. R., 7
Gibson, John, 35
Gilbert, W. S., 594
Gilchrist, Alexander, 313
Gilhooley, John J., 841
Gill, Brendan, 416, 658
Gilmour, Kathleen, 135
Gilroy, Thomas, 745
Gingrich, Newt, 32
Ginsburg, David, 521
Ginsburg, Douglas H., 883
Giscard d'Estaing, Valéry, 891
Gladstone, William, 78, 175, 290, 360, 378–79, 605–6, 769, 841, 877
Glaspie, April C., 821
Glazer, Nathan, 447
Gleason, "Battle Ax" Paddy, 41
Glenn, John, 173, 693
Godkin, Edwin L., 407
Goebbels, Joseph, 72, 309, 371, 432, 618
Goethe, Johann Wolfgang von, 247, 779
Golan, Matti, 759
Gold, Robert, 50
Gold, Vic, 97, 519, 608–9, 774
Golden, Gregg, 881

Goldman, Eric, 313, 365, 392, 452, 484, 556, 585, 739, 825, 870
Goldsmith, Oliver, 125, 443
Goldwater, Barry, 100, 130, 140, 188, 196, 223, 239, 248, 268, 270, 369–70, 399, 407, 430, 451, 458, 511, 563, 587, 657, 669, 679, 685, 709, 731, 734, 827
  AuH2O=1964, 28–29
  boring from within, 75
  campaign train, 100
  cell, 109–10
  choice, not an echo, 120–21
  daisy spot, 166
  defoliate, 173
  Eastern Establishment, 204
  extremism, 231
  heckle, 323
  house, 339
  illegitimi non carborundum, 353
  kooks, nuts and, 392
  little old ladies in tennis shoes, 415
  Mr. Republican, 468
  party loyalty, 554
  Santa Claus, nobody shoots at, 687
  Sherman statement, 700
  spontaneous demonstration, 746
  trigger-happy, 813–14
Gonzales, Oscar, 715
Goodloe, William Cassius, 739
Goodman, George J. W. See Smith, Adam
Goodman, Robert, 309
Goodwin, Richard N., 12, 292, 302, 686, 738
Gorbachev, Mikhail, 71, 283, 571, 629–30, 677, 742, 876, 886
Gordon, Charles (Chinese), 807
Gordon, Max, 739
Gordon, Slade, 404
Gore, Albert, 246, 288
Gore, Albert, Jr. (Al), 38, 153, 442, 588, 647, 805, 840
  dream ticket, 201
Göring, Hermann, 247, 308–9, 497
Gorkin, Jess, 337
Gorman, John, 642–43
Goschen, Edward, 691
Gould, Jack, 222
Gowers, Ernest, 136, 224, 353, 391
Graham, Philip, 137–38, 327

Grant, Ulysses S., 100, 125,
      213, 407, 436, 487, 496,
      519, 627, 816, 822
   boom (boomlet), 73
   deal, 169
   rotten boroughs, 672
Grassley, Charles, 364
Gray, Arthur, Jr., 43
Gray, Patrick, 821
Gray, Robert, 45
Greeley, Andrew M., 237
Greeley, Horace, 65, 103, 205,
      659, 700
Green, Archie, 575–76
Green, Dwight, 72
Green, William, 3
Greenbaum, Edward S., 27
Greenberg, Paul, 385
Greene, Graham, 825
Greene, Joe, 647
Greenfield, Jeff, 611, 733
Greenfield, Meg, 405, 588,
      640, 670, 771, 836, 858,
      861–62, 890
Greenspan, Alan, 454
Gregory, Dick, 117
Gregory XIII, Pope, 618
Grindle, Paul, 254
Griswold, Dwight, 573
Gromyko, Andrei, 70, 456
Grose, Francis, 699, 821
Gross, H. R., 1
Gross, Jerry, 445, 447
Grove, Lloyd, 34
Gruenther, Alfred M., 106,
      357
Grundy, Joe, 722
Grunwald, Henry, 795
Guidry, Vernon A., Jr., 284
Guinier, Lani, 111, 637
Gunther, John, 63, 79, 174,
      402, 680, 689, 880
Guralnik, David, 226

Haas, Lawrence J., 84
Habash, George, 595
Habib, Phil, 291
Haeckel, Ernst, 221
Hagerty, James C., 6, 115,
      400, 432, 540, 760
Hague, Frank, 214, 333, 348,
      763
Haig, Alexander M., Jr., 251,
      472, 689
Haldeman, H. R., 51, 645,
      687, 723, 750, 851, 873
Hale, E. E., 596
Hale, Matthew, 623
Haley, Alex, 496, 828
Haley, J. Evetts, 120
Hall, Bob, 289
Hall, Fawn, 327
Hall, Joseph, 156

Hall, Leonard, 41, 82, 176, 380
Halleck, Charles, 700
Halley, Rudolph, 469
Halperin, Morton, 803
Hamilton, Alexander, 426,
      678, 767, 826
   American system, 19
   contrapuntal phrases, 147
   vox populi, 848
Hamilton, E. L., 93
Hamilton, Frank, 867
Hamilton, John, 648
Hammarskjöld, Dag, 502,
      607–8, 815
Hancock, Winfield Scott, 66,
      709
Hand, Learned, 494
Handler, Bruce, 755
Hanighan, F. C., 448
Hankey, Maurice, 557
Hanna, Mark, 155, 238,
      257–58, 321, 388, 418, 852
   stand pat, 752–53
Hansen, Alvin, 488
Hanser, Richard, 263
Harcourt, William, 863
Harding, Warren G., 114,
      263, 270, 297, 330, 339,
      368, 388–89, 419, 488,
      494, 624, 626, 728
   alliteration, 13
   availability, 30
   bloc, 64
   bloviate, 66–67
   cabal, 96
   captive candidate, 105
   card metaphors, 106
   character assassin, 112
   dark horse, 167
   isolationism, 374
   normalcy, 506
   trot out the ghosts, 816
Hare, John, 306
Hare, Nathan, 61
Hargrave, W. Loftin, 43
Harkness, Richard, 784
Harlan, John Marshall, 525,
      637, 697
Harlow, Bryce, 737
Harnack, Robert, 402
Harnick, Sheldon, 416–17
Harold II, King of England,
      708
Harper, S. J., 228
Harriman, Averell, 351, 435,
      458, 530, 690, 704, 712,
      770, 811
   balanced ticket, 37–38
Harriman, Pamela, 886
Harrington, James, 116
Harrington, Michael, 482, 855
Harris, Grant, 838
Harris, Leon, 113

Harris, Louis, 792
Harris, Phil, 521
Harrison, Benjamin, 356
   boodle, 72
   campaign songs, 99
   policeman of the world, 587
Harrison, Selig, 137
Harrison, William Henry
      (Tippecanoe), 476, 502,
      643, 678
   availability, 30
   avalanche, 30
   banner district, 43–44
   campaign songs, 99
   log cabin, 418–19
Hart, A. B., 127
Hart, Gary, 245, 462, 617,
      757, 797–98, 883
   bargaining chip, 45
Hart, Johnny, 895
Harvey, George, 96, 330, 721
Hatch, Carl, 319
Hatfield, Mark, 47
Hauck, Frederick, 316
Hauge, Gabriel, 738
Haushofer, Karl, 401
Hawthorne, Nathaniel, 14
Hay, John, 130, 532, 703, 732
Hayakawa, S. I., 59, 177
Hayden, Tom, 466, 605
Haydn, Hiram, 803
Hayes, Charles, 597
Hayes, Helen, 252
Hayes, Joseph, 97
Hayes, Rutherford B., 13,
      252, 471, 496, 730
   campaign songs, 100
   dark horse, 167
   deal, 169–70
   itch to run, 375–76
Haynsworth, Clement, 8
Hazlitt, William, 264, 298, 448
Healy, Paul, 362
Hearst, Patricia, 409
Hearst, William Randolph,
      170, 323, 388–89
Heath, Edward, 57, 479
Hechler, Ken, 704, 737
Heflin, Tom, 890–91
Heiman, John, 881
Heinlein, Robert A., 268
Heisenberg, Werner Karl, 207
Heller, Walter, 74, 206, 306,
      377, 466, 488, 502, 540,
      620, 631, 687, 786,
      810–11, 840
Hellman, Geoffrey, 658
Helms, Richard, 123, 186,
      610, 747, 776
Hemingway, Ernest, 141, 244
Hench, Atcheson L., 131,
      176, 784
Henderson, John B., 700

Hendricks, Thomas A., 303
Hendrickson, Robert, 790
Henley (editor), 686
Henry, O., 696, 758, 765
Henry, Patrick, 65
Henry II, King of England, 7
Henry III, King of England, 7
Henry IV, King of France, 117, 295
Henry V, King of England, 747
Henson, Rev. J., 829
Herbert, Alan, 429
Herbert, Henry Molyneux, 28
Herblock (Herbert Block), 348, 441
Heren, Louis, 801
Hersh, Seymour M., 178, 186, 368, 747
Hershkowitz, Leo, 744–45
Herzl, Theodor, 332
Hess (cartoonist), 739
Hess, John L., 685
Hess, Karl, 231
Hess, Rudolf, 629
Hess, Stephen, 19–20, 203, 660, 737, 799
Heydrich, Reinhard, 247, 497
Hibben, Paxton, 568
Hickenlooper, Bourke, 318
Hicks, Louisa Day, 893
High, Stanley, 207, 527, 737
Highet, Gilbert, 147
Hildreth, Richard, 717
Hill, Anita, 8, 442, 883
Hill, David, 793
Hill, Joe, 575
Hill, Linda, 242
Hillary, Edmund, 702
Hilles, Charles E., 722
Hillman, Sidney, 128
Hillman, William, 737
Hilsman, Roger, 232, 361, 581, 633
Hilton, James, 742
Himmler, Heinrich, 497, 627
Hiss, Alger, 321, 652, 729
Hitler, Adolf, 139, 227, 244, 246, 371, 473, 496, 627, 640
    axis, 31
    big lie, 53
    bombing pause, 70
    Mr. Nice Guy, 468
    new order, 494
    night of the long knives, 497
    putsch, 629
    self-determination, 695
    strange bedfellows, 762–63
    war of nerves, 854
Hoagland, Jim, 468
Hobart, Alice Tinsdale, 518

Hobart, Garret A., 751
Hobart, George, 197
Hobbes, Thomas, 68, 106, 721
Hobson, Thomas, 329–30
Hoffenstein, Samuel, 156
Hoffer, Eric, 817
Hoffman, Abbie, 886
Hoffman, Clare, 726
Hoffman, David, 642
Hoffman, Paul, 41, 132, 244, 285, 639, 665, 766, 842
Hoffmann, Stanley, 522
Hofstadter, Richard, 125, 476, 794
Hogan, Frank, 315
Hogan, Lawrence, 668
Hoh, David, 844
Holland, Spessard, 627
Hollender, Al, 182
Holman, William S., 858
Holmes, Oliver Wendell, 74, 147–48, 605, 666, 830, 881
    Brahmin, 79
Holyfield, Evander, 506
Homer, 669–70
Homes, Lord, 791
Hook, Sidney, 345
Hooker, Joseph, 435
Hoover, Herbert, 139, 176, 212, 272, 356, 363, 389, 404, 407, 453, 471, 517, 524, 552, 759, 787, 813, 890
    American system, 19
    barnburners, 45
    chicken in every pot, 117
    don't change horses, 194
    grand design, 295
    grass will grow in the streets, 297
    honeymoon period, 335
    Hooverize, 335–36
    moratorium, 462
    noble experiment, 501
    playing politics, 580
    reactionary, 646
    rubber stamp, 674
    rugged individualism, 674–75
    running against Hoover, 677
    smear, 719
    war on poverty, 855
Hoover, J. Edgar, 256, 367, 393
    Byzantine, 95
Hopkins, Harry, 168, 264, 420, 600, 739
Horne, Alistair, 65
Horne, Lena, 113
Horner, Garnett, 322
Horrock, Nicholas, 382
Horton, Willie, 864

Horton, Zilphia, 867
House, Edward, 422, 531, 573, 600, 771
Houston, Tom, 670
Hoving, Thomas P. F., 113
Howar, Barbara, 873
Howard, Philip, 296
Howe, Louis, 15, 81, 298, 316, 319, 492, 509–10, 546, 600, 710
Howe, Mark DeWolfe, 674
Howe, Quincy, 811
Howells, William Dean, 325
Hower, Ralph, 94
Hua Kuo-feng, 163, 536, 821
Huang Hua, 503
Hubbard, Henry, 802–3
Hubbell, Webster, 361
Hudson, Kenneth, 318
Hudson, William C., 406, 624
Huerta, Victoriano, 858
Hughes, Charles Evans, 24, 69, 145, 354, 504, 713, 759, 776
    arena, 23–24
Hughes, E. O., 444
Hughes, Emmet John, 161, 442, 450, 544, 575, 738, 856
Hughes, Langston, 405
Hughes, Richard, 59
Hull, Cordell, 23, 168, 219, 289, 740
Humphrey, George, 488
Humphrey, Gordon J., 481
Humphrey, Hubert H., 168, 256, 317, 319, 344, 361, 372, 593, 677, 720, 817
    availability, 30
    best man, the, 49
    black capitalism, 60
    brain drain, 80
    busing to achieve racial balance, 92
    Chautauqua circuit, 115
    come now, and let us reason together, 138
    concession speech, 141
    dirty politics, 185
    Dixiecrat, 188–89
    human rights, 342
    Peace Corps, 561–62
    rhetoric, 663
    running against Washington, 677
    running mate, 679
Humphrey, Robert L., 548
Hunt, E. Howard, Jr., 172, 582
Hunt, James V., 254, 358
Hunter, Robert E., 612–13
Huntington, Samuel P., 269
Huong, Tran Van, 819

Hurd, Charles, 100, 129, 432, 516, 599, 625, 810–11
Hurley, Patrick, 119
Hurst, Steve, 521
Hursted, James M., 39
Hussein, Saddam, 269, 308, 456, 602, 607, 670, 730, 776
Huston, Tom Charles, 490
Huxley, Aldous, 567–68, 821
Huxley, J. S., 444
Hyland, John F., 655

Ickes, Harold L., 230, 292, 320, 367, 435–37, 516, 526, 632, 678, 862
  barefoot boy from Wall Street, 44
  curmudgeon, 164
Ike, Nobutake, 195
Ikeda, Hayato, 423
Iklé, Fred C., 647
Ingersoll, Robert G., 372, 782, 791
Inglehart, John K., 739
Inglis, William, 183
Innis, Roy, 344
Irving, Washington, 82, 852
Irwin, Don, 735
Iverson, Alfred, 132
Ivins, Molly, 20

Jackson, Andrew, 223, 242, 253, 277, 308, 312, 319, 397, 419, 471, 526, 546, 550–51, 643, 794
  advice and consent, 8
  caucus, 109
  clean sweep, 128
  deal, 169
  divorce issue, 188
  kitchen cabinet, 389
  manifest destiny, 433
  spoils system, 745
  war horse, 853
Jackson, Henry, 46, 250, 343, 397, 464
Jackson, James L., 248–49
Jackson, Jesse, 132, 352, 699
Jackson, Robert, 207
Jackson, Thomas Jonathan, 761
Jacob, John, 503, 846
Jacobs, Paul, 11, 393, 465
Jahn, Mike, 154
James, Esther, 36
James, Henry, 487
James, William, 199, 461
Janeway, Eliot, 35, 858
Janklow, Morton, 604
Janowitz, Morris, 664
Jaroslovsky, Rich, 860

Jarvis, Howard, 785–86
Jaspers, Karl, 809
Javits, Jacob K., 82, 127, 216, 236, 766
Jay, Peter, 206
Jefferson, Thomas, 54, 176, 247, 285, 297, 304, 308, 374, 389, 419, 448, 480, 503, 505, 556–57, 592, 619, 632, 645, 737, 754, 759, 767, 823, 893
  advice and consent, 8
  American system, 19
  bellwether, 48
  big government, 52
  cant, 102
  civil disobedience, 126
  crusade, 161
  entangling alliances, 219
  human rights, 341
  machinery of government, 427
  pay as you go, 559
  practical politics, 606
  public office is a public trust, 623
  Republican, 658
  silk stocking, 709
  war hawks, 853
  we are all, 863
  world opinion, 887
Jendrzejczyk, Mike, 877
Jenkins, Ray, 585
Jenkins, Thomas, 328
Jenkins, Walter, 730
Jenner, William, 678, 727
Jennings, Ivor, 699
Jensen, Oliver, 58, 211
Jesus, 465, 522
John Paul II, Pope, 563
Johnson, Alva, 411
Johnson, Andrew, 356, 474–75, 557–58, 670, 765
  bread-and-butter issue, 82
  satrap, 688
  stalking horse, 750
Johnson, G. L., 753
Johnson, Gabriel, 8
Johnson, George, 216
Johnson, Harold, 232
Johnson, Haynes, 594, 778, 801
Johnson, Hiram, 367
Johnson, Hugh, 367
Johnson, J. S., 745
Johnson, Lady Bird, 252, 257
Johnson, Lynda Bird, 257
Johnson, Lyndon B., 125, 219, 223, 248, 252, 257, 268, 278, 282, 291, 304, 309, 337, 339–41, 344, 352, 361, 374, 392, 400, 404, 407, 424, 432, 456, 465, 474, 487, 496, 502,

504–5, 528, 532–33, 536–37, 540–41, 556, 571, 575, 587, 591, 662, 682, 704, 720, 759, 764, 826, 858, 865, 869, 888
  alliteration, 13
  American boys, 17
  apostle of hate, 22
  arena, 24
  art of the possible, 27
  backlash, 36
  bargaining chip, 44
  Better Red Than Dead, 49–50
  bite the bullet, 57
  bleeding hearts, 63
  bombing pause, 70
  brain drain, 80
  bridge building, 83
  buck stops here, 88
  Camelot, 97
  campaign train, 100
  cant, 102
  card metaphors, 106
  caretaker, 107
  catchword, 108
  cemetery vote, 110
  chronic campaigner, 121
  coattails, 133
  come now, and let us reason together, 137–38
  common man, century of the, 139
  consensus, 143–44
  coonskin on the wall, 150
  corn pone, 152
  countdown, 153
  creative federalism, 157
  credibility gap, 157
  daisy spot, 166
  deliver, 174
  dollar diplomacy, 191
  don't change horses, 194
  electioneer, 212–13
  extremism, 231
  fence, on the, 243
  government-in-exile, 292
  Great Society, 301–3
  hatchetman, 319–20
  heartbeat away from the Presidency, 321
  high road...low road, 327–28
  initials, Presidential, 360
  intellectual-in-residence, 365–66
  Johnson treatment, 381–82
  labels, 395–96
  "let us continue," 405
  meanwhile, back at the ranch, 442
  measured response, 442
  moderate, 458

moratorium, 462
movers and shakers, 466
Nervous Nellies, 482
pacification, 543
peace feeler, 562
political animal, 589
political capital, to make, 589–90
populist, 595
President of all the people, 610
pressing the flesh, 611
progressive, 616–17
rainmaker, 642
rendezvous with destiny, 657
sitting President, 712
smell of magnolias, 720
speechwriter, 738
spend and spend..., 739
spirit of, 742
summitry, 770–71
that dog won't hunt, 790
thousand days, 796
turnout, 819
two-party system, 822
unpack, 835
war on poverty, 855–56
water's edge, 860
We Shall Overcome, 867
you never had it so good, 892
Johnson, Samuel, 164, 435, 774
Johnson, Tom Loftin, 333
Johnson, W. E. (Pussyfoot), 629
Johnston, Eric, 19
Jones, John Paul, 141
Jones, Tom, 556
Jordan, Hamilton, 370, 874
Jordan, Vernon E., Jr., 214–15, 669
Josephson, Matthew, 17–18, 627
Judd, Norman B., 791
Judson, Caly, 431
Julian, George, 303

Kaghan, Theodore, 382–83
Kahn, Alfred, 650
Kahn, Herman, 196, 223, 234, 339, 540, 613, 690–91, 836, 866
Better Red Than Dead, 50
Kalem, T. E., 10
Kampelman, Max M., 180
Kanfer, Stefan, 430
Kaplan, Fred, 171
Kaplow, Herbert, 462
Karouki, Tsuji, 298
Karr, Alphonse, 777
Katcher, Leo, 268, 648, 861

Kaufman, Arnold S., 642
Kaufman, Herbert, 654
Kaufman, Michael, 825
Keating, Kenneth B., 315, 603
Keating, William R., 54
Kefauver, Estes, 38, 150, 199, 290, 440–41, 530, 535, 613
Kelley, Edward J., 845
Kellogg, S. W., 718
Kelly, Edward, 607
Kelly, John (Honest John), 705, 782
Kelly, Walt, 819
Kemble, W. H., 557
Kemp, Jack F., 63, 215–16, 405–6, 548, 681, 700, 775, 785
Kempton, Murray, 34, 163, 335, 615–16, 655
Kendall, John, 872
Kendall, Wallace, 445–46
Kennan, George F., 318, 475, 854
    containment, 146
    Mr. X, 468–69
Kennedy, Caroline, 46
Kennedy, Edward M. (Ted), 84, 234, 292, 430, 584, 593, 642–43, 800
    character issue, 112
    charisma, 113
    high road...low road, 327
    humor, self-deprecating, 343
    inside baseball, 363
    Nobody Drowned at Watergate, 501
    pseudo-event, 622
    rubber stamp, 674
    stay the course, 757
Kennedy, Ethel, 203
Kennedy, Jacqueline, 252, 292, 665
Kennedy, James, 693
Kennedy, John F., 52, 125, 143, 162, 222, 238–39, 250, 256, 268, 270, 276, 289–90, 297, 306, 317, 357, 361, 365–66, 377, 381–82, 389, 401, 415, 420–21, 423, 441–42, 448, 475–76, 484, 488, 496, 505, 512, 530, 541, 545, 551, 560, 563, 565–66, 585, 589, 591, 613, 620, 644, 657, 673, 694, 708, 747–48, 753, 755, 759, 761, 815, 861–62, 870, 872, 874
    Alliance for Progress, 12–13
    alliteration, 13
    angry young men, 20
    arena, 24
    arrogance of power, 27
    backbencher, 32

backgrounder, 33
Bailey memorandum, 37
balanced ticket, 38
balance of power, 38–39
Bay of Pigs fiasco, 46
bellwether, 48
Better Red Than Dead, 49–50
big government, 53
bloc, 64
brinkmanship, 86
buck stops here, the, 87–88
bully pulpit, 89
busing to achieve racial balance, 92
buttons, campaign, 94
Camelot, 97
cant, 102
catchword, 108
chicken in every pot, 117
citizen of the world, 125
city on a hill, 126
contrapuntal phrases, 147–48
crusade, 162
détente, 179
dialogue, 182
dirty politics, 185
domino theory, 191
dynasty, 203
government-in-exile, 292
great debates, 300
gutter flyer, 311
heckle, 323
high road...low road, 327–28
hold still...go along, 330
hot line, 337
humor, self-deprecating, 343
Hundred Days, 345
initials, Presidential, 360
in your hands, 369
"I see" construction, 373
Kennedy Round, 386
"let us continue," 405
life is unfair, 409
limited war, 412
mainstream, 429
managed news, 432
mandate, 433
march on Washington, 438
melting pot, 447
miscalculation, 455–56
missing gap, 457–58
muzzle, 474
myth, 476–77
New Frontier, 491–93
overexposure, 539–40
party loyalty, 554
passion for anonymity, 557
Peace Corps, 561–62
power corrupts, 601

Kennedy, John F. (cont.)
President of all the people, 610
preventive war, 612
profiles in courage, 615–16
public interest, convenience and necessity, 623
Quadriad, 631
quarantine, 633
reverse bigotry, 660
rhyme, political use of, 663
rising tide lifts all the boats, 668–69
sit-ins, 711
slogan, 716
smear, 720
s.o.b., 727
spirit of, 742
stand in the doorway, 752
stroke of a pen, 768
summitry, 770–71
surgical strike, 776
task force, 784
thousand days, 796
too little and too late, 807
torch has been passed, 808
trigger-happy, 814
trot out the ghosts, 816
truth squad, 818
unpack, 835
vast wasteland, 839
victory has a thousand fathers, 841
wall, political use of, 851
war on poverty, 855
you're no JFK, 893
Kennedy, Joseph P., 263, 474, 516, 620, 720, 826, 839
Kennedy, Robert F., 127, 198, 241, 266, 268, 292, 297, 351, 429, 432, 512, 540–41, 581, 611, 712, 763–64, 811
campaign songs, 100
carpetbagger, 107
hatchetman, 319
human element, 340–41
humor, self-deprecating, 343
peace feeler, 562
power grab, 603
rap in the night, 644–45
Kennedy, Rose, 203
Kenny, Robert, 586
Kent, Edward, 325
Kent, Frank R., 78, 238, 580
Kenworthy, Tom, 651
Keogh, James, 738
Kerker, Kara B., 233
Kerouac, Jack, 498
Kerr, Clark, 711

Kerr, Philip Henry, 23
Kerr, Robert, 170
Kerrin, Porter G., 567
Kessner, Thomas, 595
Keyes, Paul, 701
Keynes, John Maynard, 21, 73–74, 488, 774, 840
Keyserling, Leon, 786–87, 855
Kharlamov, Mikhail, 337
Khomeini, Ayatollah, 515
Khrushchev, Nikita, 83, 124, 268–69, 393, 421, 553, 619, 702, 742, 817, 823, 868
cult of personality, 162–63
détente, 178–79
heckle, 322–23
kitchen debate, 390–91
peaceful coexistence, 563
revisionism, 660–61
shrimps whistle, 706
summitry, 770
troika, 815
war of national liberation, 853–54
Kiechel, Walter, 3d, 336
Kiernan, James, 81
Kiernan, Michael, 850–51
Kilgore, Bernard, 338
Kilpatrick, James J., 251, 333, 340, 655–56
King, Anthony, 566, 805
King, Edward, 182
King, Martin Luther, Jr., 9, 61, 224, 421, 505, 570, 664, 768, 874
arrogance of power, 26
black, political use of, 59
civil disobedience, 127
horse-and-buggy, 336
"I have a dream," 352–53
King, Rodney, 127
Kingsley, Sidney, 169
Kipling, Rudyard, 58, 92, 296, 830
Kirbo, Charles, 610
Kirby, Rollin, 485–86
Kirk, Claude R., 61, 344, 456–57, 653, 712, 808
Kirkland, Lane, 5
Kirkpatrick, Jeane, 686, 838
Kirkpatrick, Lyman, 124
Kirwan, Albert, 653
Kirwan, Michael J., 566
Kissinger, Henry, 11, 103, 178, 255, 342, 365, 483, 521–22, 537, 547, 566, 803, 832, 838, 843, 861, 873
autarkic, 29
back channel, 32–33
bargaining chip, 44
buzzword, 94

containment, 146
diplomacy, 185
intransigent, 366
linkage, 413
loner, 421
machismo, 428
multipolar world, 472
quiet diplomacy, 634–35
Sherman statement, 701
shuttle diplomacy, 706
step by step, 758–59
Kitchin, Rosemarie, 647
Kitman, Marvin, 806
Kjellén, Rudolf, 401
Klare, Michael T., 559
Klein, Herb, 85
Klein, Joe, 595
Klein, Woody, 273
Knebel, Fletcher, 35, 586
Knight, John S., 164, 392
Knoebl, Kuno, 114
Knowland, William, 119, 628, 667, 760
Knox, Frank, 648
Knox, Philander C., 185, 190–91
Koch, Ed, 134, 274–75, 599
Koestler, Arthur, 4, 95, 639
Kohl, Helmut, 633, 838, 868
Kokorev, Alexander A., 457
Komisar, Lucy, 428
Kondracke, Morton, 304–5
Kopechne, Mary Jo, 501
Kopkind, Andrew, 254, 359, 752
Kosygin, Alexei, 337, 742, 770, 787, 854
Kowet, Don, 240
Kraft, Joseph, 232, 451–52, 594
Kramer, Michael, 363, 792
Kranz, Eugene, 602
Krauthammer, Charles, 461
Krishna Menon, V. K., 174
Kristol, Irving, 134, 481, 485, 800
Kristol, William, 215, 860
Krock, Arthur, 3, 107, 128, 191, 211–12, 291–92, 330, 386, 424, 452, 525, 535, 540, 568–69, 589, 606, 633, 860
Krogh, Egil, 539
Krosigk, Ludwig Schwerin von, 371
Krutch, Joseph Wood, 139
Kuchel, Thomas, 254
Kudlow, Larry, 21
Kuhn, Thomas, 547
Kupcinet, Irv, 131
Kurkjian, Stephen, 152
Kurtz, Howard, 509, 886
Kusnet, David, 738

Labedz, Leopold, 5
Laffer, Arthur B., 688, 775, 785
La Follette, Robert, 195, 321, 349, 486, 535–36, 613, 753, 827, 841
  progressive, 616
  steamroller, 758
La Guardia, Fiorello, 260, 274, 310, 416, 425, 469, 595, 620
  Hizzoner, 329
  musical metaphors, 473
  two-bit politician, 822
Laird, Melvin, 141, 842
Lake, Anthony, 77
Lall, Arthur, 770
Lamartine, Alphonse de, 560
Lamb, Charles, 92
Lamkin, Raphael, 331
Lamon, Ward, 545
Lamont, Corliss, 693
LaMotte, Lawrence, 651
Lamprey, Louise, 411
Lance, Bert, 47, 279, 351–52, 470–71, 501, 614, 707, 714, 778, 881
Landau, Saul, 11, 393, 465
Landers, Ann, 425
Landon, Alfred M., 164, 250, 289, 491, 805
  alphabet agencies, 14
  American way of life, 19
  disaster metaphors, 187
  henchman, 325
  landslide, 397
Landy, Eugene, 315
Lane, Vicki, 85
Lang, George, 673
Lanzmann, Claude, 332
Laqueur, Walter, 789
Lardner, Ring, 100
Larson, Arthur, 459, 737
Laski, Harold J., 30, 302–3, 506
Lasky, Jane E., 604
Lasky, Victor, 477, 825
Lasswell, Harold, 454, 618, 876
Latimer, Hugh, 808
Lausche, Frank, 318, 655
LaVelle, Avis, 370
Lawrence, Adam Mark, 93
Lawrence, George, 594
Lawrence, Justus, 594
Lawrence, Mary Wells, 772
Lawson, Nigel, 362–63
Lawson, Wilfred, 870–71
Lazarsfeld, Paul I., 177, 466, 535
Lazarus, Emma, 447
Lear, Norman, 20

Leary, Timothy, 535
Le Carré, John, 123, 559
Leche, Richard, 294
Lechner, Ira M., 352
Lederer, William, 825
Lee, Henry (Light Horse Harry), 251
Lee, Richard Henry, 852
Lee, Robert E., 853
Lee, S., 812
Lee, Spike, 263
Lee, Susan, 67
Leggett, William, 546
Lehman, B. H., 669
Lehman, Herbert, 216, 398, 655, 811
Lehmann, John, 789
Lehrer, Jim, 447
Lehrer, Tom, 679
Lehrman, Lewis, 481
Leiser, Erwin, 332
Leland, Charles G., 67
Lelyveld, Joseph, 388, 445
L'Enfant, Pierre, 328
Lenin, Nikolai, 139, 283, 476, 563, 571, 838
Lenkowsky, Leslie, 681
Leonard, John, 547
Leonardo da Vinci, 23
Le Pen, Jean-Marie, 592
Lerner, Max, 49, 61, 133–34, 181, 241–42, 338, 414, 665, 699, 763, 817, 884–85
Lerner, Michael, 593
Lesko, Matthew, 265
L'Estrange, Roger, 388
Levi, Arrigo, 328
Leviero, Anthony, 578
Levin, Murray B., 622
Levitt, Arthur, 807
Levitt, Theodore, 382
Lewis, Anthony, 461–62, 614, 676
Lewis, C. S., 798
Lewis, Flora, 891
Lewis, John L., 3, 125, 292, 339, 367, 831
Lewis, Ted, 767
Lichty (cartoonist), 654
Liddy, G. Gordon, 582
Lieberman, Joseph I., 853
Lilienthal, David, 165
Liman, Arthur L., 721
Limbaugh, Rush, 883
Lincoln, Abraham, 82, 252, 273, 292, 300, 326, 362, 392, 435, 459, 471, 474–75, 486, 496, 545, 556, 575, 588, 620, 632, 640, 666, 737, 769, 802, 816, 818, 848, 854, 882
  black Republican, 62

  bloody shirt, 65
  candidate, 101
  coattails, 132–33
  concession speech, 142
  conservative, 144
  contrapuntal phrases, 147
  deal, 169
  don't change horses, 193
  Gettysburg address, 280–81
  house, 339
  humor, self-deprecating, 343
  in your hands, 369
  just and lasting peace, 383
  musical metaphors, 473
  pocket veto, 584
  Presidential bug, 608
  ship of state, 702
  silk stocking, 709
Lincoln, Mary Todd, 252
Lind, John, 417
Lindbergh, Anne Morrow, 862
Lindbergh, Charles A., 151, 172, 862
Lindley, Ernest K., 508, 633
Lindsay, John V., 274, 287, 298, 338, 388, 497, 522, 704, 744
  Boy Scout, 78
  buttons, campaign, 93–94
  civilian review, 127
  dead end, political, 168
  power brokers, 600
Link, R. H., 75
Linowitz, Sol, 409
Lin Piao, 163
Lippmann, Walter, 219, 302, 453–54, 474, 531, 533, 626, 801, 856–57
  Atlantic Community, 27–28
  cold war, 135–36
  community, 140
  consensus, 144
  coonskin on the wall, 150
  credibility gap, 158
  creeping socialism, 159
  deterrent, 180
  dirty tricks, 186
  graft, 294–95
  keynoter, 386
  kiss of death, 389
  mandate, 433
  official family, 516
  proletariat, 617
  speechwriter, 737
  vox populi, 848
Lipset, Seymour Martin, 640, 749, 826
Lipshutz, Robert, 370
Lisagor, Peter, 771
Livingstone, Edward, 367
Lloyd, Selwyn, 71

Lloyd George, David, 486, 807
Locke, John, 143, 341, 480
Lockwood, Daniel, 752
Lodge, Henry Cabot, 130, 175, 257–58, 378, 433, 472, 552, 759
  canvass, 104
Lodge, Henry Cabot, Jr., 38, 71, 612, 799, 888
  amateurs, 16
Logan, Andy, 134
Logan, John, 65
Lomasney, Martin, 584, 852
Lomax, Louis, 18
Lombardi, Vince, 141
London, Jack, 28
Long, Earl, 99, 674
Long, Huey P., 44, 164, 175, 228, 246, 653, 674
  Americanism, 18
  corn pone, 152
  dyed-in-the-wool, 202
  Kingfish, 387
Long, Russell, 99, 207, 246, 288, 387
Longfellow, Henry Wadsworth, 702
Longo, Luigi, 328
Longstreet, Augustus, 412
Longworth, Alice Roosevelt, 330, 436–37, 620
Lorant, Stefan, 257
Lorimer, George, 256–57
Louis XIV, King of France, 297, 348
Louis XVI, King of France, 584
Love, John A., 529
Lovelace, Mortimer, 179
Lovett, Robert A., 3, 11, 39, 204, 245, 259, 496, 533
Low, David, 762
Low, Seth, 274, 655
Lowden, Frank, 30, 167, 552, 721
Lowell, James Russell, 87, 265, 359, 680
Lowth, Robert, 661
Lubell, Samuel, 300, 756, 778–79, 819
Lucas, George, 228, 754
Lucas, Scott, 128
Luce, Clare Boothe, 42, 285, 436, 534, 808, 864
Luce, Henry R., 308, 518, 626
Luciano, Charles (Lucky), 260
Ludendorff, Erich, 809
Lukas, J. Anthony, 539
Lunt, Paul S., 225
Luntz, Frank, 709
Luther, Martin, 736
Lynch, Dennis Tilden, 418

Lynd, Staughton, 11
Lyons, Leonard, 436, 819

McAdoo, William G., 369, 573
MacArthur, Douglas, 232, 341, 456, 510, 578–79, 716
  American boys, 17
  Armageddon, 25–26
  buck stops here, the, 87–88
  limited war, 412
  no substitute for victory, 507–8
  old soldiers never die, 520–21
  privileged sanctuary, 613–14
  wrong war, 888
Macaulay, Thomas Babington, 98, 249, 264, 448, 840
McAuliffe, Christa, 629
McCallum, R. B., 622
McCann, Kevin, 738
McCarthy, Eugene F., 27, 82, 241, 442, 465, 538, 609, 712
McCarthy, Joseph R., 125, 218, 229, 254, 306–7, 313, 373, 422, 441–42, 545, 574, 591, 628, 729
  big lie, 53
  bookburners, 72
  card-carrying, 105
  character assassin, 111–12
  demagogue, 175
  point of order, 585
  pseudo-event, 622
  quoted out of context, 638
  s.o.b., 727
  twenty years of treason, 820
  yahoo, 890
McClellan, George B., 435
McClellan, George B., Jr., 713
McCloy, John J., 27, 204, 694
McConnell, Mitch, 790
McCormack, Edward, 234, 327, 622
McCormack, John, 68, 878
McCormick, Robert, 75, 335
McCoy, Donald R., 399
McCracken, Paul, 277
McCrae, John, 808–9
McCrary, John R. (Tex), 574, 749, 848
McDavid, Raven, 28
MacDiarmid, Hugh, 829
MacDonald, J. Ramsay, 367
McDonald, John B., 671–72
MacDonald, Ramsey, 700
McDuffie, John, 487
McElroy, Neil, 457
McElroy, Robert, 624
Macfadden, Bernarr, 411
McFarlane, Robert C., 82, 721

McGovern, George, 6, 297, 317, 364, 375, 391, 397, 626–27, 785, 800
  sleaze factor, 714
  stalking horse, 750
  thousand percent, 796–97
  three-martini lunch, 799
McGrory, Mary, 301, 316, 420, 430, 663
McGruder, Jeb, 620
McGuinness, Peter J., 596
Machiavelli, Niccolò, 388, 414
McIntyre, Marvin, 162
McKane, John Y., 41
McKenzie, Vernon, 446
McKeon, Michael, 25
Mackinder, Halford, 322
McKinley, William, 7, 292, 351, 411, 434, 678, 711, 774, 871
  availability, 30
  bandwagon, 43
  cowboy, 155
  front-porch campaign, 269–70
  full dinner pail, 271
  lobby, 418
  stampede, 751
Mackintosh, James, 859
McKissick, Floyd, 61, 664
McKitrick, Eric, 424–25
Mackley, J. P., 462
McLaughlin, A. C., 127
McLean, Malcolm, 569
MacLeish, Archibald, 17
MacManus, Theodore F., 578
Macmillan, Harold, 502, 560, 741, 787–88, 830, 835, 892
  winds of change, 879–80
McNamara, Robert, 153, 359, 401, 440, 457, 553, 568, 588, 865
  musical metaphors, 473
  political animal, 589
  puppet (government), 626
  Whiz Kids, 875–76
McNary, Charles, 37
McNulty, Timothy J., 757
McNutt, Paul, 128
MacPherson, Myra, 363
McVicker, C. P., 126
McWilliams, Carey, 65
Maddox, Lester, 378
Madison, Dolley, 252
Madison, James, 503, 505, 546, 612, 737, 853–54
  candidate, 101
  checks and balances, 116
Magaziner, Ira, 866, 886
Magruder, Jeb, 158
Mahbubani, Kishosre, 867
Mahe, Eddie, 249

Mahoney, David, 662
Mahoney, George, 893
Mahood (cartoonist), 510
Mailer, Norman, 18, 192, 764
Major, John, 269, 362–63
Malan, Daniel F., 695
Malcolm X, 61, 113, 496
Malmesbury, Earl, 645
Manchester, William, 34, 292, 393, 515, 665–66
Mandel, Marvin, 723
Mankiewicz, Frank, 197, 391, 743
Mann, Maurice, 206
Mann, Thomas, 387
Manning, Daniel, 406–7
Manning, Robert, 355, 432
Mansfield, Mike, 861, 870
Mao Tse-tung, 109–10, 171, 294, 345
   Cultural Revolution, 163
   Great Leap Forward, 301
   hegemony, 324
   Maoism, 437
   paper tiger, 547
   party unity, 556
   politically correct, 590
   reactionary, 646
   revisionism, 661
Marat, Jean Paul, 637
Marcantonio, Vito, 89, 367
Marchi, John, 790
Marcus, Edwin, 268, 871
Marcy, William, 619, 744–45
Marder, Murray, 157, 776
Margolin, Leo J., 618
Mariani, John F., 604
Marie Antoinette, 404, 584
Mark Antony, 574
Markham, James M., 249
Marquis, Don, 794
Marshall, Alfred, 267
Marshall, Eliot, 365, 577
Marshall, George C., 101, 245, 678
   China lobby, 119
Marshall, John, 247–48, 293, 605, 767
Marshall, Robert, 75
Marshall, Thomas, 678
Marshall, Thurgood, 888
Marshall, Will, 548
Marston, David, 51, 589, 779–80
Martin, Edward, 50
Martin, Joseph P., 37, 62, 99, 164, 193, 238, 380, 423, 439, 507, 544–45, 702, 763, 805
Martin, Ralph, 422
Martin, Robert, 682–83
Martin, William McChester, 541

Marx, Groucho, 457
Marx, Karl, 139, 350, 534, 617, 661
Mason, Noah, 459
Matalin, Mary, 314
Mathews, Mitford, 104, 516, 866
Mathias, Charles, 288, 726
Matsell, G. W., 400
Matthews, J. B., 307
Matthews, Stanley, 265
Maudling, Reginald, 722
Maury, Ann, 769
Maverick, Maury, 286–87, 515
Maverick, Samuel, 440
Maxa, Rudy, 123, 604
Maxey, C. C., 596
Maxwell, Elsa, 791
May, Mark A., 567
Mazo, Earl, 35
Mazowiecki (Polish prime minister), 388
Mead, Margaret, 568
Means, Marianne, 750
Meany, George, 416, 584
Medaris, John, 153
Medary, Samuel, 853
Meese, Ed, 233, 370, 816
Mellanby, Keith, 220
Melville, Herman, 341, 522, 570, 853
Mencken, H. L., 321, 419, 426, 496, 515–16, 613, 620, 646, 656–57, 680, 769, 772, 830, 841
   Americanisms, 19
Meredith, James, 660
Merrick, David, 46, 100
Metternich, Klemens von, 641
Metzenbaum, Howard, 430
Meyer, Karl, 12
Meyers, Victor Aloysius, 841
Michaelson, Charlie, 719
Michel, Robert H., 705
Mickels, Cathy, 352
Mies van der Rohe, Ludwig, 181
Mikheyev, Dmitri, 685
Miles, Rufus E., 620
Milholin, Gary, 692
Mill, John Stuart, 535, 541, 551
   arena, 24
Miller, Arjay, 875
Miller, Arnold, 24
Miller, Judith, 886
Miller, Lewis, 115
Millet, Kate, 883
Millett, John, 524
Mills, C. Wright, 90, 129, 203, 214, 403, 604, 623
   New Left, 493

power elite, 602
   stay-at-homes, 756
Mills, Ogden, 389
Milne, A. A., 594
Milosevic, Slobodan, 225
Mindszenty, Cardinal, 81
Minney, R. J., 183, 526
Minow, Newton, 839
Mintener, Bradshaw, 591
Mintz, Morton, 523
Mish, Fred, 739–40
Mitchel, John Purroy, 274
Mitchell, John, 51, 155, 401, 620, 642, 760–61, 873
   bug, 88
Mitchell, Margaret, 262, 412
Mockridge, Norton, 36–37
Mohr, Charles, 44, 850
Mola, Emilio, 244
Moley, Raymond, 70, 81, 157, 261, 297, 344, 357, 486, 509–10, 581, 674, 737, 768, 817
Moliére, 297
Mondale, Joan, 421
Mondale, Walter F., 27, 105, 271, 382, 421, 525, 589, 614–15, 684, 693, 801, 813, 883
   defining moment, 173
   effect, 208
   sleaze factor, 714
Monnet, Jean, 27
Monroe, James, 180, 223, 745
   doctrine, 189
Montagu, John (fourth Earl of Sandwich), 367
Montesquieu, Baron, 293
Montgomery, John, 9, 892
Moody, Blair, 300
Moore, Richard, 7, 84, 701
Moore, Victor, 800
Moos, Malcolm, 453, 737
Moran, James, 36–37
Morgan, James, 847
Morgan, Thomas B., 788
Morgenstern, Oskar, 895
Morgenthau, Hans J., 365, 601, 604
Morgenthau, Henry, 400
Morison, Samuel Eliot, 52, 63, 159, 317–18, 412, 692, 764
Morley, Christopher, 802
Morley, John, 167
Morris, J. Anthony, 872
Morris, Newbold, 260, 473
Morris, Richard, 199
Morrissey, John, 705
Morrow, Dwight, 620
Morrow, Hugh, 429
Morse, Wayne, 17, 246
Morton, Bruce, 251

Morton, Thruston, 688
Mosby, John Singleton, 730
Moscow, Warren, 110–11
Moses, George H., 732
Moses, Robert, 164
Mosher, Clint, 855
Mosk, Stanley, 415
Mowry, George E., 746
Moyers, Bill, 157–58, 598–99
Moynihan, Daniel Patrick,
    86, 242–43, 342, 482, 885
  benign neglect, 49
  if you can't stand the
      heat..., 352
  melting pot, 447
  quiet diplomacy, 635
  racism, 640
Mudd, Roger, 445, 733
Mueller, Robert Kirk, 94
Mullen, Arthur, 290
Munster, Earl of, 371
Murphy, Charles, 170, 502,
    713, 782
Murphy, Charles J., 737
Murphy, John, 382
Murphy, Robert, 408
Murphy, Thomas P., 240
Murray, "Alfalfa Bill," 152
Murray, John, 881
Murray, Philip, 22
Muskie, Edmund, 101, 467,
    484, 772–73
  blooper, 66
  Canucks, 103
Mussolini, Benito, 237, 473,
    483
  axis, 31
Myers, Dee Dee, 896
Myrdal, Gunnar, 662

Nabokov, Vladimir, 267
Nader, Ralph, 5
Naisbitt, John, 548
Napoleon Bonaparte, 141,
    349, 476, 479, 519
Nasby, Petroleum V., 57, 195,
    226–27, 486–87
Nash, Ogden, 756
Nast, Thomas, 72, 77, 213,
    271, 547, 782
  boomerang, 74
Nathan, Richard P., 885
Navasky, Victor, 170
Nehru, Jawaharlal, 272, 880
Neill, Humphrey, 148
Nelan, Bruce W., 307
Nessen, Ron, 93, 748, 813
Nethersole, Francis, 405
Neuberger, Richard L., 561,
    583
Neuhaus, Richard John, 662
Neustadt, Richard, 91, 401,
    539, 791, 860

Nevins, Allan, 492, 807
Newhouse, John, 682, 736,
    879
Newman, Edwin, 324
Nicholas I, Czar, 706
Nicolai, Walther, 371
Nietzsche, Friedrich, 774
Nikulin, Lev, 371
Nirdlinger, Charles, 252
Nixon, Patricia, 754
Nixon, Richard M., 103, 222,
    231, 249, 251, 256–57,
    272, 293, 334, 355, 361,
    365, 380, 413, 431, 450,
    459, 463, 468, 474, 496,
    526, 551, 565–66, 626,
    662, 720, 731, 744, 785,
    787, 806, 861
  American dream, 18
  arena, 24
  at that point in time, 28
  automobile metaphor, 29
  ballot-box stuffing, 41
  bargaining chip, 44
  Bircher, 56
  black capitalism, 60
  break all the china, 83
  bridge building, 83
  bring us together, 84–85
  bug, 88
  cant, 102
  card-carrying, 105
  cattle show, 109
  Checkers speech, 115–16
  China lobby, 119
  chronic campaigner, 121
  compact of Fifth Avenue,
      140–41
  concession speech, 141–42
  containment, 146
  cover-up, 155
  CREEP, 158–59
  cufflinks gang, 162
  dead end, political, 169
  détente, 179
  dope story, 197
  dream ticket, 201
  economic jargon, 206
  elitism, 214–15
  enemies list, 216–17
  evil empire, 229
  executive privilege, 229–30
  full generation of peace,
      272–73
  great debates, 300
  Great Leap Forward, 301
  gutter flyer, 310–11
  hack it, 312
  hang tough, 315
  hatchetman, 319
  heartbeat away from the
      Presidency, 321
  heartland, 322

  heckle, 323
  initials, Presidential, 360
  "I see" construction, 373
  jawboning, 377
  job seeks the man, 379
  kitchen debate, 390–91
  leaks, 401
  lift of a driving dream, 410
  machinery of government,
      427
  men of thought, 448
  New Federalism, 489–90
  Nixon Doctrine, 500–501
  Nobody Drowned at
      Watergate, 501
  -nomics, 503
  nut-cutting, 512
  one-term President, 527
  Oval Office, 538–39
  perennial candidate, 571
  play in Peoria, 580
  plumber, 582
  pointer phrases, 585
  privileged sanctuary, 614
  profiles in courage, 615–16
  Quadriad, 631
  ratfucking, 645
  rattle the cage, 645
  running against Hoover,
      677
  Saturday Night Massacre,
      689–90
  secret plan, 692–93
  silent majority, 707–9
  slush fund, 718
  smear, 719
  smoking gun, 723
  Southern strategy, 733–34
  speechwriter, 738
  stand pat, 753–54
  stonewalling, 760
  strict constructionist,
      766–67
  tilt, 803
  trigger-happy, 814
  trot out the ghosts, 816
  twisting slowly, slowly in
      the wind, 821
  umbrella symbol, 825–26
  used car salesman, 837
  veep, 840
  Vietnamization, 842
  war on poverty, 856
  war to end wars, 857
  weasel words, 864
  "who-lost" construction,
      876
  wilderness years, 877
  winning the peace, 880
  work ethic, 884–85
  workfare, 885
Nobel, Alfred B., 449
Nolan, Martin, 776

Noonan, Peggy, 387, 647, 662, 798
Noriega, Manuel, 398, 514
Norris, George, 245, 764
North, Oliver L., 82, 272, 417
Norton, Charles Eliot, 888
Norton, Charles Ledyard, 39, 279–80, 318, 358, 557, 606, 664–65, 705, 802, 828, 871
Noth, Judson, 16
Novak, Michael, 866
Novak, Robert, 27, 159, 184, 381, 398, 415, 451, 503, 541, 635, 642, 661, 767, 826, 851
    backlash, 35
    born again, 77
    break all the china, 83
    economic jargon, 206
Nunn, Sam, 165, 250–51, 781, 844
Nye, Gerald P., 99
Nye, Russell B., 616

Oberdorfer, Don, 538, 801
O'Brien, Lawrence, 206, 292, 369, 581
O'Connell, Daniel, 5, 41
O'Connor, Edwin, 397
O'Connor, Frank, 194, 216, 522–23
O'Connor, John J., 253
O'Connor, Sandra Day, 500
Odom, William E., 229
O'Donnell, Harry, 356
O'Donnell, Kenneth, 292, 319, 369, 557
O'Donnell, Peter, 120
O'Dwyer, Paul, 522
O'Dwyer, William, 36–37, 298
Ognibene, Peter, 684
O'Gorman, James, 573
O'Hara, Tom, 89
Ohga, Norio, 625
Oleszek, Walter, 541
Oliphant, Thomas, 112
Oliver, Robert T., 717
Onassis, Jacqueline Kennedy. See Kennedy, Jacqueline
O'Neill, Edward, 78
O'Neill, Thomas P. (Tip), 68, 467, 581, 589, 720–21
Oppenheimer, J. Robert, 694
Oppenheimer, Jerry, 723
Ortega Saavedra, Daniel, 713
Ortega y Gasset, José, 455
Orwell, George, 796
Osborne, David, 548
Osborne, John (columnist), 49, 687
Osborne, John (playwright), 20

O'Shaughnessy, Arthur, 466–67
O'Sullivan, John, 433–34
Oswald, Lee Harvey, 449
Otis, Harrison Grey, 367
Otten, Alan L., 74, 107, 277, 343–44, 615, 665
Ottley, Roi, 828
Owen, David, 525
Owen, Richard, 184
Owen, Robert, 159

Paar, Jack, 819
Packard, Vance, 177, 428
Packwood, Bob, 406
Paige, Satchel, 257
Paine, Thomas, 341, 480, 675, 833
Paley, William, 102
Palmer, A. Mitchell, 880
Panetta, Leon, 85
Paracelsus, Philippus Aureolus, 285–86
Park, Tongsun, 445
Parker (governor of Louisiana), 368
Parker, Alton B., 712, 757
Parker, Theodore, 349, 609
Parkinson, C. Northcote, 400
Parkinson, Gaylord E., 56, 214
Parry, Albert, 838
Parry, Robert T., 729
Partridge, Bernard, 667–68
Partridge, Eric, 42, 46, 287, 574, 691
    bloodbath, 64
Pascal, Blaise, 578
Passman, Otto, 97
Paton, Alan, 695
Patten, Chris, 518
Patterson, Ellis, 586
Patterson, Richard C., 341
Patterson, Robert, 27
Patton, Chris, 676
Patton, George, 310, 315
Paul, Leslie Allen, 20
Paul, Saint (the Apostle), 14, 113
Paul VI, Pope, 422
Payn, James, 303
Payne, Joan, 668
Payne, Lou, 110–11
Paz, Octavio, 755
Peachtree, Eustace, 802
Pearson, Drew, 465, 500, 673, 718, 726–27
Pearson, Lester, 39, 70, 484
Peck, James, 266
Peck, William G., 693
Pegler, Westbrook, 63, 367
Pei, Mario, 160, 612, 653, 843, 863

Pendergast, Thomas, 174
Pendleton, George H., 349
P'eng Te-hai, 143
Penn, William, 501
Penrose, Boise, 347
Pepper, Claude, 698
Percy, Charles, 32, 140, 174, 236, 458, 536, 752
Perelman, S. J., 480
Peres, Shimon, 249
Perle, Richard, 114
Perón, Evita, 435
Perón, Juan, 448, 726
Perot, H. Ross, 193, 195, 288, 305, 343, 572, 619, 641, 672, 691, 723, 794, 834
Perry, James M., 20, 182
Pershing, John, 62
Peter, Lawrence J., 400
Peterson, Bill, 24, 721, 790
Peterson, Val, 566, 573
Phelps, Robert, 673
Phelps, William Lyon, 626
Philip, Prince (Duke of Edinburgh), 261
Philip of Macedon, 574
Phillips, Cabell, 48, 66, 119, 196, 309, 449, 512, 610
Phillips, Howard, 350
Phillips, Kevin, 322, 771
Phillips, Leslie, 319
Phillips, Wendell, 211, 362, 526, 643, 700
Philos, Conrad D., 230
Picasso, Pablo, 198
Picker, Arnold, 217
Pierce, Franklin, 167, 356, 728
Pierson, David, 566
Pike, Otis, 442
Pinchot, Gifford, 221
Pindling, Lynden O., 749
Pinkerton, James P., 286, 548
Pinkney, Junette A., 274
Pitney, John J., Jr., 428
Pitt, William (the Elder), 568, 600–601
Pittman, Key, 175
Plato, 68, 732
Platt, Thomas C., 43, 450
Plautus, 172, 708
Pliny the Elder, 559
Plunkitt, George Washington, 33, 334, 655, 782
Podhoretz, Norman, 466
Poe, Edgar Allan, 338
Poincaré, Raymond, 64
Poindexter, John M., 82, 88, 165, 272
Polk, James K., 101, 303, 609, 670, 701, 728, 759, 769
    dark horse, 166–67
Pollack, A. J., 703, 784
Pope, Alexander, 38, 287

Porter, David, 652
Porter, Sylvia, 36
Post, Emily, 152
Potemkin, Grigori, 630
Potter, Simeon, 865
Poulson, Norris, 869
Powell, Adam Clayton, 36, 61, 371, 660, 704
Powell, Joseph L. (Jody), 149, 284, 370, 373
Powell, Lewis, 637
Powers, David, 369
Powers, John, 263
Praigg, N. T., 444
Prall, Robert, 36–37
Preston, George B., 783
Price, Raymond K., 60, 410, 689–90, 738
Pride, Thomas, 627, 676
Priest, Madison, 209
Priestley, J. B., 631–32
Procaccino, Mario, 413
Proctor, Redfield, 449
Proxmire, William, 572, 611
Pyhrr, Peter A., 894
Pyles, Thomas, 784

Qaddafi, Muammar, 124
Quadros, Janio, 292
Quay, Matthew Stanley, 557, 581
Quayle, J. Danforth (Dan), 135, 209, 215, 240–41, 300, 314, 322, 385, 577, 602, 733, 801, 840
  amiable dunce, 20
  you're no JFK, 893
Quayle, Oliver, 35, 779
Quill, Michael J., 576
Quillan, Harry W., 198
Quiller-Couch, Arthur, 238
Quincy, Josiah, 765
Quindlen, Anna, 284
Quisling, Vidkun, 635

Rabelais, 321
Radcliffe, Donnie, 886
Radford, Arthur W., 560
Rado, Gaby, 216
Rae, John, 346
Rafshoon, Gerald, 388, 625–26
Raine, Richard, 559
Raines, Howell, 173
Rajneesh, Bhagwan Shree, 405
Rakosi, Matyas, 682
Raleigh, Walter (Sir), 352
Ramsey, Ben, 381
Rand, Chandler Amy, 829–30
Randall, Gene, 145
Randall, J. G., 675–76
Randolph, A. Philip, 438

Randolph, John (of Roanoke), 366–67, 560, 853, 871
Raphael, D. D., 341
Raskob, John J., 719
Raspberry, William, 225, 333
Rather, Dan, 57, 546
Rauch, Jonathan, 796
Rauh, Joseph, 458
Ravenal, Earl, 146, 685
Rawlinson, Lord, 601
Rawls, Wendell, Jr., 51
Ray, Philip, 253
Rayburn, Sam, 68, 128, 147, 290, 297, 400, 502, 546, 552, 742–43, 767
Raymond, Henry, 608
Raymond, Jack, 337, 418
Reagan, Nancy, 252, 600
Reagan, Ronald, 8, 54, 78, 98, 157, 185, 214, 221, 247, 254, 256, 272, 300, 303–4, 308, 342, 345, 359–60, 364, 370, 416, 420, 484, 591, 634, 662, 712, 728, 742, 814, 816, 875, 877
  alliteration, 14
  amiable dunce, 20
  are you any better off...?, 24–25
  -bashing, 46
  big casino, 50–51
  big enchilada, 51
  big government, 53
  Bircher, 56
  bloodbath, 64
  briefing book, 84
  candidate, 102
  cant, 102
  cautiously optimistic, 109
  city on a hill, 126
  cowboy, 156
  crossover vote, 160
  dream ticket, 200–201
  dustbin of history, 201
  evil empire, 228
  fatally flawed, 237–38
  honeymoon period, 335
  hot property, 338
  ideology, 350
  job seeks the man, 380
  keister, 386
  let [whomever] be [whomever], 405–6
  level playing field, 406
  litmus-test issue, 414
  make my day, 430
  morning in America, 462
  -nomics, 503
  policeman of the world, 588
  secret plan, 693
  sleaze factor, 714
  sleeping giant, 715

  smoke and mirrors, 721
  South Succotash, 735
  speechwriter, 738
  stand in the doorway, 752
  star wars, 754
  stay the course, 757
  supply-side, 775
  Teflon-coated Presidency, 788
  there you go again, 792
  voodoo economics, 846–47
  waste, fraud and abuse, 858
  window of opportunity, 879
  you're no JFK, 893
Reed, James, 290
Reed, Thomas B., 350, 449, 527, 655, 823
Reeves, Richard, 132, 207, 346, 375, 793
Reeves, Rosser, 182
Regan, Donald, 364, 538
Reichel, William V., 336
Reid, T. R., 51, 710
Reiger, George, 221
Reilly, William K., 671
Reisner, Robert, 293
Remington, William T., 652
Reno, Janet, 88
Repplier, Agnes, 840
Ress, Emanuel, 93
Reston, James, 42, 158, 259, 432, 479, 540, 670, 761, 763, 892
Reuss, Henry S., 561
Reuther, Walter, 620, 647
Revel, Jean-François, 151, 809
Reynaud, Paul, 574, 749
Reynolds, Stanley, 50
Reynolds, Walter, 847
Rhatican, William F., 733
Rhee, Syngman, 341
Rhodes, Cecil, 75
Rhodes, John, 589, 697
Ribbentrop, Joachim von, 57
Ribicoff, Abraham, 379–80, 445, 660
Rice, Grantland, 141
Rice, Thomas Dartmouth, 377–78
Richards, Ann, 387
Richards, I. A., 622
Richardson, Elliot, 60, 251, 665, 689, 873
Richberg, Donald, 527, 737
Richelieu, Duc de (Armand Jean du Plessis), 298
Rickover, Hyman, 427
Ridgeway, James, 872
Ridgway, Matthew, 493
Riesman, David, 214, 427–28, 511
Riley, Pat, 281
Rinfret, Pierre, 605, 814

Riordan, William, 33, 334
Rivers, Mendel, 887
Robards, Rachel Donelson, 188
Robb, Charles S., 705
Robbins, Anthony, 715
Robbins, Tim, 462
Roberts, Chalmers, 44, 849
Roberts, Owen, 499
Roberts, Sam, 10
Roberts, Steven, 171
Robertson, Pat, 237
Robeson, George, 411
Robichaud, Jacques, 103
Robinson, Gilbert A., 185, 335, 643
Robinson, Joseph T., 192
Robinson, Paul I., 446–47
Rochau, Ludwig von, 649
Roche, John P., 292–93, 365, 602, 604
Rockefeller, Jay, 107–8, 259
Rockefeller, John D., Jr., 71
Rockefeller, Margaretta Fitler (Happy), 188
Rockefeller, Nelson, 54, 157, 162, 196, 231, 236, 280, 303, 305, 307, 310, 356, 392, 435, 458, 587, 611, 615–16, 704, 744, 811, 813
    blooper, 66
    bomfog, 71
    boring from within, 75
    candidate, 101
    compact of Fifth Avenue, 140–41
    consensus, 144
    creative federalism, 156
    divorce issue, 188
    don't waste your vote, 194
    dream ticket, 201
    edifice complex, 207
    hoopla, 335
    lightning may strike, 410
    mainstream, 429–30
    mudslinging, 471
    rally, 643–44
Rockefeller, Nelson, Jr., 188
Rockne, Knute, 621
Rodger, Walton, 499
Roe, Thomas, 706
Rogers, Lindsay, 524
Rogers, Will, 176, 192, 195, 250, 387, 463, 483, 718, 880
Rogers, Will, Jr., 586
Rogers, William P., 134, 170, 230, 585
Röhm, Ernst, 497, 627
Romagna, Jack, 726
Romano, Lois, 233

Romney, George, 184, 235–36, 261, 421, 478, 487, 529, 536, 548, 554, 589, 617, 692, 760, 880
    Boy Scout, 78
    brainwash, 81–82
    card metaphors, 106
    consensus, 144
    credibility gap, 158
Romney, Lenore, 589
Romulo, Carlos, 841
Rooney, John J., 149
Roosevelt, Eleanor, 212, 252, 341, 367, 509, 516, 616, 655
Roosevelt, Franklin D., 121, 171, 192, 214, 238, 241, 245, 256, 261, 270, 290–92, 296–97, 299, 306, 339, 350–51, 356, 385, 396, 400, 402, 415, 428, 431–32, 438, 442–43, 445, 449, 484, 494, 496, 502–4, 514, 519, 524, 526, 537, 539, 546, 557, 565, 594, 604, 607, 624, 667, 689, 695, 710–11, 742, 748–49, 755, 763, 772, 781, 856
    again and again and again, 9–10
    alphabet agencies, 14–15
    American system, 19
    appeasement, 23
    arsenal of democracy, 27
    balance of power, 38
    bald eagle, 39–40
    ballyhoo, 41
    barnstorm, 45
    black Republican, 62
    body politic, 69
    bookburners, 72
    boomerang, 74
    brain trust, 81
    bully pulpit, 89
    campaign, 98
    campaign songs, 100
    campaign train, 100
    card metaphors, 106
    catchword, 108
    cemetery vote, 110
    cigarette-holder symbol, 124–25
    citizen of the world, 125
    clear it with Sidney, 128–29
    copperhead, 151
    corn pone, 152
    crusade, 161
    cufflinks gang, 162
    day of infamy, 167–68
    defeatist, 172
    demagogue, 175
    Depression party, 176
    deterrent, 180

    don't change horses, 193–94
    draft, Presidential, 200
    economic royalists, 207
    elder statesman, 212
    Era of Good Feeling, 223
    Fala speech, 116, 235
    fireside chat, 250
    forgotten man, 261–62
    four freedoms, 263–64
    free enterprise, 267
    garden-hose analogy, 278
    Good Neighbor Policy, 289
    grand design, 295
    Happy Days Are Here Again, 316
    Happy Warrior, 316–17
    horse-and-buggy, 336
    Hundred Days, 344–45
    Hymie's ferryboat, 346
    iffy question, 351
    initials, Presidential, 360
    "I see" construction, 372
    isolationism, 374
    labels, 395
    laundry ticket, 398
    left wing, right wing, 403
    liberal, 407
    loneliest job in the world, 420
    loved for the enemies he made, 422
    love feast, 422
    loyal opposition, 423
    lunatic fringe, 425
    mandate, 433
    Martin, Barton and Fish, 439
    maverick, 440
    me too, 450
    my (use of possessive pronoun), 474
    my friends, 475–76
    New Deal, 485–87
    nine old men, 499–500
    nothing to fear but fear itself, 509–10
    one third of a nation, 527–28
    Oval Office, 538–39
    peroration, 572
    playing politics, 580
    practical politics, 606
    President of all the people, 609–10
    pump-priming, 625
    purge, 627–28
    quarantine, 632–33
    quoted out of context, 637–38
    rank and file, 644
    reactionary, 646
    rendezvous with destiny, 657

Roosevelt, Franklin D. (*cont.*)
  rider, 664
  rugged individualism, 675
  running against Hoover,
    677
  ship of state, 702
  sports metaphors, 747
  stab in the back, 749
  steamroller, 758
  That Man in the White
    House, 790–91
  traitor to his class, 810–11
  trial balloon, 811
  turnarounds, 818
  turnout, 819
  unholy alliance, 831
  United Nations, 833
  vested interests, 841
  voice from the sewer, 845
  weasel words, 863–64
  whispering campaign,
    871–72
  windfall profits, 878
  yes, but, 891
Roosevelt, Franklin D., Jr.,
    185, 194, 655, 720
Roosevelt, Theodore, 125,
    130, 180, 271, 313, 315,
    321, 325, 368, 388–89,
    397, 411, 434, 436, 449,
    471, 491, 496, 502, 550,
    575, 620, 676, 700, 757,
    762, 797, 814, 816, 841,
    864
  Americanism, 18
  arena, 24
  Armageddon, 25
  bandwagon, 43
  bread-and-butter issue,
    82–83
  bully pulpit, 89
  Byzantine, 95
  campaign oratory, 98
  campaign songs, 100
  cant, 102
  canvass, 104
  cowboy, 155
  crusade, 161
  demagogue, 175
  Democrat, 176
  do-gooder, 190
  hat in the ring, 320
  have and have-not nations,
    321
  jingoism, 378
  lunatic fringe, 425
  machine politics, 426
  malefactors of great wealth,
    431
  maverick, 440
  mess in Washington, 450
  mollycoddle, 460
  muckraker, 469–70

  mugwumps, 472
  new, political use of, 484
  New Nationalism, 494
  party of the people, 555
  policeman of the world,
    587–88
  practical politics, 606
  professional, 615
  progressive, 616
  silk stocking, 710
  sitting President, 712
  slogan, 716
  square deal, 748
  taps and bugs, 783–84
  third-party movement, 794
  thou shalt not steal, 798
  trial balloon, 811
  twisting the lion's tail, 822
  vox populi, 848
  weasel words, 863
  White House, 874
  you can't beat somebody
    with nobody, 891
Roosevelt, Theodore, Jr., 440
Root, Elihu, 204, 212, 494, 678
Roper, Elmo, 177, 593–94
Rose, George, 107, 129
Rosebery, Lord, 167
Rosenau, James, 414
Rosenberg, Michael J., 693
Rosenblatt, Roger, 12
Rosenman, Samuel I., 10, 27,
    45, 128, 168, 184, 235,
    264, 338–39, 486,
    499–500, 510, 527–28,
    638, 737, 831, 833,
    863–64, 891
  boomerang, 74
  cemetery vote, 110
  economic royalists, 207
  footnote to history, 261
  "I see" construction, 372
  New Deal, 485–87
  peroration, 572
Rosenthal, A. B., 600
Rosenthal, A. M., 314
Rosenthal, Andrew, 483
Rosow, Jerome, 884
Ross, Charles, 196
Ross, Harold, 416
Ross, Joseph, 172
Ross, Thomas B., 368
Rossi, Peter H., 237
Rossiter, Clinton, 111, 132,
    192, 466, 555, 599, 612,
    743, 756, 819
Rostenkowski, Dan, 547
Rostow, Walt Whitman, 9,
    492, 809, 865
Rothermere, Lord, 526
Rothschild, Lionel Walter
    (second Baron), 332
Rougemont (reporter), 519

Rousseau, Jean-Jacques, 68,
    404, 489
Rovere, Richard, 622
Rowell, J. H., 182
Rowen, Hobart, 180, 859
Royall, Anne, 653
Royster, Vermont, 715
Ruark, Robert, 139
Ruckelshaus, William, 251,
    689
Rudman, Warren, 130
Rumbold, Richard, 435
Ruml, Beardsley, 560
Rusher, William, 734
Rusk, Dean, 161, 198, 232,
    483, 508, 510, 588, 682,
    835, 849, 856, 865
Russel, Francis, 66
Russell, Benjamin, 223
Russell, Bertrand, 49, 612, 856
Russell, Richard, 2, 381–82
Russell, William Howard, 252
Russert, Tim, 886
Rustin, Bayard, 438, 511

Sachs, Stephen, 822
Sadat, Anwar el-, 331, 564, 759
Safire, William, 179, 229, 490,
    738
  hardball, 317
St. John, Jeffrey, 215
Sakharov, Andrei, 342
Salant, Richard, 57
Salinger, Pierre, 369, 432, 579
Salisbury, Harrison, 391, 452
Salisbury, Lord, 564, 832
Saltonstall, Leverett, 508, 554,
    727
Samuel, Lord, 691
Samuelson, Paul, 488
Samuelson, Robert J., 206
Sandburg, Carl, 208, 545,
    891
Santayana, George, 655, 880
Sargent, Alice, 283–84
Sarnoff, Robert, 300
Sartre, Jean-Paul, 138
Satchell, Michael, 571
Sauvy, Alfred, 795
Savile, George (Marquess of
    Halifax), 824
Scali, John, 232
Scammon, Richard M., 35,
    112–13, 452, 621, 857
Schaap, Dick, 273
Schaefer, William Donald, 738
Schall, James, 482
Schiff, Rosalie, 772
Schiller, Karl, 724
Schine, G. David, 72, 382–83
Schjelderup-Ebbe, Thorlief,
    567
Schlafly, Phyllis, 120, 895

Schlesinger, Arthur M., Jr.,
    229, 256, 260, 292, 317,
    327–28, 340, 343, 345,
    433, 441–42, 456–57, 475,
    491, 547, 569, 593, 610,
    621, 632, 644, 657, 690,
    738, 754, 776, 796, 832,
    867
  Bircher, 56
  bloc, 64
  buck stops here, the, 87–88
  bully pulpit, 89
  campaign oratory, 98
  centrist, 111
  come now, and let us
      reason together, 137–38
  domino theory, 191
  Eastern Establishment, 204
  imperial Presidency, 354–55
  you never had it so good,
      892
Schlesinger, James, 124, 365,
    427, 577, 650
Schmalz, Jeffrey, 233
Schmermann, Serge, 370
Schmidt, Helmut, 681
Schorenstein, Hymie, 346
Schorr, Daniel, 217, 401,
    686–87, 733
Schram, Martin, 20
Schroeder, Patricia, 445, 713,
    788
Schuette, Oswald F., 757
Schurz, Carl, 74, 205, 242,
    254, 407, 486, 627, 745,
    774, 822, 854
Schwartz, Bernard, 831
Schwartz, Harry, 294, 393, 685
Schwartz, Samuel I., 632
Schwarz, Tony, 166
Scott, Hugh, Jr., 710
Scott, John Anthony, 867
Scott, Walter, 702, 751, 881–82
Scott, Winfield, 167, 227, 436
Scowcroft, Brent, 230, 650
Scranton, William R., 96,
    120–21, 746
Sculley, John, 454
Seabury, Samuel, 416, 497
Seale, Bobby, 605
Seaton, Fred, 380
Seeger, Alan, 657
Seeger, Peter, 867
Segretti, Donald, 7, 645
Seidman, P. K., 197–98
Selden, John, 502, 764–65
Seldes, George, 117
Seldes, Gilbert, 16–17
Semple, Robert, Jr., 539
Senes, Meridyth, 768
Serrin, William, 597
Service, John, 518
Seselj, Vojislav, 225

Sevareid, Eric, 282, 298, 632,
    831
Sewall, Arthur, 568
Seward, William, 126, 326,
    473, 826
Seymore, George, 706
Seymour, Horatio, 475, 700
Shabecoff, Philip, 795
Shadegg, Stephen, 109–10
Shaftesbury, Earl of, 870
Shakespeare, William, 112,
    160, 171, 421, 435, 500,
    541, 558, 564, 584–85,
    592, 618, 633, 654, 742,
    745, 747, 764, 834, 866,
    882
  bloody shirt, 65
  candidate, 101
  stalking horse, 750
  strange bedfellows, 762
  weasel words, 863
Shalala, Donna, 210
Shalit, Ruth, 76
Shanley, Bernard, 863
Shapiro, Fred R., 44, 230, 255,
    671
Shapiro, Walter, 450
Sharif, Abdul Hamid, 736
Shaw, Albert, 43
Shaw, David, 723
Shaw, George Bernard, 589,
    601, 774
Shea, Nancy, 71
Sheehan, Edward, 758
Sheffer, Hy, 71
Shepley, James, 85
Sheppard, Samuel, 666
Sheridan, Richard Brinsley, 11
Sherman, John, 169, 243
Sherman, William Tecumseh,
    262, 609, 700, 776, 848
Sherwood, John, 375
Sherwood, Robert E., 10, 372,
    402, 439, 737, 862
Shevardnadze, Eduard A., 659
Shields, Mark, 89–90, 364
Shinn, Charles Howard,
    295–96
Shinwell, Emanuel, 359
Shirer, William L., 72, 629
Shivers, Allan, 381
Sholes, Christopher Latham,
    511
Shrapnel, Henry S., 636
Shriver, Sargent, 292
Shultz, George P., 319, 620,
    636, 686, 702, 873, 885
Sibley, J. C., 463
Sidey, Hugh, 164, 315
Sidney, Philip, 661
Siegal, Ethan H., 376
Sigiraed, King, 7
Silberman, Laurence, 170–71,

355
Silk, Leonard, 197
Sillman, Leonard, 489
Silverfarb, Edward, 744
Simpson, Alan K., 442
Simpson, Kirke, 721
Simpson, Wallis, 188
Sinclair, Harry, 375
Sirica, John, 229–30
Smith, Adam, 478–79
Smith, Adam (George J. W.
    Goodman), 286, 845
Smith, Alfred E., 70, 125, 192,
    261, 272, 369, 389,
    398–99, 404, 422, 463,
    517, 609, 620, 731, 826,
    890
  alphabet agencies, 14
  baloney, 42
  campaign songs, 100
  chicken in every pot, 117
  demagogue, 175
  doves, 199
  Happy Warrior, 316–17
  kiss of death, 388–89
  lulu, 425
  mudslinging, 471
  rank and file, 644
  red herring, 651
  ripper bill, 668
  rubber stamp, 674
  Santa Claus, nobody
      shoots at, 687
  take a walk, 781
  titular leader, 806
  unpack, 835
  whispering campaign, 871
Smith, Benjamin, II, 107
Smith, Bromley, 386
Smith, Bubba, 87
Smith, C. W., 391
Smith, Edward Conrad, 674
Smith, Hedrick, 51, 58, 410,
    427, 538
Smith, Hoke, 516
Smith, Howard (politician),
    69
Smith, Howard K., 312
Smith, Ian, 706, 768
Smith, James, 77
Smith, Margaret Chase,
    719–20
Smith, Milton, 36, 515
Smith, Perry M., 233
Smith, Robert, 736–37
Smith, Stephen, 292
Smith, Walter (Red), 317
Smoot, Dan, 369
Smuts, Jan Christiaan, 331
Smythe, William Henry, 787
Snow, C. P., 600
Snow, Edgar, 518
Snowden, Viscountess, 371

Snyder, John, 358
Sobran, Joseph, 308
Socolow, Sanford, 254
Socrates, 125
Sokolsky, George, 459
Solarz, Stephen J., 842
Solon, 732
Solzhenitsyn, Alexander, 307, 666, 685
Sonnenfeldt, Helmut, 179
Sorel, Edward, 666
Sorensen, Theodore, 8, 248, 270, 289, 292, 345, 369, 405, 423, 433, 455, 457–58, 462, 492–93, 539, 541, 557, 561, 581, 594, 612, 620, 662, 668, 711, 727, 738, 742, 770, 776, 814, 828, 875
    Alliance for Progress, 12–13
    backgrounder, 33
    Bailey memorandum, 37
    bald eagle, 39
    Bay of Pigs fiasco, 46
    buttons, campaign, 94
    calculated risk, 97
    campaign oratory, 98
    contrapuntal phrases, 148
    détente, 179
    too little and too late, 807
Sorg, Karl G., 703
Soukhanov, Anne, 640
Souter, David, 676
Souvanna Phouma, 483
Sowell, Thomas, 303
Spanjer, Ralph, 569
Specter, Arlen, 676
Speed, John, 570
Spenser, Edmund, 324
Sperber, Hans, 167, 193, 295, 419, 435, 658, 732, 752, 789
Spick, Mike, 274
Spinelli, Pier, 607–8
Spinks, Michael, 647
Spinoza, Baruch, 480, 627
Spivak, Lawrence, 748
Stalin, Joseph, 295, 604, 617, 649, 691
    cult of personality, 162–63
    strange bedfellows, 762–63
Stallybrass, Oliver, 682
Stanhope, Philip, 443
Stanley, Edward, 424
Stapleton, Ruth Carter, 76, 576
Stark, Irwin, 802
Stassen, Harold, 46, 181, 380, 571, 636, 680
    campaign train, 100
Stayskal, Wayne, 693
Stedman, Edmund Clarence, 769

Steele, Richard, 329–30
Steevens, George, 175, 270
Steffens, Lincoln, 175, 470, 654–55, 680, 748, 862
Stein, Benjamin, 536
Stein, Bruno, 387
Stein, Gertrude, 498
Stein, Herbert, 488–89, 521, 723–24, 775, 857
Stein, Howard, 217
Steinbeck, John, 421, 601
Steinem, Gloria, 701, 882
Stenholm, Charles, 69
Stephanopoulos, George, 310, 647
Stephens, Tom, 6
Stern, Howard, 764
Stern, J. David, 440
Stern, Sol, 793
Stevens, John L., 336
Stevens, Thaddeus, 568, 584
Stevenson, Adlai, 213, 245, 260, 300, 315, 363, 373, 379, 404, 407, 416, 421, 431, 435, 474, 487, 504, 512, 519, 563, 596, 598, 624, 694, 712, 730, 816, 839, 873
    alliteration, 13
    amateurs, 16
    art of the possible, 27
    automobile metaphor, 29
    barnburners, 45
    bloc, 64
    body politic, 69
    brinkmanship, 85
    candidate, 101
    cant, 102
    captive candidate, 105
    coattails, 133
    come now, and let us reason together, 137
    concession speech, 142
    cradle-to-the-grave, 156
    crusade, 162
    dialogue, 182
    dinosaur wing, 183
    divorce issue, 188
    don't let them take it away, 194
    doves, 198
    draft, Presidential, 199
    dynamic conservatism, 202
    egghead, 209
    heartbeat away from the Presidency, 321
    honeymoon period, 335
    humor, self-deprecating, 343
    "I see" construction, 373
    liberation of captive peoples, 408
    mess in Washington, 449–50

    me too, 451
    moderate, 458
    mudslinging, 471
    new, political use of, 484
    nuclear proliferation, 511–12
    one-party press, 526
    open convention, 530
    party of the people, 555–56
    political capital, to make, 589
    primary, 613
    quality of life, 632
    run scared, 679
    selling candidates like soap, 696
    soft on Communism, 729
    superpatriots, 774
    surrender on Morningside Heights, 777
    switcher, 779
    time for a change, 804–5
    titular leader, 805–6
    truth squad, 818
    volunteers, 846
    yes, but, 891
    you never had it so good, 892
Stevenson, Adlai, III, 343
Stevenson, Burton, 564
Stevenson, James, 705
Stevenson, Robert Louis, 249, 261, 815
Stewart, Potter, 118, 882
Stilwell, Joseph Warren (Vinegar Joe), 353, 567
Stimson, Henry L., 98, 204
Stockdale, James, 840
Stockman, David A., 84, 220, 672, 681, 883
Stoddard, Henry L., 41, 66, 238, 452, 730
Stoil, Michael, 505
Stokes, Thomas L., 253
Stone, Irving, 193
Stormer, John, 120
Stothard, Peter, 467
Stowe, Harriet Beecher, 1, 651, 828–29
Stowe, Leland, 244
Strachan, Gordon, 7
Straight, Michael, 215
Straus, Lewis, 8
Straus, Nathan, 546
Straus, Peter, 216, 524
Strauss, Robert, 377, 390
Streit, Clarence, 266
Stretch, C. Clinton, 895
Strong, Anna Louise, 547
Strout, Richard, 210
Stuart, J. E. B., 730
Stuckart, Franz, 247
Sturrock, John, 514

Sullivan, "Big Tim," 620
Sullivan, Kathleen M., 716
Sullivan, Mark, 238, 552, 722, 762, 891
Sullivan, Thomas P., 299
Sullivan, Walter, 878–79
Sullivan, William, 217
Sulzberger, Arthur Hays, 665
Sulzberger, C. L., 181, 249, 849, 861
Summer, William Graham, 261–62
Sumner, Charles, 623, 713
Sumner, William Graham, 380
Sununu, John, 1
Sun Yat-sen, 570
Swanson, Claude, 619, 645
Swartwout, Samuel, 778
Sweat, Noah S., Jr., 351
Sweet, John, 801
Sweet, Robert, 63
Swift, Jonathan, 715, 717, 890
Swope, Herbert Bayard, 135–36, 304, 609–10, 633
Sylvester, Arthur, 432
Sylvester, Robert, 478
Szenes, Michael M., 228

Taft, Charles P., 133
Taft, Martha, 652
Taft, Robert A., 16, 167, 288, 304, 489, 531, 535, 667, 669, 799, 805, 873
  bipartisan, 55
  can't-win technique, 102–3
  card-carrying, 105
  deal, 170
  Dewey blitz, 181
  do-nothing Congress, 193
  Eastern Establishment, 204
  Mr. Republican, 468
  packing the galleries, 544–45
  partisan, 551
  shoo-in, 704
  stalwart, 751
  surrender on Morningside Heights, 777
Taft, William Howard, 52, 315, 320, 356, 388, 450, 476, 494, 555, 581, 674, 700, 728, 757, 759
  candidate, 101
  curse of bigness, 165
  demagogue, 175
  diplomacy, 185
  dollar diplomacy, 190–91
  heir apparent, 325
  high cost of living, 325–26
  loneliest job in the world, 419
  machinery of government, 427

square deal, 748
straw man (man of straw), 763
thou shalt not steal, 798
trot out the ghosts, 816
Ta-kuang Chang, 877–78
Talleyrand-Périgord, Charles Maurice de, 308
Talmadge, Eugene, 164
Tamony, Peter, 172, 783
Tanzer, Lester, 589
Tappan, Benjamin, 400
Tarbell, Ida, 470
Tarnoff, Peter, 34
Tarsney, T. E., 259
Taufa'ahau Topou, King, IV, 595
Tauke, Thomas J., 316
Tauvin, Billy, 316
Taylor, Edmund, 593
Taylor, Maxwell, 191, 439–40, 473, 871
Taylor, Telford, 641
Taylor, Zachary, 252, 504, 765
  barnburners, 45
Teague, Olin E., 767
Tecumseh, Chief, 476
Telemachus, 639
Teng Hsiao-ping, 163, 549
Tennyson, Alfred Lord, 494–95
Thackeray, William Makepeace, 518
Thaler, Alwin, 882
Thatcher, Margaret, 152–53, 601, 650, 740
Thayer, William Roscoe, 674, 783
Theobald, Count of Champagne, 564
Theramenes, 536
Thieu, Nguyen Van, 843
Thimmesch, Nick, 172, 362
Thomas, Clarence, 8, 76, 364, 442, 481, 883
Thomas, Norman, 450, 675
Thomas, Rich, 182
Thompson, Francis, 881
Thompson, Fred, 28
Thompson, John, 153, 298–99
Thompson, Llewellyn, 682
Thompson, Tommy G., 349
Thomson, Charles, 834
Thoreau, Henry David, 126, 509
Thornburgh, Richard, 51
Thornton, Richard H., 315–16, 411, 645
Thurber, James, 97, 593
Thurmond, J. Strom, 189, 246, 378, 463, 474, 587, 731, 794
Tiemann, Norbert, 566

Tierney, George, 188, 424, 620
Tilden, Samuel J., 52, 57, 421–22, 471, 705, 728, 730
  deal, 169–70
Tillman, Benjamin (Pitchfork Ben), 762
Tinker, Jack, 356
Tocqueville, Alexis de, 502, 599, 708, 846
  coalition, 132
Tolchin, Martin, 558–59, 649
Tolchin, Susan, 559, 649
Topping, Seymour, 322
Torcaso, Roy R., 693
Tower, John, 76, 242, 512
Traheron, Bartholomew, 21
Trausch, Susan, 303
Travis, Randy, 797
Travis, William Barret, 200
Trembley, Père Joseph de, 298
Trewhitt, Henry L., 158
Tribe, Laurence, 481
Trinor, Alma, 226, 698
Trippet, Frank, 243
Trittschuh, Travis, 167, 193, 419, 658, 732, 752, 789
Trollope, Anthony, 581
Trotsky, Leon, 201, 241
Trubin, John, 216
Trudeau, Garry, 312–13
Trudeau, Pierre, 103–4, 641
Truman, Harry S., 3, 128, 147, 212, 239, 245, 253, 255, 290, 320, 327, 342, 352, 360, 370–71, 415, 435, 441, 464, 476, 496, 504, 520, 526, 533–34, 538, 541, 546, 552, 587, 593, 619, 621, 633, 645–46, 675, 748, 756, 759, 858, 860, 870, 874, 876, 888
  all things to all men, 14
  bald eagle, 40
  baloney, 42
  bolt, 70
  boom and bust, 73
  boss, bossism, 78
  buck stops here, the, 87–88
  campaign train, 100
  card metaphors, 106
  character assassin, 111
  decision-making process, 170
  deliver, 174
  demagogue, 175
  Depression party, 177
  Dixiecrat, 189
  doctrine, 189
  do-nothing Congress, 192–93
  don't waste your vote, 194
  dope story, 196
  eat crow, 205–6

Truman, Harry S. (*cont.*)
  Fair Deal, 235
  football, political, 260
  front-porch campaign,
    269–70
  give 'em hell, Harry, 282–83
  "Had Enough?," 313
  hand-picked, 315
  have and have-not nations,
    321
  hold the line, 330
  if you can't stand the
    heat..., 352
  influence peddler, 358
  Jim Crow, 378
  job seeks the man, 379
  kitchen cabinet, 389
  limited war, 412
  lobby, 418
  loneliest job in the world,
    419
  loved for the enemies he
    made, 422
  loyalty oath, 424
  mess in Washington, 449–50
  me too, 451
  mollycoddle, 460
  mossback, 463
  no substitute for victory,
    507–8
  off the reservation, 517
  open convention, 530
  partisan, 551
  party line, 554
  plant, 578–79
  police action, 587
  politician, 592
  Potomac fever, 598
  President of all the people,
    610
  pressing the flesh, 611
  privileged sanctuary, 614
  red herring, 651–52
  sellout, 696
  sitting President, 712
  smear, 719
  smoke-filled room, 722
  snollygoster, 725
  s.o.b., 726
  soft on Communism, 729
  sports metaphors, 747
  stab in the back, 749
  think tank, 793
  ticket, 802
  unfinished business, 830
  vested interests, 841
  war of national liberation,
    854
  whistlestopping, 66, 872–73
Truman, Margaret, 186
Trumbull, Jonathan, 86
Trussell, Tait, 35
Tsongas, Paul, 462

Tsuneishi, Warren M., 824
Tuchman, Barbara, 455
Tuck, Dick, 7, 323
Tucker, Josiah, 478
Tugwell, Rexford, 396
Tully, Grace, 351
Turner, Julius, 111
Turner, Stansfield, 83, 382,
  401, 689, 874
Tussaud, Marie, 863
Tutu, Desmond, 591
Tutwiler, Margaret, 761–62,
  803
Twain, Mark, 195, 422, 749,
  755, 762
  buttonhole, 92–93
  card metaphors, 106
  corn pone, 151
Tweed, William Marcy, 52, 57,
  557, 744–45
  boss, bossism, 77
Twersky, David, 376
Tydings, Joseph, 850
Tydings, Millard, 53
Tyler, John, 30, 356
Tyrrell, R. Emmet, 779
Tyson, Mike, 647

Udall, Morris, 408
Umbriet, K. B., 263
Unruh, Jesse M., 304
Urban VIII, Pope, 618
Uris, Leon, 25
U Thant, 608

Valachi, Joseph, 389
Valenti, Jack, 302, 790
Vallandigham, Clement
  Laird, 484, 487
Van Buren, John, 45, 847
Van Buren, Martin, 166, 239,
  356, 383, 418, 426, 744
  banner district, 43–44
  barnburners, 45
  campaign songs, 99
  heir apparent, 325
  silent vote, 709
  split ticket, 743
Vance, Cyrus R., 34, 232, 284,
  544, 549, 838
Van den Bark, Melvin, 265,
  669
Vandenberg, Arthur, 54–55,
  181, 371, 374, 389, 491,
  503, 536, 860
Van Gogh, Vincent, 798
Van Traa, Maarten, 838
Vaughan, Harry H., 40, 254,
  358, 370, 449, 726
Veblen, Thorstein, 787
Vergil, 834
Vesco, Robert, 642
Vick, Walter W., 178

Victoria, Queen of Great
  Britain, 49, 378, 659, 769
Vidal, Gore, 49, 655
Villard, Oswald Garrison,
  373, 808
Vincent, John, 115
Vinocur, John, 838
Vinson, Fred, 358, 424
Viorst, Milton, 66, 494–95
Voltaire, 168, 358
von Braun, Wernher, 654
Von Drehle, David, 514
von Neumann, John, 402, 895
Von Zell, Harry, 66

Wagner, Robert F., Jr., 78,
  411, 422, 468–69, 704,
  717, 766
Wald, Richard, 132
Waldheim, Kurt, 851, 859
Wales, Nym, 308
Walesa, Lech, 388
Walker, Felix, 90
Walker, Frank, 15
Walker, Herschel, 129
Walker, James J. (Jimmy),
  298, 346, 416, 469, 497,
  655
Wallace, George C., 183, 209,
  214, 226, 392, 451, 538,
  591, 653, 673, 677, 695,
  734, 794, 801
  send them a message, 697
  stand in the doorway, 752
Wallace, Henry, 38, 422, 587,
  616, 636, 794
  baloney, 42
  bellwether, 48
  common man, century of
    the, 138–39
  don't waste your vote, 194
  Hottentots, milk for,
    338–39
Wallace, Mike, 340, 611
Wallas, Graham, 302, 551
Wallop, M., 76
Walpole, Horace, 298, 823
Walpole, Robert, 620
Walsh, Mike, 566
Walters, Peter, 832
Walters, Vernon, 32
Wanamaker, John, 718
Wanniski, Jude, 681
Waple, Ben F., 222
Ward, Artemus (Charles
  Farrar Browne), 3, 195,
  592
Ward, Chester, 511
Ward, John, 433, 566
Ward, Samuel, 29
Ward, Thomas, 329
Warner, Charles Dudley, 422,
  762

Warner, W. Lloyd, 225
Warnke, Paul, 851
Warren, Earl, 38, 181, 336,
    400, 530, 543–44, 616,
    648, 749, 804, 855, 861
  reached, 646
Warren, Gerald L., 240
Warren, Jerry, 362
Warren, Robert Penn, 387,
    653
Warwick, Earl of, 388
Washburn, C. Langhorne, 43
Washington, George, 180,
    219, 239, 320, 328, 419,
    496, 537, 666, 823
  brother Jonathan, 86
  Democrat, 176
  diehards, 183
  executive privilege, 229–30
  first in war, 251–52
  liberal, 407
  partisan, 551
  politician, 592
  standard-bearer, 751–52
Watson, Jack, 1, 146–47, 546
Watson, Marvin, 319–20
Watson, Thomas J., Jr., 422
Watt, Donald Cameron, 649
Wattenberg, Ben J., 112–13,
    452, 466, 547, 621–22,
    738, 857
Wayne, John, 51
Ways, Max, 157, 642
Weaver, James B., 65, 452, 596
Weaver, Warren, 236
Webb, Walter Prescott, 491
Weber, Max, 91, 113, 884
Weber, Vin, 216
Webster, Daniel, 142,
    299–300, 318, 326, 348,
    443, 584, 605, 618, 887
Webster, Noah, 400
Webster, William, 650
Wedemeyer, Albert, 119
Weed, Thurlow, 102, 559–60
Weekly, Ernest, 866
Weicker, Lowell, 760–61
Weinberg, Sidney, 207
Weinberger, Caspar W., 171
Weiner, Richard, 363
Weinstein, Herbert T., 118
Weintal, Edward, 212
Weir, Ernest T., 238
Weisman, Steven R., 315, 329,
    340
Weismer, William, 189
Weitling, Wilhelm, 790
Welch, Joseph N., 112
Welch, Robert, Jr., 55, 141
Weld, William, 79
Weller, Charles E., 511
Welles, Sumner, 501, 749
Welliver, Judson, 738

Wells, G. Y., 147
Wells, H. G., 371, 856
Wells, Jack, 746
Wells, John A., 153, 458, 520,
    679
Wenner, Jann, 762
Wentworth, Harold, 597
Westin, Alan, 806
Westmoreland, William, 353,
    626–27
Wetmore, Edmund, 170
Whalen, Richard, 136
Wharton, Clifford, 625
Wheeler, Burton K., 17, 216
Wheeler, William, 100
Whelan, Richard, 263
White, F. Clifton, 75, 545,
    554, 700
White, Harry Dexter, 590, 694
White, John, 11
White, Theodore H., 81, 143,
    188, 196, 266, 300, 392,
    604, 709, 720, 747–48,
    752, 813–14, 861
  Eastern Establishment, 204
  power brokers, 600
  white power structure, 875
White, William Allen, 18,
    145, 303, 381, 463, 581,
    624, 721, 739, 822, 827
  cabal, 96
  dark horse, 167
  disaster metaphors, 187
  weasel words, 864
White, William S., 105, 360–61
Whitehead, Alfred North, 313
Whiteing, Richard, 131
Whitman, Alden, 658
Whitman, Walt, 418
Whitten, Les, 142
Whittier, Charles, 247
Wicker, Tom, 88, 211, 315,
    477, 527, 610, 778
Wieseltier, Leon, 630
Wilder, Billy, 376
Wilder, Thornton, 626
Wiley, Harvey W., 818
Wilhelm II, Kaiser, 578
Wilkes, John, 367
Wilkie, Curtis, 97
Will, George F., 409–10, 430,
    800
Willard, Archibald, 741
Williams, G. Mennen
    (Soapy), 611
Williams, James, 570
Williams, Joslyn, 790
Williams, Ralph, 453
Williams, Tennessee, 304
Willkie, Wendell L., 9, 37,
    164, 193, 218, 238, 420,
    435–36, 450, 476, 489,
    611, 702, 749, 805, 823

barefoot boy from Wall
    Street, 44
buttonhole, 93
campaign oratory, 98–99
candidate, 101
catchword, 108
crusade, 161
dark horse, 167
loyal opposition, 423
one world, 528–29
packing the galleries,
    544–45
party line, 553–54
vested interests, 841
weasel words, 864
wheels within wheels, 870
Wills, Garry, 758, 771
Wilson, Charles E., 52, 260,
    412, 439, 544, 807, 869
  bird dog...kennel dog,
    56–57
  boomerang, 74
Wilson, Epiphanius, 108
Wilson, George C., 47
Wilson, Harold, 57, 181,
    212–13, 345, 536, 722
  blooper, 66
Wilson, Henry, 487
Wilson, James, 435
Wilson, Pete, 845
Wilson, Samuel, 827–28
Wilson, Woodrow, 8, 235,
    339, 420, 483–84, 494,
    496, 524, 551, 555, 558,
    560, 575, 592, 600, 620,
    674, 711, 818, 833, 841,
    856, 860
  accommodation, 2–3
  boss, bossism, 77–78
  bully pulpit, 89
  Byzantine, 95
  citizen of the world, 125
  cooling-off period, 150
  entangling alliances, 219
  free enterprise, 267
  Hobson's choice, 330
  indispensable man, 356
  isolationism, 374
  John Q. Public, 380–81
  little group of wilful men,
    415
  make the world safe for
    democracy, 431
  mandate, 433
  men of thought, 448
  new, political use of, 484
  New Freedom, 490491
  open covenants, 530–31
  peace without victory, 565
  peroration, 573
  personally obnoxious, 573
  pitiless publicity, 577–78
  running mate, 678

Wilson, Woodrow (*cont.*)
  self-determination, 695
  sports metaphors, 747
  summitry, 771
  too proud to fight, 807–8
  watchful waiting, 858
  world opinion, 887
Winant, John G., 128
Winchell, Walter, 436–37
Winthrop, John, 98, 126
Winthrop, Robert C., 434
Wirthlin, Richard, 813
Wise, David, 157, 368, 492
Witcover, Jules, 47, 322, 721,
    896
Witherspoon, John, 18–19,
    475–76
Wodrow, Robert, 781
Wofford, Harris, 130–31
Wolfe, Thomas, 798
Wolfe, Tom, 550, 628
Wolfson, Louis, 155
Wollstonecraft, Mary, 429

Wood, Leonard, 30, 167, 552,
    721
Wood, William, 21
Woodcock, Leonard, 217,
    768–69
Woodward, Robert, 344, 645
Wooley, Robert W., 270
Woolf, H. B., 506
Woollacott, Martin, 844
Wooten, James, 801
Wordsworth, William, 317
Wouk, Herman, 332
Wright, Frank Lloyd, 26, 257
Wright, Quincy, 373–74
Wright, Silas, 701
Wu Han, 163
Wunderman, Sue Cott, 764
Wyclif, John, 77
Wynn, Albert R., 236

Yamamoto, Isoroku, 715
Yaqub-Kahn, Sahabzada, 283
Yates (author), 890

Yellen, Jack, 316
Yeltsin, Boris, 205, 216, 307,
    318, 521, 571, 630
Yerkes, Charles Tyson, 538
Yoder, Edwin M., Jr., 148
Young, Andrew, 77, 178, 225,
    529–30, 640
Young, David, 255, 582
Young, Frank, 47
Young, James E., 332
Young, Michael, 218–19
Young, Stephen M., 241, 667
Young, Whitney, Jr., 869

Zangwill, Israel, 447
Zeibert, Duke, 604
Ziegler, Ronald, 361–62, 501,
    676, 689, 733, 896
  backgrounder, 34
Zinsser, William, 878
Zuckerman, David, 758
Zuckerman, Mortimer, 621

ABOUT THE AUTHOR

WILLIAM SAFIRE is a man of many careers. He began as a reporter for a column in the *New York Herald Tribune* (see JOURNALESE), was a television producer (see MEDIA EVENT) and a public relations executive (see FLAK), worked as a senior speechwriter in the Nixon White House (see WORDSMITH) and escaped in time to become a political columnist for the *New York Times* (see PUNDIT).

Along the way, he has been an historian (*Before the Fall: An Inside View of the Pre-Watergate White House*) and a best-selling novelist (*Full Disclosure, Freedom*). In 1978 he was awarded the Pulitzer Prize for distinguished commentary.

To these careers, add lexicographer: the unifying thread in Safire's life has been a fascination with words. His "On Language" column in the *New York Times Magazine,* syndicated in newspapers around the world, has made him the most widely read and argued-with writer on the English language.